THE ENCYCLOPEDIA OF

UNDERSTANDING ALCOHOL AND OTHER DRUGS

THE ENCYCLOPEDIA OF

UNDERSTANDING ALCOHOL AND OTHER DRUGS

Volume I

Robert O'Brien
Morris Chafetz, M.D.
Sidney Cohen

June Lazerus
Robert Lazow,
General Editors

☑®
Facts On File, Inc.

The Encyclopedia of Understanding Alcohol and Other Drugs

Copyright © 1999 by Robert O'Brien, Morris Chafetz and Sidney Cohen

Facts On File, Inc.
11 Penn Plaza
New York NY 10001

Library of Congress Cataloging-in-Publication Data

O'Brien, Robert, 1932–
The encylopedia of undstanding alcohol and other drugs / by
Robert O'Brien, Morris Chafetz, Sidney Cohen.
p. cm.
Includes bibliographical references and index.
ISBN 0-8160-3971-2 (Vol. I)
ISBN 0-8160-3972-0 (Vol. II)
ISBN 0-8160-3970-4 (set)
1. Alcoholism—Encyclopedias. 2. Drug abuse—Encyclopedias.
I. Chafetz, Morris E. II. Cohen, Sidney, 1910– . III. Title.
HV5017.037   1998
362.29—dc21   98-22491

Facts On File books are available at special discounts when purchased in bulk quantities for businesses, associations, institutions, or sales promotions. Please call our Special Sales Department in New York at 212/967-8800 or 800/322-8755.

You can find Facts On File on the World Wide Web at http://www.factsonfile.com

Text design by Cathy Rincon
Cover design by Semadar Megged

Printed in the United States of America

MV FOF   10 9 8 7 6 5 4 3 2 1

This book is printed on acid-free paper.

CONTENTS

Volume I

A

absenteeism Absenteeism among alcohol and drug users is a major problem in industry today. Although absenteeism usually means actually being away from a job, there is another kind of absenteeism: on-the-job absenteeism, which occurs when a person is physically present but not mentally alert enough to be productive. Data from the *1993 National Household Survey on Drug Abuse* conducted by the Substance Abuse and Mental Health Services Administration (SAMHSA) indicated that 48.9% of those employed full time and 41.1% of those employed part time report some illicit drug use in their lifetime, while 12.4% and 16.2% of those two groups respectively reported illicit drug use during 1993, suggesting a total of over 12 million employed people as users of illicit drugs during that year. The cost to industry in lost production because of drug and alcohol abuse is estimated at about $116 billion annually; nearly $71 million of this has been attributed to lost employment and reduced productivity. Absenteeism is often the first indication of a drug problem and allows for early intervention by employers, teachers and union personnel. One study reported that male alcoholics had three times the number of absences as the matched control group. The U.S. Postal Service, in evaluating the relationship between recent drug use and job performance indicators, found that of 4,005 job applicants who were subsequently hired, 395 or 9% tested positive for illicit drug use and after one year were found to be absent at a rate that was 59% greater than the new

hires that tested negative (rates were 6.63% v. 4.16%).

EMPLOYEE ASSISTANCE PROGRAMS (EAPs) have been developed in both private and public employment locations to help workers with substance abuse problems. The Bureau of Labor Statistics estimated that 31% of employed Americans had access to EAPs in 1990.

National Institute on Drug Abuse (NIDA), "Research on Drugs and the Workplace," *NIDA Capsules,* cap. 87 (June 1990).

M. A. Maxwell, "A Study of Absenteeism, Accidents, and Sickness Payments in One Industry," *Quarterly Journal of Studies on Alcohol* 20 (1959): 302–307.

Substance Abuse and Mental Health Services Administration, *National Household Survey on Drug Abuse: Main Findings 1993* (Rockville, Md.: Department of Health and Human Services [DHHS]).

absinthe A flavored spirit with a dry, bitter taste, absinthe is too potent to be drunk straight. It is usually diluted with water, which changes its yellowish-green color to milky white. The name "absinthe" comes from the botanical designation of the plant *Artemisia absinthium,* more commonly known as wormwood, the basic flavoring ingredient in this beverage.

In addition to wormwood, absinthe is flavored with angelica root, star anise, dittany leaves, licorice, hyssop, sweet flag and other aromatics. These ingredients are macerated and steeped in alcohol. The final product is between 60% and 80% (usually 68%) alcohol.

The effects of excessive use of absinthe are more severe than those associated with heavy drinking in general. Due to the ingredient wormwood, absinthe is habit forming, harmful to the nerves, and can cause delirium, and sometimes, a permanent mental deterioration known as absinthism.

Absinthe was invented by a Dr. Ordinaire, a Frenchman living in Switzerland. His recipe was later bought by Henri-Louis PERNOD, who in 1797 became the first to produce absinthe commercially. Because of its grave health hazards, absinthe was banned in most western countries during the early years of the 20th century. It was outlawed in Switzerland in 1908 and in the U.S. in 1912. Although absinthe houses were very popular in Paris during the late 19th century, it was at last banned in France in 1915. After absinthe was banned, the anise-flavored apertif Pernod was produced as a substitute. Although these prohibitions have remained in effect, absinthe may still be consumed legally in some countries, including Spain.

absolute alcohol   There is always a slight amount of water in pure or absolute alcohol; commercial absolute alcohol, used only for medical or industrial purposes, contains up to 1% water. The absolute or pure alcohol in beverages is obtained by a BREWING process followed by fractional DISTILLATION.

Often the term absolute alcohol refers to the amount of pure alcohol contained in an alcoholic beverage. For example, three 1-oz drinks of 100-proof whiskey, four 8-oz glasses of beer and a half bottle of wine all contain approximately the same amount of pure alcohol—about one and a half ounces.

absorption   The process by which a chemical compound such as a drug or nutrient passes through the body membranes (intestinal lining, etc.) into the bloodstream.

abstainer   Strictly defined, one who abstains completely from alcoholic beverages and other mind-altering drugs. The application of the term or concept depends on the context in which it is used and the philosophy of the person or organization using it. For example, many agencies that report on alcohol abuse will group abstainers with moderate or social drinkers, since they are all categorized as nonusers of alcohol. ALCOHOLICS ANONYMOUS (and 12-step groups that address abuse of drugs other than alcohol) use a strict interpretation and insist upon complete abstinence. From another perspective, in cultures where the use of alcohol is proscribed or barely tolerated, such as in many Hindu and Muslim societies, abstention is the norm of social behavior, and until recent times any use of alcohol was rare. (See RECOVERY.)

abstinence   To completely refrain from the use of alcoholic beverages and/or other illicit drugs; also called total abstinence. (See ABSTAINER.)

abuse   A general term for the misuse or excessive use of alcohol and other drugs. Usually, the term applies to the use of drugs used to alter consciousness or to gratify physical needs, but abuse can also mean using drugs in forms and styles that are illegal or using drugs or alcohol without appropriate supervision. Generally speaking, abuse of alcohol and other drugs will lead to both mental and physical impairment.

Substance abuse does not necessarily mean drug or alcohol dependence (alcoholism). A person may abuse alcohol by going on drinking binges and becoming destructive, without necessarily developing the kind of psychological and/or physical dependency normally associated with alcoholism.

Substance abuse is subject to individual patterns. Some people may abuse more than one drug, such as those who misuse both alcohol and marijuana. In addition, the amount of a substance that might constitute abuse for one person might be relatively safe for another. Body weight, fat density, gender, tolerance, metabolic rate and GENETICS all play roles in the effect alcohol and drugs have on an individual. A large man might be able to consume several drinks in a sitting with no ill effects, while a small woman consuming the same amount of alcohol might become very intoxicated. Generally, older adults metabolize alcohol at a slower rate than younger adults, and women at a slower rate than men. The alcohol therefore will take longer to dilute in their systems and to break down in their systems, remaining potent for a longer period of time. Thus, when alcohol is metabolized slowly the effects of intoxication will be stronger and will last longer than when alcohol is metabolized more rapidly.

Some results of substance abuse are psychological problems, such as loss of control over drinking and/or depressive states; social problems—the breakup of a marriage, loss of employment, or involvement in criminal activities; or medical problems involving acute or chronic DISEASES such as CIRRHOSIS, ALCOHOLIC HEPATITIS or AIDS.

The Food and Drug Administration (FDA) very specifically defines *drug use* as the "taking of a drug for its intended purpose, in the appropriate amount, frequency, strength and manner"; *drug misuse* as "taking a substance for its intended purpose, but not in the appropriate amount, frequency, strength and manner"; and *drug abuse* as "deliberately taking a substance for other than its intended purpose, and in a manner that can result in damage to the person's health or his ability to function."

Substance abuse is also specifically categorized in the DSM-IV (*DIAGNOSTIC AND STATISTICAL MANUAL OF MENTAL DISORDERS*), where it defines a pattern of chronic and self-harmful misuse of alcohol/other drugs—all being the symptoms of psychological and/or physical addiction. Here it is broken down into two subcategories: *substance abuse* and *substance abuse dependence*. The criteria for a diagnosis of *substance abuse* (the less serious of the two) include continued repetitive use of a substance despite impairment in aspects of life functioning; recurrent use in situations where such use can cause physical harm; and use that results in legal problems. *Substance abuse dependence* consists of the same criteria as *substance abuse* but is characterized also by WITHDRAWAL symptoms when the individual abstains and increased TOLERANCE as well as an inability to abstain despite the negative consequences resulting from habitual use of the drug. The *INTERNATIONAL CLASSIFICATION OF DISEASES* (ICD-10) prefers the term "harmful use" to "abuse" and describes harmful use as "alcohol and other drug use that causes either physical or mental damage in the absense of dependence."

abuse liability   A psychoactive substance is susceptible to abuse if it is productive of physiological, psychological and/or social harm either to the user or to society at large. Under international drug control treaties, the World Health Organization (WHO) is responsible for determining the "abuse liability," as opposed to the "therapeutic usefulness," of all controlled substances.

World Health Organization (WHO), *Lexicon of Alcohol and Drug Terms* (Geneva, 1994).

abuse of nondependence-producing substances
This drug-related diagnostic category is included in the *ICD-10 (INTERNATIONAL CLASSIFICATION OF DISEASES)* but not in the *DSM-IV (DIAGNOSTIC AND STATISTICAL MANUAL OF MENTAL DISORDERS)*. As defined by the World Health Organization (WHO), abuse of nondependence-producing substances refers to the "repeated and inappropriate use of a substance that, though the substance (is generally) assumed to have no dependence potential, is accompanied by harmful physical or psychological effects. . . ."

The list of substances in this category includes: psychotropics, antidepressants and neuroleptics; laxatives; over-the-counter analgesics; anabolic steroids; vitamins; and antacids. These drugs do not ordinarily produce pleasurable effects but sometimes do so for individuals who become psychologically dependent on them. Getting high, or altering consciousness, however, is not usually the motivation associated with usage of these types of substances.

World Health Organization (WHO), *Lexicon of Alcohol and Drug Terms* (Geneva, 1994).

abuse potential   A drug's susceptibility to abuse or harmful use patterns.

abuse programs   Listed below are a few of the thousands of alcohol and other drug abuse programs throughout the United States. For further inquiry see Directory.

Rehabilitation and Individual Programs:
   AMERICAN MEDICAL ASSOCIATION substance-
      abuse programs
   PROJECT DARE
   DAYTOP
   SYNANON drug-free program

Indian Alcoholism Counseling and Recovery House Program:
   INDIAN HEALTH SERVICE (IHS)

Alcoholism and Substance-abuse Programs:
   NATIONAL ASSOCIATION OF BROADCASTERS
      (NAB) abuse programs

NAVY DRUG AND ALCOHOL ABUSE TREATMENT
    PROGRAM
Phoenix House
SPORTS DRUG AWARENESS PROGRAM
Women's Sports Foundation drug-use pro-
    gram

Academy of TV Arts and Sciences antidrug program   The academy has a program designed to educate its members about the danger of media glamorization and tolerance of illicit drug use. In coordination with other media efforts to deglamorize drugs, this group is committed to ending favorable or tolerant pictures of illicit drug use on television.

accidents

Alcohol and other drugs: The role drugs play in the causes of accidents is receiving increased attention today. Accidents, whether at home, in public places or on the job, usually result from one or more of the following: inhibited coordination; mental confusion; lengthened reaction time; decreased motor performance and sensory skills; or impairment of judgment, including paranoia, risk-taking behavior or ideas of grandiosity. Occupational accidents affect a significant portion of the working population. Although many types of drugs are used during working hours, of principal concern are alcohol, cocaine, amphetamines and marijuana. Between 1975 and 1985, some 50 RAILROAD ACCIDENTS were attributed to drug or alcohol-impaired workers. In those accidents, 37 people were killed, 80 injured and more than $34 million worth of property was destroyed. Since November 1988, the U.S. Department of Transportation has mandated random drug tests for the nation's 4 million private transportation workers, including airline pilots and navigators, interstate truckers, bus drivers, and railroad engineers and conductors. In postaccident testing of railroad employees in 1990, 3.2% tested positive for alcohol or other prohibited drugs. A study by the Firestone Tire and Rubber Company suggested that plant accidents were 3.6 times as likely to occur when an employee was under the influence of a drug. The study also revealed that drug users were five times as likely to file a worker's compensation claim and 2.5 times as likely to be absent longer than a week. Drug users also received three times the level of sick benefits as those who did not use drugs, and they tended to be

repeatedly involved in grievance procedures. Compared to other employees, they were estimated to function at approximately 67% of their work potential. Another major accident category is drug-related motor vehicle accidents. In 1995 CSAP (Center for Substance Abuse Prevention) estimated that alcohol and other substances were a factor in 45.1% of all fatal automobile crashes and one-fifth of all crashes involving injury. (See DRIVING WHILE IMPAIRED (DWI), MOTORCYCLE ACCIDENTS and BICYCLE ACCIDENTS.)

A significant number of accidents also occur in the home. Falls account for the majority of drug-related accidents, both at home and in public places. A 1983 study of accidental FALLS found that almost 60% of those injured had been drinking. There are no comparable figures for falls related to other drugs, or for the combination of drugs and alcohol, but because many drugs alter coordination it can be assumed that statistics would be equally high.

The use of drugs appears to be strongly involved in fires and burns. Compared to the general population, alcoholics have been found to be 10 times more likely to die in a fire. Alcohol lowers oxidation in the cells, which also increases the risk of being overcome by smoke inhalation. As alcohol is a sedative drug, it follows that other sedative drugs may have the same effect. The involvement of alcoholics and drug addicts in cigarette-related fires is three times that of fires resulting from other causes.

Although alcohol has not been directly implicated in U.S. commercial airline crashes, estimates of alcohol involvement by pilots in general aviation crashes range from 10% to 15%. In a report by the National Institute on Alcohol Abuse and Alcoholism (NIAAA), the Coast Guard estimates alcohol as being a factor in 60% of all BOATING fatalities. Drug use is also reported to play a significant role in death by drowning. Such accidents are probably the result of poor judgment, faulty coordination and confusion. In the case of alcohol and other central nervous system depressants, swallowing and breathing reflexes may also be impaired, which can make a potentially normal situation life-threatening. Another complication involving "risk-taking behavior" is that due to a depressant's "warming effect" one may stay in cold water for too long a time. This can lead to hypothermia, which can be fatal.

Alcohol: Alcohol was a contributing factor in at least 15,000 fatalities and 6 million nonfatal injuries in nonhighway settings alone, according to the NIAAA. In 1987, 30,205 Americans died from alcohol-related accidents. In a national survey of trauma centers, two-thirds of the centers estimated that the majority of their patients would test positive for alcohol intoxication at the time of their arrival. Alcohol-related injuries cost an estimated $47 billion annually and account for over 40% of medical costs in the U.S. Experiments have demonstrated that alcohol intoxication can alter a normal person's performance up to 18 hours after ingestion, and the use of alcohol prior to and during the workday is widespread. Skills begin to decline at BLOOD ALCOHOL CONCENTRATIONS as low as 0.05%. A study of railroad workers by T. A. Mannello and F. J. Seaman estimated that 30,000 workers drank on duty during one year. Alcohol-related industrial accidents may be lower than expected because of a high rate of absenteeism among those who drink heavily. Alcohol-related problems, including accidents, reduced productivity, and lost production due to absenteeism cost American industry $54.7 billion in 1987. In 1995, the federal government estimated that the annual economic cost of harmful use of, and dependence on, alcohol and other drugs was $237.5 billion: $34 billion for medical and treatment costs; $133.4 billion related to illness, injury and death; $57.2 billion for costs related to crime; and $12.9 billion for other costs. Industry has responded by sponsoring the vast number of EMPLOYEE ASSISTANCE PROGRAMS available.

Marijuana: Being under the influence of marijuana may impair the user as much as alcohol intoxication and particularly impairs spatial perception. Ability to judge distances is markedly disturbed and short-term memory is impaired. Serious skill impairment can be measured for hours after a single marijuana joint has been consumed. There is also a decline in psychomotor activities, such as hand steadiness, reaction time and attentiveness. These effects become particularly significant when an employee is operating a motor vehicle or a complex industrial machine.

Cocaine: For some time now cocaine has been a commonplace on-the-job drug, particularly in fast-paced fields, such as the stock market, where pressure and expectations are high, producing stress and feelings of insecurity on the part of employees. Although the action of cocaine is brief, many workers use it because it provides a feeling of competence and they believe it speeds up the thought process. However, tests have shown that even small amounts of cocaine snorted or smoked can disturb judgment and coordination.

Amphetamines: Commonly used because of their stimulant effects by employees who work long hours (particularly night shifts) and by truck drivers on long cross-country trips, amphetamines relieve sleepiness and fatigue. Adverse reactions can result in accidents, and even moderate doses can produce tremors of the limbs, blurred vision, impaired coordination and extreme mood swings.

Although the problem of drug-related accidents is unquestionable, it often does not receive the attention it deserves. Further study is needed to promote public awareness of the costs involved to personal life, property and industry.

Omnibus Transportation Employee Testing Act of 1991, U.S. Code, vol. 49 (part 40, updated, "Chemical Testing").

acetaldehyde The first step in the METABOLISM of alcohol results in its conversion to acetaldehyde. Acetaldehyde is even more toxic to the body than ethyl alcohol, although in the second step of metabolism acetaldehyde is converted into acetate, most of which is oxidized to carbon dioxide by the MITOCHONDRIA. Nevertheless, some escapes into the bloodstream, especially at high levels of consumption, and is thought to play a central role in the toxicity of alcohol. Alcoholics have been found to have significantly higher levels of acetaldehyde in the blood than nonalcoholics, even when both groups received the same amounts of alcohol and the BLOOD ALCOHOL CONCENTRATION (BAC) of both was the same. Apparently, alcoholics metabolize acetaldehyde less effectively, probably because of LIVER damage caused by excessive consumption of alcohol. Dr. Charles Lieber of the Mount Sinai School of Medicine in New York postulates that the alcoholic may be the victim of a vicious circle: mitochondrial function in the liver is impaired by acetaldehyde, which leads to diminished acetaldehyde metabolism, an accumulation of acetaldehyde and, consequently, further liver damage.

Acetaldehyde has been shown to affect the HEART muscle adversely and may affect other muscles as well. It may also be a contributing factor in ADDICTION to alcohol, by combining with amine neurotransmitters in the brain, which send nerve impulses from one cell to another, to form psychoactive compounds similar to certain morphine derivatives that are known for their ability to promote DEPENDENCE. This theory has yet to be confirmed.

Acetaldehyde also plays an important part in ANT-ABUSE (disulfiram) reactions. Normally, acetaldehyde, produced as a result of the initial oxidation of ethanol by the alcohol dehydrogenase of the liver, does not accumulate in the tissues because it is oxidized almost as soon as it is formed, most likely primarily by the enzyme aldehyde dehydrogenase. In the presence of disulfiram, however, the concentration of acetaldehyde rises because disulfiram seems to compete with NAD (cofactor nicotinamide adenine dinucleotide) for the active centers of the enzyme aldehyde dehydrogenase and thereby reduces the rate of oxidation of the aldehyde. When someone taking Antabuse consumes alcohol, his or her blood acetaldehyde concentrations increase five to 10 times higher than normal, resulting in a toxic reaction. The degree of intensity of the reaction depends on the concentration of disulfiram in the body, the quantity of alcohol ingested and the patient's degree of sensitivity to acetaldehyde. The consumption of only 7 mg of alcohol (0.24 oz) has produced a mild reaction in some people, and even such products as rubbing alcohol have caused reactions. The Antabuse reaction is sometimes referred to as the acetaldehyde syndrome.

Charles S. Lieber, "The Metabolism of Alcohol," *Scientific American* 234, no. 3 (March 1976): 25–33.
J. M. Ritchie, "The Aliphatic Alcohols," in L. S. Goodman and A. Gilman, *The Pharmacological Basis of Therapeutics,* 5th ed. (New York: Macmillan, 1975): 148–149.

acetone   A solvent, commonly found in plastic cements and nail polish removers, which may have euphoric effects when inhaled. Acetone is a volatile hydrocarbon.

acetylcholine   The neurotransmitter of cholinergic pathways in the parasympathetic portion of the peripheral autonomic nervous system. Dysfunction of cholinergic neurotransmission may play a role in Alzheimer's disease. Ethanol inhibits acetylcholine release, suggesting that the cholinergic system plays a role in alcohol-induced cognitive impairment.

Ackoff's model   Ackoff's model describes a method for selecting the best solution to an "evaluative" problem (such as that of placing patients in treatment) where there are alternate courses of action. Using Ackoff's model, "uncertainty conditions" of assigning patients to the most effective treatment facilities are evaluated as "risk conditions," in which the probable outcome of treatment can be assessed for specific types of patients.

acne rosacea   From the Greek *achne* (efflorescence) via New Latin + the New Latin *rosacea* (rosy, reddish). A facial skin condition usually characterized by a flushed appearance and often accompanied by puffiness and a "spider-web" effect of broken capillaries, particularly on and around the nose. Excessive consumption of alcohol over a long period of time is a frequent cause of acne rosacea. (See RHINOPHYMA.)

action therapies   Treatment designed to facilitate changes in behavior, perception or feelings. This therapy neither attempts to resolve intrapsychic conflicts, nor depends on insight to bring about the desired change. Cognitive-behavioral therapy and reality therapy are two currently popular action therapies effective with chemically dependent people. These modalities enjoy popularity because they are: (1) congruent with the beliefs of practitioners of 12-step recovery programs and (2) considered more cost-effective and so fit in with the current trend toward managed mental health care.

acupuncture   Although its origins are lost in antiquity, acupuncture has been a traditional Chinese medical treatment for over 3,000 years. In recent years it has gained popularity in the U.S. and other countries around the world. Rooted in Eastern philosophy, acupuncture is a complex system of medicine that involves *ch'i,* the vital life source or energy that is believed to flow through specific pathways in the human body. If the flow of *ch'i* is blocked or impeded, an imbalance—a surplus or deficit—can occur in an organ or area of the body and result in pain or disease. Once the nature of the imbalance is identified using a variety of diagnostic techniques, the appropriate acupuncture points on the body are stimulated by the insertion of very fine, solid needles. Moxibustion (heating with mugwort), a traditional Chinese herb, or acupressure (massage), are closely related techniques. Additionally, modern technology has contributed some new methods to the ancient practice of acupuncture, including electrical stimulation of the needles, ultrasound and laser beam stimulation.

No single explanation of the phenomenon of acupuncture is presently accepted, but the treatment is effective in most cases, particularly among patients suffering from chronic pain. However, despite overwhelming reports of its effectiveness, and its 3,000-year-plus trial period, the Food and Drug Administration and the American Medical Association still consider acupuncture to be an "experimental" treatment and research on its efficacy is only recently appearing in western scientific literature.

Acupuncture is currently used in several major treatment centers in New York City and elsewhere to facilitate withdrawal from stimulants and narcotics and as a longer-term treatment for detoxified (drug-free) individuals to help maintain abstinence from all classes of drugs including alcohol. (See Dr. Michael SMITH.) Many patients, physicians and other health professionals feel it to be an effective treatment. Acupuncture and its related therapies are relatively painless, inexpensive compared to standard western drug therapies, and virtually no dangers or negative side effects have thus far been demonstrated.

acute   The term used to describe a condition that quickly develops into a crisis, as opposed to a CHRONIC condition or disease characterized by slowly progressing symptoms. Acute conditions are usually brief, self-limiting and reversible.

acute addiction   Because addiction is usually considered a CHRONIC disease, this term is ambiguous. It could refer to intoxication, poisoning or temporary disturbances caused by excessive short-term drug use.

acute alcohol intoxication   Severe alcohol intoxication or poisoning. The term is also used to refer to a circumscribed episode of alcohol intoxication as distinct from a chronic or prolonged state of intoxication.

acute alcoholic state   A physical or mental disorder in an alcoholic associated with and which imme-

diately follows a prolonged bout of drinking. This condition can take such forms as acute KORSAKOFF'S PSYCHOSIS or DELIRIUM TREMENS. The term "acute alcoholic state" is also used, more generally, to refer to alcohol intoxication.

acute alcoholism   This term may refer to alcohol intoxication or poisoning, or to a temporary disturbance caused by excessive drinking. Because alcoholism is generally recognized as a CHRONIC disease, the term is considered ambiguous and is thus seldom used.

acute intoxication   A term used to refer to severe short-term intoxication or poisoning that results from a defined episode of intoxication, as distinct from a prolonged or chronic state of intoxication.

adaptive cell metabolism   Tissue cells may adapt to drug or alcohol exposure by requiring increasing amounts for the user to experience the same effect. This condition is called TOLERANCE. If this adaptation results in the cells requiring the presence of the drug to function normally, then DEPENDENCE has developed. When the drug is no longer supplied, the disturbance in normal cell function causes symptoms (illness) called WITHDRAWAL.

addiction   The use of the term "addiction" has changed over the years, and today there is considerable variation in (and often confusion about) its usage. In the early 20th century, the term "drug addiction" simply referred to the illicit use of drugs, without distinction between differing patterns of use and effects. Beginning in 1931, a distinction was made between drug HABITUATION and drug addiction. Drug addiction came to mean physical dependence on the effects of a drug, with illness or WITHDRAWAL occurring if the intake of the drug was severely reduced or completely stopped. Habituation came to mean a psychological dependence on a drug after a period of repeated use; withdrawal therefrom might involve emotional distress but not physiological illness.

In 1957 the Expert Committee on Addiction-Producing Drugs of the World Health Organization (WHO) defined drug addiction as:

A state of periodic or chronic intoxication, detrimental to the individual and society, produced by the repeated consumption of a drug (natural or synthetic). Its characteristics include: (1) An over-powering desire or need (compulsion) to continue taking the drug and to obtain it by any means; (2) A tendency to increase the dose; (3) A psychic (psychological) and generally a physical dependence on the effects of the drug.

Drug habituation was defined as:

A condition resulting from the repeated consumption of a drug. Its characteristics include: (1) A desire (but not a compulsion) to continue taking the drug for the sense of improved well-being it engenders; (2) Little or no tendency to increase the dose; (3) Some degree of psychic dependence on the effect of the drug, but absence of physical dependence and hence of an abstinence syndrome; (4) Detrimental effects, if any, primarily on the individual.

The definitions did not resolve the confusion surrounding these terms; for example, someone who ingested a large quantity of a stimulant drug might assault others, contradicting the fourth part of the definition of habituation. The words "addicted," "addiction" and "addict" were used benignly, as in "He's addicted to jazz," and pejoratively, as in "He's been addicted to drugs for years."

In 1965 the World Health Organization (WHO) abandoned these terms and adopted the more neutral term "drug-dependence." This term was defined in a very general way:

A state, psychic and sometimes also physical, resulting from the interaction between a living organism and a drug, characterized by behavioral and other responses that always include a compulsion to take the drug on a continuous or periodic basis in order to experience its psychic effects, and sometimes to avoid the discomfort of its absence. Tolerance may or may not be present. A person may be dependent on more than one drug.

Still used frequently today, the term "addiction" is generally employed to refer to a known physical dependence on the effects of a drug. E. M. JELLINEK (1890–1963) used the following terms in describing an addiction to alcohol: an increased tissue TOLERANCE, ADAPTIVE CELL METABOLISM, CRAVING, and LOSS OF CONTROL or INABILITY TO ABSTAIN.

However, physical dependence (the adaptive consequences of taking certain chemicals repeat-

edly) is clearly not the only aspect of addiction. As Dr. Vincent P. Dole has pointed out, physical dependence does not explain the drug-seeking behavior characteristic of addiction. People may be physically dependent on drugs without being addicted to them. For example, drugs prescribed for medicinal purposes, such as steroids, can cause physical dependence without the concurrent desire for the substance. When intake is optional, most users stop or reduce consumption. On the other hand, users who have been freed of their dependence through DETOXIFICATION still have a high risk of relapse. Unfortunately, definitions that include some concept of psychological dependence are unable to explain such behavior.

Dole, who has worked extensively as a physician, an administrator in the methadone program in New York, and in addiction research, found that former heroin users stabilized on methadone do not have the pleasure-seeking, reality-escaping traits generally associated with users. Users with a history of two or more years of addiction to heroin seem to be quite willing to sacrifice the occasional euphoria produced by the drug for a continued feeling of normality. For Dole, this finding suggested that the addictive behavior of chronic narcotics users stems less from pleasure seeking than from a need to relieve a recurring discomfort, also called NEGATIVE REINFORCEMENT. The same need may also be true for people who are unable to stop smoking or using to excess any drug, including alcohol.

Vincent P. Dole, "Addictive Behavior," *Scientific American* 243, no. 6 (December 1980): 138–154.

Frederick G. Hofmann, *A Handbook on Drug and Alcohol Abuse: The Biomedical Aspects* (New York: Oxford University Press, 1975): 21–27.

Jerome Jaffe, Robert Petersen and Ray Hodgson, *Addictions: Issues and Answers* (London: Harper & Row, 1980): 7–9.

E. M. Jellinek, *The Disease Concept of Alcoholism* (New Jersey: Hillhouse, 1979): 69–77.

A. L. Tatum and M. H. Seevers, "Theories of Drug Addiction," *The Physiological Review* 11 (1931): 187.

addiction medicine   The branch of medicine dealing with alcohol- and drug-related problems.

Addiction Research Foundation   A not-for-profit Canadian organization involved in drug-abuse prevention and research. The foundation has made notable contributions in the field and produces numerous publications, journals, newsletters, films and other audiovisual materials.

additive effect   The action attained when the combined effect of two drugs taken together is the sum of their two separate effects. (See SYNERGY and POTENTIATION.)

Adipex-P   An anorectic that contains 37.5 mg of phentermine hydrochloride, it is used for weight control. Because its activity is similar to that of AMPHETAMINES, Adipex-P has a high potential for harmful use and tolerance can develop within weeks. The user may become psychologically dependent and socially dysfunctional. An overdose can result in restlessness, tremors, rapid respiration, confusion and hallucinations.

adjustment disorder   According to the *Substance Abuse and Mental Health Statistic Sourcebook,* adjustment disorders are characterized by an inappropriate or maladaptive reaction that occurs within three months of the onset of one or more identifiable psychosocial stressors. Such stressors include family problems, divorce, career difficulties or other crises. The symptoms are in excess of a normal and expected reaction to the stressor and may impair social or occupational functioning.

People experiencing adjustment disorders are particularly vulnerable to excessive use of alcohol and other mood-altering drugs.

administration   There are various methods of administering a drug, each with advantages and disadvantages. A drug user's choice of method may involve such factors as time of onset, maximum potency and duration of effects. For example, an injected substance will have the quickest onset and usually give maximum potency, but if orally administered it will have longer-lasting effects. The main categories of drug administration are: (1) oral, which includes eating (swallowing), smoking (breathing) and sublingual ingestion (dissolving under the tongue); (2) parenteral or hypodermic injection (intravenously, intramuscularly and subcutaneously); (3) nasal inhalation, which includes spraying and snorting (sniffing); and (4) rectal (suppositories).

Other methods are sometimes tried but are generally not effective or have adverse reactions.

To exert effects on the body, a drug must be absorbed into the bloodstream and then carried to the CENTRAL NERVOUS SYSTEM (CNS). Absorption points in the body are the lungs, the gastrointestinal tract (the stomach and intestines), mucous membranes found at natural openings of the body, and the bloodstream itself.

Oral administration: Oral administration is the most common method of ingestion, whether it involves swallowing a pill, drinking a beverage, placing the substance under the tongue and letting it dissolve (sublingual), or smoking. Swallowed substances are absorbed by the gastrointestinal tract. Alcohol is largely absorbed by the stomach, while other drugs may be absorbed by the intestines. When dissolved under the tongue and absorbed by the mucous membranes, absorption time is unpredictable. When smoked and absorbed by the lungs (a method that produces faster onset of effects than absorption by the gastrointestinal tract or even injection), a portion of the drug is lost through the smoke. Tobacco and marijuana are the most commonly smoked drugs, but opium, heroin, crack cocaine, "ice" (street name for crystallized methamphetamine), DMT, DET, hashish and various herbs can also be smoked. DMT and DET (and many other substances) can be sprinkled on tobacco or marijuana in very small quantities and then smoked. The most common method of smoking is to roll the product in a cigarette paper (rolling paper) or to use a pipe or a water pipe, which cools the smoke and makes it less harsh. Some drugs, such as LSD, cannot be smoked because heat breaks down the chemical ingredients therein.

Oral administration will generally produce longer-lasting effects than either injection or smoking, but the effects are less potent and a longer onset period is required. Drugs such as cocaine cannot be taken orally, as they are not soluble in stomach fluids or they are partially metabolized by digestive juices. Oral administration can cause adverse reactions such as vomiting, but this reaction may also be beneficial if it rids the body of a toxic overdose.

Parenteral administration: This method produces a relatively quick onset of effects and more complete delivery than is possible by smoking. However, the effects do not last as long as those of a drug administered orally, and parenteral administration can have complications.

The three methods for parenterally administering a drug are: intravenous injection into a vein, intramuscular injection into a muscle (usually the upper arm or buttocks), and subcutaneous injection (also known as SKINNING, SKIN POPPING) under the skin. Injecting a drug into an artery can be particularly dangerous and should never be attempted because it may cause severe damage to the area. Whereas a drug injected into a vein is delivered from the tissue to the heart, a drug injected into an artery delivers the blood from the heart directly to an individual tissue mass—a foot or a hand, for example—where there is the possibility of centralized damage, which can cause gangrene, abscesses or visible tissue poisoning.

The greatest danger of hypodermic administration is infection from germs present on the skin, on the needle or in the substance itself. TETANUS is generally associated with subcutaneous injection because the anaerobic bacteria have low oxygen tissue—the fat cells—to grow in. AIDS and HEPATITIS are most often associated with accidental intravenous injection of a virus from a contaminated needle. Users tend to share needles, and in some cases they rent them out to raise money with which to buy more drugs. Users are often so preoccupied with getting their "fix" that little time or thought is given to sterilizing their equipment.

Heroin is the most common illegal drug administered by injection, although cocaine and some psychedelics are also administered hypodermically. A user can never be sure what additives have been put in his purchased heroin, as the drug is rarely in pure form and usually has been diluted many times and handled by several people. (See CUTTING.) Bacteria and viruses found in diluted heroin, which might easily be destroyed by stomach enzymes if the administration is oral, become dangerous when injected into the bloodstream. Heroin is often diluted with quinine or various sugars, such as lactose. In large amounts, quinine can cause blindness and can affect the central nervous system, the heart and the kidneys. Certain tablets (Ritalin, for example) have a talcum powder base that is not soluble in water and therefore can block small blood vessels in the lungs, causing fibrosis.

The differing methods of injection have a variety of effects. Intravenous injection produces the quickest onset of effects using the least amount of the drug because it is injected directly into the vein. Cocaine, amphetamines and heroin are poorly absorbed from intramuscular injections and can cause painful abscesses. Cocaine and amphetamines have poor subcutaneous absorption. Heroin can be absorbed subcutaneously but the rapid onset (RUSH) prized by many users will be lost and more heroin will be required than for an intravenous injection.

Some users are addicted as much to the act of injecting as they are to the drug itself; they may administer a drug in several small injections just for the joy of injecting. This type of needle freak may even resort to injecting plain water, sugar water or any liquid available.

Other dangers of frequent parenteral administration include collapsed, infected veins (phlebitis), endocarditis and other infections. Abscesses are common in subcutaneous injection.

Nasal administration: A substance will effectively enter the bloodstream by absorption through the small blood vessels located in the mucous membranes of the nose. Cocaine, heroin, PCP and many hallucinogens can be snorted. Frequent snorting, which is the most common method of using cocaine, frequently results in irritation of the membranes; heavy use may erode membranes and, ultimately, cause deterioration of the nasal cartilage of the septum, resulting in the need for surgery. Because cocaine acts as an anesthetic, a chronic user may not be aware of the amount of damage being done. The effects of snorting cocaine are felt within five minutes and may last from 10 to 30 minutes. The most common methods of nasal administration are by snorting through a straw (or a rolled paper, bill or matchbook), or by using a coke spoon (similar to a small salts spoon). One nostril is held closed with the finger and the cocaine is sniffed strongly through the open nostril. The process is then repeated with the other nostril. A numbing sensation is experienced as well as a sharp chemical smell and taste similar to other anesthetics such as novacaine. Depending on the purity and the adulterants added to the coke, a stinging sensation may also be experienced, followed by a rush.

Volatile substances inhaled for their intoxicating effects are also administered nasally by inhalation and are absorbed by the lungs. These include organic solvents (petroleum derivatives) and vaporous anesthetics such as chloroform, ether and nitrous oxide. The practice of placing a plastic bag over the head to enhance the effects has proved to be fatal on occasions, more often by suffocation rather than the effects of the drug. Effects of INHALATION usually last about five minutes. Frequent inhaling of volatile solvents can cause brain, heart and kidney damage.

Rectal administration: Enemas and suppositories (semisolid substances that contain a drug) are administered rectally (inserted into the anus). The drug is absorbed by the mucous membranes of the rectum. Illicit drug users rarely use this method of administration; it is used primarily by doctors on patients who are unconscious or cannot swallow.

Topical administration: Illegal drugs are rarely administered topically (placed on or rubbed into the skin) and this method is usually ineffective, although people who handle LSD have encountered accidental absorption. Blue stars, which are LSD-laced tattoos often marketed to children, are administered topically.

Effect on abuse potential: Some experts believe that the more socially acceptable (less "deviant") the method of administration, the more likely it is that a person will initiate use of a substance. Smoking (tobacco) and oral administration (alcohol, medications) are culturally accepted modes of administration, while snorting and, finally, injecting represent progressively more "deviant," or less socially acceptable, modes. While this hypothesis remains unproven, the increase in cocaine use when smokable crack cocaine became available and the fact that heroin users almost invariably begin by snorting and progress to injecting offers some support.

adolescents   Of all the age groups susceptible to harmful use of drugs in the U.S., adolescents are the most vulnerable. However, it is misleading to speak of adolescents as if they were all the same age. Adolescence is the period of development marked at the beginning by the onset of puberty and at the end by the attainment of physiological and/or psychological maturity. It should be noted that the term is not actually specific since both the onset of puberty and the precise attainment of maturity are effectively impossible to specify.

Tips for Teens: About Alcohol

1994, New York State Office of Alcoholism and Substance Abuse Services

People who are shy in social situations and turn to alcohol to loosen up frequently end up making fools of themselves and doing things they regret!

How Do I Know If I Have a Drinking Problem?

Chances are if you're even asking the question, you have a drinking problem. But here are some other factors:

Inability to control your drinking—it seems that regardless of what you decide beforehand, you frequently wind up drunk

Using alcohol to escape your problems

Changing from your usual reserved character into the "life of the party"

Change in personality—does drinking turn you from Dr. Jekyl to Mr. Hyde?

A high tolerance level—you can drink just about everybody under the table

Blackouts—sometimes you don't remember what happened when you were drinking

Problems at work or in school as a result of drinking

Concern shown by your family and friends about your drinking

If You Suspect a Friend Has a Drinking Problem:

Don't be judgmental or preachy—remember, alcoholism is a disease

Be willing to listen

Voice your concern about your friend's drinking—but don't ever do it when your friend is under the influence!

Offer your help—go to an AA meeting with your friend or offer to get him/her educational materials

Be encouraging and positive if your friend takes some initiative

---

New York State Office of Alcoholism and Substance Abuse Services, *Tips for Teens: About Alcohol* (Albany, N.Y.: New York State Office of Alcoholism and Substance Abuse Services, 1994).

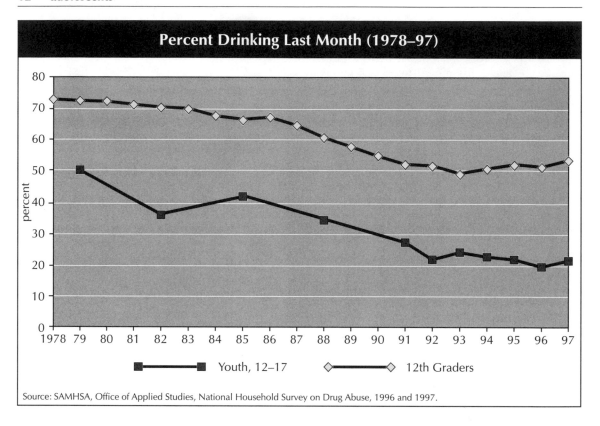

Percent Drinking Last Month (1978–97)

Source: SAMHSA, Office of Applied Studies, National Household Survey on Drug Abuse, 1996 and 1997.

Alcohol: Alcohol is the drug most widely used and abused by American teenagers. The rate of alcohol use by young people remained relatively stable but unacceptably high in the 1990s. NIDA surveys indicate that over 90% of 8th, 10th and 12th graders throughout the 1980s and 1990s have used alcohol to some extent. In 1995, 15% , 24% and 30% of 8th, 10th and 12th graders, respectively, reported having had five or more drinks on a single occasion at least once in a two week period. About 2.9% of teenagers drank on a daily basis.

Those who go on to become habitual consumers of alcohol usually start drinking before graduating from high school, even though state laws prohibit the sale or serving of alcoholic beverages to minors. Most teenagers have their first drink at age 13 or 14.

Youths and young adults cannot be judged by the same standards as adults, regarding drinking. Although alcohol-related diseases and other consequences of chronic heavy drinking are rare in young

drinkers, a substantial number of adolescents can be characterized as "problem-drinkers."

Drinking and driving: Particularly troubling is the high rate of alcohol-related automobile fatalities among young divers. Alcohol-impaired adolescent drivers usually have significantly lower BLOOD ALCOHOL CONCENTRATIONS (BAC) than adults involved in such accidents, suggesting that they are at greater risk due to both their inexperience at driving and their low tolerance for alcohol. (See MINIMUM DRINKING AGE.)

Drugs other than alcohol: Of the 10,000 emergency room visits related to marijuana in 1980, the majority of cases involved youths. A 1981 nationwide government survey showed that one out of 14 high school seniors smoked marijuana daily and in some communities adolescents who had not tried marijuana may have been in the minority. In a report published by the National Institute on Drug Abuse

Monitoring the Future Study: Drug Use among 8th-, 10th-, and 12th-Graders

HHS Press Release on Monitoring the Future Study *1997, U.S. Department of Health and Human Services*

Illicit Drug Use

Overall in 1997, 54.3% of high school seniors said they had used an illicit drug at least once in their lifetime, while 47.3% of 10th graders, and 29.4% of eighth graders said they have used an illicit drug at least once.

Marijuana: Marijuana remains the most widely used drug among adolescents. The percentage of 10th and 12th grade students who had tried marijuana at least once in their lifetime increased from 1996 to 1997. This may be affected by the fact that 12th graders in 1997 were 8th graders in 1993 and 10th graders in 1995, a time when marijuana use was increasing annually among seniors and students in the lower grades.

The percentage of students who used marijuana in the past year and past month remained unchanged for students in all three grades. However, daily marijuana use by 8th graders decreased from 1.5% in 1996 to 1.1% in 1997, and daily use among seniors increased from 4.9% in 1996 to 5.8% in 1997. The decrease in marijuana use among 8th graders is the first found by this survey for any age group since 1992.

Cocaine: Rates of cocaine use remained level for 8th and 10th grade students. Among 12th graders, however, lifetime use of cocaine in all forms increased. The percentage of seniors who had used cocaine at least once increased from 7.1% in 1996 to 8.7% in 1997, the highest rates reported since 1990.

Heroin: Past year use of heroin among 8th graders decreased from 1.6% in 1996 to 1.3% in 1997. In 1997, 2.1% of 8th, 10th and 12th graders report having used heroin at least once in their lifetime.

Stimulants: There was no change in the percentage of 8th, 10th, or 12th graders who have tried stimulants at least once. In 1997, 12.3% of 8th graders, 17.0% of 10th graders, and 16.5% of 12th graders used stimulants at least once in their lifetime. Stimulant use in the past month increased among 12th graders, but use of these drugs in the past year and in the past month decreased among 8th graders.

Cigarettes: The percentage of 8th graders reporting heavy cigarette smoking decreased between 1996 and 1997. Daily smoking in the past 30 days decreased from 10.4 to 9.0% and 8th graders smoking a half-pack or more cigarettes per day decreased from 4.3% to 3.5%. Use of cigarettes in the past month by 12th graders, however, increased from 34.0% to 36.5%. Daily cigarette use among seniors increased to 24.6%, its highest level since 1979.

Alcohol: Although rates remained mostly stable, alcohol use remains a problem among adolescents. On the positive side, the percentage of 8th graders reporting having been drunk in the past 30 days decreased from 9.6% in 1996 to 8.2% in 1997. However, the percentage of 10th graders reporting having been drunk daily increased from 0.4% in 1996 to 0.6.% in 1997. Among 12th graders, past year use of alcohol increased from 72.5% in 1996 to 74.8% in 1997. Lifetime use also increased among seniors

Students' Attitudes and Perceptions About Drug Use

The 1997 survey found that, for most drugs, adolescents' perception of the perceived risk of harm from drug use remained stable. The few exceptions include an increase in the percentage of 8th graders saying there is great risk in having five or more drinks once or twice each weekend (heavy drinking), increasing from 51.8% in 1996 to 55.6 percent in 1997, and an increase in the percentage of seniors saying there is great risk in trying heroin once or twice (52.5% in 1996 to 56.7% in 1997).

Moving in the wrong direction, however, are attitudes about drinking among 12th graders, specifically a decrease in the percentage of seniors saying there is a great risk in heavy drinking (49.5% in 1996 to 43.0% in 1997). In addition, the percentage of 8th graders saying there is great risk in trying marijuana once or twice decreased from 27.9% in 1996 to 25.3% in 1997 and the percentage of seniors saying there is great risk in taking barbiturates regularly decreased.

Disapproval of others' occasional or regular use of marijuana increased among 8th graders. There was also an increase in the percentage of 8th graders saying they disapprove of people who engage in heavy drinking including those who take one or two drinks nearly every day or have five or more drinks once or twice each weekend. Rates for the percentage of 8th and 10th graders saying they disapprove of people who smoke one or more packs of cigarettes per day increased. The percentage of 8th graders saying they disapprove of people who take cocaine powder occasionally and use smokeless tobacco regularly also increased.

Source: Department of Health and Human Services, *Monitoring the Future Study: Drug Use among 8th-, 10th-, and 12th-Graders,* 1997 HHS Fact Sheet (Washington, D.C.: U.S. Department of Health and Human Services, 1998).

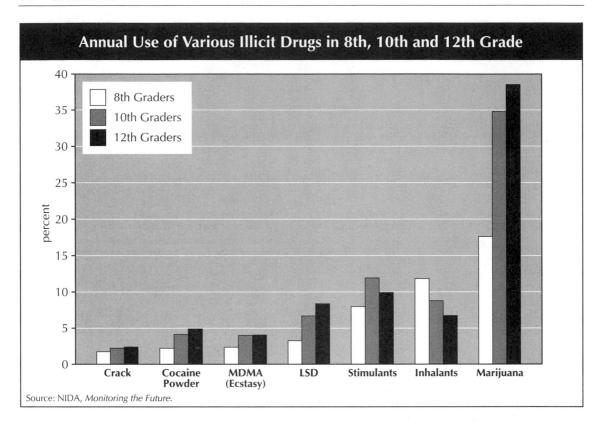

Annual Use of Various Illicit Drugs in 8th, 10th and 12th Grade

Source: NIDA, *Monitoring the Future.*

(NIDA), *Illicit drug use, smoking, and drinking by America's high school students, college students and young adults: 1975–1987,* key findings indicated that the use of many illicit drugs had declined from the peak levels of the 1970s. (The "young adults" category includes people from one to four years beyond high school but not in college.) However, NIDA's 1997 report, *Monitoring the Future Study,* on national high school drug use, indicated that illicit drug use has increased once again in the mid-1990s, among high school age youths in particular.

In the mid- to late-1970s, the NIDA survey found increasing drug use, especially marijuana use, among high school seniors. In 1978 nearly 11% of high school seniors had smoked marijuana on a daily basis; almost a decade later, in 1987, only 3.3% were daily users.

The illicit use of stimulants and sedatives had also declined among high school seniors, college students and young adults in the mid-1980s. In 1986 current use (use in the 30 days prior to the survey)

of stimulants among high school seniors was at 5.5% and dropped to 5.2% in 1987. NIDA survey data of 1986 and 1987 showed a significant drop in the use of cocaine, finding a decrease of about one-third (from 6.2% in 1986 to 4.3% in 1987) of seniors who were current users of cocaine, and a decline of about one-fifth (from 12.7% to 10.3%) of seniors who had used cocaine at least once in the past year. The downturn in cocaine use was similar for college students and young adults. The data on CRACK CO-CAINE suggested that there was also a decline in use. Among seniors in 1987, 5.6% reported having tried crack, while 4% said they used it in the past year.

Between 1991 and 1997, use of any illicit drug in the 12 months prior to the NIDA survey doubled for 8th graders (from 11% to 22.1%); almost doubled for 10th graders (from 20% to 38.5%); and rose by more than half for 12th graders (from 27% to 42%). Marijuana use in particular showed a significant increase in 1997. Between 1991 and 1997, marijuana use by 8th graders rose from 6% to 18%; among 10th grad-

Action Steps for Youth

NIDA Notes, *National Institute on Drug Abuse*

Get media wise. Discuss and analyze popular movies, music videos and television shows that promote and glamorize marijuana and other drugs. Contact the National Clearinghouse for Alcohol and Drug Information (NCADI) at 800-729-6686 for information about media literacy resources for youth. Talk with parents and other trusted adults about these issues.

Get the facts about marijuana and other drugs. Call your local health department, city or county substance abuse agency or information clearinghouses such as NCADI, to get information about marijuana and other drugs. Ask librarians to help you get answers to your questions. Order materials for yourself, friends, parents and adults, and for distribution to clubs and groups.

Speak out on youth issues about drugs. Make it a point to listen to and call in to radio stations with talk programs that discuss issues about drugs and related problems among youth. Throw your two cents in the barrel.

Influence the airwaves. Call local radio stations and talk with the station manager if you object to the music being played. As a consumer, your opinion can make a difference.

Raise community awareness. Bring information to the attention of parents, adults and community leaders about problems faced by youth in the community, e.g., the convenience store that sells drugs and/or allows underage youth to buy alcohol. Adults need to know about what youth face on a day-to-day basis so they can rally to your support.

Promote drug-free youth. Celebrate and acknowledge the drug-free lifestyle most youth already practice. Take your positive stories to newspapers, radio and TV stations, religious organizations and other groups.

Develop teen spokespersons. Organize a teen speakers bureau. Many adult groups and organizations are interested in involving youth in community prevention programs to help them develop programs that work.

Tap into the creative interests of youth. Solicit the involvement of teens who are into the arts—dancers, actors, musicians, writers and others—to help develop messages, slogans, posters, songs, print ads, T-shirts, buttons, speeches and articles that promote and address the benefits of non-use of marijuana and other drugs.

Create positive peer pressure. Do not engage in any illegal marijuana or other drug-use practices. Set an example for your friends and younger brothers and sisters. Remember, over 86% of youth ages 12-17 have never tried marijuana.

Get in the game. Sports and exercise help reduce the stress and strain of growing up. They keep you healthy and strong. When your mind and body are free from drugs, you have the performance edge.

The art of the matter. Get involved in drama, music, crafts, building things or painting. You can express your thoughts and feelings through many different art forms and share them with the world. You can grow through your dreams and creativity.

Host a party. Invite your friends to a drug-free social event and see how much fun you can have without marijuana and drugs.

Share what you have learned. Write an article for your school newspaper on the facts about marijuana. You can gather information from local libraries, or by contacting NCADI at 800-729-6686.

Source: National Institute on Drug Abuse, "Action Steps for Youth," *NIDA Notes*. n.d.

ers it rose from 15% to 35%, and among 12th graders, from 22% to 39%. The use of LSD increased for 8th, 10th and 12th graders by 1.5%, 3.0% and 3.2%, respectively. Heroin, which generally showed low usage among teenagers in the 1980s and early 1990s, showed a statistically significant increase in 1997.

While overall annual rates remain low in comparison with other drugs, they were still two to three times higher then they were in 1991. The annual use rate for all three grades were between 1.1% to 1.4%. According to the survey, a large proportion of 8th, 10th, and 12th graders, (63%, 75% and 89%, respectively) reported using heroin at least some of the time by noninjectable ADMINISTRATION, such as smoking or nasal inhalation ("SNORTING"), while 32%, 45% and 57% of the heroin users in each grade, respectively, claimed noninjectable use exclusively. The use of cocaine and crack cocaine showed gradual but statistically insignificant increases. The annual use of cocaine powder for 8th, 10th and 12th graders in 1997 was 2.2%, 4.1% and 5.0%; for crack, 1.7%, 2.2% and 2.4%.

The rate of cigarette smoking remained stable throughout the 1980s, although there has been a gradual increase in the 1990s. In 1997, 36.5% of high school seniors reported smoking cigarettes in the past 30 days—up 8% since 1991. Nineteen percent of 8th graders and 30% of 10th graders also reported smoking cigarettes in the past 30 days.

Causes of drug use: Since 1977 teenagers have consistently identified drugs as their foremost concern. Sixty percent of adolescents had put drugs at the top of their "biggest problem" list by 1989. This is a drastic increase compared to 27% in 1977. Their number-two problem after drugs, they said, was peer pressure. There are any number of theories as to why a child first experiments with drugs: pleasure, thrills, stimulation, or, to relieve boredom; to cope with questions of status and/or various other school-related problems. Most likely, the child is dealing with stress and unresolved issues in his or her home as well. Personal, social and family factors are all associated with adolescent drug use. Adolescents who use drugs have been found to express a high degree of openness to experience, tolerance of deviance, sensation seeking, unconventionality, impulsivity and rebelliousness. While developing physically and emotionally, they become vulnerable to crises of identity. Many teenagers have difficulty living up to not only the expectations that society places on them, but to the internal demands they make on themselves. Drugs offer the lure of instant gratification, feelings of euphoria and/or a numbing of any fears they may have involving their newfound independence.

According to the 1995 NIDA report, a key factor contributing to the increase in drug use is the sharp decline in perceived risk by teenagers of using not only marijuana but also crack, cocaine and LSD. Parental attitudes seem to be a factor in the increase of adolescent drug use. Parents of the 1990s, many of them alumni of the Woodstock years, seem to be less apt to talk to their children about the negative consequences of drugs, including alcohol, tobacco and prescription medications. Prevention experts also consider the ambivalent messages young people receive from the media to be a major influence in the rising rate of adolescent drug use. Rock music, movies and television present attitudes toward drugs that are often unclear or even prouse. Opponents believe the public debate over the legalization of drugs is being misinterpreted by teenagers to signify that drugs are not dangerous. Drug-using peers, parents and/or siblings often have a powerful influence on teenagers, who may therefore look upon drinking, smoking or use of other drugs as mature, adult behavior. However, sensible, moderate use of certain drugs such as alcohol, by adults, may serve as proper role models for adolescents preparing to enter adult society, where social drinking is still the norm.

Prevention and treatment: The following list is comprised of treatment methods and prevention/intervention strategies to be used during the early stages of harmful use of drugs and drug dependency:

> **Information.**   The provision of accurate, objective information about all types of drugs and their effects on the body. Parents can help inoculate their child from alcohol or other drug use by educating themselves about the signs of alcohol/other drug problems.
> **Intervention.**   The provision of assistance and support to adolescents during crisis periods, through counseling, hot lines, peer support networks, mentoring and so on
> **Education and skills-development.**   The provision of training aimed at the clarification of values and the improvement of problem-solving and coping skills through group discussions and role-plays.
> **Resilience training.**   The provision of training designed to promote confidence, self-reliance and efficacy, through challenging experiences in school and early exposure to positive

career opportunities. Many teenagers flourish when they are exposed to activities such as community restoration projects, environment preservation or work involved with helping others in any way. Whether performed voluntarily or for pay, this type of work or service empowers those involved and serves to build self esteem, improving the self-image and leading to a more productive, less self-destructive life style.

Along with numerous federal- and state-funded programs designed to educate America's youth about the dangers of harmful use of alcohol and other drugs, community concern beginning in the 1970s led to the creation of many parent and community organizations, such as FAMILIES IN ACTION (FIA) and the DO IT NOW FOUNDATION (DIN). Increasingly, parents and citizens as well as community and church leaders have been acknowledging that prevention of drug problems must extend outside the limited resources of school-based programs. Every state now has at least one drug-use prevention coordinator, usually located within the health or mental health department. Groups interested in organizing prevention programs are urged by the government to contact these coordinators.

One of the driving forces behind the evolution of parent groups is the experience of helplessness that parents feel when they realize their child has been experimenting with drugs. Many parents have no idea what actions to take and where to turn for help. One of the biggest conflicts parents face is the moment of truth when they actually find drugs in a child's possession. Should they talk it out with the child? Seize and destroy? Institute punishments? Do they (or can they) stop a child from seeing his or her friends? Compounding the problem is the unwillingness of many parents to deal with the problem head-on, due to their own guilt, anger, embarrassment and/or feelings of failure.

Professional counselors, particularly those working with school guidance programs, often carry caseloads that make it impossible to work effectively with individual children. School programs too often have no clear policy to follow, and their expectations of counselors may be unrealistic. Counselors are also under pressure because they realize they cannot "do it alone," and many parents expect them to. Misclassification of drug use can also be a problem. Many counselors treat all drug use as "dependency" and do not address the needs specific to each child. In addition, many elementary school teachers are unaware of the tremendous value of early intervention and do not devote any time to drug-related issues, presumably leaving the problem to high school staff.

Very little research has been done to determine the efficiency of prevention efforts. Comprehensive evaluations, longitudinal and qualitative studies are needed to determine the value and results of the many programs being initiated and maintained.

Treatment: Treatment of youthful alcoholics and problem drinkers is a relatively new area, as is research on its effectiveness. The success rate of adolescent treatment facilities is at least as high as that for older alcoholics, problem drinkers and users of drugs other than alcohol.

National Institute on Drug Abuse (NIDA), *Monitoring the Future: A Continuing Study of the Lifestyles and Values of Youth* (Rockville, Md.: NIDA, 1995).

D. M. Gallant, *Alcoholism: A Guide to Diagnosis, and Treatment* (New York: W.W. Norton, 1987).

Enoch Gordis, M.D., ed., *Sixth Special Report to the U.S. Congress on Alcohol and Health* (Rockville, Md.: National Institute on Alcohol Abuse and Alcoholism [NIAAA], 1987).

Enoch Gordis, M.D., ed, *Seventh Special Report to the U.S. Congress on Alcohol and Health* (Rockville, Md.: NIAAA, 1990).

Lloyd Johnston et al., *Drug Use, Drinking, and Smoking: National Survey Results from High School, College and Young Adult Populations, 1975–1988,* DHHS pub. ADM 89–01638 (Rockville, Md.: Alcohol, Drug Abuse and Mental Health Association [ADAMHA], 1989).

National Institute on Drug Abuse (NIDA), and University of Michigan Institute for Social Research, *Monitoring the Future: A Continuing Study of the Lifestyles of Youth* (Rockville, Md.: NIDA, 1990).

J. V. Rachal et al., "Alcohol Use among Adolescents," *Alcohol Consumption and Related Problems,* Alcohol and Health Monograph Series, no. 1 (Rockville, Md.: National Institute on Alcohol Abuse and Alcoholism, 1982).

Millree Williams and Jill Vejnoska, "Alcohol and Youth: State Prevention Approaches," *Alcohol Health & Research World* 6, no. 1 (Fall 1981): 2–13.

adulteration   The process by which a drug is made impure or inferior by the addition of an improper substance. Heroin is often CUT to dilute its potency and increase the volume. Drugs are often adulterated with active substances in order to increase their desirable effects or to make buyers think they are getting a more potent drug.

adverse drug reaction   A negative side effect or undesirable secondary effect of a drug; an unfavorable psychological or somatic reaction to ingesting a drug. Not only is there controversy over what constitutes an adverse reaction, but also over what exactly constitutes ACUTE as opposed to CHRONIC adverse reactions. It is theorized that "normal well-adjusted" individuals are least likely to experience adverse reactions in general. Adverse physical and psychological reactions are associated not only with hallucinogens, cocaine, amphetamines, barbiturates and alcohol, but with all other categories of licit and illicit drugs, including prescription medicines, caffeine and tobacco.

advertising
Alcohol and tobacco: The level of drug and alcohol consumption, for both medical and recreational purposes, is influenced both directly and indirectly by consumer advertising—the same advertising techniques used to market cars and toilet paper—but with serious and far-reaching consequences. Drug advertising raises ethical considerations that are difficult to resolve in light of the dual nature of the product in question: manufacturers are obligated by free enterprise to maintain and increase the profit margin on the product they sell, but drugs have the capacity to prolong life (making them more than a luxury item) or to endanger it (in the case of alcohol, cigarettes and drug overdose). Those who oppose such advertising argue that applying the profit motive with powerful, persuasive advertising techniques to chemical substances is unethical, if not dangerous. Their tenacious opposition has resulted in the abolition of television advertising for cigarettes and distilled spirits but has not affected the equally problematic areas of nonprescription drugs, pharmaceuticals and other alcoholic beverages. At an estimated $4 billion a year, cigarettes are the most heavily promoted and the most deadly consumer product in the U.S. today.

Beer and wine ads still appear on network television, while hard liquor is advertised on cable television. Advertising for cigarettes and liquor continues in other media. Both advertising and sales of alcoholic beverages have increased steadily since 1950. In 1977 the industry spent $492 million on advertising, employing the most successful agencies to develop glossy and persuasive ad campaigns. By 1982 that figure had gone up to $1,108.7 billion spent on ads for wine, beer and distilled spirits. Ad campaigns for cigarettes and alcohol typically exploit consumers' wishes and fantasies regarding sex, money, sophistication and youthfulness. Rich, beautiful and healthy young people frequently appear on the screen, billboard or magazine page, smiling seductively while grasping a glass, bottle or cigarette.

In 1988 alone, brewers spent $170 million on sports sponsorship, according to *Special Events Report* newsletter, which tracks sponsorships. Sports heroes and (increasingly) ethnic groups figure prominently in alcohol and cigarette advertising in an attempt to appeal to a broader market. In the 1990s brewers and beer distributors spent $15 million to $20 million a year marketing their products on college campuses. In the last decade or so, manufacturers of these products have recognized women as an enormous, previously unexploited market and consequently have made changes in their product lines as well as in advertising. More and more "light" beers and wines and "feminine" cigarettes appear every year, and advertising in women's magazines has increased dramatically.

One of the issues frequently raised is whether such advertising merely promotes a particular brand, or whether it promotes drinking and smoking in general. Also, most advertising of alcohol targets heavy drinkers because they account for a disproportionate share of product purchases. It is clearly in the manufacturers' interest to increase their consumption, but is it in the public interest? This concern has led to counteradvertising by various health groups and sometimes by the manufacturers themselves. Following a precedent set by the antismoking campaign, such groups as the National Council on Alcoholism have sponsored counteradvertising. Studies by the Federal Trade Commission have shown that counteradvertising has had a significant impact on reducing the number of people who start smoking and on those who quit. For countercommercials to be effective they must be aired during prime time—frequently and repeatedly—either through revision of regulations now governing public service announcements or through the purchase of air time. As with regular commercials, segmentation of the market according to drinking patterns, behavioral tendencies, value patterns and media behavior is essential for the creation of messages with maximum impact. When messages are not aired or targeted at specific populations, the results may backfire. A San Francisco countercommercial attempt failed because a high proportion of the audience thought the ads were promoting consumption. The liquor industry has been active in public education campaigns that stress moderation and responsible alcohol use. Since 1989, the alcoholic beverage industry has been required to use containers that carry warnings that pregnant women shouldn't drink and that alcohol impairs driving. Ads warning against smoking, which have decreased since TV and radio cigarette commercials were banned in 1971, may have contributed to a decrease in cigarette consumption in recent years and the increasing popularity of low-tar cigarettes over more toxic blends.

Over-the-counter medications: There are more than 300,000 over-the-counter (OTC) drugs currently on the market. Advertisements for nonprescription OTC medications flood the media, and manufacturers spend $350 million to $400 million annually to promote their products and comprise one of the biggest television advertising groups. Most of their efforts are concentrated on the daytime market and are therefore directed at women. As well as being the dominant group of television viewers during that time slot, women are also the most prevalent consumers of OTC preparations.

Ads for nonprescription drugs often epitomize the worst aspects of advertising, convincing consumers to buy products that they do not need. It is not surprising that advertisers have been called the *hidden persuaders*. Despite manufacturers' claims, most OTC preparations are relatively ineffective, treating symptoms rather than illnesses. Too often the packaging becomes the product. Recently, there was a case where one manufacturer's larger dose of aspirin was being touted as more effective than its lower dose rival. Careful wording, such as "medically proven effective"—implies much but reveals little.

Additional controls with regard to honesty in advertising have compelled manufacturers to be more forthright in warning about possible side effects and hazardous ingredients. These controls do not compel manufacturers to justify all their claims, however. The makers of Anacin, for example, do not have to admit that their "more effective" product contains nothing more than a standard aspirin preparation with caffeine. Moreover, it may be too late to correct the basic dishonesty implicit in manufacturers' attempts to persuade people that they should never suffer a moment's discomfort, and that they need OTC products to ensure that. Encouraging this kind of mentality has helped produce a drug-dependent society in which during any 24- to 36-hour period, 50%–80% of the adult population takes at least one medical drug. The fact that Americans collectively swallow 50 million aspirins daily, doubtless influences young people and contributes to our casual recreational drug habits.

Prescription drugs: Another group of drugs which sales depend on advertising and other promotion is pharmaceuticals—prescription drugs that manufacturers market to physicians to prescribe to their patients. With an extremely powerful lobby, the pharmaceutical industry has grown dramatically in the last 40 years, and expenditures for prescription drugs have tripled in the last decade. Clearly, pharmaceutical sales constitute big business and the industry has developed an extensive network through which to promote its products. A key component are sales representatives called "detailmen" who, usually without the benefit of medical or scientific training, visit doctors on a commission basis to convince them of their products' merits. Studies have shown that what detailmen say, and the order in which they describe drugs, definitely influences physicians' ideas about the medicine and therefore their prescription practices. Often the only information doctors receive about a drug is what they hear directly from the manufacturer. Patients have little choice but to trust their doctors' medical expertise and to buy the drugs prescribed for them. Doctors, however, are largely at the mercy of the pharmaceutical companies' inherently biased advertising. Some modification of advertising practices is necessary, whereby the drug manufacturers accept responsibility for providing clear, complete information about their products and—most importantly—agree not to promote the unnecessary prescription of chemical substances. To protect the public, doctors need to be informed about all medications they prescribe from objective sources that do not have vested commercial interests in the products they are describing, but so far the pharmaceutical industry has successfully prevented such a safeguard from appearing.

Medical journals, which doctors receive free, depend on advertising dollars from drug companies. Accordingly, about 45% of their content is pharmaceutical advertising. Physicians may rely heavily on such advertisements to educate themselves about available medications. Necessarily, they are relying on biased presentations of information, and medical journal advertising is at least partially responsible for the misuse and overuse of prescription drugs in this country. BENZODIAZEPINES (depressants) are heavily advertised and heavily prescribed. Ads devised to promote them encourage doctors to prescribe them for use in the most mundane anxiety-provoking situations, such as spending an evening with the in-laws. The use of SEDATIVES is also recommended to ease patient management—that is, for the staff's benefit—in nursing homes and other institutions. Repeated implications, if not assertions, that certain groups, such as women or the elderly, for instance, need specific new psychoactive drugs, fosters stereotypes that clearly affect doctors' prescription practices. Manufacturers who are reticent in advertising a drug's side effects may doubly harm a patient.

Pharmaceutical advertising is perhaps the most problematic area of drug advertising. Even though prescription drugs are less subject to the economic forces of supply and demand that govern the sale of most products, manufacturers incur great expense when they develop and introduce a new drug; therefore profits from the existing product line must compensate.

Another issue in drug advertising is the prescription of brand-name as opposed to generic drugs. When the generic-drug industry took off in the mid-1980s, brand-name pharmaceutical companies attacked with a massive campaign to raise doubts about the cheaper substitutes. Nonetheless, the number of prescriptions filled with generics climbed from less than 10% to more than 30% in a five-year period. In late 1989, the Food and Drug Administration placed 11 generic drug companies under investigation and took more than 100 generic drugs off the market because of doubts about the adequacy of product tests. As a result, the major brand-name companies mounted a fresh advertising campaign against the use of generic drugs.

affect regulation   Interventions directed at helping an individual to understand how feelings are generated, how to work with them, and how to keep them in proportion to perception and behavior. Those in recovery from chemical dependency often have lost touch with many aspects of their personalities and of their psyches. In the recovery process, individuals first learn how to identify their feelings, they then gain insight into how these emotions fit into the thinking process, and, last, they acquire the necessary skills to handle feelings in ways that are not destructive to the self or to others.

affective disorder (mood disorder)   According to the *Substance Abuse and Mental Health Statistic Sourcebook,* affective disorders are characterized by prolonged disturbances in mood that impair social, personal and occupational functioning. Disturbed mood includes depression, loss of interest in life, difficulty concentrating, irritability and excessive elation or excitement. The affective disorders may be accompanied by sleeplessness, major weight gain or loss and psychomotor agitation. Affective disorders include major depressive episodes, manic episodes, dysthymia and manic depressive illness. Manic depression is a bipolar disorder characterized by cycles of depression and excitement (mania).

The use of alcohol and drugs for self-medication by those suffering with affective disorders, although very dangerous, is not uncommon. Mood-altering substances will ultimately exacerbate the negative effects of bipolar disorders.

African-American Family Services   Formally called the Institute on Black Chemical Abuse; a not-for-profit national and international organization that addresses alcohol and other drug-use problems of all age groups in the African-American community. It offers prevention, intervention, treatment and public education programs. Training and internship seminars are available on an ongoing basis throughout the year. Materials are provided through its resource center and a free quarterly newsletter is available on request.

African Americans

Alcohol: African Americans are the largest ethnic minority in the U.S., but as with other minorities, there is a scarcity of data on drinking problems among them. A 1984 survey focusing on a national sample of African Americans found that black and white men had similar drinking patterns, although important differences did exist.

Alcohol abstention rates for black males are higher than those for white males. Surveys in 1993 showed 42.2% of black men were abstainers compared with 30.2% of white men, and 12.4% of black men were heavy drinkers compared with 17% of white men. Of black women, 66% were abstainers compared with 43% of white women, and the proportion of heavy drinkers among black women was also lower than that among white women—3% to 5%. There are also important differences within age-group categories. Heavy drinking was most prevalent among white men in the 18 to 29 age group and declined in successive age groups. In contrast, abstention rates were high among black men between 18 and 29, but rates of heavy drinking rose sharply in the thirties.

Alcoholism is a serious problem in the African-American community, particularly in urban areas, where CIRRHOSIS mortality rates are unusually high. In seven major cities (Baltimore, Chicago, Detroit, Los Angeles, New York, Philadelphia and Washington, D.C.) deaths from cirrhosis among black males aged 25 to 34 are 10 times as high as among white males of the same age group. For all ages the cirrhosis mortality rate for nonwhites is about 1.5 times that for whites. In the period from 1940 to 1973, cirrhosis rates increased rapidly, from 5.8 per 100,000 to 15 per 100,000, but by 1986 the rate had declined to 13 per 100,000.

African Americans are more susceptible to CANCER of the upper digestive tract and they suffer from a significantly higher rate of hypertension, further complicated by drinking, than do other groups. (See HEART.)

Such theorists as Frederick O. Harper, professor of psycho-educational studies at Howard University, suggest the number of liquor stores located in residential areas of African-American neighborhoods is notably high, whereas in white communities liquor stores are most often located in commercially zoned business districts. Thus, with the easy availability of liquor, drinking becomes a major source of recreation and social activity. Status is achieved by drinking certain types of liquor and by buying rounds of drinks for friends. African Americans buy 30% of the nation's scotch, a high-status liquor.

As compared to white adolescents, black adolescents report a higher abstention rate and a lower heavy-drinking rate—about one-quarter that of whites the same age. As social, familial and economic pressures increase with age, so do drinking problems.

Many African Americans are unable to pay for alcoholism treatment and are less likely to have insurance coverage for such treatment or to know about free social services. However, Melvin Porche Sr., director of the Total Community Action Alcoholism Program in New Orleans, reports that black alcoholics admitted to hospitals and clinics show stronger motivation and cooperation in treatment than do white alcoholics.

Drugs other than alcohol: The 1994 *National Drug and Alcoholism Treatment Unit Survey* reported that African Americans made up 212,400 (22.5%) of the 944,000 Americans in specialty substance-abuse treatment. In comparison, whites made up 59.9% and Hispanics 13.8% of the treatment population. According to the 1994 *Preliminary Estimates from the Drug Abuse Warning Network* (DAWN), African Americans had an estimated rate of 485.6 drug-related episodes per 100,000 emergency room visits in 1993, up from 353.2 per 100,000 in 1990. For the same reporting year (1993), Hispanics had 223.2 and whites 145.8 per 100,000. In addition, Annual Medical Examiner Data from the 1993 DAWN report indicated that African Americans accounted for 30% of the 8,541 DAWN-reported deaths related to drug use. This was slightly less than half the reported drug-related deaths for whites (56%), but almost three times as many deaths as reported for Hispanics (12%).

Treatment: Treatment programs for black users have encountered difficulties in cases where METHADONE maintenance is suggested. Some have suggested that methadone maintenance is a conspiracy against the African-American community. There are allegations that methadone renders men impotent and both men and women sterile. Although these allegations have been proven false, there is still concern among some people that methadone programs are used for repression.

Enoch Gordis, M.D., ed., *Seventh Special Report to the U.S. Congress on Alcohol and Health,* chapter 2 (Rockville, Md.: National Institute on Alcohol Abuse and Alcoholism [NIAAA], 1990).

Enoch Gordis, M.D., ed., *Eighth Special Report to the U.S. Congress on Alcohol and Health,* chapter 1 (Rockville, Md.: NIAAA, 1993).

B. Fernandez-Pol et al., "Drinking Patterns of Inner-City Black Americans and Puerto Ricans," *Journal of Studies on Alcohol* 47 (1986): 156–160.

Frederick D. Harper, "Research and Treatment with Black Alcoholics," *Alcohol Health & Research World* 4, no. 4 (Summer 1980): 10–16.

D. Herd, "The Epidemiology of Drinking Patterns and Alcohol-Related Problems among U.S. Minorities," research monograph series, no. 18, DHHS pub. ADM 89-1435 (Washington, D.C.: Government Printing Office, 1989).

NIAAA, *Quick Facts Bulletin Board* (1987).

Melvin Porche, Sr., "Report to the 29th Annual Forum of the NCA (a summary)," *U.S. Journal of Drug and Alcohol Dependencies* 5, no. 4 (May 1981): 10.

Marian Sandmaier, *The Invisible Alcoholics* (New York: McGraw-Hill, 1980).

Substance Abuse and Mental Health Administration (SAMHSA), *Preliminary Estimates from the Drug Abuse Warning Network, 1993 Preliminary Estimates of Drug-Related Emergency Department Episodes,* advanced report no. 8 (Rockville, Md., December 1994).

SAMHSA Annual Medical Examiner Data 1993, *Data From the Drug Abuse Warning Network (DAWN),* Series I, Number 13-B (Rockville, Md.).

aftercare   The package of services provided for an individual after he or she is successfully discharged from a drug-abuse treatment program. Aftercare activities include involvement in self-help groups, supported work programs and staff follow-up contacts and interventions. Aftercare is the first line of defense towards REHABILITATION and against a return to drug use.

agitation   A frequent symptom of intoxication or WITHDRAWAL from SEDATIVE HYPNOTICS such as alcohol. It is characterized by irritability, excessive restlessness, pacing, hand wringing, fidgeting and other forms of constant motor activity.

agonist, antagonist   A drug that has a pharmacological action at a receptor site of a cell is called an agonist. A drug that nullifies or prevents that action is called an antagonist. Some drugs have mixed agonist-antagonist actions. Morphine is a narcotic agonist. Naloxone is a narcotic antagonist. Talwin (pentazacine) is a narcotic agonist-antagonist.

agoraphobia   Involves fear, anxiety and the avoidance of open spaces and/or situations such as crowds, traveling or being anywhere outside the home. This anxiety concerns places or situations where panic attacks or symptoms may occur and the person feels that escape would be difficult and that help is unavailable. Some people with agoraphobia refuse to leave their homes, often for years at a time. Some are "territory-bound" and move only in a fixed route between home and work, as they cannot go outside what they consider to be their safe area without extreme fear and anxiety.

AIDS (Acquired Immune Deficiency Syndrome)
A condition caused by infection with the human immunodeficiency virus (HIV), which attacks the immune system and disables the body's capacity to fight disease. These infections are not a threat to persons whose immune systems are intact. Following initial infection, the HIV may lie dormant and people infected with it may remain healthy for ten years or longer before getting sick, or they may never acquire the disease or group of diseases that has come to be known as AIDS. When infected, in most cases, however, the HIV-infected cells replicate, destroying healthy immune-system cells. Acquired Immune Deficiency Syndrome (AIDS) is the name given to any of a group of illnesses associated with the HIV syndrome. The individual infections or diseases that are now grouped into the category known as AIDS-related infections are for the most part neither new to mankind nor to the medical profession. People have been contracting these related diseases for some time (usually when they were suffering from weakened immune systems), but until recently, there was no well known association of these illnesses and no known virus spreading these particular infections in an epidemic fashion among sectors of the population. The questions of exactly what AIDS is and why it is now widespread have yet to be answered. We do know that many things can cause

immune systems to stop functioning effectively. Extenuated drug use, unhealthy life styles, perhaps even the chemicals in the water, food, and air we breathe, may all be contributing factors. Every time we ingest a foreign chemical into our metabolism, our immune system must go to work to begin to eradicate the toxin from our system. After years of overwork in such a fashion, an immune system may naturally become weakened. Many alternative treatment approaches are now being tested. The more traditional western medical approach has met with limited success, at very great expense, in fighting this disease (or series of diseases). There are people alive today who have been diagnosed with full-blown AIDS and who appear to be leading healthy, productive lives. These people have used varied experimental approaches to achieve such results, often combining holistic approaches that include forms of psychotherapy; meditation or prayer; exercise or yoga programs; vitamin and mineral therapies; and very strict nutritional regiments. It seems that the few that have successfully conquered the AIDS illness have had to restructure their lives completely. They have shown the world, however, that it is possible to not only live but to live well with AIDS.

Transmission: HIV is transmitted through the exchange of body fluids (blood, semen, vaginal secretions or breast milk) from an infected individual to a noninfected one. The concentration of the virus in saliva is so low that kissing does not appear to be a means of transmission unless there is an open wound, creating blood-saliva contact. HIV is not spread through casual social intercourse. It is not an airborne disease (nor do mosquitoes spread it, as was rumored at one time). The belief, popular in the U.S. in the early 1980s, that AIDS was strictly a disease of gay men was mistaken. In a 1996 report, the Center for Disease Control and Prevention (CDC) noted that one-third of the 548,102 total number of AIDS cases then recorded were related to INTRAVENOUS DRUG USE (IDU) and 90% of all pediatric AIDS cases were the result of either intravenous (IV) drug use by the children's mothers themselves or the mothers' having contracted the illness through sexual contact with an intravenous drug user (IDU). Experts estimate that nearly 500,000 IV drug users take heroin regularly, while thousands more inject cocaine or amphetamines. Among IDUs, transmission of the AIDS virus most often occurs by NEEDLE SHARING.

Small amounts of contaminated blood left in the syringe carry the virus from user to user. IDUs who frequent "shooting galleries," where needles are passed between several people, are at especially high risk for HIV infection. Drug users who are not IDUs are also at greater than normal risk of HIV infection because they tend to have impaired immune systems, due to general poor health care and/or lack of nutrition, proper sleep, exercise, and so forth. Statistics show that drug users (IDUs and non-IDUs) engage in acts of unprotected sex at rates higher than normal. This behavior is often the result of impaired judgment due to the alcohol or other drugs. Additionally, drug users with severe habits will sometimes resort to selling themselves to earn money for their drug supply and engage in unprotected sex to do so. The potential spread of HIV by prostitutes is also of special concern since in one study of female, and some male, prostitutes in seven communities across the U.S., approximately one-half of the prostitutes were intravenous drug users. Prostitution contributes significantly to transmission of the HIV virus from IDUs to nonusers. Women are especially vulnerable to drug-related transmission of HIV. Of women who have AIDS, 52% are IDUs, while approximately 20% are sexual partners of IDUs.

Mother-to-child HIV transmission occurs as a result of the fetus's contact with the mother's blood during pregnancy; as a result of an exchange of blood during the birthing process; or as a result of the infant, its immune system relatively undeveloped, ingesting large amounts of infected breast milk. According to the State of New York Department of Health, taking AZT (zidovudine) during pregnancy can reduce by two-thirds the HIV infection rate of babies born to HIV-positive women. AZT must be prescribed by a doctor and should be taken from the fourth month of pregnancy through delivery. Because timely prenatal care can substantially reduce the risk that an HIV-positive mother will transmit the virus to her child, it is essential that pregnant women at risk be tested for HIV and that HIV-positive women who become pregnant seek prenatal care.

Prevalence: There are an estimated 1.1 to 1.3 million IV drug users in the U.S. and of these, 38,857 are people with AIDS. It is estimated that the New York City/New Jersey area has reported one-quarter of all diagnosed AIDS cases in the United States, including approximately 75% of drug-related cases.

(While the New York City area is hardest hit, it is important to realize that IV drug users with AIDS have been reported in all 50 states.)

Minorities are over-represented among IDUs and a disproportionate number of people with AIDS are African American and Hispanic. Although African Americans represent only 12% of the population in the U.S., they account for 28% of all people with AIDS. Hispanics account for 6% of the U.S. population and 16% of people with AIDS. Minorities account for 80% of the cases among heterosexual IV drug users, 81% of heterosexually transmitted AIDS cases and 76% of pediatric AIDS cases. Members of minority groups survive for a shorter period of time after being diagnosed with AIDS than do whites with the disease, most likely due to economic disparities. Many minority members do not have access to good health care, may delay testing longer, and thus receive care later in the course of their illness than do the more financially stable whites.

Health care workers who treat IDUs are at a very low risk of contracting HIV infection as long as they follow the CDC's AIDS precautions when handling body fluids of IV drug users and from people with the HIV virus. They must take special care when handling used needles and other paraphernalia. Because the confidentiality of HIV status is protected by federal mandate, health care workers often have no way of knowing whether or not patients are infected. All health care workers should follow universal precautions in all activities.

Prevention: In 1988 then New York City mayor Edward I. Koch began a controversial needle exchange program for IV drug users. The program met with strong objections from other officials and community leaders who felt that needle exchange programs were an irresponsible, less costly substitute for opening new drug treatment programs. At the same time, however, significant support for this first government-sponsored exchange in the nation came from health professionals and some drug treatment groups. This remained the only such program in the U.S. until November 1989, when the second program began in Portland, Oregon. Research on needle exchange programs in Tacoma, Washington; Amsterdam and London has shown that they reduced the number of HIV transmissions without treatment and without increased drug use. Unfortunately not every intravenous drug user wants to receive treat-

ment and even those who do often must wait due to the severely limited number of treatment slots available. For this reason, in many cities IDUs are being taught to flush their "works" with a dilute of one part bleach to ten parts water before they inject. Used correctly, a bleach dilute will destroy the virus left in the equipment.

AIDS and alcohol: A significant amount of HIV/AIDS prevention effort is directed toward alerting the public to alcohol's role in increasing the risk of HIV infection; even small amounts of alcohol result in DISINHIBITION, which increases the likelihood of sexual partners engaging in unprotected sex. Excessive drinking, which damages the body's natural immune system, increases the vulnerability to initial infection and compromises further the immune systems of those already infected.

To minimize the risk of transmission of HIV through sexual activity, it is recommended that one use condoms in any sexual encounter that involves the exchange of bodily fluids with a partner whose HIV-negative status cannot be ascertained. However, since condoms do not entirely eliminate the risk of infection, one should avoid any sexual practice that can cause injury to tissue and thus increase the risk of exchanging blood that may be HIV-contaminated.

Research and regulation: Research is being supported to improve the effectiveness of drug-abuse treatment and to develop other AIDS prevention strategies. The National Institute on Drug Abuse (NIDA) has funded studies to examine the spread of the AIDS virus among drug users, their sexual partners and their children. In addition, NIDA is also studying the immunosuppressive effect of many common drugs of abuse to better understand their relationship to AIDS.

Center for Infectious Diseases, Division of HIV/AIDS, *HIV/AIDS Surveillance* (Atlanta, July 1990).

John Langone, "How to Block a Killer's Path," *Time* (January 30, 1989): 60–62.

National Institute on Drug Abuse (NIDA), *Needle Sharing among Intravenous Drug Abusers, 1988,* research monograph series, no. 80 (Washington, D.C.: Department of Health and Human Services [DHHS]).

National Institute on Drug Abuse, "Drug Abuse and AIDS," *NIDA Capsules* (rev. August 1988).

Todd S. Purdom, "Dinkins to End Needle Plan for Drug Users," *New York Times* (February 14, 1990).

Al-Anon Al-Anon, officially known as Al-Anon Family Groups, is an organization designed to help relatives and friends of alcoholics. Its philosophy, program and structure correspond to the related organization ALCOHOLICS ANONYMOUS, although the two operate independently.

History: During the early days of Alcoholics Anonymous, family members of alcoholics attended the regular AA meetings. In 1951 relatives of AA members in and near New York City formed a Clearing House Committee; one of the founders was Lois Wilson, wife of AA founder Bill Wilson. The original staff members were volunteers. The committee adopted the name Al-Anon Family Groups and used a modified version of the Twelve Steps and Twelve Traditions of AA as their guiding principles. (See "The Twelve Steps" and "The Twelve Traditions" in ALCOHOLICS ANONYMOUS.) By 1954, Al-Anon had grown enormously and was publishing a monthly newsletter, *The Forum,* which had affiliations abroad.

In 1967 delegates from Al-Anon groups across North America attended the first World Service Conference, which has become an annual event. In 1970 Twelve Concepts of Service, explaining the structure of Al-Anon, were adopted. The headquarters' office is known as the World Service Office (WSO), which assists more than 30,000 registered Al-Anon and ALATEEN groups. Over 7,800 of these groups are in other countries. Al-Anon literature is available in 25 languages and there are some 5,500 Spanish-speaking Al-Anon groups worldwide.

Organization: Membership in all 12-step programs is free. If you have a relative, friend or someone you are involved with who is an alcoholic, you qualify to attend Al-Anon meetings. The alcoholic may or may not belong to AA and may or may not still be drinking. (Alcoholics may also be members of Al-Anon if they have friends or relatives who are alcoholics.) Many members of Al-Anon have stopped living with the alcoholic or are no longer closely associated, but may feel that their lives have been strongly affected by their former association and that Al-Anon can help them. Al-Anon meetings are open to all people, but in some cities there are special groups as well, composed solely of women or of gay men and lesbians.

Al-Anon meetings are structured in the same way as AA meetings. A chairman or leader opens and closes the meeting and generally leads discussion on a central theme. There are no dues; groups are self-supporting through voluntary contributions.

Although Al-Anon does have a spiritual orientation, each person is allowed their own beliefs. There are no requirements such as to the number of meetings one must attend, and whether one chooses to speak, or just to listen, in the group discussions is optional. Al-Anon provides peer counseling, support and an opportunity to understand that others share the same problems. In many ways Al-Anon offers a support system similar to that afforded in GROUP THERAPY, but free of charge and with a more casual structure. Though less is required, help is available on all levels, including individual sponsorship to newcomers by seasoned Al-Anon members.

Philosophy: Al-Anon teaches a program of "detachment with love," which sometimes is misconstrued by novices as an excuse for walking away from a situation rather than dealing with it. Members are taught that they are responsible only for their own reactions and responses to what the alcoholic does and not for the actions of the alcoholic. The primary purpose of the organization is not to stop the alcoholic from drinking but to help his or her family or friends. Members are taught neither to interfere actively with the alcoholic's drinking nor to protect the alcoholic from the consequences of drinking. The assumption is that a person cannot change another person and it is more productive to try to change yourself, thereby setting an example for others. Through seeking help from a "higher power," and through self-acceptance and self-examination, the Al-Anon member hopes that the alcoholic will be forced to a point where the effects of his or her drinking have become so severe that he or she will be motivated to stop voluntarily. Meanwhile, Al-Anon members focus on their own needs, their relationships with family members and associates, and they work on improving their own lives.

Al-Anon Family Group Headquarters, *Al-Anon Faces Alcoholism* (New York, 1977).

Al-Anon Family Group Headquarters, *Living with an Alcoholic with the Help of Al-Anon* (New York, 1978).

John Lavino and Mary Ellen Kay, "The Kemper/Al-Anon Program," *Alcoholism* 1, no. 3 (January/February 1981): 46–47.

Alaskan Natives (Inuits)   In 1985 the age-adjusted alcoholism mortality rate for NATIVE AMERICANS and Alaskan Natives was 26.1 deaths per 100,000, a significant decrease from the 1973 high of 66.1, but still four times higher than the general U.S. rate. From 1973 to 1983, the alcoholism death rate for the Inuit people remained fairly constant at 30 to 36 per 100,000, compared with seven to eight per 100,000 for white Alaskans. From 1974 to 1983, the Inuits accounted for more than half the deaths from alcoholism in Alaska, although they constituted only approximately 15% of the state's population. One study found that Alaskan Natives represented 65% of the alcohol treatment population while making up only 17% of the general population. Between 1975 and 1981, the suicide rate among Inuits dropped from 43% to 18% of all Alaskan suicides (an estimated 80% of all Native American suicide deaths are alcohol-related). Alcohol patterns and problems among this Alaskan population appear to have a strong correlation with economic factors, such as unemployment and low income, and with marital and family instability.

Indian Health Service, *Indian Health Service Chart Series Book,* Department of Health and Human Services, DHHS pub. 1988 0-218-547: QL3 (Washington, D.C.: Government Printing Office, 1988).

D. Kelso and W. DuBay, "Alaskan Natives and Alcohol: A Sociocultural and Epidemiological Review," *Alcohol Use among U.S. Ethnic Minorities,* research monograph series, no. 18, DHHS pub. ADM787-1435 (Washington, D.C.: Government Printing Office, 1987).

T. Mulu, *Status of Mental Health of Alaskan Natives* (Alaska Med., 1979).

Alateen   Alateen originated in California in 1957. A young man whose father was member of ALCOHOLICS ANONYMOUS (AA) and whose mother participated in the AL-ANON program initiated the concept of creating another similar 12-step program for teenagers. Sharing the same Twelve Steps and Twelve Traditions, it is designed for youths between the ages 12 to 20 who have been affected by a close relation or caregiver (most often a parent) with a drinking problem. The drinker does not have to be associated with AA.

Alateen meetings are conducted by teenagers, although an active adult member of Al-Anon acts as a sponsor. The sponsor, who is generally not a parent of any of the Alateen members, guides the group and shares knowledge of the Twelve Steps and Twelve Traditions. Detachment is stressed—the teenagers are taught to suspend emotional involvement with the alcoholic's problems. When older, Alateen members are encouraged to join Al-Anon.

There are now over 3,000 Alateen groups. They have their own bimonthly newsletter, *Alateen: Hope for Children of Alcoholics.* They also have conventions and Alateen Loner's Service for teens who live in isolated or rural communities where there are no groups.

Statistical information:

Predominantly white, although since 1984 there has been an increase in the number of African Americans and other ethnic groups.

The ratio of females to males is 3 to 2.

The average age of the member is 14 years.

Members report an average of 1.7 relationships with alcoholics, mostly an alcoholic parent; however, there has been a decrease in Alateen members who report relationships with alcoholic parents and an increase in those who report relationships with alcoholic relatives.

Two-thirds of Alateen members have at least one family member in AA, and three-quarters have at least one family member in Al-Anon.

Two-thirds of Alateen members attend one meeting a week.

Alateen group sponsors:

Most sponsors are female; average age—42 years old.

One-third of the Alateen groups have at least one sponsor who is a member of AA.

alcohol   There is no period in recorded history that lacks references to the production and consumption of ethanol. The history of alcohol consumption is inseparable from the history of harmful use of alcohol, and codes limiting its consumption date back to 1700 B.C. (See BEER.) Over the years, a pattern of increasing availability of alcoholic beverages has led to concern about resulting alcohol-related problems. After the failure of Prohibition in the U.S., the moral approach to the problem gave way to

World Alcohol Consumption

Total Alcohol Consumption by Country (1993–1995)
(Ranked in order of per capita consumption in 1995)

			Liters of pure alcohol		
Rank	Country	Reliability	1993	1994	1995
1	Luxembourg	🍷🍷	12.0	11.9	11.6
2	France	🍷🍷🍷	11.5	11.4	11.5
3	Portugal	🍷🍷	10.7	10.8	11.0
4	Hungary	🍷🍷	10.2	10.3	10.2
5	Spain	🍷🍷🍷	9.9	9.7	10.2
6	Czech Republic	🍷🍷	9.6	10.1	10.1
7	Denmark	🍷🍷🍷	9.7	9.9	10.0
8	Germany	🍷🍷🍷	10.4	10.3	9.9
9	Austria	🍷🍷🍷	10.1	9.8	9.8
10	Switzerland	🍷🍷🍷	10.0	9.7	9.4
11	Republic of Ireland	🍷🍷	8.3	8.6	9.2
12	Belgium	🍷🍷	9.6	9.2	9.1
13	Greece	🍷	9.6	8.9	9.0
14	Romania	🍷	8.0	6.5	9.0
15	Italy	🍷🍷🍷	8.7	8.7	8.8
16	Bulgaria	🍷	8.3	8.3	8.1
17	Netherlands	🍷🍷🍷	7.9	7.9	8.0
18	Cyprus	🍷🍷🍷	7.6	7.8	7.9
19	Slovak Republic	🍷	8.4	7.8	7.8
20	Australia	🍷🍷	7.5	7.9	7.6
21	United Kingdom	🍷🍷🍷	7.4	7.5	7.3
22	Argentina	🍷🍷🍷	7.2	7.1	7.3
23	New Zealand	🍷🍷🍷	7.3	7.2	7.0
24	USA	🍷🍷🍷	6.7	6.8	6.8
25	Japan	🍷🍷	6.6	6.6	6.6
26	Finland	🍷🍷	6.8	6.6	6.6
27	Poland	🍷🍷	6.4	6.4	6.4
28	Canada	🍷🍷🍷	6.2	6.1	6.2

(continued on next page)

World Alcohol Consumption (continued)

Total Alcohol Consumption by Country (1993–1995)
(Ranked in order of per capita consumption in 1995)

Rank	Country	Reliability	Liters of pure alcohol		
			1993	1994	1995
29	Uruguay	☛	5.6	6.3	6.1
30	Russia	☛	4.9	5.7	5.8
31	Venezuela[1]	☛	5.9	5.4	5.3
32	Sweden	☛	5.3	5.3	5.3
33	Chile	☛	5.1	5.1	5.3
34	South Africa	☛	4.5	4.8	4.9
35	Colombia[2]	☛	4.4	4.5	4.6
36	China	☛	3.2	4.4	-
37	Norway	☛	3.8	3.9	4.1
38	Cuba	☛	3.8	3.8	3.8
39	Brazil	☛	3.4	3.4	3.6
40	Iceland	☛☛☛	3.3	3.5	3.5
41	Mexico	☛	3.3	3.3	3.3
42	Paraguay[1]	☛	2.0	1.9	2.0
43	Singapore	☛☛	1.5	1.6	1.7
44	Ukraine	☛☛	3.3	2.0	1.6
45[1]	Peru[1]	☛☛	1.1	1.2	1.2
46	Turkey	☛☛	0.9	0.9	0.9
47	Israel[1]	☛	0.9	0.9	0.8
48	Thailand	☛☛	0.4	0.6	0.6
49	Malaysia[3]	☛☛	0.5	0.5	0.6
50	Tunisia[1]	☛	0.5	0.6	0.5
51	Algeria[1]	☛	0.3	0.3	0.3
52	Morocco[1]	☛	0.3	0.3	0.3
53	Vietnam[2]	☛	0.2	0.2	0.2

☛☛☛ = Very Reliable;   ☛☛ = Reliable;   ☛ = Less Reliable.
[1] Data are for beer and wine only.   [2] Data are for beer only.   [3] Data are for beer and spirits only.

Source: *World Drink Trends,* 1996 Edition

Preliminary Data—As of June 1998

Estimated Number (in Thousands) of Persons Who First Used Alcohol During Each Year 1965–1995, Their Mean Age at First Use, and Annual Age-Specific Rates of First Use (per 1000 Person-Years of Exposure), Based on 1994–1997 NHSDAs

Year	Initiates (1000s)	Mean Age	Age-Specific Rate of First Use[1]		
			12–17	18–25	26–34
1965	3121	17.7	63.5	181.0	21.0
1966	3663	17.7	66.5	224.0	43.5
1967	3734	17.5	76.3	224.9	35.3
1968	3768	18.0	76.6	208.1	49.7
1969	4231	17.7	90.7	238.9	51.2
1970	4022	17.3	89.6	240.9	32.4
1971	3638	17.5	72.8	233.1	40.6
1972	4488	16.9	103.8	257.4	33.6
1973	4420	17.0	103.5	251.1	36.5
1974	4425	17.3	105.8	253.5	34.5
1975	3988	17.0	91.8	254.4	21.7
1976	4060	16.8	102.2	238.3	19.2
1977	4575	17.5	120.7	249.0	41.4
1978	4512	16.9	124.3	244.0	37.7
1979	4048	17.3	117.2	219.0	25.1
1980	4074	17.3	117.0	241.5	25.9
1981	3627	16.6	111.1	216.1	19.4
1982	3627	17.1	110.8	202.5	34.5
1983	3600	16.8	116.5	199.0	22.0
1984	3509	16.9	111.2	196.8	30.8
1985	3335	16.6	116.6	187.5	25.3
1986	3640	17.0	121.9	210.2	39.1
1987	3285	17.1	113.1	190.6	18.6
1988	3373	17.1	115.9	188.4	31.9
1989	3071	16.3	112.7	167.5	20.2
1990	3431	16.7	119.0	204.4	17.9
1991	3477	16.7	119.1	214.3	28.5

(continued on next page)

Preliminary Data—As of June 1998 (continued)

Estimated Number (in Thousands) of Persons Who First Used Alcohol During Each Year 1965–1995, Their Mean Age at First Use, and Annual Age-Specific Rates of First Use (per 1000 Person-Years of Exposure), Based on 1994–1997 NHSDAs

Year	Initiates (1000s)	Mean Age	Age-Specific Rate of First Use[1]		
			12–17	18–25	26–34
1992	3595	16.5	132.9	208.7	23.6
1993[2]	3713	16.4	139.9	198.9	20.5
1994[3]	4150	17.2	152.8	214.9	30.1
1995[4]	4318	16.2	165.4	243.3	14.3

[1] The numerator of each rate equals the number of persons who first used the drug in the year (times 1000). The denominator of each rate equals the number of persons who were exposed to risk of first use during the year, weighted by their estimated exposure time measured in years. For example, for the age group 12–17 in 1990, the denominator is the sum of three components:

(1) those persons 12–17 years old in 1990 who first used the drug in 1989 or earlier, times a weight of zero. The weight is zero since they had zero exposure to the risk of first use in 1990.

(2) those who first used the drug in 1990 times a weight of .5. The weight of .5 assumes that these people, on average, first used the drug at midyear and consequently have a half year of exposure (i.e. the first half of the year.)

(3) those who never used, or those who first used the drug in 1991 or later, times a weight of one. The weight of one assumes their exposure to the risk of first use during 1990 was for the whole year.

Each person is also weighted by his/her sample weight.

[2] Estimated using 1995, 1996 and 1997 data only.

[3] Estimated using 1996 and 1997 data only.

[4] Estimated using 1997 data only.

Source: SAMHSA, Office of Applied Studies, National Household Survey on Drug Abuse, 1994–1997.

a scientific approach and the disease concept of alcoholism has been increasingly acknowledged. Since World War II particularly, the scope and depth of research studies have provided a wealth of information about alcohol abuse.

For the past 300 years, the term alcohol has been synonymous with spirituous liquids as well as referring specifically to the drug they contain. There are four major types of alcohol and they have one distinct chemical feature in common: the presence of an oxygen atom and a hydrogen atom bonded together to form a single unit known as a hydroxyl group. A hydroxyl group is more pre-cisely classified by the number of hydrocarbon units that it contains. Ethyl alcohol is the only alcohol type used in alcoholic beverages as the other varieties are poisonous.

Methyl alcohol (methanol):   Commonly referred to as wood alcohol, it is used commercially in the production of formaldehyde and other organic chemicals such as antifreeze and industrial solvents. It is now manufactured synthetically because distillation processes only yield limited amounts of varying purity.

Isopropyl alcohol (propanol):   Commonly referred to as "rubbing alcohol," it is now manufactured

Test Your Alcohol IQ

1993, National Institute on Alcohol Abuse and Alcoholism

1. **About how many calories are there in a six-pack of beer?**
   - a. 600
   - b. 950
   - c. 1,100
   - d. You burn calories drinking beer

2. **What drug has been linked with the highest incidence of violence and aggression in both animal and human studies?**
   - a. Crack
   - b. PCP
   - c. Alcohol
   - d. Heroin

3. **How many freshman will drop out of college due to alcohol-related causes next year?**
   - a. 10,000
   - b. 30,000
   - c. 42,000
   - d. 120,000

4. **Approximately how many of today's students will eventually die of alcohol-related causes?**
   - a. 300,000
   - b. 100,000
   - c. 50,000
   - d. 20,000

5. **What percentage of drownings are alcohol related?**
   - a. 33%
   - b. 48%
   - c. 55%
   - d. 69%

6. **Which has the most alcohol?**
   - a. Can of beer
   - b. Glass of wine
   - c. Shot of liquor
   - d. All the same

7. **In the age of university budget cuts, student expenditures for alcohol far exceed the operating costs for running the library on campus. Nationwide, students spend_____on alcohol each year.**
   - a. $2 million
   - b. $30 million
   - c. $100 million
   - d. $5.5 billion

8. **Which of these 21 year olds is likely to have more alcohol-related problems?**
   - a. Fraternity member
   - b. Honor student
   - c. Organic chemistry major
   - d. Person not in college

9. **Which 21-year-old group drinks more?**
   - a. College students
   - b. Those not attending college

10. **What is the #1 cause of headaches, sprained ankles, broken arms, car crashes, rapes, deaths and shattered dreams?**
    - a. Studying
    - b. Extracurricular activities
    - c. Dining hall food
    - d. Alcohol

Answers:
1) b 2) c 3) d 4) a 5) d 6) d 7) d 8) a 9) a 10) d

Source: National Institute on Alcohol Abuse and Alcoholism, *Test Your Alcohol IQ* (Washington, D.C.: National Institute on Alcohol Abuse and Alcoholism, 1993).

mostly from a petroleum by-product. It is used commercially in hand and shaving lotions, as an additive in shellac, lacquer and antifreeze, and as a rubbing compound.

Butyl alcohol (butanol): Produced both by fermentation and by synthesizing the petroleum by-product butene, it has perhaps the broadest range of commercial uses. In various forms it is used to produce photographic film, dye, plastic, artificial leather, safety glass and numerous other products.

Ethyl alcohol (ethanol): Produced commercially by fermentation, it is commonly called grain alcohol and is used to make alcoholic beverages. Because potable alcohol is heavily taxed, when ethyl alcohol is intended for another purpose, such as an industrial solvent, it is denatured, and rendered unfit for consumption. Denaturing is accomplished by adding a variety of toxic or nauseous chemicals that cannot be removed.

There also are a variety of high-carbon alcohols that extend beyond these four basic types. They are produced in limited quantities for more specialized uses such as jet fuels and nitroglycerin explosives.

While ethanol is not as poisonous as the other forms of alcohol described here, it is a toxin that in sufficient doses can damage virtually every organic system in the body. The degree of damage will be determined by the quantity and length of exposure, the nutritional state of the user, coexisting medical conditions and genetic factors.

Alcohol, Drug Abuse and Mental Health Association (ADAMHA)   An umbrella agency that, in addition to its own administrative staff, includes the National Institute of Mental Health (NIMH), the National Institute on Drug Abuse (NIDA) and the National Institute on Alcohol and Alcohol Abuse (NIAAA). ADAMHA is part of the Public Health Service of the U.S. Department of Health and Human Services (DHHS).

alcohol amblyopia   From Greek *amblys* (dim) + *ops* (eye). A rare disorder of the eye; alcohol amblyopia usually occurs in alcoholics who have a lengthy history of severe drinking problems. The disease begins slowly with a slight vision impairment that becomes progressively worse. The visual failure is not caused by lesions of the eye or refractive error but is believed to be due to a toxic reaction in the orbital portion of the optic nerve. The typical complaint is a painless blurring of vision over a period of several weeks with reduced sharpness for both near and distant objects. Generally, changes are relatively symmetrical in both eyes and, if not treated adequately, may be followed by optic nerve degeneration. Treatment consists of administration of VITAMINS AND MINERALS. With proper care and NUTRITION the symptoms are usually reversible. The disease is most common in male alcoholics who are also smokers.

alcohol concentration   Alcohol concentration is measured as the percentage in volume or weight of alcohol in a fluid or tissue. (See BLOOD ALCOHOL CONCENTRATION [BAC].)

alcohol control   Broadly inclusive term for various regulations and restrictions by governments of the manufacture and sale of alcoholic beverages.

alcohol dependence scale   A model for alcohol-related diagnoses that analyze multiple factors, developed by psychiatrist-researcher H. A. Skinner, based on Horn and Wanberg's Alcohol Use Inventory. Four scales from the earlier inventory are used: (1) loss of behavioral control; (2) psychophysical withdrawal symptoms; (3) psychoperceptual withdrawal symptoms; and (4) obsessive-compulsive drinking style. Skinner identified general factors that measure, in part, the alcohol dependence syndrome as outlined by Edwards and Gross (1976).

Enoch Gordis, M.D., ed., *Sixth Special Report to the U.S. Congress on Alcohol and Health* (Rockville, Md.: National Institute on Alcohol Abuse and Alcoholism, 1987): 122.

J. L. Horn, K. W. Wanberg and F. M. Forster, *The Alcohol Use Inventory (AUI)* (Denver: Center for Alcohol-Abuse Research and Evaluation, 1974).

G. Edwards and M. M. Gross, "Alcohol Dependence: Provisional Description of a Clinical Syndrome," *British Medical Journal* 1 (1976): 1058–1061.

alcohol dependence syndrome (ADS)   Researchers and clinicians have long recognized the limitations of using the blanket term "alcoholism" to describe the range of alcohol-related disabilities and the varying degrees, as well as different types, of alcohol dependence. A new trend in classification of alcohol-related pathology is to focus on the number and types of symptoms evident, as opposed to viewing alcoholism as a unitary phenomenon. In fact, in the most recent of the World Health Organization's *INTERNATIONAL CLASSIFICATION OF DISEASES (ICD-10)*, the use of the term "alcoholism" has been dropped altogether as a recommended diagnosis and the term alcohol dependence syndrome (ADS) has been substituted.

Hodgson was among the first to elaborate on this concept, and he defined the alcohol dependence syndrome according to the following factors:

(1) loss of behavioral control; (2) psychosocial withdrawal symptoms; (3) increased tolerance to alcohol; (4) repeated withdrawal symptoms; (5) relief drinking; (6) compulsion to drink; and (7) readdiction liability.

Advances in this theory have led to such diagnostic tools as the ALCOHOL DEPENDENCE SCALE, developed by Skinner. As the concept is further refined, it is hoped that clinicians will be able to plan individual treatment with a greater degree of appropriateness and success. (See CLASSIFICATION OF ALCOHOLICS.)

R. Hodgson et al., "Alcohol Dependence: The Concept, Its Utility and Measurement," *British Journal of Addiction* 73 (1978): 339–342.

alcohol discharge rate   In a hospital, the alcohol discharge rate is the ratio of alcohol-related discharges to the total number of discharges, multiplied by 100,000. (Discharge is the formal release of a patient from a hospital.) An alcohol discharge is classified by the National Center for Health Statistics as a discharge given to a person who has at least one of the following diseases:

a type of alcoholic psychosis, such as DELIRIUM TREMENS, KORSAKOFF'S PSYCHOSIS or other alcoholic hallucinosis, alcoholic paranoia or other, unspecified psychosis;
CIRRHOSIS of the LIVER;
ALCOHOLISM manifested by episodic excessive drinking, habitual excessive drinking or alcoholic ADDICTION or other, unspecified alcoholism;
toxic effect of ethyl alcohol; or acute or chronic PANCREATITIS.

The alcohol discharge rate is a significant index of harmful use of alcohol and alcoholism and, when used in conjunction with other indices, can be used to determine the approximate alcoholic population at any given time. However, it has limitations—only those who have gone for treatment are counted and some patients may go for more than one treatment.

Department of Health and Human Services (DHHS), *Utilization of Short-Stay Hospitals by Persons Discharged with Alcohol-Related Diagnoses, United States, 1976* (Hyattsville, Md., 1980): 1–34.

DHHS, *Hospital Discharges with Alcohol-Related Conditions* (Rockville, Md., 1989).

Alcohol Epidemiologic Data System (AEDS)   The National Institute on Alcohol Abuse and Alcoholism (NIAAA) established in 1977 an Alcohol Epidemiologic Data System (AEDS) that is the centralized national repository of alcohol data related to consumption, mortality, morbidity, transportation, treatment and health. The data are provided from the NATIONAL CENTER FOR HEALTH STATISTICS (NCHS), the Center for Disease Control (CDC), the NATIONAL HIGHWAY TRAFFIC SAFETY ADMINISTRATION (NHTSA), as well as from NIAAA itself. The mandate of AEDS is to identify, locate, acquire, analyze and publish alcohol-related epidemiologic information under the direction of NIAAA's Division of Biometry and Epidemiology.

alcoholic   Used as a noun, the term refers to a person who manifests signs of ALCOHOLISM. Used as an adjective, the term pertains either to the use of alcohol, as in ALCOHOLIC TREATMENT CENTER, or to the presence of alcohol, as in ALCOHOLIC BEVERAGE CONTROL LAWS.

alcoholic beverage   A beverage containing alcohol. (See individual entries for WINE, BEER, GIN and other specific beverages.)

alcoholic beverage control laws (ABC laws)   The purpose of ABC laws has always been to prevent the fraudulent sale of alcohol, ensure availability and secure revenue for the state. ABC laws date back to the Code of Hammurabi, almost 4,000 years ago.

After the repeal of PROHIBITION (THE VOLSTEAD ACT) in the U.S., emphasis was placed on the promotion of temperance and the prevention of abuse. This concern gradually changed and the primary emphasis of the ABC laws became maintaining an orderly market and collecting revenue for government agencies. With a per capita increase in alcohol consumption over the last 40 years, attention has been shifting back once again to alcohol-abuse prevention.

Regulatory controls are exercised through outlets, age restrictions, pricing and taxation regulations, and through miscellaneous controls such as laws concerning PUBLIC DRUNKENNESS and DRIVING WHILE IMPAIRED (DWI). Restrictions on outlets—both those where alcohol may be sold and those where it may be consumed—are the most frequent method employed for controlling availability. As of 1988, the federally mandated age at which alcoholic beverages may be purchased is 21.

Taxes: Regulation through pricing and taxation is unpopular with both the public and the liquor industry, but while the impact is inconclusive, there seems to be evidence that such regulations do have some beneficial effects. Some states support a doubling of the U.S. government export tax on liquor and suggest that the additional funds be used for alcoholism treatment and prevention programs. Federal, state and local taxes on alcohol vary around the country. Before his retirement in September 1989, U.S. surgeon general C. Everett Koop recommended dramatically higher federal excise taxes on beer and wine. According to this plan, the tax on a six-pack of beer, for example, would rise from 16 cents to 65 cents, and on a bottle of wine it would increase from 3 cents to 59 cents. In many states, a "sin" tax was assessed in 1990 on alcohol and tobacco.

State regulations: ABC laws vary a great deal from state to state and a large number of federal, state and local-level agencies are responsible for making and enforcing regulations. There are two major types of control systems: the monopoly system and the license system. Under the monopoly system the individual state operates all or part of the wholesale and retail sale of alcohol. Under the license system the state creates a partial monopoly for private enterprise by restricting competition. There is, as yet, no conclusive data concluding that either system is the more effective.

The role of government: There has recently been debate between those who believe that more stringent laws are necessary to curtail excessive alcohol use and those who suggest that the control laws are not very effective because they ignore the combined cultural, biological, social and psychological forces that result in problem drinking for a percentage of the population. Opponents also suggest that such laws will work in opposition to prevention programs, which promote responsible use by individuals. They further suggest that increased control will lead to the growth of an illicit alcohol trade with attendant criminality and that stricter laws will result in a loss of revenue for the legal producers and sellers, as well as lost tax resources for the government.

Supporters of increased legislation point to evidence from a number of studies that show a connection between an increase in the overall level of consumption in a population and the rate of health problems that are frequent consequences of long-term drinking such as CIRRHOSIS. These findings show a direct relationship between per capita consumption for all drinkers and the proportion of heavy users, and seem to contradict the DISEASE CONCEPT theory, which holds that alcoholism affects only people who have some underlying physical or psychological problem. Advocates of regulation believe that vulnerability to alcohol dependence is a widely shared trait. While controls on alcohol are not popular, supporters of regulation believe that it will result in a healthier life for those who might otherwise be addicted. They cite successful examples of governments intervening to safeguard public health in such related areas as food, drugs and water.

alcoholic disease   Any DISEASE, mental or physical, caused by the effects of excessive alcohol consumption, including CIRRHOSIS, DELIRIUM TREMENS (THE D.T.'S) and KORSAKOFF'S PSYCHOSIS.

alcoholic hepatitis   A DISEASE of the LIVER, characterized by inflammation and necrosis (cell death), alcoholic hepatitis may develop abruptly in alcoholics after a severe drinking bout. Its appearance is sometimes accompanied by fever, jaundice and abnormal accumulation of fluid in the abdominal cavity. Fatty infiltration and increased fibrosis of the liver are frequent but not constant symptoms of this disease. Alcoholic hyaline, a clear glassy substance, is often found in the livers of patients with alcoholic hepatitis. Hyaline deposits may be a result of the degenerative effects of alcohol on subcellular structures called microtubules, which are important to the secretory activity of the liver cells.

The mortality rate for those with severe alcoholic hepatitis is high, ranging from 10% to 30%. Even alcoholics with few or no symptoms are in danger of contracting this disease if they continue to drink. The disease can rapidly develop to CIRRHOSIS, or it can be arrested and recovery of normal liver function can be attained. Treatment of alcoholic hepatitis consists of bed rest, a high-protein diet and a multivitamin regimen. (See ALCOHOLIC LIVER DISEASE.)

alcoholic liver disease   A general category that encompasses a number of alcohol-induced liver diseases. The *Merck Manual* defines alcoholic liver disease as "a variety of syndromes and pathologic changes of the liver caused by alcohol." There is still some debate on exactly how alcohol damages the liver, but poor NUTRITION and toxicity are both known to play a role. The development of alcoholic liver disease is directly related to the quantity and duration of drinking, although there is individual variation in susceptibility.

In its initial and milder form, alcoholic liver disease is characterized by an accumulation of excess fat on the liver, called, appropriately, FATTY LIVER. This is the most common disease of the liver found in hospitalized alcoholics. A more serious form of liver disease, which may or may not be linked with a fatty liver, is known as ALCOHOLIC HEPATITIS, which has a mortality rate ranging from 10% to 30%. This disease occurs when a number of liver cells die and cause inflammation.

The most severe form of liver injury is CIRRHOSIS, which is irreversible (though not always fatal). It is characterized by scarring of the liver with fibrous tissue and breakdown of the liver structure. While the progression from hepatitis to cirrhosis is generally accepted, the relationship between alcoholic fatty liver and alcoholic hepatitis and cirrhosis is still under debate. Not all alcoholics with fatty liver develop cirrhosis, and fat buildup is not always present with cirrhosis. However, fatty infiltration is frequently seen in association with more advanced alcoholic liver diseases, and the ultrastructural changes found in the early stages of alcoholic fatty liver are identical to those evident in more severe alcoholic liver diseases.

In 1981 a team of researchers funded by the Addiction Research Foundation and headed by Dr. Yedy Israel found that when large amounts of alcohol are consumed over a long period of time, the individual liver cells expand, squeezing the fine blood vessels that form a network throughout the liver. This squeezing can block the flow of blood, causing stress on these vessels and can sometimes lead to rupture and internal bleeding. The researchers also suspect that the pressure of the swollen liver cells may trigger the formation of fibrous tissue around the blood vessels, which would prevent the exchange of materials between the bloodstream and liver cells. This presents a whole new concept about the cause of mortality from liver disease because it suggests that it is the size of the liver cells and condition of the blood vessels that indicate the health of the organ, not the presence or absence of a diagnosed liver disease, such as cirrhosis or alcoholic hepatitis. This theory also offers some hope, for while cirrhosis is not reversible, the swelling of the cells and blood vessels is, provided the alcoholic stops drinking. Researchers are continuing their studies to determine why liver cells enlarge.

Common misconceptions: There are a number of misconceptions concerning alcoholic liver disease. One is that liver damage must be accompanied by symptoms of illness after drinking. Another is that drinking is safe, provided an individual has not developed a physical DEPENDENCE on alcohol. Development of liver disease is directly related to the use of alcohol as measured by duration and dosage. Both HEAVY DRINKERS and social drinkers are at risk. A third misconception is that cheap wine and liquor are more harmful to the liver than beer. The important factor is the amount of alcohol consumed. The toxic impurities that may be present in cheap alcoholic beverages are minute in relation to the toxicity of ethanol content. The belief that an adequate diet will protect a heavy drinker from liver injury is also mistaken. While malnutrition may contribute to liver damage, many people with more than adequate diets have had severe liver disease.

Treatment: It is essential that the diseased patient stop drinking alcohol. Much of alcoholic liver disease is completely reversible, and patients with a more advanced form of the disease who stop drinking have a better chance of survival than those with a lesser degree of damage and yet continue to drink.

Liver disease and women: A study conducted in 1977 in Britain, of patients with alcoholic hepatitis or cirrhosis who continued to drink, showed that after five years, 72% of the males were alive but only 30% of female patients were still living.

alcoholic myopathy   A disease that occurs in several forms and which is associated with changes in muscle tissue. Its cause is unknown but alcohol is a primary factor in its development. The condition has only been recognized in the past 25 years. Even in severe cases, if the patient stops drinking the prognosis is good and improvement tends to occur.

Subclinical myopathy: A disease indicated by increased levels of the enzyme creatine phosphokinase, considered to be of muscle cell origin, in the blood. Frequently there is also a rise in lactic acid. The condition affects more than one-third of the alcoholic population and is difficult to detect because patients may not complain of muscular symptoms. It may progress to more severe forms of myopathy.

Acute alcoholic myopathy: Characterized by severe muscle cramps, particularly in the arms and legs, it may appear abruptly in chronic alcoholics. If the patient abstains from alcohol, recovery is possible.

Chronic alcoholic myopathy: A slowly progressive disease, it is characterized by weakness and muscle atrophy, particularly in the legs. This form of myopathy is associated with heavy drinking over an extended period of time but, as with other forms of myopathy, it can be alleviated if the patient abstains from alcohol.

Alcoholic cardiomyopathy: A progressive and often fatal condition characterized by loss of contractile strength of heart muscle fibers (cells). It can be arrested in early stages by abstaining. No other treatment is available.

alcoholic poisoning   This condition differs only in degree from a state of extreme alcohol INTOXICATION. BLOOD ALCOHOL CONCENTRATION (BAC) above 0.4% indicates the occurrence of this condition.

alcoholic polyneuropathy (peripheral neuritis)
From *poly* (many), *neuro* (nerve) + *pathy* (disease). A disease of the nervous system, alcoholic polyneuropathy is thought to be caused by a thiamine deficiency, although its origin is still undetermined. It develops slowly, over months and years, affecting first and most severely the lower legs, where numbness and pain may develop. In some cases these symptoms are absent, and diagnosis is made on the basis of muscle wasting, tenderness of the calves, and signs of impaired motor function. In time these symptoms may progress to the upper extremities as well. Recovery from this disease may take years and

frequently some permanent physical impairment remains.

alcoholic psychosis   Vague and outdated term for a severe mental disorder caused by the effects of alcohol consumption. More specific and recent terms for such mental disorders include KORSAKOFF'S PSYCHOSIS and WERNICKE'S ENCEPHALOPATHY (SYNDROME OR DISEASE).

alcoholic treatment centers (ATC)   Funded by the National Institute on Alcohol Abuse and Alcoholism (NIAAA), these centers offer treatment in three major settings: hospital (inpatient), intermediate, and outpatient. The system allows DETOXIFICATION to be followed up by longer outpatient or halfway-house care. Most clients at an ATC receive a combination of treatments. Usually, hospital care is quite short and intermediate care extends over a much longer period. Having different modes of treatment in the same place enables a center to tailor treatment to the client's needs.

David J. Armor, J. Michael Polich and Harriet B. Stambul of the Rand Corporation Social Science Department divided the types of treatment into 10 major categories, as follows:

Hospital settings:
  Inpatient hospitalization: A traditional 24-hour service based on the traditional medical model but often including psychotherapy.
  Partial hospitalization: A partial service that allows the patient to go home or to work at appropriate times.
  Detoxification: A short "drying out" period for patients with serious toxic symptoms.

Intermediate settings:
  Halfway house: Living quarters and services such as job counseling and psychotherapy for patients who need extended care but do not require hospital treatment.
  Quarterway house: Similar to a halfway house but offering intensive, often physical care under more structured conditions.
  Residential care: Living quarters but little or no other therapy provided.

Outpatient settings:

Individual counseling: Treatment sessions given by a paraprofessional (someone without a graduate degree in psychology, medicine, social work or similar relevant field).

Individual therapy: Treatment sessions given by a professional.

Group counseling: Group sessions given by a paraprofessional.

Group therapy: Group sessions given by a professional.

David J. Armor, J. Michael Polich and Harriet B. Stambul, *Alcoholism and Treatment* (New York: John Wiley & Sons, 1978): 124–126.

Alcoholics Anonymous (AA) Alcoholics Anonymous is an international nonprofessional organization of alcoholics devoted to the maintenance of the sobriety of its members through self-help and mutual support; it was founded in the United States in 1935. The organization defines its purpose as follows:

> *Alcoholics Anonymous is a fellowship of men and women who share their experience, strength, and hope with each other that they may solve their common problem and help others to recover from alcoholism.*
>
> *The only requirement for membership is a desire to stop drinking. There are no dues or fees for AA membership; we are self-supporting through our own contributions. AA is not allied with any sect, denomination, politics, organization or institution; does not wish to engage in any controversy, neither endorses nor opposes any causes. Our primary purpose is to stay sober and help other alcoholics to achieve sobriety.*

This "desire to stop drinking" is at the core of the AA program. Membership in a group is voluntary but AA groups, despite their loose organizational structure and concern for anonymity, are remarkably

\	The Twelve Steps of Alcoholics Anonymous
1	We admitted we were powerless over alcohol—that our lives had become unmanageable.
2	Came to believe that a Power greater than ourselves could restore us to sanity.
3	Made a decision to turn our will and our lives over to the care of God *as we understood Him.*
4	Made a searching and fearless moral inventory of ourselves.
5	Admitted to God, to ourselves, and to another human being[s] the exact nature of our wrongs.
6	Were entirely ready to have God remove all these defects of character.
7	Humbly asked Him to remove our shortcomings.
8	Made a list of all persons we had harmed, and became willing to make amends to them all.
9	Made direct amends to such people whenever possible, except when to do so would injure them or others.
10	Continued to take personal inventory and when we were wrong promptly admitted it.
11	Sought through prayer and meditation to improve our conscious contact with God *as we understood Him,* praying only for knowledge of His will for us and the power to carry that out.
12	Having had a spirtual awakening as a result of these steps, we tried to carry this message to a[ll] alcoholics, and to practice these principles in all our affairs.

Source: Alcoholics Anonymous World Services.

cohesive and able to provide substantial support for members in order to maintain their SOBRIETY and ensure continued attendance at meetings. (For this purpose, as in many other areas, AA has a slogan: "Don't drink and go to meetings.")

History: The history of AA begins with the story, raised almost to the level of myth, of its founder, Bill Wilson, or, as he came to be known, Bill W. Born in 1895 and raised in a "broken home," Wilson found that alcohol relaxed him socially and gave him a new sense of freedom. After a brief stint in the army and marriage, Wilson went to work on Wall Street, where he had some success. He gradually became an alcoholic and later described the years from 1930 to 1934 as an "alcoholic hell." In 1934 an old drinking friend who had sobered up introduced him to the Oxford Group, headed by the Episcopal clergyman Dr. Samuel Shoemaker. The nondenominational group stressed the importance of taking stock of oneself, confessing one's defects and a willingness to make up for past wrongs. A member also could choose his own concept of God or a "higher power." It is easy to see in these principles many of the ideas that form the basis of AA.

After attending a meeting, Wilson decided to try to dry out. He went back to his doctor, Dr. Robert Silkworth, who had dried him out several times before. Silkworth, somewhat ahead of his time, believed alcoholism was a disease and a hopeless one. He described it as an "obsession of the mind that condemns one to drink and an allergy of the body that condemns one to die." This idea of alcoholism as a disease became an important concept in AA. Wilson sank into a profound depression during his sobering up process and subsequently had a "conversion" experience. From his experience grew the idea of the hopelessness of the condition of alcoholism, "hitting bottom" as a prerequisite for changing, experiencing a conversion (this is not stressed in AA, though there is a conversion from drinking to sobriety) and realizing the importance of interaction with others, which had first impressed Wilson when his newly sober friend came to talk to him.

Wilson joined the Oxford Group and tried preaching his theories to other alcoholics with no appreciable results. On a business trip to Akron, Wilson met another member of the group, Dr. Bob (Dr. Robert Holbrook Smith), an alcoholic who was still drinking. Wilson told his story, without preaching, and stressed the disease aspect of alcoholism. Dr. Bob sobered up and Alcoholics Anonymous was founded, although not formally under that name. (AA dates its "birth" as June 10, 1935, Dr. Bob's first day of "permanent sobriety.") Wilson and Dr. Bob began talking to alcoholics in Akron. Later Wilson returned to New York and continued work there. He and his followers eventually split from the Oxford Group, rejecting their notions of absolutism and aggressive evangelism. In 1939 a third group was formed in Cleveland. At the time membership was about 100.

In 1938 and 1939, Wilson put together a collection of articles that generally reflected the ideas that formed the basis of the fledgling organization. Published by AA and entitled *Alcoholics Anonymous,* it is more commonly referred to as the "Big Book." In the process Wilson developed the Twelve Steps for recovery. The book also contained case histories of recovered members. Although it did not do well at first, it gradually gained publicity and sales increased. Since original publication, the "Big Book" has sold millions of copies and is available on the Internet. For some the "Big Book" is the basic textbook of AA, for others almost a bible. Different conflicts among the groups, such as those related to religious status, organization and anonymity, were resolved, and certain practices were formalized in 1946 in the Twelve Traditions. Headquarters were established in New York and AA began publishing books and a monthly magazine, *The Grapevine.* In 1958 there were 6,000 groups with about 150,000 members; by 1988 there were 85,270 groups worldwide, with 1,734,734 members. As of 1996, there were approximately close to 2 million members in 114 countries.

Organization: AA is incorporated as a not-for-profit organization run by two operating bodies, AA World Services, Inc. and the AA Grapevine, Inc., which are responsible to a board of trustees. Each year there is a conference attended by 91 delegates from AA areas in the U.S. and Canada; the trustees; the directors of World Services, Inc. and the Grapevine, Inc.; and the staff of the General Service Office and *The Grapevine* in New York.

On the local level, group organization is kept to a minimum, generally a few officers who arrange programs for meetings and maintain contact with the

The Twelve Traditions of Alcoholics Anonymous

1	Our common welfare should come first; personal recovery depends upon AA unity.
2	Four our group purpose there is but one ultimate authority—a loving god as He may express Himself in our group conscience. Our leaders are but trusted servants; they do not govern.
3	The only requirement for AA membership is a desire to stop drinking.
4	Each group should be autonomous except in matters affecting other groups or AA as a whole.
5	Each group has but one primary purpose—to carry its message to the alcoholic who still suffers.
6	An AA group ought never endorse, finance, or lend the AA name to any related facility or outside enterprise, lest problems of money, property, and prestige divert us from out primary purpose.
7	Every AA group ought to be fully self-supporting, declining outside contributions.
8	Alcoholics Anonymous should remain forever nonprofessional, but our service centers may employ social workers.
9	AA, as such, ought never be organized; but we may create service boards or committees directly responsible to those they serve.
10	Alcoholics Anonymous has no opinions on outside issues; hence the AA name ought never to be drawn into controversy.
11	Our public relations policy is based on attraction rather than promotion; we need always maintain personal anonymity at the level of press, radio and films.
12	Anonymity is the spiritual foundation of all our Traditions, ever reminding us to place principles before personalities.

Source: Alcoholics Anonymous World Services.

General Service Office. In all AA organizations, responsibility for leading groups is rotated.

New groups are started where there is a demand, usually by an experienced member who helps with the initial setting-up process.

Meetings: AA meetings are open to all alcoholics, whether or not they have ever attended a previous meeting. "Open" meetings are open to everyone, alcoholics and nonalcoholics. "Closed" meetings are limited to alcoholics so that members will feel free to discuss particularly difficult or intimate problems. "Step" meetings are conducted like study groups, devoted to one of the Twelve Steps. They are less spontaneous than other meetings and members are encouraged to prepare themselves beforehand.

Leadership of meetings is often self-perpetuating, since leaders are usually chosen from a nucleus of those who have successfully maintained sobriety for a long time and who are willing to serve. (Length of sobriety is of major importance in AA and anniversaries of the date when a member first became sober are important events and are celebrated at appropriate meetings, often accompanied by a small party. Conversely, if a member resumes drinking, he loses all seniority and his sobriety begins from scratch no matter how many years of previous sobriety he may have achieved.)

Speakers at AA meetings are usually drawn from within the group itself or from other groups—seldom from outside AA. Often members of one group will hold meetings for members of another group.

The Twelve Steps: The Twelve Steps stress reliance on a higher power, humility, honest admission of wrongdoing, and response to spiritual awakening by sharing with others. The first step involves the idea of despair and a breakdown of denial concerning alcohol. Second is the idea of hope, or seeing the light. Third, acceptance of the incurability of alcoholism is made, and dependence on a higher power stressed. The next steps involve making amends, continuing confirmation of a new image of oneself, and redirecting energy to help others. Much emphasis is put on this 12th step, since in the history of AA it was Bill W.'s carrying of the message to Dr. Bob that saved both of them and made the founding of AA possible. Thus attempts by AA members to help people who are drinking are known as "twelve-stepping." (See Visuals.)

The Twelve Traditions: The Twelve Traditions specify that the unity of AA is paramount, that leaders serve but not govern, that all who desire help be accepted as members and that groups are autonomous. The AA message is to be spread, but other enterprises are not endorsed and no sides are taken in controversies. Groups are self-supporting and nonprofessional, with as little formal organization as possible. Personal ambition is discouraged and anonymity is protected. However, anonymity is not required on a personal level or in small groups. (See Visuals.)

New members are asked if they have admitted to themselves that they are "powerless over alcohol" and if they are ready to accept their problem. "Surrender" is a word often used in this regard, not in the sense of capitulating to the influence of alcohol or alcoholism but of surrendering to the fact that they cannot cope with alcohol and that they must stop pretending that they can. (See DENIAL.)

Membership: New members are urged to come to 90 meetings in 90 days, a crash program designed to provide maximum support during what is regarded as a dangerous time. They are exhorted to immerse themselves thoroughly in AA participation and are warmly received for having admitted past pride and failure. They are led to recognize their need for AA and to embrace its principles enthusiastically. Skepticism, questioning of AA methods, and stories about those who have stayed sober without the help of AA are discouraged.

Each new member is urged to select a "sponsor," an experienced AA member in whom the newly-sober beginner can confide on a continuing, individual basis. Members often contact their sponsor on a daily basis, seeking advice or, of even more immediate importance, asking for help when the temptation to drink becomes intense. Another form of AA counseling is known as "twelve-stepping." Two AA members—always two to provide mutual support—will visit someone who is drinking, either a member or nonmember, and try to persuade him or her to seek help, which may or may not include medical help and professional therapy. The ultimate goal is to bring the individual into, or back into, AA and sobriety.

Meetings are generally informal sessions. After customary business, announcements and voluntary collections are taken care of, a speaker addresses the group on some aspect of alcoholism, usually from an autobiographical point of view. The talk is followed by a period in which those who wish to be heard have an opportunity to speak. Sometimes all or part of the meeting is run like an "Australian meeting," in which everyone in attendance is called upon to either speak or "pass."

Living "the AA way" includes not only regular attendance at meetings and close contact with one's sponsor but a relationship with the "higher power." In the early days of AA (and in the Twelve Steps), this higher power was identified as God ("as you understand him"). However, as AA has grown to include those whose religious beliefs range from strict fundamentalism to atheism, the concept of the higher power has been broadened for some members to include a rather general sense of spirituality or some spiritual resource within the individual. For others this new concept of the higher power has been extended to an entity outside the normal religious organizations, such as a therapy group or, particularly, AA itself.

AA members are encouraged to keep their problems as simple as possible and to avoid blowing them up to unmanageable proportions. They are not required to promise to stop drinking for all time but to "stay away from just one drink for just one day at a time." This stress on simplicity is reflected in the variety of slogans—"easy does it," "first things first," "stick to the program"—designed to help the alcoholic stay out of situations that might hurt him or cause him anxiety or anger. New members are urged not to make serious changes in their lives, except those aspects that would endanger their sobriety. Major career changes, possibly stressful or complicated new personal relationships, and situations where alcohol is served or even available are to be avoided. The new member is encouraged to focus his or her social activity on AA and, whenever possible, to place strict limits on their outside social contacts. At the end of each successful day, they are urged to thank their higher power.

Membership statistics: The membership figures listed below are based on reports to the General Service Office as of January 1, 1998, plus an average allowance for groups that have not reported membership. There is no practical way of counting members who are not affiliated with a local group.

Groups in U.S.	50,997
Members in U.S.	1,166,079
Groups in Canada	5,277
Members in Canada	102,499
Groups Overseas	38,895
Members Overseas	636,306
Internationalists	108
Lone Members	312

Groups in Correctional Facilities:	
U.S. & Canada	2,399
Total Groups Reported	97,568
Total Members Reported	1,967,433

Approximately 145 merchant marines, or men and women in the naval service on sea duty, describe themselves as "AA Internationalists." Staff members of the U.S./Canada General Service Office correspond with these members and make it possible for them to correspond with each other. Internationalists have been responsible for starting and encouraging local AA groups in many foreign ports.

AA and its critics: Within AA there is mistrust, sometimes considerable, of professionals and others outside the organization who work in the treatment of alcoholics. It is felt that professionals who are not alcoholics do not know what alcoholism is really about. Even professionals who are themselves alcoholics are sometimes resented for failing to recognize that the only successful cure for alcoholism is AA.

The organization views alcoholism as a permanent state that may only be controlled, not corrected. The heavy emphasis placed upon this philosophy promotes a prolonged, even permanent, group dependency. All life situations are recast in terms of a member's sobriety or alcoholism. A preoccupation with non-drinking replaces a preoccupation with drinking. For example, *The Grapevine,* AA's monthly publication in the United States, is filled with jokes about the stupidity of people who are drunk. Simple formulas and slogans, supplemented by an abundant variety of AA literature, are used to combat negative feelings that may lead to a resumption of drinking. Perhaps most important is the emphasis on the AA "program" centered around "doing the steps"—the Twelve Steps. This progress, from one step to another, is the essence of the program and entire meetings are often devoted to the study and analysis of a single step. Doing the steps gives the AA member a sense of participation and progress.

Critics have pointed out that this ingrown aspect of AA can lead to conflict in the mind of the member. Alcoholics Anonymous not only helps maintain sobriety—it *is* sobriety and, without it, sobriety is unattainable. The individual may not learn to cope with his disease or gain self-reliance because the program encourages dependency and discourages outside interests that would in any way diminish the central place of AA in the life of the member. Even the name—Alcoholics *Anonymous*—diminishes individual identity. (At meetings, members traditionally identify themselves as follows: "Hello. My name is [first name], and I'm an alcoholic.") The anonymity was originally justified as a way of protecting members against a society hostile to alcoholics and accustomed to discriminating against them. Even with more widespread acceptance of alcoholism as a disease, there is still some hostility and discrimination today. But in the eyes of its critics, AA perpetuates itself by maintaining this gulf; by stripping members of their names and, hence, their identities and leaving them only the label "alcoholic," AA increases their dependence on the organization. Since there is no known cure for alcoholism and

Common Drugs: Symptoms of Abuse of Alcohol

Alcohol. A depressant that slows down the central nervous system.

Drug Name	Street Names	Method of Use	Sign and Symptoms	Hazards of Use
Ethanol—Includes Beer, Wine, Wine Coolers, Distilled Spirits.	Booze, Hooch, Juice, Brew, Taste, Sauce.	Swolled in liquid form.	Impaired muscle coordination and judgement. Slurred speech. Blackouts.	Heart and liver damage with prolonged extensive use. Death from overdose and accidents, addiction.

Source: New York State Office of Alcoholism and Substance Abuse Services.

since AA does not consider itself a treatment program with an eventual end, the fellowship is therefore permanent and self-perpetuating. Dropping out is, in the eyes of many AA members, almost tantamount to the resumption of drinking. Nevertheless relatively few members remain in AA for 10 years or more.

AA views alcohol as the alcoholic's "solution" to an uncomfortable state. This discomfort stems from a sense of failure caused by unrealistic goals and expectations and, often, a tendency to fantasize. The inevitable failures lead to a loss of self-esteem and then to uncontrolled drinking. This view is not unique to AA, but others feel that to focus exclusively on this aspect of a broader problem oversimplifies it.

There are other criticisms of AA. Meetings have been called exclusionary and their tone conventional and middle class; to some they are offensively inspirational and anti-intellectual.

However, most critics recognize the success that Alcoholics Anonymous has had. While pointing out that neither the achievements nor failures of AA can be proven because there are no membership records to document them, they agree that the organization helps and sustains vast numbers of alcoholics who would otherwise be without support or hope. Regardless of its shortcomings, if they are shortcomings, AA has virtually created an entirely new concept in organized healing programs, which is based on service, fellowship and asking help of a higher power. The fact that AA's doors are open to

all, and at no cost, without judgment and without strict rules, has made it a very great success in a time when most treatment is very expensive and/or requires that the patient give up much more time and make a much stricter commitment. AA, and the Twelve-Step concept, has broad appeal that transcends gender, race, lifestyle, even nationality, as shown by its phenomenal worldwide growth.

Alcoholics Anonymous World Services, *Alcoholics Anonymous*, 3rd ed. (New York, 1978).

General Service Office of Alcoholics Anonymous, *Analysis of the 1988 Survey of the Membership of AA* (1989).

Margaret Bean, "Alcoholics *Anonymous*," *Psychiatric Annals* 5, no. 3 (March 1975): 3–64.

Ernest Kurtz, *Not-God: A History of Alcoholics Anonymous*, (Center City, Minn.: Hazelden, 1979).

Robert Thomsen, *Bill W.* (New York: Popular Library, 1975).

alcoholism   A chronic disorder associated with excessive consumption of alcohol over a period of time. The earliest known use of the term "alcoholism" was by a Swedish scientist, Magnus Huss of Stockholm. Huss published a treatise, *Chronische Alkohols-Krankheit* (Chronic Alcohol Disease, Sweden, 1849; Germany, 1852), in which he identified a condition involving abuse of alcohol and labeled it *Alkoholismus chronicus*. However, the DISEASE CONCEPT of alcoholism is much older. References to it have been found in the works of the 18th century American physician Dr. Benjamin RUSH, Geoffrey Chaucer and the Roman philosopher Seneca. E. M. JELLINEK has been credited with creating the first scientific typology that was developed into a theory of alcoholism as a disease, but perhaps the first official recognition of alcoholism as a disease was a resolution by the American Medical Association in 1956. This landmark resolution, along with a similar one by the American Bar Association, had a profound impact upon alcoholism-related state and federal laws, program financing, insurance coverage and hospital admissions policies, and the legal status of alcoholics.

There is a continuing discussion over the cause, nature and characteristics of this disorder and, consequently, there are many definitions. Most authorities now recognize alcoholism as a "DISEASE," but this position is challenged in some medical circles on the grounds that a self-inflicted condition cannot properly be designated a disease. (See ALCOHOL DEPENDENCE SYNDROME [ADS].) There are a variety of other arguments against the disease concept: alcoholism cannot be a disease because there is no anatomic structural abnormality; irresponsible people will abuse the legal and medical benefits given them as "sick" people; alcoholism is a label that stigmatizes patients; the concept dignifies and excuses drunkenness; the concept does not satisfactorily deal with a wide variety of categories, including heavy-drinking nonalcoholics, borderline alcoholics, periodic alcoholics. Certain RELIGIOUS groups, particularly fundamentalist Protestants, continue to view alcoholism as drunkenness and, therefore, a "sin." Some social scientists engaged in the study of ETIOLOGICAL THEORIES OF ALCOHOLISM AND OTHER DRUG DEPENDENCE, believe the term "alcoholism" inadequately describes a social dysfunction. They claim that to call it a disease is to label it nothing more than a medical-psychiatric problem and that the medical approach is constricted and, often, ineffective.

The counterargument is that the solution to the problem, if there is one, is not to reject the medical-psychiatric approach but to supplement it.

Thomas F. Babor, a professor and scientific director at the Alcohol Research Center at the University of Connecticut School of Medicine, describes two basic types of alcoholics, which correspond to two categories that have been labeled by other scholars as either type A, also called MILIEU-LIMITED (TYPE ONE) ALCOHOL-ISM, and type B (or type two). (For further details on type one and type two, see GENETICS.)

According to Babor:

Alcoholic subtypes can be categorized within two broad groups, called the Apollonian and Dionysian types, based on recurrent characteristics of the drinkers. This means that, for example, type A alcoholics are basically the same as milieu-limited or delta alcoholics, with some differences between these types resulting from the different methods and defining criteria used to establish the typologies.

The Apollonian-Dionysian distinction has been used to summarize the commonalties among alcoholic subtypes. Greek and Roman mythology attributes the characteristics of contemplation, intellect, artistic creativity, and self-restraint to the god Apollo. As suggested in the subtypes grouped under this designation, when alcohol dependence develops in such an individual, typically after years of socially approved heavy drinking, it presents in a more benign form. Consequently Apollonian subtypes include alcoholics who are characterized by later onset, a slower disease course, fewer complications, less psychological IMPAIRMENT, and a better prognosis. In contrast, the god Dionysius was known for his drunken revelry, sexual abandonment, and physical aggression. When alcoholic dependence develops in this type of personality, it can be identified by the subtype characteristics of pathological drinking and drunken comportment. Thus, Dionysian subtypes of alcoholics are characterized by early onset, more severe symptomatology, greater psychological vulnerability, and more personality disturbance. . . .

Confirmation on the hypothesis that only two broad categories of alcoholics exist would represent an important breakthrough for theory development and treatment matching. For example, research on the etiology of alcoholism might be informed by the possibility that two different paths may lead to alcohol dependence—one originating primarily in environmental influences and the other genetic and personality factors. Treatment matching and patient placement also might profit from this knowledge, provided that different therapeutic approaches and treatment settings prove to be differentially effective with different types of alcoholics.

(See ADDICTION, DEPENDENCE, INABILITY TO ABSTAIN, LOSS OF CONTROL, RELEASE and TOLERANCE.)

Thomas F. Babor, "The Classification of Alcohlics: Typology Theories from the 19th Century to the Present," *Alcohol Health & Research World* 20, no. 1 (1996): 6, 11.

alcoholist   Although rarely used in the U.S., in Scandinavian countries this term is frequently used to refer to a person whose drinking results in the excessive use of alcohol. The definition varies; it is also used to describe a heavy drinker who is not necessarily an alcoholic.

alcohol pathology   The scientific study of physical damage caused by the direct or indirect effects of alcohol consumption and the chronic use or ABUSE of alcohol.

alcoolisation   The French use this term to describe a pattern of large daily consumption of alcohol, particularly wine, which has harmful effects on health and contributes to a shortened life span, but which does not result in either physical or psychological *dependence*.

alcoolist   A person who follows the pattern of ALCOOLISATION, a term used by the French to describe someone who drinks daily and heavily to the extent that his or her life span may be shortened, but who is not physically or psychologically dependent upon alcohol.

ale   A BEER brewed by TOP FERMENTATION that has a more bitter taste and a slightly higher alcohol content than lager beer. The name is derived from the Old Norwegian *ol* and has been transformed by English dialectical usage. In Britain, ale and beer are synonymous; elsewhere ale has a variety of popular usage not strictly related to beers or malt liquors produced by top fermentation.

Fermentation of ale in Britain, the country with which it is traditionally associated, was a common practice by the time of the Roman invasions during the first century A.D. At that time, however, ale was less popular than fermented meads and ciders, both of which were more easily produced by the predominantly nomadic inhabitants. The Roman influence encouraged permanent settlements, which had the effect of encouraging permanent *tabernae,* or ale-houses, where fermented malt liquors were both produced and sold. The Anglo-Saxon invasion in the fifth century brought Britain under the control of a people already familiar with brewing techniques, and it was at this point that ale first became a prominent feature of daily British life.

Thereafter, ale became the subject of early legal legislation in Britain. The first alehouses in the country to be licensed were those authorized during the reign of King Edgar, who ruled until 975. By 1100 Henry II had levied the first taxes on malt liquor, the term by which ale was then known, and by 1300 Richard II had required all licensed alehouses to display identifying signs. The first brewery to receive a royal charter was the City Brewing Company of London, which was given its commission in 1437 and retained an official monopoly on ale production for some time. However, most ale brewing remained a cottage industry, one presided over by women who closely oversaw the drawn-out fermentation process. The product was a beer brewed exclusively from malt barley and commonly mixed with spices to counteract its extremely sweet taste. As one dietary book of 1542 noted, "Ale is made of malt and water; and they the which do put any other thing to ale than rehearsed . . . doth sofysticate their ale."

A major change in ale brewing came in the late 16th century, when hops were first imported from Bavaria to flavor the sweet brew produced by grains and natural sugars. Hops, the female flowers of the *Humulus lupus* vine, probably arrived in Britain via Flemish immigrants to Kent during the reign of King Henry VIII. Since that time, they have remained an essential ingredient in the mash from which ale is brewed. They were first used by the large family brewers, such as the Whitbreads, the Barclays and the Courages, who for a time competed with the brewers chartered by the crown and have since replaced them.

Because of top fermentation, true ale is generally bitterer and "heavier" to the taste than lager beer, which is made by BOTTOM FERMENTATION. This process employs a different yeast than that used in bottom fermentation and takes place at higher temperatures and is faster than the lager-making process. Today, three principal types of ale are brewed commercially in Britain: mild ale is generally dark and very "hoppy" in taste; pale ale is lighter in color and drier in taste; and bitter, the most common type, is a compromise between the other two in both appearance and taste.

alienation   It is a state characterized by feelings of powerlessness, depersonalization, isolation and meaninglessness; dissociation or estrangement from the surrounding society.

alkaloid   A diverse group of some 5,000 bitter compounds of plant origin that contain nitrogen in their molecules, as well as carbon, oxygen and hydrogen. They are usually physiologically or pharmacologically active (that is, producing mind-altering or toxic effects). Examples include morphine, nicotine, caffeine, strychnine, atropine and mescaline. The word is often a synonym for *active ingredient.*

alkyl nitrites   Organic nitrites, usually amyl, butyl or isobuytl nitrite. Amyl nitrite was originally used as a coronary vasodilator for angina; it was prepared in ampules covered with mesh that were crushed in the hand and inhaled for anginal chest pains. Butyl was legally manufactured as a room deodorizer.

The street term "snappers" or "poppers" comes from the snapping or popping sound made when an ampule is crushed. More recently these volatile nitrites have been sold in small, dark bottles and used for sexual enhancement and to produce a "high." When these substances are inhaled immediately before orgasm, they seem to slow the passage of time and prolong climax.

The long-term uses of these substances run the health risks of developing the eye disease glaucoma and red blood cell damage.

allergy   It has been suggested that an allergy to alcohol may be the cause of alcoholism. The theory, which was published in Alcoholics Anonymous literature, was first presented in 1937 by William D. Silkworth of the Charles R. Towns Hospital in New York. There is no medical evidence to support the theory, however, and the American Medical Association (AMA) states: "There is no similarity between the signs and symptoms of alcoholism and those of known allergies." There is the possibility that a person may be allergic to ingredients contained in alcohol beverages such as CONGENERS. A hypersensitivity to alcohol, known as pathological intoxication, exists in a small number of individu-

als. It consists of intoxication and sometimes aggressiveness following ingestion of minute quantities of alcohol.

allobarbital   An intermediate-acting BARBITURATE.

allopathy   The main system of western medical practice as practiced by most medical doctors, based on the concept of treating an illness by counteracting its symptoms and pathology by creating a condition antagonistic to the pathology itself. A prime example is the use of antibiotics to treat a bacterial infection. The antibiotic is antagonistic to the bacteria in that the antibiotic attacks and weakens the microbe's wall, leaving the microbe vulnerable to the body's immune system.

Allopathy is contrasted with the homeopathic approach, which seeks to increase the body's natural resistance through the introduction of minute amounts of substances that in larger amounts would have symptoms similar to the symptoms of the illness itself. (See HOMEOPATHIC MEDICINE.)

Another school of medicine, osteopathy, employs various methods of diagnosis and treatment but places special emphasis on the interrelationship of the musculo-skeletal system to all other body systems.

allyl isothiocyanate   Oil of mustard. Following the glue sniffing fad in the 1960s, the largest manufacturer of plastic cement, the Testor Corporation, announced the addition of allyl isothiocyanate to its basic formula as a method of controlling the problem. When oil of mustard is sniffed, it severely irritates the nostrils.

alpha alcoholism   The first of five categories of alcoholism defined by E. M. JELLINEK, "*alpha alcoholism is a purely psychological continual dependence* or reliance upon the effect of alcohol to relieve bodily or emotional pain." Alpha alcoholism does not lead to LOSS OF CONTROL but it may damage the subject's family or social relationships. There are no WITHDRAWAL effects and no signs of a progressive process. Alpha alcoholism is not an illness per se, but it signifies some other underlying disturbance. Alpha alcoholism may develop into GAMMA ALCOHOLISM, but it is often seen for years without any signs of progression. Alpha alcoholism is sometimes known as problem drinking, but that term is also used to indicate physical dependence upon alcohol. (See PROBLEM DRINKER.)

alpha-chloralose   An alcohol form of a chloral derivative. It is converted in the body to CHLORAL HYDRATE.

alphaprodine   A synthetic analgesic that has morphine-like effects but is neither as potent nor as long-lasting as morphine. It is a Schedule II drug.

altered state of consciousness (ASC)   A broad term that covers a variety of states induced by a variety of drugs and autosuggestive techniques, including intoxication, delirium, meditative and visionary states, and the phases of sleep and dreaming. During such psychological states the perception of time, space and reality is altered.

alurate   A sedative hypnotic and intermediate-acting depressant containing the BARBITURATE aprobarbital. It is used for insomnia and daytime sedation and may be habit-forming. It has a 20% alcohol content.

ambivalence   In the chemical dependency recovery process, there often exists ambivalent emotions about drugs or alcohol, resulting in the urge to hold on to maladaptive behaviors while also recognizing their dysfunctional aspects. Therapy assists recovering people to recognize and work through these conflicting feelings. In this process, it is vital for individuals to learn to conceptualize and accept recovery as an on-going process rather than an event.

ambulatory/outpatient services   As defined by the Substance Abuse and Mental Health Services Administration (SAMHSA), the term ambulatory services refers to those outpatient services provided to a client who does not reside in a treatment facility. Such services include treatment, recovery, aftercare or rehabilitation services for mental illness, drugs or alcoholism. Home care is included in this category. Ambulatory services also are known in the alcoholism field as nonresidential services.

Beatrice A Rouse, ed., *Substance Abuse and Mental Health Statistics Sourcebook* (Washington, D.C.: Substance Abuse and Mental Health Services Administration, 1995).

American Civil Liberties Union (ACLU)   The ACLU is a nonpartisan organization devoted to the preservation and extension of the basic rights set forth in the U.S. Constitution. Founded in 1920 by such prominent figures as Jane Addams, Helen Keller, Judah Magnus and Norman Thomas, the ACLU grew out of earlier groups that had defended the rights of conscientious objectors during World War I. Its program is directed toward three major areas of civil liberties: inquiry and expression, including freedom of speech, press, assembly and religion; equality before the law for everyone, regardless of race, nationality, sex, political opinion or religious belief; and due process of law for all. Since its founding, the ACLU has participated directly or indirectly in almost every major civil liberties case contested in American courts.

The organization has criticized the concept of using drug testing to "diagnose" drug use and opposes those who would "permit urine searches to creep into our schools on the coattails of forced medical examinations." The ACLU argues that drug use is not an illness but "plain old criminal conduct," and trying to combat it with "forced medical exams is a great intrusion on the individual's privacy." In August 1985, a high school in Becton, New Jersey, tried to make drug testing part of the complete medical examination required of all its students. Five students challenged the policy in the courts and on December 9, 1985, the New Jersey State Superior Court ruled against Becton's school board. This decision was reversed, however, in a landmark decision in 1996. (See DRUG TESTING.)

In January 1997 the ACLU filed an *amicus curiae* grief requesting the U.S. Supreme Court to strike down a Georgian law that requires candidates for statewide office to submit to, and pass, a urine test before qualifying, believing that this law stands in violation of the Fourth Amendment's protection against "suspicionless searches." Advocating drug sentencing reform in a 1995 press release, the ACLU commended the U.S. Sentencing Commission for moving in the direction of ending the disparity between crack and cocaine. In 1997 the organization criticized Congress and the president for "blocking the Commission's recommendation regarding the disparity."

Gilda Berger, *Drug Testing* (New York: Franklin Watts, 1987): 49, 67.

American Council for Drug Education (CDE)
Formerly the American Council on Marijuana and Other Psychoactive Drugs (ACM), it changed its name in 1983 to better reflect the council's aim—that of educating the public about the health hazards associated with the use of psychoactive drugs. Established in 1977, the council believes an educated public is the best defense against harmful use of drugs; consequently it promotes scientific findings, organizes conferences and seminars, provides media resources and publishes educational materials.

American Council on Alcohol Problems (ACAP)
A not-for-profit organization that provides a medium through which individuals, churches and social agencies can cooperate to find a moral and scientific solution to the alcohol problem and promote abstinence in the U.S. It has been in operation since 1895 under various names: the Anti-Saloon League of America, the Temperance League of America and the National Temperance League.

American Medical Association (AMA) substance abuse programs
In 1974 the AMA adopted guidelines affirming that physicians have a responsibility to meet the needs of alcohol- and other drug-abuse patients by providing care at one of three levels: (1) diagnosis and referral (designated as the minimum acceptable level of care); (2) limited responsibility for treatment (restoration of the patient to a point of being capable of participating in a long-term treatment program); or (3) responsibility for long-term treatment and follow-up care.

Physicians are expected to have knowledge of and skills in the care of substance-abusing patients, including common terminology and diagnostic criteria; epidemiology and natural history; familial, sociocultural, genetic and biologic risk factors; basic pharmacology and pathophysiology; patient evaluation techniques; referral and appropriate referral resources; long-term care needs; legal and regulatory requirements about prescribing to and treatments of alcohol- and drug-abusing patients; release of information; and consent to care.

The AMA also encourages all physicians to consider the degree to which they are personally at risk of developing alcohol- and other drug-related problems, together with their ethical obligation to intervene with a colleague who gives evidence of such impairment. Since these guidelines were issued, many of the barriers to physician involvement in the prevention, early identification, and treatment of harmful use of alcohol and other drugs have been recognized.

Bonnie B. Wilford, "Stopping Silent Losses," *Alcohol Health & Research World* 13, no. 1 (1989): 69.

American Medical Students Association (AMSA)
An independent professional organization representing the concerns and interests of some 30,000 physicians-in-training. Since the 1970s, AMSA has conducted programs aimed at enhancing medical curricula on alcohol and drug use, and at protecting the health of its members, their future patients and their physician colleagues. The association has members at over 140 allopathic and osteopathic medical schools throughout the United States.

AMSA publishes a monthly journal, *The New Physician,* which, in collaboration with the National Institute on Alcohol and Alcoholism (NIAAA) and four primary care specialty societies, published the *Directory of Training Sites for Medical Student Education in Chemical Dependency.*

AMSA's Aid to Impaired Medical Students (AIMS) programs are a major initiative in the area of student well-being. These programs, run by medical students, are designed to help identify maladaptive behaviors including impairment by drugs and alcohol, refer medical students for treatment, and prevent harmful use of drugs and alcohol by medical students. In 1988, with support from the Office for Substance Abuse Prevention (OSAP), AMSA launched a project that uses medical students to teach alcohol- and other drug-abuse prevention to adolescents in communities surrounding their medical schools.

American military
Conditions of military life traditionally have been such that soldiers often resort to mind-altering substances, primarily alcohol, to relieve homesickness, loneliness, frustration, bore-

dom, fear, and even hunger and cold. Also, drinking is a socially-conditioned fraternal behavior. Since the American Revolution, heavy alcohol use has been a problem among enlisted men, though not the only example of drug use. Drug problems have not resulted solely from enlistees' efforts to intoxicate themselves. The American Civil War broke out shortly after the invention in 1853 of the hypodermic syringe. Many of the physicians serving both Union and Confederate troops mistakenly believed, along with the rest of the medical profession, that intravenous administration of morphine circumvented the danger of addiction to the drug since it bypassed the stomach. Consequently, they administered morphine freely to wounded soldiers and often provided them with their own personal drug supplies and syringes. Doctors also routinely distributed other opium preparations to relieve dysentery and diarrhea. In the years following the war, their error in judgment became apparent. Some 400,000 Civil War veterans showed evidence of morphine addiction: it came to be known as "the army disease."

In the early 20th century, when American military forces occupied the Panama Canal Zone, government authorities became concerned about heavy and widespread marijuana smoking among military personnel stationed there. Up to 20% of enlisted men admitted a marijuana habit consisting of an average of five joints (marijuana cigarettes) a day over the previous 14 months. A military investigation into the matter concluded that such individuals were "constitutional psychopaths and morons." Later studies confirmed that there were underlying personality deficiencies involved, but found they had little effect on military performance.

Marijuana use in the ranks persisted during World War II, by which time it had also gained significant popularity among civilians, but it received little attention and was not considered a serious problem. During the Korean conflict, military personnel in the Far East took advantage of local availability to experiment with heroin and other narcotics, but few addictions or other problems developed.

Recent history has shown that drug trends in American society are reflected in even the strictest military environments and may be exacerbated by factors unique to wartime circumstances. Drug offenses at the military and naval academies (such as West Point and Annapolis) have increased markedly in the 1980s and early 1990s, as have court-martial and dishonorable discharges for such infractions. Moreover, during the unpopular war in Vietnam, the scope of military drug use and addiction enlarged dramatically, forcing authorities (after their rather late recognition of the problem) to establish educational, treatment and rehabilitation programs. These programs, which included surprise urinalysis to test for drugs, met with some success.

American soldiers stationed in Vietnam, particularly those involved in heavy combat, found themselves in an ambivalent situation that rendered them especially vulnerable to harmful use of drugs. They fought in a dubious war, which their civilian peers vocally opposed, and many undoubtedly questioned their own participation. Combat increased their stress. Many of those men who enlisted late in the war had already developed patterns of drug use in civilian society, where drug popularity was increasing. Finally, in Vietnam, extremely potent marijuana and pure heroin were readily and inexpensively available. Abuse of these drugs was less obvious than alcohol intoxication, which was subject to severe penalties. In light of these factors, the development of heavy drug consumption among enlisted personnel was not surprising.

Alcohol, marijuana and heroin were the drugs most commonly used by soldiers in Vietnam combat zones, and most who indulged in drugs used a combination of several. On their return home, almost all veterans said they drank while in Vietnam and about 11% admitted to having alcohol-related problems; 69% said they had smoked marijuana during their tours of duty and most consumed very large doses. One-third quit smoking marijuana after their return. Many complained that they were unaffected by the less potent marijuana available in the U.S. The THC content of the marijuana available in Vietnam reached 10% to 14%, making it even stronger than hashish.

The years following 1970 saw a dramatic increase in heroin use. In a study of soldiers returning to the U.S. in September 1971, 34% admitted that they used heroin during their stay in Vietnam. Since abundance made economic considerations (the usual impetus for injecting) unimportant, most users smoked or sniffed the heroin. It was 92%–94% pure. Although reported average daily consumption exceeded an astounding 1,000 mg, the method of administration and relatively short duration of regular use (most enlistees were in Vietnam for only a year) limited the development of heroin addictions. Upon their return home over two-thirds of those who had used narcotics quickly discontinued their habits. Lack of parenteral use by many, relatively short duration of use (approximately one year), and mostly the fact that they were once again in an environment containing far less stress and conflict, have been suggested as factors facilitating this discontinuance.

The armed forces tend to reflect drug use in American society at large, and soldiers generally exhibit no more tendency than the rest of the American people to misuse drugs, except perhaps under extraordinary conditions such as those found in Vietnam. Nevertheless, drug use in the military, especially in combat situations, presents a more serious problem than in the general population. Combat fighting demands that soldiers, who represent and defend an entire nation's interests, be alert, attentive and fully responsive.

Since 1981 regulations include irregular urine testing and breathometer tests for alcohol. The military currently gives about 3 million drug tests a year to its 2.14 million soldiers, sailors and marines. According to the Defense Department, the military drug program costs over $47 million a year. Evidence of marijuana and other drugs, including alcohol in intoxicating amounts, may lead to discharge if rehabilitation fails. During the Persian Gulf conflict, illegal drugs and alcohol were difficult to obtain and Pentagon officials noted fewer disciplinary problems among the troops during the Persian Gulf conflict than during the Vietnam War. The military's efforts to eliminate drug use among its personnel appear to have had an impact. The *Worldwide Survey of Substance Abuse and Health Behavior among Military Personnel* reported in 1980 that 27.6% of military respondents polled reported illegal drug use during the past month. This percentage fell to 3.4% in 1992.

American Nurses Association (ANA)   Founded in 1896, over the years ANA's members have made important contributions to the diagnosis, treatment and rehabilitation of people dependent on alcohol and other drugs. It is the ANA's position that, ideally,

all nurses should have the knowledge and skills to support intervention throughout the continuum of alcohol abuse and alcoholism treatment. The organization, along with other nurses' groups of addiction specialists, works to better serve clients and patients through an improved understanding of actual and potential nursing roles in prevention, treatment and rehabilitation, and through ongoing programs that strengthen and increase the presence and visibility of nurses.

In collaboration with the National Nurses Society on Addictions (NNSA), the ANA has recently completed *Standards of Addictions Nursing Practice with Selected Diagnoses and Criteria*. The document establishes twelve standards for the specialty of addiction nursing.

Edith M. Heismemann and Agnes L. Hoffman, "Nurse Educators Look at Alcohol Education for the Profession," *Alcohol Health & Research World* 13, no. 1 (1989): 48–51.

Madeline A. Naegle, "Targets for Change in Alcohol and Drug Education for Nursing Roles," *Alcohol Health & Research World* 13, no. 1 (1989): 52–55.

American Society of Addiction Medicine (ASAM) ASAM members are physicians from all medical specialties and subspecialties. Many are also involved in research and medical education. The group has more than 3,500 physician members who are concerned with the disease of alcoholism and other drug dependencies as well as other problems associated with psychoactive drug use and how it affects public health. The society extends and disseminates knowledge in these fields; enlightens and informs medical personnel and the public; and encourages research, teaching and the delivery of better care to chemically dependent people and their families. A certification examination is offered for members so that they may assess their knowledge of alcoholism, drug dependence and the care and management of patients.

ASAM was admitted to the American Medical Association (AMA) House of Delegates as a voting member in June 1988, and in June 1990 the AMA added addiction medicine (ADM) to its list of designated specialties.

History: ASAM has its roots in research and clinical traditions that predate its founding in the early

1950s, when Dr. Ruth Fox began regular meetings with other physicians interested in alcoholism and its treatment at the New York Academy of Medicine. In 1954 these physicians established the New York City Medical Society on Alcoholism with Dr. Fox as its first president. As the organization grew, it was subsequently named the American Medical Society on Alcoholism (AMSA). Interest in addiction medicine grew with the establishment of the NIDA/NIAAA (National Institute on Drug Abuse/National Institute on Alcohol and Alcoholism) Career Teacher Program for medical school faculty (1970), the creation of the California Society for the Treatment of Alcoholism and Other Drug Dependencies, and the California Specialty Society for Physicians, devoting significant time to treatment of chemically dependent patients. In 1982 the American Academy of Addictionology was incorporated and began efforts to achieve recognition for this new field within medicine. In April 1983 a single national organization was formed; all of these groups merged with AMSA.

In 1989, to reflect the society's concern with all drugs of addiction as well as its interest in establishing addiction medicine as part of mainstream medicine, the organization was renamed the American Society of Addiction Medicine (ASAM).

Americans with Disabilities Act (ADA)   The act is applicable to people with alcohol problems because such people are significantly more prevalent among the disabled population. One reason for this is that the regular use of prescribed medications (both psychoactive and nonpsychoactive) among disabled people may serve as a catalyst to increase the effects of alcohol.

Passed by Congress in 1990 to eliminate major forms of discrimination against people with disabilities, the act makes illegal the following types of discrimination:

Outright intentional exclusions;
Overprotective rules and policies;
Segregation or regulation to lesser services or programming;
Architectural, transportation and communication barriers.

amethystic   From the Greek *amethystos* (not drunken). The Greeks believed that amethyst, the semiprecious stone, could prevent intoxication. Today, the term "amethystic" refers to a substance or treatment method that could accelerate the normal sobering process or offset the effects of alcohol on the body. A number of researchers, particularly Ronald L. Alkana and Ernest P. Noble of California, have searched for an agent that would counteract the effects of alcohol on the CENTRAL NERVOUS SYSTEM (CNS), but progress is slow. Of primary concern to researchers are the possibilities that such an amethystic agent could be used both in treating medical emergencies caused by an overdose of alcohol and its potential uses in the prevention of automobile accidents.

Thus far, no effective antidote for acute intoxication has been found. Such an antidote would need to be fast acting, free of toxic side effects, inexpensive, and capable of being stored and administered conveniently.

Since it is unlikely that any drug now known could hasten the METABOLISM of ethanol the 10 to 20 times needed to achieve rapid sobriety in an intoxicated person, research efforts have focused on finding agents that counteract the effects of ethanol on the central nervous system. Recent findings indicate that chemical stimulation of noradrenalin (a neurotransmitter substance in the brain) can reverse some of alcohol's depressive effects.

ammonium chloride   The administration of ammonium chloride in a 1% or 2% solution is a method of treatment for PCP overdose. PCP is readily excreted in acid fluids and ammonium chloride increases the acidity of the urine.

amnesia   A loss of memory that may be temporary or permanent. In one of the typical warning signs of alcoholism known as a BLACKOUT, there is a temporary amnesia during which a person is conscious but cannot later recall what transpired. In Korsakoff's (alcoholic) Amnestic Syndrome, which is a result of long-term chronic alcohol use, only recent memory is affected. In syndromes with causes that are not directly related to alcohol use (Alzheimer's disease or multi-infarct dementia), all memory may be lost over time.

amobarbital   An intermediate-acting BARBITURATE commonly sought by drug users. (See AMYTAL.)

amotivational syndrome   A condition associated with heavy regular marijuana use, characterized by loss of effectiveness and apathy and by a reduced capacity to carry out long-term plans, endure frustrations, follow routines or concentrate for long periods of time. The syndrome was first described in a study of unemployed men who smoked marijuana continuously in a West Indian drug subculture.

amphetamines   Amphetamines are central nervous system (CNS) STIMULANTS with actions resembling those of the naturally occurring substance adrenaline.

History: Amphetamine was first synthesized in 1887. Over the past 40 years it has been manufactured in two chemical forms. Its clinical use as a decongestant under the trade name Benzedrine began in the early 1930s. Soon after, the drug's CNS-stimulating properties became known and by the end of the decade it was prescribed primarily as an analeptic drug. Later, dextroamphetamine (DEXEDRINE) was marketed as a more potent form (on a weight basis) of amphetamine. The pharmacological effects of both are identical.

Methamphetamine, commonly called "speed" or "meth," is a derivative that stimulates the central nervous system more powerfully than amphetamine. In the 1960s it became popular for users in the U.S. to inject large doses of amphetamine (usually methamphetamine) intravenously. ICE, a smokable and more harmful form of methamphetamine, appeared in the late 1980s in Hawaii and the Far East. Ice quickly made its way to California and, more slowly, across the United States. Ice is to methamphetamine what crack is to cocaine. Ice and crack, both smokable, are more concentrated and more potent, fast-acting, of shorter duration, produce greater dependency and are more deleterious to the health of the users than their parent drugs.

Statistics: Amphetamines and BARBITURATES are Schedule II drugs according to the Controlled Substances Act of 1970, and are the third most widely used class of illicit drug in the U.S., following marijuana and cocaine. The *1994 National Household Survey on Drug Abuse* from the Substance Abuse and Mental Health Services Administration (SAMHSA) estimates that 10.8% of Americans over the age of 12 used an illicit drug during that year, and 34% of Americans have used drugs at least once in their lives. By contrast, one study by the National Institute on Drug Abuse (NIDA) noted that 3% of those surveyed over the age of 14 reported having used illegal stimulants (including amphetamine) within the previous six months. In 1993 there were 5,602 emergency-room-related incidences involving amphetamines, approximately 1,500 more than in 1988. Between 1993 and 1995, lifetime use of stimulants by 8th graders rose from 11.8% to 13.1% and from 14.9% to 17.4% for 10th graders, but remained relatively stable for 12th graders (15.1% in 1993 and 15.3% in 1995). Unfortunately, the increase in methamphetamine use in the mid-1990s far outstripped that of amphetamines. Methamphetamine accounted for 10,052 emergency room cases in 1993, up by over 1,000 cases in 1988. In 1994, 3.4% of high school seniors had used crystal methamphetamine at least once in their lives, up from 2.7% in 1990.

Usage: Although now rarely prescribed by physicians because of negative side effects and high potential for dependency, amphetamines were once widely prescribed for conditions such as obesity, depression, hyperactivity in minimally brain-damaged children and narcolepsy (uncontrolled fits of sleep). The DEA (Drug Enforcement Administration) has tightened controls but unfortunately there are still many doctors who write prescriptions for amphetamines on demand. Amphetamines are commonly used illicitly for "starvation dieting," and for inducing euphoria and self-confidence. They are used by students to increase their concentration and duration of study time, by truck drivers who need to stay awake on long trips, and by employees who have to endure very long work shifts. Chronic users are known as "speed freaks." For reasons not fully understood, these drugs seem to have the reverse effect on hyperactive children, actually calming them.

Intravenous use: Injection of amphetamine, usually methamphetamine, yields a higher drug concentration in the blood than oral usage, and often results in a different pattern of harmful use. Most intravenous users experience sensations almost instantly upon injection (the "rush" or "flash"), which they compare to a sexual orgasm or an electric shock. After "shooting up," users feel energetic and self-confident. They may have feelings of enhanced sexuality, and orgasm tends to be delayed, sometimes indefinitely, for both men and women. As frequent users become eager to re-experience the initial rush, intervals between injections tend to grow shorter (in some cases less than two hours).

One pattern of abuse is known as a "run," which consists of a two-to-five-day period of continuous amphetamine use. On the first day a user is generally euphoric, sociable and self-confident. By the second day, the user has difficulty concentrating and experiences mood swings. Dose size increases considerably as a run progresses and there is a tendency to increase the amount of the drug used over a period of weeks or months. After the ingestion or injection of large doses of amphetamine, a paranoid psychotic state called "amphetamine psychosis" may develop. A combination of this suspicious, anxious state with feelings of great energy may lead to violence. The feeling that bugs are crawling on the skin, teeth grinding and frightening visions also occur. Eventually the run ends and the user sinks into an exhausted sleep or "crash." Following the crash, the user generally feels lethargic, fatigued and has a large appetite due to food deprivation. This may last several days and its length is proportional to the duration of the run. Users may crash because they have run out of drugs or the drugs no longer give the desired effect. At this point significant depressive symptoms may occur: the user may attempt suicide or become delusional. Such depressive states may be brief or may last for months, requiring psychiatric hospitalization.

Whereas the chronic user of alcohol or barbiturates becomes increasingly uncoordinated, easily distracted and has clouded thinking, amphetamine use increases coordination and the user feels especially clear-headed. This makes amphetamine psychosis particularly dangerous, as the potential aggressor is more apt to achieve his or her desired ends. After the user stops taking the drug, the psychosis usually subsides within a week, however, 5% to 15% of amphetamine users fail to recover completely and may exhibit disturbances for months or years after the last episode of drug use.

Amphetamines and alcohol: Amphetamine users have been known to drink alcohol to help them fall asleep or counter the wired-up feeling produced by large amounts of amphetamines. Conversely, alcohol users have been known to take amphetamines to counter the depressant effects of alcohol. Although the amphetamines may reduce the drowsiness caused by the alcohol, there is no improvement of impaired motor coordination. Not only can the combination of alcohol and amphetamines cause gastrointestinal upset, there is also the danger of producing a false sense of security, which can lead to carelessness and accidents. Amphetamines and alcohol are a dangerous combination because the safeguard against overdosing with alcohol—unconsciousness—is evaded. Some alcoholic beverages, Chianti wine for example, contain tyramine, a white crystalline base derived from the amino acid tyrosine. The combination of tyramine and amphetamine can cause an excessive rise in blood pressure. The belief that amphetamines will increase the brief high of alcohol is mistaken.

Effects: When amphetamines are taken orally at low doses (often prescribed therapeutically), physical effects include increased breathing and heart rate, rise in blood pressure, reduction of appetite and dilation of pupils. Users may exhibit brisk reflexes and fine tremors of the limbs. Higher doses may result in dry mouth, fever, sweating, blurred vision and dizziness. Users often have difficulty eating and urinating and may develop nonhealing ulcers and brittle fingernails, possibly due to malnutrition. Very high doses may cause flushing, pallor, very rapid or irregular heartbeat, tremors, loss of coordination and collapse. A chronic speed user may have any number of these symptoms and may lose 20 to 30 pounds or more. With mild amphetamine use there is generally no hangover on awakening; however, with continued usage, hangovers do occur, often with increasing severity. Psychological effects of short-term use include euphoria, enhanced self-confidence, heightened alertness, greater energy and increased concentration. With continued use psychological effects include restlessness and garrulousness; users often become irritable or manic. They may become increasingly suspicious of everyone, have difficulty concentrating and have memory problems.

Fatalities: Fatalities from an overdose of amphetamine are fairly rare. Symptoms of a lethal overdose are convulsions, coma and cerebral hemorrhage. Fatalities may also occur from infectious diseases caused by nonsterile needles. Since habitual users can ingest much more than nonusers, the size of a lethal dose varies from person to person. Death resulting directly from amphetamine use is most often the consequence of burst blood vessels in the brain, heart failure or a very high fever.

Tolerance and dependence: Tolerance to the cardiovascular effects of amphetamines is suggested by the fact that habitual users can survive single intravenous doses of 1,000 mg or more with only occasional negative physiological effects, while a nonuser taking this dose would be at considerable risk. Profoundly habituating, research has shown that the use of amphetamines frequently results in addictive behavior and *psychological* DEPENDENCE. Certain studies comparing the effects of amphetamines and heroin have indicated that addiction to amphetamines may be a more severe type of psychological addiction than that to heroin. The data concerning amphetamine consumption and *physical* dependence is less clear. While it is generally believed that the use, of amphetamines does not cause physical dependence, researchers continue to look for scientific evidence that the hangover and depression, often consequent to heavy use, are actually symptoms of physical WITHDRAWAL.

Availability: In the 1990s, amphetamine is marketed in a variety of forms in the U.S., with tablets and capsules the most common. Methamphetamine usually appears in powder or crystal form and is usually illicitly made. Pharmacologically similar drugs with different chemical structures include benzphetamine   (DIDREX,   PHENMETRAZINE, PRELUDIN), phendimetrazine (PLEGINE), methylphenidate (RITALIN), diethylpropion (TENUATE) and chlorphentermine (PRESATE). Preparations of phenolpropylenolamine (PPAs), which are known as "legal speed" because they are available without prescription, are weaker than amphetamines but, when taken in large quantities mimic the effects of amphetamines. Advertisements for PPAs tend to target the young.

Sources: Often produced legally in other countries, amphetamines are smuggled into the U.S. from Colombia and Mexico. There are also a number of clandestine laboratories in the U.S. that manufacture amphetamine and methamphetamine for domestic consumption. Demand greatly exceeds supply and a large number of amphetamine look-alikes have appeared on the market.

Synonyms: speed, crystal, meth, bennies, dexies, ups, uppers, pep pills, diet pills, hearts, footballs, cranks, splash and many others.

amphetamines with alcohol   Some people may take amphetamines in combination with alcohol to try to counter the depressant effects of the alcohol or in the mistaken belief that amphetamines will increase the brief high of alcohol. While there may in fact be some possible antagonism of the depressant effects of alcohol on the central nervous system (CNS), amphetamines do not improve motor coordination impaired by alcohol consumption, and the combination of alcohol and amphetamines may provide a false sense of security. Both alcohol and amphetamines may cause gastrointestinal upset. If amphetamines are taken with a beverage containing tyramine (a white crystalline base derived from the amino acid tyrosine), such as Chianti wine, an excessive rise in blood pressure may occur. (See DRUGS.)

amyl alcohol   The chief constituent of fuel oil, amyl alcohol is used as a source of amyl compounds, such as AMYL NITRITE. It is a colorless liquid with a burning taste. Not to be confused with ETHANOL, the type of alcohol used in alcoholic beverages.

amyl nitrite   An inhalant used for vasodilatation and to lower blood pressure and occasionally in the treatment of asthma and convulsions. Discovered in 1857, it was first used to treat angina pectoris. Amyl nitrite causes a sudden lowering of the blood pressure by dilating blood vessels; the lowering of blood pressure causes the heart to pump rapidly. It is supplied in glass vials (ampules) that are then broken open and inhaled. A very quick-acting drug, it takes effect in 15 to 30 seconds and its effects lasts approximately three minutes. It is only active when inhaled.

Amyl nitrite is used to produce an intense, but brief, euphoric high and is prized among drug users for its purported sexual stimulation and ability to intensify orgasm. Tolerance may occur but dependency is rare. Unpleasant side effects such as vomiting and nausea sometimes occur, and it is a particularly dangerous drug for anyone suffering with a heart problem. Long-term harmful use has also been cited as a risk factor for glaucoma and Kaposi's Sarcoma, which is a common disease among AIDS patients. A disproportionate number of AIDS patients were known to have been frequent amyl nitrite users, so this drug may severely damage the immune system.

Synonyms: pearls, poppers, snappers. (See ALKYL NITRITES.)

amytal   A sedative-hypnotic DEPRESSANT containing the moderately rapid-acting BARBITURATE amobarbital. It is used for the control of convulsions and as a diagnostic aid in schizophrenia. Also it is used for insomnia, daytime sedation and as a preanesthetic medication. An overdose can cause central nervous system (CNS) depression. Symptoms of an overdose include respiratory depression, reduction in reflexes, pupil dilation or constriction, decreased urine formation, reduced body temperature and coma. It can be administered intravenously or intramuscularly, but administration should be closely supervised. When used with alcohol or other CNS depressants it can have a potentiating effect. It is occasionally used for nonmedical purposes.

anabolic steroids   Street term for androgenic anabolic steroids, synthetic derivatives of the male hormone testosterone used to promote growth of skeletal muscle and increase lean body mass. The term "androgenic" means "promoting masculine characteristics"; "anabolic" means "building"; and "steroids" identifies the class of drugs to which they belong. First used nonmedically by elite athletes seeking to enhance performance, anabolic steroids are currently used by athletes and nonathletes (to improve physical appearance and strength). Although their popularity among high school athletes is on the wane, they remain a topic of serious concern to the drug-use prevention specialists.

Steroids are taken orally or by injection, usually in cycles of weeks or even months (rather than continuously), a pattern called cycling. "Stacking" is the process of combining various types of anabolic steroids to maximize effectiveness and minimize side effects.

Negative effects of harmful use of steroids include: liver tumors, jaundice, fluid retention, high blood pressure as well as a number of sex-related effects, such as shrinking of the testicles, infertility, reduction in sperm count and the development of breasts in men and facial hair growth and deepening

voice in women. Most, but not all, of these adverse reactions appear to be reversible. The most serious health threat to teens is from the artificial acceleration of pubertal changes that may permanently stunt normal growth. There is evidence to support concern over possible psychiatric effects of abuse: manic mood swings leading to violent and even homicidal episodes, depression, paranoid jealousy, delusions and impaired judgment, as a result of drug-induced feelings of invincibility.

Secondary health risks from anabolic steroids include possible infection with HIV (human immunodeficiency virus) from needle sharing and the unknown consequences of using illegally manufactured steroids of questionable purity.

The use of steroids is proscribed at national and international athletic competitions. The nonmedical distribution and use of anabolic steroids is a federal crime in the U.S., and possession is punishable by up to one year in prison; distribution by up to five years in prison and a fine of up to $250,000.

analeptics   A class of drugs that stimulates the central nervous system (CNS) and counteract drowsiness. They have the opposite effect of sedatives. Caffeine and amphetamines are analeptics.

analgesic   A drug used for the relief of varying degrees of pain without the loss of consciousness. Some analgesics will produce sedation.

anesthetics   Substances, usually gases, used to produce anesthesia (coma) for surgical procedures. Although anesthetics have undeniably made medical treatment more humane, anesthetics also have a long history of abuse. (See NITROUS OXIDE, ETHER, CHLOROFORM and INHALANTS.)

Anexsia-D   A narcotic opiate containing the CODEINE derivative hydrocodone bitartrate, used as an analgesic. Its habit-forming potential is greater than that of codeine and less than that of morphine. It also contains aspirin, caffeine and phenacetin. It is a Schedule III drug.

angiitis, nectrotizing   A disease characterized by inflammation of small- and medium-sized arteries and segmental necrosis (death of living tissue in a localized area). It is associated with viral infections such as hepatitis and the intravenous use of such drugs as methamphetamines and heroin. The disease usually terminates in the failure of vital organs and is generally fatal.

anileridine A synthetic NARCOTIC that has activity similar to that of meperidine and has morphinelike effects. It is a Schedule II drug.

animal models of alcoholism Many alcohol-related problems cannot be closely studied in humans. Alcoholics have numerous biomedical and psychosocial problems, in addition to their alcoholism, that may interfere with studies of the causes and consequences of excessive alcohol consumption. Factors such as poor nutrition, liver damage, psychiatric illness and drug use can make it difficult to determine which factors are caused by alcohol consumption and which are the result of these other problems. Animal models are one way that the effects of alcohol use can be isolated and examined. Animal models may also be used to study the role played by GENETICS in alcoholism, though great progress has been made in this field by studying adopted human twins.

Theodore J. Cicero of the Department of Psychiatry, Washington University School of Medicine in St. Louis, has made an extensive review of existing animal models. He cites four main objectives of animal studies in the field of alcoholism: to examine the biomedical complexities associated with chronic alcohol consumption, such as LIVER damage and BRAIN dysfunction; to evaluate therapeutic methods that may be useful in the management of alcohol WITHDRAWAL syndrome; to study the mechanisms underlying TOLERANCE to and physical DEPENDENCE on alcohol; and to investigate the factors that lead to and maintain excessive consumption of alcohol.

To be a true analogue of human alcoholism, an animal must meet a number of criteria. It must self-administer alcohol in pharmacologically significant amounts; TOLERANCE should be demonstrable following a period of continuous consumption; and dependence should develop. Psychological dependence cannot be examined to any significant degree in an animal. Physical dependence is defined by those responses expressed during withdrawal.

At present no animal meets all the criteria for a true analogue of human alcoholism. For example, in many cases there are difficulties with self-administration. However, for studies of the neurobiological mechanisms underlying tolerance and dependence, forced administration of alcohol is usually sufficient to meet criteria.

Today there is a growing and already very powerful movement favoring animal rights. Most advocates of animal rights are opposed to the use of animals in any testing procedures, claiming that the animals suffer hardship, torture and abuse. It has also been poignantly argued that many possible testing alternatives now exist, which include the use of organic compounds in test tubes and the use of human genes and molecules rather than animals. These techniques may be even more effective and can be conducted without involving the pain and discomfort imposed on animals during scientific testing procedures. There is a growing base of people in society who believe that our species, although dominant, does not have the right to abuse another species or even to upset the ecological balance of the planet, unless it is done in an extremely thoughtful and productive way that will benefit the earth as a whole, and not just one small percentage of it, namely the human species, at the expense of the others. In the long run it may be extremely beneficial to science and to humanity to discover new methods of researching diseases and disorders without having to harm any creatures. Learning to respect all life on the planet may be just as important and may even aid in discovering the etiological causes of human diseases and disorders.

Theodore J. Cicero, "A Critique of Animal Analogues of Alcoholism," in *Biochemistry and Pharmacology of Ethanol,* ed. Edward Majchrowicz and Ernest P. Noble, vol. 2 (New York: Plenum, 1979): 533–560.

anisette A liqueur produced from aniseed (the seeds of anise) and other herbs such as cinnamon and coriander combined with alcohol. The result is a clear liquid of approximately 60 proof with a sweet, licorice flavor derived from the aniseed.

Anisette is primarily a French liqueur. The best-known variety originates in Bordeaux.

anorectics Drugs used as appetite suppressants in the treatment of obesity and for weight control. In recent years a number of anorectics have come on the market to replace AMPHETAMINES, and though they are less potent they have many of the same effects as amphetamines and have a high potential for harmful use. Common anorectics include benzphetamine, chlorphentermine, diethylpropion, fenfluramine, mazindol, phenmetrazine, phendimetrazine and phentermine.

Anstie's Law   In 1862 Sir Francis Anstie made public Anstie's Law of Safe Drinking: 1½ oz of absolute alcohol per day was the upper limit of safe drinking. Anstie was a British psychiatrist who established the first women's medical school in England. Even today his law is viewed as a good general guideline for the average drinker. One-and-a-half ounces of absolute alcohol is equivalent to four 8-oz glasses of beer, a half bottle of wine or three 1-oz drinks of 100 proof liquor. It must be remembered, of course, that some people cannot tolerate any alcohol, so the law is not necessarily an appropriate guideline for everyone.

Antabuse   Antabuse (brand name of the drug disulfiram) has been prescribed to deter consumption of alcohol by patients in treatment for alcoholism. By itself, Antabuse has little effect in the body. However, if a patient taking Antabuse consumes alcohol, he or she will have a severe reaction to it, exhibiting such symptoms as headache, vomiting, breathing difficulty and, occasionally, collapse and coma. Reaction to Antabuse begins within five to 10 minutes after ingesting alcohol and may last from 30 minutes to several hours, depending on the amount of alcohol in the body.

No longer recommended for use alone in treating alcoholism, Antabuse is possibly effective in solidifying abstinent behavior until the patient seeks to establish an initial program of recovery, but even in this case it appears to be a rather extreme measure considering the many negative side effects.

Antabuse interferes with the METABOLISM of alcohol in the liver by causing a toxic buildup of ACETALDEHYDE. Care should be taken when prescribing Antabuse for alcoholics who have such physical conditions as arteriosclerotic heart disease, hypertension, diabetes mellitus, cirrhosis or any other illness that might make them unable to tolerate acetaldehyde poisoning. In addition, the action of

Antabuse may alter the metabolism of some other medicines.

The usual dosage of Antabuse was 500 mg a day for five to seven days and 250 mg a day thereafter. Patients have been treated for 17 years without bad effect (unless they drank). However, some people have experienced certain adverse reactions, including slight drowsiness, headache, temporary impotence and psychotic reactions. This drug should definitely not be used during pregnancy. (See PHARMACOTHERAPY AND ALCOHOL ABUSE.)

Anti-Drug Abuse Act of 1986   In 1986 Congress passed and President Ronald Reagan signed the Anti-Drug Abuse Act of 1986. One requirement of that legislation was the establishment of a White House Conference for a Drug Free America. The president appointed 127 citizens as conferees on the basis of their experience and commitment to a drug-free society. Chairman of the conference was Lois Haight Hessington, a former U.S. deputy attorney general. The conference held six regional meetings in 1987. A national meeting took place in Washington, D.C., from February 28 to March 3, 1988. A final report was issued in June 1988 and included findings and recommendations, as well as proposals for legislative action necessary to implement such recommendations.

anti-inflammatory medication   A group of medications, including aspirin, ibuprofen, acetaminophen, indomethacin, phenylbutazone, keterolac and naproxen, which have both analgesic and anti-inflammatory effects because they block the generation of peripheral pain impulses by inhibiting the synthesis and release of prostaglandins. Gastric irritation limits their long-term use.

Anti-Saloon League   The Anti-Saloon League of America was founded in 1895 as a political solution to issues related to saloon and liquor traffic, such as drunkenness, violence and the disintegration of family life. Funded by money collected from church congregations, the league worked as a political pressure group, launching publicity against saloons, electing political candidates who supported the anti-saloon cause, and running local prohibition campaigns. It gained support in the early 1900s and between 1905 and 1915 the number of churches cooperating with it increased from 19,000 to 40,000. The Anti-Saloon League emphasized the economic advantages of prohibition and argued that alcohol made the working man inefficient and careless.

Larry Engelmann, *Intemperance: The Lost War against Liquor* (New York: The Free Press, 1979): 10–19.

anticholinergic   A drug that blocks cholinergic (or parasympathetic) nerve transmission. Anticholinergics dilate the pupils. Dry mouth, and sometimes delirium, can occur. It also can cause the gastrointestinal tract to stop its movements. Medical drugs with anticholinergic properties include anti-Parkinsonian agents, antispasmodics, some antihistamines, antidepressants and antipsychotic drugs. Atropine is a classic example of an anticholinergic drug. It is sometimes used for its psychoactive properties. Belladona is a toxic, potent, naturally occurring anticholinergic.

antidepressant   A major classification of drugs developed in recent times to medically relieve symptoms in severely depressed patients. Antidepressant drugs are rarely used recreationally because although they seem to have a stimulant effect in cases of pathologic depression, they appear to have little immediate pleasurable effect on normal mood states. In fact, amitriptyline (Elavil) is occasionally used for its sedative effect. Antidepressants are subdivided into various classifications, including tricyclic antidepressants (TCA) and MONOAMINE OXIDASE (MAO) INHIBITORS.

antihistamines   Drugs used as histamine antagonists. They are usually prescribed for allergies, runny nose, sneezing and motion sickness. They have central nervous system (CNS) DEPRESSANT properties and when used with alcohol or other CNS depressants (narcotics, barbiturates, tranquilizers) they have an ADDITIVE EFFECT. Some antihistamines are combined with codeine or pentazocine (Talwin). This combination is called T's and Blues, which are sought after by drug users for their sedative effects. Alcohol, found in some antihistamines, has a synergistic effect that increases the sedative properties of both the alcohol and antihistamine.

antilirium   A drug containing physostigmine, a salicylic acid derivative of an alkaloid extracted from the seeds of the calabar bean (*Physostigma venenosum*). It is used to reverse toxic effects on the central nervous system (CNS) caused by anticholinergic drugs that result in hallucinations, delirium, disorientation and coma.

antipsychotics   Also referred to as neuroleptics, ANTIDEPRESSANTS and, previously, as major tranquilizers; drugs in this category are rarely used nonmedically because they have unpleasant side effects and do not produce euphoria

antitussive   A drug used to relieve or prevent coughing, such as codeine or dextromethorphan. Antitussives frequently are narcotics.

anxiolytic   A minor tranquilizer that reduces anxiety.

apathy   A lack of feeling or passion such that a person does not respond, even to very strong emotional stimuli. In the course of active chemical dependency, the user often displays apathy toward the crises brought on by the use of chemicals and denies the seriousness to himself or herself as well as to the significant people in his or her life. Because a chemically dependent person's main preoccupation is with the substance of abuse, they are often incapable of responding appropriately to other stressors in their life and therefore are not able to resolve or remove the sources of the stress.

aperitif   French, *aperitif* (appetizer). In its broadest sense, an aperitif is any drink taken before a meal to stimulate the appetite. The more popular alcoholic beverages used for this purpose are champagne, vermouth, gin, sherry, mild whiskey and Cognac. These are usually referred to as cocktails.

Certain beverages are manufactured specifically as aperitifs. Such drinks are intended to be sipped and are often associated with moderation. They usually have a high alcohol content and may have a bitter taste, the degree of bitterness depending on the type of plant used as a flavoring. Among the bitter plants used in the distillation of aperitifs are roots of parsley, fennel, asparagus and butcher's broom. Those with a milder bitter flavor include roots of maidenhair, couch grass, thistle and the strawberry plant.

Four well-known French wines sold as aperitifs are Dubonnet, St. Raphael, Byrrh (pronounced beer) and Lillet. Although sometimes used in mixed drinks, they are usually drunk by themselves. The flavor of these wines is more pronounced than that of ordinary wines because of the special flavorings (roots, barks, and flowers of bitter plants) added to them. Dubonnet, for example, is red wine with bitter bark and quinine added. Byrrh and St. Raphael are also flavored with bitter bark and quinine but are fortified with brandy as well.

ABSINTHE, now illegal because of the severe health hazards it poses, was a popular aperitif in France during the late 19th and early 20th centuries. It was flavored with wormwood. Pernod is now a popular substitute, especially in southern France.

aphrodisiac   A substance that enhances or heightens SEXUAL arousal or activity.

apomorphine   A chemical derivative of morphine used to induce vomiting. Unlike morphine, it does not produce dependency and has no euphoric effects. It is also used in AVERSION THERAPY in the treatment of alcoholism.

appetite suppressant   Psychoactive agent used to facilitate weight loss by decreasing the user's desire to eat and, consequently, the quantity of food he or she will eat. Unfortunately, the appetite suppressants so far developed are limited in their long-term use by side effects that include insomnia, irritability and a potential for dependence. (See ANORECTICS.)

applejack   The American name for apple brandy, applejack is the equivalent of French CALVADOS, although the term is sometimes used loosely to refer to hard cider. Its alcohol content ranges from 80 to 100 proof.

Applejack is usually made by distilling hard or fermented cider or fermented apple pomace. Another method, now rarely used, consists of freezing hard cider; concentrating the alcohol in the center, where it remains unfrozen; removing the ice and pouring off the alcoholic center.

Applejack was one of the most popular drinks among the early settlers in North America, who sometimes referred to it as "essence of lockjaw." It is still popular in rural areas and the South.

It has been suggested that the risk of cancer of the esophagus from daily consumption of alcohol is increased if the beverage has an apple base.

A. J. Tuyns, G. Pequignot and J. S. Abbatucci, "Oesophageal Cancer and Alcohol Consumption," *International Journal of Cancer* 23 (1979): 443–447.

aprobarbital   An intermediate-acting barbiturate generally used for sedation and to induce sleep. (See ALURATE.)

aquavit   A Scandinavian alcoholic beverage distilled from grain or potatoes and flavored with caraway seeds. The name "aquavit" (also spelled *akuavit*, *akvavit* and *akavit*) is the Scandinavian form of *aqua vitae* (WATER OF LIFE), the Latin term used in the late Middle Ages to refer to any distilled spirit.

Aquavit is particularly associated with Denmark, where it is also sometimes referred to as SCHNAPPS; in Sweden it is also known as *snaps*. *Linie Aquavit* (equator aquavit) is a Norwegian variety that gets its name from the fact that it is shipped south from Norway and across the equator twice while still in casks. The exposure to the high temperatures of the equatorial zone is believed to improve its flavor, much like the heating process used in the making of MADEIRA wine.

Aquavit is generally between 86 and 90 proof. Since it is usually not aged, it is normally colorless. Aged aquavit has a light brown color.

Aquavit is most often drunk straight as an aperitif. It is customarily swigged from a small glass, sometimes with beer as a chaser.

arecoline   An alkaloid found in the nut of the betal palm *Areca catechu* native to Malaya. It has mild stimulant effects when chewed or sucked.

Argentina   Second to Brazil among South American countries in both size and population, Argentina is a predominantly Catholic, Spanish-speaking country, largely peopled by Caucasians of European descent. The majority of this Caucasian population is descended from Spaniards and Italians, and the country as a whole has to some extent adopted the drinking habits of those nationalities. Trafficking and consumption of illegal drugs in Argentina is located in the *departement* of Gers in southwest France. Armagnac is somewhat stronger and drier in taste than Cognac and is distilled by a different method. Whereas Cognac is distilled by a two-part process, the distillation of Armagnac is one continual operation. It comes from the still at approximately 104 proof (Cognac is between 140 and 150 proof at this stage) with less of the raw product distilled. Armagnac is aged in casks made of black Gascon oak and marketed at around 80 proof.

asarone   A drug found in the roots of a marsh herb called sweet flag, which grows wild in the U.S. It is purported to have hallucinogenic effects similar to MESCALINE.

Ascriptin with Codeine   A narcotic opiate containing CODEINE and aspirin. An analgesic used for moderate to severe pain, Ascriptin also contains Maalox, an antacid medication, which keeps aspirin-induced gastric distress at a minimum. Also available without codeine, it is often used for arthritic conditions and can be habit-forming.

Asian Americans   Asian Americans comprise a number of diverse groups, making generalizations difficult. They are one of the less visible populations in the U.S. because of their comparatively small numbers (though this is changing as a result of increased immigration), geographic distribution (heavy concentration on the West Coast and in Hawaii), housing patterns (segregated) and low-profile life style.

Traditionally, there has been a low incidence of alcohol abuse among Asian Americans, although their use of alcohol may be increasing as a result of assimilation and acculturation. Nonetheless, the amount of drinking in this group is lower than that among other ethnic groups, and Asian Americans are more likely than other racial groups to be abstainers.

Asian Americans have some cultural taboos against drinking. Recent studies have indicated that many Asians develop a skin flush after drinking very small amounts of alcohol. This physiological response, which occurs in a high proportion of Asian people, is characterized by headaches, dizziness, rapid heart rate, itching or other feelings of discomfort.

Both Chinese Americans and Japanese Americans (who as groups have minimal arrest records, according to FBI statistics) are most likely to be charged with an alcohol-related violation if arrested. In 1988 arrests for driving under the influence accounted for nearly 12% of the total arrests of Asian Americans.

Asian Americans use alcohol treatment facilities less than most other ethnic groups, mainly because of a philosophy that the family can best take care of its members. Other reasons include a cultural sensitivity to stigma, fear of losing face, lack of awareness of existing services, and cultural and language problems. Most Asian Americans do not recognize alcoholism as a problem except when it occurs in their own families, and then there may be a tendency to hide or deny it.

Enoch Gordis, M.D., ed, *Eighth Special Report to the U.S. Congress on Alcohol and Health* (Rockville Md.: National Institute on Alcohol Abuse and Alcoholism [NIAAA], 1993).

Enoch Gordis, M.D., ed., *Seventh Special Report to the U.S. Congress on Alcohol and Health* chapter 2 (Rockville, Md.: NIAAA, 1990).

H. L. Kitano, "Asian American Drinking Patterns," *NIAAA, Special Population Issues,* Alcohol and Health Monograph Series, no. 4. (Rockville, Md., n.d.).

P. H. Wolff, "Ethnic Differences in Alcohol Sensitivity," *Science* 175 (1972): 449–50.

Asian drug trade   In the drug-trafficking countries of Burma (now Myanmar), Laos and Thailand, the Golden Triangle in Southeast Asia, political turmoil and favorable climate have provided conditions for increased narcotics production and trafficking. The U.S. DEA (Drug Enforcement Administration) reported in August 1995 that Southeast Asian heroin is dominating the U.S. heroin market, with Myanmar being a principal source. In April 1989 David L. Westrate, then assistant administrator of the DEA, reported to a congressional subcommittee that "in addition to Myanmar being a major source country for narcotics transiting Thailand, it is expected that there will be an increase in opiate products from Myanmar transiting China, India, Laos, and Bangladesh." Because of police efforts, Thailand's opium production fluctuated significantly from 1985 to 1995, although U.S. government agencies estimate that 50% of the heroin bound for the U.S. from the Golden Triangle passes through Thailand. While the something of a wild card: unlike many of its neighbors, Argentina is not a major producer of narcotics, but its role as both a transit source to Europe and an internal consumer of narcotics expanded steadily in the 1990s.

Alcohol: In 1985 per capita consumption of wine was 60.1 liters. For the same year, per capita consumption in liters of ABSOLUTE ALCOHOL, was 8.8 liters from all beverages consumed. Beer consumption in Argentina measured 13.0 liters per capita. By 1995 the per capita consumption of wine had decreased to 43.8 liters, placing Argentina fifth out of 52 leading consumer countries. In that same year, the per capita consumption of absolute alcohol decreased to 7.3 liters. Argentina's per capita consumption of beer in 1993 had jumped to 27.7 liters, but then lowered to 20.0 liters the following year.

The national drinking pattern is characterized by toleration of daily consumption of alcoholic beverages with effective cultural discouragement of public drunkenness. Most drinking takes place in the home, usually in conjunction with meals, and the inhibition of drunkenness is thus provided for by the family structure. Drinking outside the home generally takes place in family-oriented restaurants, which have the same inhibitory effect on drunkenness. Modern trends affecting this established pattern are heavier drinking among the middle and upper classes, increased acceptance of drinking by women and higher rates of harmful use of alcohol in rural areas than in urban areas. The country has few legal restrictions on advertising of alcoholic beverages, hours of sale or minimum age for purchase.

The cost of alcoholism to the country has not yet been statistically researched, but authorities acknowledge the presence of rising drunkenness in the workplace, family problems and social aberrations related to alcohol abuse.

It was not until 1977 that Argentina formed a national body, known as the Advisory Technical Committee on Alcoholism (CO.TE.SAL.), to study alcohol problems and their effects. Its authority to plan programs for prevention, treatment and rehabilitation, however, is limited by the country's constitution, which grants virtual autonomy to each of the 22 provinces, and by Argentina's recent history of severe economic and political problems. Furthermore, the Argentine wine industry, which is completely in private hands, is a powerful opponent of

legislative restrictions on alcohol production and distribution. As a result, most treatment facilities for alcohol problems consist of small general medical and psychiatric centers in the major cities of individual provinces. A major concern is the general lack of cooperation between these facilities and most of the country's nonpsychiatric physicians. But an equally important problem is the general reluctance to diagnose maladies as alcohol-related or seek specific antialcoholism treatment. The principal efforts to combat this attitude are provided by the ALCOHOLICS ANONYMOUS, AL-ANON, and ALATEEN organizations in Argentina's larger cities.

Drugs other than alcohol: As of the mid-1990s, Argentina faced a growing problem both with the trafficking of illegal narcotics through the country and the internal rate of consumption. The Argentine government has taken a hard-nosed legislative position against drug manufacture, distribution and use. However, few actual controls exist to support this stand.

Argentina is neither a major narcotics producer (in crop cultivation or drug refining) nor a critical drug transshipment country. Still, with radar control rare outside the Buenos Aires area, large shipments of cocaine from Bolivia enter the country at any of its thousands of uncontrolled airfields or its many small municipal airports on their way to Europe and, to a lesser extent, the U.S. Drugs can pass undisturbed through Argentina by railroad because of shipping regulations that bar inspection of sealed containers bound for third-country destinations. Narcotics are also shipped by river transport from Paraguay and Brazil—the ports of Buenos Aires offer a convenient exit point for narcotics concealed in containerized cargo.

Brewers and Licensed Retailers Association, *1993 Annual Report* (London, 1995).

Hoeveel alcoholhoude dranken worden er in de wereld gedronken? (How many alcoholic beverages are being consumed throughout the world?), 27th ed. (Schiedam, Netherlands: Produktschap Voor Gedistilleerde Dranken, 1987).

United States Dept. of State, Bureau for International Narcotics and Law Enforcement Affairs, *International Narcotics Control Strategy Report March 1996.*

Armagnac The best-known French brandy after Cognac, it takes its name from the Armagnac region,

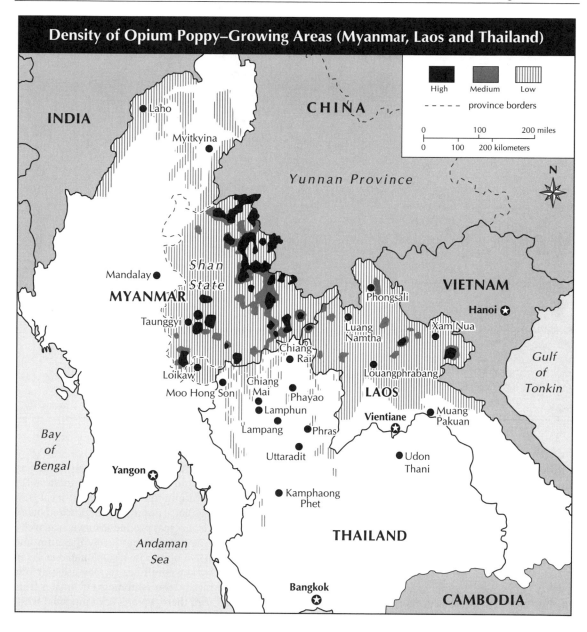

Density of Opium Poppy–Growing Areas (Myanmar, Laos and Thailand)

effect of regulation has been impressive (from a high of 200 metric tons in the 1970s to 25 metric tons in 1995), numbers are once again on the rise (up 8 metric tons in 1995 from an all-time low of 17 metric tons in 1994).

Cannabis is cultivated and smuggled out of Cambodia. The Philippines continues to serve as a transit and transshipment point for Southeast Asian marijuana and heroin destined for the U.S. and Hong Kong—the third leading financial center in the

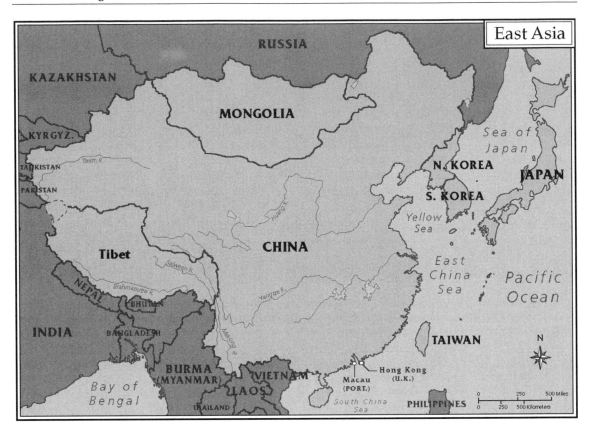

world—which continues to be a safe haven for narcotics-generated funds because of bank secrecy and weak currency control laws.

Opium poppy cultivation in 1987 and 1988 in Pakistan's Northwest Frontier Province yielded approximately 205 metric tons of opium each year. In September 1988 the U.S. and Pakistan signed the Tribal Areas Agreement, which provided for the gradual enforcement of an opium production ban. The five-year program was designed to eliminate all poppy production in the Mohmand and Bajaur regions of the Northwest Frontier Province. Government enforcement efforts in Pakistan, however, have been unimpressive. Production dropped initially to 130 metric tons in 1989, rose steadily to a high of 180 metric tons in 1991, dropped to 140 metric tons in 1993, but rose to 160 metric tons in 1994 and 155 metric tons in 1995. India, on the other hand, remains concerned about its role as a transit country

for narcotics produced in neighboring countries, particularly Pakistan and Afghanistan. India is the world's largest traditional supplier of legal raw opium, although illegal poppy production and diversion of opium from legal production exists as well.

Afghanistan is a major producer of opium and hashish, with 1995 opium yields estimated at 1,250 metric tons. Turkey continues to play a major role in the trafficking and transshipments of opiates from South Asia. From there, opiates are smuggled westward through Bulgaria and Yugoslavia into western Europe and to the U.S.

Elaine Sciolino, "Drug Production Rising Worldwide," *New York Times* (March 2, 1989).

U.S. Department of Justice, *Drug Enforcement Administration (DEA) Briefing Book* (1989).

United States Dept. of State, Bureau for International Narcotics and Law Enforcement Affairs, *International Narcotics Control Strategy Report March 1996.*

Eastern Europe

Asian skin-flush reaction   Elevated levels of acetaldehyde, the first metabolic product of alcohol, have been implicated as the cause of the alcohol skin-flush reaction common in Asians. The physiological response, which occurs in a high proportion of Asian people, is characterized by headaches, dizziness, rapid heart rate, itching or other feelings of discomfort.

aspergillosis   Many samples of marijuana are contaminated by the fungus *Aspergillus*. However only a few instances of pulmonary aspergillosis have been reported from smoking marijuana, presumably because heat destroys most or all of the fungus, and the healthy person is unlikely to become ill from a minor invasion of *Aspergillus* fungi.

aspirin and alcohol   Aspirin is not a risk-free drug, and the combination of aspirin and alcohol carries an increased risk of gastric bleeding, as discussed in several National Institute on Alcohol Abuse and Alcoholism (NIAAA) special reports to the U.S. Congress. Aspirin might possibly retard the teratogenic effects of alcohol. Investigators point out that further work is needed to demonstrate conclusively that aspirin reduces alcohol-related birth defects. Nonetheless it must be remembered that any alcohol consumption during pregnancy (with or without aspirins) will place the fetus in grave danger. (See FETAL ALCOHOL SYNDROME.)

Enoch Gordis, M.D., ed., *Sixth Special Report to the U.S. Congress on Alcohol and Health* (Rockville, Md.: National Institute on Alcohol Abuse and Alcoholism, 1987): 92.

Association for Medical Education and Research in Substance Abuse (AMERSA)   Founded in 1976 by the Career Teachers in Alcohol and Drug Abuse organization, AMERSA is in the forefront of national agencies that address the unique interests and concerns of medical educators in the area of alcohol and other drug use. The group has concentrated recently on training issues relating to primary care and has formed working alliances with the national leadership in psychiatry, pediatrics, family medicine, internal medicine, emergency medicine, obstetrics and gynecology.

AMERSA hosts an annual national conference, usually held in November in the Washington, D.C., area. In 1982 the organization held its first international conference on medical education in Berkeley, California. Cosponsors of the conference were the World Health Organization (WHO), the National Institute on Alcohol Abuse and Alcoholism (NIAAA) and the National Institute on Drug Abuse (NIDA).

AMERSA publishes the quarterly journal *Substance Abuse,* which is distributed to more than 400 members (all faculty members of U.S. medical schools) and to some 350 subscribers. The association maintains both a speakers and a consultants bureau available to organizations and institutions involved in or interested in advancing medical education in the harmful use of alcohol and other drugs. Recently, AMERSA joined with other national groups to define the availability of standards for fellowship training in the addictions.

asthmador   A cigarette containing stramonium and atropine and once used by asthma sufferers. It is now obsolete. Along with relieving bronchial spasms, in large doses it also produced hallucinogenic effects.

at-risk populations   Groups within the general population that have been identified as particularly susceptible to harmful use of drugs or alcohol because of risk factors such as age, environment and/or being a child of an alcoholic or drug user. At-risk populations include adolescents, the elderly and certain minority groups such as African Americans, Native Americans and Hispanic Americans. Such groups are generally targeted by drug-abuse and drug-prevention organizations.

ataraxic drugs   Drugs used as tranquilizers. Also called ataractics. (See SEDATIVE HYPNOTICS.)

atropine   Extracted from the plant BELLADONNA (also known as deadly nightshade), this alkaloid is generally used as an antispasmodic because it relaxes smooth muscle. It is also used as an antidote to certain poisons. In large doses it is toxic and since ancient times has been used as a sedative and poison. There have been fatalities among children who have eaten deadly nightshade.

attack therapy   A group therapy model in which individuals are verbally (never physically) attacked in the expectation that their defensiveness, rationalizations and denials will be broken down. They are vigorously confronted with their inappropriate or "junkie" thinking and behavior so that they are compelled to examine themselves stripped of their defensive armor. Some therapeutic communities place the person under attack on a "hot seat" at the center of the group for greater focus.

Following the attack, the individual is given considerable group support and understanding so that he or she can reconstitute his or her shattered psychological defenses into something more honest, realistic and resilient. (See INTERVENTION.)

Australia Australia's problems with alcohol and other drug use are painfully similar to those of English-speaking nations in the West. Excessive drinking is the major drug problem in Australia. While government surveys show that marijuana is the illegal drug most often used in the country's various states, harmful use of other illicit drugs (amphetamines, in particular) is on the rise.

Australia's primary concern regarding alcohol and other drugs (ATOD) has been consumption, as opposed to production or trafficking. Marijuana, amphetamines and methaqualone, produced locally, are the most commonly used illegal substances. Heroin has been a consistent problem over the years, while the early 1990s witnessed an increasing trade in cocaine smuggled in from South America and the U.S. Use of barbiturates and LSD, popular in the late 1960s, has declined significantly.

In recent years, Australia has approached its alcohol and other drug problems with greater emphasis on abuse as a medical problem. Government programs now focus on education, treatment and rehabilitation along with continued law enforcement. Drug-abuse treatment is provided, in one form or another, at all public hospitals. There are also voluntary community organizations in all states and territories that give additional help that the more rigid federal government is unable to provide.

In 1969 the government established a nationally coordinated approach to drug-abuse control—the National Standing Control Committee on Drug Dependence, comprised of federal and state members. In 1970 the Drug Education Sub-Committee was established, made up of state and territorial health members with expertise in education, law enforcement and management fields. It has developed a National Drug Education Program aimed at incorporating drug education into the wider concept of health education in the community.

The Royal Commission of Inquiry into Drugs is sponsored by the federal government. In Australia, the responsibility for drug prevention is shared by the federal and state governments; the federal government acts primarily as a coordinator and advisor, while state governments are responsible for implementing policies and programs in their areas. Evidence presented to the Royal Commission of Inquiry into Drugs in the early 1970s showed illegal drug use was confined to certain community groups; by 1979 surveys showed a spread to almost every social, economic, cultural and age group, with the exception of the state of Tasmania. The latter was probably due to Tasmania's small population and its isolation from the mainland. (Tasmania actually has a licit opium poppy industry, effectively blocked from illegal diversion into the black market by government control.)

Law enforcement with respect to drugs in Australia is handled mainly by the following three bodies: the Australian Federal Police, which polices Commonwealth laws; state and territory police, which work in conjunction with Commonwealth authorities; and the Bureau of Customs, which has the responsibility of enforcing regulations in the importing and exporting of drugs. All state governments have agreed to a uniform code of penalties based on those applicable under Commonwealth government legislation. The Australian Federal Police serve as the national agency for the systematic collection, collation, evaluation and dissemination of information concerning illicit drug traffic and use in the country.

Government surveys carried out during the 1970s are still useful for understanding drug use in Australia. The majority of drug users were between the ages of 16 and 35 and, within this range, the 18–24 age group predominated. The predominance of young users was particularly noticeable in relation to heroin, which was more prevalent among people who had left school than those still attending. While these patterns originally applied to marijuana use too, there has been a steady increase in use among older high school students. Moreover, although the 18–24 age group predominated, use of marijuana by well-educated people over the age of 30 was not uncommon. Males outnumbered female users of all drugs. Few surveys attempted to determine a connection between drug use and socioeconomic background and the few that did were generally inconclusive. Findings did indicate, however, a higher rate of drug use among middle-class children than working-class children. Children of unskilled workers were more likely to become intravenous users than their middle-class counterparts. There was also a higher trend of drug use among the unemployed. Although few surveys considered ethnic background and nationality, a 1972 study showed that the highest rates of harmful use were among those who came to Australia from the British Isles and western Europe. Immigrants from southern and eastern Europe and Asia reported using drugs one third as often. Midway between the two groups were those born in Australia. Although there was an indication that illegal drug use was more common among those who profess no religion than among those of a particular faith, here again, the surveys were inconclusive.

The Australian Institute of Health and Welfare estimated that in 1995, 17.6% of men and 10.8% of women, aged 18 and over, consumed alcohol, tobacco and illicit drugs at levels hazardous or harmful to their health. The same report estimated abstinence rates of 12.6% of men and 24.7% of women, while the remaining adult population (69.9% of men and 64.6% of women) consumed alcohol within safe limits. It was also estimated that death from harmful alcohol consumption in 1995 was 2,521 (3.8%) for men and 1,139 (2.0%) for women. Cigarette smoking (exclusive of passive smoking) accounted for 13,857 (21.0%) male deaths and 5,063 (8.8%) female deaths. The 1995 estimated illicit-drug-related deaths were 384 (0.6%) for men and 104 (0.2%) for women. When you compare (in approximate figures for men in one year) illicit drug deaths (384), alcohol-related deaths (2,500) and tobacco deaths (14,000), you see that in Australia as elsewhere, tobacco, though legal, is far and away the substance having the deadliest impact on the health and mortality of citizens.

Alcohol: First acknowledged by its Alcohol and Drug Addicts Treatment Act of 1961, Australia has endured widespread chronic alcohol use throughout its diversified population. The dominant cause of the problem, according to several government reports on the subject, is that excessive consumption of alcoholic beverages (most often beer) is not only accepted, but is actually expected and encouraged by the majority of the people. Although there is significant variation of the drinking pattern in urban and rural areas of the country, the nation as a whole is prone to associate heavy drinking with civil liberty, a pioneer identity, and other images of pride and freedom embedded in the Australian concept of "mateship." While these characteristics are most dominant among the population descended from English and Irish settlers, the condition of the native aboriginal population in regard to alcohol is even more precarious due to poverty and the lack of opportunity available to these people.

Beer consumption decreased 10% from 1975 to 1985. Annual per capita consumption of beer further decreased between 1985 (114.5 liters) and 1993 (97.5 liters), although it still ranked 10th in consumption of the top 52 consumer nations. On the rise in the 1970s, annual per capita wine consumption has been dropping (from 21.5 liters in 1985 to 18.2 liters in 1995). In 1985 Australia ranked 15th among reporting nations in annual per capita consumption of all alcoholic beverages (7.2 liters of absolute alcohol). Consumption declined to 7.6 liters in 1995, although Australia's ranking among nations worldwide dropped from 15th in 1985 to 20th in 1995. All figures are based on total population.

Treatment: Federal hospital and treatment services are funded on a cost-shared basis with state governments. Many private organizations and hospitals also receive financial support from the government. As no single form of treatment is appropriate to all forms of drug dependence, a variety of programs and treatments are offered by the various institutions: (1) counseling and consultation; (2) detoxification with both chemical and psychological support; (3) controlled maintenance through methadone with the support of therapy; (4) psychiatric treatment; (5) participation in therapeutic communities; and (6) attendance at "drop-in" centers with advisory service. There is also continuing rehabilitation in the form of vocational guidance and counseling.

Australian Institute of Health and Welfare, 1997.

Brewers and Licensed Retailers Association, *1993 Annual Report* (London, 1995).

United States Dept. of State, Bureau for International Narcotics and Law Enforcement Affairs, *International Narcotics Control Strategy Report March 1996.*

Hoeveel alcoholhoude dranken worden er in de wereld gedronken? (How many alcoholic beverages are being consumed throughout the world?), 25th ed. (Schiedam, Netherlands: Produktschap Voor Gedistilleerde Dranken, 1987).

M. M. Horgan et al., *International Survey: Alcoholic Beverage Taxation and Control Policies,* 6th ed. (Toronto: Brewers Association of Canada).

aversion therapy   A behavior therapy based on the experiments of Ivan Pavlov (1849–1936), a Russian scientist who worked extensively in the field of conditioned reflexes. Typically in aversion therapy, after detoxification, a patient might be given a powerful nausea-producing drug, such as emetine or APOMORPHINE, and then a shot of liquor. The liquor must be drunk just before the drug-induced nausea occurs in order for the therapy to be successful. Once a patient undergoes this therapy a few times, he or she begins to associate the nausea with the liquor. Conditioning sessions last 30 to 60 minutes and are given on alternate days for a total of four to six treatments. Reinforcement is given any time a patient develops a desire to drink.

Electric shock may sometimes be applied in the same way, a jolt of electricity given with a shot of liquor. However, this procedure has gradually become discredited and is not much used today. Another variation is the verbally induced aversion, also known as covert sensitization therapy.

It is stressed that alcoholics treated by aversion therapy must also be provided with alternative ways of securing gratification while sober, if abstinence is to be maintained.

There is disagreement over whether aversion provides any long-lasting cure. It seems to be more effective with some personality types than with others; Robert S. Wallerstein feels that the best results are achieved with depressed patients because the "punishing aspect helps to alleviate guilt and externalize aggressive charge." He suggests that patients who are paranoid, antisocial, hostile or passive-aggressive are not helped by aversion therapy. There is also the danger that a patient will have a serious physical reaction if the treatment is not carefully supervised by a medical specialist. Many patients drop out of this type of treatment because it is unpleasant, if not painful. Aversion therapy is popular in some eastern European countries, but it is not widely used in the U.S.

David J. Armor, J. Michael Polich and Harriet B. Stambul, *Alcoholism and Treatment* (New York: John Wiley & Sons, 1978): 33–34.

Albert Bandura, *Principles of Behavior Modification* (New York: Holt, Rinehart & Winston, 1969).

Morris E. Chafetz and Harold W. Demone Jr., *Alcoholism and Society* (New York: Oxford University Press, 1962): 204–207.

John Langone, *Bombed, Buzzed, Smashed, or . . . Sober: A Book about Alcohol* (Boston: Little, Brown, 1976): 132–133.

Robert S. Wallerstein, "Comparative Study of Treatment Methods for Chronic Alcoholism: The Alcoholism Research Project at Winter V.A. Hospital," *American Journal of Psychiatry* 113 (1956): 228–233.

ayahuasca   A psychedelic beverage brewed by the Amazonian Chama Indians of Peru. It is prepared from the bark of various vines and sometimes the leaves of *Banisteriopsis, esp. B. caapi.* of the malphigia family. The active alkaloid is HARMINE. Ayahuasca also refers to any of these vines.

Synonyms: caapi, natema, yage.

B

B & B   A dark-colored 86-proof liqueur, B & B consists of one part BENEDICTINE and one part brandy (often Cognac). It is a drier version of straight Benedictine and is a preferred drink in the U.S.

B & O Supprettes   A narcotic analgesic containing powdered OPIUM and BELLADONNA extract. It is used rectally to treat minor to severe pain and can be habit-forming. Overdosage results in respiratory depression.

babies, drug-addicted and -exposed   Concern about drug-addicted babies has prompted a loose confederation of fetal-protection advocates made up of physicians, social workers, prosecutors and even some prospective fathers dedicated to protecting unborn children against dangerous actions such as drug use by their pregnant mothers. Some advocates are using the civil laws in an attempt to expand their efforts beyond cases of drug use. Although this is a very sensitive issue since the mothers involved in drug use may be victims in their own right and may be powerless to control their addictions, nonetheless a growing number of women and men, both pro-choice advocates as well as anti-abortionists, in light of the exposure of rampant child abuse and neglect, strongly feel that the health and well-being of a child that a mother intends to give birth to should be protected from any harm or injury at all costs, and that it is society's responsibility to do this, just as it is society's duty to protect all of its citizens against harm or injury from other persons. Women's rights advocates, along with the American Civil Liberties Union (ACLU), protest that the rush to protect the fetus will backfire and could deter women from coming forward for treatment.

Meanwhile, it remains legal to smoke tobacco, drink alcohol, inject caffeine, and take prescription and over-the-counter medications, or in many other ways injure an unborn child. Not surprisingly, health authorities face an epidemic of drug-affected infants. Each year, according to the National Institute on Drug Abuse (NIDA) researchers, more than 300,000 infants are born with traces of illegal drugs in their systems. More women than men are now reported using crack in several major American cities, and drug experts say a large number of the new users are young pregnant women. Medical findings show that effects on drug-exposed babies can include retarded growth, stiff limbs, hyperirritability, a higher risk of crib death (now commonly referred to as SIDS—sudden infant death syndrome), strokes and seizures, malformed or missing organs, facial deformities, mental retardation and more. An alarming rate of infants are born each year, suffering from the debilitating effects of FETAL ALCOHOL SYNDROME.

The rise of cocaine use, especially crack, led to a proportionate rise in pregnant addicts. Consequently, reports of infants born with evidence of drug exposure increased across the country. Fetuses exposed to cocaine through their mother's use are

68

more likely to die before birth or to come to term prematurely; they are also at increased risk of deformities. Such newborns tend to be abnormally small at birth, especially their heads. They also appear to be more susceptible to SIDS.

A massive campaign by various federal agencies on the risks of prenatal drug use seems to be paying off in reducing drug use among women of childbearing age. According to the *1997 National Household Survey on Drug Abuse* conducted by the Substance Abuse and Mental Health Services Administration (SAMHSA), 6.8% of all women aged 15 to 44 had used an illicit drug within the last month, while only 2.5% of pregnant women had used one. By contrast, a 1988 survey of women having babies at 36 hospitals around the country found that on average 11% were exposing their unborn babies to illegal drugs, most commonly cocaine. (Rates at each hospital varied from less than 1% to 27%; the study included both urban and rural hospitals, with some serving the poor and others serving higher-income groups.)

By comparison, however, 333,000 (14.1%) of the women tested positive for alcohol and 469,000 (19.9%) for nicotine. In light of the risks of perinatal use of either of these legal drugs, the NIDA study suggests that alcohol and tobacco use, although legal, remain the most potentially dangerous drugs for pregnant women and their unborn children. The study also broke down perinatal drug use by racial and ethnic groups: 5.4% of African-American women, 2.4% of white women and 1.2% of Hispanic women.

Jane Brody, "Cocaine: Litany of Fetal Risks Grows," *New York Times* (September 6, 1988).

Center for Substance Abuse Prevention, "Alcohol, Tobacco and Other Drugs and Pregnancy and Parenthood," *Making the Link* ML006 (Spring, 1995).

Ted Gest, "The Pregnancy Police, on Patrol," *U.S. News & World Report,* (February 6, 1989).

National Institute of Health, *Maternal Drug Abuse and Drug Exposed Children: Understanding the Problem* (Rockville, Md., 1992).

Substance Abuse and Mental Health Services Administration, *Preliminary Estimates from the Drug Abuse Warning Network, 1993 Preliminary Estimates of Drug-Related Emergency Department Episodes,* advanced report no. 8 (Rockville, Md., December 1994).

bacarate A brand of phendimetrazine tartrate, which was used as an ANORECTIC for weight control, and is no longer available in the U.S. The drug elevates blood pressure and stimulates the central nervous system. Its activity is similar to that of AMPHETAMINES, and tolerance to its effects can build up within a few weeks. Overdosage results in rapid respiration, restlessness, tremors and hallucinations.

Bacchus The god of wine in Roman mythology, identified with the Greek god Dionysus. A "son of Bacchus" is a heavy drinker.

bad trip Drug users' slang for a negative experience resulting from the use of a mind-altering drug, usually a hallucinogen or stimulant. Determinants of a "bad trip" include: feelings of loss of control, hallucinations, sudden dread of insanity or death, and suicidal thoughts; physiological sensations include heart palpitations, nausea and sweating.

BAL Blood alcohol level. See BLOOD ALCOHOL CONCENTRATION.

balloon effect A term that refers to the substitution, by users, of one type of drug for another when authorities clamp down on the original drug of choice. The phenomenon is likened to the squeezing of a balloon in one direction, which causes it to expand in another. The crackdown on Mexican marijuana in southern California, for instance, was said to have resulted in an increase in heroin use, although this theory seems somewhat unlikely.

banana smoking In the mid-1960s, a widespread rumor reported that smoking the scrapings of the inside of a dried banana peel would produce a marijuana-like high. It was a hoax played on narcotics authorities, who would have found it impossible to prohibit the sale of bananas. Banana peels do not intoxicate but they do apparently contain a poisonous substance.

bancap A narcotic opiate containing CODEINE, which is used as an analgesic for minor pain. It may be habit-forming and overdosage can cause excitability.

History of Barbiturates

1864	Two German scientists, von Mering and Fischer, synthesize barbital, a derivative of barbituric acid.
1903	Barbital is introduced to medicine under the trade name Veronal.
1912	Phenobarbital, a second derivative, is introduced under the trade name Luminal.
1930s	Barbiturates are widely prescribed in the U.S.
1940s	Studies show that barbiturates are intoxicating and addictive, and that withdrawal symptoms appear when use is stopped.
1942	First major campaign against nonmedical use of "thrill pills" is launched. States begin passing laws against nonprescription barbiturates, and black market becomes profitable.
1950s	Barbiturates become one of the major abused drugs in the U.S.
1960s	Abuse spreads to youth.
1970s–1980s	Barbiturates still widely prescribed and abused. Benzodiazepine mostly replaced the medical use of barbiturates. Government estimates that 20% of legally manufactured barbiturates is diverted into illicit channels. A 1988 survey by the National Institute on Drug Abuse indicated that 3.5% of the population had used sedatives without a prescription.
1990s	Government estimates on illicit barbiturate use in the mid-decade were at 3.4%.

Source: Robert O'Brien and Morris Chefetz, *The Encyclopedia of Alcoholism*, New York: Facts On File, 1982.

bar   In its broader usage, a bar is a shop where alcoholic beverages are sold and drunk. Meals are not usually served. In this sense, bar is synonymous with SALOON. More specifically, a bar is the counter at which drinks are served. (See BAR DRINKER.)

bar drinker   One who habitually consumes alcoholic beverages in public establishments, rather than at social functions or at home. A pronounced tendency to drink mostly in bars, saloons and other public places can be caused by any number of reasons. To name a few, drinking in the home may be discouraged or prohibited for religious or other reasons; an alcoholic may be trying to hide their drinking problem from family or friends; or the drinker may be a minor who does not have parental approval to drink.

One characteristic of bar drinking is its convivial anonymity: most bar relationships are transient, lim-

ited to the confines of the bar, and unscheduled, that is, confined to chance encounters (or the "normal" routines of bar socializing). It has been suggested that alcoholics with past patterns of bar drinking are more receptive to help from socially-oriented support groups such as ALCOHOLICS ANONYMOUS than are SOLITARY DRINKERS.

barbital   A long-acting BARBITURATE with an onset time of up to one hour and a duration of up to 16 hours.

barbiturates   Sedative (calming), hypnotic (sleep-inducing) drugs that act as central nervous system (CNS) depressants. They slow down or decrease the activity of the nerves that control the emotions, breathing, heart action and a number of other body functions.

The first barbiturate was synthesized in 1864 from barbituric acid (malonylurea). In 1882 it was manufactured and used in medicine as barbital and was released under the trade name Veronal in 1903. Initially, barbiturates were used to induce sleep, replacing such aids as alcohol, bromides and opiates such as laudanum. Since the appearance of Luminal (a phenobarbital) in 1912, several thousand barbituric acid derivatives have been synthesized. Each of the 80 or so brand names manufactured come in a variety of forms: tablets, capsules, suppositories, liquids for injection, and in combination with many other drugs. However, the medical profession considers five or six types sufficient for clinical use.

Usage: Barbiturates are used medically to induce sleep, to provide day-long sedation in the treatment of tension and anxiety problems, and in combination with other drugs in the treatment of epilepsy and other convulsive and neurological conditions. They are also used in withdrawal treatment for alcoholism and addiction to other sedatives. According to one study, the elderly (especially women) received the most prescriptions for sedative hypnotics. Since age decreases the speed with which drugs are metabolized, people over 65 are particularly vulnerable to their toxic effects and the development of dependence. In addition, some of the effects of these drugs are often mistaken for senility.

There has been a marked increase in harmful use of barbiturates and other sedative hypnotic drugs among young people—even those in grade school. One Canadian study revealed that 12.8% of students in grades 7 to 12 had used prescribed barbiturates and 6.8% had used nonprescribed pills.

Activity: Barbiturates are metabolized (broken down chemically) in the liver and eliminated by the kidneys at varying speeds according to their types: slow- or long-acting (mostly phenobarbital and barbital); intermediate and short-acting (mostly secobarbital and pentobarbital); and ultra-fast (thiopental).

Slow- or long-acting barbiturates: take one to two hours to reach the brain through the bloodstream. Their effects last 6 to 24 hours, with a half-life of 48 hours for phenobarbital and 24 hours for barbital brands. They are metabolized slowly and pass through the liver unchanged, leaving most of the work of detoxification to the kidneys. They are the preferred type for patients with liver problems. Those who consume barbiturates illegally want quick action, and thus are seldom attracted to slow- or long-acting brands; therefore, this group of drugs rarely makes its way onto the black market.

Intermediate and short-acting barbiturates: take effect in 20 to 45 minutes and are very much alike. They are metabolized rapidly by the liver, placing much less strain on the kidneys and are consequently preferred for patients with kidney problems. *Short-acting barbiturates* are the type commonly known as "sleeping pills." Their effects last only five or six hours. They are used medically as sedatives in obstetrics, in the treatment of insomnia, anxiety neuroses, high blood pressure, coronary artery disease and for various diagnostic procedures. Because of the speed with which they take effect, short-acting barbiturates are invariably the choice of users and are most likely to produce dependence. According to the DEA (Drug Enforcement Administration), the four types of barbiturates that are most in demand, are Nembutal (pentobarbital), Amytal (amobarbital), Seconal (secobarbital) and Tuinal (secobarbital and amobarbital combined). Tuinal, however, is no longer legally available in the U.S. They are most like alcohol in the speed with which they take effect, in the kind of intoxication produced by their use, and in the addiction that can result. These are the "sleeping pills" used most often in suicides.

Ultra-fast-acting barbiturates: These fast-acting barbiturates produce unconsciousness in a very few minutes. Sodium pentothal (thiopental) is perhaps the best known of this variety. It is used almost exclusively in hospitals as an anesthetic in minor surgery and to induce anesthesia before the administration of a longer-acting anesthetic such as nitrous oxide. Ultra-fast-acting barbiturates are rarely found outside of medical channels and present no harmful use problems.

Effects: The effect of these drugs varies with the strength of the dose; individual tolerance depending on previous use and the environment and circumstances in which they are taken. Whereas a prescribed dose at bedtime will merely induce sleep, intoxication results when they are taken in larger doses in a social setting, such as at a party or in a bar, especially when combined with alcohol. With mild intoxication there is a feeling of well-being (euphoria), a heightening of self-esteem and a lowering of inhibitions. Increasing intoxication produces reactions exactly like those of alcohol intoxication—staggering due to loss of muscular control, short temper, the "fighting drunk" syndrome of aggressiveness and violence, or, in some individuals, depression and withdrawal. Barbiturate users suffer the same "morning-after" hangover miseries as alcoholics, including headache, nausea, dizziness, depression and drowsiness, which may persist for hours. Impairment of judgment, poor motor control and mood swings may last many more hours, making chronic users unfit to drive or operate machinery. Very high doses increase blood pressure and depress respiration so that less oxygen reaches the heart and brain. Such doses may result in acute poisoning, with all the classic signs of shock: shallow breathing, weak pulse, cold and clammy skin, depressed reflexes. Coma and finally death—usually from respiratory failure—may occur unless hospital care is available in time.

Interaction with other drugs: Barbiturate users often take other drugs as well. A common use pattern is to take AMPHETAMINES to wake up and offset the morning-after barbiturate hangover. Then more barbiturates are needed to fall asleep, and as the barbiturate doses increase, so does the need for more amphetamines, and a vicious cycle develops. Alcohol and barbiturates are another common and dangerous mixture: each one enhances the effect of the other so that a dose of either one—not fatal when taken alone—can cause death. (See SYNERGY.) Other drugs that interact with barbiturates are tranquilizers, antihistamines and opiates, which also depress the brain's control over breathing and increase the risk of respiratory failure.

Barbiturates and pregnancy: A woman who uses barbiturates regularly during pregnancy, especially in high doses, may endanger her baby. Congenital defects and abnormal behavior have been observed in such children. The drug is carried from the mother's bloodstream into the child's through the placenta, and after birth the baby suffers the same withdrawal symptoms that are produced by all central nervous system depressants. These may include feeding difficulties, disturbed sleep patterns, breathing problems, irritability and fever.

Tolerance: With regular use, the body gets so accustomed to the presence of barbiturates that ever larger and/or more frequent doses are needed to get the desired effects. Unfortunately, tolerance to the lethal level does not develop, and as time goes on chronic users may find themselves close to a fatal dose before they get any effect at all. Accidental death may occur when the user is not certain about how much to take because of his or her increased tolerance; he or she may also become confused and either not remember taking a previous dose or not remember how much was taken. Two kinds of dependence (addiction) may develop with chronic or excessive use. Psychological (psychic) dependence, which can develop very quickly, occurs when there is a compulsive desire for the relaxing or hypnotic effects of the drug—a feeling that well-being or sleep is not possible without it. Physical dependence on barbiturates and other sedative hypnotic drugs takes longer to develop, but is one of the most dangerous of all drug dependencies. It occurs when the body has grown so used to the presence of the drug that it reacts violently if the drug is suddenly withdrawn or sharply reduced.

Withdrawal symptoms: Once physical dependence has developed, suddenly stopping or sharply reducing daily barbiturate doses causes very severe withdrawal symptoms—worse than those that follow morphine or heroin withdrawal. They include anxiety, progressive weakness and restlessness, dizziness, visual distortion, nausea, vomiting, delirium and severe convulsions. With fast-acting barbiturates, reactions come to a peak in about two to three days. Reactions to withdrawal of slow-acting types take seven or eight days to reach their height. When dependence on barbiturates has been very severe, symptoms can last for several months. Treatment consists of slowly reducing the daily intake. While this does not eliminate suffering, it at least decreases the severity of symptoms and lessens the danger of death while the body slowly adjusts. Death occurs in about 5% to 7% percent of those attempting withdrawal without treatment.

Trafficking: As with other dangerous drugs, illegal possession of barbiturates is a criminal offense.

Without proof of intent to sell, however, sentences for those arrested on charges of possession are often light.

Availability: Barbiturates are legitimately available only by prescription. Their manufacture is strictly controlled by the DEA under Schedule II of the Controlled Substances Act. Unlike amphetamines and narcotics, barbiturates are not illicitly manufactured in clandestine laboratories. The supplies that reach the black market are generally stolen or smuggled into the country from Colombia or Mexico. Government agencies estimate that about 20% of legally produced barbiturates are diverted through illicit channels.

Synonyms: barbs, downers, block busters, goof balls and numerous others. Terms tied in with the color of the capsules include: blues or blue devils (Amytal); Mexican reds, red birds or red devils (Seconal); yellow jackets (Nembutal); rainbows or Christmas trees (Tuinal); and purple hearts (Luminal).

Beaujolais A French wine that takes its name from the Beaujolais region in southern Burgundy, where it is produced. Although there are several varieties and qualities of Beaujolais wine, 99% of them are red and have a fruity taste. These wines are intended to be drunk when they are young and fresh (or by the time they are three years old). Their alcoholic content is usually 12% or more, although it may be as low as 10%. *Beaujolais nouveau,* which is sold prior to completion of fermentation and marketed as a seasonal wine, developed a trendy following in the U.S. in the 1980s and 1990s.

beer An alcoholic beverage produced by fermenting and aging (BREWING) a mash of malted cereal grain and hops. Alterations in the proportion of cereal and hop ingredients and variations in the fermentation process account for the wide variety of beers. These include lagers, ales, stouts, porters, malt beers (malt liquors), bock beers and pilsners. The alcohol content of most beers varies from 3% to 6%, with malt beers slightly exceeding that proportion. The caloric value depends on the variety, but in most cases falls between 12 and 14 calories per ounce. Nutritionally, beer is high in carbohydrates and low in fats and has a relatively low proportion of B vitamins.

The origins of beer date back to prehistoric times. It was undoubtedly among the earliest alcoholic beverages known to man. The first recorded producers of beer were the Egyptians and Mesopotamians, both of whom are known to have fermented some forms of "barley-water" long before 2000 B.C., with one Mesopotamian record dating back to 4000 B.C. The Babylonian Code of Hammurabi in 1800 B.C. included an injunction against drunkenness that in all likelihood was provoked by a prevalence of beer consumption.

From Egypt, beer traveled to Greece—where it was produced in substantial quantities as early as 600 B.C.—and later to Rome. In both the classical Greek and Roman societies, however, beer was considered a rather crude and even barbaric beverage in comparison with wine. It was left to the Gauls, in their colder climates, to pursue the refinement of brewing techniques, which they began to do as early as the first century A.D., according to Tacitus. To a large extent, this reinforced the association of beer with barbarism and wine with culture, which, on some level, survives today in our culture.

During the same time span, knowledge of beer brewing passed south from Egypt throughout most of Africa; north and east to regions that became part of Russia, where it was called *quass;* and into China and Japan, where it became known as *samshu* and *sake,* respectively. When beer finally spread north and west to Europe, however, the greatest quantitative and qualitative advances in brewing were achieved. Just as its early history began in regions that were too warm and dry for widespread production of wine grapes, its later evolution occurred in lands too cold and damp for such cultivation, particularly Germany and Britain. Originally done in homes and monasteries in western Europe, brewing became commercialized during the 16th century. For a short time, before the introduction of coffee and tea, some form of beer was one of the few available and affordable alternatives to water or milk for the majority of the population.

The tradition of beer consumption was easily transported to the New World by western European settlers and soon caught on in the Commonwealth, and throughout the American continent. In, *World Drink Trends 1995,* the U.S. ranked 14th worldwide

Per Capita Beer Consumption in Leading Countries

Consumption of beer by country between 1992 and 1994: in liters/inhabitant

Country	1992	1993	1994	Country	1992	1993	1994
Czech Republic	145.0	150.0	160.0	Mexico	47.0	50.4	49.8
Germany	144.2	138.1	139.6	Norway	49.49	49.2	49.0
Irish Republic	130.8	126.5	135.2	Greece	40.0	42.6	42.0
Luxembourg	120.8	122.0	122.9	Romania	46.4	43.8	41.7
Denmark	121.01	120.14	121.46	Brazil	38.0	38.0	38.0
Austria	124.1	116.7	117.0	Cuba	34.1	34.0	34.0
Slovakia	110.0	110.0	103.9	France	40.3	39.2	40.0
Hungary	100.8	103.8	103.0	Poland	38.6	33.0	33.0
United Kingdom	102.3	100.0	102.3	Paraguay	35.0	35.0	32.9
New Zealand	104.0	101.8	102.1	Iceland	21.4	22.0	27.0
Australia	103.4	102.1	?	Italy	25.9	25.1	26.2
Belgium	112.0	109.5	101.6	Chile	24.0	26.5	25.3
Netherlands	90.2	85.2	86.0	Uruguay	25.6	25.2	25.3
USA	86.2	85.5	85.2	Peru	30.2	20.6	21.5
Finland	88.6	86.7	83.7	Singapore	19.9	20.0	21.0
Portugal	65.3	80.3	77.1	Argentina	28.8	27.1	20.0
Venezuela	77.0	78.5	76.0	Russia	18.8	17.1	19.8
Canada	69.4	68.5	68.1	China	8.6	10.0	12.5
Spain	70.5	67.1	66.2	Ukraine	17.8	13.0	10.8
Switzerland	68.6	65.0	64.3	Thailand	5.8	6.0	10.0
Sweden	62.6	63.2	64.2	Malaysia	8.9	8.9	9.1
Colombia	50.9	57.4	57.7	Israel	9.0	9.3	9.0
Japan	55.13	55.0	57.30	Turkey	6.7	7.7	7.8
South Africa	56.5	54.7	56.9	Tunisia	4.2	5.0	4.9
Bulgaria	61.0	58.3	56.3	Vietnam	2.3	3.2	3.4
Cyprus	59.2	53.8	56.3	Morocco	2.7	2.7	2.7
				Algeria	1.5	1.5	1.5

References: *1. World Drink Trends 1995,* International Beverage Alcohol Consumption and Production Trends. Produktschap voor Gedistilleerde Dranken, in association with NTC Publications LTD.

Source: *World Drink* Trends 1995 Edition

in annual per capita beer consumption (85.2 liters). Meanwhile, it has not lost its popularity in western Europe.

behavior modification Behavior modification, also known as behavior modification therapy, focuses on the behavior of the individual alcoholic or drug user rather than on underlying and perhaps deeply buried causes of the behavior. After it is determined what types of behavior are not useful, techniques are used to manipulate these in a beneficial manner to possibly prevent future deviations.

There are two main goals of behavior therapy in the treatment of chemical dependency. The first is to eliminate excessive consumption as a primary response to stress or other uncomfortable situations. The second is to establish alternative methods of coping with stressful situations. Initially, the addiction cycle must be broken and then new habits must be established. Many approaches today concentrate only on the first goal, which constitutes only partial treatment.

The best-known behavior modification technique is that of AVERSION THERAPY, in which a negative value is associated with the consumption of alcohol. Another technique is discrimination training based on internal cues, although this type of training is being questioned because of doubts about the ability of users to estimate their own level of inebriation. Other techniques include assertiveness training and biofeedback.

Some behavior therapies employ a number of techniques. Individualized behavior therapy, for instance, has four major components: shock avoidance procedures; videotaped self-confrontation with drunken behavior; availability of the drug as part of the treatment program; and individualized talk therapy focused on developing problem-solving skills. Unfortunately, with this program, to date there are no conclusive studies indicating which of the therapies employed are most effective.

One of the most recent trends in behavior modification is an attempt to teach controlled drinking as an alternative to alcoholic drinking. This approach is highly controversial since it directly contradicts the traditional LOSS OF CONTROL model of alcoholism. Because excessive consumption is viewed as learned behavior rather than an irreversible process, controlled drinking is seen as a viable alternative for some alcoholics. This is flatly denied by most opponents of MODERATE DRINKING. (See RAND REPORT.)

Advocates of behavior modification point out that it is a much more efficient mode of treatment than psychoanalytic approaches, which can take years and often still do not succeed in uncovering the deep-seated causes of drug dependency. Opponents of behavior modification feel that it is a superficial treatment that does not really solve the problem, that its record to date is unimpressive, and that symptoms frequently reappear.

David J. Armor, J. Michael Polich and Harriet B. Stambul, *Alcoholism and Treatment* (New York: John Wiley & Sons, 1978).

Don Cahalan, *Understanding America's Drinking Problem* (San Francisco: Jossey-Bass, 1987).

John R. DeLuca, ed., *Fourth Special Report to the U.S. Congress on Alcohol and Health* (Rockville, Md.: National Institute on Alcohol Abuse and Alcoholism, 1981): 152–153.

Cyril M. Franks, "Behavior Modification and the Treatment of the Alcoholic," in *Alcoholism: Behavioral Research, Therapeutic Approaches,* ed. Ruth Fox (New York: Springer, 1967): 186–203.

A. Marlatt, "The Controlled-Drinking Controversy: A Commentary," *American Psychologist* 38 (October 1983): 1097–1110.

M. Pendery, I. Maltzman and L. West, "Controlled Drinking by Alcoholics? New Findings and a Re-evaluation of a Major Affirmative Study," *Science* 217 (1982):169–175.

R. Roizen, "The Great Controlled Drinking Controversy," in *Recent Developments in Alcoholism,* ed. M. Galanter, vol. 5 (New York: Plenum, 1987).

M. B. Sobell and L. C. Sobell, *Behavioral Treatment of Alcohol Problems* (New York: Plenum, 1978).

behavioral toxicity Behavior that is both apparent and destructive to the individual or those around him. With mild or even chronic use of alcohol or another drug, one's behavior can remain relatively stable for long periods of time, if not indefinitely, in many cases. However, when aberrant, damaging behavior is due to drug intoxication, withdrawal or overdose, it becomes obvious that the impaired perceptions, mood changes and destructive actions are caused by harmful use or misuse of a mind-altering substance. For instance, if a person experiences auditory or visual hallucinations and does not act upon them, they go undetected by those around him, whereas if he responds visibly the behavior becomes evident to others and action may be taken, in some cases leading to the incarceration of the user.

beinsa   *Mitragyna speciosa,* a plant native to Burma (now Myanmar). There are claims that it can produce sedative effects when chewed or brewed into a tea.

Belgium

Alcohol: Although alcohol retains an important place in the social life of Belgians, the country experiences only limited alcohol-abuse problems. One reason is the national preference for beer over all other alcoholic beverages: In 1984 fully 56% of all alcohol consumed was taken in the form of beer, followed by smaller amounts of wine and very small amounts of distilled spirits. According to the Brewers and Licensed Retailers Association's *Statistical Handbook 1993,* Belgium/Luxembourg ranked 6th in beer consumption among leading countries in the world (108.1 liters per person per year), 11th in wine consumption (22.6 liters per person per year) and about 10th in spirits consumption (2.4 liters). This country is 9th in overall alcohol consumption (9.9 liters). Rates for all types of alcohol consumption fluctuated a little more or less than 1% between 1985 and 1993. The established drinking pattern also plays a part in limiting alcohol use. Alcohol is seldom drunk before meals, and heavy drinking during special family and social occasions is rare. The Flemish northern population and the French southern population, both predominantly Roman Catholic, display a generally controlled acceptance of alcohol. One useful indicator of the national attitude toward alcohol is the law that permits sale of distilled spirits in grocery stores, but only in quantities larger than two liters, which are not conducive to the casual drinking associated with smaller, cheaper and more portable quantities.

Using the E. M. JELLINEK formulation, authorities in Belgium calculated the number of alcoholics in the country at about 1% of the total population of 10 million in 1980. Legal regulations on alcohol consumption include a 1939 law against public drunkenness and a 1968 drunken driving law that was modified in 1975 to lower the permissible level of alcohol in the blood to 0.8 gm of ethanol per 1,000 gm of blood.

The agencies charged with addressing harmful use of alcohol in Belgium are the National Committee for Study and Prevention of Alcoholism and Other Drug Addictions; the National Federation of Consulting Bureaux and Institutions for the Care of Alcoholics and Other Drug Addicts; and the Volksbond (People United) Against the Abuse of Alcohol. All are private bodies working in close cooperation with one another. The National Committee, established in 1949, concentrates on statistical records; the National Federation, established in 1972, on hospital care; and the Volksbond, established in 1972, on secondary school prevention programs. In 1980 the National Committee on Alcohol and Other Drugs was established to help coordinate funding and redistribute activities among the three existing agencies.

Drugs other than alcohol: According to a March 1996 report by the U.S. Department of State's Bureau of International Narcotics and Law Enforcement Affairs, "Belgium is not a significant producer of illicit drugs or precursor chemicals used to manufacture illicit drugs, but both transit Belgium in significant quantities bound for the rest of Europe. . . . Belgian authorities believe increasing drug shipments arrive from Asia and the Middle East through eastern Europe and the former Soviet republics. . . . The government of Belgium does not maintain drug-use statistics, but authorities believe the number of heroin users has reached a plateau. Cocaine seizures continue to decline steadily. However, synthetic drug consumption—particularly ecstasy and LSD— has been on the rise among young Belgians."

Hoeveel alcoholhoude dranken worden er in de wereld gedronken? (How many alcoholic beverages are being consumed throughout the world?), 27th ed. (Schiedam, Netherlands: Produktschap Voor Gedistilleerde Dranken, 1987).

belladonna   A plant, *Atropa belladonna,* also called deadly nightshade, that has been known since the Middle Ages as both a sedative and a poison. The Romans considered the pupil dilation caused by belladonna a mark of beauty. It can produce hallucinations with severe adverse reactions and sometimes even extremely small doses can prove toxic. As little as 120 mg of plant material (less than the amount of material in one marijuana joint) may result in coma or death. There have been fatalities among children who have eaten deadly nightshade. It contains the alkaloids ATROPINE, HYOSCYAMINE and SCOPOLAMINE, and these extracts are used today as ingredients in proprietary drugs. Other plants containing belladonna alkaloids are DATURA, HENBANE, MANDRAKE and PITURI.

bender A drinking spree or bout, as in, *He is on a bender.*

Benedictine Benedictine, an amber-colored French liqueur, was first manufactured by monks of the Benedictine Order at the Abbey Fecamp in Normandy. It contains approximately 43% alcohol by volume and has a somewhat sweet taste. Like other liqueurs, it is meant to be sipped in a relaxed manner as a digestive. Although the exact recipe is a carefully guarded secret, Benedictine includes among its ingredients honey, sugar, fruit peels and brandy (generally Cognac) and at least 30 different aromatic plants. At one time it also contained China tea.

Benedictine is said to have been invented during the early 16th century (possibly 1510) by Dom Bernardo Vincelli, one of the monks at the Abbey Fecamp. It was produced there until 1793, when the abbey was destroyed during the French Revolution. The recipe was preserved among the monastic documents entrusted to the *procureur fiscal* (civil administrator). More than 70 years later, one of the *procureur*'s descendants, Alexandre le Grand, established a distillery at the same site where the abbey had been. Benedictine is still manufactured there today although it is no longer associated with the religious order.

Benzadrine A brand of AMPHETAMINE sulfate no longer legally distributed in the U.S. Generally used for weight control, it has a high potential for harmful use and TOLERANCE, and extreme PSYCHOLOGICAL DEPENDENCE often occurs. Insomnia, irritability and personality changes are all symptoms of overdosage.

Synonyms: bennies, benz, peaches, roses, whites.

benzene C6H6, a toxic volatile hydrocarbon found in dyes, paints, paint and varnish removers, gasolines, insecticides, plastics, motor fuels, solvents and numerous detergents. It is a clear, flammable, poisonous, aromatic liquid and has an intoxicating effect when inhaled. Prolonged inhalation can result in acute poisoning and liver damage. Its use in industry is decreasing.

benzodiazepine The chemical source of the class of DEPRESSANT drugs known as minor tranquilizers (or anxiolytics) that includes chlordiazepoxide (Librium), diazepam (Valium), oxazepam (Serax), clorazepate dipotassium (Tranxene) and others. Flurazepam (Dalmane), which is a sedative hypnotic, is also a benzodiazepine derivative. Stronger than meprobamate and tybamate, the benzodiazepine derivatives have gained popularity as safer substitutes for BARBITURATES. Australian authorities credit the replacement of barbiturates with benzodiazepine derivatives for the fall in the Australian suicide rate between 1962 and 1973.

Usage: Medical applications of the benzodiazepine derivatives cover a wide range. Their most common use is as anxiolytics in the relief of symptoms of tension and anxiety resulting from neurosis or stressful circumstances. Other applications include treatment of convulsive disorders, neuromuscular and cardiovascular conditions, and gastrointestinal distress related to anxiety.

Knowledge of the advantages of the minor tranquilizers over barbiturates has spread beyond the medical community to drug users, and many of these drugs are available illicitly. Because they produce less euphoria and intoxication than barbiturates, users often take them in dangerous combination with other drugs, particularly alcohol: 10% of drivers arrested for DRIVING WHILE IMPAIRED (DWI) have both alcohol and minor tranquilizers in their systems. Similarly, the minor tranquilizers have been used successfully in suicides (and accidental deaths) when ingested with alcohol. In early 1996, the federal government officially banned the importation of Rohypnol (flunitrazepam), a sedative reportedly 10 times more powerful than Valium. Users make numerous claims for Rohypnol's effects and uses. It is considered "a cheap drunk," an antidote for hangovers, and is frequently used in combination with marijuana and cocaine.

Activity: The benzodiazepine derivatives are readily absorbed in the gastrointestinal tract and quickly though unevenly distributed in the body. Most are metabolized in the liver and slowly excreted in the urine. They are central nervous system (CNS) depressants and act on the brain's limbic system, the center of emotional response. Their usual half-life is about one day.

Effects: The effects of the benzodiazepine derivatives closely resemble those of the barbiturates, though they produce less euphoria. The drugs relieve tension, muscular tension, and anxiety, due to emotional stress. They have very little effect on REM sleep in ordinary amounts. They are useful in treatment of seizure disorders.

Adverse reactions are rare but can include drowsiness, loss of coordination, confusion, constipation, rash, jaundice, tremors and—in large doses—fainting. Paradoxical hostility has also been reported.

Tolerance and dependence: Use of benzodiazepine derivatives were erroneously thought to involve a low risk of tolerance or the development of physical or psychological dependence. This was another factor in doctors' preference for these drugs over barbiturates. When dependence does occur and use of the drug is stopped, withdrawal symptoms are similar to but less severe than those seen in barbiturate and alcohol addiction; symptoms include convulsions, tremors, muscular and abdominal cramps, vomiting, sweating, insomnia, loss of appetite, and the recurrence and aggravation of the patient's neurosis. These symptoms can last 7–10 days.

The mild tranquilizers exhibit a CROSS-TOLERANCE to alcohol and other CNS depressants, as well as a SYNERGISTIC REACTION and therefore should not be administered in combination with these drugs.

Synonyms: Rohypnol is sold on the street as rophies, roofies, ruffies and many others.

benzoylecgonine   A cocaine metabolite looked for when testing an individual for drug use. Benzoylecgonine is invariably found in the urine of a cocaine user whether or not cocaine itself is present.

benzphetamine   A sympathomimetic amine with pharmacological activity similar to AMPHETAMINES,

used as an anorectic for weight control and in the treatment of narcolepsy. It has significant potential for harmful use. (See DIDREX.)

beta alcoholism   The second of five categories of alcoholism defined by E. M. JELLINEK (1890–1963). Although chronic alcohol users included in this classification may eventually develop medical complications such as ALCOHOLIC POLYNEUROPATHY or CIRRHOSIS, beta alcoholism is not associated with either physical or psychological dependence on alcohol and WITHDRAWAL symptoms do not emerge. The combination of heavy drinking in conjunction with poor nutritional habits may be the cause of this type of alcoholism.

Although beta alcoholism can develop into GAMMA ALCOHOLISM, this transition is more likely to occur in the case of ALPHA ALCOHOLISM.

bicycle accidents   According to the NHTSA (National Highway Traffic Safety Administration, 1985), alcohol is a significant factor in bicyclist fatalities, as shown by blood alcohol test results obtained from 41% of such victims. In about 42% of the tests, the blood alcohol concentration (BAC) exceeded 0.10%. and in 23% of the tests, the BAC was 0.20% or higher. Precise figures for the number of alcohol-related bicyclist fatalities are not available, but the U.S. averages more than 1,000 deaths per year for bicycle riders, with about 1.2 deaths per 100,000 bicycles.

binge drinking   Pattern of heavy drinking characterized by alternating periods of drinking to excess and periods of moderate drinking or abstinence. The negative effects of binge drinking can be as physically, psychologically, socially and/or professionally devastating as daily alcohol use, and according to the *DSM-IV (DIAGNOSTIC AND STATISTICAL MANUAL OF MENTAL DISORDERS)* a pattern of binge drinking is one of the criteria for a diagnosis of abuse. When binge drinkers display the tendency to focus on the periods in which they do not drink, they may resist reducing consumption or seeking treatment.

Binge drinking is a persistent problem on college campuses, where a recent study revealed that up to 50% of men and 39% of women admitted to at least one bout of heavy drinking within the two weeks preceding the survey. College campuses are also plagued by a second, even more serious kind of periodic drinking: each year, a few students die of alcoholic respiratory failure during a commonly practiced hazing ritual in which fraternity candidates are forced to consume vast amounts of hard liquor in a short period of time.

biofeedback   A treatment method applied during withdrawal and rehabilitation from alcohol and other drug dependence. The goals in biofeedback treatment are to increase the individual's motivation to tolerate withdrawal and to decrease tension after physical withdrawal is complete. The patient is presented with ongoing biological information (such as heart rate) by means of biofeedback machines using meters, lights, auditory signals and so on. The treatment then centers on the patient using this information to self-regulate the biological process and control certain autonomic functions. This method of self-regulation has similarities to the ancient practice of yoga. The technique is not completely understood and the Biofeedback Society of America, founded in 1969, along with other medical organizations, is continuing to research the subject.

biphetamine   A central nervous system stimulant that contains AMPHETAMINE and DEXTROAM-PHETAMINE. No longer legally available in the U.S.; due to widespread harmful use, biphetamines were used medically as anorectics for weight control. Tolerance can develop within a few weeks and psychological dependence as well as signs of social disability often occur with usage. Overdosage results in restlessness, tremors, hallucinations and coma.

Synonyms: black beauties, blackbirds, black mollies and many others.

bipolar disorder and substance abuse   Also known as manic-depression, bipolar disorder is a condition in which manic and depressed states occur, either separately or together (as a mixed state). In the DSM-IV (*DIAGNOSTIC AND STATISTICAL MANUAL OF MENTAL DISORDERS*) a variant called bipolar II is added that signifies an illness with less severe, or hypomanic, swings in elevated mood.

Compulsive drug use during manic episodes, when judgment is usually severely impaired, is common and is frequently an attempt at self-medication. In those suffering from DUAL DIAGNOSIS, the self-pre-

scribed use of any mind-altering substances renders pharmacotherapy treatment less effective, resulting in greater morbidity. Many patients desire the euphoria and increased sense of power and importance accompanying a manic mood state (either arrived at naturally or drug induced) and so often resist taking the mood-stabilizing medications offered in treatment, such as lithium, carbamazepine and valproic acid. Use of a number of drugs can generate manic symptoms, including cocaine, amphetamines, phencyclidine, LSD and occasionally marijuana. When the drug use is identified as the proximal cause of the mania, a diagnosis of substance-induced mood disorder is made rather than bipolar disorder.

blackout   A chemically induced period of amnesia commonly suffered by chronic alcoholics and not uncommonly by nonalcoholics in conjunction with bouts of heavy drinking over a short period of time. A blackout is the inability to recall entire blocks of time during which one was fully conscious. The condition appears to be related to the impairment of the brain's ability to transfer information to long-term memory stores and is an early sign of progressive alcoholism. The risk of blackout is increased by factors such as fatigue and stress, and severely increased by the combination of alcohol with other sedatives, tranquilizers and marijuana.

blood alcohol concentration (or content) (BAC) The degree of intoxication that can be measured by the concentration of alcohol in the bloodstream. When a blood sample is tested for alcohol, the findings are reported in the form of blood alcohol concentration (BAC), also called blood alcohol level (BAL), which measures in percentages the weight of the alcohol in a fixed volume of blood. In certain countries, including the U.S. BAC for 7 parts alcohol per 10,000 parts blood is expressed as .07%. In Canada and some other nations the equivalent would be 70 mg per 100 ml of blood, expressed as 70%. In Sweden it would be recorded as 0.7 promille. Each system records the same percentage of alcohol.

While medical facilities and alcohol treatment centers use BACs as guides for immediate treatment of a presumably inebriated patient, BAC tests are most often given to motorists suspected of DRIVING WHILE IMPAIRED (DWI). In Idaho and Utah any driver with a BAC over .08% is considered legally intoxicated. In other areas of the U.S., including the District of Columbia, the figure is .10% (though many critics consider this level abnormally high and permissive). In Canada the limit is 80%; while in Sweden 0.5 promille is evidence of second-degree drunken driving and 1.5 promille of first degree, a very serious offense.

The amount of alcohol ingested may be determined by testing a person's urine, breath or blood. Breath alcohol has a constant ratio to blood alcohol levels. Breath alcohol levels are multiplied by a factor of 2,300 to obtain blood alcohol levels. Urine tests are difficult to administer and are rarely used. Blood tests are both difficult to perform and often unsatisfactory since the analysis frequently cannot be made for up to two hours after the suspect is apprehended. However, through the use of mobile blood laboratories, the results of blood tests can often be given within minutes. Despite past legal difficulties and problems of accuracy, BREATHALYZERS are in common use, particularly for preliminary, on-the-spot analysis.

BAC varies according to a number of factors:

Gender: Pound for pound of body weight, the increase in BAC per drink is less for men than for women, because men generally have more muscle than women. Women have a larger percentage of fatty tissue, which has a smaller blood supply than muscle tissue. Consequently, given persons of equal weight, the ingestion of equal amounts of alcohol will result in higher blood concentrations (higher amounts of alcohol stored in lesser amounts of blood) in women than in men.

Weight: In general the larger (and heavier) a person is, the greater the blood supply is and, thus, the more alcohol can be accommodated. But as noted above, in men and women of equal weight, fatty tissue is a major determinant of BAC levels. The same is true for overweight people. Since their excess weight is stored in the form of fat, their blood supply is not increased in proportion to the additional weight. Therefore someone who is overweight at 170 pounds will have a higher BAC from a given amount of alcohol than a lean person of the same weight.

Duration of consumption: On average, unless consumption is limited to less than one full drink an hour, BAC will continue to rise. The body will slowly excrete the alcohol as follows: oxidization by the liver, 95%; breath, 2%; urine, 2%; perspiration, 1%.

Food consumption: A "full" stomach will retard the absorption of alcohol but less so than is commonly believed. Furthermore, the effect of food on BAC varies according to the individual.

Quantity: Two to four 1½-oz shots of 86-proof liquor or an equivalent amount of wine or beer approaches the danger limit for drivers.

blood sugar   Consumption of alcohol can affect blood sugar levels. The effects vary depending upon the body's physical state when alcohol is consumed. If carbohydrate stores in the LIVER are adequate, ETHANOL appears to bring about a rise in blood glucose levels (hyperglycemia). If carbohydrate reserves are low, as when the body is fasting, the opposite effect, low blood sugar (hypoglycemia), occurs. This condition is apparently due to the interference of alcohol with the normal conversion of carbohydrates into sugar. Alcohol may also indirectly stimulate the hormone insulin, which works to lower blood sugar. An adequate supply of blood sugar from a meal or snack is generally protection against the effects of low blood sugar produced by the consumption of alcohol. However, when alcohol and sugar are taken together, such as in a gin and tonic, the combination may increase stimulation of insulin production and thereby produce a hypoglycemic effect.

Alcoholics are often hypoglycemic, due to inadequate food intake. Another possible cause is the impairment of liver function, caused by heavy drinking, which may interfere with the ability to metabolize glucose. Alcoholics who have stopped drinking often experience a craving for sweets. Low blood sugar may cause HANGOVERS as well. (See DIABETES, and NUTRITION.)

blunt   Marijuana-filled cigar; a fad in U.S. urban centers during the early 1990s and credited, at least partially, for a resurgence in marijuana use. Blunt-smoking is often accompanied by drinking a 40-oz malt liquor, giving birth to the street term *40 and a blunt.*

B'nai B'rith International   An international service organization established in 1843 to unite world Jewry for the advancement of the Jewish people and to help create a better world for all. Community Volunteer Services (CVS) is a branch of B'nai B'rith dedicated to the prevention of alcohol and other drug abuse; its mass-media information campaign includes the distribution of literature directed to the Jewish community and to society at large.

boating accidents   Boat operators' peripheral vision, balance and reaction time are impaired by alcohol consumption as well as the use of other mind-altering drugs. Studies show that the ability to operate a boat safely is significantly affected at a BAC (blood alcohol concentration) of 0.035%. In most states, it is unlawful to operate a recreational boat while under the influence of alcohol, but many states have not defined the level of intoxication for operators of vessels and most states can't perform tests without consent.

In 1983 the U.S. Coast Guard received reports of 5,569 recreational boating accidents that resulted in 1,241 fatalities and 2,913 injuries. In 1988 the death rate had dropped to 5.5 fatalities per 100,000 boats—or 946 people killed in recreational boating accidents. However, the Coast Guard estimates that it receives reports of only 5% to 10% of all reportable accidents that do not involve fatalities. Studies by California, Maryland and North Carolina indicate that the full extent of alcohol involvement in boating accidents is grossly under-reported, as is the extent of illicit drug use. They also show that 75% to 80% of boating accidents and deaths were alcohol-related; and, in Maryland in 1986–87, 60% of the fatally injured victims were legally drunk (with BACs of 1.008% or higher). The Coast Guard has estimated that 40% of boaters carry alcohol on their outings. A review of literature analyzing drownings associated with boat use suggested that at least 17% to 31% of boaters who drowned had consumed alcohol. A study by the U.S. Department of Health reported the following about drowning deaths: the rate of alcohol involvement in drownings appears to vary by gender, age and activity type; alcohol was less likely to be detected in teenage victims than in adult victims; BAC was positively associated with age; alcohol involvement was more likely among male (59%) than female (40%) drowning victims; and alcohol was present in about half the drownings associated with swimming, boating or rafting.

National Transportation Safety Board (NTSB), "Safety Study: Recreational Boating and Safety and Alcohol," NTSB No. 55-83-02, NTIS No. PB 83-917006 (Washington, D.C.: NTSB, 1983).

J. Howland and R. Hongson, "Alcohol as a Risk Factor for Drowning: A Review of the Literature 1950–1985," *Public Health Rep* (1987): 475–483.

Lori Sharn, "States to Boaters: Lakes, Rivers not Watering Holes," *USA Today* (August 15, 1989): 5A.

G. J. Wintermute et al., "Alcohol and Drowning: An Analysis of Contributing Factors and a Discussion of Criteria from Case Selection," *Accident Analysis Prevention* 22 (1993): 291–296.

S. J. Wright, "SOS: Alcohol, Drugs, and Boating," *Alcohol Health & Research World* 9, no. 4 (1985): 28–33.

boats and drugs   Drugs pay for about one of every three recreational boats in Miami and maybe 50% carry some kind of contraband sometimes. Drug TRAFFICKING is also behind the piracy of many recreational boats off the Florida coast. Some stolen boats are used to transport drugs, while others are illegally seized because they are mistaken for craft belonging to rival drug gangs. Dealers in security equipment, including guns, actually tout their wares at national boat shows in Florida. According to a 1994 report by the DEA (Drug Enforcement Administration), shipping by water continues to be a key conduit for the importation of illicit drugs into the U.S. Cocaine smugglers continue to use intermodal means of transport and often conceal larger shipments in commercial maritime containerized or bulk cargo. Traffickers also are believed to have experimented with the use of semi-submersible and fully-submersible vessels in conjunction with cocaine SMUGGLING operations from Colombia to Northern Caribbean Islands or Puerto Rico. Traffickers from Colombia, the Caribbean and the Far East use cargo vessels, pleasure boats and fishing boats to transport marijuana via traditional maritime routes. Sometimes, boaters get involved in drug-trafficking themselves. On August 29, 1987, powerboat-racing champion Benjamin Kramer was arrested for running a drug ring involving the distribution of approximately 550,000 lbs (250,000 kg) of marijuana between early 1980 and mid-1987. The grand jury noted that Kramer was the "organizer, supervisor, and manager" of the smuggling operation, which did business in Florida, Illinois and elsewhere in the U.S.

T. D. Allman, *Miami: City of the Future* (New York: Atlantic Monthly, 1987): 83.

Gilda Berger, *Drug Abuse: The Impact on Society* (New York: Franklin Watts, 1988): 82–83.

Drug Enforcement Administration, *The Supply of Illicit Drugs to the United States* (Washington, D.C., 1995).

James A. Inciardi, *The War On Drugs* (Palo Alto: Mayfield, 1986): 184–191.

bock beer   A seasonal beer. Its which name derives from the German *Einbecker Bier* (literally, beer from Einbeck), shortened in the dialect of Bavaria, where it originated, to *Bockbier*. Bock beer, sometimes simply called bock, is brewed in winter from the residue collected from vats before they are cleaned for another year's brewing. Stronger and sweeter in taste than most lagers, of which it is a variety, true bock beer is dark and has a life of about six weeks. The day on which the product is first ready for consumption, Bock Beer Day, is traditionally associated with the coming of spring.

Boggs Amendment   An amendment to the HARRISON ACT of 1914, the Narcotic Drugs Import and Export Act of 1922 and the Marijuana Tax Act of 1937. Enacted in 1951, the amendment increased the penalties for all drug violations. Reflecting the increased concern over drug addiction after World War II, it lumped together—for the first-time—marijuana and narcotic drugs and established uniform penalties for offenses: a mandatory minimum sentence of two years for first time "narcotic" violators and up to 10 years of imprisonment for repeat offenders. These penalties were raised in 1956 by the Narcotic Drug Control Act. (See LEGAL ASPECTS OF MARIJUANA, AND OTHER DRUG CONTROLS.)

BOL-148   A congener of LSD-25, d-2-bromolysergic acid tartrate is a hallucinogen.

Bolivia   Coca cultivation and consumption have been traditional for centuries in Bolivia, but licit demands for coca account for only a minuscule amount of the estimated amount produced annually (85,000 metric tons in 1995, down from 89,800 metric tons in 1994, but marking an otherwise steady increase—up from 80,300 metric tons in

1992, and 78,400 in 1988). Along with Peru and Colombia, Bolivia is responsible for the majority of cocaine on the world market, with approximately 30% net production in 1993. Most of the coca cultivated in Bolivia is processed and distributed by Colombia.

On average, Bolivia's government has changed more than once per year since the republic was founded in 1825; after each change, attempts by the U.S. government to resume coca control must begin all over again. Narcotics assistance programs were begun in Bolivia in 1972, for instance, and in 1977 there was an agreement that provided for narcotics control assistance and a study of alternate crops. But in 1980, a coup by General Garcia Meza—who allegedly had the support of a Mafia group that dominated the cocaine trade—halted these activities. Some years later, the Bureau of International Narcotics Matters attempted an eradication program designed to reduce Bolivia's coca cultivation. The program included both voluntary and mandatory crop eradication and controls. The large number of landowners complicates the eradication problem: in 1989 there were an estimated 23,000 farm families growing coca, usually on small holdings of one hectare (2.47 acres) or less. One official estimate contends that $300 million to $500 million a year is needed to develop legitimate alternatives for coca-farming peasants. President Bush's so-called Andean initiative proposed between $100 million and $270 million to finance antidrug campaigns in Bolivia, Peru and Colombia. The 1994 National Drug Control Strategy shifted interdiction emphasis from activities primarily focused on the transit zones to a stronger focus on the source countries.

The situation in Bolivia remains mixed. The country was granted "vital national interest" certification in 1994 because of the U.S. assessment that some key counternarcotics performance deficiencies precluded a "full" certification. As of 1996 Bolivia was the second highest producer of cocaine in South America.

White House, *National Drug Control Strategy: Strengthening Communities' Response to Drugs and Crime* (Washington, D.C., 1995).

Bontril PDM   A brand of phendimetrazine tartrate, a stimulant used as an anorectic for weight control. Its activity is similar to that of AMPHETA-

MINES and tolerance to its effects develops within a few weeks. It has a potential for harmful use and can cause personality changes, insomnia, irritability, and hyperactivity. Overdosage can result in rapid respiration, hallucinations, restlessness and tremor.

boom towns   In communities that either spring up almost overnight or become prosperous suddenly because of some new industry or the discovery of a valuable resource, the incidence of harmful use of alcohol and other drugs usually jumps markedly. In new communities, it establishes itself at a level well above the norm for other communities of similar size. U.S. studies from the mid- and late-1970s show that the pattern was repeated in community after community, with the increase in alcohol use considerably higher than the rise in drug use (which was overwhelmingly marijuana).

The characteristics of these boom towns are very similar. There is an influx of young, often blue-collar males (single or without their wives) to an area where the social fabric is strained by economic and population changes. Wages and prices are high, and amenities, including recreational facilities, are scarce or nonexistent. Drinking is the only major social activity and is done in bars. Prostitution often flourishes. Treatment for alcohol-related problems generally rises but the pattern is erratic and hard to measure. Alcohol-related arrests show a marked increase, particularly those for DRIVING WHILE IMPAIRED (DWI). (See DEPRESSED COMMUNITIES.)

booting   Attempting to prolong the initial effects of a HEROIN injection by injecting a small amount, then withdrawing blood back into the syringe and repeating the process.

bootlegging   A possible derivation of the term "bootlegging," referring to traffic in illegal whiskey, dates back to the post-Revolutionary period, when the government first started imposing taxes on whiskey. Distillers were required to buy tax stamps and display them on their whiskey barrels. To avoid the tax, some distillers had their delivery men remove the stamps from the barrels after the whiskey was delivered and return them in their bootlegs for use on the next shipment.

In 1880, when Kansas incorporated prohibition into its constitution, "bootlegging"—apparently the practice of carrying flasks of whiskey concealed in boot tops—gained widespread popularity. Later, other areas of the country established similar laws, resulting in an increase in bootlegging from wet communities to dry ones. From 1920 to 1933, during PROHIBITION, bootlegging became a major racket as well as a familiar term across the nation. In the early days of Prohibition a great deal of liquor was smuggled into the U.S. across the Canadian and Mexican borders and from ships anchored off the coast. As the Coast Guard increased its campaign in the sea, bootleggers began to rely more on industrial alcohol, which they washed of noxious chemicals, diluted with water and sometimes flavored with a small amount of potable liquor. Alcohol was also obtained from government-supervised warehouses, where it was being held for medical use or for export. Although the small-scale bootlegger was usually not a gangster, the liquor had to be delivered to speakeasies, which were usually controlled by gangsters. Bootlegging continued after Prohibition and still exists today.

Although the practice is generally associated with the U.S., other nations have had similar issues with bootlegging. During World War I, the Russian government banned the sale of vodka as a war measure. The post-war Communist regime continued the prohibition, but by 1925 bootlegging was so widespread that the government rescinded the ban on vodka. In the late 1980s, the government again restricted the sale of vodka—and bootlegging once more is a widespread practice among the Russians.

Alice Fleming, *Alcohol: The Delightful Poison* (New York: Dell, 1975): 34.

"Bootlegging," *Encyclopedia Britannica* (USA: William Benton, 1972).

booty (asset forfeiture)   In their crackdown on drug traffickers, especially major drug lords, beginning in the 1980s, federal authorities have taken possession of a wide range of properties and other assets bought with proceeds from illegal drug sales. Law enforcement officials have seized boats, cars, aircraft, businesses and even real estate purchased by drug kingpins with their profits. In fiscal year 1986, the total income of the U.S. Department of Justice Assets Forfeiture Fund was about $90 million; under provisions of the 1984 Comprehensive Crime Control Act, some $25 million in cash and property forfeited in federal cases in 1986 was shared with the state and local criminal justice agencies that participated in those cases. Gross seizures by the federal government mushroomed to approximately $647 million in 1994, due largely to efforts by U.S. Justice Department agencies and the U.S. Customs Service.

"Asset forfeiture is among the most effective and powerful tools in the fight against drug trafficking and money laundering and, as such, is a critical component of this nation's anti-drug efforts," stated a 1995 report on drug control from the White House. "The ability of the government—as part of its investigative and prosecutive strategy—to remove the proceeds of crime from individuals and to destroy the economic infrastructure of criminal organizations is essential to drug law enforcement. . . . Once forfeited, property is sold or retained for official use by law enforcement. . . . To date, the program has distributed hundreds of millions of dollars to State and local law enforcement agencies to fund drug law enforcement endeavors."

In fiscal year 1994, federal authorities made 13,631 seizures of nondrug property (currency and other financial instruments, real property, 3,744 vehicles, 146 vessels, 37 aircraft, and so forth). Forfeitures at the national level are coordinated by the Federalwide Drug Seizure System (FDSS), a coalition of FBI (Federal Bureau of Investigation), DEA (Drug Enforcement Administration), U.S. Customs and U.S. Coast Guard drug-control forces.

Sharing of proceeds from seizures assets with state and local law enforcement officials began in August 1985, following authorization by Congress in the Comprehensive Crime Control Act of 1984. State and local law enforcement agencies share property forfeited to the federal government in proportion to their participation in particular cases—and are thus encouraged to help federal officials make "big busts." Funds are used to purchase vehicles, firearms and surveillance equipment, as well as to support overtime pay for narcotics officers, funding for informants, and new investigative units to go after major drug traffickers.

There is some concern that asset seizure has resulted in unfair criminal sentencing practices, that is, relatively small, street-level drug dealers are being sentenced according to stringent, mandated minimums, while drug kingpins may be "buying" their way out of long sentences by forfeiting portions of their astronomical fortunes. Defense attorneys object to the aggressive asset seizure policy, since it can be used to keep ill-gotten drug profits from being used to pay attorneys (either by freezing of assets of the accused in pretrial proceedings so that attorneys cannot be paid, or by seizing fees allegedly paid from drug proceeds at a later time). Some legal authorities say the practice of seized fees violates the Sixth Amendment right to counsel of choice, interferes with the attorney-client relationship, and precludes an effective defense because such cases require specialized expertise.

In a 5–4 ruling in June 1989, the U.S. Supreme Court temporarily quashed the debate when it ruled as permissible the seizure of assets by federal prosecutors of those indicted for dealing drugs, including money used to hire a lawyer. Justice Byron White said Congress made no exception for attorney's fees when it allowed seizure of assets. No right exists, the court stated, "to spend another person's money for services rendered by an attorney." The ruling gives prosecutors a powerful tool against drug dealers who hire high-priced lawyers to keep them out of jail.

Early in 1996, however, the asset forfeiture policy was dealt a temporary blow as a result of a case brought before the Supreme Court by a federal prisoner who has been teaching himself law while serving out a life sentence. The case is known now as the "$405," a shortened version of the $405,000 he won on behalf of his client, a fellow inmate whose assets were seized following his conviction for dealing drugs. The inmate successfully argued that the seizure of assets, heard in a civil court following the original sentencing, represents a violation of the constitutional protection against double jeopardy, namely, being tried for the same case twice. In June 1996, however, the Supreme Court overruled the local decision in favor of the "$405," ensuring state and federal rights to forfeitures.

As the "$405" case proved, asset forfeiture is not impervious to attack. In light of the decision against that case, and given the intensity of concern about illicit drug sales and use, it is likely that asset-seizure programs will grow more important in the effort to control the distribution of drugs other than alcohol.

The United Nations Convention against Illicit Traffic in Narcotic Drugs and Psychotropic Substances of 1988 marked the first decisive step in mobilizing the international community for the fight against drug trafficking. In the U.S., several states have followed the lead of Arizona and Florida, which have both developed sophisticated seizure capabilities. The Police Executive Research Forum and the National Criminal Justice Association have developed and are presently maintaining a training program for local criminal justice investigators using the tools and techniques for financial investigations in asset seizure and forfeiture cases. The training is funded by the Bureau of Justice Assistance.

National Institute of Justice (NIJ), "Research in Action," *NIJ Reports* SN1202 (March/April 1987): 2.

booze   Formerly spelled "boose" but pronounced "booze," from early Germanic sources via the early modern Dutch *buisen* and Middle English *bousen*.

Booze has always been a slang term for drinking excessively, usually to get drunk quickly. As a verb it means to guzzle; to drink to excess. As a noun it is the alcoholic beverage, often whiskey, such as that made around 1840 by a Philadelphia distiller named E. G. Booze (although both the verb and the noun predate Mr. Booze by many centuries). From booze comes "boozing it up," "boozer," "boozy" and other such terms.

booze fighter   One for whom BOOZE has become a habit, a compulsion, or an addiction and who is determined to "fight" the habit. The term implies an ongoing, and therefore unsuccessful, battle with a continuous stream of good intentions and broken resolutions. (See BOOZE HOUND.)

booze hound   A heavy drinker whose life is greatly influenced by, even dedicated to, the consumption of alcoholic beverages. (See BOOZE FIGHTER.)

borderline personality disorder   A disorder wherein enduring personality traits result in maladaptive behavior and subjective distress. Those with the disorder characteristically have unstable interpersonal relationships that vacillate between over-idealization and devaluation, and their fears of abandonment, real or imagined, can lead to uncontrollable anger and attempts at self-mutilation. They also have a marked difficulty in modulating emotional states, and may engage in impulsive behavior with potentially harmful consequences. Suicidal ges-

tures and attempts are common, among other acts such as gambling, substance abuse, binge eating and engagement in unsafe sex. The prevailing mood of those with borderline personality disorder is dysphoric, with chronic feelings of emptiness and boredom, punctuated by intense states of anxiety, depression, depersonalization and paranoia when confronted with rejection or abandonment. The sense of self is disturbed, frequently considered evil, and unstable with regard to future plans, goals and identity.

bottom fermentation   Fermentation of a hop wort (plant) with a yeast that sinks as sediment in the course of brewing lager beer. Beer yeasts are selected strains of bacterial enzymes that flocculate, or separate themselves from the brewing beer, so that they may be drawn off at the end of the process. This process, in conjunction with the different blend of cereal grains employed, accounts for the lighter flavor of lager beers in comparison with that of ales which are brewed by a process called TOP FERMENTATION. Bottom fermentation is typically carried out at temperatures between 38° and 48° F. It ordinarily takes between seven and 11 days for the yeast to convert the soluble sugar of the grains into the desired level of alcohol content.

bourbon   A spirit distilled from a fermented mash of grain that is at least 51% corn (Indian maize), bourbon is the most distinctly American of all whiskeys. Particularly regional in origin and history, it continues to be produced almost exclusively in north central Kentucky.

Of the three principal types of American whiskey—rye, corn whiskey and bourbon—both rye and corn whiskey predate bourbon, which to some extent is a compromise between these earlier spirits. Bourbon is distilled in a process identical to that used to produce RYE WHISKEY, but the mash from which it is distilled contains a high proportion of corn to which other grains, such as rye, have been added. In fact, according to one apocryphal story, bourbon originated when the rye whiskey distillers of Kentucky were faced with a crop failure of their preferred grain.

Most histories date the origin of bourbon to 1789 and credit its invention to Elijah Craig, a Baptist minister in the village of Georgetown in Bourbon

County, then a part of Virginia. The harsh taste of the early bourbons was in keeping with the frontier life style of that region (which was settled from Virginia through the Cumberland Gap after the American Revolution), but it also made this spirit a poor competitor with rye and rum elsewhere in the U.S. Up until the Civil War, bourbon production remained at a level of about 1,000 barrels per year, most of which came from family distilleries catering to local markets. After the war, however, the highly publicized exposure of a *whiskey ring* with connections to President Ulysses S. Grant's administration brought about sudden government regulation of the bourbon trade. Such regulation tended to reduce the distinct qualities of the various individual brands of bourbon, but it also modernized production of the whiskey and increased its availability in mass markets.

Today, production of bourbon begins with the cleaning and milling of the basic grain—corn kernels that are crushed and then soaked, traditionally in limestone water—before additional grains such as rye and malted barley are mixed in. In the *sweet-mash* method, an unusually high proportion of malted barley is added to encourage fermentation. In the *sour-mash* method, fermentation is encouraged by adding a *slop* of residue from a previous DISTILLATION. The grain mash is then poured into open-topped fermenting vats and yeast is added. Once fermentation has produced enough alcohol to qualify the mash as *distiller's beer,* distillation is begun. Originally carried out in pot stills, distillation of bourbons is now almost exclusively done in patent stills. Because of the content of the grain mash, distilled bourbon is considered a *heavy* whiskey and requires two or three years more aging than Scotch whiskey or Irish whiskey.

Most commercially sold bourbon is blended before bottling, a process that involves mixing a single distillate with at least one other distillate and sometimes with flavorless or *neutral* spirits. Less commonly, bourbon is sold as *bottled in bond,* a designation that indicates a *straight* bourbon produced by a single distillation.

Bowery   A street and neighborhood in lower Manhattan, New York City, that was once notorious for its cheap theaters, dance halls and beer gardens. Later it became populated in large part by indigents who lived on the streets or in one of the numerous SRO (single room occupancy) hotels. Today most of the hotels have shut down but the Bowery still includes a SKID ROW section. The term "Bowery bum," meaning hobo, or derelict, is still used to describe down-and-out alcoholics.

brain   A part of the CENTRAL NERVOUS SYSTEM (CNS), which is made up of the brain and spinal cord. The brain controls almost all the functions of the body through its regulation of endocrine hormones and through its nerve-cell network, which reaches all the tissues.

The brain consists of some 12 billion cells and has a complex chemistry that is only now being explored. Stimulation of a neuron results in an electrical transmission through the long cell axons that extend from the nerve cell. Transmission from one neuron to another is a chemical process across a microscopic gap (or synaptic cleft) between the cells. We are aware of numerous neurotransmitters (also called biogenic amines) that carry the signal across the gap. They include dopamine, norepinephrine, serotonin and acetylcholine. It is suspected that hundreds of neurochemicals are present in various parts of the brain.

Not all substances in the bloodstream enter the neuron. A blood-brain barrier exists that keeps certain molecules out—proteins, for example. All drugs that have an effect on brain function will, of course, pass the blood barrier. The drugs that tend to be abused usually affect synaptic transmission, while others affect the permeability of the cell membrane.

Alcoholism was first linked to brain damage more than 100 years ago, when three patients were described as suffering from delirium, visual problems, imbalance in walking and muscle tremors. Their condition came to be known as WERNICKE'S ENCEPHALOPATHY (SYNDROME OR DISEASE). In 1887 another form of brain damage was linked to alcoholism— KORSAKOFF'S PSYCHOSIS, characterized by disorientation, memory failure and a tendency to recite imagined occurrences.

Today, there is substantial evidence indicating that prolonged heavy consumption of alcohol as well as other drugs has a negative effect on the brain. CAT scans of heavy drinkers and other drug users who were not noticeably ill have shown brain atrophy (loss of brain cells) and other mutations. O. A.

Parsons, for example, in 1977, concluded that 50% to 100% of the alcoholics in any given sample have suffered brain atrophy. Tests have shown deficits in cognition and perception in drug users similar to those in patients with brain damage not related to drug use. However, there seems to be a continuum of effects on the brain, ranging from little or no effect in light "social" drinkers or brief drug experimenters to moderate or severe impairment in late-stage alcoholics and drug-addicted individuals. With alcohol, at least, there is evidence that some brain damage may be partly reversible.

Innovative imaging techniques in drug research are being used to study brain structure and function. One such is positron emission tomography (PET), a noninvasive technique that measures the localized brain metabolism of substances such as glucose. The images reflect local rates of glucose metabolism instead of anatomical detail and provide information about subcortical as well as cortical processes. CAT scans are limited in this respect. PET scans also allow the measurement of biochemical and metabolic processes in the living brain and have been used to study brain receptors.

PET and other new techniques promise to advance the correlation of neurochemical and anatomic changes with behavioral and physiological responses to alcohol. This will aid greatly in research on central nervous system deficits associated with drug-induced brain damage.

Alcohol: Alcohol inhibits the brain's ability to use oxygen and reduces its capacity to utilize glucose. Nerve cell transmission and the transport of ions in and out of brain cells are affected. Insufficient oxygen in the brain may cause its cells to die, and excessive alcohol intake can result in permanently impaired brain function, although several studies show that partial reversal of atrophy and impairment can occur in abstinent alcoholics. For very moderate drinkers there is no clear evidence that alcohol harms the brain. NUTRITIONAL deficiencies associated with alcoholism may also play a role in brain damage.

According to experiments cited in the U.S. Department of Health and Human Services report to Congress in December 1983, the alteration of electrical charges and neurotransmitters is different after chronic exposure to alcohol than after a single acute dose.

RNA and protein synthesis in the brain both affect learning and memory. Studies by Drs. Sujata Tewari and Ernest Noble of the University of California at Irvine have shown that alcohol may interfere with the manufacture of RNA and protein. This effect may be partly responsible for alcoholic BLACKOUT.

The ACETALDEHYDE produced when alcohol is METABOLIZED may also affect the brain, and investigators have suggested that acetaldehyde may be responsible for the DEPENDENCE that characterizes alcohol addiction. The mechanisms of this effect are still unclear. Researchers at the University of California at Irvine found that excessive drinking led to brainstem abnormalities in 40% of the alcoholic patients they studied, in addition to causing atrophy of the brain. The brainstem connects the brain to the spinal cord and controls such vital functions as respiration, heart rate and blood pressure. Abnormalities of these functions appear to have a strong link to alcohol use and are most prevalent in older patients who have already shown neurological complications resulting from extended alcohol use. A correlation between brainstem abnormalities and cerebral atrophy has been found.

Cannabis: The precise way in which MARIJUANA affects the brain is not known. Many mental functions are affected by marijuana intoxication, including immediate recall, sensory perception, tracking and attention span. The heavy, consistent ingestion of marijuana produces a chronic cannabis syndrome (amotivational syndrome) in certain people. Since it is LIPID SOLUBLE and the nerve cell membrane is lipid, the drug seems to be retained in the brain for longer periods than alcohol. Studies that show structure are suggestive of marijuana's effect, but further work is needed.

brandy An alcoholic beverage distilled from the fermented juice of grapes (wine) or other fruits. The term "brandy," without further qualification, usually refers to grape brandy. When fruits other than grapes are used, the name of the fruit precedes the term "brandy" (apricot brandy, cherry brandy, orange brandy or apple brandy, particularly the French CALVADOS and the American APPLEJACK). Many of these fruits go through a "wine stage" similar to that of the grape, and several are actually made into wines such as apple wine or elderberry wine.

Sometimes the term brandy is extended to include what the French call *marc* (pronounced *mar*) and the Italians refer to as *grappa* inexpensive brandies made from the stems, pips and skins of grapes after the juice has been pressed from them to make wine.

Brandies are produced all over the world, chiefly in France and the U.S., but also in Greece, Spain, Portugal, Italy, Peru and South Africa. The name, therefore, is often also qualified by the country or region where it is produced (for example, French brandy, California brandy). The best known brandy is COGNAC, named after the town of Cognac in southwestern France. Another popular French brandy is ARMAGNAC, also named for the region that produces it.

Brandy production can be traced back to the 13th century, and it is thought to be the oldest of the distilled alcoholic beverages. The art of distillation itself originated in the eastern world. It was first introduced to the Italians, who produced *acqua di vite* or *arzente*. From Italy the technique traveled to France, where its results were known as EAU DE VIE, and then to Spain. By the end of the 17th century the production of brandy had spread throughout Europe.

It is not known when the name "brandy" was first applied to distilled wine. However, it was originally a compound term: brandywine, brandewine or brandwine, which came from the Dutch *brantewijn* (from *branden,* to burn, and *wijn,* wine).

The first step in the production of grape brandy is to press the grapes in the usual way to make wine. The wine is then stored in casks until it is distilled into brandy. It takes approximately 10 casks of wine to produce one cask of brandy. In the distillation process, the wine is placed in pots constructed to retain the impurities, or CONGENERS, which give brandy its characteristic flavor and aroma. The congeners in brandy include normal propyl alcohol, normal butyl alcohol, amyl alcohol, hexyl alcohol, ethyl acetate and oenanthic ether; the latter provides one of the main taste characteristics that distinguishes brandy from other distilled liquors, such as whiskey or rum.

When first distilled, brandy is a colorless liquid with a very high alcoholic content, which exact percentage at this stage of production varies among the different brandies. California brandy, for example, is approximately 102 proof, while Cognac is between 140 and 150 proof. Before being bottled, brandy is aged in wooden casks for at least three years. As it ages, it mellows and acquires a yellow color that grows darker the longer the brandy remains in the casks. However, depth of color is not an accurate indicator of age, for producers often artificially color brandy with caramel. Brandy also loses some of its alcoholic content in the aging process and frequently through the addition of distilled water. Bottled Cognac, for example, is between 68 and 80 proof.

Brandy is usually drunk by itself as an after-dinner drink. It is also sometimes used in mixed drinks, such as cocktails, punches and so-called dessert drinks, and as a flavoring in coffee and foods.

Breathalyzers   Machines that detect and measure the BLOOD ALCOHOL CONCENTRATION (BAC). Used for a number of years by law-enforcement agencies in an effort to crack down on drunken drivers, the readings are based on a solid-state semi-conductor reaction to alcohol present in the breath. Breath-alcohol has a constant ratio to blood alcohol levels. Breath alcohol levels are multiplied by a factor of 2,300 to obtain blood alcohol levels.

Breathalyzers are being utilized increasingly by the military and in other industries, such as transportation and construction, where public safety may be jeopardized by the careless actions of intoxicated operators. In addition, the development of a portable, hand-held Breathalyzer encouraged the introduction of breath analysis into high schools. A number of schools admit to a reluctance to use them, but hope that their presence and the students' awareness of the fact will deter alcohol use during school hours. There have been questions raised whether breath analysis in schools is a violation of students' constitutional rights, but the 1996 Supreme Court decision in favor of allowing drug testing in high schools presumably silenced such challenges.

breech births   Studies have shown that breech births, in which a fetus emerges with the buttocks, knees or feet appearing first, are significantly higher among mothers addicted to narcotics. (See PREGNANCY for other effects of narcotic use among pregnant women.)

Brevital Sodium An intravenous anesthetic containing methohexital sodium. A rapid, ultra-short-acting BARBITURATE, it is used for quick surgical procedures. It may be habit-forming, but the rapid onset of effects and brief duration of action makes it less desirable for harmful use.

brewing A process that combines cereal grains, water, hops and yeasts to produce beer or ale. Records of early brewing processes for creating "barley water" appear on a Mesopotamian clay tablet from 4000 B.C. and on a wooden model of a brewery in Thebes from 2000 B.C. The Egyptians developed the most extensive primitive brewing techniques, which were later adopted by the Greeks and ultimately brought to western Europe by the Romans. Early European brewing was based principally in monasteries and homes until the 16th century, when significant commercial breweries emerged. Gradually, there evolved a process of brewing that has remained essential to the production of all commercial beers—lager, ale, stout and porter.

The first stage in the process is the preparation of a cereal mash. The principal grain used is barley, which is malted by milling it, soaking it until it germinates, and then drying it. Most beers also contain a blend of other cereal grains, which are soaked separately and then mixed with the malted barley. Then the grain content is cooked in water, which liquefies the starches present and converts them into soluble sugars, chiefly maltose and dextrin, which are essential to fermentation. The result, once filtered, is a liquid called wort.

In the next stage, the wort is combined with hops, which are the ripened cones found on the female hop vine, in a brew kettle (traditionally a copper one) and boiled for several hours. Technically, the term "brewing" refers to just this stage of beer production, but the term is commonly used to describe the entire process. The brew is then strained through a hop separator and the result is known as hop wort.

The third stage is fermentation, a process carried out in a fermenting tank and initiated by adding yeast enzymes to the sugar-rich hop wort. Fermentation is carried out at temperatures between 40° and 60° F, and requires anywhere from five to 11 days to complete. The yeast employed must produce sufficient fermentation to create the desired alcohol content, and it must also flocculate (separate itself from the beer) to enable its removal at the end of the process. Two types of brewing yeast have these properties. One type rises in the beer during fermentation (TOP FERMENTATION) and results in a product known as ale. The second type sinks during fermentation, and the result of this BOTTOM FERMENTATION process is lager. During both processes, gases emitted by the beer are collected and returned to the liquid for carbonation. "Krausened" beers are entirely carbonated by naturally active yeasts, but most beers are carbonated, at least in part, by the introduction of carbon dioxide.

The final stages of the process are aging and packaging. All beers are kept in chilled aging tanks for the last stages of fermentation. Once aged, beer is filtered to remove most of its yeast content and placed in barrels or in smaller consumer containers, such as cans or bottles. If barreled, usually in aluminum kegs, beer requires no further processing and has a short storage life. To extend their shelf life, bottled and canned beers are usually pasteurized to destroy the remaining yeast enzymes and prevent further fermentation.

Two popular brewing trends of the 1990s are "homebrewing" (often by upper-middle-class urbanites) and "microbreweries"—small-scale producers of high-quality beer that are sometimes attached to an upscale bar/eatery, usually located in the same facility.

brief intervention A treatment strategy in which structured therapy of short duration (typically five to 30 sessions) is offered with the aim of assisting an individual to cease or reduce the use of a psychoactive substance.

British Road Safety Act of 1967 The British Road Safety Act of 1967, which established drunken-driving laws, received renewed support in 1975 after a much-publicized media campaign called the "Cheshire Blitz." After the campaign, there was a statistically significant decline in serious auto crashes.

The British System In Great Britain, the treatment of opiate users is medically oriented and addicts are allowed to obtain and use opiates legally. Widely praised by advocates of heroin maintenance, the system has been recommended as a model for implementation in the U.S. The British System has been credited with limiting the use of heroin, preventing the development of a black market, reducing drug-related crimes and enabling addicts to lead more useful lives.

Before 1967 the system was simply a policy that allowed private physicians to prescribe maintenance doses to opiate users. As heroin use increased during the 1960s, however, the approach was altered, resulting in the establishment of a government-sponsored program. The new program imposed stricter controls on the manufacture, sale and possession of opiate drugs, and required addicts to be registered and treated through clinics or specially licensed physicians.

Yet the British System remains highly controversial, and while some observers view government clinics as a sensible and humane approach to the problem, others maintain that the clinics are not abstinence-oriented and do not remedy the problem of addiction. The AIDS crisis, however, refueled support for a maintenance approach as a means of minimizing the risk of HIV transmission through shared needles and contaminated apparatus related to intravenous drug taking.

The British System of heroin maintenance seems to have become mostly a methadone maintenance system. In 1980, 2,095 of the 2,846 patients in treatment received methadone alone; others received methadone in combination with other drugs; and only 53 patients were given heroin alone. (See UNITED KINGDOM.)

bromides   A group of synthetic sedative-hypnotic DEPRESSANTS derived from bromine. Introduced to medicine in 1857 as a treatment for epilepsy, bromides were later widely prescribed as sedatives, though rarely used as hypnotics. Bromides are now considered obsolete and have been replaced by BARBITURATES and BENZODIAZEPINES.

Classification: Bromides are not subject to the Controlled Substances Act.

Usage: Used medically as antiemetics (to suppress vomiting), aphrodisiacs or anticonvulsants.

Activity: Readily absorbed into the bloodstream, bromides have a 12-day half-life. They appear in mother's milk and cross the placental barrier.

Effects: Bromides depress the central nervous system, but, like paraldehyde, have little or no effect on the medullary centers and thus do not affect breathing or circulation. In low doses bromides have a typical sedative effect, causing drowsiness and loss of muscular coordination. The substance is cumulatively toxic and larger doses can cause confusion and agitation.

Dependence: Dependence, when it occurs, results in a disease similar to alcoholism, called bromism, with symptoms that include tremors, skin rashes, dizziness, delirium and lethargy. Overdosage can result in coma and death.

brompton cocktail   A variable mixture of drugs used in British and American hospices to control pain associated with terminal cancer. Traditionally, it contained heroin, cocaine and an antiemetic (used to suppress vomiting), like Thorazine. Morphine is now used as effectively as heroin, when given orally, after dosage adjustment. Cocaine has been dropped from the formulation in many hospices

Buff-A-Comp   A buffered analgesic containing aspirin, caffeine, phenacetin and an intermediate-acting BARBITURATE called butalbital. Possibly habit-forming and having a potential for harmful use, it is no longer legally available in the U.S.

bufotenine   A HALLUCINOGEN found in the skin glands of certain toads, as well as in several plant species. In Haiti and parts of Central and South America, natives use a snuff, Cohoba, which contains bufotenine as well as DMT and other hallucinogens. Bufotenine produces an LSD-like experience, though the illusionary disturbances are less complex. Physical effects are pronounced and typically appear first: the user may experience walking difficulties and paralysis, and the face may swell and redden. As the effects wane, the user falls into a stupor-like sleep.

Synonyms: Yopo (for Cohoba).

buprenorphine   Buprenorphine is an opioid AGONIST and NARCOTIC ANTAGONIST that may prove to be a valuable adjunct for the detoxification and maintenance treatment of heroin- and methadone-dependent persons. It offers the possibility of being acceptable to opiate-abusing patients seeking treatment, helping to decrease their heroin use and having a better safety profile than pure agonists such as METHADONE. Buprenorphine does not produce a clinically significant level of physical dependence; thus, discontinuing it is easier than detoxification from methadone.

Bureau of Alcohol, Tobacco and Firearms (ATF)

The ATF is a branch of the Treasury Department, responsible for enforcing federal laws and regulations pertaining to alcohol, tobacco, firearms, explosives and arson. In this capacity, the ATF has pursued drug traffickers who use or deal in firearms. Historically, the ATF traces its roots to the act of July 1, 1862, that created the Internal Revenue Service and imposed a tax on distilled spirits. The tax became an important part of the federal revenue system, and in 1863 Congress authorized the hiring of three detectives to enforce the act.

In the 20th century, the ATF was directly involved in the enforcement of Prohibition, which was instituted by the ratification of the 18th Amendment to the Constitution in 1919. The Volstead Act that enforced this amendment forbid the manufacture, sale and transport of alcohol. The commissioner of the Internal Revenue Service, through a newly created Prohibition Unit, was given responsibility for enforcing this act. With the repeal of Prohibition in 1933, the Bureau of Prohibition, which had been moved to the Justice Department, turned over its responsibilities to the newly created Alcohol Tax Unit (ATU) within the Internal Revenue Service in the Treasury Department.

In 1935 the Federal Alcohol Administration Act (FAA) was passed, creating licensing and permit requirements and establishing fair-market regulations for the sale of alcoholic beverages. In 1940 the FAA was merged with the ATU to combine alcohol-associated law-enforcement and regulatory authority.

In 1942 because of its experience in both law enforcement and industry regulation, the ATU was made responsible for administering the National Firearms Act (NFA) of 1934 and the Federal Firearms Act (FFA) of 1938. The NFA controlled the sale of machine guns and sawed-off shotguns, and the FFA established regulation of the firearms industry and made it a federal crime for felons and fugitives to receive firearms in interstate commerce. In 1951 tobacco tax responsibilities were also given to the ATU. In 1952 the ATU had its name changed to the Alcohol and Tobacco Tax Division (ATTD) of the Internal Revenue Service.

The 1968 Gun Control Act added bombs and other destructive devices as items controlled by the federal government. Enforcement of the act came under the ATTD's jurisdiction. The name was then changed to the Alcohol, Tobacco, and Firearms Division (ATFD) of the Internal Revenue Service. In 1970 the Organized Crime Control Act was passed, which created strict regulations on the explosives industry and established certain bombings and arson cases as federal crimes. The ATFD was given a lead role in the act's enforcement. In 1972 the ATFD was separated from the Internal Revenue Service and turned into the Bureau of Alcohol, Tobacco and Firearms. Since that time, the BATF has been involved in enforcing the Contraband Cigarette Act of 1978, the Gun Control Act of 1986 and the Brady Gun Law of 1994, as well as continuing to ensure the payment of taxes on alcohol and tobacco.

Bureau of Health Care, Delivery and Assistance (BHCDA)

As one of the three organizational components of the Health Resources and Services Administration (HRSA), the BHCDA works to improve access to quality health care for populations that are underserved because of social, economic and cultural factors. It conducts a number of alcohol- and drug-abuse activities by funding a network of 565 community and migrant health centers, which in turn work to improve the care of close to 6 million clients who exhibit problems with alcohol and other drugs. The BHCDA has also increased public awareness through extensive community education and prevention activities, cooperation with local alcohol and drug agencies, and distribution of resource directories and prevention brochures. As a component of HRSA, the organization falls under the jurisdiction of the Public Health Service (PHS) in the U.S. Department of Health and Human Services (DHSS).

Bureau of Narcotics and Dangerous Drugs (BNDD)

A law enforcement agency of the U.S. Department of Justice, created in 1968 and replaced in 1973 by the Drug Enforcement Administration (DEA).

Annual Cost of U.S. Alcohol, Tobacco and Other Drug (ATOD) Problems

1992 Estimates and Inflation- and Population-Adjusted Costs of Alcohol and Drug Abuse for 1995
(millions of current-year dollars)

	Alcohol		Drugs	
	1992	1995	1992	1995
Specialty alcohol and drug services	$5,573	$6,660	$4,400	$5,258
Medical consequences	13,247	15,830	5,531	6,623
Lost earnings—premature death	31,327	34,921	14,575	16,247
Lost earnings—illness	69,209	77,150	15,682	17,481
Lost earnings—crime/victims	6,461	7,231	39,164	43,829
Crashes, fires, criminal justice, etc.	22,204	24,752	18,307	20,407
Total	**$148,021**	**$166,543**	**$97,659**	**$109,832**

Note: Components may not sum to totals because of rounding.
Source: National Institute on Drug Abuse; National Institute on Alcohol Abuse and Alcoholism based on analysis by the Lewin Group

burns   A 1983 study found 2.4% of the violent deaths of alcoholics were caused by fires, a figure that was 26 times the expected rate. A review of the medical records of 70 burn patients over the age of 14 showed that 46% had been using alcohol at the time of injury. Fifty-seven percent of burns took place near vehicles. Males victims were likely to have been drinking at the time of injury—a rate of 58% was indicated—with a rate of 36% for female victims. In a 1989 study, the breathalyzer readings of 25% of fire-related emergency room admissions tested positive. Another study from 1991 cited alcohol as a factor in 43% of fire-related, unintentional injury deaths.

Reports concerning burn deaths resulting from the use of drugs other than alcohol is more elusive. Careless smoking is associated with drinking and plays a large role in such deaths. The practice of freebasing cocaine, as well as crack smoking, are also distinct burn risks. Comedian Richard Pryor nearly died from burns sustained from such activity.

T. Comes-Orme et al., "Violent Deaths among Alcoholics: A Descriptive Study," *Journal of Studies on Alcohol* 44 (1983): 938–949.

K. Voughtsberger and R. Taylor, "Psychosocial Factors in Burn Injury," *Texas Medicine* 80 (1984): 4346.

business   The annual costs of drug use to the U.S. business and the economy are astronomical: in 1995 the economic cost to the nation from the use and harmful use of alcohol, tobacco and other drugs was estimated at $275 billion. Costs can be broken down into the following categories: lost productivity (ABSENTEEISM, impaired judgment and creativity, and the loss of employees due to drug-related deaths, imprisonment and/or the premature "retirement" of workers who leave in search of more lucrative activities, often criminal, with which to support their habits); medical expenses (increased utilization of medical benefits for drug-use treatment, as well as treatment of the physical and the psychological consequences of drug use); the research, training and administration of the EMPLOYEE ASSISTANCE PRO-GRAMS that exist, in large part, to handle drug-use problems; and drug-related CRIME (court, police and incarceration costs at the federal, state and local levels, and drug-related crime prevention systems such as locks, alarm systems and so forth, and the destruction of property during drug-related criminal acts). (See DISEASES.)

Historical overview of drug-related business losses: Alcohol use by employees was not always viewed in a negative light. At one time, it was common in some industries to distribute beer to workers while they were on the job, presumably to lift their spirits. The first major acknowledgment of alcohol abuse within industry seems to have occurred in the 1930s and 1940s. After calculating the costs of this abuse, John D. Rockefeller became an early and influential supporter of Bill WILSON in an effort to popularize ALCOHOLICS ANONYMOUS. The concept of the employment assistance program was developed around that time, principally to address the burgeoning issue of harmful use of alcohol. By the 1980s, attention shifted to include the illicit use of cocaine, heroin, marijuana and prescription drugs.

Prevalence: The harmful use of alcohol and other drugs is not confined to any one socioeconomic class, ethnic background or gender, and occurs in virtually all occupations. Presently, issues related to employee impairment are not the only cause for concern. Because such drugs are illegal, they are used in secret, making it extremely difficult to identify or assist the employees in question. Management may perform in a sloppy and erratic manner, while their staff are similarly wreaking havoc within the company through substandard record- or bookkeeping. High-level executives may snort cocaine in the morning to "get going" and continue to use the drug during the day to "stay on top." The "three-martini lunch" is a favored tradition used to court prospective clients in certain industries; less discussed, however, is the lost productivity on the afternoons following these sessions. Office personnel commonly use drugs such as marijuana on a lunch break; night-shift workers take amphetamines to stay awake. Medical and health-care professionals, the primary providers of drug *treatment,* are not above drug abuse. In fact, a number of risk factors specific to the field, including stress, long hours, exposure to human suffering, and the availability of drugs, contribute to the vulnerability of health care workers. As many as 12% of doctors and nurses may be abusing drugs, proving that there are no exemptions among the various professional levels—doctors, nurses, support staff, emergency medical workers and cleaning staff—all are affected by this temptation. (See HEALTH CARE PROFESSIONALS AND ADDICTION.)

Unlike alcohol, illicit drugs are frequently more costly than a user can handle on his or her salary. Individuals as well as the companies they work for pay a high price when employees fall victim to drug-related financial stress. The quality of work will suffer from emotional strain and possibly resultant family problems. There is also an increased chance that the worker will then accept kickbacks, engage in property theft or even embezzlement to pay off rapidly accumulating debts. One survey stated that police officers, teachers and child care workers had the lowest reported use of illicit drugs within the last month (1.0%, 2.3% and 2.6%, respectively), compared to construction workers, food-preparation workers and restaurant servers, who reported the highest rates (17.3%, 16.3% and 15.4%, respectively). Heavy alcohol use (five or more drinks on five or more occasions during the past 30 days) was highest among construction workers (20.6%), laborers (19.5%), auto mechanics (16.3%), food-preparation workers (16.3%) and light-truck drivers (15.1%). The lowest rate of alcohol consumption was reported among data clerks (0.8%), personnel specialists (1.1%) and secretaries (1.4%). Drug-abusing employees perform at only 67% of their ability, according to government-sponsored research.

It is estimated that as much as $100 billion (2.5% of the GNP and 8% of discretionary spending) may be diverted from legitimate business enterprises to buy illegal drugs, while the cost to individual companies usually exceeds 2.5% of payroll. An ongoing study by the U.S. Postal Service has tracked the job performance of drug users vs. nonusers. Users show a 66% higher rate of absenteeism, 84% greater utilization of medical benefits and 90% more disciplinary actions than nonusers. A study conducted by the National Transportation Safety Board found that in commercial truck accidents, 22% of fatally injured drivers had one or more illegal drugs in their blood.

Drug abuse among workers appears to be declining. The *1993 National Household Survey on Drug Abuse* reported a drop of more than one-half since the mid-1980s in the rate of workers' harmful use of alcohol and other drugs. Among full-time personnel there was a decline from 16.7% in 1985 to 7.0% in 1993; and among part-time employees, from 15% to 7.0% during the same time period. (See ACCIDENTS, ECONOMIC IMPACT and WORKPLACE.)

Prevention and the business community: Until the implementation of drug-abuse prevention systems beginning in the mid-1980s in the U.S. automobile industry, there was widespread quality loss due to rampant harmful use of alcohol and other drugs by workers on the assembly lines. Increasingly, companies are employing drug-detection tests (blood and urine tests) to prevent wide-scale loss due to harmful use of alcohol and other drugs. Tests are generally performed on employees who arrive late to work excessively, take numerous sick days, and make frequent requests to leave early or to take time off. Substance users are also more likely to file a workmen's compensation claim in case of accidents. Other telltale signs among drug users are pupil changes, odors, chain smoking filterless cigarettes and constant licking of the lips. Investigations are also instigated by fellow employees who may be tired of "covering" for their coworkers.

Working within government guidelines, IBM, AT&T and 3M are among the private companies who have implemented regular testing. Unless a worker has union backing or an employment contract that will help defend him, he has little legal protection against drug tests or "the right to search." Workers have occasionally sued for "invasion of privacy" and "defamation of character." Such court battles are time-consuming and expensive for both parties, but the courts have often ruled that the corporation's practices were negligent. A 1988 federal ruling mandated random testing of transportation employees in what are classified as "safety-sensitive" jobs. High costs and the opposition of labor unions are two factors that discourage more industries from initiating similar programs.

EAPs (employee assistance programs):   The implementation of EAPs can save very large corporations billions of dollars annually. Dr. Robert G. Wiencek of General Motors stated that "for every $1 invested in treatment, GM can identify $3 in return for full-time employees who recover completely." In 1991 the U.S. Department of Labor estimated even greater savings from the enactment of EAPs: $5 to $16 for every dollar invested. A growing number of companies are now looking to Employee Assistance Programs to help control skyrocketing health care costs. EAP services are generally free and they seem to be an effective solution to industry's drug-related problems. The General Motors program has been widely acclaimed; the company set up its original alcohol-based programs in 1972, and in 1975 expanded them to include assistance with personal issues as well as matters involving the harmful use of other drugs. Unfortunately, despite high success rates, due to the fact that the monetary gain of treatment programs is difficult to evaluate, and because companies often do not have the capital to make the initial investment required, medium-sized industries in particular appear to be reluctant to adopt such programs.

Partnership For A Drug Free America, *The Impact of Illegal Drugs on America and Our Most Critical Domestic Issues* (New York, 1994).

Substance Abuse and Mental Health Services Administration, "Drug Use among U.S. Workers: Prevalence and Trends by Occupation and Industry Categories," *National House Hold Survey on Drug Abuse: Main Findings 1993* (Rockville, Md., 1995).

Department of Labor, *What Works: Workplaces without Drugs* (Washington, D.C., 1991).

Department of Labor, "Working Partners: Confronting Substance Abuse in Small Business," *National Conference Proceedings Report* (Washington, D.C., 1992).

butabarbital   An intermediate-acting barbiturate that produces mild sedation and has muscle-relaxing properties. (See BARBITURATES.)

butalbital   An intermediate-acting barbiturate used as a sedative hypnotic. (See BARBITURATES and BUFF-A-COMP.)

buticaps   A central nervous system depressant containing the intermediate-acting BARBITURATE sodium butabarbital. It is used for sedation and hypnotic purposes, and users are susceptible to psychological dependence. Overdosage can result in severe respiratory depression. It is no longer distributed in the U.S.

butisol sodium   A central nervous system depressant that contains the intermediate-acting BARBITURATE sodium butabarbital. It is used for sedation and hypnotic purposes, and may be habit-forming or create a psychological dependence. Overdosage can result in severe respiratory depression.

butyl alcohol   A solvent made by the fermentation of glucose. It should not be confused with ETHANOL, the principal chemical in alcoholic beverages.

butyl nitrite   An inhalant drug that first appeared in 1969 and is similar to AMYL NITRITE. Classified as a volatile inhalant, butyl nitrite inhalation produces a brief but intense lightheaded feeling, which is the result of lowered blood pressure and relaxation of the smooth (involuntary) muscles of the body.

C

caffeine   A naturally occurring alkaloid found in many plants throughout the world, caffeine was first isolated from coffee in 1820 and from tea leaves in 1827. Both "coffee" and "caffeine" are derived from the Arabic word *gahweh* (pronounced "kehveh" in Turkish).

Caffeine is a STIMULANT of the CENTRAL NERVOUS SYSTEM (CNS). When taken in beverage form, it begins to reach all the body tissues within five minutes; peak blood levels are reached in about 30 minutes. Caffeine has a half-life of about three and a half hours, and it is rapidly and completely absorbed from the gastrointestinal tract. Little can be recovered unchanged in urine, and there is no day-to-day accumulation of the drug in the body.

Caffeine increases the heart rate and rhythm, affects the circulatory system and acts as a diuretic. It also stimulates gastric acid secretion. There may be an elevation in blood pressure, especially during stress. Caffeine inhibits glucose metabolism and may thereby raise blood sugar levels.

As a behavioral stimulant it postpones fatigue. Caffeine appears to interact with stress—improving intellectual performance in extroverts and impairing it in introverts. When taken before bedtime, caffeine usually delays the onset of sleep, shortens sleep time and reduces the average "depth of sleep." It also increases the amount of dream sleep (REM) early in the night while reducing it overall.

Fatalities resulting from caffeine poisoning are rare: only seven deaths have been recorded to date. The lowest known fatal dose is 3.2 gm, administered intravenously. The fatal oral dose appears to be on the order of 10 gm.

While caffeine in moderate doses can increase alertness and verbal effusion and decrease fatigue, regular use of 350 mg or more a day results in a form of physical dependence. Interruption of such use can result in withdrawal symptoms, the most prominent of which may be severe headaches—which can be relieved by taking caffeine. Irritability and fatigue are other symptoms. Criteria for the actual diagnosis of caffeine dependency includes the persistent and continued use of this substance, despite knowledge of its causing physical and/or psychological problems, a persistent desire to stop its use, or development of a tolerance to this substance's effects, accompanied by increased use. Regular use of caffeine produces partial tolerance to some or all of its effects.

Regular use of more than 600 mg a day (approximately eight cups of percolated coffee) may cause chronic caffeine intoxication or poisoning, a condition known as caffeinism. Common symptoms of caffeinism are chronic insomnia, breathlessness, persistent anxiety and depression, mild delirium and stomach upset. Additionally, at a toxic level this condition can produce tremors, headache, ear ringing, irregular heartbeat, blood pressure fluctuations, diarrhea and ulcers, stomach pain, nausea and reflux. It may also cause heart disease; researchers at Johns Hopkins University School of Hygiene and Public Health found a modest association between heavy coffee drinking (considered to be five cups or more per day) and a myocardial infarction in young women (a condition in the heart muscle resulting from the formation of a blood clot in the coronary arterial system). Excessive use of caffeine has been suspected as a factor in cancer of the bladder and renal pelvis, but the evidence is inconclusive. In addition, caffeine consumption has been linked to fibrocystic disease in women, but again, the evidence so far is inconclusive.

Studies have also indicated that heavy use of caffeine in amounts equivalent to eight or more regular cups of coffee a day is responsible for an increased incidence of spontaneous abortions and stillbirths, breech deliveries, and cyanosis at birth.

Caffeine is probably the most popular drug in the world. It is primarily consumed in tea and coffee but is also present in cola drinks, cocoa, certain headache pills and aspirins, diet pills and patent stimulants such as Vivarin and Nodoz. Caffeine belongs to the family of methylxanthines. Theophylline and theobromine are closely related compounds, but caffeine is the most potent of the group.

Sara J. Carrillo, "Caffeine Versus the Body," *PharmChem Newsletter* 10, no. 3 (April 1981).

"Facts about Caffeine" (Toronto: Addiction Research Foundation of Ontario, January 1980).

M. B. McGee, "Caffeine Poisoning in a 19-Year-Old Female," *Journal of Forensic Sciences* 24, no. 1 (January 1980).

Mark Wenneker, "Breast Lumps: Is Caffeine the Culprit?" *Nutrition Action* (Center for Science in the Public Interest, August 1980).

caines   A group of synthetic local anesthetics frequently used as adulterants of cocaine. They include novocaine, pontocaine and lidocaine and provide the numbness and perhaps a very small amount of the euphoria of cocaine. They are found among the "legal cocaines" advertised in publications that specialize in drug paraphernalia as cocaine look-alikes and sound-alikes with brand names like Cococaine, Snowcaine and so on.

calabar bean   Seeds of the plant *Physostigma venenosum,* which is native to the West Indies. The seeds contain physostigmine (an inhibitor of the enzyme that breaks down acetylcholine). It therefore can cause severe adverse reactions.

California, drug cases in   Alcohol and other drug use makes headlines when Hollywood celebrities are involved. But the problem is also widespread among workers in other industries. According to Dr. Howard Frankel, medical director of Rockwell's space shuttle division from 1981 to 1983, 20% to 25% of Rockwell employees at the Palmdale, California, plant (the final assembly point for U.S. space shuttles) were high on the job from drugs, alcohol, or both. A single police raid at the plant resulted in the firing of nine workers.

Another California problem is the CLANDESTINE LABORATORIES now flourishing in the southern part of the state. The labs produce "crystal meth" and other forms of speed, PCP, and even synthetic heroin. State and federal authorities raided 647 clandestine drug labs nationwide in 1987, three-quarters of which were located in southern California. This was a marked increase from the 479 labs seized during 1986, although the number of seizures declined in the 10 years following. In 1994, the U.S. Drug Enforcement Administration (DEA) reported seizing 306 laboratories.

Clandestine drug labs have been a factor in California's drug underworld since the mid-1960s, when the Hell's Angels began setting up operations to produce methamphetamine. For a total investment of less than $5,000, an underground chemist can make about 10 pounds of crystal meth. Each pound sells for $10,000 to $15,000 wholesale, or up to $150,000 for a 10-pound amount—retail (on the street) prices may be as much as $15 million.

According to a 1995 DEA report, Northern California is, in all likelihood, a prime location of laboratories producing LSD. The same report also names California as one of five states with a significant amount of domestic outdoor cannabis cultivation, most of which occurs in remote locations and occasionally on public lands.

Gilda Berger, *Drug Abuse: The Impact on Society* (New York: Franklin Watts, 1988): 13, 66, 102, 117.

Michael A. Lerner, "An Explosion of Drug Labs," *Time* (April 25, 1988): 25.

Drug Enforcement Administration (DEA), "The Supply of Illicit Drugs to the United States," *National Narcotics Intelligence Consumers Committee* (August 1995).

California poppy   There are unconfirmed claims that smoking the poppy *Eschscholtzia californica* can produce narcoticlike effects.

calorie   A unit of measure used to express the heat- or energy-producing value of food when it is metabolized in the body. ABSOLUTE ALCOHOL, on average, contains about 150 to 200 calories an ounce. Calories contained in alcohol are so-called empty calories because they cannot be stored and do not produce essential vitamins for the body's nutritional needs. The body burns alcohol before it burns food. Food is stored and used as fat. Prolonged consumption of heavy amounts of alcohol while cutting down on food can lead to malnutrition and avitamenosis, a condition frequently seen in alcoholics.

Calvados   A famous French apple brandy from the Normandy region of the same name. The production of alcohol from apples was first developed by the Vikings who settled in Normandy over a thousand years ago. After being distilled from apple cider or sometimes apple pulp, Calvados is then aged in oak casks for six years. Bottled at around 80 proof, it has a distinct, applelike flavor.

Campari   An alcoholic beverage made in Milan, Italy, Campari belongs to the class of drinks known as bitters. It is 48 proof, reddish in color and has a somewhat bitter flavor. In Italy, Campari is one of the most popular APERITIFS. It is drunk either neat (without ice), with soda as a chaser or mixed in cocktails.

Canada   Most likely because of geographical proximity, the patterns and trends of harmful use and dependency of alcohol and other drugs in Canada tend to follow those of the U.S., although to a lesser extent. As in the U.S., smoking and drinking are the two major health problems.

Alcohol: Overall rates for the consumption of alcohol in Canada are on the decline. In 1993, 74.4% of Canadians over the age of 15 reported drinking compared to 79% in 1990. In the 1993 survey, 84.6% of those aged 20 to 24 identified themselves as current drinkers. This was the highest rate of any age group surveyed. Consumption of alcohol was lowest in those 75 or older, with 42% in this age group reporting consumption. Between 1950 and 1987 there was an increase in drinking among youth and women—groups that in the past did not generally drink—and the number of abstainers may have dropped by 50%. Canada's drinking pattern is one of increased consumption on weekends and holidays, though only one-sixth of the consumption takes place in public places. Proportions of alcoholic beverages consumed have changed between 1987 and 1993. Consumption of beer, the most popular beverage, increased from 50% to 56.4%, distilled spirits decreased markedly from 40% to 28.4%, and wine increased from 10% to 15.2%. Per capita consumption on a national level rose 34% between 1966 and 1974. In 1984 consumption per person among those 15 years and older showed Canada with 105.9 liters (1 liter equals 1.06 quarts) for beer, 12.5 for wine and 3.4 for spirits (pure alcohol). In 1992 consumption fell to 4.63 liters for beer, 12.6 for wine and 2.51 for spirits. The nation's total alcohol consumption per person among those over 15 years old was 10.2 liters in 1984. This decreased to 7.97 liters in 1992. Between 1975 and 1979, sales of alcoholic beverages by value rose 46% from $2.9 billion to $4.37 billion.

A conservative estimate of the entire country put the total number of alcoholics at 503,000 in 1984. The prevalence of alcoholism was 1,800 per 100,000 persons. This rate remained the same in 1990; however, in actual numbers, there was a slight decrease to 490,700. In 1993 nearly one in 10 Canadians 15 or older (9.2%) reported a problem with alcohol. The most commonly reported problem was with health (5.1%). In the most recent survey, alcohol-related deaths have increased slightly. In 1988 there were 10.8 deaths per 100,000 persons, and in 1991 there were 11.6 deaths per 100,000. In 1986 there were 150,571 alcohol-related traffic offenses, and 1,277 fatally injured drivers who used alcohol. The number of alcohol-related accidents and fatalities decreased after that year. In 1987 there were 7.7 accidents per 100,000, and in 1991 6.0 accidents per 100,000. Fatalities decreased slightly from 1,413 in 1987 to 1,180 in 1991. Of those Canadians surveyed, 5.1% reported alcohol-related health problems. Cirrhosis accounted for 69.1% of the deaths directly attributable to alcohol. In 1985 there were 880 divorces attributed to alcohol-related problems. While actual divorce was not surveyed in 1993, 9.3% of current drinkers surveyed reported family or marital problems.

Alcoholism treatment: There is an acknowledged need for comprehensive training programs to deal with the problem of harmful use of alcohol and alcoholism and there are responsible agencies on both the federal and provincial levels. But while most of the provinces maintain research foundations, health facilities and education programs, formal policies aimed at reducing chronic alcohol use appear to be lacking. In many provinces, voluntary and charitable organizations such as the Salvation Army and Alcoholics Anonymous have been the most successful in addressing the problem. Most Canadians surveyed in 1993 believed that self-help programs such as AA, emergency telephone hot lines, community prevention programs and professional treatment programs were moderately to very effective, with AA being seen as the most effective. Additionally, the overwhelming majority (79%) saw drug use as the most important issue for government to deal with.

Drugs other than alcohol: Overall, use of marijuana, heroin, codeine, cocaine and methaqualone decreased in the 1990s. However, overall rates can be deceiving in that they mask the increase in the use of some drugs among particular age groups and in some geographic locations. A 1993 government survey identified aspirin as the most commonly used legal substance in Canada, with 69.8% of the population reporting having used it in the month prior to that survey. Codeine, which is legal in Canada, was the most popular psychoactive drug, with at least 8.2% of the population using it one month before the survey.

In 1987 an estimated 1.8 million Canadians (9.5% of the total population of 20 million) reported using marijuana at some time. This rate dropped to 5.0% of the population in 1990 and 4.2% in 1993. However, the rate of marijuana increased for 15- to 19-year-olds to 10.3% in 1993. A government survey in 1973 reported 45,000 *known* users and more than 10,000 convictions on marijuana-related charges. While the number of known users as identified by marijuana offenses only decreased to 43,917 in 1984, it decreased significantly (to 34,005) in 1993. Between 1984 and 1992, the number of offenses for cocaine increased from 4,119 to 13,459. This increase may be reflective of increased police or prosecutorial actions and not a significant increase in use. Government surveys actually show a decrease in

cocaine use: while rising from 0.9% in 1985 to 1.4% in 1989, it dropped to 0.3% in 1993. The survey also reported 10,000 known users of other hallucinogens, particularly LSD, PCP and MDA. According to Canadian government surveys, the use of heroin, speed and LSD has remained at an almost constant low rate of 0.4% in 1989 and 0.3% in 1993. (These rates were based on moderate samples and therefore can be questionable.) Concurrently, and possibly reflecting their continued low use, the number of offenses for these drugs has decreased from 7,457 to 4,615. The use of inhalants was also reported but to a far lesser degree. However, an earlier survey had shown an increase in the use of methaqualone, which led to the establishment of a methaqualone treatment program in 1971.

As in the U.S., there is a movement in Canada toward the legalization of marijuana. The federal Commission of Inquiry into the Non-Medical Use of Drugs (commonly called the Le Dain Commission) is conducting a continuing study and has suggested that, while marijuana should not be legalized, penalties for possession cases should be reduced (namely, eliminating jail sentences for first-time offenders) and research on the subject should be continued and expanded. As a result of the study, considerable discretion is now used in possession cases. However, convictions for trafficking, importing, exporting and growing marijuana can result in prison terms of up to seven years. If the charges concern narcotics or other dangerous drugs, the penalty can be seven years to life imprisonment.

Substance abuse treatment: Drug treatment programs in Canada generally center around the problem of heroin addiction; methadone maintenance is generally used. It should be noted, however, that there has been an increase in methadone use recently.

Canadian Centre on Substance Abuse, *Canadian Profile, Alcohol, Tobacco and Other Drugs* (Toronto: Addiction Research Foundation of Ontario, 1995).

Brewers and Licensed Retailers Association, *Statistical Handbook 1995* (London, 1995).

Canadian whiskey   An alcoholic beverage produced in Canada by distilling a fermented mash of barley, rye and corn. The distilled alcohol is subjected to secondary extraction and rectification proc-

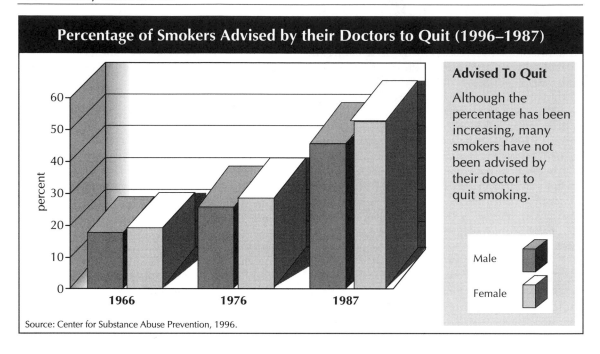

Percentage of Smokers Advised by their Doctors to Quit (1996–1987)

Advised To Quit

Although the percentage has been increasing, many smokers have not been advised by their doctor to quit smoking.

Male

Female

Source: Center for Substance Abuse Prevention, 1996.

ess that leaves it with a very low level of heavy CONGENERS. For that reason it is known as the lightest of all whiskeys. Individual Canadian whiskeys are aged for four, eight or 12 years and then blended with other whiskeys before final filtering and bottling. They are sold at 86.6 proof.

The origins of Canadian whiskey are not known, but it is assumed that distillation of grains in Canada was begun by Irish and Scottish settlers around the end of the 18th century. Although the whiskey was no doubt prized by pioneers, particularly during the harsh Canadian winters, effective temperance movements controlled its distribution throughout the 19th century. There were also several provincial prohibitions on alcohol distillation in Canada, and consequently, the country's whiskey industry developed much later than its American counterpart.

A law banning the distillation of alcohol in Canada was being drafted when Prohibition was enacted in the U.S. with the passage of the Volstead Act in 1919. Bolstered by the sudden lack of competition from America, distillers in Canada prevailed on the government to abandon its plans for instituting prohibition there. Canadian whiskey subsequently became enormously popular in the U.S. as the cheapest

safe alternative to "bathtub gin" and other illegal distillates, and the Canadian liquor industry boomed. When Prohibition ended in the U.S. in 1933, Canadian distillers were able to extend their syndicates across the border before producers of domestic brands of whiskey could establish themselves.

Canary Island broom   *Genista canariensis.* There are claims that when smoked or taken orally, this plant can produce narcotic-like effects. However it is poisonous even in low doses.

cancer   The primary drugs of that seem to be directly related to cancer are alcohol and tobacco—the two most widely used drugs in the U.S. Recent studies have shown that heavy drinkers who also smoke have a higher incidence of cancer than drinkers who do not smoke or smokers who do not drink. Compared to the rest of the population, alcoholics and heavy drinkers show a high incidence of mortality from cancer of the mouth, pharynx, larynx, esophagus, liver and lungs. Cancer associated with alcohol accounts for 6.1% to 27.9% of the total incidence of all cancer. It has been difficult to separate the effects of drinking from the effects of smoking, because most heavy drinkers are also heavy smokers. Alcohol itself has not been shown to be an independent carcinogen, but it is thought to act as a cocarcinogen—a substance that promotes cancer in conduction with a carcinogen. Studies have indicated that alcohol and cigarettes act synergistically to increase carcinogenic potential, particularly in cancers of the mouth and throat. It has been suggested that the combination of drinking and smoking increases the risk of throat and mouth cancer 15 times above that of the nonsmoking nondrinking population. Studies of marijuana smokers and the incidence of cancer are few and inconclusive; in fact, THC (the active ingredient in marijuana) is sometimes prescribed for cancer patients as a treatment for the nausea and vomiting caused by chemotherapy.

During the 1950s and 1960s, extensive studies provided conclusive evidence that cigarette smoking was directly related to lung cancer, heart disease, emphysema and chronic bronchitis. It was further shown that NICOTINE use during pregnancy was hazardous to the unborn child.

In 1989, then-U.S. surgeon general C. Everett Koop released a report on the consequences of smoking that attributed 390,000 deaths to smoking tobacco in 1985. The report stated that major smoking-related diseases were cancer, heart disease, respiratory disease and other conditions such as stomach ulcers. It indicated that since 1986, lung cancer has exceeded breast cancer as the leading cause of cancer death in women—the relative risk of lung cancer among women smokers has increased more than four times since the early 1960s. It has been estimated by the U.S. Environmental Protection Agency (EPA) that tobacco is responsible for 3,000 cases of lung cancer a year. Additionally, the EPA has identified nonsmokers who are in consistent, close contact with smokers as "passive smokers," who have a 34% increased risk for lung cancer. The EPA estimates that 20% of lung-cancer deaths among nonsmokers are due to passive cigarette smoke. The EPA has labeled tobacco as a class A carcinogenic substance. The American Cancer Society in 1994 estimated that lung cancer accounted for more than 153,000 deaths a year. Smoking, according to Dr. Koop, now causes more than one of every six deaths in the U.S.

Esophagus: The cancer-causing role of alcohol among smokers was found to be even greater in cases of cancer of the esophagus than in those of cancer of the mouth and larynx. There is an increased risk of esophageal cancer among all drinkers, although it is apparently greater for whiskey drinkers than for wine or beer drinkers. Between 60% and 80% of

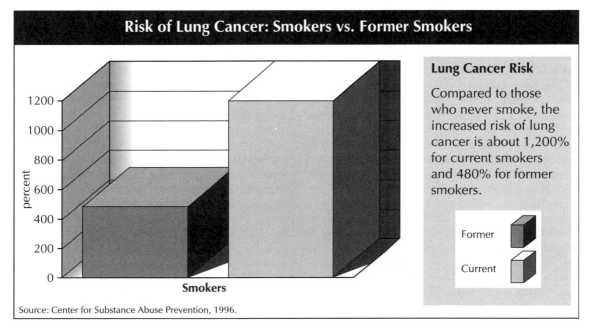

Risk of Lung Cancer: Smokers vs. Former Smokers

Lung Cancer Risk

Compared to those who never smoke, the increased risk of lung cancer is about 1,200% for current smokers and 480% for former smokers.

Former

Current

Source: Center for Substance Abuse Prevention, 1996.

patients who develop cancer of the esophagus have a history of heavy alcohol use. Alcohol may destroy the chemical barriers in the esophagus, exposing susceptible cells to carcinogens. A study done in France in 1977 showed that the risk of esophageal cancer is 44 times greater for heavy users of both alcohol and tobacco than for abstainers from both drugs, compared with 18 times greater for heavy users of alcohol and five times greater for heavy users of tobacco.

Liver: Primary liver cancer (hepatoma) is very often accompanied by and probably preceded by CIRRHOSIS. In a study cited in the *Sixth Special Report to the U.S. Congress on Alcohol and Health,* the prevalence of cirrhosis in patients with liver cancer was found to be between 55% and 80%. There are possibly two stages involved in liver cancer: liver damage due to alcoholism, followed by intervention of a secondary agent setting off the actual malignancy. Some studies suggest that the hepatitis C virus, which is an important risk factor for alcoholic cirrhosis, was a significant predictor for the development of heptocellular carcinoma.

In several broad-based studies, alcohol was shown to slightly increase the risk of cancer with an intake of alcohol of more than one drink a day. Other research has not been conclusive. In 1985 Dr. Nicholas Pace, one of the nation's leading alcoholism treatment specialists and founder of Pace Health Services in Manhattan, told reporter Lucinda Franks, "If we thought yesterday's alcoholic was haunted by internal conflict, we know that today's is primarily haunted by his liver."

There are several risks for alcoholic patients who have cancer, including the development of WITHDRAWAL as a postoperative complication. Such patients have poorer chances of survival and greater chances of developing another primary tumor than other patients with the same type of cancer.

More research on the exact relationship between alcohol and cancer is needed. Cell study tests are currently being conducted to detect precancerous cells at sites associated with alcohol consumption. A number of theories seek to explain the increased incidence of cancer in alcoholics and/or smokers. Inadequate nutrition is one of them: lack of nutritious food weakens the body's immune defense system, leaving it vulnerable to cancer-causing agents. Another theory suggests that alcohol itself causes cancer. Known carcinogens have been found in many alcoholic beverages; beer, for example, has been found to contain asbestos fibers from the filters used in its manufacture. Alcohol has also been shown to have an effect on the cell membranes, possibly increasing the ability of carcinogens to affect the cells themselves. Alcohol may also dissolve water-insoluble carcinogens, making them more available to various organs.

American Association for Cancer Research, "Alcohol and Cancer Workshop," *Cancer Research* 39, no. 7 (July 1979).

Lucinda Franks, "A New Attack on Alcoholism," *New York Times Magazine* (October 20, 1985).

American Cancer Society, *Cancer Facts and Figures—1994* (Atlanta, November 1994).

Richard L. Berke, "U.S. Report Raises Estimate of Smoking Toll," *New York Times* (January 11, 1989): A20.

Enoch Gordis, M.D., ed., "Eighth Special Report to Congress on Alcohol and Health," *National Institute on Alcohol Abuse and Alcoholism (NIAAA) (September 1993).*

cannabinoids   Derivatives of CANNABIS. Cannabis contains some 60 cannabinoids.

capital with codeine suspension   A narcotic opiate containing 325 mg of acetaminophen and 30 mg of codeine, used as an analgesic for mild to moderate pain. It can produce effects similar to morphine and therefore has a potential for harmful use and dependency. When used with alcohol or other central nervous system depressants, it can have an ADDITIVE EFFECT. Symptoms of overdosage include respiratory depression, cold and clammy skin, muscle flaccidity and extreme somnolence leading to stupor or coma.

carbohydrate   Alcohol affects carbohydrate metabolism and may increase or decrease blood sugar depending on the state of nutrition in the body. It appears that when hepatic (liver) carbohydrate stores are adequate, ethanol induces hyperglycemia, whereas when they are low, hypoglycemia results. (See BLOOD SUGAR.)

Although it contains calories and carbohydrates, alcohol has no nutritional value. Beer is very high in carbohydrates as well as calories; wine contains some carbohydrates; and most distilled liquors, such as gin and whiskey, have almost none. This lack of carbohydrates in hard liquor has become the basis for some fad diets, such as "the drinking man's diet." However, hard liquor has a lot of "empty calories" that must be metabolized before food calories (such as those in carbohydrates), which are then stored as fat. Therefore, if someone drinks large amounts of alcohol and eats, he or she is likely to gain rather than lose weight.

carbon tetrachloride   A toxic hydrocarbon that was once a common ingredient in many cleaning fluids, but has been barred from consumer products because of its toxic properties. Although it was sometimes inhaled for the intoxicating effect produced, it is extremely dangerous: inhalation can result in headache, confusion, vomiting, and coma or death. Large quantities may cause damage to the nervous system, heart, liver and kidneys. It is especially dangerous when combined with alcohol.

Career Teacher Program (CTP)   Jointly sponsored by the NATIONAL INSTITUTE ON ALCOHOL ABUSE AND ALCOHOLISM (NIAAA) and the NATIONAL INSTITUTE ON DRUG ABUSE (NIDA), this program has been the impetus for many of the new courses or expanded substance-abuse curricula at 60 medical education institutions. The problems of harmful use of alcohol and other drugs are, at long last, receiving increased emphasis in many medical school curricula. This has been an area of long-standing criticism of medical professional programs. The CTP was instituted in 1986–87 and is an ongoing endeavor by NIAAA and NIDA.

catalytic antibodies   Catalytic enzymes are synthetic molecules developed within the last decade and designed to recognize and bind to a specific molecule. Unlike naturally occurring antibodies, however, catalytic antibodies function as enzymes by inducing the molecules to which they bind to undergo a chemical reaction. Most other strategies for developing cocaine-addiction treatment medication target dopamine receptors (the brain cell molecules that are over-stimulated during cocaine use), but catalytic enzymes work by neutralizing the drug in the bloodstream and reducing the amount available for brain uptake. This method would limit adverse side effects as a result of increased activity on the brain and also reverse some of cocaine's toxic effects, including decreased blood flow and reduced oxygen delivery to the brain.

catnip   An herb, *Nepeta cataria*. There are claims that when smoked it can produce marijuanalike effects, but this is not the case. It does, however, appear to have a psychoactive effect when ingested by cats, who are especially fond of this herb. It is available in most pet stores.

celebrity alcohol and other drug use   A number of famous singers, musicians, dancers and actors have made headlines when heavy alcohol or other drug use ruined their careers and, in some cases, cost them their lives. Most authorities believe that this notoriety affects the behavior of impressionable young people and their attitude toward drugs, because such personalities are often role models for the country's youth. When a prominent athlete, actor or rock star uses drugs, it seems to send out a message to youngsters that "drugs are okay, they're cool."

Alcohol and other drugs have figured in the tragic deaths of many well-known celebrities, including: basketball star Len Bias, baseball legend Micky Mantle, comedian John Belushi, and rock stars Janis Joplin and Kurt Cobain. Richard Pryor, the actor-comedian, frankly admits that drugs almost killed him. Others who have spoken out about their drug-use problems include: Elizabeth Taylor, Gelsey Kirkland, Carrie Fisher, Liza Minnelli, Drew Barrymore, Suzanne Sommers, New York Giants football star Lawrence Taylor, outfielder Darryl Strawberry and former Pittsburgh Pirates pitching ace Dock Ellis.

Many celebrities have urged fans through talk shows, books, interviews and audience appeals to help in the fight against illicit drug use. Others have contributed their time to public service programs and announcements.

Center for Substance Abuse Prevention (CSAP) In 1992, the Office for Substance Abuse Prevention (OSAP) became CSAP because of a reorganization of the Alcohol, Drug Abuse and Mental Health Administration. CSAP leads the federal government's efforts in the prevention and intervention of alcohol, tobacco and other drug problems.

Center for Substance Abuse Treatment (CSAT)
CSAT is the federal agency responsible for funding residential and nonresidential treatment programs. It provides grants to states for drug and alcohol services, counselor training programs, rehabilitation programs in the criminal justice system and national demonstration projects.

central nervous system (CNS)   The network of neurons (nerve cells) concentrated in the BRAIN and spinal cord that conduct electrical sensory and motor impulses to and from all parts of the body via the peripheral nervous system (PNS). The PNS also includes the autonomic nervous system, which is divided anatomically and functionally into the sympathetic and parasympathetic branches.

Nerve fibers called axons lead away from neurons and produce and store neurohormones, such as norepinephrine, serotonin and acetylcholine. Transmission of an impulse occurs when neurohormones cross the synaptic gap to a neuron or its attached dendrite (a nerve fiber that carries impulses toward a neuron).

The brain is divided into a number of areas that exert control over specific functions: in the brainstem, the medulla oblongata is the center of respiratory, cardiac and vasomotor functions; the reticular activating system, a network of specialized nerve cells within the brainstem, controls alertness. The brainstem also includes the pons and mesencephalon (midbrain), collections of nerve fiber bundles that relay impulses.

Located above the brainstem, the thalamus acts as a central switchboard, directing impulses between the body and brain and within the subcortical area. Projecting from the thalamus, the hypothalamus affects emotional balance, regulates the autonomic nervous system, body temperature and water balance, and controls the dichotomous pleasure/pain and hunger/satiety reactions. Attached to and behind the brainstem, the cerebellum controls coordination, equilibrium and muscle tone. The most highly evolved part of the human brain is the approximately 6 mm outside layer called the cerebral cortex. It controls intellectual functions (including memory), certain motor functions, language and speech, auditory, visual and other sensory skills.

Drugs and other toxic substances can alter nervous system function by inhibiting, stimulating or imitating neurohormones, by disturbing their metabolism or affecting structures involved in the neurological process. Drugs also specifically affect different parts of the brain and therefore predictably impair certain functions. Drug use can cause permanent organic damage.

Depressants: Depressant drugs, including alcohol and opiates, interfere with neurohormonal production and absorption by the postsynaptic membrane and exert their principal effect on the medulla. This action explains the danger of respiratory failure that can accompany use of these drugs. They also affect the reticular activating system, including sleep and other areas of the cerebral cortex, and can result in structural damage, such as cerebral edema, congestion and hemorrhage.

One of the best-documented categories of drug-use pathology is that of brain damage related to alcoholism, though the mechanisms of many of these disorders are not fully understood. Alcoholics commonly suffer from impairment of judgment, concentration and memory. In their early stages, these symptoms can disappear with abstinence, which does not, however, always reverse brain atrophy that occurs as more and more brain cells are destroyed by alcohol.

Factors associated with alcoholism, such as malnutrition, also contribute to the development of both reversible and irreversible brain damage; thiamine deficiency, in particular, is at least partially responsible for a number of common alcoholic brain disorders. Victims of WERNICKE'S ENCEPHALOPATHY (SYNDROME OR DISEASE) and KORSAKOFF'S PSYCHOSIS, for example, exhibit delirium tremens, visual impairment, inability to maintain balance and memory failure. Thiamine deficiency also contributes to ALCOHOLIC POLYNEUROPATHY, another relatively common condition that involves numbness, pain, wasting and impaired function of the limbs, beginning with the legs. ALCOHOL AMBLYOPIA provides another example. This disorder consists of visual impairment, which sometimes involves degeneration of the optic nerves. Heavy alcohol use affects protein and nucleic-acid synthesis in the brain, which may be related to disturbances in learning, mental deficiencies and malformation in children with FETAL ALCOHOL SYNDROME. Brain injuries also result from accidents attributable to intoxication from alcohol.

Stimulants: Stimulant substances generally accelerate production and release of neurohormones. Nicotine overloads the nerve cells and blocks synapses by mimicking acetycholine. Stimulants seem to focus on the autonomic nervous system, increasing heartbeat and blood pressure. Hypertension and tachycardia leading to cerebral hemorrhage are risks associated with the harmful use of amphetamines and other stimulants. These drugs also keep the user awake by stimulating the reticular activating system and appear to stimulate the pleasure and satiety centers located in the hypothalamus. Altered patterns of thinking, such as the exaggerated attention to insignificant detail that often occurs on an amphetamine binge, may indicate that there is an effect on the cerebral cortex as well. Cumulative nervous-system degeneration has been associated with chronic stimulant use.

Cocaine is a very strong CNS stimulant. Specific physical effects include constricted peripheral blood vessels, dilated pupils and increased temperature, heart rate and blood pressure. Cocaine's immediate euphoric effects, which include hyperstimulation, reduced fatigue and mental clarity, last approximately 30 to 60 minutes. Cocaine used at high doses or chronically can have toxic effects. Overdose deaths are a result of seizures followed by respiratory arrest and coma, or sometimes by cardiac arrest or stroke.

Opiates: Heroin and other opiates act primarily on the thalamus, medulla and cerebral cortex. Large doses stimulate the hypothalamic pleasure center to produce immediate euphoria that is often likened to a "complete body orgasm." Opiates also appear to stimulate or mimic activity of the parasympathetic division of the autonomic nervous system and generally depress the function of affected areas. Opiate overdose sometimes involves coma and cerebral edema.

Hallucinogens: Hallucinogens such as LSD excite a collection of structures known as the limbic system, which plays a large role in emotional response and is closely connected to the thalamus and hypothalamus. They also seem to affect those areas of the brain that control auditory and visual reflexes and speech skills. Psychedelics may inhibit nerve impulses by antagonizing the neurohormone serotonin and possibly by mimicking norepinephrine. Reports

of permanent brain damage resulting from the use of LSD have been largely unsubstantiated, but long-term psychotic reactions are occasionally reported.

Many studies have been conducted to determine the relationship of chronic marijuana use to the loss of short-term memory, but none has sufficiently explained this phenomenon. It has been postulated that chronic marijuana smoking inhibits production of DNA, which chemically stores information. To date, there has been no conclusive evidence that structural brain damage, including cerebral atrophy, can result from chronic cannabis consumption.

central pontine myelinolysis   A rare disease of unknown origin that occurs in a group of brain nerve fibers known as the pons. It is most often found in long-time alcoholics suffering from malnutrition. Difficult to diagnose, the principal symptoms are a progressive weakness in the muscles extending from the lowest part of the brain to the spinal cord, an inability to swallow, and an absence of the gag reflex. As the disease progresses, the patient experiences drowsiness and ultimately becomes comatose.

cerebral atrophy   Decreased BRAIN size (cerebral and cortical atrophy) has been a rather recent and major finding in studies of alcoholic patients. It has been demonstrated repeatedly by autopsy examination and computerized axialtomography (CAT scan). Widespread atrophy has been revealed (along with cell loss) in many brain regions. Damage can result in INTELLECTUAL IMPAIRMENT, including memory disorders such as Wernicke-Korsakoff syndrome. The reversibility of alcohol-induced organic brain damage and neuropsychological impairment remains one of the most controversial yet important issues in all of alcohol-related research.

charas   The Indian term for the resin produced by the flowering top of the female plant *Cannabis sativa.* It is far more potent than ganja, which comprises the leaves, stems and twigs all ground up and mixed in with the flowering top.

chaser   A mild liquid, such as water or beer, taken after a drink of strong liquor (often ordered accompanying a *shot* of some strong spirit such as whiskey). The term and perhaps the custom derive from the French *chaser.* In France a *chasse-cafe* is a liqueur used to "chase" coffee. It is served as a *digestif* after a meal. The chaser has something of a soothing effect after a jolt of hard liquor, but its major use is to provide a contrast—a distinct, opposite sensation—just as the *chasse-cafe* contrasts with coffee.

chat   See KHAT.

Chemical Awareness Training Institute   A not-for-profit national organization specializing in student assistance program training for grades seven through 12. The institute trains educators and other interested adults to provide student assistance and act as group facilitators. It also offers technical assistance to schools, regarding alcohol and drug use programs and other related student problems. Training materials and student assistance manuals are available through the institute.

Chemical Diversion and Trafficking Act of 1988
Passed by Congress and signed by President Ronald Reagan on November 18, 1988, the act provides the Drug Enforcement Administration (DEA) with the major authority to mount a "revitalized attack against the clandestine manufacture of controlled substances and to pursue an aggressive program against those who divert certain precursor and essential chemicals for illicit purposes."

The act regulates the distribution of 20 listed chemicals used in the clandestine manufacture of controlled substances, such as methamphetamine, LSD, PCP, cocaine and heroin. More than 2,000 chemical manufacturers, distributors, importers and exporters are required to report all suspicious orders for these chemicals to the DEA; to maintain sales and distribution records; and to make these records available for inspection.

Importers and exporters are required to adhere to criteria regulating the importation and exportation of listed chemicals. An advance notice and declaration system for all imports and exports of these chemicals enables the DEA to identify consignees and shipments to and from the U.S. The act also provides penalties for certain actions related to the diversion of listed chemicals.

Drug Enforcement Administration, *Drug Enforcement Administration Briefing Book,* from a statement by David L. Weintraub, (April 1989): 44.

chia seeds   The term is applied to seeds from any plant that belongs to the genus *Salvia*. There have been claims that they produce a marijuanalike effect when smoked.

children of alcoholics (COA's) and substance users
Alcohol: It is estimated that there are 29 million Americans who can be categorized as children of alcoholics (COA's). Of this population, approximately 7 million are under 18 years old. Unfortunately, the best way to predict the future drinking habits of a child is to study the drinking pattern of his or her parents: one of the most negative effects of having an alcoholic parent is that it predisposes a child to harmful use of alcohol. Alcoholic mothers seem to exert more influence in this way than alcoholic fathers, as daughters of alcoholics become alcoholic 20%–50% of the time. Studies have also shown that even if a daughter of an alcoholic parent escapes becoming an alcoholic, she is likely to marry one. (See COADDICT.)

Half the Al-Anon members (spouses of alcoholics) in one west coast city had an alcoholic parent, and characteristic brain electrical patterns have been found in subjects who are not alcoholic, but are judged to be at high risk for alcoholism if their fathers or mothers are alcoholics. Fast EEG activity and deficiencies in alpha, theta and delta EEG activity have been reported in the high-risk sons of alcoholics. Also, investigators in the field suggest that electroencephalography may be the most sensitive indicator of fetal alcohol toxicity. It is also possible that the electroencephalographic disturbances noted could be a sign of alcohol withdrawal in the infant rather than toxicity; however, the persistence and precise meaning of these EEG changes are not known.

Children of alcoholics generally do not completely understand the problem and are confused about their own responsibility for their parent's behavior. The alcoholic parent often shifts between being overly affectionate to neglectful or abusive. Inconsistency is very deleterious to child development—children cannot understand this treatment in terms of their own behavior and become frightened and anxious. The alcoholic parent is often unavailable to the children because of drinking, and the spouse is unavailable because of his or her preoccupation with the alcoholic. The children may be used by one parent in maneuvers against the other, or they may blame themselves for their parent's drinking.

Some children may appear to cope with their parent's drinking and not really suffer because of it. However, as Claudia Black, family program coordinator for Raleigh Hills Hospitals in Irvine, California, points out, the children of alcoholics run a high risk of developing a variety of problems, and even those who appear to handle the situation well are deeply affected by parental alcoholism. The ways in which such children have learned to adjust may eventually be the source of problems later in life. A child who takes the responsible role, attempting to care for the parents, the siblings and himself or herself, may be unable to depend on others in later life and will always need to be in control of a situation. A child who adjusts to a drinking parent's mood changes and the commotion occurring in the family may later continue to allow himself to be manipulated by others and lose his or her self-esteem. A child who always tries to smooth over conflicts and help others in the family feel at ease may later fear and deny his or her own feelings of anger and constantly be trying to please or placate others. The roles that seemed positive in childhood often have negative consequences in adulthood.

Drugs other than alcohol: Most of the studies concerning other drugs have centered on how drug use affects PREGNANCY (the unborn child) and the consequent symptoms of withdrawal at birth. However, it would follow that the negative effects of having an alcoholic parent would also be true of having a parent addicted to heroin, cocaine, amphetamines, barbiturates or any mind-altering substance. In a situation where a parent is not rational at all times, the same neglect, unstable home life and abusive treatment will be present.

Child abuse: Of the estimated one million cases of child abuse and neglect each year in the U.S., it has been suggested that one-third are alcohol-related. How many are attributable to other drug use is not known. Child abuse in the family can be a vicious circle. It is not always the alcoholic parent who abuses a child; often the alcoholic will abuse the spouse who, in turn, will abuse the children as a means of releasing frustration. When a parent is undergoing WITHDRAWAL symptoms from any drug,

his or her irritability threshold is very low and this may also lead to child abuse.

The exact connection between child abuse and drug use is not known, but studies have shown repetitive cycles from generation to generation. If an adult has been abused as a child, he or she will be more apt to continue the abuse pattern. In regard to alcohol, it was found that nearly one-third of all reported cases of father-daughter incest were attributed to alcohol dependence. Even when drug use is not considered the major factor in child abuse, it may aggravate the problem.

As the incidence of child abuse grows, so does public awareness of the problem. Adults who were abused children are now more open about discussing their childhood, both as a way of helping others who have suffered child abuse and as a way of dealing with their own emotional problems. A number of national self-help organizations have been established to help children of alcoholics—both adult COA's and those still in their adolescent years. Neighbors and relatives of battered children are also more forthcoming with reports, and school officials, law enforcement agencies and hospitals are finally more conscious of the problem. The number of cases reported, however, is still thought to represent only the tip of the iceberg.

It is important that the whole family be involved in treatment. In the past, children who have been neglected by alcoholic parents have often been sent to foster homes. Today, it is recognized that this approach is not always the answer. A child who is sent away may feel increased guilt, possibly believing that he or she has failed completely. Furthermore, a mother who fears that her child will be taken away is less likely to enter into treatment.

Rehabilitation: Family life does not immediately get better after an alcoholic parent stops drinking. A child may meet a parent's sobriety with resentment or hostility, having grown accustomed to living without rules and doing what he or she pleases. The child may also be upset that the parent can no longer be used as the scapegoat for misbehavior. A family needs time to adjust to the new situation.

ALCOHOLICS ANONYMOUS sponsors ALATEEN, a group designed primarily to help the children of alcoholics.

Claudia Black, "Innocent Bystanders at Risk: The Children of Alcoholics," *Alcoholism* 1, no. 3 (January/February 1981): 22–25.

Geraldine Youcha, *A Dangerous Pleasure* (New York: Hawthorn, 1978).

Office of Substance Abuse Prevention, *Some Questions and Answers about Children of Alcoholics,* DHHS pub. ADM-92-1914 (Rockville, Md.: National Clearinghouse For Alcohol and Drug Abuse Information, 1992).

Janet G. Woititz, *Adult Children of Alcoholics* (Deerfield Beach, Fla.: Health Communications, 1983).

China   The cultivation and use of opium has been a tradition in China for centuries. The Chinese and British fought two OPIUM wars during the 19th century because Britain was bringing opium into China from India and undercutting the local competition. The Chinese government, however, contends that the Opium Wars were fought to combat the consumption of opium. In the 1850s and 1860s, when Chinese laborers were brought to the U.S. to work on the railroads, they were said to have introduced the practice of opium smoking, which rapidly gained popularity. It was the prevalence of "opium dens" that prompted San Francisco to enact the first narcotics ordinance in 1875.

The cultivation of the opium poppy is a laborious undertaking (the short, 10-day harvest season alone can require hundreds of hours), and so commercial production tends to flourish in economically deprived countries that have cheap sources of labor available on short-term notice.

Drugs and mainland China: According to the U.S. Department of State's Bureau for International Narcotics and Law Enforcement Affairs (1996), "China is one of the two principal transit routes for Southeast Asian HEROIN smuggled to the U.S. and other overseas markets. . . . China's geographic position offers a tempting route to the west for heroin and other opiates from the narcotics-producing countries of the GOLDEN TRIANGLE. Its transport and communications links, which are improving due to economic development, facilitate movement of narcotics as well as legitimate goods." While most of the opium smuggled out of Burma (now Myanmar) travels by road to Hong Kong for overseas distribution, the use of air and rail routes continues to grow. Despite its long history involving opium, China is no longer a source. Opium cultivation is presently limited to small crops in rural areas where sole distribution is domestic.

As a result of China's increasing role in international drug trafficking, violent crime and drug addiction are growing social concerns for this vast nation. The laws against drug trafficking are harsh, and the death penalty is applied in cases that involve more than 50 gm of heroin. Addicts are encouraged to register and receive treatment at the government's growing network of treatment facilities. The increase in HIV infection cases, up to 75% of which may be due to intravenous drug use, is yet another negative consequence of China's increasing role in the international drug trade.

An alcohol problem in China is acknowledged to exist, but to what extent is unknown.

Drugs and Taiwan: Taiwan is more urban than China, but also faces a growing problem with heroin trafficking. The frantic level of activity in its bustling ports make it almost impossible to monitor containerized cargo that may be concealing narcotics. Taiwan is also struggling to control a rise in heroin addiction cases, as well as an amphetamine epidemic that is afflicting many modernized countries.

chloral alcoholate   A chloral derivative converted to CHLORAL HYDRATE in the body.

chloral betaine   A synthetic chloral derivative similar to CHLORAL HYDRATE but said to cause less gastric distress. It is used as a sedative.

chloral derivatives   CHLORAL HYDRATE, chloral betaine, chlorobutanol, triclofos sodium and CHLORAL ALCOHOLATE.

chloral hydrate   A nonbarbiturate sedative hypnotic that acts as a depressant on the central nervous system. It is produced by passing chlorine gas through ethyl alcohol. The first synthetic sedative hypnotic, it was introduced in 1869 by Oskar Liebreich and was widely used both medically and recreationally. Today it has been largely replaced by newer drugs and is a Schedule IV drug under the Controlled Substance Act.

Usage: Chloral hydrate interferes with anticoagulants and should be used cautiously in combination with other drugs. Medically, it serves as a post- and preoperative sedative and hypnotic, particularly in combination with barbiturates. It is also used in the first stages of labor, as a nocturnal sedative in the treatment of insomnia, and in the treatment of certain convulsive disorders. Like other sedatives, it is frequently used in treating withdrawal from other drugs, such as alcohol, barbiturates and narcotics.

Recreationally, it is used to produce the same euphoria and intoxication derived from the use of alcohol and barbiturates, although its use in this regard is infrequent. Morphine and heroin addicts use it as a substitute when their habitual drugs are unavailable.

Dosage: The average lethal dose of chloral hydrate is 10 gm. As little as 3 gm have proved fatal, and up to 30 gm have been survived. The recommended sedative dosage is 250 mg, three times a day after meals. The usual hypnotic dose is .5 gm to 1 gm, approximately 15–30 minutes before bedtime.

Appearance and availability: Chloral hydrate appears as colorless or white transparent crystals soluble in water, olive oil and alcohol. It is available in liquid, capsule or tablet form for oral use and in suppositories and olive oil enemas for rectal use. The substance decomposes quickly when exposed to light and in liquid form quickly develops mold. It has a bitter taste and unpleasant odor.

Activity: Chloral hydrate is absorbed into the bloodstream from the intestinal tract and evenly distributed through the body. It appears in breast milk and crosses the placental barrier; like the barbiturates, it is not advised for use during pregnancy and nursing. The drug's half-life is four to eight hours.

Effects: Like other DEPRESSANTS, chloral hydrate inhibits the transmission of nerve impulses in the ascending reticular formation of the brain, thereby affecting such functions as breathing. As a hypnotic, it acts very quickly, producing immediate drowsiness and—within 15–30 minutes—a sound sleep that lasts four to eight hours. Chloral hydrate is considered safer than other hypnotics, particularly BARBITURATES, because it interferes very little with REM sleep and has less effect on the respiratory center in the brain.

In sedative doses, chloral hydrate's effects are similar to those of alcohol and barbiturates: euphoria

leading to intoxication and usually resulting in a slight hangover. Common side effects include gastrointestinal irritation and loss of muscular coordination. Overdoses can result in falling temperature, pupil constriction followed by dilation, irregular pulse, delirium, coma, and death within five to 10 hours. The combination of chloral hydrate and alcohol increases the depressant activity of both drugs, causing a SYNERGISTIC reaction, intensifying the euphoria and intoxication as well as slowing the breathing and accentuating loss of muscular coordination. Coma and death can result.

Tolerance and dependence: Users are susceptible to developing a tolerance, as well as physical and psychological dependence; consequently, it is not recommended for long-term use, especially for patients with histories of drug addiction or harmful use. However, the abuse risk for chloral hydrate is only low to moderate, probably because of its bad taste and gastric effects. Drug users generally prefer barbiturates and the newer nonbarbiturates, such as glutethimide and ethchlorvynol.

Synonyms: The potentially lethal combination of alcohol with chloral hydrate preparations has earned the nicknames "knockout drops," "Mickeys" and "Mickey Finns."

chlordiazepoxide Best known under the trade name LIBRIUM, this drug is one of the most commonly prescribed sedatives in the U.S., and is a Schedule IV drug under the Controlled Substances Act. Chlordiazepoxide hydrochloride is a benzodiazepine derivative very similar to diazepam (Valium) and oxazepam (Serax).

Usage: Like the other sedatives, it calms symptoms of anxiety and tension resulting from emotional stress. One of its principal applications is the treatment of alcohol-withdrawal symptoms, especially delirium tremens (D.T.'s).

Dosage: In the form of Librium, it is prescribed in two or four daily doses of 5–50 mg and sometimes ranging as high as 100 mg. At prescribed doses, chlordiazepoxide produces less euphoria than meprobamate, opiates or barbiturates, so psychological dependence may be less of a risk. But doses 10 times larger than the recommended therapeutic dose (around 300–600 mg) can produce physical dependence, as well as the kind of intoxication induced by barbiturates. This makes the drug attractive to users, and it has also been used in a large number of suicide attempts.

Appearance: Chlordiazepoxide hydrochloride appears as a colorless crystalline substance that is water soluble.

Activity: It is absorbed in the gastrointestinal tract and depresses the limbic system—the center of emotional response. Metabolized chiefly in the liver, it is excreted in the urine and crosses the placental barrier. After oral administration, its effects manifest in about half an hour and peak in two to four hours. Onset after intramuscular injection occurs in 15–30 minutes and in 3–15 minutes after intravenous administration. It has a 24–48 hour half-life.

Effects: Withdrawal symptoms for physical dependence are convulsions, insomnia, loss of appetite, tremors and the recurrence of previous symptoms of anxiety. Like other benzodiazepine derivatives, it is additive to and produces a SYNERGISTIC EFFECT to other depressant drugs and when taken simultaneously the result can be fatal respiratory depression.

chlormezanone   A DEPRESSANT drug used as a tranquilizer in the treatment of mild anxiety and tension. It acts without impairing the patient's clarity of consciousness. (See TRANCOPAL.)

chloroform   A vaporous ANESTHETIC, more potent than ether, but no longer used therapeutically because it produces serious adverse effects on the liver.

chlorphentermine hydrochloride   A sympathomimetic amine with pharmacologic activities similar to AMPHETAMINES. (See PRESATE.)

chocolate   A very mild stimulant containing 1.0% CAFFEINE; made from cocoa beans.

chromatography   A technique used for urine testing for drugs. Both thin-layer and gas chromatographic methods of urine testing are considered the most useful techniques for detecting drugs with the exception of LSD. (Methods for detecting LSD in both blood and urine are presently restricted to research laboratories.)

chronic   A descriptive term for a condition or disease characterized by slowly progressing symptoms, often irreversible, and continuing for a long time, often a lifetime. It is usually due to multiple or unknown causes as opposed to an ACUTE disease or condition that has a known or singular cause (often a virus or bacteria). Acute conditions are brief, self-limiting and may improve with treatment.

chronic alcohol intoxication   A state of intoxication maintained by repeated consumption of alcohol before or just after previously taken alcohol has been metabolized. The term is also used generally to refer to ALCOHOLISM, in this sense referring to the continued and prolonged practice of drinking, not to one continuous drinking binge. In this more generalized sense, a "chronic user" (of alcohol or another substance) refers to one who continues to use the drug to excess over a period of time.

chronic alcoholism   A redundant term since alcoholism is itself a chronic disorder. The term "chronic alcoholism" is sometimes used to refer to alcoholism without complications or to a long-lasting alcoholic disorder in order to distinguish it from more severe phases of the disease. (See ACUTE ALCOHOLISM..)

chug-a-lug   A slang term for drinking a glassful of a beverage in one gulp or in a series of uninterrupted swallows. The practice is somewhat popular among students, who have "chug-a-lug" contests, usually with beer.

Chug-a-lugging is a drinking fad, along with a number of other similar practices, such as "one-a-minute," in which a drinker consumes beer nonstop for an hour. These contests and styles of drinking are generally part of a tradition in which virility and social acceptance are equated with the ability to consume large amounts of alcohol. Aside from producing rapid intoxication, these contests can be quite dangerous and may result in severe intoxication, coma or death, particularly when hard liquor is consumed.

Church of England Temperance Society   The largest British temperance society, it was founded in

1862 and reconstituted in 1873 with the dual goal of promoting total abstinence and general anti-intemperance. The society supported measures to reform control of alcohol traffic and to reduce licenses to sell alcohol, rather than prohibition. It had an extensive publications department, educational courses, missions and homes for inebriates, and its comparative moderation contrasted with the extreme stance of many other temperance societies. In 1909 total membership was 636,233, including 485,888 members of the juvenile division. The numerical strength of several temperance societies at this time was provided by juvenile contingents.

cirrhosis From the Greek *kirrhos* (orange-colored)—the color of a cirrhotic liver. The U.S. Department of Health and Human Services defines cirrhosis as "a chronic inflammatory disease of the LIVER in which functioning liver cells are replaced by scar tissue." It involves a disruption of the liver structure by fibrous tissue and nodule formation, which results in impaired liver function.

Cirrhosis is the result of the normal reaction of the liver to injury, whatever the cause. The vast majority of cases, particularly in the U.S., are caused by chronic alcohol use. Usually it takes from five to seven years of steady drinking to develop cirrhosis. Each time alcohol is used, the liver is injured only mildly, but continuous use has a cumulative effect over the years. The liver cells are slowly replaced by fibrous scar tissue, resulting in irreparable damage and leaving a smaller and smaller fraction of the liver to carry on the organ's normal functions (including the detoxification of alcohol).

Although the majority of cirrhotic deaths are related to alcoholism, no more than approximately 10% of alcoholics develop cirrhosis, so there is reason to believe that genetic factors, as well as NUTRITION, may play a role in the contraction of or immunity from cirrhosis.

Malnutrition, from which many alcoholics suffer, can increase the severity and degree of alcoholic FATTY LIVER development. However, studies have shown that even with an adequate diet, high alcohol consumption damages the liver.

Different racial groups are affected differently—American JEWS tend to have a lower-than-average incidence of cirrhosis, whereas among NATIVE AMERICANS the rate is considerably higher. According to 1986 figures compiled by the U.S. Department of Health and Human Services, cirrhosis mortality is 1.5 times as high for nonwhites as for whites; and the rate for nonwhite males aged 25 to 34 is nearly three times as high as that for white males in the same age group.

Cirrhosis is the final stage of liver injury in alcoholics. Heavy drinking over a period of years can produce a fatty liver, which, as the name indicates, is characterized by a buildup of increased amounts of fat on the liver. However, if the patient abstains from alcohol, the abnormal accumulation of fat will disappear. If drinking continues, fatty liver, in most people, will evolve into more severe liver diseases, such as ALCOHOLIC HEPATITIS and irreversible cirrhosis. Exactly why the liver may lose its ability to adapt to alcohol has not been clearly established. Symptoms of cirrhosis usually become apparent after a person reaches 30 and more severe problems appear after 40.

There are many types of cirrhosis, but one type—portal cirrhosis—is predominant and most frequently affects alcoholics. Portal cirrhosis is named for the large vein that transports blood from the stomach and spleen to the liver, where it is dispersed into the capillaries. Portal cirrhosis, also known as Laennec's, nutritional or alcoholic cirrhosis, is characterized by small, diffuse nodules and, usually in the alcoholic, extensive fatty infiltration of the liver. Frequently there are also signs of considerable inflammation. Because of the size of the nodules, this type of cirrhosis has recently been classified by some as micronodular cirrhosis.

The onset of cirrhosis is associated with such nonspecific complaints as weakness and fatigability. As the disease progresses, some of the associated effects may include:

jaundice, because bilirubin pigment (a reddish-yellow pigment) can no longer be removed by the liver;

fluid accumulation in the legs (edema) or in the abdomen (ascites), because the liver cannot make enough albumin, which normally holds this fluid in the body's vessels;

uncontrolled bleeding due to a decrease in clotting factors in the blood; and

increased sensitivity to drugs because the liver cannot inactivate them.

No successful therapeutic treatment has been developed for cirrhosis. Long-term survival of patients with portal cirrhosis is markedly improved by abstinence from alcohol. In a study, the five-year survival rate after diagnosis of portal cirrhosis was 63% for abstainers, compared with 40.5% for those who continued to drink.

Research conducted in 1981 by a team under the direction of Yedy Israel and funded by the Addiction Research Foundation in Toronto may lead to significant progress in the understanding of cirrhosis. The researchers found that prolonged heavy drinking causes liver cells to swell, which in turn can block the flow of blood in the organ. They feel that the relative health of the liver is indicated by the size of its cells and the condition of the blood vessels and not by the presence or absence of cirrhosis. Backing up this theory are figures that show about 10% of the alcoholics seen by the researchers had completely normal liver function and yet had full-grown cirrhosis; on the other hand, alcoholics who are free of cirrhosis can die of portal hypertension or hepatic coma (caused by swollen liver cells that squeeze the fine blood vessels and block the flow of blood). Since the swelling of the liver cells is reversible with abstinence—while cirrhosis is not—the finding of the research team indicates some hope for cirrhotic patients.

There are many varieties of cirrhosis less common than portal cirrhosis. One that may also affect alcoholics is called postnecrotic cirrhosis, which follows liver damage caused by toxic or viral hepatitis. The difference between portal cirrhosis and postnecrotic cirrhosis is that in the latter the nodules are larger and more widely spaced. Because of the larger nodules, postnecrotic cirrhosis is sometimes classified as macronodular cirrhosis.

Among the types of cirrhosis not related to alcoholism are several that affect children and two types of biliary cirrhosis: primary biliary, a rare form of unknown etiology affecting chiefly middle-aged women; and secondary biliary, resulting from obstruction or infection of the bile ducts.

"Cirrhosis in Women Is Up," The Journal 10, no. 6 (Toronto, June 1, 1981): 6.

Charles S. Lieber, "The Metabolism of Alcohol," Scientific American 234, no. 3 (March 1976): 25–33.

L. M. DeCarli and E. Rubin, "Sequential Production of Fatty Liver, Hepatitis, and Cirrhosis in Subhuman Primates Fed with Adequate Diets," Proceedings of the National Academy of Sciences 72, no. 2 (February 1975): 437–441.

"Liver Ailments—Part 1: Cirrhosis," The Harvard Medical School Health Letter 6, no. 3 (January 1981).

Pat Ohlendorf, "Key to Liver Dysfunction Spotted?" The Journal 10, no. 3 (Toronto, March 1, 1981): 1–2.

citronella   A pungent oil with a lemonlike odor made from citronella grass. Generally used as an insect repellent, there are unconfirmed claims that it can produce intoxicating effects when inhaled.

clandestine laboratories   The past 25 years have seen a rise in the number of illicit, clandestine laboratories. They were first noticed in California in the mid-1960s, when the Hell's Angels motorcycle gang set up operations to produce "speed." They have since been encountered in virtually every part of the U.S. Government actions to control the legitimate manufacture and distribution of dangerous drugs contributed to the growth of these labs as demand for psychoactive drugs—stimulants, depressants and hallucinogens—mushroomed.

Clandestine laboratories have also proliferated because of the limited skill needed to operate them, the ease of production, and the potential for enormous profits. The overall risks are minimal, despite sporadic fires and explosions, and the threat of discovery and arrest.

Some clandestine laboratories synthesize analogues of controlled substances. Known popularly as "designer drugs," these analogues usually retain the pharmacological properties of controlled substances, but because of slight variations in chemical structure, they are not specifically listed as controlled substances. They carry increased health risks because of their unknown purity, toxicity and potency. The emergency scheduling provisions of the Comprehensive Crime Control Act of 1984 and the Controlled Substance Analogue Enforcement Act of 1986 are aimed at closing legal loopholes used by individuals who manufacture and distribute these drugs.

Nationwide, federal and state authorities raided 647 clandestine labs in 1987, up from 479 during the previous year. In 1994, 306 labs were seized, a number lower than in 1986 but reportedly higher than in 1989. Of the laboratories seized in 1994, 263 produced METHAMPHETAMINE. They were located primarily in rural areas of the western and south-western U.S., and three-quarters of them were in Southern California. Laboratories were found in a variety of locations, including underground hide-aways, motel kitchens, bathrooms and garages.

Department of Justice, Drug Enforcement Administration, *Drugs of Abuse,* by John C. Lawn, 1988 edition (Washington, D.C.: Government Printing Office (1988): 53.

classification of alcoholics and other drug users

Addiction is not a single illness that affects everyone in the same way or with the same intensity. Accurate diagnosis of the problem is a critical factor in determining the most appropriate treatment for each individual. In the majority of western countries, diagnosis and classification of alcohol and other drug problems relies on one of two texts: the *DSM-IV (DIAGNOSTIC AND STATISTICAL MANUAL OF MENTAL DISORDERS)*, which is published by the American Psychiatric Press, and the *INTERNATIONAL CLASSIFI-CATION OF DISEASES (ICD-10)*, sponsored jointly by the Substance Abuse and Mental Health Services Administration (U.S.) and the World Health Organization (WHO). Both texts identify several categories of chemical dependency (abuse, dependence, disabilities and so on), each of which is useful for particular purposes and populations. There is, however, no single classification that can adequately represent the full range of problems related to harmful use of alcohol and other drugs. The similarities apparent among drug-affected individuals is receiving ongoing attention, and concepts and measurements appropriate to such heterogeneity are being developed. Regarding alcoholism, the ALCOHOL DE-PENDENCE SYNDROME (ADS) concept, which strongly supports an individualized approach to treatment planning, has gained a measure of acceptance. Approaches tailored to the individual are also recommended in working with those who are addicted to drugs other than alcohol.

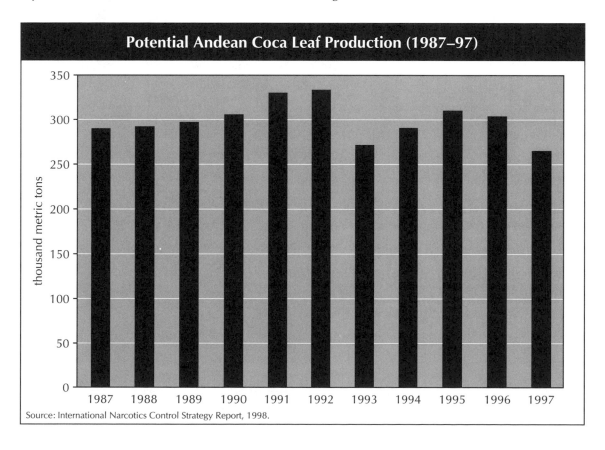

Potential Andean Coca Leaf Production (1987–97)

Source: International Narcotics Control Strategy Report, 1998.

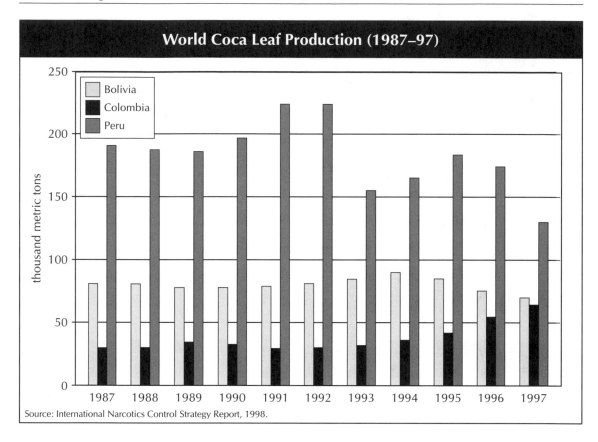

World Coca Leaf Production (1987–97)

Legend: Bolivia, Colombia, Peru

Source: International Narcotics Control Strategy Report, 1998.

cleaning fluids   Although they are toxic and have the potential to produce brain, liver and kidney damage, cleaning fluids are sometimes inhaled by those seeking an intoxicating effect. (See INHALANTS.)

clonidine   A drug widely used to treat narcotic withdrawal that was also reported to have success in curbing tobacco cravings. Recent studies do not confirm this claim. Clonidine was first used in the treatment of hypertension. It is now sold illicitly and may have some abuse potential.

clorazepate dipotassium   A synthetic BENZODIAZEPINE used in the treatment of anxiety. (See TRANXENE.)

clortermine   A sympathomimetic amine with pharmacologic activity similar to that of AMPHETAMINES. It is used as an anorectic. (See VORANIL.)

coca   *Erthroxylon coca,* a bush that grows in South America. The alkaloid COCAINE makes up 0.65% to 1.25% (by weight) of its leaves. South American Indians, particularly those in the mountains of Peru and Bolivia, mix the leaves with lime to release the cocaine, then chew them for a stimulant effect and a variety of medicinal and religious purposes. Coca was an ingredient of Coca-Cola until the U.S. government prohibited its use in 1906. In 1914, its use was controlled by the Harrison Act, which incorrectly classified it as a narcotic. Now, the coca leaves are decocainized before being used as a flavoring in cola drinks. In 1989 the maximum estimated production of coca was: 319 tons in Ecuador; 26,620 tons in Colombia; 87,604 tons in Bolivia; and 138,446 tons in Peru, according to figures supplied by the Congressional Research Service, the U.S. State Department and the Drug Enforcement Administration (DEA). According to the U.S. State Department's 1997 International Control Strategy Report, Colombia's coca production was 63,600 metric tons; Boliva's, 70,100 metric tons; and Peru's, 130,200 metric tons. The last year of data for Ecuador was 1993, which at that time had an estimated production rate of 100 metric tons.

coca paste The first extract produced during the manufacture of cocaine from coca leaves, it is made by adding sulfuric acid and kerosene to the leaves. In South America, cocaine is not processed into FREEBASE before smoking; it is smoked in the form of coca paste. Smoking coca paste is extremely dangerous due to the impurities it contains.

cocaine Cocaine is an alkaloid found in the leaves of the coca bush (*Erthroxylon coca*). Cocaine affects the central nervous system and induces feelings of euphoria.

Classification:

History: The known use of the coca leaf as a stimulant dates back to the Inca Empire in the Andean Mountain region of Peru, a civilization that flourished for hundreds of years until the arrival of Europeans in the 1500s. Originally, chewing coca leaves was a mark of the aristocracy. Inca priests and nobles ingested them to achieve and enhance their religious experiences; gradually, other members of the male Inca population took up the habit. Chewing coca, the Incas noted, not

only helped the quest for religious truths, but it also prolonged physical endurance, retarded fatigue and hunger, and induced euphoria. As a result, coca was widely used by the men who worked in mines located at very high altitudes. Currently, it is estimated that fully 90% of adult male Indians in the region regularly use coca. They chew the leaves along with an alkali such as lime, which, when mixed with saliva, acts as an agent to release the cocaine.

The processed chemical substance is far more potent and toxic than the coca leaf in its natural form. Purity of cocaine from a 20-to-50-mg coca leaf dose is between 0.5% to 1%, while purity from a 20- to-25-mg dose of powder cocaine snorted through the nose is between 20% to 80%. The pure cocaine substance benzoylmethylecognine was first identified and extracted from the leaves of the coca bush in the 1850s by the German chemist Albert Niemann, although this form of cocaine was not used until the 1880s, when it was given to Bavarian soldiers to help them gain endurance and retard fatigue. Shortly afterward, cocaine was touted in medical circles as a highly effective local anesthetic for certain operations. Experiments were conducted to discover what other disorders and maladies cocaine could cure or soothe, and a small circle of professional people began taking the drug themselves. Sigmund Freud insisted it helped him in his work. In a series of papers, he commented favorably on the drug's beneficial properties as a cure for morphine addiction, depression, overeating and alcoholism. However, Freud immediately ceased taking the drug after reports began surfacing of cases of cocaine addiction and death by overdose.

Common Drugs: Symptoms of Abuse of Cocaine

Cocaine. A stimulant drug.

Drug Name	Street Names	Method of Use	Sign and Symptoms	Hazards of Use
benzoylmethylecognine	Coke, Snow, Toot, White Lady, Blow Rock, CRACK, Girl, Uptown, Perico	Most often smoked or inhaled; also injected or swallowed in powder, pill or rock form.	Extreme euphoria; illusion of increased strength and heightened tolerance for pain; diminished desire for food or sleep; sweating, dilated pupils, rapid heartbeat and paranoia	Delirium hallucination, muscle spasm, chest pain; impotence; deterioration of nasal cartilage; death from respiratory arrest, heart failure, convulsions or stroke

Source: New York State Office of Alcoholism and Substance Abuse Services.

Preliminary Data—As of June 1998

Estimated Number (in Thousands) of Persons Who First Used Cocaine During Each Year 1965–1996,
Their Mean Age at First Use, and Annual Age-Specific Rates of First Use
(per 1000 Person-Years of Exposure), Based on 1994–1997 NHSDAs

| Year | Initiates (1000s) | Mean Age | Age-Specific Rate of First Use[1] | | |
			12–17	18–25	26–34
1965	*	*	**	0.6	**
1966	*	23.6	0.5	1.2	1.1
1967	*	*	0.6	0.5	**
1968	77	19.7	0.5	2.1	0.3
1969	180	18.3	1.5	5.1	0.3
1970	296	19.7	2.1	7.3	1.6
1971	343	19.4	4.2	6.8	1.0
1972	270	19.1	3.0	6.0	0.4
1973	477	20.2	4.1	11.2	1.6
1974	673	21.2	3.9	17.6	1.1
1975	808	21.7	4.0	17.4	6.0
1976	646	21.2	5.5	12.3	3.2
1977	950	21.5	4.7	22.6	4.4
1978	1041	21.1	7.6	20.9	5.0
1979	999	21.8	7.0	18.8	5.5
1980	1345	21.1	7.6	29.8	6.7
1981	1383	21.7	9.5	27.6	8.8
1982	1389	21.8	9.1	28.3	9.6
1983	1220	22.0	8.7	24.3	8.2
1984	1230	21.9	9.7	23.2	10.1
1985	1174	22.5	6.4	25.5	9.6
1986	1210	23.1	8.3	26.0	6.6
1987	961	22.6	7.5	20.7	6.1

(continued on next page)

Preliminary Data—As of June 1998 (continued)

Estimated Number (in Thousands) of Persons Who First Used Cocaine During Each Year 1965–1996,
Their Mean Age at First Use, and Annual Age-Specific Rates of First Use
(per 1000 Person-Years of Exposure), Based on 1994–1997 NHSDAs

			Age-Specific Rate of First Use[1]		
Year	Initiates (1000s)	Mean Age	12–17	18–25	26–34
1988	776	21.4	5.7	18.8	4.3
1989	762	21.9	6.5	17.2	4.7
1990	631	22.7	5.7	12.9	4.4
1991	480	21.4	4.0	11.7	2.2
1992	488	21.0	5.8	10.3	2.6
1993	553	22.4	5.9	11.8	2.4
1994[2]	537	21.7	7.7	10.0	1.5
1995[3]	653	19.5	9.3	14.3	2.2
1996[4]	675	18.7	11.3	14.8	1.6

*   Low precision; no estimate reported.
** Estimate rounds to zero.
[1] The numerator of each rate equals the number of persons who first used the drug in the year (times 1000). The denominator of each rate equals the number of persons who were exposed to risk of first use during the year, weighted by their estimated exposure time measured in years. For example, for the age group 12–17 in 1990, the denominator is the sum of three components:
(1) those persons 12–17 years old in 1990 who first used the drug in 1989 or earlier, times a weight of zero. The weight is zero since they had zero exposure to the risk of first use in 1990.
(2) those who first used the drug in 1990 times a weight of .5. The weight of .5 assumes that these people, on average, first used the drug at midyear and consequently have a half year of exposure (i.e. the first half of the year.)
(3) those who never used, or those who first used the drug in 1991 or later, times a weight of one. The weight of one assumes their exposure to the risk of first use during 1990 was for the whole year.
Each person is also weighted by his/her sample weight.
[2] Estimated using 1995, 1996 and 1997 data only.
[3] Estimated using 1996 and 1997 data only.
[4] Estimated using 1997 date only.

Source: SAMHSA, Office of Applied Studies, National Household Survey on Drug Abuse, 1994–1997.

In the early 1900s, cocaine found new distribution through patent medicines like Vin Mariani. A great deal of cocaine was produced for use in potions and beverages. Coca-Cola contained cocaine until 1906, when the company removed the ingredient from its recipe at the insistence of the U.S. government. Not long after, the Canadian government (in 1911) and the U.S. government (in 1914) put legal restrictions on the sale of the drug. Cocaine use diminished significantly in the years following, but moved back into public awareness in the 1960s, probably due to the burgeoning popularity of amphetamines and the similarity between the effects of the two drugs.

Usage: There are several methods of taking cocaine hydrochloride or crystal cocaine. The most common is by "snorting" it into the nostrils through a straw. A rolled paper or a tiny "coke spoon" created specifically for this purpose can also be used. Another method, favored by some heavy users, is to inject the substance directly into the bloodstream—sometimes mixing or following it up with a shot of heroin. Heroin and cocaine mixtures are sometimes called "speedballs," and are also ingested nasally. Cocaine can also be taken by applying it to the mucous lining of the mouth, rectum or vagina. Oral ingestion of the drug decreases its potency. FREEBASE and CRACK are smokable forms of cocaine. Crack, which is derived from cocaine hydrochloride in a conversion process that makes use of baking soda and ammonia, is sold in small vials or aluminum foil and resembles soap shavings or tiny rocks. It is smoked in pipes or mixed with a marijuana or tobacco cigarette. More recently, crack has been "cut" with PCP, a dissociative sedative. Crack first appeared in New York City in late 1985 and moved into the national drug scene in early 1986. It is inexpensive, but its highly addictive properties make it a very expensive habit for those who wind up taking it continuously.

Prevalence: Studies by the Substance Abuse and Mental Health Administration indicate an overall decline in cocaine use since the 1980s. Past-year use by adults aged 26 and older declined from 9.3% in 1985 to 1.5% in 1997. In that same period, use by youths (12 to 17 years of age) also decreased from 3.9% to 2.2%. Past-year use of cocaine among high school seniors peaked in 1985 at 13.1%, decreased to a low of 3.1% in 1992, then rose in 1997 to 5.2%. The number of past-year crack users, however, remained constant between 1988 and 1997 (about .5%, or 1 million people). The rate of past-year crack use is higher among adults aged 18 to 34 than for 12- to 17-year-olds and those over 35.

Indications are that Europe is on the verge of a cocaine explosion reminiscent of the U.S. epidemic in the 1980s. Romolo Urcioli, deputy chief of Italy's

Central Anti-drug Service, warned, "What was only a threat a few years ago is now a reality." Lists of cocaine seizures in recent years in Europe support this view: 1,034 lbs in central France; 770 lbs in Madrid, Spain; 230 lbs in Milan, Italy; 460 lbs in Rotterdam, the Netherlands.

Effects: The effects of cocaine are similar to those of amphetamine, but they only last a very short time. Cocaine directly affects the central nervous system, causing a definite stimulative sensation. Small doses will bring about sensations of extreme euphoria, the illusion of increased mental and physical strength, sensory awareness and tolerance for pain, as well as a severely diminished desire for food and sleep. Large doses significantly magnify these effects, sometimes causing irrational behavior. For heavy users, the heightened euphoria is often accompanied by intensified heartbeat, sweating, dilation of the pupils and a rise in body temperature. Euphoria can be followed by irritability, depression, insomnia and an extreme condition of paranoia also known as cocaine psychosis. Psychosis from large doses of cocaine may cause the user to feel and imagine insects crawling under the skin (a condition known as formication). In some cases, a state similar to amphetamine poisoning may occur and the user will experience delirium, hallucinations, muscle spasms and pain in the chest, in addition to feelings of extreme restlessness and anxiety. Malnutrition and anemia may eventually be experienced because of decreased appetite. Males who are chronic, heavy users sometimes become impotent or incapable of ejaculation. If the drug is injected, abscesses may appear on the skin. Many of these symptoms can be reversed simply by discontinuing use of the drug. In the case of nasal administration, both heavy and light users eventually develop a chronic runny nose, eczema around the nostrils and gradual deterioration of the nasal cartilage. Death can occur from either heavy or light cocaine use, and usually results from respiratory arrest, heart rhythm disturbances, heart failure, convulsions or stroke.

Tolerance and dependence: Cocaine users quickly build up tolerance to the drug, often increasing the dosage frequently. A lethal dose can be as small as 1.2 gm intravenously, but a user with an extremely high tolerance could, through frequent small doses, ingest as much as 10 grams in a day. Physical dependence, though once thought not to occur, may occur. Continued use may make the brain more sensitive to the drug so that even low doses can cause a convulsion or other severe reaction. This sensitization is known as a "kindling effect." Additionally, when heavy use ceases, the likely results are: hunger, irritability, extreme fatigue, depression, anxiety and prolonged periods of restless sleep. Psychological dependence is common. Many users become "hooked" on the feeling of euphoria induced by cocaine and their entire being begins to revolve around the next dose. If dependence is severe, a user will experience a deep depression when the effects of a dose wear off.

Sources: Approximately 70% of the cocaine entering the U.S. comes from COLOMBIA and passes through south Florida. Colombia is also responsible for 50% of the world's supply. The drug is also transported to the U.S. via Mexico and the Caribbean to distribution centers in southern California, Texas, New York City and southern Florida. According to the DEA, it is available in every major U.S. city and is distributed mainly through organized gangs.

Synonyms: coke, snow, blow, leaf, stardust, flake, C, girl, lady and many others.

United States Dept. of State, Bureau for International Narcotics and Law Enforcement Affairs, *International Narcotics Control Strategy Report March 1996.*

Gordon Wilkin and Stephen J. Hedges, "The Coming Cocaine Plague in Europe," *U.S. News & World Report* (February 20, 1989): 34–36.

cocaine substitutes In 1982, the Food and Drug Administration (FDA) issued a warning against cocaine substitutes—white powders that look like cocaine and are sold openly to members of the drug culture through the U.S. mail and in HEAD SHOPS. Many of these substitutes contain local anesthetics such as lidocaine, procaine and tetracaine, and can be as hazardous as cocaine itself. Although they arenot controlled substances, they are subject to regulation and the FDA has asked all manufacturers and distributors to help stop their dissemination. Adverse reactions can include collapsed blood vessels, lowered blood pressure and depressed heart-muscle strength. Some of the trade names for these cocaine substitutes are: Toot, Florida Snow, Supercaine and Ultracaine.

cocktail A drink that is a mixture of a distilled spirit and an aperitif or other flavoring. A cocktail is usually shaken or stirred with ice and then strained into a glass. The origin of the term is unknown, although there are various theories. It came into popular usage in the U.S. in the 1920s and is considered an American term, although it is now widely used throughout the world. Probably the most common cocktail is the martini, which was traditionally made with a mixture of gin and vermouth, and was served in a very cold "martini" glass, usually with a green olive. More recently it has become popular to substitute vodka for the gin.

cocktail hour A term referring to the time when COCKTAILS are usually served, either at a social gathering (such as a late-afternoon or early-evening cocktail party) or a designated hour at a restaurant, bar or lounge. A similar term, "happy hour," has also become popular in recent years.

cocoa *Theobroma cacao,* a bush that grows in Central and South America. The seeds are used to make cocoa powder and chocolate. Cocoa is a mild stimulant containing 1.0% CAFFEINE by weight.

CODAP (Client Oriented Data Acquisition Program) This reporting system provides demographic, diagnostic, and outcome data on patients in federally supported drug treatment facilities and is conducted by NIDA (the National Institute on Drug Abuse).

codeine (morphine 3-methyl ether) A narcotic analgesic, codeine was discovered in 1832 and takes its name from the Greek word *kodeia,* meaning "poppyhead." Like morphine, it is an opiate, a natural opium alkaloid, and appears in the juices of the unripe white poppy pod. The natural yield is rather small (about .5%), so codeine is also synthesized through the methylization of morphine (and is sometimes called methyl morphine).

Usage: Codeine's most common medical use is as an antitussive in cough syrups, often in combination with non-narcotic pain relievers such as aspirin or Tylenol. Codeine is used for this purpose more than any other drug and is thus widely prescribed. Other medical applications include relief of various kinds of minor pain and of constipation (though large doses can exacerbate the latter problem).

Codeine and alcohol: The combination of codeine and alcohol can be dangerous and can result in respiratory arrest and depressed brain activity.

Dosage: Codeine can be taken orally, subcutaneously or intramuscularly. As an ANTITUSSIVE it is prescribed in doses ranging from 5–10 mg; the usual analgesic dose is 15–60 mg. Taking more than 60 mg can have stimulatory rather than sedative effects. In hypodermic administration, 120 mg of codeine is equivalent to 10 mg of morphine. Death from codeine is very rare, and the lethal dose has not been determined.

Appearance: Codeine appears in two forms. The first, codeine phosphate, is an odorless, white crystalline powder, soluble in water and slightly soluble in alcohol. The second, codeine sulfate, appears as white crystals slightly soluble in water and freely soluble in alcohol. Being more soluble in water, codeine phosphate is used most often in elixirs and in injectable form. Codeine sulfate appears in pill form.

Activity: Taken orally, codeine is absorbed (more rapidly than morphine) from the gastrointestinal tract. It is biodegraded in the liver and appears in the urine. Codeine's effects peak in 30–60 minutes and last three to four hours. It has a half-life of three to five hours. About 10% of the substance converts to morphine in the body. Codeine crosses the placental barrier and therefore affects the fetus.

Effects: Codeine's analgesic effects are very similar to morphine's, although it has only about one-sixth to one-tenth the potency. It relieves minor pain, producing a mild euphoria and drowsiness. Codeine also dries the respiratory mucosa and affects the autonomic nervous system. Large doses intensify these effects.

Tolerance and dependence: Tolerance to the drug's sedative effects does develop, but codeine is considered only moderately physically addictive; psychological dependence is more common. In addition to the desired euphoria, addicts experience loss of appetite, depressed sexual drive, itchiness and, most often, constipation and nau-

sea. Withdrawal symptoms are relatively mild. Since large doses are required to achieve and maintain the kind of "high" users seek, brand-name codeine products, which often contain other drugs, are not satisfactory for this purpose. In the 1960s, however, teenagers drank codeine cough syrups in large quantities for their euphoric effects, and studies have shown that many addicts of harder drugs first experimented with codeine syrups.

codeine with alcohol   A dangerous combination, the possible effects of which include respiratory arrest and depression of brain activity. The same effects can result from combining alcohol with other narcotic analgesics, such as morphine, Demerol and methadone. (See DRUGS and SYNERGY.)

coercive treatment   When a drug-dependent person is forced into a treatment situation, it is considered coercive treatment. The pressure may arise from a court ("Get into treatment or go to jail"), from an employer ("If you don't stop drinking, you will be fired") or from other sources.

Since the entry into treatment is not voluntary, the person may have little or no motivation to change, and if a therapist is involved, he or she must attempt to induce the desire. It has been found in some cases that if the threat of punishment is maintained, the results of coercion are as good as those for voluntary participation in treatment programs.

coffee   See CAFFEINE.

Cognac   Under French law, the name "Cognac" may be given only to BRANDY produced in an officially defined region in and around Cognac, a town in the Charente *departement* of southwestern France. The Cognac region is divided into seven subregions according to the quality of brandy produced in each. A Cognac is usually a blend of two or more Cognacs from different subregions. Blends with the highest proportion of Cognac produced in the Grande Champagne subregion are thought to be the best. Differences in quality are due to differences in the soil, which ultimately affects the quality of the grapes used in the production.

Cognac undergoes a double-distillation process known as the *methode charentaise.* The product of the first distillation is called *brouillis,* which is a liquid between 50 and 60 proof. The *brouillis* is then returned to the still for a second distillation, resulting in raw Cognac, or *bonne chauffe,* whose proof is between 140 and 150.

The *bonne chauffe* is placed in specially made oaken casks to age. Standard Cognacs are normally aged from five to 20 years; the finest may be aged for as long as 50 to 100 years. As it ages, Cognac loses some of its alcoholic content, which may be further reduced through the addition of distilled water. Most bottled Cognac is between 68 and 80 proof.

Like other brandies, Cognac is usually sipped as an after-dinner drink.

cognitive impairment Deficiencies in perception, such as absent-mindedness, poor concentration and/or inattentiveness that can be a consequence of alcohol or other drug use. Although some cognitive impairment, like delirium, is reversible when the harmful use ceases, others, like dementia, are irreversible. Most cognitive impairment due to drinking improves significantly within a year or two after abstinence is achieved. (See PROTRACTED ABSTINENCE SYNDROME, WERNICKE'S ENCEPHALOPATHY [SYNDROME OR DISEASE], and KORSAKOFF'S PSYCHOSIS.) As of the mid-1990s, there was only limited information about cognitive impairment due to crack use; that is, the long-term effects on users, as well as on the of women addicted to crack. (See FETAL ALCOHOL SYNDROME.)

cola, kola The kola tree is native to Africa and belongs to the Sterculiaceae family. The seeds, kola nuts, contain 2% CAFFEINE and are used to make a mildly stimulative beverage. Kola nuts are an ingredient in the carbonated soft drinks Coca-Cola and Pepsi Cola.

cold turkey An expression meaning that one has suddenly and completely stopped using a drug one is addicted to, as opposed to withdrawing from the drug gradually. (See WITHDRAWAL.)

collapsed veins A common condition among HEROIN addicts caused by frequent injections over a long period of time. When a vein becomes swollen and blocked (collapsed) because of infections known as thrombophlebitis, or venous thrombosis, an addict will have to start using another vein. As more commonly used veins collapse, long-term addicts have been known to use veins in the neck, penis, between the toes and even under the tongue.

Colombia Colombia has the dubious distinction of being the world's principal drug source, a fact that may be attributed to its strategic location on the South American continent and to its geographic makeup, as well as to its experience as a well-ordered trafficking community. As the major processing and transshipment center for Peruvian and Bolivian coca, Colombia is responsible for 70% of the cocaine entering the U.S. and 50% of the world's supply. U.S. drug enforcement officials estimate that 44 tons of cocaine (with a street value of $29 billion) are annually smuggled into the U.S. from Colombia. The country also cultivates coca on some 7,200 acres that yielded an estimated four tons of cocaine in 1994. The country produced 35,000 metric tons of coca leaves in 1994 (as opposed to 20,000 in 1983), and 4,138 metric tons of marijuana in 1994 (compared to 2,700 in 1983). An estimated 80% of other dangerous drugs entering the U.S., particularly methaqualone, are supplied through Colombia. Opium poppy cultivation has also been found on a limited scale in the country, and in 1995 it was reported that Colombia had been increasingly supplying heroin to the U.S.

Most of the illicit drug traffic passes by way of Mexico and the Caribbean islands through south Florida, Southern California, the Gulf of Mexico and East Coast port areas. Trafficking in cocaine and marijuana, the top-two illicit industries, has a value to the Colombian economy of an estimated $1 billion to $1.5 billion, perhaps $500 million of which stays in the country and—untaxed and inflationary—undermines the legitimate economy.

While cocaine processing is big business in Colombia, it is interesting to note that three of the chemicals considered essential to the processing of coca into cocaine—ether, hydrochloric acid and acetone—are not produced in the country. Until recently, Colombia's principal suppliers for these chemicals were the Netherlands, Germany and the U.S. Colombia, in turn, supplies these countries with the majority of their cocaine. On January 4, 1983, the Colombian Minister of Economic Development banned the importation of these chemicals in an effort aimed at curbing cocaine smuggling into the U.S.

Although the Colombian government and public do not perceive drug use as a major problem, outside observers have noted an increase in the use of cocaine, marijuana and methaqualone among Colombian youth—hardly surprising, given the availability of these drugs in Colombia. In 1981 Colombia's National Council on Dangerous Drugs initiated a program to reduce the domestic demand for narcotics. With the continuing political unrest in the country, it is difficult to foresee what government efforts and actions will be effective. Guerrilla groups are rumored to be trafficking drugs to earn money to pay for arms shipments.

After the August 18, 1989, murder of Senator Luis Carlos Galan, who was at the time one of Colombia's leading presidential candidates, then-president Virgilio Barco vowed to drive the drug dealers out of his country. Eduardo Martinez Romero, a reputed money manager for the Medellin cocaine cartel was the first victim of Barco's executive order, reviving a U.S.-Colombia extradition treaty invalidated by the Colombian Supreme Court in 1987. Since June 1995, three Cali cocaine cartel gang leaders—Gilberto Rodriguez-Orejuela, Jose Santacruz-Londono and Miguel Rodriguez-Orejuela—have been arrested by Colombian authorities.

The drug lords of Colombia vowed to fight back against both their government's and the U.S. government's crackdown. Then-president George Bush moved promptly to assure U.S. reinforcement of President Barco's imperiled government with an emergency grant of $65 million worth of weapons and military training equipment. The U.S. National Drug Control Strategy includes additional funds to assist Colombia, Peru and Bolivia in the fight against drugs. In February 1996 the U.S. economically decertified Colombia, ending most U.S. aid and U.S.-backed loan guarantees. This came after the U.S. government accused Colombia's president, Ernesto Samper, of accepting monetary bribes from drug cartels, resulting in a decrease in the prosecution of drug traffickers.

This decertification did not automatically stop funds to help Colombia in its actions against illegal drug production and trafficking.

colorines   *Erythrina flabelliformis,* a tropical shrub of the Leguminosae family. There are claims that the seeds are a hallucinogen; in fact, they are toxic.

coma   A state of unconsciousness. A person in a coma cannot be aroused even by powerful stimulation.

Committees of Correspondence   A not-for-profit, government-approved drug-education resource organization that disseminates up-to-date information relating to drug-use issues. Among the items available are a basic information kit containing educational fact sheets, pamphlets and brochures, and a 125-page drug-prevention resource manual, including age-appropriate reading and audio/visual recommendations plus special resources for parents, educators, librarians and health professionals.

Community Mental Health Centers Act of 1963   In 1963 the U.S. government initiated a program that funded and established community mental health centers throughout the country. As established by the act, each center would serve a region containing between 70,000 and 80,000 people. By 1980 there were 798 centers providing services for more than half the U.S. The centers provided inpatient and outpatient services, 24-hour emergency services, partial hospitalization, consultation and education. The Community Mental Health Centers Act Amendments of 1968 provided federal funding to, and specifically mandated services for, chemical dependency treatment at the centers. Persons with addiction problems were treated because they were seen as having a "mental illness." Thus, this was the first instance in which federal funding was provided for the treatment of chemical addictions.

Since the inception of the centers in 1963, successive federal administrations have taken varying views as to the appropriateness of the government funding of the centers' operations. In 1981 the Reagan Administration (under Public Law 97-35, the 1981 Omnibus Budget Reconciliation Act) repealed the legislation authorizing community mental health centers. Additionally, the administration consolidated all federal funds for mental health and alcohol and drug use into block grants funded at 21% less than the previous year's appropriation. Community Mental Health Centers were no longer recognized as a special category of programs; although some still bore the title. For the most part they became free-standing psychiatric clinics and outpatient/inpatient multiservice treatment facilities dependent on funds from state and local governments and from private health insurance plans.

Compazine   A brand of prochlorperozine used for severe neuropsychiatric conditions and nausea. The drug is rarely used illicitly as its effects do not produce euphoria.

compulsion   A psychological term used to refer to a desire that compels a person to act against his or her own will or better judgment. When used in regard to alcohol and other drug use it means, specifically, the desire to maintain drug-induced feelings of well-being or pleasure, as well as to decrease feelings of anxiety and depression. It is the need to avoid reality through use of chemical substances. The term is often used interchangeably with the word CRAVING. Compulsion is different from the type of behavior exhibited during physical withdrawal from a drug, when the need for the drug stems from physical reactions to the removal of the drug. As a reason for an individual's continued substance use, compulsion and psychological dependence are increasingly being seen as equal to, if not more serious than, physical dependence.

confabulation   The tendency in instances of recent memory loss to cover up the lapse with tales or exploits that are fantastically untrue and seem devoid of insight, introspection or good judgment. Confabulation is common with psychiatrically-impaired alcoholics and other drug users, but is also a symptom of Wernicke-Korsakoff syndrome, a condition involving organic impairment. (See WERNICKE'S [ENCEPHALOPATHY] SYNDROME and KORSAKOFF'S PSYCHOSIS.)

confidentiality   In drug-abuse treatment programs, confidentiality—the assured anonymity of participants—is protected by federal and state regulations. Records may be disclosed only with the prior written consent of the person seeking treatment.

congeners   The organic alcohols and salts formed in the manufacture of alcoholic beverages that provide the distinctive flavor and pungency of various beverages. Different liquors have different congener contents; vodkas contain the least; bourbons and brandies, the most.

Congeners have been suspected of contributing to the HANGOVER effect, but because of the small amounts used, their importance is debatable. They may compete with ethanol for its metabolizing enzyme, alcohol dehydrogenase, resulting in the buildup of unmetabolized alcohols in the body, producing a toxic effect. However, pure ethanol has been shown to be the major cause of hangovers.

Congeners may play some part in the development of CANCER, but again, how much is not known. A study published in 1979 showed that the risk of cancer of the esophagus was more pronounced in alcoholics who drank apple brandy, which has a high congener content, and less apparent in those who drank beer and wine.

A. J. Tuyns, G. Pequinot and J. S. Abbatucci, "Oesophageal Cancer and Alcohol Consumption," *International Journal of Cancer* 23 (1979): 443–447.

consumption   There are two principal ways of estimating consumption of alcohol: apparent consumption, which is derived from official reports of states, tax records and, in some cases, reports of sales by the alcoholic beverage industry; and self-reported consumption, which is derived from responses to surveys by individuals.

In the U.S. from 1934 to 1978, apparent consumption of beer, wine and distilled spirits increased at varying rates, depending on the given period and type of beverage. During the 1960s, there was a rapid rise in apparent consumption, as the relatively stable rate of two gallons of 100% ethanol (ABSOLUTE ALCOHOL) per person per year of the 1950s grew to 2.5 gallons by 1970, a 25% increase. In the 1970s, the rate of growth in apparent consumption slowed to 8%, and according to the industry trade publications, alcoholic beverage sales have been declining since the early 1980s. A consistent decrease of about 8%

was witnessed from 1980 to 1987, and sales of distilled products fell 4.2% in 1988, compared to 1987.

Apparent consumption in the U.S. averaged 2.54 gallons in 1982, slightly less than 1 oz of 100% ethanol (approximately two drinks) per day for each person 14 years of age and older. Since approximately one-third of the U.S. adult population reported abstaining, daily average consumption for those who drink is higher, 1.5 oz of 100% ethanol (three drinks). This average is still somewhat misleading, because a small proportion of adults drink far more than the average and the majority drink less. It has been estimated that more than 16 million adults 18 years and older (approximately 11% of the adult population) consume about half of all beverages sold in the U.S. In 1987, the gallons of alcohol consumed per year per person had dropped back to 2.54 from an estimate of 2.76 in both 1981 and 1982. In 1989, consumption decreased further to 2.43 gallons, the lowest level since 1967.

Beer consumption has remained relatively level from 1978 to 1989. The most recent apparent per-capita rate for the population 14 years and older is 1.34 gallons in absolute alcohol, which is nearly 30 actual gallons. For the first time in 10 years, at the end of the same period, wine consumption did not increase (.039 gallons in 1989). Consumption of distilled spirits experienced a consistent decline from 1978 to 1989 (from just under 1.1 gallons in 1978 to just under 0.8 gallons in 1989). An increasingly conservative social climate may have contributed to this turning away from beverages with a high alcohol content. In 1988, vodka was the best-selling liquor, at 38 million cases, up from 21 million in 1970.

Nevada was the leading state in per capita apparent consumption, just ahead of Washington, D.C., although both have substantial nonresident sales that may inflate values. New Hampshire and Alaska followed in having the highest rates of per capita alcohol consumption in the U.S. in 1989. From 1977 to 1987, Connecticut, Ohio, Delaware and Alaska showed the largest percentage increases in per capita consumption. The greatest decreases in consumption in this period came in Nevada, Wyoming, New Hampshire and Hawaii.

In 1987 the drinking habits of men according to self-reported consumption indicated that 14% were heavier drinkers, 36% moderate drinkers, 28% light drinkers and 22% abstainers. In 1989 there was an increase in all categories of use: 19%, 37% and 44% respectively. Abstainers also increased significantly to 32%. Among women, the percentage of drinkers ran from 7% listed as heavier, 21% moderate, 40% light and 32% abstainers. By 1989 the percentage of heavy drinkers remained at 7%, while 29% were listed as moderate and 64% as light. Abstainers increased to 53%. These figures are based on basic data from the National Institute on Alcohol and Alcoholism (NIAAA), stipulating that abstainers consume 0–12 drinks per year, light drinkers have 3 drinks per week, moderate drinkers have 4–13 drinks per week, and heavy drinkers consume 14 or more drinks per week.

Per capita consumption of alcohol is lower in the U.S. than in many countries. In 1987, a report published in the Netherlands ranked the U.S. 21st out of 47 countries surveyed, with a per capita consumption of 7.6 liters of 100% ethanol. The same year, the consumption level in France was 13.0 liters. In 1993 the U.S. ranked 18th of the 52 leading alcohol-consuming countries, while actual consumption barely increased to 7.7 liters. The move in ranking may be reflective of an increase in the number of countries surveyed and a decrease in overall alcohol consumption internationally.

There has been a debate in recent years over the relationship between the general level of alcohol consumption in a population and the percentage of heavy drinkers. This issue is still unresolved. While in some countries where there has been increased per capita consumption, there has also been a corresponding increase in hospital admission rates for patients diagnosed with alcoholism or alcoholic psychosis. There has so far been little evidence of a decrease in hospital admission rates in countries where there has been decreased consumption.

Laura Z. Chatfield, "Alcoholic Beverage Sales Staggered by Baby Boomers," *USA Today* (August 17, 1989).

W. B. Clark and L. Midanik, "Alcohol Use and Alcohol Problems among U.S. Adults," *Alcohol Consumption and Related Problems,* Alcohol and Health Monograph Series, no. 1 (Rockville, Md.: National Institute on Alcohol Abuse and Alcoholism [NIAAA]).

Enoch Gordis, M.D., ed., *Seventh Special Report to the U.S. Congress on Alcohol and Health,* chapter 2 (Rockville, Md.: NIAAA, 1990).

Enoch Gordis, M.D., ed., *Eighth Special Report to the U.S. Congress on Alcohol and Health,* chapter 1 (Rockville, Md.: NIAAA, 1993).

Hoeveel alcoholhoude dranken worden er in de wereld gedronken? (How many alcoholic beverages are being consumed throughout the world?), 27th ed. (Schiedam, Netherlands: Produktschap Voor Gedistilleerde Dranken, 1987).

H. Malin et al., "An Epidemiologic Perspective on Alcohol Use and Abuse in the United States," *Alcohol Consumption and Related Problems,* Alcohol and Health Monograph Series, no. 1 (Rockville, Md.: NIAAA, in press).

Joy Moser, *Prevention of Alcohol-Related Problems* (Toronto: World Health Organization, 1980): 50–53.

NIAAA, *Apparent Per Capita Alcohol Consumption National, State and Regional Trends, 1977–1987,* Surveillance Report, no. 13 (1989).

Brewers and Licensed Retailers Association, *Alcohol Consumption* (London, 1994).

contingency A behavior modification procedure frequently used in residential drug-abuse treatment settings. Specifically agreed-upon behavior and activities are rewarded; failure to act in the way agreed upon is punished. Under this system, the continuation of specified rewards is contingent upon continuation of agreed-upon behaviors.

controlled drugs Drugs that are strictly controlled on the federal and state government levels through the CONTROLLED SUBSTANCES ACT. Although alcoholic beverages are sometimes said to be controlled, they are only "regulated" by federal and state laws that govern their sale and purchase. Unlike controlled drugs, the manufacturers and suppliers of alcoholic beverages are not held accountable for every ounce of the substances involved in their business. (See CONTROLLED SUBSTANCE.)

controlled substance A psychoactive drug, such as a narcotic, that is strictly controlled by law. Stringent requirements govern the prescribing and dispensing of these substances, as well as their manufacture, storage and transport, and an exact inventory of the quantities on hand and dispensed must be maintained at all times.

Although alcoholic beverages are sometimes said to be "controlled," they are not; they are regulated. Most countries and states have laws governing the sale and purchase of alcoholic beverages, but from manufacture through retail sales there is no strict enforcement, and suppliers are not held accountable for every ounce of the substance they handle. (See CONTROLLED SUBSTANCES ACT.)

Controlled Substances Act The familiar name for The Comprehensive Drug Abuse Prevention and Control Act of 1970 (Public Law 91-513), Title II. It is the legal foundation of a federal strategy aimed at reducing the consumption of illicit drugs. The Controlled Substances Act (CSA) attempted to bring up to date and consolidate all federal drug laws since the nation's first law regarding narcotics regulation, which was passed in 1914 (the HARRISON ACT). The DEA (Drug Enforcement Administration) of the Department of Justice is responsible for enforcing the provisions of the act. The following material is quoted from *Drugs of Abuse* (vol. 6, no. 2, July 1979), published by the DEA:

Criteria by which drugs are scheduled: The CSA sets forth the findings that must be made to put a substance in any of the five schedules. These are as follows (Section 202b):

SCHEDULE I:
(A) The drug or other substance has a high potential for abuse.
(B) The drug or other substance has no currently accepted medical use in treatment in the U.S.
(C) There is a lack of accepted safety for use of the drug or other substance under medical supervision.

SCHEDULE II:
(A) The drug or other substance has a high potential for abuse.
(B) The drug or other substance has a currently accepted medical use in treatment in the U.S. or a currently accepted medical use with severe restrictions.
(C) Abuse of the drug or other substance may lead to severe psychological or physical dependence.

SCHEDULE III:
(A) The drug or other substance has a potential for abuse less than the drugs or other substances in Schedules I and II.

Schedule of Controlled Substances—Regulatory Requirements

Schedule	I	II	III	IV	V
Abuse Potential	**High**	**High**	**Less Than I and II**	**Low**	**Lower Than IV**
Use	may lead to severe dependence	may lead to severe dependence	may lead to moderate physical or high psychological dependence	may lead to limited physical or psychological dependence	may lead to limited physical or psychological dependence
Medicinal value (U.S.)	none; unsafe without proper supervision	yes	yes	yes	yes
Prescriptions		require dr.'s signature, must be typewritten or indelible; cannot be refilled	6-month limit; can be refilled up to five times		
Examples	heroin, LSD, peyote, psilocybin, bufotenine, mescaline, THC/hashish, PCP analogues, methaqualone	opium, morphine, cocaine, codeine, methamphetamine Benzedrine, Dexedrine, methadone, pentobarbital, PCP	paregoric, nalorphine, glutethimide	chloral hydrate, diazepam (Valium), paraldehyde, phenobarbital, Darvon, other less addicting barbiturates	preparations containing limited amounts of narcotics, like cough medicines: Robitussin A-C, Cheracol
Registration	required	required	required	required	required
Recordkeeping	separate	separate	readily retrievable	records required	records required
Distribution Restrictions	order forms	order forms	records required	readily retrievable	readily retrievable
Dispensing Limits	research use only	Rx: written; no refills	Rx: written or oral; refills (with medical authorization, refills up to 5 in 6 months)	Rx: written or oral; refills (with medical authorization, refills up to 5 in 6 months)	OTC—(Rx drugs limited to M.D.'s order)
Manufacturing Security	vault/safe	vault/safe	secure storage area	secure storage area	secure storage area
Manufacturing Quotas	yes	yes	No but some drugs limited by Schedule II	No but some drugs limited by Schedule II	No but some drugs limited by Schedule II
Import/Export Narcotic	permit	permit	permit	permit	permit to import; declaration to export

(continued on next page)

Schedule of Controlled Substances - Regulatory Requirements (continued)

Schedule	I	II	III	IV	V
Abuse Potential	High	High	Less Than I and II	Low	Lower Than IV
Import/Export Nonnarcotic	permit	permit	Permit for some drugs, declaration for others	declaration	declaration
Reports to DEA by Manufacturer/ Distributor Narcotic	yes	yes	yes	manufacturer only	manufacturer only
Reports to DEA by Manufacturer/ Distributor Nonnarcotic	yes	yes	Manufacturer reports required for specific drugs	Manufacturer reports required for specific drugs	no

Source: United States Drug Enforcement Administration

(B) The drug or other substance has a currently accepted medical use in treatment in the U.S.

(C) Abuse of the drug or other substance may lead to moderate or low physical dependence or high psychological dependence.

SCHEDULE IV:

(A) The drug or other substance has a low potential for abuse relative to the drugs or other substances in Schedule III.

(B) The drug or other substance has currently accepted medical use in treatment in the U.S.

(C) Abuse of the drug or other substance may lead to limited physical dependence or psychological dependence relative to the drugs or other substances in Schedule III.

SCHEDULE V:

(A) The drug or other substance has a low potential for abuse relative to the drugs or other substances in Schedule IV.

(B) The drug or other substance has a currently accepted medical use in treatment in the U.S.

(C) Abuse of the drug or other substance may lead to limited physical dependence or psychological dependence relative to the drugs or other substances in Schedule IV.

There are eight specific factors that the DEA and the Department of Health and Human Services (DHHS) are directed to consider when including a drug or other substance in a particular schedule, or when transferring or removing a substance entirely from the schedules. As published by the DEA in *Drugs of Abuse:* (Vol. 6, No. 2, July 1979), these criteria are:

Its actual or relative potential for abuse.
Scientific evidence of its pharmacological effect, if known.
The state of current scientific knowledge regarding the drug or other substance.
Its history and current pattern of abuse.
The scope, duration, and significance of abuse.
What, if any, risk there is to public health.
Its psychic or physiological dependence liability.
Whether the substance is an immediate precursor of a substance already controlled under this title.

Under the Controlled Substances Act, nine major control mechanisms are imposed on manufacturing, purchasing and distributing controlled substances:

Registration of handlers: Any person who handles or intends to handle controlled substances must obtain a registration issued by the DEA, which assigns a unique number to legitimate handlers: importers, exporters, manufacturers, wholesalers, hospitals, pharmacies, physicians and researchers. Prior to the purchase of a controlled substance, the number must be made available to the supplier by the customer, thus diminishing the opportunity for unauthorized transactions.

Recordkeeping requirements: Full records must be kept of all quantities manufactured, and of all purchases, sales and inventories of all controlled substances, regardless of the schedule in which they are placed. Limited exemptions are available to physicians and researchers. Because they are highly abusable substances, records for Schedule I and II drugs must be kept separate from all other records by the handler, if there is call for expeditious investigations. The system of control makes it possible to trace the flow of any drug from the time it is first manufactured or imported to the actual person who receives it. It also serves as an international check for large corporations, which must be concerned about employee pilferage. The mere existence of this requirement can discourage forms of harmful use.

Quotas on manufacturing: The DEA limits the quantity of controlled substances listed in Schedules I and II that may be produced during any calendar year. Although the statute speaks exclusively in terms of Schedules I and II, certain drugs in Schedules III, IV and V derive from materials listed in Schedule II. Codeine syrups, for example, are made by combining codeine (a Schedule II drug) with other ingredients in a special diluted form. Therefore, many narcotic products in Schedules III and V, as well as certain barbiturate combination drugs in Schedule III, are in fact subject to quotas as well. The DEA uses available data on sales and inventories of Schedule I and II substances and, taking into account Food and Drug Administration (FDA) estimates of drug usage, establishes aggregate production quotas, which set the national limits of production. The overall production limits are subdivided into manufacturing quotas, which are granted to the registered manufacturers. To set manufacturing quotas, it is necessary to determine how much of a controlled substance will be purchased in bulk by those companies engaged only in the formulation of dosage units. Formulating companies are granted procurement quotas, based on their past usage.

Restrictions on distribution: Record keeping is required for the distribution of a controlled substance from one manufacturer to another, from manufacturer to wholesaler, from importer to wholesaler, and from wholesaler to dispenser. In the case of Schedule I and II drugs, the supplier must have a special order form from the customer. This form is issued only by the DEA (form 222) to those who are properly registered, and is preprinted with the name and address of the customer. The drug must be shipped only to that person. This reinforcement of the registration requirement makes certain that only authorized persons may receive Schedule I and II drugs. No order form is necessary for Schedule III, IV and V drugs, but the supplier is held fully accountable for any drug shipped to a purchaser who does not have a valid registration.

Restrictions on dispensing: There are also restrictions on the dispensing or delivery of a controlled substance to the ultimate user, who may be a patient or research subject. Schedule I drugs may be used only in research situations, as currently they have no accepted medical use in the U.S. A prescription order is required for Schedule II, III and IV medications under the Federal Food, Drug and Cosmetic Act. The determination to place drugs on prescription is within the jurisdiction of the FDA. Schedule II drugs are subject to additional special restrictions: prescription orders must be written and signed by the practitioner and may not be telephoned in except in an emergency. In addition, these prescriptions may not be refilled; the patients must see the doctor again in order to get more drugs. Schedule III and IV drug orders may be prescribed with either written or oral notice, and with the doctor's authorization may be refilled up to five times within six months of the initial dispensing. Schedule V drugs include many over-the-counter (OTC) narcotic preparations, antitussives and antidiarrheals, and here too restrictions are imposed. The patient must be 18 years old, have some form of identification, and have his name entered into a special log maintained by the pharmacist.

Limitations on imports and exports: International transactions involving any drug in Schedule I or II or a narcotic drug in Schedule III must have prior approval of the DEA; international transactions involving a nonnarcotic in Schedule III or any drug in Schedule IV or V do not need approval but prior notice must be given to the DEA. Approval to import a Schedule I or II drug is not given unless an importer can show that there is an insufficient domestic supply with no adequate competition. Similarly, exportation of Schedule I and II drugs and narcotic drugs in Schedule III is severely limited: exporters must demonstrate that the drugs are going to a country where they will actually be used and will not be re-exported.

Conditions for storage of drugs: The DEA sets requirements for the security of premises where controlled substances are stored. Among the requirements for Schedule I and II drugs are specially constructed vault and alarm systems. For Schedule III, IV and V drugs, a vault is optional and the handler may segregate the controlled substance in a secure area under constant supervision. These requirements do not apply to qualified researchers, physicians, exporters and wholesalers who handle small quantities of controlled substances. The DEA is presently reviewing requirements for shippers, as well as employees who have access to controlled drugs.

Reports of transactions to the government: The monitoring of all drugs in Schedules I and II and narcotic drugs in Schedule III is carried out by the Automation of Reports and Consolidated Orders System (AR-COS), established in January 1974. Manufacturers, wholesalers, importers and exporters of these drugs must report all manufacturing activities, importations, exportations and all other distributions to the DEA. Inventories must also be filed annually.

Criminal, civil and administrative penalties for illegal acts: Trafficking is defined as the unauthorized manufacture or distribution (delivery by sale, gift or otherwise) of any controlled substance, or possession of the substance with intent to distribute. For narcotics in Schedules I and II, a first offense is punishable by up to life in prison and up to a $4 million fine. For trafficking in a Schedule I and II non-narcotic drug or any Schedule III drug, the penalty is up to five years, imprisonment and a $250,000 fine. Trafficking in a Schedule IV drug is punishable by a maximum of three years and up to $250,000. Trafficking in a Schedule V drug is a misdemeanor punishable by up to one year and up to $100,000. Second and subsequent offenses are punishable by twice the penalty imposed for the first offense. The CSA carefully distinguishes between trafficking offenses (those who supply illicit drugs to users) and use offenses (those possessing drugs solely for personal use). A use offense is always a misdemeanor on the first offense, punishable by one year and up to $5,000.

Procedures for controlling substances: The various procedures for controlling a substance under the CSA are set forth in Section 201 of the act. Proceedings may be initiated by DHHS, the DEA or petition from any interested person or group: the manufacturer of a drug, a medical society or association; a pharmacy association, a public interest group concerned with harmful use of drugs or a state or local government agency. When a petition is received by the DEA, the agency begins its own investigation of the drug. In most cases this process has led to a report and recommendation to HEW.

International obligations: The CSA further provides that if control of any drug is required by U.S. obligation under international treaty arrangements, the drug shall be placed under the schedule deemed most appropriate to carry out these obligations. As cited in the CSA, the U.S. is a party to the Single Convention on Narcotic Drugs of 1961, designed to establish effective control over international and domestic traffic in narcotics: coca leaf, cocaine and cannabis are included within the legal definitions. A second treaty, the Convention on Psychotropic Substances of 1971, which became enforceable in 1976, is designed to establish comparable control over such drugs as LSD, amphetamines, certain barbiturates and other depressants. Legislation has been passed by Congress authorizing the U.S. to become a signatory to this treaty. Congress ratified this treaty in 1980.

conventions, international drug   According to the World Health Organization in 1994, international drug conventions and treaties are concerned with the control of production and distribution of psychoactive drugs, including alcohol.

convulsions   Involuntary spasmodic contractions of muscles. Convulsions can occur in cases of stimulant OVERDOSE and during central nervous system depressant WITHDRAWAL. With heavy alcohol use, withdrawal convulsions can begin 12 hours after the start of ABSTINENCE, but more often appear during the second or third day after an alcoholic stops drinking. The number of seizures and their duration vary from individual to individual. To prevent convulsions, medications such as benzodiazepines are administered during detoxification. (See DELIRIUM TREMENS.)

cordial   From the Latin *cor* (heart). Broadly defined, a cordial is any medicine, food or beverage believed to steady or stimulate the heart. In the case of alcoholic beverages, "cordial" is now used simply as another name for LIQUEUR. These beverages are made by adding the flavor of fruits, herbs, roots, flowers or juices to an alcohol base. In addition, they are sweetened and, in most cases, colored. Most cordials are between 40 and 80 proof. They are sold under the name of their particular flavor, preceding the word "cordial" (blackberry cordial, clove cordial, mint cordial and so forth).

corn whiskey   A spirit distilled from a fermented mash that is at least 80% corn (Indian maize). Along with rye and bourbon, corn whiskey is a distinctly American spirit. Until the early part of the 19th century, it rivaled the other two types in popularity, but since then a preference for less harsh whiskeys has made it commercially unfeasible. Corn whiskey is a colorless spirit bottled without aging, which gives it an extremely raw taste similar to that of neutral grain spirits.

coronary heart disease   See HEART.

Costa Rica   The smallest and one of the least-populated countries in Central America, Costa Rica has for some time supported one of the more advanced antialcohol programs in the hemisphere. A state committee on alcoholism has existed since 1954, when alcoholism was declared a disease by presidential decree in order to facilitate treatment in public health centers. Since 1973, there has been a complete ban on consumption of alcoholic beverages in government buildings, and legal penalties for alcohol-related offenses are severe.

Seventy-two percent of the population was considered abstinent in 1982, and although total alcohol consumption in the country remains low, some harmful use of alcohol is reported among this relatively small drinking population. The preferred beverages are gin, dark rum and *aguardiente,* a distilled alcohol common in Hispanic countries; all are potent, with an typical ethanol content of roughly 35%.

The government maintains a monopoly on distilled alcohol production but the production of beer and wine is done privately. A significant amount of illegal alcohol is distilled from fermented sugarcane in rural areas. One report estimated annual consumption of this *guaro contrabando* at 4 million liters, and in an isolated area one in three houses were found to be engaged in the production of this home-brewed liquor.

The government has estimated that there are nearly 100,000 "abnormal drinkers" in Costa Rica, or about one out of every 20 persons. The incidence of alcoholism is higher in rural than in urban areas, and the highest incidence of heavy drinking is among males who began to drink between ages 15 and 19 and are unemployed or have experienced unemployment.

Treatment: Treatment of alcoholism in Costa Rica comes under the authority of the National Institute on Alcoholism and the Center for Studies on Alcoholism, which are attached to the country's Ministry of Health and operate in cooperation with the Ministry of Public Education. Enforced treatment of alcoholism is made possible by a 1970 addition to the penal code that defines the alcoholic as a patient in need of protection and rehabilitation. The Social Security Institution guarantees financial assistance to alcoholics and their families. Costa Rica's alcoholism prevention measures include mass media campaigns, primary school education sessions, and training programs for teachers, nurses, police and social workers. These programs and others are currently being expanded, and all are monitored by the National Institute on Alcoholism.

cough medicine Cough medicines are often abused because of their high alcohol content. Some nighttime cough medicines have more than twice the amount of alcohol found in wine and only 15% less than the amount found in various hard liquors. Comtrex Nighttime and Vick's Nyquil Cold Medicine both contain 25% alcohol; Vick's Formula 44D has 10% alcohol; Pertussin Cough Syrup for Children, 8% alcohol; Chlor-Trimeton Allergy Syrup, 7%; and Robitussin Cough Formula, 3.5%.

Many cough medicines are also abused because of the CODEINE they contain. These can only be obtained with a prescription. An effective antitussive, codeine resembles MORPHINE, but its effects are milder. Although it is considered only mildly addictive and instances of addiction are rare, it is often abused for its sedative and mild euphoric properties. Codeine is a Schedule II drug and it is more difficult

to obtain a cough medicine containing codeine than it is an over-the-counter (OTC) cough medicine with a high alcohol content. Dextromethorphan, contained in Ramilar and most other OTC cough preparations, has a lower harmful use potential than codeine, but has been taken infrequently in large quantities for nonmedical purposes.

counseling Although forms of psychotherapy and counseling are ubiquitous in the modern treatment of alcoholics and other drug users, there is little scientific certainty regarding the effectiveness of such procedures. Because of the key role played by counselors and therapists in substance-abuse treatment, much additional empirical study of which methods and approaches are most beneficial is necessary. S. R. Valle, for example, has shown that an active rather than passive interaction between a counselor and his or her client results in the client showing fewer relapses, fewer relapse days and less use of alcohol during the two years after treatment.

Abstention from alcohol and other psychoactive drugs continues to be the treatment goal for those diagnosed as chemically dependent, and counseling often not only provides the support system, but offers the appropriate procedures required to attain that goal.

Enoch Gordis, M.D., ed., *Sixth Special Report to the U.S. Congress on Alcohol and Health* (Rockville, Md.: NIAAA, 1987).

S. R. Valle, "Interpersonal Functioning of Alcoholism Counselors and Treatment Outcome," *Journal of Studies on Alcohol* 42 (1981): 783–790.

counterculture A culture that rejects key norms and values of society at large, or which views run counter to the accepted "status quo." The term was coined in the 1960s and was often used to describe first the "beatniks" and later the "hippies." Anyone who was not opposed to the use of drugs such as LSD, mescaline or marijuana, who was politically "left wing" or "liberal" or who lived an alternative lifestyle qualified as a member of the counterculture. (This included most artists, musicians and a great many college students of that time.) Frequently the term was applied to groups whose ideology was opposed to the prevalent practices of the government and the police. During that period there was a great deal of political strife and controversy involving the rapidly changing mores of society, including environmentalism, civil rights and feminism (known then as "women's liberation"). A key issue of controversy was the role the U.S. was playing in foreign affairs, particularly the war in Vietnam. The mass protests against the war were not only against that particular war with all of its shortcomings, but most of the protesters were against all violence and wars in general. Peace and Love were the standard slogans of the day. The term counterculture was often applied to the young adults and so called "bohemians" living in urban and/or university neighborhoods such as HAIGHT-ASHBURY in San Francisco and Greenwich Village in New York City. This period indeed spawned a social and cultural revolution. People went to great extremes to express their beliefs, and there were those who died in protest; some who were involved in dangerous work for civil rights were murdered, and, of course, prominent leaders who took an unpopular stand. Marches and protests were frequent and often gathered large crowds of people who traveled great distances to attend. Many things that we take for granted today, just a few decades later, were not accepted or available then. The country was sharply divided into two distinct factions that were bitterly opposed to each other's views and lifestyles. Over time, for the most part, these two sides have come to meet somewhere near the middle. Among the many sociocultural aspects of our lives that were heavily influenced by the counterculture of the 1960s are the foods we eat, the language we speak, the music we listen to, the television shows we watch, the films we see, dress codes in schools and offices,womens' roles and issues, politics (including America's role in foreign affairs), education, civil rights, Native American and Hispanic issues, gay rights, animal rights, our views towards the environment, changing trends in business and how it operates, the arts . . . virtually every aspect of our culture has somehow been influenced by the social, nonviolent revolution that was led by thousands of young idealists who wanted to change the world.

couples   Couples in recovery (couples in which one or both members are recovering from alcohol or other drug use) are frequently distinguished by a number of interrelational problems, including: poor communication and problem-solving skills; a high degree of negative or hostile verbal and nonverbal exchange; and a low degree of intimacy, free time or quality time spent together. The usual treatment recommendation is for the chemically dependent partner to attend AA (or a similar 12-step program that deals with the drug of his/or her choice) and the nonaddicted spouse/significant other to attend Al-Anon or a similar program. Also beneficial for both partners is a didactic group designed to explain the family disease concept of alcoholism and other drug use, and the value of involving all family members in the recovery process.

crack cocaine   First reported in Los Angeles, San Diego and Houston in 1981, crack cocaine is cocaine in smokable (free base) form. It became a serious problem in New York City in 1985 and became prevalent on the U.S. drug scene in early 1986; by 1988 crack was reported in 28 states and the District of Columbia.

Each year, according to the National Institute on Drug Abuse (NIDA) researchers, more than 300,000 infants are born with traces of illegal drugs in their systems. No one is yet certain how many are being exposed specifically to crack, but few doubt that the needs of these babies will present a challenge to schools, future employers and society. More women than men are now reported using crack in several major American cities, and drug experts say a large number of the new users are young pregnant women.

Usage: Crack is smoked in a pipe or mixed in a marijuana or tobacco cigarette. The term "crack" comes from the crackling sound made when it is smoked, or from its occasional resemblance to cracked paint chips or plaster. Users pulverize the chips into "pebbles" prior to smoking.

Statistics: Data from the SAMHSA *1985 National Household Survey on Drug Abuse* showed that 21% of the people who have ever used cocaine used free base, and 8% used cocaine intravenously. In 1997 one-third of the more than 4 million persons who had used crack in their lifetime had used it in the past year. The *1997 National Household Survey* reported that from 1988 through 1997, the percent of cocaine users who have used crack has remained relatively constant, between 31% and 36%. The number of past-year crack users has also remained constant between 1988 and 1997, at 1 million persons or 0.6% of the surveyed population. Among high school seniors in the class of 1987, 5.6% reported having tried crack, 4% in the past year. In the class of 1994 these rates declined: 3.0% of seniors reported having tried crack, 1.9% in the past year.

The *1985 National Household Survey* indicates that among youth aged 12–17, lifetime and past-year prevalence of cocaine is highest for Hispanics (7% and 6%), compared to whites (6% and 5%) and blacks (3% and 3%). While use for all ethnic groups in this age range declined in the 1997 survey, it remained higher for Latinos (1.1% and 1.0%), compared to whites (0.5% and 1.1%) and blacks (0.1% and 0.1%). Among young adults (age 18–25), the rates in 1985 were highest for whites (28% and 18%), compared to Hispanics (15% and 12%) and blacks (14% and 11%). In 1997 it was still highest among whites (2.3% and 1.2%), compared to Latinos (2.1% and 1.5%) and blacks (1.0% and 0.9%). Among older adults (age 26–34), these rates in 1985 were highest among blacks (7% and 3%), as compared to whites (4% and 1%) and Latinos (3% and 1%). In 1997 the rates were still highest among blacks (3.1% and 1.8%), compared to Hispanics (1.4% and 0.9%) and whites (1.3% and 0.7%).

The percentage of people admitted to treatment for a primary cause of cocaine abuse, and who reported smoking cocaine as their primary route of administration, increased from 1.4% in 1979 to 18.7% in 1984. Between 1984 and 1986, the proportion of cocaine-related hospital emergency-room episodes involving smoking of the drug increased from 1 in 15 patients to 1 in 5.

Demographic data for cocaine-related emergency-room patients from the DAWN (Drug Abuse Warning Network) system in 1989 suggest a predominance of males (66%) and adult patients aged 26–35 (117.4 per 100,000). Fewer whites than Hispanics and blacks were seen in emergency rooms for cocaine emergencies in 1990 (14, 34.4 and 172 per 100,000, respectively). In the 1993 DAWN report, cocaine was the second most frequently mentioned substance after alcohol in an emergency room, representing 27.1% of drug mentions. Males still were predominant, but at a higher rate than in 1987 (74.5%). Adults aged 26–35 accounted for the majority of emergency room incidents (139.3 per 100,000). Blacks were still the largest group seen in

emergency rooms in 1993 for cocaine-related incidents of 263.4 per 100,000, followed by Hispanics (57.1 per 100,000) and then whites (19.1 per 100,000).

Demographic data on cocaine-related death in 1987 were similar to data shown for cocaine emergencies, except that the number of whites and blacks were similar (39% and 47%, respectively), while 11% were Latinos. Eighty percent were male and 79% were 20–39 years of age. In 1991, cocaine-related deaths accounted for .2% of emergency room episodes.

In July 1989, the National Institute on Drug Abuse (NIDA) estimated that the number of Americans using *any* illegal drug on a "current" basis (at least once in a 30-day period preceding the survey) dropped 37%, from 23 million in 1985 to 14.5 million in 1988. In 1993 of the 207 million people in the population of the *1989 National Household Survey*, 12 million persons had used an illicit drug in the past month.

The above-noted report stated, however, that crack is responsible for the explosion in recent drug-related medical emergencies—a 28-fold increase in hospital admissions involving smoked cocaine since 1984.

Crack babies: Crack may produce these negative effects by altering fundamental neurological pathways in the baby's brain, researchers say. The drug crosses the placenta during the first trimester of pregnancy, when the brain is forming. The pleasure-and-reward pathway, based on the brain chemical dopamine, is especially vulnerable to cocaine. Experts believe this might explain the flat (lethargic) moods and emotional poverty seen in some crack babies. Research groups are doing follow-up studies on this phenomenon at the Perinatal Center for Chemical Dependency at Northwest University School of Medicine in Chicago and at the University of California, Los Angeles. Another devastating result stemming from crack use is the drug's serious effect on babies born to mothers using the drug. Studies have indicated thus far that prenatal exposure to crack may result in some permanent impairment. Experts say that while the babies themselves are free of drugs not long after birth, prenatal exposure and postnatal deprivation are likely to take a severe toll. Crack and cocaine can cause seizures, cardiac arrest, arrhythmia heart attack, stroke or respiratory arrest. Effects of an overdose include agitation, increase in body temperature, hallucinations, convulsions and possible death.

Appearance: Cocaine HCL (cocaine hydrochloride) is made from leaves of the coca plant (grown primarily in Bolivia and Peru) that are turned into coca paste. This paste is converted chemically into dried cocaine base by being dissolved in ethyl ethers, acetone, or a mixture of both, then filtered to remove solid impurities. A mixture of acetone and concentrated hydrochloric acid or ethanol and concentrated hydrochloric acid is added to precipitate the cocaine hydrochloride, and the precipitate is then filtered and dried carefully using bright light to produce the white crystalline powder substance.

Because cocaine HCL will largely decompose if smoked directly, the HCL must be converted back to a relatively pure base state, or freebase, before it is suitable for smoking. Traditionally, freebase is made by mixing cocaine HCL with distilled water, a solvent (volatile chemicals), and ether, and then putting the mixture over a high flame. "Crack" is produced by heating a mixture of cocaine HCL, water and baking soda in a pan. Once all the impurities have been cooked out, what remains is a pancake that is cracked into little pieces to be used or sold.

Availability: Cocaine hydrochloride, otherwise known as cocaine, is available at 55% purity for $100 per gram; crack cocaine is available at 75% to 90% purity for $10 per one-tenth of a gram. In early 1990, crack was selling for $3 to $20 a vial (less than 1 gm). This amount provides a "high" lasting approximately 20 to 30 minutes.

Synonyms: Street names include: base, baseball, black rock, cloud nine, conan, crack, crank (also the name for speed or methamphetamine in the Northeast U.S.), freebase, gravel, handball, lido, rock, Roxanne, Serpico, snow, toke, space basing (crack doused with liquid PCP and smoked—also called ghost-busters), super white, white cloud, white tornado and many others.

Sandra Blakeslee, "Crack's Toll among Babies: A Joyless View, Even of Toys," *New York Times* (September 17, 1989).
Maurice L. Hill, *Drug Enforcement Administration Briefing Book: DEA Mission* (Department of Justice, June 1988).
Drug Enforcement Administration (DEA), *Drugs of Abuse,* by John C. Long, 1988 edition (Washington, D.C.: Government Printing Office, 1988).
Office of National Drug Control Policy, Executive Office of the President, *National Drug Control Strategy; Strengthening Communities Response to Drugs and Crime* (Washington, D.C.: White House, February 1995).
Substance Abuse and Mental Health Services Administration, *National Household Survey on Drug Abuse Population Estimates, 1994* (Rockville, Md.: Department of Health and Human Services [DHHS], September 1995).

crackhead   Derogatory street term for one addicted to crack.

crackhouse   Location where crack is routinely sold and/or used. Some crackhouses are open to all users, while others are homes to a group of users organized according to a familylike structure, where roles and responsibilities are clearly delineated among the member-residents.

craving   "Craving" is often associated with alcoholism and other drug use and can be divided into two types: "physiological," otherwise referred to as physical DEPENDENCE and "psychological." Physical craving occurs in those who have been drinking or using certain other drugs to excess over a long period of time. They are manifested by the symptoms of WITHDRAWAL. Such cravings arise out of a need for relief from the distress of withdrawal rather than from an actual desire for the drug.

Psychological craving is thought to account for the initial substance abuse, as well as for any relapses after the start of abstinence. During a period of abstinence there may either be a buildup of psychological tension provoking a desire for the individual's drug of choice as a means of relief, or the desire/craving may be intermittent.

crime   The seriousness of the federal government's commitment to controlling criminal drug activities is reflected in the money it has earmarked to do so. In 1997, drug control was allotted $15.1 billion, of which $8.3 billion was to be used for law enforcement. This is almost 10 times the amount allotted in 1981 ($1.5 billion). These funds are part of the so-called "War on Drugs," which is also a war on drug-related crime. To understand the link between

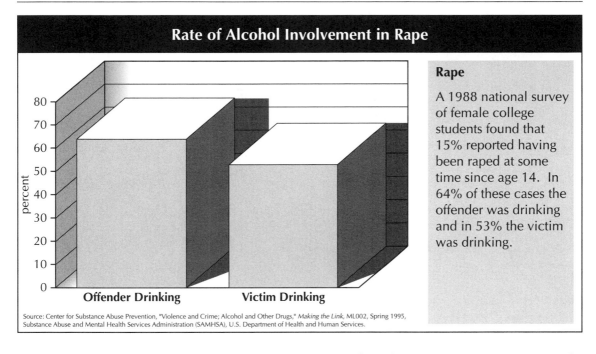

Rate of Alcohol Involvement in Rape

percent
80 70 60 50 40 30 20 10 0

Offender Drinking   **Victim Drinking**

Rape

A 1988 national survey of female college students found that 15% reported having been raped at some time since age 14. In 64% of these cases the offender was drinking and in 53% the victim was drinking.

Source: Center for Substance Abuse Prevention, "Violence and Crime; Alcohol and Other Drugs," *Making the Link*, ML002, Spring 1995, Substance Abuse and Mental Health Services Administration (SAMHSA), U.S. Department of Health and Human Services.

crime and drug use, one must distinguish between the three categories of criminal activity included in that link. First, it is a crime to be involved in an illegal activity such as cultivation, manufacture, transportation, sale, purchase or use, involving any controlled substance. The second category includes crimes committed in order to obtain money to buy drugs for personal use (in order to sustain a habit). The third category in the drug crime are crimes or felonies committed when the perpetrator is under the influence of a mood-altering substance. (See DRIVING WHILE IMPAIRED, SPOUSE ABUSE and CHILDREN OF ALCOHOLICS AND SUBSTANCE ABUSERS.)

Crimes related to the manufacture, sale and illegal possession/use of drugs: The most visible group of crimes under the first category are the acts of violence and murder by traffickers competing for shares of the illicit drug market or disputing thefts of money, drugs and so forth. The popularization of crack cocaine in the 1980s and 1990s introduced violent intergang warfare, very different from the quasi-professionalism with which the Mafia traditionally has run its heroin distribution network or the homespun, communal flavor of the more loosely-organized marijuana network. The arrival of crack resulted in a huge rise in convictions for *pos-*

session of the drug. Within this category too is the manufacture, sale and use of prescription drugs for *nonmedicinal* purposes, although of course it is legal to perform any of these activities for *medicinal* purposes, if you are licensed to do so.

Crimes committed to obtain drugs: A drug user needs a vast amount of money in order to support a habit—usually more than he or she has access to by legal means. According to a report by the Bureau of Justice Statistics in 1991, 27% of federal inmates, 27% of state inmates and 32% of local inmates claimed to have committed a robbery in order to obtain drugs; 32% of federal, 30% of state and 31% of local inmates claimed to have committed a burglary for the same purpose. In an 11-year longitudinal study funded by the NATIONAL INSTITUTE ON DRUG ABUSE (NIDA), 243 male heroin addicts committed more than 473,738 crimes during their years on the street (when they were not incarcerated or in residential treatment). Crimes frequently committed by drug users to obtain the money needed to support their habits include: theft, drug dealing (buying and selling), confidence games, gambling, forgery, pimping and prostitution. According to studies conducted by NIDA, many drug users commit more than one type of crime although they tend to specialize in a

Violence and Crime; Alcohol and Other Drugs

Making the Link, Spring 1995, Center for Substance Abuse Prevention

"In both animal and human studies, alcohol, more than any other drug, has been linked with a high incidence of violence and aggression."

—Seventh Special Report to the U.S. Congress on Alcohol and Health (Secretary of Health and Human Services, January 1990).

Crime is inextricably related to alcohol and other drugs (AOD). More than 1.1 million annual arrests for illicit drug violations, almost 1.4 million arrests for driving while intoxicated, 480,000 arrests for liquor law violations and 704,000 arrests for drunkenness come to a total of 4.3 million arrests for alcohol and other drug statutory crimes. That total accounts for over one-third of all arrests in this country.[1, 2]

The impaired judgment and violence induced by alcohol contribute to alcohol-related crime. Rapes, fights, and assaults leading to injury, manslaughter, and homicide often are linked with alcohol because the perpetrator, the victim, or both, were drinking. The economic cost of AOD-related crime is $61.8 billion annually.[3]

Many perpetrators of violent crime were also using illicit drugs. Some of these drugs, such as PCP and steroids, may induce violence. These drugs can also be a catalyst for aggressive-prone individuals who exhibit violent behavior as a result of taking them.

The need for preventing alcohol and other drug problems is clear when the following statistics are examined:

Alcohol is a key factor in up to 68% of manslaughters, 62% of assaults, 54% of murders/attempted murders, 48% of robberies, and 44% of burglaries.[4]

Among jail inmates, 42.2% of those convicted of rape reported being under the influence of alcohol or alcohol and other drugs at the time of the offense.[5]

Over 60% of men and 50% of women arrested for property crimes (burglary, larceny, robbery) in 1990, who were voluntarily tested, tested positive for illicit drug use.[2]

In 1987, 64% of all reported child abuse and neglect cases in New York City were associated with parental AOD abuse.[6]

We cannot put a monetary value on the human lives and suffering associated with alcohol and other drug problems. But we know the child welfare and court costs needed to deal with the consequences of these problems are substantial. The cost to arrest, try, sentence, and incarcerate those found guilty for these 4.3 million alcohol and other drug-related offenses is a tremendous drain on our nation's resources.

Prevention works to reduce the problems associated with alcohol, tobacco, an other drug use. For more information, call the National Clearinghouse for Alcohol and Drug Information at 1-800-729-6686.

[1] U.S. Department of Justice, Bureau of Justice Statistics, Crime in the United States 1991, Washington, DC, 1992.
[2] U.S. Department of Justice, Bureau of Justice Statistics, Drugs, Crime, and the Justice System: A National Report, Washington, DC, 1992.
[3] Institute for Health Policy Brandeis University, Substance Abuse: The Nation's Number One Health Problem: Key Indicators for Policy, Robert Wood Johnson Foundation, October 1993.
[4] U.S. Department of Health and Human Services, National Institute on Alcohol Abuse and Alcoholism, Alcohol and Health: Sixth Special Report to Congress on Alcohol and Health from the Secretary of Health and Human Services, 1987.
[5] Collins, J. J. and Messerschmidt, P. M., Epidemiology of Alcohol-Related Violence, Alcohol Health and Research World, 17 (2): 93–100. National Institute on Alcohol Abuse and Alcoholism, 1993.
[6] Chasnoff, I. J., Drugs, Alcohol, Pregnancy and Parenting, Northwestern University Medical School, Departments of Pediatrics and Psychiatry and Behavioral Sciences, Hingham, MA, Kluwer Academic Publishers, 1988.

Center for Substance Abuse Prevention, "Violence and Crime; Alcohol and Other Drugs," *Making the Link, ML002* Spring 1995, (Substance Abuse and Mental Health Services Administration; U.S. Department of Health and Human Services).

particular field. A user's drug of addiction seems to play a role in the kind of crime in which he or she engages. Crimes related to crack tend to be more violent than those related to heroin, for instance. The seriousness of the crimes grows greater with the age of the perpetrator, and those who become addicted to drugs at younger ages tend to commit crimes more frequently later on. Crimes most common to youthful addicts include mugging and purse snatching; to older addicts, robberies. Stolen merchandise sold on the black market will net only one-fourth of its retail value. Unfortunately, *hot* items find a ready market from members of the public who welcome the opportunity to buy goods at bargain prices. Loss due to theft is one of many areas of drug-related crimes that impacts the business community. Often small machinery and supplies are pilfered by lower-level employees in order to pay for their drugs, while funds are embezzled by white collar executives for the same purpose.

Crimes committed under the influence: Although drugs are involved in a majority of crimes, the precise role they play is not always the same. Tests and studies indicate that a majority of felons used alcohol or another drug immediately prior to committing a crime. The statistics do not indicate, however, the quantity ingested and for what purpose. Many felons have a beer or two to give them the courage to go through with their crime; others commit violent, unplanned crimes as a result of alcohol or other drugs having intensified angry feelings and provoked loss of control. The statistics do not differentiate the difference between the two situations.

Drugs and violence are a particular concern, although statistics do not always establish the link. Depending on the study, in cases of rape, as few as 13% and as many as 50% of perpetrators have been drinking as have 6% to 31% of the victims; 26% to 86% of homicide perpetrators and 14% to 87% of their victims have ingested alcohol. Alcohol can magnify angry feelings, hence, a number of theories have been offered to make a link between alcohol and criminal violence. Alcohol both releases inhibitions and intensifies certain negative mood states. The ADDITIVE EFFECT as well as the SYNERGISTIC effect of alcohol when combined with other drugs, such as BARBITURATES, may produce confused or violent feelings which can lead to acts of crime.

The habitual use of cocaine, crack and other stimulants can result in mental disorder, confusion, paranoia and other changes in behavior that can lead to criminal and/or violent behavior. Barbiturates, which are classified as "sedative hypnotics," mimic the affects of alcohol and tend to make chronic users argumentative, overactive and irritable. Studies have found, for example, that members of motorcycle gangs frequently take barbiturates ("downers") before engaging in violent confrontations. HEROIN has the reverse effect, and tends to diminish aggressive behavior, which is why heroin addicts (at least, when they are high) are not prone to violence. Other criminogenic affects of drug use include paranoid thought disorders; bursts of violent hyperactivity; feelings of persecution or suspiciousness; or conversely, omnipotence and bravado. Whether or not criminal behavior results from drug use depends on a number of factors, including the dosage taken and the level of tolerance that has been developed to the drug. Other variables include the setting in which a drug is taken, the user's personality and his or her state of mind at the time of use.

The role of marijuana as a stimulus for criminal activity raises many questions and fewer answers. Although a number of felons are regular or chronic marijuana smokers, no research has shown the drug to be a potentiator of violent acts. METHADONE maintenance was traditionally administered according to the belief that prescribing it to heroin users will reduce crime. Yet methadone has given birth to another drug-related crime: its illegal distribution by patients who sell their doses on the streets to support their addictions to other drugs.

The above information suggests a need for greater clarification about the different categories of drug-related crimes. Each of the different behaviors within those categories should be reviewed in order to measure the harm potential inherent to the general public. The criminalization of all illegal drug-related activities, most of which are of a nonviolent nature, and the use of imprisonment as the sole deterrent require grave reconsideration in light of the apparent failure of this approach; namely, the revolving door system of the prisons and the astronomical cost per day of incarceration. The current alternatives, such as the assignment of offenders to treatment and rehabilitation are now receiving support from criminal courts. Far less costly to society, the results appear to be excellent in many cases. Drug abuse PREVENTION MODELS provide another area for future development. Efforts must go beyond the level of the individual "Just Say No" approach, and look instead to more realistic solutions incorporating change into the environmental conditions of poverty, lack of opportunity and quality education, disintegration of family and community life, and the absence of personal fulfillment in the lives of the increasing number of legal and illicit drug users in each economic strata of society.

Drug Enforcement Administration, National Narcotics Intelligence Consumers Committee 1994, *The Supply of Illicit Drugs to the United States* (Washington, D.C.: 1995).

Bureau of Justice Statistics, *Drugs and Crime Facts, 1994* (Washington, D.C.: 1994).

White House, *Crime Control and Law Enforcement Act of 1994* (Washington, D.C.: 1995).

crisis intervention   The process of diagnosing and arresting such conditions as overdose, suicide attempts and panic reactions in drug-crisis situations. Unconsciousness, a low breathing rate, respiratory arrest, fever, extreme high or low pulse rate, muscle rigidity and vomiting in either a conscious or semiconscious state are signs indicating overdose and the need for immediate drug-crisis intervention.

cross-addiction   A term used to describe a mutual or interchangeable addiction (or CROSS-TOLERANCE) between drugs within the same group. A person addicted to alcohol, which belongs to the classification of drugs known as sedatives, will have some degree of addiction to all other sedatives. Therefore, an alcoholic could prevent withdrawal symptoms by taking sufficient quantities of another sedative, such as Librium, and someone addicted to Librium could stem withdrawal by taking alcohol. However, for someone addicted to a sedative, no drug from another category, such as a narcotic (like heroin or morphine), would be effective.

cross-dependence   A term used to describe a mutual or interchangeable dependence between drugs within the same group, such as sedatives. For example, alcohol and Librium, both sedatives, are cross-dependent. (See CROSS-TOLERANCE.)

cross-tolerance   If tolerance has developed to one drug it will carry over to another drug in the same category. Alcoholics or heavy drinkers will have a TOLERANCE for other sedative drugs; they will be more difficult to anesthetize with ether, for example. Cross-tolerance may be caused either by an increased ability to metabolize another drug (metabolic tolerance) or by changes in the tissues of the central nervous system (CNS) that make the system less responsive to the drug (cellular tolerance). Both increased metabolic ability and changes in CNS tissue result from prolonged heavy ingestion of alcohol and other drugs.

cultural etiological theories of alcoholism Several studies, while recognizing the importance of physiological and psychological factors, have shown that alcoholism is related more to ethnic and social background. Cultural etiological theories, also known as SOCIOCULTURAL ETIOLOGICAL THEORIES, suggest that individual attitudes toward alcohol and alcoholism to a large extent reflect the attitudes of the culture as a whole. Customs and codes of behavior regulating drinking, environmental support for drinking, and the level of intoxication considered "appropriate" are largely determined by cultural setting. For example, the low rates of alcoholism among Jews and Muslims can be traced to cultural proscriptions against the use or abuse of alcohol, whereas the extremely high rate of alcoholism consumption among the French and the Irish may be attributed to cultural support for excessive use of alcohol.

D. Cahalan, I. H. Cisin and H. M. Crossley, *American Drinking Practices: A National Survey of Behavior and Attitudes,* Rutgers Center of Alcohol Studies Monograph Series, no. 6 (1969).

W. McCord, J. McCord and J. Goodman, *Origins of Alcoholism* (Stanford: Stanford University Press, 1960).

cultural stress etiological theories   Some theorists feel that the incidence of alcoholism and other drug-abuse problems in a society may be related to the degree of stress produced by the culture. In 1946, R. F. Bales suggested that if the use of alcohol in particular is accepted under the societal norms, then it will be used to reduce the anxiety and tension produced by that society. Bales listed three major factors affecting the rate of alcoholism in a given society: the degree of stress and inner tension produced by the culture; the attitudes toward drinking held by the culture; and the opportunity for alternative means of satisfaction and coping with anxiety. In 1943, after studying the relation between social stress and alcohol consumption in primitive societies, D. Horton found that where alcohol use was sanctioned, there was a correlation between a high degree of anxiety and a high level of consumption.

David J. Armor, J. Michael Polich and Harriet B. Stambul, *Alcoholism and Treatment* (New York: John Wiley & Sons, 1978).

R. F. Bales, "Cultural Differences in Rates of Alcoholism," *Quarterly Journal of Studies on Alcohol* 6 (1946): 480–499.

D. Horton, "The Functions of Alcohol in Primitive Societies: A Cross-Cultural Study," *Quarterly Journal of Studies on Alcohol* 4 (1943): 199–320.

cutting The act of adding to or diluting a potent drug, often with milk sugar or another relatively harmless substance that is similar in appearance to the drug being adulterated. The exporter, importer and street dealer, often each in turn, add their cut so as to increase their profits. Trends change in the amount of cutting that is acceptable at a given time for a given drug, according to availability and demand. HEROIN, for example, is far more potent these days than it was even five or 10 years ago, and CRACK is a more potent version of its parent drug, cocaine, even though it does not cost more. (See CAINES.) A drug that has been cut has been "stepped on." In the drug business it is assumed that unless drugs such as cocaine and heroin are purchased directly from the grower or processor that they will have been cut. Many various methods and tests are applied for determining how pure a drug is. One method involves heating the substance, as different chemical ingredients melt at different temperatures. Many veteran drug dealers simply test the drug by trying it, but it is important for them to know that the sample being tested is representative of the entire batch being purchased.

Marijuana is frequently "stepped on." This is done by adding an inferior grade to a more potent grade; by adding "shake" (loose particles of marijuana as opposed to whole buds or flowers); even small twigs and pebbles will be added to large batches to increase size and weight. Other herbs can be mixed in as well, but this is not a common occurrence.

cyclazocine A NARCOTIC ANTAGONIST used in the treatment of heroin addiction. An addict who has been withdrawn from heroin and then treated with cyclazocine will not feel the effects of an ordinary dose of heroin. The drug can cause dependence, but withdrawal is milder than heroin withdrawal. Cyclazocine has not been used since NALTREXONE, a more effective and longer-lasting antagonist, has become available.

cycling A pattern of discontinuous anabolic STEROID abuse that consists of alternating a specified period of multiple doses with periods of nonuse.

cyclobarbital A short-acting BARBITURATE used mainly in hypnosis. Because of the rapid onset of its effects and their short duration, it is undesirable to most drug users.

Cylert A STIMULANT of the central nervous system generally used for children with minimal brain dysfunction (attention deficit disorder, or ADD). It is a brand of pemoline that, although pharmacologically similar to AMPHETAMINES, does not have a high potential for abuse. Overdosage can result in agitation, restlessness and hallucinations.

Cystospaz-SR A depressant containing the intermediate-acting BARBITURATE butabarbital. It is used as an antispasmodic sedative and may be habit-forming.

cytisine An extremely poisonous alkaloid found in many plants of the pea family. It was once used as a cathartic and diuretic. Canary Island broom, Spanish broom and Scotch broom, which are sometimes smoked or taken orally, all contain cytisine.

D

d-3 Copamine receptor currently under investigation by National Institute on Drug Abuse (NIDA) as a potential target for cocaine treatment development. (See RECEPTOR SITES.)

Dalmane A sedative, benzodiazepine flurazepam hydrochloride; prescribed as a hypnotic agent in the treatment of insomnia. Due to its widespread abuse, it is no longer legally available in the U.S. When taken in combination with alcohol or other central nervous system depressants, it has an additive effect. Symptoms of an overdose include somnolence, confusion and coma.

damiana *Turnera diffusa,* a tropical American plant of the Turneraceae family. There are claims that the smoked leaves can have a marijuanalike effect, and it is purported to be a mild aphrodisiac.

Darvon An analgesic widely prescribed for moderate pain, Darvon has the pharmacological properties of a NARCOTIC but does not compare with narcotics in analgesic potency. It is often abused and the user may become physically dependent. It contains propoxyphene hydrochloride. Combining Darvon with alcohol or other central nervous system depressants can have additive effects. Symptoms of an overdose include respiratory depression, convulsions, circulatory collapse, pupil constriction and extreme somnolence leading to stupor and coma. Cardiac arrest and death have also resulted.

Darvon-N A drug that contains propoxyphene napsylate, which is similar to propoxyphene hydrochloride (DARVON), but differs in that it allows more stable, longer-acting liquid and tablet forms. Like Darvon, it is a mild analgesic structurally related to the narcotics but is less potent. The user may become physically dependent and there is potential for abuse. Overdose symptoms are the same as those for Darvon. Darvon-N is prescribed for detoxification of opiate-dependent patients.

Data Center and Clearinghouse for Drugs and Crime Established in 1986 but absorbed by the larger OFFICE OF NATIONAL DRUG ABUSE CONTROL POLICY (ONDCP), the agency was funded by the Bureau of Justice Assistance and directed by the Bureau of Justice Statistics of the U.S. Department of Justice. The center served a variety of purposes: it responded to requests for drug and crime data; advised about new drugs and crime data reports; conducted bibliographic searches upon request for specific drugs and crime topics; and published special reports on subjects such as assets forfeiture and seizure, economic costs of drug-related crime, drugs and violence, drug laws of the 50 states, drug abuse and corrections, and innovative law enforcement reactions to drugs and crime. The center also prepared a comprehensive, concise report bringing together an array of data to trace and quantify the complete flow of illicit drugs.

datura *Datura stramonium;* a HALLUCINOGEN found in the poisonous jimson weed plant and a member of the potato family. The active ingredients are the BELLADONNA alkaloids: atropine, scopolamine and hyoscyamine. Leaves and seeds of this extremely toxic plant have been used as poisons and hallucinogens for centuries. Users smoke the dried leaves. The leaves have also been used in asthma powders and in the antiasthma cigarette Asthmador.

Synonyms: angel's trumpet, devil's apple, devil's weed, Jamestown weed, jimson-weed, stinkweed, stramonium, thorn apple.

dawamesk A green cake popular in North Africa, made from sugar, spices, orange juice and the tops of the MARIJUANA plant, eaten for its psychoactive effects. It was in the form of dawamesk that cannabis was first introduced to Europe in the mid-1800s.

Daytop The oldest and largest drug-free therapeutic program in the U.S. The program features a residential center for persons 13 years old and older who have a severe drug-abuse problem, outreach centers that treat adolescents who have a moderate drug problem, and specialized services, such as an adolescent program, a young women's group, a siblings group and an adult outpatient service.

de-alcoholized beverage A beer or wine from which the brewery or winery has removed most of the alcohol, resulting in a beer- or winelike beverage with a very low alcohol content. Since the alcohol content of de-alcoholized beverages is less than 0.5%, they are not classified as alcoholic beverages for purposes of taxation or for regulation of sale and consumption. There are two principal types of de-alcoholized beverages: malt beverages (formerly known as NEAR BEER) and wines—red, white and sparkling.

Many alcoholics as well as moderate drinkers and abstainers drink de-alcoholized beverages. Most people agree that the substitution of a nonaddictive beverage is a harmless, even beneficial way for an alcoholic to fill the void left by the elimination of alcohol, yet there are those who argue that the consumption of substitute "beer" and "wine" reinforces old drinking patterns and may lead to the resumption of drinking. Most likely the individual alcoholic would have to see for himself or herself whether or

not an alcoholic substitute was indeed just that or a temptation to return to old habits.

deafness Alcohol and drug use by hearing-impaired people is a serious problem that only recently received attention by treatment personnel and government funding agencies. A number of factors complicate the prevention and treatment of chemical dependence in hearing-impaired people. Because the hearing-impaired are often cut off from traditional media, they frequently cannot be reached by traditional prevention messages. The isolation from the mainstream experienced by many deaf people puts them at risk for abuse of mind-altering drugs. Those who suffer hearing-impairment may also have trouble finding treatment facilities that can adapt to their special needs, such as providing sign-language interpreters.

In 1990, the Minnesota Chemical Dependency Program opened. Funded by the Center for Substance Abuse Treatment's critical populations demonstration grants, and organized around the 12-step model of Alcoholics Anonymous, the Minnesota Program has become the prototype for many of the treatment approaches developed since then that serve the deaf community.

debauch A drinking and/or other drug spree or bout that usually includes excessive sexual activity.

decriminalization Lifting of laws, bans or other forms or regulations that define a behavior as criminal. The term may also refer to a reduction in the penalties, rather than a complete removal of legal restrictions, as distinct from legalization, which means the repeal of any definition of criminality.

delirium tremens (the D.T.'s) Although this term is also used, more casually, to refer to "the shakes"—a frequent hangover symptom, in the lexicon of substance abuse, the term indicates one of the most dramatic and serious conditions associated with alcoholism and dependence on sedatives including barbiturates. Delirium tremens (commonly referred to as "the *D.T.'s*") is the last and severest stage of WITHDRAWAL.

Chronic alcohol or sedative users are at risk of developing the D.T.'s on the second or third day of abstinence following a period of heavy drinking or drug taking. Because the D.T.'s have a 10% mortality rate, this condition is a medical emergency and the patient should be hospitalized immediately. Symptoms include profound confusion; disorientation; severe agitation and restlessness; insomnia; fever; vivid and terrifying auditory, visual and tactile hallucinations; and abnormally rapid heartbeat. Although sedation may be necessary, it should be done with extreme caution to avoid over-sedation: the dosage required to suppress all the symptoms of a sedative-tolerant drug user in this state would be high enough to seriously depress respiration.

The D.T.'s may last for three to four days or persist intermittently for several weeks. A small percentage of patients do not recover and remain in a psychotic state. There have been reported cases of delirium tremens after surgery, trauma and severe illness in patients who claimed to have abstained from alcohol for several months. More research is needed to determine the exact nature of this condition and the circumstances under which it appears.

delta alcoholism   The fourth of five categories of alcoholism defined by E. M. JELLINEK (1890–1963). Delta alcoholism, like GAMMA ALCOHOLISM, is characterized by an acquired tissue tolerance of alcohol, adaptive cell METABOLISM and WITHDRAWAL symptoms. However, instead of the LOSS OF CONTROL found in gamma alcoholism, there is an INABILITY TO ABSTAIN. The delta alcoholic cannot stop drinking for even a few days without showing some withdrawal symptoms; however, the amount of intake on any given occasion can be controlled. Consumption of alcohol, though large, is steady over a long period of time and less "explosive" than that of gamma alcoholism. Delta alcoholism is the predominant form of alcoholism in FRANCE and in some other countries with a significant wine consumption.

delusions   A belief or firm fixed idea not amenable to reason, rationality or evidence to the contrary. Delusions are common among those who are under the influence of a hallucinogen or large doses of stimulants and are quite dangerous. During the "LSD Era" a number of people died because of delusions that they could walk on water or fly. Drug-induced delusions are often persecutory or grandiose in quality.

demand reduction   Policies intended to reduce consumer interest in a particular psychoactive drug by such means as education and treatment. By contrast, law enforcement strategies are classified as supply reduction.

dementia   A condition described by the DSM-IV (DIAGNOSTIC AND STATISTICAL MANUAL OF MENTAL DISORDERS) as "characterized by multiple cognitive deficits that include impairment in memory . . . sufficiently severe to cause impairment in occupational or social functioning and . . . a decline from a previously higher level of functioning." These deficits are multifaceted and involve memory, judgment, abstract thought and other cortical functions. Dementia is further characterized by changes in intellect, personality and behavior. Alcoholism, or the nutritional deficiencies associated with it, are two of its many possible causes. Early symptoms vary and deterioration of personality and intellect may be slow. Ultimately, it affects judgment, insight, speech and motor activity. Personal habits deteriorate and, in the later stages of the illness, the patient may require total nursing care.

Demerol   A narcotic (a brand of MEPERIDINE hydrochloride) prescribed as a sedative and as an analgesic for moderate to severe pain. Its activity is similar to that of morphine: it can cause the same type of dependence and it has a high potential for abuse. Symptoms of an overdose include respiratory depression. If Demerol is combined with alcohol or other central nervous system depressants the effects can be additive. Use and withdrawal at high dosages can cause seizures. (This symptom is unique to Demerol; it is not seen with other narcotics.)

denatured alcohol   ETHANOL made unfit for drinking by the addition of a substance such as METHANOL.

denial   This term refers to the psychological defense mechanism most characteristic of people dependent on alcohol or other drugs: a refusal to admit to problems related to their alcohol or drug use. Denial is one of the main methods chemically dependent people use to deal with life. They deny their emotional problems and their dependence on drugs, claiming that they do not have a problem or that they use drugs only in moderation. The situation is further complicated for those dependent on illegal drugs who must find a way to rationalize the illegality of their behavior and the risk of arrest and physical harm that they expose themselves to when purchasing and using drugs. When confronted with their drug-affected behavior, the substance user is likely to respond that he or she can stop at any time.

One of the initial signs of denial is concealment of the amount of alcohol and other drugs consumed. This posture distinguishes the alcohol- or drug-dependent person from the social drinker, or, looking past its illegality, the so-called recreational drug user. Society's negative attitude toward alcoholics and other drug users encourages denial: many alcohol- or drug-dependent people hide their problem rather than confront the stigma associated with alcoholism and other drug use.

Denial is pervasive in American society. Spouses, relatives and friends may deny a problem on the part of an alcoholic or other drug user, often to protect him or her from the scorn of friends and neighbors. Employers may ignore an uneven work record or fire a chemically dependent employee rather than to discuss and try to find a solution to the problem. Physicians may prescribe tranquilizers rather than confront an alcohol- or drug-dependent patient.

In treatment, denial should be dealt with quickly; otherwise the patient may sustain severe physical and psychological damage over time. Recognition of denial allows the chemically dependent person to be more aware of his or her problem and his or her role in its resolution. (See INTERVENTION and ENABLING.)

Denmark   There is a liberal attitude toward alcohol consumption in Denmark, and the country experiences few problems with alcohol abuse. Abuse of other drugs has been an acknowledged problem in Denmark since 1940 or the start of World War II.

Alcohol: The national drinking pattern is characterized by frequent but temperate consumption of alcoholic beverages, mostly beer. The majority of consumption takes place in the home; initial drinking by adolescents usually takes place in the presence of adults; and there is little increase in drinking on weekends or holidays. Alcoholic beverages, including distilled spirits, are sold in virtually all retail food outlets. These patterns have remained relatively sta-

ble for many years, although authorities note some increase in preference for distilled spirits over beers.

According to the Brewers and Licensed Retailers Association's *Statistical Handbook 1993,* Danish annual per capita consumption of alcoholic beverages, computed as ABSOLUTE ALCOHOL, was 9.9 liters. This reflects an increase from 8.8 liters in 1975, compared with an increase of about 50% in the decade from 1967 to 1977. Between 1975 and 1985, per capita consumption of beer increased less than 1% from 129.0 to 129.8 liters and per capita consumption of spirits declined from 1.7 to 1.1 liters, while wine consumption increased from 11.5 to 20.7 liters. According to the *Statistical Handbook 1995,* Denmark ranked only 50th (39.0 liters) worldwide in annual per capita beer consumption but ninth in total overall alcohol consumption

Based on World Health Organization guidelines, the country reported a mortality rate from alcohol abuse of 18.4 men and 9.1 women per 100,000 population in 1987.

The Danish government believes that regulation of alcohol consumption is suitable only if agreeable to a majority of the population. For this reason it limits controls on consumption to taxation of alcoholic beverages and licensing of public drinking places. Further action is left to private health and charitable organizations. There is a National Commission on Alcohol and Narcotics, but its role is primarily advisory.

Treatment: Public responsibility for prevention and treatment of alcohol-related problems remains in the hands of county-level government. The only government spokesmen for antialcohol causes are appointees with limited advisory status within existing government agencies such as the Ministry of Education.

Drugs other than alcohol: Beginning in 1940, the use of other drugs, particularly morphine, became increasingly widespread in Denmark. In an attempt to stem the problem, the government passed the Euphoric Drugs Act of 1955, which empowered the Minister of the Interior to limit the use of certain drugs to medicinal purposes. In the 1960s, as the use of illicit drugs spread (including cannabis, amphetamines and morphine) government policy focused on dealers rather than users. In 1965 stiff penal rules for convicted drug offenders were introduced. In 1968,

42,000 out of Denmark's 350,000 school-age youths admitted having used illegal drugs—cannabis being the drug of choice in 90% of the cases. However, a follow-up study in 1970 showed that while the use of marijuana and other illegal drugs continued to rise, its increase was on a smaller scale than before.

Between the mid-1970s and 1990, the number of addicts in Denmark stabilized at around 6,000–10,000 out of a population of 6 million. Heroin, brought in from Southwest Asia, dominated the drug scene, which also included the use of barbiturates, amphetamines and cannabis. Use of LSD, at one time common, virtually disappeared in the late 1980s. Studies in this period set the average age of initiating heavy drug use at 18 and the average age of users at between 26–27. The consequences of drug use rose significantly during this period: New arrests put a strain on penal institutions. The number of offenses against property rose, and the presence of organized crime—a new development in Denmark—increased. The number of drug-related deaths among young people was second only to the number of vehicular fatalities.

The *International Narcotics Control Strategy March 1996* issued by the U.S. Department of State's Bureau for International Narcotics and Law Enforcement Affairs describes the current illicit drug situation in Denmark as follows: "Denmark is a convenient gateway for narcotics to the Nordic region . . . Traffickers bring illicit drugs for consumption and transshipment to the other Nordic countries. Heroin from southern Asia is transshipped to western Europe and the U.S., while South American cocaine is transshipped to western Europe." Danish authorities estimate that there were 10,000 users of hard drugs in 1995. While hashish remains the drug of choice, the availability of cocaine has been growing steadily. In the "free city" of Christiana, an enclave of Copenhagen, the open sale and use of hashish have been long established.

Treatment: Despite the imposition by the Danish government of increasingly severe penalties aimed at curbing distribution, the attitude in Denmark toward use of drugs other than alcohol is similar to that in the United Kingdom. Addiction is perceived first and foremost as a medical problem, that it is: (1) a manifestation of a disease; and (2) a public health problem, which, if not controlled, leads to more serious challenges to national well-being such as HIV and AIDS. A relatively large number of addicts, unlike the system in the U.S., seek treatment from general practitioners. Drug-abuse treatment in Denmark generally takes place in a large number of institutions throughout Denmark. In addition to free inpatient care at most hospitals, there are free outpatient programs in hospitals, youth crisis centers and special out-clinics.

Hoeveel alcoholhoude dranken worden er in de wereld gedronken? (How many alcoholic beverages are being consumed throughout the world?), 27th ed. (Scheidam, Netherlands: Produktschap Voor Gedistilleerde Dranken, 1987).

dentistry   Proper dental care is rarely a high priority for active alcoholics and other substance users. Because of chaotic lifestyles, disordered personal finances and impaired self-esteem, inadequate health care is a common problem among chemically dependent people. Actively chemically dependent people tend to seek dental care only in emergencies, while people in recovery often see a dentist not long into successful abstinence.

Dentists should learn to recognize the signs of alcoholism and other drug use: for example alcoholics often have enlarged, but otherwise asymptomatic, parotid glands (the largest salivary glands), and alcoholics also have a rate of permanent tooth loss three times greater than that of the general population. Dentists should watch for such warning signs so that they can refer chemically dependent patients for proper treatment of substance abuse problems. Alcoholics and users of other drugs should have routine dental exams to counter the long-term neglect of the teeth as evidenced by coated tongue, heavy plaque formation, deposits of calculus and bium loss. Combining drugs (including alcohol) with tobacco can have a synergistic effect and is associated with an increased susceptibility to cancers of the head and neck. Many alcoholics and other drug users are also heavy smokers and thus have an increased tendency toward cancers of the throat and mouth.

Dentists should be cautious when administering anesthetics to patients who have alcohol or other drug problems. SYNERGISTIC effects can result from combinations of anesthetics and other substances. If the patient has alcohol or a related drug in his or her system while undergoing surgery, the initial phase of anesthesia may be followed by a synergistic interaction resulting in a deeper and possibly more dangerous narcosis and an increase in sleeping time. Also, alcoholics and users of related drugs are more resistant to the effects of anesthesia, and a CROSS-TOLERANCE with both chloroform and ether has long been observed. In addition, dentists must take care to prescribe nonaddictive medications to minimize the risk of relapse in their clients who are in recovery. After surgery, healing may take longer than normal. There is an increased incidence of infection among substance users, who are often malnourished or have otherwise impaired immune systems. Any dental surgical procedure should be avoided if possible. If surgery on an actively chemically dependent person is elective, he or she should be completely detoxified because the stress of surgery may precipitate WITH-DRAWAL.

"Alcohol-Drug Interactions," *Anesthesia Progress* 26, no. 5 (September/October 1979): 129–132.

Charles E. Becker, "Review of Pharmacologic and Toxicologic Effects of Alcohol," *Journal of the American Dental Association* 99 (September 1979): 494–500.

Marc A. Shuckit, "Overview of Alcoholism," *Journal of the American Dental Association* 99 (September 1979): 489–493.

Department of Defense, drug testing Because officials believe that the nation's security calls for drug-free personnel, the military now gives over 3 million drug tests a year to its approximately 2.5 million soldiers, sailors and marines. These tests detect six types of drugs: cocaine, marijuana, amphetamines, barbiturates, opiates and PCP. In 1987 the Department of Defense estimated that its military drug program costs over $47 million a year. It was the first and is the most thorough drug-testing program in the U.S.: half the drug tests in the nation are conducted by the armed forces.

Since "blanket testing" began in 1981, drug use is reported to have declined significantly in all military services. While advocates contend that these results indicate that testing leads people to stop using drugs, opponents argue that these results are misleading. There is discussion of extending the military's drug-testing program to the space and defense industries. However, across-the-board drug testing in privately owned businesses and in nonmilitary

agencies of the government raises a special set of legal and ethical questions.

Gilda Berger, *Drug Testing* (New York: Franklin Watts, 1987).

dependence The *DSM-IV (DIAGNOSTIC AND STATISTICAL MANUAL OF MENTAL DISORDERS)* distinguishes between those people who "abuse" mind-altering substances, including alcohol, from those who are "dependent" on them. Dependence is defined as a "maladaptive pattern of substance use, leading to clinically significant impairment or distress, as manifested by three or more of the following symptoms which may appear at any time in the same twelve-month period: TOLERANCE; WITHDRAWAL symptoms; loss of control; unsuccessful desire to cut down; increasing amount of time spent to obtain the substance or recover from its use; reduction of non-substance-related social, occupational or recreational activities; and inability to stop using the substance despite knowledge of its consequences." Symptoms may include severe anxiety, tremors and nausea, such as those that appear when an alcoholic stops drinking or the physical pains of heroin withdrawal, and may also include such behavioral symptoms as the need to have a drink or use a drug "in order to function" or "to relieve stress." Some people become dependent very rapidly and others gradually, over years. Because some people manifest withdrawal symptoms after detoxification, once there is no longer a physiological basis for dependence, or in situations involving substances not known to produce physical dependence, it is believed that dependence can be psychological as well as physical. (See ADDICTION.)

depressants Drugs that act on and slow down ("depress") the action of the CENTRAL NERVOUS SYSTEM (CNS), diminishing or stopping vital body functions. OPIATES, BARBITURATES, ALCOHOL and INHALANTS are depressants. Alcohol and sedatives are the most commonly used and abused depressant drugs. Their action is irregular because they do not depress all parts of the CNS at once. They work primarily on the brain, depressing psychomotor activity and relieving tension and anxiety. After the initial effects begin to wane, the sedative levels in the blood begin to fall and psychomotor activity again increases, producing agitation. The term "depressant" is misleading because, initially, such drugs actually elevate a person's mood (as opposed to causing depression).

depressed communities Communities in which population and economic growth decline tend to experience an increase in alcohol and drug use, although less so than BOOM TOWNS. A study of depressed towns during the mid- and late-1970s showed that, as in the case of boom towns, the rise in alcohol use was higher than that in drug use.

Unlike boom towns, however, depressed communities are usually stable and long-established areas in which the economy and population have declined over a period of time. Since young people tend to leave such areas in search of employment, the populations tend to be older and more established. Increases in alcohol are related to a variety of factors, such as responses to personal difficulties, the ethnic and religious makeup of the community, and the social class of the individuals affected. The rate of arrests for DRIVING WHILE IMPAIRED (DWI) tend to be erratically (but often substantially) higher than in more prosperous communities, and treatment for alcoholism declines or falls off sharply. Although there is less money to spend, and presumably less to be spent on alcohol, liquor provides short-term relief, and drinking is often considered to be a cheaper form of recreation than the alternatives.

National Institute on Drug Abuse (NIDA), *Drug and Alcohol Abuse in Booming and Depressed Communities,* DHEW pub. ADM 80-960 (Washington, D.C., 1980).

depression Depression is a mood or state variously described as feeling "down," "blue," "sad" or "low." The *DSM-IV (DIAGNOSTIC AND STATISTICAL MANUAL OF MENTAL DISORDERS)* describes several disorders associated with depression, including major depression, dysthymia, bipolar disorder and cyclothymia.

Although depression is a normal response to loss, a diagnosis of major depression is applied when symptoms are prolonged, intense and associated with anhedonia (a lack of pleasure or interest in usual activities), guilty thoughts, hopelessness, decreased energy and difficulty concentrating. Major depression is often identifiable by the presence of vegetative signs including changes in appetite, sleep, bowel and sexual function. Psychotic symptoms

such as delusions and hallucinations and extreme psychomotor retardation (for example, "catatonia") herald the most severe manifestations of major depression.

Other depressive disorders include: dysthymia, a depressive condition in which symptoms are less florid than those of major depression but appear over a period of two or more years; bipolar disorder, in which depressive and manic episodes alternate or appear simultaneously for what is called a "mixed state"; and cyclothymia (a milder form of bipolar disorder). Variations of pattern and timing of symptoms further define and distinguish between types of depressive disorder (such as atypical, melancholic, seasonal and post-partum variants).

No single cause of depression has been identified. Genetic, psychological and biological theories of etiology have been explored. Treatments founded on the biological model and treatments founded on the psychological models have been equally effective in eliminating or reducing the symptoms of depression.

Depression in chemically dependent people: For many, depression is a distinct and separate disorder. In others, the drinking or drug taking itself causes the depression. Stimulants, especially cocaine, are often used to combat feelings of low energy and listlessness. The direct pharmacological action of cocaine is an increase in dopaminergic and noradrenergic neurotransmission in the BRAIN, producing short-term elevations in mood, energy and concentration. Continued use, however, results in a net depletion of these neurotransmitters, resulting, nearly inevitably, in depression. Similarly, many people use alcohol, successfully at first, to relieve dysphoric feelings; used habitually, alcohol itself induces depression. More than one half of all alcohol- and cocaine-dependent people meet the criteria for depression. Opiate and, less frequently, marijuana users are also at risk for depressive reactions.

Depression is a symptom common to withdrawal from most mood-altering drugs, including caffeine and nicotine. In the case of heroin withdrawal, depression can last for years and is a leading cause of relapse.

Depression is associated with serious impairment in social and occupational functioning. Depressed people are at greater risk of suicide than nondepressed people, and attempts to take their own lives are frequent among substance users, both during active use and after withdrawal. In a study conducted at Duke, 26 out of 29 people who had attempted suicide were intoxicated at the time. In other studies, as many as 40% of the completed suicides were by people who had been drinking or had a history of alcohol abuse. Depression is common after detoxification from alcohol and other drugs, but will often lift without psychopharmacologic intervention after several weeks of sustained sobriety. Severely depressed people and those who are actively suicidal may require hospitalization.

Treatment: Psychotherapy and a variety of medications can help in treating depression. Most first-line antidepressants work by increasing norepinephrine or serotonin neurotransmission. Such agents include the heterocyclic compounds, monoamine oxidase inhibitors and the relatively newer serotonin reuptake inhibitors. Adjunctive agents for treating resistant depression include lithium, thyroid hormone and stimulants, as well as combinations of first-line drugs. (See DOPAMINE.)

Because depression often masks all emotions, frequently someone suffering from depression will feel very little, and will not even be aware of their depression. There is a great danger in that, and it is important to recognize depression by signs such as lack of motivation, procrastination, feelings of insecurity and self-doubt, weakness, lethargy, weight gain or loss, various forms of physical illness, withdrawal from family and friends, lack of sleep—too much sleep—or being unable to get out of bed in the morning. First and foremost it is important to know that depression is curable. Drug treatments should not be seen as a cure, but should be used only in emergency situations, that is, to get the depressed person through a crisis period. Often they can be used effectively when the client first seeks treatment, and is still "at the bottom." The therapist or counselor should actively explore the source of the patient's problems and find productive solutions and applicable answers. Many therapists rely on drug treatment rather than tackling the far more difficult task of actively participating in a patient's complete recovery from all forms of abuse, including chemical dependency of any kind. Twelve-step programs often offer enough support and community for a depressed person to recover, without any fees or medication. Religion also has proved extremely effective for many people suffering from depression as well as substance abuse. Whatever approach is tried, it is vital that the depressed person reach out to others, discusses their feelings and does not remain in isolation. Reaching out is the first step toward recovery.

deprivation A major psychological theory suggesting that deprivation and disturbance are the cause of addiction in early infancy. According to this theory, addiction results from the absence or failure of a significant emotional relationship during an individual's formative years. Deprived of a warm relationship with a mother figure (resulting, for example, from the mother's death or her emotional or physical absence), the individual may remain fixed in the oral stage of development. This object loss early in life causes the addict to have primitive, excessive and insatiable demands. As a result, he or she may experience repeated failure involving interpersonal relationships. Long suppressed feelings of loss and rejection will reawaken and, rather than destroy another, the person will turn his anger inward or obliterate it by drug use. Deprivation, however, can clearly be a result of growing up in a family where addiction is present. Research indicates that one's concept of reality, how healthy or dysfuncional one is psychologically and emotionally, issues of self esteem and even one's values are predominantly shaped and formed during the first six years of life.

desensitization A technique employed during rehabilitation or treatment aimed at decreasing tension in situations that can lead to the use of drugs. Patients are repeatedly subjected to situations that would ordinarily make them tense and reduce their self-control, such as being offered a "fix" by an old friend. They are then taught to practice methods that will allow them to relax.

designer drug A term popularized in the 1980s for synthesized, man-made psychoactive drugs, many of which find their audience in fashionable social gathering places such as bars and discos. According to the National Institute on Drug Abuse (NIDA), "A designer drug is an analogue, a chemical compound that is similar in structure and effect to another drug of abuse but differs very slightly in structure. Designer drugs are produced in clandestine laboratories to mimic the effects of controlled drugs. . . . The street names of designer drugs vary according to time, place and manufacture, and change frequently."

Designer drugs are also synthesized for legitimate medicinal purposes.

desoxyn gradumet tablets   A highly potent central nervous system stimulant containing methamphetamine hydrochloride, prescribed primarily as an anorectic for weight control. A member of the AMPHETAMINE group of sympathomimetic amines, it has a high potential for abuse. Users may develop tolerance, severe psychological dependence and social disability. Symptoms of an overdose include restlessness, tremors, rapid respiration and hallucinations.

DET   (diethyltryptamine) A completely synthetic HALLUCINOGEN similar to DMT except that it is milder and of even shorter duration. Like DMT, the drug is easily manufactured in home laboratories.

detoxification   From the Latin *de* (reversing or undoing) + *toxicum* (poison). A treatment process by which a patient addicted to a drug is withdrawn from it under supervision; also known as detoxication. The symptoms that appear during this WITHDRAWAL vary with the type of drug involved, the length of use and the kind of services provided during withdrawal. After detoxification, the patient is able to abstain from the drug without severe physical discomfort and is no longer *physically* dependent upon it.

Decisions about where and how a patient is detoxified should be based on a number of factors. The severity of the withdrawal symptoms is a primary consideration; those with severe symptoms require close medical supervision and management, usually in a hospital. Patients who have alcohol- or nonalcohol-related complications, such as cardiac disease or hypertension, also generally require hospitalization. However, those with mild or moderate withdrawal symptoms and no complications may not need the care of a hospital and may be able to go through the detoxification process in a more social setting. As alternatives to hospitalization, some states provide nonhospital detoxification centers.

There has been some interest in the possibility of limited use of ambulatory detoxification for carefully screened patients. In such a program, the patient would return daily to a clinic for medication and counseling, and participation by family and friends would be encouraged.

Detoxification is generally accomplished during a short confinement (five to ten days) in a general hospital. Hospitalization has several advantages: it removes the chemically dependent person from the environment he or she associates with compulsive drug use, forces the patient to see that his or her behavior has medical consequences that can be deadly, protects the patient from the sometimes fatal effects of withdrawal, and gives him or her an opportunity to commence REHABILITATION. In a hospital, a chemically dependent patient is usually given an appropriate sedative or other medication to control withdrawal symptoms.

Opinions vary among researchers and clinicians as to which medications should be prescribed to support withdrawal when using PHARMACOTHERAPY. All medications are discontinued before discharge. In an inpatient detoxification facility, patients receive education about their drug use. They are also introduced to ALCOHOLICS ANONYMOUS or other 12-step programs specific to the drug they abuse. Before patients are released, they usually work out a discharge plan, including such elements as outpatient GROUP THERAPY, and referral to a rehabilitation center.

Detoxification centers in inner-city settings are often in particular demand during the winter, less as a gateway to recovery than as a temporary respite from the cold. (See INPATIENT TREATMENT, OUTPATIENT TREATMENT.)

Dexedrine   An AMPHETAMINE (a brand of dextroamphetamine sulfate) usually prescribed as an anorectic for weight control. Classified as a Schedule II drug, it has been extensively abused and can cause extreme psychological dependence and social disability.

dextroamphetamine   A synthetic AMPHETAMINE; a central nervous system stimulant prescribed in the treatment of narcolepsy, minimal brain dysfunction in children, and as an anorectic. (See DEXEDRINE.)

dextromoramide   An analgesic with a potency greater than morphine. It is a synthetic OPIATE and is classified as a Schedule II drug.

diabetes There is controversy over whether diabetics should include alcoholic beverages in their diets, and therefore all diabetics should consult their physicians about the advisability in light of their own condition. Proper diet is of primary importance in achieving control of hyperglycemia (high blood sugar), the principal manifestation of diabetes mellitus. While the effects of alcohol vary from one person to another and depend on kind, dosage and whether consumed in the fasting state or after having eaten, small amounts of alcohol consumed close to or with a meal generally cause little change in the blood sugar levels of diabetics whose disease is under control. However, excessive alcohol can cause many problems if consumed in a fasting state or if sweet dessert wines, port, or liqueurs are consumed. These beverages contain high amounts of sugar (up to 50%).

If alcohol is consumed in a fasting state, it can precipitate hypoglycemia (low blood sugar) and can enhance the blood-sugar-lowering action of insulin and interfere with the body's ability to produce its own glucose. Insulin-dependent diabetics in a fasting state are especially susceptible to hypoglycemia. Because the symptoms are similar to those of intoxication, a hypoglycemic reaction may not be recognized, and necessary treatment may therefore be delayed. If alcohol is consumed, it is essential that it accompany food or be consumed shortly before or after a meal. Alcohol ingestion raises the level of triglyceride (a type of fat) in the blood. Excessive levels of this fat, known as hypertriglyceridemia, are believed to be a major cause of atherosclerosis. Hypertriglyceridemia is more common in diabetics than in nondiabetics, and anyone with high triglyceride levels should be discouraged from drinking.

Alcohol can cause a reaction in diabetics using oral glucose-lowering agents that are sulfonyl derivatives (Orinase, Diabinese). Possible symptoms include dizziness, flushing and nausea.

The sugar content of wine varies a great deal. Information about sugar content can be obtained by writing to the quality control laboratories of wineries. An alternative is to use the reducing sugar tablets, which measure the percentage of glucose and fructose (Clinitest) to determine sugar concentration. Since wine contains sugars other than glucose,

tests that measure only glucose (Tes-Tape, Diastix, Clinistix) should not be used.

On the simplest level, alcohol may disrupt diet control, provide extra calories and stimulate the appetite. Alcohol should not contribute more than 6% of the total CALORIES consumed per day by a diabetic. For a 70-kg (154-lb) man this standard amounts to approximately 160 kcal (kilogram calories) per day, or two 4-oz glasses of dry wine. Alcohol is considered a "fat exchange," or a food with the nutritive equivalent of fat, in the "food-exchange" terminology used in diabetic nutritional texts. The following formulas may be used to compute the alcohol calories in one serving of a beverage:

$0.8 \times$ proof $\times$ ounces per serving = kcal.

Example: A 2-oz serving of 80-proof whiskey equals 128 kcal (0.8×80 proof $\times 2$ ounces = 128 kcal).

When the alcohol content is expressed as a percentage, such as in wines and beers, double the percentage and apply the same formula.

$0.8 \times$ double the percentage of alcohol listed on the bottle $\times$ ounces per serving = kcal from alcohol.

Example: A 4-oz serving of wine containing 14% alcohol equals 89.6 kcal. 0.8×28 (double the percentage of alcohol) $\times 4$ (ounces) = 89.6 kcal.

Any carbohydrate kcal (in beer, wine, mixers) should be added to the alcohol kcal for total kcal.

Janet McDonald, "Alcohol and Diabetes," *Diabetes Care* 3, no. 5 (September/October 1980): 629–637.

"Whiskey or Water?" *Diabetes Forecast* (November/December 1980): 17–20, 42.

diacetylmorphine Known universally as HEROIN this semisynthetic opiate derivative was first produced in 1898.

diazepam A minor tranquilizer, diazepam is best known under the brand name VALIUM, which was at one time the most prescribed drug in the U.S. In 1974, Americans spent $500 million on 50 million prescriptions. Valium's liberal dispensation for anxiety and as a sleeping aid made it a socially acceptable drug of abuse: it has been known to play as large a role in middle-class American life at cocktail parties and little league baseball.

Appearance: Diazepam appears as a colorless crystalline powder insoluble in water and slightly soluble in alcohol.

Classification: Diazepam is a Schedule IV drug under the Controlled Substances Act.

Activity: After oral administration it is quickly and completely absorbed by the gastrointestinal tract, with effects manifesting in 15–30 minutes. The onset of effects from intramuscular injection is erratic. There is immediate onset of effects by intravenous injection. Diazepam is detoxified in the liver and metabolites are excreted in the urine and feces. The drug acts on the brain's limbic system, but does not interfere with the peripheral autonomic system. It has a half-life of 20–50 hours and crosses the placental barrier.

Usage: Diazepam is prescribed to alleviate neurotic tension and anxiety that prevent a person from coping with daily life. It is also prescribed as a sleeping pill. Its anticonvulsive properties warrant its use, alone and in conjunction with other drugs, to control muscle spasms in such conditions as cerebral palsy, paraplegia, petit mal and myoclonic seizures. It is also prescribed to treat the symptoms of alcohol withdrawal. Both physicians and "street drug users" use diazepam to calm anxiety and panic induced by hallucinogenic drugs.

Dosage: For mild to moderate anxiety it is prescribed in two or three daily doses of 2–5 mg, and in severe anxiety three or four daily doses of 5–10 mg are prescribed. It is ineffective for suicidal purposes except in combination with other central nervous system (CNS) depressants, which make it highly lethal.

Effects: A benzodiazepine derivative, diazepam common has side effects that include initial drowsiness, unsteadiness and weakness. High doses cause intoxication similar to that caused by alcohol and barbiturates. When taken with alcohol or other central nervous system depressants it can have an ADDITIVE EFFECT.

Tolerance and dependence: The user may develop tolerance along with physical and psychological dependence. Withdrawal symptoms include convulsions, tremors, cramps and sweating.

Although over 200 times the normal dose of Valium has been survived, the drug is still often used in suicide attempts. Some of these attempts have been successful, particularly in cases where alcohol was combined with the Valium.

Availability: Valium (the major brand name under which diazepam is known) is a favorite drug of substance users. It is available illicitly, but probably a bigger problem is the fact that it is over-prescribed for minimal anxiety. Doctors have been known to prescribe it freely to patients who insist they require a tranquilizer. Matters are complicated when a prescription is not limited to a certain number of refills, and Valium users have been known to take them freely when they know they will be well supplied. Supervision of the patient on diazepam or other benzodiazepines is essential. Situational anxiety does not seem to warrant constant tranquilization. Another issue in the Valium controversy is whether, in the absence of Valium, a patient would resort to barbiturates or alcohol—which are much more dangerous—or not use any drug at all.

Illicit Valium is frequently taken in large quantities by users to achieve maximum intoxication. These bootleg pills are often referred to as "Vs." Valium may also be taken to ease the crash experienced after amphetamine or cocaine use.

DiClemente and Prochaska   The originators of the much-cited model of recovery from addictive/compulsive behaviors. People, they posit, are usually ambivalent about wanting to conquer their addictions. Prior to changing, the user is in a state of "contemplation" about stopping the negative behavior and will have to move into a phase of "readiness to change" in order to proceed with the process. DiClemente and Prochaska's model is the linchpin in MOTIVATIONAL INTERVIEWING, a model of treatment that puts much of the onus on the therapist to propel (or motivate) the client out of contemplation state and into one of readiness to change. According to DiClemente and Prochaska's model, the process begins all over again in the event of a relapse.

Didrex   A central nervous system stimulant that contains benzphetamine hydrochloride and has a pharmacological and chemical activity similar to that of the AMPHETAMINES. It is prescribed as an anorectic for weight control. It can cause psychological dependence and social disability and has a potential for abuse.

diethylpropion   A synthetic drug similar to the AMPHETAMINES in its activity but with less central nervous system stimulation. It is usually prescribed as an anorectic. (See TENUATE.)

differential assessment   Refers to the detailed evaluation of the client's substance-abuse disorder in terms of etiology, presenting symptoms, substance-related problems and other associated features.

digestion   Alcohol, when taken in very small quantities, may aid digestion if gastric motility is impaired. It allows freer salivation in "dry mouth" associated with stress, which in turn triggers increased gastric motility, the gentle motion that is beneficial to digestion and empties the stomach. Wine in particular is thought to be good for this purpose because the type of acid in wine is close to that in the gastric juices. Heavier doses, however—more than a glass or two—can cause increased acid secretion causing gastritis and peptic ulceration. (See CORDIALS.)

dihydrocodeine   A semisynthetic narcotic analgesic that is related to codeine and has a similar activity. (See SYNALGOS.)

dihydrocodeinone   A synthetic codeine derivative, also called oxycodone. (See PERCODAN.)

dihydromorphinone   An opium derivative prescribed as an analgesic; also called hydromorphone. (See DILAUDID.)

Dilaudid   A narcotic analgesic that contains hydromorphone, a MORPHINE derivative. It is prescribed for moderate to severe pain. It is habit-forming and the user can become physically dependent. Although it has the same activity as morphine, Dilaudid is much more potent and does not cause such adverse reactions as nausea and vomiting and is therefore highly sought after by narcotics users. Dilaudid is considered by some to be the ultimate psychoactive drug experience.

dill   There are claims that when they are dried and smoked, dill seeds can produce a mild high. This is unlikely.

dimethyltryptamine   A psychedelic drug manufactured synthetically in England. (See DMT.)

diphenoxylate hydrochloride   A Schedule V drug that is chemically related to the narcotic MEPERIDINE. It may be habit-forming. Prescribed in the management of diarrhea, it slows intestinal motility. (See LOMOTIL.)

dipipanone   A synthetic OPIATE prescribed as an analgesic. Although less potent than morphine, the user can become dependent. It is a Schedule II drug.

dipsomania   From the Greek *dipsa* (thirst) + *mania* (madness). An obsolete term that refers to an uncontrollable CRAVING for alcohol, often of a periodic nature. (See EPSILON ALCOHOLISM.) Dipsomania is also improperly used as a synonym for persistent drunkenness or alcoholism. The slang word "dipso" means drunkard.

disability, alcohol- or other drug-related   Consequences of alcohol and other drug use that render the user unable to perform at a normal level in social and economic activities. Interestingly, people who suffer from alcoholism, which is officially recognized by the American Medical Association (AMA), are protected from discrimination by the terms of the Federal Americans with Disability Act (ADA). People addicted to other drugs are not protected from discrimination because the AMA has yet to identify as a disease addiction to drugs other than alcohol.

disease concept   The disease concept provides the basis for most of the current approaches to the treatment of ALCOHOLISM and, by extension, to treatment of abuse of other drugs. It describes a somewhat predictable course in genetically marked people subjected to environmental stressors.

According to the *Seventh Special Report to the U.S. Congress on Alcohol and Health,* "Alcohol dependence, like hypertension, diabetes and coronary artery disease, may be characterized as a biologically based disease in which a genetic predisposition is activated by environmental factors." The disease concept is the foundation of the philosophy of ALCOHOLICS ANONYMOUS since it shifts the emphasis from alcoholism as a moral issue to alcoholism as a medical illness with a distinct biopsychosocial symptomatology. The disease concept seeks to rehabilitate the alcoholic rather than punish him or her. It does not look for causes but advocates treatment, identification of the individual as a recovering person, and peer support in recovery through participation in AA.

There is a misconception that the disease concept is of recent origin, perhaps because only recently has it gained widespread acceptance. Actually, the concept has a long and controversial history. Mark Keller of the Rutgers Center for Alcohol Studies pointed out that as early as the first century the Roman philosopher Seneca distinguished between "a man who is drunk" and one who "has no control over himself . . . who is accustomed to get drunk, and is a slave to the habit." The 18th-century American physician Benjamin Rush said of drunkenness that it "resembles certain hereditary, family and contagious diseases." The idea of alcoholism as a disease was accepted in the 19th century by a large part of the medical community. Similarly, in 1804, the British physician Thomas Trotter wrote, "In medical language, I consider drunkenness, strictly speaking, to be a disease."

In 1952 E. M. JELLINEK (1890–1963) defined alcohol addiction as a distinct diagnostic category and elaborated a developmental course of the addiction process. While his theoretical progression of the major symptoms has been seriously questioned, most authorities still affirm the major elements of the disease concept. Since the rapid growth of other recovery programs to treat other addictions, the disease concept has been "borrowed" to explain them. One justification for classifying dependency on alcohol and other drugs as a disease is the theory of "self-medication," in which the substance user is believed to take drugs to relieve the symptoms of a mental disorder biochemical or genetic in origin. The disease model has also been applied to compulsive gambling, spending and working. Critics attack this usage because they believe it trivializes the concept.

Both the American Medical Association and the World Health Organization regard alcohol dependence as a specific disease entity. Recently, both organizations reevaluated their classifications of alcohol dependence, effectively eliminating the blanket term "alcoholism" as a clinical descriptor. The ALCOHOL DEPENDENCE SYNDROME (ADS) construct has been gaining influence in this regard. (See CLASSIFICATION OF ALCOHOLICS.)

Whether or not alcoholism and substance abuse is, in fact, a disease, acceptance of the alcoholic and other drug users as victims of illnesses that require medical and psychological treatment has paved the way for improved treatment and tolerance of these shamed and stigmatized people. It has also influenced the funding of programs designed to resolve many of the problems that contribute to, result from or help sustain individuals' dependence, for example, lack of education or vocational training, homelessness and alienation from their families. When alcohol- and drug-abuse are classified as medical problems, treatment is subject to reimbursement of some personal economic costs through INSURANCE, disability payments and workers' compensation.

There are a number of arguments against the disease model: It may overemphasize the medical aspects, leading to the (probably erroneous) assumption that alcoholism is essentially a singular entity, like tuberculosis, and ignores the fact that alcoholism may be a symptom of a number of quite separate problems. Some doctors feel that for alcoholism to be classified as a disease there must be some manifest abnormality of the anatomic structure. But this requirement would eliminate all behavioral disorders from the classification of disease.

It is also thought that the disease model takes inadequate account of the sociocultural factors that may play a causal role, and fosters irresponsibility in the patient, allowing him or her to be passive. Another danger with this model is that alcoholism may be considered an all-or-nothing disease entity, with no degrees in between.

Discoveries of anomalous brain waves in children of alcoholic fathers as well as recent research into GENETIC markers for a predisposition to alcoholism are helping to build a stronger case for the disease model. However, none of these studies has come close to ruling out the significant role that sociocultural and other environmental factors play in contributing to alcoholism.

David J. Armor, J. Michael Polich and Harriet B. Stambul, *Alcoholism and Treatment* (New York: John Wiley & Sons, 1978): 9–11.

R. Williams, "Nature, Nurture, and Family Predisposition," *New England Journal of Medicine* 318, no. 12 (1988): 770–771.

diseases   There are numerous diseases caused by extended, heavy use of alcohol and other drugs, as well as others in which their use plays a significant role. Alcohol and tobacco are major contributors to various diseases of the HEART, LIVER, LUNGS, PANCREAS and STOMACH. Heavy use of any drug may damage the BRAIN and CENTRAL NERVOUS SYSTEM (CNS), while intravenous drug use is a frequent factor in TETANUS, HEPATITIS and AIDS (ACQUIRED IMMUNE DEFICIENCY SYNDROME). Not only can drug use harm the individual, it can also harm the fetus of a pregnant woman who uses any drug, including alcohol, tobacco, illicit drugs and many prescription and over-the-counter remedies. FETAL ALCOHOL SYNDROME is currently the third leading cause in the U.S. of birth defects, including mental retardation. Of the three, it is the only one totally preventable. About 1 in 750 live births, or 4,800 babies per year, are born in this country with fetal alcohol syndrome. Each year 36,000 newborns are affected by a range of less severe alcohol-related "fetal alcohol effects." (See BABIES, DRUG-ADDICTED AND -EXPOSED and PREGNANCY.)

Despite focus by the media on the use of illicit drugs, use of alcohol and tobacco (the legal drugs) account for a much higher percentage of the substance-related diseases, partly because they are used by a much greater portion of the population. Cancer (of the lungs, esophagus and mouth) and emphysema are the primary diseases caused by tobacco. Although tobacco with NICOTINE is by far the number-one killer, the illnesses related to alcohol use are more numerous. According to the New York State Office of Substance Abuse Services, "Alcohol abuse ranks third among cause of illness and disability in this country and accounts for 10% of all deaths. . . . Each year, thousands of responsible people develop liver disease, respiratory problems, anemia, obesity and malnutrition due to abusive drinking. Even pneumonia and influenza may be linked to misuse of alcohol." Chronic alcohol abuse is associated with greater susceptibility to several diseases, including certain types of cancer, evidently because of alcohol's ability to interfere with the body's immune system. Even minimal alcohol intake increases the drinker's risk of contracting sexually transmitted diseases, including HIV, since alcohol's disinhibiting effect increases the chance of people having unprotected sex.

Diseases of the liver caused by drinking include: ALCOHOLIC LIVER DISEASE, CIRRHOSIS, FATTY LIVER and ALCOHOLIC HEPATITIS. Damage to the brain and central nervous system related to heavy drinking includes: DELIRIUM TREMENS (THE D.T.'S), KORSAKOFF'S SYNDROME, WERNICKE'S ENCEPHALOPATHY (SYNDROME OR DISEASE) and ALCOHOLIC POLYNEUROPATHY, as well as less common diseases such as MARCHIAFAVA-BIGNAMI DISEASE and CENTRAL PONTINE MYELINOLYSIS. Other diseases resulting from excessive alcohol consumption include ALCOHOL AMBLYOPIA, ALCOHOLIC MYOPATHY, HEMOCHROMATOSIS, RHINOPHYMA and ACNE ROSACEA.

disinhibition   Defined by the World Health Organization as "a state of release from internal constraints on an individual's behavior," disinhibition is often the result of using a psychoactive drug. The disinhibiting effect of alcohol has become a matter of potentially life-threatening importance since the advent of the HIV/AIDS epidemic. Even a few drinks reduces the likelihood of drinkers observing safe-sex precautions. Alcohol intoxication may also increase the likelihood of needle sharing among intravenous drug users

disorientation   A condition of mental confusion with respect to time, place, situation or identity. A variety of drugs—stimulants, alcohol and other depressants, hallucinogens—can have this effect. Accidental deaths may result from disorientation, in which the individual has no idea when, or even if, he or she took a previous dose of a drug.

distillation   The process of separating or purifying liquids by boiling them, collecting the vapors emitted, and recondensing the vapors into liquid form. Distillation is used for a variety of purposes, ranging from oil refining to desalinization of sea water. It takes place naturally in the cycle by which groundwater evaporates into clouds and then recondenses to fall as rainwater.

In the production of alcoholic beverages, distillation involves heating a fermented mash, collecting the alcohol, which vaporizes before the water because it has a lower boiling point, and then collecting the recondensed alcohol as a distillate.

Distillation of alcoholic beverages is believed to have been a discovery of Arab cultures, although they never fully refined the technique because of Muslim strictures against consumption of alcohol. Classical Greek and Roman societies used distillation processes to purify water but apparently never distilled their wines into spirits to any great extent. It was not until after A.D. 1,000 that distillation of alcoholic beverages became common in Europe, with the first spirits probably being crude brandies distilled from wines in Italy. The procedure also has a long history in Ireland, where the fermented material was a mash of grains rather than wine.

The early motivation for distillation may have been economic: producers of wines or beers could reduce the cost of transport if they shifted to smaller quantities of more potent alcoholic beverages, and distilled spirits are also more stable than wines or beers. A preference for the more potent beverages developed, and continental Europe's early *aqua fortis* (strong water) and Ireland's *uisce beathadh* (water of life) were prized for their superior powers as intoxicants before their recorded histories began in the early 16th century.

Today, distillation of potable spirits begins with the production of a fermented mash. Grains are the most common material employed, and they are generally malted, or germinated, to make soluble sugars. Once yeast is introduced, these sugars convert into alcohols, creating a fermented "wash," or "wort," from which the alcohol content is distilled. Two types of apparatus are used for distillation: the traditional pot still or the newer and more efficient patent still, sometimes called the continuous still. In either case, the alcohol distillate is the base from which any number of potable spirits are produced by various flavoring, dilution and aging processes.

Distilled Spirits Council of the U.S. (DISCUS)
The Washington, D.C.–based trade group representing the country's liquor industry; it monitors such things as ADVERTISING, marketing, sales, consumption and promotion. In 1975, DISCUS adopted an advertising code for the industry called "The Code of Good Practice."

diviner's sage   *Salvia divinorum,* a plant belonging to the mint family. The Mazatec Indians of Mexico chew the leaves or brew them as a beverage for their hallucinogenic effects.

d-lysergic acid diethylamide tartrate 25   LSD 25. (See LSD.)

DMT   A fast-acting HALLUCINOGEN (N-dimethyltryptamine) similar in structure to psilocin and its congener, PSILOCYBIN. Organic DMT is found in the seeds of the shrubs *Piptadenia,* in the flesh of the climbing vine *Banisteriopsis caapi* and in the roots of *Mimosa hostilis.* It can also be easily synthesized. DET and DPT are close chemical variants.

Effects: Within five to ten minutes after ingestion, DMT produces an LSD-like experience that lasts from 30 to 60 minutes. Because the effects do not last long, DMT is sometimes referred to as the "businessman's LSD" or the "businessman's lunch-time high." Unlike LSD, it affects only visual perceptions, not auditory and tactile ones. It can cause lack of coordination and spasticity, physical effects not associated with LSD. Physical and psychic effects appear simultaneously. The DMT experience can be quite intense and, for many who try it, frightening and nightmarish.

Tolerance and dependence: As with all hallucinogens, short-term reversible tolerance to the drug does rapidly develop, but physical DEPENDENCE does not.

Sources: Easily synthesized, DMT is manufactured in "basement" laboratories and sold illicitly. Its use has declined in recent years as has that of other hallucinogens. It is an important component of cohaba, a snuff used in Haiti and parts of Central and South America, which also contains BUFOTENINE.

Synonyms: businessman's LSD, businessman's lunch-time high.

DNA   Deoxyribonucleic acid. Along with RNA, DNA is one of the two main types of nucleic acid, an organic substance found in the chromosomes of all living cells. DNA plays an important role in the storage and replication of hereditary information and protein synthesis and is an extremely complex molecule composed of substructures of phosphates, bases and sugars. The particular sequence of these subunits determines the genetic information carried by the chromosomes and regulates all metabolism.

During the 1960s and 1970s (the HIPPIE years), rumors circulated widely, warning of permanent GENETIC impairment resulting from excessive drug-use, particularly from LSD. There are, however, no scientific data to support these rumors.

Do It Now Foundation (DIN)   A not-for-profit publisher of low-cost drug, alcohol and health education materials distributed nationally and internationally. Founded in 1968 and supported entirely by its sales, DIN distributes approximately seven million pieces of literature a year. The foundation believes that ignorance about drugs can be as dangerous to an individual as drugs themselves, and consequently publishes materials on both primary and secondary prevention techniques and approaches, as well as general information.

doctor   Slang for a person who sells liquor at higher prices when bars and liquor stores are closed. When used as a verb, the term also refers to the addition of alcohol to a drink, often without the drinker's knowledge.

dolene   A depressant that contains phenazopyridine hydrochloride, hyoscyamine hydrobromide and the short- to intermediate-acting BARBITURATE butabarbital. It may be habit-forming. Prescribed for inflammation of the lower urinary tract, it is no longer available in the U.S.

dolophine hydrochloride   A synthetic narcotic analgesic that contains METHADONE hydrochloride and has multiple actions similar to MORPHINE. It is prescribed for severe pain and for detoxification and maintenance in the treatment of narcotic addiction. The user may develop a dependence, similar to morphine dependence. Dolophine has the potential for abuse.

DOM (STP)   The synthesis of DOM (2, 5-dimethoxy-4-methyl amphetamine) was reported in the chemical literature in 1964 and first came to

public attention in 1967 when Food and Drug Administration (FDA) chemists identified it as one of the active constituents of STP. Today, STP is a common synonym for DOM, although the original STP was a variety of drug mixtures and not all of them contained DOM.

Classification: A synthetic HALLUCINOGEN with a structural resemblance to both AMPHETAMINES and MESCALINE, DOM is sometimes classified as an adrenergic hallucinogen because it causes physiological changes typical of such adrenergic agents as epinephrine.

Usage: DOM is considerably more potent than either amphetamines or mescaline, which it resembles in chemical structure. On a weight-for-weight basis it is less potent than LSD but the effects last longer: effects are perceptible about one hour after ingestion and reach their highest intensity three to five hours after ingestion. They subside after 12 to 18 hours. Psychological effects the next day are only rarely reported.

Effects and dosage: Physiological changes include an increase in heart rate and systolic blood pressure, dilation of the pupils, and a slight rise in body temperature. Other changes may include nausea, tremors and perspiration. The intensity of these changes appears to be related to the dosage. Psychological effects also vary with the dosage. Doses of approximately 3 mg result in euphoria and "enhanced self-awareness," while doses over 5 mg cause hallucinations. Some users may experience vivid visual imagery on closing their eyes along with a change in their perception of time. Eventually, they may see these images with eyes open. The predominant emotional state of the user is usually one of happiness. The experience is clear to the user after it is over and insight is retained throughout.

Tolerance and dependence: It is similar to other hallucinogens in that tolerance to its effects develops with regular use. This tolerance develops rapidly but is also rapidly reversed when use stops. Physical dependence does not develop to DOM.

Availability: It is difficult to know how much DOM is available today. Users may buy DOM and receive some other drug, or they may receive DOM when they think they are buying something else.

Sources: DOM is manufactured by "basement" chemists who supply the illegal drug market.

Frederick G. Hofman, *A Handbook on Drug and Alcohol Abuse* (New York: Oxford University Press, 1975): 171–173.

Richard R. Lingeman, *Drugs from A to Z* (New York: McGraw-Hill, 1974): 236–238.

Dona Ana   A cactus, *Coryphantha macromeris*, native to Texas and Mexico, which contains the psychedelic alkaloid macromerine. It is eaten or brewed into a tea and has about one-fifth the potency of mescaline.

dopamine   The immediate precursor of norepinephrine in the body, dopamine is found most commonly in the adrenal glands and exhibits adrenergic effects. It is a neurotransmitter and is important in the action of amphetamines and cocaine. Dopamine deficiency is thought to be a primary defect in Parkinson's disease. Dopamine hydrochloride is a synthetic drug that affects the autonomic nervous system and is prescribed in the treatment of shock syndrome and congestive heart failure. Cocaine and amphetamines are thought to have their major effects by disturbing dopamine transmission.

Doriden   A nonbarbiturate HYPNOTIC that contains glutethimide and is prescribed for insomnia. Because it does not cause respiratory depression it is also administered as a preanesthetic. The user can become physically and psychologically dependent. Symptoms of an overdose, which is difficult to treat, include pupil dilation, loss of tendon reflexes, central nervous system (CNS) depression and coma. Combining Doriden with alcohol or other CNS depressants, can have additive effects. It is no longer available in the U.S.

Dover's powder   An obsolete remedy that contained 10% opium and ipecac. It was given to induce sweating during a febrile illness.

doxepin   A tricyclic ANTIDEPRESSANT manufactured as Apapini and Sinequan.

DPT   A little-known synthetic HALLUCINOGEN (dipropyltryptamine); chemically related to DMT and DET.

dram   From the weight of the ancient Greek coin the drachma. In modern fluid measurement, 1 dram = $1/8$ oz. Although a dram is too small a portion to have ever been used seriously as a measurement of liquor, it was a common measure of medicine (1 teaspoon = $1 1/3$ drams), with which it was first associated, and liquor has often been euphemistically referred to as "medicine." "Taking a dram" (like "having a wee nip") is a way of playing down the amount of alcohol consumed. Usually a dram, like a SHOT (which is what the word "dram" most often means today), is downed in a single gulp. As early as the 17th century, "dram-drinking" and "dramming" were terms usually reserved for habitual drinking to the point of mild intoxication. (See DRAM SHOP LAW.)

Dram Shop Law   A law that imposes legal liability upon a person, usually a tavern keeper, who supplies alcoholic beverages to a one who becomes intoxicated and causes injuries or damages to himself or another as a result.

Drinamyl   A drug manufactured in England that combines amphetamine sulfate and amobarbital. It is not legally distributed in the U.S.

drinker   A person who consumes alcoholic beverages, as opposed to someone who abstains. In popular usage the term "drinker" also refers to an alcoholic or heavy drinker.

drinking   Consuming alcoholic beverages; as opposed to abstaining.

driving while impaired (DWI)

Alcohol: Each year nearly 50,000 people die on U.S. highways and a significant number of these fatalities are alcohol related. In 1997 alcohol-related crashes claimed 16,189 lives, about one-quarter of these fatalities were people under the age of 25. Alcohol-related injuries in 1997 account for 327,000 people (an average of one person injured every two minutes).

Alcohol is almost always one of the drugs found in highway accidents in which the driver has taken more than one drug. About 75% of single-vehicle accidents are alcohol- or drug-related. Studies indicate that people with severe drinking problems are

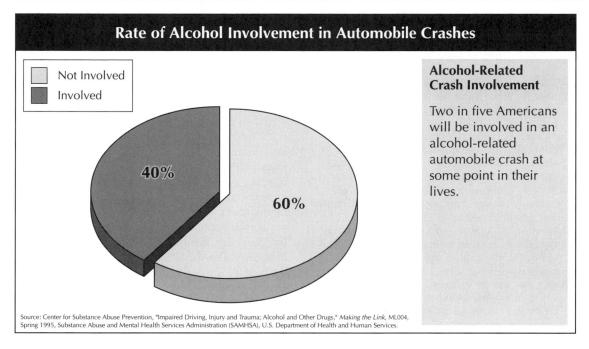

Rate of Alcohol Involvement in Automobile Crashes

Not Involved
Involved

40%
60%

Alcohol-Related Crash Involvement

Two in five Americans will be involved in an alcohol-related automobile crash at some point in their lives.

Source: Center for Substance Abuse Prevention, "Impaired Driving, Injury and Trauma; Alcohol and Other Drugs," *Making the Link,* ML004, Spring 1995, Substance Abuse and Mental Health Services Administration (SAMHSA), U.S. Department of Health and Human Services.

disproportionately involved in all kinds of crashes. Of known alcoholics who drive, some 24% to 40% have had at least one traffic crash previously on their driving records. The biggest menace on the highway is the PROBLEM DRINKER who has been arrested at least once for offenses involving alcohol.

It is generally believed that to reduce traffic fatalities and accidents the amount of drinking-and-driving must be reduced. Factors that might deter drinking and driving include: a higher risk of arrest through the use of targeting patrols by day, time and location; breath tests that are easier to administer both legally and physically; simplification of the process for making a DWI arrest; and increased motivation for police to make such arrests. On the other hand, increasing the severity of penalties might result in fewer arrests, fewer convictions and more plea bargaining as well as lengthier trials and appeals that could cost the taxpayer more. Public education may reduce the amount of drinking and driving, although so far there is no strong evidence to support this.

Some states require people arrested for driving while intoxicated to attend a drinking driver program. More extensive programs may be needed for drivers recognized to be problem drinkers. In many places there are citizen action groups, such as MOTHERS AGAINST DRUNK DRIVING, that work not only to educate drivers but to put pressure on law enforcement agencies to strictly enforce driving laws. Federal efforts have been increased with the establishment in 1982 of a presidential commission on drunken driving.

There are many problems related to enforcing drinking-and-driving laws. Only motorists driving in an erratic or illegal manner or who become involved in a crash are likely to be apprehended for driving under the influence or while intoxicated. And after an intoxicated motorist is stopped, there are several loopholes through which he or she can escape. A recent study showed that experienced police failed to recognize approximately 40% of the drivers who were over the 0.10% BAC level.

Studies have shown that alcohol causes degeneration of driving skills, including reaction time, coordination, attention, visual awareness and judgment. In most states the determination of whether or not someone is intoxicated is based on BLOOD ALCOHOL CONCENTRATION (BAC), as measured by a breath tester, urinalysis or direct analysis of the blood. The Breathalyzer, used frequently today, is a chemical photometric device that determines BAC by testing

Facts about Drinking

*1993, National Institute on
Alcohol Abuse and Alcoholism*

Student drinking is the number-one health problem on the nation's college and university campuses.

The amount of alcohol consumed by college students annually is enough to fill 3,500 Olympic sized swimming pools—roughly one for every college and university in this country.

Each year, "college beer cans" could litter every federally assisted highway in the United States at a rate of almost one can per foot.

Alcohol consumption, misuse, and its consequences have been estimated to cost our society $26 billion more than the cost of Desert Storm.

During the war in Vietnam, over twice as many Americans were killed in automobile crashes by alcohol-impaired drivers than were killed by the Viet Cong.

240,000 to 360,000 of the current college student body will eventually die of alcohol-related causes, comparable to the entire undergraduate body of the Big Ten dropping dead.

Various cancers are associated with drinking, including cancers of the lip, oral cavity, pharynx, larynx, esophagus, stomach, colon, rectum, tongue, lung, pancreas, and liver.

Chronic alcohol consumption can cause breast enlargement in men and menstrual disturbances, loss of secondary sex characteristics, and infertility in women.

Source: National Institute on Alcohol Abuse and Alcoholism, *Facts about Drinking* (Washington, D.C.: National Institute on Alcohol Abuse and Alcoholism, 1993).

bicyclist) has registered a BAC of 0.01% or above. (This is the legal limit for intoxication in most jurisdictions.)

The National Center for Statistics and Analysis estimated that the risk of a fatal crash, per mile driven, could be at least eight times higher for drunken drivers than sober drivers. At a BAC of 0.15% the risk is 10 times higher than normal; at 0.20%, 20 times. Apparently alcohol consumption also diminishes a driver's ability to avoid the mistakes of others on the road. In a University of Vermont study, 18% of fatally injured drivers not at fault were found to have BAC levels above 0.10%. (This figure is very high when you consider that only 2% of the total population were on the road at the time, but those not involved in accidents were found to have BACs above 0.10%.) Of those at fault, 50% had BACs at or above the 0.10% level. The majority of alcohol-related accidents occur at night and a larger proportion of men than women are involved, perhaps in part due to differences in drinking patterns (for example, women are more likely to drink at home).

Roadside breath tests, while not always accurate, improve the probability of detection. Notwithstanding, even under an implied consent law, drivers can refuse to take the test. And in Connecticut, for example, no one was convicted of refusing to take the test for a period of at least 10 years. Furthermore, revocation of a driver's license often fails to prevent a person from driving. All 50 states have laws against driving under the influence of alcohol (DUI) and impose various penalties for the offense. In most states, a BAC level of 0.10% is considered evidence of intoxication. Idaho and Utah are two of five states where the level is 0.08%. A few states have two levels: 0.10%, with less severe penalties, and 0.15%, with harsher penalties. Maine's 1981 drunken-driving law is considered one of the toughest in the U.S. The law introduced a civil charge for driving while intoxicated (DWI) so that the state needed to prove only preponderance of evidence rather than guilt beyond a reasonable doubt; a BAC of 0.10% became per se evidence of driving under the influence of alcohol. Repeat offender alcohol-impaired drivers were denied second jury trials, and minimum mandatory penalties were established. The first year after the law was passed, DWI conviction rates increased 85%. During the first two years after the law was in

a sample of breath from deep inside the lungs. In many states there is an implied consent law that requires a motorist to submit to a BAC test upon request or face fines or suspension of his or her driving privileges.

In an average person, some degree of impairment can usually be observed at a BAC of 0.05%; above 0.08% the risk of an accident rises appreciably. The National Highway Traffic Safety Administration (NHTSA) defines a traffic crash or fatality as alcohol-related when a participant (driver, pedestrian or

Impaired Driving, Injury and Trauma, Alcohol and Other Drugs

Making the Link, Spring 1995, Center for Substance Abuse Prevention

"Half of all injuries could be avoided by not drinking when you are driving, boating, operating machinery, feeling angry, or using a firearm."

—*Louis W. Sullivan, M.D., former secretary of Health and Human Services, March 1992.*

The role of alcohol and other drugs in automobile crash deaths and injuries is widely acknowledged. Alcohol and other drugs also have been linked to an array of serious and fatal injuries, including spinal cord injuries, drownings, bicycle crashes, and intentional injury. Intoxication is frequently found in trauma victims, and a history of trauma is a marker for the early identification of alcohol abuse.

Alcohol and other drugs are a factor in 45.1% of all fatal automobile crashes and one-fifth of all crashes involving injury. In 1992, impaired driving crashes claimed the lives of more than 17,000 Americans and injured 1.2 million others. Of those killed, close to one-third were under 25 years of age.[1]

More than 40% of all deaths of 15-20 year olds result from motor vehicle crashes. In 1993, 40% of the 5,905 traffic fatalities of 15-20 year olds were alcohol-related.[1]

Of 936 patients admitted to the University of California at San Diego Medical Center for Trauma Unit in 1988 who underwent a toxicology screening, 65% were found to be positive for one or more drugs. Of the positives, 50% were for alcohol alone, 20% were for illicit drugs only, and the remaining 30% were positive for two or more drugs. Over 75% of patients admitted who were between the ages of 21 and 30 tested positive.[2]

Between 47% and 65% of adult drownings and 59% of fatal falls are associated with alcohol.[3]

The estimated relative risk of accidental death is 2.5 to eight times greater among males defined as heavy drinkers or alcohol dependent than among the general population. Alcoholics are nearly five times more likely to die in motor vehicle crashes, 16 times more likely to die in falls, and 10 times more likely to become fire or burn victims.[3]

The impact of alcohol- and other drug-related injury and death takes a tremendous toll on our society. The number of potential years of life lost to alcohol- and other drug-related injuries equals those lost to cancer and surpasses those lost to heart disease, the two leading causes of death in the U.S.

Beyond the tragedy of lost lives, these incidents exact a huge economic cost. Alcohol-related injuries alone cost an estimated $47 billion annually. And, according to a recent study, illnesses and injuries caused by the use of alcohol, tobacco, and other drugs accounted for nearly 40% of the medical costs at one large metropolitan hospital.[4]

For more information, contact the National Clearinghouse for Alcohol and Drug Information at 1-800-729-6686.

[1] EARS, National Highway Traffic Safety Administration, 1993 and 1994.
[2] Bailey, D. N., Drug Use in Patients Admitted to a University Trauma Center, Journal of Analytical Toxicology 14, January/February 1990.
[3] Eighth Special Report to the U.S. Congress on Alcohol and Health, National Institute on Alcohol Abuse and Alcoholism, 1993.
[4] Center for Substance Abuse Prevention's Discussion Paper on Preventing Alcohol, Tobacco, and Other Drug Problems, September 1993.

Source: Center for Substance Abuse Prevention, "Impaired Driving, Injury and Trauma, Alcohol and Other Drugs," *Making the Link, ML004,* Spring 1995. (Substance Abuse and Mental Health Services Administration; U.S. Department of Health and Human Services).

force, fatal crashes and single-vehicle nighttime crashes declined 35%. Three years after the law's enactment, however, fatal accidents returned to the pre-1981 level. Thus, the law did not achieve a sustained reduction in alcohol-related fatal crashes. However, the public no longer regards the state's penalties for DWI as severe.

Most countries have similar legal limits, and a few, such as the Russian Federation and other eastern European countries, completely prohibit alcohol consumption before and while driving. The Scandinavian countries have the strictest laws in the world, some calling for automatic imprisonment and loss of driver's license. Although early studies of these laws found no significant changes in the rate of fatal motor vehicle crashes after they went into effect, the laws have not yet been adequately evaluated and are still under study. It has generally been found that strict penalties in themselves do little to prevent drunken driving unless they are enforced and perceived to be enforced. Surveys have shown that severe laws that are highly publicized work well at first, but if drivers learn that the actual level of arrests and convictions is very low, within a few months the laws have little deterrent effect.

Administrative License Revocation (ALR) laws are another option used by 33 states and the District of Columbia as of 1993 to enforce drunken driving laws. ALR allows an arresting officer to immediately confiscate the driver's license of a driver who has a BAC over the legal limit or who refuses to take a BAC test. The officer usually then issues a temporary driver's permit valid for a short time (10 to 15 days), and the driver is notified of his or her rights for an administrative hearing to appeal the license revocation. If there is no appeal, the revocation is upheld and the driver loses their license. (Ninety days for a first offense and longer for subsequent offenses in most states where ALR laws exist.)

In addition to laws against drunken driving, there a number of actions and programs that seek to reduce the overall use of alcohol in order to limit drunken driving. The most notable of these is the federal government's setting of the national minimum purchase for alcoholic beverages at 21 in 1988. Federal legislation was passed in 1987 to withhold highway construction funds from states that did not adopt this age standard. As of 1996, all 50 states have complied with the federal standard. It should be noted that in 1996 Louisiana actually reduced its age minimum to 18, after an appeal to a state court. However, in July 1996, the Louisiana Supreme Court reversed the lower court, making 21 Louisiana's minimum age for purchasing alcoholic beverages.

The designated driver program is another method to reduce the number of people who drink and drive. This program encourages people who drink to select one member of their group to abstain from alcohol in order to drive the other group members to their destinations. A 1991 Roper Poll found that 37% of adults reported that they had served as a designated driver.

Some states have instituted responsible beverage service programs. These programs seek to change the environment surrounding drinking by establishing in bars, restaurants and hotels strict age identification practices; the discouragement of intoxication; improved customer service; and the provision of nonalcoholic beverages.

Young people: About 50% of all fatally injured drinking drivers are less than 30 years old. More than 40% of all ADOLESCENT (in this case, 15–19 years old) deaths result from motor vehicle crashes. Alcohol is a factor in 40%–60% of all fatal crashes involving young people. Young people are inexperienced in both drinking and driving and, therefore, are at a particularly high risk of being involved in a traffic accident. In addition they are more likely to combine alcohol with other drugs which may cause a synergistic effect. This effect is far more severe than that caused by either alcohol or another drug alone.

Drugs other than alcohol: Drugs taken in combination (even in therapeutic doses) can also have an ADDITIVE EFFECT on concentration levels, coordination and, consequently, on driving skills. The consumption of alcohol, for example, increases the depressant effect that over-the-counter sleeping aids have on the central nervous system

While a lot has been written on the effects of alcohol and driving, there is less information available about driving and the use of illegal drugs. Several factors contribute to this. One reason may be that there are fewer people who use illegal drugs (5% of the frequency of alcohol). Another reason is that in contrast to alcohol testing of drivers, in most states there are legal limitations placed on drug testing. Also, drug use often goes undetected since no apparatus measures other drug use as efficiently as the on-site breathlyzer. Drivers who have been drinking can be seen leaving bars and getting into their cars, while users of other drugs naturally tend to be more discreet about their drug use.

One 1981 NHTSA study covered 497 drivers injured in motor vehicle accidents and treated at a hospital. The results were considered conservative because only drivers who consented to blood analysis were included in the sample. The results of the study showed 38% of the drivers had alcohol or some other drug in their system: alcohol was found in 25% of the drivers; THC (TETRAHYDROCANNABINOL) —the active agent in marijuana—in 9.5%; and tranquilizers in 7.5%. Two or more drugs had been ingested by 10% of the drivers. A negligence rate of 74% was found in drivers who were legally intoxicated (BAC of 0.10%). Drivers with lower alcohol levels had a negligence rate of 54%, and those with THC in their system had a rate of 53%. Drivers with tranquilizers in their system were considered negligent in 22% of their accidents. By comparison, drug-free drivers had a negligence rate of 34%. This evidence, along with the results of similar studies, strongly suggests that marijuana interferes with driving skills, perception, coordination, attention, visual awareness and reaction time. Unlike alcohol, however, the effects of which dissipate quickly when consumed in reasonable amounts, marijuana may impair performance in decrements that persist for some time, possibly hours beyond the time that someone actually considers himself or herslf to be "high." The danger is that someone in this condition would drive without realizing that their ability was still impaired. Because the effects of cannabis are so different from the effects of alcohol (one does not have the tendency to act recklessly, or thoughtlessly after smoking), it is common for marijuana smokers to be unaware of their impaired driving ability—perhaps thinking that due to their increased concentration and the fact that they may be driving even more slowly than usual, that it is safe for them to be on the road. Studies, however, have conclusively proved that this is not the case.

Robert D. Arnold, "Effect of Raising the Legal Drinking Age on Driver Involvement in Fatal Crashes: The Experience of Thirteen States," NHTSA Technical Report no. DOS HS 806 902 (Washington, D.C.: National Highway Transportation Safety Administration [NHTSA], 1985).

John R. DeLuca, ed., *Fourth Special Report to the U.S. Congress on Alcohol and Health* (Rockville, Md.: National Institute on Alcohol Abuse and Alcoholism, 1981): 81, 82, 131, 132, 157, 158.

Enoch Gordis, M.D., ed., *Seventh Special Report to the U.S. Congress on Alcohol and Health* (Rockville, Md.: NIAAA, 1990).

R. Hingson et al., "Effects of Maine's 1981 and Massachusetts' 1982 Driving-Under-the-Influence Legislation," *American Journal of Public Health* 77, no. 5 (1987): 593–597.

Insurance Institute for Highway Safety, *To Prevent Harm* (Washington, D.C., 1978).

H. Kletta, "On the Possibilities for the Police to Detect Low Blood Alcohol Concentrations," *Alcohol and Highway Safety*, Swedish Government Committee Report (1970): 61.

Joy Moser, *Prevention of Alcohol-Related Problems* (Toronto: World Health Organization, 1980): 211–218.

National Highway Traffic Safety Administration (NHTSA), National Center for Statistics and Analysis, *Drunk Driving Facts* (Washington, D.C., 1988).

M. W. Perrine, J. A. Waller and L. S Harris, *Alcohol and Highway Safety: Behavioral and Medical Aspects, Department of Transportation NHTSA Technical Report* (Washington, D.C., 1971).

dropper   A medicine dropper used for injecting heroin when a needle is attached to its tip. The bulb acts as a plunger and the glass portion acts as the barrel. A dropper is sometimes favored over a regular hypodermic because it gives an addict more control over injecting the heroin. They are also commonly used when no hypodermic is available.

drowning   Drowning is the third leading cause of accidental death in the U.S., with alcohol involved in an estimated 38% of deaths by drowning. Of the 946 boating fatalities in 1988, 788 or 83% were the result of drowning. Research has shown that a person under the influence of alcohol is much more susceptible to drowning than a person who is sober. Reasons for this include disorientation, exacerbated thermal responses to water temperature, and impairment of psychomotor skills and breath-holding time. (See BOATING ACCIDENTS.)

Centers for Disease Control, *Morbidity and Mortality Weekly Report* 39, no. 11 (March 23, 1990).

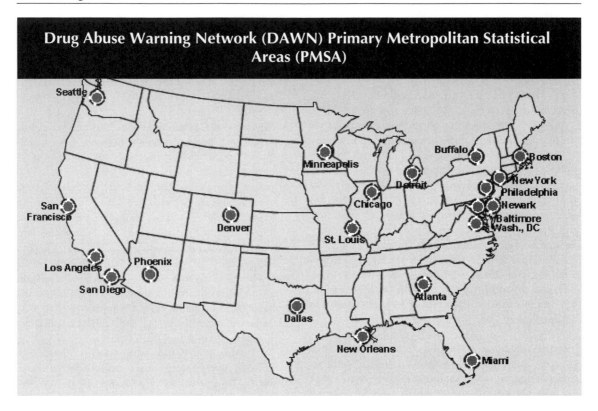

Drug Abuse Warning Network (DAWN) Primary Metropolitan Statistical Areas (PMSA)

National Transportation Safety Board (NTSB), *Safety Study: Recreational Boating Safety and Alcohol,* NTSB no. 55-83-02, NTIS no. PB83-917006 (Washington, D.C.: NTSB, 1983).

U.S. Coast Guard (USCG), *Boating Statistics,* 1988 (Washington, D.C., 1989).

Drug Abuse Control Amendment of 1956   This act established the Bureau of Drug Abuse Control within the U.S. Department of Health Education and Welfare (subsequently transformed into two departments: the Department of Health and Human Services and the Department of Education) with the goal of regulating hypnotics and stimulants such as barbiturates and amphetamines. The act shifted the constitutional basis of drug-control responsibilities from the government's taxing power, vested in the Treasury Department, to that of the government's power to control interstate commerce. (See MARIJUANA.)

Drug Abuse Warning Network (DAWN)   A network founded in 1972 by the Bureau of Narcotics and Dangerous Drugs to provide information on medical and psychological problems associated with the effects of drug use. The network identifies patterns and trends in drug use and pinpoints those drugs that are bringing users into emergency facilities. Data are received from such sources as general hospital emergency rooms, medical examiners and coroners, and crisis intervention centers and fed into DAWN. There are approximately 15,000 new case descriptions a month. The network issues quarterly reports describing current drug emergencies and whether or not the people concerned are in treatment. Presently funded and administered by the National Institute on Drug Abuse (NIDA), it derives information from 26 metropolitan areas and detects trends such as which drugs are being taken for what purposes and by whom.

drug addiction in the movies   The Hays Commission, America's early film censor, forbade depictions of drug addiction in movies. As a result, the Sherlock Holmes movie series completely omitted the famed detective's addiction to opium. Since the end of the Hays Commission, three perspectives on drug use have predominated: the hard-hitting drama about the tragedy of drug abuse (*The Man with the Golden Arm, A Hatful of Rain* and *Panic in Needle Park*) thrillers about international drug control agents (*The French Connection*) and atmospheric depiction of the drugged state (films such as *Easy Rider, The Trip,* and *Drugstore Cowboy*).

drug automatism   Taking drugs without being aware of the amounts; as often happens with heavy barbiturate use when tolerance has developed. In order to induce sleep, the user takes more of the drug because of an amnesia about the amount previously taken.

drug control   Defined by the World Health Organization as "The regulation, by a system of laws and agencies, of the production, distribution, sale, and use of specific psychoactive drugs (controlled substances) locally, nationally, or internationally."

Drug Enforcement Administration (DEA)   The lead agency in narcotic and dangerous drug suppression programs at the national and international levels and in federal drug law enforcement. Established in 1973 to replace the Bureau of Narcotics and Dangerous Drugs (BNDD), the DEA was created to enforce the controlled substances laws and regulations. To this end, it investigates and prosecutes organizations and people involved in the growing, manufacture and distribution of controlled substances destined for illicit traffic in the U.S. To expand its facilities and become more efficient, the DEA began working with the FEDERAL BUREAU OF INVESTIGATION (FBI) in January 1982.

drug interaction   See DRUGS and SYNERGY.

drug testing   Testing a urine sample taken from an individual suspected of using illegal drugs or screening large groups of people for drug use. Both practices are common today. Many U.S. companies (the U.S. Bureau of Labor Statistics reported 43% of the

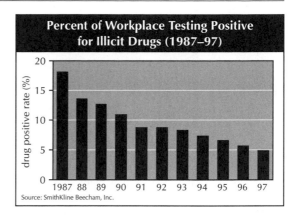

Percent of Workplace Testing Positive for Illicit Drugs (1987–97)

Source: SmithKline Beecham, Inc.

nation's largest firms) had implemented drug-screening programs for job applicants, employees or both. A 1986 executive order signed by then-president Ronald Reagan authorized drug testing throughout the federal government. More than 50 government agencies, including the agriculture and interior departments, have moved to start up testing programs. In addition, the federal government now requires a urine test of railroad employees involved in serious accidents.

This proliferation of drug testing of both public and private sector workers has, however, initiated a growing number of legal challenges from civil libertarians and labor leaders who view the antidrug campaign as an ominous invasion of privacy. They argue that such testing is an "unreasonable search" barred by the Fourth Amendment to the U.S. Constitution. In February 1989, the U.S. Supreme Court, in its first rulings on the drug-testing issue, upheld, by a 7-to-2 vote, the constitutionality of the government regulations that require railroad crews involved in accidents to submit to prompt urinalysis and blood tests. The court also upheld, 5 to 4, urine tests for U.S. Customs Service employees seeking drug enforcement positions.

The U.S. armed services conduct about half the drug tests in the nation. According to the Defense Department, the military drug program costs over $47 million a year. Blanket testing for military personnel began in 1981 and today the military gives more than 3 million drug tests a year to its soldiers, sailors, marines and airmen. Urine testing first became a part of military life during the Vietnam War. Thus far, random drug testing has survived all challenges in the military courts, including *Murray v. Haldeman* in 1983 and *Committee for GI Rights v. Callaway* in 1975. It is assumed that random drug testing was a primary catalyst behind the major drop in illegal drug use in the armed forces from an estimated 27% in 1980 to 9% in the fall of 1985.

In spite of controversy, the practice of drug testing continues to grow among U.S. companies as a result of liability awards against companies held responsible for the acts of impaired employees, anti-drug media campaigns and other factors. A 1995 survey by the American Management Association reveals that approximately 78% of American businesses had implemented drug-testing policies. Also, transportation companies have stepped up the frequency of random (or unannounced) testing. Even so, the rate of employees and prospective employees testing positive continues to drop. Drug testing has even been introduced into the school system despite legal challenges. In 1995 the U.S. Supreme Court approved random testing of high school athletes. Drug-testing policy is affected by advances in technology as well as by legal issues. HAIR ANALYSIS may someday replace urine testing. Presently, hair tests are more accurate, easier to handle and store, less invasive than urine testing and provide information on the presence of most drugs used, including alcohol, over the previous three months (as opposed to urine tests, which, with most drugs, monitor only the previous 24 hours). Its use currently is limited by its high price. Researchers are investigating a drug-testing method that uses human sweat. (See GAS CHROMATOGRAPHY/MASS SPECTROMETRY; RADIOIMMUNOASSAY; SUPREME COURT DRUG DECISIONS, U.S. and THIN LAYER CHROMATOGRAPHY.)

Robert Augoroia, "Protect Safety, Not Drug Abuse," *American Bar Association Journal* (August 1, 1986): 35.
Gilda Berger, *Drug Testing* (New York: Franklin Watts, 1987): 76–87, 100–114.
Alain Sanders, "A Boost for Drug Testing," *Time* (April 3, 1989): 62.

Drug Use Forecasting System   A program developed by the National Institute of Justice in the U.S. Department of Justice that collects vital statistics and drug-use data based on urine tests of people arrested in eleven cities. The program's purpose is to track drug-use trends among urban defendants suspected of dangerous crimes. The Drug Use Forecasting System (DUF) conducted the urine tests on a sample of more than 2,000 arrestees between June 1987 and November 1987.

James K. Stewart, National Institute of Justice (NIJ), *NIJ Reports*, SNI208 (March/April 1988).

drugs   Chemical substances used to diagnose, treat or prevent disease or other abnormal conditions, to relieve pain or to alter the state of body or mind. NICOTINE and CAFFEINE are both drugs in the STIMULANT classification. Alcohol is classified as a drug. Pharmacologically it is a member of a group of compounds generally known as sedatives that act as depressants on the central nervous system. These compounds include barbiturates, "minor tranquilizers" such as Valium, and general anesthetic agents, such as ether. The patterns of misuse of alcohol are similar to those of other drugs.

In the past 40 years, the use and abuse of alcohol and other drugs—prescription, illicit and over-the-counter—has become increasingly widespread, resulting in a significant increase in dual or multiple addiction. A survey conducted by ALCOHOLICS ANONYMOUS (AA) in 1986 showed that 38% of alcoholics in AA were addicted to one or more other drugs. This was especially true of women—46% of women as opposed to 37% of men. Eighteen-year-olds had the highest level of combined drug and alcohol addiction, at 80%. A 1988 study noted that almost 20% of people addicted to alcohol are also addicted to at least one other drug.

Another major problem with combined drug and alcohol use is the danger that arises from the interaction of the two within the body. The *Third Special Report to the U.S. Congress on Alcohol and Health* defined an interaction between alcohol and a drug as "any alteration in the pharmacologic properties of either due to the presence of the other." The report classified three different types of interactions:

1. *Antagonistic, in which the effects of one or both drugs are blocked or reduced;*
2. ADDITIVE, *in which the effect is the sum of the effects of each;*
3. *Supra-additive (synergistic or potentiating), in which the effects of the two drugs in combination is greater than it would be if the effects were additive.*

The supra-additive effect (also known as SYN-ERGY) is the most dangerous because even safe levels of both alcohol and drugs can prove fatal when combined. When alcohol and another drug are present in the system, the alcohol competes for the enzymes that normally would metabolize the drug. The drug then accumulates in the body, when it would normally be breaking down and losing its potency, thus having a much greater impact than it would normally have. This effect most commonly appears when alcohol is combined with barbiturates, which, like alcohol, are central nervous system depressants. Although not quite as dangerous as the synergistic effect, the antagonistic effect can be hazardous when the needed therapeutic effects of a prescription drug are reduced by the presence of alcohol.

Drugs also have a half-life, which is the amount of time it takes for the body to remove half the drug from the system. For drugs with a half-life of 24 hours or more, such as Valium, half the first dose will still be in the body when the next dose is taken. After several days the buildup in the body can be fairly large and the result of taking a drink or another sedative at this point can be devastating.

drunk   Slang for a person who is intoxicated or under the influence of alcohol; also an alcoholic. The state of being intoxicated. (See INTOXICATION.)

dry   Prohibiting the manufacture or sale of alcoholic beverages, as opposed to "wet." A dry county; town. Drys, (plural and colloquial) are prohibitionists. When applied to an alcoholic, it means abstinent. The term also refers, particularly in ALCOHOLICS ANONYMOUS, to someone who is marginally sober and abstinent but who may relapse at any time. Such a person is also called a "dry drunk." (See SOBRIETY.)

dry drunk   One who has stopped drinking but who still craves alcohol. The term, particularly as used by ALCOHOLICS ANONYMOUS, refers to a person who has not achieved real SOBRIETY but exists in a sort of "white-knuckled sobriety," gritting the teeth and trying hard not to drink. Such sobriety is seen as a temporary condition, with an inevitable return to drinking unless the person accepts

help. The term "dry drunk" is also used to describe an experience in which the alcoholic participates, without consuming any alcohol, in a social and emotional occasion (usually in a drinking environment) that he or she associates with excessive drinking. If the psychological impact and aftermath of an experience have many of the aspects and symptoms of a drunken spree, or if the person involved is acting intoxicated in spite of the fact that they have abstained, then both the individual and/or the experience may be referred to as a dry drunk.

DSM-IV (Diagnostic and Statistical Manual of Mental Disorders)   The fourth edition of *Diagnostic and Statistical Manual of Mental Disorders* (including chemical dependency). Like its predecessors, the *DSM-IV* is written and published by the American Psychiatric Society. It is prepared by a vast army of specialists who contribute as editors, assessors, expert advisors, field researchers and so forth. It is intended to standardize diagnoses, and the creators go to great lengths to minimize biases concerning etiology, treatment and prognosis. The *DSM-IV* is the generally accepted diagnostic standard in the U.S. A variety of substance-abuse conditions are included. As with previous editions, the *DSM-IV* is considered a work in process, and planning for a *DSM-V* began before the actual publication of the *DSM-IV*.

dual diagnosis   Two distinct but simultaneous mental illnesses. (See MENTALLY ILL CHEMICAL ABUSER.)

DUI   Driving under the influence. (See DRIVING WHILE IMPAIRED [DWI].)

Duradyne DHC   A NARCOTIC analgesic, containing dihydrocodeinone bitartrate along with aspirin, caffeine and acetaminophen, prescribed for moderate to severe pain. It may be habit-forming and repeated administration can cause dependence. If Duradyne DHC is combined with alcohol or other central nervous system depressants, there will be an ADDITIVE EFFECT. It is a Schedule III drug.

dynorphin   A potent ENDORPHIN found in the pituitary gland of cows. It is about 200 times more powerful than morphine and is one of the most potent endorphins yet discovered.

dysphoria   A generalized feeling of discomfort, malaise or unhappiness that accompanies WITHDRAWAL. All abused drugs occasionally cause a dysphoric state. Antonym: euphoria. (See HANGOVER.)

early intervention   A PREVENTION STRATEGY whereby treatment is offered before the alcohol or other drug user has either developed serious problems (such as physical dependence or major psychosocial dysfunction) or sought treatment on his or her own. Early INTERVENTION is a proactive strategy, and a component of the HARM REDUCTION and risk-management movements.

eau de vie   French, "water of life." Any spirit distilled from wine, especially BRANDY.

ebriate   From Latin *ebriare* (to intoxicate); to inebriate.

ebriety   From Latin *ebrius* (intoxicated). See IN-EBRIETY.

economic impact   The economic costs of alcohol and other drug use to American society is on the rise, both from a decrease in normal production levels and an increase in spending for health and social services, police activities and fire fighting.

A 1985 Research Triangle Institute (RTI) report, "Social and Economic Costs of Alcohol Abuse and Alcoholism," estimated the economic cost at $116.9 billion during the year 1983. The report attributes $71 billion of this to lost employment and reduced productivity, and $15 billion to alcoholism treatment expenditures. The economic cost of alcohol- and drug-abuse rose to $136.3 billion by 1990. In

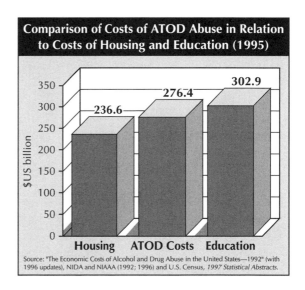

Comparison of Costs of ATOD Abuse in Relation to Costs of Housing and Education (1995)

Source: "The Economic Costs of Alcohol and Drug Abuse in the United States—1992" (with 1996 updates), NIDA and NIAAA (1992; 1996) and U.S. Census, *1997 Statistical Abstracts.*

1995, the federal government estimated that the annual economic cost of alcohol and other drug-abuse was $276.4 billion: $34 billion for medical and treatment costs; $145.8 billion related to illness, injury and death; $51.1 billion for costs related to crime; and $45.2 billion for other costs. (See BUSINESS.)

Enoch Gordis, M.D., ed., *Seventh Special Report to the U.S. Congress on Alcohol and Health,* chapter 7 (Rockville, Md.: National Institute on Alcohol Abuse and Alcoholism, 1990).

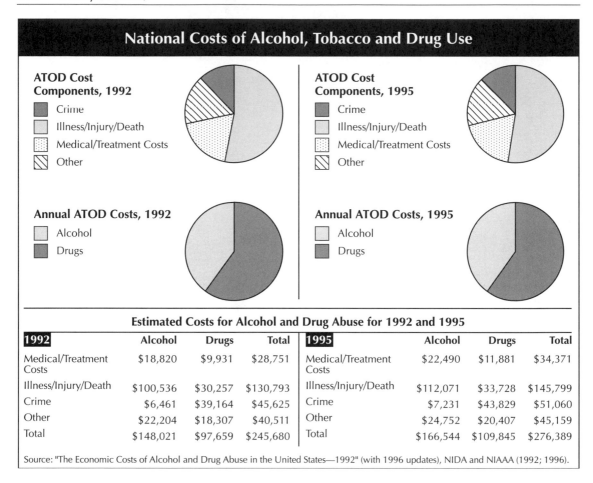

National Costs of Alcohol, Tobacco and Drug Use

ATOD Cost Components, 1992
- Crime
- Illness/Injury/Death
- Medical/Treatment Costs
- Other

ATOD Cost Components, 1995
- Crime
- Illness/Injury/Death
- Medical/Treatment Costs
- Other

Annual ATOD Costs, 1992
- Alcohol
- Drugs

Annual ATOD Costs, 1995
- Alcohol
- Drugs

Estimated Costs for Alcohol and Drug Abuse for 1992 and 1995

1992	Alcohol	Drugs	Total	1995	Alcohol	Drugs	Total
Medical/Treatment Costs	$18,820	$9,931	$28,751	Medical/Treatment Costs	$22,490	$11,881	$34,371
Illness/Injury/Death	$100,536	$30,257	$130,793	Illness/Injury/Death	$112,071	$33,728	$145,799
Crime	$6,461	$39,164	$45,625	Crime	$7,231	$43,829	$51,060
Other	$22,204	$18,307	$40,511	Other	$24,752	$20,407	$45,159
Total	$148,021	$97,659	$245,680	Total	$166,544	$109,845	$276,389

Source: "The Economic Costs of Alcohol and Drug Abuse in the United States—1992" (with 1996 updates), NIDA and NIAAA (1992; 1996).

Henrick J. Harwood et al., *Social and Economic Costs of Alcohol Abuse and Alcoholism* (Research Triangle, N.C.: Research Triangle Institute, June 1985).

L. G. Schifrin, C. E. Hartsog and D. H. Brand, "Costs of Alcoholism and Alcohol Abuse and Their Reaction to Alcohol Research," in *Alcoholism and Related Problems: Opportunities for Research* (Washington, D.C.: Institute of Medicine of the National Academy of Sciences, 1980).

ecstasy (MDMA)   The street name given to 314 methylenedioxymethamphetamine (MDMA), which was first synthesized in the early 1900s. It is currently illegal. A combination stimulant and hallucinogen, its chemical structure is very similar to two other synthetic drugs: MDA (the "love drug") and METHAMPHETAMINE ("speed"), which is believed to cause brain damage.

Called "Adam," "ecstasy" or "XTC" on the street, this is a synthetic psychoactive drug with hallucinogenic and amphetamine-like properties. MDMA is a so-called designer drug, which, according to the Drug Enforcement Administration (DEA), became a nationwide problem as well as a serious health threat in the 1980s, and was implicated in several deaths. Promoted by a few individuals as an aid to psychotherapy, it became the focus of a short-lived controversy, but has not been accepted or approved by any responsible group of psychotherapists.

In March 1989, the West German chemical company Imhausen-Chemie was found by German prosecutors to have been involved in the illegal production and sale of MDMA. Authorities said the firm had supplied U.S. drug traffickers with 374 pounds of MDMA, worth up to $27 million on the

Health Care Costs, the Deficit, Alcohol, Tobacco and Other Drugs

Making the Link, Spring 1995, Center for Substance Abuse Prevention

Alcohol, tobacco, and other drug (ATOD) use contributes significantly to the nation's health care bill as well as the deficit. Consider the following facts:

Former Secretary of Health, Education, and Welfare Joseph A. Califano, Jr. (currently chairman and president of the Center on Addiction and Substance Abuse at Columbia University) estimates that in 1993, the cost to society of alcohol, tobacco, and other drugs was nearly $400 billion—about $1,608 for every man, woman and child in the nation.[1]

Alcohol and other drug use has been implicated as a factor in many of this country's most serious and expensive problems, including violence, injury, child and spousal abuse, HIV/AIDS and other sexually transmitted diseases, teen pregnancy, school failure, car crashes, escalating health care costs, low worker productivity, and homelessness.

A large part of the national health care bill is for alcohol, tobacco, and other drug-related medical expenses. For example, 25% to 40% of all Americans in general hospital beds (that is not in a maternity or intensive care unit bed) are being treated for complications of alcoholism.[1]

28% of all admissions to one large metropolitan hospital's intensive care units (ICUs) were related to ATOD problems (9% alcohol, 14% tobacco, and 5% other drugs). The ATOD-related admissions were much more severe than the other 72% of admissions, requiring 4.2 days in ICU versus 2.8 days as well as much more expensive—about

63% greater than the average cost for other ICU admissions.[1]

Health care costs related to substance abuse are not limited to the abuser. Children of alcoholics average 62% more hospital days than do other children. These increased hospital days result from 24% more inpatient admissions and 29% longer stays when admitted.

The Center on Addiction and Substance Abuse at Columbia University estimates that at least one of every five dollars Medicaid spends on hospital care and one in every five Medicaid hospital days are attributable to substance abuse.[1]

Alcohol is the drug most frequently used by 12–17 year olds—and the one that causes the most negative health consequences. More than four million adolescents under the legal drinking age consume alcohol in any given month. Alcohol-related car crashes are the number one killer of teens. Alcohol use also is associated with homicides, suicides, and drownings—the other three leading causes of death among youth.[1]

Prevention does work. However, different ATOD prevention programs yield economic benefits at various times. For example, if alcohol and drug-taking behavior is reduced among pregnant women, the payoff will be realized within a year. In contrast, the benefits of a successful preschool program may not accrue to society for a decade or more—when these youngsters become adolescents and begin making choices about ATOD use.

For more information, contact the National Clearinghouse for Alcohol and Drug Information at 1-800-729-6686.

[1] Center on Addiction and Substance Abuse, Columbia University, The Cost of Substance Abuse to America's Health Care System, Report 1: Medicaid Hospital Costs, 1993.

Source: Center for Substance Abuse Prevention. "Health Care Costs, the Deficit, Alcohol, Tobacco and Other Drugs," *Making the Link, ML007,* Spring 1995 (Substance Abuse and Mental Health Services Administration; U.S. Department of Health and Human Services).

street. Company officials claimed they were unaware the substance was illegal.

educational campaigns and programs   In recent years there has been a noticeable increase in educational programs and MEDIA CAMPAIGNS designed to build awareness, expand knowledge, change attitudes and modify behavior of the general public regarding alcohol- and other drug-related problems. These various, ongoing programs may be successful, especially in the long run, but the National Institute on Alcohol Abuse and Alcoholism (NIAAA) and the

National Institute on Drug Abuse (NIDA) both believe that more research is needed in this area.

Moreover, studies have shown that efforts to educate drunken drivers are less effective than license revocation. Controversy continues, as well, over the role of ADVERTISING in alcohol consumption and tobacco use. Occupational programs have reported highly positive results and are being expanded into EMPLOYEE ASSISTANCE PROGRAMS (EAPs) offering counseling and referral services for alcohol and other drug use problems detected in the workplace. PARENT EDUCATION is also being studied.

Encouraging progress has been made in increasing physicians' awareness of the importance of early detection, and federal and private initiatives have increased the emphasis on alcohol-abuse education in the medical school curricula. (See HEALTH CARE PROVIDERS.)

effective dose of a drug (ED50)   This term refers to the dosage of a drug that has a certain effect in 50% of the people tested, whereas 25% of those tested require a higher dosage and 25% require a lesser dosage for the same effect.

Eighteenth Amendment   The Eighteenth Amendment (1919), also known as NATIONAL PROHIBITION banned the manufacture, transportation and sale of intoxicating beverages. The Volstead Act provided the mechanism for its enforcement. The Eighteenth Amendment was repealed in 1933 by the TWENTY-FIRST AMENDMENT.

Elavil   An ANTIDEPRESSANT with sedative effects that contains amitriptyline. While the mechanism of its action is not known, Elavil is prescribed to alleviate endogenous depression. When taken with central nervous system depressants it can have an additive effect. Although abrupt cessation can cause mild nausea, headache and malaise, these withdrawal symptoms are not indicative of addiction. Patients who are potentially suicidal should not have access to large quantities of the drug as a severe overdose can result in convulsions, congestive heart failure, coma and death.

elderly   Current statistics reveal that "senior citizens," people over 65 years of age, comprise 14% of American society. By the year 2000, the percentage will have grown to 18%. In view of this increase and the fact that most of us will one day belong to this age group, it is important to recognize the special substance-abuse problems facing the elderly.

Misuse and abuse of medications and other drugs, is common among people over 65 for several reasons. Many older people suffer from a variety of physical ailments for which they receive prescription medications and for which they also self-prescribe nonprescription, over-the-counter drugs. Old age is also often fraught with emotional problems that may prompt further medication. In addition to experiencing frustration as a result of physical deterioration, older people frequently have a new lifestyle forced on them by retirement and respond, not unnaturally, with feelings of loneliness, boredom and uselessness. Lowered incomes and the acute awareness of mortality that comes when more and more of one's friends and relatives die add to their distress. As a result, many older people request and receive tranquilizers and other sedative medicines and many resort to alcohol to alleviate their anxiety. POLYDRUG USE may result from the practice of the elderly person visiting more than one physician without telling one physician what was prescribed by another physician. Additionally, the elderly person may borrow a prescription or OTC drugs from a companion in the hope of saving money on the cost of a physician's visit or prescription. Doctors often fail to explain adequately the purpose and effects of the drugs they prescribe. Forgetfulness may also lead them to take larger than safe quantities of drugs or fail to take doses of an essential drug. People over 65 consume more than 25% of all prescription drugs, at a cost between $2.5 billion and $3 billion a year and even more nonprescription, over-the-counter preparations.

Many older people, then, regularly ingest significant quantities of several drugs. Unconscious, habitual drug taking can have seriously debilitating effects, especially in old age when the system is more sensitive. People over 60 experience adverse drug reactions twice as frequently as the rest of the population. And because the body of an elderly person has a higher fat content than that of a younger person, fat soluble drugs remain in the system longer. Less effective metabolism in old age also contributes to the accumulation of such substances, making the elderly particularly vulnerable to drug interactions.

Older Adults & Alcohol

*OASAS Facts, 1992, New York State Office of
Alcoholism and Substance Abuse Services*

In 1989 older Americans (65 and above) represented 12.5% of the total population. This is a 9.4% increase from the previous 10 years. By the year 2025, older adults will account for 20% of the population. (Update, Alert)

Older adults use 30% of all prescription drugs sold in the United States. Alcohol use in combination with prescription or over-the-counter drugs can cause serious health problems. The combination of these substances can intensify a person's reaction to alcohol, leading to more rapid intoxication. (Illinois)

Statistics show that between two and 10% of the older adult population have alcohol-related problems. Alcohol-related problems are highest among older adults of lower socioeconomic status. (Illinois, Update, Prevention)

Two-thirds of older alcoholics have used alcohol excessively throughout their lives. They are referred to as "early onset" alcoholics. (Older Adults)

Older adults who have developed abusive drinking patterns later in life are referred to as "late onset" alcoholics. Elderly women are more likely than their male counterparts to begin heavy drinking later in life. Late onset alcoholism appears more frequently among older adults of higher socioeconomic status. (Older Adults)

Physiological changes in older adults make them more susceptible to the effects of alcohol. Because of a decrease in muscle tissue and an increase in fatty tissue, older adults are less able to absorb and dispose of alcohol in their body resulting in a decreased tolerance to alcohol. (Special Needs, Illinois, Update)

Older men are four times as likely to have alcohol problems as are their female counterparts. (Illinois)

The criteria used to measure alcohol abuse with the younger population may be inappropriate for older people. Many researchers suggest that alcohol abuse is underreported by the elderly population. They display higher levels of denial. Indicators such as poor work performance and attendance, or driving under the influence are usually not appropriate. More appropriate indicators might include housing problems, falls or accidents, poor nutrition, inadequate self care, social isolation, and new stressors in their life. (Alcohol & Health, Prevention, Update)

Within the elderly population, symptoms of alcoholism are often misdiagnosed as stereotypical signs of aging such as dementia, depression, disorientation, forgetfulness, or confusion. This can sometimes lead to unnecessary institutionalization. (Illinois, Special Needs, NIAAA)

Older adults tend to stay with treatment programs for the duration. In one New York State survey, 70% of the clients over 60 completed the 28-day rehabilitation program compared to 40% of younger alcoholics. (Update, Times)

In a New York State survey, 19% of the males over 65 years old reported heavy drinking (2 or more drinks per day). 0.7% of females 65 years old and over reported heavy drinking. 65% of males in this age group report drinking occasionally, while 48% of females report drinking occasionally. (Alcohol Use)

In 1990 5% of adults 65 years and older admitted to hospitals with Hospital Intervention Services screened positive for alcohol problems. This is a higher rate than for people 19 and younger. (OASAS Bureau of Workplace & Institutional Intervention Services)

(*continued on next page*)

Lack of communication between older patients and their doctors (often they have several doctors) can result in the prescription of contradictory medication—sometimes with serious results.

Alcohol: One of the most dangerous effects of interaction arises with the use of alcohol, the fore-

most form of substance abuse among older people. Research has consistently indicated that alcohol consumption levels are lower and alcohol abuse is less prevalent among people over 60 than among any younger age group. Half of all elderly abstain from all alcohol use. This proportion is even higher in women. Nonetheless, in the U.S. and other countries, alcohol abuse among the elderly is a serious

References

Update: 1992 *Update to the Five-Year Comprehensive Plan for Alcoholism Services in New York State,* Albany, NY: New York State Division of Alcoholism and Alcohol Abuse, 1992.

Alert: National Institute on Alcohol Abuse and Alcoholism, *Alcohol Alert: Alcohol and Aging,* Washington, D.C.: U.S. Department of Health and Human Services, 1988.

Illinois: Illinois Prevention Resource Center, *Prevention Forum,* Springfield, IL: Illinois Department of Alcoholism and Substance Abuse, 1991.

Prevention: University of California, San Diego, *Prevention File: Alcohol, Tobacco and Other Drugs,* 1991.

Older Adults: *Alcohol Abuse and Older Adults,* State of Ohio Department of Liquor Control, n. d.

Special Needs: Jan Heist, RN, *Special Needs for the Chemically Dependent Older Adult,* Wernersville, PA: Caron Foundation.

Alcohol and Health: National Institute on Alcohol Abuse and Alcoholism, *Seventh Special Report to the U.S. Congress on Alcohol and Health,* Washington, D.C.: U.S. Department of Health and Human Services, 1991.

NIAAA: National Institute on Alcohol Abuse and Alcoholism, *Research on the Prevention of Alcohol Abuse in the Older Population,* Washington, D.C.: U.S. Department of Health and Human Services, 1990.

Times: Robert Whitaker, "Alcohol Ruins Golden Years for Some," *Sunday Times Union,* Statistics from Conifer Park, August 20, 1989. Albany, NY.

Alcohol Use: Grace M. Barnes, Ph.D., and John Welte, Ph.D. *Alcohol Use and Abuse among Adults in New York State,* New York State Division of Alcoholism and Alcohol Abuse, Buffalo, NY: Research Institute on Alcoholism, 1988.

Source: New York State Office of Alcoholism and Substance Abuse Services, "Older Adults & Alcohol," *OASAS Facts* (1992).

and growing problem. Survey estimates of the number of alcoholics 65 and over in the U.S. range from 2% to 10% and by the year 2000, it is estimated that 337,000 elderly people will have a major problem with alcoholism. Alcohol-related problems, including alcoholism, are often ignored in the elderly for a number of reasons. DENIAL of an alcohol problem is greater in the elderly and is more likely to be encouraged (or, at least overlooked) by relatives and friends who feel that alcohol is one of the few pleasures left in old age. Alcoholism and alcohol abuse are also difficult to diagnose in the elderly because their manifestations may be perceived as the result of frailty, senility or just the unsteadiness of old age. The symptoms exhibited by alcoholics are very similar to those of nonalcoholic suffering deterioration of cerebral function because of advanced age. And alcohol-related illness may be difficult to distinguish from other chronic illness and from adverse side effects of medicines.

As noted in the Eighth Special Report by the National Institute on Alcohol Abuse and Alcoholism (NIAAA), alcoholism among the elderly has been differentiated into two categories, early-onset and late-onset. Early-onset alcoholism, which accounts for two-thirds of elderly alcoholics, is the continuation of a lifelong drinking problem. The early-onset alcoholic may have engaged in a continuous uninterrupted drinking pattern or may have had periods of sobriety. These elderly alcoholics usually have personality traits and drinking styles similar to younger alcoholics. As a result of more effective treatment, such as proper NUTRITION and antibiotics, more people with histories of alcoholism now survive into old age than in the past. Late-onset alcoholism accounts for one-third of elderly people with alcoholism problems. This group becomes addicted to alcohol after retirement as a result of loneliness, boredom, feelings of being unneeded or through participation in recreational or social activities at which alcohol is frequently served. Additionally, these people may have had little or no experience with alcohol previous to retirement. Stressful situations, such as bereavement, separation from children and physical deterioration, multiply in old age. The elderly who begin abusing alcohol late in life generally have fewer deep-seated psychological problems and are more amenable to counseling than those who become alcoholics at a younger age. Alcoholism is higher among elderly men than among elderly women and highest among widowers and the divorced.

According to NIAAA's *Sixth Special Report,* one study found that around 5% of men over age 60 suffered alcohol problems as compared to about

1% in women over 60. About one-fourth of the people in this country over age 65 take prescribed medications, and the interactions of these drugs with alcohol may pose significant health risks.

Alcohol has a somewhat different effect on the elderly than on the rest of the adult population. Older people generally consume less alcohol, although they are more likely to drink every day, possibly because the slower metabolism associated with aging may induce WITHDRAWAL symptoms in those who have become dependent on alcohol, thus increasing the frequency of alcohol intake. Furthermore, the ratio of body fat to body water increases with age, and as alcohol is almost completely soluble in water but not in fat, the same amount of alcohol intake per body weight consumed by older people results in higher concentrations in the blood and brain.

Treatment: There are several problems related to treatment of alcoholism and alcohol abuse among the elderly. Social agencies for the aged are usually poorly equipped to treat alcohol problems and many alcohol treatment centers are geared to a younger patient population. In addition to staying in the body longer, both alcohol and other drugs tend to have a more prolonged and toxic effect on elderly people. Alcohol also masks pain and other warning signs of illness and disease and can interfere with the therapeutic effects of prescription DRUGS that older people frequently must take. The possible existence of cardiovascular difficulties in the aged person often restricts or prevents the use of such alcohol antagonist drugs as ANTABUSE and TEMPOSIL in the treatment of alcoholism.

Drugs other than alcohol: Chemical abuse in nursing homes is a particularly sensitive issue for the elderly. Less than 5% of the elderly are currently confined to such institutions; two-thirds are women, and their average age is 82. There have been a number of reports in recent years of over-medication of nursing home patients with high-power tranquilizers and antidepressants for purposes of "patient management" (i. e., the convenience of the nursing home staff), rather than because the patients needed these medications. Constant tranquilization can seriously incapacitate a patient as well as simulate symptoms of

senility or physical ailments from which he has not previously suffered. The tranquilizer Thorazine, for example, induces symptoms of Parkinson's disease. Such deceptive symptoms may prompt attending physicians, insufficiently aware of the medication's effect or patient's condition, to prescribe more medication. Advertisements for some drugs promote this misuse of medication by stressing the product's value in "patient management," rather than patient care. In *The Tranquilizing of America,* Richard Hughes and Robert Brewin labeled this practice "the chemical pacification of the elderly." They blamed doctors for their negligence, irresponsibility and general lack of knowledge about geriatric medical problems. Geriatric specialists are few in the U.S., and doctors who treat all age groups are sometimes impatient with their older patients, who generally have numerous complaints and consequently demand a great deal of time and attention. The elderly frequently have little chance of recovery and little money. Sometimes doctors terminate the visits and silence the complaints of what they consider a cantankerous group by simply writing prescriptions that are not really necessary. Hopefully, with increasing postgraduate education in geriatrics, this practice may be on the decline.

A recent phenomenon to come out of the U.S. drug scene is older people selling drugs. The elderly, law enforcement officials say, are being lured into the drug trade by the big money involved. And, say authorities, their relative age is "the best cover around." In Baltimore recently, three men, ages 65 to 69, were arrested at their social club on drug conspiracy charges after police found 308 bags of cocaine worth $7,700.

Other police reports around the country have revealed instances of drug dealing by seniors in Washington, D.C.; Putnam, Connecticut; Trenton, New Jersey; and Jacksonville, Florida. In New York, a 70-year-old man was linked to an intercity drug ring after authorities seized 850 pounds of Asian heroin. And in Puerto Rico, a 90-year-old man and his 70-year-old wife were arrested after police found $45,000 worth of cocaine and heroin in their home.

George Sunderland of The American Association of Retired Persons (AARP) acknowledges that senior citizens are being drawn into the drug scene. Among the reasons are money, excitement, less severe punishment if caught and "feeling back in the mainstream—a big-time operator." Northeastern University criminologist James Fox notes that "as the population is getting older, so is the criminal population." It is possible that many of these elderly drug dealers were involved in drugs for some time but were not apprehended earlier. People who may have first become involved with drugs in the early 1960s (for instance, at age 30 or 35) could be in their 60s or early 70s today.

Sam Meddis, "Seniors' New Deal: Drugs," *USA Today* (June 29, 1989).

electric shock   Also known as electroshock shock treatment. A form of shock therapy in which an electric current is passed through the brain. It may result in convulsions or coma. In the treatment of alcoholism, conditioning with electric shock was once administered in AVERSION THERAPY. Therapy by electric shock is currently used to treat patients suffering from depression, especially those unresponsive to antidepressant medication.

elemicin   An alkaloid found in NUTMEG and believed to have mild hallucinogenic effects.

emetine   An emetic drug (inducing nausea). It is administered in AVERSION THERAPY.

empirin compound with codeine   A habit-forming analgesic prescribed for moderate pain. A Schedule III drug; it contains aspirin, caffeine and phenacetin, along with codeine. No. 1 contains 1/8 grain codeine; No. 2, 1/4 grain; No. 3, 1/2 grain; and No. 4 contains 1 grain (65 mg).

Employee Assistance Programs (EAPs)   Also known as occupational alcoholism programs, employee assistance programs (EAPs) were begun in the 1930s and 1940s, first by DuPont and Kodak and later by a small number of progressive companies. Between 1950 and 1973, the number of EAPs increased from about 50 to 500. By 1989, some 10,000 firms and public agencies, including 70% of the Fortune 500 companies, had EAPs that addressed both alcohol and other drug problems.

According to the U.S. Department of Health and Human Services (DHHS), the highest rate of recovery from alcoholism is found in the office or factory rather than the clinic or hospital program. According to the U.S. National Council on Alcoholism, the average alcoholic will allow his or her family ties to disintegrate five years before he or she loses a job. The rate of recovery for EAP referrals is between 50% and 85%. Critics say these success statistics are exaggerated and maintain best estimates are that only 12% to 25% of patients manage to stay on the wagon for three years.

The National Institute on Alcohol Abuse and Alcoholism (NIAAA) has estimated that 50% of people with job performance problems suffer from alcoholism. Because it is a progressive disease, alcoholism frequently takes as long as 10 to 15 years to reach its middle stages. At this point the worker is often occupying a position of responsibility. Richard Bickerton, a spokesman for the Employee Assistance Professionals Association in Arlington, Virginia, notes that for every dollar spent on an EAP, employers can expect to recover $3 to $5 of loss.

Among the organizations that provide programs for employees with alcohol and other drug-abuse problems are voluntary associations, labor unions and organizations for employees in both the public and private sectors. A variety of counseling services are offered but the basic orientation of most programs is alcoholism identification and intervention. The workplace provides structures for effective early intervention and confrontation. Poor job performance is the best indicator of a possible drinking problem. The rationale underlying the modern approach to employee alcoholism is that any alcoholic, even one in the early stages of the disease, will tend to exhibit a pattern of deteriorating job performance observable by an alert individual. A return to adequate job performance should be regarded as the criterion for judging whether or not treatment has been a success.

There are 120 million workers in the U.S., 15% of the workforce (excluding the military) is in the public sector. Few public sector programs existed before 1972, but gradually, partly because of legislation, their numbers have been increasing. Today, 98% of all U.S. government installations report having alcoholism counseling services.

While many organizations are well served by EAPs, up to two-thirds of workers still do not have access to such programs. This deficit in service is most pronounced among employees of small- and medium-sized businesses. There is also a strong need for programs to help women and minorities. In Canada, women make up about one-third of the alcoholic population, but according to Louise Nadeau, director of the University of Montreal's training program in addiction, only about 5% of them are referred for treatment through assistance programs. Women have a double problem on the job: drinking is part of the process of becoming accepted by male coworkers, but women also have to deal with men's ambivalence about competing with them (as well as their own identity conflicts).

Another group of hard-to-reach employees are those holding senior or high-income positions. Such employees often work in an isolated or insulated environment, frequently change job location, work with minimal supervision or are responsible to multiple supervisors, and have a flexible work schedule. Supervisors often cover up problems they see in senior personnel, and those in senior positions may feel that EAPs are only for lower-level employees. The key to reaching these people is to involve them in the development of the programs, in the advisory and policy-making processes, and in educational awareness programs. When this is not possible, the best approach is through peers and colleagues.

Despite the gain in numbers of EAPs and increase in treatment facilities in the U.S., the vast majority of alcoholics and other substance users are still untreated. Only a meager 15% to 20% of alcoholics get any treatment at all.

Rhonda Birenbaum, "EAPs Failing Female Alcoholics," report of a speech given by Louise Nadeau, director of the University of Montreal's training program in addiction, to the 4th Biennial Canadian Conference on Alcohol and Addiction Problems in the Workplace, Ottawa, *The Journal* 10, no. 12 (December 1, 1981): 3.

William Dunkin, "The EAP Movement, Past and Present," *Alcoholism* 1, no. 4 (March/April): 27–28.

"EAPs Neglect Execs, Shift Workers," report of a speech given by John Harder, director of the Canadian Forces Addiction Rehabilitation Centre, Kingston Ontario, to the 4th Biennial Canadian Conference on Alcohol and Addiction Problems in the Workplace, Ottawa,

The Journal (Toronto) 10, no. 12 (December 1, 1981): 12.

Alan Massam, "EAPs Have Highest Alcoholism Recovery Rates," report of a speech given by Dale A. Masi, director of employee and counseling services, for the U.S. Department of Health and Human Services, to the World Conference on Alcoholism, London, *The Journal* (Toronto) 11, no. 1 (January 1982): 12.

enabling   Enabling refers to the actions of those who attempt to protect substance users from the consequences of their actions. Although these attempts are generally aimed at helping the user, they allow the problem to persist. Any member of society can be an enabler—family members and friends can provide reassurance and sympathy; an employer may find ways of keeping a substance user on the job; doctors and counselors may be overly protective or blind to the condition; law enforcement officials may choose not to penalize offenders. These methods "enable" substance users to continue on their destructive course unchecked. (See CHILDREN OF ALCOHOLICS AND SUBSTANCE ABUSERS and COADDICTS.)

endocrine etiological theories   A physiological approach to the causes of alcoholism, endocrine etiological theories hypothesize that dysfunction of the endocrine system may lead to the development of alcoholism. A pituitary-adrenocortical deficiency resulting in hypoglycemia is believed to cause symptoms that stimulate drinking. Alcohol temporarily relieves the hypoglycemia by elevating blood sugar, but ultimately it intensifies the hypoglycemic condition, causing dependence on increasing amounts of alcohol. To date there is no strong evidence to support this view. (See PHYSIOLOGICAL MODELS OF ETIOLOGY.)

endorphins   Any of several peptides secreted in the brain that have a pain-relieving effect like that of morphine. Other "opioid" peptides include the enkephalins and the dynorphins. The parent compound, proopiomelanocortin, comes from the pituitary and hypothalamus. Beta-endorphin, the major endorphin derivative, is a one amino-acid compound with a potency 1,000 times that of morphine. A variety of behavioral effects are linked to these naturally occurring chemicals, including respiratory depression, analgesia and a sense of well-being. It is thought they may also have psychological effects on blood pressure, temperature regulation, appetite, sex drive and lymphocyte proliferation. Ethanol has been reported to decrease beta-endorphin releases.

enkephalins   Short-chain amino acids that have opioid actions. Endorphin is becoming a collective name for the long-chain and short-chain endogenous opioids.

environment   See GENETICS, SOCIOCULTURAL ETIOLOGICAL THEORIES and CULTURAL ETIOLOGICAL THEORIES.

enzyme multiplied immunoassay technique (EMIT)   Manufactured by the Syna Corporation; a rapid urine screening test to detect the use of drugs.

epena   The Waika Indians of Brazil grind up the bark of the epena tree to make a snuff that has hallucinogenic effects.

ephedrine   A synthetic cardiac and central nervous system stimulant prescribed for asthma, allergies, hypotension and narcolepsy. It is taken mainly as a bronchial dilator and vasoconstrictor of the nasal membranes.

epidemiology   From the Greek *epidemos* (among the people); *epi* (in), *demos* (people) + *logy* (discourse). It is the study of the causes of diseases and epidemics in a population. Epidemiologists research public health and are concerned with causes, frequency of occurrence (incidence), the extent of occurrence (prevalence) and the distribution of health events within society. Epidemiology uses biostatistical tools and methods to quantify and analyze data. A major tool used to study the occurrence of drug and alcohol problems in the U.S.; epidemiological research is sponsored on a continuing basis by the U.S. Department of Health and Human Services (DHHS) through the Substance Abuse and Mental Health Services Administration (SAMHSA) to monitor trends and the extent of drug use over time, based on age, gender, race, grade level (if in school) and geographic location. The leading report on such research is the *National Household Survey on Drug Abuse*.

epsilon alcoholism   The fifth of five categories of alcoholism defined by E. M. JELLINEK. Epsilon alcoholism refers to periodic alcoholism. Less is known about the causes of epsilon alcoholism than about any of the other categories.

Equanil   A minor tranquilizer that contains MEPROBAMATE. It has a potential for abuse and may cause physical and psychological dependence. Symptoms of an overdose include the rapid onset of sleep, and reduction of pulse, blood pressure and respiratory rates to basal levels.

erogenics   Synonymous with STIMULANTS; drugs that stimulate the central nervous system (CNS) and appear to increase the user's capacity for physical and mental functioning.

erthroxylon coca   The coca bush containing the alkaloid COCAINE.

esgic   An analgesic with a mild sedative effect that contains caffeine, acetaminophen and the BARBITURATE butalbital. It is generally prescribed for headache pain and may be habit-forming.

esophagus   In comparison with the general population, smokers, heavy drinkers and alcoholics show a high incidence of esophageal CANCER. Patients with cirrhosis of the liver have blockages of the veins that return blood from the abdominal cavity to the heart. In an effort to overcome the obstruction, esophageal varicosities develop. These enlarged veins rupture easily, causing bleeding that can be profuse. The esophagus itself may tear as a result of irritation and vomiting associated with alcoholism.

ethanol   The active ingredient in distilled spirits, wine and beer, ethanol is a highly soluble, colorless, inflammable liquid produced by the reaction of fermenting sugar with yeast spores. Distillation can produce 96%–100% ethanol, also called ABSOLUTE ALCOHOL. It can also be produced in small amounts in the human intestines when dietary sugars are fermented, but it is then detoxified by a liver enzyme called alcohol dehydrogenase.

ethchlorvynol   Brand name: Playcidyl. A nonbarbiturate sedative hypnotic. Symptoms of an overdose are similar to those of BARBITURATES and the user can become dependent. It is frequently abused and is sometimes detectable because it gives the breath an applelike odor.

ether   A volatile anesthetic produced by distilling alcohol with sulfuric acid. Its medical usage began in the early 1800s and because of its euphoriant effects (similar to alcohol), ether sniffing became quite popular. It was also taken orally as a less expensive intoxicant than alcohol. Ether is seldom used today

ethical issues, drugs and   In *Drug Abuse: The Impact on Society*, Gilda Berger discusses at length the fundamental question: "Is violating people's rights justifiable when protecting the community against drugs? Or is it better to stick to the letter of the law and risk letting drug criminals get away?"

Various national polls show that the American public considers drug use the nation's number-one problem. Government officials at all levels—national, state and local—have increased efforts and taken stronger measures to combat drugs. Despite notable victories, most authorities (including William J. Bennett, director of the Office of National Drug Control Policy during the Bush Administration) seemed to agree that the war against drugs and drug use is being lost. This led to even tougher strategies, some of which have been sharply criticized. Chief among them are drug testing and greater penalties (including seizure of personal assets of drug dealers and, in some instances, users) for drug violators. (See BOOTY.) Certain state governors, big-city mayors and other lawmakers have urged the U.S. Congress to create a death penalty for drug dealers. The purpose of the various stronger measures under consideration is to send a powerful message to both drug sellers and users that the country is serious in its determination to control the drug epidemic. Critics say measures that violate individual rights when attempting to protect communities from the drug scourge are wrong. Opponents to more severe punishment admit that the nation has serious problems of drug abuse, but argue that more effective methods must be found to prevent drug abuse and to help users live productive, noncriminal lives. Historically, enforcement has been of negligible value in controlling or eliminating drug use.

Advocates of the legalization or decriminalization of drugs see drug use as a health problem, not a criminal problem. Accordingly, drug users should be offered treatment, not incarceration. They argue that the drug policies of the criminal justice system have not stemmed illicit drug use, while the costs associated with these policies have continued to rise. On the federal level, costs have risen form $1.5 billion in 1981 to $13.2 billion in 1995. Proponents of legalization further argue that the costs for police, prisons and judicial costs would decrease as a result of legalization; these funds could then be freed up to be spent on treatment. Additionally, they argue that violence and other crime related to drug trafficking would be reduced if not completely eliminated because the profitability of illegal drug dealing would be minimal once the costs of formerly illegal substances were lowered due to their availability. Advocates for this view frequently point to the example of the prohibition of alcohol and the rise in alcohol-related trafficking crimes in the U.S. in the 1920s and early 1930s as a basis for their argument. This argument is often countered with the claim that there would be an enormous rise in costs related to health and economic productivity, as well as social cost to the community. The decriminalization of heroin sale and use in a designated park in Switzerland is given as an example of such a policy's dramatic failure. The rate of heroin-related deaths in Switzerland became the highest in Europe; the park experiment was discontinued. However, ongoing alternatives are being initiated and have been established in England, the Netherlands and elsewhere with greater success.

Gilda Berger, *Drug Abuse: The Impact on Society* (New York: Franklin Watts, 1988): 119–127.

ethinamate   A nonbarbiturate mild sedative hypnotic used when deep hypnosis is not needed. (See VALMID.)

ethnopharmacology   The study of human beings in relation to drug use, with special emphasis on the social, cultural and historical aspects of the subject.

ethylmorphone hydrochloride   An OPIUM derivative.

etiological theories of alcoholism and other drug dependence   Because of the complex nature of alcoholism and other drug dependence, there are numerous theories as to its cause. To date much is still unknown regarding the etiology of alcoholism and other drug dependence and no one theory completely explains the syndrome. The current theories generally can be divided into three main categories.

One main category is PHYSIOLOGICAL MODELS OF ETIOLOGY. Theories in this category postulate that people are predisposed to develop alcoholism in particular because of some organic defect. They include ETIOLOGICAL THEORIES, ENDOCRINE ETIOLOGICAL THEORIES and GENETIC theories.

A second main category is PSYCHOLOGICAL MODELS OF ETIOLOGY. Most psychological theories postulate that some flaw in the personality structure leads to the development of alcoholism and other drug dependence. Among these is the theory, originally advanced by Freud, of ORAL FIXATION. Behavioral learning theories are another psychological model.

A third category of theories on the causes of alcoholism and other drug dependence is SOCIOCULTURAL ETIOLOGICAL THEORIES, also known as CULTURAL ETIOLOGICAL THEORIES. These theories postulate relationships between various factors in society, such as ethnic and cultural differences, and the incidence of alcohol and other drug use. Also in this category are CULTURAL STRESS ETIOLOGICAL THEORIES.

In addition, there is a category known as Moral Etiological Theory, which holds that alcoholism and other drug use and dependency is either a moral fault or a sin of the alcoholic or drug user. Once almost universally embraced in western countries, this theory is now most commonly held by fundamentalist religious organizations.

etiology   From the Greek *aitia* (cause) + *logos* (discourse). The science of causes, especially the investigation of the causes and origins of disease.

ETOH, Alcohol & Alcohol Problems Science Database   ETOH, the Alcohol and Alcohol Problems Science database produced by the National Institute on Alcohol Abuse and Alcoholism (NIAAA) is the most comprehensive online resource coverage of alcohol-related and behavioral research. The information it provides consists of bibliographic records with abstracts of scientific references from U.S. and foreign sources. Included are journal articles, books and monographs, selected book chapters, reports, conference papers and proceedings, unpublished papers and dissertation abstracts. ETOH covers all aspects of alcoholism research: psychology, psychiatry, physiology, biochemistry, epidemiology, sociology, animal studies, treatment, prevention, education, accidents and safety, legislation, employee assistance programs, drinking & driving, health services research and public policy from 1968 to the present.

euphoria   After consuming alcoholic beverages or using other drugs, a user may feel elated, worry-free, and fearless. For an alcoholic or someone who is dependent on other drugs such as heroin, however, the euphoric effect may be reduced because TOLERANCE has developed. While the desire to re-experience the euphoric effect may start new drinkers or drug users on the road to alcoholism or other drug dependency, there is debate as to why they continue to use mind-altering substances. One theory posits that they *have not* yet reached the desired level of euphoria, and therefore, continue to use alcohol or other drugs in hope of eventually reaching that level. The other theory states that because they *have* attained the pleasure they sought, they continue to use drugs to keep experiencing it.

The effect of drinking alcohol on the human brain is almost identical to the effect of ether or most other surgical anesthetics. The first stage, usually corresponding to two or three drinks, is generally one of relaxation and euphoria, not unlike the first couple of whiffs of ether.

Eve (MDEA)   Street name given to 3,4-methylnedioxyethylamphetamine, a combination stimulant and hallucinogen related to methamphetamine and ecstasy (31d4 methylenedioxymethamphetamine, or MDMA).

ex-addict   The term is generally applied to someone who is no longer addicted to a drug. It usually implies abstinence for some minimum length of time (for example, six months, one year or two years), rather than detoxification alone. It also signifies a change in lifestyle, characterized by such indicators as employment, lack of arrests, school enrollment, improved relationships and continuing or completing treatment. The term is felt by many clinicians to be inaccurate, since addiction is considered to be a chronic condition. The term recovering addict is suggested by many as more accurate.

exogenous opioids   Opioid substances produced externally, such as those found in milk and plant proteins. Also called "exorphins."

experimental drug use   A short-term nonpatterned trial period of drug use, usually motivated by curiosity or by the desire to assess anticipated drug effects. Experimental use of drugs happens most often in the company of one or more friends or social acquaintances. It may or may not lead to a heavier involvement in drug use.

eyes   Traditionally considered the "windows to the soul," the eyes can reveal a good deal about a person's drug use. Bloodshot eyes, for example, may betray the use of marijuana or heavy alcohol consumption, while dilated pupils are the classic telltale sign of LSD and stimulant ingestion. Although most types of drugs exert some effect on the eyes, no ocular diseases or other damage to the eyes seems to be precipitated by short- or long-term use of most recreational drugs, with the notable exception of alcoholic amblyopia. This rare disease appears most commonly in male alcoholics who also smoke. It involves painless, progressive blurring of the vision thought to be the result of a toxic reaction in the orbital portion of the optic nerve. If unchecked, the disease may progress to include degeneration of the optic nerve, but it is otherwise reversible with abstinence and a vitamin and mineral treatment program.

By affecting areas of the brain that control sensory perceptions, large doses of alcohol disturb the vision and other senses. Alcohol congests blood vessels in the eyes, causing "red eye." It also relaxes certain eye muscles, thereby interfering with the eyes' ability to focus, and slows adjustment reactions. These two effects result in double vision—common in those who are intoxicated. Nystagmus, involuntary oscillation of the eyeball, may also be present in cases of sedative intoxication. Horizontal nystagmus is most common in barbiturate and other sedative intoxications, but PCP can also cause vertical nystagmus.

Constricted pupils accompany opiate use, but extreme tearing, dilated pupils and double vision occur during withdrawal. Dilated pupils, which can cause photophobia, result from using hallucinogens, certain solvents and stimulants.

Psychedelic drugs cause intense visual hallucinations, often consisting of brightly colored geometric designs seen especially when the eyes are closed. These hallucinations, prolonged afterimages and sensory interaction such as hearing colors and seeing sounds (synesthesis), all seem to be manifestations of the drug's effect on the central nervous system.

Cocaine gained international recognition in the 19th century after Freud and his colleague Koller endorsed it as a local anesthetic for eye surgery. The drug acts directly to anesthetize the corneal sensory nerve, but is rarely used medically any more. THC (the active ingredient in marijuana), however, is beginning to enjoy professional approval in the treatment of open angle glaucoma, which it relieves by lowering pressure within the eyeball.

F

falls Falls, a major cause of trauma, account for more accidental deaths than any other cause except automobile ACCIDENTS and for over 60% of all accidental injuries. All fall injuries in which the victim has a BLOOD ALCOHOL CONCENTRATION (BAC) above 0.10% are considered to have been caused by alcohol. A 1987 review of the literature on falls indicated that alcohol played a role in 17% to 53% of fatal falls and between 21% to 77% of nonfatal falls. A study of over 300 emergency room patients who had suffered accidental falls found that 60% had detectable levels of alcohol in their blood, and 53% of these fall victims had BAC above 0.2%. Risk estimates in this study showed a steep rise in relative risk of accidental falls with increasing BAC. Other studies have shown that alcoholics are more likely to suffer falls that result in death than the general population.

Statistical data relating to the role of drugs other than alcohol as a cause of falls is more elusive, buried within the data intended to underscore the overall risk and illegality of using such drugs.

B. Honkanen et al., "The role of alcohol in accidental falls," *Journal of Studies on Alcohol* 44 (1983): 231–245.

R. Hingson and J. Howland. "Alcohol as a risk factor for injury and death resulting from accidental falls: A review of the literature," *Journal of Studies on Alcohol* 48 (1987): 212–219.

false negative, false positive These terms are used to indicate erroneous results in tests that use measuring techniques. In a screening for drugs, for example, the presence of drugs would be a positive and the absence of drugs would be a negative. A *false positive* would mean that the test indicated the presence of a drug when in fact none was there, and a *false negative* would mean the reverse. Whether a result of personal or computer error, errors associated with the collection or transportation of specimens, or improperly performed tests, all drug-testing techniques are susceptible to false or erroneous test results, especially when improper techniques, identification or storage occurs. The possibility of false positives and the associated legal consequences are one of the primary civil rights arguments used against blanket testing for illegal drug use.

familial etiological theories A sociocultural approach to the etiology of alcoholism and other drugs, these theories place emphasis on the role of the family in providing models and social learning experiences for children. Children tend to follow the parental mode of coping with problems of depression, feelings of inadequacy and rejection. Studies of the family backgrounds of alcoholics have shown an unusually high incidence of familial alcoholism. While this finding may suggest a GENETIC interpretation, the pattern of drinking and the range of circumstances under which such drinking happens are usually the same for both parents and offspring, giving weight to a social learning component.

The family plays an important role in the development of personality and behavior. In various studies it was found that the prevalence of alcoholism among parents of alcoholics was two to ten times that of parents of nonalcoholics. Among siblings of alcoholics there was a prevalence of two to fourteen times that of siblings of nonalcoholics. The rate of abuse of drugs other than alcohol among children of alcoholics is also higher than that of children from nonalcoholic homes, giving further credence to both the genetic heritability of drug-related mental disorders and the negative effects of alcoholic family dynamics on the emotional well-being of children from those families. (See SOCIOCULTURAL ETIOLOGICAL THEORIES.)

David J. Amor, J. Michael Polich and Harriet B. Stambul, *Alcoholism and Treatment* (New York: John Wiley & Sons, 1978): 25–26.

James G. Rankin, ed. *Alcohol, Drugs and Brain Damage* (Toronto: Alcoholism and Drug Addiction Research Foundation of Ontario, 1975.)

Families in Action (FIA)   The nation's first community-based parents group formed to prevent drug use among children and teenagers. Founded in De Kalb County, Georgia, in 1977 to collect and distribute relevant information about young people and drugs, and to conduct research on the effects of drugs, FIA established the Drug Information Data Base.

family therapy intervention   A systematic plan designed to effect change by working with key family members, creatively using the anxiety aroused from disrupting the family homeostasis or status quo. The Johnson Institute model is a more aggressively confrontational approach because it "preps" the family members and key persons in four or five educational sessions in preparation for confronting the chemically dependent person. There are risks involved in this approach. Another family therapy INTERVENTION approach draws on the theoretical concepts of Murray Browen, who said that you can intervene in a dysfunctional family system most effectively by working with the most motivated person to change how he or she responds to the substance abuse. This approach, though slower, is a more subtle process and is considered to involve a lesser degree of risk.

Fastin   An anorectic prescribed for weight control that contains phentermine hydrochloride and has a pharmacological activity similar to that of AMPHETAMINES. Because of this similarity, Fastin has a significant potential for abuse and tolerance develops quickly. Symptoms of an overdose include restlessness, rapid respiration, confusion and hallucinations.

fatty liver   A type of liver damage characterized by an accumulation of fat in the liver. Alcohol upsets the normal METABOLISM of fat in the liver, resulting in an accumulation of fatty acids and can cause changes in the liver after only a few days of heavy drinking. The underlying cause is not well understood, but the primary result may be damage to the liver MITOCHONDRIA, which break down chemical bonds in the complex molecules of nutrients during oxidation. Damage to the mitochondria causes an impairment of the oxidation of fatty acids and results in fatty acid accumulation. When alcohol is consumed with a high-fat diet, the fatty acids that accumulate are derived primarily from the diet; when alcohol is consumed with a low-fat diet, the fatty acids are synthesized within the liver. A low-fat diet is nevertheless preferable to a high-fat diet. (See NUTRITION.)

In one liver biopsy study of chronic alcoholics, 90% had fatty liver. In recent years, the incidence of this disease has been increasing both in the U.S. and Europe. Patients with fatty liver may be quite asymptomatic, and an uncomplicated case is generally considered to be a relatively mild condition and fully reversible. However, in a number of autopsies performed on alcoholics, particularly younger alcoholics, the only common finding was a massive fatty liver.

Federal Bureau of Investigation (FBI)   On January 21, 1982, the U.S. attorney general announced that the FBI and the Drug Enforcement Administration (DEA) would have concurrent jurisdiction over violations of the federal drug laws. The announcement was a result of the serious drug-trafficking problem in the U.S. and the need for a more concentrated effort at all levels. Under the new alliance, the DEA reports to the director of the FBI and the FBI is given concurrent jurisdiction with the DEA for investigations of violations of the Controlled Substances Act. The DEA remains the lead organization in the federal government's assault on drug traffickers and assists state and local enforcement. Drug-enforcement investigators now have the backing of trained FBI agents. They also have access to ISIS, the Investigative Support Information System of the FBI, and the OCIS, the Organized Crime Information System, which retrieves, organizes and analyzes information developed in organized crime investigations.

In the first few months of the alliance, FBI narcotics investigations increased from 100 to over 800, and joint FBI/DEA investigations increased from a handful to about 200. Only seven years into the alliance, the DEA reported a 200% increase in arrests of drug traffickers and dealers and a 300% increase in the rate of prosecutions.

Federal Bureau of Narcotics   A government agency within the Treasury Department, created in 1930. Its goal was to investigate, detect and prevent violations of laws prohibiting unauthorized possession, sale or transfer of opium, opium derivatives, synthetic opiates, cocaine and marijuana. Transferred in 1968 to the Department of Justice, it was merged with the Bureau of Drug Abuse Control to form the Bureau of Narcotics and Dangerous Drugs (BNDD). This bureau, in turn, was replaced by the Drug Enforcement Administration (DEA).

fenfluramine hydrochloride   A synthetic drug chemically related to the AMPHETAMINES. It is prescribed as an anorectic. (See PONDIMIN.)

Fentanyl   A narcotic analgesic and opium derivative. Fentanyl is about 100 times more potent than morphine. It is generally administered intravenously as a preoperative anesthetic for brief anesthesia or for postoperative pain. In terms of drug abuse, the self-administration of Fentanyl by anesthesiologists and nurses has become a matter of great concern in hospitals around the country, particularly after the highly publicized, accidental death of a promising medical resident at New York City's Bellevue Hospital in 1995. Compulsive use is a constant threat with Fentanyl since it cannot be detected by routine drug tests due to the microscopic amounts needed to produce psychoactive effects. Fentanyl is also the basis for the manufacture of "china white" (methyl-

fentanyl), which is even more potent and is a street drug, frequently used as a heroin substitute. Due to its extreme potency, overdose is far more likely to occur with this drug than with other narcotics. (See SUBLIMAZE).

fetal alcohol syndrome (FAS)   The risk to the fetus from excessive maternal drinking is hardly a recent discovery. The ancient Greeks noted that alcohol abuse by pregnant women often resulted in harmful effects to their unborn children. The so-called "gin epidemic" in London during the 1700s drew attention to a connection between alcohol abuse and inflated rates of birth defects. However, fetal alcohol syndrome was only recognized as a clinical entity in 1973, through the efforts of Kenneth L. Jones and David W. Smith of the University of Washington in Seattle (who utilized studies done a few years earlier by Christie Ulleland, also of the University of Washington).

FAS is a major global health problem. In the U.S., alcohol-related birth defects are among the leading causes of congenital mental disorders, ranking with Down's Syndrome and Spina Bifida. Of the three, only alcohol-related defects are preventable. Treatment costs for FAS in the U.S. were estimated at nearly a third of a billion dollars per year in 1988 and have continued to rise. In 1976 French investigators reported worldwide stillbirth rates (associated with maternal drinking) of 9.9 per 1,000 for light drinkers, 25.5 per 1,000 for heavy drinkers, and 50.5 per 1,000 for women who both drank and smoked heavily. On the basis of a survey of 19 published worldwide epidemiological studies on FAS frequency, it was estimated that the incidence of FAS is 1.9 cases per 1,000 live births. Reported rates were higher in North America than in Europe (2.9 vs. 1.1 per 1,000). As of 1998, the revised estimate was lowered to 1 FAS case per 750 live births. (The exclusion of data on certain high-risk groups in the later study may explain the disparity in the analyses). The numbers of FAS cases could be as much as three times higher than current estimates, which are based on criteria that are restrictive and exclusive.

When a woman drinks alcohol during pregnancy, she puts her child at risk of being born with fetal alcohol syndrome, with any or all of a series of abnormalities, including growth deficiencies, physical malformations and mental retardation. (Because

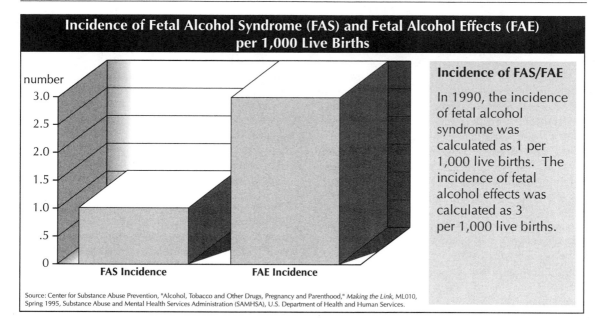

Incidence of Fetal Alcohol Syndrome (FAS) and Fetal Alcohol Effects (FAE) per 1,000 Live Births

Incidence of FAS/FAE

In 1990, the incidence of fetal alcohol syndrome was calculated as 1 per 1,000 live births. The incidence of fetal alcohol effects was calculated as 3 per 1,000 live births.

Source: Center for Substance Abuse Prevention, "Alcohol, Tobacco and Other Drugs, Pregnancy and Parenthood," *Making the Link*, ML010, Spring 1995, Substance Abuse and Mental Health Services Administration (SAMHSA), U.S. Department of Health and Human Services.

FAS is not based on one single feature observable in all cases, it is sometimes appropriately referred to as "fetal alcohol effects," FAE.) Certain features, however, are common to most cases of FAS. Newborn babies and fetuses frequently fail to reach normal length. At age one, children with FAS are, on average, only 65% of normal length. They are also below normal weight, tend to remain thin and small as they get older and have unusually small head circumference. Most have elongated folds in their eyelids, causing eye slits. Other physical abnormalities that appear frequently include low nasal bridge, short nose, indistinct philtrum (the vertical groove between the nose and mouth), narrow upper lip, small chin and flat midface. About 30% of children with FAS have heart defects. The effects of FAS on the central nervous system include retarded mental and motor development, tremors, hyperactivity and poor attention span. The average IQ of children with FAS is approximately 68 (as opposed to 100 for nonafflicted children). Varying degrees of mental deficiency are the most common signs of FAS. Such children show no improvement with time, even when placed in supportive atmospheres.

Effects: When a pregnant woman drinks, alcohol passes freely across the placental barrier into the baby's bloodstream in concentrations at least as high as those in the mother. (See BLOOD ALCOHOL CONCENTRATION.) The metabolic system of the fetus, however, is not as equipped to handle the effects of alcohol as is the mother's system. The undeveloped liver of the unborn baby burns up alcohol at less than half the rate of the adult liver, so that alcohol remains in the fetal system longer. Deficiencies of VITAMINS AND MINERALS resulting from maternal drinking will be harmful to the fetus. Alcoholic women commonly suffer from insufficient amounts of calcium, magnesium, zinc, folic acid and thiamine, all of which play an important role in fetal development. Low zinc content in certain infant diets has resulted in limited growth. Deficiencies of folic acid and thiamine may play a role in fetal malformations and central nervous system lesions. Research in this area is still in its early stages.

Sudden WITHDRAWAL from alcohol by the mother during pregnancy may subject the fetus to major metabolic and physiologic disturbances. However, withdrawal under controlled conditions with progressively reduced doses of alcohol will be far more advantageous for the fetus than continued drinking. Controlled withdrawal can result in rebound growth in the infant, compensating for an earlier disruption. Heavy drinking is often associated with heavy SMOKING, which can also impair the development of the fetus. Smoking mothers generally have a high percentage of low-birth-weight infants.

How much alcohol is safe?   Although most documented cases of FAS have been children of women whose drinking meets the criteria of alcoholism, it is not yet known exactly how much alcohol is harmful to the fetus. Many organizations, such as the National Institute on Alcohol Abuse and Alcoholism (NIAAA) and the American Medical Association Panel on Alcoholism, recommend complete abstinence from alcohol during pregnancy. The March of Dimes, which once held that such a prohibition unnecessarily frightened women, now recommends total abstinence as well.

Researchers currently believe that the harmful effects of prenatal exposure to alcohol exist on a continuum, ranging from extreme structural defects at one end to very subtle cognitive-behavioral dysfunction at the other. The inability to test for a "threshold dose" above which FAS or FAE is a danger leads most experts and organizations to prescribe extreme caution until more is known about whether or not any level of alcohol intake is safe. (See BABIES, DRUG-ADDICTED AND -EXPOSED.)

E. L. Abel, *Fetal Alcohol Syndrome (FAS) and Fetal Alcohol Effects* (New York: Plenum, 1984).

E. L. Abel and R. J Sokol, "Incidence of Fetal Alcohol Syndrome and Economic Impact of FAS-Related Anomalies," *Drug and Alcohol Dependence* 19 (1987): 51–70.

E. L. Abel and R. J. Sokol, "A Revised Conservative Estimate of the Incidence of FAS and its Economic Impact," *Alcohol and Clinical Experimental Research* 15 (1991): 514–524.

Judy Dobbie and Philippa Bell, *Fetal Alcohol Syndrome* (Toronto: Addiction Research Foundation of Ontario, 1978).

Enoch Gordis, M.D., ed., *Seventh Special Report to the U.S. Congress on Alcohol and Health,* chapter VI (Rockville, Md.: National Institute on Alcohol Abuse and Alcoholism, 1990).

G. C. Robinson, J. L. Conry and R. F. Conry, "Clinical Profile and Prevalence of FAS in an Isolated Community in British Columbia," *Canadian Medical Association Journal* 137 (1987): 203–207.

Henry L Rosett, "Clinical Pharmacology of the Fetal Alcohol Syndrome," in *Biochemistry and Pharmacology of Ethanol,* ed. Edward Majchrowicz and Ernest P. Noble, vol. 2 (New York: Plenum, 1979): 485–509.

K. Warren, "Alcohol-Related Birth Defects: Current Trends in Research," *Alcohol Health & Research World* (Fall 1985): 4.

Finland   The government of Finland has taken a particularly active role in dealing with its problems of alcohol and other drug use. National policy has addressed both supply and treatment.

Alcohol: The per capita consumption of alcohol in Finland is in line with that of most other European nations, but for a variety of reasons specific to this country it has nevertheless been a cause for concern. This concern led in 1959 to the consolidation of studies on alcohol consumption issues, previously handled by various temperance societies, within a national Foundation for Alcohol Studies, a branch of the State Alcohol Monopoly, which regulates liquor sales throughout the country.

A popular drink in Finland is a distilled vodka called *viina.* In liters of ABSOLUTE ALCOHOL based on total population, the apparent per capita consumption rate was 6.8 liters, placing Finland 17th among the leading countries included in the 1993 survey of international drinking patterns. Interestingly, Finland places only about 15th among survey countries for consumption of distilled spirits, with a total per capita rate of 1.9 liters for 1993, a decline of 45% from 1985, when the annual per capita rate was 2.8 liters. The per capita consumption rate of wine has jumped from 4.5 liters in 1987 to 8.3 liters in 1993, and to 86.1 liters of beer in 1993 (up from 61.7 liters in 1985), making it the 11th highest internationally in beer consumption.

A tradition of illegal distilling for home use continues in most rural areas; estimates suggest that perhaps 10% of the alcohol consumed in Finland is distilled illegally. Since the country abolished its experiment with total prohibition following a referendum in 1931, legal distribution has been controlled solely by the State Alcohol Monopoly, which maintains restricted distribution centers in cities but has eliminated them entirely in rural areas. To some extent these measures have unintentionally encouraged the national pattern of occasional but heavy drinking that prevails today.

Statistics on alcohol poisoning, recorded by the government since 1802, are particularly high because of the traditional acceptance of illegally distilled liquor. In 1981 (most recent available figures), the rate of death from alcohol poisoning was 5.7 per 100,000 population.

A special area of concern is the territory of Lapland, in the northern part of the country. Deprived of liquor stores by the State Alcohol Monopoly, the Lapps, heavy drinkers, travel great distances to purchase liquor legally or drink dangerous varieties of home-brewed alcohol. Many alcoholics among the Lapps are also known to drink industrial and medicinal alcohol products. One problem confronting those who travel to legal liquor stores is that the trip takes, on average, a full day. These trips are themselves occasions for ritualistic and excessive drinking. Experiments have been conducted to test the effect of local liquor distribution on the Lapps' drinking habits. In these experiments, legal alcohol replaced illegal brews in large proportions, but the overall problem of excessive drinking and drunkenness remained virtually unchanged.

Alcoholism treatment: Beginning in 1962, care of alcoholics in Finland has been regulated by a special "Act Governing the Treatment of Misusers of Intoxicants." However, the Finnish government has provided institutions for the care of alcoholics since 1937. In addition to hospitals, these include outpatient clinics managed by the National Board of Social Welfare and, in eight large cities, voluntary admission A-clinics maintained since 1955 by an independent government foundation. There are also a variety of homes for skid row alcoholics, nursing homes for chronic users of alcohol and halfway houses for young alcoholics. The Finnish Temperance Movement privately funds several programs for the treatment of alcoholism.

Given the acknowledged failure of its experiment with total prohibition, the primary task facing this country of sporadic but excessive drinkers is to encourage moderation, perhaps by finding a way to shift consumption habits away from strong liquors toward beers and wines. At the same time, the country is aware of the danger of changing its citizens from occasional to habitual consumers of alcoholic beverages. Emphasis at present is on increased governmental supervision of public drinking places, such as licensed restaurants, where drinking habits and cultural alcohol trends are most likely to be formed.

Drugs other than alcohol: The use of cannabis, LSD and amphetamines was first detected in Finland during the late 1960s. At that time, the use of barbiturates and minor tranquilizers also increased. In 1968 the National Board of Health withdrew amphetamines from the market and doctors were required to obtain a special license in order to prescribe their use in individual cases. These legal restrictions, however, led to illicit smuggling and illegal manufacture. Cannabis became popular, particularly among youths, and was often combined with alcohol. Increases in drug use led to an extensive study by the National Board of Health in 1971. As a result, rules for prescribing were re-evaluated and a permanent system to monitor drug use was established.

A follow-up study in 1977 showed a decrease in consumption of barbiturates and minor tranquilizers, but a compensatory rise in use of antidepressants and neuroleptics (major tranquilizers). In 1979 to 1980, the use of neuroleptics once again showed an increase.

There is a high incidence of respiratory ailments in Finland due to the cold moist climate, and treatment traditionally has centered on cough remedies containing codeine. As a result, codeine accounted for 80% to 90% of narcotic use in Finland until 1972, at which time the Board of Health revised the control of codeine, significantly decreasing the rate of its consumption. As the use of methaqualone increased, it too was placed under the same sort of control, and doctors had to follow certain rules in prescribing the drug (for example, keeping detailed records of the patients for whom it was prescribed). In 1977, the Board of Health restricted methaqualone use to hospitals. The government's concern and actions have led to a decrease or leveling off in the use of most drugs, and it continues to monitor the situation closely.

According to the U.S. Dept. of State's *International Narcotics Control Strategy Report March 1996:*

Although the rate of narcotics consumption, demand, arrests and seizures rose in 1995 from that of 1994, law enforcement kept pace with the challenge. As a result, narcotics trafficking and use remain only a minor problem for Finnish authorities. There is some concern, however, about an increased flow of drugs from the former Soviet Union, as well as increased use of the Helsinki international airport as a transit point for couriers in the Nigerian narcotics network. Despite some rise in heroin use, Finland's rate remains well below that of neighboring Norway and Sweden, probably due to the success of Finnish authorities in uncovering and preventing attempts to establish local laboratories for processing illegal drugs.

Substance abuse treatment: Finnish social policy emphasizes treatment over punishment for drug users and the development of educational and prevention programs, targeting youths aged 10–14.

Brewers and Licensed Retailers Association, *1993 Annual Report* (London, 1995).

United States Dept. of State, Bureau for International Narcotics and Law Enforcement Affairs, *International Narcotics Control Strategy Report March 1996.*

Hoeveel alcoholhoude dranken worden er in de wereld gedronken? (How many alcoholic beverages are being consumed throughout the world?), 27th ed. (Schiedam, Netherlands: Produktschap Voor Gedistilleerde Dranken, 1987).

M. M. Horgan et al., *International Survey: Alcoholic Beverage Taxation and Control Policies,* 6th ed. (Toronto: Brewers Association of Canada, 1986).

E. J. Immonen, "New Trends in the Alcohol Problem in Finland," *Social Psychiatry* 4, no. 4 (1969): 173–176.

Kari Poikolainen, "Increase in Alcohol-Related Hospitalizations in Finland 1969–1975," *British Journal of Addiction* 75 (1980): 281–291.

Fiorinal An analgesic prescribed for tension (or muscle contraction) headaches. It contains aspirin, phenacetin, caffeine and Sandoptal (the BARBITURATE butalbital). It may be habit-forming and the user may become psychologically dependent. Symptoms of an overdose include respiratory depression, confusion, hypotension and coma.

flashback A little-understood phenomenon of the MEMORY, reported by a small percentage of users of hallucinogenic drugs, whereby the individual re-experiences the drug state, days, weeks or months after the original experience. Stressful or other dissociative states, such as falling asleep or waking up, may precipitate flashbacks. They may represent a form of state-dependent learning: when the nervous system is aroused and ego functioning is diminished, the physical and psychological state induced by LSD or other hallucinogens is reproduced and intensified. Visual and other perceptions experienced and stored during the drug "trip" surface. Since the body eliminates LSD within 24 hours after ingestion, prolonged retention of the substance cannot explain the flashback phenomenon. Nor does the drug affect the brain's structure in any way.

Flashback has been known to result from large doses of amphetamines and may be provoked by marijuana and such substances as antihistamines, nitrous oxide and even caffeine.

Florida, drug cases in According to a 1986 article in *U.S. News & World Report* entitled "America on Drugs," by John Lang and Ronald Taylor, in Florida, TRAFFICKING had grown so phenomenally that it had become the biggest source of income in the state. (See BOATS AND DRUGS.) That year in Florida, cocaine arrests rose 80%, and the burglary rate, 30%. Between 1986 and 1996, other crimes that generate enough cash for a quick fix had also risen in areas of the state where crack is sold.

Until the federal crackdown on money LAUNDERING in 1994, Miami was known as the capital of the money-laundering industry. At one time, Florida banks routinely reported cash surpluses of $6 billion to $8 billion a year—more than double that of other

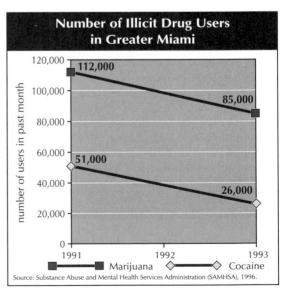

Number of Illicit Drug Users in Greater Miami

Source: Substance Abuse and Mental Health Services Administration (SAMHSA), 1996.

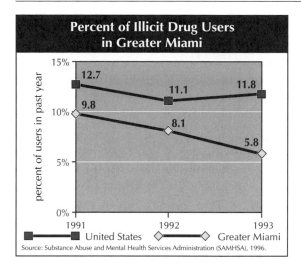

Percent of Illicit Drug Users in Greater Miami

Source: Substance Abuse and Mental Health Services Administration (SAMHSA), 1996.

state banking systems around the country. Agents of the U.S. Treasury Department believe that more than one-third of all Miami banks shared in the huge profits made in laundering illegal drug money. Most of the laundered money, of course, ended up in the pockets of the international drug lords. In 1982 the Drug Enforcement Administration (DEA) found the Great American Bank guilty of money laundering an estimated $94 million in illegal drug profits during a 14-month period.

Gilda Berger, *Drug Abuse: The Impact on Society* (New York: Franklin Watts, 1988).

fluorocarbons   A group of hydrocarbons, chlorinated or fluorinated, now used chiefly as refrigerants. They were widely used as aerosol propellants prior to 1978 and were subject to abuse because of their intoxicating effects when inhaled. In 1978 the U.S. Environmental Protection Agency under the Toxic Substance Control Act banned fluorocarbons and chlorofluorocarbons from use in household consumer products.

Flurazepan   A BENZODIAZEPINE derivative. (See DALMANE.)

fly agaric   A HALLUCINOGEN obtained from the *Amanita muscaria* mushroom. The mushroom is also used as a fly poison, which explains the origin of the drug's name.

Effects: Fly agaric causes various PSY-CHOTOMIMETIC reactions similar to but less intense than those caused by LSD and PSILOCYBIN. As mentioned in the entry on HALLUCINOGENS, it is suspected that the Norse tribesmen used this drug to stimulate warlike rage before going into battle.

The mushroom is consumed whole or mixed with milk or water. As the hallucinogen passes through the system, it remains chemically unchanged. Thus, it is a practice among some users to "recycle" the urine of a person who is intoxicated.

Food, Drug, and Cosmetic Act (FDC) of 1938
The FDC replaced the Pure Food and Drug Act of 1906. This came about as a result of mounting deaths from the use of elixir of sulfanilamide. This product, the first antibiotic, was sold over the counter and had not been tested for safety. Among other things, the FDC Act required that new drugs and medical devices had to be approved for safety; cosmetics had to be proven safe; drug labeling had to include warnings needed to ensure safe use; drugs that were not safe for self-treatment were to be restricted to prescription use; drug manufacturing plants had to be registered and inspected by the Food and Drug Administration (FDA); and medications and colors used in foods, drugs and cosmetics had to be tested in FDA laboratories before their sale. The FDA was empowered to enforce this act.

Food and Drug Administration (FDA)   The FDA is part of the U.S. Public Health Service, a basic unit of the U.S. Department of Health and Human Services (DHHS). The FDA's main function is to protect the public from health hazards involving food, drugs, cosmetics and medical devices. The FDA sets industry standards, conducts inspections of production facilities to ensure regulation compliance, and evaluates and approves drugs and medical devices that require premarket clearance. In this capacity, the FDA has responsibility for approving and monitoring all psychoactive medications. It also initiates enforcement actions and helps inform and educate the public and professionals. The roots of the FDA are in the Bureau of Chemistry of the Department of Agriculture, which was given responsibility for enforcing the Pure Food and Drug Act of 1906. The FDA was formerly established within the Department of Agriculture in 1927 and then transferred to the Federal Security Agency (now the Department of Health and Human Services) in 1940.

formaldehyde   Formaldehyde is a colorless pungent gas formed in the oxidation of methyl alcohol, which is produced naturally in the body in small amounts. Formaldehyde is even more toxic than the ACETALDEHYDE produced by the METABOLISM of ethyl alcohol, but normally the LIVER has ample capacity to break down both formaldehyde and acetaldehyde into nontoxic units. However, if the liver is flooded with ethyl alcohol, as happens when someone has had a great deal to drink, the liver works first to metabolize the ethyl alcohol, at a rate 16 times faster than it breaks down the methyl alcohol. Therefore, methyl alcohol builds up as the liver acts on the excess ethyl alcohol. When the methyl alcohol is finally metabolized, a considerable amount of formaldehyde is produced. This may be responsible for WITHDRAWAL symptoms and may also be at least partially responsible for the HANGOVER effect, which has been shown to begin as soon as all the ethanol has been metabolized.

fortified wine   Wine to which another alcoholic substance, usually grape brandy, has been added during the vinification process. This addition not only increases the alcoholic content of the wine to between 16% to 23% alcohol, but also changes its flavor and character by interfering with the normal fermentation process. The principal fortified wines are PORT, SHERRY, MADEIRA and VERMOUTH.

Fourth Amendment and drug use   The chief legal argument against the practice of "blanket" DRUG TESTING is that it violates the Fourth Amendment, which protects against "unreasonable searches." The Fourth Amendment to the U.S. Constitution states:

> The right of the people to be secure in their persons, houses, papers and effects, against unreasonable searches and seizures, shall not be violated, and no warrants shall issue, but upon probable cause, supported by oath or affirmation, and particularly describing the place to be searched, and the persons or things to be seized.

The Fourth Amendment applies *only* to government searches. It does not legally limit the power of private employers or school officials, except if the principle of fairness—the idea that general searches of innocent people are unfair and unreasonable—is violated.

An exception to the Fourth Amendment is the "administrative search." For example, airport, border, courthouse and certain regulated industry searches have all been determined permissible under the Constitution. Administrative searches (to justify blanket searches) in drug cases have been repeatedly rejected by federal and state courts. Prisons are the only institutions that have the Supreme Court's permission to conduct blanket searches.

Gilda Berger, *Drug Testing* (New York: Franklin Watts, 1987): 50–54.

Fox, Ruth, M.D. (1897–1989)   A prominent psychoanalyst who, in 1959, became the first medical director of the National Council on Alcoholism. A native New Yorker, Dr. Fox performed pioneering research on the use of Antabuse, a chemical once prescribed widely in alcoholism treatment. In 1954 she was founder and first president of the American Medical Society on Alcoholism and Other Drug Dependencies, a forerunner of the American Society of Addictive Medicine. Writer, researcher and lecturer, Dr. Fox also maintained a private practice and was one of the first psychoanalysts willing to accept alcoholics as patients. She was a fellow of several groups: the American Psychiatric Association, the New York Academy of Medicine, the American Academy of Psychoanalysis, the American Health Association and the American Society of Clinical Hypnosis. A graduate of Rush Medical College, Chicago, she also studied in Paris, Vienna and Frankfurt and interned at the Rockefeller Foundation in Beijing. Dr. Ruth Fox won many national and international honors. She died at a nursing home in Washington at age 93 on March 24, 1989.

France   Until recently, recreational drug use in France consisted primarily of the use of alcohol, particularly wine, and tobacco. Changing cultural habits, however, are altering the pattern to include a broad range of narcotics, marijuana, amphetamines and barbiturates. This is not to say that drugs were not previously used (hashish was introduced in the 19th century), only that they have recently gained in popularity.

Alcohol: Throughout the history of France, some brands of alcohol, but especially wines, have played a very important role culturally, socially and financially, and France is still a large-scale producer of wine and other alcoholic beverages. While there are controls on production, the amount of wine produced far exceeds demand despite rising rates of exportation. There is some illicit brewing, principally of rums and aperitifs, both in homes and in larger operations.

The French have a liberal attitude toward the use of alcohol and abstinence is unusual. Any concern over consumption is more likely to focus upon a reduction of drinking to moderate levels than upon abstinence. The French view alcohol as a natural part of their daily diet. Nonalcoholic drinks are often considered too sweet to be consumed with meals or to quench thirst, and in cafes wine is much cheaper than fruit juice or soft drinks. In 1980 (most recent available statistics), one Frenchmen in 10 derived his income directly or indirectly from the alcoholic beverage industry, and one in five French parliamentarians represented the industry.

According to the Brewers and Licensed Retailers Association's *Statistical Handbook 1993,* the French had the highest rate of alcohol consumption in the world (12.3 liters per capita annually, although the rate had dropped from 17.2 liters in 1970). Per capita consumption of ABSOLUTE ALCOHOL was 2.5 liters annually, tying France with Japan as the sixth highest consumption rate worldwide. As might be expected, wine is the most popular beverage and France continues to have the highest per capita level of any country for wine consumption even though wine consumption is decreasing (67.01 liters annually; followed by Portugal, 60.9 liters; and Italy, 52.0 liters). Moreover, while overall consumption of absolute alcohol continues to decline, alcoholic beverages still represented a significant amount of the total of all drinks consumed in France (80%) in the early 1980s. The French drink eight times as much alcohol as fruit juice. After cardiovascular diseases and cancer, alcohol-related diseases are the leading cause of death in France.

Prevention: Because of a growing awareness of the problem, the French government, under Valery Giscard d'Estaing, announced a drive against alcoholism in December 1980. The campaign represented a new political backing for a cause that had traditionally been unpopular. Politically, alcohol abuse has never been a "noble subject," partly because of the enormous power of the wine and spirits industry. As part of this early drive, a committee was set up to study the problem of alcoholism and determine what could be done to reduce it. Aiming to cut alcohol consumption by 20% in five years, the government passed 35 measures in the program to combat alcoholism, including higher taxes on alcohol, stricter application of breath tests for motorists, prohibition of store sales to minors and a publicity campaign.

Drugs other than alcohol: The pattern of drug use in France generally resembles the patterns in other western countries. Nearly all drugs of abuse are found in France, particularly in the metropolitan areas and around the southern ports. Marseilles, in particular, achieved worldwide notoriety during the days of the FRENCH CONNECTION, and there is reason to believe that heavy trafficking and clandestine laboratories still exist in the area. France's long Mediterranean coastline facilitates smuggling and provides almost ideal conditions for the illicit drug trade. During the 1960s and 1970s, most of the heroin for the U.S. market came through France—an estimated 10 tons annually. Morphine base and opium from Turkey and other Middle Eastern countries were converted to heroin in French laboratories and then shipped out. At the time, most of the heroin was exported and little was consumed in France itself. This pattern has now changed and since the early 1980s, heroin has played an increasingly important role as a drug of choice.

Cannabis use (especially hashish) has spread to all ages and social groups and the use of cocaine has also increased. France is a primary point of entry to Europe for cocaine traffickers (generally arriving by way of commercial airliner or boats and ships from South America), and much of this cocaine now stays within the country.

Hallucinogens and psychedelic drugs are rare in France. PCP, which has been a problem in the U.S., has barely made an appearance on the illicit market. The pattern of amphetamine and barbiturate use follows the steady increase found in other European countries but has not reached the magnitude seen in the U.S.

France has also become active in worldwide organizations aimed at stemming drug use, particularly the United Nations Commission on Narcotics.

INTERPOL (THE INTERNATIONAL CRIMINAL POLICE ORGANIZATION) is headquartered in Paris.

Although drug use in France has continued to increase in recent years, particularly in the over-25 age group, there has been a decrease in the likelihood that teenagers will indulge in heavy drug use—an encouraging sign for the future.

Treatment: The government of France is at the forefront of European countries opposing the decriminalization of drugs although support for decriminalization appears to be growing among younger French citizens. In 1995 the French government budgeted $200 million for preventative drug education and continued to expand its experimental methadone treatment program.

Brewers and Licensed Retailers Association, *1993 Annual Report* (London, 1995).

United States Dept. of State, Bureau for International Narcotics and Law Enforcement Affairs, *International Narcotics Control Strategy Report March 1996.*

Hoeveel alcoholhoude dranken worden er in de wereld gedronken? (How many alcoholic beverages are being consumed throughout the world?), 27th ed. (Schiedam, Netherlands: Produktschap Voor Gedistilleerde Dranken, 1987).

freebase, cocaine   In its normal street form, cocaine hydrochloride is not effective when smoked; an alkali and solvent are required to convert it to cocaine alkaloid, called "freebase." The process involves heating ether, lighter fluid or a similar flammable solvent with cocaine—a potentially dangerous process that could lead to burns. It can also be manufactured by adding bicarbonate of soda (baking soda) and ether to street cocaine and smoking the mixture. The result is a purified cocaine base that is smoked in a special pipe with wire screens, or sprinkled on a marijuana or tobacco cigarette. When smoked it causes a sudden and intense high that lasts for less than two minutes.

Crack cocaine is the preprocessed smokable form of cocaine and after conversion to a purified form known as "freebase" can be highly potent and addictive.

Freebase has a lower vaporizing temperature than cocaine hydrochloride, therefore smoking does not destroy it. It is rapidly absorbed by the lungs and carried to the brain in a few seconds. The brief euphoria that results is quickly replaced by a feeling of restless irritability. The post-high after freebase can be so uncomfortable, in fact, that in order to maintain the high, users often continue smoking until they either run out of cocaine or they are completely exhausted.

The custom of smoking cocaine originated in the 1970s in Peru and quickly spread through the South American countries and into the U.S. In South America, cocaine is not processed into freebase before smoking; it is smoked in the form of coca paste, the extract produced during the manufacture of cocaine from coca leaves. Smoking coca paste is extremely dangerous because of the impurities it contains.

Synonyms: white tornado, base, freebase, baseball, snowflake.

freestanding nonresidential facility   A facility that only provides treatment services to clients who visit the facility but who live at home. Freestanding means that no other health care or mental health programs operate at the same location.

French Connection   Led by Jean Jehan, the French Connection was a group of French underworld figures who were the major suppliers of heroin to the U.S. from the 1930s until 1973 when a concentrated international law enforcement effort smashed the ring. Jehan was later arrested in France but was held only briefly, then released.

While it was flourishing, the French Connection dominated heroin trafficking; it had control of smuggling and a monopoly on heroin laboratories. It also had a working relationship with Italian criminals that guaranteed the American market to the French; apparently the agreement was to the effect that if the French sold only to the Italians in America, the Italians in Europe would stay out of the traffic. Of necessity, this agreement required the closest understanding between the highest levels of the criminal underworld in Italy and its counterparts in the U.S.

Although the French Connection operation was allegedly dismantled, it has been suggested that it is not really dead. Heroin laboratories were found in France in February of 1978 and September of 1979; two months later a French chemist was arrested at a clandestine heroin laboratory in Italy. In March 1980, another small lab was seized outside Marseilles, France. Among those who were in contact with the people managing the laboratory was Jean Jehan. In June 1980, three laboratories were seized in and near Milan, Italy; following the raids the French police arrested Jehan at Marseilles. Jehan was released in September of 1980, at the age of 82, for reasons of ill health.

freon   A FLUOROCARBON. It was frequently used as a propellant for aerosols prior to 1978 when fluorocarbons were banned from use in household consumer products.

Friends for Sobriety (FFS)   A recovery support group; Friends for Sobriety was organized by five recovering alcoholics in March 1980 to help people addicted to mood-altering chemicals, including alcohol. FFS offers an alternative, nontheistic recovery program in the belief that most people cannot endure a crisis of religious conscience and the crisis of confronting their alcoholism at the same time. Groups meet for one hour, three times a week, to hold open discussions structured around a nine-step recovery booklet. Emphasis is on both the emotional needs of the recovering individual and the necessity of assuming personal responsibility for one's behavior. FFS is not in competition with other recovery or support programs and encourages members to attend such programs as needed for maintaining their sobriety. The group is headquartered in Paradise Valley, Arizona.

fructose   A sugar that appears naturally in fruits and honey; fructose may help to speed up the metabolic rate at which ethanol is metabolized, but the degree of acceleration of metabolism is thought to be relatively small. The mechanism by which the rate of elimination is increased is unknown. Although adding fructose to the diet may somewhat reduce the HANGOVER effect, it is not generally considered to be a practical or effective sobering agent.

fumo d'Angola   Brazilian for MARIJUANA. This Brazilian reference to Angola, a Portuguese colony in Africa, supports the theory that African slaves may have been the first to bring cannabis to South America.

functional impairment   A person with functional impairment has difficulties that substantially interfere with or limit functioning in one or more major life activities. These activities include basic daily skills, instrumental living skills and functioning in social, family, vocational and education contexts. Examples of daily living skills include eating, bathing and dressing. Examples of instrumental living skills include maintaining a household, managing money, maneuvering successfully within the community, and taking prescribed medication responsibly. The term functional impairment, when applied to children or adolescents, refers to difficulties that substantially interfere with or limit the achievement or maintenance of one or more developmentally appropriate social, behavioral, cognitive, communicative or adaptive skills.

Functional impairment is one criteria for a *DSM-IV (DIAGNOSTIC AND STATISTICAL MANUAL OF MENTAL DISORDERS)* diagnosis of alcohol or other drug use.

G

gamma alcoholism   The third of five categories of alcoholism defined by E. M. JELLINEK (1890–1963), the term *gamma alcoholism* refers to that category of alcoholism characterized by (1) acquired increased tissue tolerance to alcohol; (2) adaptive cell metabolism; (3) withdrawal symptoms and craving, that is, physical dependence; and (4) loss of control. There is a progression from psychological DEPENDENCE to physical ADDICTION. This type of alcoholism does the most damage to both the individual's interpersonal relationships and his or her health. Gamma alcoholism is the dominant form of alcoholism in the U.S. and is the type generally recognized by ALCOHOLICS ANONYMOUS. (See LOSS OF CONTROL, METABOLISM and WITHDRAWAL.)

gamma-amubytric acid (GABA)   GABA, formed from glutamate, is thought to be a major inhibitory neurotransmitter in the brain. Present in relatively large amounts in the central nervous system (CNS), GABA is not found elsewhere in the body. GABA receptors are an important locus of action for the benzodiazepines and the barbiturates, although each has a somewhat different action.

gas chromatography/mass spectrometry (GC/MS)   A drug-screening test that is alleged to be 99.9% accurate. GC/MS is considered as effective in recognizing chemicals as fingerprints are in identifying people. It is the only test accepted in most courts of law as proof of drug use beyond a reasonable doubt.

The GC/MS machine, which costs around $15,000, must be operated by highly skilled, specially trained technicians. To run the test, a tiny amount of urine is injected into a port in the gas chromatograph. The moving gas then carries the sample through a long narrow tube packed with a special chemical. As it passes through the tube, the various molecules in the sample are attracted, whether strongly or weakly, to the chemical in the tube. The various molecules arrive at the end of the tube at different times.

The molecules then pass into a mass spectrometer, which ionizes the molecules and sends them through an electromagnetic field that pulls on the individual molecules with varying force (depending on the mass, weight and electric charge of each ion). Thus, they're further separated. At the end, the machine draws a chart indicating which molecules are present in the urine and the specific amount of each kind of molecule.

The GC/MS test can cost as much as $80 per sample. It is strictly a laboratory tool and cannot be used conveniently on location, for example, in a factory, plant or at an army base.

Simple, fast and relatively accurate new tests for drug use are presently being developed for on-site use in doctors' offices, clinics, corporations, factories and for use in the home.

Gilda Berger, *Drug Testing* (Franklin Watts: New York, 1987): 38–41.

gaseous anesthetics   See NITROUS OXIDE.

gasoline   Inhaling gasoline fumes can have an intoxicating effect similar to that of alcohol and INHALANTS. Extensive inhalation can cause hallucinations, confusion, delirium, lead poisoning, coma and death.

gastrointestinal tract   The gastrointestinal tract (also known as the GI tract) consists of the organs from the MOUTH to the rectum that are associated with digestion. Alcohol passes from the mouth to the stomach, where about 20% of it is absorbed. The rest is absorbed in the upper small intestine. The presence of food in the stomach decreases the rate of alcohol absorption.

Alcohol is eliminated from the body chiefly through METABOLISM in the liver. Less than 10% of the amount consumed is lost through the kidneys, lungs and skin. Consumption of alcohol has a number of deleterious effects on the gastrointestinal tract, depending on the quantity ingested and the susceptibility of the individual.

In addition to the damaging effects of chronic alcohol ingestion on the GI tract itself, alcohol impairs the absorption of certain VITAMINS AND MINERALS and interferes with the NUTRITIONAL process, adversely affecting the entire body.

For the effects of alcohol on the various parts of the GI tract, see STOMACH, LIVER and PANCREAS.

For the effects of other drugs on the various parts of the GI tract, see ADMINISTRATION and the individual drug entries.

gateway drug   A licit or illicit drug perceived as leading the way to use and abuse of other, more problematic drugs. Alcohol and marijuana are widely viewed as gateway drugs. This somewhat biased assumption is based largely on statistical data indicating that people who become dependent on drugs such as heroin and cocaine are initiated into drug use by their use of alcohol or marijuana. This argument could be taken even further: every day drugs such as nicotine, caffeine and even perhaps sugar (which effects metabolism and temperament) could be said to lead to the use of harder drugs. What remains to be studied, however, is the number of people who begin with alcohol or marijuana and never go on to use other drugs and how many of those who develop problems with other drugs might have initiated drug use with other substances if marijuana or alcohol had not been available.

generics   When used to refer to drugs, the term means the chemical name of the drug, as opposed to a commercial brand or trade name for the same compound. For example, diazepam is the generic name for the drug with the brand name Valium. Meperidine hydrochloride is the generic name of the NARCOTIC analgesic, known by the brand name DEMEROL, and fluoxetine is commonly called by its brand name, Prozac.

genetics   Researchers have known for many years that alcoholism runs in families, and research over the last 30 years has begun to confirm the fact that many aspects of alcoholism are due to heredity rather than environmental factors. Currently, most scientists agree that alcoholism arises from a complex mixture of genetic, cultural and social factors. Much of the current evidence for a genetic contribution to alcoholism is derived from Scandinavian studies of the incidence and patterns of the disease among children who were adopted away from their biological parents, as well as that of adopted twins who were separated at birth. Scientists continue to find evidence of a genetic role in a wide variety of studies, including analyses of similarities between certain brain wave phenomena of alcoholic fathers and their sons; examination of hereditary psychological deficits; and studies of biochemical markers for a predisposition to alcoholism.

In April 1990, it was reported in the *Journal of the American Medical Association (JAMA)* that a research team, headed by Dr. Ernest P. Noble of the University of California at Los Angeles and Dr. Kenneth Blum of the University of Texas Health Science Center in San Antonio, had identified a gene that they believed to be linked to a higher risk of alcoholism. The gene, located on chromosome 11, is the "D2" receptor gene for dopamine, a chemical tied to pleasure-seeking behavior, and was found in 77% of the brains of 35 people who had died of alcoholism. The gene was present in only 28% of the brains of non-alcoholics. This statistical evidence is promising, and this study bodes well for future clinical testing for genetic susceptibility to alcoholism, but studies using a larger number of alcoholics need to be conducted. A new National Institution on Alcohol Abuse and Alcoholism (NIAAA) study published in the December 1990 issue of the same *Journal of the American Medical Association* questioned the theory of the proposed genetic predisposition to alcoholism.

Annabel M. Boles, M.D., chief, Section on Genetic Studies, NIAAA, argued that this new study does not support a widespread or consistent association between the (dopamine) receptor gene and alcoholism. The study tested for association in a large population (the control group); in two families with multigenerational alcoholism; and in a group of 40 *living* alcoholics who had been characterized as to age of onset, severity, presence of ASP (antisocial personality disorder) and family history.

In addition to the alcoholics, the authors examined 127 racially mixed controls and two white families with eight alcoholics and six unaffected members. Two different tests were used to detect the specific dopamine receptor gene. The authors wrote: "There was no significant difference in the Al allele frequency between any alcoholic sub-population and the control group. Furthermore, there was also no significant difference between the fraction of alcoholics and controls positive for the Al allele."

In the test results from the two families, close linkage of the dopamine gene to alcoholism was ruled out. Furthermore, there was no significant difference in the frequency of the allele found in those alcoholics who were the offspring of an alcoholic and those who were not.

This study supports the derisive response to the Blum-Noble study by geneticists when the study was released in April.

The most frequently cited studies supporting a genetic role in alcoholism are the Scandinavian adoption studies, which consistently show biological susceptibility to alcoholism even when children are separated from their biological families. These studies have become increasingly sophisticated since the landmark 1960 Swedish finding that of identical twins separated at birth, the chance was on the order of 74% that if one twin became an alcoholic, the other would as well. (In contrast, the concordance of alcoholism between fraternal twins was found to be 26%.) Among the most compelling findings of these adoption studies, was that the biological sons of alcoholics, as well as the biological daughters of

alcoholic mothers, were three times as likely as other adoptees to develop alcoholism. The most recent research in this area has focused on heritability of specific drinking behaviors, such as frequency, quantity and regularity of drinking at particular times. Interestingly, the heritability estimates for these behaviors have been found to range from 36% to 40%.

Among the most important adoption studies was the analysis of Swedish research that revealed the existence of two types of genetic predisposition to alcoholism. The more common type, called MILIEU-LIMITED (or type one) alcoholism, accounts for most cases. It appears in both men and women, is usually not severe, and is associated with mild, adult-onset abuse in either biological parent. Its occurrence is thought to be heavily influenced by the postnatal environment. A more severe type of alcoholism, accounting for 25% of male alcoholics, is called male-limited (or type two) alcoholism. This type of susceptibility was associated with severe alcoholism in the biological fathers of males, and its transmission seems unaffected by environment, leading to the conclusion that it is caused by genetic makeup.

Another line of inquiry is the study of brain wave activity as a potential neurophysiological marker for a genetic predisposition. The most exciting studies have focused on two new electroencephalographic (EEG) techniques for examining deficits in the brain: event-related potential (ERP) and evoked potential (EP) techniques. One particular ERP feature, the P3 wave, was found to have a reduced amplitude in chronic alcoholics. A most startling discovery was that a group of young boys who were the sons of alcoholics, and who had yet to drink alcohol or use drugs, were found to have a similar flattening of the amplitude of the P3 wave.

Other important research has focused on biochemical markers for susceptibility to alcoholism. Numerous reports have been published on the enzyme monoamine oxidase (MAO) found in lower levels in the blood platelets of alcoholics. Another platelet enzyme, adenylate cyclase (AC) has been found to react to stimulation differently among alcoholics.

Much genetic variation has been found in the characteristics of two enzymes crucial to alcohol metabolism in the liver—alcohol dehydrogenase (ADH), which converts ethanol to acetaldehyde, and aldehyde dehydrogenase (ALDH), which converts the ACETALDEHYDE to acetate to facilitate elimination. Researchers have found that genetic variations in these enzymes can profoundly effect the rate of alcohol elimination in the body and hypothesize that this may be an important factor in one's susceptibility to alcoholism.

Despite mounting evidence for a causal relationship between heredity and alcohol problems, researchers agree that it is the interaction of genetic factors and the familial, social and cultural environment that truly determines the course of the disease. Thus, research is likely to focus less on proving a genetic contribution, than on determining how exactly genetics and environment interact.

Lawrence K. Altman, "Scientists See a Link Between Alcoholism and a Specific Gene," *New York Times* (April 18, 1990): 1.

H. Begleiter and B. Porjesz, "Potential Biological Markers in Individuals at High Risk for Developing Alcoholism," *Alcoholism* 12 (1977): 488–493.

K.M. Fillmore, "The 1980s Dominant Theory of Alcohol Problems—Genetic Predisposition to Alcoholism: Where Is It Leading Us?" *Drugs and Society* 2 (1988): 69–87.

Kathleen Whalen FitzGerald, *Alcoholism: The Genetic Inheritance* (New York: Doubleday, 1988).

Enoch Gordis, M.D., ed., *Seventh Special Report to the U.S. Congress on Alcohol and Health* (Rockville, Md.: National Institute on Alcohol Abuse and Alcoholism, 1990): chapter 3.

genetotropic etiological theory A theory, first advanced by R. J. Williams, that suggests that alcoholism is related to a genetically determined biochemical defect—the desire to drink is an inner urge mediated by nervous structures, perhaps in the hypothalamus of the brain. These nervous structures, according to Williams's theory, are disrupted by alcohol and malnutrition. Williams believes that satisfaction of all nutritional needs will end an individual's desire for alcohol. Although his methods and studies have been criticized, it is acknowledged that NUTRITION plays a role in the etiology of alcoholism.

Germany, Federal Republic of (FRG)
Alcohol: The FRG reports one of the highest levels of consumption of alcohol in the world. The annual level of consumption in West Germany, according

to a 1980 report, was approximately 13.3 liters per person. By 1993 that figure had dropped to 11.9 liters per person. In 1980 the annual per capita beer consumption was 285 liters. By 1993 it had dropped significantly to 138 liters. In that same year, Germany's wine consumption was 17.5 liters, still well behind many leading countries, with France being the number-one consumer of wine (67.0 liters per capita in 1993).

A report by the Institute fur Demoskopie Allensbach attributed the drop in consumption to the public's increased awareness of the problem of alcohol abuse. Causes for alcohol abuse in Germany are the same problems that exist in many countries today: divorce, unhappy marriages, lack of fulfillment in personal life and work, and feelings of hopelessness and inadequacy. World War II gravely affected the generation whose formative years coincided with the war period. The reunification of East and West Germany may also have been a factor in the drop in consumption rates, due to the fact that many families were no longer separated and an entire population previously watched, guarded and forbidden to leave was given their freedom at long last.

Alcoholism treatment: In the mid-1970s, the first centralized center for the intoxicated opened in Hamburg. The center was designed primarily to provide a place where people whom the police suspected of being drunk could sober up overnight. Such a center was felt to be necessary due to reported incidents of people actually dying in police "coolers" because they were in need of medical attention. At the Hamburg center a doctor examines each person brought in by the police. Those in need of medical care are taken to a hospital, and those who are merely drunk are kept in the center over night at their own expense.

Among the other German cities considering opening such treatment centers are Stuttgart, Frankfurt, Dusseldorf and Cologne.

Today many of the programs providing assistance to alcoholics tend to fall into three categories: self-help groups, advice bureaus (*Beratungsstellen*) and treatment centers. Among the best known of the self-help groups is Anonymen Alkoholiker (ALCOHOLICS ANONYMOUS). Modeled on the American organization of the same name, Anonymen Alkoholiker has approximately 2,000 chapters in Germany. In Frankfurt there are several programs for the families of alcoholics. Among these are the Al-Anon Familiengruppen and the Elternkreise des Jugenberatung und Jugendhilfe, a program for the parents of young alcoholics. In many towns, an organization known as the Freundeskreise ("Circle of Friends") provides assistance to families of alcoholics. None of the aforementioned programs are affiliated with any religious or political groups.

Self-help groups with a religious affiliation include the Protestant Blaue Kreuz ("Blue Cross"), the Catholic Kreuzbund ("League of the Cross") and the Jewish Guttempler ("Good Templar").

Advice bureaus are usually located in health services, churches, clubs and other organizations. Frankfurt lists among its advice bureaus the Sozialpadagogischen Dienst der Stadt ("Social-Educational Service of the City"), the Beratungsstellen von Evangelischen Regionalverband ("Advisory Board of the Protestant Regional Alliance") and, for young people, the Vereins Arbeits- und Erziehungshilfe ("Society for Work and Educational Assistance").

In Hamburg, an organization known as Das Kreisgesundheitgesamt Hamburg ("The District Health Agency of Hamburg") has developed a program in which a doctor, a social worker and a self-help group work together with individual alcoholics.

Drugs other than alcohol: According to the *International Narcotics Control Strategy Report March 1996* published by the USDS (U.S. Department of State):

> The FRG is not a major narcotics producing country, but an important consumer and transit country. . . . Heroin abuse appears to be on the decline, although it remains a significant problem. The use of cocaine, amphetamines and ecstasy, is growing, and LSD also appears to be on the rise.

In 1970 the German government initiated a crash program to deal with drug use. In-depth surveys were begun and funding was made available for research. Law enforcement was strengthened to try to halt illegal trafficking; a system of public education on the dangers of narcotics was set up; and the quality of medical care available to drug users was improved. In the late 1970s, the program was further expanded, and cooperation increased with neighboring countries regarding border control.

In the late 1980s, officials were alarmed by a renewed wave of cocaine abuse. In 1988, 1,302 lbs of cocaine were seized, up from 638 lbs in 1987. At the time, a U.S. DEA official noted that Germany, in fact all of western Europe, was only about five years behind the U.S. in cocaine use and availability. In the mid-1990s, Colombian drug cartels increased cocaine trafficking and, consequently, consumption in the FRG. In this lucrative European market, cocaine sells for considerably higher prices than in the U.S.

In the late 1980s and early 1990s, flunitrazepam (Rohypol) "roofies" became a serious problem. A benzodiazepine prescribed as a short-term treatment for insomnia and as a sedative hypnotic and preanesthetic medication, the drug is ten times more potent than DIAZEPAM (Valium). Because of increasing abuse in FRG, in 1995 the drug's manufacturer (Roche) removed from the market the 2 mg dosage formerly available through retail distributors, restricting its sale to hospitals. In 1994 the German Supreme Court decided to "tolerate" (although not, technically, to legalize) possession of small amounts of cannabis. Individual states in the federation have the right to interpret what constitutes "a small amount." This has created further controversy.

Substance abuse treatment and prevention: Since the initial crash program of the early 1970s, numerous institutions have been available to users for long-term therapy. Former drug users have access to vocational rehabilitation institutions and under federal law employers may be reimbursed for 60%–80% of salary for up to two years if they employ a former drug user. In the 1990s, FRG began to implement a program for heroin users combining methadone and psychotherapy treatment.

The Federal Center for Health Education, an agency subordinate to the Federal Ministry for Youth, Family Affairs, and Health published pamphlets aimed at combating drug use, and has attempted to educate the public through television advertising. Future government plans call for an intensification of these existing programs, particularly with regard to epidemiological research. A recent government study revealed that those particularly vulnerable to drug dependence are those who feel they do not belong to any society and believe they are getting "too little from life." The government targets the following groups with its public health education measures: children prior to at-risk age (8–12 years); young people in high-risk groups (13–17 years); parents with children in these two age groups; "mediators" who work with these age groups and parents; and representatives of institutions responsible for structuring and implementing preventive measures.

Hoeveel alcoholhoude dranken worden er in de wereld gedronken? (How many alcoholic beverages are being consumed throughout the world?) 27th ed. Schiedam, Netherlands: Produktschap Voor Gedistilleerde Dranken, 1987.

gin An alcoholic beverage made from distilled fermented grains (chiefly rye, but also corn, barley and oats) and flavored with juniper berries. Most gin is colorless and its alcohol content is usually between 80 and 94 proof.

The name "gin" is an Anglicized and abbreviated form of *jenever* (sometimes spelled *genever* or *geneva*), one of the terms that the Dutch used for gin. The Dutch term is an altered form of the French *genievre,* meaning juniper.

The word "gin" has been used in a number of popular expressions, particularly during the 20th century. Among the best known is the card game. At the turn of the century the expression "ginned up," meaning "drunk," came into use. Ginned up was shortened to "ginned" in the 1920s. During the same period, cheap saloons, bars and nightclubs were sometimes referred to as "gin mills," an expression that is still used. Cirrhosis of the liver has sometimes been referred to as "gin drinker's liver."

Gin was first invented in the Netherlands during the 17th century by Dr. Franciscus Sylvius, also known as Franciscus de la Boe (1614–1672), a professor of medicine at Leyden University. Dr. Sylvius was attempting to find a prophylactic against certain tropical diseases by distilling spirits with juniper berries.

Since the origins of gin were medicinal, it was at first available only in apothecary shops. As its popularity increased, many apothecary shops set up their own distilleries. By the end of the 18th century, the Dutch were producing approximately 14 million gallons of gin each year, of which around 10 million were exported.

The taste for gin was brought to England in the 17th century by soldiers returning from wars on the continent. It was officially introduced there by William of Orange, who reigned from 1686 to 1702. He thought that gin would be an acceptable substitute for French brandy, since at that time the English considered the French their enemies.

Gin rapidly acquired popularity in England. Within 40 years of its introduction there, annual production rose from a half million to 20 million gallons. Gin's popularity in the early years of the 18th century has been attributed in part to the fact that it was more refined than the spirits made by English distillers from beer and wine lees (dregs). Perhaps a more important reason was its low cost. Both William of Orange and his successor, Queen Anne, who reigned from 1702 until 1714, raised the duties and taxes on imported goods and lowered the excise on home products. In addition, during their reigns, anyone who applied to the excise bureau was allowed to establish a distillery, making it very easy to manufacture gin.

For many of the poor in England during the 18th century, there was almost no alternative alcoholic drink. Gin was given the nickname "mother's ruin" because so many women could be seen lying in the streets drunk on gin. Gin was also sometimes referred to as "Dutch courage," a term still used for bravery (or perhaps foolhardiness) inspired by alcohol.

Today most countries that distill spirits produce gin. Its chief manufacturers are the Netherlands, Britain and the U.S. Despite the many local variations, there are basically only two types of gin: Dutch gin, referred to variously as Geneva, Genever, Schiedam or Hollands; and London dry gin, which is distilled in both Britain and the U.S. Another gin, so-called Plymouth gin, is manufactured only in Plymouth, England. Today, Plymouth gin and London dry gin are about the same, but at one time the gin made in Plymouth was midway between London dry gin, which is only lightly flavored with juniper berries, and Dutch gin, which is more heavily flavored with juniper. The other differences between the two are the distillation processes and the ingredients.

Dutch gin is doubly distilled. First a low-proof spirit is distilled from a fermented mash consisting of approximately two-thirds rye meal. This low-proof spirit is then rectified and flavored with juniper berries, salt and other agents. The resultant spirits are then redistilled, producing a gin between 94 and 98 proof.

Dutch gins are not aged, which accounts for their lack of color, and have a strong, malty aroma, which makes them unsuitable for mixing in cocktails. Consequently, they are usually chilled and drunk straight.

Manufactuers of English and American gin begin by rectifying a high-proof (about 190) grain whiskey to a completely pure and flavor-free spirit. The spirit is then distilled off at approximately 160 proof, which is further decreased to around 114.2 by adding water. This product is placed in a pot still with various flavoring agents and redistilled. The resultant gin is reduced to either 80, 86 or 94 proof. Although gin is usually bottled immediately, some types produced in the U.S. are aged, giving them a pale golden color.

In addition to juniper berries, English and American gins usually contain other botanicals in varying proportions, including orris, angelica and licorice roots; bitter almonds, caraway, coriander, cardamom, anise and fennel seeds; lemon and sweet and bitter orange peels, cassis bark and calamus. The kinds and proportions of these flavorings account for the differences between the various brands of gin.

English and American gins have a dry, astringent taste, which makes them less likely to be drunk straight. In varying proportions they are frequently combined with dry vermouth to make martinis. They are also mixed with tonic water and with water and angostura bitters. Some ordinary gins are given a fruit flavor, such as orange, lemon or pineapple. Old Tom gin is slightly sweetened.

Sloe gin is not gin in the usual sense but a liqueur made by steeping sloe berries—small bluish-black plums with a sour, astringent taste—in gin.

glutethimide   A nonbarbiturate hypnotic usually prescribed for insomnia. It has a rapid onset. (See DORIDEN.)

glycine   An inhibitory neurotransmitter; structurally the simplest amino acid. Although ubiquitous in mammalian tissues, glycine appears to act as a neurotransmitter in more circumscribed regions of the central nervous system than GABA (a major inhibitory neurotransmitter in the brain). Inhibitory activity in the spinal cord, brainstem and retina has been identified experimentally.

Golden Crescent   In the late 1970s, following a drop in production of illicit opium in the GOLDEN TRIANGLE, three Southwest Asian countries emerged as the leading opium producers in the world: Pakistan, Afghanistan and Iran. Most of the trafficking of Southwest Asian heroin is carried on by Turkish nationals who smuggle heroin processed in illicit laboratories in eastern Turkey and western Iran. Current trends indicate that increasing numbers of other Southwest Asian nationals (Lebanese and Syrians) are moving into the European heroin market. Southwest Asian heroin has enjoyed great success in Europe because it is less expensive and of higher quality than that from Southeast Asia. Production is down slightly in one of the Crescent's countries, Pakistan, which in 1994 produced 160 metric tons of opium, down from 180 metric tons in 1991. However, Afghanistan's production rose from 570 metric tons in 1991 to 950 in 1994. Total Southwest Asian production also rose from 750 to 1,992 metric tons.

The Federal Republic of Germany has become the major market for Turkish traffickers (partly because of the large number of Turkish guest workers there), although the Netherlands has also experienced a recent influx of smuggled heroin. Italy is beginning to play an increasingly important role in international heroin trafficking. Not only is it a key transit point for Southwest Asian heroin headed for western Europe, the U.S. and destinations within Italy (which has become an important consumer country for heroin as well), but Italy also has created a number of heroin conversion laboratories. Italian authorities estimate that between 40,000 and 50,000 Italians use heroin on a daily basis.

For years the governments of Southwest Asian countries viewed the abuse of heroin as an American problem. Although narcotics have been used in Asia throughout history, there are now more addicts in Asia than there are in the U.S., and heroin addiction is quickly becoming epidemic. The trend troubles local governments, making them take a closer look at international policing efforts aimed at narcotics. There are several reasons for the increase of heroin abuse in the area. In addition to such factors as

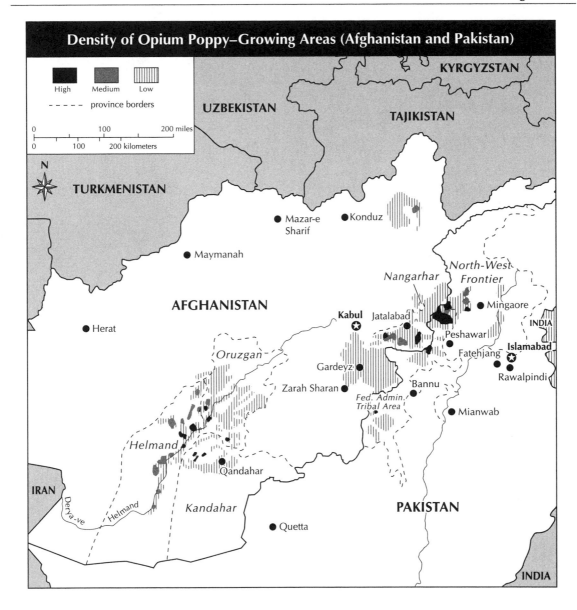

Density of Opium Poppy–Growing Areas (Afghanistan and Pakistan)

plentiful supplies and low prices, in recent years Asians have become more open to drug use: there has been a shift in population from rural to urban areas; people have started to earn more money and have become alienated from traditional ways; and in many households both parents now work, leaving children unsupervised. In Burma (now Myanmar), Thailand, Pakistan and Afghanistan, traffickers are often government insurgents or independent tribal leaders who are almost impossible to control. Furthermore, the refining of heroin is increasingly taking place in Asian laboratories.

It is estimated that Asia already accounts for 60% of world heroin use, and addiction among people under 21 is growing at an alarming rate.

Golden Triangle   An area in Southeast Asia that includes regions in eastern Burma (now Myanmar),

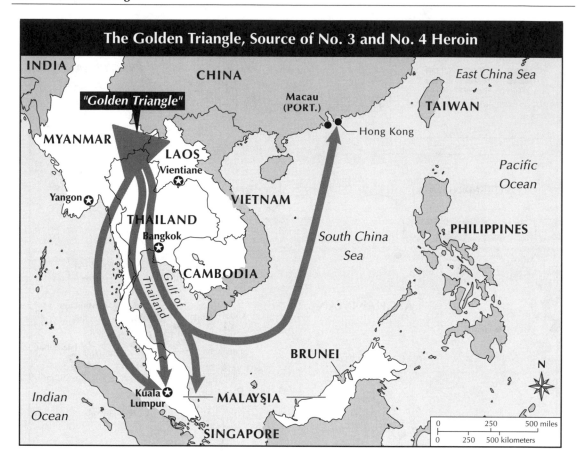

The Golden Triangle, Source of No. 3 and No. 4 Heroin

northern Laos and Thailand. It emerged in the 1960s and 1970s as the largest producer of illicit opium in the world and, until recently, dominated the heroin market in western Europe. The growing of opium poppies is thought to have been introduced to the region by Chinese political refugees and further encouraged by Europeans as a source of revenue. Chinese traffickers, using the Netherlands as the main importation and distribution area, virtually controlled the heroin market; arranging for the purchase of raw opium, overseeing its conversion (usually in laboratories in and around Bangkok and Hong Kong) and managing an international smuggling network. In the late 1970s there was a reduction in trafficking due to several factors: rivalry among the various Chinese crime syndicates, law enforcement efforts against major Asian traffickers, and a drop in opium production because of poor crops.

With the reduced supply of heroin from Southeast Asia, control of the European market was successfully challenged by other traffickers, mostly Turkish nationals smuggling heroin converted from opium grown in Southwest Asia (the GOLDEN CRESCENT) and processed in western Iran and eastern Turkey. Since the late 1970s, Southwest Asian heroin has enjoyed great success because it is less expensive and generally more potent than heroin from the Golden Triangle. Although the production of opium in Southeast Asia was down from 2,650 metric tons in 1991 to 2,157 in 1994 because of drought, it remains the major center for the production of opium and a primary supplier of heroin to the United States. Myanmar is the major producer of opium in this region and in the world. In 1994 it produced 2,030 metric tons of opium, slightly down from its 1991 production of 2,350 metric tons. Laos's production decreased dramatically, from 265 metric tons in 1991, to 85 metric tons in 1994. Thailand between 1991 and 1994 produced the least opium in the area, from 35 metric tons down to 17 metric tons.

government corruption, drugs and   In certain drug TRAFFICKING areas, government corruption is widespread. In south Florida, for instance, drug-related corruption among law enforcement personnel has been commonplace; so much so, in fact, that new scandals are rarely considered newsworthy.

Drug traffickers in some countries have even tried to take over governments. In 1980, for example, Bolivia's General Luis Garcia Menza, a major cocaine trafficker, staged a military coup and established close ties between the government and the nation's drug enterprises. Both major political parties reportedly had ties to the principal drug dealers; police and armed forces personnel did not act, either from fear or because they, too, had taken bribes.

Bolivian attorney general Carlos Mavro Hoyos summed up the role of traffickers in politics: "Narcotics traffickers are becoming a super-state because of their enormous wealth. But if we allow ourselves to be intimidated by fear or by the power of these people, our future will be more and more uncertain."

Some traffickers have links with international terrorist groups, such as the Palestine Liberation Organization, M-19 leftist rebels in Colombia and Peru's Maoist Shining Path guerrillas. Governments in several countries—Bolivia, Colombia, Thailand, Pakistan—have reportedly used weapons provided for antidrug activities to kill those who happen to disagree with their politics.

U.S. government officials were apparently aware of the fact that Panamanian leader General Manuel Antonio Noriega accepted payoffs in the millions of dollars to allow drug shipments to pass through his country en route to the U.S., yet Noriega was put on the payroll of the U.S. Central Intelligence Agency in the mid-1970s as the then-head of his country's intelligence service and considered an ally. In 1988 he fell from grace with the U.S. government—federal prosecutors in Miami won indictments accusing him of helping Colombian drug lords smuggle tons of cocaine into the U.S., and the U.S. promptly deposed him using military force. (Many innocent Panamanians were killed by U.S. troops in the endeavor.) In January 1990 the deposed dictator surrendered in Panama to U.S. officials of the Justice Department and was flown to Miami, where he was incarcerated in the city's federal courthouse and convicted on drug trafficking charges. He claims that he was betrayed by the U.S. government, who was supportive of his activities.

In July 1989 Cuba announced that four high-ranking army officers had been executed after conviction by court-martial of conspiracy to ship tons of cocaine and marijuana to the U.S. The four included General Arnaldo T. Ochoa Sanchez, a highly decorated war hero. The death sentence imposed by special military tribunal represented the biggest scandal since Fidel Castro took power in Cuba 30 years ago. Evidence presented at the trial suggested that Castro's brother, Raul, Cuba's defense minister, may have been aware of the drug trafficking. Fidel Castro complained that the U.S. withheld information that could have helped his government uncover the drug ring sooner. In 1996 the president of Colombia was accused of accepting campaign contributions from drug cartels.

grand mal convulsions   Convulsive seizures that can occur during WITHDRAWAL from alcohol, barbiturates or, less frequently, from Demerol. (It is extremely rare for such convulsions to occur during withdrawal from narcotics.) They generally appear 24 to 48 hours after cessation of drinking, and a third of those who experience convulsions also experience DELIRIUM TREMENS (THE D.T.'S). Grand mal convulsions are less common in barbiturate withdrawal and do not appear as quickly. Convulsions can also accompany a drug OVERDOSE.

grog   A mixture of rum and water. In 1740 a British admiral, Edward Vernon (1684–1757), concerned that his men were becoming habitually intoxicated on their daily rum ration, ordered the rum to be diluted with water. The resulting mixture was named for the admiral's sobriquet "Old Grog" (which he earned for his habit of braving inclement weather in a coat made of a wool-silk-mohair combination known as grogham). Vernon's practice of diluting rum was soon widely imitated, and some captains found a way to line their pockets by watering the grog further. Sailors, unhappy with "half and half grog," were incensed by the even weaker "seven-water grog." From the term "grog" are derived "groggy," "groggily," "grogginess," "grogged" and "grog-fight" (drinking party).

George Washington's brother, Lawrence, served under Admiral Vernon, and the Washingtons' Virginia estate, Mount Vernon, was named after him.

grog blossom   From GROG. A pimple or red coloration of the nose often attributed to excessive drinking over a prolonged period. (See RHINOPHYMA.)

group therapy   A psychotherapy and counseling modality considered an essential component in the treatment and rehabilitation of chemically dependent patients. Working with patients in a group rather than individually emphasizes that a patient's problems are not unique. Usually fewer than a dozen patients are involved in a group, allowing for maximum participation, and the group is generally led by a psychiatrist, a psychologist or a social worker. Members reveal their problems to the scrutiny of others and discuss them as a group. This communal therapy also allows members to benefit vicariously from the resolution of other members' problems. Group therapy with alcohol and other drug-abusing clients provides an effective complement to participation in the larger, self-help (or leaderless) group meetings of 12-step programs such as Alcoholics Anonymous or Narcotics Anonymous, where opportunities for extensive and intimate exploration of a problem may be limited.

gum opium   Raw OPIUM.

habit A dependency on drugs. (See ADDICTION.)

habit-forming Manufacturers of drugs use the phrase "Warning: May be habit-forming" if there is a possibility that the user may develop a tolerance and if the user can become physically or psychologically dependent on the substance. Many other drugs, such as caffeine and nicotine, and even modes of behavior, can be habit-forming.

habituation Accommodation or adaptation to a stimulus or to a response. The term is often used to refer to the process of forming a habit and is sometimes used synonymously with TOLERANCE. Habituation is closely linked to ADDICTION, however one may become habituated to a substance or to an activity without necessarily being addicted psychologically or physically. Habituation is often closely dependent upon external forces such as environment and lifestyle; when these factors are changed, the habit often disappears. The majority of U.S. soldiers in Vietnam that were supposedly addicted to heroin while serving in Vietnam were no longer "addicted," nor did they have the desire for the drug once they were returned to their previous lifestyles and environments in the United States. When one travels, habits are frequently adjusted to the culture, climate and environment of the place being visited.

Hague Conferences of 1911 and 1913 The first International Conference on Opium was held in the Hague, Netherlands, to discuss the restriction of worldwide opium and cocaine production. The conference ratified an international agreement or "convention" to develop, enact and enforce domestic legislation that would require the control of all phases of the preparation and distribution of medical opium, morphine, heroin and cocaine as well as any new narcotic derivatives. Further, the countries involved agreed to control their own international traffic in such substances and to respect the laws of other countries in this regard. In 1913 a second Hague Conference was held to consider the progress of the ratification of the convention by the international community. By the time of the 1913 conference, 34 nations had signed this agreement, including the 12 original conference participants. The convention, which was ratified by the U.S. Congress and signed by the U.S. in 1913, was a significant factor in the passage of the Harrison Act in 1914.

Haight-Ashbury A district in San Francisco, California, that during the mid-1960s was a gathering spot for counterculture youths (known as hippies). The center of this area (also known as "the Haight") is where Haight Street crosses Ashbury Street. This was the main gathering spot for the hippies, whose lives often involved the use of marijuana and sometimes the hallucinogenic drugs, such as mescaline, psilocybin and LSD. Haight Ashbury still has a significant hippie population, and the area attracts students, artists, musicians and the like. As in the 1960s, there are still numerous cafes, restaurants, bars and trendy boutiques.

hair analysis   Hair analysis, while still in the testing stage, promises a complementary system of drug detection for various criminal justice and forensic applications and provides information about drug use over a longer period of time than urinalysis, which is limited to detecting drugs consumed within the previous three days.

The technique of hair analysis is essentially the same as that used in radioimmunoassay (urine analysis), and offers the same general detection sensitivity. Over time a growing hair absorbs drugs and their metabolites into its structure from the circulatory system. Metabolites are the biochemical products of drugs that have metabolized within the body. For cocaine, both urine testing and hair testing detect the drug metabolites rather than the illegal drug itself. The utility of radioimmunoassay of hair (RIAOH) is due to the fact that once a drug metabolite is embedded in the hair shaft, a process which appears to take place while the hair is being formed in its follicle, the metabolite is very nearly permanent: as the hair shaft grows, it forms a longitudinal record of the compounds it has absorbed. Drug metabolites appear in detectable levels in hair approximately a week after ingestion. Hair grows at an average rate of about half an inch every 30 days.

According to the National Institute of Justice (NIJ), presently engaged in research, it appears that present laboratory-based hair analysis methods will be refined and made more amenable to larger scale applications. If this happens, hair analysis will become a technique complementary to urinalysis, expanding the criminal justice system's ability to detect and monitor illicit drug use.

U.S. Department of Justice, National Institute of Justice, *NIJ Reports/SNI 202* (March/April 1987): 4.

Mieczkowski et al., "Testing Hair for Illicit Drug Use" *Research in Brief,* National Institute of Justice, 1993.

Haldol   A major tranquilizer and SEDATIVE-HYPNOTIC that contains haloperidol and is prescribed in the treatment of acute or chronic psychosis. It is an antipsychotic drug classified chemically as a butyrophenone. When combined with alcohol or other central nervous system depressants it can have an ADDITIVE EFFECT. Symptoms of an overdose include respiratory depression and hypotension.

Hale House   A child care agency in the Harlem district of New York City for young children born dependent on alcohol or other drugs or infected with the AIDS virus. It was founded in 1969 by Mother Clara Hale, who devoted her life to helping children born to drug users. Other Hale House activities include a housing and education program for recovering mothers and their children; an apprenticeship that works with juveniles just beginning to find themselves in trouble; a home for HIV-positive mothers and infants; a facility for teenage mothers and their children; and a place where over-stressed parents who feel at risk of abusing their children may leave their children for a few days. Mother Hale died in 1992, but her daughter, Dr. Lorraine Hale, carries on her mother's mission.

half-life of drugs   The amount of time it takes for the body to remove half of a drug dose from the system. For drugs with a half-life of 24 hours or more, such as Valium, half of the first dose may still be in the body when the next dose is taken 24 hours later. After several days, the accumulation in the body may be fairly large and if alcohol or another central nervous system depressant is taken, the result can be SYNERGICTIC and extremely dangerous. Accumulation levels off within a week.

halfway house   A home for formerly institutionalized people, such as alcoholics or other chemically dependent people, mental patients or ex-prisoners. It is a transition point as they move from inpatient care to outside life. The halfway house movement developed in the 1970s and mushroomed in the 1980s. To be effective such houses should have only a small number of residents and maintain an informal "homelike" atmosphere. Primarily for the homeless who need support and protection rather than medical care until they can again take their place in the community, halfway houses are generally staffed by nonprofessionals and provide residents with food, shelter and a therapeutic environment. Professionals are available for any needed medical care. Halfway houses are sometimes referred to as transitional housing for recovering drug users and alcoholics, who may need or want

Common Drugs: Symptoms of Abuse of Hallucinogens

Hallucinogens. Drugs that alter perception of reality.

Drug Name	Street Names	Method of Use	Sign and Symptoms	Hazards of Use
PCP (Phencyclidine)	Angel Dust, Killer Hog, Weed, Supergrass, PeaCee Pill	Most often smoked, can also be inhaled (snorted), injected or swallowed in tablets.	Slurred speech, blurred vision, incoordination. Confusion, agitation, aggression.	Anxiety, depression, impaired memory and perception. Uncontrolled aggression. Death from accidents or overdose.
LSD	Acid, Cubes, Purple Haze, Tabs, Blotter, Micro Dot	Usually swallowed.	Dilated pupils, sweating, trembling, illusions, hallucinations, mood swings.	Breaks from reality, emotional breakdown, flashback.
Mescaline, Psilocybin	Mesc, Cactus, Magic Mushrooms	Usually swallowed in their natural form.	Dilated pupils, sweating, trembling, illusions, hallucinations, mood swings.	Breaks from reality, emotional breakdown, flashback.

New York State Office of Alcoholism and Substance Abuse Services

ongoing therapy as they make their transition back into society.

hallucinogens   From *hallucination*—a sensory experience that does not relate to external reality. Hallucinogens are drugs that act on the central nervous system and cause mood changes and perceptual changes varying from sensory illusion to visual and auditory hallucinations. Because some of these drugs have the ability to "mimic" psychotic reactions—loss of contact with reality, mania and schizophrenia—they are sometimes called psychotomimetic drugs. The term psychotogenic, which refers to the production of a psychoticlike state, is also used. In addition, because of their perceptual effects, the hallucinogens are called psychedelics.

Numerous pharmaceuticals and other drugs can cause hallucinogenic reactions. Such drugs are not classified as hallucinogens, however, since the primary reaction sought from them is not hallucination.

Hallucinogenic drugs have been in use for at least 5,000 years. In many parts of the world they have traditionally been used on religious and ceremonial occasions and continue to be so used today. The peyote cactus, which contains mescaline, was first used by the Aztec Indians of Mexico and is still used by the members of the Native American Church as a sacrament in religious ceremonies.

The Indians of Central America and Mexico have long used *Psilocyba mexicana*, a mushroom that contains the hallucinogens psilocin and psilocybin. They call it "food of the gods." It is believed that Norse tribesmen used *Amanita muscaria* mushrooms to bring on a rage before going into battle. This mushroom, also known as FLY AGARIC, contains hallucinogenic agents with effects similar to those of LSD. The word berserk comes from the bearskin shirt that these warriors wore in battle.

More recently, because many of these drugs mimic psychoses, it has been hoped that they could be beneficial in the research and treatment of various mental illnesses. But while many therapeutic claims have been made for these drugs, as yet none have proven safe or effective in the treatment of mental disorders.

Classification: Hallucinogens are classified as Schedule I drugs under the CONTROLLED SUBSTANCES ACT, and include LSD, MESCALINE, PEYOTE, DMT, PSILOCYBIN, and MARIJUANA or THC (TETRAHYDROCANNABINOL).

Usage: Apart from marijuana and THC (which have not quite appropriately been placed in this class although they can have some mild psychedelic effects), the most widely used of the hallucinogens are LSD, mescaline, DOM (STP) and psilocybin/psilocin. LSD and DOM (STP) are synthetic compounds, as are other hallucinogens such as MDA, MDMA and TMA. Mescaline and psilocybin are naturally occurring substances that can also be synthesized. Some of the less widely used hallucinogens occur only in plant materials such as MORNING GLORY SEEDS, NUTMEG and certain varieties of mushrooms.

Effects: Most drugs affect individual users differently depending on the amount taken, past experience of the user, the method of administration and whether the drug is used concurrently with another substance. Reactions to the hallucinogens are particularly variable and often depend on the context and environment in which the drugs are taken and the mental and physical state of the user. Variations in composition and purity also contribute to the idiosyncratic effects of these drugs.

In low doses, hallucinogens alter moods and perceptions, though they do not necessarily cause hallucinations or other psychotic symptoms. Mood changes range from euphoria to depression. Perceptual changes may be pleasant and quasi-mystical or frightening and unpleasant. Typically, sensory perceptions are heightened, and in high doses hallucinogens may also cause hallucinations; some substances more than others.

The onset of the auditory and/or visual hallucinogenic experience may be fast or slow depending on the drug itself and the manner in which it is used. Duration is also variable. Occasionally the user will experience a prolonged reaction or a recurring reaction to a hallucinogen. In such cases, the effects may continue for an extended period after the drug is taken or there may be a spontaneous FLASHBACK of the original experience weeks or even months later.

Interestingly, a user is generally aware to a greater or lesser extent, that his or her experiences are distortions of reality. With some of the more powerful hallucinogens, however, the user may lose all sense of reality. Though this state usually passes quickly, in a few cases users have become permanently psychotic, perhaps because of the stress of the experience or the precipitation of an underlying schizophrenic disorder.

Physical effects of hallucinogens are also wide-ranging. Adverse effects such as headache, nausea and vomiting, blurred vision, sleeplessness and dilation of the pupils are all common. Other effects include loss of appetite, trembling, dizziness, profuse perspiration, increased body temperature, lowered or raised blood pressure, decreased or increased heart or respiratory activity, and numbness of extremities. Some of the hallucinogens are also known to occasionally cause convulsions.

Though hallucinogens are relatively nontoxic—there are no known cases of death caused by heavy doses—individual psychological reactions to them can be life-threatening. BAD TRIPS and prolonged or recurring reactions have brought on delusions that have caused serious accidents, even suicides and homicides. And though not confirmed conclusively, research suggests LSD increases the risk of spontaneous abortion among pregnant women.

Among drug users, it is a common belief that the perceptual effects of LSD and other hallucinogens stimulate creativity. This has not been confirmed by objective studies. Studies conducted with marijuana have actually demonstrated that musicians, when comparing recordings they made under and not under the influence of the drug, consistently rated their "straight" session as having a higher quality.

Tolerance and dependence: Regular use of certain hallucinogens, such as LSD, will rapidly produce tolerance but it disappears after a few days' abstinence. Tolerance is not generally an issue as few people would use a drug such as LSD or mescaline on a daily basis. However, users tolerant to the effects of LSD exhibit CROSS-TOLERANCE to mescaline and psilocybin. Research states that tolerance to hashish and marijuana do not develop. Because of the very long half-life of CANNABINOIDS, regular use leads to a state where even a *smaller* than initial dose may raise an existing steady blood level and produce the high. Regular users need less, not more, to feel the effects. Nonetheless, many users do increase the amounts they consume over time and appear to build up a noticeable tolerance. This may be because they have learned to function in an altered state and need to increase use to feel "higher." Chronic users of hallucinogens can become psychologically dependent on these drugs, but it is generally agreed that no physical DEPENDENCE develops. Even after long use, no WITHDRAWAL symptoms are known to develop when hallucinogens are given up. Psychological dependence is manifested by a compelling need to use the drug involved. The mental state induced by the drug becomes so much a part of the user's life that to be without it seems abnormal. Thus the user craves the mental state induced by the drug. New studies indicate that there may be a withdrawal process associated with chronic use of the cannabinoids, however.

Sources: Only limited amounts of certain hallucinogens are produced commercially in government-authorized laboratories for research or treatment. Most of the synthetic hallucinogens can be readily manufactured and both these and naturally occurring hallucinogens are sold illicitly.

Trafficking: Because they have a potential for abuse and no accepted medical benefits, most hallucinogens are federally regulated under Schedule I of the CONTROLLED SUBSTANCES ACT (CSA). The drugs under Schedule I are research substances for which there is no known or accepted medical use in the U.S. By law, they can be manufactured only in federally regulated laboratories for research purposes. They cannot be sold by prescription. Researchers using the drugs must administer the substances directly to their subjects, although small amounts of THC have been given to cancer patients to take home for the treatment of nausea from chemotherapy. (See LEGAL ASPECTS OF MARIJUANA, AND OTHER DRUG CONTROLS.)

Morning glory seeds, nutmeg, jimson weed and the like are not subject to any specific legal regulations. Peyote is used legally by members of the Native American Church.

Synonyms: psychedelics, illusionogenics, psychotomimetics, psychotogenics, mind-expanding or mind-manifesting drugs.

Samuel M. Levine, *Narcotics and Drug Abuse* (Cincinnati: the W. H. Anderson Company, 1973).

Robert J. Wicks and Jerome J. Platt, *Drug Abuse: A Criminal Justice Primer* (Beverly Hills, Calif.: Enziger Bruce & Glencoe, Inc., 1977).

hangover   In this sense "hang" means "linger," from the Gothic *hahan* via the Anglo-Saxon *hangian*. The term hangover is an Americanism introduced in the early 20th century. The use of the word "hang" to describe the unpleasant aftereffects of excessive drinking is similar to that in "just *hang*ing around," in the sense of aimless lingering.

A hangover generally follows intoxication by eight to twelve hours. Some common effects are: splitting headaches; sensitivity to movement, bright light or loud sounds; nausea and vomiting; dizziness; sweating; loss of appetite and dry mouth; and the D.T.'s (the shakes). These are accompanied by general malaise or tiredness and, often, anxiety, depression or both.

The causes of hangovers are not completely understood, but there are probably a number of factors involved. For most drinkers the stress of intoxication has been compounded by other contributing elements, such as heavy smoking, lack of sleep and feelings of guilt resulting from uninhibited behavior. The changes expected in the body following a stress reaction are seen in the signs of hangover. Another factor at work may be low BLOOD SUGAR, or hypoglycemia. Blood glucose levels are at their lowest during the height of a hangover; many symptoms of a hangover are similar to those of hypoglycemia.

When alcohol is consumed, its METABOLISM by the liver causes an accumulation of organic acids and ketones in the blood, known as ketoacidosis. The degree of ketoacidosis corresponds fairly well to the intensity of the hangover and may be partially responsible for its onset. Water balance is also altered when alcohol is consumed. Increased urinary excretion, sweating, vomiting and diarrhea can lead to dehydration, which appears as dry mouth and thirst. On the other hand, a drop in BLOOD ALCOHOL CONCENTRATION can stimulate an antidiuretic hormone, so that hyperhydration can also develop during a hangover. CONGENERS, the organic alcohols and salts other than ethanol formed when alcoholic beverages are manufactured, have been thought to play a role in the hangover effect, but it has been well demonstrated that pure ethanol can by itself cause a hangover. The role of congeners in causing hangovers is probably small. Irritation of the STOMACH lining may be the cause of the nausea and vomiting that accompany a hangover.

It has not been proven that the amount of alcohol consumed is related to the appearance and severity of a hangover, although this is generally thought to be the case. The hangover experience varies from person to person. Some consider the hangover syndrome a symptom of early WITHDRAWAL. According to this theory, a certain DEPENDENCE has been established by overdrinking, and the body is reacting because it needs more alcohol. The fact that resumption of drinking will reverse or alleviate some hangover symptoms is evidence in support of this concept. Hence the expression "have a hair of the dog that bit you."

The traditional use of a small amount of alcohol to correct the metabolic rebound brought on by a hangover may be justified as long as it does not lead to another round of overindulgence. For those who suffer from alcohol dependence it is best to abstain completely. To correct acidosis, water balance disturbance and low blood sugar, fruit juice, such as orange juice, may be of help. Aspirin may be taken for a headache, but sedatives and tranquilizers should be avoided. Rest and time will correct the other unpleasant effects.

Sidney Cohen, "Hangover," *Drug Abuse and Alcoholism Newsletter* 9, no. 8 (October 1980).

hard drugs and narcotics   Hard drugs are potent, illegal substances that tend to lead to physical or psychological dependency and debilitation with repeated use. Drugs in this category include opium, morphine and their derivatives (such as heroin), which are NARCOTICS, and cocaine, crack cocaine, and methamphetamine (ice), which are stimulants. Marijuana and nonopiates, on the other hand, are sometimes referred to as soft drugs. When used over an extended period of time, or in sufficient quantities, the so-called soft drugs, like alcohol and tobacco, can be equally if not more dangerous than the hard drugs. Withdrawal from a severe alcohol habit may be the most dangerous withdrawal syndrome associated with any of the abused substances. More people die each year from tobacco-related causes than from all of the illegal drugs, alcohol, car accidents, AIDS, homicides, suicides and fires, combined.

When we spend vast amounts of taxpayer dollars on our so-called War on Drugs, we should be certain that we are fighting the actual enemy, as opposed to focusing our resources and attention on the drugs and the drug dealers that make the headlines and bring in the votes. There will never be a legitimate "War on Drugs" unless the pharmaceutical companies and the tobacco industry are included among the list of enemy forces; along with the international drug traffickers (often legitimate businesses operating on two levels); the politicians or law enforcers who are paid off or look the other way; and the banks that continue to launder the money. The local crack dealers of the inner cities are very small players in a very large and profitable game.

harm reduction   According to the World Health Organization, "Policies or programs that focus directly on reducing the harm resulting from the use of alcohol or other drugs" as opposed to a focus directed at prohibition or cessation of use. Models of harm reduction include: needle exchange programs for intravenous drugs users and mandated air bags in all new cars to minimize the risks of driving under the influence of alcohol and other drugs. The concept holds that drug policies need to focus on *reducing crime,* whether engendered by drugs or resulting from the prohibition of drugs. It holds that disease and death will be diminished even among people who can't, or won't, stop taking drugs. This approach is being experimented with or has been implemented in the Netherlands, Switzerland, Australia, parts of Germany, Austria, Britain and a growing number of other countries.

harmal   *Peganum harmal,* an herb containing psychedelic alkaloids including HARMALINE. The plant is native to India and countries of the eastern Mediterranean.

harmaline   A psychedelic alkaloid found in the herb HARMAL.

harmine   A psychedelic alkaloid ($C_{13}H_{12}N_2O$), found in *Banisteriopsis esp. B. caapi,* of the malphigia family, a vine native to the Amazon River basin. Harmine causes reactions similar to those induced by LSD and mescaline. South American Indians drink AYAHUASCA (a beverage containing this substance) during religious ceremonies, and it is also used as a healing agent.

Harris-Dodd Act   A drug-abuse control act passed in 1965 that has since been superseded. (See CONTROLLED SUBSTANCES ACT.)

Harrison Act   The first law in the U.S. to regulate narcotics. Passed in December 1914, it took effect in 1915 and was intended primarily to control the flow of opium and coca leaves (and their derivatives) and to record their transfer. Forms issued by the Collector of Internal Revenue were required for all transfers of the drugs between manufacturer, wholesaler, retailer and doctor. A tax was also levied on narcotics. The act required the registration of all those who dealt in the production or transfer of narcotics, with the exception of warehousemen and common carriers, nurses who were under a doctor's supervision, and government officials who had drugs in their possession for official duties. The Federal Bureau of Narcotics was not in existence in 1915 and enforcement of the act was carried out by the Collector of Internal Revenue and the Narcotic Unit of the Bureau of Prohibition, both agencies of the Treasury Department. Under the law, the only way an unregistered person could legally possess one of these was when he had obtained it through a doctor's prescription.

Haschischins, Le club des   A French club attended by literary men for the purpose of experimenting with hashish. It was founded in 1844 by the French novelist Theophile Gautier.

hash oil   HASHISH is made from only the resin of the plant *Cannabis sativa;* hash oil (liquid hashish) is made from plant material that is ground or chopped up and distilled into liquid form. Considerably more potent in liquid form, as little as one drop can produce a HIGH. It can be smoked (a very small amount is put on a cigarette) or taken orally, but when ingested orally, due to its potency it has to be used in cooking or mixed into wine or other liquid and drunk.

hashish   From the Arabic *hashish,* "dry grass," the word "hashish" is also associated with a semilegendary religious cult in eleventh-century Persia. The cult was headed by Al-Hasan ibn-al Sabbah, the so-called Old Man of the Mountain, who led a branch of the Isma'ili sect of Shi'ite Muslims in a number of terrorist murders committed for political and religious reasons. Known as the Hashishi, the sect has been linked to the use of hashish, though there is no concrete evidence for this. Our word "assassin" comes from the name of this sect.

Hashish is the resinous extract of the hemp plant *Cannabis sativa.* It is obtained by boiling in a solvent the parts of the plant that are covered with resin or by scraping the resin from the plant. The resin, which contains the active compound THC (TETRAHYDROCANNABINOL), is then formed into cakes or lumps that range in color from golden brown to black. Hashish is a very potent form of cannabis; its THC content may range from 5%–12% by weight compared with 5%–10% for the most potent forms of commercial grade and Jamaican MARIJUANA (the very potent sinsemilla has a higher THC content) and roughly 1% for Mexican marijuana. An even more potent form of cannabis with a THC content of about 20%–80% is known as liquid hashish (HASH OIL).

In America, hashish is usually smoked in a pipe, sometimes in a water pipe, which regulates the intake and cools the smoke. In Europe, where hash has traditionally been more available than marijuana, it is mixed into large, hand-rolled, cone-shaped tobacco cigarettes. In North Africa, hashish is smoked or eaten in a confection known as *majoon* or DAWAMESK, a sort of cake made of sugar, vanilla, almonds, pistachios and spices, along with the hashish. In India, hashish is known as *charas.*

The effects of hashish, like those of marijuana, depend a great deal on the user, on the dosage and particularly on the potency of the drug. In the 19th century a group of French literary figures, including Gautier, Baudelaire, Hugo, Balzac and de Nerval, formed a group known as LE CLUB DES HASCHISCHINS. They ingested hashish in the dawamesk form, a more unpredictable way of consuming it than smoking because it is difficult to control the dose. The effects that these men describe in their writings vary a great deal and were almost certainly linked to their individual imaginations and personalities and the atmosphere in which they took the drug. Gautier had hallucinations of "hybrid creatures, formless mixtures of men, beasts, and utensils; monks with wheels for feet and cauldrons for bellies," while Baudelaire saw "an exquisite harmony of proportion . . . through space." Although the effects experienced by most users are similar to those caused by smoking potent marijuana, large amounts of ingested hashish can lead to such a degree of intoxication that extreme perceptual distortion and anxiety may result. Psychotic episodes rarely last for more than 48 hours after the hashish has been ingested.

A typical American hashish user is white, male, aged 18 to 25, with some college education. Use is limited almost exclusively to those who also use marijuana. In spite of its relative scarcity, use of hashish has increased in the U.S. because of a growing preference for higher potency cannabis.

Hashish is a potent product made from the resin of the upper leaves and flowering tops of the female marijuana plant. Marijuana and all other cannabis drugs come from this one species, but different varieties and different growing climates affect the potency. Hashish is usually produced from plants grown in areas of fairly high altitude and high temperature because they tend to yield more resin. The principal psychoactive ingredient in all forms of cannabis is delta-9 tetrahydrocannabinol, or THC, found in the resin on the under surface of the flowers and leaves.

Classification: Hashish is perhaps inappropriately classified as a hallucinogen; a Schedule I classification under the CONTROLLED SUBSTANCES ACT.

Effects: The effects may include distorted perception, depersonalization or "double consciousness," spatial and time distortions, intensification of scents, tastes, colors and sounds, and mild visual hallucinations. The effects are similar to those produced by marijuana, but usually they are more intense because of the higher potency of hashish.

Tolerance and dependence: Tolerance to hashish does not develop. Because of high blood levels of THC, someone who has smoked hashish regularly will need a smaller dose to achieve the same "high." Psychological dependence is a danger; this has been seen primarily in North Africa and India, where use is quite heavy, but is infrequent in the U.S. Recent studies may indicate that cannabis and hashish are more addictive than was previously thought, and that there may be withdrawal symptoms associated with the cessation of prolonged use.

Sources: Most of the hashish in the U.S. is smuggled in from Morocco, Nepal, Pakistan, Afghanistan and Lebanon. According to the U.S. State Depart-

ment, cultivation and sale of cannabis account for much of the economic base of northern Morocco, which devoted 74,000 hectares to cannabis cultivation. Most of this cannabis is processed into hashish. Moroccan cannabis resin (hashish) accounted for a major part of the resin seized in Europe, upward from 44% in 1993 to 70% in 1994. The principal suppliers of marijuana to the U.S. market, Mexico, Colombia and Jamaica, do not produce significant quantities of hashish. This is probably due to differences in the quantity of resin yielded by the plants in varying climates (more resin is produced in dry areas at high altitudes) and also to cultural and traditional practices.

Trafficking: The use of hashish in the U.S. is on the rise, but it is difficult to estimate how much is being used because seizures by authorities fluctuate widely from year to year: from 700 lbs in 1970 to 50,000 lbs in 1973–74. One large seizure will completely change the figures for a given year. In 1978, for instance, 2,999 lbs were seized; but in 1979, a total of 43,233 lbs were taken, which included one huge seizure of 41,676 lbs of suspected Lebanese hashish from a ship off Sandy Hook, New Jersey. In May 1988 the DEA (Drug Enforcement Administration) seized a record amount of 75,000 lbs in San Francisco. The 1990s witnessed a further upswing in hashish seizures: in 1993, 11.4 tons and 72 tons in 1995.

The *1993 National Household Survey on Drug Abuse* conducted by SAMHSA (Substance Abuse and Mental Health Services Administration) combined hashish with marijuana use in its estimates. The survey estimates that people aged 12 and up had a lifetime hashish/marijuana use rate of 9.0%. Adults aged 26 and older were the only group that had an increased rate of use, from 12.9% in 1976 to 34.3% in 1993.

Synonyms: hash, Goma de Mota, soles, charas.

International Narcotics Control Commission, *Report to the United Nations* (Vienna, 1995)

Substance Abuse and Mental Health Services Administration, *National Household Survey on Drug Abuse: Main Findings 1993* (Rockville, Md.: Department of Health and Human Services [DHHS]).

United States Dept. of State, Bureau for International Narcotics and Law Enforcement Affairs, *International Narcotics Control Strategy Report March 1996.*

Hawaii

Alcohol: The mixture of populations in Hawaii offers a unique opportunity for comparing alcohol use and abuse patterns among people of differing ethnic backgrounds. A survey of alcohol consumption by the four major ethnic groups in Hawaii suggests that native Hawaiians drink less alcohol than Caucasians but significantly more than Japanese or Filipinos. In all groups, men drink more than women. The proportion of heavy drinkers (defined in this study as those who regularly consume two or more drinks per day) among native Hawaiians is approximately 11%, compared with 14% for Caucasians, 7% for Filipinos and 5% for Japanese. More than half the Japanese and Filipinos are abstainers, compared with 41% of native Hawaiians and 31% of Caucasians.

Between 1975 and 1980, native Hawaiians were at less risk than Caucasians for liver CIRRHOSIS, with an estimated 6.8 deaths per 100,000 population versus 12.1 per 100,000 for Caucasians. During this period, native Hawaiians were at greater risk than the general state population for such causes of death related to alcohol as homicide, motor vehicle accidents and SUICIDE. (See CRIME and DRIVING WHILE IMPAIRED.)

Drugs other than alcohol: Illicit drug distribution and sales in Hawaii are, as in other states, a source of major concern.

Treatment: A 1995 study of state alcohol- and drug-treatment and prevention resources noted the following areas of particular concern to Hawaii state authorities: a rise in the use of crystal METHAMPHETAMINE; a worsening in the economic situations of families and a corresponding increase in drug use; the recent establishment of organized business dealing in crack cocaine; and the problems common to small rural states related to efficient use of treatment funds and the location of treatment sites with a population both far-flung and diffuse.

Historically, native Hawaiians have been underrepresented in treatment facilities in proportion to their estimated numbers of heavy drinkers. In a 1979 study, for example, 41% of heavy drinkers in Hawaii were Caucasian, yet they represented 71% of treatment admissions. Native Hawaiians accounted for 19% of the state's chronic alcohol users that year but only 10% of admissions.

F. M. Ahern, *Alcohol Use and Abuse among Four Ethnic Groups in Hawaii: Native Hawaiians, Japanese, Filipinos, and Caucasians,* in National Institute on Alcohol Abuse and Alcoholism's *Alcohol Use Among U.S. Ethnic Minorities,* research monograph series no. 18, DHHS pub. ADM 87-1435 (Washington, D.C.: U.S. Government Printing Office, 1995).

Hawaiian wood rose, baby   A plant, native to Hawaii and Asia, the seeds of which contain lysergic acid amide. When eaten they produce psychedelic effects similar to but milder than those of LSD.

Hawaiian wood rose, large   Similar to baby HAWAIIAN WOOD ROSE, but only half as potent.

head shop   Head shops, which have sprung up across the country since the 1960s (there are an estimated 15,000 to 30,000), sell assorted drug paraphernalia. Their stock includes everything from roach clips and water pipes to hypodermic syringes and cocaine spoons. They also carry books and publications advising which drugs to buy and how much to pay and offer "how to's" on growing your own marijuana and mushrooms. They also sell kits to convert street cocaine to FREEBASE. Not only are head shops sometimes a place to make contacts for the purchase of an illicit drug, they also occasionally sell certain uncontrolled drugs. For example, butyl nitrite (which is technically not a drug and is usually sold as a room deodorizer) is sold as an inhalant. A vasodilator, it expands blood vessels and produces a three- to five-minute "high." The Food and Drug Administration (FDA) has no control over this substance and it is sold in head shops under brand names such as Bullet and Rush. They also may sell legal COCAINE SUBSTITUTES.

The head shop business is a multimillion dollar industry. Some states have attempted to control the sale of drug paraphernalia, but these laws are usually ineffective. The Drug Enforcement Administration (DEA) drafted a Model Drug Paraphernalia Act, which covers the control of all equipment, products and materials of any kind that are used, intended for use or designated for use in planting, propagating, cultivating, growing, harvesting, manufacturing, compounding, converting, producing, processing, preparing, testing, analyzing, packaging, repackaging, storing, containing, concealing, injecting, ingesting, inhaling or otherwise introducing into the body a controlled substance in violation of the Controlled Substances Act. The act further amends the offenses and penalties section of the Controlled Substances Act to cover the possession of such drug paraphernalia. It has been adopted by a number of municipalities and states and is being considered by others.

health care costs of alcohol abuse   See ECONOMIC IMPACT.

health care professionals and addiction   By some estimates, as many as one in eight physicians is or will become chemically dependent. The percentages in other health care professions are believed to be equally high. Some theorize that this phenomenon is due to medical workers' constant exposure and easy access to addictive substances.

In 1972 the American Medical Association (AMA) launched the "impaired physician movement" that called on doctors to report debilitated colleagues and recommended that state and local medical societies oversee treatment. Today, all 50 state medical societies have impaired-physicians committees. Nurses, dentists and other professional groups have followed suit.

The AMA currently lists well over 100 programs to which doctors are referred by state committees, including many that specialize in medical addicts. The AMA estimates that roughly 85% to 90% of impaired physicians stay "clean" for at least two years after treatment. A Mayo Clinic study put the recovery rate at 83%.

Some critics say there is still too much denial on the subject among professionals and urge more candor about the problem, beginning with frank discussion in medical schools. As a result, the rehabilitation of addicted health care professionals has become a significant sub-specialty of the drug-treatment field.

David Gelman, Andrew Murr and Regina Elam, "Docs in Need of Detox," *Newsweek* (May 29, 1989): 61–62.

health care providers   All primary health care providers—physicians, nurses, nurse practitioners, physician assistants—have a responsibility to increase their knowledge of and skills in treating substance abuse for the purpose of improving therapeutic care of alcoholic and chemically dependent patients. Primary care providers often provide the initial treatment for patients' health problems. However, their record on alcohol- and other drug-abuse problems has been extremely disappointing. One study found that only 45% of problem drinkers visiting a doctor were even asked about their alcohol consumption, and only 25% of those who were asked were told to reduce their drinking or warned about alcohol-related health dangers. Only 3% (a rather alarming rate) of heavy drinkers were referred to a treatment program. These findings were corroborated by a second study, which found that misdiagnosis or oversight of alcohol-related problems is common among primary care physicians. Doctors often collude with their patients' DENIAL either by ignoring symptoms of alcohol and other drug use or too quickly accepting patients' dismissal of questions about drinking and substance use.

The fact that many doctors suffer from substance abuse themselves (see HEALTH CARE PROFESSIONALS AND ADDICTION) and that they are not held accountable for their lack of proper diagnoses and treatment, not to mention that the more patients a private practitioner sees in the shortest amount of time, the more money he or she makes, all contribute to the lack of proper health care available under the current system. An average doctor visit requires more time spent waiting in the waiting room to see the physician than actually spent with the physician, regardless of the severity of illness. In hospitals doctors are frequently required to work abnormally long shifts and attend to far too many patients, all of which impairs their judgment, puts their own health at risk from exhaustion and fatigue, and does not allow them to spend the proper amount of time and to do the proper research required to treat patients with optimal care. Other factors that can combine to obstruct appropriate treatment include inadequate medical school training in alcoholism and other drug dependence, patient resistance and the financial pressures and the overall mismanagement of the health care system. Sometimes, physicians' own attitudes toward addiction interfere with their ability to diagnose accurately.

In the 1970s, however, the American Medical Association mandated inclusion of alcohol abuse and alcoholism information into all medical school curricula. The CAREER TEACHER PROGRAM, jointly sponsored by the NATIONAL INSTITUTE ON ALCOHOL ABUSE AND ALCOHOLISM (NIAAA) and the NATIONAL INSTITUTE ON DRUG ABUSE (NIDA), led to the addition of new courses and expanded substance-abuse curricula at U.S. medical education institutions and the HIV-AIDS crisis directed new attention to the problem of substance abuse, particularly INTRAVENOUS DRUG USE (IDU).

S. Clement, "The Identification of Alcohol Related Problems by General Practitioners," *British Journal of Addiction* 81 (1986): 257–264.

R. Hingson et al., "Seeking Help for Drinking Problems: A Study in the Boston Metropolitan Area," *Journal of Studies on Alcohol* 42 (1982): 273–288.

C. Holden, "Medical Schools Confront Another Taboo," *New Physician* 40 (1986): 17–20.

Enoch Gordis, M.D., ed., *Sixth Special Report to the U.S. Congress on Alcohol and Health* (Rockville, Md.: National Institute on Alcohol Abuse and Alcoholism, 1987).

Healthy People 2000: National Health Promotion and Disease Prevention Objectives In 1990 the U.S. Public Health Service established a national strategy to promote three basic goals: (1) increase the span of healthy life for Americans; (2) reduce health disparities among Americans; and (3) achieve access to prevention services for all Americans. Within these basic goals were objectives that included 19 specific to use of alcohol and other drugs.

Department of Health & Human Services, *Healthy People 2000: National Health Promotion and Disease Prevention Objectives* (Washington, D.C.: 1990).

heart A muscular organ that rhythmically contracts and relaxes to pump blood throughout the body. The heart is one of the body's most complex organs and is susceptible to temporary and permanent damage from a variety of causes, including short- and long-term use of alcohol and other drugs.

Long-term use of alcohol is directly related to diseases and abnormalities of the heart, including hypertension, diminished heart muscle contractility and arrhythmia. Long-term abuse of other drugs is perceived to be less frequently associated with heart disease, a perception that may be due in part because alcohol is used and abused 2,000% more frequently than all other illegal drugs combined. Another factor that may contribute to this perception is the paucity of research on the topic.

Alcohol:

Cardiac arrhythmia: The most frequent complication of drinking alcohol is *cardiac arrhythmia,* an irregularity in heartbeat that can appear both as a result of a pattern of active drinking and as a complication of withdrawal from drinking. The most common form in patients with a previous history of heart disease has come to be known as the "holiday heart syndrome." Cardiac arrhythmia is seen in people who show up in emergency rooms between Sunday and Tuesday or around holidays associated with high alcohol ingestion. They generally report palpitations, sharp left chest pain or "passing out" spells. Both the direct effects of alcohol on the heart muscle and the effects of either alcohol or acetaldehyde on the heart's conduction system are the likely cause of arrhythmia, although some studies suggest that mild alcohol withdrawal or some neurological factor may also be at fault. In most cases, the recommended treatment is at least a few days of abstinence.

Hypertension: Long-term alcohol use is associated with *hypertension* (high blood pressure). Other factors, such as stress, psychosocial factors or hereditary predisposition, can exacerbate the link between alcohol and high blood pressure. While further study is needed in this area, the medical hierarchy currently takes the position that ingestion of three or more drinks per day may have a direct causal effect on elevated blood pressure.

Alcoholic cardiomyopathy: Heavy alcohol consumption causes *alcoholic cardiomyopathy,* a disease of the heart muscle associated with the development of coronary artery disease. In victims of alcoholic cardiomyopathy, which can appear in those who drink excessively over a long period of time regardless of the level of nutrition, the heart appears large and flabby, although the arteries and valves look normal. In such cases, the tissue of the heart is remarkably similar to tissue seen in ALCOHOLIC LIVER DISEASE. Exactly how the heart muscle is affected is unknown. A 1975 study by A. I. Cederbaum and E. Rubin, supported by more recent studies, indicated that ACETALDEHYDE, the first METABOLITE of ethanol, damages the mitochondria of the heart muscle and may play a key role in the development of alcoholic cardiomyopathy. While the evidence is not definite, it probably takes about 10 years of heavy drinking to cause serious damage to the heart. If the damage is detected in time and if the patient stops drinking alcohol completely, there is a fairly good chance of recovery. If severe heart failure has occurred, however, the outlook is usually poor.

There appears to be great variation in individual susceptibility to alcoholic cardiomyopathy. It usually occurs in men 25 to 50 years of age. Common early symptoms are difficult or labored breathing, swelling of feet and ankles, fatigue, and palpitations or chest pain. If excessive alcohol consumption continues, the disease often progresses to heart failure.

A very rare form of cardiomyopathy, known as beriberi heart disease, is seen only in alcoholics who are suffering from extreme nutritional deficiencies and is thought to be due to a lack of thiamine. (See NUTRITION.)

Coronary heart disease: Coronary heart disease results from atherosclerosis, which is characterized by the localized accumulation of lipids on the inner lining of the large- and medium-sized arteries serving the heart. Several pioneering studies, including one by Charles Hennekens and associates in 1973 and 1974, maintain that the consumption of alcohol in small amounts (up to 2 oz of ABSOLUTE ALCOHOL per day) decreases the risk of coronary heart disease. More recently, studies that correlate moderate alcohol consumption with reduced risk of coronary heart disease have come under attack. Critics argue that moderate use of alcohol is less a biological factor than a sign of a lifestyle that may also include balanced diet, exercise and more relaxed attitudes. There is also concern that widespread support of the benefits of moderate drinking may lead to experimentation and eventual relapse if attempted by people in abstinence-based recovery programs.

Drugs other than alcohol: While the correlation of heavy drinking with harm to the heart has long been recognized, the use of many other mood-altering drugs appears to affect the heart in more subtle ways.

Hallucinogens: LSD and other hallucinogens can cause temporary tachycardia (increased heart rate), as well as bradycardia (lowered heart rate). One of the most consistent effects of smoking marijuana is increased pulse, probably caused by increased secretion of the neurotransmitter epinephrine. Inhalation of aerosols and solvents can cause cardiac arrest which is usually fatal.

Narcotics: Heroin and other narcotics generally reduce heart rate, although vast fluctuations can take place during heroin withdrawal. More importantly, however, heroin addiction exposes the heart and liver to diseases attributable to the method of administration rather than to the drug itself. Endocarditis, an infectious inflammation of the heart's inner lining and valves, usually appears in addicts with some history of heart problems and is caused by staphylococcus and other antibiotic-resistant bacteria and fungi. Antibiotics are prescribed in the treatment of this disease, but their effectiveness can be compromised by the presence of the human immunodeficiency virus (HIV), which, since the early 1980s, has cut a broad swath across the ranks of heroin addicts worldwide because of widespread sharing of hypodermic needles. (See AIDS.) HIV itself affects the workings of the heart, besides diminishing the body's natural immune response to the diseases that commonly appear in drug addicts.

Stimulants: Stimulants such as cocaine and amphetamines can drastically speed up heart rate, exposing users to numerous forms of heart disease. Amphetamines have the added effect of strengthening myocardial contraction. Cardiac arrhythmia occurs with these drugs in direct proportion to their overall toxicity, and cardiac arrest is a frequent result of their abuse.

Nicotine: Although nicotine is not strictly speaking a stimulant, it does have both stimulant and depressant properties. Nicotine is the most widely abused and is said to be the hardest drug to quit. It causes heart disease and other circulatory problems such as coronary artery disease, arteriosclerosis and hypertension. Nicotine mimics acetylcholine, blocking the impulses that acetylcholine normally transmits and affecting nerve synapses to cause greater excitability. Nicotine also releases epinephrine to overwork the heart

B. M. Altura, "Introduction to the Symposium and Overview," *Alcoholism* 10, no. 6 (1986): 557–559.

G. E. Burch, "Alcoholic Cardiomyopathy," *Comprehensive Therapy* 3, no. 8 (August 1977): 10–15.

A. I. Cederbaum and E. Rubin, "Molecular Injury to Mitochondria Produced by Ethanol and Acetaldehyde," *Federation Proceedings* 34, no. 11 (1975).

"Drinkers and the 'Holiday Heart' Syndrome," *Medical World News* (December 27, 1976): 19.

Charles Hennekens et al., "Effects of Beer, Wine, and Liquor in Coronary Deaths," *Journal of the American Medical Association* 242, no. 18 (November 2, 1979).

A. L. Klatsky "The Cardiovascular Effects of Alcohol," *Alcohol* 22, Suppl. 1 (1988): 117–124.

A. G. Shaper et al., "Alcohol and Ischaemic Heart Disease in Middle Aged British Men," *British Medical Journal* (1987).

heavy drinker A person who drinks beyond the normal limits of moderation as defined by the society in which he or she lives. Often a heavy drinker is in danger of becoming, or indeed is well on his or her way to becoming, an ALCOHOLIC. Many heavy drinkers, however, do not become alcoholics, although the figure is probably much higher than those revealed in the available studies since numerous alcoholics have never been diagnosed as such. Some heavy drinkers escape most of the criteria for a PROBLEM DRINKER, but most cannot escape the cumulative effects of alcohol upon the human body, which result from consumption at a given time or over a period of time rather than from dependence. For statistical purposes, a heavy drinker has been defined as an individual with a consumption level "averaging above 3.82 ounces of 90-proof whiskey daily." This level amounts to an average daily consumption of 1.72 oz of ABSOLUTE ALCOHOL. (See ANSTIE'S LAW.)

hedonistic A term meaning "pleasure-seeking" that has been used to describe the motivations of chronic drug users. This term would be more apt if describing occasional BINGE DRINKING, or sessions of debauchery (see DEBAUCH). There is little justification in referring to addicts as hedonists since by the time a user becomes an addict, generally he or she is no longer using the drug to attain pleasure, but is requiring it to alleviate pain or discomfort (a process known as negative reinforcement).

heliotrope A plant of the genus *Heliotropium.* There are claims that when the flowers are brewed as a tea they produce a beverage that has a tranquilizing effect.

hemochromatosis A little-understood and relatively uncommon disorder that involves excessive deposition of iron within the body tissues and terminates after many years of widespread tissue damage. Victims often suffer from liver disease, diabetes and a bronze pigmentation of the skin.

The cause of hemochromatosis is not known, but one theory is that it may not be a single disease entity but rather a type of CIRRHOSIS, in which two conditions occur simultaneously—an excess buildup of ingested iron and liver disease caused by alcohol consumption and malnutrition. At Boston City Hospital, hemochromatosis was found to be most prevalent in patients who were heavy and chronic drinkers of wine, which contains large amounts of iron.

henbane *Hyoscyamus niger,* a fetid Old World herb. Its leaves yield an extract containing hyoscyamine, which has properties similar to BELLADONNA.

hepatitis An inflammation of the liver that appears frequently in alcoholics and addicts who administer drugs with used syringes. In the case of alcoholics, the inflammation is due to consumption of alcohol and with abstinence usually subsides quickly. Intravenous drug users get hepatitis from viruses. This type is contagious and can be much more serious, causing permanent LIVER damage and possibly death.

hepatoma Also known as hepatocarcinoma; hepatoma is a cellular CANCER of the liver, often associated with CIRRHOSIS.

herbal detoxification Newly popular but ancient treatment for detoxification and relaxation. Herbal mixtures help relieve the physical symptoms of anxiety concomitant to detoxification of drug-dependent people. They can also reduce insomnia. Herbs prescribed for detoxification are not habit-forming, are not vulnerable to overdose or misuse and may be administered even hourly if necessary.

herbals Certain plants were dried and used as medicinal agents long before modern medicine emerged. The herbals are now enjoying renewed interest as part of the movement toward natural foods and remedies. Some herbals have psychoactive effects, while some are inert and may be used as teas. Potentially toxic herbals include poke root and ginseng preparations. Instances of lead and pyrolizidine poisoning have been reported.

heredity   The sum of qualities and potentialities genetically handed down through families. Studies of natural and adopted children have been conducted to try to determine in what ways environment and genetics contribute to a predisposition to alcoholism. The results strongly suggest that a vulnerability to alcoholism is inherited. It is a recognized fact that alcoholism is common in certain families and studies point to both GENETIC and environmental factors. In addition, it has been shown that inherited traits may ward off alcoholism; possibly because of excessive production of acetaldehyde in the metabolic process. East Asians show a low incidence of alcoholism and a high level of acetaldehyde. Although heredity may play a primary role, it is generally agreed that other factors are also involved for the development of alcoholism.

Several studies have been conducted to determine the genetic or heredity susceptibility to drugs other than alcohol, but they are as yet inconclusive.

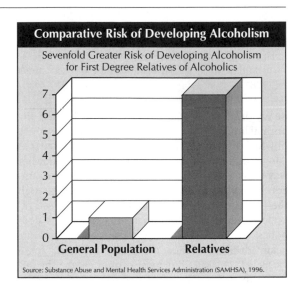

Comparative Risk of Developing Alcoholism

Sevenfold Greater Risk of Developing Alcoholism for First Degree Relatives of Alcoholics

General Population   Relatives

Source: Substance Abuse and Mental Health Services Administration (SAMHSA), 1996.

heroin   A narcotic, diacetylmorphine, derived from morphine, which it greatly resembles. Heroin is a central nervous system depressant that also relieves pain. It was developed in 1898 by the Bayer Company in Germany. Found to be more potent than morphine, its name comes from the German word *heroisch* (powerful, heroic). Originally, the drug was considered a better analgesic than morphine, a more efficient cough suppressant and a nonaddictive cure for morphine and opium withdrawal symptoms. It took some 12 years for the medical profession to realize that heroin was at least as addictive as morphine.

The Harrison Act of 1914 was the first attempt to control the use of heroin medically. By 1924 its manufacture in the U.S. was prohibited and law enforcement agencies were made responsible for its control. Nevertheless, more than 20 years went by before all existing stocks were surrendered. The dangers involved in heroin use became recognized worldwide and by 1963 it was prescribed medically in only five countries and legally manufactured in only three.

Meanwhile, heroin was steadily replacing opium and morphine on the street. International cultivation and well-organized smuggling operations with associated underground laboratories grew rapidly. Two things made such operations fairly easy—the comparatively simple chemical equipment needed to convert morphine to heroin, and the reduced bulk of heroin as compared to morphine.

Classification: Heroin is classified as a Schedule I drug under the Controlled Substances Act of 1970. It is illegal in the U.S. and is considered to have no medical value. Its manufacture, importation and use are illegal, but in spite of strenuous control efforts an international black market flourishes.

Usage: While abuse of alcohol and barbiturates can increase belligerent behavior by removing inhibitions, heroin acts to depress aggression as well as appetite and sexual drive. Depending on the method of administration, heroin induces varying degrees of euphoria; orgasmic reactions have been reported to follow intravenous injection. After a "fix," a sense of well-being replaces feelings of depression or low self-esteem, and this is followed by a semiconscious dreamy state—"going on the nod."

In 1989, however, users started to snort cocaine, a stimulant, and then quickly snort heroin, or mix the two together and then snort it (the "speedball"). Authorities say the speedball has the potential for catching on with whitecollar drug addicts.

Although once concentrated in metropolitan areas, heroin use has spread to all levels of society from inner-city ghettos to prosperous suburbs. Narcotics have become a problem on college campuses as well as in rural and city high schools. No class, race, educational level or community is free from the problems of heroin abuse. The most visible social evils, and criminal activities, however, are concentrated in large cities. A heroin habit is expensive: in one city it was estimated to average $10,000 a year. For the addict who must support his habit through theft, this means stealing some $50,000 worth of goods because they can be fenced for only one-fifth their value. Unlike barbiturate users and crack users, heroin addicts are not apt to commit violent crimes but many already have criminal records before they become dependent on drugs.

In the *1997 National Household Survey on Drug Abuse* published by the Substance Abuse and Mental Health Services Administration (SAMHSA), it was estimated that 2 million of the 216 million people represented had used heroin in their lifetime. It was further estimated that 597,00 people used heroin in the past year. Trends in actual use rose between 1985 and 1997, with an actual increase in estimated use among those aged 18 to 25 (0.6% to 0.8%). However, heroin-related deaths increased 18% between 1981 and 1988, when 1,100 people in the U.S. died from the drug. Additionally, data from the Drug Abuse Warning Network (DAWN) Report of 1994 indicated that the number of hospital emergency service visits related to heroin rose from 38,000 in 1988 to 63,000 in 1993, an increase of 65%. The report also showed a 35% increase in heroin-related emergency visits between 1992 and 1993 for people aged 18 to 25 (5,900 to 7,900). Significantly, the number of emergency visits related to the snorting and sniffing heroin jumped 470% between 1988 and 1993, from 1,100 to 6,000. The rise in this category may reflect growth in the popularity of snorting heroin, along with heroin smoking as alternatives to injecting. For many heroin users, injection carries

History of Heroin

1874	Heroin is isolated from morphine.
1898	Bayer Company of Germany produces heroin commercially and it is found to be more potent than morphine.
1900	Heroin is recognized as being addictive, though it was originally thought to be a cure for opium and morphine addiction. U.S. authorities estimate 250,000 to 1 million users.
1914	Harrison Narcotics Act taxes maufacture, importation and distribution of heroin.
1924	Manufacture is prohibited in the U.S. and heroin becomes available on the black market.
1930s	Abuse becomes widespread and the French Connection becomes main supplier of U.S. market until broken up in 1973.
1965	Drs. Dole and Nyswander present methadone maintenance program to treat heroin addiction.
1970	Controlled Substances Act classifies heroin as a Schedule I drug.
1980s	Government authorities estimate 400[,000]–750,000 users in the U.S. Southwest Asia becomes the major supplier. Heroin-related hospital emergencies rose 9.5% from 1987 to 1988.
1990s	Government authorities estimate a lifetime heroin prevalance of 2 million, with an estimated number of current users at 325,000 in the U.S. as of 1997. Emergency room visits rose to 72,221 in 1995 (13.9% of all drug-related emergency visits)

Source: Substance Abuse and Mental Health Services Administration (SAMSHA) *National Household Survey on Drug Abuse* (Rockville, MD): Department of Health and Human Services 1995)

Preliminary Data—As of June 1998

Estimated Number (in Thousands) of Persons Who First Used Heroin During Each Year 1965–1996,
Their Mean Age at First Use, and Annual Age-Specific Rates of First Use
(per 1000 Person-Years of Exposure), Based on 1994–1997 NHSDAs

Year	Initiates (1000s)	Mean Age	Age-Specific Rate of First Use[1]		
			12–17	18–25	26–34
1965	*	*	**	0.5	**
1966	*	*	**	0.5	**
1967	*	*	0.2	0.3	0.9
1968	*	*	0.3	0.2	0.3
1969	93	17.0	2.3	1.2	0.1
1970	106	19.4	0.4	3.3	0.1
1971	137	18.0	1.5	3.3	**
1972	137	17.3	1.7	2.9	0.1
1973	70	18.6	1.1	1.3	**
1974	86	22.6	0.4	1.5	1.1
1975	83	19.0	0.3	2.4	**
1976	68	18.7	0.9	0.9	0.5
1977	104	21.8	0.8	1.6	1.1
1978	54	20.9	0.2	1.1	0.3
1979	66	21.0	0.6	1.2	0.3
1980	49	20.6	0.3	0.8	0.1
1981	62	20.6	0.4	1.3	0.2
1982	50	21.6	0.1	1.0	0.3
1983	67	25.1	0.4	1.0	0.1
1984	91	27.0	0.3	0.9	0.9
1985	39	23.3	0.1	0.9	0.2
1986	55	20.1	1.0	0.9	0.1
1987	53	20.5	0.3	1.3	0.1

(continued on next page)

Preliminary Data—As of June 1998 (continued)

Estimated Number (in Thousands) of Persons Who First Used Heroin During Each Year 1965–1996, Their Mean Age at First Use, and Annual Age-Specific Rates of First Use (per 1000 Person-Years of Exposure), Based on 1994–1997 NHSDAs

Year	Initiates (1000s)	Mean Age	Age-Specific Rate of First Use[1]		
			12–17	18–25	26–34
1988	78	26.2	0.2	1.2	0.3
1989	55	24.3	0.5	0.9	0.3
1990	58	25.9	0.3	0.6	0.6
1991	53	23.5	0.4	0.7	0.6
1992	32	19.6	0.4	0.6	0.2
1993	61	20.2	1.1	0.7	0.4
1994[2]	93	19.5	1.5	1.5	0.4
1995[3]	117	19.4	2.2	2.2	0.2
1996[4]	171	18.1	3.9	2.3	0.4

*   Low precision; no estimate reported.
** Estimate rounds to zero.
[1] The numerator of each rate equals the number of persons who first used the drug in the year (times 1000). The denominator of each rate equals the number of persons who were exposed to risk of first use during the year, weighted by their estimated exposure time measured in years. For example, for the age group 12–17 in 1990, the denominator is the sum of three components:
  (1) those persons 12–17 years old in 1990 who first used the drug in 1989 or earlier, times a weight of zero. The weight is zero since they had zero exposure to the risk of first use in 1990.
  (2) those who first used the drug in 1990 times a weight of .5. The weight of .5 assumes that these people, on average, first used the drug at midyear and consequently have a half year of exposure (i.e. the first half of the year.)
  (3) those who never used, or those who first used the drug in 1991 or later, times a weight of one. The weight of one assumes their exposure to the risk of first use during 1990 was for the whole year.
  Each person is also weighted by his/her sample weight.
[2] Estimated using 1995, 1996 and 1997 data only.
[3] Estimated using 1996 and 1997 data only.
[4] Estimated using 1997 data only.

Source: SAMHSA, Office of Applied Studies, National Household Survey on Drug Abuse, 1994–1997.

the stigma associated with the stereotype of the "junkie." It is also known to spread of HIV. The purity of street-bought heroin has increased significantly so that the risk of overdose from snorting and smoking has increased as well. According to the DEA (U.S. Drug Enforcement Administration), the purity of an ounce of street heroin has risen from 34% in 1990 to 60% in 1993.

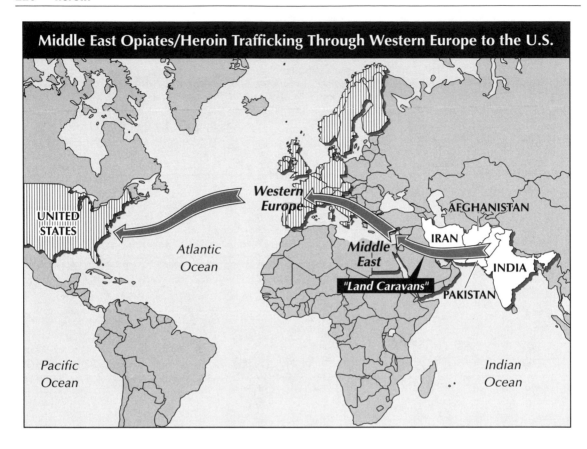

Middle East Opiates/Heroin Trafficking Through Western Europe to the U.S.

Administration and dosage: Addicts usually inject ("shoot up" or "mainline") heroin into a vein. Although it can also be mixed with a liquid and swallowed, sniffed like cocaine, placed under the tongue and even smoked—as it was occasionally in Vietnam, where it was cheap, potent and plentiful—these methods of ADMINISTRATION are rarely used in the U.S. due to the high cost of the drug and the fact that addicts need a number of fixes a day and want the maximum effect from their supply. Also, heroin has a disagreeable taste and the "rush" that addicts crave follows only intravenous injection.

Many people "snort" in an attempt to avoid becoming addicted. The cautious first-time user who tries swallowing or snorting heroin often graduates to "skin popping" or "joy popping" (subcutaneous injection of heroin), but the effects are comparatively mild and again there is no rush. Some users continue at this level, trying to avoid addiction but they are not always successful. Most people who become addicted have already begun mainlining.

Before preparing the powder for injection, the user measures out the usual dose. This can be difficult to estimate because the heroin sold on the street has been adulterated ("cut") many times as it passes down the line from the large distributor to the street dealer. To prepare an injection, the addict dilutes the heroin powder in a little water, puts it into a spoon or other device known as a "cooker" and holds it over a match, candle, cigarette lighter or other single flame until the mixture has boiled for a few seconds. After the liquid is filtered through a piece of cotton to remove any solid impurities and drawn up into a syringe or medicine dropper attached to a hollow needle, it is ready for injection. If the user is skin popping, the needle is pushed under the skin in any convenient place; if mainlining, the usual area that is chosen is the large vein inside the elbow. A tourniquet is applied between the vein and the heart, the needle is inserted and the syringe is pulled up to draw blood (a step called "verifying" or "registering") to make sure the needle is in a vein and not in muscle tissue or flesh. The bulb or syringe is then pushed down to inject the heroin and the rush follows immediately. Some users employ the process of BOOTING to prolong the initial effects. When heroin is booted, a small amount is injected and then blood is withdrawn back into the syringe and the process is repeated.

Since an epidemic of malaria among addicts in the 1940s, QUININE has often been used to cut heroin. Quinine enhances the "rush" effect, and in heroin that has been cut with milk sugar, quinine replaces the bitter taste of heroin that has been somewhat lost. Other adulterants include mannitol (a mild laxative) and various vitamins (inositol) and local anesthetics (lidocaine). Talcum powder is sometimes used as an adulterant and can be extremely dangerous because it does not dissolve in the bloodstream.

Appearance: Pure heroin is a white, crystalline powder with a bitter taste. It is soluble in water. Until recently, most heroin smuggled into the U.S. was supplied by Southeast Asian (GOLDEN TRIANGLE) opium sources and converted to heroin in clandestine laboratories in the area of Marseilles, France. After this supply route was curtailed, production of the drug increased in Mexico. Simpler, faster methods than those used in Marseilles resulted in impurities, which gave the Mexican heroin a brown color.

Activity: Heroin depresses the central nervous system in a way similar to alcohol and barbiturates but, unlike those drugs, it also relieves pain.

Effects: While numerous studies have indicated that heroin is not physiologically harmful, and does not cause brain deterioration, it is characteristic of addicts to neglect their health. Because the drug suppresses hunger, malnutrition is common and chronic bronchitis often develops as a result of suppression of the cough reflex. Addicts are also prone to accidents and violent death, living as they often do in contact with the underworld that controls the distribution of heroin. Many must become small-time pushers themselves to earn their own supply.

The greatest danger of heroin use is death from what the media call an overdose. Actually, the heroin sold on the street has been adulterated so much the addict is unlikely to get a large enough amount to suppress respiration. Most deaths are due to what medical examiners now call acute reactions. These include hypersensitivity with pulmonary edema, infections, complications associated with the adulterants used and the combination of heroin with alcohol or barbiturates. (See SYNDROME X.) In New York City on February 4th, 1991, it was reported that at least a dozen heroin addicts had been killed by a batch of heroin that contained the tranquilizer methyl fentanyl that made it 27 times more powerful than heroin alone.

Abscesses at the site of injection are common and the preferred vein may inflame after repeated use. Veins in the thigh, wrist or foot may then be used. Addicts who have run out of usable veins may resort to skin popping and end up covered with sores. One of the great dangers in mainlining is the chance of hitting an artery instead of a vein. The result is extreme pain at best, and permanent necrosis and scarring of the arm or leg at worst. Infection from unsterilized needles is an ever-present danger. Along with abscesses, serum hepatitis, tetanus and endocarditis (infection of the heart lining) can also appear, as well as the HIV virus communicated by sharing dirty needles.

Heroin and pregnancy: Women addicts run a high risk of complications during pregnancy and childbirth. The most common medical problems are anemia, heart disease, hepatitis and pneumonia. Children born to addicted mothers have a significantly higher mortality rate, are smaller than average and often show signs of acute infection. Some are also born physically addicted because they develop varying degrees of withdrawal symptoms within a short time after birth and require detoxification. (See BABIES, DRUG-ADDICTED AND -EXPOSED.)

Tolerance and dependence: Tolerance to heroin builds rapidly and stronger doses and more frequent shots are needed to produce the effects craved. Some addicts inject "speedballs" (heroin and amphetamines or cocaine), increasing the danger of acute reactions and death. Unlike barbiturates, virtually unlimited tolerance to heroin can build up, but there is still always a lethal dosage. Tolerance to heroin carries over to other opiates (all drugs derived from opium) as well as to opioids (synthetic drugs that resemble opium alkaloids and their derivatives). Both psychological and physical dependence develop rapidly with regular use of heroin. In psychological dependence there is an uncontrollable craving for the drug's effects. In physical dependence the body comes to rely on the drug to avoid withdrawal sickness.

Withdrawal symptoms: Although withdrawal symptoms from heroin are neither as severe nor as dangerous as those associated with depressants, especially alcohol and barbiturates, they are bad enough. Their severity depends on several factors—how long an addiction has lasted, how frequently a fix is needed, the general state of health and whether withdrawal is forced or voluntary. The first symptoms are usually noticed just before the time for the next regular shot. They include restless sleep, gooseflesh (from quitting "cold turkey"), tremors, yawning, irritability, joint and muscle pains, abdominal cramps, chills alternating with profuse sweating, runny nose, nausea, vomiting, diarrhea, urinary incontinence, shortness of breath and muscle spasms ("kicking the habit"). Reactions usually peak in a few days and linger for about one week. Although physical withdrawal symptoms subside in a week or so, psychological craving can continue for months and even years, making treatment difficult and causing many addicts to resume their habits. A protracted abstinence syndrome has been observed, in which for many months detoxified addicts experience sleep disturbance, anxiety and physical discomfort.

Treatment: Treatment for heroin addiction other than simple detoxification has changed greatly in recent years. Long-term residential centers (Daytop, Synanon, Phoenix House), now modified to address the problems of multiple drug use, including alcohol, still exist and are the most restrictive and longest duration treatments. Shorter-term residential programs of one to three months are becoming more common and are structured similarly to alcohol rehabilitation centers providing detoxification, education and the development of habits, skills and strategies useful in recovery. An approach based on a chemical dependency, not a single substance dependency, is becoming more accepted as most ex-heroin users have been found to develop problems with alcohol. Methadone maintenance provides opiate addicts with a long acting, orally administered,

affordable and, when administered properly, nonintoxicating dose of a prescribed narcotic. For a portion of patients treated it is effective. By breaking the drug procuring cycle it has been useful in allowing people to lead stable, productive lives. Another portion of patients use methadone for a short period of time and then detoxify. For many patients the results are less positive and they remain drug-involved, with chaotic lives and all the attendant risks. The factors in selecting good candidates for methadone and how best to use it, how much and what types of counseling and other services to provide remain obscure and are often debated.

Trafficking: When the manufacture and smuggling of heroin from Southeast Asia through Marseilles, the well-known FRENCH CONNECTION, was curtailed, many operations shifted to Mexico. Between 1986 and 1988 the amount of Mexican heroin entering the U.S. doubled, according to the National Narcotics Intelligence Consumers Committee. Most of the heroin supplying the U.S. market today comes from Southwest Asia (the GOLDEN CRESCENT). It has enjoyed great success because it is more potent and less expensive than heroin from Southeast Asia.

Smuggling by land and sea is very difficult to control. When enforcement efforts are increased in one border area or seaport, drug smugglers quickly switch to another. The profits of the illicit drug trade are so great that the risk of being caught is disregarded and others are always waiting to take the place of those arrested. To make things more difficult, worldwide organized crime is deeply involved in heroin manufacture, smuggling, distribution and laundering, as well as in prostitution and other crimes that many users commit to support their habits.

Synonyms: H, big H, horse, Harry, hairy, junk, joy powder, Mexican brown or mud, smack, white stuff, thing and many others.

Edward M. Brecher, ed., *Licit and Illicit Drugs* (Boston: Little, Brown and Company, 1972).

Sidney Cohen, *The Substance Abuse Problems* (New York: The Haworth Press, 1981).

"Facts About Opiates" (Toronto: Addiction Research Foundation of Ontario, 1980).

Richard R. Lingeman, *Drugs from A to Z* (New York: McGraw-Hill Book Company, 1974): 101–112.

Jack Margolis, *Complete Book of Recreational Drugs* (Los Angeles: Price/Stern/Sloan Publishers, Inc., 1978): 227–231.

Mike McQueen, "Heroin Cracks Cocaine Market," *USA Today* (July 7, 1989): 3A.

Substance Abuse and Mental Health Services Administration, *National Household Survey on Drug Abuse: Main Findings 1993* (Rockville, Md.: Department of Health and Human Services [DHHS]).

Substance Abuse and Mental Health Services Administration, *Preliminary Estimates from the Drug Abuse Warning Network, 1993 Preliminary Estimates of Drug-Related Emergency Department Episodes,* advanced report no. 8 (Rockville, Md., December 1994).

hexane   A major volatile solvent found in plastic cement. (See INHALANTS.)

hexobarbitol   A short-acting BARBITURATE. Its rapid onset and short duration of action makes it undesirable for purposes of abuse. It is sold under the trade name Sombulex.

high   Slang for being under the influence of alcohol or a drug, especially marijuana. The term "high" usually refers to a state of pleasurable intoxication, not to the point of unconsciousness. The "high" associated with alcohol, often expressed in uninhibited behavior, is an ironic effect of the sedative nature of the drug. The "high" phase of the effect is actually the result of the sedation of those areas of the brain that guard against abnormal behavior by producing inhibitions. The high from alcohol is thus the opposite of a high from such stimulants as amphetamines or cocaine, which are over-stimulating the central nervous system, giving the user a false sense of self-confidence and well-being.

high blood pressure   Also referred to as HYPERTENSION. A number of studies have linked high blood pressure to heavy alcohol consumption. (See HEART.)

hippie   A member of the nonconformist social movement of the mid- to late-1960s, often referred to as the "COUNTERCULTURE." The hippie subculture developed in the Haight-Ashbury section of San Francisco and in New York City in Greenwich Village and in the East Village, then rapidly spread to cities and universities across the country and throughout the world.

Hippies rejected many of the predominant values of mainstream American culture, which they characterized as "The Establishment." Pacifism, communal living and rejection of material ambitions were emphasized. Nonconformist modes of dress were encouraged, including long hair and beads. Hippies advocated use of drugs, particularly marijuana and hashish, and to a lesser extent, hallucinogens, as a means of increasing awareness.

Hispanics (Latinos)   Government projections predict Hispanics by 2010 will surpass the African-American population as the nation's largest minority. The Hispanic population is not uniform but composed of many subgroups; Mexican Americans form the largest subgroup, followed by Puerto Ricans, Cubans, Central Americans, South Americans and those of Spanish ancestry. Unfortunately, most statistical data fail to take into account any culturally linked behavioral differences between the various subgroups. As a result, statistical information about "Hispanics" can be misleading and therefore less useful than hoped for in the identification of problems and the planning of interventions. The following statement demonstrates the problem of generalizing about subgroups within the field of alcohol and other drug use. "Alcoholism is identified as a leading public health problem among the Hispanic population in the U.S." is a true statement when applied to the Hispanic population at large, but takes on a second meaning when one learns that the rates of both problem drinking and abstinence among Mexican Americans are higher than those of Puerto Ricans or Cubans. Regrettably, the information that follows is based on the only data available and does not take into account distinctions between Hispanic subgroups.

Alcohol: In 1983 about 18% of Hispanic men and 6% of Hispanic women suffered at least one alcohol-related problem. In Los Angeles over half the deaths of Hispanic males between the ages of 30 and 60 were from disorders of the LIVER. Studies note that Latinos have a higher than average rate of arrests for public drunkenness and drunken driving. Accidents while driving under the influence are also higher among Hispanics than among the general population.

A national sample of Hispanics in 1984 pointed to the vast differences in alcohol consumption between men and women. More than 70% of Hispanic women drink less than once a month or not at all; the numbers are reversed for Hispanic men, more than 70% of whom are drinkers. Hispanic men, like African-American men, show heavier drinking rates in their thirties but the rate declines thereafter. The *1993 National Household Survey on Drug Abuse* report by SAMHSA (Substance Abuse and Mental Health Services Administration) added depth to an understanding of Hispanic drinking patterns: 78.2% of Hispanic women reported having used alcohol in their lifetime compared to 96.4% of Hispanic men. Just 42% of Hispanic women reported past-month use—substantially less than the 69% of Hispanic men in this category. The percentage of drinkers is lower and the percentage of abstainers is higher among Hispanic teenagers than among their Anglo counterparts. The numbers shift, however, for Hispanic adults, who report higher rates of alcohol use and abuse than do Anglo adults.

Drugs other than alcohol: In the *1993 National Household Survey on Drug Abuse*, the rate of past-year illicit drug use by Latinos was slightly higher (12.2%) than that of either African Americans (12.1%) or whites (11.8%). More significantly, the rate of past-year use had increased (from 10.8%) in the year since 1992. Increases that year in past-year drug use were greatest among people aged 12 to 17 (12.7% to 17.6%) and those 35+ (4.1% to 6.8%). Hispanics were second highest (6.2%) in past-month illicit drug use compared to African Americans, who had the highest rate (6.6%), and whites, who had the lowest rate (5.5%). Young Hispanic males, 12–17, reported higher levels of lifetime, past-year and current marijuana use compared to their white age-mates: 15.7%, 13.2% and 6.7%, respectively. This same group also had greater lifetime, past-year and current cocaine use than their age counterparts among blacks and whites. Overall, Hispanics had the highest in past-year use (3.1% compared to 2.9% for blacks and 2.0% for whites), second in lifetime use (9.5% compared to 12.0% for whites and 9.4% for blacks), and second for past-month use (1.1% compared to 1.3% for blacks and 0.5% for whites) for cocaine use.

Causes: Poverty, inadequate health care, problems of acculturation, language difficulties, discrimi-

nation and feelings of failure, alienation and disappointment have been suggested as factors contributing to the high rate of drug use among Hispanics. In the case of alcohol consumption, culturally ingrained attitudes toward drinking and drunkenness, gender roles and public behavior may affect patterns significantly, regardless of any particularly negative social condition.

Treatment: While there is a belief that Hispanics are less likely than others to seek treatment for alcohol and other drug-use problems, data from two sources—the *1993 National Association of State Alcohol and Drug Abuse Directors' report* and the *1993 National Household Survey* indicated that Hispanics comprised 12.0% of drug client admissions, 0.1% more than whites and only 0.2% less than African Americans. Factors that may deter Latinos from seeking treatment include: cultural attitudes that alcohol problems are a moral weakness and not a disease, ignorance about the availability of treatment among newly arrived Hispanics, and less access to services because of income constraints or a lack of community services. While Spanish-speaking AA (Alcoholics Anonymous) and NA (Narcotics Anonymous) groups exist, culturally sensitive treatment services that are staffed with bilingual personnel remain in short supply.

R. Caetano, "Alcohol Use Among Hispanic Groups in the United States," *American Journal of Drug and Alcohol Abuse* 14 (1988): 273–311.

H. Edmandson, "Mexican-American Alcoholism and Deaths at LAC-USC Medical Center," testimony before the Subcommittee on Alcoholism of the California Senate Health and Welfare Committee (February 17, 1975).

Enoch Gordis, M.D., ed., *Seventh Special Report to the U.S. Congress on Alcohol and Health* (Rockville, Md.: National Institute on Alcohol Abuse and Alcoholism, 1990): 52.

Enoch Gordis, M.D., ed., *Seventh Special Report to the U.S. Congress on Alcohol and Health* (Rockville, Md.: National Institute on Alcohol Abuse and Alcoholism, 1990): 52.

Johns S. Gustafson et.al. *National Association of State Alcohol and Drug Abuse Directors, Inc., State Resources and Services Related to Alcohol and Other Drug Problems* (Washington, D.C., 1993).

Antonio Melus, "Culture and Language in the Treatment of Alcoholism: The Hispanic Perspective," *Alcohol Health and Research World* 4, no. 4 (Summer 1980): 19–20.

Richard Roth and David Fernandez, "Historic Accord between Hispanic Alcoholism Community and NIAAA," *Alcoholism* 1, no. 2 (November–December 1980): 20–22.

Substance Abuse and Mental Health Services Administration, *National Household Survey on Drug Abuse: Main Findings 1993* (Rockville, Md.: Department of Health and Human Services, June 1995): 95-3020.

histamine   A compound found in human tissue and highly concentrated in the skin, lungs and stomach. It is responsible for the dilation and increased permeability of blood vessels and plays a major role in allergic reactions. It is also a potent stimulator of gastric acid secretion. Release of histamine takes place very quickly after an intravenous injection of heroin, morphine or codeine, and can cause intense itching, sometimes over the entire body. Histamine can also cause a reddening of the eyes and a fall in blood pressure. The latter can result in dizziness and sometimes shock.

holiday heart syndrome   An irregularity or disturbance in the HEART (arrhythmia) that can occur after a period of heavy alcohol consumption.

holistic medicine   A medical approach that addresses a patient's whole complex of needs rather than treating a diseased or malfunctioning part of the body in isolation. The lifestyle of the patient is examined in depth. This includes diet; sleeping patterns; physical, mental or emotional stress; employment; relationships; physical and psychological history and so forth. Along with traditional biomedical techniques and nutrition, holistic medicine employs exercise plans, diet regimes, methods of self-healing, and suggests less stressful ways of living. Frequently, several health care specialists are involved in a patient's treatment.

homelessness   The U.S. Department of Housing and Urban Development estimates that at any given time roughly 250,000 to 350,000 people in the U.S. are homeless—and that these numbers are increasing. Although homeless people have usually been perceived as alcoholics, drug addicts and transients, this group now includes increasing proportions of the elderly, women, children, minorities, the unemployed, displaced families and the mentally ill. A host of factors adds to increases in the number of homeless people, but alcohol abuse remains high on the list.

Surveys in eight cities found that alcohol abuse among the homeless ranged from less than 20% to 45%. A recent review of health problems among 30,000 clients of the national Health Care for the Homeless (HCH) program revealed that 45% of men and 15% of women seeking health care were alcohol dependent. Two studies including significant numbers of women found overall problem drinking rates of 25% to 32%.

The coexistence of alcohol abuse, drug abuse and mental illness among the homeless is striking. In the HCH study, more than one-fourth of alcohol-abusing women and nearly one-fifth of men abused other drugs in addition to alcohol. Mental illness was diagnosed in more than half of female users and in one-fourth of male users.

Homeless people who drink heavily are especially susceptible to certain health problems, such as thermoregulatory disorders, peripheral vascular disorders and general physical debilitation. The homeless exhibit active tuberculosis rates 100 to 200 times that of the general population. Heavy drinkers are considered at greater risk for tuberculosis because of their generally more debilitated condition, and sharing of bottles is one possible source of tubercular infection.

A 1984 study of 1,000 homeless people in Ohio found that those with alcohol problems were more likely than the total sample to be men (94% versus 78%), were older (median age 41 years versus 33 years), were more likely to be divorced (45% versus 20%), were less likely to be currently married (3% versus 11%), and were more likely to have been in jail (87% versus 51%). The group with alcohol problems had been homeless twice as long; 24% of the alcohol users had been homeless for two years or more, compared with 13% of the others in the study.

E. M. Corrigan and S. C. Anderson, "Homeless Alcoholic Women on Skid Row," *American Journal of Drug and Alcohol Abuse* 10 (1984): 535–549.

V. Mulkern and R. Spence, *Alcohol Abuse/Alcoholism among Homeless Persons: A Review of the Literature* (Washington, D.C.: U.S. Government Printing Office, 1984).

D. Roth and J. Beau, *Alcohol and Homelessness: Findings from the Ohio Study (Summary)*, in F. D. Wittman, ed., *The Homeless with Alcohol-Related Problems: Proceedings of a Meeting to Provide Research Recommendations to the NIAAA (1985)* (Rockville, Md.: NIAAA, 1985): 5–11.

J. D. Wright et al., "Ailments and Alcohol: Health Status among the Drinking Homeless," *Alcohol Health and Research World* 11 (2) 1987.

homeopathic medicine   Homeopathic medicine is based on the "law of similars," the theory that symptoms of disease can be cured by substances that induce symptoms similar to the disease itself in healthy people. The principles of this theory were formulated by Samuel Hahnemann (1755–1843), who believed that diseases represent a disturbance in the body's ability to heal itself and that only minute amounts of a homeopathic drug are needed to stimulate the body to self-heal. A basic tenet of homeopathy is the smaller the amount of a medicine the more powerful the effect, contrary to the prevailing view of present-day allopathic physicians, who believe in objectively finding a proven drug effect by using the scientific method. Homeopathic preparations, if soluble, are diluted 1 part to 9 or 99 parts water or alcohol. If insoluble, the substance is pulverized and mixed with powdered lactose in similar proportions to soluble preparations. These preparations may be further diluted until a specified concentration is reached. Over 1,000 homeopathic substances are listed in the Homeopathic Pharmacopoeia of the U.S.

At the turn of the century in the U.S., there were 14,000 practitioners and 22 schools of homeopathy. However, as the competing theories of allopathic medicine evolved into what became so-called scientifically based medicine and medical education, homeopathic medicine declined in the U.S. Its medical schools closed or converted to the teachings of allopathic medicine. Today, homeopathy is still practiced either by physicians (M.D.'s), the descendants of the allopaths, or by dentists, nurses, chiropractors or naturopaths. Homeopathic remedies are still used and were given legal status by the Federal Food, Drug and Cosmetic Act of 1938. These remedies are available from practitioners, health food stores, pharmacies and mail-order houses. Most homeopathic substances have not been scientifically tested for their effectiveness. The Food and Drug Administration (FDA) has taken action against manufacturers who have made grand claims as to the effectiveness of homeopathic remedies for serious diseases. However, the FDA has generally presumed that homeopathic substances are safe because the active ingredients in the substances are diluted to undetectable and possibly nontestable amounts. As with vitamins, the FDA has not required that homeopathic substances be proven effective. In recent times there has been a willingness on the part of the public to try alternative forms of medicine, largely due to the fact that Americans have been rapidly losing faith in the entire health care system, from the doctors, to the hospitals, to the insurance companies, all of which seem to be more interested in turning over profits than in providing the solid, beneficial, personal and effective health care that should be available to all tax-paying citizens.

M. Kaufman, *Homeopathy in America* (Baltimore: The Johns Hopkins University Press, 1971).

homosexuals (gay men and lesbians)   The needs of chemically dependent gay men and lesbians are specifically addressed in certain specialized treatment centers. Much has been written about elevated rates of chemical dependency among gay men and lesbians, but these previous "statistics" were established by self-report surveys and by observing treatment populations. There are no valid statistics on what percentage of the population is homosexual. It has been conservatively estimated that one out of every four homosexuals in the U.S. is an alcoholic, compared with a rate of approximately one out of every ten in the general population. A study found that approximately one-third of the total gay and lesbian population of Los Angeles County abuses alcohol on a regular basis.

Factors contributing to alcoholism and drug use may be related to the stigma society has attached to homosexuality. Gay men and lesbians may feel alienated from society and from themselves as a result of this stigma. In the 1970s and early 1980s, a significant segment of the homosexual community used bars as a focal point for social activity (as did large segments of society in general), which undoubtedly encouraged excessive drinking. In the wake of the AIDS crisis, however, alternative lifestyles are in the process of undergoing significant transformations. It is unclear what impact this will have on the relationship of homosexuals and alcohol abuse.

Marian Sandmaier reports that lesbians are more likely to have alcohol-related problems than gay men. One study found that 35% of lesbians had problems with alcohol at some point in their lives compared with 28% of gay men and only 5% of heterosexual women. Alcohol-dependent lesbians suffer from both the stigmas attached to homosexuality and to WOMEN who drink.

Treatment: Currently, some authorities believe that gay men and lesbians may have more difficulty gaining access to treatment and may have socially complicated recoveries. Whether gay men and lesbians have higher rates of chemical dependency than other groups is not known.

The majority of treatment centers are not geared to the specific chemical dependency problems of gay men and lesbians, and in certain parts of the U.S. there are treatment centers that may have a negative attitude toward them. Some centers may even refuse to treat homosexuals or try to cure their sexual orientation rather than their alcoholism or drug problem.

There is a need for recovery programs oriented toward people with alternative lifestyles. Alcoholics Anonymous has a few gay and lesbian groups in urban areas. In Boston, the Homophile Alcohol Treatment Service (HATS), funded in part by the Massachusetts Division of Alcoholism, helps homosexuals with alcohol problems. The National Association of Lesbian and Gay Alcoholism Professionals publishes a newsletter and works to improve treatment for alcoholic clients, and the *Pride Institute* in Minnesota, California and Pennsylvania is a valuable resource for information and referral sources for gay men and lesbians.

Lilene Fifield, "Introductory Address to the National Council on Alcoholism Forum Session on Alcohol Abuse in the Gay Community," *National Institute on Alcohol Abuse and Alcoholism (NIAAA) Information and Feature Service,* no. 75 (September 3, 1980).

Marian Sandmaier, *The Invisible Alcoholics* (New York: McGraw-Hill Book Company, 1980): 179–183.

Bryan Stephens, "Alcoholism: The Dark Side of Gay," *The Magazine* 6, no. 3 (Fall 1980).

hooch   Short form of *Hoochinoo,* a variation of *Hutsnuwu,* the name of an Alaskan Tlingit tribe. The name was applied to a liquor secretly produced by the tribe. Slang for liquor or whiskey, especially inferior, homemade or cheap varieties, or alcohol obtained surreptitiously. The term "hooch" became common during Prohibition, when it was used to refer to bootlegged whiskey of unknown origin. Today the term is rarely used.

hops   Cones formed on the female *Humulus lupulus* vine. The cones are green with a surface of broad scales and a base that includes twin blossoms. When ripe, they are dried and used as an essential ingredient in the production of virtually all beers. It is the hop that produces the distinctively bitter, or "hoppy," flavor of beer, and the proportion of hops used in brewing is an important factor in creating distinct varieties of beer. First cultivated in Bavaria for use in beer, hops have been successfully transplanted to other areas for the same purpose. The shoots of the vine are also sometimes eaten as a vegetable and are especially popular in Belgium.

hormone   A body chemical formed in some organ of the body, such as the adrenal glands or the pituitary, and carried by a body fluid to another organ or tissue, which brings about specific effects. Now it is often prepared synthetically.

hormones, male sex   Many male alcoholics show signs of sexual impotence, loss of libido and symptoms of hypogonadism (diminished function of the sex glands). Consumption of alcohol lowers testosterone levels, resulting in breast enlargement, loss of facial hair and testicular atrophy. The lower levels may be due to either of two direct causes: increased breakdown of testosterone or reduced synthesis.

Breakdown of testosterone: It appears that alcohol increases the synthesis of LIVER enzymes called 5-alpha-reductases, which are responsible for the degradation of testosterone by converting it to dehydrotestosterone. There is also evidence that administration of alcohol over a long period of time causes estrogen levels to rise, and this increase correlates with an increase in the level of a liver enzyme called hepatic aromatase, which is involved in the conversion of androgens (male sex hormones) to estrogens (female sex hormones). It has also been shown that there is an increased rate of conversion of testosterone to its respective estrogen. The signs of "feminization" in male chronic alcoholics are probably due to a simultaneous reduction in androgens and an increase in estrogens.

Reduced testosterone synthesis: In addition, there is evidence to indicate that alcohol administered acutely or chronically depresses testosterone synthesis in the testes. The levels of testosterone are lowest three to five hours after a high level of alcohol consumption and become normal or higher than normal six to eight hours later, when BLOOD ALCOHOL CONCENTRATION is very low. Apparently the effect of alcohol is biphasic—low doses increase testosterone levels and high doses depress them.

Most researchers have found that heavy use of alcohol over a long period of time has a strong toxic effect on the testes. Serum testosterone levels are low in chronic alcoholics, and it appears that repeated and persistent alcohol use eventually causes irreversible damage to the structural and biochemical composition of the testes. Several recent studies have shown that the toxic agent may be ACETALDEHYDE, the metabolic product of ethanol, rather than the ethanol itself. In one recent study, alcoholic men healthy in other respects experienced decreases in plasma testosterone levels after a 10-day administration of alcohol. It has long been known that chronic alcoholics experience impotence and this is probably due to inhibition of testosterone production.

Enoch Gordis, M.D., ed., *Seventh Special Report to the U.S. Congress on Alcohol and Health* (Rockville, Md.: National Institute on Alcohol Abuse and Alcoholism,1990): 66–67.

hot lines   Telephone numbers that can be called for information and help. They are usually toll-free and generally operate on a 24-hour basis. Hot lines cover a wide range of problems—from battered women, runaways and child abuse, to mental health, suicide and drug problems. Some are very specific, such as the cocaine hot line and the hot line for Alcoholics Anonymous.

Hughes Act   The act that established the National Institute on Alcohol Abuse and Alcoholism in 1970. This federal legislation was named after its sponsor, Senator Harold Hughes.

Hycodan   A narcotic ANTITUSSIVE prescribed as a cough suppressant that contains hydrocodone bitartrate (a CODEINE derivative) and homatropine methylbromide. It has a potential for abuse and can cause drug dependence. When combined with alcohol or other central nervous system depressants it can have an ADDITIVE EFFECT. Symptoms of an overdose include depressed respiration, somnolence and muscle flaccidity; an extreme overdose can cause cardiac arrest and death.

Hycomine   A narcotic ANTITUSSIVE prescribed as a cough suppressant. It contains hydrocodone bitartrate (a CODEINE derivative) and phenylpropanolamine for nasal congestion. It has the potential for abuse and can cause dependence.

hydrocodone   A synthetic CODEINE derivative prescribed as an ANTITUSSIVE. It is a Schedule II drug and an ingredient in HYCODAN.

hydromorphone   A semisynthetic MORPHINE derivative. Prescribed as an analgesic, its potency exceeds that of morphine. (See DILAUDID.)

hyoscine, hyoscyamine   See SCOPOLAMINE.

hyperactive   A condition of excessive or pathological activity, most often seen in young children. It is also called attention deficit disorder (ADD). Their hyperactivity is characterized by constantly moving, handling, touching and otherwise drawing attention (usually critical) to themselves. Stimulant drugs are sometimes prescribed in the treatment of children and adults with ADD. It is paradoxical that stimulants can be helpful in a condition where hyperactivity is present, but studies have shown that the use of stimulants can decrease aggressive behavior and hyperactivity and improve concentration and attention. Since a deficit in concentration may be the cause of the hyperactivity, this improvement in concentration may be the key action of the stimulant. This use of stimulants is controversial, however, and some authorities suggest that hyperactivity may be due to situational or personality factors, and that stimulants may aggravate the condition they were prescribed to alleviate. It has been suggested that use of stimulants may condition children to psychotropic drug use in later years, but this has not been proven. Another belief is that adequate treatment of ADD may reduce probability of later chemical dependency.

hyperglycemia   Unusually high BLOOD SUGAR level, the principal condition of DIABETES.

hypertension   High blood pressure. This condition has been associated with excessive consumption of alcohol. PCP, cocaine and amphetamines cause temporary hypertension. (See HEART.)

hypnosis   In recent years, hypnosis has gained popularity as a way of controlling unwanted habits, particularly among smokers. Originally identified with the work of Anton Mesmer in the 1770s, hypnosis gained a certain respectability in 1843 when James Braid published a book entitled *Neurypnology,* which served to remove the taint of "occultism" from the procedure. Hypnosis has been questioned right up to the present, however. Today it is recognized as a process, not a therapy, but one that can be successfully utilized in combination with alcohol and other drug treatment. More popular, however, is the use of self-hypnosis: patients are taught these techniques in recovery as part of a program of stress management and relaxation.

The recent popularity of hypnosis has led to an increase in untrained and incompetent practitioners entering the field, which has prompted the American Society of Clinical Hypnosis and the International Society of Hypnosis to take a strong stand against unskilled hypnotists. Lacking training, they are unaware of the importance of trance states and there can be untoward and possibly dangerous consequences.

(Hypnosis also refers to sleep, and drugs that induce sleep are called HYPNOTICS.)

hypnotic   A drug prescribed to induce sleep. Hypnotics slow down the action of the central nervous system. This group of drugs includes BARBITURATES and some nonbarbiturates.

hypoglycemia   Low BLOOD SUGAR; a condition sometimes seen in alcoholics.

hypotension   Abnormally low blood pressure. Hypotension may be caused by use of drugs, especially narcotics, sedatives and diuretics.

I

iatrogenic addiction   Addiction to a drug that has resulted from the drug being prescribed by a physician for medical purposes.

ibogaine   A psychedelic alkaloid found in the roots, stems and leaves of *Tabernanthe iboga* and also in the plants *Peschiera lundii, Stemmademia donnellsmithi, S. galleottiama* and *Conopharyngia durissma,* which are native to Africa, Asia and South America. It is a STIMULANT, and it has hallucinogenic effects similar to those of LSD. The alkaloid was isolated in 1901 and synthesized in 1966. Iboga extracts, or ibogaine, are still sold in Europe in tonics and stimulants. Used in Africa by hunters stalking game, iboga has the effect of allowing the user to remain motionless for long periods of time while remaining conscious and mentally alert. Indian tribes in South America use iboga in a rite of passage into adulthood and it is known as the *ordeal bean.*

In the early 1990s researchers began to explore ibogaine's potential role in the treatment of addictions. Advocates believe that ibogaine: (1) acts to suppress the multiple symptoms and physical discomfort of narcotic withdrawal; (2) interrupts the psychological drive (or craving) to use; and (3) is free of any iatrogenic side effects.

ice   Like crack, ice is not a new drug but a smokable version (methamphetamine hydrochloride) of an old one—crystallized methamphetamine, better known as "meth" "crystal meth" and "speed." During the 1960s and 1970s, meth was usually taken in pill form or injected. There is still a high rate of methamphetamine use by injection reported in California. The first appearance of ice in the U.S. was in Hawaii (1989), and by 1990 it was on the U.S. mainland. Ice has now become Hawaii's number-one drug problem.

Usage: Ice was reported to be making serious inroads in the U.S., and some officials predicted it would soon outstrip crack cocaine in overall use. This possible epidemic is as of yet difficult to document and may not occur. The fact that methamphetamine already exists in the U.S. in a relatively cheap and available form (pills and "crystal") may make ice less of a marketing phenomenon than crack. The DEA (Drug Enforcement Administration) stated in 1995 that although the production and distribution of methamphetamine had spread even to the rural regions of the eastern U.S., such as southern Pennsylvania (as ice), it had not emerged as a major drug problem outside of Hawaii. However, in the *Monitoring the Future Study* conducted by the National Institute on Drug Abuse (NIDA), 26.6% of high school seniors reported that they could fairly easily obtain ice. Additionally, 3.4% reported having used this substance at least once in their lifetime, an increase of 2.7% from 1990. The report also indicated that 1.8% of seniors had used ice in 1994, an increase of 1.3% from 1990.

Dosage: Methamphetamine sold for around $50 in cellophane packets ("paper") that contain about a tenth of a gram, good for one or two "hits," which last longer than the brief (less than 30 minutes) high for crack cocaine.

Effects: According to NIDA, ice is as addictive as crack and produces similar bouts of severe depression, anxiety and paranoia, as well as convulsions, increased wakefulness, increased physical activity, increased respiration, hyperthermia, euphoria, irritability, confusion, tremors and convulsions. Hyperthermia and convulsions can result in death. Cardiovascular side effects include chest pain and hypertension and can also result in cardiovascular collapse and death. In addition, the substance can increase heart rate and cause hypertension, resulting in blood vessel damage and possible stroke. It is possible that prolonged stimulant use can result in long-lasting psychological damage. Other side effects: aggressive behavior, hallucinations and fatal kidney failure.

The little that is known about ice's effects on newborns is alarming. As with cocaine babies, ice babies tend to be irritable and have difficulty with early bonding. Some have severe tremors and cry for 24 hours without stopping; they have to be swaddled to be held.

Trafficking: Methamphetamine is smuggled in from illegal labs in South Korea and the Philippines. It is produced in clandestine labs across the U.S., but primarily in California, Oregon and Texas. Hawaii's ice trail can be traced back to South Korea (where it's called *hiroppon*), which, along with Taiwan, leads the world in the manufacture and export of the drug. Koreans learned about methamphetamine from the Japanese, who invented the stimulant in 1893. Japan banned use of the drug they call *shabu* in the 1950s, and though use in recent years has leveled off in that country, it remains the drug's largest market.

Treatment: Most clinics are treating ice addiction as they would cocaine and other stimulant addiction but report that ice addiction is proving more difficult to "kick."

idiosyncratic reaction   A unpredictable and unique response to a mind-altering substance.

illusions   Distorted or mistaken perceptions that differ from hallucinations and delusions because they *always* involve the misrepresentation of exter-

nal stimulus. Illusions may include distortions of space, perspective and movement. For a person suffering from illusions, a crack in a wall may, for example, be seen as a crawling snake.

immune system   Chronic alcohol abuse can lead to increased susceptibility to several DISEASES and certain types of CANCER. Several immune deficiencies have been observed in alcoholics at the time of admission for treatment. For example, 4% to 8% of admitted patients have decreased circulating levels of white blood cells called neutrophils, indicating that the ability to destroy (phagocytize) bacteria is reduced.

Acute and chronic consumption of alcohol has been shown to suppress the immune defense system, though it is not yet proved that alcohol is involved in the progression of disease in persons who have been infected with the virus responsible for AIDS (ACQUIRED IMMUNE DEFICIENCY SYNDROME).

National Institute on Alcohol Abuse and Alcoholism, *The Effects of Alcohol on the Immune System,* summary of a workshop to provide policy and research recommendations to the National Institute on Alcohol Abuse and Alcoholism, Alcohol Research Utilization System Working Document no. 85-02 (Rockville, Md., 1986).

impairment   From the Latin *in* (intensive) + *pejorare* (to make worse). Impaired functioning or damage to an individual as a result of the use of alcohol or other drugs. There is a tendency on the part of society to associate impairment with illicit drug use rather than with alcohol abuse. This is most likely due to the common belief that alcohol is not a drug. This view is related to the legality of alcohol and its subsequent acceptance and integration within the general culture. Impairment must be measured on an individual basis because there are people who consume large amounts of alcohol or take other substances and exhibit little indications of abuse, whereas others are strongly affected by small amounts. The term impairment is used to describe both short- and long-term effects of substance abuse. For a person on a drinking bout, for example, it may mean difficulty in walking and/or talking, confusion and drowsiness or even unconsciousness. Impairment is also used to determine whether or not a person is an alcoholic, since alcoholism can rarely be measured in terms of consumption alone.

According to David J. Armor, J. Michael Polich and Harriet B. Stambul of the Rand Corporation (see RAND REPORT), major signs of behavioral impairment that indicate a diagnosis of alcoholism are:

Tremors (shakes)
Alcoholic blackouts (loss of memory)
Missing meals due to drinking
Drinking on awakening
Being drunk
Missing work days because of drinking
Difficulty in sleeping
Quarreling with others while drinking
Drinking on the job
Continuous drinking
Drinking alone

If one is continually high, missing work or social activities, and/or having problems with family or with other interpersonal relationships, then alcohol or other drug use most likely is interfering with the ability to function in society, and this signifies that one is suffering from impairment.

David J. Armor, J. Michael Polich and Harriet B. Stambul, *Alcoholism and Treatment* (New York: John Wiley & Sons, 1978): 89.

inability to abstain   A characteristic of E. M. JEL-LINEK's fourth category of alcoholism (DELTA ALCO-HOLISM); the term is used to describe someone who, although unable to abstain from drinking for even a day, can sometimes control the amount consumed on any given occasion.

India   Although there have been partially successful attempts to abolish the caste system in India, alcoholism and drug use are still conditioned by the system, which is based on religion and affluence. There are a number of individual patterns even within the various religions. The Islamic religion forbids drinking, but some Muslims drink; Sikhism forbids smoking, but some Sikhs smoke; Christianity permits the use of alcohol, but some Christians abstain. The Brahmins, the highest caste among Hindus, are not allowed alcohol but are permitted to use ganja. Thus there is no single pattern of substance use and abuse.

Alcohol: India claims that alcohol is the most commonly abused drug, but the term "abuse" has a much wider connotation in India than in other countries and includes not only addiction but also occasional and experimental use of alcohol. By most western standards "experimental" and "occasional" is more *use* than abuse. Compared with other nations, India actually has a low rate of alcohol abuse—somewhere in the range of 0.2%–1.9% of the total population. But when you consider the lack of money and facilities available for treatment, these figures represent an enormous burden.

Thus far the Indian government is focusing a substantial portion of its study of drug and alcohol problems on the student population. This group is more readily available to the centers conducting the research and is easier to communicate with than the rest of the population. There is also a higher incidence of drug use among college students than among other groups.

Drugs other than alcohol: Although no comprehensive survey has been taken to assess the magnitude of drug use in India, research studies sponsored by the Ministry of Social Welfare in selected cities showed alcohol and tobacco to be the most commonly abused drugs. Although the prevalence rate of drugs such as cannabis, LSD, heroin and opium was very small, it should be noted that cannabis, in various potent forms, is often used in religious ceremonies. While there has been an increase in the use of ganja (a form of cannabis midway in potency between charas and bhang) among college students in recent years, the drug has been mostly used for experimental purposes. Previously, drug use was associated with the more impoverished sections of the population.

Charas, a potent form of cannabis, has been forbidden since the mid-1940s. There is heavy smuggling of the drug from Tibet, though, and most of the supplies pass through India before being channeled into other countries. An increase in trade has prompted the Indian government to consider stronger penalties for smuggling.

Treatment: As of the late 1980s there were few centers in the country devoted exclusively to the treatment of drug and alcohol abuse. Although there are limited inpatient facilities in mental and psychiatric departments of general hospitals, the government tends to feel that "it is not desirable to promote specific and separate treatment facilities for drug addicts." In outpatient programs, the principal method of treatment emphasizes the use of antagonistic drugs.

Indian Alcoholism Counseling and Recovery House Program   A private not-for-profit drug and alcoholism residential treatment program for Native Americans of all ages. The program works with youths and parents to provide education and guidance about Amerindian traditions through a combination of classes, alternative activities, culturally specific programs, support groups and community functions. Parenting and life-skills training classes are also provided for all ages.

Indian Health Service (IHS) alcoholism and substance abuse programs   The IHS is an agency of the U.S. Department of Health and Human Services (DHHS), which provides primary health care for approximately 800,000 Amerindians and Inuits through a system of some 200 hospitals, clinics and health stations. The IHS also assists in funding several urban Native American health clinics. More than 300 alcohol- and drug-abuse programs providing prevention, education, outpatient, inpatient, aftercare, halfway house and drop-in center services are funded by the IHS and contracted by tribes and native organizations. Through this specialized health care delivery system, approximately 800 physicians and 2,000 hospital, clinic and public health nurses respond daily to the many consequences of alcohol and other drug use, abuse and dependence. The IHS now conducts a training program for its professional staff members. This effort was accelerated with enactment of Public Law 99-570, the Anti-Drug Abuse Act of 1986.

Eva Marie Smith, M.D., "Service for Native Americans," *Alcohol Health & Research World* 13, no. 1 (1989): 94–96.

inebriate   An alcoholic. See INEBRIETY.

inebriety   Standard terminology in the late 19th century for habitual intoxication or excessive drinking. Usually applied to the habitual state of ALCOHOLISM. Still used by the World Health Organization (WHO) and applied in legal contexts ("Public inebriates" and "Chronic inebriates").

infancy   In addition to the serious danger of being exposed to excessive amounts of alcohol or other drugs as a developing fetus, an infant is also at risk if the mother drinks excessively or uses other drugs after giving birth. Alcohol and other drugs enter the breast milk at the same level that they enter the mother's bloodstream, endangering breast-fed infants. Ingesting breast milk that contains alcohol may cause pseudo-Cushing syndrome, which is characterized by high levels of the hormone cortisol and of glucose in the blood as well as obesity, purple striations on the abdomen, easy bruising and a "moon" face. The long-term effects are unknown. It has also been shown that alcohol inhibits the milk-ejection reflex and may cause a reduction in the milk supplied to the nursing infant. (See FETAL ALCOHOL SYNDROME, CHILDREN OF ALCOHOLICS [COA'S] AND SUBSTANCE ABUSERS and PREGNANCY.)

infection   Infection from unsterile needles is a serious danger to intravenous drug users (IDUs). Two of the most common diseases associated with unclean needles are AIDS (ACQUIRED IMMUNE DEFICIENCY SYNDROME) and HEPATITIS. Thrombophlebitis and bloodstream infections from contaminated injections are also a hazard. (See ADMINISTRATION and LIVER.)

Chronic alcohol abuse weakens the IMMUNE SYSTEM and increases susceptibility to myriad infectious diseases, including certain types of cancer. Among these: tuberculosis, pneumonia, yellow fever, cholera, bacteremia, bacterial peritonitis, head and neck cancer and hepatitis.

inhalants   Inhaling substances for their euphoric and intoxicating effects has had a long history of use and abuse. Thousands of years ago people inhaled the vapors from burning spices and herbs, particularly in religious ceremonies. Today people use commercial inhalants that are usually broken down into two categories: anesthetic gases and volatile hydrocarbons. Inhalants are absorbed through the lungs and their effects have a rapid onset but are usually of short duration.

Anesthetics: The anesthetics NITROUS OXIDE, ETHER and CHLOROFORM were used recreationally long before they were used medically. Discovered in the 1700s, they were most often abused by students and physicians, and "inhalant parties" were popular during the 19th century. Although some abuse of

Preliminary Data—As of June 1998

Estimated Number (in Thousands) of Persons Who First Used Any Inhalant During Each Year 1965–1996, Their Mean Age at First Use, and Annual Age-Specific Rates of First Use (per 1000 Person-Years of Exposure), Based on 1994–1997 NHSDAs

Year	Initiates (1000s)	Mean Age	Age-Specific Rate of First Use[1]		
			12–17	18–25	26–34
1965	119	14.9	2.2	2.0	**
1966	93	18.8	3.1	**	**
1967	166	15.4	5.2	1.5	**
1968	160	16.9	2.6	2.6	0.7
1969	115	15.7	3.6	0.9	0.1
1970	201	18.0	5.1	1.7	**
1971	283	15.9	7.1	3.3	**
1972	274	19.3	4.3	2.7	2.9
1973	240	16.9	4.6	3.7	0.2
1974	341	19.1	6.0	3.9	0.2
1975	326	17.2	7.0	4.0	0.5
1976	435	18.7	7.8	5.7	1.0
1977	443	18.7	8.4	4.6	1.4
1978	558	18.2	9.6	8.3	1.0
1979	436	18.3	9.0	4.7	1.9
1980	485	17.9	9.6	6.4	0.5
1981	447	19.1	7.1	5.9	1.9
1982	391	17.9	7.7	5.0	0.9
1983	439	19.3	7.1	5.3	1.4
1984	384	17.9	8.7	3.9	1.6
1985	364	16.8	9.1	4.8	0.2
1986	365	17.0	9.3	4.4	0.6
1987	384	18.1	9.3	4.8	0.5

(continued on next page)

Preliminary Data—As of June 1998 (continued)

Estimated Number (in Thousands) of Persons Who First Used Any Inhalant During Each Year 1965–1996, Their Mean Age at First Use, and Annual Age-Specific Rates of First Use (per 1000 Person-Years of Exposure), Based on 1994–1997 NHSDAs

Year	Initiates (1000s)	Mean Age	Age-Specific Rate of First Use[1]		
			12–17	18–25	26–34
1988	462	18.8	10.9	5.3	1.5
1989	361	16.9	9.5	4.0	0.8
1990	385	16.5	10.1	4.5	0.7
1991	382	15.4	10.3	4.6	**
1992	460	16.7	12.2	6.4	0.4
1993	605	16.4	16.4	8.7	0.2
1994[2]	613	16.3	17.6	7.8	0.1
1995[3]	634	15.8	19.8	7.5	0.2
1996[4]	805	16.3	21.0	12.4	0.5

** Estimate rounds to zero.

[1] The numerator of each rate equals the number of persons who first used the drug in the year (times 1000). The denominator of each rate equals the number of persons who were exposed to risk of first use during the year, weighted by their estimated exposure time measured in years. For example, for the age group 12–17 in 1990, the denominator is the sum of three components:

(1) those persons 12–17 years old in 1990 who first used the drug in 1989 or earlier, times a weight of zero. The weight is zero since they had zero exposure to the risk of first use in 1990.

(2) those who first used the drug in 1990 times a weight of .5. The weight of .5 assumes that these people, on average, first used the drug at midyear and consequently have a half year of exposure (i.e. the first half of the year.)

(3) those who never used, or those who first used the drug in 1991 or later, times a weight of one. The weight of one assumes their exposure to the risk of first use during 1990 was for the whole year.

Each person is also weighted by his/her sample weight.

[2] Estimated using 1995, 1996 and 1997 data only.

[3] Estimated using 1996 and 1997 data only.

[4] Estimated using 1997 data only.

Source: SAMHSA, Office of Applied Studies, National Household Survey on Drug Abuse, 1994–1997.

gaseous and vaporous anesthetics, which produce effects similar to alcohol intoxication, still exist today, the trend now is toward the use of volatile hydrocarbons and organic solvents.

In the 1960s, glue sniffing became a nationwide concern as numerous deaths were reported. A campaign was mounted against it and received mass media coverage. Studies reported that most deaths

Common Drugs: Symptoms of Abuse of Inhalants

Inhalants. Substances abused by sniffing.

Drug Name	Street Names	Method of Use	Sign and Symptoms	Hazards of Use
Gasoline, Airplane Glue, Paint Thinner, Dry Cleaner Fluid		Inhaled or sniffed, often with use of paper or plastic bag or rag.	Poor motor coordination, impaired vision, memory, and thought.	High risk of sudden death. Drastic weight loss. Brain, liver and bone marrow damage.
Nitrous Oxide	Laughing Gas, Whippets	Inhaled or sniffed by mask or balloons.	Slowed thought, headache.	Death by anorexia. Neuropathy, muscle weakness.
Amyl Nitrate, Butyl Nitrate	Poppers, Snappers, Rush, Locker Room	Inhaled or sniffed from gauze or ampules.	Abusive violent behavior, light-headedness.	Anemia, death by anorexia.

Source: New York State Office of Alcoholism and Substance Abuse Services.

(approximately six out of nine) were actually the result of asphyxiation because the person (usually a child) placed a plastic bag over his head to intensify the effects of the fumes. It has been suggested that the nationwide attention given to the campaign may have actually alerted potential users to the substance and contributed to the extensive abuse.

Volatile hydrocarbons and organic solvents: Volatile hydrocarbons, used commercially as aerosols and solvents, are compounds of distilled petroleum and natural gas and include gasoline, kerosene, benzene and other related chemicals. Varnish, varnish removers, paint thinners and lacquers, lighter fluid, nail polish remover, cleaning solutions, spot removers, glues and cements and various aerosols are common household products containing organic solvents. Toluene, acetone, naphtha, cyclohexane, carbon tetrachloride and various alcohols are some of the active chemicals found in these products.

Classification: Local and state governments now prohibit minors from purchasing certain substances, particularly plastic model glues. The abuse of organic solvents will most likely continue, however, because of the large variety of household products on the market that contain them.

Usage: Inhalants are absorbed through the lungs, one of the most rapid routes to obtaining a "high." Various methods are employed, including putting the substance on a piece of cloth and then inhaling the fumes; spraying or placing the substance in a paper bag and then inhaling (known as "huffing"); and, in the case of pressurized gases, filling a balloon and waiting for the vapor to warm before inhaling. Recreational use of inhalants is usually seen in young teenagers (particularly boys) between the ages of 13 and 15, probably because they have access to many common household products that contain organic solvents and do not have access to the more conventional drugs. Consistent inhalant users tend to be disturbed individuals. The use of inhalants by prisoners in institutions, retarded and mentally ill people, and people in economically deprived communities has also been reported, probably because common household products are the only substances readily available. Alcoholics who are trying to forestall withdrawal symptoms are also known to inhale solvents when alcohol is not available. In some countries, such as Ireland, inhalant use among teenagers is more widespread than in the U.S.

Tobacco and MARIJUANA, as well as various other substances inhaled through smoke and absorbed through the lungs, are classified as inhalants. (See SMOKING AND ALCOHOL.) Cocaine is also often referred to as an inhalant although it is sniffed and actually absorbed through the membranes of the nostrils.

AMYL NITRITE, a rapidly acting stimulant inhalant that dilates the blood vessels and is used particularly to intensify and prolong sexual orgasm, is also often classified as an inhalant although it, too, is absorbed through the membranes of the nostrils.

NIDA reported that the rate of inhalant use among high school seniors has seen a slight increase. In 1997 the rate of use for this group was 6.7%. This was an increase from 6.6% in 1991. In 1997, 2.5% of high school seniors reported using inhalants in the last 30 days. This was an increase from 2.4% in 1991. The lifetime rate of use for seniors in 1997 was 16.1%, a 1.5% decrease from 1991. Alarmingly, 8th graders reported a 21.0% use rate. This was an increase of 3.4% from 1991. The high rate among this group would appear to indicate the ease of access that young children have to inhalants. In 1997, 23.8% of high school seniors reported that they had fairly easy access to amyl and butyl nitrates.

Activity: Absorbed by the lungs, vapors rapidly enter the bloodstream and are then distributed to the brain and liver. Because most solvents are fat soluble they are quickly absorbed into the central nervous system and consequently depress such body functions as heartbeat and respiration. In fatty tissue, accumulation occurs less rapidly. The kidneys metabolize and excrete some solvents; others are eliminated unaltered, primarily through the lungs. When the lungs are the route of elimination the solvent odor will linger on the breath for several hours.

Effects: After the quick onset of effects, the duration can usually be measured in minutes; maximum duration is probably an hour depending on the substance and the dosage. Among the effects generally felt are excitement, the lowering of inhibitions, restlessness, uncoordination, confusion and disorientation, and—after prolonged inhalation—delirium and coma. The effects are similar to alcohol and other sedative intoxication, though some inhalants are reported to produce psychedeliclike effects. In industrial settings, where chemicals are inhaled for prolonged periods in unventilated areas, they become toxic. Prolonged exposure can result in nau-

sea, vomiting, muscular weakness, fatigue and weight loss. There also can be extensive damage to the kidneys, liver, bone marrow and brain. Most people who inhale substances for their giddy and intoxicating effects stop long before these more serious symptoms appear.

In moderate doses inhalants can produce sedation, changes in perception, impaired judgment, fright and panic—symptoms that in some cases have resulted in accidental deaths. Some inhalants seem to be capable of sensitizing the heart to adrenaline, a substance that is present in the body and is manufactured in greater quantities in times of stress. This has been thought to be a cause of cardiac arrhythmia fatalities in some cases. In larger doses inhalants produce sleep, unconsciousness and even seizures. The long-term known effects of inhaling are usually reversible after drug use is stopped, although permanent brain, liver or kidney impairment can occur. Chromosome damage among inhalant users is still under study by researchers and the effects of blood abnormalities are still not proven. Another area needing research is the effect of inhalant use on the immune system. There has been a high incidence of certain inhalant use and the human immunodeficiency virus (HIV), which seems to be caused by a weakened immune system.

Inhalants are often referred to as "deliriants," drugs capable of producing illusions, hallucinations and mental disturbances.

Tolerance and dependence: Tolerance can develop and a user will need a larger dose in order to get the same effect. Physical and psychological dependence have occurred in cases of long-term abuse, but solvents are not considered as dangerous as other DEPRESSANTS, such as alcohol and barbiturates. There have also been reports of withdrawal symptoms among solvent users, such as hallucinations, chills, abdominal cramps and delirium tremens. Studies have shown that a cross-tolerance can develop between solvents and other central nervous system depressants, such as alcohol. In addition, there is a synergistic or ADDITIVE EFFECT when alcohol or barbiturates are taken with certain solvents.

inpatient treatment   Alcoholism and drug treatment services have increased in recent years. More than 1.43 million persons were treated in 1987; with 15% in an inpatient setting and 85% as active outpatients (see OUTPATIENT TREATMENT). In 1993 there were 47,962 inpatient treatment admissions for alcohol and 21,538 for drugs in hospitals, and 284,912 alcohol and 97,030 drug admissions to free-standing residential facilities. In that same year, the number of inpatient rehabilitation admissions for both alcohol and drugs was 141,015. State and local government control of in-hospital treatment units decreased by 17% from 1978 to 1984 while for-profit ownership of such units increased by 342%. Other drug use, alcohol or drugs, was recorded as a discharge diagnosis on 1.13 million (2.7%) of all discharges for short-term hospitals in 1983.

Continuing attention needs to be paid to the heterogeneity apparent among alcoholics, and attempts are being made to develop concepts and measurements appropriate to such heterogeneity. The alcohol-dependence syndrome concept has been researched extensively. Possible applications of this concept involve approaches to individualized treatment planning.

Studies of inpatient and outpatient treatment indicate that some alcoholics do not require inpatient treatment. In fact, detoxification can be accomplished safely and effectively in both social settings and medical settings. Although inpatient treatment costs eight times as much as outpatient treatment, a recent study found that detoxification was completed by 95% of inpatients but only 72% of outpatients. Before advising against a medical detoxification, however, the patient's complete medical and psychiatric condition must be evaluated.

The practice of patient-treatment matching—where patients are assigned to different treatments based on various characteristics, and the treatments are later correlated with outcomes—continues to be of considerable interest.

There have been a number of interesting changes and some advances in PHARMACOTHERAPY for alcoholics. Interest continues in possible uses of disulfiram (Antabuse) as an adjunct to more comprehensive treatment. Lithium carbonate has been a therapy for some alcoholics, mainly those with coexisting affective disorders. Benzodiazepines have been used for the clinically anxious alcoholics without significant findings. In addition, there is a concern for the appropriateness of medication groups for alcoholics, given that benzodiazepines can be addictive. There is recent indication that antidepressant medications, such as fluoxetine (Prozac), that reduce the uptake of the neurochemical serotonin and nonbenzodiazepine antianxiety drugs such as busiprone, have had a significant impact on decreasing alcohol abuse. There is also some research and treatment with the medication naltrexone, which blocks the opiate receptor sites in the brain and reduces alcohol craving.

More studies are under way to better determine which treatment—inpatient or outpatient—is most suitable for which alcoholics.

Recovery rates for alcoholism and other drug dependencies vary considerably according to various studies. A study of 1,001 adults treated for chemical dependency in five Minneapolis–St. Paul clinics in 1983–1984 found that 58% of the patients maintained continuous abstinence for two years following treatment; only 28% relapsed to multiple or prolonged periods of substance abuse.

With regard to cost, all treatment expenditures, including a substantial portion for treatment of the medical consequences of alcoholism, are estimated at $15 billion a year in the U.S. Alcoholism treatment is effective for many persons. Favorable cost-benefit ratios that show reduced general health care expenditures in treated alcoholics indicate that alcoholism treatment is an effective means of containing HEALTH CARE COSTS throughout the health care system.

There is a downward trend on the number of days allowed for inpatient stays. This is a result of the questioned cost effectiveness of inpatient vs. outpatient treatment as well as cost containment efforts on the part of INSURANCE companies and the federal and state governments. As a result, 30-day inpatient stays have often been reduced to one week or even less.

Additional research is needed to develop objective and reliable markers of treatment outcome. Continuing treatment goal studies indicate that for most substance users, abstention from alcohol (and other psychoactive drugs) is still the most reasonable treatment goal for diagnosed alcoholics in light of current scientific and clinical information. In some cases, an ability to adopt a lifestyle incorporating moderate usage can be acquired, and may be appropriate, in other cases pharmacotherapy or other therapies may be needed for the interval following initial treatment and preceding complete recovery. In a smaller percentage of cases some form of therapy may be required for the duration of the user's life.

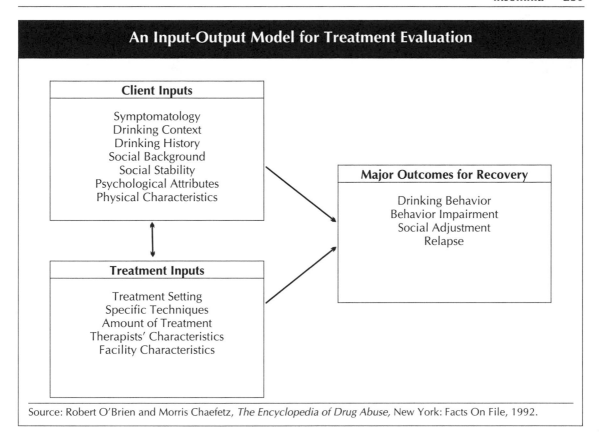

An Input-Output Model for Treatment Evaluation

Client Inputs

Symptomatology
Drinking Context
Drinking History
Social Background
Social Stability
Psychological Attributes
Physical Characteristics

Treatment Inputs

Treatment Setting
Specific Techniques
Amount of Treatment
Therapists' Characteristics
Facility Characteristics

Major Outcomes for Recovery

Drinking Behavior
Behavior Impairment
Social Adjustment
Relapse

Source: Robert O'Brien and Morris Chaefetz, *The Encyclopedia of Drug Abuse,* New York: Facts On File, 1992.

Raymond F. Anton, "Medications for Treating Alcoholism," *Alcohol Health & Research World* 18, no. 4 (1994): 265–267.

Enoch Gordis, M.D., ed., *Sixth Special Report to the U.S. Congress on Alcohol and Health* (Rockville, Md.: National Institute on Alcohol Abuse and Alcoholism [NIAAA], 1987).

Seventh Special Report to the U.S. Congress on Alcohol and Health (Rockville, Md.: NIAAA, 1990): 408.

John S. Gustafson et.al. *State Resources and Services Related to Alcohol and Other Drug Problems, Fiscal Year 1993: An Analysis of State Alcohol and Drug Abuse Profile Data* (Washington, D.C.: NASADAD, January 1995): 21.

National Clearinghouse for Alcohol and Drug Information (NCADI), *Fact Sheet* (Rockville, Md.: NCADI, June 1987).

input-output model for treatment   A method of matching alcoholic clients with the most suitable treatment center for successful results. It was pro-posed by the authors of the RAND REPORT. "Input" is divided into two categories: client and treatment inputs. The first group lists client characteristics, such as symptoms, drinking history, social background and physical characteristics, that might be relevant in determining the best type of treatment. The second group lists the type and amount of treatment available at a particular center, such as the techniques used and the characteristics of the therapists and the facility. The success of the treatment (the "output") depends on the appropriateness of the treatment chosen.

Although designed for use in the treatment of alcohol abuse, the model is also relevant to the treatment of other substance users.

insomnia   A disturbance of the biologic rhythm of waking and sleeping, insomnia is characterized by insufficient or poor sleep and fatigue during waking hours. Common complaints of insomniacs include difficulty falling asleep and frequent awakenings during the night. A detailed study of a person's insomnia is generally not made because sleeping pills can usually provide a simple, apparently effective but very short-term cure. Although true insomnia does exist, there can be numerous other causes such as depression, misinformation about sleep requirements and a preoccupation about getting enough sleep. Certain drugs, such as amphetamines, will also cause insomnia. Alcohol can cause sleeplessness in some individuals and relaxation and sleep in others. Although when the effects of alcohol are still strong it can make one drowsy and put one to sleep; when the effects wear off an AGITATION occurs, which is a symptom of alcohol withdrawal. This can cause the user to wake up and then be unable to return to sleep. (See SEDATIVE HYPNOTICS for a detailed explanation of this syndrome.)

Insomnia is a common complaint of chemically dependent people in varying stages of recovery and is considered a symptom of PROTRACTED ABSTINENCE SYNDROME. It almost always resolves in recovery, although complete resolution of the problem may take months or even one or two years.

instability and crisis etiological theory   One of a number of SOCIOCULTURAL ETIOLOGICAL THEORIES, the instability and crisis etiological theory posits that alcohol and other drug (AOD) abuse is sometimes the result of stressful social factors upon the individual, especially during crisis periods when significant changes have occurred. Although mood-altering substances are consumed in this context to alleviate stress, heavy consumption ultimately exacerbates the condition, creating a cycle whereby stressful events lead to drug use, which in turn increases stress levels.

Institute for Social Research   Located at the University of Michigan in Ann Arbor, the institute reports annually on the drug use and related attitudes of America's high school seniors and young adults. The findings come from an ongoing national research and reporting program entitled *Monitoring the Future: A Continuing Study of the Lifestyles and Values of Youth*. The program is funded by the National Institute on Drug Abuse (NIDA).

insurance   Although insurance companies paid out large sums during the first half of the 20th century to cover complications and secondary manifestations of alcoholism, the disorder of alcoholism itself went undiagnosed and untreated. The Kemper Insurance Companies and Wausau became the first, in 1964, to provide coverage for the treatment of alcoholism, and other companies began to follow suit. Early coverage was generally restricted to inpatient care, and it wasn't until the mid-1970s that it began to be extended to some outpatient facilities. Kemper was again the leader in providing group health coverage for outpatient treatment in qualifying nonhospital alcoholism centers. By 1979, 24 states had enacted legislation concerning the coverage of alcoholism; some mandated coverage, others required coverage to be available as an option. Insurance coverage for the treatment of other substance abuse was still ignored, however, and it wasn't until recently that it was recognized as an area where coverage was needed. Treatment for those addicted to heroin, cocaine and other drugs is still often limited to EMPLOYEE ASSISTANCE PROGRAMS, and these programs, in turn, are often limited to companies that can afford to finance them.

Today many companies provide some form of coverage for alcoholism, but a number of issues related to this type of insurance have yet to be solved.

The insurance coverage matter is extremely difficult to summarize because state regulations, as well as individual employer plans, vary so greatly. Most major health insurance plans cover some inpatient and outpatient treatment. According to a report by the Substance Abuse and Mental Health Services Administration, private medical insurance in 1990 covered about 80% of Americans for alcoholism and 74% for drug dependency, including 70% of workers in companies with more than 100 employees. Some 10,000 firms and public agencies, including 70% of the Fortune 500 companies, now have to help alcohol/drug-use victims pull their lives together and return to work. The logic of acting on a chemical-dependency problem sooner rather than later is slowly being recognized throughout corporate America.

The unevenness of insurance reimbursement for chemical dependency is one of the major problems faced by consumers in dealing with private insurance companies. There are insurance plans that have only provided coverage for treatment related to traditional physician and hospital care. Other plans have limited reimbursement to inpatient detoxification for alcoholism, but not reimbursed for cocaine or heroin abuse. Many plans have not provided coverage for alternative modes of treatment, such as outpatient services, residential programs, therapeutic communities, halfway houses and alternative forms of medicine such as acupuncture and homeopathy. Additionally, in states where it is not required by law, there are health insurance plans in which chemical dependency treatment services have not been included in the basic coverage package and must be purchased through extended premiums as an extra. In 1990, 84% of those persons privately insured were covered for outpatient services, while 94% were covered for inpatient care.

The resistance of insurance plans to provide coverage for treatment in alternative programs may not be cost-effective. Alternative programs have often been less expensive and less disruptive to employed individuals and may be as effective as, if not more so, than hospital treatment. Estimated costs for one patient day of treatment can run from as low as $40 in alternative models to well over $200 in more traditional inpatient hospital base settings. The National Institute on Alcohol Abuse and Alcoholism (NIAAA) estimated that the cost of treatment per year, per client, is $13,730 for hospital alcoholism treatment; $20,780 for hospital detoxification; $4,730 for an intermediate long-term alcoholism treatment service; and $740 for an outpatient treatment program. More recently, as the treatment outcomes for long-term inpatient treatment have come into question, a number of major insurance companies have shifted their coverage to emphasize outpatient care. This shift has been exercised by decreasing the number of days of inpatient coverage from 30 to as low as three or in some cases no days, while increasing the coverage days for outpatient care.

In addition to private insurance, the federal, state and county governments through the Medicare and Medicaid programs are also providers of health care coverage for chemical-dependency treatment. The focus of these programs is to ensure that health care services are provided to the indigent, disabled and persons aged 65+.

Medicare was instituted by the federal government in 1966 and provides a range of health care benefits to people over 65 who are covered by Social Security; people over 65 who are not cov-

ered by Social Security, but are willing to pay premiums; and to persons who are disabled. Part A of Medicare covers services given in hospitals, extended-care facilities and a person's home. It is financed by mandatory payroll deductions and from Social Security funds. Part B is a voluntary part of the plan that covers physician and other medical services. Costs for Part B are paid for by general tax revenue and premiums paid by persons choosing to participate in this part of Medicare. Part B is also paid for by Medicaid for people who are disabled and cannot afford to pay the Part B premiums. Medicare enrollees can also choose to purchase MediGap plans from private insurance carriers to cover the Medicare deductibles and copayments as well as other noncovered expenses. Medicare Part A benefits for chemical-dependency services are the same as for general medical services. Inpatient hospital services are limited to 190 days in a lifetime, 150 of which can be used in any one benefit period, 90 days are held in reserve. Physician services under Part B are unlimited. Outpatient physician services and chemical-dependency treatment were initially limited to 50% of charges or $250, whichever was less. However, in 1987, Congress expanded these benefits to $2,000 annually with a 50% copayment charge to the patient. (By 1995, reimbursement had increased to $2,300.) Additionally, in 1987, limits and special copayments were removed for the medical management of patients receiving psychopharmacological medications. There is now no visit limits for chemical-dependency treatment and the same $20 copayment charged to medical patients is charged to chemical-dependency patients. Payments for chemical dependency services combined with mental health services remain a relatively small part of the Medicare budget, about 3%. This reflects the limited coverage for such services, along with the possible reluctance of older persons, because of fear of stigma and lack of knowledge, to seek such services.

Medicaid, the second major form of publicly financed health care coverage, is financed by federal, state and, in most cases, county governments. It was instituted in 1967 and provides health care benefits to public assistance recipients; the blind; one-parent families with dependent children; adults unable to work; the physically disabled; the mentally disabled; the homeless; migrant laborers and their families;

rural residents lacking regular health services; and those persons considered disabled because of chemical dependency. The federal government funds 50% of the program, with states paying in some cases the other 50%, but in most instances requiring counties to contribute between 10% to 25% of the costs. States are required to include health care coverage for: inpatient and outpatient services, including family planning, laboratory and X-ray services, physician services, long-term care or rehabilitation services for persons over 21. States have the option, but are not required, to provide services such as prescription drugs, eyeglasses and dental care. Additionally, states may limit the type and amount of services received by the mentally ill and chemically dependent. It should be noted that states have leeway in defining who is indigent (poor) and therefore eligible for services. Consequently, 60% of those who are indigent in the U.S. are left out of this program. Included in this number are many persons with alcohol and other drug-use problems.

Beginning in the mid-1980s and accelerating in the 1990s, insurance companies and the government began to alter or significantly modify coverage and payment systems for chemical-dependency treatment services as well as general medical services. These actions were in direct relation to the increasing cost not only of chemical-dependency programs, but all health care in the U.S. in the 1970s, 80s and 90s. In 1996, it was estimated that health care accounted for 14% of the U.S.'s gross national product (GNP) and had almost doubled from 1970 when it was 7.6% of the GNP. This growth in costs exceeded the overall U.S. inflation rate. Corresponding to these increases was the doubling, during this same time period, of the health care expenditures of the private insurance companies who accounted for over one-third of health care funding. This rise in insurance expenditures was increasingly being reflected in the rising insurance premiums paid by employers and by the rise in government spending for Medicaid and Medicare.

Up until October 1, 1983, Medicare, like most private insurance carriers, provided insurance through prospective payment plans or, as commonly known, indemnity plans. In such plans, the insurer is billed by the service provider or patient for the cost of services after the services have been rendered. The charges for services are usually determined by the provider, based on what the market will bear or what are reasonable and customary charges. Additionally, in the classic private indemnity plan the patient must cover a deductible payment (on average the first $300 of charges per year) and a 20% copayment. Indemnity plans can be costly to the government and private insurers if the provider determines how much is paid out for health care. The tendency in some situations is for the provider to overbill to increase revenues. To counter this, the federal government instituted a new hospital reimbursement system. Under the new system, referred to as the *prospective payment plan,* hospitals were reimbursed with fixed payments, determined in advance, rather than the previous cost-based payment method.

The preset rates of the new system were based on an extensive list of Diagnosis Related Groups (DRGs) that cover most illnesses. The Federal Health Care Finance Administration (HCFA) established 470 DRGs based on specific diagnosis, patient age and sex, treatment procedure, and clinical and statistical analysis of all cases treated. Additionally, the DRG rate for individual hospitals were weighted or adjusted to cover the cost of geographic differentials such as construction costs, wages, whether in a rural or urban location, and the amount of care given to indigent populations. The hospital's costs in providing medical education or conducting research were also factored in. The DRG schedule applied only to inpatient operating costs. Physician and outpatient and emergency services were originally excluded from this schedule. However, the Omnibus Budget Reconciliation Act of 1989 instituted a national fee schedule that went into effect in 1992 for what physicians are paid for their services, whether on an inpatient or outpatient basis. The schedule is based on the relative value of the time, skill and intensity of the procedure as adjusted for geographic location. Under this system, physicians are limited as to what they can charge a patient above the amount Medicare reimburses. HCFA exempted alcohol/drug-use treatment services provided at psychiatric facilities *if* they met HCFA criteria (a key criterion is that the unit be under the direction of a psychiatrist).

While the DRG system was designed to curb the rapid growth of costs, according to authorities in the field of substance-abuse treatment, it most likely negated any advances in treatment achieved in the past. The DRG system did not allow for continuing care and neglected the fact that different modes of approach and treatment are required by different patients. Additionally, the DRG system was one of the first payment systems to begin limiting the average length of an inpatient stay. Where the average length of stay in a hospital, including detoxification, had been 28.5 days, Medicare payments, however, were based on an average 11.3-day stay. Addiction authorities contended that the treatment of alcoholism could not be restricted to an 11-day regimen and suggested that the patient's family is the ultimate victim as it was left to pay additional treatment bills.

The DRG system has mostly been phased out in most states in favor of letting the *market forces* control health care costs, namely letting hospitals set their own fees. The delivery of health care services has become competitive. This is due to an oversupply of hospital beds and in turn a surplus of hospitals. Hospitals are now competing with each other for patients and are reducing their fees to attract these patients as well as insurance companies. This has resulted from a number of factors that include insurance companies negotiating contracts to exclusively send their insured clients to the most cost/effective hospitals in a cost containment system that is known as managed care. Managed care as well as the older DRG system created the stimulus for hospitals to reduce their own costs by reducing the length of hospital stays and in developing technology that permitted a shift in doing many medical procedures from an expensive inpatient to a less costly outpatient service.

Private insurance carriers as noted have attempted to decrease their own costs. They have done this by increasing the premiums charged to employers or have cut back on the number of days that are reimbursed for inpatient stays, such as for detox services. A number of these insurers have also in the past adopted the DRG-based payment methodology. Most significantly, private insurers are now seeking to contain their costs through the previously mentioned system of managed care. Although there are different models of managed care, it can be defined as a set of procedures that manage health care costs by influencing, and in some cases controlling, patient care decision-making through a case-by-case assessment of the appropriateness of the care prior to its delivery. Its goal is to eliminate unnecessary or inappropriate care and therefore reduce health care

costs found in prospective payment plans. In 1996 over 100 million Americans were enrolled in some form of managed care health insurance program.

The most prominent type of managed care is the health maintenance organization (HMO). The HMO offers services to a defined population of enrollees usually through their employer. HMOs contract with a group of physicians known as an independent practice association (IPA) or with individual physicians, hospitals and other health care providers to offer a full array of health care services to the HMOs enrollees. Payment to the health care provider is at a previously agreed upon prospective rate per enrollee cared for by that provider. The rate is based on a payment formula. This is known as a capitated rate. In some situations the provider is paid at an agreed upon discounted rate, a rate less than what the provider would normally charge for each patient seen. These providers, known as panel members, must first be certified by the HMO before being the provider in the plan. Certification is based on professional training and credentialing. In some cases HMOs directly employ health care providers and own the hospitals. Enrollees are provided or are assigned a primary care physician. An HMO enrollee cannot directly seek the services of a specialist, including those of a chemical-dependency specialist. The patient must be referred by the primary care physician, if that physician sees this referral as appropriate. This is known as *gatekeeping*. Additionally, if a specialist or hospitalization is needed, it must be preapproved by the HMO. The patient benefits from belonging to an HMO because there is no office visit payment or only a small copayment ($5 to $10) per visit and usually no hospital costs. The employer benefits because HMO premiums are lower than traditional (indemnity) insurance plans. The HMO benefits because, as an insurer, expenses are kept down through the limiting of what in theory are inappropriate or unnecessary services and through reduced payments to providers. Chemical-abuse-treatment inpatient services have been increasingly limited under the HMO model. It is rare that a patient could receive 30 days for inpatient detoxification. Many stays are limited to three to seven days. In addition, as has been the case with many health insurance plans, inpatient stays for substances other than alcohol may not be covered at all. Outpatient visits for chemical dependency are also tightly managed by the HMO. Although benefits for outpatient visits might cover 52 weeks, the HMO might require that the provider have prior approval from the HMO for any additional visits after an initial five visits. This is known as *recertification*, and the HMO may decide not to agree to it because it is believed to be clinically unnecessary, although the addiction specialist and the patient believe otherwise. The provider and patient must then provide additional clinical evidence that continued services are necessary, but may still be turned down for recertification.

Another form of managed care is the Preferred Provider Organization (PPO). Like the HMO, the PPO serves a defined population of enrollees. While there are a number of variations of the PPO model, all offer some organized network of health care providers who agree to see the enrollees of the PPO at a discounted rate. The enrollees are free to select their primary care physician through a list of participating panel members. PPO patients pay a small copayment for each outpatient visit. PPOs vary in their requirements that enrollees see a primary care physician or receive prior PPO approval in order to see a specialist. As with HMOs, PPOs have limited the number of outpatient and inpatient visits for chemical-dependency treatment.

A variation of the PPO is the point-of-service plan (POS). In the POS, the enrollee is allowed to go out of the PPO's network for services. Like the traditional indemnity plan, the enrollee pays a deductible and office visit payment. However, unlike the traditional plan, the POS's deductible is usually 30% instead of 20% as a way of discouraging out-of-network services. Point-of-service plans are used as a way of encouraging people, who would not give up a traditional plan, to sign up for a managed care plan. Its selling point is the offer of choice of going out of the plan's network. PPOs are attractive to employers, enrollees and insurance companies for the same reasons found in an HMO—reduced costs.

Many managed care companies do not offer chemical dependency treatment services within their own provider networks. Rather they *carve out* these services and subcontract them to managed care companies that specialize in chemical dependency and mental health services.

More recently, state governments have turned to the HMO model as a way to decrease Medicaid

costs. As of 1995 there were 15 states in the process of incrementally implementing a managed care plan for chemical dependency, as well as all health care services.

A criticism of the coverage, either through Medicare and Medicaid systems or through private managed care insurance carriers, is that these plans do not reflect the needs of people with chemical dependency problems such as the recent upsurge in DUAL DIAGNOSIS, which requires longer detoxification. Many women alcoholics fall within this category. The limit on coverage for detoxification services, however, which is now often a matter of days, may not be adequate to treat dual diagnosis. There is also the concern that the responsibility for clinical decision-making in managed care has been taken away from the treatment provider and patient, and transferred to the treatment review structure of the managed care company, with the result that the inpatient or outpatient services needs of the patient are determined by financial and not clinical decisions. There are additional concerns that managed care companies will not be able to determine what is appropriate, cost-effective treatment in programs that provide methadone maintenance services, or are therapeutic communities or community-based, and will find it difficult to evaluate nontraditional treatment modes.

There has also been concerns on the part of insurers and employers as to the consistency of chemical-dependency programs because of how they are now accredited. Some are accredited by the Joint Commission on Accreditation of Hospitals (JCAH) and some are accredited by various states. Corporate occupational program directors can also evaluate local treatment programs. Different accreditation policies can create different criteria for what is effective programming, further confusing the understanding of what is cost-effective care on the part of government and managed care companies.

More than half of all company insurance policies cover only the individual and not the family, although the family is often involved in an alcoholic's problem.

Data seem to indicate that treatment of a chemically-dependent person and his or her family will decrease subsequent health care costs. Accordingly, it may prove to the insurer's advantage to encourage their clients to use occupational substance-abuse programs and other treatment so as to prevent the progression of the disease and its costly effects.

Donald M. Gallant, *Alcoholism: A Guide to Diagnosis, Intervention, and Treatment* (New York: W.W. Norton, 1987).

Gary Graham, "Occupational Programs and Their Relation to Health Insurance Coverage for Alcoholism," *Alcohol Health & Research World* 5, no. 4 (Summer 1981): 31–34.

Sandra S. Sternberger and Helen Drew, "Women, Health Insurance and Alcoholism," *Alcohol Health & Research World* 5, no. 4 (Summer 1981): 37–38.

Charles D. Watts, "Health Insurance Coverage for Underserved Populations," *Alcohol Health & Research World* 5, no. 4 (Summer 1981): 35–36.

William G. Williams, "Nature and Benefit Packages in Health Insurance Coverage for Alcoholism Treatment 1995," *Alcohol Health & Research World* 5, no. 4 (Summer 1981): 5–11.

intellectual impairment   Findings of recent studies support the view that chronic alcohol ingestion and use of other drugs (especially CRACK) leads to cell alterations and loss in the central nervous system. These alterations are probably related to the functional impairment often noted in CHRONIC ALCOHOL INTOXICATION.

In the case of alcohol, decreased brain size (cerebral or cortical atrophy)—demonstrated repeatedly by autopsy examination and computerized axial tomography (CAT scan)—has been a major finding in studies of alcoholic patients. Autopsy examination has revealed widespread atrophy and cell loss in many brain regions, including at least two areas of the diencephalon: (1) the mammillary bodies of the hypothalamus; and (2) the middle and frontal area of the thalamus. Damage to these structures has been reported in various memory disorders, including WERNICKE'S ENCEPHALOPATHY (SYNDROME OR DISEASE).

There is still controversy as to whether moderate alcohol consumption causes any permanent structural brain damage. The reversibility of alcohol-induced organic brain damage and neuropsychological impairment remains one of the most controversial yet important issues in all alcohol-related research.

Enoch Gordis, M.D., ed., *Sixth Special Report to the U.S. Congress on Alcohol and Health* (Rockville, Md.: National Institute on Alcohol Abuse and Alcoholism [NIAAA], 1987).

intemperance   Excessive or habitual drinking.

intensive outpatient services   According to the *Substance Abuse and Mental Health Statistic Sourcebook*, "Intensive outpatient services are client services that last two or more hours per day for three or more days per week."

In recent years, the use of intensive outpatient treatment of alcohol and other drug-use disorders has increased dramatically, while the use of extended inpatient treatment has dropped.

Internal Revenue Service (IRS)   The IRS is a unit of the Treasury Department that has primary responsibility for regulating and enforcing revenue tax codes and collecting federal taxes. In this capacity, the IRS has conducted investigations and gathered intelligence on the untaxed profits made by individuals and organizations through the illegal trafficking of drugs. The information gathered by the IRS is used to prosecute drug dealers for income tax evasion. (See BUREAU OF ALCOHOL, TOBACCO AND FIREARMS and BOOTY.)

International Classification of Diseases (ICD)   The World Health Organization (WHO) publishes the *International Classification of Diseases (ICD)* and has played a major part in formalizing definitions of alcoholism and abuse of other drugs.

In the 1950s, WHO formulated criteria for a definition of alcoholism, which remained the standard definition for the next 20 years. This definition was still used in "Other Nonpsychotic Mental Disorders" in the *International Classification of Diseases (ICD-8)* published in 1974.

In *ICD-9* (1978), the term alcoholism was completely redefined and the concept of ALCOHOL DEPENDENCE SYNDROME (ADS) was introduced. ADS is described in terms of factors that characterize increasing levels of dependence. *ICD-10* was introduced for worldwide use in 1994. This edition finally synthesized its diagnostic categories relating to substance use with those set forth by the American Psychiatric Association system in its *Diagnostic and Statistical Manual of Mental Disorders*. (See CLASSIFICATION OF ALCOHOLICS AND OTHER DRUG USERS.)

Estimated Worldwide Potential Illicit Drug
(tons)

Country	1997	1996	1995	1994	1993
Opium					
Afghanistan	1,265	1,230	1,250	950	685
India	30	47	77	90	-
Iran	-	-	-	-	-
Pakistan	85	75	155	160	140
Total SW Asia	**1,380**	**1,352**	**1,482**	**1,200**	**825**
Burma	2,365	2,560	2,340	2,030	2,575
China	-	-	19	25	-
Laos	210	200	180	85	180
Thailand	25	30	25	17	42
Total SE Asia	**2,600**	**2,790**	**2,564**	**1,157**	**2,797**
Colombia	66	63	65	-	-
Lebanon	-	1	1	-	4
Guatemala	-	-	-	-	-
Mexico	46	54	53	60	49
Vietnam	45	25	-	-	-
Total Above	**157**	**143**	**119**	**60**	**53**
Total Opium Gum	**4,137**	**4,285**	**4,165**	**3,417**	**3,675**
Coca Leaf					
Boliva	70,100	75,100	85,000	89,800	84,400
Colombia	63,600	53,800	40,800	35,800	31,700
Peru	130,200	174,700	183,600	165,300	155,500
Ecuador	-	-	-	-	100
Total Coca Leaf	**263,900**	**303,600**	**309,400**	**290,900**	**271,700**
Cannabis					
Mexico	2,500	3,400	3,650	5,540	6,280
Colombia	4,133	4,133	4,133	4,138	4,125
Jamaica	214	356	206	208	502
Belize	0	0	0	0	0
Others	3,500	3,500	3,500	3,500	3,500
Total Cannabis	**10,347**	**11,389**	**11,489**	**13,386**	**14,407**

* While there is no solid information on Iranian opium production, the U.S.government estimates that Iran may potentially produce
Source: International Afghani Narcotics Control Strategy Report, 1998

Net Production 1987–1997 (tons)					
1992	**1991**	**1990**	**1989**	**1988**	**1987**
640	570	415	585	750	600
-	-	-	-	-	-
-	-	-	-	-	300
175	180	165	130	205	205
815	**750**	**580**	**715**	**955**	**1,105**
2,280	2,350	2,255	2,430	1,280	835
-	-	-	-	-	-
230	265	275	380	255	225
24	35	40	50	25	24
2,534	**2,650**	**2,570**	**2,860**	**1,560**	**1,084**
-	-	-	-	-	-
-	34	32	45	-	-
-	11	13	12	8	3
40	41	62	66	67	50
-	-	-	-	-	-
40	**86**	107	123	75	53
3,389	**3,486**	3,257	3,698	2,590	2,242
80,300	78,000	77,000	77,600	78,400	79,200
29,600	30,000	32,100	33,900	27,200	20,500
223,900	222,700	196,900	186,300	187,700	191,000
100	40	170	270	400	400
333,900	330,740	306,170	298,070	293,700	291,100
7,795	7,775	19,715	30,200	5,655	5,933
1,650	1,650	1,500	2,800	7,775	5,600
263	641	825	190	405	460
0	49	60	65	120	200
3,500	3,500	3,500	3,500	3,500	1,500
13,208	13,615	25,600	36,755	17,455	13,693

between 35–75 MT of opium gum annually.

National Institute on Alcohol Abuse and Alcoholism, "Epidemiologic Bulletin no. 20," *Alcohol Health & Research World* 13, no. 1 (1989): 80–81.

World Health Organization (WHO), *Mental Disorders: Glossary and Guide to their Classification in Accordance with the Ninth Revision of the International Classification of Diseases* (Geneva: World Health Organization, 1978).

International Commission for the Prevention of Alcoholism and Drug Dependence (ICPA)

Founded in 1952, ICPA is a nonsectarian, nonpolitical organization of the United Nations, operated exclusively for scientific and educational purposes. It seeks to reveal the impact of alcohol and other drug dependencies upon the economic, political, social and religious life of nations and to present effective preventive actions. The commission is made up of 250 prominent men and women from around the world. The number of invited representatives is based upon the population of a country.

international drug control   High-level meetings on international drug policy were held during the White House Conference meeting, February 28 to March 2, 1988, in Washington, D.C. Attending were experts from the international community, the U.S. government and the private sector, plus conferees and White House Conference participants. They discussed ways to improve the effectiveness of the U.S. international drug policy.

Participants concluded that international enforcement and diplomatic activities initiated by the United States are only part of the solution and will never be sufficient to eradicate the illicit drug trade. The U.S. currently is the world's largest consumer of illicit drugs: 60% of all such drugs now produced in the world are being used in this nation. So long as this country provides such a lucrative market for illicit drugs, it was decided, no amount of federal resources will be enough to stop the flow of illicit drugs from foreign lands. The conclusion was that the long-term, permanent solution is reduction in the demand for illegal drugs by Americans.

It was stressed, too, that many policy questions relate to issues of individual responsibility and the protection of the individual, which are fundamental to a democratic society. Any antidrug policy that is to have widespread public support must carefully balance the wide latitude given to individuals in U.S. society against the need for society to protect itself from that which could destroy it.

Six general recommendations were made by conference attendees:

International narcotics issues must be given a much higher priority in the formulation of U.S. foreign policy.

U.S. drug-eradication programs overseas must be refocused and strengthened.

Congress should review the legislation creating the narcotics certification process.

The activities of U.S. law enforcement officials engaged in narcotics enforcement overseas should be strengthened.

The U.S. Department of Treasury should convene a meeting, or series of meetings, on international drug money laundering to develop specific suggestions for improving international cooperation in the investigation and confiscation of illicit, drug-related assets and profits.

The U.S. should intensify its efforts to exchange expertise and information with other countries on effective prevention and treatment programs in order to combat illegal drug use.

The above recommendations were included in the final report of the White House Conference for a Drug-Free America, issued in June 1988, by then Chairman Lois Haight Herrington.

Since that time, it appears U.S. efforts to slow cocaine traffic from Peru, Bolivia and Colombia have been ineffective. This effort had cost U.S. taxpayers roughly $72 million between 1972 and 1988. In late July 1989, the U.S. Department of State's inspector general, Sherman Funk, told a Senate subcommittee that coca production in Peru and Bolivia has increased every year—with less than 1% of the illegal drugs being seized. Eradication efforts were equally unsuccessful.

In addition, the inspector general's audit, updated through July 1989, found: inadequate security to protect U.S. drug agents, no contingency plans to evacuate the agents and useless intelligence data.

At the same time, Assistant Secretary of Defense Stephen Duncan stated that the military is ready for a greater role in the drug war abroad. Congress called for using U.S. military to join the effort in Peru, Bolivia and Colombia. All this came in the wake of then drug czar William Bennett's declaration that crack cocaine was the number-one target of his drug policy recommendations to President George Bush—issued in a special report in early September 1989.

In 1993 the Clinton Administration, as part of an overall staff reduction effort in the Executive Branch of Government, cut the staff of the White House Office of National Drug Control Policy (ONDCP) from 146 to 25. The Administration reduced the ONDCP 1994 budget from $101.2 million to $5.8 million. The number of agents in the DEA (Drug Enforcement Administration) was reduced and the Caribbean drug-interdiction program was cut by $200 million. The State Department's Bureau of International Narcotics' budget also fell during this time. Clinton's original 1995 budget called for a further reduction in drug interdiction efforts, including funds for treatment programs, by 94.3 million (a cut of 7.3%). The U.S.'s foreign allies may have read these budgets as a sign that the U.S. was backing away from its commitment to strong drug control policy. However, considering the vast amounts of tax dollars being spent previously to no effect (with little reduction in drug-related crime, consumption, and trafficking), it might also have been viewed as improved efficiency in government spending and deficit reduction. There is some indication that there was a shift in the Clinton Administration's policy; the Administration looked to increase spending for drug interdiction in its 1996 budget.

intervention   A term used to describe the action taken when confronting an alcoholic or other drug-dependent individual with their substance-abuse problem. Effective intervention can be achieved by someone who plays a significant role in the substance user's life, usually a member of the immediate family, a close friend or an employer. Even more effective is confrontation by two or more persons genuinely concerned about the welfare of the user and directly affected by the consequences of the drug use. The subject must be sober and clearheaded and the most effective time for intervention is during a crisis, when defenses are apt to be lowered. During a crisis that is the result of their own doing, the user is more apt to see clearly that they are on the wrong

path and that a change is needed. At this time the user will be more vulnerable, that is open to self-analysis and less defensive. The user then is presented with factual data about their behavior and the consequences that their behavior is having on themselves and those around them. It is important during a time of crisis to take advantage of the situation in a calm, rational manner, without malice. The substance user should be made aware of the fact that it was their behavior that caused the crisis and that it is therefore their responsibility to enter treatment. When forced to face the consequences of their actions, they may become more depressed and seem to regress. Such a reaction, however, is often a first step toward acceptance of the fact that they need treatment. Those confronting the individual should be supportive, patient, and should be prepared to help the user to find suitable treatment.

It is not enough for the individual to make promises to change and to do better; despite good intentions, the situation is generally not within his or her control. The subject must be made to accept professional help to establish new patterns of behavior.

Donald M. Gallant, *Alcoholism: A Guide to Diagnosis, Intervention, and Treatment* (New York: W.W. Norton, 1987).

interview, structured   An interview with a client or subject that follows a set form, usually for purposes of systematic data collection. No deviation from the series of questions is permitted.

interview, unstructured   An interview format that uses the responses of the client or subject as a stimulus for subsequent inquiries. This method of questioning exploits unusual answers and attempts to obtain in-depth data on pertinent issues.

intestine   Direct effects of alcohol on the small intestines can include changes in intestinal motility, metabolism, blood circulation and cellular structure. Studies indicate that injury to the intestinal tract may also take the form of varices (twisted and dilated veins or arteries) in the colon, which, though rare, may cause sudden massive rectal bleeding in patients with CIRRHOSIS. Alcohol also may have direct effects on colonic motility and morphology. An increased incidence of colon cancer also has been reported in alcoholics. Indeed, the range and complexity of alcohol's effects on the body are immense and constitute a picture puzzle that still has many missingpieces.

Charles S. Lieber, ed., "Medical Disorders of Alcoholism: Pathogenesis and Treatment," in *Major Problems in Internal Medicine* 22 (Philadelphia: Saunders, 1982).

intoxication   From the Latin *in* + *toxicum* (poison). An abnormal state produced by ingesting alcohol (or another drug) that can range from exhilaration to stupor. Degree and experience of intoxication vary from individual to individual. Recent studies have indicated that intoxication may have as much or more to do with psychological processes as with physical processes. Psychologists G. Alan Marlatt and Damaris J. Rohsenow of the University of Wisconsin used a "balanced placebo" experiment to determine the physical effects of drinking alcohol as distinguished from the expected or imagined effects on someone who *thinks* he is drinking alcohol. Marlatt and Rohsenow divided subjects into four groups: one expecting alcohol and receiving alcohol; one expecting alcohol and receiving tonic; one expecting tonic and receiving alcohol; and one expecting tonic and receiving tonic. The groups then were observed, with the focus being on social behavior, aggression and sexual arousal.

The study showed that men who mistakenly believed they had been drinking alcohol became less anxious in social situations. On the other hand, WOMEN in the same group became more anxious, possibly because their drinking experience and expectancies were different from those of the men.

Alcoholics were found to experience the same craving after taking one or two placebo drinks as they did after drinking real alcohol, but they reported little or no craving when they were given drinks containing alcohol that they believed were nonalcoholic.

Men became more aggressive when they drank tonic that they believed contained vodka, and relatively less aggressive when they drank vodka believing they were getting only tonic. Men tended to become more sexually aroused when they believed they were drinking alcohol but actually were drinking only tonic. Women reported feeling more aroused when they believed they had been drinking alcohol, but a measure of vaginal blood flow showed that physically they were becoming less aroused.

The authors of this study reported that more than 25 other published experiments using the balanced placebo design had also found the "expectancy effect" in the use of alcohol. These studies suggest that people have strong beliefs about what alcohol does, and react accordingly. They indicate that women, whose experiences with alcohol and expectancies about its effects differ from those of men, will not react to alcohol in the same way as men. In most states a person with a BLOOD ALCOHOL CONCENTRATION (BAC) of 0.10% is considered intoxicated. While the level of intoxication varies from individual to individual, depending on such factors as the amount of food in the stomach, body weight and individual tolerance, most people with a BAC of 0.15% are definitely intoxicated. Their voluntary motor action is affected, they are unable to walk properly and they have lost some control over their emotions. At a BAC of 0.20%, which can be achieved by drinking about 10 oz of distilled spirits in a few hours, there generally is severe impairment, and behavior is incoherent and emotionally confused. At 0.30% the deeper areas of the brain are affected and the drinker becomes stuporous, and at 0.40% he or she becomes unconscious. Death can occur between 0.40% and 0.70%, but this is rare because most drinkers have lapsed into unconsciousness at these levels.

John Langone, *Bombed, Buzzed, Smashed, or . . . Sober: A Book about Alcohol* (Boston: Little, Brown, 1976): 78–80.

Alan G. Marlatt and Damaris J. Rohsenow, "The Think-Drink Effect," *Psychology Today* 15, no. 12 (December 1981): 60–69, 93.

intravenous drug use (IDU)   IDU is a term applied both to the injection of drugs (intramuscular, subcutaneous or intravenous) or to the injecting user (intravenous drug user). (See ADMINISTRATION.)

ionamin   A central nervous system stimulant that contains phentermine resin and is used as an anorectic for weight control. It is chemically and pharmacologically related to AMPHETAMINES and consequently has a significant potential for abuse. Overdosage can result in rapid respiration, tremors, confusion and hallucinations.

ipecac A syrup used as an emetic to induce vomiting in cases of poisoning. If it is absorbed instead of vomited it can exert a cardiotoxic effect.

Iran Opium abuse has long been widespread in Iran, although traditionally in a different form from that known in the United States. Opium in Iran is eaten or smoked. The goals of the users also differ in the two countries. Iranians do not seek opium's euphoric, mind-altering effects; they use it mainly to deaden the realities of life among the poor. Use is particularly widespread in rural areas among poor farmers. Opium also is used extensively among the sick and aged to numb pain.

In 1972 it was estimated that there were 110,000 registered and 200,000 unregistered opium addicts. After 1980 heroin use in Iran became increasingly widespread (driven even more underground, of course, by the reactionary and restrictive government), as it has in other Asian countries.

Large amounts of cannabis, which is either cultivated in Iran or imported from neighboring countries, also are used, usually in the form of hashish and ganja. The hashish is more potent than most types of marijuana used in the U.S.

In the past, Iran responded favorably to requests from other countries to cut back on the amount of opium it produced and exported. While Iran was ruled by the Shah, constructive steps were taken; in 1955 he imposed a ban on domestic opium production, although he later permitted some legal production to meet the requirements of registered addicts. In 1969 the cultivation of the opium poppy was made a government monopoly and very stringent laws imposed harsh fines and prison sentences for possession, trafficking, importing and exporting of opium and hashish.

As the Shah's hold on Iran weakened, law and order began to break down; the ban on cultivation began to erode, and there was a major increase in illicit export. In 1979, when the Shah and his government were overthrown by the Ayatollah Khomeini regime, the government structure that had held production and trafficking in check over the years collapsed. Police and military forces who had enforced the narcotics laws were diverted from their primary tasks and became involved in internal security. In addition, many of those who had staffed law enforcement units became political outcasts and were considered enemies of the people.

Since 1979 Iran has become a major player in the GOLDEN CRESCENT, the primary source of heroin smuggled into Europe and on to the United States. The political chaos in Iran has diverted government attention to other priorities, and trafficking has increased. In addition to Iran's role as a major source and transit country, it also has become a significant producer of heroin and morphine base in clandestine laboratories.

In 1989 Iran was third among the major suppliers of opium, producing over 300 metric tons. It ranks behind Burma (now Myanmar) and Afghanistan, and just ahead of Laos, as a major world supplier of opium.

If the current turmoil in Southwest Asian countries continues, it can be expected that traffickers will continue to exploit the situation and that the flow of heroin probably will continue to increase.

Ireland

Drugs other than alcohol: Ireland lies just outside the mainstream of drug trafficking in Europe, but there has been an upward trend in drug use during the last few years. It has been suggested that the increase is due to the relatively recent industrialization of Ireland; others theorize that it is due to recent restrictive government measures concerning drug use and a rebellion among the people who feel their rights are now being impinged. Still others attribute the increase to the country's political unrest. According to the U.S. Dept. of State's *International Narcotics Control Strategy Report March 1996,* "ecstasy use skyrocketed in 1995, with Irish officials confirming reports of its widespread availability throughout the country. Heroin abuse remains a significant social problem in Ireland, particularly in depressed urban areas in and around Dublin."

Government recognition of the problem led to the Misuse of Drugs Act of 1977, which strictly defined controlled substances but which is more flexible than previous legislation. Under the law, heavier penalties were to be enforced for serious offenses, while penalties to minor offenses were to be less severe. In cases where drug dealing or possession is suspected, the 1977 law supersedes normal provisions that protect individuals from warrantless search and seizure.

Although the Irish are striving for more effective methods to control drug use, they have not yet found any satisfactory solutions.

Substance abuse treatment and prevention: Treatment facilities are inadequate to the country's needs, particularly the availability of methadone maintenance treatment slots. One response to the drug problem in Ireland has been an increased investment in demand reduction, namely, an intensive school-based antidrug education program, including anti-heroin programs for schools in areas where heroin abuse is most prevalent.

Alcohol: The abuse of alcohol in Ireland far exceeds the abuse of other drugs. It is a common belief that the Irish are prone to alcohol-related problems. The mere thought of Ireland is likely to conjure up images of beer drinking in public houses, Irish whiskey and boisterous celebrations. Surprisingly, however, by international standards alcohol consumption in Ireland (adjusted for total population) is comparatively low among the leading alcohol-consuming countries. According to a 1987 study, apparent per capita consumption of ABSOLUTE ALCOHOL in that year was 5.4 liters, placing the Irish 30th among 47 reporting countries. In a 1995 survey, while Ireland's consumption rose to 9.2 liters, it was 11th among 53 alcohol-consuming countries, basically remaining consistent in its consumption relative to other countries. It should be noted that Luxembourg's per capita alcohol consumption was 11.6 liters in 1995, placing it first among consuming countries. Interestingly, in keeping its reputation for beer consumption, the country's consumption for that beverage rose from 109 liters per capita in 1985, to 135.2 liters in 1995. By contrast, in 1995 the Czech Republic consumed 160.0 liters per capita; Americans consumed 85.2 liters. Although beer has long been the traditional drink in Ireland, the consumption of wine and distilled spirits has increased in recent years

Alcohol consumption rose steadily from 1950 to 1979 (by a factor of 115%). However, in the 1980s it declined. In 1985 per capita consumption had fallen to 6.6 liters, and by 1987 the consumption rate had fallen again by 3.6%. However, in 1989 consumption began to rise again. In that year it stood at 7.0 liters. Consumption continued to rise, so that by 1995, as noted, it was 9.2 liters.

Drinking is relatively expensive in Ireland, but cost does not seem to hinder those who drink. Evidence suggests that the expenditure on drink rises in proportion to income, and higher alcohol prices result in higher expenditures on drink rather than decreased consumption. The Irish spend 12% of their income on alcoholic beverages, a higher percentage than any other country. This probably is due to the high excise tax on alcohol, which the government treasury is heavily dependent on as a source of revenue.

The high percentage of abstainers in Ireland is probably due to the number of temperance movements and reaction to the high rate of alcoholism among alcohol users. These movements were very common in the 19th century, and one in particular had disastrous results. In the 1840s a vigorous crusade led by a Catholic priest resulted in thousands pledging never to drink. There was a physician in Draperstown, Northern Ireland, however, who had been experimenting with the use of ether, and the news quickly spread that it was a pleasant substitute for alcohol. Not only was it cheap, because unlike alcohol it was not subject to tax, the effects were quick and even when used several times a day there were no hangover effects. In fact, the effects wore off so quickly that a person exhibiting signs of drunkenness was usually sober even before he reached a police station. The sniffing of ether in Draperstown and in other parts of Ireland became epidemic for some time, and it wasn't until the 1920s that ether abuse finally died out.

Most drinking in Ireland is done in public houses rather than at home, a contributing factor to the proportion of traffic accidents caused by alcohol, around 50%, which is close to the percentage in the United States. Premises where alcoholic beverages are sold must be licensed by the state, and the number allowed is related to the population of an area and the existing distribution of already licensed premises.

Treatment: The Irish are searching for effective ways to control alcohol abuse but have not yet found satisfactory solutions. As noted, the high cost of alcohol does not seem to prevent people from purchasing alcohol so that raising the price probably would have no effect. Restrictive social measures often impinge on the rights of drinkers who do not abuse alcohol, and resistance to these measures may result in increased abuse. One area that might warrant more attention is heavier penalization for drunk drivers and for those whose alcoholism causes absence from work. However, as Ireland has changed from a nation where drinking was polarized (heavy drinkers vs. abstainers) to one where there is increased social drinking, alcoholism problems have become more complex.

Admissions to mental hospitals for the treatment of alcoholism increased by over 300% from 1965 to 1977, and the upper socioeconomic group has one of the highest hospital admission rates. The average hospital stay, however, is much shorter for this group than for the average unskilled worker.

Brewers and Licensed Retailers Association, *1993 Annual Report* (London, 1995).

United States Dept. of State, Bureau for International Narcotics and Law Enforcement Affairs, *International Narcotics Control Strategy Report March 1996.*

Hoeveel alcoholhoude dranken worden er in de wereld gedronken? (How many alcoholic beverages are being consumed throughout the world?), 27th ed. (Schiedam, Netherlands: Produktschap Voor Gedistilleerde Dranken, 1987).

Brendan M. Walsh, *Drinking in Ireland* (Dublin: The Economic and Social Research Institute, 1980).

Irish Americans Ethnic background and generational status are both important determinants of drinking patterns in the U.S. It has been reported that Irish Americans have a rate of problem drinking two or three times as high as that of other ethnic groups. The Irish in general do not strongly disapprove of drunkenness, and a drunken man is frequently looked upon with amusement rather than pity or disgust. Intoxication often is deliberately sought. Many in this community look upon drinking as fulfilling a functional need to relieve stress, and it is not used in a ritualistic way, as with some ethnic groups. Irish Americans are likely to drink in public bars, to drink beer and to drink with members of their own sex. According to a study by the National Opinion Research Center, 40% of Irish Americans reported that there was a drinking problem in their homes when they were children.

Morris E. Chafetz and Harold W. Demone, Jr., *Alcoholism and Society* (New York: Oxford University Press, 1962): 76–80.

Barry Glassner, "Differences in Ethnic Drinking Habits," *Alcoholism* 1, no. 4 (March/April 1981): 19–21.

John Langone, *Bombed, Buzzed, Smashed, or . . . Sober: A Book about Alcohol* (Boston: Little, Brown, 1976): 47–49.

Irish whiskey Irish whiskey is a distilled spirit made from mixed grains. Production of Irish whiskey differs from that of Scotch whiskey in three ways: the fermented grain mixture contains a lower proportion of malted barley, the malted barley used is cured with charcoal rather than peat (to avoid giving it the smoky flavor generated from the burning peat), and the fermented mash is most often triple distilled in pot stills that are larger than those used to make Scotch. Triple distillation is a drawn-out process that reduces the quantity produced, strengthens it and brings it to an unusually high degree of rectification. The result is a drier and more subtle spirit than most varieties of Scotch whiskey. As in the case of Scotch whisky, the product usually is blended with any number of whiskeys from other distillations to broaden its appeal in the marketplace and to ensure consistency of taste. Aging generally is done in casks that previously have held sherry or other whiskeys and continues for a minimum of three years, but most exported Irish whiskey is between 10 and 12 years old.

The Irish were in all likelihood the first people of the British Isles to distill grain spirits, although the precise date is unknown. Some legends attribute the importation of distilling techniques to missionary monks from Europe who arrived after St. Patrick, sometime between A.D. 500 and 600. By about A.D. 1200, the Irish were known more for their *uisce beathadh* (water of life) than for anything except perhaps their Catholicism. The English word *whiskey* is an Anglicization of the Gaelic *uisce*.

In 1608, on the bank of the River Bush, Sir Thomas Phillips established the first distillery in Ireland, chartered by the English crown. Bushmills, as the distillery was called, has remained the trade name of the leading whiskey of Northern Ireland. Despite English efforts to regulate and tax the trade, Irish whiskey remained a notorious cottage industry through Elizabethan times, producing an erratic product heavy with congeners. Even today, in response to high taxes on whiskey levied by the government of Ireland, home distilling remains a right insisted upon by the Irish in defiance of the authorities. The most common illegal distillate is poteen, a spirit that is colorless and raw to the taste because of a lack of aging. Poteen currently is available throughout the rural districts of Ireland, and often it is offered to visitors instead of licensed distillates as a gesture more in keeping with the Irish culture and heritage.

In the 18th century, efforts to evade British regulations took the form of a division of labor: "sugar bakers" assumed charge of fermenting the grain mash, an entirely legal activity at the time, and they then exchanged the mash with independent distillers for a quantity of the finished spirit. Realizing that measures to control the trade had failed, the British decided to charter a number of Irish distilleries. Between 1779 and 1829 virtually all the major Irish whiskey distillers other than Bushmills came into existence: John Jameson in 1780, John Power in 1791, Daly in 1807, Murphy Brothers in 1825 and Tullamore in 1829.

The national industry underwent a major transformation during the 1960s, when most distillers merged to form the Irish Distillers Limited, a conglomerate that manufactures separate brand names and distinct distillates at a central location.

isocarboxazid   See MONOAMINE OXIDASE (MAO) INHIBITORS.

isopropyl alcohol   Also known as isopropanol and 2-propanol, isopropyl alcohol is a colorless liquid that can be mixed with water. Poisonous if taken internally, it is a major component of rubbing alcohol and has replaced ethanol for many uses because it is cheaper and has similar solvent properties.

Israel

Alcohol: Apparent per capita consumption of all alcoholic beverages in 1983–85 (in liters of ABSOLUTE ALCOHOL and based on total population) was only 1.0 liters. Israel's alcohol consumption remains very small. In a 1993 survey, it did not even show up among alcohol consuming countries. This is among the lowest known rate among countries who regularly report data. Israelis are known to have a relatively low incidence of alcoholism, but the Israeli government now recognizes that there is a problem of alcohol use within the country. Although by no

means epidemic, the incidence of alcoholism in Israel is high enough to have attracted the attention of the Ministry of Labour and Social Affairs and the Ministry of Social Welfare. Their investigations have isolated factors that tend to encourage alcoholism, despite the cultural restraints inhibiting the disease among the Jewish people.

When Israel was established in 1948, only about 650,000 Jews lived within its borders. Today that figure is well over 3 million. The people who immigrated to Israel during these years came from about 80 different countries, and they brought with them as many different attitudes toward alcohol consumption as there were countries of origin. The traditional image of abstemious consumption of alcohol is for the most part derived from the habits of European Jews. This portion of the population brought with it virtually no habits of alcohol abuse, largely because drinking had been socially inhibited to avoid confrontations with the non-Jewish segments among which it had formerly lived.

Those Jews who immigrated from Asia and North Africa, however, brought with them a relatively casual attitude toward alcohol consumption because they had come from predominantly Islamic countries, which had prohibitions on the use of alcohol. In the past they therefore had less need to separate themselves from a non-Jewish population who drank—they had less fear of confrontations with antagonists as a result of alcohol abuse. Moreover, once these Asian and North African immigrants entered Israel, they were forced to relinquish vestiges of their patriarchal culture, alter their traditional family structure and accept a lower position in the class system than they had formerly enjoyed. The trauma of this integration into what was for these immigrants a secularized Israeli culture caused some of them to degenerate from moderate to excessive drinkers. By 1980 this group of Asian and North African immigrants accounted for more than half of the alcoholics in Israel.

Statistics on drunk-driving offenses, drinking among youth and the incidence of alcoholism among women all suggest that alcohol abuse is worsening in Israel. In 1980 it was estimated that there were 6,000 alcoholics in the country. The figure represented the end result of years of neglect of the problem, an increasing acceptance of European social and dietary habits, and a gradual loss of the special sense of mission associated with the early years of the state of Israel. Of the 6,000, 55.3% were immigrants from Asia and North Africa; and 80% of the alcoholics born in Israel were descended from this same group of immigrants.

Drugs other than alcohol: According to the *International Narcotics Control Strategy Report March 1996* issued by the U.S. Department of State (USDS), abuse of drugs other than alcohol (including hard drugs, which had not been seen in Israel before) rose significantly in the early 1990s. The Government of Israel reported that drug use by young people doubled (from 9.2% to 4.8%) between 1992 and 1995. Heroin and cannabis traditionally have been the prime drugs of abuse in Israel. The demand for cocaine, LSD and amphetamines increased, however, during the first half of the 1990s. Ironically, the Government is concerned that a rise in drug trafficking due to enhanced regional ties may be one unanticipated negative effect of the recent Mideast peace initiatives.

Italian Americans Italian Americans have strong attitudes against drunkenness, apply little social pressure to participate in social drinking, but usually consume alcohol with meals. Wine is a staple in the diet of Italian Americans and most have their first drink between six and 10 years of age. First-generation Italian Americans drink frequently but have few alcohol-related problems; later generations have higher rates of heavy drinking, and they consume more distilled spirits than either Italians in Italy or first-generation Italians in America. When there is drunkenness, it generally occurs during festive occasions where a group is present that includes members of both sexes (as opposed to Irish-American drinking customs, which are not connected solely with festivity). As Italians become more Americanized, they may begin to lose the protective Italian drinking traditions and develop more drinking problems, but the rate of alcoholism among them is still significantly low compared to that of other groups, such as Irish Americans, Hispanics and African Americans.

Morris E. Chafetz and Harold W. Demone, Jr., *Alcoholism and Society* (New York: Oxford University Press, 1962): 80–84.

Italy
Alcohol: Exportation of wine is increasing, and wine that previously was shipped to France to be mixed with French wine now is simply exported directly to other countries. This situation has triggered a French-Italian wine war, one that continues to escalate.

Historically, alcohol use has not been a major problem in Italy. Because drinking in Italy traditionally is associated with wine, and wine consumption generally is associated with meals and is an integral part of family life, public drunkenness is not a common occurrence. Moreover, alcohol control laws do not regulate wine or beer because they are not considered alcoholic beverages—a reflection of the traditional wine culture of the country.

Despite Italy's place as one of the top wine-producing countries in the world, per capita wine consumption in the country itself has fluctuated widely over the last several years. In 1968 per capita consumption was 116 liters; in 1980 per capita consumption had decreased to 92.9 liters. In 1993 per capita wine consumption had decreased to 52.0 liters annually, although Italy still ranked as number three in per capita consumption among the 52 top wine-consuming countries. At the same time, there has been an increase in the consumption of beer, from 11.3 liters in 1970 to 25.1 liters in 1993. It should be noted, however, that Italy's total alcohol consumption has decreased from 1985—when it stood at 12.5 liters to 8.0 liters in 1993.

Alcoholism treatment and prevention: The government of Italy does not recognize alcohol abuse as a major health care concern, and since 1979, when health care was nationalized, alcohol abuse has become a relatively "forgotten problem," with the only treatment usually found in private facilities.

While no recent surveys have been conducted on alcohol abuse, and research into social attitudes is lacking, there is a bill pending in the Italian Parliament to restrict advertising for distilled spirits. There also is an attempt to form a permanent national commission on alcohol problems that would collect data and suggest reforms. Because alcohol consumption is so closely tied to the family and home, the history and background of this aspect of Italian culture will have to be extensively explored before contemporary problems of alcohol abuse can be dealt with.

Drugs other than alcohol: Aside from alcohol, abuse of drugs in Italy is a relatively new occurrence. Probably because it is less expensive than other drugs, hashish has long been the most commonly abused drug in Italy, although abuse of cocaine and heroin also is problematic, particularly in urban areas. Government studies showed a 600% rise in the use of heroin between 1975 and 1985. By 1995 the government estimated the number of heroin addicts in Italy at 150,000, and regular users of cocaine at 200,000. There is a surprisingly strong movement in Italy in favor of legalizing marijuana despite the opposition of all the major political parties.

Substance abuse treatment: Until new legislation was passed in 1973 to alter the definition, drug addiction in Italy was considered a criminal act, not a disease. Subsequent laws established harsher penalties for traffickers and pushers in order to discourage sales and set up protocols for treating addicts as "sick individuals." Treatment programs in Italy during the early 1970s focused on individuals addicted to hashish and marijuana, although doctors were obligated to report persons using narcotics. In 1979 general health care was nationalized in Italy. Medical care therefore is virtually free, but a scarcity of bed space has historically limited drug-abuse treatment to detoxification, or drying out, followed by an immediate release. As heroin abuse increased, however, the Italian Government established a network of specialized treatment services, with an emphasis on therapeutic communities.

Trafficking: The Italian Government works proactively to control narcotics distribution. Faced with a sudden increase in domestic cocaine use in 1988, Italy's Central Anti-Drug Service broke up a major clandestine laboratory near Genoa, seized 230 lbs of cocaine in a single raid near Milan, and in total seized 2,832 lbs of cocaine, a significant increase from the 708 lbs seized the year before. The Italian Anti-Drug Service faces the unenviable challenge of confronting Italy's many organized crime groups (the Sicilian Mafia, the Neapolitan Camorra and the Calabrian Ndrangheta) and their links with the South American cocaine cartels and other large-scale smuggling organizations. Repeated raids on cocaine shipments from Latin America by government forces in the early 1990s are believed to have driven the cocaine trafficking out of the Italian ports, which had served for years as their European transit point. At least through the first half of the 1990s, however, Italy continued to function as a key transit point for Southwest Asian heroin on its way to Europe and the U.S. Evidence also suggests that Italy, where anabolic steroids are not covered by antinarcotics laws, became a key shipping point for steroids bound for the U.S.

Italy has a long and interesting history of drug trafficking and trafficking control. Heavy trafficking and processing of heroin in the late 1950s led to the establishment of a Rome branch office of the U.S. BUREAU OF NARCOTICS AND DANGEROUS DRUGS (BNDD). The office was moved to Paris, France, in 1969, when it was believed that activity had shifted to that area. The FRENCH CONNECTION, active from the 1930s to the 1970s, involved Italian underground criminals; raids of clandestine heroin laboratories in Italy during 1980 suggested either that the French Connection was not really dead or that it has been replaced by a Franco-Italian Connection.

M. M. Horgan et al., *International Survey: Alcoholic Beverage Taxation and Control Policies,* 6th ed. (Toronto: Brewers Association of Canada, 1986).

United States Dept. of State, Bureau for International Narcotics and Law Enforcement Affairs, *International Narcotics Control Strategy Report March 1996.*

J

J.M. Foundation Created in 1924 by philanthropist Jeremiah Milbank (1887–1972) to enhance the nation's health, rehabilitation and educational programs, the J.M. Foundation began funding projects related to alcohol and other drug use in 1983. Since then the organization has funded 88 projects (totaling $2.75 million) involving children of alcoholics, medical education, national voluntary organizations and public policy. The foundation also has initiated several grant-writing conferences on alcohol and other drug issues. The J.M. Foundation Medical Student Scholarship Program in Alcohol and Other Drug Dependencies, begun in 1985, is the foundation's most prominent alcohol-related project.

jackroller SKID ROW slang for a thief, usually one who robs indigent, homeless alcoholics.

Jamaica For over 100 years, the cultivation and use of *ganja,* as marijuana is called locally, has been a tradition in Jamaica and is thought to have been introduced by indentured laborers from India. In the past, it generally was smoked only by isolated social groups, but in recent years use has spread to all ages and segments of society; an estimated 60%–70% of the island's population now uses marijuana in one form or another. Although the Jamaican government has made attempts to control usage (it has been illegal since 1913), due to the fact that marijuana may be the basis of the Jamaican economy and that usage is so much a part of the lifestyle, most law enforcers turn their backs on incidents of cultivation, use and possession. The U.S. government claims that 10% of the U.S. marijuana market comes from Jamaica. The usual route is through South Florida, both by plane and boat.

Alcohol: As in other countries throughout the world, Jamaica also has an alcoholism problem. Jamaican rum, known the world over, is inexpensive and readily available. The consumption of rum by all socioeconomic classes is a major problem.

Drugs other than alcohol: In 1995 Jamaican authorities seized triple the amount of cocaine seized in 1994, suggesting more efficiency on the part of the Jamaican police and reconfirming Jamaica's status as a significant cocaine transit country. Like marijuana, cocaine is smuggled out of the country by a vast network of *mules* (smugglers) to markets in the U.S., Canada and Europe.

Marijuana (known in Jamaica as "ganja"): In 1989 Jamaica was one of the top-three suppliers of marijuana to the U.S., with their total production being 400 metric tons. Only Mexico and Colombia produced more, which is not surprising, considering the relative size of this island. According to the U.S. State Department, Bureau for International Narcotics and Law Enforcement Affairs, "Jamaica's climate, soil, and rainfall are ideal for the cultivation of cannabis, which offers more profit to the farmer than any other local crop. The most commonly grown

257

varieties are indica and sinsemilla, four to six crops of which can be grown each year."

Marijuana is particularly important to the RASTAFARIANS and their way of life. Reggae music, which popularizes Rastafarianism, is known worldwide, and many of the lyrics encourage the use of ganja. Popular Rastafarian musicians, including the late Bob Marley, are idols of young people in the U.S. and throughout Europe, who are influenced by the songs praising the "mystical herb."

The use of cannabis is more widespread among men than women, although both women and children are known to consume it in a beverage called "green tea."

Members of Jamaica's medical profession are more than aware of the health hazards involved in the widespread use of marijuana, although often they are criticized as having a "middle-class bias." Dr. John Hall, consultant physician with the Jamaica Ministry of Health, researched the effects of marijuana for years. Among his clinical observations are the facts that the seasonal upsurges in stomach hemorrhages tend to occur during the twice-yearly marijuana harvests and that the whites of the eyes often turn brown among heavy users of marijuana. Apathy, or AMOTIVATIONAL SYNDROME, and a tendency to retreat from reality are common among heavy users, as well as impotence, low blood sugar and a bronchitis-type of cough. The extensive poverty in Jamaica may contribute to the use of marijuana as an escape from problems, but as with all chemical dependency, a vicious circle ensues when users become dependent and lose all power to overcome economic conditions.

U.S. Dept. of State, Bureau for International Narcotics and Law Enforcement Affairs, *International Narcotics Control Strategy Report March 1996.*

Japan

Alcohol: There is a deeply ingrained acceptance of social consumption of alcoholic beverages in Japan that has led to a national pattern of infrequent but heavy drinking on special occasions. There is some actual encouragement of drunkenness during festive celebrations, and expensive distilled spirits are favored as gifts to hosts. In one survey, 52% of the Japanese polled considered alcohol to be a part of their lives, while 35% of those polled went so far as

to say that they considered abstinence harmful to social life.

Japan's drinking patterns have a lengthy history. Although the majority of Japanese are nominal adherents to Buddhism or the native Shintoism, these religions have long been secularized in respect to prohibitions on alcohol consumption. Recent increases in the level of drinking (especially among women and youth), due to wider advertisement of alcoholic beverages and a general trend toward westernization, have, since World War II, weakened the traditional hierarchical society.

In *World Drink Trends 1995*, Japan ranked 25th worldwide in annual per capita consumption of alcohol, having increased from 4.8 liters annually in 1970 to 6.6 liters in 1995. It is interesting to note that annual consumption of wine (this category does not include sake, which technically is not a wine) was almost negligible in Japan. Sake, a fermented rice beverage usually sold in varieties that average 16% absolute alcohol, has traditionally been the preferred drink in Japan. The popularity of sake, however, has gradually been declining, presumably due to increasing commercial and social contact with western influences. Ironically, the West is now discovering sake, and its popularity (along with Japanese food) continues to increase. Japanese restaurants are proliferating not only in the U.S. but in places like Mexico City.

The amount of illegal fermented or distilled beverages produced in the country is negligible. Most of the whiskey and beer in Japan is made by large corporations or is imported. Sake is produced by smaller, more local companies.

Alcoholism treatment: The Liaison Conference for Alcoholic Problems, an organization funded by the Ministry of Health and Welfare, coordinates alcoholism prevention and treatment programs, including the efforts of the Japanese Medical Society on Alcohol Studies and the All Nippon Sobriety Society, Japan's version of Alcoholics Anonymous. Significant contributions also are being made by the Christian Women's Temperance Association and the Salvation Army.

Drugs other than alcohol: Prior to 1945 drugabuse problems were virtually nonexistent in Japan, although cocaine and opium addicts were not unknown. After World War II, however, serious problems arose that can be divided into three separate periods.

The first phase occurred immediately following World War II, during Japan's reconstruction period. Stimulants were in great demand, particularly among students, night laborers and entertainers. Abuse of stimulants began in the major cities but soon spread, becoming prevalent throughout the country. The government enacted the Stimulants Control Law (1951) and amended its Mental Health Law to provide for compulsory hospitalization of those addicted to stimulants. The increased law enforcement, treatment of addicts and intensive public campaigns proved to be effective by the late 1950s. However, just when the stimulant problem was brought under control, widespread heroin abuse appeared. While some heroin abuse existed throughout the time after World War II, its popularity spread suddenly, and by 1961 the number of heroin addicts in Japan was estimated at 40,000. Government countermeasures included the strengthening of penalties for offenders and compulsory hospitalization of addicts. After 1964 heroin abuse decreased sharply and the country enjoyed a period of declining drug problems.

In the 1970s stimulant abuse surfaced again, spreading rapidly throughout the country. The government amended the Stimulants Control Law, increasing the penalties for violation to the same level as those for heroin offenses. As a result, abuse dropped 30% in 1974, but the decrease proved to be only temporary. Stimulant abuse remains the most serious drug problem. Japan has been especially hard hit by the worldwide crisis centered around METHAMPHETHAMINE, with the number of Japanese addicts estimated at 400,000 to 600,000. According to the *International Narcotics Control Strategy Report March 1996:*

> *Methamphetamine in Japan usually is administered by injection. Trafficking of methamphetamine is considered to be Japan's most significant drug problem, with Japanese organized crime groups controlling over 95% of its smuggling and distribution. There is negligible illicit domestic manufacture, and little is diverted from licit channels. Public health and social problems have resulted from the widespread stimulant abuse. An individual's economic and social life is seriously hampered by his psychological dependence on the drug. In addition, "am-phetamine psychosis," or the occurrence of hallucinations and illusions, has been responsible for a marked increase in traffic accidents, arson and murder.*

Opium abuse has never constituted a problem in Japan; most offenses involve ignorance of the law when poppies are grown for ornamental purposes. Under the Opium Law of 1954, the cultivation of the opium poppy is permitted only under license, and the government monopolizes its import, export and domestic purchase. Cocaine and heroin use, however, is small but growing. The arrest in 1995 of Aum Shinrikyo cult leader Shoko Asahara exposed a whole new source of concern for government officials when it was learned that he had ordered the production of narcotics and hallucinogens (including LSD and mescaline).

Substance abuse treatment and prevention:　The Japanese government's measures to reduce drug use have included a nationwide eradication campaign, the establishment of a council to check the dependence-producing properties of new drugs and harsher penalties for users. On an international level, Japan cooperates with the United Nations in the field of drug abuse.

U.S. Dept. of State, Bureau for International Narcotics and Law Enforcement Affairs, *International Narcotics Control Strategy Report March 1996.*

NTC Publications LTD, *World Drink Trends 1995* (London, 1997).

Hoeveel alcoholhoude dranken worden er in de wereld gedronken? (How many alcoholic beverages are being consumed throughout the world?), 27th ed. (Schiedam, Netherlands: Produktschap Voor Gedistilleerde Dranken, 1987).

Jellinek, E. M. (1890–1963)　The founder of the Center of Alcohol Studies and Summer School of Alcohol Studies, formerly at Yale University and now centered at Rutgers University. Jellinek also was a cofounder of the National Council on Alcoholism and a consultant on alcoholism for the World Health Organization (WHO). He was the author of *The Disease Concept of Alcoholism.* In this influential study, Jellinek distinguished between five categories of alcoholism, which he referred to as alpha, beta, delta, epsilon and gamma.

Alpha alcoholism: Sometimes known as "problem drinking," it represents a continual, purely psychological dependence or reliance upon alcohol's effects to relieve emotional or bodily pain. It can develop into gamma alcoholism, but often continues in the same state for years with no signs of progression. The damage it causes is usually limited to disturbances in the person's family or social relationships and does not lead to loss of control. There are no withdrawal effects.

Beta alcoholism: The person who suffers from this kind of alcoholism, possibly as a result of poor nutritional habits or of the customs of certain social groups, eventually develops medical complications such as cirrhosis or alcoholic polyneuropathy. Beta alcoholism is not associated with physical or psychological dependence, and withdrawal symptoms do not appear, but the condition can develop into gamma alcoholism.

Gamma alcoholism: This type of alcoholism causes the most damage to an individual's health and to his interpersonal relationships. Recognized by Alcoholics Anonymous, it apparently is considered to be the dominant form of alcoholism in the U.S. It is characterized by acquired increased tissue tolerance, adaptive cell metabolism, physical dependence (craving and withdrawal symptoms) and loss of control. When suffering with gamma alcoholism, psychological dependence progresses to physical dependence.

Delta alcoholism: The predominant form of alcoholism in France and other countries where there is significant wine consumption, delta alcoholism is characterized by an acquired tolerance to alcohol. Unlike gamma alcoholism, which is characterized by loss of control, delta alcoholism involves the inability to abstain. The intake can be controlled but one cannot stop drinking even for a few days; consumption, although heavy, is steady, not "explosive."

Epsilon alcoholism: The term refers to periodic alcoholism. Less is known about this category than the other four.

Though clinicians tend to no longer make use of Jellinek's categories to refer to the different types of alcoholism, the patterns he described and the research he performed are still useful and valid today.

The current definitions of alcoholism are less prone to differentiate physiological from psychological dependence. (See ALCOHOLISM.)

Jews   Research has indicated that Jews have lower rates of alcoholism than most other ethnic groups; a study by the National Opinion Research Center found that only 4% of Jews reported a drinking problem in their homes, as compared to approximately 9% in the general population. (Two or more drinks per day was considered heavy drinking.) Although Jews as a group largely have avoided alcoholism for over 2,500 years, it is false to believe that they are somehow immune to alcoholism. A 1992 OASAS (New York State Office of Alcoholism and Substance Abuse Services) study, surveying 6,000 homes in New York State, estimated that 12% of the population suffered from drug and alcohol abuse problems, and this same percentage applied to Jews.

The vast majority of Jews drink on a fairly regular basis; only 5% are abstainers. Drinking is first introduced to children in a family context, which has been shown to be a strong force in determining later drinking habits. Alcoholic beverages are used in positive settings, including religious rituals and mixed social gatherings, rather than as a means of coping with stress. When a baby is circumcised he is given a few drops of wine, and wine is served at bar mitzvahs and weddings. Consumption of wine is a part of the Sabbath ceremony, and all family members partake. Sobriety is a factor in Jewish identity, and intoxication generally is not tolerated.

One study revealed that among Jewish men, the more orthodox the participant, the lower the incidence of intoxication—the most orthodox drank most frequently but also had the lowest incidences of intoxication. However, there are orthodox Jewish rabbis who are alcoholics, and religious disaffiliation is not necessarily an indication of a drinking problem. Rates of alcoholism are low among reform Jews as well as orthodox Jews, but there appears to be a correlation between a move away from orthodoxy and an increase in the incidence of alcoholism. Identification with Judaism generally seems to act as a protective factor against alcoholism and an aid in recovery from alcoholism when it develops.

In a 1975 study, researchers W. Schmidt and R. E. Popham found that four types of coping mechanisms are used by Jews to deal with their alcoholism:

(1) denial—"Since I'm a Jew, I can't be an alcoholic"; (2) disaffiliation—"Since I'm an alcoholic, I can't be much of a Jew"; (3) rationalization—"I drink to excess, but so do most Jews"; and (4) acceptance—"I drink excessively, and I am Jewish."

Difficulties in treating Jews who have drinking problems stem from a generalized DENIAL of the problem by the Jewish community and a lack of tolerance, which make alcoholics feel isolated from their community and may worsen their situation. In addition, ALCOHOLICS ANONYMOUS meetings often are held in churches, where Jews may feel uncomfortable. Though alcoholism is less of a problem among Jews than among most other ethnic groups, increased awareness of the problem may be needed to eliminate the element of denial. Holding more AA meetings in synagogues also might serve to aid in the recovery process.

Sheila Blume, Dee Dropkin and Lloyd Sokolow, "The Jewish Alcoholic: A Descriptive Study," *Alcohol Health and Research World* 4, no. 4 (Summer 1980): 21–26.

Morris Chafetz and Harold W. Demone, Jr., *Alcoholism and Society* (New York: Oxford University Press, 1962): 84–88.

Barry Glassner, "Irish Bars and Jewish Living Rooms: Differences in Ethnic Drinking Habits," *Alcoholism* 1, no. 4 (March/April 1981): 19–21.

W. Schmidt and R. E. Popham, "Impressions of Jewish Alcoholics," *Quarterly Journal of Studies on Alcohol* 37 (1976): 931–934.

C. R. Snyder, *Alcohol and the Jews: A Cultural Study of Drinking and Sobriety*, Yale Center of Alcohol Studies Monograph Series, no. 1 (New Haven, 1958).

Joint Commission on Accreditation of Hospitals (JCAH) Specific alcoholism program accreditation was initiated in 1975 by JCAH, under contract with the NATIONAL INSTITUTE ON ALCOHOL ABUSE AND ALCOHOLISM (NIAAA). In the years since, however, some authorities have complained that alcoholism program identity has become increasingly diffused, first subsumed under psychiatric standards and now in danger of being absorbed under JCAH's general hospital standards.

The ad hoc Commission on Accreditation of Rehabilitation Facilities (CARF), a competitive agency, is planning standards for treatment programs as an alternative to the JCAH standards, ostensibly to give more emphasis to nonhospital care. CARF points out in its newsletter that the uncertainty about standards has worked a special hardship on nonhospital programs. Don Cahalan, in his book *Understanding America's Drinking Problem,* writes, "Since the issue of certification is vital to determining which treatment organizations get funded for what kinds of treatment, the controversy over turf (between such interests as the hospital-based programs and freestanding programs, and among various groups of professionals caught in the middle) is likely to delay the settlement of the certification-of-facilities issue for a while longer."

D. Cahalan, *Understanding America's Drinking Problem: How to Combat the Hazards of Alcohol* (San Francisco: Jossey-Bass, 1987): 169.

J. Lewis, *The Alcoholism Report* (a subscription newsletter), vols. 10 through 14 (1982–86).

Jones Miller Act (1922) Federal legislation that established fines of up to $5,000 and imprisonment of up to 10 years for anyone involved in the trafficking of narcotics. At the time, drug use, especially heroin, was considered a national epidemic. As finally adopted, Jones Miller, or the Narcotics Drug Import and Export Act, approved on May 26, 1922, led to the establishment of the Federal Narcotics Control Board, composed of the secretaries of state, treasury and commerce. A key measure of the act was the prohibition of in-transit shipments of narcotics.

Just Say No Foundation A not-for-profit national and international research-based drug prevention program for children and teenagers. The program offers young people the opportunity to join Just Say No clubs, where members gain information skills and support to help them resist peer pressure and other influences to use drugs. It provides educational, recreational and service activities designed to foster and reinforce the attitude of intolerance toward drugs and drug use. The foundation supports and offers clubs materials, handbooks, a club book, a quarterly newsletter, on-site training and coordination of events such as the annual Walk Against Drugs.

katzenjammers Slang for DELIRIUM TREMENS (THE D.T.'S).

kava A beverage made from the roots of the shrub *Piper methysticum,* which produces a mild, marijuanalike high. It also has a sedative action, and if enough is consumed, will produce sleep. The roots are sometimes chewed for similar effect.

Kefauver-Harris Amendments, 1962 This act amended the Food, Drug and Cosmetic Act of 1938. Among the Act's more notable points:

> Manufacturers were required to provide substantial evidence to the Food and Drug Administration (FDA) that a new drug was safe and effective before it could be approved;
>
> The FDA was given the right to remove previously approved drugs from the market if those drugs proved to be hazardous;
>
> All drug products were required to be registered annually with the FDA;
>
> More specific labeling was required for drugs, including the drug's generic name and the quantity of each active ingredient;
>
> Prescription drug advertisements were required to include a summary of side effects, counter-indications and effectiveness;
>
> The FDA was given increased oversight authority over all drugs.

Keller, Mark A colleague of E. M. JELLINEK (1890–1963) at Yale University and founding editor of the *Journal of Studies on Alcohol.* The first issue of the publication, then called the *Quarterly Journal of Alcohol Studies,* appeared in June 1940. One of the country's foremost authorities in the field of alcoholism, Mark Keller was for many years associated with RUTGERS CENTER OF ALCOHOLIC STUDIES.

Kenya

Alcohol: The drinking patterns in Kenya, an independent member of the British Commonwealth since 1963, parallel those of other equatorial African nations. Approximately 90% of the population is composed of African ethnic groups living in rural areas where alcoholic beverages are often home brews and drinking occasions are related to the cultural activities of various tribal societies. Imported liquors and bottled beers are sold through licensed retail stores, but there is widespread and unregulated consumption of *busaa,* a fermented beverage made from maize flour and sugar honey, and *chang'aa,* a beverage similar to gin distilled from a variety of fermented brews. Consumption of such alcoholic beverages is an integral part of social celebrations, settlements of disputes, agrarian festivals and hunting expeditions. Assistance from distant neighbors in the construction and repair of rural farms and homes usually is rewarded with alcoholic beverages, and in certain places consumption of alcohol has become a part of sacrificial rites within communities.

In Nairobi and Mombasa there is a greater availability of imported wines and liquors, such as brandy, whiskey and gin, and the number of public bars has risen in recent years. Drinking of imported alcoholic beverages, as in other developing nations, is most common among educated people and is considered a mark of high social status. As Kenyan society has become more modernized, and cultural restraints on drinking have been relaxed, licensed drinking premises have tended to replace the communal gatherings to which drinking once was limited.

There is growing concern in Kenya about the spread of alcoholism resulting from this process of modernization. Figures on consumption are unreliable due to the amount of noncommercial alcoholic beverage production. It is also difficult to collect statistics because of increased migration within the country, which has further loosened social inhibitions on drinking as a result of the loss of traditional environments. Heavy costs to the country in lowered productivity have been attributed to the susceptibility of economically depressed peoples to drunkenness and the availability of inexpensive, home-brewed alcoholic beverages.

Drugs other than alcohol: The U.S. Department of State's *International Narcotics Control Strategy Report March 1996* stated that, "Due to its geographic location, ports, facilities and comparatively well-developed transportation and telecommunications infrastructure, Kenya serves as a transit point for hashish from Pakistan and heroin from Asia [en route to Europe]." Kenya also is a transit point for methaqualone from India on its way to Southern Africa. Cannabis (called "bhang") is cultivated illegally in Kenya; KHAT is grown and sold legally.

In 1995 Government authorities reported the concern that drug use (namely, heroin, cocaine and methaqualone) was perceived to be widespread and growing, especially in Nairobi, Mombasa and other urban centers. Still, estimates by the Kenyan police set the number of heroin addicts nationwide at only 1,000 (out of a population of 28 million). Specific drug rehabilitation centers were unknown in Kenya at that time; drug-abuse cases were treated in the psychiatric units of provincial hospitals.

Ketaject   A nonbarbiturate, rapid-acting general anesthetic that normally is used for short surgical procedures; with additional doses, however, it can be used for longer operations. It contains ketamine hydrochloride, which is related to phencyclidine, and has the potential for abuse. Ketaject is supplied in vials for injection. (See KETAMINE HYDROCHLORIDE.)

ketalar   Contains ketamine hydrochloride and is the same as KETAJECT. See KETAMINE HYDROCHLORIDE for abuse potential.

ketamine hydrochloride   A   nonbarbiturate, rapid-acting general anesthetic that normally is used for short surgical procedures. Discovered in 1961, it was used frequently during the Vietnam War. Manufactured as KETAJECT and KETALAR, it is supplied in vials for injection. It is an abused drug but not in its liquid form since injection only produces a rapid onset of sleep. Users evaporate the liquid by heating it and reducing it to a fine white powder. It is then sprinkled on marijuana or tobacco and smoked, or it is snorted. The crystalline powder is called "green" and has both depressant and psychedelic effects similar to those of phencyclidine, but of much shorter duration. It relieves tension and anxiety, is purported to be a sexual stimulant, and intensifies sounds and colors. Large doses produce delusions and hallucinations. When taken with alcohol or other central nervous system depressants, the drug can have an ADDITIVE EFFECT. It frequently is a drug of abuse of medical personnel.

khat   An East African plant, *Catha edulis* (also spelled "chat," "q'at" and "kat"). The leaves and buds are chewed or brewed as a beverage. It is said to produce stimulant effects similar to, but milder than, those induced by amphetamines, and psychological dependence can develop. In addition to dependence, opponents claim it suppresses appetite and prevents sleep. Advocates of this drug claim that it eases symptoms of diabetes, asthma and stomach/intestinal tract disorders.

It was, until recently, classified as a Schedule IV substance by the Drug Enforcement Administration (DEA). Cathine, a psychoactive ingredient in khat is still a Schedule IV substance—having a low potential for abuse. Cathinone, a more potent substance found in fresh picked khat (picked within the first 48 hours), is a Schedule I narcotic.

Khat has primarily been used by the populations of East Africa, the Arabian Peninsula and throughout the Middle East. It should be noted, however, that in 1993 the New York State Office of Alcoholism and Substance Abuse Services reported that khat was becoming increasingly available in the United States, particularly in New York, Washington, D.C., Los Angeles, Boston, Dallas and Detroit.

Korsakoff's psychosis (syndrome, disease)

Named after Sergei Korsakoff (1854–1900), a Russian psychiatrist who founded the Moscow School of Psychiatry and was the first to identify this form of psychosis in 1897. The disease was officially named Korsakoff's psychosis at the 12th International Medical Congress in Moscow in 1897.

Korsakoff's psychosis is primarily a mental disorder characterized by confusion, memory failure and a tendency to recite imaginary occurrences. Other symptoms include disorientation in time, emotional apathy and loss of insight, or awareness of the disability. Patients often are moderately cheerful and noncomprehending. The disease usually affects only those who have been drinking steadily for years, although it has been known to appear in nonalcoholics suffering from severe nutritional deficiencies. Thiamine deficiency is suspected to be partly responsible. Treatment consists of nutritional supplements, including VITAMINS AND MINERALS, but Korsakoff's psychosis is usually irreversible. Often it is preceded by WERNICKE'S ENCEPHALOPATHY (SYNDROME OR DISEASE) and given the single designation Wernicke-Korsakoff syndrome.

La Guardia Report   In 1938 New York City mayor Fiorello La Guardia commissioned a study on marijuana use. The report suggested that marijuana might have valuable therapeutic applications and found no evidence that its use might lead to the use of opiates. The report since has been succeeded by more contemporary studies, but when it was published in 1944 as *The Marijuana Problem in the City of New York, by the Mayor's Committee on Marijuana,* it was a landmark study. It still is cited today, especially by those who favor the legalization of marijuana.

LAAM (levo-alpha-acetylmethadol)   A narcotic analgesic AGONIST, LAAM is an opioid that has been tried as an alternative to METHADONE. Unlike methadone, which must be taken daily, LAAM, which suppresses the signs and symptoms of opiate withdrawal for 48 to 72 hours, is taken only three times a week. LAAM was approved by the FDA in 1993, after two decades of study.

lacquer thinner   Sometimes inhaled for its intoxicating effects, lacquer thinners contain highly toxic liquid hydrocarbons such as TOLUENE and acetone.

lactose   A white chrystalline disaccharide found in milk and prepared by evaporation of the whey, leaving the crystallized sugar. It is used in infant foods, medicine and as a cutting agent or adulterant in illicit drugs. (A disaccharide is any of a group of sugars with a common formula, such as maltose, sucrose and lactose.) See MILK SUGAR.

lager   A light, foamy BEER brewed by means of BOTTOM FERMENTATION. The procedure utilizes a yeast that sinks to the bottom of the brewing vat and bubbles up through the liquid. The name "lager" is derived from the German *Lagern,* meaning "to rest," in reference to the yeast. Lager beer usually is aged for several months in a cool place to clear it of sediment.

Lager beer first was brewed in Bavaria, and the process has remained the principal brewing method for German beers. Since that time it also has become the dominant process used by the American brewing industry. The first known lager brewery in the U.S. was started in Philadelphia some time prior to 1840. Initially, it served the German-American population of that city, but lager beers quickly became popular across the country and were the basis of the major American brewing industries established in Milwaukee and St. Louis. In the U.S., the influence of German lager beer has completely eclipsed that of English ALE.

laudanum   In the early 1500s, the physician Paracelsus created what he called laudanum, a tincture of powdered opium dissolved in alcohol. It was the first medicinal form of opium. In Europe laudanum was used to relieve pain, control dysentery, and as a cough suppressant and sedative. It remained a standard drug until the end of the 19th century, when its use began to decline. Several other opium mixtures were developed in the 1700s and 1800s but the most important was paregoric, a tincture of opium combined with camphor. Although considered an old-fashioned remedy today, it is still used to control diarrhea and is listed in Schedule III of the Controlled Substances Act.

Formerly, laudanum referred to any of various preparations of opium, particularly the hydroalcoholic tincture. The term laudanum now exclusively refers to the tincture (an alcoholic solution) of opium. By the mid-1800s, before it was discovered to be highly addictive, opium, either in the form of laudanum or in a form suitable for smoking, was a popular "remedy" for every imaginable ailment—and some imaginary ones, and was sold as an over-the-counter (OTC) medication in pharmacies. Later when opium's addictive potential became known, morphine was introduced to the medical profession, and was hailed as a powerful analgesic, effective in the relief of all kinds of pain and, falsely, as it turned out, as a cure for opium addiction. Morphine quickly replaced opium in many applications, though it did not cure opium addiction. Those addicted to laudanum very likely represented the group hardest hit by the enactment of the HARRISON ACT, which took effect in 1915. By eliminating legal access to the drug without providing a treatment alternative, the act forced those addicted to seek illegal supplies of the drug and, in effect, created a whole new class of criminals. (See DECRIMINALIZATION and LEGAL ASPECTS OF MARIJUANA, AND OTHER DRUG CONTROLS.)

laundering   Drug dealers and others involved in criminal activities, when successful, have the problem of hiding the massive amounts of money they collect. "Laundering" involves converting "dirty" money (acquired through illicit means) into "clean" money (earned from legitimate sources). Money laundering is always illegal, yet due to the volume that can be involved, banks often cooperate in these operations, which entails feeding huge amounts of small bills into high-speed money counters. When the volume is extremely high, they may just weigh the money. For example, 300 lbs (136 kg) of $20 bills is worth $3.6 million.

Money-laundering schemes are complex and thus difficult to uncover; it is as difficult to gather the evidence required as it is to prosecute those involved. Criminal violations can result in a maximum penalty of five years in prison and a $500,000 fine.

With the cocaine influx of the 1980s, Miami, Florida, gained a reputation for being the capital of the nation's money-laundering business. Until the introduction of strict legislation in 1994, one source estimated that Miami's posh Brickwell Avenue housed offices of more than 100 banks from 25 to 30 different countries. In addition, over 40 branches of overseas and out-of-state banks, plus some 50 agencies, representing foreign banks. At that time, Miami was thought to have more banks than supermarkets. Agents of the U.S. Treasury Department estimated that over one-third of all Miami banks shared in the huge profits made in money-laundering schemes.

In recent years, money-laundering centers have sprung up around the world, in such places as Hong Kong, Panama, the Cayman Islands, Montevideo (Uruguay), Nassau (Bahamas) and the Netherlands Antilles, offering services ranging from secret accounts to dummy corporations with hidden ownership. UN members, however, increasingly have joined forces to stem the tide of the growing drug-related international money-laundering outfits.

New opportunities continue to open up at home. In 1994, money launderers' exploitation of casinos continued to grow, as a proliferation of casinos in the U.S. was not matched by a growth in the resources to monitor them. Riverboat casinos became popular and Native Americans opened casinos in almost every state. Nevada's casinos are exempt from federal currency transaction reporting. Various ethnic groups in the U.S., new to money laundering, have invented their own methods or have revised established ones.

According to police and launderers, the basic rate paid for recycling money of dubious origin is 4%, while the rate paid for laundering drug cash and other "hot" money is 7% to 10% of the total.

Gilda Berger commented in *Drug Abuse: The Impact on Society,* "Not only is the drug trade extracting a great deal of money from drug users and robbing the government of millions of dollars in tax revenues, it is also buying its way into the very heart of American's trade and industry."

Gilda Berger, *Drug Abuse: The Impact on Society* (New York: Franklin Watts, 1988): 71–74.

Drug Enforcement Administration, *The Supply of Illicit Drugs to the United States* (Washington, D.C., 1995).

laxatives   Agents to promote bowel movements or soften stools; laxatives are helpful for occasional use, especially for those individuals with health problems or who take medications that cause constipation. This is particularly the case with people who are on pain medication such as codeine or morphine. Laxatives also are a frequently misused and abused class of drug. Abuse has been particularly noted among two groups of people: young women (often anorexic or bulimic) who are compulsively engaged in weight-loss activities and older adults who may have unrealistic expectations or are overly concerned about maintaining a regular bowel movement. Continuous usage for six months or longer on a weekly basis indicates abuse, and various estimates suggest that from 5% to 15% of the U.S. population misuse or abuse laxatives.

l-dopa (levodopa)   A drug mimicking the neurotransmitter dopamine that is currently used in the treatment of Parkinson's disease. It has been used experimentally, without particular success, as a possible counteragent to the acute effects of alcohol intoxication, alcoholism and cocaine craving.

learning disorder   Learning disabilities, which are present in 10% to 20% of school-aged children, represent a complex group of disorders with diverse etiologies. Learning problems are not always linked to detectable brain damage. Although some learning disabilities appear to be inherited, others are caused by prenatal problems or early injury to the nervous system, both of which can be the result of alcohol and other drug use. Babies sometimes suffer overt signs of nicotine addiction and withdrawal, and often they are afflicted with related mental and physical impairments. Lactating mothers excrete nicotine directly through breast milk, and pregnant women transport it through their blood supply to the fetus.

When a woman drinks alcohol during pregnancy, she puts her child at risk of being born with FETAL ALCOHOL SYNDROME (FAS), any or all of a series of abnormalities that includes growth deficiencies, physical malformations and mental retardation. The effects of FAS on the central nervous system include retarded mental and motor development, tremors, hyperactivity and poor attention span. The average IQ of children with FAS is approximately 68 (as opposed to 100 for nonafflicted children). Varying degrees of mental deficiency are the most common signs of FAS. Such children show no improvement with time, even when placed in supportive atmospheres.

At present there is an epidemic of drug-affected infants. Emerging medical findings indicate that effects on drug-exposed babies can include retarded growth, stiff limbs, hyper-irritability, tendency to stop breathing with higher risk of crib death, strokes and seizures, malformed or missing organs, facial deformities and mental retardation. (See BABIES, DRUG-ADDICTED AND -EXPOSED.)

Leary, Timothy   Prominent 1960s prodrug social psychologist who coined the expression "Turn on, tune in, and drop out" to describe the change of consciousness brought on by drug use. When he first uttered the expression, he was indeed describing a common phenomenon of that era. (See HIPPIES.) Dr. Leary, then a Harvard professor, was dedicated to establishing the unhindered use of psychedelics for "seekers of self-knowledge." He proposed that useful self-knowledge was obtained by the use of psychedelics. While he profited economically from publishing royalties and paid speaking engagements, his ideas are not necessarily considered psychologically or philosophically sophisticated.

Dr. Leary again drew media attention in 1995–96, when, weakened by inoperable and fatal illness, he turned his sickroom into a salon and place of celebration with friends. Dr. Leary died in 1996.

legal aspects of alcohol abuse   Historically, alcohol abuse was considered a criminal justice matter, and chronic users were imprisoned under legislation forbidding PUBLIC DRUNKENNESS. This approach was not very successful; abusers would be arrested repeatedly with no improvement in their condition. Prior to 1971, the alcoholic population was estimated to account for one-third of all arrests excluding traffic violations.

In the last 20 years, the criminal justice philosophy has been replaced by a more humane, public-health-problem approach that calls for treatment and rehabilitation rather than incarceration. In 1971 the Uniform Alcoholism and Intoxication Treatment Act was adopted by the National Conference of Commissioners on Uniform State Laws. This act declares that alcoholics and intoxicated persons may not be subjected to criminal prosecution because of their consumption of alcoholic beverages but should instead be provided with appropriate treatment. (These laws however are often skirted by local policies against "public nuisances," a vague description that can be interpreted to include drunken behavior.)

The major piece of social legislation dealing with problems of alcohol abuse and alcoholism is the Comprehensive Alcohol Abuse and Alcoholism Prevention, Treatment, and Rehabilitation Act of 1970, also known as the Hughes Act. This act created the NATIONAL INSTITUTE ON ALCOHOL ABUSE AND ALCOHOLISM (NIAAA) and was amended in 1973 to establish the Alcohol, Drug Abuse, and Mental Health Administration, of which NIAAA became a part.

Each state has its own particular set of laws concerning the purchase and sale of alcoholic beverages and business hours for establishments that sell liquor. (See ALCOHOLIC BEVERAGE CONTROL LAWS.) States also determine their own regulations regarding DRIVING WHILE IMPAIRED (DWI).

The year 1988 saw a new wave of product-liability suits in federal courts in Pennsylvania and Washington State, charging that alcohol caused serious birth defects or fatal illnesses. These new cases were based on plaintiffs' arguments that "moderate drinking" caused harm and that companies should have warned them of the danger. In early 1989, Congress passed a bill requiring "health-warning labels" on beer, wine and liquor containers (not unlike the surgeon general's warning on cigarette packages) that "pregnant women should not drink" alcohol because of risks of birth defects, and that alcohol "may cause other health problems." It is now a federal law.

In a landmark decision handed down on April 20, 1988, the Supreme Court ruled four to three that the Veterans Administration can continue to deny disability and other benefits to most veterans disabled by alcoholism because their condition is caused by "willful misconduct." The decision, which directly concerns only veterans, stressed the majority's view of what Congress intended in two ambiguously worded statutes (in 1977 and 1978) that define who is entitled to veterans' benefits and that prohibit discrimination against handicapped people.

Both the majority and the dissent stressed the view expressed by Associate Justice Byron R. White (who wrote for the majority) that "this litigation does not require the Court to decide whether alcoholism is a disease whose course its victims cannot control."

Writing for the majority in the case *Traynor* v. *Turnage,* No. 86-622 and 86-737, Justice White noted that the Veterans Administration policy with regard to alcoholism as a disability had been consistent since at least 1964. Marcus A. Rothschild, M.D., editor of *Alcoholism: Clinical and Experimental Research,* the Journal of the American Medical Society on Alcoholism, said that the Supreme Court decision was discouraging. "The ruling," he told the *New York Times* "will lend itself to misinterpretation. To consider this genetic-inherited trait as willful misconduct is to deny all our more recent knowledge and advances."

The 1990s saw a number of new policy issues raised concerning alcohol distribution. Research indicating the positive effects of very moderate drinking (such as a glass of wine daily) in preventing heart attacks resulted in a debate over whether or not wine distributors could advertise such a claim. African-American, Latino and Native American lobby groups have been trying, so far unsuccessfully, to introduce legislation restricting ethnically targeted marketing programs.

National Institute on Alcohol Abuse and Alcoholism, *Federal Activities on Alcohol Abuse and Alcoholism: FY 1977 Final Report,* (Silver Spring, Md.: Marco Systems, 1978): 4–6.

Stuart Taylor, Jr., "Denial of V.A. Benefits to Alcoholics Upheld," *New York Times* (April 21, 1988).

legal aspects of marijuana, and other drug controls   The legal foundation for the government's strategy for combating abuse of drugs and other substances is the CONTROLLED SUBSTANCES ACT of 1970. The basic provisions of the law were strengthened by the Congress in 1984 and again with the Anti-Drug Abuse Act of 1986. A major segment of the latter, the Narcotics Penalties and Enforcement Act, provides for mandatory minimum sentences. The most common and well-known control mechanism is the criminal penalty for trafficking. Trafficking is defined as the unauthorized manufacture, distribution or possession of a drug with intent to distribute. Criminal penalties are based on the drug "Schedules" listed in the act.

Federal trafficking penalties for Schedule I and II controlled substances such as heroin, cocaine base, PCP, LSD, Fentanyl and Fentanyl Analogues (dependent on such factors as first or second offense and quantity/mixture, vary greatly. For example, the penalty for trafficking in cocaine, first offense, 500–4,999 gm mixture) is not less than five and not more than 40 years. If death or serious injury results, it is not less than 20 years and not more than life. Fines of not more than $2 million individual, $5 million other than individual, may be levied. (See BOOTY.)

Federal trafficking penalties for marijuana, hashish and hashish oil also vary considerably. For instance, the penalty for a first offense when the quantity involved is 50–100 kg is not more than 20 years; if death or serious injury occurs, it is not less than 20 years, not more than life. Fines go up to $1 million (individual), $5 million (other than individual). Marijuana is a Schedule I controlled substance. A Schedule IV drug offense is punishable by a maximum of three years in jail and up to a $250,000 fine (individual), $1 million (not individual). Trafficking in a Schedule V drug is punishable by up to one year in prison and up to a $100,000 fine (individual), $250,000 (not individual). Second and subsequent offenses are punishable by twice the penalty imposed for the first offense. The Controlled Substances Act carefully distinguishes between trafficking offenses (those that supply illicit drugs to users) and use offenses (when drugs are possessed solely for personal use). Possession for one's own use of any controlled substance in any Schedule is always a misdemeanor on the first offense, and is punishable by one year in jail and up to a $5,000 fine. A first offender under the age of 21 may receive up to one year probation and thereafter motion court for expungement of all records. When compared to some countries, particularly Turkey, where not only the penalties but the jails themselves have a reputation for harshness, and China, where the punishment can be death, or Singapore (death by hanging), the U.S. is considered lenient.

During the 1990s, pro-marijuana advocates challenged the ban on marijuana when used for medicinal purposes, that is, to stimulate the appetite of patients undergoing radiation and as a painkiller for patients who are unresponsive to other antipain remedies.

The NATIONAL ORGANIZATION FOR THE REFORM OF MARIJUANA LAWS (NORML) is the most active group attempting to decriminalize the use of marijuana and remove the country's estimated 30 million marijuana users from the domain of the criminal justice system. In recent years some states have changed their laws and no longer treat possession of a small quantity of marijuana for personal use by adults as a felony: Alaska, California, Colorado, Maine, Massachusetts, Minnesota, Mississippi, Nebraska, New York, North Carolina, Ohio and Oregon now provide written citations for offenses and charge small fines or extend probation. This procedure replaces the system of arrest, prosecution and jail sentences. In Alaska there are no state laws prohibiting the private possession and cultivation of marijuana for personal use in the home by adults. As a result of follow-up surveys in these states, NORML cites substantial monetary savings to the criminal justice system, public approval of the new laws, only a slight increase in the number of first-time marijuana users and a decline in frequency of use. The move toward decriminalization appears to have halted recently, as research uncovers a number of adverse consequences of marijuana use.

As of November 1982, 33 states had enacted legislation authorizing programs of legal access to THC (tetrahydrocannabinol—the principal psychoactive ingredient in all forms of cannabis) for victims of cancer and glaucoma. In addition, three state supreme courts, those of Washington, Illinois and Michigan, have held marijuana penalties to be unconstitutional, stating that marijuana is improperly classified as a Schedule I drug. According to the CONTROLLED SUBSTANCES ACT (CSA), which was enacted in 1970, and still dictates the government's policy regarding all controlled substances, Schedule I drugs have the highest abuse potential, have no recognized medicinal value in the U.S. and no prescriptions may be written for this category of drugs. Drugs of this class include heroin, LSD and PCP analogues. Oddly enough, crack cocaine and PCP are classified as Schedule II drugs.

In June 1982 a committee appointed by the National Academy of Sciences released a detailed report that endorsed marijuana decriminalization. The report concluded, however, that marijuana is not a single drug but a complex preparation containing many biologically active chemicals, and recommended that comprehensive studies of the effects on the health of the American public be undertaken. Both the president of the academy and the director of the National Institute on Drug Abuse (NIDA) rejected the committee's recommendation to eliminate criminal penalties.

The increased cost of importing marijuana due to interdiction has stimulated domestic production. At the same time, the total amount consumed by Americans has been rising slowly but steadily since 1986. The three largest marijuana-producing states are Oregon, California and Kentucky. One official has said that the marijuana growers are the bootleggers of the 1980s and 1990s.

The only legal marijuana farm in the U.S. is located in Faulkner County, Mississippi. It is operated by scientists from the Research Institute of Pharmaceutical Sciences of the University of Mississippi. A 5.6-acre farm with more than 100 varieties of cannabis plants, it has been under contract to NIDA since 1968. The drug is grown under carefully controlled conditions for general research and to further study marijuana's therapeutic properties. A sophisticated analysis laboratory is located nearby where the crude plant material is extracted and filtered off to yield a resin extract that is then dissolved in ethanol. Various levels of the cannabinoids in each specimen are pinpointed; some are then isolated and synthesized. All crude plant material is carefully labeled as to seed origin, plant sex and dates of planting and harvest, so that uniform study results can be obtained.

legal high   A term for mind-altering substances that produce a HIGH of some sort (though they may be extremely toxic) and are legally available without a prescription. NUTMEG, MOUTHWASHES with a high alcohol content, and INHALANTS such as CLEANING FLUIDS, airplane glues, and so on, are all examples of "legal highs."

legalization   In the late 1980s, the concept of legalizing or decriminalizing the use of currently illicit

drugs was hotly debated. Due to drug-related crime many so-called conservatives began to consider decriminalization as a possible step to reducing crime. The parallel was noted between the current drug-related crime epidemic and the similar alcohol-related crime epidemic rampant during Prohibition. (Legalization would still call for regulation, the way alcohol and cigarettes are currently regulated.)

Many general opinion surveys reveal a significant increase in the number of people who believe the measure would reduce crime and violence. Statistics and studies suggest that incarceration does not serve as either a deterrent or a cure for drug selling or drug using. The objective of our prison system was to punish and possibly cure prisoners, yet the result has been to create an ever growing subculture of repeat offenders who have come to view the prison system as a way of life, thus the popular term "revolving door" has come into our vocabulary. Studies do indicate, however, that many treatment and rehabilitation programs can and do prevent drug-involved individuals from returning to criminal activities related to drugs. They also have established that various types of PREVENTION MODELS are proving to be effective in involving youth. Prevention and rehabilitation programs studied thus far cost far less to build, implement and run than jails, which are phenomenally expensive per suspect/prisoner and are paid for with taxpayer dollars. The entire court system leading up to, or in lieu of, prison, is prohibitively costly and in regard to drug-related activities, appears to be ineffectual. Whether or not legalization would be more effectual is a question that needs to be studied. Many approaches have been and are being experimented in nations around the world, however, it must be remembered that each nation has a distinct population with very different sociological histories and patterns. A severe approach that may yield excellent results in Singapore, for instance, may prove disastrous in Amsterdam, where an extremely tolerant approach may yield equally favorable results.

Lemmon   The manufacturer of the pills called QUAALUDES, which were nonbarbiturate sedative hypnotics that became extremely popular on the illicit market, particularly in the club scene. The company produced these large white tablets with their name stamped on them. A Lemmon 714 was the 300-mg size. On the street these came to be known as "Lemmons," "714s" or "ludes." Fake Quaaludes (sometimes called "bootlegs" or "boots") were widely adulterated with substances other than methaqualone. This drug was eventually withdrawn from the pharmaceutical market by the manufacturer (Lemmon) due to its widespread misuse.

lethal dose
Alcohol: It is difficult to die from an overdose of alcohol, as people usually lose consciousness before they are able to drink themselves to death. However, death from alcohol overdose has occurred during drinking contests. For death to result, more than a quart of whiskey or its equivalent must be drunk in a short time.

Unconsciousness usually results from a BLOOD ALCOHOL CONCENTRATION (BAC) of 0.4% or higher. Deep coma sets in at about 0.5%, depending on one's gender, size and tolerance, and at 0.6% death may result from suppression of the nerve centers that control the heartbeat and breathing. (See CENTRAL NERVOUS SYSTEM.)

Drugs other than alcohol: The lethal dose of drugs other than alcohol depends on so many factors—the amount taken, the purity of the drug, what it was taken in combination with, the physical state of the person taking it and so on—that it is impossible to say what actually constitutes a "lethal" dose. The amount of a lethal dose can be profoundly affected by the materials with which the pure drug has been adulterated—depending on the conditions, it could be an extremely small amount. (See ADDITIVE EFFECT and SYNERGY.)

lettuce There are claims that both wild lettuce and head lettuce sold in supermarkets can produce marijuanalike effects when dried and smoked. This is extremely doubtful, however, and any effects that are felt may be a result either of the person hyperventilating while smoking or of a psychological placebo effect.

levallorphan A NARCOTIC ANTAGONIST used to lessen respiratory depression caused by the use of narcotics. (See LORFAN.)

levo-dromoran A synthetic NARCOTIC that contains levorphanol tartrate and acts as a highly potent analgesic for moderate to severe pain. With an addictive potential similar to morphine, it can be habit-forming. It is no longer available in the U.S.

levorphanol An OPIOID NARCOTIC analgesic, similar to but more potent than morphine. Levorphanol tartrate is used in many of the same ways as other opioids—to relieve moderate to severe pain in cases of renal or biliary colic, myocardial infarction and pain associated with cancer. It also supplements nitrous oxide in pre- and postoperative anesthesia. The effects of levorphanol peak in 60–90 minutes and last from four to eight hours. It is prescribed in quantities of 2–3 mg, to be taken orally or subcutaneously; this is equivalent to 10 mg of morphine.

Although levorphanol achieves the same analgesic effects as morphine, the side effects typical of morphine, such as nausea, constipation and vomiting, occur less frequently. The drug can cause respiratory depression, in which case NARCOTIC ANTAGONISTS may be called for to counteract it.

Available from Roche in tablets as well as in ampules and vials for injection, it is marketed as LEVO-DROMORAN and is a Schedule II drug under the Controlled Substances Act. Although tolerance and dependence do occur, levorphanol is not subject to great abuse.

Librax A SEDATIVE HYPNOTIC and so-called minor tranquilizer (DEPRESSANT) that combines Librium (chlordiazepoxide hydrochloride) and Quarzan (clidnium bromide, an anticholinergic drug), both developments of Roche research. Dependence can occur if the recommended dosage is exceeded. When taken with alcohol or other central nervous system depressants it can have an ADDITIVE EFFECT. Somnolence, confusion and coma are results of overdosage.

Libritabs A sedative tranquilizer that contains chlordiazepoxide, a BENZODIAZEPINE derivative. Both psychological and physical dependence are possible if the recommended dosage is exceeded. When taken with alcohol or other central nervous system depressants it can have an ADDITIVE EFFECT. Possible results of overdose are diminished reflexes, somnolence, confusion and coma.

Librium   One of the most widely prescribed sedative tranquilizers. It contains chlordiazepoxide hydrochloride (a BENZODIAZEPINE derivative) and is used to reduce both simple and severe forms of tension, anxiety and fear. It also is used to detoxify alcoholics and other sedative-dependent drug users. Chemically and pharmacologically it is similar to diazepam (Valium) and oxazepam (Serax). Physical and psychological dependence can occur if the recommended dosage is exceeded, and it has a significant potential for abuse. As is the case with other central nervous system (CNS) drugs, use with alcohol or other depressants produces an ADDITIVE EFFECT. Possible results of overdose are diminished reflexes, somnolence, confusion and coma.

lidocaine   A synthetic local anesthetic that has a relatively weak effect on the central nervous system and consequently has little potential for abuse.

life-skills training   Treatment modality based on the observation that many alcohol- and other drug-abusing individuals have deficits in the basic tasks of adult living, such as self-care, financial planning, interpersonal relations and work-related skills. Additionally, it is thought that life-skill deficiencies are major contributors to the potential for relapse. This training may also include relaxation techniques, job-search skills, assertiveness training and cognitive behavioral techniques of relapse prevention.

lipid soluble   A substance such as THC (tetrahydrocannabinol, the active ingredient in marijuana) that is soluble in fats and fatty tissues. Lipid solubility usually is synonymous with insolubility in water.

liqueur   An alcoholic beverage, usually from 35 to 60 proof, produced by combining a distilled spirit with strong flavorings and, in most cases, a sweetener. Liqueurs are sometimes known as "cordials" in the U.S.; in the U.S. and elsewhere they are often referred to as fruit brandies. (See DISTILLATION.)

Today's liqueurs have, in all likelihood, evolved from the flavored wines popular in earlier times, when fermentation processes were erratic and vintages were sometimes scarcely potable. Liqueurs that were based on distilled spirits, rather than on WINES, probably originated in Italy during the 15th century; their present name derives from the Italian *liquori*,

corrupted by later French usage. Benedictine, a liqueur that is still produced today, may have been made as early as 1510 in a monastery in Fecamp, France. Early liqueurs were produced exclusively by monasteries for their reputed medicinal powers. Monks in the Middle Ages were experienced herbalists, and it is likely that they switched from a wine base to a distilled spirit base in the hope of increasing the potency of their remedies.

The distilled spirit base of a liqueur and the flavoring additive are combined by one of two methods. The first is percolation, in which alcohol vapors are circulated through flavoring herbs, spices or fruit and then recondensed by cooling. The second is infusion, in which the flavoring additives are simply soaked in a distilled spirit and filtered out once the flavor has been absorbed. In either case, the flavored distillate is generally rectified for greater strength, sweetened, artificially colored and aged before being bottled for distribution.

Liqueurs are produced from virtually every combination of spirit and flavoring imaginable, and the precise ingredients and proportions in any given liqueur are usually a matter of long tradition and professional secrecy. The spirit bases vary according to country of origin, with France and Italy being known for grape brandy liqueurs, Scotland and Ireland for whiskey liqueurs, and many other countries for a variety of grain and potato spirit liqueurs. The flavorings used are even more varied, although the majority are natural produce used in combination with each other, such as fruit and fruit rinds, herbs, spices, roots and even flowers. The most common liqueurs are those flavored principally with oranges, strawberries, almonds or honey, all of which are marketed under a number of different brand names.

liquor   The Latin term for liquidity in general. In its earliest English usage, the term liquor was used to refer to any mixed liquid, such as "neat liquor," or to any measured solution of a solid in liquid. It was only in the 17th century that the term came to be associated specifically with alcoholic beverages. Today the term liquor refers to any and all alcoholic beverages, but commonly is used in reference to high potency spirits (hard liquor) created by a DISTILLATION process.

lithium An alkali metallic element and mood stabilizing medication effective in the treatment of mania and depression.

While mixed results in early research studies of lithium carbonate therapy generated some interest, later studies ruled it out as a pharmacological adjunct to treatment of alcoholism and other drug use where there was no co-occurring bipolar disorder. (See PHARMACOTHERAPY AND ALCOHOL ABUSE.)

liver The liver is located in the upper right-hand side of the abdomen, and is partially protected by the lower rib cage. Weighing about three pounds in adults, it is the largest and most metabolically complex organ in the human body. Its functions include circulation, metabolism, excretion, immunology and detoxification. Seventy-five percent of the blood carried to the liver comes from the intestinal tract; the liver is, therefore, the first to receive digested material.

Alcohol abuse has directly harmful effects on the liver. Ninety percent of the alcohol a person consumes must be oxidized or detoxified in the liver, and both alcohol and acetaldehyde (a metabolic product of alcohol) can scar the liver and break down its tissues. This damage affects all parts of the body, since the liver can no longer convert vitamins and foods into forms usable by the other organs and tissues, or perform its many other functions.

There are several distinct types of ALCOHOLIC LIVER DISEASES that can result from heavy drinking. The mildest and most common form of liver disease found in hospitalized alcoholics is characterized by an accumulation of fat in the liver. ALCOHOLIC HEPATITIS is a more acute and serious form of the disease. It involves inflammation of the liver and cell death and can be accompanied by fever, jaundice and an abnormal accumulation of fluid in the abdominal cavity. Alcoholic hepatitis has a mortality rate of 10% or more. The most serious form of alcoholic liver disease is CIRRHOSIS, which is characterized by scarring of the liver with fibrous tissue and breakdown of the liver structure. This disease is irreversible, though not always fatal.

One does not have to be an alcoholic to fall victim to an alcoholic liver disease—heavy social drinking also can result in damage to the liver. An adequate diet will not protect a heavy drinker from liver injury, as many people believe, though malnutrition may certainly contribute to liver damage. The liver can repair itself to a remarkable degree, however, and with the exception of cirrhosis, most liver diseases can be corrected to some extent through proper diet (high protein, high vitamin content) and rest—provided the individual stops drinking.

Acute hepatitis: Inflammation of the liver, or hepatitis, is the most common medical complication that results from injecting drugs such as heroin or methedrine and is transmitted through the use of contaminated needles. Narcotics themselves seem to have little direct effect on the liver. In one study, 76% of addicts with a history of hepatitis had their first episode within 24 months of starting to use a needle and 50% within the first year. Some 30% of addicts who get hepatitis have recurring bouts of the disease. The first symptoms of hepatitis are nausea, vomiting, jaundice and pain in the upper right side of the body.

Liver dysfunction has been reported in adolescents who have abused inhalants, particularly cleaning fluid preparations. However, abuse of glue, the most popular inhalant among young users, does not seem to affect the liver.

In studies of the effects of cannabis on the liver, no laboratory evidence was found of liver dysfunction in heavy users, with the exception of individuals who used marijuana in conjunction with alcohol.

The use of LSD and other psychedelic drugs does not seem to result in liver damage. In the case of cocaine, studies have shown that from 10% to 20% of the cocaine administered was excreted unchanged in the urine, and that the liver can detoxify one minimal lethal dose of cocaine in an hour.

Ralph W. Richter, ed., *Medical Aspects of Drug Abuse* (New York: Harper & Row, 1975): 61.

lobelia There have been claims that smoking the dried leaves of the plant *Lobelia inflata* can produce a marijuanalike effect. However, it does not have a significant potential for abuse due to extremely unpleasant side effects, such as nausea and vomiting.

Lomotil An antidiarrhetic. A synthetic drug containing diphenoxylate hydrochloride and atropine sulfate; it is chemically related to the narcotic MEPERIDINE. Because of its similarity to meperidine it has addiction potential, and the prescribed dosage should be strictly followed. Overdosage can result in severe or even fatal respiratory depression.

lophophorine   An alkaloid contained in PEYOTE.

lorfan   A NARCOTIC ANTAGONIST that contains levallorphan tartrate. It is used in cases of deliberate and accidental opioid overdose for the treatment of respiratory depression. If used in the absence of a narcotic, it can cause respiratory depression; if the respiratory depression has been caused by a barbiturate or other non-narcotic agent, it can increase the depression. Lorfan is no longer available in the U.S.

loss of control   A major symptom of addiction, loss of control is the inability on the part of an alcoholic or other drug user to refrain from using a drug. There are two types of loss of control: the first type is the inability to refrain from trying the drug for the first time. The second type refers to the inability to stop using a drug after using even once. Loss of control does not mean that every time the drug is used it is used to excess. The symptoms may appear only sporadically. However, at certain times, the addicted individual is powerless to resist use or to control the extent of use. The stimulus may be outside of the user's conscious awareness, and at some point the drug itself may become the stimulus.

The unpredictable nature of this symptom has been used to bolster the concept of absolute ABSTINENCE for alcoholics and other drug users, since, the argument goes, there can be no loss of control if the addicted individual can refrain from use completely. In the case of alcohol, there have been studies such as the RAND REPORT, which examine the possibility of MODERATE DRINKING for some alcoholics under certain conditions, suggesting reasons to reconceptualize alcoholism, not as the generic disorder of popular conception, but as a syndrome with causes, manifestations and appropriate treatment models that vary according to the individual. In other words, the theory states that whereas total abstinence may be the most appropriate solution for some substance users, controlled use is possibly more attainable and beneficial to others.

lotusate   A short-acting BARBITURATE, that contains talbutal and is used as a hypnotic sedative. It

can produce dependence and has a high potential for abuse. Lotusate is no longer available in the U.S.

low birth weight   Recent studies show that use of any drug, including alcohol, tobacco and caffeine, can be related to low birth weight. Effects of prenatal exposure to alcohol are measurable over a broad range of maternal drinking levels, including even "social drinking." The best advice for pregnant women continues to be to abstain from alcohol, tobacco and all illegal, prescription and over-the-counter drugs, including caffeine.

For more information regarding associations between alcohol and other drugs and adverse pregnancy outcome, see BABIES, DRUG-ADDICTED AND -EXPOSED, FETAL ALCOHOL SYNDROME (FAS) and PREGNANCY.

LSD   A semisynthetic drug derived from the alkaloid lysergic acid that is found in ergot, a parasitic fungus or "rust" that grows on rye and other grains (d-lysergic acid diethylamide, lysergide, LSD-25).

LSD was originally synthesized in 1938 by two Swiss chemists. Five years later, in the spring of 1943, one of its codiscoverers, Dr. Albert Hofmann, inadvertently ingested some of the drug. He experienced restlessness and dizziness followed by a mild delirium in which he experienced "fantastic visions of extraordinary vividness accompanied by a kaleidoscopic play of intense coloration." To make certain that LSD was the source of these visions, Hofmann took another dose, 25 mg, which today is considered to be two and a half times the normal dose for a major trip. He again experienced intense visual changes and also synesthesia, or the merging of senses: "sounds were transposed into visual sensations so that from each tone or noise a comparable colored picture was evoked, changing in form and color kaleidoscopically."

According to Edward M. Brecher, after 1943 LSD was "a drug in search of a use." The U.S. Army tested it for use as a brainwashing agent and as a way of making prisoners talk more readily, and it was stockpiled by the armed forces for possible use in disabling an enemy. Psychiatrists, believing that its effects mimicked a psychotic state, used LSD on themselves and on staff members of mental hospitals in order to better understand mental illness. LSD came into widespread use as an adjunct to psychotherapy in the late 1940s and early 1950s in the U.S., England and Europe. It was used on chronically withdrawn, seriously ill mental patients and showed initially promising results. Longer-term and more careful follow-up studies were not as favorable, but the ultimate scientific proof of its effectiveness in psychotherapy has not been established.

Until the 1960s, self-administration of LSD was mostly restricted to a small number of intellectuals. Writer Aldous Huxley's favorable reports of his experiences with MESCALINE, another hallucinogen whose effects are similar to those of LSD, encouraged others to explore the possibilities of mystical visions and the potential for increased creativity. The illicit use of LSD on a broad national scale began in the U.S. around 1962. Prior to this time, almost all the LSD available in the U.S. and Canada was produced by Sandoz Laboratories. New Food and Drug Administration (FDA) laws and restrictions on LSD and other investigational drugs were followed by an *increase* in the availability and use of LSD. This was helped by Dr. Timothy Leary, an instructor at Harvard University, who left Harvard in 1963 under a cloud of scandal because of his activities involving LSD. He became a media figure overnight and used his newfound fame to propagandize his famous slogan ("turn on, tune in, and drop out") promoting LSD on a national and international scale.

Classification: LSD is classified as a HALLUCINO-GEN, a Schedule I drug under the CONTROLLED SUBSTANCES ACT.

Appearance: LSD commonly is prepared as a tartrate salt that is soluble in water. When pure, it is a white, odorless, crystalline material, but street preparations are generally mixed with colored substances.

Usage: The subjective experiences that LSD induces can be spectacular. Sensory perceptions are altered and intensified so that colors appear brighter and sounds become magnified or are perceived as patterns; there is a merging of senses (synesthesia) so that sounds become swirling patterns of vivid color; perceptions of time and space are distorted so that seconds may seem like an eternity and objects become fluid and shifting. The user may experience himself as being both within and without himself, or as merged with an object or another person. Hallu-

cinations, visions, religious revelations and personality insights have all been reported. The majority of users have both pleasant and unpleasant reactions to the drug, but for those whose overall reaction has been positive, the unpleasant side effects are seen as both transitory and valuable in terms of self-knowledge.

Early typical users of LSD were generally college students and hippies. Regular users in the late 1970s and the 1980s were not confined to these groups—in one comparative study of regular users of LSD, occupations included plumbers, longshoremen, janitors and tractor mechanics.

As the use of LSD became more widespread in the 1960s, the incidence of "bad trips" also increased. On a "bad trip," the user may feel that he no longer has control of the psychological effects experienced and may want to end the drug state immediately. The most common reaction to a bad trip is one of acute anxiety or panic, often accompanied by terrifying hallucinations and/or a fear of insanity. Confusion, depression and paranoia also may result.

One widely publicized adverse effect of LSD is the FLASHBACK—a re-experiencing of the effects of the drug weeks or even months after taking it. There are a few theories that seek to explain flashbacks, but none of them are conclusive; one is that flashbacks are induced by stress, fatigue or the use of other drugs. Flashbacks seem to occur most frequently in people who have used LSD repeatedly.

Use of LSD peaked in the late 1960s and, after a steady decline, seemed to have stabilized in the 1970s. In the early 1980s there appeared to be increasing interest in LSD, but there was little hard evidence that there was much increase in the actual use of the drug. In a nationwide comparison of drug trends among high school students in 1975–1980, the Institute for Social Research found that 9.3% of high school seniors used hallucinogenic drugs at some time in 1980 compared to a rate of 11.2% in 1975.

Prevalence rates for LSD did not change significantly for any age group. NIDA's *Monitoring the Future Study,* from 1975–1994, found that the prevalence rate for LSD use among 12th graders had increased from 5.2% in 1991 to 6.9%. in 1994. Lifetime use during the same time period for this group increased from 8.8% to 10.5%. Between 1985 and 1988, lifetime prevalence was highest among 26-

to 34-year-olds (18%). The SAMHSA (Substance Abuse and Mental Health Services Administration) Population Estimates of the *1994 National Household Survey on Drug Abuse* found that this same age group had dropped to second place in lifetime use of hallucinogenic drug use, with an estimated lifetime rate of 13.1% (18- to 25-year-olds had the highest rate of use: 15.1%).

Dosage: LSD is one of the most potent drugs known to man: dosages are measured in micrograms—millionths of a gram—and 25–150 micrograms constitute a dose. Because such small amounts are required, LSD often is impregnated on sugar cubes, blotter paper or small gelatin squares. In relation to other psychedelic drugs, LSD is considered to be 200 times as potent as psilocybin and 5,000 times as potent as mescaline. The size of a lethal dose of LSD is not known, and so far there are no well-documented reports of human deaths attributable to the action of LSD. In 1967 it was reported that the drug caused damage to white-blood-cell chromosomes in test tubes; however, subsequent studies produced mixed results and to date there has not been any conclusive evidence of its deleterious effects on chromosomes. Also, it has not been proven that brain damage or other permanent psychological or physical change is caused by LSD.

Activity: When taken orally the effects of LSD usually are felt within an hour. They can last from six to 12 hours and usually peak after three to five hours. LSD can be considered "the king of psychedelics," because it produces the most intense effects of "mind-expansion," with little or no adverse physical side effects. LSD is quickly distributed to the brain and throughout the body. It acts on the central and autonomic nervous systems. All traces of LSD are gone from the brain after 20 minutes, although its effects last for many more hours. It is metabolized in the liver and kidneys and excreted in the feces.

Effects: The effects of LSD depend on the quality of the drug and, largely, on the psychological and emotional state of the user and the setting in which the drug is taken. Effects also can vary in an individual, so that one experience may be pleasant and the next unpleasant.

There is no evidence that even long-term, high-dosage use of LSD results in any permanent damage to the body or brain. However, like all other drugs, it is particularly dangerous when taken by people who are unstable or have psychotic tendencies.

Use of LSD appears to be related to an increased risk of spontaneous abortion among pregnant women. It may also be linked to a higher-than-normal incidence of congenital abnormalities in newborns. However, as chronic users of LSD also are likely to be users of other drugs, it is difficult to establish what effects are due to each particular drug.

Physiological effects are associated almost entirely with the central and autonomic nervous systems. These include increased blood pressure, a rise in body temperature, dilated pupils and a rapid heartbeat. Occasionally, trembling, nausea, loss of interest in food, chills and flushing occur. Body motor skills may also be impaired. (See SEROTONIN.)

Psychological effects: Organic hallucinogenic drugs producing LSD-like effects have been used by people throughout the world, especially in North and South America, for thousands of years in religious ceremonies, because of the mystical experience they offer, purportedly bringing the user closer to God and nature. They are called "mind-expanding" drugs because that is what they do—break down the barriers that keep an individual locked into his "normal" perception of the world and free his mind to other ways of perceiving the universe. Users have reported experiences ranging from hallucinations, visions, synesthesia, great euphoria and feelings of well-being and "oneness" with the world, to anxiety, panic, fear, depression and despair. Prolonged anxiety and psychotic reactions following the use of LSD have occurred.

Tolerance and dependence: If used daily, tolerance to the effects of LSD can develop rapidly, but it will disappear after a few days' abstinence. Physical DEPENDENCE does not develop with LSD.

Availability: LSD may be manufactured in capsule, tablet or liquid form. It is always taken orally, but it has been injected in clinical situations.

Sources: "Basement chemists" have been readily able to obtain the materials for synthesis of LSD, and it is fairly easily made. Supply has equaled demand.

Synonyms: acid, the beast, blotter acid, blue cheer, Blue Star, California sunshine, chocolate chips, cubes, dots, the ghost, the hawk, microdots, pellets, sacrament, windowpane.

E. M. Brecher and the editors of *Consumer Reports, Licit and Illicit Drugs* (Boston: Little, Brown, 1972).

Aldous Huxley, *The Doors of Perception* (New York: Harper & Row, 1954).

R. R. Lingeman, *Drugs from A to Z* (New York: McGraw-Hill, 1974).

Office of Applied Studies, *Preliminary Estimates from the 1994 National Household Survey on Drug Abuse* (Washington, D.C.: Substance Abuse and Mental Health Services Administration, 1994).

LSM   Lysergic acid morpholide; a chemical substance related to LSD.

Luminal   A hypnotic sedative and long-acting BARBITURATE that contains phenobarbital. It is often used to control seizures. Physical dependence can occur, as the drug can be habit-forming, and tolerance will develop. Luminal is no longer available in the U.S.

lungs   The two conical, sacklike organs, where respiration, or the exchange of gases between blood and the external atmosphere, takes place. Cartilaged passageways of smooth muscle, called bronchi, conduct air to smaller bronchioles, which terminate in alveoli. It is in the alveoli, tiny membranous air sacs filled with vast networks of blood vessels and capillaries, that the absorption of oxygen and the emission of carbon dioxide occur. The sympathetic and parasympathetic nerve fibers regulate respiration through their respective effects on the blood vessels and bronchi of the lungs.

Although sedatives do not seem to inflict direct damage to the lungs, their effect on the medulla, the brain's respiratory center, explains the danger of death by respiratory failure that may result from the abuse of these drugs. High doses of barbiturates, volatile solvents, tranquilizers and alcohol can cause oxygen deficiency and difficulty in breathing that can result in *apnea*, temporary suspension of breathing, and death by suffocation. Many alcoholics also are smokers, and a correlation between alcohol abuse and respiratory disorders such as bronchitis and emphysema has been established through association with heavy smoking.

STIMULANTS such as amphetamines, cocaine, caffeine and nicotine increase respiratory rate and depth, causing labored breathing. In the case of an overdose, however, their effects during the depressive phase can cause death from respiratory failure. The long-term effects on the lungs from smoking cocaine freebase are unknown.

Abuse of the addictive stimulant nicotine, through smoking, definitely leads to serious lung damage, though this is attributable to the particulate and gaseous contents of tobacco smoke rather than to the action of nicotine. Tars and other particles in the smoke damage the lungs in several ways. By trapping air they cause alveolar ruptures, scarring and inflammation. The decreased surface area of the lungs severely inhibits exchange of gases and causes emphysema victims to suffer from very labored breathing, which can make them barrel-chested. Twenty thousand American smokers die from emphysema each year. Furthermore, the hydrocarbons in cigarette tar contain carcinogens and cocarcinogens that promote the development of cancerous cells in the lungs and other parts of the body. Cancerous cells eventually replace functioning respiratory cells. Lung cancer, which is the second major cause of deaths from smoking (after coronary heart disease), claims approximately 84,000 Americans annually.

Cigarette smokers risk even further damage to the lungs from such gases as ammonia, formaldehyde, acetaldehyde and hydrogen cyanide, which are contained in cigarette smoke and irritate and eventually kill the mucus-producing and ciliary cells lining the respiratory tract. This destruction of the respiratory system's protective mechanisms sharply increases the smoker's susceptibility to bronchial inflammation (bronchitis) and other infectious diseases.

Heroin abuse increases the likelihood of pulmonary infections such as abscesses and pneumonia, not because of the drug itself but because of the unsanitary conditions under which heroin often is administered—unsterilized or shared needles. Usually attributable to staphylococcus, such diseases are common among addicts. In addition, "street" heroin often is contaminated or adulterated with binding agents, such as talc or cellulose, which can lodge in the small vessels of the lungs and cause fibrosis and thrombosis. Heroin itself can depress respiration and decrease the volume and diffusing capacity of the lungs. Pulmonary hypertension and even cardiopulmonary collapse can follow the reduction of lung function. Narcotic overdose can involve abnormally fast or slow breathing, congestion and edema. This last condition manifests as froth that fills the bronchial tree, comes out through the nose and mouth and can cause death by suffocation. Autopsies of overdose victims have revealed fluid-filled lungs weighing five and six times the normal weight.

In general, psychedelic drugs produce no characteristic adverse effects on the lungs or on respiration. There have been reported cases of LSD precipitating asthma, but it is not known if the individuals involved suffered from asthma before taking the drug, in which case the asthma may have been the result of a panic reaction to the LSD.

The effects of marijuana smoking on the lungs have not yet been satisfactorily established. No causal relationship has been established between marijuana use and emphysema or lung cancer. In fact, until early in this century marijuana was used in the U.S. to treat a variety of illnesses, including asthma. Like tobacco, marijuana contains tars that may conceivably produce deleterious effects, and cancer-causing chemicals in marijuana smoke are present in amounts 50%–70% higher than in old-fashioned, high-tar cigarettes. Furthermore, the marijuana smoker deliberately inhales and holds the smoke in his lungs as long as possible, placing the irritants and carcinogens in long and direct contact with lung tissue. As people continue to use marijuana over the period of years that it takes to develop a symptomatic lung cancer, we may see primary malignancies on the lungs due to cannabis. Chronic heavy daily use can significantly impair lung function. Excessive smoking of hashish and other forms of potent marijuana have produced bronchial irritation, asthma and chronic catarrhal laryngitis.

M

mace An aromatic spice, usually ground, made from the dried arillode (outer covering) of the nutmeg seed. It is mixed with hot water to form a beverage that has psychedelic properties. (Not to be confused with chemical Mace, the trademark name for a chemical compound having the combined effect of a tear gas and a nerve gas.)

macromerine An alkaloid found in the cactus DONA ANA. It has psychedelic properties similar to, but far less potent than, mescaline, which is found in the head of the peyote cactus.

macronodular cirrhosis A contemporary classification of a type of cirrhosis that is similar to POST-NECROTIC CIRRHOSIS, which follows LIVER inflammation or hepatitis.

Madagascar periwinkle *Catharanthus roseus.* The leaves of this plant produce stimulant and hallucinogenic effects when smoked but can cause extremely severe adverse reactions as well.

Madeira The name given to any of several fortified wines made on Madeira, a Portuguese-owned island located in the Atlantic Ocean about 400 miles off the northwestern coast of Africa.

There are four basic types of Madeira: Malmsey, a very sweet, dark brown wine that is usually drunk as a dessert wine; Bual (or Boal), a golden-brown wine that is only slightly less sweet than Malmsey and also drunk as a dessert wine; Verdelho, a golden wine that is less sweet than either Malmsey or Bual and drunk either with dessert or as an aperitif; and Sercial, a pale gold wine that is the driest of the four and generally is drunk as an aperitif. In addition to these four types there is a blend of different Sercial wines called Rainwater Madeira. The alcohol content of Madeira wines usually falls between approximately 18.5% and 19.5% by volume.

The wines made on Madeira are fortified with brandy, which is added during the fermentation process. The brandy serves to slow down and gradually halt fermentation. The longer the wine is allowed to ferment before the brandy is added, the drier it will be.

After fermentation is complete, the wine is subjected to a special heating process unique to the production of the Madeira wines. The fermented wine is placed in a heated chamber called an *estufa,* where its temperature gradually is raised to 140° F. It is held at this temperature for six weeks, then gradually reduced again. The process is intended to simulate the effects of a slow sea voyage through the tropics. Madeira wine has been subjected to this procedure since the 18th century, when it was discovered that such a voyage had actually improved the flavor of the wine.

mainline, mainlining   Injecting heroin into a vein, particularly the main arterial vein of the arm. (See ADMINISTRATION.)

maintenance therapy   See METHADONE.

malaria   A disease once suffered by a significant number of narcotic addicts. The last epidemic of malaria, spread by contaminated needles, occurred in New York City in 1939. At that time QUININE became a popular dilutant of heroin on the East Coast because it suppresses malarial symptoms. Nonetheless, the reason why very few cases of heroin-related malaria are seen today is due to the fact that the malarial plasmodium has been eradicated in North America and the causative agent of any new outbreak would have to be introduced into the country from abroad.

Mallory-Weiss syndrome   A condition caused by frequent vomiting that results in laceration of the gastroesophageal junction and, in turn, massive hemorrhage. Many victims of the syndrome are alcoholics, as the local toxic and irritating effects of alcohol may result in frequent morning nausea and vomiting. The syndrome, however, is not restricted to alcoholics, and the bleeding may accompany any condition associated with frequent vomiting. Prognosis is excellent once the bleeding has been stopped, although surgery usually is necessary to stop the bleeding.

malt   A grain, almost invariably barley, steeped in water until it germinates, or "malts," and produces the soluble sugar maltose. It is then spread and dried to produce pure malt. Pure malt is a highly nutritive ingredient of certain nonalcoholic beverages and many cereal foods, but it has traditionally been used in brewing or distilling processes. In fact it is one of the oldest ingredients of alcoholic beverages, dating back to the ancient Egyptians, who used it to produce beer. Malted barley is found in nearly all lager, ale, stout, porter and bock beers. It also is mixed with other ingredients to make most types of whiskey. In Scotland a nearly 100% malt whiskey is produced, but it is rarely consumed in this form.

The drying process for malt is especially important, and several different methods of turning the malt during drying have been developed. In the traditional method, drying is accomplished on a malting floor large enough to scatter the grain, which is turned with hand shovels to disperse the heat generated by germination and to speed the drying process. In the more modern Saladin technique, the grain is strewn along troughs and turned by mechanical blades. Some malters employ a procedure known as the "drum method," in which the grain is poured into barrels that can be rotated and ventilated with cool air.

Whatever method is used, malting is a very delicate process that continues for up to two weeks until the germinated sprout has reached the desired length.

malt beverage   A beerlike beverage made from MALT. Most malt beverages are about the same as NEAR BEER. Popular during Prohibition, they began to reappear in the 1970s as a refreshment for those who enjoyed the taste of beer but did not want the effects of the alcohol in beer. For this reason malt beverages have enjoyed some popularity among alcoholics who no longer consume alcohol. (See DEALCOHOLIZED BEVERAGE.)

malt liquor   An alcoholic beverage similar to BEER but with a higher alcohol content (6.5% to 7.0%).

mandrake   *Mandragora officinarum.* An herb that grows in southern Europe and northern Africa. It contains anticholinergic belladonna alkaloids and can cause severe adverse reaction.

Marchiafava-Bignami disease   This disease was first detected in Italy in 1903 by two pathologists, Ettore Marchiafava (1847–1935) and Amico Bignami (1862–1929), among heavy drinkers of wine. It mainly afflicts middle-age alcoholic males, although only a few cases have been reported. The disease can take several months to develop. Symptoms include agitation, confusion, hallucinations, memory disturbances and disorientation. The exact causes of this disease are unknown, but it has been seen in conjunction with WERNICKE'S ENCEPHALOPATHY (SYNDROME OR DISEASE) and ALCOHOL AMBLYOPIA and may be due to malnutrition.

marijuana (cannabis)   The Indian hemp plant, *Cannabis sativa.* The resin, flowering tops, leaves and

History of Marijuana

c. 2737 B.C.	Reference to marijuana in Chinese pharmacology treatise.
c. 2000 B.C.	Reference to marijuana found in India.
c. 500 B.C.–1500 A.D.	500 B.C. urn containing marijuana found near Berlin, Germany. Cloth made from hemp in Europe.
1545	Hemp plant introduced to Chile.
1611	Hemp is cultivated by early colonists in Virginia.
1850	U.S. Pharmacopoeia lists marijuana as a recognized medicine.
1856	Putnam's Magazine publishes an account of Fitz Hugh Ludlow's marijuana-eating experiences.
c. 1875	"Hasheesh houses" modeled after opium dens begin to appear.
1920s–1930s	Commerce in marijuana for recreational use begins to increase during Prohibition. "Tea pads" spring up in major cities. Marijuana linked to crime wave of the 1930s.
1937	Marijuana Tax Act outlaws nonmedical, untaxed possession or sale.
1944	La Guardia Report in NYC clears the drug of being criminogenic and attests to its relative harmlessness.
1950s–1960s	Recreational use grows in the 1950s and becomes widespread in the 1960s on college and high school campuses.
1970	Controlled Substances Act lists marijuana as a Schedule 1 drug, and makes possession a misdemeanor, sale, transfer and intent to sell are felonies.
1970s–1980s	Use spreads to all segments of society and increases each year until 1978–79. In 1979 35.4% of young adults (aged 18–25) report use in past month; in 1982 27.4% report past month use. In 1988, 28 million Americans (14%) had used marijuana, cocaine or other illicit drugs at least once in the past year. The lifetime rate of marijuana use for youths (12 to 17) was 17%; the rate for young adults (18 to 25) was 56%.
1990s	Marijuana producers appear set to be the "bootleggers" and "moonshiners" of the decade. Marijuana use is beginning to rise again as 5.1% of the general population report having used it in the past month, as compared to 4.7% in 1992. Past month use has not dramatically risen in the group aged 12 to 17. As of 1997, 9.4% of that group reported use, as compared to 3.4% in 1992.

Source: National Institute on Drug Abuse

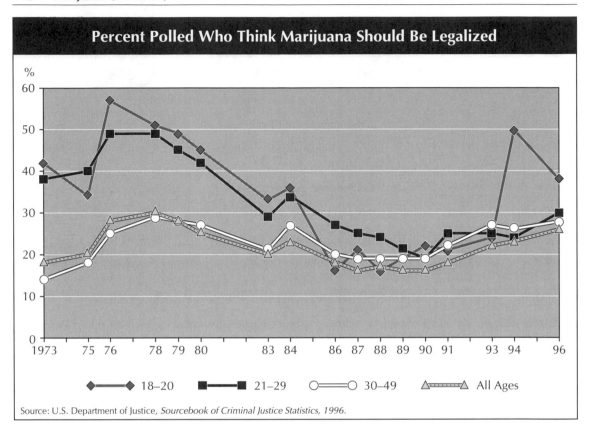

Percent Polled Who Think Marijuana Should Be Legalized

18–20   21–29   30–49   All Ages

Source: U.S. Department of Justice, *Sourcebook of Criminal Justice Statistics, 1996.*

stems contain the psychoactive substance delta-9-THC (TETRAHYDROCANNABINOL).

Marijuana is a tall, leafy weed that grows wild practically anywhere, but flourishes in temperate and tropical climates like Central Asia, where it probably originated. The resin contains the highest concentration of THC; and plants grown in very hot, dry climates produce the most resin and are therefore most potent. It grows wild, however, in most parts of the world. An herbaceous annual with palmlike leaves, male and female plants occur separately. The female plant is taller, broader and longer-lived than the male, producing more leaves and resin. Although the plant can reach 30 feet, average height is four to eight feet, and it has a hollow, six-sided base that is at least two inches in diameter at maturity.

Cannabis occurs in a variety of grades, depending on climate and method of cultivation, and can be processed to yield several different forms of gradu-

ated strength. Plants cultivated for the hemp fiber contain only .05% THC. The name marijuana refers to the leaves and flowering tops, which are dried and shredded and usually consumed orally—either smoked in cigarettes or pipes, or prepared in foods or beverages such as tea. Cannabis typically contains 0.5%–5% THC. Ghanja (known in the U.S. as "Jamaican") contains about 10% THC and is cultivated and consumed primarily in Jamaica. It is made from the flowering tops, leaves and top stems of a specially cultivated female plant. SINSEMILLA can contain up to 20% THC levels, and HASH OIL, (liquid HASHISH), the most potent form of cannabis, may have a THC content of 20% to 80%.

The cannabis family, Cannabinaceae, has one other member, *Humulus lupulus*, the HOPS of which are used to flavor beer and ale.

History: Probably the oldest cultivated nonfood plant, the hemp plant, from which marijuana is

Preliminary Data—As of June 1998

Estimated Number (in Thousands) of Persons Who First Used Marijuana During Each Year 1965–1996,
Their Mean Age at First Use, and Annual Age-Specific Rates of First Use
(per 1000 Person-Years of Exposure), Based on 1994–1997 NHSDAs

Year	Initiates (1000s)	Mean Age	Age-Specific Rate of First Use[1]		
			12–17	18–25	26–34
1965	617	18.8	9.2	13.4	4.9
1966	900	20.3	11.2	23.4	2.7
1967	1467	19.9	15.2	40.9	6.9
1968	1590	19.1	18.5	44.8	3.7
1969	2218	19.2	32.2	52.3	5.4
1970	2668	19.3	35.8	64.8	10.7
1971	2799	18.8	42.5	66.7	12.5
1972	2897	18.4	52.0	63.5	9.5
1973	2782	18.2	55.5	58.4	8.0
1974	3008	18.6	57.2	62.0	9.9
1975	3185	18.8	69.4	55.1	12.8
1976	2824	18.5	61.3	53.4	10.4
1977	2884	19.3	66.5	48.6	10.1
1978	2879	17.8	76.9	50.7	7.1
1979	2585	18.0	61.4	55.4	4.1
1980	2492	18.6	58.2	57.1	5.3
1981	2218	17.8	57.0	46.2	4.8
1982	2080	18.2	50.5	45.8	9.1
1983	2044	17.8	54.9	42.4	3.5
1984	1994	19.6	51.2	38.8	3.9
1985	1767	17.8	48.7	39.1	1.5
1986	1871	19.4	50.4	41.9	3.0
1987	1817	17.9	49.2	43.2	2.3

(continued on next page)

Preliminary Data—As of June 1998 (continued)

Estimated Number (in Thousands) of Persons Who First Used Marijuana During Each Year 1965–1996, Their Mean Age at First Use, and Annual Age-Specific Rates of First Use (per 1000 Person-Years of Exposure), Based on 1994–1997 NHSDAs

Year	Initiates (1000s)	Mean Age	Age-Specific Rate of First Use[1]		
			12–17	18–25	26–34
1988	1526	17.3	43.0	37.7	1.7
1989	1413	17.8	37.6	34.2	2.4
1990	1401	17.3	37.2	37.0	1.4
1991	1376	17.5	36.6	33.9	1.7
1992	1701	17.7	45.5	39.3	2.8
1993	1949	17.0	53.9	46.3	2.2
1994[2]	2393	16.7	73.3	47.9	2.7
1995[3]	2406	16.6	74.6	50.7	2.4
1996[4]	2540	16.4	83.2	53.6	1.3

[1] The numerator of each rate equals the number of persons who first used the drug in the year (times 1000). The denominator of each rate equals the number of persons who were exposed to risk of first use during the year, weighted by their estimated exposure time measured in years. For example, for the age group 12–17 in 1990, the denominator is the sum of three components:
(1) those persons 12–17 years old in 1990 who first used the drug in 1989 or earlier, times a weight of zero. The weight is zero since they had zero exposure to the risk of first use in 1990.
(2) those who first used the drug in 1990 times a weight of .5. The weight of .5 assumes that these people, on average, first used the drug at midyear and consequently have a half year of exposure (i.e. the first half of the year.)
(3) those who never used, or those who first used the drug in 1991 or later, times a weight of one. The weight of one assumes their exposure to the risk of first use during 1990 was for the whole year.
Each person is also weighted by his/her sample weight.
[2] Estimated using 1995, 1996 and 1997 data only.
[3] Estimated using 1996 and 1997 data only.
[4] Estimated using 1997 data only.

Source: SAMHSA, Office of Applied Studies, National Household Survey on Drug Abuse, 1994–1997.

derived, has been a valuable source of products for man's commercial, medical, religious and recreational use for thousands of years. Its cultivation in the Eastern Hemisphere, both for its fibers and its psychoactive properties, has been widely chronicled. The earliest known written reference occurs in a Chinese pharmacological treatise dating from 2737 B.C. and is attributed to the Emperor Shen Nung,

Common Drugs: Symptoms of Abuse of Marijuana and Hashish

Drug Name	Street Names	Method of Use	Sign and Symptoms	Hazards of Use
Tetrahydrocannabinol (THC)	Pot, Grass, Reefer, Pasto, Weed, Colombian, Hash, Hash Oil, Sinsemilla, Joint, Chiba, Herb, Splitt, Smoke	Most often smoked, can also be swallowed in solid form.	Sweet, burnt odor, red eyes; lethargy; lack of coordination. Chronic heavy use may lead to losss of interest & motivation, possible weight change.	Impaired memory perception, interference with psychological maturation. Possible damage to lungs, heart, reproductive & immune systems. Psychological dependence.

Source: New York State Office of Alcoholism and Substance Abuse Services.

who, according to tradition, was the first to teach his people the medicinal value of cannabis. In India, the first known reference to marijuana is found in the *Atharva Veda,* which probably dates back to the second millennium B.C. There are references to marijuana on cuneiform tablets from Asia Minor dating back to 650 B.C., and some believe there are references to the drug in the Bible, in Homer, Herodotus, Pliny, Dioscorides, *The Arabian Nights* and Marco Polo's writings. It is not known exactly when hemp was introduced to western Europe but it must have been very early; an urn found near Berlin, Germany, containing marijuana leaves and seeds is believed to date back to 500 B.C. Marijuana was also in early use in all parts of Africa.

The first record of marijuana in the New World dates from 1545, when the Spaniards introduced it to Chile, although it has been suggested that African slaves who used marijuana as an intoxicant and as a medicine brought it to Brazil earlier in the 16th century. It is not known if the Pilgrims brought hemp to Plymouth, but the plant was introduced to Virginia in 1611 and cultivated as a source of fiber for cloth and rope. It was brought to New England in 1629, and until the end of the Civil War it was a major crop in North America and played an important role in colonial economic policy. In 1765 George Washington was growing hemp at Mount Vernon, presumably for its fiber, though some say Washington was interested in the medicinal as well as the intoxicating qualities of his plants.

Raised for thousands of years as a source of fiber, the hemp plant has also been used medicinally throughout the centuries to treat such conditions as open wounds, scorpion bites and skin inflammations; as a sedative in cases of mania and hysteria; and as an anticonvulsant. During the latter half of the 19th century, American doctors used hemp in the treatment of pain, convulsive disorders, hysteria, asthma, rheumatism and labor pains. The U.S. PHARMACOPEIA (USP) listed it as a recognized medicine in 1850 under the name *Extractum Cannabis* (extract of cannabis) and it appeared in the list until 1942. Marijuana also was used recreationally during the last half of the 19th century and became quite popular in the early part of the 20th century. In 1856 *Putman's Magazine* published an account of hashish-eating by a 16-year-old Poughkeepsie, New York, resident named Fitz Hugh Ludlow, who had read and been influenced by De Quincey's *Confessions of an English Opium Eater.* Ludlow continued to experiment with hashish and marijuana extracts over the next few years and published an expanded account of his experiences in *The Hasheesh Eater.* Marijuana "tea pads," resembling opium dens, were established in New York about 1920. They were tolerated in much the same way as speakeasies were tolerated, and by the 1930s there were an estimated 500 of them in New York City alone. During the 1920s New Orleans was another center of marijuana use, as black musicians made it part of the jazz scene. Prohibition and the unrestrained lifestyles of the Roaring Twenties contributed to the spread of marijuana

Marijuana: Facts for Teens

National Institute on Drug Abuse

Q: What is marijuana? Aren't there different kinds?

A: Marijuana is a green or brown mixture of dried, shredded flowers and leaves of the hemp plant *Cannabis sativa.* You may hear marijuana called by street names such as pot, herb, weed or Mary Jane. There are more than 200 slang terms for marijuana.

Sinsemilla *(sin-seh-me-yah; it's a Spanish word)* is a very strong or potent form of marijuana. Hashish *("hash" for short),* and hash oil, also are very potent and are made from the marijuana plant.

All forms of marijuana are mind-altering. This means they change how the brain works. They all contain THC *(delta-9-tetrahydrocannabinol),* the main active chemical in marijuana. But there are also 400 other chemicals in the marijuana plant.

Q: How is marijuana used?

A: Marijuana is usually smoked as a cigarette *(called a joint)* or in a pipe or a bong.

Recently, it has appeared in cigars called blunts, which are larger and therefore more dangerous.

Q: How long does marijuana stay in the user's body?

A: THC in marijuana is strongly absorbed by fatty tissues in various organs. Generally, traces *(metabolites)* of THC can be detected by standard urine testing methods several days after a smoking session. However, in heavy chronic users, traces can sometimes be detected for weeks after they have stopped using marijuana.

Q: How many teens smoke marijuana?

A: Contrary to popular belief most teenagers have not used marijuana and never will. Among students surveyed in a yearly national survey, about one in six 10th-graders report they are current marijuana users *(that is, used marijuana within the past month).* Fewer than one in five high school seniors are current marijuana users.

Q: Why do young people use marijuana?

A: There are many reasons why some children and young teens start using marijuana. Most young people use marijuana because they have friends or brothers and sisters who use marijuana and pressure them to try it. Some young people use it because they see older people in the family using it.

Other users may think it's cool to use marijuana because they hear about it in music and see it used in TV and movies.

But no matter how many shirts and caps you see printed with the marijuana leaf, or how many groups sing about it, you should know this fact: **You don't have to use marijuana just because you think everybody else is doing it. Most teens *(four out of five)* do not use marijuana!**

Q: What happens if you smoke marijuana?

A: The effects of the drug on each person depend on the user's experience, **as well as:**

how strong the marijuana is *(how much THC it has)*;
what the user expects to happen;
the place where the drug is used;
how it is taken; and
whether the user is drinking alcohol or using other drugs.

(continued on next page)

Marijuana: Facts for Teens (continued)

Some people feel nothing at all when they smoke marijuana. Others may feel relaxed or high. Sometimes marijuana makes users feel thirsty and very hungry—an effect called "the munchies."

Some users can get bad effects from marijuana. They may suffer sudden feelings of anxiety and have paranoid thoughts. This is more likely to happen when a more potent variety of marijuana is used.

Q: What are the short-term effects of marijuana use?

A: The short-term effects of marijuana include:

problems with memory and learning;
distorted perception *(sights, sounds, time, touch)*;
trouble with thinking and problem-solving;

loss of coordination; and
increased heart rate, anxiety, panic attacks.

These risks are even greater when other drugs are mixed with the marijuana; and users do not always know what drugs are given to them.

Q: Does marijuana affect school, sports or other activities?

A: One of the biggest hazards of marijuana for teens is this: the drug can make you mess up in school, in sports or clubs, or with your friends. If you're high on marijuana, you are more likely to make stupid mistakes that could embarrass or even hurt you. If you use marijuana a lot, you could start to lose energy and lose interest in how you look and how you're getting along at school or work. In addition, there is a strong link between drug use and unsafe sex and the spread of HIV, the virus that causes AIDS.

Q: What are the long-term effects of marijuana use?

A: Findings so far show that regular use of marijuana or THC may play a role in some kinds of cancer and in problems with the respiratory, immune and reproductive systems.

Cancer. It's hard to know for sure whether regular marijuana use causes cancer. But it is known that marijuana smoke contains some of the same, and sometimes even more, cancer-causing chemicals as tobacco smoke. Studies show that someone who smokes five joints per week may be taking in as many cancer-causing chemicals as someone who smokes a full pack of cigarettes every day.

Lungs and airways. People who smoke marijuana often tend to develop the same kinds of breathing problems that cigarette smokers have. They suffer frequent coughing, phlegm production and wheezing, and they tend to have more chest colds than nonusers.

Immune system. Animal studies have found that THC can damage the cells and tissues that help protect people from disease.

Reproductive system. Heavy use of marijuana can affect both male and female hormones. Young men could have delayed puberty because of THC effects. Young women may find the drug disturbs their monthly cycle (ovulation and menstrual periods).

Q: Does marijuana lead to the use of other drugs?

A: Long-term studies of high school students and their patterns of drug use show that very few young people use other illegal drugs without first trying marijuana. Using marijuana puts children and teens in contact with people who are users and sellers of other drugs.

So there is more of a risk that a marijuana user will be exposed to and urged to try more drugs. However, most marijuana users do not go on to use other illegal drugs.

(continued on next page)

(*continued from previous page*)

Q: How can you tell if someone has been using marijuana?

A: If someone is high on marijuana, he or she might:

> seem dizzy and have trouble walking;
> seem silly and giggly for no reason;
> have very red, bloodshot eyes; and
> have a hard time remembering things that just happened.

When the early effects fade, over a few hours, the user can become very sleepy.

Q: How does marijuana affect driving?

A: Marijuana has serious harmful effects on the skills needed for driving a car. Timing, coordination, alertness and performance are all affected. For instance, the marijuana user may have trouble judging distances and may have delayed reactions to sights and sounds that drivers need to notice.

There are data showing that marijuana has played a role in crashes. A study of patients who had been in traffic accidents revealed that 15% of those who had been driving a car or motorcycle had been smoking marijuana, and another 17% had both THC and alcohol in their blood.

Q: Is marijuana sometimes used as a medicine?

A: Under U.S. law enacted in 1970, marijuana is a Schedule I controlled substance. This means that the drug, at least in its smoked form, has no commonly accepted medical use. However, at present this ruling is being widely debated, and marijuana may be legal in some states, for medical purposes only, if prescribed by a doctor. THC that is manufactured into a pill can be used legally for treating the nausea and vomiting that occur with certain cancer treatments. The oral THC can be used to help AIDS patients eat more to keep up their weight, as well.

Source: *Marijuana: Facts for Teens* (National Institute on Drug Abuse, n.d.).

use, until it was linked (predominantly by the sensationalist reports of yellow journalism) to the crime wave that swept the country during the 1930s. This link was largely considered to be innocuous. The belief that the nationwide upsurge of depraved criminal behavior was closely linked to the growing use of marijuana was particularly encouraged by Harry Anslinger, commissioner of the Federal Bureau of Narcotics. He conducted a personal campaign (felt by some individuals to be primarily an effort to gain political power) against the "killer weed," which resulted in state legislation banning marijuana. It also resulted in the passage of the 1937 Marijuana Tax Act, which, while it did not actually ban marijuana on a federal level, outlawed the nonmedical, untaxed possession or sale of the drug. Up until that time marijuana preparations were on the shelves of every pharmacy and were widely prescribed. Anslinger's campaign was based on the contention that marijuana was "criminogenic," that is, it directly caused criminal behavior. In 1939 Mayor Fiorello La Guardia appointed a committee to study the use of marijuana in New York City. In the LA GUARDIA REPORT the committee cleared the drug of the criminogenic charge and further testified to its relative harmlessness. The report was not published until 1944, however, when stereotypes fostered by Anslinger and such propaganda films as *Reefer Madness* were already strongly imbedded in the consciousness of the American people—who were too preoccupied with World War II to pay it much attention anyway. During the 1955 Senate committee hearing, Anslinger testified that marijuana use inevitably led to heroin addiction—an apparently false allegation that stuck in the public mind. (This premise is still being put forward by some, see GATEWAY DRUG.)

Its legitimate cultivation in the U.S. peaked during World War II, when Asian sources were cut off by Japanese military conquests. Despite the lurid stories of sexually depraved and criminal behavior that resulted from smoking marijuana, cannabis use continued to spread. Encouraged by the "Beat Generation," represented by such authors as Jack Kerouac, during the 1950s marijuana found a broad new audience: the intelligentsia. In the 1960s it gained widespread popularity on college and high school campuses, becoming almost a symbol of American youth and the generation gap that separated young people from their parents.

Meanwhile, with the first production of synthetic THC by Mechaulam at the Hebrew University in Israel in 1966, medical research progressed rapidly. One new possible medical application was to use it to relieve pressure on the eyeballs in the treatment of glaucoma. Its most widespread current use has been as an antiemetic for the nausea and vomiting of cancer chemotherapy. Cannabidiolic acid, a cannabis alkaloid, is a topical antibiotic.

During the 1970s, 1980s and 1990s, as the younger generation grew older, for the first time, marijuana use spread to all strata of American society and to all age groups. The increase in its popularity has brought with it a growing lobby for its legalization, which recent legislation reflects.

Today, hemp fiber has been largely replaced in commercial use by nylon. Other commercial cannabis products include oil for soap and cooking. The seeds are used in bird seed, fish bait and fertilizer.

Classification: Cannabis has been not quite appropriately classified as a HALLUCINOGEN. Although it is true that it *can* produce mild psychedelic effects in very high doses, it also exhibits some of the characteristics of depressants (sedation), narcotics (analgesia) and even stimulants (enhanced perception). Its defiance of previously established categories may be one of the reasons it has erroneously been classified as a Schedule I drug under the CONTROLLED SUBSTANCES ACT of 1970.

The Controlled Substances Act of 1970 deems marijuana a Schedule I drug (no known medical use), and makes possession of it a misdemeanor. The sale, transfer and intent to sell marijuana are felonies. A 1972 presidential commission suggested that the government focus on controlling traffic of the drug rather than on prosecuting recreational users of it. President Nixon rejected the recommendation. In 1996 citizens in the state of California voted to permit the medically related use of marijuana as a treatment for a variety of illnesses, particularly as an antidote to glaucoma, and to relieve the side effects from chemotherapy for cancer. In many states the law remains unchanged, while actual enforcement policies testify to a diminishing concern among police officers about recreational users of marijuana. (See LEGAL ASPECTS OF MARIJUANA, AND OTHER DRUG CONTROLS.)

Usage: During 1982 three major agencies reviewed research findings: the Institute of Medicine (IOM), World Health Organization (WHO) and the National Institute on Drug Abuse (NIDA). Their general conclusions were similar and are best summarized in the NIDA study on marijuana, which makes the following points: adolescents are beginning to smoke marijuana at an earlier age; marijuana is used intensively by adolescents of both sexes; and the marijuana available is five to 10 times more potent than it was a half-dozen years before. Adolescence is a vulnerable period when coping mechanisms are learned and psychological maturation should be taking place. Instead, the report states, many youngsters are intoxicated on marijuana during a good part of their waking hours. According to data from the SAMHSA (Substance Abuse and Mental Health Services Administration) *1997 National Household Survey on Drug Abuse,* use of marijuana, over the year preceding the survey, was greatest among those between the ages of 18 to 25 (22.3% of the general population). It was lowest among those over 35.

After caffeine, nicotine and alcohol, marijuana is the most popular mind-altering substance in the world. Despite its illegal status in the U.S., an estimated 19,446,000 persons used this substance at least once during 1997, and over 10 million used it 12 or more days. During the 1980s, the two most reliable surveys, the *High School Senior Survey* and the SAMHSA *National Household Survey on Drug Abuse* show significant drops in marijuana use in the general population but a rise in specific age groups. For example, in 1977 nearly 17% of all 12- to 17-year-olds reported past-month use of marijuana; this figure dropped to 11.5% during the month prior to the 1982 survey. In 1992 the use rate for this age group dropped to its lowest point, 4.0%. However, in 1997 it rose to 9.4%. This increase represents a possible renewed interest in and corresponding use of marijuana as a recreational substance by teenagers. There may be a similar pattern for young adults. In the 1979 survey, 35.4% of all young adults (aged 18–25) reported past-month use (an all-time high), but by 1992 this figure had dropped to 11.0%. In 1997, it rose to 12.8%. Among adults 26 and older, 3.3% reported using marijuana at least once in the past month in 1997, down from 6.0% in 1985. This decrease in use is attributed to a change in attitude among young people. In 1978, 35% felt that regular marijuana use was associated with great risk; by 1982 this figure had risen to 60%. Economist Mark A. R. Kleiman, of Harvard's Kennedy School of Government says that the total amount of THC consumed by Americans actually rose 22% from 1982 to 1986.

Dosage: It is impossible to say how much marijuana constitutes an effective dose, since different varieties contain different concentrations of THC. The THC content can vary from 1% to 20% and more. When smoked, THC's effects manifest in a few minutes, peak in 10–30 minutes and last two to three hours (depending on the potency). About 50% of the THC content of a marijuana cigarette is lost in burning and in the side stream smoke; the rest is available for absorption if the roach is consumed. If a joint contains 1000 mg of 1% THC, it has 10 mg of the active ingredient and about 5 mg available for absorption. Since the brain receives its share only by weight, approximately 0.05 mg of THC would arrive in the brain during the first few minutes.

After eating THC, effects materialize in 30–60 minutes, peak in two to three hours and last three to five hours. THC is only one-half to one-third as effective when eaten as it is when smoked. A lethal dose has never been established since no deaths directly related to the action of marijuana have been reported. Research indicates that for a human weighing approximately 154 pounds, a lethal dose of marijuana containing 1% THC would be 15 pounds smoked or 30 pounds eaten—all at once.

Activity: The active principal in *Cannabis sativa* is delta-9-tetrahydrocannabinol (THC). It is most concentrated in the resin but is distributed throughout the plant, except in the root and seeds. Absorbed slowly and incompletely by the stomach, THC is much more effective when smoked and absorbed by the lungs. It is distributed to all the organs and almost completely metabolized in the liver. It is LIPID SOLUBLE, and deposits form in fatty tissues. It crosses the placental barrier and is excreted in the urine and feces. THC is insoluble in water and destroyed by heat. Its half-life, the time required to eliminate half of the dose from the body, is 28–56 hours.

Effects: The effects of marijuana are highly subjective and are affected by a number of variables such as the quality of the drug, the dosage, the experience and expectations of the user, the environment and if it is combined with another mind-altering substance, such as alcohol. In very high doses, THC can produce hypnotic and psychedelic effects, including time and space distortions, enhanced sensory perceptions, euphoria and free-flowing thoughts. Adverse psychological reactions such as anxiety and paranoia can occur, usually in novice users. Some writers have described an "AMOTIVATIONAL SYNDROME," which occurs with regular marijuana use. They claim that research has shown some chronic smokers to became lethargic and lose their ambition and interest in everything except smoking marijuana.

The most common physiological effects reported with moderate use are dryness of the mouth and throat, an increase in pulse rate and heart action (tachycardia), increase in appetite (especially for sweets), red eyes, slight impairment of reflexes and psychomotor coordinated tasks such as driving, sleepiness and sometimes nausea due to dizziness or anxiety. These symptoms are transitory and disappear after a few hours except for impaired driving skills, and lack of energy, which can last up to 10 hours. Different people react differently, and not all people appear to lose energy, becoming lethargic and slowing down. Some users report increased energy with use. Many report a brief period of increased energy, often lasting approximately one to two hours, followed by decreased energy and the desire to lay down or sleep.

The 1982 research findings by the Institute of Medicine (IOM), concluded: "What little we know now about the effects of marijuana on human health—and all we have reason to suspect—justifies serious national concern." The WHO summary states that "intermittent use of low potency cannabis is not generally associated with obvious symptoms of toxicity. Daily or more frequent use, especially of the highly potent preparations, may produce a chronic intoxication that may take several weeks to clear after drug use is discontinued." Subsequent research has demonstrated marked disturbances in depth perception, time judgment and coordination during cannabis use. Coupled with surveys indicating that many traffic accidents occur due to people using cannabis derivatives, these facts raise a significant public health concern about driving vehicles or operating machinery after use.

A Canadian study on the effects of marijuana on the fetus found a link between marijuana smoking and temporary exaggerated tremors, vision problems and startle reflexes among the babies of mothers smoking five or more marijuana cigarettes per week during pregnancy. There are sparse reports of evidence of a fetal cannabis syndrome that resembles the fetal alcohol syndrome. (See PREGNANCY.)

Marijuana and alcohol: People who smoke marijuana also are apt to drink alcohol. According to findings of the National Commission on Marijuana and Drug Abuse, alcohol and tobacco are the two substances most commonly used by regular marijuana smokers. When alcohol is taken with marijuana there is greater impairment of motor and mental skills than with either drug alone. (See SYNERGY.) Among the young (under 21) there seems to be a growing trend toward the combined use of alcohol and marijuana.

Tolerance and dependence: Studies have shown that moderate and infrequent use of marijuana does not produce tolerance. Most experts agree, however, that heavy daily use produces tolerance to the tachycardia. "Reverse tolerance" has been suggested, a syndrome characterized by the user needing progressively smaller doses to achieve a HIGH. This phenomenon has been attributed to (1) the theory that smoking marijuana is a learned behavior, in the sense that with use the smoker learns how to smoke more efficiently and to recognize the effects of the drug more quickly and (2) the fact that because of the very long excretion period of the drug and its lipid solubility, blood levels may remain at a subintoxification level but be rapidly raised by small additional quantities used. The use of marijuana produces not physical dependence but psychological dependence, presumably on marijuana's euphoric and sedative effects. Abstinence may result in feelings of irritability, nervousness or insomnia. Recent studies, however, indicate that marijuana may have addictive properties and may produce a withdrawal effect.

Trafficking and cultivation: The U.S. Drug Enforcement Administration (DEA) in 1995 identified marijuana as the most widely used and readily available illegal drug in the U.S. It notes a resurgence in trafficking, with an increase of the smoking of marijuana-filled cigars known as blunts. More than 50% of the marijuana used in the U.S. was supplied by Mexican sources (whether grown in-country or transshipped from other countries). While Mexico has led in worldwide marijuana production, its production actually decreased from 7,775 metric tons in 1991 to 2,500 metric tons in 1997. However, there was an increase of shipments to the U.S. from Colombia, which ranked as the second largest producer of marijuana. There also was an increase of marijuana shipments from Venezuela and possibly from Jamaica, which produced 406 metric tons in 1989. In the U.S., major outdoor cannabis cultivation took place in Alabama, Hawaii, Kentucky, Tennessee and California in remote locations (occasionally on public lands). The street value of a pound of commercial-grade marijuana rose in price between the mid-1980s and 1990s. Prices that ranged, in accordance with quality, from $400 to $600 a pound in 1984, rose to as high as $4,000 a pound in 1994. Sinsemilla (often grown domestically), a very potent form of marijuana, sold for $1,200 to $2,500 per pound in 1984 and $900 to $9,500 per pound in 1994. John P. Sutton of the DEA stated that Americans now grow "the most potent marijuana in the world."

Substance Abuse and Mental Health Services Administration, *National Household Survey on Drug Abuse: Population Estimates 1994* (Rockville, Md.: Department of Health and Human Services [DHHS], 1995).

Drug Enforcement Administration, *The Supply of Illicit Drugs to the United States* (Washington, D.C., 1995).

Mark A. R. Kleiman, *Marijuana: Costs of Abuse, Costs of Control* (Westport, Conn.: AVI Publishing Company, 1989).

Massachusetts Society for the Suppression of Intemperance   One of the earliest temperance societies in America, founded in Andover, Massachusetts, in 1813. It was organized by a number of Calvinist ministers and included other prominent community members. They published a number of antialcohol tracts and spread their message around the country.

mazindol   A stimulant drug whose activity is similar to that of amphetamines. Some patients notice mild sedation from it. It is found in the anorectic SANOREX.

MDA (3, 4-methylenedioxyamphetamine)   A semisynthetic drug produced by modifying the major psychoactive components of nutmeg and mace. It also can be produced from safrole, the oil of sassafras. The drug first was synthesized in 1910.

Usage: The effects of MDA combine some of the properties of MESCALINE and AMPHETAMINES. A sense of physical well-being with heightened tactile sensations may occur with low doses, as well as pupil dilation and increased blood pressure and pulse rate. High doses may result in increased body temperature, profuse sweating, muscular rigidity, illusions and hallucinations. Subjective reports emphasize "warm loving feelings" and the desire for close communication and increased reflectiveness, hence, its nicknames "the love drug" and "speed for lovers." Once believed by some to induce age regression, it was used experimentally in psychotherapy as a way of helping patients to relive specific childhood experiences, although it was not found to be effective.

Dosage: The average dose of MDA is from 50 to 150 mg. The effects begin to be felt about 30 to 60 minutes after ingestion and they last approximately eight hours. Mental and physical exhaustion may follow use. It can be highly toxic—even fatal—in various dosages, depending on the individual's sensitivity to the drug.

Tolerance: Tolerance to MDA does not develop. No physical or psychological dependence has been conclusively demonstrated. See ECSTASY (MDMA).

mead   A beverage made of fermented honey, water and spices. Although it is often incorrectly identified as a kind of beer, mead is essentially a honey wine. It is considered to have been among the earliest alcoholic beverages developed, along with fermented fruit juice (wine) and fermented grains (beer). Little is known about the history of mead, but it has been especially associated with the Anglo-Saxon and Teutonic cultures of the early Middle Ages. The name "mead" also has been used to refer to numerous other beverages, some containing no alcohol, and others having no honey content.

mebaral   A long-acting BARBITURATE that contains mephobarbital. It is used as a sedative hypnotic, particularly in the treatment of epilepsy; its anticonvulsive action being much stronger than its hypnotic effect. Physical and psychological dependence can occur, and when used with alcohol or other central nervous system depressants it has an additive effect. One result of overdosage is respiratory depression; severe overdosage may result in coma and death.

media and entertainment, drug use in   The White House Conference for a Drug Free America's final report in June 1988 stated: "For too long some media have glamorized illicit drugs and portrayed their use as socially acceptable." Members of the film and television industries, musicians and gatekeepers of national news, the report said, "were often viewed as unresponsive to attempts to fight illicit drug use." The report went on to explain that although the media certainly has been part of the problem, they must now become an "ever-growing" part of the solution. To accomplish this end, the conference set forth eight recommendations:

Every segment of the media and entertainment industries must ensure or continue to ensure that its programming avoids any positive portrayal of illicit drug use, and that responsible industry executives reject as unacceptable any programming that does not meet this standard.

Every segment of the media must establish a comprehensive public campaign against illicit drug use.

Media employers must adopt for all media workplaces a strong antidrug work policy that covers every employee.

Local media must work closely with community leaders and citizens groups to combat the use of illicit drugs.

Media messages also must increasingly target people who do not now use illicit drugs and minority populations.

The movie rating system, conducted by the Motion Picture Association of America, must take a stronger stance against the use of illicit drugs.

The media must adhere to existing guidelines restricting alcohol and tobacco advertising that targets youth.

Student-run media, including high school newspapers and college print and broadcast outlets, must actively disseminate accurate information about illicit drug use.

medication   Alcohol is a basic ingredient in many liquid medications. (See COUGH MEDICINE.) Historically, alcohol alone was used as a medicine; for instance, before the introduction of antibiotics, physicians prescribed small doses of whiskey for infants suffering from pneumonia. Today it is still dispensed in some chronic disease wards as a sedative.

melfiat   An ANORECTIC drug containing phendimetrazine tartrate that is used for weight control. Its activity is similar to that of AMPHETAMINES. Tolerance develops within a few weeks, and psychological dependence and social disability can occur. As with other anorectics it has a high potential for abuse. Results of overdosage are restlessness, tremors, rapid respiration, confusion and hallucinations.

Mellaril   An antipsychotic that contains thioridazine and is used for acute or chronic psychosis. When taken with alcohol or other central nervous system depressants, it will have an additive effect.

memory   Memory is defined as the power or process of reproducing or recalling what has been learned in the past and retained. In this literal sense, what is remembered can be given a more or less sharply defined position in time and space.

Neither the mechanisms of memory itself, nor those of memory loss induced by drugs or other factors, are well understood at present, but both continue to be the subject of much scientific study. The memory process includes immediate short-term and long-term storage and retrieval faculties that appear to be centered in the brain's limbic system. Electrical stimulation of this area has enabled some patients to recall long-forgotten events and other information.

Information storage seems to be related to such chemical structures as proteins and nucleic acids. Pituitary hormones also may contribute to the memory process. Information appears to be filed chronologically and by sense; that is, there is a separate memory "file" for vision, hearing, taste and so on.

Important Information About Giving Nonprescription Medicine to Your Children

The U.S. Food and Drug Administration

Today's nonprescription, over-the-counter (OTC) drugs are safe and effective treatments. And they are serious medicines—no less so for children than adults. With that in mind, the U.S. Food and Drug Administration (FDA), working with manufacturers of OTC drugs, developed this important advice for parents:

Never guess on the amount of medicine given. Kids aren't just small adults—half an adult dose may be more than your child needs—or not enough to help.

Always check for the proper dose. Read the label—every time.

Know the abbreviations for tablespoon (Tbsp.) and teaspoon (Tsp.). Don't confuse them.

Avoid making conversions. If the label says two teaspoons and you're using a dosing cup with ounces only, get another measuring device.

Never play doctor. Twice the dose is not appropriate just because your child seems twice as sick as last time.

Talk to your doctor or pharmacist before giving two medicines at the same time.

Always follow the age-limit recommendations. If the label says don't give to children under two, don't do it. Call your doctor.

Always use the child-resistant cap, and relock the cap after each use.

Heed the "keep out of reach" warning. We've come a long way since cod liver oil and nose holding to get the medicine down. Today's medicines are often flavored—all the more reason to store all drugs out of reach.

As with any medicine, always check the package and the medicine itself for signs of tampering. Don't use any medicine from a package that shows cuts, tears, slices or other imperfections. If you notice anything suspicious, tell the pharmacist or store manager.

The U.S. Food and Drug Administration, *Important Information about Giving Nonprescription Medicine to Your Children* (Washington, D.C., U.S. Food and Drug Administration, n.d.).

Alcohol and other drugs: Symptoms of memory loss, regardless of the cause, include inability to concentrate, absent-mindedness, poor sequence retention and general temporal confusion. A number of recreational drugs interfere, probably chemically, with the transfer of information from short-term to long-term memory, preventing users from storing and remembering information received while intoxicated. Scientists have been studying a theory known as "state dependency"; it postulates that information received under intoxication can be recalled only when that state is reproduced, but so far findings have been inconsistent. Storage blockage is known to occur with the use of alcohol, marijuana, heroin and other depressants. Furthermore, information that is stored during drug intoxication may be distorted and therefore disturb the reasoning process.

Alcohol: Alcoholics and nonalcoholics alike commonly report an experience of impaired memory function after consumption of a large quantity of alcohol. While the effects of alcohol on memory have been studied, they are difficult to measure objectively because of such factors as the uniqueness of each person's memory and the difficulty of obtaining controls in studies; for example, it is difficult to determine if a recovered alcoholic would have a better memory if he or she had never had a drink or how much better that memory would be.

Investigation of the relationship between alcohol and memory has centered on two areas. The first concern is to determine the impact on memory produced by the state of intoxication: How does the memory function during intoxication? The second aspect is to ascertain the long-term effects of chronic alcohol use on memory: Are there different degrees of impairment for different levels of consumption? What aspects of memory are affected? Is any of the damage reversible?

Among the factors that must be assessed when investigating the effects of intoxication are the dose size; the kind of memory impaired—recent or remote or both; the impact, if any, of rising or falling BLOOD ALCOHOL CONCENTRATION; the effect on storage of information or the ability to recall information previously stored (retrieval); and the sex of the participant. When studying the impact of alcohol on memory over a long period of time, the duration of alcoholism as well as the age and sex of the subject must be considered.

Alcohol dosage: For some kinds of memory function it appears that a greater amount of alcohol consumed in a sitting causes a corresponding impairment of memory. Researchers Ben Morgan Jones and Marilyn K. Jones tested two groups, one of which was given a high dose of alcohol and the other a low dose, for immediate and short-term memory examination. To test immediate memory, subjects were given six lists of 12 words each and tested for immediate memory after each list. To test short-term memory the subjects were given five minutes to recall words from all six lists in any order. It was found that on the short-term memory test a high dose of alcohol (1.04 gm of ethanol per kilogram of body weight) caused a significantly greater level of impairment than a low dose (0.52 gm per kg). On the test of immediate memory, however, there were no significant differences in the amount of impairment caused by high and low doses.

Rising or falling blood alcohol concentration: When someone has a drink, his or her blood alcohol concentration rises to a peak and then gradually falls off. Acute alcohol doses can seriously disrupt memory according to the resultant blood alcohol concentration (BAC). A BAC as low as .04 gm per 100 ml of blood depresses memory functions, and the disruption increases as the BAC rises, causing increasing levels of amnesia.

Storage and retrieval: When the mind receives information, it must first construct an internal representation of the data (encoding). The translation of encodings into a permanent form (consolidation) must take place before data can be stored in the memory. Later, in order to use such information, the representation that has been stored must be searched for and found, a process known as retrieval. It is possible to have information stored in the memory that is not available for immediate retrieval; this is demonstrated by the "tip of the tongue" phenomenon—someone is sure he or she knows a fact but, at the moment, is unable to recall it. When an individual is able to remember something learned previously, it is assumed that first the information was consolidated in the storage process and that later it was searched for and retrieved. In the case of an individual who cannot recall information previously learned, researchers studying the affects of alcohol on memory must determine whether the encoding storage or the retrieval phase of memory has been affected. Most researchers today agree that alcohol impairs the encoding of information and not its consolidation or retrieval. This conclusion is supported by the work of Isabel M. Birnbaum and Elizabeth S. Parker, who found that information previously learned in the sober state could be retrieved equally well under sober and intoxicated conditions. Parker's more recent research with Weingartner has analyzed amnesia after acute doses of alcohol and has suggested that alcohol has its primary effect on encoding activities, rather than other memory processes. In fact, it has been found that alcohol facilitates memory consolidation once an event has been encoded.

Sex difference: Jones and Jones report that males and females given equal doses of alcohol adjusted for body weight perform equally well on immediate memory tests, but that females experienced greater impairment than males on memory tests that required a delayed response. The researchers are continuing their study of this area.

Long-term effects of alcohol use: Many alcoholics, when they finally submit to treatment, complain of memory disturbances. In studies of those who submitted to neuropsychological tests, it was reported that 45% to 75% of alcoholics show specific deficits in cognitive functions such as memory. It is known that prolonged overuse of alcohol affects the BRAIN. If alcoholism has reached the stage of diagnosable organic brain syndrome, memory disturbance typically is present; often it is one of the primary symptoms leading to such a diagnosis. The most notable example of such a state is KORSAKOFF'S PSYCHOSIS, characterized by loss of recall of recent events and the inability to learn new data or tasks. Recent research of this syndrome has also focused on victims' difficulty in retrieving information from long-term memory that was stored before the onset of illness. In some alcoholics with this condition, immediate memory of information is relatively unimpaired, but the same information appears to be inaccessible after even short periods of delay. Alcoholics with a history of 10 or more years of heavy drinking perform significantly worse on abstracting tasks than those with a history of less than 10 years of such drinking. Age appears to exacerbate the loss of memory by alcoholics—those around age 50 per-

form considerably worse than those around 40, even when the duration of alcoholism is the same. Both age and alcoholism can result in failure of the cognitive system to process information in sufficient depth or with sufficient elaboration.

Jones and Jones found that drinking habits and age have an ADDITIVE EFFECT in female social drinkers. Alcohol had a significantly greater impact on the short-term memory scores of middle-aged women than on those of young women, and on the scores of female moderate drinkers than on those of female light drinkers. These findings suggest that social drinking may lead to certain types of cognitive impairment that increase as a woman ages and as she drinks more alcohol.

For the alcoholic without severe brain damage there is often marked improvement of memory function after three or more weeks of abstinence, although this improvement generally does not reach the extent of nondrinking controls. Research is proceeding to ascertain the reversibility of cognitive impairments in alcoholics who abstain. However, alcohol withdrawal symptoms often obscure the interpretation of findings concerning such reversibility.

Blackout: Perhaps the most dramatic disturbance in memory function associated with alcoholism is BLACKOUT, a loss of memory by an individual for events during a period when he or she was completely conscious. About two-thirds of chronic alcoholics frequently experience blackouts while drinking; these generally occur midway or late in the course of alcoholism, and rarely after the ingestion of moderate amounts of alcohol.

State dependency: In some cases it has been reported that information learned in one state—either sober or intoxicated—is recalled better in that state than in the other state. This phenomenon is known as state dependency. State-dependent retrieval is demonstrated most readily using moderate doses of alcohol—high doses often produce severe retention deficits and low doses are not sufficient either to greatly inhibit or facilitate the memory process. State dependency has been under investigation only since the mid-1960s. There have been several reports of alcohol-related state dependency, but to date the findings are not consistent. This too is attributed to severe impairment of information storage facilities and can happen to anyone—not just alcohol-ics—when very large quantities of alcohol are in-gested quickly. Risk of blackout is increased by fatigue and by the combination of alcohol and other sedative drugs.

Drugs other than alcohol: Myriad studies on the effect of marijuana on memory processes have yielded a variety of results. Some have shown that only immediate recall is affected during intoxication and that this is due to the user's inability to concen-trate. Other reports state that the transfer of informa-tion from short-term to long-term memory is impaired while the user is high but that there are no long-term effects. Marijuana's suppression of nucleic acid synthesis may be responsible for this effect, which is significant in light of the large numbers of students of both high school and college age who smoke marijuana during school hours. If memory storage is impaired, information received while the person is high will not be remembered—clearly, learning cannot take place at the student's full capac-ity. However, marijuana smoking is a learned behav-ior in a number of ways, and many users have reported being able to overcome the drug's effects on memory storage by concentrating harder on the material at hand.

Use of hallucinogens like LSD has caused a rare but well-known phenomenon of memory distur-bance known as FLASHBACK, in which the user's drug experience is so vivid and impressive that it becomes firmly implanted in the memory and can be re-expe-rienced long afterward. No satisfactory explanation for flashbacks has been developed. The perceptual distortion that results from taking psychedelic drugs has also included temporal confusion, in which the user projects a memory into his present situation.

Isabel M. Birnbaum and Elizabeth S. Parker, "Acute Effects of Alcohol on Storage and Retrieval," in *Alcohol and Human Memory,* ed. Isabel M. Birnbaum and Elizabeth S. Parker (New Jersey: Lawrence Erlbaum, 1977): 99–108.

N. Butters, "Alcoholic Korsakoff's Syndrome: Some Unre-solved Issues . . ." *Journal of Clinical and Experimental Neuropsychology* 7 (1983): 181–210.

R. V. Esposito et al., "Enkephalinegic-dopaminergic 're-ward pathways,'" *Substance and Alcohol Actions and Misuse* 5 (1984): 111–119.

M. S. Goldman et al., "Neuropsychological Recovery in Alcoholics: Endogenous and Exogenous Processes," *Al-coholism* 10, no. 2 (1986): 136–144.

Enoch Gordis, M.D., ed., *Seventh Special Report to the U.S. Congress on Alcohol and Health* (Rockville, Md.: Na-tional Institute on Alcohol Abuse and Alcoholism, 1990).

Ben Morgan Jones and Marilyn K. Jones, "Alcohol and Memory Impairment in Male and Female Social Drink-ers," in *Alcohol and Human Memory,* ed. Isabel M. Birn-baum and Elizabeth S. Parker (New Jersey: Lawrence Erlbaum, 1977): 127–138.

Hardin and Helen Jones, *Sensual Drugs* (New York: Cam-bridge University Press, 1977).

Elizabeth Loftus, *Memory* (Reading, Mass.: Addison-Wesley, 1980).

Robert O'Brien and Morris Chafetz, *The Encyclopedia of Alcoholism* (New York: Facts On File, 1982).

Elizabeth S. Parker, "Alcohol and Cognition," *Psychophar-macology Bulletin* 20 (1984): 494–496.

mentally ill chemical abuser (MICA) This is the designation given to an individual with mental ill-ness who also qualifies for a substance-abuse diag-nosis. Synonyms include PISA (psychiatrically ill substance user) and CAMI (chemically-abusing mentally ill person). Substance abuse complicates the diagnosis and treatment of most mental disorders and is well known as a hindrance to the proper care of the chronic mentally ill. It is important, where possible, to establish the relationship between the disorders; that is, whether one contributed to the development of the other, whether each developed independently, or whether both developed from a common factor. The recognition and treatment of these individuals is further complicated by the usual segregation of service for the mentally ill, drug-abus-ing and alcoholic patient. MICA patients represent as many as one-half of those presenting to psychiat-ric emergency rooms.

meperidine A NARCOTIC analgesic, meperidine hydrochloride is best known by the brand name DEMEROL. It is an OPIOID (a synthetic opiate), similar pharmacologically but not structurally to morphine, and is one-tenth as potent. Eislab and Schaumann introduced the drug, also known as penthidine, to the medical profession in 1939, proclaiming its use-fulness in reducing spasms of the smooth muscles of the stomach and small intestine. The discovery of its analgesic properties some time afterward produced a wave of excitement among doctors, who believed that the drug had morphine's effects without being addictive. This supposition subsequently was proven false.

Usage: Used medically for the short-term relief of moderate to severe pain, meperidine often serves, in combination with other drugs, as a preoperative analgesic, particularly in obstetrics. After morphine, meperidine is the second most widely used analgesic for severe pain.

Recreational use of and addiction to meperidine occurs most frequently, though not exclusively, among members of the medical profession, to whom the drug is most readily available.

Dosage: For pain relief, meperidine is administered orally, intramuscularly or subcutaneously every three to four hours in doses of 50–200 mg. The lethal dose has not yet been determined; 1,200 mg have been fatal and 2,000 mg have been survived. Cases of extreme tolerance have been recorded in which the addict's daily habit reached 3,000–4,000 mg. Intravenous administration should be slow and in diluted solution to accommodate the higher potency of the drug through that route.

Appearance: Meperidine hydrochloride appears as a fine white crystalline powder. It is odorless, soluble in water and alcohol, and slightly soluble in ether. Its melting point is between 186°–189° F.

Activity: Rapidly absorbed and metabolized in the liver, meperidine brings relief in 15 minutes when taken orally and in 10 minutes when administered hypodermically. The effects of morphine last longer than the effects of meperidine, which peak in one hour and last two to four hours, with a half-life of three to four hours. Meperidine crosses the placental barrier and appears in mother's milk.

Effects: Meperidine relieves moderate to severe pain and produces a euphoric effect less intense than that of morphine. It is a respiratory depressant and has proved fatal when administered to patients suffering asthmatic attacks. In therapeutic doses meperidine causes the side effects usually associated with narcotic drugs, such as dizziness, nausea and

sweating. Larger doses can cause tremors, twitches and seizures.

Tolerance and dependence: Tolerance to meperidine's sedative effects develops more quickly than tolerance to its analgesic action. The drug's short duration necessitates repeated administration to maintain euphoria; this accounts in part for the uncommon development of meperidine dependence. Special care should be exercised with patients receiving other narcotic-analgesic and sedative-hypnotic drugs. Symptoms of addiction include extreme drowsiness, respiratory depression and cold clammy skin. Overdoses can result in circulatory collapse, cardiac arrest and death. Withdrawal symptoms are dose-related, as with all opiates. Unlike other opiates, meperidine withdrawal may produce seizures.

Availability: Winthrop manufactures meperidine hydrochloride in tablet form under the brand name Demerol. The drug also is available in syrups and in an injectable form.

mephobarbital A long-acting BARBITURATE that exerts a strong sedative and anticonvulsive action but has a relatively mild hypnotic effect. Onset of action is from 30 to 60 minutes; duration is from 10 to 16 hours. It is manufactured as MEBARAL and appears in tablet form. It is converted in the liver to PHENOBARBITAL but is less effective as a sedative than phenobarbital. Mephobarbital is used in the treatment of epilepsy, anxiety, tension and apprehension.

meprobamate A sedative hypnotic, first marketed under the name MILTOWN in tribute to the New Jersey town where it was developed in the early 1950s.

Usage: Meprobamate was heralded as a unique drug that relieved anxiety without producing undue sedation. It enjoyed instant popularity, and liberal prescriptions were given to patients suffering from anxiety and tension. As early as 1956 reports of addiction appeared, encouraging caution in its prescription but curbing its use only slightly. In the late 1960s over a million pounds of meprobamate were manufactured and distributed. Less potent than the minor tranquilizers derived from benzodiazepines (Librium, Valium), meprobamate is used for muscle relaxation and sedation. It is prescribed for the short-term relief of symptoms of anxiety.

Dosage: Usual oral doses range from 1,200–1,600 mg daily, divided into three or four doses. A dose of 800 mg taken at one time may cause sleep and daily doses above 2,400 mg are not recommended. No lethal dose has been established, however, although 20,000–40,000 mg doses have been survived.

Appearance: Meprobamate is a bitter white powder, slightly soluble in water and freely soluble in alcohol.

Activity: The drug depresses the central nervous system, with effects peaking in two hours. It has a half-life of four to ten hours. Meprobamate exhibits cross tolerance to barbiturates and is potentiated by other central nervous system depressants. Readily absorbed in the gastrointestinal tract and rapidly distributed throughout the body, meprobamate is metabolized by the liver and excreted by the kidneys. It crosses the placental barrier and appears in mother's milk; cases of congenital malformation associated with meprobamate use by pregnant women have been reported.

Effects: Large doses can result in euphoria and intoxication similar to that induced by BARBITURATES, including such symptoms as slurred speech and loss of coordination and muscular control. Adverse reactions include drowsiness, dizziness, headache, visual impairment, nausea, vomiting, rash, prickly or burning sensations and diarrhea. Withdrawal symptoms include tremors, insomnia, gastrointestinal distress, convulsions and hallucinations, as well as the recurrence, in magnified degree, of the symptoms of anxiety that lead to the use of the drug. Overdose can cause respiratory depression, coma and death. Accidental deaths have occurred from combinations of meprobamate and other depressants, and it has been used in suicide attempts—usually unsuccessfully.

Tolerance and dependence: Along with physical and psychological dependence, tolerance can develop with meprobamate use.

Meprospan A nonbarbiturate minor tranquilizer or SEDATIVE HYPNOTIC that contains MEPROBAMATE. It is used for the relief of tension and anxiety and as a muscle relaxant. Tolerance, as well as physical and psychological dependence, may develop. When taken with alcohol or other central nervous system depressants, it has an additive effect. Overdosage can result in drowsiness, stupor, coma and respiratory collapse.

mescal A slang term for PEYOTE. Mescal buttons (or peyote) are chewed for their hallucinogenic effects, particularly in the religious ceremonies of some Mexican Indians as well as certain Native-American tribes, and come from a small spineless cactus (*Lophorphora williamsii*) growing in the southwestern U.S., with rounded stems and button-like tops. Another usage of the word refers to an alcoholic liquor of Mexico, made from pulque, maguey or other fermented juice from the plants of the *Agave* genus. It is colorless like tequila, but lower in quality and cruder in taste.

mescaline The principal alkaloid in the peyote cactus, *Lophorphora williamsii,* found in northern Mexico and Texas.

Mescaline was one of the first hallucinogens to be chemically isolated. Arthur Heffter (1860–1925), a German chemist and professor of pharmacology, was studying peyote and individually tested four alkaloids that were isolated from the cactus. On November 23, 1896, Heffter took 150 mg of mescaline hydrochloride and reported: "2:00 p.m. Violet and green spots appear on the paper during readings. When the eyes are kept shut the following visual images occur . . . carpet patterns, ribbed vaulting, etc. . . . Later on, landscapes, halls, architectural scenes (e.g., pillars decorated with flowers) also appear. The images can be observed until about 5:30 p.m. Nausea and dizziness are at times very distressing. . . . In the evening well-being and appetite are undisturbed and there is no sign of sleeplessness."

The chemical structure of mescaline was determined in 1918. Mescaline attracted widespread intellectual interest in the early part of the century by such people as Havelock Ellis, Weir Mitchell and Aldous Huxley, but today it is rarely available illicitly.

Mescaline usually is taken orally, but it can be inhaled by smoking ground peyote buttons, or, more rarely, it can be injected. It is considerably less potent than LSD. Of the alleged mescaline samples analyzed at the Addiction Research Foundation in Toronto, Canada, nearly 90% were not mescaline; usually they contained either PCP or LSD combined with PCP.

Classification: Mescaline is classified as a HALLU-CINOGEN, a Schedule I drug under the CONTROLLED SUBSTANCES ACT. It is in the same chemical group of drugs as TMA and MDA and is chemically related to adrenaline.

Usage: Mescaline offers the user the opportunity to achieve a hallucinogenic state without undergoing all of the preliminary emetic effects of peyote, and to achieve it more rapidly. The hallucinatory effects of peyote and mescaline are reported to be fairly similar to the effects of LSD. Common mental effects include euphoria; heightened sensory perception; a dreamlike state, sometimes with hallucinations or synesthesia; and difficulty with linear thinking (and enhanced ability with lateral thinking).

Dosage: Average doses range from 300 to 500 mg.

Effects: At low doses the effects appear within one to three hours and last for four to 12 hours or more. Physical effects include dilation of the pupils, an increase in body temperature, some muscular relaxation and sometimes vomiting. At higher doses mescaline may induce headache, fever, low blood pressure and depressed heart and respiratory activity.

Tolerance and dependence: Tolerance to mescaline, as to all hallucinogens, develops rapidly and is very short-lived. Mescaline is rarely taken on the kind of regular basis that would allow tolerance to develop. When tolerance is observed, CROSS-TOLER-ANCE to other hallucinogens occurs. No physical dependence on the effects of mescaline develops, regardless of the frequency of usage.

Sources: Mescaline can be made synthetically but it is also contained in the peyote cactus. The heads or "buttons" of the cactus are dried and then sliced, chopped or ground and sometimes put into capsules.

Jan G. Bruhn, "Three Men and a Drug: Peyote Research in the 1890s," *The Cactus and Succulent Journal of Great Britain,* vol. 30, no. 2, (1977): 27–30.

"Facts about Hallucinogens," pamphlet (Toronto: Addiction Research Foundation of Ontario, 1980).

Frederick G. Hofmann, *A Handbook on Drug and Alcohol Abuse* (New York: Oxford University Press, 1975): 169–171.

Jerome Jaffe, Rovert Petersen and Ray Hodgson, *Addictions: Issues and Answers* (New York: Harper and Row Publishers, 1980): 61–61.

metabolic deficiency Etiological theory of alcoholism/chemical dependency that emphasizes abnormalities of body functioning, genetic factors and studies of high-risks groups. It is believed that male children of alcoholics have the highest likelihood of becoming alcoholic, followed by daughters of alcoholics and people with a history of depression in their family of origin.

metabolism The process by which the body uses food, water and oxygen to sustain itself. The process begins with absorption of a substance, such as food or a drug, into the system and continues until the substance is excreted. There are two metabolic processes: anabolism and catabolism. Anabolism is the chemical change that turns the introduced substance into the complex substances of which the body is built. Catabolism involves the breaking-down process of energy production. (See entries on individual drugs for their specific metabolic patterns.)

Alcohol: Once ingested, alcohol is absorbed into the bloodstream from the stomach, duodenum and gastrointestinal tract by a process of passive diffusion. It is then carried in the blood through the circulatory system from the digestive organs to the LIVER. The rest is excreted through sweat, saliva and breath. Unlike fat and most carbohydrates, which can be metabolized by almost all tissues, more than 90% of the alcohol absorbed into the body is metabolized in the liver, a process that accounts for many of the damaging effects alcohol can have on that organ.

The primary pathway of metabolism of ethyl alcohol consists of a series of reactions. The first reaction is catalyzed by the enzyme alcohol dehydrogenase, that removes two hydrogen atoms from each molecule of ethyl alcohol to form acetaldehyde, which is even more toxic to the body than ethyl alcohol before the enzyme catalysis, but is quickly oxidized to form acetic acid. Acetic acid eventually is converted to carbon dioxide and water.

A number of the metabolic effects of alcohol on the body are linked to the products of oxidation. One consequence of heavy alcohol consumption is a metabolic derangement called alcoholic ketoacidosis—the production of excess blood acidity. The excessive breakdown of fatty acids causes a buildup of the intermediate acidic products of the breakdown, which normally would be burned to carbon dioxide. These intermediate compounds back up into the bloodstream, increase blood acidity and produce toxic effects. Susceptibility to alcoholic ketoacidosis varies from individual to individual. It appears to be more prevalent in women than in men.

Another effect of alcohol is that the excess hydrogen given off in the first reaction upsets the liver cell's chemical balance. The cell must get rid of the excess hydrogen, and one way in which it does this involves the formation of lipids (fats). The hydrogen is used in the synthesis of the precursors of the lipids that accumulate and result in alcoholic FATTY LIVER. In addition, the liver uses the excess hydrogen from the alcohol as a fuel instead of metabolizing fat, which would be the normal method, again causing an accumulation of lipids leading to fatty liver.

The excess acetaldehyde produced in the reactions may have direct toxic effects on the liver. Acetaldehyde also affects the heart and other muscles and, possibly, the brain. Some researchers suggest that acetaldehyde may play a part in the development of a DEPENDENCE.

A secondary metabolic pathway occurs at high levels of alcohol consumption. This pathway utilizes the microsomal system of structures within the cells, which also works to metabolize certain drugs. As a result, alcohol competes with other drugs normally metabolized by this system, thereby delaying their metabolism and increasing their effect; this is also called SYNERGY.

A figure frequently cited for the rate at which alcohol can be metabolized is 7 gm, or about three quarters of an ounce of alcohol per hour, for a man weighing 70 kg or 150 lbs. (See BLOOD ALCOHOL CONCENTRATION [BAC].) However, this rate can vary as much as +/-50%. There is a widespread belief (if little hard evidence) that heavy drinkers can develop an increased metabolic rate or TOLERANCE, and that in time, the rate of metabolism for an alcoholic without liver disease may be doubled. (If the alcohol were being metabolized with greater speed, the in-

toxicating effects would be lessened.) Nevertheless, the rate of alcohol metabolism is decreased in those with liver disease. (See GENETICS and ALCOHOLIC LIVER DISEASE.)

Although most drugs are excreted by the kidneys, drugs also may be excreted in feces, mother's milk, saliva, bile, sweat and breath. Anesthetic gases in particular are excreted through the lungs.

Lucinda Franks, "A New Attack on Alcoholism," *New York Times Magazine* (October 20, 1985).

Charles S. Lieber, "The Metabolism of Alcohol," *Scientific American* 234, no. 3 (March 1976): 25–33.

methadone   An OPIOID and a synthetic NARCOTIC analgesic; methadone was first introduced during World War II, when it was developed by German chemists (the brand name DOLOPHINE is a tribute to Adolph Hitler). Though structurally dissimilar to morphine, it shares its effects. Methadone is best known for its application in the controversial methadone maintenance program, which some experts believe has been our most useful tool in the treatment and rehabilitation of heroin addicts.

The positive aspects of methadone treatment are the following: cross-tolerance may reduce craving and block opiate effects. The oral administration of methadone is especially important, because it breaks the ritual of injecting and eliminates infection. Finally, and perhaps most significantly, methadone can be obtained legally. The heroin addict can satisfy his dependence without reverting to criminal activities and, at the same time, work under a controlled program to free himself of his addiction. This same argument has been used for the legalization of all controlled substances, and the approach is now being experimented with to varying degrees in a number of European countries.

Statistics on the success of the methadone maintenance programs differ, and it remains a controversial issue. New problems have arisen as a result of the program: large quantities of legal methadone are diverted to the illicit drug market each year, for example, and in 1973 there were more methadone-related deaths than heroin-related deaths in New York City. On the other hand, the treatment developed by Drs. Dole and Nyswander certainly has enabled large numbers of heroin addicts to reshape their lives and to rejoin society.

Some critics argue that methadone maintenance is little more than "chemical slavery" and say it does not give addicts the hope of being drug-free. (In 1996, there were an estimated 500,000 heroin addicts in the U.S.) Researchers counter that if it is a choice between lifelong addiction to a drug that poses no danger as opposed to addiction to a dangerous drug, such as cocaine or heroin, the choice is clear.

Usage: Methadone is used to relieve pain of moderate to severe intensity. Methadone also is useful as an antitussive and as a detoxicant for patients withdrawing from heroin and morphine. The drug's primary use today is in methadone maintenance programs aimed at helping heroin addicts to overcome their addiction and accompanying destructive lifestyle. The two-fold method employed is to wean the addict away from heroin and to provide the counseling and training necessary for the user to rejoin society in a constructive capacity. The program has been applied at numerous rehabilitation centers all over the U.S. and abroad, and its philosophy and results have been the subject of a long-standing debate.

Appearance: Methadone is an odorless white crystalline powder that is soluble in water, alcohol and chloroform and insoluble in ether.

Activity: The body absorbs and responds to the substance in much the same way as it does to MORPHINE.

Effects: The effects of methadone resemble those of morphine and heroin in most respects. The drug produces the same euphoria and drowsiness but does not slow the respiration as much as heroin. Most importantly, it produces cross-tolerance to that drug, thereby blocking its effects. It is this quality that makes the drug useful in heroin addiction therapy. It also reduces the craving for opiates. Methadone is as likely as heroin to produce dependence and withdrawal symptoms are more prolonged. Symptoms include pain in the bones, sweating and diarrhea.

Dosage and tolerance: As an ANTITUSSIVE, methadone is prescribed in 1–2 mg doses to be taken every four to six hours. For pain relief, 2.5–20 mg are prescribed intramuscularly or orally every three to

four hours. There are two types of programs: the original high-dose model, developed in the early 1960s by Drs. Vincent Dole and Marie Nyswander, and the low-dose model. Both models use the oral administration method; the dose generally is in liquid form and dissolved in fruit drinks. In the high-dose model, the treatment begins by increasing the patient's tolerance until a daily dosage of between 50 and 120 mg can be accommodated. The low-dose model stabilizes the patient on 30 mg or less a day.

The patient leaves urine samples, which are tested for signs of morphine (heroin is excreted as morphine) and other drugs. Although methadone blocks heroin's effects, some patients continue to use heroin and other opiates. Abuse of cocaine, alcohol and barbiturates has been well documented among methadone patients. Once responsibility and commitment to rehabilitation is demonstrated, the patient is allowed to take home a one- and later a three- or six-day supply of methadone. (See LAAM.)

Dependence: Detoxification is effected by gradually reducing the methadone content of the mixture. Some patients, however, find their psychological dependence more difficult to overcome than their physical addiction. Many either revert to their heroin habit or require indefinite methadone supplies. Opponents of the programs focus their arguments on the fact that it replaces one addiction with another and that it is doubtful that the patient will ever withdraw from methadone.

Methadone and alcohol: Investigations have revealed a considerable amount of crossover between the use of alcohol and heroin. Alcoholism among heroin addicts is frequent. Studies have suggested that alcohol is the drug most frequently used before the initial use of heroin—that alcohol addiction has usually occurred before the addiction to heroin. When heroin is not available, addicts often use alcohol as a substitute to relieve their withdrawal symptoms. The figures on the prevalence of alcoholism among methadone-maintained addicts vary from 20% to 50%.

Alcoholism among methadone-maintained addicts not only interferes with the rehabilitation process, but the combination of METHADONE WITH ALCOHOL causes dangerous side effects.

Methadone and AIDS: According to some researchers, a patient who is on methadone has a better-functioning immune system than a heroin addict (because he or she is less likely to be "running the streets" and more likely to be getting proper nourishment, rest and medical care). Additionally, for IDUs (intravenous drug users) already infected with HIV, methadone maintenance eliminates the risk of infection with other HIV strains, which they would face if they were still actively using heroin and sharing needles. Maintaining the lifestyle of heroin addiction imposes extraordinary stress on the body of the user—stress that is likely to wear down the HIV-infected individual's already impaired immune system faster and more severely than the more regulated lifestyle made possible with opioid substitution therapy. Moreover, according to *Treatment for HIV-Infected Alcohol and Other Drug Abusers:*

> *Opioid substitution therapy has been proposed because it frequently involves daily attendance at a clinic that may offer access to medical care, psychiatric consultation, and social services. . . . Studies have shown that substitution therapy programs that provide medical and psychiatric care, social work assistance, family therapy and employment counseling promote several positive outcomes with regard to alcohol and other drug (AOD) use, criminal involvement, family relations, the need for emergency services, psychiatric status and employment.*

Availability: Methadone is manufactured in tablets, syrups and injectable forms.

B. Bihari, "Alcoholism and Methadone Maintenance," *American Journal of Drug and Alcohol Abuse* 1 (1974): 79–89.

J. M. McCann et al., eds., *Treatment of Opiate Addiction with Methadone: A Counselor Manual, Treatment Assistance Publication Series,* no. 7 (Rockville, Md.: Center for Substance Abuse Treatment, 1994).

M. W. Parrino, "Overview: Current Treatment Realities and Future Trends," *State Methadone Treatment Guidelines,* Treatment Improvement Protocol (TIP) Series, no. 1. (Rockville, Md.: Center for Substance Abuse Treatment, 1993).

P. A. Selwyn and S. L. Batki, consensus panel co-chairs, "Treatment for HIV-Infected Alcohol and Other Drug Abusers," *Treatment Assistance Publication Series,* no. 15 (Rockville, Md.: Center for Substance Abuse Treatment, 1995).

Barry Stimmel, "Methadone Maintenance and Alcohol Use," in *Drug and Alcohol Abuse: Implications for Treatment* (Rockville, Md.: National Institute on Drug Abuse [NIDA], 1981).

methadone "clone" A therapeutic agent designed to break a cocaine user's physical and psychological dependence on the drug. An idea championed by Senator Daniel Patrick Moynihan (D-NY) and given the catchphrase "methadone clone," it has yielded few encouraging results.

Research into the biology of cocaine addiction is beginning to show that a methadonelike substance for cocaine addicts will be neither simple to develop nor necessarily effective. Cocaine does not produce the kind of easily duplicated physical tolerance and dependence of heroin.

The idea behind providing methadone, with its narcotic activity, is that it reduces the craving for heroin. Both heroin and methadone are opiates and tolerance develops to opiates. However, when the body is subjected to cocainelike stimulants, stable narcoticlike tolerance does *not* develop, so a chemical as similar to cocaine as methadone is to heroin could overstimulate nerve cells the way cocaine itself does, significantly affecting the way a person acts or thinks.

Researchers seem to agree, though, that pharmacological agents combined with various nonchemical therapies could be useful. Current treatment methods, which rely heavily on self-help group sessions and one-on-one counseling, have produced mixed results.

The new therapeutic drugs under development are intended not as a replacement for cocaine but to help addicts past the initial anxiety, depression and craving associated with going "COLD TURKEY"—and to give support structures and therapy a chance to work. Agents that have shown success thus far include: antidepressants, and antiepileptic drugs that block the erratic nerve-cell firing that results from cocaine use.

Joanne Silberner, "A Technical Fix for Cocaine Addiction," *U.S. News & World Report* (April 17, 1989): 61.

methadone hydrochloride diskettes A synthetic narcotic analgesic, which activity is similar to that of morphine. It is used for detoxification and maintenance treatment in cases of narcotic addiction. It is long-acting and, when doses are given daily, its effects last 24 to 48 hours. The drug has a high potential for abuse and tolerance will develop as well as physical and psychological dependency. Overdosage can result in respiratory depression; circulatory collapse, cardiac arrest and death. It is a Schedule II drug under the CONTROLLED SUBSTANCES ACT.

methadone with alcohol   It is a common but false belief that there is an absence of alcoholism among heroin addicts. People who ingest large quantities of either alcohol or heroin have a tendency to use other drugs, and investigators have found a considerable amount of crossover between the use of these agents. Increasing evidence suggests a relationship between alcohol and opiate dependency, and there may be a specific interaction between the two drugs. Studies by Dr. Barry Stimmel of the Mount Sinai School of Medicine in New York suggest that alcohol is the drug initially and most frequently abused before heroin is first used and before addiction occurs. In addition, when heroin or other opiates are not available, alcohol is the drug most often sought as a substitute to relieve symptoms of anxiety and discomfort brought on by withdrawal.

Methadone is an opium derivative that blocks the euphoric effects of heroin. In maintenance programs it is administered in controlled doses that allow the addict to function normally. Such programs are thought to help prevent the criminal activity through which addicts get money to buy heroin.

Figures on the prevalence of alcoholism among methadone-maintained addicts vary. For example, it has been estimated that 40% of such patients consume excessive amounts of alcohol, and 5% are severe alcoholics, but other estimates of the proportion of methadone patients who drink excessively have been as low as 12%. These rates, however, are no greater and may even be less than those for similar socioeconomic populations of nonaddicts. Alcoholism does not develop as a result of methadone maintenance. However, the medical consequences of consuming large quantities of alcohol are considerable for persons on methadone maintenance. The majority of heroin addicts have had an episode of viral hepatitis and, if such a pre-existing liver condition is aggravated by alcohol abuse, a rapid progression to FATTY LIVER or CIRRHOSIS may occur. There

is also the danger of a significant increase in the depressant effects of alcohol when combined with methadone, as a synergistic reaction will occur. (See SYNERGY.) Mortality rates are much higher for alcoholic methadone patients than for those patients who are not alcoholic.

Alcoholism interferes with the rehabilitative process and may be responsible for the termination of methadone therapy; a client suffering from alcoholism is likely to become aggressive and refuse to follow clinic rules. This refusal, and the complexities of his CROSS-ADDICTION, may lead to improper detoxification and premature discharge from the program.

Withdrawal from methadone does not necessarily alleviate alcoholism and, in fact, may have the opposite effect, especially if rehabilitation has not progressed to a sufficient degree. After complete detoxification, alcoholism appears to be the single most important obstacle preventing an individual from functioning well in society.

Treatment: It is difficult, if not impossible, to refer alcoholic methadone patients for treatment, because most alcoholism programs will not accept methadone-maintained patients. Therefore, methadone programs must be geared toward recognizing alcoholism and treating it. Both psychological and biological tests can help to identify the problem drinker as well as the potential problem drinker. Treatment should be geared to the individual's needs, and the highest rates of success have been achieved with patients who were offered a number of different treatment modalities.

B. Bihari, "Alcoholism and Methadone Maintenance," *American Journal of Drug and Alcohol Abuse* 1 (1974): 79–89.

Barry Stimmel, "Methadone Maintenance and Alcohol Use," in *Drug and Alcohol Abuse: Implications for Treatment* (Rockville, Md.: National Institute on Drug Abuse [NIDA], 1981).

methamphetamine   A very high potency, synthetic amphetamine used as an ANORECTIC. (See DESOXYN, GRADUMET TABLETS, AMPHETAMINES and ICE.)

methanol   Methanol (also known as methyl alcohol or wood alcohol) is a colorless, flammable liquid that can be mixed with water in all proportions. It is a poison, and because it oxidizes more slowly than ethyl alcohol, the formaldehyde produced may cause blindness, even in small doses. When used as a denaturant for ethanol it makes the latter unfit for drinking. Methanol also is called wood alcohol because at one time it was produced primarily as a by-product of wood distillation. Today, methanol is produced synthetically and is generally used as a solvent or antifreeze. People have died from unknowingly drinking wood alcohol in bootleg whiskey or moonshine. Others have died after knowingly consuming it in the absence of their usual alcoholic beverages (initially it has intoxicating effects).

methaqualone   First synthesized in 1951 in India as an antimalarial drug, methaqualone (2-Methyl-3-[2-methyl- phenyl]=4[3H]quinazolinone) was introduced to the American medical market in the mid-1960s for the treatment of insomnia and anxiety and was believed to have none of the abuse potential of short-acting barbiturates. Because it was alleged to be safe and nonaddictive, it became quite popular with individuals looking for a new, safe high. Since that time, however, many instances of addiction and overdose have been reported and its high abuse potential has been documented in scientific research.

Classification: Methaqualone is a nonbarbiturate sedative hypnotic. LEMMON, the last manufacturer of methaqualone under the brand names Quaalude and Mequin, removed the drug from the market in the early 1980s because of its widespread abuse. Methaqualone was classified as a Schedule II drug under the CONTROLLED SUBSTANCES ACT in 1973, then rescheduled to Schedule I in 1984.

Usage: Users experience a pleasant sense of well-being, an increased pain threshold, loss of muscle coordination and a prickling of the fingers, lips and tongue. Although the "high" is reputed to enhance sexual performance, there is little evidence to support this. It is more likely that, like alcohol, the drug acts on the central cortex of the brain to release normal inhibitions. Intoxication from methaqualone is similar to intoxication from barbiturates and alcohol. The risks are the same: death by overdose, accidents due to confusion and impaired motor coordination. As more doctors became aware of the

abuse and addictive potential of methaqualone, their willingness to prescribe it declined. This resulted in a large traffic in illicitly produced tablets. The most commonly produced imitations were of the brands Quaalude and Mequin, both of which, before they were withdrawn from the market, contained 300 mg of methaqualone. The imitations may contain between 10 and 150 mg of methaqualone, between 20 and 300 mg of diazepam (Valium) or combinations of other substances. The level of diazepam found in just one tablet may at times be enough to render a user unconscious. Other imitations may be so weak that a small handful of pills are needed in order to get high—a danger if someone accustomed to a weak form unknowingly obtains an identical-looking but much more potent product. Overdose can result in delirium, restlessness, excessive tension and muscle spasms leading to convulsions. An addict should not discontinue the drug abruptly, and to avoid the risk of convulsions during withdrawal, a patient should be detoxified in a hospital. The heaviest concentration of users of illicit methaqualone is between high school age and the mid-thirties.

Dosage: Users who take the drug for pleasure typically resist its sedative effects in order to achieve a dissociative high similar to that induced by barbiturates. They generally take larger doses, 600–900 mg, or more if TOLERANCE has developed. Coma has been known to occur following 2.4 gm of methaqualone; 8 to 20 gm have produced severe toxicity and death.

Appearance: Methaqualone is a white crystalline powder with little or no odor and a bitter taste. It is stable in light and air and soluble in alcohol and ether. It is slightly soluble in water.

Activity: Like barbiturates, methaqualone has a synergistic effect when used with alcohol and other central nervous system depressants. Methaqualone is readily absorbed from the gastrointestinal tract. It is transported in the plasma and is distributed in the body fat, the liver and the brain tissue. (See SYNERGY.)

Effects: Relatively low doses (75 mg, four times a day) lead to sleep. With hypnotic (sleep-inducing) doses there may be transient "pins and needles" sensations prior to sleep. Excessive dreaming and sleepwalking sometimes occur. Hangover is frequent. Side effects can include nausea, vomiting, stomach discomfort, sweating, hives, rapid heartbeat and lack of appetite.

Tolerance and dependence: Tolerance to the drug's euphoric effects develops at a more rapid rate than tolerance to its respiratory depressant effects, increasing the danger of overdose. Psychological dependence occurs with methaqualone. Physical dependence also develops, producing distinctive WITHDRAWAL symptoms similar to those occurring with barbiturate dependence: headaches, severe cramps, convulsions and tremors. Symptoms of withdrawal also include irritability and sleeplessness, followed by mania and delirium tremens. Many authorities believe that the potential for addiction and abuse with methaqualone is as serious as that associated with the use of barbiturates and heroin.

Sources: Legitimate supplies are currently unavailable in the U.S., although there is a strong black market of look-alike (or bootleg) capsules or tablets that may or may not contain actual methaqualone. A large amount of illicit methaqualone arrives in the U.S. from Colombia. Mandrax is a European name for methaqualone in combination with an antihistamine.

metharbital   A long-acting BARBITURATE, with anticonvulsant properties similar to those of MEPHOBARBITAL and PHENOBARBITAL; used in the treatment of grand mal, petit mal, myoclonic and mixed types of seizures. Metharbital is a derivative of BARBITAL, to which it is converted in the liver. Milder and less toxic than phenobarbital, it is manufactured under the brand name of Gemonil.

methyldihydromorphinone   An analgesic. A semisynthetic MORPHINE derivative used mainly in the treatment of cancer, it is a Schedule II drug and is more potent than morphine. It is also known as Metopon.

methylphenidate   A central nervous system stimulant, with action somewhat like that of the AMPHETAMINES. It is used in the treatment of narcolepsy and also in the treatment of hyperkinetic children. (See RITALIN.)

methyphenobarbital   A long-acting barbiturate, with an onset time of up to one hour and duration of action up to 16 hours. It also is known as MEPHOBARBITAL. (See BARBITURATES and MEBARAL.)

methyprylon   A central nervous system depressant and hypnotic used in the treatment of insomnia. Its action is similar to that of the BARBITURATES, but it is chemically unrelated. (See NOLUDAR.)

Mexico   For thousands of years indigenous peoples used "native" hallucinogens in religious rites. Peyote and sacred mushrooms were the most common. In recent years the use of these substances has dwindled in Mexico, but an interest in these hallucinogens has sprung up in other countries, possibly influenced in part by author Carlos Casteneda's popular writings about Mexican sorcerers. Consequently, the Mexican government has to contend with trafficking in esoteric indigenous drugs, as well as the more popular marijuana, cocaine and heroin.

Since 1970 there have been several investigations aimed at estimating the prevalence of drug use in Mexico. Surveys were conducted in hospitals, treatment centers, among the general population through household surveys, schools and prisons, and among other high-risk groups. It was reported that inhalants were the most commonly abused substances, followed by amphetamines, cannabis and tranquilizers. Use of heroin, LSD and cocaine were reported by only a small percentage of the population in Mexico City and the northern regions. Although the surveys uncover certain problem areas, the government has acknowledged that they are far from comprehensive and that the actual number of users is unknown.

The kinds of drugs that are abused vary greatly among different groups and in different geographical areas. Abuse of illicit drugs is greatest among males under 25 years of age, whereas the abuse of medically used drugs is most frequent among the female population of the same age. It should be noted that most surveys are carried out in metropolitan areas and not in the numerous rural communities.

Alcohol: In a 1970 international survey, Mexico's annual alcohol consumption was 1.9 liters per person (1 liter equals 1.06 quarts). In 1995 it increased to 3.3 liters. Consumption of beer has risen steadily, from 29.1 liters in 1970 to 49.8 liters in 1994.

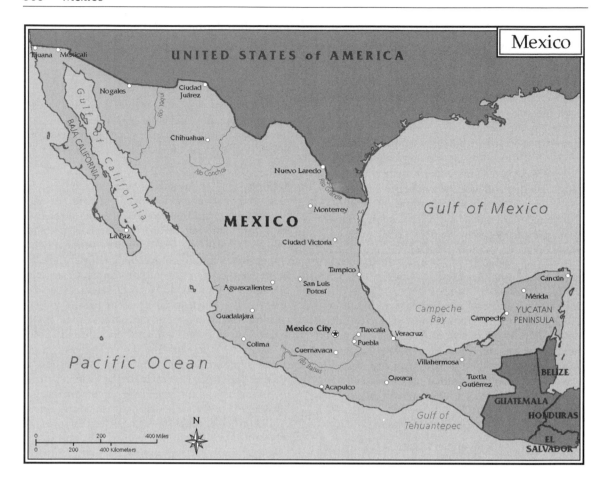

Drugs other than alcohol: In a 1980 survey carried out among 14- to 18-year-olds (a representative sample of the school population of Mexico City and its metropolitan area), 12.3% of the students reported some pattern of abuse. This figure was further broken down as follows: 10.7% light users; 1.1% moderate users; and .5% heavy users. The percentage of heavy users increased to 5.6% when alcohol and tobacco were included. When compared to a 1976 survey, the frequency of regular use did not show a significant increase. There was an increase, however, in the percentage who had "ever used" a drug. A recent study carried out in Mexico City among younger children (11–14 years old) reported that 27% had used inhalants.

According to the Mexican Government, drug use among the general population of Mexico remained low through the early and mid-1990s except in the area near the Mexican-U.S. border. Mexico's drug treatment authorities in 1995, however, were concerned that their depressed economy would spur an increase in drug use throughout the country.

Trafficking: Because it borders the U.S., Mexico has long been a prime drug trafficker to the U.S. Since the late 1980s Mexico has been the primary source for the U.S. marijuana market. In 1989 it became a top producer of marijuana as well (4,750 metric tons), surpassing Colombia (2,700 metric tons), which was the primary marijuana producer from the mid-1970s through most of the '80s. In 1992 Mexico produced 7,795 metric tons of marijuana, declining in 1994 to 5,549 metric tons, though still the top producer. By the mid-1990s, Mexican sources, whether grown in-country or

Density of Opium Poppy–Growing Areas (Mexico and Colombia)

shipped through Mexico (transshipped) from other countries, supplied more than 50% of the marijuana used in the U.S.

Mexican poppy cultivation dates back to World War II. Shipments from Europe were all but cut off due to the war, and the New York Mafia began to finance Mexican production. Poppy cultivation in Mexico declined until its brief comeback in the mid-1970s. Opium fields are still cultivated today in

rural areas but only an insignificant amount of the drug is exported.

It should be noted that during the 1980s and early '90s Mexico also become a major transit point for South American–produced cocaine. In 1969 the U.S. and Mexico signed an agreement calling for joint action against drug trafficking. Called "Operation Cooperation," it resulted in the confiscation of many tons of drugs, particularly marijuana, and the arrest of many smugglers. Since that time there have been numerous agreements between these two countries in an attempt to curb drug trafficking. In 1995 both countries agreed to share information on criminal investigations and currency matters regarding illicit drugs.

When the FRENCH CONNECTION fell apart, Mexico became a main supplier of heroin to the U.S. During the mid-1970s it was estimated that 60% of the heroin consumed in the U.S. was of Mexican origin. Mexican "brown" heroin was at that time assayed at about 17% heroin—a high percentage when compared with the other heroin available, which assayed at about 2%–3%. Mexico had a corner on the market for only a short time though, and has since been replaced by the GOLDEN CRESCENT. However, Mexico has become, in the mid-1990s, a major transit point for the shipment of heroin from foreign regions, such as the Golden Crescent, into the U.S.

There is significant traffic in amphetamine powder and other illicit drugs to Europe and the U.S. either from Mexico or through Mexico from other sources. Additionally, Mexican trafficking organizations dominate the illicit manufacture, sale and distribution of methaqualone.

Penalties for drug use and possession have also undergone changes. There is no bail or bond now for individuals charged with a narcotics crime; they must stand trial and, if convicted, there is no parole or suspended sentence. Long pretrial imprisonment can be expected in Mexico because the courts are backed up with pending cases.

In 1989 Mexico, under President Carlos Salinas de Gortari, prosecuted some formerly untouchable drug lords and officials, notably Jose Antonio Zovilla Perez, former chief of the Federal Security Directorate. The Mexican Government in the mid-1990s continued to pursue drug lords and government officials involved directly or indirectly in trafficking.

Treatment: Nearly all health institutions in Mexico provide some sort of service for drug users. In the mid-1990s the Mexican Government reported that the number of community organizations involved in drug prevention increased, although due to depressed economic conditions and budget constraints, the ability of these organizations to provide services was constrained. There have been over the last two decades a number of small pilot programs in which new approaches to the treatment of high risk groups have been

tried and evaluated—with particular attention given to those who use inhalants. An example of such programs is Centros de Integracion Juvenil, one of the biggest organizations using treatment facilities to have received government funding. Since 1970 the association has established 32 centers in 28 cities. Before 1981 every young person who asked for treatment was accepted; after 1981 the admission policy had to be modified due to the large number of applicants—now only the most severe cases are accepted.

United States Dept. of State, Bureau for International Narcotics and Law Enforcement Affairs, *International Narcotics Control Strategy Report, March 1996.*

Michigan Alcoholism Screening Test (MAST) A formal questionnaire that allows for scoring or measuring a history of alcoholism problems, including self-reported daily alcohol intake during the preceding two weeks, nutrition, other drug use and medical and obstetric information. MAST may be used as part of a routine health maintenance visit. The MAST has a high sensitivity to drinking problems (95%), so it has been quite successful at pointing to problem drinking, even among alcoholics that may be in a state of DENIAL.

micronodular cirrhosis A contemporary classification for a kind of CIRRHOSIS that is similar to PORTAL CIRRHOSIS, the most common cirrhosis found among alcoholics.

milieu-limited (type one) alcoholism Adoption studies traditionally have been viewed as offering the most promise for proving a genetic component in alcoholism, because these studies can clearly differentiate between the hereditary and environmental factors in a given subject's drinking. In 1981 researchers made a breakthrough in their analysis of Swedish adoption studies by revealing the existence of two types of GENETIC predisposition toward alcoholism. Type one, or milieu-limited alcoholism, fit most closely into existing etiological paradigms for alcoholism. This type was found to occur in both sexes (that is, it could be transmitted by either biological parent and could be passed to children of either sex) and was implicated in most cases of alcoholism. It was associated with low-level, late-onset drinking behavior in either biological parent and little parental criminal behavior (a further indicator of a lower severity of drinking behavior).

minimum drinking age

Adoptees with this type of predisposition were reported to be heavily influenced in their drinking behavior by factors in their postnatal environment—or milieu—rather than exclusively by the genes they inherited from their biological parents.

Type two alcoholism was said to be male-limited, as it was transmitted exclusively from father to son and accounted for approximately 25% of male alcoholics. This type of susceptibility was found to be unaffected by environment. In cases of severe alcoholism in the biological father, for example, as evidenced by early-onset drinking as well as increased criminal behavior and extensive treatment, adopted sons, regardless of their postnatal environment, were nine times more likely than controls to abuse alcohol. Despite the strong heritability of this type of alcoholism, some environmental influence was suspected in the severity of alcohol abuse, as the sons tended to be less alcoholic than their fathers.

Recently, Cloninger has suggested other traits that can be associated with these types of alcohol heritability: novelty seeking, harm avoidance and reward dependence. Type one behaviors will tend to represent low levels of novelty seeking and exhibit traits of a "passive dependent personality," as well as high harm avoidance and concern for others' feelings (high reward dependence). Type two behaviors, in contrast, are more strongly antisocial and exhibit high levels of novelty seeking and impulsivity, uninhibited behavior (low harm avoidance) and little reward dependence; that is, weak development of social relations.

C. Robert Cloninger, "Neurogenetic Adaptive Mechanisms in Alcoholism," *Science* 236 (1987): 410–416.

C. Robert Cloninger, M. Bohman and S. Sigvardsson, "Inheritance of Alcohol Abuse," *Archives of General Psychiatry* 38 (1981): 861–868.

milieu therapy A socioenvironmental therapy that is an essential part of inpatient treatment. In this therapy the behavior and attitudes of the staff and the activities prescribed for a patient are determined by the patient's interpersonal and emotional needs. This interaction between patient and staff includes learning how to interact with others without letting anger turn to violence; learning to talk to people about things other than drugs; and learning to ask for help when it is needed.

milk sugar Lactose crystals that are often used to adulterate heroin. It closely resembles heroin in appearance.

miltown A widely used minor tranquilizer that contains MEPROBAMATE and is used for the relief of tension and anxiety. It has a significant potential for abuse, and both physical and psychological dependence can occur. When taken with alcohol or other central nervous system depressants it can have an additive effect. Overdosage can result in drowsiness, stupor, respiratory collapse, coma, shock and death.

Miltrate A minor tranquilizer that contains MEPROBAMATE (for tension and anxiety) and pentaerythritol tetranitrate (to relax smooth muscles). Used for the relief of pain associated with coronary artery disease, Miltrate has the potential for abuse, and both physical and psychological dependence occur if this drug is taken over periods of time. When taken with alcohol or other central nervous system depressants an ADDITIVE EFFECT results.

minimum drinking age In the 1970s many states lowered their legal minimum drinking ages, usually to 18, resulting in notable increases in alcohol-related accidents among drivers 18 to 20. By 1984 legislation was passed to withhold federal highway funds from states that did not raise their drinking ages to 21. By 1988 all 50 states and the District of Columbia had raised the minimum drinking age to 21, and this same year (1988) the National Highway Traffic Safety Administration (NHTSA) reported that approximately 40% of all teenage deaths (ages 15 to 19) occurred in motor vehicle accidents.

In 1972, when Michigan reduced the minimum legal driving age from 21 to 18 years, among 18- to 20-year-old drinking drivers there was a 32% increase in fatal accidents and a 21% increase in nonfatal personal injury accidents, according to a five-year follow-up report by the University of Michigan's Highway Safety Institute. During this five-year period, the number of newly licensed 18- to 20-year-old drivers increased by only 9%. Similar data are available from Massachusetts and Ontario, Canada.

In 1987 Donald M. Gallant, M.D., the director of medical student education in psychiatry, Tulane University of Medicine, noted that "well-docu-

A Policy Worth 16,513 Lives

History of the Minimum Legal Drinking Age Policy (MLDA)

Pre-1970s	Most adult privileges, including the right to vote and, in most States, the right to drink alcohol legally, are reserved for those 21 years and older.
1971	The right to vote is granted to 18-year-olds by amendment to the Constitution; in most States, a parellel effort lowers the MLDA.
1983	Dramatic increases in traffic deaths among young people—particularly along "blood borders," or heavily trafficked areas between States with different MLDAs.
1984	Legislation threatens to withhold Federal highway funds from States with MLDAs under 21.
1996	The National Highway Traffic Safety Administration estimates that 16,513 young lives have been saved because of the higher MLDA.

Source: *NHTSA Technical Report,* National Highway Traffic Safety Administration, March 1997.

mented reports reveal and confirm the consistent correlation between minimum legal drinking ages and traffic morbidity and mortality rates in young people with high blood-alcohol concentrations at the time of the accident."

National Highway Traffic Safety Administration (NHTSA), *Alcohol Involvement in Fatal Traffic Crashes, 1986,* technical report DOT HS 807 268 (Springfield, Va.: National Technical Information Service [NTIS], 1988).

A. C. Wagenaar and R. K. Douglass, "An Evaluation of Changing the Legal Drinking Age," *The Bottom Line* 4 (1980): 16–17.

Minnesota Multiphasic Personality Inventory (MMPI)   The MMPI-II is the most current version of a psychological assessment instrument. Subjects complete a lengthy multiple choice questionnaire. The results indicate the general characteristics of the subject based on the characteristics of other individuals who answered particular groups of questions in a similar way. The McAndrew Alcoholism Scale, derived from the first MMPI, has been used as a detection instrument to assess early symptoms of alcoholism as well as the psychological and social functioning of the alcoholic patient.

Personality inventories, including both MMPIs, will always have a margin of error. The first version

MMPI, for example, noted that alcoholics tend to score high on the "psychopathic deviant" scale. This trait, however, is found among other groups such as criminals and heroin addicts and does not appear to be unique to alcoholics.

Donald M. Gallant, *Alcoholism: A Guide to Diagnosis, Intervention, and Treatment* (New York: W.W. Norton, 1987).

misuse   The use of any legal, prescription or over-the-counter (OTC) drug for a purpose that it was not originally intended for (for example, drinking alcohol in order to sleep). The initial misuse of alcohol, prescription medications or over-the-counter medications is in most cases how a vulnerable person becomes addicted or cross-addicted; the underlying problem goes unidentified and unresolved and the drug becomes ever more necessary as a means of coping with the unresolved problem.

mitochondria   The part of the cell that supplies the organism with energy by breaking down the chemical bonds in the molecules of complex nutrients. Mitosis is cell division, in which the chromosomes split, with one-half of each chromosome going to the daughter cell.

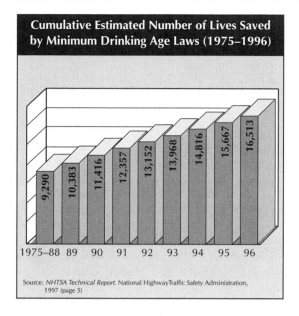

Cumulative Estimated Number of Lives Saved by Minimum Drinking Age Laws (1975–1996)

9,290 — 1975–88
10,383 — 89
11,416 — 90
12,357 — 91
13,152 — 92
13,968 — 93
14,816 — 94
15,667 — 95
16,513 — 96

Source: *NHTSA Technical Report.* National HighwayTraffic Safety Administration, 1997 (page 5)

mixed cirrhosis   Any combination of macronodular and MICRONODULAR CIRRHOSIS. (See CIRRHOSIS.)

mixing drinks   Contrary to popular belief, and to what many an experienced drinker will swear, research has indicated that mixing, or changing, alcoholic beverages in the course of a drinking session does not in itself cause a HANGOVER. It is rather the alcohol content and concentration of the drinks consumed that are to blame. In addition, the CONGENERS in the various beverages may intensify the hangover. Regardless of research, many people who have mixed such combinations as beer and champagne to any large degree, may have regretted it the following day.

In some cases the order in which drinks are mixed produces a different effect. If beer, for instance, is taken before whiskey, the first alcohol entering the bloodstream (in the form of beer) has already been diluted and is therefore less potent. Beer takes up volume in the stomach, which slows the absorption of whiskey, diluting it and delaying its effects.

If whiskey is followed by beer, the effect is a concentrated rush of alcohol to the bloodstream, with the alcohol in the whiskey reinforced by the alcohol in the beer. This combination, known as a "boilermaker," is more dangerous to the drinker and results in more rapid intoxication.

MMDA   A derivative of the alkaloid myristicin found in nutmeg. It has psychedelic properties and purportedly intensifies present experiences, as opposed to MDA, which intensifies experiences in the user's past. It is the same as MDA except that its chemical formula includes a 3-methoxy group.

moderate drinking   Occasional drinking or a regular habit of drinking small amounts of alcohol, perhaps a drink or two; a level and frequency of drinking consistent with the pattern in the community and resulting in no pathological behavior or consequences. According to statistics published in the *Second Report to the U.S. Congress on Alcohol and Health* (1974), moderate drinkers, as a group, live longer than ex-drinkers, heavy drinkers or abstainers. (See ANSTIE'S LAW.) Studies in the 1970s, 1980s and more strongly in the 1990s suggest that moderate drinking, even on a daily basis, can protect drinkers from coronary heart disease and result in a longer life. The studies came under attack for not having adequately controlled for other lifestyle factors, such as exercise and healthy eating habits. There was concern about the studies done in the 1990s because it was believed by some treatment professionals that the studies' results might encourage abstaining alcoholics to drink. Additionally, the concern was for persons who, not previously exposed to alcohol but now encouraged to drink as a health measure, would be at risk of alcoholism. To date the question is not settled, and controversy still surrounds the issue. (See HEART.)

Moderation Management   One of several self-help groups and/or treatment modalities that achieved notoriety in the early 1990s by endorsing controlled drinking and suggesting that abstinence may not be the only, or even the best, solution for all people with problems related to excessive drinking. Moderation Management borrows the group-support model from Alcoholics Anonymous, but groups are utilized to support the control required to limit, rather than eliminate, their drinking.

Moderation advocates distinguish between "problem drinkers" (individuals who might benefit from a treatment approach that teaches them to reduce their drinking rather than eliminate it altogether) and "chronic drinkers," for whom AA-style abstinence is the treatment of choice. Despite such reassurances, organizations such as Moderation Management drew protests from alcoholism hard-liners such as the National Council on Alcohol and Drug Dependencies, which fear that chronic drinkers may see the movement as an excuse to resume their drinking.

monoamine oxidase (MAO) inhibitors   Central nervous system stimulants that are used in the treatment of moderate to severe depressive states. The main types are isocarboxazid (Marplan), phenelzine (Nardil) and tranylcypromine (Parnate). Although they are effective, adverse reactions can be extremely severe. When used in combination with many other types of drugs—depressants, stimulants, narcotics—such an intense additive effect can be produced that death may result. The same is true when MAO inhibitors are taken with common foods that contain tyramine, such as cheese, herring, salami and chocolate. MAO inhibitors are considered extremely dangerous drugs and usually are administered only under close medical supervision.

moonshine   Moonshine is the name given to corn whiskey that is not aged to any extent. It has the clear color and raw taste of pure alcohol, and its other name, "white lightning," is well merited. Moonshine dates back to the year when the government first started to impose taxes on whiskey—1791. Distillers and private whiskey-makers sought to avoid paying government taxes by producing whiskey secretly. They set up stills in out-of-the-way places and usually worked at night by moonlight. This illegal production became known as moonshining, and the product was called "moonshine."

Moonshining is still common in Tennessee, Kentucky, North Carolina and other parts of the rural South. Moonshine is said to be the preferred drink of some Americans and is now legally available in some areas. However, illegal manufacture continues. A major incentive for moonshining is the opportunity to make an extra profit by not paying customs and/or excise taxes. If the government substantially increases taxes on legally produced liquor, the public may rebel and encourage moonshiners.

John A. Ewing and Beatrice A. Rouse, "Drinks, Drinkers, and Drinking," in *Drinking,* ed. Rouse and Ewing (Chicago: Nelson-Hall, 1978): 12–13.

morning drinking   Sometimes engaged in to relieve the symptoms of a HANGOVER; morning drink-

ing is a significant warning sign indicating probable alcoholism.

morning glory seeds   The seeds of certain members of the bindweed family Convolvulaceae, which contain HALLUCINOGENIC substances similar to those found in LSD—principally lysergic acid amides, d-isolysergic acid amide, chanoclavine and clymoclavine. All of these substances also are found in the fungus ergot *Clavicips purpurea,* from which LSD first was synthesized. The active ingredients in morning glory seeds have about one-tenth the potency of LSD.

As with so many of the organic hallucinogens, morning glory seeds have long been used by native peoples of America in religious ceremonies and as healing agents. The Aztecs were the first to discover their hallucinogenic possibilities, and the Aztec word *ololiuqui* now is used to refer to all varieties of the seeds. It is believed that the Aztecs used the word only when referring to the seeds of one species, *Rivea corymbosa. Tlitliltzen,* it is thought, was the Aztec name for morning glories of the genus *Ipomoea.*

Effects: As might be expected, the effects of morning glory seeds are somewhat like those of LSD. The user may experience perceptual disturbances, mood changes and even psychomimetic reactions. Physical effects are wide-ranging: nausea, vomiting, intense headache, drowsiness, diarrhea, chills, impaired vision, decreased blood pressure and even shock can result from their use. Onset of effects occur 20–45 minutes after ingestion, and duration can be upwards of six hours. Cases of prolonged reactions or FLASHBACKS following ingestion of morning glory seeds have been reported.

Sources: Several seed varieties commonly planted in gardens are used, including heavenly blue, pearly gates, blue star, flying saucers and wedding bells, but those sold commercially often are covered with methyl mercury to prevent spoilage. Some may also be covered with vomit-inducers, which have been applied to discourage psychotropic use. As a result, many users grow their own seeds.

The appearance of morning glory seeds on the illicit drug market is rare, as LSD is readily available and preferred. When the seeds are used, they are first pulverized or ground and then soaked in water. The liquid is strained and drunk.

History of Morphine

c. 1803	Serturner, German pharmacist, isolates morphine from opium.
1825	Morphine is first used in medicine as an analgesic and is thought to be a cure for opium addiction.
1853	Hypodermic needle is introduced and used to inject morphine.
1866	Morphine use during Civil War in U.S. creates an estimated 400,000 addicts.
1870s	Franco-Prussian War in Europe creates morphine addicts.
1874	Heroin is isolated from morphine.
1906–1920	Legislation regulates cultivation and distribution of opium, outlaws prescriptions of narcotics to addicts and imposes criminal penalties.
1920s	Heroin, because of its higher potency and illicit availability, becomes favored over morphine.
1952	Complete synthesis of morphine is achieved.
1970	Prescriptions containing morphine are classified as Schedules II and III drugs under the Controlled Substances Act.
1980s–1990s	Morphine rarely appears on the illicit market and addicts are generally members of the medical profession or hospital personnel.

Source: Robert O'Brien and Morris Chafetz, *The Encyclopedia of Drug Abuse,* New York: Facts On File, 1992.

Trafficking: No laws regulate the sale of morning glory seeds.

Synonyms: ololiuqui, bador, loquetico, tlitliltzen, bindweed, heavenly blue, pearly gates, blue star, flying saucers, wedding bells.

morning shot For an alcoholic, the first drink of the day. (See MORNING DRINKING.) For an intravenous drug user (IDU), the first injection of the day.

morphine Morphine is a NARCOTIC analgesic, the principal alkaloid of OPIUM. It is a Schedule II drug under the CONTROLLED SUBSTANCES ACT.

The isolation of morphine around 1802 is usually attributed to Serturner, who named the drug for Morpheus, the god of sleep and dreams. The most potent naturally occurring medication known for pain relief, it remains the standard by which all other analgesics are judged. Complete synthesis of morphine was achieved in 1952.

Opium (the coagulated exudate of the poppy plant *Papaver somniferum*) is made up of morphine (about 10% by weight), codeine and about 20 other alkaloids.

Usage: When morphine was introduced to the medical profession, it was hailed as a powerful analgesic, effective in the relief of all kinds of pain and, falsely, as it turned out, as a cure for opium addiction. Opium, either in the form of LAUDANUM (a hydroalcoholic tincture) or in a form suitable for smoking, was already a popular "remedy" for every imaginable ailment—and some imaginary ones. Morphine quickly replaced opium in many applications, though it did not cure opium addiction. In the 1850s, with the advent of the hypodermic syringe (which made possible almost immediate relief from pain and anxiety), morphine proved especially valuable and doctors prescribed it liberally. Unfortunately, the new drug proved equally popular among recreational users, particularly in conjunction with the hypodermic needle. Morphine could be purchased at the local drugstore or through the mail, in powder, tablet or liquid form. Hypodermic kits also were readily available. Compared to alcohol it was a "respectable" intoxicant and was heartily recommended by many of those who tried it. During the Civil War it served as a priceless surgical anesthetic and analgesic. Doctors distributed supplies of the drug, along with hypodermic syringes, to soldiers for use at home to ease the continuing pain of battle wounds. It was not until several decades after the war that doctors realized their mistake in assuming that injections of morphine carried no risk of addiction, because when administered in this way the drug bypasses the digestive tract. Approximately 2% of the population (400,000 people) was estimated to be suffering from the "army disease"—opiate or morphine addiction. Many of the addicts were doctors.

Today opiate addicts prefer the more potent and shorter-acting heroin. Morphine rarely appears on the illicit market, and most addicts today are probably members of the medical profession (including hospital personnel) who have access to the drug. Morphine generally is used as a sulfate rather than in its pure form. It is often taken in combination with stimulant drugs such as amphetamines or cocaine, in order to counteract the depression, weakness and dizziness it produces, as well as to increase the analgesic effect.

Currently morphine is applied medically as a preanesthetic for the relief of fear and anxiety associated with surgery and to reduce the amount of anesthetic needed. It is also used for cough suppression, to relieve diarrhea and for severe pain relief. It is not recommended for patients suffering from bronchial asthma or other respiratory depression.

Dosage: Recommended dosage for relief of moderate to severe pain is 10 mg per 70 kg (approximately 154 lbs) body weight. When taken orally, morphine produces longer-lasting effects but it is only about one-tenth as potent as when it is injected intramuscularly. With subcutaneous injection, pain relief manifests in 20–60 minutes and lasts four or five hours. Intravenous ADMINISTRATION brings almost immediate pain relief and effects peak within 20 minutes. Analgesia lasts a much shorter time when morphine is injected intravenously.

Toxic and lethal doses vary with individual tolerance; 120 mg taken orally and 30 mg injected intra-

venously have caused no toxic reactions in a nonaddicted person, though less than 30 mg have caused death by respiratory depression on some occasions. Addicts have been known to take daily doses of up to 5,000 mg due to their high TOLERANCE.

Appearance and availability: Because pure morphine is only slightly soluble in water, morphine sulfate is the form most commonly used, both medically and recreationally. It appears as odorless white crystals, or white crystalline powder, which loses water on exposure to air and darkens on exposure to light. Morphine sulfate is soluble in water, slightly soluble in alcohol and insoluble in chloroform and ether. Morphine hydrochloride also is used occasionally in injections. Recreational users inject the drug, take it orally in capsules or liquid solution, heat and inhale it, or absorb it from rectal suppositories.

Activity: Readily but slowly absorbed from the gastrointestinal tract, morphine acts directly on the central nervous system, specifically affecting pain-receptor neurons. After initial stimulation, the drug depresses the cerebral cortex and medullary centers.

Within 24 hours, 90% of the total excretion process is complete. Like other narcotics and depressant drugs, morphine crosses the placental barrier. Babies of addicted mothers usually exhibit withdrawal symptoms soon after birth.

Effects: Morphine is prized for its ability to relieve almost any kind of pain—particularly dull, continuous pain—along with the fear and anxiety associated with such suffering. In addition to analgesia, the drug produces drowsiness (and, in sufficient doses, sleep) and euphoria, though it impairs mental and physical performance. When given to people who are not experiencing pain, initial doses can produce dysphoria—heightened fear and anxiety—rather than euphoria. Vomiting after the first dose is common. Morphine decreases the motility of the genitourinary and gastrointestinal tracts (causing constipation), depresses respiration and decreases hunger. It can diminish the sex drive, although in some people, especially women, it can enhance sexuality by disinhibition. It may also have the effect of delaying ejaculation in men. (It has been suggested that opium's popularity in 19th-century India was largely due to that effect.) In women, morphine use can cause menstruation to become irregular; with daily use some women stop menstruating altogether. Studies indicate that narcotic use also decreases the likelihood of pregnancy.

Typical adverse effects include nausea, vomiting and sweating. Yawning, lowered body temperature, flushing of the skin, a heavy feeling in the limbs and itchiness around the face and nose are usually also present, along with pupillary constriction and consequent dimming of vision.

In overdose, the effects described above are magnified. Respiratory depression can be severe enough to cause coma and death—respiratory failure (apnea) is in fact the principal danger of morphine abuse. The skin of overdose victims is cold, clammy and bluish, and the pupils are so constricted that they become a pinpoint. Skeletal muscles become flaccid. Overdose also frequently involves pulmonary congestion and edema. Until the patient can be admitted to emergency hospital care, he should be kept awake by walking, administering smelling salts and by stimulating the skin. NALOXONE (Narcan) is a specific antidote for opiate overdose. Given intravenously it will restore a comatose, barely breathing patient to consciousness within seconds.

Tolerance and dependence: Tolerance and severe psychological and physical dependence develop quickly with regular use of morphine. Psychological dependence develops before actual physical craving. Tolerance, however, develops only to morphine's depressant effects and not to other physical effects such as constriction of the pupils. Morphine exhibits CROSS-TOLERANCE and dependence to other narcotics, and its depressant effects are prolonged and intensified when used with other depressants.

Up to a threshold of 500 mg a day, the severity and duration of WITHDRAWAL symptoms from morphine depends upon the quantity of the drug regularly ingested. Usual symptoms include nausea, lacrimation, yawning and sweating alternating with chills. Withdrawal from morphine generally lasts 36–73 hours.

Synonyms: M., morph, dreamer, Miss Emma, M.S.

morpholinylethylmorphine   Another name for PHOLCODINE, a semisynthetic morphine derivative.

mortality   Clinical research has shown that alcoholics/other drug-addicted individuals have a higher mortality rate than that of the general population. The mortality rate for men with alcohol problems, for example, is two to six times higher than that for men without alcohol problems.

An increase in the general CONSUMPTION level of the overall population usually results in an increase in the number of individuals with diseases related to the abused substance and, consequently, an increase in mortality. A demonstration of this effect can be seen in the dramatic drops in deaths from cirrhosis during times of war or prohibition when alcohol was not available.

There are two major causes of alcohol and/or other drug-related mortality. Substance abuse is directly responsible for a number of DISEASES resulting in death, and it is indirectly involved in deaths from ACCIDENTS and aberrant behavior. (See SUICIDE, DRIVING WHILE IMPAIRED [DWI] and CRIME.)

Ernest P. Noble, ed., *Third Special Report to the U.S. Congress on Alcohol and Health* (Rockville, Md.: National Institute on Alcohol Abuse and Alcoholism, 1978): 17–20.

Mothers Against Drunk Driving (MADD)   A community action group organized to fight drunk driving, the organization was begun by Candy Lightner in 1979 after her daughter was killed by a drunk driver with a record of five drunk-driving arrests since 1976. MADD seeks to change the climate of acceptance and tolerance of the drunk driver and to change the response of the legal system toward drunk driving. It also serves to advocate for, and to support, those who have been victimized by drunk drivers. Headquartered in Hurst, Texas, the organization has gained nationwide attention: petitions instigated by MADD have been instrumental in the rise in the legal drinking age to 21 in all states.

motivational interviewing   Treatment approach incorporating techniques that start during the intake interview. Drawing on the "readiness to change" model pioneered by DiClemente and Prochaska, the goal of motivational interviewing is to help clients resolve ambivalence and commit themselves to change. This approach utilizes strategies from client-centered counseling, cognitive therapy, systems theory and the social psychology of persuasion.

Comparative Death Rate from Alcohol, Tobacco, Other Drugs and Causes

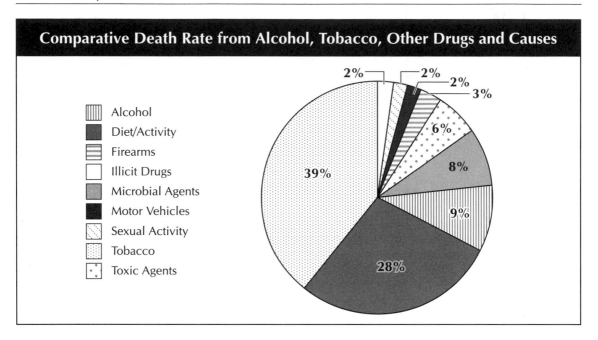

Alcohol
Diet/Activity
Firearms
Illicit Drugs
Microbial Agents
Motor Vehicles
Sexual Activity
Tobacco
Toxic Agents

2%   2%   2%   3%   6%   8%   9%   39%   28%

Motivational interviewing sessions are client-centered. The counselor maintains a strong sense of purpose and direction, actively choosing the right moments to intervene in incisive ways. This method combines elements of directive and nondirective approaches, and can be integrated with a broad range of strategies. It also can be used to prepare a motivational foundation for other approaches, including behavioral training, cognitive therapy, 12-steps groups and medication.

C. C. DiClemente and J. O. Prochaska, "Coping and Consequences in the Smoking Behavior Change," in *Coping and Substance Abuse: Processes of Change,* ed. S. Shiffman and T. A. Wills (San Diego: Academic Press, 1985).

W. R. Miller and S. Rollnick, *Motivational Interviewing: Preparing People to Change Addictive Behavior* (New York: Guilford, 1991).

motorcycle accidents   Of the total deaths from motor vehicle accidents, more than 60% involve passenger cars; motorcycles and motor scooters account for 8%. In 1986 alcohol was involved in nearly 54% of fatal motorcycle accidents, compared with 35% of drivers of passenger cars. One trauma-center study of victims of motorcycle crashes over an 18-month period found a 25% incidence of intoxication. Intoxicated motorcyclists were responsible for the crash 50% more often than those who were not intoxicated, and their mortality rate was four times higher. Although intoxicated motorcyclists constituted only 25% of the crash victims, they sustained 39% of the severe head injuries and 57% of the mortalities. Furthermore, intoxicated motorcyclists wore helmets one-third as often and sustained head injuries twice as frequently.

Data on other drug-use and motorcycle accidents has usually been inaccurate or nonexistent because it is harder to identify the drug user. Drug use is an illicit activity in itself, and therefore drug users usually hide its use and are not cooperative in being tested for drugs.

National Highway Traffic Safety Administration, *Alcohol Involvement in Fatal Crashes, 1986* (Washington, D.C., 1988).

mouth   The mouth is the entry into the digestive tract, and any impairment to its functions (mastication, salivation, swallowing, tasting, speaking) will subsequently affect the functioning of the digestive system.

Of all recreational drugs, alcohol and tobacco have the most directly harmful effects on the mouth. Alcohol alone has not been proved to be carcinogenic but it is believed to act as a "cocarcinogen" in conjunction with a substance that is carcinogenic, such as tobacco. Studies have shown that alcohol and cigarettes act synergistically to increase the potential for cancer, especially in the mouth and throat. (See SYNERGY.) Most heavy drinkers also are heavy smokers, and it is estimated that people who drink and smoke heavily run a 15-times-greater risk of developing cancer than that of nondrinkers and nonsmokers. One theory states that the carcinogens in tobacco have easier access to the mucous membranes of the mouth if the cells are bathed in alcohol, with its solvent effects. Another theory suggests that alcohol and tobacco independently affect the mucous membranes. Tobacco may contribute to cancers of the roof of the mouth, of the nasopharynx (which connects with the nostrils), of the larynx and of the lungs. Pipe and cigar smoking increase the incidence of cancer of the lip and jaw. Smokeless tobacco products, including both chewing tobacco and snuff, have been associated with a precancerous condition know as leukoplatsius, white patches that occur on the mucous membrane in the mouth. This can convert to malignant conditions. The presence of carcinogenic compounds in tobacco are responsible for the development of malignancies. These compounds include polonium-210, polycyclic aromatic hydrocarbons and netrosaminos. Alcohol plays more of a role in cancers of the floor of the mouth, the lower pharynx and the esophagus—areas where contact is most direct.

Few other drugs of abuse produce directly harmful effects on the mouth. Marijuana smoking often produces dryness in the mouth and throat, and many users of amphetamines and other stimulants have experienced teeth-grinding, but these symptoms disappear quickly after cessation of use.

Many opiate users neglect oral and personal hygiene, and this results in rampant tooth decay. However, a large segment of the population—particularly the poor—receives unsatisfactory dental care, so it is difficult to establish if dental neglect is due to poverty or drug use.

mouthwash   Numerous mouthwashes contain high percentages of alcohol. Listerine, for example, has 26.9%, while most hard liquor (gin, vodka, whiskey) contains about 40% alcohol. While they do have a potential for abuse, the main concern posed by mouthwashes containing alcohol is that an alcoholic who legitimately uses one may develop a craving for more. In addition, an alcoholic who is abstinent may be started on a relapse by drinking mouthwash. Mouthwashes may also produce adverse reactions in people taking ANTABUSE. Other mouthwashes with a high alcohol content are: Cepacol, 14%; Scope, 18.5%; and Signal, 15.5%. Mouthwash may also be excessively used by persons seeking to hide their misuse or abuse of alcohol.

MPTP   A synthetic, heroinlike designer drug that produces permanent symptoms closely resembling the stiffness and tremors of Parkinson's disease. Ironically, an outbreak of MPTP-induced Parkinson's in California has led to a breakthrough in medical knowledge and treatment of the disease, which afflicts many Americans.

multihabituation   See POLYDRUG USE.

multimodality programs   A drug treatment program that uses a variety of treatment approaches. Such a program would seek to meet the mental, physical, social and vocational needs of the patient through an array of services. These programs frequently provide: medical services specific to TB and AIDS testing and counseling; urine testing; medical detoxification; long-term outpatient mental health care, including counseling, psychotherapy, pharmacology treatment for co-occurring psychiatric problems; and NARCOTIC ANTAGONISTS treatment; chemotherapy for addiction problems such as methadone maintenance; and social and vocational rehabilitation. In addition, programs would provide access to general inpatient and outpatient medical care, either on their own premises or at transitional care facilities such as residential centers.

muscles   The effects of drug use on the muscles range from a slight muscular weakness that allegedly follows marijuana use to the severe, permanent muscular damage that can result from ALCOHOLIC and heroin abuse. The mechanisms of most of these disorders remain unclear, although the symptoms are well known and frequently encountered.

Sedatives: Tranquilizers such as VALIUM (diazepam) act as muscle relaxants and are commonly used in the treatment of spastic disorders. Cumulative effects of chronic use of such depressants (including barbiturates, alcohol, sedatives and narcotics) can cause muscular necrosis, or cell death. Alcohol abuse in particular has been recognized as a causative agent in the development of muscle disease. In the early stages, muscle diseases thus caused can be reversed through abstinence.

Alcoholic myopathy: This disease is probably a direct effect of ethanol or acetaldehyde on the muscle cells. The subclinical form of alcoholic myopathy develops in as much as one-third of the alcoholic population and is indicated by abnormally high levels of the enzyme creatine phosphokinase, which is produced by muscle cells. Lactic acid levels also rise, and victims may suffer muscle cramps and tenderness. Unless the patient stops drinking, the condition may worsen.

Sudden severe muscle cramps, pain or swelling of the arms and legs after heavy alcohol consumption are usually signs of acute alcohol myopathy, a localized, benign condition that also improves with abstinence. Myoglobinuria, a condition characterized by muscle fiber necrosis, fluid leakage and high enzyme levels may appear later. If undetected, it can progress and cause renal insufficiency and death.

Chronic alcoholic myopathy progresses slowly, often painlessly and without myoglobinuria, and involves weakness and atrophy of the limbs (usually the legs).

Alcoholic cardiac myopathy: This is a progressive weakening of the heart muscle fibers that often leads to severe disability and death.

Stimulants: Wasting of the muscles also occurs with the abuse of AMPHETAMINES, accompanying and partially resulting from weight loss. Amphetamines and other stimulants increase skeletal muscle tension while relaxing smooth muscles of the bronchi and intestine. After several days of a speed run, the user experiences pain in the muscles and joints and distinct tremors. These involuntary movements, which also have been noted in connection with alcohol and other sedative abuse, sometimes temporarily continue to trouble the individual after he or she has stopped using the drug.

Narcotics: Heroin's usual effect on the muscles is to reduce muscular activity of the hollow organs. Muscle spasms are a well-known, recognizable symptom of withdrawal from narcotic drugs and can involve the facial muscles as well as entire limbs (hence the expression "kicking the habit"). Muscular rigidity is a usual condition in babies born of addicted mothers.

It is still unclear whether disorders related to heroin abuse constitute toxic or allergic reactions. Several disorders seem to be associated with the adulterants used as cutting agents in street heroin. Acute rhabdomyolysis, for example, manifests within a few hours after injection as skeletal muscular pain, tenderness, swelling and weakness in the extremities. In this condition, muscular fibers can undergo structural change with or without necrosis. Random or total necrosis also can occur, sometimes accompanied by edema and hemorrhage.

Years of subcutaneous or intramuscular heroin injection also can cause muscular fibrosis or abscesses, as well as chronic infections. Permanent muscular contractions—"frozen" limbs or extremities—can result from muscular scarring.

Bacterial infection is a common complication of heroin use in unsanitary conditions. It strikes the muscles in the form of pyomyositis, which involves fever and swelling and tenderness of the limbs. Extensive areas of dead muscle have been found in some cases. Muscular rigidity and convulsions are frequently present during tetanus infections and can interfere with respiration.

Another muscular disorder associated with heroin addition is the "crush syndrome," which afflicts overdose victims. It sometimes appears as a massive swelling of the extremity that received the injection. Localized limb compression has been seen in individuals who lost consciousness.

Hallucinogens: Marijuana and hallucinogenic drugs have only a slight effect on the muscles. The muscular weakness previously mentioned in connection with marijuana smoking is not universally accepted as an effect of cannabis use, although the drug has been used medically as a muscle relaxant since the mid-19th century. Extremely high doses of cannabis may, however, cause involuntary jerking of the muscles and the lower extremities and some-times other parts of the body.

LSD and other psychedelics generally constrict smooth muscles of the uterus, blood vessels and bronchioles. Skeletal muscles may show tremor and weakness but, again, these effects do not commonly result from the use of hallucinogens

mushrooms   Several varieties of mushrooms with hallucinogenic properties have been used for centuries by Mexican Indians in religious rites and ceremonies. When eaten, the mushrooms affect mood and perception in a way similar to LSD and MESCA-LINE. They contain the active alkaloids PSILOCYBIN and psilocin. In 1958 Dr. Albert Hofmann, who synthesized LSD, isolated psilocybin and later synthesized it. The psilocybin that is sold in chemical form on the illicit market today is more often than not another chemical compound, such as LSD or PCP.

Another name for sacred mushrooms is *teonanactl*, which means "flesh of the gods" or "god's flesh." The most common types of mushrooms are *Psilocybe mexicana, Conocybe siliginoides, Psilocybe aztecorum, Psilocybe zapotecorum, Philocybe caerulescens* and *Stropharia cubensis*. Effects begin 20–30 minutes after ingestion and the duration can be from six to 12 hours. Peak effects usually are felt in one hour and may include visual hallucinations. The mushrooms can be lethal in large doses. Psilocybin, which is expensive to synthesize, is a Schedule I drug under the CONTROLLED SUBSTANCES ACT.

music and drugs   It has been suggested that currently popular music and currently popular drugs go hand-in-hand. This suggestion of a link between the two dates back to the 1880–1920 era, a time of widespread poverty when the great majority could obtain only inexpensive drugs, such as alcohol and tobacco, and an inexpensive form of entertainment—in this case "the blues"—because it was basically guitar or piano music requiring only one performer.

Dixieland jazz, which was popular during the Blues Era but came into its own after World War I, is associated with the use of alcohol and the limited use of cocaine (a habit brought home by some World War I servicemen). The National Prohibition Act of 1919, aimed at curtailing the use of alcohol, actually enhanced the desire for it; people would drink anything that even resembled it, such as wood alcohol.

From 1930 to 1942, the "Swing Era" was prominent and coincided with the repeal of Prohibition. The availability of alcohol and an atmosphere of permissiveness led to a boom in legitimate dance halls and nightclubs. This also was a time when many Americans, musicians included, were called into service for World War II and newly developed "music and dance rooms" in many popular hotels were forced to close. Those who could afford it and who were not involved in the war effort attended private "jam sessions," and the small groups that evolved developed "bop" music. With the development of bop music, which was somewhat restless and angular compared to previous forms, came an increase in heroin use.

The interaction of music and drugs was further demonstrated in the decade from the late 1940s to the late 1950s when the soft, intimate sounds of the newly evolved "cool" music was enjoyed by a host of marijuana users who preferred quiet intoxication.

In the 1960s "electric" sounds became popular and there was an increase in the use of hallucinogens; acid rock parties centered around the use of LSD. As the drug's popularity waned in the 1970s, the use of amphetamines, barbiturates, cocaine and other hazardous drugs took over. People continued to use alcohol, which became known as the gateway drug. A number of musicians who were popular in the 1960s such as Jimi Hendrix, Janis Joplin and Jim Morrison, died of drug overdoses.

Musicians and singers have long inhabited an environment that is conducive to drug use: along with the irregular pay and working hours, frequent traveling and contact with the criminal underworld in order to get bookings, there is the pressure and tension inherent in performing itself. Musicians also are apt to use drugs because of their desire to perceive "life" more deeply and to come up with unusual insights that they can express through their music. The lyrics of songs often contain references to LSD, marijuana, alcohol and cocaine and the "highs" they can produce. Adolescents in particular are greatly influenced by popular singers and by song lyrics, sometimes even on subliminal levels. They often model their own lifestyles on those of their idols. Recently many of the same entertainment people who once used illicit drugs have undergone treatment and are now encouraging their fans to achieve a natural high. (See RASTAFARIANS.)

mydriasis   Dilation of the pupils that occurs with intoxication from hallucinogens, scopolamine, atropine, cocaine and amphetamines. It also is a symptom of opiate withdrawal. Mydriasis does not occur from the use of marijuana, barbiturates or alcohol. (See EYES.)

myoglobinuria   A syndrome characterized by severe muscle pain, weakness, tenderness and swelling. It can be accompanied by cardiac arrhythmia, respiratory failure and renal insufficiency (the latter possibly leading to death). Depressant drugs (barbiturates, alcohol, narcotics) have been known to cause muscle necrosis resulting in myoglobinuria. There also is a syndrome referred to as "heroin user's myoglobinuria," which is thought to be related to heroin that has been adulterated with other chemicals ingredients.

myristicin   An alkaloid found in NUTMEG and thought to produce hallucinogenic effects.

nail polish remover A mixture of acetone, a volatile hydrocarbon, that is sometimes inhaled for its intoxicating effects. (See INHALANTS.)

nalbuphine A synthetic narcotic AGONIST/ANTAGONIST analgesic chemically related to oxymorphone and naloxone. (See NUBAIN.)

Nalline NARCOTIC ANTAGONIST that is no longer available. It contained nalorphine hydrochloride and was used to treat opiate drug overdose. It counters respiratory and central nervous system depression caused by opiates, but not barbiturates or other drugs. Small doses of Nalline were used to ease withdrawal symptoms. The drug was used in the NALLINE TEST to determine whether ex-addicts had resumed using narcotics.

Nalline test This is a test using the NARCOTIC ANTAGONIST Nalline to determine whether an addict is taking drugs. NALLINE reverses the effects of a narcotic and causes pupil dilation. The Nalline test has been replaced by the NARCAN TEST.

nalorphine A semisynthetic morphine ANTAGONIST. (See NALLINE.)

naloxone A nearly pure NARCOTIC ANTAGONIST used to reverse the effects of opiate overdoses, particularly respiratory depression. It does not act on barbiturates and takes a few minutes to take effect. (See NARCAN.)

Naloxone Challenge Test See NARCAN TEST.

naltrexone A nearly pure opiate or NARCOTIC ANTAGONIST developed in 1963. It is long-acting, effective orally, has very few side effects and does not induce withdrawal symptoms when suddenly discontinued. When taken regularly, it discourages opiate use by inhibiting intoxification. In the early 1990s, studies also showed that naltrexone reduced alcohol cravings. As treatment for alcohol dependence, it was marketed under the name Revia. Naltrexone is also the main ingredient of Trexan.

nanogram A billionth of a gram. Laboratory testing of certain drugs, such as THC, is often recorded in nanograms per milliliter (a thousandth of a liter).

Narcan A NARCOTIC ANTAGONIST that contains naloxone hydrochloride. It reverses depression caused by natural and synthetic opiates (but not nonopiate drugs) and indicates recent use of narcotics. Unlike many other narcotic antagonists it does not produce respiratory depression. If narcotics are absent it produces relatively little pharmacological activity.

Common Drugs: Symptoms of Abuse of Narcotics

Narcotics. Natural or synthetic drugs that contain or resemble opium.

Drug Name	Street Names	Method of Use	Sign and Symptoms	Hazards of Use
Dilaudid, Percodan, Demerol, Methadone, Vicodin, Percocet, Darvocet	Dogs, K-4	Swallowed in pill or liquid form, injected.	Drowsiness, lethargy. Constricted pupils, slurred speech.	Addiciton with severe withdrawal symptoms. Loss of appetite, death from overdose.
Codeine	School boy, Licorice	Swallowed in pill or liquid form.	Drowsiness, lethargy. Constricted pupils, slurred speech.	Addiciton with severe withdrawal symptoms. Loss of appetite, death from overdose.
Morphine, Heroin	Dope, Smack, Boy, Scug	Injected, smoked, or snorted.	Needle marks, constricted pupils, neglected appearance.	Addiction with severe withdrawal symptoms. Loss of appetite, death from overdose.

Source: New York State Office of Alcoholism and substance Abuse Services.

Narcan test   Similar to the NALLINE TEST, it is used to determine opiate dependence. Both tests are NARCOTIC ANTAGONISTIC and cause pupil dilation.

narcologist   A person, often a psychiatrist or psychologist, who studies and treats alcohol and drug addiction. The term is mostly used in Europe and Asia, particularly in the countries of the former Soviet Union.

narcology   According to the World Health Organization's *Lexicon of Alcohol and Drug Terms,* narcology is "the study and science of phenomena relating to psychoactive substances as well as a medical specialty dealing with such problems." In the U.S., this is called "addiction medicine" or "addictionology."

narcotic   Narcotics are central nervous system depressants with analgesic and sedative properties. The U.S. government defines narcotics as addictive drugs that produce physical and psychological dependence. They include opium and its derivatives, heroin, morphine and codeine, as well as synthetic substances, such as Demerol and methadone. Both narcotics and non-narcotics are included under the CONTROLLED SUBSTANCES ACT. Under the Harrison Act of 1914, the first U.S. law regulating narcotics, cocaine, which is not an opiate or opiatelike substance, was included in the classification, but has been removed under contemporary legislation although they are still classified as narcotics in some states.

Narcotic Addict Rehabilitation Act (NARA)   This 1966 federal law, which has since been repealed, established guidelines for judges and prosecutors to funnel drug users into in-hospital treatment programs and aftercare programs in their home communities. The federal hospitals at Lexington and Fort Worth, established under the law, have been closed. This act also provided assistance and support to states and municipalities in developing facilities and treatment programs. Title I of the act covered addicts charged with certain federal offenses and committed for treatment in lieu of prosecution. Title II covered addicts convicted of federal crimes and committed as part of their sentences. Title III covered addicts who applied voluntarily. The National Institute on Drug Abuse (NIDA) administered Title I. The U.S. Department of Justice administered Titles II and III.

narcotic antagonist   A drug that counteracts or blocks the effects of opiate narcotics. In sufficient doses, these drugs can counter physical dependency and reverse or prevent toxic effects. Several narcotic antagonists were developed by creating isotopes of natural or synthetic opiates or chemically altering them. Low doses of antagonists cause dilation of the pupils in addicts and have been employed to identify persons who are physically dependent. (See NALLINE TEST and NARCAN TEST.) Among the best known antagonists are naloxone (NARCAN and NALTREXONE).

Narcotics Anonymous (NA)   A self-help organization of persons who meet regularly to help each other recover from drug addiction. Their rehabilitation involves a 12-step program almost identical to the one used by Alcoholics Anonymous and is centered around the therapy of addicts helping addicts. The organization, founded in 1953, also publishes informational pamphlets and a quarterly publication, *Voices of Narcotics Anonymous.* There are more than 12,000 chapters in the U.S. and around the world. The group is open to all and has no dues or fees.

narrowing of the drinking/other drug repertoire   According to the World Health Organization (WHO) *Lexicon of Alcohol and Drug Terms,* this expression refers to "the tendency of substance use to become progressively stereotyped around a self-imposed routine of custom and ritual, characterized by reduced variability of dosage and type of substance taken, and of time, place, and manner of self-administration."

nasal septum   The dividing wall between the nostrils. Persons who regularly snort COCAINE or heroin often develop severe nasal problems, including erosions and perforations of the septum.

National Asian Pacific American Families against Substance Abuse (NAPAFASA)   A not-for-profit organization based in Monterey, California, committed to eliminating alcohol and other drug use and abuse among Asian-Pacific-American families.

National Association of Broadcasters (NAB) abuse programs   This professional organization currently has 17 antidrug and antialcohol abuse campaigns, including Team Up Against Drugs; Project Workplace: America Responds to AIDS; and Stations Target Alcohol Abuse Reduction, Alcoholism and Underage Drinking. These programs are cospon-sored by various social service organizations, federal and state governments, corporations, small businesses, schools and parent groups.

National Association of State Alcohol and Drug Abuse Directors (NASADAD)   Founded in 1978, this group is composed of directors of state alcoholism agencies (SAAs) and single state agencies (SSAs) for drug-abuse prevention. NASADAD represents and promotes the interests of these agencies before Congress and federal agencies and lobbies for the development and financing of comprehensive programs in each state. The organization was formed by the merger of the National Association of State Drug Program Coordinators, established in 1971, and the Council of State and Territorial Alcoholism Authorities, established in 1974.

National Center for Health Statistics (NCHS)   One of several organizations that provide databases for analyzing patterns and trends in consumption, morbidity and mortality from alcohol and drug use. The center, located in Hyattsville, Maryland, provides specialized information to researchers, administrators and planners.

National Clearinghouse for Alcohol and Drug Information (NCADI)   The NCADI, established in 1988, collects, classifies and disseminates drug-use information. This federal agency maintains an inventory of more than 300 publications and distributes them without charge. It also supports the Regional Alcohol and Drug Abuse Resources (RADAR) program, which maintains satellite information centers affiliated with federal, state and local government agencies and colleges and universities.

National Coalition of Hispanic Health and Human Services Organizations   A Washington, D.C.–based, not-for-profit organization (also known as COSSMHO) that promotes the health and well-being of the Hispanic community. It conducts substance abuse demonstration and training and operates a development program that provides books, brochures, curricula and training materials. Its *Reporter* newsletter reports on its activities and contains health-related information.

National Collegiate Athletic Association (NCAA) drug education program   The NCAA finances drug education for student athletes and helps sponsor drug education conferences. It stresses drug prevention in its various youth programs, such as YES (Youth Education through Sports) Clinics and National Youth Sports Programs. It distributes drug education material each year to more than 100,000 freshmen in member institutions. It also conducts comprehensive drug testing of student athletes participating in its national championships and postseason football bowl games.

National Commission on Marijuana and Drug Abuse   Established by President Nixon in 1971, the commission was comprised of nationally prominent citizens who undertook a two-year examination of drug use, misuse and abuse. They concluded that old attitudes and definitions required a new set of terms and perspectives. The commission issued two reports (1972, 1973) that defined the issues, provided data on drug-using behavior, assessed its social impact and suggested a coherent social policy regarding illicit drugs. It also recommended the decriminalization of marijuana, which Nixon rejected. (See LEGAL ASPECTS OF MARIJUANA, AND OTHER DRUG CONTROLS and MARIJUANA.)

National Council on Alcoholism and Drug Dependency (NCADD)   Founded by Marty Mann in 1944 as the National Committee for Education on Alcoholism, it was known until the 1990s as the National Council on Alcoholism. Mann, a captivating speaker, joined Alcoholics Anonymous (AA) in 1939. At her death in 1980, she held the record for continuous sobriety of any woman in the group. In 1943 Mann studied at the newly founded Yale School of Alcohol Studies, the country's first such education program.

The National Council on Alcoholism and Drug Dependence was the first nationwide volunteer agency in the field of alcoholism. Today, it works for the prevention and control of alcoholism and drug dependence through public and professional educational programs, provides medical and scientific information and advocates public policy.

National Crime Prevention Council (NCPC)   This council offers several drug-abuse prevention materials and publishes a monthly newsletter for adults. A free multimedia drug-abuse prevention kit is distributed for elementary school children, which contains cassettes, puzzles, games and activity sheets. The Drug Prevention and Child Protection Program uses puppets and songs to deliver its anti-drug message to children from kindergarten through grade six (the McGruff Puppet Program). The full-year curriculum includes 12 drug or alcohol abuse prevention lessons for each grade level.

National Federation of Parents for Drug Free Youth (NFP)   A not-for-profit organization of parents and others committed to preventing alcohol and drug use by young people. The federation has a parent networking component, a materials clearinghouse and sponsors a youth training seminar called Reach America.

National Highway Traffic Safety Administration (NHTSA)   This federal agency provides information on passenger protection, such as safety belts, child safety seats and auto recalls. NHTSA, headquartered in Washington, D.C., analyzes patterns and trends relating to drinking and driving, minimum drinking age and driving, and traffic accidents and fatalities. It collects alcohol-related data dealing with traffic safety for drivers, passengers, pedestrians and bicyclists, and refers consumers to appropriate government agencies for questions on warranties, service and auto safety regulations.

National Hospital Discharge Survey (NHDS)   Continuously conducted since 1964 by the NATIONAL CENTER FOR HEALTH STATISTICS (NCHS), NHDS collects data from a sample of nonfederal hospitals with six or more beds and an average length of stay of under 30 days. The random samples are broken down by geographic region and hospital size.

Each entry describes the hospital episode of one patient and includes age, sex, race, marital status, length of stay, condition, treatment and surgical procedures.

Estimates of alcohol-related morbidity based on the NHDS sample are underestimates, because the sample is limited and does not account for the morbidity of those who seek outpatient treatment or no treatment at all. In addition, some health professionals are reluctant to report or make alcohol-related diagnoses.

F. S. Stinson, M. DuFour, M.D., and D. Bertolucci, "Alcohol-Related Morbidity in the Aging Population," *Alcohol Health & Research World* 13, no. 1, epidemiologic bulletin no. 20, NIAAA (1989): 80–87.

National Institute of Mental Health (NIMH)
One of several major organizations that analyze patterns and trends in consumption, morbidity and mortality of alcohol use and abuse. NIMH also has an in-progress Epidemiologic Catchment Area (ECA) program that assesses the prevalence and incidence of psychiatric disorders among adults in specific geographic areas.

National Institute on Alcohol Abuse and Alcoholism (NIAAA)
NIAAA, established in 1971, predates its administrative parent, the Substance Abuse and Mental Health Services Administration (SAMHSA). The institute develops policies and goals for the prevention, control and treatment of alcohol abuse and alcoholism. It conducts and supports research on the biological, psychological, sociological and epidemiological aspects of alcoholism; helps train professionals and paraprofessionals in the field; supports the development of alcoholism services, programs and projects; provides technical assistance to state and local government agencies and community organizations; and supports programs that provide care, treatment and rehabilitation of alcoholics. It also administers alcoholism detection, referral and treatment programs for federal civilian employees.

As part of its information program, NIAAA has submitted eight special reports to Congress on alcohol and health since 1971.

NIAAA has also funded various research projects. Perhaps the best-known and most controversial is an ongoing study, conducted by the Rand Corporation, designed "to assess the nature of treatment outcomes." The findings of this study have been published in the first RAND REPORT, and in RAND REPORT II.

National Institute on Drug Abuse (NIDA)
Established in 1972, NIDA is a component institute of the Substance Abuse and Mental Health Services Administration (SAMHSA). Its mandate is similar to

that of the NATIONAL INSTITUTE ON ALCOHOL ABUSE AND ALCOHOLISM (NIAAA). NIDA is charged with providing "leadership, policies, and goals for the federal effort in the prevention, control, and treatment of narcotic addiction and drug use, and the rehabilitation of affected individuals." Although drug-abuse services are administered primarily at the state level under the Alcohol, Drug Abuse and Mental Health block grant, NIDA provides leadership in the areas of research, research training, data collection and analysis, information dissemination and technical assistance. It is the lead agency responsible for federal efforts to reduce the demand for drugs.

National Nurses Society on Addictions (NNSA)
Begun in 1975 as the National Nurses Society on Alcoholism, NNSA, with the American Nurses Association (ANA), published *Standards of Addiction Nursing Practice with Selected Diagnoses and Criteria.* The document established 12 standards for the specialty of addiction nursing. NNSA also employs these objectives:

assure quality of care;
provide credentials for employers and third-party payers;
expand opportunities for advancement;
motivate nurses to participate in continuing education in order to expand knowledge and alternatives in approaches to nursing practice;
inject a greater measure of prestige and peer recognition into clinical practice.

NNSA also selects candidates for professional-in-residence scholarships to the Betty Ford Treatment Center in Rancho Mirage, California. The scholarships, funded by the center, are designed to augment nurse's awareness of alcoholism and drug addiction.

National Organization for the Reform of Marijuana Laws (NORML)
A volunteer citizen action group founded in 1970 to seek changes in U.S. laws regarding marijuana. NORML lobbies for legislative reform, disburses educational material and provides speakers in an effort to end criminal penalties for the possession, use and cultivation of marijuana. NORML has brought legal action against the Federal Drug Enforcement Administration (DEA) to make marijuana legally available for medical uses, and it

was instrumental in the passage of legislation that now allows marijuana to be used for medicinal purposes in a majority of states. In 1989 NORML failed in its petition to the DEA to reclassify marijuana as a Schedule II drug (it is currently a Schedule I drug) to make it easier to obtain for medical purposes. (See LEGAL ASPECTS OF MARIJUANA, AND OTHER DRUG CONTROLS.)

National Parents' Resource Institute for Drug Education, Inc. (PRIDE)   Based at Georgia State University, PRIDE is a not-for-profit organization that provides parents, educators, physicians, counselors and other concerned citizens with the most current research information on drug use. It also helps in the organization of parent groups, parent-school teams and citizen action groups.

National Temperance League   A British TEMPERANCE organization.

Native Americans (American Indians)
Alcohol: Alcoholic beverages were unknown to most Native Americans before the arrival of the European colonists. A few tribes fermented alcohol from corn and cactus for spiritual purposes. Whites used alcohol to their advantage when signing treaties or trading. The practice of intoxicating the Native Americans and cheating them out of their land and goods became so prevalent that some tribal leaders requested the enactment of federal laws to prohibit the sale of alcoholic beverages to their people. The first such law was passed in 1832 and not only banned the sale of liquor to Amerinds but made it illegal for them to drink in public. Some of these laws remained in effect until 1953. Today 408 out of 482 recognized tribes still prohibit the sale of alcoholic beverages on their land.

Because the Native American population is diverse and scattered around the country, drinking statistics are generally rough estimates.

Statistics: Alcoholism is among the major health problems of Amerinds, including the Inuits. In 1988 accidental injuries, chronic liver disease, CIRRHOSIS, homicide and suicide were the 10 leading causes of death among Native Americans and almost certainly reflect the wide-range of alcohol-related problems. From 1984 to 1986 the suicide rate for Native Americans aged 15 to 24 was almost twice the national rate

for that age group, and in 1985 the homicide rate for Amerinds aged 24 to 44 was nearly twice the national rate. In 1988, 28% of all Native American arrests were due to drunkenness or driving while intoxicated. On a reservation in Maine, 47% of all deaths over a 20-year period were alcohol-related, and every Native American in the state prison was there for an alcohol-related offense. The mortality rate from cirrhosis among these people was nearly three times the national average in 1986, and accidental deaths more than double the national average. It has been estimated that 30% of the male and 15% of the female Native American population are alcoholics.

Youth: Drinking begins early, sometimes as early as age 10. Children often are raised on a reservation in one culture until school age, when they are sent to boarding school, where they must give up that style of life. The most problematic age begins at 15, adolescence, when they are the most conformist and the least occupied. Many drop out of school and are either too young to work or unable to find jobs. The prevalence of drinking among older people sets an example for the youth.

Urban populations: Urban Native Americans have special problems, living in a setting where they are generally economically, educationally and socially disadvantaged and where they do not have the support of family and familiar customs. The Seattle Indian Health Board estimates that 80% (16,000) of the adult Native American population of Seattle are problem drinkers. The arrest rate for urban Native Americans was more than 40 times higher than that for the nation as a whole in 1980 (38,461 per 100,000 vs. 930 per 100,000).

Women: Native American women account for almost half of the deaths from liver cirrhosis among Amerindians, compared with one-third of cirrhosis deaths among both blacks and whites. Native American women also were more likely to die of liver cirrhosis at a younger age than either white or black women and died of cirrhosis at nine times the rate of white women.

Various studies on several reservations in the Plains, the Southwest and Canada have found that between 5% and 25% of children whose mothers drank heavily during pregnancy were born with FETAL ALCOHOL SYNDROME (FAS).

Worldwide, the rate at which children are born with FAS is 1% or less.

The Inter-Tribal Alcoholism Center in Sheridan, Wyoming, reports that 25% to 35% of its clients are women and believes that many others, because of their family responsibilities, are afraid to seek help. Many Amerind men won't do housework or take care of the children, tasks they consider unmanly or counter to tradition. Some women, the center said, fear that while they are seeking help, their children will be neglected and taken by child welfare officials and placed in foster homes.

Treatment: Native American women with drinking problems can receive help from the North American Indian Women's Council on Chemical Dependencies.

The Indian Health Service (IHS) has been the primary resource for handling the alcoholism-related problems and provides direct health services through 43 hospitals, 67 health centers, 78 service units and 55 health stations. Currently, the IHS funds more than 300 alcohol treatment programs.

The most promising avenue of treatment is helping Native Americans plan their own local programs with therapists and counselors sensitive to tribal cultures and the variations from tribe to tribe. Some specifically Native American Alcoholics Anonymous groups have integrated elements of their traditional cultures into the AA setting and have achieved more success than standard AA programs.

Causes: Numerous attempts have been made to explain why alcoholism is so high among Native Americans, who are really many distinct peoples with unique cultures and world views. There are several myths about their drinking, such as once they taste liquor they develop an uncontrollable craving for it. But their psychological or physiological reactions to alcohol do not appear to be different from those of other racial groups. While there are genetic differences, there is no evidence that they metabolize ethanol differently than other racial groups. But, the pattern of drinking among Native Americans rarely has a middle ground. Generally, they are heavy drinkers or teetotalers.

In the Passamaquoddy Indian language no words or phrases exist to describe social or moderate drinking. There are only terms to describe someone on a drinking binge—*sputsuwin*—or someone who is habitually drunk—*kotuhsomuin.*

Because alcohol was entirely new to Native American culture, no socially established norms for its use had developed and they did not perceive its potential destructiveness. When they were later prohibited from drinking, they had to gulp quickly to avoid being seen, forcing them to ingest larger quantities of liquor in a short time. The laws against drinking also may have created a fatalistic attitude toward alcohol—"If it is prohibited to me, it must be because I have no control."

Native Americans generally do not condemn the drinkers among them. They believe a drunk person is not himself and, therefore, not responsible for his behavior. Consequently they often are unwilling to testify against someone accused of committing a crime while drunk, creating problems for law enforcement officials. There is also heavy peer pressure to drink, and as with food, it is polite to share alcohol and to accept what is offered. Abstainers are sometimes accused of trying to be better than their peers.

One cause of the widespread drinking problems is probably due to sociocultural stress. Many cannot identify with the mainstream white-oriented society because they have been prevented from enjoying its fruits in terms of education, opportunity and social and economic status. Amerind traditions have been weakened and family relations have been disturbed. There are strong feelings of powerlessness and anxiety due to conflicts between their ways and the ways of the white man. They have been placed on reservations, their religions and cultures have been undermined, and their children have been placed in schools that do not teach them about their own rich heritage, and in no way respect the fact that they were indeed the guardians of this continent for many thousands of years before Europeans made their appearance. Under their watch the land remained rich, the animal populations flourished and the water remained pure.

Enoch Gordis, M.D., ed., *Seventh Special Report to the U.S. Congress on Alcohol and Health,* chap. 2 (Rockville, Md.: National Institute on Alcohol Abuse and Alcoholism, 1990).

Indian Health Services, *Indian Health Service, chart series,* DHHS pub. 1988 0-218-547: QL3 (Washington, D.C.: U.S. Government Printing Office, 1986).

Indian Health Services, *Trends in Indian Health, 1989* (Washington, D.C.: U.S. Government Print. Off., 1989).

Bruce Johansen, "The Tepees Are Empty and the Bars Are Full," *Alcoholism* 1, no. 2 (November/December, 1980): 33–38.

Gina Kolata, "Alcohol Abuse by Pregnant Indians Is Crippling a Generation of Children," *New York Times* (July 19, 1989).

Marian Sandmaier, *The Invisible Alcoholics* (New York: McGraw-Hill Book Company, 1980): 145–146.

Susan M. Stevens, "Alcohol and World View: A Study of Passamaquoddy Alcohol Use," *Journal of Studies on Alcohol,* supplement no. 9 (January 1981): 122–142.

Dale R. Walker, "Treatment Strategies in an Urban Indian Alcoholism Program," *Journal of Studies on Alcohol,* supplement no. 9 (January 1981): 171–184.

natural recovery   Contemporary, holistic approaches to the health, nutritional and lifestyle needs of the recovering person, including relaxation therapies, acupuncture, vitamin and herbal treatments, biofeedback, yoga and meditation. These approaches are becoming increasingly popular. "Wholeness" of mind/body/spirit are widely recognized as important components in long-term sobriety. (See HOLISTIC MEDICINE, ACUPUNCTURE and Dr.Michael SMITH.)

Navy Drug and Alcohol Abuse Treatment Program   This program provides both outpatient and residential treatment for U.S. Navy and Marine Corps personnel diagnosed with drug or alcohol abuse or dependency. Patients are accepted from military installations across the U.S.

near beer   Beer with an alcoholic content of less than 0.5%. Near beer is not considered an alcoholic beverage for purposes of taxation or for the regulation of sale or consumption. During PROHIBITION (the Volstead Act) much near beer was manufactured and sold, but because of its weakness or poor quality, or both, it was generally ridiculed even by those who drank it. When Prohibition ended, near beer all but disappeared until the 1970s, when it surfaced under a new and less objectionable name: MALT BEVERAGE. (See DE-ALCOHOLIZED BEVERAGE.)

needle sharing   A common and dangerous practice among intravenous drug users (IDUs), in which a shared syringe, dropper, cotton or other apparatus is used for injection. Needle sharing dramatically increases the risk of transmission of blood-borne

viruses, including hepatitis B and the human immunodeficiency virus (HIV), which often causes Acquired Immune Deficiency Syndrome (AIDS). Ironically, while strict controls on the sale of hypodermic equipment possibly may curtail illegal drug use, it also has the disastrous effect of exacerbating the spread of AIDS among intravenous drug users. In response to this dilemma, some public health officials, doctors, nurses, social workers, addicts and addicts' advocacy groups have launched education efforts to encourage intravenous drug users to sterilize needles and have begun needle-exchange programs, where IDUs get new needles in exchange for used ones. They have also mounted efforts to encourage heroin addicts to enter methadone maintenance programs and lobbied for laws that would make it legal to obtain hypodermic paraphernalia without a prescription. (See HARM REDUCTION.)

Nembutal   A BARBITURATE sedative containing pentobarbital sodium, Nembutal is a hypnotic and a preanesthetic medication. It is psychoactive and habit-forming and has the potential for abuse. Both psychological and physiological dependency can occur. An overdose can result in circulatory collapse, respiratory depression, diminished reflexes and coma.

Synonyms: nebbies, nemmies, nemish, nimby, nimbies, yellow bullets, yellow dolls, yellow jackets, yellows, and the little yellow death.

Netherlands, The
Alcohol: Alcohol has an important place in the lifestyle of most Dutch citizens. According to one study, 93% of the male population and 82% of the female population in the Netherlands are drinkers. Even more striking is that only 3% of the population recommended abstinence from alcoholic beverages, and that an overwhelming majority approve of drinking for adolescents, who reach the legal age of 16 years. Surprisingly, alcohol abuse, which is declining, is only a minor problem in the Netherlands. More than two-thirds of the nation's total consumption takes place in the home, where familial restrictions are effective controls. Although some consumption of alcohol is widespread, less than one-quarter of the population drinks daily.

Beer is the alcoholic beverage of choice for the vast majority citizens. In 1985 the estimated per capita rate of consumption of ABSOLUTE ALCOHOL in the Netherlands was at 8.3 liters per annum, which dropped to 7.1 liters by 1993. In 1993 the per capita rate for beer consumption was 85.2 liters per annum, compared to 84.3 liters in 1985; for wine, 16 liters, compared to 14.61 liters in 1989; and 1.8 liters of distilled spirits, compared to 1.9 liters in 1987. The 1986 rate of mortality from liver cirrhosis (6.7 males and 4.2 females per 100,000) was a marked drop from 1976, when the rate was 18.4 male and 7.6 female deaths per 100,000. However, the growing abuse of drugs is a matter of great national concern.

Drugs other than alcohol: International trafficking of illicit drugs is on the rise. Because of its centralized location and highly developed transportation and financial infrastructure, this small country is a key transit point for cocaine and heroin destined for locations throughout Europe. A major player in the legitimate international chemical industry, the Netherlands is also a production/export site for illegal amphetamines and synthetic drugs, such as ecstasy. The Dutch government has made combating this illicit drug trade a priority.

In 1974 the Dutch Public Prosecutor eliminated prosecution involving less than 30 grams of cannabis. This gave rise to "coffeehouses," where cannabis products for personal use are sold legally.

Meanwhile, one of the world's most comprehensive HARM REDUCTION programs has been implemented. As a result, the government is able to minimize the risk of the potential harm to the public. The program involves provision of adequate health care to drug addicts, needle-exchange programs and sufficient public assistance to discourage drug-related crime. Authorities stay in contact with about 75% of the country's hard-drug addicts. The government also makes available several treatment alternatives, including methadone maintenance, and sponsors drug education and prevention programs targeted at young people.

Brewers and Licensed Retailers Association, *1993 Annual Report* (London, England: 1995).

Bureau for International Narcotics and Law Enforcement Affairs, *International Narcotic Control Strategy Report March 1996* (Washington, D.C.: 1996).

New Zealand

Alcohol: Alcoholism is recognized as one of New Zealand's major public health problems. The pattern of drinking in New Zealand is one of excessive consumption, usually of beer, in homes and clubs. Fully half the country's alcohol consumption takes place in private residences and facilities that are not liable to normal legislative restrictions. As a result of this heavy alcohol consumption in private places, adolescents have easy access to alcohol. New Zealand's Alcohol Liquor Advisory Council, created in 1976, cites ignorance of the dangers of excessive consumption as an important factor contributing to the country's drinking problems. Government efforts have focused on DEMAND REDUCTION and treatment programs in an effort to reduce the rate of alcohol-related road fatalities (45% of all vehicle-related deaths in 1977) and the high rate of hospital admissions due to alcohol-related emergencies.

Between 1976 and 1985, per capita consumption of ABSOLUTE ALCOHOL rose 27%, to 7.9 liters. By 1993, however, the rate dropped to 7.4 liters annually, or 15th highest among nations worldwide. New Zealanders placed 7th in beer consumption in 1993 (102.5 liters), a drop from 104.8 liters in 1985. Per capita wine consumption came to 16.9 liters per annum (16th worldwide), and spirits consumption to 1.3 liters.

Drugs other than alcohol: Aside from alcohol and tobacco, cannabis is the most widely used drug. Most of it is produced locally, as are most of the other illegal drugs consumed in the country, with the exception of LSD and methamphetamines. Due to its relative isolation, New Zealand is not likely to become a major producing or trafficking country. Heroin abuse is down, principally because the drug is in short supply, although a synthetic known as "homebake" is produced for local consumption. Amphetamine and barbiturate use is fairly widespread and difficult to monitor. Deaths classified as "drug-related" usually involved these two drugs.

In 1977 the New Zealand government established a Caucus Committee to recommend legislative and administrative action to control the misuse of drugs. Laws enacted the following year substantially increased the penalties for drug sales and possession. The maximum penalty for selling drugs is now life imprisonment.

One of the government's most important, though circumscribed powers is the use of listening devices. This power was introduced in 1979 and is invaluable in monitoring the activities of those thought to be trafficking in drugs. In a 12-month period, ending March 1982, successful prosecutions resulted from nearly all wiretap warrants issued. If it had not been for the use of listening devices, officials said several of the biggest drug importers in New Zealand would not have been apprehended.

In the 1990s, all police officers are trained in drug identification and expected to handle drug offenses in the course of their normal duties. Along with stepping up police action, the government is pushing drug education and the field of addiction treatment and rehabilitation.

British Distillers and Licensed Retailers Association, *1993 Annual Report* (London, England: 1995).

Hoeveel alcoholhoude dranken worden er in de wereld gedronken? (How many alcoholic beverages are being consumed throughout the world?) 27th ed. (Schiedam, Netherlands: Produktschap Voor Gedistilleerde Dranken, 1987).

United States Dept. of State, Bureau for International Narcotics and Law Enforcement Affairs, *International Narcotics Control Strategy Report March 1996.*

nicotine   Nicotine is a potent, oily alkaloid found in concentrations of 2%–5% in the tobacco plant *Nicotiana tabacum.* Native to South America, the plant is cultivated throughout the world. Volatilized somewhat by heat, nicotine is inhaled as smoke from cigarettes, cigars and pipes. It also is ingested through chewing and snuffing tobacco. An estimated 45 million Americans use tobacco, in smokable or chewable form, making it the most popular addictive drug in the U.S.

History: Used for centuries by natives of the Americas, nicotine ($C_{11}HV_{14}N_2$) was first encountered by Europeans during the 15th century. It was named in honor of Jean Nicot, who claimed that it had great medicinal potential. Columbus noted that Native Americans "drank the smoke" from dried tobacco leaves, not for medicinal purposes, but rather for the paradoxical stimulant-sedative effects it had on the mind and body. To date no therapeutic or healthful applications of nicotine have been found.

Since colonial times, nicotine has supported a large and prosperous tobacco industry. Despite its ill effects, it was consumed as fast as it could be supplied. One observer in 1662 indicated that "the common people are so given up to the abuse that they imagine they cannot live without several pipes

of tobacco a day—thus squandering in these necessitous times the pennies they need for their daily bread." The use of tobacco was prohibited by the Roman Catholic Church as early as the 17th century, and Russian czars were known to torture smokers. The Sultan of Constantinople imposed the death penalty for smoking in 1633, but "even the fear of death was of no avail with the passionate devotees of the habit."

Before the 20th century most nicotine was ingested by chewing tobacco, smoking pipes and cigars, and inhaling snuff. In the early 1900s, cigarettes became the most popular method of taking nicotine. This popularity came about for several reasons. First, public health warnings stated that chewing tobacco had been shown to cause tuberculosis. Unaware of the high risks of cigarette smoking—irreparable damage to the lungs, heart, blood and nervous system—people switched to smoking instead. Second, the cigarette industry began to use automatic machinery for mass production, which lowered the price of cigarettes. The industry also embarked on extensive advertising campaigns. Third, and probably the foremost reason for the public switch, was the fact that a new "milder" type of Virginia tobacco was used in cigarettes and allowed for deeper inhalation.

As cigarette smoking increased in popularity so did the number of antismoking leagues and campaigns. Several states enacted cigarette prohibition laws and other states passed laws prohibiting the sale of cigarettes to young people. Despite the campaigns and regulations, however, the production of cigarettes increased from 4.2 billion (1900–1909) to 80 billion (1920–1929); by 1970 the figure had jumped to 583 billion.

In 1964 the first Surgeon General's report was issued on the dangerous effects of smoking. Entitled *Report of the Surgeon General's Advisory Committee on Smoking and Health,* it received extensive media coverage and convinced many smokers of the risks they were taking. For a while, cigarette sales dropped. President Johnson signed legislation, effective on January 1, 1966, requiring all cigarette packs and cartons to carry the statement: "Caution: Cigarette smoking may be hazardous to your health." In 1971 cigarette advertising was banned from radio and television. The ban resulted in increased print advertising, and in 1977 the U.S. Department of Agricul-

Preliminary Data—As of June 1998

Estimated Number (in Thousands) of Persons Who Began Daily Cigarette Use
During Each Year 1965–1996, Their Mean Age at First Daily Use, and Annual Age-Specific Rates
of First Daily Use
(per 1000 Person-Years of Exposure), Based on 1994–1997 NHSDAs

Year	Initiates (1000s)	Mean Age	Age-Specific Rate of First Use[1]		
			12–17	18–25	26–34
1965	1606	17.9	44.0	106.2	7.9
1966	1716	17.9	42.6	117.0	6.0
1967	1741	18.7	48.1	100.8	14.8
1968	2268	18.5	49.7	155.2	6.4
1969	2055	18.0	57.1	116.4	18.0
1970	1910	17.3	52.5	101.9	6.5
1971	2175	18.0	58.0	117.9	15.0
1972	2004	17.9	57.7	95.4	25.4
1973	2276	17.9	65.3	106.5	25.6
1974	2403	18.9	66.2	109.2	23.7
1975	1811	18.4	49.4	87.1	14.5
1976	1976	18.1	54.8	93.1	17.6
1977	2284	18.4	66.8	108.0	12.9
1978	1984	18.3	59.6	88.1	14.4
1979	1955	19.0	54.7	92.5	16.7
1980	1704	18.7	51.6	81.7	10.5
1981	1757	19.1	56.4	73.3	14.1
1982	1586	18.7	49.2	73.3	11.9
1983	1527	18.3	43.8	73.9	13.3
1984	1547	18.4	52.3	65.4	11.1
1985	1497	18.7	50.2	66.2	10.8
1986	1561	18.0	56.7	69.5	10.0
1987	1482	18.4	51.8	68.0	10.4

(continued on next page)

Preliminary Data—As of June 1998 (continued)

Estimated Number (in Thousands) of Persons Who Began Daily Cigarette Use
During Each Year 1965–1996, Their Mean Age at First Daily Use, and Annual Age-Specific Rates
of First Daily Use
(per 1000 Person-Years of Exposure), Based on 1994–1997 NHSDAs

Year	Initiates (1000s)	Mean Age	Age-Specific Rate of First Use[1]		
			12–17	18–25	26–34
1988	1384	18.5	51.2	60.8	11.4
1989	1436	18.7	53.8	61.4	7.1
1990	1503	18.3	57.8	63.6	13.9
1991	1464	18.1	57.6	58.0	13.3
1992	1651	18.2	61.9	69.1	11.9
1993	1578	18.8	58.7	60.0	12.6
1994[2]	1747	17.9	67.7	68.9	10.4
1995[3]	1797	17.8	71.8	62.3	11.3
1996[4]	1851	17.3	77.8	68.4	7.5

[1] The numerator of each rate equals the number of persons who first used the drug in the year (times 1000). The denominator of each rate equals the number of persons who were exposed to risk of first use during the year, weighted by their estimated exposure time measured in years. For example, for the age group 12–17 in 1990, the denominator is the sum of three components:

(1) those persons 12–17 years old in 1990 who first used the drug in 1989 or earlier, times a weight of zero. The weight is zero since they had zero exposure to the risk of first use in 1990.

(2) those who first used the drug in 1990 times a weight of .5. The weight of .5 assumes that these people, on average, first used the drug at midyear and consequently have a half year of exposure (i.e. the first half of the year.)

(3) those who never used, or those who first used the drug in 1991 or later, times a weight of one. The weight of one assumes their exposure to the risk of first use during 1990 was for the whole year.

Each person is also weighted by his/her sample weight.

[2] Estimated using 1995, 1996 and 1997 data only.

[3] Estimated using 1996 and 1997 data only.

[4] Estimated using 1997 data only.

Source: SAMHSA, Office of Applied Studies, National Household Survey on Drug Abuse, 1994–1997.

ture reported that cigarette companies had spent $779 million in that year alone on promotion and advertising, and cigarette production is now one of the world's wealthiest industries.

In early 1989 then U.S. surgeon general C. Everett Koop issued a federal report that set the number of deaths attributed to smoking in 1985 at 390,000. Smoking, the report said, was a major cause of stroke

Preliminary Data—As of June 1998

Estimated Number (in Thousands) of Persons Who First Used a Cigarette
During Each Year 1965–1996, Their Mean Age at First Use, and Annual Age-Specific Rates of First Use
(per 1000 Person-Years of Exposure), Based on 1994–1997 NHSDAs

Year	Initiates (1000s)	Mean Age	Age-Specific Rate of First Use[1]		
			12–17	18–25	26–34
1965	2974	16.0	101.3	112.9	19.8
1966	2843	16.2	88.3	125.4	13.8
1967	3229	15.6	112.9	114.6	9.5
1968	3166	15.4	101.6	114.6	16.8
1969	3362	15.5	111.0	122.3	8.3
1970	3574	15.7	113.7	112.9	21.0
1971	3472	15.2	119.3	102.1	9.4
1972	3794	15.3	129.6	107.9	22.4
1973	3395	15.5	114.8	87.2	16.8
1974	3708	15.0	132.2	84.3	7.9
1975	3650	15.2	125.0	95.7	7.3
1976	3492	15.5	124.8	87.6	9.8
1977	3428	15.7	126.9	87.8	14.6
1978	3031	15.6	112.0	72.7	8.4
1979	2997	15.7	111.0	83.8	9.7
1980	2753	15.6	105.1	70.0	6.5
1981	2735	15.6	107.0	66.7	7.0
1982	2750	15.5	102.4	67.2	11.2
1983	2739	15.1	106.0	64.5	4.5
1984	2679	15.5	99.4	71.1	7.7
1985	2816	15.5	111.3	69.4	7.8
1986	2782	15.5	107.0	77.2	5.4
1987	2566	16.1	98.6	66.1	12.6

(continued on next page)

Preliminary Data—As of June 1998 (continued)

Estimated Number (in Thousands) of Persons Who First Used a Cigarette
During Each Year 1965–1996, Their Mean Age at First Use, and Annual Age-Specific Rates of First Use
(per 1000 Person-Years of Exposure), Based on 1994–1997 NHSDAs

Year	Initiates (1000s)	Mean Age	Age-Specific Rate of First Use[1]		
			12–17	18–25	26–34
1988	2484	15.3	107.0	58.6	7.1
1989	2503	16.3	99.5	60.9	8.5
1990	2645	15.5	101.6	71.3	7.9
1991	2567	16.0	100.5	66.4	11.1
1992	2707	15.7	115.0	64.7	9.2
1993[2]	2897	16.1	121.4	70.1	6.7
1994[3]	3178	16.0	131.0	82.0	4.6
1995[4]	3263	15.6	139.1	85.8	7.6

[1] The numerator of each rate equals the number of persons who first used the drug in the year (times 1000). The denominator of each rate equals the number of persons who were exposed to risk of first use during the year, weighted by their estimated exposure time measured in years. For example, for the age group 12–17 in 1990, the denominator is the sum of three components:

(1) those persons 12–17 years old in 1990 who first used the drug in 1989 or earlier, times a weight of zero. The weight is zero since they had zero exposure to the risk of first use in 1990.

(2) those who first used the drug in 1990 times a weight of .5. The weight of .5 assumes that these people, on average, first used the drug at midyear and consequently have a half year of exposure (i.e. the first half of the year.)

(3) those who never used, or those who first used the drug in 1991 or later, times a weight of one. The weight of one assumes their exposure to the risk of first use during 1990 was for the whole year.

Each person is also weighted by his/her sample weight.

[2] Estimated using 1995, 1996 and 1997 data only.

[3] Estimated using 1996 and 1997 data only.

[4] Estimated using 1997 data only.

Source: SAMHSA, Office of Applied Studies, National Household Survey on Drug Abuse, 1994–1997.

and the third leading cause of death in the U.S. An estimated 50 million Americans continued to smoke. By mid-1988, more than 320 local communities adopted laws or regulations restricting smoking. New state laws enacted in 1987 to restrict smoking in public places exceeded the number of tobacco-control rulings passed in any preceding year. Two major differences between the 1964 report and Dr. Koop's 1989 report were that in the first report there was no mention of the hazards of inhaling smoke from others' cigarettes (passive smoking), nor of the fact that smoking was conclusively a cause of heart disease.

In 1996 the Clinton Administration issued an Executive Order that would put the regulation of tobacco under the Food and Drug Administration (FDA). The FDA had, in turn, claimed authority over cigarettes by defining them as a delivery system for addictive drugs. As a result, the FDA proposed that the purchase of cigarettes require a photo I.D. confirming proof of age, that tobacco ads be limited to black-and-white text with no photos, and that they be allowed only in magazines not read by significant numbers of teenagers. Also, the same regulations would be applied to billboards, which would be banned within 1,000 feet of schools or playgrounds. Additionally, sporting events could not be sponsored by tobacco companies, and cigarette logos and other advertising would be banned from T-shirts, hats, athletic bags and other sports paraphernalia.

There was an increase in the 1990s in the manufacture of filter and low-tar, low-nicotine cigarettes in response to increasing public concern for the health risks of nicotine. Brands of cigarettes now on the market have tar and nicotine yields ranging from 1 mg to 20 mg. Although low-tar and nicotine cigarettes may be safer, there is no such thing as a "safe" cigarette. Because of the smaller amount of nicotine, according to some, people may become less dependent and eventually stop smoking altogether. Others argue that smokers will find them less satisfying and simply smoke more of them, which will make the health risk even greater.

Appearance: Pure nicotine is colorless and has a strong odor and acrid taste. It is highly poisonous and, when dissolved in water, has been used as a potent insecticide.

Classification: Nicotine is both a transient STIMULANT and a sedative to the central nervous system and to both voluntary and involuntary muscle systems.

Usage: Studies have shown that smokers are more likely to use other drugs, particularly alcohol and marijuana. This is especially disturbing in the light of teenage smoking statistics. Millions of teenagers smoke, and it is thought that peer pressure, the "kick" of risk-taking and parental use of cigarettes

are the main reasons why they begin. School and government-funded antismoking programs have had mixed success in reducing the number of teenage smokers.

The campaign against smoking has tended to minimize both the popularity and the health and sanitation risks of using tobacco in its chewable form. Professional baseball players can be seen partaking generously during televised baseball games, providing millions of dollars of free advertising for so-called smokeless tobacco during the six-month baseball season.

Smoking among women increased dramatically during World War II, when women began "doing men's work." It is estimated that slightly under 30% of the adult women in the U.S. are smokers. While the number of male smokers has dropped sharply over the last 20 years, there has been no similar decline for women. The number of teenage girls who smoke is larger than the number of teenage boys.

Dosage: Pure nicotine is highly poisonous, and only a drop or two (about 50 mg) on the tongue can kill a person within minutes. Ingesting a cigarette or cigar whole may well prove lethal or, at the least, produce serious physical and mental reactions. There are approximately 15–20 mg of nicotine in a typical cigarette (although some of the newer low-nicotine brands contain as little as 0.5), but usually less than 1 mg reaches the bloodstream. The amount can vary according to how frequently the smoker inhales, whether or not the cigarette is filtered, the type of filter and so on.

Activity: Nicotine taken in smoke takes only 60 seconds to reach the brain, but has a direct effect on the body for up to 30 minutes. For this reason, smokers who are dependent on nicotine—and virtually all regular smokers are—generally find that they need at least one cigarette every half hour. This can add up to about a pack and a half per day. The ingestion of nicotine results in a transient stimulation or "kick," because it causes a discharge of epinephrine from the adrenal cortex. This stimulates the central nervous system, as well as other endocrine glands, causing a sudden release of glucose ("blood sugar"). Stimulation is followed by depression and fatigue, leading the user to seek more nicotine to restimulate the adrenals. Meanwhile, stress causes a rise in the acidity level of urine, thus enhancing the elimination rate of nicotine and the further need for more. Many people cannot break this vicious cycle and become further depressed. Perhaps the most devastating social effect of nicotine is that it leaves its countless addicts feeling guilty and/or powerless.

Effects: It is difficult to discern the exact effects of nicotine, since it is taken in combination with many other substances found in tobacco. Cigarette smoke is mainly comprised of a dozen gases (particularly carbon monoxide) and the particulate matter, nicotine and tar. The tar in a cigarette (approximately 15 mg, though as little as half this amount is found in low-tar brands) disposes the user to a high expectancy rate of lung cancer, emphysema and bronchial disorders. The carbon monoxide in the smoke increases the chances of being vulnerable to cardiovascular diseases. In any case, nicotine plays a significant role in many serious diseases, most of which have high fatality rates. Bronchial and cardiovascular disorders are increased by the effects that nicotine has on bronchial and heart muscles and the arteries. Chronic bronchitis and emphysema are particularly common among smokers. Nine-tenths of those who suffer Buerger's disease are smokers: this affliction involves the progressive constriction of the vascular system, particularly in the legs. By impeding blood circulation, it eventually leads to arterial occlusions. These cause gangrenous conditions that often lead to amputation. For much the same reason, users of nicotine have at least a 70% greater chance of suffering from coronary and cerebral occlusions, which manifest as heart attacks and strokes.

The risk of congestive heart failure also is increased by the effects of nicotine. Coronary and cerebral thromboses (blood clots in the blood vessels of the heart or brain) and emboli (dislodged particles that break off from a main clot and travel through the vascular system) also are precipitated indirectly by nicotine, since the vasoconstriction increases the possibility of blood-flow interference. Bronchial and pulmonary dysfunction are caused partly by the displacement of oxygen by the carbon monoxide in cigarette smoke (especially in the case of emphysema) and by the irritant effect of the tars.

The most specific and serious of all long-term effects of smoking is lung cancer, which proves to be fatal in more than 90% of cases. Relatively rare in the early 1900s, today lung cancer is a leading cause of death from cancer. An average male smoker runs a 10 times greater risk of death from lung cancer than a nonsmoker; women smokers run a 5 times greater risk. The tar in a cigarette contains many constituents known to cause cancer. The hairlike cilia on the membranes of the lungs (which work to keep the lungs clean) can become damaged or paralyzed by the tar, and when the cilia are not working properly the lungs become vulnerable to pneumonia and chronic obstructive pulmonary disease. Cancer of the esophagus, mouth, lips and larynx also are associated with cigarette smoking.

Nicotine has many deleterious effects on pregnant women and lactating mothers. Women who smoke run two times the risk of having a stillborn infant. Most babies born of women smokers are smaller than normal and frequently premature. There are indications that babies born to parents who smoke have a greater risk for sudden infant death syndrome (SIDS). Babies sometimes suffer overt signs of nicotine addiction and withdrawal and are often afflicted with mental and physical impairments. Miscarriages are much more likely among smokers, and congenital heart defects (those occurring at birth) are more likely if the father smokes. In addition, women who smoke generally have earlier menopause and, if they also take oral contraceptives, are even more prone to cardiovascular and cerebrovascular diseases (this is especially true for women over 30). Lactating mothers excrete nicotine directly through breast milk, and pregnant women transport it through their blood supply to the fetus.

Besides the many serious long-term effects of nicotine, there are also less severe short-term effects. They include sweating, vomiting, throat irritation and others that typically lead to more serious conditions: increased heart rate and blood pressure, leading to myocardial dysfunctions and arteriosclerosis; a drop in skin temperature accompanied by increased respiration, which may cause chronic hyperventilation; and dimness or blurring of vision culminating in blindness, a condition known as Tobacco Amblyopia.

Cigar and pipe smoking do not have as great an effect on health as cigarette smoking, probably because the smoke is usually not inhaled. Pipe and cigar smokers do run a greater risk of cancer of the oral cavity, however, and lip cancer is increased by pipe smoking.

Effects on nonsmokers: Research studies indicate that the health of nonsmokers can be affected by the toxic substances, particularly carbon monoxide, that are released in the air around them by smokers. Nonsmokers also are subject to headaches, as well as eye, nose and throat irritation from cigarette smoke. In many parts of the U.S. recent legislation and regulations now restrict smoking to certain areas or prohibit it altogether.

Tolerance and dependence: The body rapidly develops tolerance to the short-term effects of nicotine, thus making it more likely that the habit will take hold. Increased and more frequent dosages, taken in order to satisfy the craving for nicotine, are also quickly adapted to.

Addictive aspects: It is physically and psychologically addictive and some studies indicate that it is even more addictive than heroin. Casual use of even small amounts of nicotine (three or four cigarettes, for example) can develop into a definite physical and psychological dependence on the drug in just a matter of days. The dependence increases until it reaches a fairly stable level, at which the user stays for many years, often for the rest of his or her life. At least 75% of smokers attempt to overcome their addiction. Interruption of nicotine use leads to a WITHDRAWAL syndrome, featuring irritability, depression and preoccupation with the thought of smoking. It generally takes a full year to break the habit. Fatigue, dizziness, headache and shortness of breath are physical characteristics of withdrawal, which usually subside rapidly. Because smoking sometimes is used as a tranquilizer during periods of stress, or as a pleasure enhancer after meals, during coffee breaks and in such social situations as parties, the psychological difficulties involved in withdrawal (quitting) can be far worse than the physical difficulties.

Treatment: To help people break their dependency on the drug, a number of nicotine "congeners" (chemically similar substances) have been developed to displace it. Lobeline is the most common of these. It is used in Nikoban and marketed as an aid to breaking the habit, but is thought by many to be little more than a placebo. Nicotine chewing gums and pills have also been employed in this way, but usually they give the user as much nicotine as he gets

from smoking and hence have little effect on breaking the nicotine habit unless used in a programmed, tapering-dose regimen.

Smoking-withdrawal clinics and support groups have become particularly popular in the last 15 or 20 years, although the majority of people who stop smoking still tend to do it on their own without outside help. The National Clearinghouse for Smoking and Health reports that from 1966 to 1970 the number of ex-cigarette smokers in the adult population rose by 10 million; from 19 million in 1966 to 29 million in 1970. Nearly half of all living adults who ever smoked have quit, according to Dr. Koop's 1989 report. Smoking has been reduced from 40% of adults in 1965 to 29% in 1987.

Nigeria

Alcohol: The most populous country in Africa, Nigeria in the late 1980s experienced a period of relative economic boom from oil and natural gas production. Newfound prosperity, however, brought with it an increase in the manufacture and consumption of alcoholic beverages, particularly beer. This increase compounded the well-established permissive attitude of Nigerians toward alcohol and resulted in a rise in consumption. Drinking and even drunkenness generally are tolerated, and both social and family gatherings are now considered incomplete without alcohol. Even representatives of the older tribal society, such as the traditional "healers," are commonly incorporating alcohol drinking into their functions. The general pattern is one of heavy consumption, with the unusual feature of virtually indistinguishable drinking habits among both adolescents and adults. Consumption is high during traditional festivals and nontraditional holidays, with the heaviest consumption of all among skilled laborers and factory workers occurring on nontraditional occasions. This rising use of alcoholic beverages has completely outpaced governmental efforts and mechanisms to control it.

The preferred alcoholic beverage in Nigeria is beer, including various kinds of stout. There are no prohibitions on home brewing and distilling in Nigeria, and enormous quantities of palm wine are fermented from local trees. This beverage is also distilled into native gin in large quantities. Thus, availability of alcoholic beverages is so widespread that it is difficult to measure precisely.

The Nigerian government has acknowledged alcoholism as a major medical problem, but the country has no method of documenting its extent. Limited hospital facilities and a general reluctance to contact those that exist render statistics on alcohol-related clinical admissions completely inadequate. Similarly, the country maintains poor police records on traffic fatalities and incidents of alcohol-related public disorder. Most sources, however, agree on the widespread and increasing prevalence of alcoholic psychosis, DELIRIUM TREMENS and gastric and malnutrition problems resulting from alcohol use.

Despite its acknowledgment as a medical problem in Nigeria, alcoholism has been given a low priority because of the country's other pressing problems.

Drugs other than alcohol: According to a 1996 report, Nigeria is the focal point for most West African drug trafficking: heroin to the U.S. and Europe; cocaine from South America, destined for Nigeria, South Africa and Europe; and Nigerian-grown cannabis to Europe and other West Africa countries. Nigerian traffickers are among the leading carriers of heroin from Southeast and Southwest Asia into the U.S. In 1995 INTERPOL (The International Criminal Police Organiztions) listed Nigerian couriers as the third-largest heroin smuggling network in the world.

As a result of Nigeria's growth as a trafficking center, the country is experiencing a rise in domestic drug use. The government appears to have been caught unaware and, as of 1995, had not yet implemented any significant demand reduction program.

United States Dept. of State, Bureau for International Narcotics and Law Enforcement Affairs, *International Narcotics Control Strategy Report March 1996.*

niopo   Pods from the plant *Acacia niopo,* which grows in Venezuela. They are ground up and used as a snuff that produces psychedelic effects.

nitrous oxide   (N2O) A general anesthetic normally used in dentistry. It is also called nitrogen oxide and is commonly called "laughing gas." When supplemented with other agents it is used for surgical anesthesia. It had been previously used as a propellant for canned whipped toppings but has been discontinued due to abuse for its euphoric effects (which sometimes include mild hallucinations). Sustained inhalation of nitrous oxide without adequate oxygen can result in anoxia (arrested respiration) and death.

noctec   A sedative hypnotic that contains CHLORAL HYDRATE and is used for nocturnal sedation and as a pre- and postoperative medication. It may be habit-forming, and when taken with alcohol or other central nervous system depressants, it can have an ADDITIVE EFFECT.

noludar   A sedative hypnotic that contains METHYPRYLON and is used for insomnia. Physical and psychological dependence can occur, and it has the potential for abuse. When taken with alcohol or other central nervous system depressants, it can have an additive effect. Overdosage can result in somnolence, respiratory depression, confusion and coma. Not available in the U.S.

nonaddictive abuser   A person who on occasion misuses or overuses alcohol or other drugs but generally does not lose control or become compulsive.

nonaddictive pathological drinker   Someone who drinks excessively as a way of handling problems. Although probably in some way impaired by this drinking, the individual still does not have the overwhelming need, compulsion or LOSS OF CONTROL characteristic of alcohol ADDICTION.

norepinephrine   Derived from dopamine and stored in nerve terminals in the brain, norepinephrine acts at adrenergic receptors in the sympathetic division of the autonomic nervous system, in the brain, heart and at other target organs throughout the body. A deficiency of norepinephrine is hypothesized to underlie depression, although other neurotransmitters likely play a role as well. Of medications used to treat depression, tricyclic and heterocyclic compounds, stimulants and monoamine oxidase (MAO) inhibitors all act to increase norepinephrine levels in the brain. Amphetamines and cocaine block reuptake and cause increased release of norepinephrine and dopamine into intercellular spaces, resulting in elevated mood. Prolonged use of these substances, however, results in depletion of norepinephrine stores.

North Conway Institute (NCI) Founded in 1951 by a group of clergy and lay persons, the institute is an outgrowth of the Yale University School of Alcohol Studies. It is an interfaith, ecumenical, not-for-profit organization, governed by a board of church people. It works as a catalyst with religious and secular organizations in all areas of alcohol and drug problems. In addition to holding an annual seminar, NCI serves as a resource center.

Norway

Alcohol: As reported by the British Distillers, the country's annual per capita consumption of ABSOLUTE ALCOHOL in 1995 equaled 4.1 liters annually, a relatively low rate compared to other countries. Beer consumption accounts for most of alcohol consumption, with a per capita rate of 49 liters annually as of 1994. Norway ranks near the bottom among reporting countries for consumption of wine and spirits.

Norway has one of the most stringent approaches to drunk driving in the world. Police conduct spot tests on motorists, and drivers have come to expect them about once a month. Any driver found with a BLOOD ALCOHOL CONCENTRATION of 0.05% or more is required to serve a minimum prison sentence of three weeks. In addition, a judge may extend the sentence and impose a fine at his discretion; in certain cases the judge may substitute a fine for the prison term. Any person convicted of drunk driving will have his license suspended for at least a year and sometimes permanently. About 7,000 Norwegians serve time in prison each year for drunk driving.

Insurance regulations in Norway penalize drunk driving too. If a person causes an accident while drunk, he receives no compensation. Furthermore no insurance is paid to his estate if the accident is fatal.

Norway's severe penalties for drunk driving have been effective in curtailing accidents and discouraging people from driving under the influence of alcohol. However, arrests for drunk driving began to rise gradually in the first half of the 1980s, perhaps reflecting the increase in the number of cars in operation.

The Norwegian government was one of the first countries to implement stringent limits on advertising as a way of controlling a rise in alcohol consumption. In 1975 the Storting (Parliament) passed a bill banning the advertising of alcoholic beverages in the print media. In 1980 the Norwegian government proposed over 30 measures to reduce the consumption of alcohol by providing information, altering licensing and pricing policies, and creating a greater awareness of the alcohol problem. The measures proposed included a ban on wine-making in the home, a complete ban on strong beers (5.5% alcohol content), a lowering of the alcohol content in mild beers (from 4.7% to 3.5%) and stricter control of all these areas by police, customs officers and licensing authorities.

Alcoholism treatment: Cases involving alcohol abuse are handled by Temperance Committees. Under the Act concerning Temperance Committees and the Treatment of Alcohol Addicts passed in 1932, a Temperance Committee was set up in almost every municipality. In municipalities where there is no temperance committee, a Social Welfare Board serves the same purpose.

The Temperance Committees have four main functions: 1) to take care of persons who abuse alcohol and making decisions (as necessary) about their possible committal to hospitals or sanatoria; 2) to give advice and assistance to the families of alcohol abusers; 3) to promote education and information concerning the use and abuse of alcohol in schools and other areas of life; and 4) to submit proposals and recommendations to municipal authorities for implementing committee programs.

With respect to the individual alcohol user, a Temperance Committee may act either at the request of someone functioning on behalf of the user or on its own initiative. Courses of action open to Temperance Committees are counseling, ANTABUSE treatment, selection of a person to support a discharged alcoholic patient, suggestion that an alcoholic join a temperance society and imposition of restrictions on the way an alcoholic spends his wages.

The bureau's statistical report lists the following types of institutions where treatment may be obtained:

Detoxification stations
Sections for medical treatment
A-clinics
Sanatoria
Supervision homes
Protection homes
Psychiatric clinics and hospitals

These institutions may be owned either by the central government or by private concerns licensed by the government.

A-clinics are generally run by private organizations. Patients are admitted on the same basis as in ordinary hospitals. These A-clinics are financed according to the regulations of the Hospital Act. Many patients discharged from sanatoria and A-clinics are placed in supervision homes. In such homes patients live and receive treatment while working. Supervision homes that are connected with A-clinics are also financed under the Hospital Act. Those that are not attached to A-clinics are financed in part by the National Insurance Fund and in part by either a municipality, if it referred the patient, or by the patient himself. Protection homes are for those patients who have been judged not capable of being rehabilitated to working life. The financing of these homes is somewhat similar to that of the supervision homes that are not attached to A-clinics.

Drugs other than alcohol: Although Norway has one of the most stringent approaches to alcohol consumption (and drunk driving) in the world, the government's attitude toward the abuse of other drugs has not changed in recent years, even though there has been an increase in use. According to the government, existing programs will be continued and general preventive measures will be taken but no new treatment programs will be implemented. This is because the government looks upon the drug-use problem as a symptom of personal, family and social problems.

Up to 1940, drug dependence was not considered a problem in Norway. During the 1940s there was an increase in the use of tranquilizers, particularly in the middle and older age groups. By 1965, use of drugs had spread to younger people and the favorite substance usually was marijuana or hashish. Abuse of tranquilizers continued, and amphetamines began to make their appearance.

Illicit trade in drugs was not always an issue in Norway. Up until 1976, the government reported no problems with heroin, although methadone and some morphine-based drugs had gained in popularity. Doctors were specifically warned not to prescribe methadone. According to the Bureau for International Narcotics and Law Enforcement Affairs, drug use has become a serious problem in Norway. During 1995 the price of heroin dropped, demand increased, drug-related deaths rose and schools reported an alarming rise in drug use among students. The greatest increase occurred among teens aged 16–20. Officials also noted an increasing popularity of the use of hashish, amphetamines, LSD and cocaine, as well as designer drugs such as ecstasy (MDMA).

Narcotics production is rare in Norway, but the first half of the 1990s witnessed an increase in drugs transiting Norway via the Balkan route. Routes have changed as a result of the conflict in the former Yugoslavia. Instead of using the Near East route via Greece-Yugoslavia-Germany-Scandinavia, traffickers bring drugs into Scandinavia via air and water from the Near East via Turkey, the Czech Republic, Slovakia, Poland and Germany. The increase in drug trafficking in Norway has produced an increase in drug-related violence, primarily targeted at police agents and their families.

Substance abuse treatment: Addicts with complex and serious addiction problems receive treatment in mental health institutions. But because the government believes that drug dependency is not an illness but a symptom of personal or social problems, a generally accepted treatment model for drug dependency does not exist. Instead, the problem is approached from the standpoint of prevention. Along with educational programs, the government believes in implementing programs that help the youth of the country channel its energies in new directions.

Developments since 1975 have included the establishment of therapeutic communities modeled after Daytop and Phoenix House in the U.S. Regional contact groups have been set up in various counties to establish contact between country doctors, schools, social services, and the police and prison systems in an effort to coordinate information and help on drug-use questions. Tighter pharmaceutical control also has been implemented, and these recent controls may be an indication that dependency on drugs other than alcohol is being acknowledged as a specific problem in need of special attention.

Brewers and Licensed Retailers Association, *1993 Annual Report* (London, England).

Hoeveel alcoholhoude dranken worden er in de wereld gedronken? (How many alcoholic beverages are being consumed throughout the world?) 27th ed. (Schiedam, Netherlands: Produktschap Voor Gedistilleerde Dranken, 1987).

United States Dept. of State, Bureau for International Narcotics and Law Enforcement Affairs, *International Narcotics Control Strategy Report March 1996.*

noscapine   An opium alkaloid used as a cough suppressant in cough medicines. It is a Schedule IV drug under the CONTROLLED SUBSTANCES ACT.

nubain   A synthetic NARCOTIC agonist-antagonist analgesic that is chemically related both to OXYMORPHONE HYDROCHLORIDE and NALOXONE. A potent analgesic, it is used for the relief of moderate to severe pain, as a preoperative analgesic and as a supplement to surgical anesthesia. Nubain contains nalbuphine hydrochloride and caution should be used in prescribing it to a person with a history of narcotic abuse because psychological and physical dependence, along with tolerance, can develop. Nubain is supplied in ampules for injection. If it is administered intravenously, onset of effects occurs in two to three minutes; onset time is less than 15 minutes if administered intramuscularly or subcutaneously. Analgesic activity ranges from three to six hours.

numorphan   A potent analgesic that contains the opium derivative OXYMORPHONE HYDROCHLORIDE and is similar to morphine in its effect. It may be habit-forming and physical dependence can occur. It is listed as a Schedule II drug under the CONTROLLED SUBSTANCES ACT.

nursing mothers   In 1989 Harold Kaminetzky of the American College of Obstetricians and Gynecologists reported findings indicating that nursing mothers who regularly drink moderate amounts of alcohol (one drink a day) may put their babies at a slight risk, delaying development of motor skills. His research, reported in the *New England Journal of Medicine,* followed 400 infants and correlated alcohol use during breast-feeding with scores on a psychomotor test and a mental developmental test given to the infants when they were about 12 months old. Dr. Kaminetzky noted that moderate drinking appears to be more significant than an occasional "binge" of four or five drinks. In an unrelated study, a team of researchers at the University of Michigan found infants exposed to at least one drink a day scored five points lower on the motor test than

infants exposed to less alcohol, but demonstrated no differences in mental development. The Michigan team concluded that larger tests are needed to see if there exists a consistent pattern related to alcohol.

Nursing mothers, intravenous drug use and HIV: While the research remains unclear about the risks to infants from nursing mothers who drink alcohol, there is considerable evidence that HIV can be transmitted to infants through the breast milk of infected mothers. AIDS (ACQUIRED IMMUNE DEFICIENCY SYNDROME) prevention efforts are now targeting new mothers and women of child-bearing age who are themselves IDUs (intravenous drug users) or have unprotected sex with IDU partners.

nutmeg   The dried seed of *Myristica fragrans,* an evergreen tree indigenous to East India. MACE, its seed coat, has similar properties. Both are common cooking spices as well as HALLUCINOGENS. The two hallucinogenic substances in both nutmeg and mace are elemicin and myristicin, which are closely related to MESCALINE and TMA.

Usage: Because of their unpleasant side effects, nutmeg and mace have limited popularity. They are used chiefly by prison inmates who have little access to other drugs and by teenagers as substitutes for illegal drugs.

In their powdered forms the substances may be brewed into a tea and then drunk or added to a hot beverage such as hot chocolate. Some users add them to orange juice or to mashed potatoes.

Dosage: A normal dose is one to two tablespoons, or about 10 grams. Occasionally these substances are snorted but they are poorly absorbed when used this way and can be irritating and mildly painful. They also can be obtained in an oil form, which is nearly unpalatable.

Effects: Commonly, nutmeg and mace produce a euphoric or intoxicating effect not unlike a mescaline high, in conjunction with unpleasant physical effects such as nausea and dizziness. In high doses—over 20 grams—the substances can produce more intense effects, ranging from strong visual hallucinations to feelings of fear, anxiety and sometimes acute panic. Physical reactions intensify with higher doses. Vomiting, rapid heartbeat, excessive thirst, bloodshot eyes, temporary constipation and difficulty in urinating are all typical. Physical reactions may begin within 45 minutes after ingestion; psychological effects usually occur after one to two hours. The effects generally last two to four hours and then begin to subside, although the user may experience residual effects for up to 24 hours.

Sources: Nutmeg and mace are common grocery store items and are found on the spice shelves of most households and eating establishments.

Trafficking: No laws regulate the sale of these substances.

nutrition   Nutrition plays a role in many aspects of the abuse and treatment of alcohol and other drugs.

Alcohol: Unlike other drugs, alcohol has a high caloric value. A gram of alcohol provides 7.1 calories, compared with 4 calories provided by a gram of carbohydrates and 9 calories provided by a gram of fat. Twenty ounces, slightly more than one pint, of an 86-proof beverage contains about 1,500 calories, or from one-half to two-thirds of a person's normal daily caloric requirement. While a small dose of alcohol may stimulate the appetite, a larger intake often diminishes appetite. Alcoholics are likely to devote more time and energy to drinking than eating. Alcohol not only contains no protein, vitamins or minerals, but interferes with the body's ability to metabolize those that it does ingest from other sources. As a result, a person who consumes large quantities of alcohol is likely to receive insufficient amounts of essential nutrients. The calories in alcohol may provide energy but cannot be stored for future use. They also do not aid in building body tissue, as do carbohydrates, fats and proteins. As a result, alcoholics often suffer from primary malnutrition in addition to the directly damaging effects of alcohol itself. Individuals who consume larger quantities of nutritionally empty alcohol calories than their bodies can use will, in fact, gain weight, but in fatty, flaccid deposits around the abdomen (beer bellies).

Heavy consumption of alcohol causes inflammation of the stomach, pancreas and intestine, which can impair the digestion of food and the absorption of nutrients into the blood, resulting in secondary malnutrition. Alcohol inhibits the transport of nutri-

ents to the GASTROINTESTINAL TRACT and adversely affects nutrient absorption even when a balanced diet is maintained. Alcoholics exhibit poor absorption of a number of essential nutrients, including vitamins B_{11} and B_{12}. Malnutrition can in turn cause a sluggish intestine.

Alcohol also may interfere with the activation of vitamins by the liver cells, often resulting in deficiency diseases. VITAMIN AND MINERAL deficiencies, such as zinc or thiamine deficiency, common in alcoholics, may contribute to a decreased desire for food. Malnutrition can play a role in the LIVER damage associated with alcoholism, although a heavy drinker who is well nourished can also develop ALCOHOLIC LIVER DISEASE. A low-fat diet, however, may have some effect in the prevention of a FATTY LIVER. A study conducted by Charles S. Leiber and N. Spritz showed that for a given alcohol intake there was more abnormal fat formation on the liver with a diet of normal fat content than with a diet low in fat. There is some evidence that the development of CANCER may also be influenced by the direct consequences of alcoholism resulting from malnutrition. Deficiencies of various vitamins and minerals associated with alcoholism may play a role in carcinogenesis.

Some researchers have theorized that vitamin deficiencies play a role in the initial development of alcoholism. So far, however, there is little proof of this theory, and most nutritional deficiencies in alcoholics appear to be a result of the disease rather than the cause.

Nutrition also plays an important role in the rate that alcohol is absorbed into the body tissues and blood. (See BLOOD ALCOHOL CONCENTRATION.) Two factors are involved: the quantity and the type of food in the stomach. Alcohol is absorbed rapidly from an empty stomach and more slowly from a full stomach. A high-carbohydrate meal has been shown to reduce alcohol absorption more than a high-fat or high-protein meal. In addition, different alcoholic beverages are absorbed at different rates, perhaps because of ingredients other than alcohol.

In the treatment of alcoholism, nutrition plays an important role. For treatment of cirrhosis and other liver diseases, a high-protein diet and massive amounts of B vitamins are prescribed. Regularly scheduled meals, especially breakfast, are important for an alcoholic, because the lowering of blood sugar at any time of day increases the desire for alcohol. An alcoholic who is properly nourished may find it easier to abstain from alcohol, although good nutrition in itself is not a cure for alcoholism. Drinkers often fail to account for the high caloric value of all alcoholic beverages. Although beer and wine contain some carbohydrates and vitamins, distilled spirits have none.

Drugs other than alcohol: Nutritional deficiencies often accompany prolonged use of drugs. Drugs may decrease the appetite; change the sense of smell and taste; and alter metabolic processes, resulting in hindered absorption, hastened excretion and impaired use and storage of nutrients.

Addicts in drug-induced states are often disinterested in food, and when funds are limited, an alcoholic or addict generally will use money for alcohol and/or drugs rather than food. The neglect of good eating habits also is a consequence of the disorganized lives addicts lead, and street addicts often experience large weight loss. Drugs do not contain vitamins or minerals, so replacing food intake with drugs will obviously cause problems.

The use of marijuana often brings on periods of increased appetite; the same is true of morphine early in the addictive process. The foods craved, however, are usually high in carbohydrates and low in nutrition ("junk" foods such as soda, candy and other sweets). These foods are often picked for their convenience and low cost.

Some drugs actually are taken to depress the appetite. When taken in large doses, ANORECTICS, particularly cocaine and amphetamines, can lead to ketosis—the process in which a low carbohydrate diet causes the body's fat stores to be broken down for energy faster than they can be used by the body. Body protein can eventually waste away during prolonged and heavy amphetamine or cocaine use.

Barbiturate users experience a decrease in the absorption of thiamine and an increase in urinary ascorbic acid. Barbiturate and heroin users also have low serum B vitamin levels. A bad diet, especially insufficient consumption of leafy green vegetables, can cause low folate (folic acid) levels, further complicating their B-complex deficiencies. Heroin users frequently suffer from acute and chronic infections, which can alter their nutritional needs. Hepatitis, a common occurrence among heroin users, can cause decreased appetite and nausea.

Some drugs, however, will increase appetite and result in weight gain. This is particularly true of phenothiazines, such as Thorazine.

Use of some narcotics, as with alcohol, also can impair the digestion of food and the absorption of nutrients into the blood, thus causing malnutrition. As with alcohol, the correction of maladaptive diets due to drug use is an important part of rehabilitation.

Daphne A. Roe, *Alcohol and the diet* (Westport, Conn.: AVI Publishing Company, 1979).

Charles S. Lieber, "Alcohol-Nutrition Interaction—An Update," *Alcohol* 1 (1984): 151–157.

nystagmus Involuntary rapid eye movement. It is a common symptom of toxic reaction resulting from PCP or sedative use. (See EYES.)

O

Odyssey Resources, Inc. Founded in 1966 as a treatment center for adult drug addicts in New York City, Odyssey Houses are now located in other parts of the U.S. as well as in Australia and New Zealand. They are drug-free, therapeutic communities that are psychiatrically oriented and hold the belief that personal growth can replace the need for drugs. Odyssey Houses now treat a wide range of patients: adolescents, alcoholics, female addicts with children and child-abuse victims.

Office of Disease Prevention and Health Promotion (ODPHP) This agency assists the public in locating health information and resources through an inquiry and referral service. Formerly the National Health Information Clearinghouse, the center also prepares and distributes publications and directories on health promotion and disease prevention topics.

Office of National Drug Control Policy (ONDCP) ONDCP operates within the White House and is charged with providing a policy on drug use that includes the efforts of federal, state and local government agencies, as well as the private sector. The office is headed by a presidential appointee who is often referred to in the media as the "drug czar." Formerly known as the Data Center and Clearinghouse for Drugs and Crime, the ONDCP Drugs & Crime Clearinghouse is funded by the Office of National Drug Control Policy to support drug control policy research. The clearinghouse is managed by the U.S. Department of Justice, Bureau of Justice Statistics, and is a component of the National Criminal Justice Reference Service. The clearinghouse responds to requests for drug and crime data; advises about new drugs and crime data reports; conducts special bibliographic searches upon request for specific drugs and crime topics; and publishes special reports on subjects such as assets forfeiture and seizure, economic costs of drug-related crime, drugs and violence, drug laws of the 50 states, drug abuse and corrections, and innovative law enforcement reactions. It also prepares a comprehensive, concise report that brings together an array of data to trace and quantify the complete flow of illicit drugs.

onset In drug research, the term refers to the first time a person uses a particular drug. It also is used to refer to the initiation of the "withdrawal syndrome." Age of onset is often studied by epidemiologists as a major variable and also in its relation to other variables.

on the wagon A phrase meaning "abstinence from alcoholic beverages." The term probably was first used by the American Army during the 19th century to refer to the water wagon taken by soldiers on extended trips, on which, presumably, they had no access to liquor.

Operation Primavera A 10-day campaign by Colombian authorities in early 1984 that became the most successful bust of cocaine laboratories in Colombian history. The successful operation netted a total of 26 plants capable of producing 6.6 tons of cocaine per week. Authorities confiscated 1.3 tons of cocaine in base and finished form, plus unprecedented quantities of chemicals used in the manufacture of cocaine. Enough chemicals were seized to make 104 tons of cocaine, a third of the estimated annual cocaine output of Colombia, Bolivia and Peru combined. The seizures underscored a little-noted but crucial fact of life in the $130 billion cocaine business: the drug trade is a two-way street. That is, the cocaine flows from mostly Third World producers to the U.S. and other industrialized nations, but the chemicals and other materials needed to turn coca leaves into cocaine—ether acetone, methyl ethyl ketone, potassium per manganate—flow from the industrialized nations to the third world.

William R. Doesner, "The Chemical Connection," *Time* (February 20, 1989): 44–45.

Operation Snowcap An important mutual action initiative in which the U.S. Drug Enforcement Administration (DEA) has been involved since 1987. Operation Snowcap is a multifaceted campaign created to significantly reduce the supply of illicit cocaine reaching the U.S. from Latin America. It was developed by the DEA and the U.S. State Department's Bureau of International Narcotics Matters (INM), and has been closely coordinated with appropriate U.S. agencies. The overall strategy is to extend to other Latin American countries various interrelated aerial, waterway and ground enforcement/reduction programs that were previously proven successful in coca-reduction efforts under Operation Stop Prop/Blast Furnace in Bolivia. At present, Snowcap operations are coordinated with law enforcement officials in 12 Latin American countries.

U.S. Department of Justice, Drug Enforcement Administration, Statement of David L. Westrate before U.S. Senate Subcommittee on Terrorism, Narcotics and International Operations, *Drug Enforcement Administration Briefing Book* (Washington, D.C., 1989): 3.

opiates Specifically refers to the two opium alkaloids, MORPHINE and CODEINE, and the semisynthetic drugs derived from them, such as HEROIN (diacetylmorphine) and Dilaudid (hydromorphine hydrochloride). Morphine and codeine, along with opium, sometimes are referred to as "natural" opiates, and their derivatives as "semisynthetic" opiates. All opiates are classified as narcotic analgesic agonists.

opioids Synthetic drugs with characteristics similar to OPIATES.

opium Opium is made by air-drying the juice extracted from the unripe seed pods of the Oriental poppy *Papaver somniferum*. The resulting brownish gum is then formed into bricks or cakes that eventually harden.

History: Opium has probably been used since prehistoric times. The opium poppy is thought to have originated in Asia Minor and was first used medicinally in Egypt. From there, its use spread to Greece. Arab traders carried it to India and China, where it was used to control dysentery and for its euphoric and sedative effects. Opium use became so widespread in China and was considered so harmful that the Chinese government tried to control its importation, sale and use. This was opposed by the British because it interfered with their profitable trade in opium grown in India, and led to the Opium War (1839–42). The British won the war and as a result, opium cultivation and importation was legalized in China. Chinese immigrants carried the habit of opium smoking to the U.S. and elsewhere.

In the early 1500s, the physician Paracelsus made a tincture of opium (powdered opium dissolved in alcohol), which he called LAUDANUM. It was the first medicinal form of opium. In Europe, laudanum was used to relieve pain and control dysentery, and as a cough suppressant and sedative. It remained a standard drug until the end of the 19th century, when its use began to decline. Several other opium mixtures were developed in the 1700s and 1800s, but the most important was paregoric, a tincture of opium combined with camphor. Although considered an old-fashioned remedy today, it is still used to control diarrhea and is listed in Schedule III of the CONTROLLED SUBSTANCES ACT. However, it is obtainable in some places without a prescription and heroin addicts are known to resort to it when they cannot get their usual "fix."

History of Opium

5000 B.C.	Opium is known in Mesopotamia and mentioned in Assyrian medical texts.
1500 B.C.	Used as an anesthetic by Egyptian physicians.
c. 7th century A.D.	Opium poppy is brought to China via Middle East and India.
1200	Used in the Middle East as a medicine and an intoxicant.
1541	Paracelsus, Swiss alchemist, introduces laudanum and it becomes popular throughout Europe.
1650	Opium smoking becomes rampant in China.
c. 1803	Morphine is isolated from opium and used medically in 1825.
1839–1842	Opium War between China and England.
1866	Use of opium and morphine during Civil War in U.S. creates estimated 400,000 addicts.
1870s	Sales of patent medicines containing opium proliferate in Europe and America.
1875	San Francisco passes first ordinance against opium den.
1909	Legislation is passed making opium smoking a criminal offense.
1914	Harrison Narcotics Act taxes manufacture, importation and distribution of opium and products containg opium.
1920s	Opium dens operate in most U.S. cities.
1930s	Opium abuse almost completely replaced by heroin.
1931	Agreement for Control of Opium Smoking in the Far East is signed at Bangkok.
1942	Opium Poppy Control Act prohibits cultivation except under license in U.S.
1946	Iran prohibits opium cultivation.
1948	World Health Organization becomes responsible for narcotics control. Only a few nations are allowed to cultivate opium for export.
1970	Controlled Substances Act classifies medicines containing opium as Schedules II, III and V drugs.
1971	Turkey agrees to stop cultivation of opium poppies in 1972.
1980s–1990s	Opium itself is not a major abuse problem in the U.S. In the Middle and Far East it is still smoked or eaten.

Source: Robert O'Brien et al., *The Encyclopedia of Drug Abuse,* New York: Facts On File, 1992.

Opium Cultivation and Production

LATIN AMERICA

	1993	1994	1995	1996	1997
Net cultivation (hectares)	**40,438**	**40,050**	**13,119**	**12,600**	**13,200**
Mexico	3,960	5,796	5,050	5,100	4,000
Guatemala	438	50	39	0	0
Colombia	20,000	20,000	6,540	6,300	6,600
Potential production (metric tons)	**49**	**60**	**118**	**117**	**112**
Mexico	49	60	53	54	46
Guatemala	...	...	...	...	...
Colombia	...	...	65	63	66

SOUTHEAST ASIA

	1993	1994	1995	1996	1997
Net cultivation (hectares)	167,230	**177,795**	**176,745**	**190,520**	**184,950**
Myanmar (Burma)	146,600	154,070	154,070	163,100	155,150
Laos	18,520	19,650	19,650	25,250	28,150
Thailand	2,110	2,110	1,750	2,170	1,650
China	...	1,965	1,275	...	...
Potential production (metric tons)	**2,797**	**2,157**	**2,564**	**2,790**	**2,600**
Myanmar (Burma)	2,575	2,030	2,340	2,560	2,365
Laos	180	85	180	200	210
Thailand	42	17	25	30	25
China	...	25	19	...	...

SOUTHWEST ASIA

	1993	1994	1995	1996	1997
Net cultivation (hectares)	25,480	**34,680**	**50,440**	**44,450**	45,300
Afghanistan	21,080	29,180	38,740	37,950	39,150
India	4,400	5,500	4,750	3,100	2,050
Pakistan	0	0	6,950	3,400	4,100
Potential production (metric tons)	**825**	1,200	1,482	1,352	1,380
Afghanistan	685	950	1,250	1,230	1,265
India	...	90	77	47	30
Pakistan	140	160	155	75	85

Source: United States Dept. of State, Bureau for International Narcotics and Law Enforcement Affairs, International Narcotics Control Strategy Report, March 1996.

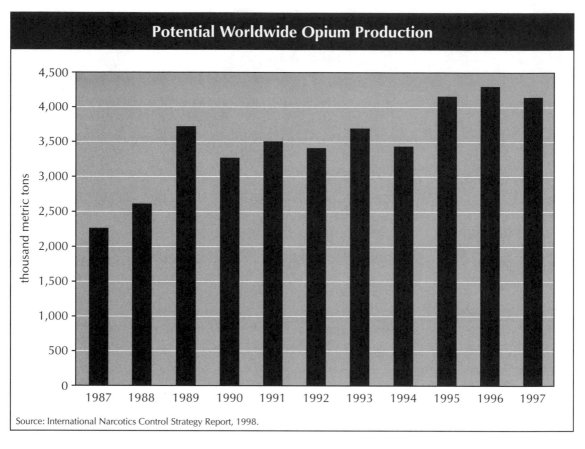

Potential Worldwide Opium Production

Source: International Narcotics Control Strategy Report, 1998.

The danger of developing a dependence on these staple opium remedies was not well understood and by the end of the 19th century many people, including famous poets and writers, had become addicted. After doctors became aware of the problem, laws were passed making opium and its derivatives available only by prescription. The first of these was the 1914 Harrison Act, which placed opium under strict federal control. Other legislation followed, culminating in the Controlled Substances Act of 1970, which regulated all drugs likely to be abused. The drugs are listed under five schedules according to their abuse potential. Although they are both narcotics and opiates, heroin is a Schedule I drug, and opium is listed in Schedule II.

The chemical substance (alkaloid) in opium that causes its mind-altering effects is morphine. Morphine was extracted from opium for the first time in 1803, after which the medical use of opium began to decline. Except for a few prescription drugs, opium is rarely used medically today. Only two of the alkaloids extracted from opium—morphine and the milder codeine—are still in clinical use.

When heroin, a derivative of morphine, was developed in 1898, it was heralded as a better painkiller than morphine and a highly effective cough suppressant. Considering it to be nonaddictive, physicians used heroin to treat opium and morphine addicts until its even worse addictive effects were recognized. By that time, addicts (whose opium and morphine supplies had been cut off by stringent laws) and the underworld had discovered the greater potency and availability of heroin. By the early 1900s, heroin had replaced both opium and morphine on the street, and the era of the "junkie" was born. Today, in the U.S., the manufacture and use of heroin is completely illegal, and heroin is considered to have no medical use.

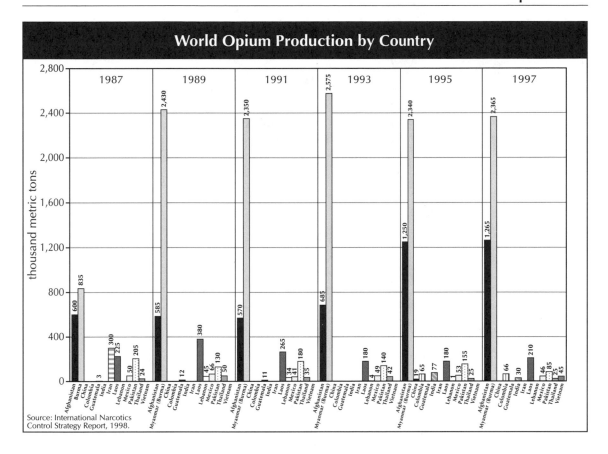

World Opium Production by Country

thousand metric tons

Source: International Narcotics Control Strategy Report, 1998.

Classification: A narcotic that acts as a depressant on the central nervous system (CNS). Unlike other CNS depressants, such as barbiturates and alcohol, narcotics are also analgesics (they relieve pain).

Usage: Opium smoking, the most common method of opium use, is practiced mostly in China, Hong Kong and Southeast Asia. Some American soldiers acquired the habit during the war in Vietnam. The use of opium per se is not a major drug problem in America—the main problems stem primarily from morphine and its derivative heroin.

Appearance: Raw opium comes in a solid mass of varying shape, weighing from one-half to five pounds. It varies in color from yellow gold to deep brownish black and sometimes has a heavy, gummy texture. It is processed in several ways:

Although now rarely used, granulated opium is a medically approved drug for treating diarrhea.

Powdered opium is more finely ground than the granulated variety. It is used in the manufacture of a few prescription drugs, notably PANTOPON and B & O SUPPRETTES.

Dissolved in water, filtered, then boiled down into a sticky paste, the substance becomes the preparation used by opium smokers.

Dissolved in alcohol, the substance becomes the tincture of opium used in making laudanum and paregoric.

Broken down chemically into its alkaloids (chemical substances found in all plants), the substance yields morphine, codeine and papaverine.

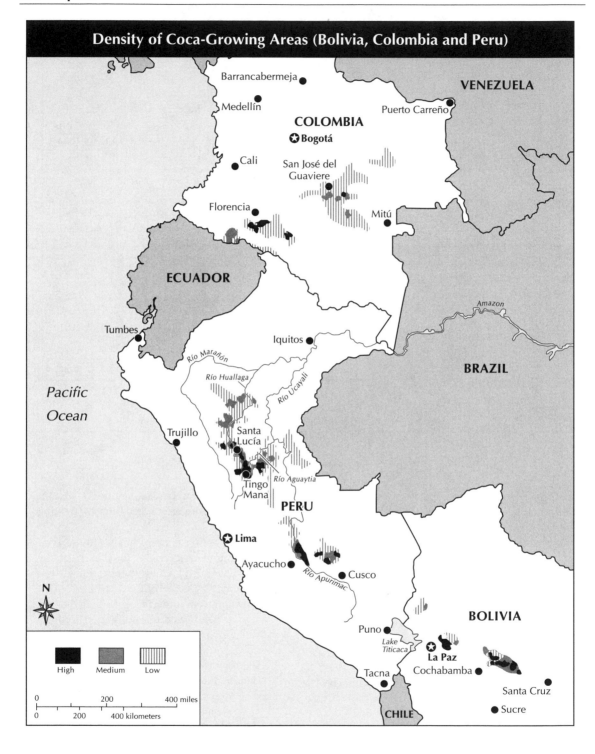

Density of Coca-Growing Areas (Bolivia, Colombia and Peru)

VENEZUELA

COLOMBIA

Barrancabermeja

Medellín

Puerto Carreño

✪ Bogotá

Cali

San José del Guaviere

Florencia

Mitú

ECUADOR

Tumbes

Amazon

Iquitos

BRAZIL

Río Marañón

Río Huallaga

Río Ucayali

Pacific

Ocean

Trujillo

Santa Lucía

Tingo Mana

Río Aguaytia

PERU

✪ Lima

Ayacucho

Río Apurímac

Cusco

BOLIVIA

Puno

Lake Titicaca

✪ La Paz

Tacna

Cochabamba

Santa Cruz

CHILE

Sucre

N

High   Medium   Low

0   200   400 miles

0   200   400 kilometers

Effects: Used medically, opium dulls sensations of pain, controls diarrhea because it has a constipating action, suppresses coughing, induces drowsiness, alleviates anxiety and gives a feeling of euphoria or well-being. It is the drug's euphoric effect that the opium user is seeking, as well as its ability to produce indifference to hunger, sexual urges, tension and anxiety. Unlike barbiturates, alcohol and other drugs, narcotics do not trigger aggressive behavior. On the contrary, they usually make the user docile and dreamy.

There also can be unpleasant side effects with opium use, such as nausea and vomiting, but the user is normally indifferent to these reactions because they are quickly followed by sedation and euphoria.

Tolerance and dependence: Opium tolerance develops as inexorably as tolerance to barbiturates and other central nervous system drugs. With regular use, dosage must be steadily increased to achieve the desired effects. As dosage increases, dependence can develop. Long-term use of opium can cause both psychological and physical dependence. With psychological dependence, the user has a craving for the drug and feels that life is not worth living without it. With physical dependence, the body grows to rely on the drug to take over some of its normal functions. When the drug is stopped or sharply reduced, physical reactions of varying degrees of severity follow.

Withdrawal: When physical dependence has developed, opium users experience a number of withdrawal symptoms if the drug is suddenly stopped. These develop rapidly and reach their height in two or three days; they continue for a week or more before subsiding, although it may take as long as six months for some effects to wear off. There are occasional fatalities among deeply dependent users who are in poor health, but opium withdrawal is much less dangerous to life than barbiturate or severe alcohol withdrawal.

The symptoms of opium withdrawal are the same as those for other narcotics: anxiety, restlessness, yawning, tears, runny nose, nausea, diarrhea, cramps, general body aches, gooseflesh and dehydration.

Production and trafficking: In 1989 the four major producers of opium in the world, in metric tons,

were Burma (now Myanmar), 1,300; Afghanistan, 750; Iran, 300; and Laos, 250. According to a report by the U.S. Department of State, overall world opium production has greatly increased. In 1997 it was at 4,137 metric tons. That year, Myanmar alone produced 2,365 metric tons of opium, making it the world's top producer, followed by Afghanistan (1,265 metric tons), Laos (210 metric tons) and Pakistan (85 metric tons). By region, Southeast Asia produced 2,600 metric tons, followed by Southwest Asia with 1,380 metric tons.

Raw opium is too bulky for profitable long-distance smuggling and does not present a major traffic and control problem in the U.S. Even morphine is in the form of a solid block before it is processed into a soluble salt. In North America the real problem is heroin. It has only half the bulk of morphine and control of smuggling is extremely difficult and requires international cooperation.

Sources: The opium poppy is grown in China, Southeast Asia, Mexico, Turkey, Lebanon and now Colombia. The amount of raw opium required by legitimate drug houses to manufacture morphine and other prescription drugs is only a fraction of the supply available. The rest makes its way into black market laboratories in Europe and elsewhere to produce illicit heroin and morphine.

Synonyms: O, op, black pills, black stuff, gum, hop, tar.

oral fixation A psychoanalytic theory on the cause of alcoholism. According to this theory, trauma affects the infant in the earliest stage of psychosexual development, a time when his sole means of achieving security and release from tension is through stimulation of the oral cavity. During this stage the child feels omnipotent, and through his mouth he is given sustenance and expresses his love and hate. However, as a result of an absent or uncaring mother, the infant is deprived of a warm relationship with a mother figure and subsequently continues to seek gratification of his primary emotional hunger. There is fixation at this oral stage of development and an unconscious desire for warmth and nurturance that cannot be satisfied in normal interpersonal relationships. This theory postulates that as the infant seeks through ingestion to fill his emptiness, so does the alcoholic. Alcohol is a liquid nourishment that generates a sensation of warmth and satisfaction. The alcoholic's feelings of anger and rage at his parents, who failed him, coupled with an intense fear of losing them and a need to obtain some sort of gratification, cause him to redirect his rage from his parents (or, later, other people who cannot meet his excessive needs) to himself, and so he consumes his rage in alcohol.

The theory of oral fixation also has been applied to other drugs of abuse, particularly those that are smoked, such as marijuana and tobacco, and to eating disorders.

David J. Armor, J. Michael Polich and Harriet B. Stambul, *Alcoholism and Treatment* (New York: John Wiley and Sons, 1978): 17.

Morris E. Chafetz and Harold W. Demone, Jr., *Alcoholism and Society* (New York: Oxford University Press, 1962): 21–25, 220–223.

Order of Good Templars   The first international TEMPERANCE organization, the Order of Good Templars began in 1851 in Utica, New York. Started by a society of abstainers, it spread throughout the U.S. and Canada, and in 1868 it was introduced into Britain. Some years later the organization emerged in Scandinavia and other countries. The first international conference was held in 1885 in Antwerp, Belgium.

organic disorder   A group of disorders that are the result of known or hypothesized pathological changes in the tissues, as opposed to functional disorders (conditions in which one or more of the normal activities of the organism cannot be properly performed, but where there is no known pathological change in organic structure). Often, organic disorders are related to the nutritional deficiencies consequent to severe alcohol or other chemical abuse. Usually, a diagnosis of organic disorder is based on the type of damage done to the brain and the resultant neurological, cognitive, behavioral and intellectual impairments that have occurred. DEMENTIA, WERNICKE'S SYNDROME and KORSAKOFF'S PSYCHOSIS are all examples of organic disorders.

organized crime   Organized crime will forever be linked to illicit drug trafficking, largely because it is extremely lucrative and extremely dangerous. Nationwide, according to the U.S. Department of Jus-

tice, drug dealers took in an estimated $130 billion in 1987. At least four organized gangs in Los Angeles ran cocaine operations, netting more than $1 million per week.

Organized crime reaped the bulk of these profits—more than a 100% increase from 1977—through large-scale, highly sophisticated operations. "Big time" drug dealers have to obtain the illicit substances (usually overseas), smuggle them into the country, arrange for the cutting of pure drugs, and then distribute them through often elaborate trafficking networks. Drug money is often "laundered" or passed through legitimate businesses, some of which are "fronts" in major enterprises, (including large banks) before it is put back into the drug trade.

Two new nontraditional groups have emerged in organized crime in the last two decades: prison gangs that operate inside and outside of prison and outlaw motorcycle gangs. Other drug operations that have recently appeared are Colombian groups such as the Medellin and Cali cartels and several Southeast Asian groups.

The DEA reported in 1995 that crime groups varied from large, sophisticated organizations that controlled cultivation, processing and interstate trafficking, to small, independent local traffickers. Groups of 10 to 15 individuals controlled retail distribution on the streets, which is both lucrative and dangerous. In 1981, 25% of all homicides in Dade County, Florida, were the result of drug groups carrying out machine gun assassinations in public places. Violence among gangs in Los Angeles rose 88% in 1987 alone. These gangs have now spread from their original neighborhoods to smaller urban areas across the U.S., with one estimate placing Los Angeles street gang members in 49 American cities. The U.S. Department of Justice reported that in 1991, 15% of students ages 12 to 19 reported the presence of gangs in their schools, compared to 66% who said gangs were not present. Of students who reported gang presence, 78% said drugs were available at their schools. In a 1991 survey of inmates in state correctional facilities, 6% of state prison inmates belonged to a gang. In that same year, 25% of federal offenders involved in illegal drug activities identified themselves as belonging to an organization engaged in such activities. Approximately 11% were leaders or middlemen in these organizations.

Organized crime also engages in weapons trafficking, prostitution, gambling, pornography and other activities. There are also reports of public officials at all levels who are being corrupted by drug money, particularly rural police officers who accept large sums to "look the other way" during smuggling operations.

To combat organized crime, the Drug Enforcement Administration (DEA) was reorganized; and for the first time the FBI was brought into the so-called war on drugs. The navy, Coast Guard and U.S. customs officials are also cooperating in interdicting smuggling operations. In 1988, the DEA made 23,972 drug arrests; 14,116 for cocaine alone. In 1994 the DEA made 13,631 domestic seizures of nondrug property with a value of $647 million, which belonged to criminals involved in illegal drug activities. Drug-related arrests have increased dramatically from the mid-1980s through the mid-1990s. In 1993 there were 1,126,300 state and local arrests for drug violations, up 59% from 1984, when 708,400 arrests were made.

Orphan Drug Act of 1983 This act was passed to facilitate the development of new drugs for the treatment of rare diseases (diseases effecting fewer than 200,000 people). Underlying the act was the assumption that few drug companies are willing to invest the millions of research dollars to develop a new drug when its potential market is small, namely because these "orphan diseases" affect relatively few individuals. Drug companies receive incentives for research, development and manufacturing. Incentives include tax deductions for three-fourths of the cost of clinical trials and the exclusivity of marketing rights for the first seven years after the drug's approval by the FDA. The act authorized the money needed to cover the costs of the incentives.

outpatient treatment In recent years, alcohol and other drug treatment programs have proliferated across the U.S. More than 1.43 million persons were treated in the 12-month period ending October 30, 1989, with 15% of those in INPATIENT TREATMENT or residential settings and 85% as active outpatients. In 1993, 1.97 million persons received treatment for alcohol- or drug-related problems with 93% in outpatient care.

Just as alcoholics and drug users do not always feel they need formal treatment to recover, many treated for alcohol or drug use do not always require intensive or long-term inpatient treatment. Studies of inpatient-outpatient treatment indicate that some chemically dependent individuals do not require inpatient treatment. The severity of drug dependence and withdrawal symptoms, general medical condition, psychiatric condition and other factors determine which setting is most appropriate for DETOXIFICATION. Matching patients with the right treatment is an ongoing area of research. The American Society of Addiction Medicine has developed assessment guidelines to standardize patient/treatment matchup.

As a rule, patients who are married, employed, free of severe psychological impairments, and of higher socioeconomic status respond most favorably to treatment. However, many patients in outpatient facilities for the treatment of alcoholism drop out soon after admission. E. J. Larkin compiled a summary of characteristics of people who terminate their treatment. He found they were more restless, nomadic, impulsive and rigid in their attitudes, and less dependable and less inhibited by anxiety than patients who remained in treatment. They also were less willing to reveal personal feelings or to express ideas spontaneously. Aside from personality characteristics, lower-economic-class patients were more likely to terminate psychotherapy prematurely than patients from higher economic classes.

The cost of treatment varies. A four-week "drying-out" regimen can cost anywhere from $4,000 to $20,000 for inpatient care and, given that most studies have been unable to uncover significant differences in outcome among inpatient and outpatient programs, for most patients it is likely that outpatient programs will continue to serve the majority of alcoholics receiving treatment.

E. J. Larkin, *The Treatment of Alcoholism* (Toronto: Addiction Research Foundation of Ontario, 1974): 31–36.

W. R. Miller and R. K. Hester, "Treating the Problem Drinker: Modern Approaches," in *The Addictive Behaviors: Treatment of Alcoholism, Drug Abuse, Smoking and Obesity* ed. W.R. Miller (Oxford: Pergamon Press, 1980): 11–141.

John S. Gustafson et. al. *State Resources and Services Related to Alcohol and Drug Related Services for Fiscal Year 1993; An Analysis of State Alcohol and Drug Abuse profile Data*

(Washington D.C.: National Association of State Alcohol and Drug Abuse Directors, January 1995).

outreach   The effort to reach out to a drug- or alcohol-dependent person who does not voluntarily enter a treatment situation is called outreach. It may be made by street workers who are recovered addicts, or by health care workers visiting places where addicts are found. It is also done by public media, such as television, radio and magazines.

over-the-counter medications (OTC)   Drugs sold without prescriptions are over-the-counter drugs (OTC). Many of the estimated 350,000 OTC products are subject to abuse, particularly those that contain analgesic, sedative or stimulant ingredients. Among the OTC medications most frequently abused are cough syrups, sleeping aids and appetite depressants (diet pills). Annual sales of OTC drugs total somewhere between $5 billion and $7 billion.

overdose   The ingestion of a drug in an amount larger than the body's system can handle. Whether accidental or deliberate, an overdose poses a real danger.

A deliberate overdose of a drug, particularly a short-acting barbiturate such as amobarbital, secobarbital or pentobarbital, is a widely used method of suicide. Studies have shown that a high percentage of those who use this method are also alcoholics. Although the amount of a barbiturate required to produce a lethal dose can vary from person to person, it is usually 10 to 15 times a normal dose. Cardiovascular collapse precedes respiratory depression and is followed by coma and death.

Accidental overdose can result from a variety of factors. In recent years the increase in polydrug use has been a leading factor in overdoses, particularly the use of alcohol with other drugs. Because of the synergistic effect, even a small, normal dose of a drug can prove fatal when taken with alcohol. The combination of barbiturates and amphetamines, often taken by amphetamine-dependent people to bring themselves down from a "wired-up" state or to ward off withdrawal symptoms, also can prove fatal. A person can never be completely certain what his or her reaction will be to a combination of drugs, and overdoses are common with polydrug use.

An overdose of an amphetamine, which is a central nervous system stimulant, is characterized by hyperactivity, restlessness, tremulousness and mental confusion. In severe overdose the symptoms are delirium, stroke, cardiac arrhythmia and convulsions, followed by circulatory collapse and coma. The lethal dose of an amphetamine is not known, but it is estimated to be 5–10 mg per kg of body weight for a nontolerant person. Among some individuals, however, a much smaller dose can prove fatal, while a habitual user who has developed tolerance can consume a much larger dose. Tolerance to amphetamines builds quickly, and the need for larger amounts is the primary factor in overdose.

Overdose of cocaine, also a central nervous system stimulant, has symptoms similar to amphetamine overdose. In cases of acute toxicity, death can occur in as little as two to three minutes. Lethal doses vary according to the method of administration. Ingested cocaine is less toxic than cocaine that is injected; 120 mg taken intravenously is said to be a lethal dose, but as little as 20 mg applied to mucous membranes can also be lethal in sensitive individuals.

Overdoses of barbiturates—which normally act as central nervous system depressants, relieve tension and anxiety and produce drowsiness and sleep—are common. When the desired effect is not achieved by a normal dose, a user often will increase the dosage. Another cause of overdose occurs when a user takes repeated doses because he is in a state of mental confusion and cannot remember how many doses he already has taken. Symptoms of overdose include cold sweaty skin, a weak rapid pulse, breathing that is either slow or rapid and shallow, and coma. Treatment for barbiturate overdose by support of breathing and heart action usually is effective if the person is discovered in time.

Heroin overdose is characterized initially by lethargy and stupor, followed by a prolonged coma. Death from an overdose sometimes can be prevented by an injection of a NARCOTIC ANTAGONIST. Reports of death by heroin overdoses are generally inaccurate. Because death from heroin is a slow process, the sudden death of an addict is more likely to be caused by such complications as a combination of heroin and alcohol or a sensitivity to an adulterant. (See SYNDROME X.) Overdose patients admitted to hospitals often show signs of pulmonary edema, pneumonia, shallow breathing and coma. A lethal dose of heroin is related to a person's tolerance level and increases as tolerance increases. A lethal dose for a nonaddict has been variously estimated at between 120 and 500 mg. Addicts have been known to survive injections of 1,800 milligrams. Overdoses have occurred when an addict's tolerance is low, and also in cases when he has taken heroin that is unusually potent. Addicts can never be sure what percentage of the mixture they have purchased is pure heroin. Sometimes a dealer will give a buyer a "hot shot"—a deliberate overdose—if the latter is suspected of being an informer or thief.

There is no known lethal dose of marijuana, although it can produce highly toxic reactions whether it is taken orally or injected. Prolonged heavy use can result in chronic bronchitis, asthma and pulmonary disorders.

An overdose of hallucinogens (LSD, mescaline, psilocybin and so on) is not likely to be fatal. Large doses can produce unconsciousness, however. One of the great dangers associated with the use of hallucinogens is that they impair the user's judgment, and deaths have been reported while a person was under the influence of such a drug. Temporary panic states can occur, and sometimes chronic psychoses occur that last for months.

Deaths have resulted from the use of inhalants but, as in the case of glue sniffing, the cause of death is most likely to be from suffocation because a plastic bag has been placed over the head to enhance the effects. In the case of solvents, a high dose can produce general sedative-anesthetic effects—drowsiness, stupor, respiratory depression and unconsciousness. In extremely heavy use, death has been reported from inhibited breathing. The fluorocarbons in aerosols have been associated with deaths due to cardiac arrhythmia.

oxazepam   A BENZODIAZEPINE derivative that has a relatively slow onset of action but long-lasting effects. It is used to relieve tension, anxiety and muscle spasm, to produce sedation and to prevent convulsions. (See SERAX.)

Oxford Group   Originally called The First Century Christian Fellowship, the Oxford Group was founded in 1908 by Frank Buchman. Its popularity under the name the "Oxford Group"—from Buchman's preaching among the students at Oxford—peaked in the late 1920s and early 1930s. It was a nondenominational, theologically conservative, evangelical attempt to recapture the spirit of what its members understood to be primitive Christianity.

Bill WILSON, founder of ALCOHOLICS ANONYMOUS (AA), became familiar with the Oxford Group while he was still drinking. He amalgamated a number of its principles (self-survey, confession, restitution and giving of oneself in service to others) into the philosophy of AA.

oxycodone   A semisynthetic MORPHINE derivative, it is a narcotic used as an analgesic. Its potency is similar to that of morphine. It produces sedation as a side effect. (See PERCOCET-5 and PERCODAN.)

oxymorphine hydrochloride   A semisynthetic MORPHINE derivative, which has an analgesic potency much higher than that of morphine. It is sold under the trade name Numorphan.

P

Pacific Institute for Research and Evaluation Health Professionals as Preventors An organization concerned with the prevention of alcohol and other drug use. Since 1985 a team of researchers and program development specialists has sought to extend prevention and early intervention to settings that offered access to youth, demonstrated a keen interest in the welfare of young people, and did not consistently address youth alcohol and other drug prevention and early intervention issues.

The group works with officials at the Substance Abuse and Mental Health Services Administration (SAMHSA) to locate potential funding sources. Grants supporting the project have come from such sources as The Pew Charitable Trusts, The J. M. Foundation and IBM.

The basic philosophy of the group is that all health professionals, as a crucial component of the national effort to combat these problems, can and should help young people avoid alcohol and drug use and the related problems.

Pakistan

Drugs other than alcohol: According to a report by the Bureau for International Narcotics and Law Enforcement Affairs, "Pakistan has a substantial problem with the abuse of drugs other than alcohol." A United Nations study, published in 1993, reported that Pakistan had 3 million addicts of all kinds, including 1.5 million heroin addicts. At the time of the study, most heroin addicts were smoking the drug, but subsequent research indicates the number of needle users in large cities was on the rise.

Pakistan is a significant producer and transit country for opiates and hashish. Intelligence information and seizures indicate that considerable amounts of Afghan opiate and cannabis products are consumed by its significant addict population or pass through on their way to the world's markets. Morphine base is produced in the tribal areas for refining abroad, and heroin is produced for domestic use and export. Not only has the poppy, the source of opium, been cultivated since time immemorial, the cannabis plant grows wild in the northern areas of the country. In the face of small land holdings, the absence of employment opportunities, depleted soil and inadequate irrigation, it is not hard to understand the temptation to sell and gain an easy profit from these products.

The government of Pakistan, aware of the complexity, magnitude and repercussions of drug use within the country, as well as the serious implications of illicit exportation, set up a Pakistan Narcotics Control Board in 1973. In 1979 the Prohibition (Enforcement of Hadd) Ordinance was put into effect by the government: it imposed a complete ban on the production, processing, manufacture, sale and use of all intoxicating drugs. The ordinance introduced Islamic disciplines into the domain of drug abuse and the deeply religious bent of the people has helped to assure their determination to combat the drug problems. Demand reduction is an integral part of Pakistan's five-year master plan for drug control. In the early 1990s, the government expanded its demand-reduction efforts, including the education of religious leaders about drug use. The government has been cooperating with agencies from the UN, the U.S. and other foreign nations to step up their supply-reduction efforts.

Treatment: Public efforts against addiction are limited to detoxification without any follow-up treatment. Private clinics use a variety of treatment methods, but relapse rates are high for all of them.

Cultivation: Poppy cultivation in Pakistan formerly was divided into three diverse areas: (1) settled districts, (2) merged areas and (3) tribal areas. In settled areas, poppy cultivation was under license of the government (licensed production now is forbidden by law); it was understood that the entire harvest would be turned over to the government and after processing would be issued by the government opium factory for scientific, medical and quasi-medical uses. In merged and tribal areas, cultivation was not governed by licensing and was largely administered according to tribal customs. Following the enactment of the Prohibition Ordinance, the government of Pakistan appealed to tribal elders to respect the drug and alcohol law according to Islamic injunctions against the use of intoxicants.

The withdrawal of poppy cultivation has imposed an enormous socioeconomic hardship, particularly in neglected areas of the country. One of the major problems facing the Pakistan government is to find a viable alternative crop that will produce a sufficient economic return. The U.S. designated an aid program package to help in the development of rural areas. In the late 1980s, the Buner Project, a development previously implemented in Thailand, was introduced in Pakistan. Projects have included road-building, providing water supplies for villages and crops, supplying farm credit, land leveling and terracing, and improving livestock health and production.

Trafficking: During the 1960s, only a fraction of the total production of opium and cannabis was consumed within the country; the majority found its way into illicit foreign trade. Substantial amounts of morphine base have been identified moving from southwestern Pakistan to the Arabian Sea for trans-

port to refineries in Turkey. Most of these opiates are loaded either in Karachi or off the Makran Coast of Baluchistan. Another route moves opium and refined products from eastern Pakistan to Turkey. Some opium is processed locally for home and international markets, and some heroin is transported to India.

United States Dept. of State, Bureau for International Narcotics and Law Enforcement Affairs, *International Narcotics Control Strategy Report March 1996.*

pancreas A small glandular organ located below and behind the stomach and connected to the small intestine at the duodenum. The pancreas secretes insulin and glucagon—hormones that regulate the blood's glucose level—and enzymes necessary for the digestion of proteins, carbohydrates and fats. A failure to produce sufficient insulin results in diabetes mellitus.

Most drugs have little direct effect on the pancreas, whether taken in therapeutic or abusive doses. Alcohol, however, appears to stimulate pancreatic secretion while prompting spasms that obstruct pancreatic duct outflow. The pressure on the pancreatic ducts causes tissues in the organ to swell, and the resulting condition is pancreatitis.

Malnutrition may also be partly responsible for pancreatitis, which can occur after bouts of heavy drinking but more frequently develops after years of excessive alcohol consumption. Chronic alcoholics show a particularly high incidence of both acute and chronic pancreatitis. Chronic relapsing pancreatitis is relatively common among alcoholics, who are also more likely than the rest of the population to develop carcinoma of the pancreas. Pancreatitis is rare in nonalcoholics. It does not develop in all alcoholics, however. Cirrhotic patients are more than twice as likely to develop pancreatitis as those without cirrhosis.

Symptoms of pancreatitis include severe abdominal pain, nausea, vomiting, abdominal bleeding, digestive distress and diabetes mellitus, in varying degrees of severity. Abstinence from alcohol and a low-fat diet can relieve the acute state of the disease, which is evidenced by abnormally high concentrations of serum amylase. Pancreatitis can sometimes produce striking mental changes due to electrolyte disruptions in the suffering individual. More severe cases can involve pancreatic necrosis, hemorrhage and scarring.

pancreatitis   Inflammation of the PANCREAS.

panic disorder   According to Beatrice A. Rouse, the essential feature of panic disorder is the presence of recurrent, unexpected panic attacks and significant behavioral change (such as severely life-threatening activities). A panic attack is an episode of intense fear accompanied by physical symptoms such as pounding heartbeat, sweating, dizziness and nausea. The sensation is so terrifying that there is a constant dread of another panic attack and one may go to great lengths to avoid any situation that seems likely to trigger it. During a panic attack one is usually terrified and may believe that they are having a heart attack, dying or going crazy. The criteria for panic disorders are: recurrent and unexpected panic attacks followed by at least one month of persistent concern about having another attack; worry about the possible implications or consequences of the panic attacks; or significant behavioral change related to the attacks.

Many individuals suffering from panic disorders mistakenly self-medicate themselves with alcohol or other mood-altering substances. Ultimately, however, these nonprescribed drugs almost always exacerbate the condition.

Beatrice A. Rouse, ed., *Substance Abuse and Mental Health Statistics Sourcebook* (Washington, D.C.: Substance Abuse and Mental Health Services Administration, 1995).

pantopon   A narcotic analgesic that contains hydrochlorides of OPIUM alkaloids. It is used in place of morphine for the relief of severe pain. In addition to the action of morphine, it exhibits the action of codeine and the other alkaloids present in opium. It can be habit-forming, and dependency can occur. Pantopon is not available in the U.S.

Papaver somniferum   The Oriental opium poppy plant from which opium and its derivatives are produced.

papaverine   An alkaloid of opium in the benzylisoquinoline class that has no analgesic effect, as it does not depress the central nervous system. Usu-

ally used as a cough suppressant and in the treatment of cardiovascular disease. Because it does not produce euphoric effects, it is not an abused drug. Dependency does not develop.

para-addict (usually, coaddict)   A person who has a close relationship with an addict (a parent, spouse, or employer, for example) and because of the relationship also is an indirect victim of the disease and its effects. A coaddict (or para-addict) also needs counseling in many cases and often will find that his or her needs have been vicariously served by the relationship in some way. There is often an attempt by coaddicts to assign blame, particularly in the case of wives who feel at fault because of their husbands' addiction. Denial of a person's addiction problem may also be a fault of coaddicts. Denial only delays the treatment, which should begin immediately. Problems for a coaddict also can continue after a person stops using. During the time an addict is using, his or her spouse will often take control of the household; when the addiction stops the addict is no longer dependent, and the coaddict may feel unnecessary, unneeded, and unappreciated. NARCOTICS ANONYMOUS (NA) and AL-ANON are organizations that help the friends and relatives of addicts and alcoholics in these types of situations.

parahexyl   A synthetic cannabinoid resembling THC.

paraldehyde   A synthetic nonbarbiturate sedative hypnotic. Discovered in 1829, it was first used medically in 1881 and was long considered to be one of the safest hypnotics. It enjoyed widespread use.

Appearance: Paraldehyde appears as a colorless, inflammable liquid with a strong bitter taste and odor.

Usage: Paraldehyde has been used most commonly in connection with withdrawal treatments for alcoholics, particularly those suffering from delirium tremens. It also can be used to treat insomnia, convulsions and tetanus, and as an obstetric anesthetic and analgesic. It is now thought to be inconvenient and slightly dangerous, and has largely been replaced by barbiturates and benzodiazepines.

Despite its addictive qualities, paraldehyde is not commonly abused, probably because of its bitter taste, unpleasant and identifiable odor, and its burning effect on the mucous membranes.

Dosage: Paraldehyde is administered in doses ranging between 5–30 mg. As little as 12 mg has proved fatal to patients with liver disease, and doses of more than 100 mg have been survived.

Activity: Taken orally or by injection, it is rapidly absorbed by the body and metabolized in the liver. Up to 28% of the substance is exhaled, which gives the breath a characteristic pungent odor. Paraldehyde crosses the placental barrier, and large doses can depress neonatal respiration.

A problem encountered with paraldehyde relates to the substance's quick absorption of oxygen. When exposed to air, it oxidizes to strong acetic acid and loses a great deal of its effectiveness. Since the products of decomposition can be very dangerous, sometimes causing death, strict guidelines for the storage of paraldehyde must be observed. It is stored in amounts no greater than 30 mg and at temperatures no higher than 25° C. It must be discarded if not used within 24 hours after exposure to air.

Effects: Although paraldehyde acts much more quickly than chloral hydrate, barbiturates, alcohol and other depressants, its effects are very similar, including intoxication and diminished reflexes. Hypnotic doses induce sleep in as little as 10 minutes, and the drug's effects last from four to eight hours. Respiration is not significantly depressed nor is circulation affected. Oral administration causes burning of the mucous membranes, and intramuscular injection causes severe permanent injury if the injection is close to the sciatic nerve. Intravenous administration is both difficult and dangerous: difficult, because paraldehyde reacts with plastic syringes, and dangerous because the minimal injectable anesthetic dosage and the lethal dosage are extremely close in measurement.

Tolerance and dependence: Tolerance as well as or CROSS-TOLERANCE to other depressants develops with the use of paraldehyde. Dependence also can occur, especially in the case of alcoholics who receive the drug in withdrawal treatment. Abusive doses can cause stomach bleeding, blood dysfunctions and, in some cases, a deep coma similar to ether anesthesia. Symptoms of WITHDRAWAL from paraldehyde are similar to those of alcohol withdrawal.

Availability: Paraldehyde is available as a liquid to be administered orally with juice, as rectal suppositories, in olive oil or cottonseed oil enemas and in injectable form. It is a Schedule IV drug under the CONTROLLED SUBSTANCES ACT.

paranoia Users of illegal drugs often live in constant fear of arrest, bodily harm or financial misdoings before, during and after the purchase of drugs. This may lead to excessive fear and paranoia. Much of this anxiety, however, may be based on actual threat. A paranoid state is a serious mental disorder characterized by well-rationalized delusions of persecution or of grandeur. This state can result from the use of a drug or during withdrawal from amphetamines, cocaine, phencyclidine and hallucinogens. There is a mild form of paranoia often associated with marijuana and hashish; for this reason many who have tried this substance have discontinued use.

paraquat A herbicide that at one time was used (but later abandoned) by the Drug Enforcement Administration (DEA) to eradicate marijuana crops on federal land areas in the U.S. The U.S. government also encouraged the spraying of paraquat in Latin American countries.

In July 1979 the United Nations Narcotics Laboratory issued the following statement about paraquat:

> . . . the toxic properties of paraquat are such that the handling of the concentrate requires care. Although fibrosis of the lung can result from the ingestion of paraquat, there is no known instance of this occurring in humans following the ingestion of paraquat. Furthermore, residues of sprayed formulations on cannabis would not be sufficient to cause toxic effects to the marijuana user.

Opponents of paraquat use included the National Organization for Reform of Marijuana Laws (NORML), the Sierra Club, Friends of the Earth, the National Coalition Against the Misuse of Pesticides and several citizen action groups, which argued that the spraying poses a serious health threat to the estimated twenty-nine million marijuana smokers in the U.S. The government claimed that it was not paraquat, but rather marijuana itself that caused the harm. They further claimed that farmers were using an estimated four million pounds of paraquat annually over an estimated 10.7 million acres for the control of weeds among crops. A suit brought against the DEA by the above-mentioned groups resulted in a court order on September 13, 1983, temporarily restraining paraquat spraying because the DEA had not assessed the environmental impact before beginning the operation. The day after the court ruling, the Reagan Administration announced that spraying would be suspended for the rest of the 1983 growing season. It has not been reinstated. Subsequent studies sponsored by the Centers for Disease Control (CDC) in Atlanta state that the original fear of the health consequences of paraquat spraying was an overreaction. One can argue that it could hardly be called an overreaction, when in fact a toxic chemical was being sprayed on a substance that would be ingested by thousands, if not millions of citizens, and its deleterious effects were not yet known. If the government decided to put a toxic chemical in all alcoholic beverages to discourage use, there would surely be an outcry from the public. One could say that because marijuana is illegal, the government has this right, however, in recent years a number of states have changed their laws and no longer treat possession of a small quantity of marijuana for personal use by adults as a felony. Laws and customs continue to change. Alcohol was illegal in this country during Prohibition and is still outlawed in a number of Muslim countries. The Brahmins, the highest caste among Hindus, are not permitted to drink alcohol, but are permitted to use marijuana.

paregoric   Paregoric is an opium tincture (powdered opium dissolved in alcohol) combined with camphor, and it has an alcohol content equivalent to 90-proof whiskey. It has been used medically since its introduction in the early 1700s. In the 19th century the danger of addiction to opium-containing medicines was not well understood, and abuse of paregoric and LAUDANUM (an earlier tincture of opium) was common. Countless people, including a number of famous poets and writers, developed at least psychological, and more often physical dependence on them.

Well into the 20th century, mothers gave paregoric to their babies not only to control infant diarrhea but also to quiet their crying and put them to sleep. There is no way of estimating the harm this practice

caused before the Narcotics Act of 1914 placed opium and its products under federal control, making them available only by prescription. Paregoric is a Schedule III drug under the CONTROLLED SUBSTANCES ACT of 1970.

Usage and dosage: Although considered an old-fashioned remedy, it is still medically accepted and used principally to treat diarrhea and to detoxify newborns addicted to narcotics.

Paregoric is used by some heroin addicts when heroin is not available. Paregoric is a liquid and most addicts drink it, requiring about a quart a day to get the effects they need. Others inject it intravenously after processing it to remove the camphor and alcohol. At one time, addicts sometimes added antihistamines to paregoric for a mixture referred to as "Blue Velvet." Because the intravenous injection of Blue Velvet resulted in plugged veins and sometimes death, its popularity quickly waned.

Effects: See OPIUM.

Tolerance and dependence: Tolerance and physical dependence can develop with use over a long period of time. If it does, stopping suddenly or sharply reducing the accustomed dosage can bring on the same symptoms as those that follow opium withdrawal.

Richard R. Lingeman, *Drugs from A to Z* (New York: McGraw-Hill, 1974): 203.

Jack Margolis, *Recreational Drugs* (Los Angeles: Price Stern Sloan, 1978): 311–312.

parent education   Research has shown that involving parents in alcohol and other drug prevention is an effective strategy. A review of 127 evaluations of drug-abuse prevention programs suggested that programs built around peers and parents are more effective than those using only teachers. Prevention programs that aim to train parents to help shape positive health behavior in their children should be tailored to address cultural differences. Such EDUCATIONAL CAMPAIGNS AND PROGRAMS will undoubtedly prove successful, especially in the long run, but more research is needed to determine precisely which methods are most effective in this area.

E. Schaps et al., "Primary Prevention Evaluation Research: A Review of 127 Impact Studies," *Journal of Drug Issues* 11 (1980): 14–17.

Action Steps for Parents and Caregivers

1994, Substance Abuse and Mental Health Services Administration

Talk with your children about marijuana and other drugs and listen to their pressures and problems. Be clear and consistent in your "no-use" rules and messages.

Be aware of the connection between marijuana and other risky behaviors. Car crashes, sexually transmitted diseases, HIV/AIDS and injuries have all been linked to marijuana use.

Help your child deal with peer pressure. Practice ways for him or her to refuse drugs in ways that fit your child's personality.

Help children and adolescents learn the health, safety and legal consequences of using marijuana and other drugs. Be sure they understand that marijuana can be as dangerous as other illegal drugs.

Model and encourage good health practices: serve balanced and nutritious meals at regular times and plan fun family activities. Encourage individual expression and creativity.

Be sure children have easy access to a wide range of appealing, drug-free, alternative activities and safe, monitored areas where they can gather; work with others in your community—clubs, schools, churches and neighborhood groups—to sponsor and promote safe, healthy activities.

Discuss pro-use marijuana and drug images that youth see in movies and on TV, and hear on CDs and radio. Ask what they think about these messages. Do they understand their purpose? Do they recognize that these messages do not teach the harmful effects of these products?

Be a positive role model. Do not engage in any illegal, unhealthy or dangerous drug-use practices. Provide an example consistent with your messages to youth.

Be tolerant of a child's individuality. Accept a child for his or her talents and personality. Provide love, support and encouragement to the child or children in your life.

Source: Substance Abuse and Mental Health Services Administration, *Action Steps for Parents and Caregivers* (Rockville, Md.: Substance Abuse and Mental Health Services Administration, 1994).

parenteral   The injection of a substance, either intravenously, intramuscularly or subcutaneously, as opposed to oral ingestion. (See ADMINISTRATION.)

parest   A rapid-acting sedative hypnotic that contained METHAQUALONE hydrochloride and was used for sedation and sleep. It was taken off the market due to its widespread abuse.

parica   A psychedelic snuff used by the Yekwana Indians in Venezuela. It is made from the bark of the virola tree.

Partnership for a Drug-Free America, Inc. Organization responsible for the development and distribution of some of the most sophisticated drug awareness messages. Millions of dollars worth of media time has been generated to disseminate well-designed, effective public service announcements. The partnership also conducts research to help target these messages.

passion flower   *Passiflora incarnata.* The leaves and stems of this plant contain a small amount of the alkaloid HARMINE. There are claims that it produces mild psychedelic effects when smoked or brewed in a tea.

passive smoking   Smoke enter the lungs of nonsmokers when they are in the presence of tobacco or marijuana smokers. It is unlikely that one will get "high" from passive inhalation of marijuana. Any "contact high" is usually the result of psychological identification with the smoker rather than THC intoxication.

Despite a media fascination with deaths from illicit drugs (media fascinations translate to political campaigns), death rates from these drugs are significantly lower than those related to tobacco. According to a poster distributed by the Coalition for a Smoke-Free America and based on 1992 EPA (Environmental Protection Agency) figures, there were 25,000 deaths from heroin-morphine abuse and

3,300 deaths from crack-cocaine use vs. 418,690 deaths due to tobacco use and *53,000* deaths annually as a result of secondhand smoke. These astounding numbers mean that as many people die each year from passive smoking as from all of illicit drug use combined. An American is 17 times more likely to die from tobacco-related causes than from illicit-drug related causes.

There has been increasing concern over the adverse health effects of "secondary" or passive inhalation of tobacco smoke since the U.S. surgeon general's report on smoking and tobacco was issued in early 1989.

In a preliminary report issued in May 1990, the EPA alerted Americans to the risk of lung cancer for non-smokers from secondhand cigarette smoke. The increased concern has resulted in activity in several policy making areas: smoking restrictions in public places by some states, cities and federal agencies, smoking restrictions in the workplace and on all commercial domestic flights under six hours duration, lawsuits against tobacco manufacturers, warning labels and even proposed bans on print advertising of tobacco products. In the early 1990s, a number of civil employees successfully sued their employers for the negative health consequences of job-related exposure to smoke.

An Australian Federal Court ruled in February 1991 that an advertisement by the Tobacco Institute claiming that there was "Little evidence and nothing which proved scientifically that cigarette smoking causes disease in nonsmokers" was false, and that scientific evidence demonstrated that secondhand smoke could cause respiratory diseases in children, asthma attacks and lung cancer.

pathibamate   A sedative that contains tridihexethyl chloride and MEPROBAMATE. It is used in the treatment of peptic ulcers and colon disorders, particularly when they are accompanied by tension and anxiety. It has the potential for abuse. Physical and psychological dependence can occur, especially when taken with alcohol or other central nervous system depressants. Overdosage can result in stupor, coma and respiratory collapse. It is not sold in the U.S.

pathological drinker   Someone who drinks excessively as a means of handling unconscious problems; an alcoholic or PROBLEM DRINKER.

pathological intoxication   The World Health Organization defines pathological intoxication as a "syndrome characterized by extreme excitement with aggressive and violent features and, frequently, ideas of persecution, after consumption of disproportionately little alcohol. . . . A controversial entity primarily used in a forensic context."

World Health Organization (WHO), *Lexicon of Alcohol and Drug Terms* (Geneva, 1994).

PCP   Phencyclidine hydrochloride; chemical name: 1- (1-phenylcyclohexyl) piperdine. PCP (often referred to as angel dust) first was developed in 1959 as one of a new class of anesthetic agents, known as dissociative anesthetics because they detach or dissociate patients from all bodily sensations so that no pain is felt during surgery. It was found that patients often became agitated, delusional and irrational while recovering from the anesthetic effects of PCP and its use was discontinued. It was used in veterinary medicine until the late 1970s when it was replaced by an equally effective anesthetic with fewer side effects.

PCP was first introduced in the latter part of the 1960s as a street drug and quickly gained a reputation as a dangerous and hazardous chemical. It was then used as an adulterant in other drugs that were more expensive or more difficult to synthesize.

In the 1960s PCP was commonly sold as THC, which is costly to manufacture and rarely available. As ersatz THC, the drug spread nationwide, and increasingly users began wanting PCP itself. In 1985 past-month use reached an all-time high of 672,000, declined to its lowest point in 1990 (50,000), but increased steadily again until 1994 (201,000).

Classification: PCP is a dissociative anesthetic with mixed neurologic and autonomic activity, originally developed as an anesthetic. It is difficult to classify accurately, as different doses produce different effects, sometimes resembling a sedative, stimulant, analgesic, anesthetic or HALLUCINOGEN. PCP is in a class by itself—the Student Organization for the Study of Hallucinogens has called it a "delusionogen."

Usage: PCP has more undesirable reactions than any other commonly used psychoactive drug. Dr. Ronald Siegel, a Los Angeles psychologist, tested and interviewed 310 adult users, who all said there were unpleasant negative aspects to the PCP experience. But despite its many bizarre and unpleasant effects, it has enough desirable qualities to create a demand. The positive effects included heightened sensitivity to outside stimuli, dissociation, elevation in mood, inebriation and relaxation. Only one in 12 reported experiencing euphoria. The incidence of male users is higher than female users (3.6% vs. 2.1%), according to the SAMHSA (Substance Abuse and Mental Health Services Administration) *1994 National Household Survey on Drug Abuse*. PCP users come from all ethnic backgrounds.

Appearance: PCP is a white crystalline powder that is readily soluble in water or alcohol. It has a distinctive bitter chemical taste. It can be easily mixed with dyes and turns up on the illicit drug market in a variety of tablets, capsules and colored powders. It can be snorted, smoked, eaten or injected, but it is not often used this way. When smoked it is most often mixed with another substance such as mint leaves, parsley, tobacco or marijuana.

Effects: At low to moderate doses, physiological effects include a slight increase in breathing rate and a more pronounced rise in blood pressure and pulse rate. Respiration becomes shallow, and flushing and profuse sweating frequently occur. Generalized numbness of the extremities and muscular uncoordination may also develop. At high doses there is a drop in blood pressure, pulse rate and respiration. This may be accompanied by nausea, vomiting, blurred vision, vertical nystagmus (flicking up and down of the eyes), drooling, loss of balance and dizziness. Large amounts of the drug can cause convulsions and coma; several deaths have been associated with PCP use.

Psychological effects with small doses include distinct changes in body awareness, similar to those associated with alcohol intoxication. Effects of higher doses mimic certain primary symptoms of schizophrenia, such as delusions, mental turmoil and a sensation of distance from one's environment. Illusions and hallucinations, usually auditory, occasionally visual, have also been reported following administration of large amounts of the drug. Bizarre behavior of many types sometimes occurs in response to them. Speech often is blocked and to the outsider may appear meaningless. Paranoid thinking

is common. Users may react with frightening violence in response to imagined threats. Because PCP has anesthetic action, touch and pain sensations are dulled, and the user may severely injure himself without knowing it. Users may be difficult to control in a hospital situation. Voluntary patients at Metropolitan State Hospital with a history of PCP abuse without current major behavioral, mental or physical disorders said they experienced the following effects during PCP abuse:

80% reported organicity—forgetfulness, difficulty in concentrating, thinking clearly and understanding;

75% reported behavior dyscontrol—physical violence, aggression and agitation;

74% reported estrangement—feelings of derealization and depersonalization;

60% reported paranoia—transient suspiciousness;

55% reported altered mood states—elation to depression;

41% reported hallucinations—tactile, visual or auditory;

20% reported suicidal impulses.

PCP has sedative effects, and interactions with other CENTRAL NERVOUS SYSTEM depressants such as ALCOHOL and BENZODIAZEPINES can lead to coma or accidental overdose. Use of PCP among adolescents may interfere with hormones related to normal growth and development as well as with the learning process.

Tolerance and dependence: In two studies published in 1978, tolerance was reported, making increased doses of PCP necessary to produce the same effects. The degree of tolerance developed is still unknown. The popularity of PCP indicates some degree of psychological dependence. Physical dependence and WITHDRAWAL in humans has not been observed.

Availability: PCP is easily manufactured and is in plentiful supply wherever there is a demand. It also is commonly found as an adulterant in mescaline, psilocybin and LSD. Most THC sold on the streets is actually PCP. Marijuana is sometimes "dusted" with PCP to increase its market appeal. Crack cocaine mixed with PCP is known as Bazooka or Space Base. Less frequently it is found as a substitute for cocaine and heroin or as an adulterant in these drugs and is difficult to detect. It is sold by at least 100 different street names.

Sources: PCP is difficult to control by law because it is easily and inexpensively synthesized. The starting chemicals are in widespread industrial use, very simple equipment is needed, and no special skill is required. The drug is manufactured only in illicit laboratories within the U.S., and efforts to control the precursors have been only partly successful.

Synonyms: angel dust, horse tranquilizer, animal tranquilizer, tic, dust, crystal, superweed, rocket fuel, street drug, peace pill, Shermans.

pedestrian accidents Alcohol plays a significant role in pedestrian traffic fatalities. The NATIONAL HIGHWAY TRAFFIC SAFETY ADMINISTRATION estimates that 50% to 55% of all fatal ACCIDENTS involve either a driver or a pedestrian who is drunk. Although less studied because total national prevalence of drug abuse is only 5% that of alcohol, the use of other drugs also plays a role in both driver and pedestrian fatalities. (See DRIVING WHILE IMPAIRED [DWI].)

E. C. Cerelle, *Alcohol in Fatal Accidents: National Estimates—USA Executive Summary,* NHTSA tech. note DOTHS 806 746 (Springfield, Va.: National Technical Information Service, 1985).

peer pressure ADOLESCENTS are perhaps the group most vulnerable to the growing social acceptance of drug use in the U.S. Peer pressure, the desire and need to belong to a certain group and to show that one belongs, has long been cited as a reason for drug use and abuse among youths.

Peers pressure adolescents to try drugs at this particularly vulnerable stage when their sense of individual identity is still being developed and the need to be accepted is very strong. Adolescents may also use drugs in order to relax and be comfortable, as much as from the pressure to conform to the dictates of the group. Younger children also are likely to adopt the group's attitude toward drugs.

In 1993 there were 15,439 emergency room visits related to the use of marijuana; 2,439 involving adolescents. Cocaine accounted for 1,583 emergency room visits by young people. A 1994 nationwide survey conducted for the National Institute on Drug Abuse (NIDA) reported that 80.4% of senior high school students had tried alcohol at least once (down from 91% in 1989) and 28% had consumed five or more drinks in a row within the last two-week period (down from 33% in 1989).

pemoline A central nervous system stimulant that is most commonly used in the treatment of minimal brain dysfunction. Because it has an activity similar to that of AMPHETAMINES, dependency can occur. (See CYLERT.)

pentazocine A potent ANALGESIC and mild NARCOTIC ANTAGONIST first synthesized in 1961 by Sterling-Winthrop. Pentazocine resembles codeine and morphine in most of its properties. The drug is best known by the brand names TALWIN and Talwin NX (Winthrop) and is one of the 100 most-prescribed drugs.

Classification: It is a Schedule IV drug under the Controlled Substances Act.

Usage: It is used for the relief of moderate to severe pain and as a supplement to anesthetics. When given to a patient who has previously received a narcotic, it may act as a narcotic antagonist and withdrawal symptoms are experienced. Talwin's abuse is related to its medical use and is partially a result of over-prescription. It is abused on the street in a combination of Talwin and pyribenzamine ("T's and blues"), often intravenously.

Dosage: Talwin is prescribed orally in doses of 30–50 mg every three or four hours. In intravenous administration, 30 mg is equivalent to 10 mg of morphine, but the duration of the effects may be less than those of morphine.

Appearance: Pentazocine is a white crystalline substance soluble in acidic aqueous solution.

Activity: It is extensively metabolized in the body, with only 13% appearing in the urine. The tablets recently have been reformulated to contain NALOXONE, and now they are sold as Talwin NX to make intravenous use undesirable, because if injected the Naloxone will negate the effects of the Talwin, but if taken orally the Talwin will be effective.

Effects: Pentazocine's analgesic effects materialize more quickly than morphine's—in as little as 15–30 minutes with oral administration and in two to three minutes with intravenous administration. They include euphoria and the usual range of narcotic effects. Like DARVON, the drug can cause hallucinations, disorientation and confusion.

Tolerance and dependence: Talwin itself will produce withdrawal in individuals dependent on opiates due to its partial antagonist properties. It should never be given to methadone-maintained or actively narcotic-addicted individuals. Overdoses and deaths from the drug have been reported.

pentobarbital A short-acting barbiturate that is used as a sedative hypnotic. In the depressant category, it is one of the most sought-after drugs by users. It is sold under the trade name NEMBUTAL. (See BARBITURATES.)

pentothal A short-acting central nervous system depressant that contains thiopental sodium. It is used intravenously to induce hypnosis and as an anesthesia for brief procedures. It is also used in the control of convulsive states and for narcoanalysis in psychiatric disorders. Overdosage can result in respiratory depression and paralysis. No longer used in the U.S.

Percocet-5 A semisynthetic narcotic analgesic that is used for sedation and for mild to moderate pain. It contains oxycodone hydrochloride and acetaminophen. It can produce morphine-type drug dependency and has a potential for abuse. When taken with alcohol or other central nervous system depressants it can have an additive effect.

Percodan A semisynthetic narcotic analgesic that contains OXYCODONE HYDROCHLORIDE. Its activity is similar to morphine and it is usually used for analgesia and sedation. It may be habit-forming and has a significant potential for abuse. Tolerance, along with physical and psychological dependence, can develop. When used with alcohol or other central nervous system depressants it can have an ADDITIVE EFFECT. Overdosage can result in respiratory depression, muscle flaccidity, somnolence and coma; severe overdosage can result in circulatory collapse, cardiac arrest and death.

Percodan is sold and sought after on the street. Most street varieties come from pharmacies that are involved in illicit selling of drugs (pill mills).

periodic alcoholism A form of alcoholism characterized by bouts of excessive drinking with intervals of abstinence or moderate drinking. Periodic alcoholism also is known as EPSILON ALCOHOLISM.

Pernod An anise-flavored aperitif named after Henri-Louis Pernod, the first manufacturer of AB-SINTHE. Pernod was initially produced as a substitute for absinthe when the latter was banned for health reasons because it contained the poisonous wormwood.

When diluted with water, Pernod takes on a cloudy appearance. In comparison with absinthe, it is lower in alcoholic content (45% as compared with 60% to 80%) and contains no wormwood.

personality disorder and substance abuse Individuals who abuse substances are often diagnosed with personality disorders, especially antisocial and borderline disorders. Drug abuse and the resultant dysfunctional lifestyle are among the criteria used to diagnose personality disorders. Some disorders signify a poorer prognosis for recovery from substance abuse.

personality trait theories Personality trait theories may one day be used to determine a set of characteristics associated with the development of alcohol and/or other drug abuse. Although studies have not identified a particular set of personality traits that distinguish drug users from other groups, the following traits were most often observed: low thresholds for frustration; ambiguity and dissonance; high levels of hopelessness, anxiety and helplessness; negative self-image; and feelings of isolation and depression. It is often difficult to determine whether these traits preceded drug use or were a consequence of it. However, several studies have clearly supported the emergence of these traits after the onset of addiction.

Peru For more than 2,000 years Peruvians have grown and chewed coca. Today the government permits and licenses substantial cultivation of coca for traditional domestic use as well as for pharmaceutical purposes. Despite government controls, however, coca cultivation expanded in 1989 to an estimated 186,000 metric tons, rose to 223,900 metric tons in 1992, but dropped to 155,500 metric tons in 1993. About half of the cocaine consumed in the U.S. is synthesized from coca grown in Peru; most of it processed and distributed by Colombians. Peru suffers from a weak economy and runaway inflation.

The smoking of coca paste is of particular concern to the Peruvian government. In this semirefined state, coca contains harmful impurities, such as cement, large amounts of coca alkaloids and kerosene, and inhaling it into the lungs can be extremely dangerous. Recent reports show an increase in smoking coca paste among high school youths.

Peru was part of President George Bush's September 1989 National Drug Control Strategy, which proposed that $100 million to $270 million go into a superfund to finance the so-called Andean—Peru, Colombia and Bolivia—Initiative. In 1995 President Clinton praised the efforts of the Fujimori Administration to counter Peru's illegal drug industry. The outlawing of the cultivation of opium-producing poppies, along with the effects on international drug exportation of the capture of Colombian drug-kingpins, has also broken down some of Peru's drug industry.

Cultivation: Cocaine trafficking provides several hundred million dollars and is the principal and often only income for thousands of farmers—an income that is many times the daily wage for growing other crops. Coca is an attractive crop because it is a deep-rooted plant with a life span of about 30 years. In addition, it can be harvested three to six times a year and can be grown in poor soil unsuitable for other crops. Officials admit to having difficulty developing legitimate alternatives for coca farming unless economic growth opens markets for alternative products.

In 1980 the government doubled its resource commitment to curbing production in excess of that used for legal purposes. In a cooperative effort with the U.S., 1,500 acres of coca were eradicated in 1980, and 57 laboratories were destroyed. In 1981 a five-year eradication and enforcement project was initiated by the Bureau of International Narcotics Matters (INM), concurrently with a five-year plan by the Agency for International Development (AID) to diversify agricultural development. By mid-1982

about 5% of coca cultivation had been abandoned, and other cultivations were not being fully harvested.

White House, *National Drug Control Strategy: Strengthening Communities' Response to Drugs and Crime* (Washington, D.C., 1995).

pethidine   A generic name for MEPERIDINE.

Pew Charitable Trusts, The   A Philadelphia-based national foundation with a long-term interest in the health field. The Trusts awarded its first grants to train health professionals in the area of alcohol and other drug use in 1971. The foundation established health professional training as one of three primary components of its drug and alcohol abuse programs, which include prevention and early intervention programs for children and youth and research on prevention. The Trusts supported the development of Johns Hopkins University's establishment of a center for teaching and clinical practice in alcoholism, as well as the Society of General Internal Medicine through the American College of Physicians, for a curriculum in alcohol- and drug-use education for general internal medicine faculty. The George Washington University School of Medicine and Health Sciences also receives support from the Trusts to educate health professionals to meet the challenge of alcohol and other drug use.

peyote   *Lophophora williamsii;* a spineless cactus native to central and northern Mexico, whose top crown or button contains a hallucinogenic drug. The button is dried, then ingested by holding it in the mouth until it is soft and then swallowed whole. Generally it takes three to four buttons to achieve a "trip." The buttons also are cut up and eaten in pieces or cooked into a slush and then mixed with juices or drunk alone.

Peyote was first used by the Aztecs and then by other Mexican Indians to enhance awareness in religious ceremonies. It is a very nauseating drug and vomiting is considered a part of the purgation by Native American Peyotists. Users say peyote produces a deep insight into reality, along with highly complex sensory experiences. The richly colored "kaleidoscope" type of hallucination is one of its most sought-after effects.

In the 1800s the use of peyote spread northward and "peyote cults" began to spring up. A total abstinence from alcohol was required. This was a time when alcohol use was becoming epidemic among the Native Americans, so many tribal leaders, striving to maintain peace with "the white man," encouraged the use of peyote because those using it were less hostile.

An attempt, particularly by missionaries, to have peyote outlawed by the various western states gained some success, but many state legislatures that enacted such laws eventually repealed them to permit ritual use in religious services.

Although peyote has long since been declared illegal, during the 1950s and early 1960s it was a simple matter to purchase peyote buttons. Mail-order companies advertised them in numerous publications. The drug's availability led to widespread use, particularly among college students. LSD also became popular during the 1960s and the government's attitude and public hostility toward its use influenced the attitude toward peyote. Investigations were conducted into the possible dangerous effects of peyote.

In 1969 the federal government granted the Native American Church of North America the legal right to consume peyote in religious services. The church claims some 250,000 members in the U.S. and Canada. The principal supporters of this move were anthropologists and psychiatrists. They suggested that there is something to be learned from the long use of peyote among Native Americans. Their ability to take a potentially dangerous drug and to use it without suffering harmful side effects warranted continued study. When peyote is taken, the Native Americans use safeguards far greater than those employed by some LSD users. Peyote services are held at strictly defined times; no one is allowed to leave a meeting, so consequently a hallucinating person is not allowed to wander off. Customarily the meetings last until the following morning, well after the drug's effects have worn off.

Peyote currently is the only hallucinogen whose use is sanctioned by the U.S. government, but only for the Native Church of North America. In 1990 however, the Supreme Court, upholding an Oregon law, held that states had the right to ban peyote use even when used for religious purposes.

pharmaceuticals   Pills, capsules, liquids, medicinal suppositories, lotions and other preparations that have a medical use.

pharmacogenic orgasm   The pleasurable sensation or "RUSH" felt by a HEROIN addict directly after intravenous injection. (See ADMINISTRATION.)

pharmacokinetics   A study, made over a period of time, of a drug's action and movement through the body. The processes studied include the dynamics of absorption, distribution and excretion.

pharmacological etiology (iatrogenic addiction)
Drug addiction as a result of the medical administration of drugs can and has been a cause of drug abuse. The majority of physicians are now quite aware of the addictive qualities of drugs, although some are still inclined to prescribe them freely, simply because it is easier to cover symptoms than to take the time to treat, if possible, the causes of an illness, and many unethical doctors make a large proportion of their income by prescribing addictive medicines to their patients. On the other hand, some patients have been known to complain that physicians are overcautious in the prescription of drugs, a complaint common among patients recovering from surgery and in extreme pain. No extensive studies have been made to determine the effects of medical narcotic use for short periods of time (several days to a couple of weeks), to discover the extent of withdrawal symptoms when a drug is stopped, or to find out if patients develop a craving or substitute other drugs for the one that has been withdrawn. It is known, however, that after a week of full doses of a narcotic, tolerance and some degree of withdrawal may be seen. With barbiturates the process may take a few weeks; with the BENZODIAZEPINES it can take months.

pharmacotherapy and alcohol abuse   Pharmacotherapeutic agents continue to be used as adjuncts for limited purposes in the treatment of alcohol dependence. Various agents have been tested over the years, but no pharmacotherapy has emerged as being effective in ameliorating long-term drinking behavior. In the early 1990s, research revealed promising results at controlling the cravings and consequent relapses common to early abstinence from the use of NALTREXONE, which is marketed under the name Revia. Because it seems useful only in the short term, has deleterious side effects and is very dangerous, ANTABUSE (disulfiram) is no longer recommended for use alone in treating alcoholism. Under certain controlled conditions Antabuse may be effective in solidifying abstinent behavior until the patient can establish an appropriate program of recovery.

Enoch Gordis, M.D., ed., *Sixth Special Report to the U.S. Congress on Alcohol and Health* (Rockville, Md.: NIAAA, 1987): 125–126.

Phenacetin   A central nervous system depressant and synthetic analgesic used to relieve minor pain (headache and neuralgia) and to reduce fever. In prescription drugs it is generally combined with other drugs such as butalbital and codeine. Phenacetin in large amounts can cause kidney damage.

Phenaphen with Codeine   A narcotic analgesic that contains codeine phosphate and acetaminophen. Available in varying strengths, No. 2 and No. 3 are used for mild to moderate pain; No. 4 is used for moderate to severe pain. Tolerance, along with psychological and physical dependence, can develop. It has a significant potential for abuse and, when taken with alcohol or other central nervous system depressants there will be an ADDITIVE EFFECT. Overdosage will cause respiratory depression, somnolence, muscle flaccidity and possibly coma.

phenazocine   A synthetic narcotic analgesic, derived from OPIUM, that is used for acute and chronic pain. Classified as a Schedule II drug, it has a potency that exceeds morphine.

phencyclidine   Developed as an anesthetic agent in the 1950s, phencyclidine (PCP) was removed from the market in 1965 after reports of agitated and psychotic reaction, often prolonged, that occurred in patients given it prior to surgery. PCP gained appeal as a drug of abuse in the 1970s, and the popularity of "angel dust," as it is most commonly known on the street, has waxed and waned since then. Users frequently end up in the emergency room. Signs of toxicity from PCP include nystagmus, delirium agitation, seizure and psychosis resembling that seen in schizophrenia. Coma and death can result from high serum levels. Lower levels result in withdrawal,

negativism, autistic, idiosyncratic and bizarre responses, along with disorders of attention and perception. The effects of PCP on emotions and behavior are so similar to the psychotic symptoms of the schizophrenic that PCP has been used as a study model for this disorder.

phendimetrazine tartrate   A central nervous system stimulant, whose activity is similar to that of AMPHETAMINES. It is used as an ANORECTIC for weight control and has a significant potential for abuse. Tolerance can develop within a few weeks. Phendimetrazine tartrate is found in many marketed anorectics.

phenmetrazine   A central nervous system stimulant that is used as an ANORECTIC for weight control. Its activity is similar to that of AMPHETAMINES and it has a significant potential for abuse. (See PRELUDIN.)

phenobarbital   A long-acting BARBITURATE with an onset time of up to one hour and a duration of action up to 16 hours. It is used as a sedative hypnotic and anticonvulsant.

phentermine   A central nervous system stimulant, which activity is similar to that of AMPHETAMINES. It is used as an ANORECTIC for weight control and has a significant potential for abuse. (See IONAMIN.)

phenylpropanolamine   A synthetic drug that affects the autonomic nervous system. Used as a mucous membrane decongestant and as a treatment for allergic conditions, it is found in over-the-counter preparations for colds and weight control. It has significant stimulant effects and is a frequent drug of abuse among adolescents, who often purchase it on a mail-order basis.

phenytoin   A central nervous system depressant that is used mainly as an anticonvulsant in the treatment of epilepsy. Its highly selective action affects only motor centers, and it has little or no hypnotic or sedative action. The use and dosage of phenytoin should be carefully monitored because of numerous severe side effects. It is marketed as Dilantin and appears to have no abuse potential.

phobia Phobias are more than extreme fears, they are intense and irrational fears that are out of proportion to any actual danger. Phobias occur in several forms. Simple phobia is a fear of a particular object or situation. Social phobia is a fear of being painfully embarrassed in a social setting. AGORAPHOBIA is a fear of being in any open space or situation that might provoke a panic attack or from which escape might be difficult.

Beatrice A. Rouse, ed., *Substance Abuse and Mental Health Statistics Sourcebook* (Washington, D.C.: Substance Abuse and Mental Health Services Administration, 1995).

pholcodine An OPIATE derivative that is used as a cough suppressant in England and France.

Phrenilin An analgesic used for head pain associated with tension and upper respiratory infection. It contains the BARBITURATE sodium butabarbital, acetaminophen and caffeine. Because it contains a barbiturate, Phrenilin may be habit-forming.

Physicians' Desk Reference (PDR) An annual volume for health care professionals, listing all of the brand name prescription drugs. There are photographs of each drug and information on usage, dosage and so forth. Illicit drug users refer to it as well, for pill identification and drug descriptions. A PDR for nonprescription drugs also is available, and the publisher, Merck, now distributes home versions of both books.

physiological models of etiology In reference to substance abuse, theories in this category postulate that some individuals are predisposed to develop alcoholism and other drug dependency because of an organic defect. In the case of alcohol, an underlying biological malfunction results in a craving that in turn leads to alcoholism. Models in this group include ENDOCRINE ETIOLOGICAL THEORIES and GENETIC theories.

It is difficult to measure physiological differences between addicted and nonaddicted individuals, in part because "addiction" remains ill-defined. Those addicted are more easily identified and usually become the subjects of the majority of research studies. Tests may show consequences of alcohol/drug use rather than any physiological differences antecedent to that abuse. To date there is little clear evidence as to what role physiological variables play in addiction. (See also PSYCHOLOGICAL MODELS OF ETIOLOGY and SOCIOCULTURAL MODELS OF ETIOLOGY.)

physostigmine An acid derivative of an alkaloid extracted from the seeds of the calabar bean. It is used to reverse toxic effects on the central nervous system, such as hallucinations, delirium and disorientation, caused by drugs that have produced anticholinergic poisoning. (See ANTILIRIUM.)

Pil-Anon Family Program A self-help support organization founded in 1978 and sponsored by PILLS ANONYMOUS WORLD SERVICE, for the families of chemically dependent people. It is based on the 12-step program of Alcoholics Anonymous and Al-Anon, which is an organization for families of AA members.

Pills Anonymous World Service (PA) A self-help, self-supporting group with a 12-step program based on that of Alcoholics Anonymous. The only requirement for membership is a desire to stop taking pills and/or other mood-altering chemicals. Founded in 1975, the group also sponsors PIL-ANON FAMILY PROGRAM for the families of those who are chemically dependent.

piloerection The involuntary bristling or erection of hair (gooseflesh), which is an objective diagnostic sign of opioid withdrawal and therefore opioid dependency.

pilsner beer Now generally used as a generic name for any light lager beer, the term originally was applied only to a product brewed in Pilsen (Plzen), in what is now the Czech Republic.

Pilsner beer originated during the Middle Ages, when Slavic peoples developed an especially light beer because of a lack of barley, which forced them to combine a high proportion of wheat with the malted barley in the cereal mash from which they brewed their beer. At the time, private brewing rights were an especially sensitive issue in Bohemia (which is today the western Czech Republic). Attempts to restrict private trade in beer resulted in the brief Parsons War of the 14th century, a struggle by monasteries to protect their brewing rights.

Modern pilsner beer dates from the 19th century, when, in response to similar restrictions, families in Pilsen joined together to form a cooperative brewery. That venture lasted until World War II ended its ability to export and brought about its collapse. Today the only true pilsner beer is brewed under the brand name "Pilsner Urquell," but because of its long and distinguished reputation other brewers have adopted the label "pilsner" to describe their finest beers.

piptadenia   A hallucinogenic snuff used by Native Americans in Venezuela and Colombia. It is made from the seeds of shrubs in the mimosa family *Leguminosae.*

pituri   *Duboisia hopwoodii,* a plant that grows in Australia and whose leaves are chewed by Aborigines for a stimulating effect. After the initial stimulation, there are often severe adverse effects.

placidyl   A sedative hypnotic that contains ethchlorvynol and is used for insomnia. It has the potential for abuse, and when taken with alcohol or other central nervous system depressants can produce an additive effect. Overdosage can result in severe respiratory depression and deep coma.

Plegine   A brand of phendimetrazine tartrate that is used as an ANORECTIC for weight control. Chemically and pharmacologically similar to AMPHETAMINES, it has a high potential for abuse and can cause psychological dependence and social dysfunction. Overdosage can result in restlessness, confusion, hallucinations and coma.

plexonal   A BARBITURATE sedative that is used for anxiety, tension and insomnia. It contains barbital sodium, butalbital sodium, phenobarbital sodium, scopolamine and dihydroergotamine. Tolerance may develop along with physical and psychological dependence, and it has a significant potential for abuse. Overdosage can result in shallow respiration, coma and possibly death. It is not available in the U.S.

PMB 200 & PMB 400   A sedative preparation that contains Premarin (conjugated estrogens) and MEPROBAMATE. Usually it is used for menopausal

syndrome when accompanied by tension and anxiety. It has a potential for abuse and can produce physical and psychological dependence. When overdosage occurs, sleep ensues rapidly and blood pressure, pulse and respiratory rates are reduced to basal levels. No longer available in the U.S.

Poland

Alcohol: According to a 1995 survey, Poland's annual per capita consumption of spirits is one of the 10 highest worldwide, probably because of the Polish preference for vodka and other liquors. The country ranked significantly lower in consumption of wine and beer.

Little information is available concerning alcohol abuse in Poland. According to a 1981 report in the *New York Times,* the consumption of alcohol in Poland had been increasing for several decades. At the time of the report, the Polish people consumed seven times as much alcohol as they did a decade before. In 1987 the rate of cirrhosis was 13.4 per 100,000 men and 6.8 per 100,000 women, slightly lower than the U.S. rate.

Until the 1980s, Poland had no comprehensive program to combat alcoholism. However, spurred in part by attacks by leaders of the independent labor movement, the Communist government then in power launched a national campaign against alcohol abuse.

Drugs other than alcohol: In 1995 the Polish Ministry of Health estimated the country had only 40,000 drug users. But independent experts estimated 100,000 addicts and another 200,000 casual users. Poppy seed compote is the most prevalent. Production of a poppy seed compote, made from opium poppy illegally diverted from legal government supplies, is common among farmers. Amphetamines are the second most prevalent drug of abuse. Local marijuana cultivation is on the decline.

One-third of Poland's IDUs (intravenous drug users) are HIV-infected, and contaminated needle use is the leading cause of AIDS in Poland. The government is slowly increasing prevention and treatment efforts.

According to a report by the Bureau of Narcotics and Law Enforcement Affairs, "In 1995, Poland has emerged as a major producer of illicit amphetamines, and a significant transit point for cocaine, heroin, and cannabis destined for the western European market. . . . The Cali cartel is stepping up efforts to target Poland both by sea and air. Heroin traffickers, including those from Nigeria, Turkey, India and Pakistan are also attempting to use routes through Poland. . . . Ethnic Chinese crime gangs are also establishing themselves in Poland."

In terms of local drug manufacturing, Poland may now be the largest producer of amphetamines in Europe.

Brewers and Licensed Retailers Association, *1993 Annual Report* (London, 1995).

United States Dept. of State, Bureau for International Narcotics and Law Enforcement Affairs, *International Narcotics Control Strategy Report March 1996.*

polydrug use   The use of two or more drugs simultaneously. This may be done to enhance or potentiate one drug's effects, to neutralize or counteract undesirable effects of a particular drug, or to achieve a less expensive HIGH by combining an inexpensive drug with a small amount of an expensive one. The practice of polydrug use has become so common that single-drug users appear to be in the minority. There are an infinite number of combinations, including marijuana and alcohol, or cocaine and alcohol. Other favorites are barbiturates and alcohol, barbiturates and amphetamines, cocaine and heroin, analgesics with tranquilizers or sedatives, and more recently, sleeping pills and codeine. Heroin users will supplement their habit with barbiturates if the only heroin they can obtain is highly diluted. The practice of polydrug use is also known as multihabituation. (See POTENTIATION)

polystyrene cement   Model airplane glue; sniffed for its intoxicating effects.

Pondimin   An ANORECTIC used for weight control. It is a brand of fenfluramine hydrochloride. Unlike other anorectics that have an amphetamine activity, Pondimin produces more central nervous system (CNS) depression than stimulation. When taken with alcohol or other CNS depressants it can have an additive effect. It has a significant potential for abuse and psychological dependence can occur. Overdosage can result in agitation, confusion, hyperventilation and pupil dilation.

port   A fortified wine (18% to 20% alcohol) traditionally associated with the town of Oporto on the upper Douro river in Portugal. It now is produced in the United States, Australia and South Africa as a varietal wine.

Fermentation of port wine grapes begins when they are pressed and the grape sugars and juice combine. The process is then halted at an early stage, and brandy is added to the mixture of grape juice and wine. The mixture is then aged in bottles or in casks.

When the quality of the grape harvest is exceptional, the grapes are reserved for a vintage port. In this case the mixture of grape juice, wine and brandy is kept for one year and then refortified and bottled. Vintage port is aged in bottles for 15 to 20 years in order to produce the desired strength and flavor. Further aging is considered a mark of distinction, and vintage ports survive in the bottle for more than 40 years before separating and deteriorating.

When the quality of the harvest is less exceptional, the grapes are used to make tawny port, the only variety produced outside of Portugal. Tawny port is the product of a blend of grapes from several years aged in wooden casks for periods shorter than those for vintage port. After 12 years of aging the wine is considered tawny port, but it is commonly bottled earlier and sold as ruby port. These wines usually survive less than five years in the bottle.

Port from Oporto is usually bottled and sold in Britain, where a taste for it developed when wars with France halted importation of French wines. There are a number of different blends and types, including a white port. It is often drunk like wine but, because of its alcoholic strength, it also is commonly mixed with lemon or tonic water and poured over ice.

portal cirrhosis   Named for the portal vein that transports blood from the stomach, intestines and spleen to the liver, it is the most prominent type of cirrhosis and the one most frequently found among alcoholics. It is also known as Laennec's, nutritional or alcoholic cirrhosis.

porter   A dark and sweet ALE that is in effect a combination of ale and stout, although more carbonated than stout. Porter is supposed to have originated in response to the demands of 18th-century market porters in London for a "half and half" potion of ale and stout. Now generally referred to as "dark ale," "porter" remains the designation of stouts in Ireland that are more carbonated than those intended for bottling and exportation.

Porter Narcotics Bill of 1929   This bill established prisons or "farms" as an alternative form of detention for convicted addicts. The Lexington Farm was established in 1935 and the Fort Worth Farm in 1938. The farms were operated by the U.S. Public Health Service under the supervision of the Justice Department and the Federal Bureau of Prisons. The farms stressed the medical treatment approach to addiction as opposed to punishment. Both institutions served as major training facilities for psychiatrists and other physicians interested in the problems of addiction.

postintoxicated state   This term refers to the agitated state immediately following a drinking bout. It may refer to a HANGOVER or to the symptoms attributed to WITHDRAWAL. (See DELIRIUM TREMENS [THE D.T.'S] and BINGE DRINKING.)

postnecrotic cirrhosis   A form of CIRRHOSIS that follows hepatitis or other inflammations of the liver, which often occurs in alcoholics.

pot still   A primitive form of still used especially in the DISTILLATION of Irish grain whiskey and Scotch malt whiskey. The heat of the fire is applied directly to the pot containing the mash.

potentiation   The ability of one drug to increase the activity of another drug taken simultaneously. The ADDITIVE EFFECT is when two or more drugs including alcohol are combined, and the total effect that they produce equals the added effects of each drug taken alone. Potentiation, also called supra-additive, and SYNERGY, produces a greater effect than the total effect of each drug combined. The combination creates a change in the effects of at least one of the drugs, increasing its potency in the system. Put in another way, when one substance is combined with another substance, such as alcohol, the first substance may suddenly become hundreds of times more potent than it would be ordinarily, and the unsuspecting user may go into a coma or worse; it can result in death.

predisposition   See GENETICS.

pregnancy   When a woman is pregnant, her health and nutrition are crucial not only to her own well-being but also to the developing baby's. Almost everything that a pregnant woman ingests passes directly from her bloodstream through the placenta to the fetus. Accordingly, since there is no chemical known that has proved to be entirely harmless during all phases of pregnancy, most doctors today advise women not to take *any* drug during pregnancy unless there is a specific need for it, and then only under the strictest medical supervision. This restriction on drug intake applies not only to illicit drugs and medically prescribed drugs, but also to self-prescribed remedies such as aspirin and to legal drugs such as alcohol, caffeine and nicotine. Alcohol, nicotine and other drugs pose a serious health risk not only to the developing fetus but to the pregnant woman as well.

Alcohol: There is incontrovertible evidence that alcohol consumption during pregnancy is dangerous to the fetus. When a pregnant woman drinks, the alcohol passes through the placenta and reaches the bloodstream of the fetus in about the same concentrations as in the mother. Since the fetus lacks the mature metabolism and elimination capabilities of an adult, alcohol is many times more toxic to its system. The most severe damage to a developing fetus caused by alcohol consumption is known as FETAL ALCOHOL SYNDROME, which is characterized by growth deficiencies, physical malformations and mental retardation. The problem is especially severe among Native Americans. Studies show that on some reservations in the Plains, the Southwest and Canada, 5% to 25% of the children are affected. Worldwide, the rate at which children are born with disabilities caused by alcohol is 1% or less, experts say. A safe limit of alcohol consumption during pregnancy has not been established. Many experts and organizations such as the NATIONAL INSTITUTE ON ALCOHOL ABUSE AND ALCOHOLISM recommend complete abstinence during pregnancy, arguing that since the effects of even small amounts of alcohol are unknown, the wisest course is to abstain completely. Others point out that millions of moderate social drinkers (whose alcohol intake is three ounces or less per day of ABSOLUTE ALCOHOL) have perfectly healthy babies. These experts and organizations prefer not to frighten patients whose custom may be to have a drink or two in the evening, but rather to counsel them on the potential dangers of this habit.

Obstetrical drugs: Another aspect to be considered regarding the use of drugs during pregnancy concerns the administration of analgesics and anesthetics to women in labor and during childbirth itself. All these drugs, which are intended to make birth easier for the mother and to help in emergency situations, directly affect the fetus, and many of these drugs have recently been discovered to be unsafe. The combination of obstetrical drugs with whatever recreational or self-prescribed drugs a woman may be using can have an interactive effect that can stupefy the infant throughout the first days of its life.

Opiates: Babies born to women addicted to opiates such as heroin suffer great consequences. Complications during pregnancy, such as toxemia, abruptio placentae, retained placenta, postpartum hemorrhage, premature births by weight, breech deliveries, high neonatal morbidity and even mortality are often the result. One hospital study of 22 addicted women showed a low birth weight in 56.5% of their infants (compared to 13.7% for the hospital as a whole) and a mortality rate at the time of birth of 17.4% compared with 2.2% for infants of nonaddicted mothers. The deaths were attributed directly to the infants' low birth weight, poor nutrition and lack of prenatal care. These complications, however, are also associated with poverty—a condition that affects many women addicts in the U.S. Such babies, born with "monkeys on their backs," often display withdrawal symptoms soon after birth. Tremors, sneezing, twitching, irritability, shrill crying, restlessness, yawning, fever, vomiting and watery stools can be expected. The severity of the symptoms appear to be in direct proportion to the amount of heroin consumed on a daily basis by the mother.

Barbiturates and amphetamines: Babies born to mothers who are addicted to barbiturates and tranquilizers also experience withdrawal symptoms. Severe central nervous system damage at birth, due to the effects of amphetamines in the womb, can be of long duration or even permanent.

Cocaine: Equally severe central nervous system damage to the fetus can also be caused by cocaine use, and also can be of long duration or permanent.

A survey compiled by the National Association for Prenatal Addiction Research and Education in 1988 indicated that health consequences of prenatal cocaine exposure could cause premature birth, retarded fetal growth, seizures after birth, breathing lapses, absence of part of the gut, abnormalities in genital and urinary organs and lasting brain damage. In 1990 the first of the "crack babies" (babies born to crack/cocaine-abusing women) attended school, and it is still too early to tell the long-term developmental effects crack will have on children.

Tobacco: Studies have shown that women who smoke are two to three times more likely to have premature babies than nonsmoking mothers and on average the babies are 150–240 grams lighter. In addition, babies of mothers who smoke during pregnancy are twice as likely to be aborted, to be stillborn or to die soon after birth from such conditions as *sudden infant death syndrome* (SIDS).

LSD: During the 1960s and 1970s there was much publicity linking the use of LSD to birth defects and chromosome damage. While studies have not ruled out the possibility, there has been no conclusive evidence that use of LSD by either the mother or father increases such risks. However, one study found evidence that the incidence of spontaneous abortion (miscarriage) is higher among women who use LSD.

Marijuana: In 1978–1983 the first extensive research on the effects of marijuana on the human fetus was conducted by professor of psychology Dr. Peter A. Fried, at Carleton University in Canada. He stated that the babies of mothers who smoked five or more marijuana cigarettes per week "consistently display many more tremors in their arms, legs, and lower jaw than do infants of non-users." He also reported a tendency to display more startle reflexes in the absence of obvious external causes, and in a test given three days after birth, babies showed abnormal responses in reacting or habituating to a light that was shone on them, which suggests "subtle alterations in the nervous system." All of these symptoms disappeared within a month. Although there was no increase in stillbirths or risk of miscarriage, mothers who smoked marijuana gave birth a few weeks early. Research has also shown that the chemical THC in marijuana crosses the placental barrier, where it effects the central nervous system of the fetus. (See BABIES, DRUG-ADDICTED AND -EXPOSED.)

Jane E. Brody, "Widespread Abuse of Drugs by Pregnant Women Is Found," *New York Times* (August 30, 1988).

Gina Kolata, "Alcohol Abuse by Pregnant Indians Is Crippling a Generation of Children," *New York Times* (July 19, 1989).

George Blinick, Robert C. Wallach, and Eulogio Jerez, "Pregnancy and Menstrual Function in Narcotics Addicts Treated with Methadone," *American Journal of Obstetrics and Gynecology* (December 15, 1969).

C. M. Fletcher and Daniel Horn, *Smoking and Health* (World Health Organization, 1970).

Preludin   An ANORECTIC that is used for weight control. A brand of phenmetrazine hydrochloride, its activity is similar to that of AMPHETAMINES and tolerance develops within a few weeks. It has a high potential for abuse, and psychological dependence and social dysfunction can occur. Symptoms of overdosage are rapid respiration, confusion and hallucinations.

presate   An ANORECTIC that contains chlorphentermine hydrochloride and used for weight control. Its activity is similar to that of the amphetamines and has the potential for abuse. Dependency can occur. Overdosage results in restlessness, aggressiveness, hallucinations and panic, and can progress to convulsions and coma. It is no longer distributed in the U.S.

prevalence   An understanding of "prevalence" is necessary for anyone interested in reviewing or generating research in the field of alcohol and other drug use. Beatrice A. Rouse offers the following explanation for prevalence: "The prevalence of a condition is the number of, or rate at which, individuals have the specified condition at a given point or period of time. For example, the past-year prevalence of a particular (chemical dependence) is the number of persons who met criteria for that disorder in the past year, regardless of when they developed the disorder. The prevalence rate is different from the incidence rate. The incidence rate is the rate of only those cases that were new during the specified period of time."

Current prevalence: The current prevalence of a condition is the percentage or rate of those who have the condition or who recently had the condition. Studies on substance abuse and mental disorders vary in the time period used for current prevalence. In the *Substance Abuse and Mental Health Statistics Sourcebook,* the time period for current prevalence is defined whenever it is used. In the SAMHSA (Substance Abuse and Mental Health Services Administration) *National Household Survey on Drug Abuse,* current drug use refers to use of a drug at least once in the past month. In the *National Comorbidity Study,* the measure of current prevalence for mental disorders is the prevalence of 30-day disorders. The 30-day prevalence is the percentage of the sample who experienced the disorder at some time in the 30 days before the study interview. Some studies use the past two weeks as the period for current prevalence.

Lifetime prevalence: The lifetime prevalence of a condition is the number or rate of those who have ever had the condition in their lifetime. In the SAMHSA *National Household Survey on Drug Abuse,* the lifetime drug prevalence is the percentage of people who *ever* have used the drug, regardless of the number of times they may have used it. In the *National Comorbidity Study,* the lifetime prevalence of mental disorder is the percentage of the sample who have ever experienced any of the mental disorders.

prevention models   Activities that reduce the number of new cases of chemical dependency. These

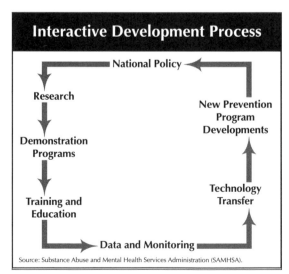

Interactive Development Process

National Policy

Research

Demonstration Programs

Training and Education

Data and Monitoring

New Prevention Program Developments

Technology Transfer

Source: Substance Abuse and Mental Health Services Administration (SAMHSA).

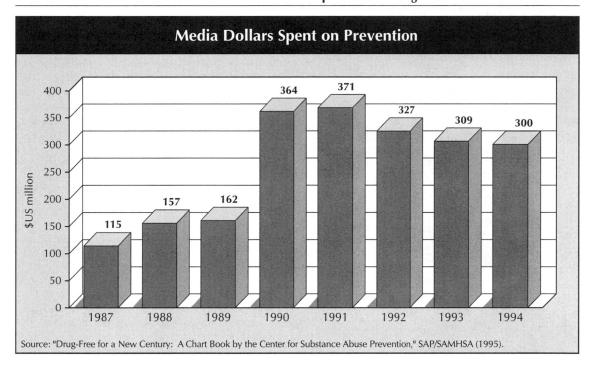

Media Dollars Spent on Prevention

Source: "Drug-Free for a New Century: A Chart Book by the Center for Substance Abuse Prevention," SAP/SAMHSA (1995).

may include public information and education, legislation and regulatory or economic measures. Prevention models are aimed especially at high-risk groups: adolescents, children of alcoholics and drug users, pregnant women and minorities. Most recently, prevention models have successfully targeted intravenous drug users and their sexual partners in order to reduce the transmission of the AIDS virus. (See PUBLIC HEALTH MODEL and PREVENTION STRATEGIES FOR SUBSTANCE ABUSE.)

prevention strategies for substance abuse   The *Substance Abuse and Mental Health Statistics Sourcebook* breaks down substance abuse prevention strategies into the following categories:

Alternatives: Provides for the participation of target populations in constructive and health activities that exclude alcohol, tobacco and other drug use. Constructive and healthy activities offset the attraction to, or otherwise meet the needs usually addressed by alcohol and other drugs. Some examples include (1) drug-free dances and parties; (2) youth/adult leadership activities; (3) community drop-in centers; and (4) community service activities.

Community-based process: Enhances the ability of the community to more effectively provide prevention and treatment services for alcohol, tobacco and drug-abuse disorders. Activities in this category include organizing, planning, enhancing efficiency and effectiveness of services implementation, inter-agency collaboration, coalition building and networking. Some examples include (1) community and volunteer training (neighborhood action training, training of key people in the system, staff/officials training); (2) systematic planning; (3) multiagency coordination and collaboration; (4) accessing services and funding; and (5) community building.

Early intervention: Uses activities designed to come between an early substance user and his or her actions in order to modify behavior. It includes a wide spectrum of activities, ranging from user education to formal intervention, and referral to treatment from a substance-abuse professional.

Education: Builds critical life and social skills through structured learning processes. Critical life and social skills include decision making, peer resistance, coping with stress, problem solving, interper-

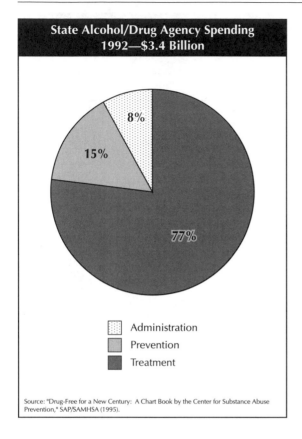

**State Alcohol/Drug Agency Spending
1992—$3.4 Billion**

8%

15%

77%

▫ Administration

▪ Prevention

■ Treatment

Source: "Drug-Free for a New Century: A Chart Book by the Center for Substance Abuse
Prevention," SAP/SAMHSA (1995).

sonal communication, and systematic and judgmental abilities. Some examples include (1) classroom and/or small group sessions; (2) parenting and family management classes; (3) peer leader/helper programs; (4) education programs for youth groups; and (5) children of substance abusers groups.

Environment: Establishes activities to change written and unwritten community standards, codes and attitudes that tend to tolerate, accept or support the abuse of alcohol, tobacco and other drugs used in the general population. This strategy is divided into two subcategories to permit distinction between activities that center on legal and regulatory initiatives and those that relate to the service and action-oriented initiatives. Some examples include (1) promoting the review of alcohol, tobacco and drug-use policies in schools; (2) technical assistance to communities, to maximize local enforcement procedures governing availability and distribution of alcohol, tobacco and other drugs; (3) modifying alcohol

and tobacco advertising practices; and (4) product pricing strategies.

Information: Provides knowledge and increases awareness of the nature and extent of alcohol and other drug use, abuse addiction and their effects on individuals, families and communities. This strategy also provides knowledge and increases awareness of available prevention and treatment programs and services. Some examples include the following: (1) clearinghouse/information resource center(s); (2) resource directories; (3) media campaigns; (4) brochures; (5) radio/TV public service announcements; (6) speaking engagements; (7) health fairs/health promotion; and (8) information lines.

Problem identification and referral: Includes activities to identify those who have engaged in illegal or age-inappropriate use of tobacco or alcohol and persons who have begun to use illicit drugs. This strategy assesses whether this early alcohol and drug use can be reversed through education. It does not include any activity designed to determine if a person is in need of treatment. Notable examples include (1) employee assistance programs (EAPs); (2) student assistance programs; and (3) driving while-under-the-influence/driving-while-intoxicated education programs. (See PUBLIC HEALTH MODELS.)

Beatrice A. Rouse, ed., *Substance Abuse and Mental Health Statistics Sourcebook* (Washington, D.C.: Substance Abuse and Mental Health Services Administration, 1995).

Pride Institute   America's only inpatient facility devoted exclusively to the treatment of HOMOSEXUAL and bisexual persons with mental health and addiction problems that has been accredited by the Joint Commission on Accreditation of Healthcare Organizations (JCAHO). In addition to traditional alcohol and other drug therapies, treatment includes building clients' self-esteem and working through any internalized homophobia that may be interfering with their recovery.

primary progressive disease   The tendency over time for symptoms of dysfunctionality to emerge in the drinking individual that affect health, psychological functioning, family, wellness and ability to deal with stress. The progression from social drinking to problem drinking to alcoholism is a process that usually occurs within 10–15 years from the beginning of drinking in genetically marked individuals who have not been educated about alcoholism and who have peer support for drinking. It is extremely rare for a person who has progressed in this way to alcoholism to reverse the process and return to social drinking. Alcoholics commonly delude themselves into believing that they can return to social drinking; a goal of treatment is to dispel that delusion.

prisoners and drug use   According to a 1986 survey of inmates in 275 state correctional facilities, 35% of 13,711 prisoners reported being under the influence of drugs at the time they committed their current offense (compared to 32% in a 1979 survey). In the 1986 survey, 43% of state prison inmates were using illegal drugs on a daily or near daily basis one month before their current offense; 19% were using a major drug—heroin, methadone, cocaine, PCP or LSD—on a daily or near-daily basis. In 1991, 50% of the inmates surveyed were using drugs on a daily or near-daily basis; 49.9% of this was major drug use. Many inmates said they began to use drugs, particularly major drugs, only after their criminal careers started. Half of the inmates who had ever used a major drug and three-fifths of those who used a major drug regularly did not do so until after their first arrest.

Other findings of the survey:

In both the 1986 and 1991 surveys, inmates were more likely to report that they were under the influence of cocaine but less likely to report using heroin at the time of the offense than in earlier surveys. Alcohol, marijuana and hashish were the drugs most frequently used at the time of the offense.

In the 1986 survey, almost 80% of inmates reported that they had used drugs at some time in their lives; 52% said they had used a major drug. The results in the 1991 survey were similar, with 79.4% of the inmates reporting drug use in their lifetime; of that group, almost 50% reported major drug use. Interestingly, in both surveys white inmates and female inmates were more likely than others to have been regular major drug users at some time in the past.

Among those who had used drugs, about half said that they began using by age 15.

The majority of inmates in the 1986 (81%) and 1991 (82.3%) surveys were not daily major drug users in the month before they committed the offense for which they were sentenced to prison. About one-seventh (13%) of inmates appeared to have committed crimes for gain in 1986; this category rose to almost 40% in the 1991 survey.

Of state prisoners sentenced for robbery, burglary, larceny or a drug offense, 50% were daily drug users in 1986, the figure rose to 69% in 1991. About 40% were under the influence of an illegal drug at the time they committed the crime in 1986, decreasing to 31% in 1991. These proportions were higher than those reported by inmates convicted of other crimes.

In addition, in the 1986 survey, the greater an offender's use of major drugs, the more prior convictions the inmate reported; less than 13% of those who had never used a major drug had six or more prior convictions, compared to about 30% of daily users of major drugs.

Major drug users among prisoners surveyed were more likely than nonusers to report that they had received income from illegal activities during the time they were last free (48% vs. 10%).

In 1986, 28% of inmates reported a past drug dependency or habit. The drugs most frequently mentioned were heroin (14%), cocaine (10%) and marijuana or hashish (9%). In 1981 the most frequently used drug was cocaine/crack (31.9%), heroin (15.3%) and marijuana (51.9%).

In 1986, 30% of inmates said they had participated in a drug treatment program at some time—12%, more than once. In 1991 this category rose to 43.3%—with a decline in the category of those who had been in treatment more than once to 8.4%. In 1986 about 50% of the inmates who had taken part in a program had received their most recent treatment while they were incarcerated; this rate dropped to 35.7% in 1991.

Caroline Wolf Harlow, *Comparing Federal and State Prison Inmates, 1991,* NCJ-145864 (Bureau of Justice Statistics, September 1994).

Christopher A. Innes, "Drug Use and Crime," *State Prison Inmate Survey 1986,* NCJ-111940 (Bureau of Justice Statistics, July 1988).

Pro-Children Act of 1994   U.S. Congressional Act (March 31, 1994) that prohibits smoking in virtually all indoor, federally funded kindergartens, elementary or secondary schools and libraries.

problem drinker   A vague and mostly outdated term for one who experiences personal, social, vocational and/or health problems whenever he or she drinks. Problem drinkers almost always are HEAVY DRINKERS, but there are exceptions. Often the distinction between problem drinking and alcohol dependence is a matter of degree, or depends on whether tolerance is present and whether withdrawal symptoms appear when drinking is stopped. Newer definitions of alcohol dependence do not require tolerance and withdrawal to be present and therefore may include problem drinkers.

People tend to react to drugs including alcohol in very distinctive and individualistic ways. Whereas alcohol may make one person happy, silly and carefree, it may make another cynical, angry or even violent. A drinker who consistently reacts adversely to alcohol is sometimes referred to as a "bad drunk."

procaine   A local anesthetic known as Novocain; its action prevents the initiation and transmission of nerve impulses. It has a rapid onset (two to five minutes), and its duration is one- to one-and-a-half hours depending on the type of nerve block, the concentration and the individual patient. Procaine is sometimes used as an adulterant in cocaine. Procaine, sometimes in combination with cortisone, also has been used in sports events to allow a participant who is in pain to continue in a contest.

progression   The risk of moving from experimental or occasional drug use to regular social and recreational use and on to dysfunctional use. It has been suggested that the use of "soft" drugs, such as marijuana, may lead to the use of "hard" drugs, such as heroin. The progression risk is also found in the manner of administration of a drug; when applied to heroin it can be the escalation from intramuscular or subcutaneous injection to mainlining (intravenous use). (See HARD DRUGS AND NARCOTICS.)

Prohibition (the Volstead Act)   The National Prohibition Act, popularly known as the Volstead Act, provided for the enforcement of wartime prohibition and constitutional prohibition as established by the EIGHTEENTH AMENDMENT to the U.S. Constitution.

The bill, introduced in the House of Representatives on May 17, 1919, was quickly adopted by both the House and Senate but was vetoed by President Woodrow Wilson on the ground that since the emergency of war had long since passed, the section authorizing wartime prohibition was unnecessary. Wilson's veto was overruled by the House on October 27 and by the Senate on the next day.

The Volstead Act consisted of three titles: Title I provided for the enforcement of wartime prohibition; Title II banned intoxicating beverages; and Title III contained technical provisions for users of industrial alcohol.

Title II comprised the general provisions for the enforcement of constitutional prohibition. The text of this title follows:

Title II. Prohibition of Intoxicating Beverages.

Sec. I . . . (1) the word "liquor" or the phrase "intoxicating liquor" shall be construed to include alcohol, brandy, whiskey, rum, gin, beer, ale, porter, and wine, and in addition thereto any spirituous, vinous, malt, or fermented liquor, liquids, and compounds, whether medicated, proprietary, patented, or not, and by whatever name called, containing one-half of 1 per centum or more of alcohol by volume which are fit for use for beverage purposes. . . .

Sec. 2. The Commissioner of Internal Revenue, his assistants, agents, and inspectors shall investigate and report violations of this act to the United States Attorney for the district in which committed . . .

Sec. 3. No person shall on or after the date when the Eighteenth Amendment to the Constitution of the United States goes into effect, manufacture, sell, barter, transport, import, export, deliver, furnish or possess any intoxicating liquor except as authorized in this act, and all the provisions of this act shall be liberally construed to the end that the use of intoxicating liquor as a beverage may be prevented.

Liquor for nonbeverage purposes and wine for sacramental purposes may be manufactured, purchased, sold, bartered, transported, imported, exported, delivered, furnished and possessed, but only as herein provided.

Sec. 4. The articles enumerated in this section shall not, after having been manufactured and prepared for the market, be subject to the provisions of this act if they correspond with the following descriptions and limitations, namely: (a) Denatured alcohol or denatured rum produced and used as provided by laws and regulations now or hereafter in force. (b) Medicinal preparations manufactured in accordance with formulas prescribed by the United States Pharmacopoeia, National Formulary, or the American Institute of Homeopathy that are unfit for use for beverage purposes. (c) Patented, patent, and proprietary medicines that are unfit for use for beverage purposes. (d) Toilet, medicinal, and antiseptic preparations and solutions that are unfit for use for beverage purposes. (e) Flavoring extracts and syrups that are unfit for use as a beverage, or for intoxicating purposes. (f) Vinegar and preserved sweet cider. A person who manufactures any of the articles mentioned in this section may purchase and possess liquor for that purpose, but he shall secure permits to manufacture such articles and to purchase such liquor, give the bonds, keep the records, and make the reports specified in this act and as directed by the Commissioner. No such manufacturer shall sell, use, or dispose of any liquor otherwise than as an ingredient of the articles authorized to be manufactured therefrom. No more alcohol shall be used in the manufacture of any extract, syrup, or the articles named in paragraph b, c, and d of this section, which may be used for beverage purposes, than the quantity necessary for extraction or solution of the elements contained therein and for the preservation of the article.

Sec. 6. No one shall manufacture, sell, purchase, transport, or prescribe any liquor without first obtaining a permit from the Commissioner so to do, except that a person may, without a permit, purchase and use liquor for medicinal purposes when prescribed by a physician as herein provided, and except that any person who in the opinion of the

Commissioner is conducting a bona fide hospital or sanatorium engaged in the treatment of persons suffering from alcoholism, may, under such rules, regulations, and conditions as the Commissioner shall prescribe, purchase, and use, in accordance with the methods in use in such institution, liquor, to be administered to the patients of such institution under the direction of a duly qualified physician employed by such institution. . . . Nothing in this title shall be held to apply to the manufacture, sale, transportation, importation, possession, or distribution of wine for sacramental purposes, or like religious rites . . .

Sec. 7. No one but a physician holding a permit to prescribe liquor shall issue any prescription for liquor . . .

Sec. 11. All manufacturers and wholesale or retail druggists shall keep as a part of the records required of them a copy of all permits to purchase on which a sale of any liquor is made . . .

Sec. 17. It shall be unlawful to advertise anywhere, or by any means or method, liquor, or the manufacture, sale, keeping for sale, or furnishing of the same, or where, how, from whom, or at what price the same may be obtained. No one shall permit any sign or billboard containing such advertisement to remain upon one's premises. But nothing herein shall prohibit manufacturers and wholesale druggists holding permits to sell liquor from furnishing price lists, with description of liquor for sale, to persons permitted to purchase liquor, or from advertising alcohol in business publications, or trade journals circulating generally among manufacturers of lawful alcoholic perfumes, toilet preparations, flavoring extracts, medicinal preparations, and like articles . . .

Sec. 20. Any person who shall be injured in person, property, means of support, or otherwise by any intoxicated person, or by reason of the intoxication of any person, whether resulting in his death or not, shall have a right of action against any person who shall, by unlawfully selling to or unlawfully assisting in procuring liquor for such intoxicated person, have caused or contributed to such intoxication, and in any such action such person shall have a right to recover actual and exemplary damages. In case of the death of either party, the action or the right of action given by this section shall survive to or against his or her executor or administrator, and the amount so recovered by either wife or child shall be his or her sole and separate property. Such action may be brought in any court of competent jurisdiction. In any case where parents shall be entitled to such damages, either the father or the mother may sue alone therefor, but recovery by one of the parties shall be a bar to suit brought by the other.

Sec. 21. Any room, house, building, boat, vehicle, structure, or place where intoxicating liquor is manufactured, sold, kept, or bartered in violation of this title, and all intoxicating liquor and property kept and used in maintaining the same, is hereby declared to be a common nuisance, and any person who maintains such a common nuisance shall be guilty of a misdemeanor and upon conviction thereof shall be fined not more than $1,000, or be imprisoned for not more than one year, or both . . .

Sec. 26. When the Commissioner, his assistants, inspectors, or any officer of the law shall discover any person in the act of transporting in violation of the law, intoxicating liquors in any wagon, buggy, automobile, water or air craft, or other vehicle, it shall be his duty to seize any and all intoxicating liquors found therein being transported contrary to law . . .

Sec. 29. Any person who manufactures or sells liquor in violation of this title shall for a first offense be fined not more than $1,000, or imprisoned not exceeding six months, and for a second or subsequent offense shall be fined not less than $200 nor more than $2,000, and be imprisoned not less than one month nor more than five years . . .

Sec. 33. After February 1, 1920, the possession of liquors by any person not legally permitted under this title to possess liquor shall be prima facie evidence that such liquor is kept for the purpose of being sold, bartered, exchanged, given away, furnished, or otherwise disposed of in violation of the provision of this title . . .

Project Cork Institute   Project Cork, created in 1977–78 grew out of a program of the Kroc Foundation called Operation Cork. The project began as a limited effort by Dartmouth Medical School to develop a model curriculum on alcohol-related issues for undergraduate medical education. In 1978 a resource center, with more than 9,000 items and a computer-based cataloging system, was created. The

creation of the bimonthly newsletter *Alcohol Clinical Update* in the early 1980s greatly expanded the institute's role in the alcoholism education movement in the U.S.

Starting in 1981, Dartmouth Medical School provided the support necessary to maintain the project's identity, and a gift from the Joan B. Kroc Foundation in 1984 provided funds for the establishment of the Project Cork Institute. The institute now is an autonomous entity on the Dartmouth Medical School campus in Hanover, New Hampshire. It has an independent board and promotes the education and training of physicians and other health service professionals in the diagnosis and treatment of individuals and families affected by alcoholism and other forms of chemical dependency.

Project Cork Institute's historical involvement with the Dartmouth Health Service has expanded to collaboration with the American College Health Association (ACHA) for the creation of alcohol and drug-use standards for member institutions. The institute also has contractual arrangements to assist other organizations, such as the INDIAN HEALTH SERVICE, in devising curriculum and support materials for the training of primary care clinicians.

Project DARE (Drug Abuse Resistance Program)   A cooperative law enforcement and education effort through which police officers provide classroom lessons and presentations on drug use in the elementary schools throughout the Los Angeles metropolitan area. The program has been cited as an example of effective and innovative collaboration between criminal justice personnel and community-based alcohol and other drug (AOD) prevention resources.

prolixin   An antipsychotic that contains fluphenazine hydrochloride and is generally used for psychotic disorders. Prolixin is not an abused drug.

proof   A measure of the amount of ABSOLUTE ALCOHOL in a distilled spirit. As early as the 15th century, drinkers demanded "proof" that a liquor was fit (had a high enough alcohol content) for human consumption. To this end various tests were devised. Oil was floated on liquor; if it sank, that was "proof" of the spirit's strength. If a liquor-soaked cloth could be easily and satisfactorily ignited, that was sufficient "proof." If a mixture of liquor and gunpowder burned smoothly with a blue flame, it was exactly on the mark; if it blew up, it was over "proof."

John Clarke in 1725 and Bartholomew Sikes in 1803 pioneered modern measurements of proof in Britain with the use of hydrometers. The height at which the hydrometer floated in the liquor determined the proof.

The British and the Americans use different systems for measuring proof. The British system is based upon a comparison of equal volumes of water and liquor at 51° F. If the liquor weighs $^{12}/_{13}$ths as much as the water, it is 100 proof. In Britain, liquor bottled for home consumption has a lower proof and a slightly lower alcohol content than that intended for export. For example, Scotch whiskey meant for the domestic market is bottled at 70 proof (40% alcohol), but that exported to the U.S. is 86.8 proof (43.4% alcohol) under the American system.

The American system is based upon the percentage of absolute alcohol in the liquor at 60° F. The proof measurement is double the percentage of alcohol: 100 proof = 50% alcohol.

propoxyphene A synthetic analgesic, propoxyphene hydrochloride first was synthesized in 1953 by Pohland and Sullivan. It first was marketed in 1957 as DARVON by Lilly & Co., who claimed the new drug was as effective as codeine but did not share its side effects or addictive nature.

Classification: Propoxyphene is a Schedule IV drug under the Controlled Substances Act.

Usage: Propoxyphene is in fact very similar to codeine and methadone, except that it lacks an antitussive effect. Nearly 20 million prescriptions for Darvon are written annually, making it one of America's most widely used narcotics. Darvon and other forms of propoxyphene produce the drowsiness and euphoria typically associated with morphine and codeine, as well as pain relief. Propoxyphene is used medically to relieve mild to moderate pain and occasionally for withdrawal treatment for morphine and heroin addiction. Recreational use does occur, but very large doses (over 500 mg) are required to achieve and maintain a "high" and hallucinations may also occur. Such high levels of ingestion are dangerous and can result in severe side effects.

Dosage: Propoxyphene is prescribed in 32–65 mg doses, to be taken three or four times daily: 90–120 mg is equivalent to 60 mg of codeine, and 100 mg of the napsylate form is equivalent to 65 mg of the hydrochloride form. The drug is not prescribed for children. Intravenous administration is not recommended either—it is very irritating and results in damage to the veins and soft tissue.

Appearance: Propoxyphene hydrochloride is an odorless, bitter-tasting white crystalline solid, soluble in water and slightly soluble in alcohol. It also occurs as propoxyphene napsylate, which is not water-soluble.

Activity: The effects of the drug peak in two to two-and-a-half hours. This drug should not be taken during pregnancy.

Effects: The drug acts as a central nervous system (CNS) depressant and has side effects such as dizziness, headache and nausea. It brings on withdrawal symptoms when given to addicts of heroin and other opiates. Overdosage can result in gastrointestinal distress, circulatory collapse, depressed respiration, convulsions, psychosis, coma and death. In cases of overdose, a NARCOTIC ANTAGONIST, such as NALOXONE, should be administered.

Tolerance and dependence: Tolerance as well as physical and psychological dependence can develop. It is clearly addictive and has high abuse potential.

Availability: Propoxyphene hydrochloride is commercially available as Darvon. Darvon is known on the street as "pinks" or "red and grays." The drug is also available in combination with aspirin and other drugs, in capsule or tablet form. DOLENE is another brand name, while Darvon-N and such variations refer to the napsylate form.

propoxyphene napsylate This substance differs from propoxyphene hydrochloride in that it allows for more stable liquid dosage forms and tablet formations. It is also longer acting than the hydrochloride form. (See PROPOXYPHENE.)

prostitution Many women and men obtain money for drugs through prostitution. Some work on their own, others are associated with ORGANIZED CRIME. There is a high incidence of AIDS and other sexually transmitted diseases among addicts involved in prostitution. An addict who supports a habit in this way is also apt to become more deeply addicted. Drug use provides an escape from a dismal life.

Although the likelihood of pregnancy may be reduced for addicts due to a decrease in fertility, when it occurs, the effects of addiction are often passed on to the child. (See PREGNANCY and BABIES, DRUG-ADDICTED AND -EXPOSED.)

protopine   A crystalline alkaloid found in small quantities in opium and some papaveraceous plants.

protracted abstinence syndrome   Long-term alcohol and other drug (AOD) abuse causes changes in the central nervous system that persist even after the user has achieved abstinence. *Protracted abstinence syndrome* is the name given to those effects that persist several months or even years after the individual has ceased his or her alcohol or drug use. In some instances, symptoms manifest only when provoked, for example, following re-exposure to the drug. Symptoms can include: hypersensitivity to sensory stimuli, irritability, impaired concentration, feelings of derealization or depersonalization, disordered sleeping, panic attacks, generalized anxiety and depression.

psilocybin   The active hallucinogenic ingredient of the MUSHROOM *Psilocybe mexicana* and some of the other psilocybe and conocybe species. Ritual use of psilocybin among native Mexican and Central American cultures dates back to at least 1500 B.C. These mushrooms were considered to be sacred and were named *teonanacatl,* or "flesh of the gods."

In 1958 Albert Hofmann, a Swiss chemist, isolated psilocybin and its congener, psilocin, from *Psilocybe mexicana.* Psilocybin is the only naturally occurring hallucinogen identified thus far that contains phosphorus.

Classification: Psilocybin is a hallucinogen. It shows cross-tolerance to LSD and mescaline.

Appearance: In pure form, psilocybin is a white crystalline material, but it may also be distributed as fresh raw mushrooms, intact dried mushrooms or as a capsule containing the powdered mushroom.

Usage: These mushrooms are usually taken orally. When eaten, they are sometimes coated with honey or sweetened condensed milk to mask the rather unpleasant taste. They may be injected if they have been synthesized into an injectable form, but this method is rare. Doses generally vary from 4 mg to 5 mg, although 20–60 mg is not unusual. The potency of psilocybin lies somewhere between that of mescaline and LSD, and the effects are reported to be similar to those of LSD but the hallucinations are not as intense or frequent.

Effects: When taken orally, psilocybin is one of the most rapid-acting hallucinogens: initial effects may be felt 10 to 15 minutes after ingestion. Reactions often reach maximum intensity after about 90 minutes and do not begin to subside until two to three hours later. The effects of psilocybin usually last five to six hours in all, but doses larger than 8 mg probably prolong the duration. Physiological effects include increased pulse rate, respiratory rate and body temperature, dilated pupils and elevation of systolic blood pressure. Larger doses, 13 mg or more, can produce dizziness, lightheadedness, abdominal discomfort, numbness of tongue, lips or mouth, nausea, anxiety and shivering. Psychological effects with small doses may include mental and physical relaxation, detachment from surroundings and sometimes coexisting feelings of anxiety or elation. With larger doses individuals may experience difficulty in thinking and concentrating, visual distortions and other changes in perception.

Tolerance and dependence: Physical DEPENDENCE on psilocybin has not been reported. Tolerance to psilocybin does develop, and there is a CROSS-TOLERANCE to the effects of LSD and MESCALINE. As with all hallucinogens, tolerance develops rapidly and rapidly passes with cessation of use.

Sources: It is difficult to estimate how much psilocybin is available to users. Sometimes the active ingredient may be extracted from the mushrooms for street sale, and sometimes it is synthesized. Some users and sellers grow their own mushrooms. Psilocybin can be bought as a liquid or powder or as whole mushrooms. In Mexico these mushrooms grow wild in cow manure and are plentiful in certain rural areas. Much of what is sold as psilocybin is actually PCP and, sometimes, LSD.

Synonyms: shrooms, sacred mushroom, magic mushroom.

psychiatrist   A medical doctor specializing in the treatment of mental disorders. A psychiatrist must complete a medical education and post-M.D. (doctor of medicine) or D.O. (doctor of osteopathy) residency in psychiatry in a clinic or hospital setting.

psychoactive   Drugs that alter thinking, perception, emotions or consciousness are termed psychoactive. They are sought after by drug users.

psychodrama   A form of GROUP THERAPY in which individuals act out their problems before a group under the direction of a therapist. Usually a member with a problem portrays himself while a different member takes the role (father, wife, boss) of another person associated with the member and his problem. The two (or more) "performers" then act out their roles. Sometimes roles will be reversed, with the member acting out a role other than his own. The purpose of psychodrama is to heighten the member's awareness of his problem through performance, giving it an immediacy that simple discussion cannot provide.

Because of its emphasis on actions rather than words, psychodrama can be a particularly useful component in the treatment of chronic alcohol and other drug users, who, as a group, are prone to be out of touch with and unable to articulate their feelings. Role playing and other techniques of psychodrama have proved to be very effective in providing a good framework to help individuals in recovery to practice new ways of behaving and interrelating.

psychological dependence   A broad term that refers to a craving or compulsion to continue the use of a drug because it gives a feeling of well-being and satisfaction. The term HABITUATION is frequently used interchangeably with *psychological dependence;* the syndrome is also known as *behavioral, psychic* or *emotional* dependence.

In chronic drug use, psychological dependence is considered more serious and more difficult to deal with than physical dependence. Psychological dependence can vary in intensity from a mild preference for a drug to a strong craving for it. The World Health Organization defines psychic dependence as "a feeling of satisfaction and a psychic drive that requires periodic or continuous administration of a drug to produce a desired effect or to avoid discomfort." An individual can be psychologically dependent on a drug and not physically dependent and the reverse also is true (but rarely occurs).

Beatrice A. Rouse, ed., *Substance Abuse and Mental Health Statistics Sourcebook* (Washington, D.C.: Substance Abuse and Mental Health Services Administration, 1995).

psychological models of etiology   A category of theories, including sociocultural theories and physiological theories, on the etiology of alcoholism and other drug use. Most psychological theories are based on the assumption that some element in the personality structure leads to the development of addiction. In the case of alcoholism, there have been studies designed to identify an "alcoholic personality," that is, one with a characterological vulnerability to the development of alcoholism. To date, studies have failed to find any specific personality traits that clearly differentiate alcoholics from either "normal" people, from those addicted to drugs other than alcohol, or from those with psychological problems unrelated to addiction. There is evidence that once drinking patterns have been established, alcoholics and other drug-addicted individuals display certain common traits. Some of these traits (such as concern with the drug of choice that supersedes all other relationships or responsibilities, and impaired impulse control) are common among those with any substance-addictions; others (the paranoia and hypersexuality that sometimes accompanies addiction to cocaine and other stimulants) are specific to particular classes of drugs. Since the majority of studies have focused on addicted individuals, however, it remains unclear whether these traits precede addiction or are a result of it.

There are several different psychological models of etiology regarding addiction. Under the psychodynamic model, addiction results from unconscious tendencies that are expressed in excessive consumption of alcohol or other drug use. (The abuse of drugs other than alcohol, because they are illegal, can be a symptom of sociopathy not relevant to the use of alcohol, which is legal.) Writing about alcohol (although the theory can just as easily be applied to the addiction to drugs other than alcohol),

Freud suggested that alcoholism is related to a traumatic experience in early childhood caused by a poor parent-child relationship. The loss or absence of the object of love, usually the mother, in the oral stage creates demands in the alcoholic that are insatiable. As a result, interpersonal relations eventually fail and are interpreted as rejection. A consequent loss of self-esteem develops and there is an enormous rage stemming from the original rejection by the parent figure. He or she turns a desire to destroy that figure upon himself and consumes his or her rage in alcohol. (See ORAL FIXATION.) Other theories that are "ego" focused hold that addicted individuals suffer from strong feelings of inferiority and powerlessness, what Eric Ericson refers to as "shame for self." The same individuals are often inhibited from expressing their hostility or aggression. Drugs allow addicted individuals to avoid the feelings of inferiority and shame and at the same time provide a false sense of competence and control of these feelings. Mind-altering substances will also allow them to release their inhibitions and express their impulses.

It has also been postulated that addicts experience unusually strong conflicts between dependency needs and a desire for autonomy. Drug use allows for dependency through sociability and dependence on the drug, even as it fosters feelings of independence and strength.

Behavioral models propose that addiction is a conditioned behavioral response that can be helped through modification of stimuli and reinforcement in the environment.

David J. Armor, J. Michael Polich and Harriet B. Stambul, *Alcoholism and Treatment* (New York: John Wiley and Sons, 1978): 17–29.

Morris E. Chafetz and Harold W. Demone, Jr., *Alcoholism and Society* (New York: Oxford University Press, 1962): 19–29, 39–56.

psychologist   A person who holds an advanced degree in psychology, usually a Ph.D. or Psy.D., from an approved institution of higher education and who has passed a state licensing examination.

psychopathology   The study of abnormal behavior and of the signs, symptoms and causes of mental disorder and illness.

psychosis   A mental state characterized by defective or lost contact with reality. In toxic psychosis, acute or chronic psychoticlike behavior results from impairment of brain-cell function. Symptoms can include extreme confusion, hallucinations, disorientation, depression and aggressive behavior. Schizophrenic and manic-depressive psychosis are examples of functional psychoses (not caused by drugs or a separate physical dysfunction such as fever).

psychostimulant   See STIMULANT.

psychotherapeutic drugs   Psychotherapeutic drugs include prescription medications, analgesics, sedatives, stimulants and tranquilizers and are frequently used nonmedically, namely, to get high or to achieve mental effects for purposes other than curative.

psychotherapist   A term describing an individual who is trained specifically in the practice of psychotherapy. Psychotherapists may have been trained in a university setting as a psychologist, social worker, or school counselor, or in psychotherapy institutes.

psychotherapy   The techniques, procedures and professional services utilized by trained psychotherapists (specialized counselors) that provide relief from mental, emotional or behavioral disorders.

psychotic ideation   According to the Substance Abuse and Mental Health Services Administration (SAMHSA), "Psychotic ideation are those thoughts that are out of touch with reality. Persons with psychotic ideation have difficulty separating real from unreal experiences." Certain drugs of abuse can induce psychotic ideation in users. (See PCP and COCAINE.)

Beatrice A. Rouse, ed., *Substance Abuse and Mental Health Statistics Sourcebook* (Washington, D.C.: Substance Abuse and Mental Health Services Administration, 1995).

psychotogenic   Drugs that frequently produce hallucinations and delusions when taken in large doses. In smaller doses they produce euphoric effects.

psychotomimetic   Drugs such as LSD and mescaline that can produce hallucinations, symptoms of a psychotic state and sometimes chromosomal breaks. Psychotomimetic drugs usually are psychedelics or hallucinogen-stimulant combinations.

psychotropic   The term is used more or less interchangeably with psychoactive and is applied to drugs that alter consciousness.

Public Affairs Committee   A not-for-profit educational organization founded in 1935 to "develop a new technique to educate the American public on vital economic and social problems and to issue concise and interesting pamphlets dealing with such problems." The committee offered an extensive variety of pamphlets dealing with substance abuse and its consequences.

public drunkenness   The public inebriate is the most visible alcoholic and therefore has symbolic importance for all alcoholics. Public intoxication has been regarded as a legal matter ever since the English Parliament prescribed punishment in 1606 for that "loathesome and odious sin of drunkenness" that is "the root and foundation of many other sins." This approach was brought to America and remained the general rule for three centuries. Around 1910 the merit of treating alcoholics as criminals was questioned and attempts were made to develop alternative facilities. These attempts failed, and local police departments continued to be responsible for public inebriates. Several other attempts were made through the years to provide treatment for public inebriates, but without success. By 1965 arrests for public drunkenness numbered more than 1.5 million annually, accounting for approximately 40% of all nontraffic arrests. In the 1960s alcoholism gradually came to be regarded as a disease, and in the early 1970s the Uniform Alcoholism and Intoxication Act was established, which provided the states with "a legal framework within which to approach alcoholism and public intoxication from a health standpoint." The Declaration Policy of the Uniform Act states, "It is the policy of this State that alcoholics and intoxicated persons may not be subjected to criminal prosecution because of their consumption of alcoholic beverages but rather should be afforded a continuum of treatment in order that they may lead

normal lives as productive members of society" (National Conference of Commissioners on Uniform State Laws). To date, this act, which decriminalizes public drunkenness, has been adopted by a majority of states and the District of Columbia.

While the Uniform Act has worked to reduce the number of alcoholics incarcerated for drunkenness, it has not sufficiently reduced the public inebriate problem. The act has helped to destigmatize alcoholism and to increase access to treatment, but it has not brought chronic public inebriates into treatment voluntarily or kept them in treatment. Skid row programs in particular are often given low priority, and public inebriates are frequently written off by treatment programs as unlikely to recover.

John R. DeLuca, ed., *Fourth Special Report to the U.S. Congress on Alcohol and Health* (Rockville, Md.: National Institute on Alcohol Abuse and Alcoholism, 1981): 155–156.

P. Finn, "Decriminalization of public drunkenness: Response of the Health Care System," *Journal of Studies on Alcohol* 46 (1985): 7–23.

N. R. Kurtz and M. Regier, "The Uniform Alcoholism and Intoxication Treatment Act: The Compromising Process of Social Policy Formulation," *Journal of Studies on Alcohol* 36, no. 11 (1975): 1421–1441.

National Conference of Commissioners on Uniform State Laws, *Uniform Alcoholism and Intoxication Treatment Act* (Washington, D.C.: Government Printing Office, 1973).

NIAAA Information and Feature Service, *Client Funds Contribute to Public Inebriate Program* (July 18, 1980).

NIAAA Information and Feature Service, *Public Inebriate Conference Addresses Range of Issues* (August 28, 1981): 3.

Ernest P. Noble, ed., *Third Special Report to the U.S. Congress on Alcohol and Health* (Rockville, Md.: NIAAA, 1978): 329–330.

Federal Bureau of Investigation, *Uniform Crime Reports for the United States, 1965* (Washington, D.C.: Government Printing Office, 1965).

public health model   The public health model is a concept of health that views disease and injury as well as health itself as being the result of complex interactions between hosts (people), agents (elements of disease or illness) and their environments. Therapeutic health care such as clinical medicine differs from the public health model in that therapeutic health care is more concerned with the diagnosis and treatment of health problems after they have occurred (for example, operating to remove a lung after cancer has been diagnosed). While the public health model is inclusive of therapeutic interventions, it places more emphasis on changing or preventing those factors in an environment or population (the factors that cause lung cancer in the first place). Consequently, while the professions of therapeutic health care are usually medicine, nursing, psychology, dentistry, physical therapy and the biological sciences, the professions involving public health include all of these, as well as those of law, sanitation, the environment, conservation, politics, sociology and local and federal administrations. The public health model is often applied to the problem of alcohol and drug use and the goal is to establish primary intervention activities, which may take place at any point within the parameters of the model, in order to prevent or eliminate occurrences of the particular problem.

Host: In the public health model, the host is identified as the individual, including his or her socio-economic status, gender, ethnic origins, family interactions, education, beliefs and attitudes that put him or her at risk for disease. In the area of alcohol/other drug use, these risk factors include the individual's biological and psychological states.

Prevention activities targeted toward the host include drug education programs sponsored by schools, employers, religious and community organizations, and government agencies. These programs employ a combination of skill-building strategies such as problem solving and interpersonal coping skills to help individuals cope with the problems of substance abuse. Clients are taught methods for fostering self-awareness and self-efficacy. Prevention programs aim to help reduce the risks of abuse by promoting responsible alcohol use, while revealing the harm potential related to the abuse of illicit drugs and alcohol. Teenagers are shown how to resist the peer pressure that drives them to experiment with alcohol/other drugs, and adults learn how to deal productively with the psychosocial stresses. Additionally, host-centered activities include over-the-counter and prescription drug-labeling education the purpose of avoiding negative side effects or toxic drug-alcohol interactions.

Agent: The agent refers to the drug or substance itself; its pharmacological makeup; its psycho-neurological and other physical effects, and its availability and use.

Public health activities targeted at substances are usually aimed at reducing the substances' availability or potency. Agent-directed interventions include federal and state laws that prohibit the cultivation or manufacturing, importation, distribution, sale or possession of illicit drugs within the U.S. These laws have become, in many cases, stricter in terms of sentencing guidelines and penalties. Other agent-focused prevention activities include diplomatic efforts, economic incentives and international law enforcement cooperation projects aimed at encouraging foreign countries to eradicate illicit drug crops and prosecuting individuals and organizations involved in drug trafficking. Interventions have also focused on reducing alcohol abuse by setting the minimum age requirement for the sale of alcohol in all states at 21. Similar methods have been used in most states to reduce the sale of cigarettes and other tobacco products. Setting taxes on tobacco and alcohol products, limiting the retail sale to certain geographic locations, and placing restrictions on advertising methods are additional ways that federal and state governments discourage alcohol and tobacco use. To prevent the misuse of psychoactive pharmaceuticals, federal laws require that these drugs be accounted for and controlled. Physicians are required by law to exercise caution in the prescribing of all psychoactive drugs. Unfortunately this law is rarely enforced, and consequently there may be more prescription drug addicts in the U.S. than there are illicit drug addicts.

Environment: In applying the public health model to the problem of alcohol and other drug use, the "environment" is defined as the setting in which misuse and abuse of the drug occurs. Schools, neighborhoods and places of work are possible drug-use environments. Economics, law enforcement, politics, community values, group culture as well as the media are usually influencing factors. Some neighborhoods may lack the economic, educational and social activities to provide constructive alternatives to drug use and drug trafficking. Other social groups may be ambivalent in their attitudes toward illicit drug use. Movies or television may inadvertently glorify smoking, drinking or drug use.

Prevention interventions on environmental factors related to the abuse of alcohol and other drugs include: government, voluntary and private sector programs and initiatives aimed at improving the social and economic status of impoverished communities; the banning or limiting of advertisements for alcohol and tobacco; and campaigning for the voluntary de-emphasis of alcohol/other drug use by television, movie and publishing companies. The development of community-wide coalitions to coordinate the activities of businesses, schools, religious institutions, law enforcement, community service and local government agencies is still another approach. These coalitions advocate tougher drug laws or more government funding for prevention education, and they try to achieve their goal by the establishment of voluntary parent support groups, education programs and citizen neighborhood-watch programs that report street drug trafficking to the police.

Center for Substance Abuse Prevention, Substance Abuse and Mental Health Services Administration (SAMHSA), *Prevention Plus II: Tools for Creating and Sustaining Drug Free Communities,* DHHS pub. ADM 89-1649 (Washington, D.C.: Government Printing Office, 1993): 181–84.

Center for Substance Abuse Prevention, SAMHSA, *Signs of Effectiveness II- Preventing Alcohol, Tobacco, and Other Drug Use: A Risk Factor /Resiliency-Based Approach,* DHHS pub. SAM-94-2098 (Washington, D.C.: Government Printing Office, 1993).

Pure Food and Drug Act of 1906 The act was passed in response to growing public concern about the safety of food and drugs. Public awareness of the safety issues related to food and drugs were the result of exposes in popular magazines such as *Collier's* and the publication in 1905 of Upton Sinclair's novel *The Jungle.* This book revealed the unsanitary conditions in Chicago meat-packing plants. Additionally, the combined crusading efforts of Dr. Harvey Wiley of the U.S. Agricultural Department's Bureau of Chemistry, the American Medical Association and the American Pharmaceutical Association brought attention to the uncontrolled use of opiates and alcohol in patent medicines with the resultant risks of addiction. The act resulted in a program to supervise and control the manufacture, labeling and sale of food to ensure that it was pure and unadulterated. Additionally, the act sought to control addiction by requiring that all patent medicines containing narcotics shipped in interstate commerce have the medicine's narcotic content identified on labels. "Narcotic" drugs included not only opium, but morphine, marijuana, cocaine and alcohol as well. Additionally, the act required that medicines meet standards of purity, and any imported drug that was considered dangerous was banned.

pyrahexyl A semisynthetic derivative of cannabis that has similar effects.

pyribenzamine An antihistamine manufactured by Geigy (also called PBZ). Its generic name is tripelennamine. There was a short-lived fad of injecting "Blue Velvet," a mixture of pulverized pyribenzamine tablets and boiled paregoric. There were numerous deaths from plugged veins, thought to have been a result of the talc used as a filler in the tablets. Pyribenzamine has been combined with TALWIN as "Ts and blues," the "blues" referring to the color of the scored 50-mg tablets. The combination is injected intravenously. (See TRIPELENNAMINE HYDROCHLORIDE.)

Q

Quaalude A nonbarbiturate sedative hypnotic that contained METHAQUALONE. It was prescribed as a sleeping medication, as well as for daytime sedation, and was once thought to be nonaddictive. The manufacturer, Lemmon Company, removed this drug from the market in the early 1980s because of its widespread abuse. Illicit methaqualone (or counterfeit Quaaludes) today resemble the original Quaaludes to varying degrees. They are classed as Schedule II drugs under the Controlled Substances Act.

quibron A bronchodilator that contains theophylline, guaifenesin, ephedrine and butabarbital and is usually used in the treatment of bronchial asthma, bronchitis and emphysema. It may be habit-forming and is available in yellow capsules and as an elixir.

quinine A bitter crystalline alkaloid, derived from the bark of the cinchona tree, which is used as an antipyretic, antimalarial medicine. After an outbreak of malaria among heroin addicts in New York City in the 1930s, quinine became a popular dilutant of heroin. In the amounts found in street heroin, quinine cannot cure malaria, but when the solution is dissolved for injection the quinine may kill the malaria parasite. Quinine is also added because it is thought to enhance the "RUSH " felt after injection. Heroin is frequently diluted with milk sugar (lactose), which masks its bitter taste, so when quinine is added it provides the bitterness in case a user taste-tests the heroin to ensure its quality before buying. Some deaths labeled "heroin overdose" are thought to be due to sensitivity to intravenous quinine. (See SYNDROME X.)

RADAR Network Support   RADAR is the acronym for Regional Alcohol and Drug Awareness Resource. The National Clearinghouse for Alcohol and Drug Information (NCADI) is the hub of the RADAR Network, which consists of the state clearinghouses, information centers of national voluntary organizations and the Department of Education's regional training centers. Network members use NCADI products and services to respond to local needs for information and technical assistance. Individuals can obtain information from NCADI on how to contact the RADAR center in their state.

radioimmunoassay (RIA)   Similar to the EIA (enzyme immunoassay) drug-testing method, the radioimmunoassay (RIA) machine adds to the urine antibodies that are specific to the target drug. These added antibodies attach to any drug molecules that are present. The antibodies are "tagged" with radioactive molecules and can be located because of this radioactivity. The emission of radiation during the test indicates the presence of the drug. A widely used RIA test is marketed under the trade name Abuscreen, and its biggest client is the U.S. military. The RIA machine is a more complex piece of equipment than the EIA, thus requiring more training for its technicians. It can, however, do more drug tests in less time than most other methods.

Gilda Berger, *Drug Testing* (New York: Franklin Watts, 1987).

railroad accidents   A 1979 study of drinking practices among 234,000 railroad employees suggested that 44,000 (19%) of the workers were problem drinkers. Between 1975 and 1984, alcohol- or drug-impaired employees were implicated in 48 train accidents/incidents that resulted in 37 deaths, 80 nonfatal injuries and $34.2 million in damage. In postaccident testing of railroad employees in 1990, 3.2% tested positive for alcohol or other prohibited drugs. The NATIONAL INSTITUTE ON ALCOHOL ABUSE AND ALCOHOLISM believes that "because of the existing latitude in the current reporting system, alcohol and drug involvement in railroad accidents and injuries is very likely to go undetected or unreported in a significant number of cases." The *Federal Register* concedes that their figures probably understate alcohol and drug use among railroad workers.

Since November 1988, the U.S. Department of Transportation has mandated random drug tests for the nation's 4 million private transportation workers, including airline pilots and navigators, interstate truckers, bus drivers and railroad engineers and conductors.

Omnibus Transportation Employee Testing Act of 1991, U.S. Code, vol. 49 (updated, part 40, "Chemical Testing").

Rand Report   In June 1976 the Rand Corporation of Santa Monica, California, issued a highly controversial report on alcoholism. The report was sponsored and subsidized by the National Institute on Alcohol Abuse and Alcoholism (NIAAA), which contracted with the Rand Corporation, an independent, not-for-profit research organization, to participate in an analysis of its comprehensive alcoholism treatment program begun in 1971, to codify and examine the results and to release the findings. The Rand Corporation published its report under the title *Alcoholism and Treatment.*

While many aspects of the report were attacked, two conclusions in particular drew outraged response. The first was that after treatment some alcoholics were able to resume "normal" drinking. The second was that the rate of relapse for alcoholics who resumed normal drinking was no higher than the rate for alcoholics who adopted a program of complete abstinence.

Challenges came from all quarters. Dr. Marvin A. Block, former head of the Committee on Alcoholism of the American Medical Association, stated that "an addict trying to use the drug alcohol again runs the risk of becoming addicted again." The National Council on Alcoholism and the American Medical Association's Committee on Alcoholism jointly stated, "Abstinence from alcohol is necessary to recovery from the disease of alcoholism." Alcoholics Anonymous declined comment but quoted from its own "Big Book," "We have seen the truth demonstrated again and again; once an alcoholic; always an alcoholic. . . . Commencing to drink after a period of sobriety, we are in a short time as bad as ever." Other adverse comments about the report from professionals in the field ranged from "almost criminal" to "death on the installment plan" to "haphazard study."

Dr. Ernest P. Noble, who was the director of the NIAAA at the time the findings were released (but not when the study was funded), expressed his concern over "the manner in which the results of this report have been isolated and construed to suggest that recovered alcoholic people can return to moderate drinking with limited risk." He added that "until further definite scientific evidence exists to the contrary, I feel that abstinence must continue as the appropriate goal in the treatment of alcoholism. Furthermore, it would be extremely unwise for a recovered alcoholic to even try to experiment with controlled drinking."

Supporters of the report emphasized the scientific professionalism of its approach and findings, hailing the fact that some long-accepted dogma was receiving much-needed scrutiny. They saw this challenge as an opportunity, a new, unemotional step toward more productive research and a continuing dialogue between those who held opposing points of view. Yet in a generally favorable review of the report, Drs. Samuel B. Guze and Spencer T. Olin of Washington University, St. Louis, pointed out that the report's "initial distribution to the news media and its tone of exaggerated optimism . . . raise misgivings which the authors could easily have avoided."

Conclusions and considerations of the Rand Report: The major conclusions and considerations were as follows:

Treatment: Clients who underwent treatment had a slightly higher rate of remission than those who had a single contact with a treatment center, with some slight additional advantage as the amount of treatment increased. ("Single contact" and "untreated" are used synonymously throughout the report.)

Remission rates: Untreated clients; "natural" remission: 50%
Untreated clients with AA attendance: almost 70%
Treated clients: 70%.

The remission results for treated clients varied little from one treatment program to another.

The report contained a new definition of remission that includes both abstention and "normal" drinking. Normal drinking means consumption in moderate quantities commonly found in the general nonalcoholic population, provided no serious signs of impairment are present.

Relapse analysis: Relapse rates for normal drinkers are no higher than those for long-term abstainers;

For some alcoholics moderate drinking is not necessarily a prelude to full relapse.

Other conclusions: The study was unable to find a pattern upon which to conclude that one program was best for one type of client and another was best for another client.

It was found that "recovery from alcohol dependency may depend upon mechanisms quite unrelated to the factors that led to excessive drinking in the first place."

Future considerations: Total abstinence is not the only goal of treatment *if* future research confirms the initial conclusions of the survey.

If the survey's initial conclusions are confirmed, research is needed to determine which alcoholics can return to normal drinking.

If the theory that the results of most programs are uniform is true, as applied not only to an individual's drinking but to other behavior patterns as well, less expensive methods of treatment can be used.

Throughout the report, the authors pointed out the limitations of their sample: that the size of the sample was small and the time frame of the study was limited; that the conclusions about behavior were based on observation and not on controlled, experimental data; and that future behavior would not necessarily conform to the data in the survey.

Critics' conclusions: Critics of the report seized upon the limitations noted by the authors. What the authors viewed as a careful delineation of the limitations of their survey was seen by its detractors as factors that made the report not merely worthless but actively harmful. They claimed that the facts did not support the conclusions and that the result was a "legitimized" report that deluded alcoholics into believing that they could resume drinking, with disastrous results. A summary of some of their objections follows:

Size of sample: Critics of the report challenged its use of "on the basis of over 1000 subjects . . ." and countered that the Rand sample was" (actually a subsample of only 161 former patients, not randomly selected and from only 8 out of 45 government alcoholism treatment centers) with about 74% of all interviews at 4 sites (a large proportion over the phone by opinion interviewers who had 2-weeks training)."

Time period: Noting that "the time period for the Rand study *was 18 months after entering treatment*" [emphasis theirs], critics pointed out that Drs. D. L. Davies and John A. Ewing had examined the possibilities of alcoholics resuming social drinking in in-

dependent studies over substantially longer periods and had rejected them.

Makeup of sample: Critics have questioned whether all the clients in the Rand sample were in fact alcoholics.

The ongoing controversy: In January 1980 a second *Rand Report,* "The Course of Alcoholism: Four Years after Treatment," was published. In this new study (actually a continuation of the previous one) many of the conclusions of the original report were modified, although it was not, as some of the original report's critics claimed, a "retraction." The authors suggested a greater complexity of the issues involved than originally reported and characterized the report as another phase of a continuing program of study by the Rand Corporation. (See RAND REPORT II.)

Rand Report II   The National Institute on Alcohol Abuse and Alcoholism (NIAAA) funded the Rand Institute to conduct a follow-up study to the first RAND REPORT because critics pointed out two major defects: the study's follow-up period of six months was too short (a substantial number of clients were still in treatment) and only about one-quarter of all clients in the study responded to the six-month follow-up interviews. The results of this second study, known as *Rand Report II,* were published in January 1980. NIAAA contracted Rand to make follow-up studies of a sample of clients who were involved in the first Rand study. The subjects were to be interviewed after 18 months of treatment and again four years after treatment was initiated. The second report was completed by the same three doctors who had worked on the first report: J. Michael Polich, David J. Armor and Harriet B. Stambul. This four-year study of alcoholism, which cost about $500,000, was the most extensive and comprehensive of its kind to date.

The findings of the study were published in a 361-page report entitled *The Course of Alcoholism: Four Years after Treatment.* This second report received much less criticism and press coverage than the first *Rand Report,* and the picture that emerged from it was less optimistic than that of the earlier report. While the first report concluded that "clients of NIAAA treatment centers show substantial improvement on a number of outcome indices," the second stated that "although there is a frequent improvement there is also frequent relapse and much instability."

The second *Rand Report* nevertheless confirmed the earlier finding that some alcoholics are able to return to social drinking. But for most, the study showed, total abstinence seemed to be the surest method of maintaining remission. The second report substantiated the need for a more flexible definition of "recovering from alcoholism," while significantly refining the earlier report's conclusions.

Rand Report II found that there were at least two different types of alcoholics and that what worked best for one type might not work as well for another. In general the second report showed that alcoholics who were under 40 years old and who had shown relatively few symptoms of alcohol dependence within the month previous to treatment were less likely to relapse into alcoholism if they resumed social drinking. Those under 40 who attempted total abstinence were more likely to relapse. For alcoholics over 40 with strong symptoms of alcohol dependence, total abstinence offered the best prognosis. (Dependence symptoms included tremors and shakes, morning drinking, blackouts, missed meals because of drinking, loss of control while drinking and continuous drinking for 12 hours or more.)

In other words, for younger unmarried alcoholics who often are under social pressures to drink, the attempts to maintain abstinence may be more stressful than nonproblem social drinking; older married alcoholics are more likely to be encouraged by their spouses to remain abstinent and less likely to relapse than if they attempted controlled drinking.

Remission rates: Four years after entering treatment at one of eight centers around the country, 46% of the approximately 900 men studied were found to be "in remission" from the symptoms of alcoholism, with 28% abstaining and 18% drinking socially. Among those engaged in social drinking, half consumed more than four drinks a day and half drank less than that.

The study showed that alcoholics who entered treatment programs were highly unstable in their ability to refrain indefinitely from problem drinking. Many relapsed several times during the four years, and most entered other treatment programs from time to time. Only 28% of the respondents were free of alcohol-related problems both at 18 months and at four years after they first entered treatment, and

only 15% were in continuous remission for the entire four years. (Of the latter, 7.5% maintained abstinence for the entire four-year study period, and 7% maintained low amounts of consumption or a mixture of abstinence and low consumption without adverse consequences or symptoms.) Fifty-four percent had drinking problems four years after they first started treatment. Nevertheless there was some improvement, since upon admission to treatment at least 90% were drinking with more serious problems.

Alcoholic men who regularly attended AA meetings had the highest rate of long-term abstinence (57%). (Permanent abstinence is fairly infrequent, even for regular AA members.) Alcoholics who abstained for less than six months had the worst prognosis; these "short-term" abstainers had a much higher rate of relapse and many more alcohol-related deaths than either long-term abstainers or social drinkers. However, while regular attendance at AA sessions offered the best chance for recovery from alcoholism, those who attended the sessions were just as likely to have relapsed as those who had not attended.

The authors of the second *Rand Report* emphasized again that the study "does not recommend a particular treatment approach and does not recommend that any alcoholic resume drinking." It does, however, raise questions about the nature and treatment of alcoholism.

Rastafarians   The first Rastafarians appeared in JAMAICA in 1930, when Ras Tafari was crowned emperor of Ethiopia and took the name Haile Selassie. Until his death, Rastafarians looked to Selassie as their messiah. Their objective was—and still is—to revitalize and promote their African heritage.

The Rasta god is called Jah, and some orthodox followers grow dreadlocks (long unaltered locks formed by washing the hair and allowing it to dry without combing) as a symbol of their devotion. The Rastafarians believe the smoking of ganja (the Jamaican word for marijuana, appropriated from the Hindu term) is one of their strongest shared experiences and look on ganja as a divine herb important to their spiritual, mental and physical health. Most probably, marijuana was introduced to Jamaica by indentured laborers from India in the mid-1800s, and there are estimates that between 60% and 70%

of the island's population ingests ganja in one form or another. Although the "herb" (as it is often referred to) has been illegal to use, possess and sell since 1913, the police have traditionally turned a blind eye, unofficially tolerating the ganja trade. In the early 1990s, however, the Jamaican government, believing that the enormous marijuana industry had grown out of control, sought assistance from the U.S. Drug Enforcement Administration (the DEA).

The Rastafarians smoke ganja in "spliffs," approximately five-inch cone-shaped rolls made from paper or corn husks. It is also brewed in a green tea. This method is often preferred by women and children and is also used as a major folk remedy for treating rheumatism, allergies, sleeping difficulties, male impotence and as an external tonic for wounds and infections. Kali (after the Hindu black goddess of strength) is the term denoting the most potent grade of ganja.

Reggae music brought the Rastafarians to worldwide attention in the late 1960s, especially through the music of the late Bob Marley. The lyrics of many reggae songs reflect the near-worship of the "mystical herb," as the Rastas frequently refer to it.

rational emotive therapy (RET)   Sometimes used to treat alcoholics and other drug users undergoing REHABILITATION, rational emotive therapy (RET) is an educational, rather than psychodynamic or medical, model of psychotherapy. RET, developed by Albert Ellis and Robert A. Harper, asserts that people have choice in their lives, that most of their conditioning consists of self-conditioning and that the therapist serves to help them see a range of alternatives to their behavior. RET stresses a semantic approach to understanding; change in semantic usage is stressed so as to concomitantly change thinking, emotions and behavior. The therapy shows people how they behave self-defeatingly and how they can get themselves to change. Both individual and small-group therapy as well as large workshops and lectures are used.

Rational Recovery (RR)   Abstinence-based alternative to Alcoholics Anonymous, founded by Jack Trimpey in 1985 and based on Albert Ellis's RATIONAL EMOTIVE THERAPY techniques.

Rauwolfia serpentina   A DEPRESSANT obtained from the dried root of a small climbing shrub of the Apocynaceae family, which is native to India and known in English as *snakeroot*. Indians have used it for 2,500 years in powdered form as a tranquilizer for such conditions as snakebite, hypertension, insomnia and insanity. It is the source of the drug RESERPINE.

Usage: The Indians who first ground up the *Rauwolfia serpentina* root and used it to treat hypertension and insanity applied the substance wisely. It is still used in the treatment of mild hypertension and, with additional drugs, for more severe hypertension. It should not be used in patients who are suffering from or prone to depression; it induces a depression that has been known to be severe enough to result in suicide, particularly after withdrawal from the drug.

Dosage: The recommended dose for hypertension is 0.5–3.0 mg, and the dosage suggested for emotional disorders is 0.1–2.0 mg

Activity: *Rauwolfia serpentina* is rapidly absorbed from the gastrointestinal tract, widely distributed throughout the body, and excreted slowly in the urine and feces. It depresses the central nervous system (CNS) at the hypothalamic level, suppressing the sympathetic branch of the autonomic system. *Rauwolfia serpentina* crosses the placental barrier and also appears in breast milk.

Effects: *Rauwolfia serpentina* is an antihypertensive drug that calms symptoms of anxiety, such as headache and palpitations, without analgesia. It lowers the blood pressure, slows the pulse, causes pupil constriction and increases gastrointestinal secretion (and should therefore be used cautiously in patients with peptic ulcers and ulcerative colitis). Unlike the minor tranquilizers, *Rauwolfia serpentina* does not potentiate other CNS depressants, nor does its use lead to tolerance or physical or psychological dependence.

Side effects reported in conjunction with the use of *Rauwolfia serpentina* include infrequent paradoxical excitation, increased respiratory secretions, gastrointestinal hypersecretion, nasal congestion, nausea, vomiting, diarrhea, drowsiness, depression, rash, impotence and anorexia in babies of women treated with the drug.

Availability: *Rauwolfia serpentina* is manufactured as tablets under the name of the root and Raudixin and Harmonyl. It is also available in tablets mixed with thiazides and potassium chloride.

reality therapy   Developed by a psychiatrist, Dr. William Glasser, who has worked extensively in corrections and education, reality therapy is based on the theory that behavior is generated by what happens in the mind rather than what happens in the real world. Individuals attempt to control the world outside through use of a control system made up of millions of perceptions, including perceptions of what is ideal. A gap between the perceived world and the ideal world is called a "perceptual error" and is sensed through comparison. Actions are adjusted so that the perception from the real world eventually corresponds with the mind's idealization. Alcohol (and by extension, other drugs), according to Glasser, blots out perceptual error and destroys the comparing system that shows the difference between what a person wants and what he or she gets. In reality therapy, drug users are taught alternative solutions to drug use and learn to fulfill their needs (and narrow the gap between the world in their minds and the "real" world) through ALCOHOLICS ANONYMOUS, various 12-step programs and/or through other forms of REHABILITATION.

Anita Diamant, "Reality Therapy," *U.S. Journal of Drug and Alcohol Dependence* 5, no. 9 (November 1981): 13.

reassurance   A simple therapeutic method of decreasing a client's anxieties or fears by assuring him that his reactions are excessive or his fears groundless. Reassurance is given with sincerity and certainty, along with positive, realistic evidence of the needlessness for the anxiety that is being experienced.

receptor sites   Sites within the body, where chemical substances interact to produce pharmacological actions. Receptors recognize a substance by its chemical configuration and electrical charge, distinguish it from others, and transmit the signal indicating the presence of the substance that brings about pharmacological action in the target tissue. Opiate receptor sites have been identified in the brain, intestines and spinal cord. Endogenous opioid peptides, or ENDORPHINS, were discovered in 1975,

and the discovery of others has followed. Very little is known, however, about where and how the endorphins are produced and what their exact role is in modulating pain and mood. Receptors have also been identified for benzodiazepines, and some interesting studies involving alcoholics are under way. (See GENETICS.)

recovery   Defining recovery from alcoholism or other drug addiction is not a simple matter, since there is no clear-cut definition for either "alcoholism" or "addiction." Recovery is defined differently by different groups. Those who espouse the philosophy of ALCOHOLICS ANONYMOUS, NARCOTICS ANONYMOUS or other similar self-help groups believe that recovery is a never-ending process, characterized by complete abstinence from mind-altering drugs (with the exception of caffeine and nicotine) and a willingness to continue to pursue personal growth. AA introduced the term (and it also is a common practice in similar groups) to refer to members as "recovering," which emphasizes the concept of recovery as a continuing process.

Other schools of thought, however, disagree with the AA model and are open to the notion that once the psychological causes of alcoholism/other drug addiction have been removed and reconditioning has been achieved—a formerly drug dependent individual can recover. Some professionals believe that a recovered alcoholic can return to nonalcoholic, social drinking, and studies do substantiate this theory, with some, but not all, "recovered" alcoholics.

The best definition of recovery appears to be a stable REMISSION of symptoms over a period of time. This means that for a relatively long period the patient has exhibited no alcohol/other drug-abusing behavior. Recovery seems to be a distinct stage in the course of drug dependency. A great deal of the recovery process appears to depend on the individual, who must recognize the costs of his or her drug-related behavior, allow a breakdown of the defenses that have prolonged it, and commit him- or herself to change. (See DENIAL.)

David J. Armor, J. Michael Polich and Harriet B. Stambul, *Alcoholism and Treatment* (New York: John Wiley & Sons, 1978).

recreational drug use   The U.S. Commission on Marijuana and Drug Abuse defines recreational/social drug use as that which occurs in social settings among friends or acquaintances who wish to share a pleasurable experience. Unlike EXPERIMENTAL DRUG USE, recreational and social use tends to have more of a pattern, but individuals' patterns vary widely in terms of frequency, duration and intensity. Regardless of the duration of use, it tends not to escalate in either intensity or frequency.

However, William J. Bennett, then-director of the Office of National Drug Control Policy, challenged the commission's largely benign view of recreational drug use in his September 1989 *National Drug Control Strategy Report to the President*. Nonaddicted casual and regular users of drugs represent "a grave issue of national concern," he declared. According to Bennett, so-called nonaddicted recreational users of illicit drugs numbered in the millions, "and each represents a potential agent of infection for the non-users in his personal ambit."

red eye   See EYES.

red wine   Red WINE is produced by fermenting grape juice with the grape skins and a certain quantity of grape stems. It is the presence of the skins, in particular, that gives red wines their color, for the juice of virtually all grapes is colorless. Unlike red wines, white wines are produced by fermenting grape juice without the grape skins, and rosé wines usually are produced by fermenting grape juice that has had limited contact with grape skins. The alcohol content of red wines ranges from 10% to 14%.

Once grapes intended for red wines have been gathered, they are crushed and loaded into fermenting tanks with the skins and, according to the tannin content desired, some amount of stems from the vine. This wine "must" is then mixed with less than one part per thousand of an antiseptic, usually sulfur dioxide, to eliminate all but the alcohol-tolerant natural yeasts in the grapes. Other active yeast cultures sometimes are added at this stage to assist fermentation.

In the fermentation process the sugars in the grapes are converted into alcohol and carbonic gas by the yeasts. The skins and the stems are forced to the surface of the fermenting must by the gas (some red wine vinters use a grill to keep this "cap" submerged in the fermenting vat for greater flavor and color). Fermentation of red wines lasts anywhere

from two days to two weeks, with wines that are intended for long aging being fermented the longest. When the grape juice has attained the desired level of alcohol content and has extracted the desired level of tannin from the skins and stems, the solids are separated and the process follows the same steps used in the production of white and rosé wines.

Most experts agree that the finest red wines in the world are those bottled in the Bordeaux district of France. Located in the southeastern part of the country, this area is officially about 90 miles from north to south and about 60 miles from east to west. The soil is an especially favorable one for growing grapes, consisting of a sandy topsoil and a clay subsoil, and it is drained by the Garonne and Dordogne rivers that meet to form the Gironde, a term sometimes considered synonymous with Bordeaux. The principal subdivisions of the region include Medoc, Saint-Emilion and Pomerol, which produce red wines exclusively, and Graves, which produces both red and white wines. Second only to Bordeaux is Burgundy, located in eastern France, which holds the distinction of being the oldest wine-producing region in the country. There are more hills than in Bordeaux, and the finest vineyards in Burgundy are those located midway up the slopes of the hills. The most famous vineyards in the region are those of the Cote d'Or, a range of low hills to the southwest of Dijon. Among the notable Cote d'Or red wines is Beaujolais, a fruity red wine usually drunk young. Each year it is sold after incomplete fermentation as a less-expensive (but usually having a quite acceptable quality and taste) seasonal wine known as *Beaujolais nouveau*. The other principal red wine regions of France are the Rhone Valley in the southeast and the Loire Valley in the southwest.

Besides French wines the famous European red wines are mostly Italian. These include the northern Piedmont wines, such as Barbaresco, Barbera and Barolo; the Tuscany wines from central Italy known as Chianti; and wines from the Lago di Garda region, such as Bardolino and Valpolicella. Other leading European red wines include the Riojas from Spain, the Dao red wines from Portugal and the Tokay wines from Hungary. Numerous red wines are also produced in places as far apart as Rumania and South America, and the wine regions of the U.S. have for many years produced red wines from grape vines imported from Europe.

reggae music and drugs   Reggae music makes positive and frequent reference to marijuana use and the Rastafarian lifestyle. It also describes poverty and oppression in the West Indies. It was reggae music that called attention to the Rastafari in the late 1960s—the first Rastafarians appeared in Jamaica and looked to the late emperor of Ethiopia, Haile Selassie, as their messiah. The lyrics of many reggae tunes reflect the near worship of the "mystical herb," as the Rastas refer to ganja, the Hindi word for marijuana. (See RASTAFARIANS.)

rehabilitation   After DETOXIFICATION a patient is physically free of alcohol and/or other drug dependence, but his or her behavior patterns and needs have not been changed. Therefore some sort of follow-up treatment usually is necessary to enable the patient to function soberly in society without relapsing into alcoholism. Patients may be encouraged to go to ALCOHOLICS ANONYMOUS meetings or other self-help groups, to individual or group therapy or to both. Some enter special rehabilitation centers for a certain length of time in order to establish ways of living without alcohol or other drugs.

The same facilities may provide detoxification and rehabilitation services, but generally these services are offered in different places. Detoxification usually takes place in a hospital setting and lasts about a week. Rehabilitation normally is accomplished in a special environment, where patients dress in their everyday clothes (as opposed to hospital clothing) and keep regular hours. The duration of rehabilitation in private treatment centers varies, but usually the stay is longer than for detoxification, often up to four weeks. Many private treatment centers are located in nonhospital settings, often in rural areas or other pleasant surroundings. Some, however, are in general hospitals.

Modes of treatment also vary, but almost all emphasize the value of Alcoholics Anonymous and AL-ANON or the 12-step groups appropriate for an individual's drug of choice. Chemical dependence is treated as a disease, patient responsibility is stressed and abstinence is a primary aim. During rehabilitation patients receive a good deal of instruction about drugs and living without them. Most programs encourage family involvement and aftercare following the inpatient stay, either through therapy, 12-step membership or both.

In a private rehabilitation treatment center the patient is surrounded by an enormous support system. He also is removed from the pressures of daily life and the presence of drugs and is surrounded by people who understand the problem. This environment may help him to restructure his life, but because it is so sheltered a return to normal living may be difficult. There, with the availability of liquor stores and bars or drug dealers plus a drug-related culture and the daily pressures of work and social life, he may soon return to drinking. Or the opposite may occur: the user may feel that he is cured and free of drug problems and therefore can return to using normally, the so-called "flight into health," which generally leads to a relapse. This is one reason why aftercare is stressed and why it is important to involve the family. (See RAND REPORT II.)

rehabilitation counselor   Usually a master's-level professional who assists recovering persons in vocational assessment, planning and job reentry. Counselors may also work in some inpatient settings to assist in day treatment programs or programs for dually diagnosed MENTALLY ILL CHEMICAL ABUSERS in recovery.

reinforcement, positive and negative   The behavioral theories of psychology consider human behavior to be strongly influenced by a system of rewards and punishments within the environment of family, school, neighborhood and work. Most often one will repeat a behavior when it is rewarded. This pattern of repeated behavior is known as *reinforcement*. When the pattern of repeated behavior continues, it is called *conditioning*. If there is no reinforcement, or if a punishment is issued instead of a reward, one will tend to discontinue the behavior.

However, reinforcement may be *positive* and/or *negative*. For the drug user the reward for taking a drug is the pleasurable effect (the high) experienced soon after the drug is ingested. This immediate rewarding effect, in turn, encourages the user to repeat the behavior of taking the drug. This process is known as positive reinforcement. The reward is the addition of the pleasurable, or positive effect. Negative reinforcement is also rewarded behavior, but the reward is the removal of a negative effect. For example, alcohol cravings associated with withdrawal usually arise out of the need for relief from the distress of withdrawal rather than from an actual desire for the drug. To ingest a drug to relieve headaches, stress and anxiety—to alleviate negative symptoms—is considered negative reinforcement. (See CRAVING.)

relapse   A return to uncontrolled drug use by an alcoholic or user of other drugs during a stage of recovery. Recovery may mean complete abstinence or the ability of a user to partake moderately without LOSS OF CONTROL. Addiction is a disorder characterized by a tendency to relapse.

Relapse seems related to a number of factors, including personality, environmental influences, physiology, social attitudes and the availability of the substance one is addicted to. Social pressures during treatment that tempt the user to break abstinence are particularly important. Individual problems or even positive achievement may lead to relapse. Overconfidence after making progress in treatment and attempting to tackle difficult situations that one is not yet ready to handle may cause a return to drug use. Or relapse may occur because of depression or frustration. But an addict generally is not considered to be completely recovered until he or she is able to maintain continued abstinence without relapse. (See RAND REPORT II.)

relaxation training   Any number of techniques that are used to achieve relaxation, usually concentrated in part on muscle tightness. Anxiety states may be contributed to by muscles that are in a state of chronic tension. A feedback loop exists between tensed muscles and psychological tensions. If muscle tension can be relaxed by biofeedback, self-hypnosis or progressive muscle-relaxation exercises, it can reduce anxiety. Even when drugs are required for anxiety reduction, relaxation training improves the effect of the antianxiety drugs. Psychological techniques to effect thought content and images also are utilized.

Release   Based in England, with headquarters in London, Release is a national 24-hour welfare and advice agency that specializes in urgent problems, particularly in the area of drugs and criminal law. Staffed by both professionals and volunteers, Release provides counseling, advice, education and information on drug use and abuse.

religion   The attitudes of different religious groups toward the use of alcoholic beverages vary widely. A number of religious groups regard drinking alcohol as immoral or sinful; total abstinence is the accepted norm in these groups. Other religions permit members to use alcohol socially, as well as in such ceremonies as Holy Communion, which may involve the drinking of wine. All the major religions frown on drunkenness. Following are the views on alcoholism of most of the major religions in the U.S.:

Roman Catholics: The Roman Catholic Church permits the use of alcoholic beverages by all except those who are diagnosed as alcoholic. Use is considered to be appropriate on holidays and during celebrations. Alcoholism is considered a disease involving the physical, mental and spiritual components of man. The church recommends INTERVENTION and treatment followed by membership in ALCOHOLICS ANONYMOUS.

A national study of American drinking practices conducted in 1969 by the Rutgers Center for Alcohol Studies found relatively high proportions of drinkers and heavy drinkers among Catholics. Those who attended church more often were more likely to report infrequent drinking and consumed less per occasion. The incidence of alcoholism among Catholics appears to be determined by ethnic background; both Irish Americans and Italian Americans are primarily Catholic, yet Irish Americans have a higher rate of drinking problems.

Greek Orthodox: The Greek Orthodox Archdiocese permits the use of alcoholic beverages and finds them traditionally appropriate following a wedding or baptism. Occasional overindulgence of alcoholic beverages is tolerated but not condoned. Alcoholism is considered an illness to be understood and treated.

Jews: Judaism permits the use of any alcoholic beverage that conforms to the laws of *kashruth*. The only prohibition against drinking is during fast days (when consumption of food is prohibited as well). There are several religious ceremonies that require the use of wine, including the Passover seder and certain rites of passage. People who do not consume alcoholic beverages may substitute grape juice on occasions when wine is required. Purim is the one holiday during the year when excessive intake of alcohol is permissible.

Jews have the lowest percentage of abstainers of any of the major American religions. They also have a very high proportion of light drinkers and the lowest proportion of heavy drinkers. The rate of alcoholism among Jews is believed to be relatively low.

Protestants: The Protestant position on the use of alcohol varies from sect to sect. Many sects that preached abstinence at one time have switched to an emphasis on moderation. In one survey liberal Protestants demonstrated a drinking pattern somewhat similar to that of Catholics, although there were fewer heavy drinkers. Conservative Protestants had a large proportion of abstainers and a low proportion of heavy drinkers.

Presbyterians: In 1970 the General Assembly of the Presbyterian Church noted the obligation of persons to make responsible decisions regarding the use of alcoholic beverages, the danger of excessive drinking and the responsibility to seek constructive solutions for social problems related to the use of alcoholic beverages.

Jehovah's Witnesses: Jehovah's Witnesses allow the use of alcohol, since according to their teachings, God's word does not require total abstinence. Wine is a symbol of happiness in the Bible; therefore it is not forbidden to mankind. However, the Witnesses caution strongly against alcohol dependence and abuse.

Methodists: The Methodist Church is the largest American church proscribing the use of alcohol. In a 1980 position paper, the United Methodist Church stated: "We affirm our long-standing support of abstinence from alcohol as a faithful witness to God's liberating and redeeming love for persons. The drug dependent person is an individual of infinite human worth in need of treatment and rehabilitation and misuse should be viewed as a symptom of underlying disorders for which remedies should be sought." An increasing number of younger Methodists, however, are using alcohol, sometimes in an extreme manner.

Baptists: The American Baptist Association forbids the use of alcoholic beverages and considers alcoholism to be a sin rather than a disease, a "violation of God's will and word toward man." The Christian Life Commission of the Southern Baptist Convention also holds that use of alcohol is immoral but it advocates the demonstration of "love, patience, and forgiveness of God in dealing with alcoholics."

Mormons: The Mormons recommend strongly against the use of alcohol. Only 21% of Mormon males who attend church weekly consume alcohol.

Friends United Meeting (Quakers):   The position of the Friends toward the use of alcohol is based on the belief that the human body is the temple of the Lord and that to mar it is to dishonor him. Any pleasurable or exhilarating effects produced by intoxicants are temporary and tend to react injuriously on both mind and body. Total abstinence is advocated, and the entire liquor traffic is considered to be detrimental to human welfare.

Seventh-Day Adventists: Seventh-Day Adventists forbid the use of alcohol. Temperance is considered to be a way of life and is equated with self-control through Jesus Christ.

Native-American Church: As one of many Native American religions, all of which have differing practices, members of the Native-American Church use mescal buttons as part of their religious rituals. The buttons contain mescaline—a psychoactive hallucinogenic substance found in the PEYOTE cactus. Although mescal is illegal to use (it is a Schedule I controlled substance), it has been legal for members of the Native-American Church to take in conjunction with their rituals since 1969.

Morris E. Chafetz and Harold W. Demone Jr., *Alcoholism and Society* (New York: Oxford University Press, 1962): 84–99.

John Langone, *Bombed, Buzzed, Smashed, or . . . Sober: A Book about Alcohol* (Boston: Little, Brown, 1976): 48–49.

Jennifer James, *Peyote and Mescaline: A History and Use of the Sacred Cactus* (Tempe, Arizona: December 1990).

REM (rapid eye movement)   One of the various stages of sleep; the stage in which a person dreams. All the orders of the sleep cycle are biologically essential and, deprived of REM, a person may become hostile, irritable and anxious. Barbiturates and other sedatives suppress REM, and alcohol, at higher consumption levels, also reduces REM sleep.

remission   Remission is defined as "a relatively prolonged lessening or disappearance of the symptoms of a disease," according to *Webster's New World Dictionary* (Second College Edition, 1984). In the field of alcohol/other drug use, the term "remission" often is used instead of "RECOVERY," since it is extremely difficult to say when someone has completely recovered from the addictive use of a mind-altering substance. Remission generally is measured in terms of drinking/drug use behavior as opposed to social behavior.

There are two conflicting schools of thought on what constitutes remission. One school, represented by ALCOHOLICS ANONYMOUS and other 12-Step programs, believes that remission exists only when an alcoholic/drug user is in a state of complete abstinence. Another school, which includes the authors of the RAND REPORT, expands the definition of remission to cover an individual who is able, in the case of alcohol, to maintain a course of "normal drinking," defined as a daily consumption of less than three ounces of ABSOLUTE ALCOHOL with no serious symptoms related to drinking, such as tremors, frequent episodes of blackouts, absences from work and/or drunkenness. Both abstainers and those who drink at normal levels without showing signs of alcoholism are considered to be in remission. Moderate use of other drugs is even more difficult to define, since the vast majority of people who are regular users and/or chemically dependent on legal drugs, including nicotine, caffeine and prescription medications are not necessarily aware of the level of their addiction or the existent danger to their mental and physical health, and when they are aware of the problem, they often choose to ignore or conceal the extent of their drug use. The moderate nonmedical use of illegally procured drugs is difficult to assess since the practice, although widespread, remains a criminal act.

repan   A sedative and analgesic that contains 50 mg of butalbital (an intermediate-acting BARBITURATE), caffeine, phenacetin and acetaminophen. It is used for the relief of pain associated with nervous tension. Because it contains a barbiturate it is habit-forming and may result in dependence.

reproductive functions   Drugs, and particularly alcohol, take a toll on the entire endocrine system, including reproductive functioning. Disturbances in the menstrual cycle, infertility and loss of secondary sex characteristics are often witnessed in alcoholic women. A study of a national sample of women revealed that heavy menstrual flow, dysmenorrhea (painful menstruation) and premenstrual discomfort increase with drinking. It is known that chronic intoxication can lead to amenorrhea (absence of menstruation) and can also result in pathological changes in the ovaries and ovulation. A history of miscarriage or still-birth, premature birth, birth defects and infertility was found to be associated with high levels of alcohol consumption. Drinking and other drug use during pregnancy can also lead to mental retardation in children. (See FETAL ALCOHOL SYNDROME and BABIES, DRUG-ADDICTED AND -EXPOSED.)

Alcoholism can also lead to marked reproductive dysfunction in men, including impotence, low testosterone production and sperm counts, and testicular atrophy. Alcohol-related changes in hormone levels have also been associated with enlargement of breasts in male alcoholics. Even acute or periodic heavy drinking may result in impotence and reduced levels of testosterone. (See SEX.)

T. J. Cicero, "Alcohol-induced Deficits in the Hypothalmic-Pituitary-Luteinizing Hormone Axis in the Male," *Alcoholism* 6 (1982): 207–215.

R. W. Wilsnack, S. C. Wilsnack and A. D. Klassav, "Drinking and Reproductive Dysfunction among Women in a 1981 National Survey," *Alcoholism: Clinical and Experimental Research* 8 (1984): 451–458.

reserpine   A DEPRESSANT and SEDATIVE HYPNOTIC, reserpine is an alkaloid of *RAUWOLFIA SERPENTINA* and can also be synthesized. In the last 20 years, it and other *Rauwolfia* derivatives have been significant in the treatment of patients suffering from psychotic disorders.

Usage: Like *Rauwolfia serpentina*, reserpine is used to relieve hypertension. It is no longer used psychiatrically due to the very significant depression it can induce. It has a low abuse potential and is not sold on the black market.

Dosage: Recommended dosages of reserpine range from 0.1–1.0 mg, with 0.5 mg daily suggested for hypertension. Administered intravenously, effects begin to manifest in one hour and last six to eight hours. The onset of effects with intramuscular injection is slower, but can last 10–12 hours.

Appearance and activity: Reserpine is an odorless white, off-white or yellowish crystalline powder. It is insoluble in water, slightly soluble in alcohol and freely soluble in acetic acid. Rapidly absorbed in the gastrointestinal tract and widely distributed throughout the body, reserpine crosses the placental barrier, appears in breast milk and is excreted in the urine and feces.

Effects: Reserpine's effects resemble those of *Rauwolfia serpentina*. The drug alleviates anxiety and tension without causing disequilibrium or loss of motor control. It lowers blood pressure. Reserpine does not have anticonvulsant or antihistaminic properties. Tolerance and dependence do not develop. The drug can induce depression, and its cardiovascular and central nervous system depressant effects continue after use of the drug has stopped.

Availability: Reserpine is manufactured as tablets under the brand names Diutensen, Diupres, Hydropres, Regroton and Reserpine, and in injectable form under the brand name Serpasil.

resilience   Term frequently occurring in prevention texts, usually in the context of lists of protective factors, which appear to predispose some individuals toward being less susceptible to addiction of alcohol and other drugs. Resilience can be characterological or attained as a result of a number of different environmental factors. The environmental factors include: (1) living in a socioeconomically healthy community, where unemployment is low, housing is adequate, schools are well-run, good health care is accessible and there is easy access to social services; and (2) a positive family environment, where there is adequate nurturing, support for education, a multi-generational kinship network, supportive role models, adequate child care alternatives, few chronic or excessively stressful life events, close relationship with a parent, minimal marital conflict and clear behavioral guidelines. Characterological qualities in children favoring resilience include: (1) constitutional strengths, including sufficient sensorimotor development, physical robustness and no

temperamental impairment; and (2) easy, affectionate temperament, flexibility, optimism, self-discipline and internal locus of control.

reverse tolerance   A condition in which the response to a certain dose of a drug increases with repeated use. In marijuana use, consistent users sometimes claim to require lesser amounts to achieve the desired effect. Some experts attribute this more to efficient smoking and earlier identification of the effects of marijuana than to reverse tolerance. However, having TCH (tetrahydrocannabinol—the active ingredient in marijuana) in the blood consistently, over long periods, may result in circulation blood levels that are raised higher than they would normally be, by small additional ingested quantities, resulting in the appearance of reverse tolerance.

rhinophyma   New Latin, from Greek *rhinos* (nose) + *phyma* (swelling). A skin condition of the nose characterized by swelling, redness and often, broken capillaries. It is sometimes, but not always, caused by heavy drinking over a prolonged period. W. C. Fields was a well-known victim of rhinophyma; in his case it was called by its popular name: "whiskey nose." (See ACNE ROSACEA.)

risk management   See HARM REDUCTION.

Ritalin   A central nervous system stimulant that contains METHYLPHENIDATE hydrochloride. It is used in the treatment of narcolepsy; minimal brain dysfunction; to treat patients showing withdrawn senile behavior; and also in the treatment of hyperkinetic children. Chemically similar to amphetamines, tolerance will develop, physical and psychological dependence can occur, and there is abuse potential. Results of overdosage are agitation, tremors, convulsions and hallucinations.

RNA   Ribonucleic acid. One of the two main types of nucleic acid; the other being DNA. RNA is an organic substance found in the chromosomes of all living cells and plays an important part in the storage and replication of hereditary information and in protein synthesis.

***Robinson v. California,* 370 U.S. 660, 1962**   The Supreme Court in this ruling reiterated its view of

Resilience/Protective Factors

Prevention Primer, Center for Substance Abuse Prevention

Many youths, although living in high-risk environments, seem to possess personal resilience that helps them avoid alcohol, tobacco and other drug problems. One current challenge to the prevention field is to identify these protective factors and determine how they can be instilled in all youth in high-risk environments.

The following is a checklist of youth protective factors:

1. Community Environment
Middle or upper class
Low unemployment
Adequate housing
Pleasant neighborhood
Low prevalence of neighborhood crime
Good school
School that promotes learning, participation and responsibility
High-quality health care
Easy access to adequate social services
Flexible social service providers who put clients' needs first

2. Family Environment
Adequate family income
Structured and nurturing family
Parents promote learning
Fewer than four children in family
Two or more years between the birth of each child
Few chronic stressful life events
Multigenerational kinship network
Non-kin support network, e.g., supportive role models, dependable substitute child care
Warm, close personal relationship with parent(s) and/or other adult(s)
Little marital conflict
Family stability and cohesiveness
Plenty of attention during first year of life
Sibling as caretaker/confidante
Clear behavior guidelines

3. Constitutional Strengths
Adequate early sensorimotor and language development
High intelligence
Physically robust
No emotional or temperamental impairments

4. Personality of the Child
Affectionate/endearing
Easy temperament
Autonomous
Adaptable and flexible
Positive outlook
Healthy expectations
Self-efficacy
Self-discipline
Internal locus of control
Problem-solving skills
Socially adept
Tolerance of people and situations

If the high-risk environment is the family itself, for instance if children are growing up in an alcoholic or drug-abusing family, studies suggest that they have a better chance of growing into healthy adulthood if they:

Can learn to do one thing well that is valued by themselves, their friends and their community
Are required to be helpful as they grow up
Are able to ask for help for themselves
Are able to elicit positive responses from others in their environment
Are able to distance themselves from their dysfunctional families so that the family is not their sole frame of reference
Are able to bond with some socially valued, positive entity, such as the family, school, community groups, or church
Are able to interact with a (perceived to be) caring adult who provides consistent caring responses

Resiliency factors, along with risk factors, need to be more widely publicized for the use of parents, gatekeepers and prevention planners. While many of the factors listed are the result of external forces, those factors that may be taught or instilled in children can provide some protection to youths at high risk for alcohol, tobacco or other drug problems.

Sources
Youth at High Risk for Substance Abuse (1990) BKD06.
Using Community-Wide Collaboration to Foster Resiliency in Kids. A Conceptual Framework (Portland, Oreg.: Northwest Regional Educational Laboratory, 1993).

Source: Center for Substance Abuse Prevention, *Prevention Primer: Resilience/Protective Factors* (Rockville, Md.: Center for Substance Abuse Prevention, n.d.).

drug addiction as being a medical problem and not a criminal one.

Robitussin   An expectorant and cough suppressant that contains guaifenesin and codeine phosphate. It is supplied as an amber-colored elixir with 3.5% alcohol content and can be habit-forming.

role models, drug use by   When prominent people, be they athletes, actors, musicians or singers, make headlines because of drug use, young people who are working hard to develop their own professional skills may become disillusioned. Some youngsters may then start to distrust their own ambitions and question their goals.

In recent years, prominent athletes, rock stars, actors and, on occasion, political and government leaders or their spouses have been found to be heavily dependent on drugs. Their notoriety may influence the public's behavior and attitude about alcohol and other drugs. Some of these celebrities go on to use their experiences to try to prevent others from experiencing the problems they have had. Perhaps the most noted—and notable—example of the latter is Betty Ford, wife of former president Gerald Ford. In 1982 the former first lady established a treatment center in her name in Mirage, California. Mrs. Ford had courageously admitted to the American people that she was in recovery from alcohol and drug dependency. In 1989 Kitty Dukakis, wife of Democratic presidential candidate Michael Dukakis, governor of Massachusetts, revealed that she had entered a treatment program for alcoholism following her husband's national election defeat. Former Senator John Tower (R-Tex.) on the other hand, with a reputation for hard drinking, never publicly acknowledged his drinking problem or alcoholism, despite his rejection by the Senate Armed Services Committee as U.S. Secretary of Defense. Most committee members agreed that the major issue in their deliberations was Tower's drinking.

While considerable good may come from celebrities announcing that they have had alcohol or other drug problems and have resolved them, the opposite effect may result from prominent personalities who are unable to "come clean," thereby missing an opportunity to serve as a role model and to transform what would appear to be an entirely negative circum-

stance into something with long-reaching positive repercussions.

rose wine   Having an alcohol content from 12% to 15%, rose WINE is produced by fermenting grape juice that has had limited contact with grape skins. Since the juice of virtually all grapes is colorless, the difference in color between red and white wines stems from the fact that the former is fermented in a "must" that includes grape skins and the latter is fermented in a "must" of pure grape juice.

Once grapes intended for rose wines have been gathered, they are crushed to extract their juice, which is allowed to mix with the grape skins for a period of 12 to 36 hours. Then the solids are separated and the process continues through steps similar to those used to produce red or white wines. Today some inexpensive rose wines are produced in bulk simply by adding a tasteless red coloring, called *cochineal,* to finished white wines. The product is a wine that resembles true rose in color but lacks the flavoring tannins extracted from the grape skins in the traditional process.

The most prized rose wines come from the Anjou, Bordeaux and Tavel wine districts of France. The south Tyrol region of Italy also is noted for its rose wines, and both Portugal and Spain produce rose wines in virtually all of their wine districts. A number of rose wines from California are considered to be comparable to the European brands. Inexpensive varieties are produced in nearly all wine-producing countries, often by means of artificial coloring, as a way to dispose of marginal wines.

rubbing alcohol   A nondrinkable solution made with isopropyl alcohol rather than ethyl alcohol, or ethanol (the type of alcohol found in potable beverages). Rubbing alcohol is used externally for medicinal purposes and is poisonous when ingested.

rum   An alcoholic beverage made from the distillation of fermented products of sugarcane. Most frequently rum is produced by distilling molasses, but also it is sometimes made from the juice of sugarcane.

It is thought that the term "rum" has its origins in the British word "rumbullion" (meaning tumult or uproar), or possibly "rumbustion" (meaning rambunctious). When rum was first manufactured in the

West Indies during the early 17th century, it was referred to as "kill devil" and, later, "rumbullion." By 1667 "rumbullion" had been abbreviated to "rum."

Rum often is thought of as the drink of romantics and adventurers. In the 18th century, British sailors used rum as the base of their daily GROG, which consisted of rum, water and lemon juice. Rum also was the alcoholic beverage consumed in the largest quantities by the American colonists just before the Revolutionary War. It has been estimated that at that time the colonists, women and children included, drank three and three-quarters gallons of rum per person per year.

Throughout the 17th and 18th centuries until the time of the Revolution, rum was the key item of trade in what was dubbed the New England Rum Triangle, a trade route between New England, Africa and the West Indies. In this trade route, rum manufactured in New England was shipped to Africa, where it was exchanged for slaves. The slaves in turn were taken to the West Indies, where they were traded for the molasses needed to make rum. This trade route was a major source of revenue for New England ship owners. Their business as well as that of the rum manufacturers thus suffered greatly during the Revolutionary War, when molasses supplies were cut off from Cuba and the West Indies. At the time that the American rum business began to suffer, the newly emerging American WHISKEY business began to flourish, since it did not depend upon foreign trade for its essential ingredients. The rum business never fully recovered, and whiskey gradually replaced rum as the most popular alcoholic beverage in the U.S. (See RYE and BOURBON WHISKEY.)

In the 19th century, rum acquired a rather low reputation in the U.S. Its name became a synonym for intoxicating beverages in general, and a hard drinker was referred to as a "rum sucker" in the 1850s and a "rummy" or "rummie" in the 1860s. In addition, cheap saloons sometimes were called "rum holes" (1830s). During the 20th century, "rumdum" (1920s) and "rumbag" (1940s) became slang expressions for a "drunkard." The popular card game gin rummy made references to both GIN and rum.

Although rum is produced in most countries where sugarcane is grown, the chief producers on an international scale are the islands in the West Indies, of which the more important sources are Barbados, Jamaica, Trinidad, Cuba, Puerto Rico, Haiti and the Virgin Islands. Other important producers of rum are Indonesia, Australia, South Africa, Germany and the U.S.

Basically there are two kinds of rum: white rum, which is usually dry and light-bodied; and dark rum, a richer, sweeter, more full-bodied product that ranges in color from amber to mahogany. The best-known white rums are made in Puerto Rico, Cuba and the Virgin Islands, and the best-known dark or heavier rums are made in Jamaica, Barbados and Guyana (formerly British Guiana). In the U.S., white rum is preferred, but in other northern countries, such as Britain and Germany, heavier rums are favored.

The many variations within the two basic types of rum are the result of differences in the quality of the ingredients used and in the methods of fermentation, distillation and aging. The two most common fermentation techniques are the Demerara (the name of a river and an early name for Georgetown in Guyana) method and the Jamaican method. In the Demerara method, which takes approximately 48 hours, the molasses or sugarcane is prepared into a liquid known as wash, to which sulfuric acid and ammonium sulfate are added to encourage fermentation of the alcohol yeasts. In the Jamaican method, neither sulfuric acid nor ammonium sulfate is added to the alcohol yeasts in the wash to hasten fermentation. As a result fermentation by this method takes 10 to 12 days.

Distillation may take place either in a pot still or a continuous still. If a pot still is used, two distillations are required, as the product of the first distillation is too weak for consumption. Distillation in a continuous still is more economical and the product can be brought to any strength with only one distillation.

All rum is colorless when first distilled. Many rums, especially those sold in the U.S., are not aged, or aged only for a year. These rums often are colored by the addition of artificial caramel coloring. The better rums are aged in oak casks for three to 20 years, during which time they acquire some of their color, but even these more expensive rums are subjected to artificial coloring. The proof of rum ranges from 80 to 150.

In the U.S., rum most often is used in mixed drinks, especially those made with fruit juices, although occasionally it is drunk straight. It also is employed as a flavoring agent in meat marinade, dessert sauces and ice cream.

Reay Tannahill, *Food in History* (New York: Stein & Day, 1973).

rum fits (withdrawal seizures)   GRAND MAL CONVULSIONS or seizures, whereby one experiences loss of consciousness. They are associated with withdrawal from alcohol and appear to develop in a minority of alcoholics. Rum fits often appear in clusters and can start as early as 12 hours after reduced intake or abstinence. Named for withdrawal seizures seen in sailors when ships ran out of rum, they are also seen with withdrawal from other sedatives, especially barbiturates. They may be associated with DELIRIUM TREMENS (THE D.T.'S). (See STATUS EPILEPTICUS.)

rush   The immediate, intense and pleasurable effect that intravenous drug users (IVUs) experience following the injection of drugs such as heroin, morphine and cocaine. This term can also be used to describe the sensation of an immediate onset of effects following a snort of cocaine or a deep inhalation of pot, crack cocaine or any other smokable psychoactive substance.

Rush, Dr. Benjamin   One of the signers of the Declaration of Independence, Rush was a Philadelphian and arguably the most respected American physician of his time. He was the first American to call chronic drunkenness a distinct, progressive disease. His powerful tract, "An Inquiry into the Effects of Ardent Spirits on the Human Mind and Body," published in 1784, identified alcohol as addictive and claimed that once an "appetite" or "craving" for it became fixed, the victim lost all control over his drinking. His argument that drunkenness was the fault of the drinker only in the early stages of the disease, before alcohol took command, was a radical departure from previous thinking. It became a classic in temperance literature.

Rutgers Center of Alcoholic Studies   One of the nation's foremost centers for the study of alcohol abuse and alcoholism, and a central source of research information, the Rutgers Center of Alcohol Studies is located in Piscataway, New Jersey. (See YALE UNIVERSITY CENTER OF ALCOHOL STUDIES.)

rye whiskey   A spirit distilled from a grain mash that contains at least 51% rye. The production of rye, along with that of bourbon and corn whiskeys, is an American adaptation of European distilling practices. Today most Canadian whiskey also is produced from a grain mixture such as that used to make American rye.

Rye probably was the first grain whiskey to be distilled in America. Its beginnings date from the arrival of Irish and Scottish immigrants in colonial Pennsylvania. Because of the difficulty involved in transporting grain to market, distillation of grain into whiskey became economically advantageous. Nevertheless, during colonial times rye was slow to challenge rum in popularity. During the American Revolution rum distillers were forced to shut down for lack of foreign sugarcane supplies, and rye distillers, who required only domestic products, came into prominence.

As a result of abundant grain supplies, the popularity of rye whiskey rose steadily during the 1790s and quickly attracted the interest of the new government as a source of revenue. In 1791 the first whiskey tax was levied. A segment of the population, however, firmly believed that having won independence from Britain, they had a right to distill whiskey. The result of this conflict was the Whiskey Rebellion of 1794, in which distillers based in western Pennsylvania refused to pay the new tax. President George Washington was forced to dispatch a military contingent to confront the distillers in Pittsburgh, but the distillers dispersed and their leader, David Bradford, fled the state. Thus rye whiskey was the provocation of one of the first domestic political crises in American history and the means by which the new government demonstrated its federal authority.

Rye remained the leading spirit in the U.S. through the Civil War years. Its principal domestic competitor, after the decline of rum, was corn whiskey, a raw-tasting, colorless spirit that was sold without aging. Rye's appeal was advanced during the early 19th century, when distillers began to age the product in charred barrels. This process moderated the alcoholic taste of rye and gave it an amber color. After the Civil War, bourbon began to rise in popularity. Distilled like rye, but from a greater proportion of corn grains, bourbon was originally a compromise between harsh corn whiskey and smoother but more expensive rye.

Rye distillers usually buy malted barley from specialized manufacturers rather than malt their own, as in Scotland and Ireland. The grain mixture, predominantly rye filled out with barleys, corns and oats, is cooked into a mash called "slurry," either by atmospheric cooking in an open vat, pressure cooking or a continuous cooking method that utilizes steam. Once cooked, the slurry is cooled and poured into fermentation tanks, which traditionally have been made of wood but today usually are stainless steel. Yeast is then added, and fermentation produces the "distiller's beer" from which the spirit can be distilled, generally in large patent stills. The rectified spirit then is barreled in charred white oak. Rye is almost always blended, a process that involves combining the products of several distillations, for consistency of flavor and appeal to a broad market.

S

safety belts and alcohol use Alcohol use is correlated with a lower rate of safety-belt use. Although only 7.2% of sober drivers involved in fatal accidents in 1984 were wearing safety belts, a significantly smaller proportion of the drivers who had been drinking (2.2%) wore such restraints, according to the National Highway Transportation Safety Administration. (See DRIVING WHILE IMPAIRED.)

sake A "rice wine" fermented from a mixture of rice and malted barley. Sake is not a true wine because a raw material other than grapes is used, but since the fermented beverage is colorless or amber in color and slightly sweet, it resembles a wine both in appearance and in taste.

Sake, which has an alcohol content of about 17%, is the traditional alcoholic beverage of Japan; it probably originated as an outgrowth of the brewery fermentation of beers there. Generally, it is served in ceramic cups, usually heated.

saloon (From the French *salon* drawing room, lounge; the Italian *salone* hall.) Generally speaking, a saloon is a place to which the public may go for any specified purpose, such as billiards, boxing or other recreation. The word also refers to a large lounge or ballroom on a ship. In the U.S. the most common usage of saloon is the old-fashioned meaning; of a place where alcoholic beverages are sold to be drunk on the premises, usually without meals. (See BAR.) In the West particularly, bars were called saloons, and were often gambling houses as well. In many

western towns you can still find traditional "Wild West"–type saloons, which generally have a long bar at one side, swinging doors at the entrance, and tables and chairs throughout, sometimes with a pool table and frequently a dartboard in the rear. Live entertainment was commonly featured in the past and today live country music will often be found in western-style saloons located in any part of the country.

In Britain, the expression "saloon bar" is used to refer to the best of the bars in an ordinary public house. "Bar" in this sense simply means the counter over which drinks are sold.

Salvia divinorum A plant belonging to the mint family. Its leaves are chewed or brewed into a tea for their hallucinogenic effects.

San Pedro cactus *Trichocereus pachanoi.* A native of Peru and Ecuador, the stem of the plant is peeled and eaten or brewed into a beverage for its psychedelic effects.

sanorex An ANORECTIC that contains mazindol and is used for weight control. Its activity is similar to that of the AMPHETAMINES. Tolerance and psychological dependence can develop within a few weeks. It has a significant potential for abuse. Overdosage can cause restlessness, tremors and rapid respiration.

sansert A sympatholytic ANTAGONIST to epinephrine and similar drugs. Used for the prevention or reduction of intense, frequent vascular headaches, it causes vasodilation and increases the tone of alimentary tract muscles and other smooth muscle tissue. It contains methysergide maleate. Chemically related to LSD, in large amounts it can produce similar effects and therefore may have the potential for abuse.

sassafras *Sassafras officinal albidum.* Though there are claims that it has psychedelic properties, none are known. The plant does contains the toxic ether safrole.

schizophrenia Schizophrenia is a relatively common disorder affecting nearly 1% of the population of most countries. Occurrence is uncommon before late adolescence. Individuals with schizophrenia suffer from an array of symptoms varying from person to person. The extent of this variation is so great that schizophrenia is often referred to as a "syndrome" rather than a disorder. The symptoms for this syndrome are divided into two categories: "positive" also referred to as "acute," and "negative." Persons diagnosed with schizophrenia will not have all of the symptoms in each category, but will usually have a combination from both categories and several symptoms will have been presently active for at least a month.

"Positive" symptoms include: *Disturbance of thought:* Also known as delusion, this is characterized by false beliefs relating to sound, sight or experiences. For example, one may actually believe that people are after them when it is not the case, or that their mind is being read by aliens from space. *Auditory hallucinations:* Schizophrenics often hear voices when no other person is present. These voices commonly convey negative messages about themselves or others. *Language disorder:* Speech patterns are often disorganized. Speaking in non sequiturs, (phrasing language in unrelated patterns, where a group of sentences do not relate to the next) is common. This symptom is also referred to as a "thought disorder," as it is assumed that the disassociated speech patterns originate in disordered thought patterns. *Behavior:* An adult may act like a young child. For example, they may not be able to adequately dress themselves, they may appear on a cold day without an overcoat or on a hot day in layers of sweaters. There is a tendency to neglect their

personal hygiene, maintaining a dirty and disheveled appearance.

More enduring, "negative" symptoms are chronic or long lasting in nature. These symptoms are distinguished by the *Blunted affect:* This can be described as a lack of emotion in speech, body movement or facial expression. One may say that they are happy, yet have a flat expression on their face or a sad, empty tone in their voice. *Lack of motivation:* The inability to initiate an activity or complete a task without supervision. *Associality:* Asocial behavior manifesting in an apparent lack of interest in work or social activities, and in extreme cases, in total isolation from others.

Although the acute or positive symptoms are often responsive to treatment with antipsychotic medications, unfortunately the negative symptoms are not as responsive to medication and are the more crippling characteristics of this syndrome. Negative symptoms require both psychological and social interventions that must be available on an ongoing basis to effect change. Treatment programs must provide counseling with the patients receiving education in both vocational and social skills. Many programs provide persons who are schizophrenic with community residences or apartments, which are supervised by professional staff.

There is a well-documented increase in risk of illness for individuals who have a close relative with schizophrenia. Both genetic and environmental influences have been identified as potential etiologic factors. Recent research has identified structural and functional abnormalities in the brains of those with schizophrenia, particularly, enlarged ventricular spaces and decreased activation of the frontal areas when completing tasks which, in normal persons, activate these regions. The significance of these findings is being studied at present with techniques of brain imaging that have become available in recent years. Chemical abuse frequently coexists in persons with schizophrenia. One hypothesis for this is that drugs (including alcohol) are misused in an attempt to self-medicate or to suppress "positive" symptoms (such as auditory hallucinations) and/or to combat "negative" symptoms (such as blunted affect). (See PARANOIA.)

schnapps German *schnaps* (spirits, brandy, gin or liquor). A broad term that may refer to any distilled alcoholic beverage. Often the beverages called schnapps resemble Holland GIN. Usually, they are a colorless grain distillate and have a fiery taste. Schnapps is particularly associated with Sweden, Norway, Denmark, the Netherlands and northern Germany, each of which produces its own variety. In Scandinavia the term "schnapps" sometimes is used to mean AQUAVIT.

Alternate spellings of schnapps include *schnaps* (Denmark) and *snaps* (Sweden).

School Program to Educate and Control Drug Abuse (SPECDA)

SPECDA is a cooperative program of the New York City Board of Education and the police department. Police help to provide classes and presentations on drug abuse while simultaneously concentrating on enforcement efforts within a two-block radius of schools so as to create a drug-free corridor.

scopolamine

A belladonna alkaloid. It is a non-barbiturate sedative hypnotic that has been used as a "truth serum." Large doses can produce hallucinations and are accompanied by adverse toxic reactions such as blurred vision, confusion, delirium and heart effects. Scopolamine generally is used to dry up secretions. It appears as scopolamine hydrobromide in several nonprescription sedatives such as Sominex, although there is no evidence that the amount contained in these medications successfully aids in producing sleep.

Scotch broom

Cytisus scoparius, a toxic plant containing CYTISINE.

Scotch whiskey

A spirit distilled in Scotland from a fermented mash of cereal grains. Scotch whiskey is considered by many to be the finest in the world. Unlike American, Canadian or Irish whiskeys, true Scotch whiskey usually is identified by the region where it is produced. There are four principal regional varieties: Highland malts, Lowland malts, Campbeltowns and Islays. They all differ subtly because of their various water sources, grain contents, methods of malting and distillation processes.

Although the precise origins are obscure, methods of distilling grain whiskeys probably came to Scotland directly from Europe, rather than from Europe through Ireland as many believe. This must have taken place during the early Middle Ages, although there is no written record of whiskey in Scotland until the Scottish Exchequer Rolls of 1494. By that time the liquor was already accepted as a legal unit for business transactions.

The Scottish Parliament, then independent of England, first attempted to tax whiskey as a source of public revenue in 1644. The trade proved impossible to control and illicit distillation became a matter of fierce local pride. Increasing English intervention in Scotland brought further attempts to tax the whisky trade, which eventually led to riots in Edinburgh in 1713. England's control over Scotland became complete with its victory at the Battle of Culloden in 1746, giving the English control over the Scottish Highlands and the especially prized malt whiskeys produced there. In 1823 the Duke of Gordon proposed legalization of local distillation and taxation of the trade at a new lower rate. Once in effect, this program slowly eroded the illegal whisky trade. In 1860 the first organized exportation of Scotch whiskey to England began, and since that time whiskey has become one of Scotland's most valuable exports.

There are two principal types of Scotch whiskey: POT STILL, and patent still, distinguished by the methods used to produce them. Pot-still malt whiskeys are the most traditional sort. The only grain employed in their manufacture is barley that has been malted over peat, making them smokier in taste than the Irish malt whiskeys, which are cured over charcoal. Pot-still Scotch whiskeys are nevertheless extremely heavy in taste and usually blended with the lighter, patent-still types. Only a small amount of pot-still Scotch whiskey, intended for a limited but affluent market of aficionados, is bottled. Most commercial Scotch whiskeys are produced by patent stills and employ a mixture of grains that includes only a portion of malted barley. The different grain content and distillation process of patent-still Scotch yields a lighter and clearer product, which for a time was challenged by some as not deserving of the designation "Scotch" or "Scotch whiskey." Both pot-still and patent-still distillates are matured in casks made either of new wood or of woods previously used to age sherry or whiskey. Virtually all Scotch whiskeys commercially available are blends of several types and distillations; only those called "self-whiskeys" are the yield of a single distillation.

Common Drugs: Symptoms of Abuse of Sedatives

Sedatives. Depressant drugs that slow down the central nervous system.

Drug Name	Street Names	Method of Use	Sign and Symptoms	Hazards of Use
Benzodiazepines— Valium, Xanax, halicon.	Tranks, Sleepers, Vs or Vees	Swallowed in pill form or injected.	Drowsiness, confusion, impaired judgement, slurred speech, needle marks, constricted pupils.	Infection, addiction with severe withdrawal symptoms, loss of appetite, nausea, death from overdose.
Barbiturates— Pentobarbital, Secobarbital, Amobarbital	Barbs, Downers, Yellow Jackets, Nembies, Red Devils, Blue Devils	Swallowed in pill form or injected.	Impaired judgement and performance, also drowsiness, slurred speech.	Death from overdose, injury or car accident; synergistic effects of interaction with alcohol.

Source: New York State Office of Alcoholism and Substance Abuse Services.

seconal A sedative hypnotic that contains secobarbital sodium, a short-acting BARBITURATE. It is used for insomnia and for preoperative sedation. It can be habit-forming and when taken with alcohol or other central nervous system depressants can have an ADDITIVE EFFECT. Both physical and psychological dependence can occur, and it has a high potential for abuse. Results of overdosage are respiratory depression, depression of reflexes, lowered body temperature and coma.

Secular Organizations for Sobriety (SOS) An International recovery movement and alternative to AA, SOS was founded in 1985 by James Christopher, the son of an alcoholic and a sober alcoholic himself. Seventeen years after achieving and then maintaining abstinence through AA, Christopher finally gave voice to his discomfort with the concepts of powerlessness over alcohol and a surrender to a higher power that are the mainstays of the AA philosophy. Unlike AA, SOS, in their own words: "takes a reasonable, secular approach to recovery and maintains that sobriety is a separate issue from religion or spirituality." SOS credits the individual for taking the responsibility him- or herself to choose and maintain abstinence; and acknowledges and "encourages the validity of the scientific method to understand alcoholism." However, SOS borrows heavily from AA's 12 Traditions for its organizational structure: the offer of membership open to anyone seeking sobriety; reliance on members' donations for financial support; an insistence on neutrality on all matters other than those related to the cessation of drinking; a recognition of the benefits of both anonymity and group support; and rules to protect members from hurting each other.

sedapap A sedative hypnotic that contains acetaminophen and butabarbital (a short-acting BARBITURATE). Generally, it is used as an analgesic for arthritic and rheumatic conditions and for tension headaches. It can be habit-forming and steady usage may result in dependence.

sedative hypnotic Any of a number of substances, including alcohol, that acts as an irregular depressant of the central nervous system (CNS). A depressant is a substance that diminishes or stops normal body function. Sedatives are irregular because they do not depress all parts of the CNS at once, but work first on the cerebrum and cerebellum, second on the spinal cord and finally on the vital centers. Sedatives (or soporifics) include liquid substances, such as alcohol; solid drugs, such as barbiturates; and gases, such as ether and chloroform. All these belong to a group of compounds that produce similar pharmacological behavior. All sedatives are potentially addicting compounds with associated severe withdrawal syndromes. However, for physical dependence to develop, the daily intake of each drug must exceed a certain threshold level. After nicotine, sedatives are probably the most widely abused drugs in the western nations.

When alcohol or other sedatives enter the system, they first work on the brain to depress psychomotor activity, thereby relieving anxiety and tension. For approximately two to three hours the blood alcohol (or sedative) level rises and a sedative, or calming effect, is produced. Then the level of alcohol or sedative in the blood begins to fall and the psychomotor activity level increases. This second effect usually lasts for about 12 hours after consumption of a large drink. Thus the sedative effect always is followed by an agitating effect, which often leaves the subject more tense than before he or she began drinking. This is one reason why people who have been drinking often crave another drink and also why a drink can relieve some of the agitating effects of a hangover. The agitation is multiplied with each pill or drink, and at high levels of consumption the individual may become tremulous, have hallucinations or—at extreme levels, when unable to get another drink—experience DELIRIUM TREMENS (THE D.T.'S) and WITHDRAWAL.

Aside from alcohol, the most commonly used (and abused) sedatives are barbiturates and the so-called minor tranquilizers, such as Librium and Valium, which were at first believed to be safer than barbiturates but subsequently were found to produce similar patterns of addiction and withdrawal. Barbiturates are currently prescribed for medical and psychiatric purposes as hypnotics, sedatives, anesthetics and anticonvulsants. However, because they are so readily available for legitimate purposes, they also are abused and therefore used illicitly. The most commonly abused barbiturates are short-acting agents, such as pentobarbital (Nembutal), secobarbital (Seconal) and amobarbital (Amytal).

The first barbiturate (barbital) was made available for medical use in 1903, followed by a second (phenobarbital) in 1912. By 1914 the German medical literature already contained a description of barbiturate withdrawal syndrome.

Valium is one of the most widely prescribed drugs in North America. Dependence on Valium can develop even at prescribed doses. After 10 to 14 weeks larger doses may be required to maintain a patient's feeling of well-being. By four to six months, abrupt cessation may result in physical withdrawal symptoms. Discomforts, such as tremors, agitation, stomach cramps and sweating, can occur for two to four weeks. Xanax (Alprazolam), a newer benzodiazepine, has partially replaced Valium as a prescribed tranquilizer for anxiety disorders. Dependence on this drug can also develop. Rohypnol (flunitrazepam), another one of the newer benzodiazepines, has effects similar to those of Valium, but is 10 times more potent, and longer-lasting, according to the DEA (Drug Enforcement Administration). Neither manufactured nor sold in the U.S., it is manufactured and legally prescribed in Europe and Latin America, primarily for use as a preoperative hypnotic and for the treatment of insomnia. It was reported in 1995 that increasingly it was being smuggled into the U.S. It is frequently ingested in conjunction with alcohol or other mind-altering substances.

Perhaps the most dangerous effect of barbiturates and other sedatives occurs when they are used in combination with alcohol, which multiplies the potency and dangers of each drug. (See SYNERGY.) In humans a level of 100 mg of ethanol (alcohol) per 100 ml of blood combined with a level of 0.5 mg of barbiturate per 500 ml of blood has proved fatal. When each of these substances is taken alone, a higher dose of each would be required to reach dangerous levels in the bloodstream, that is levels of alcohol alone of 100 to 800 mg per 100 ml of blood and of phenobarbital (a barbiturate) alone of 10 to 29 mg per 100 ml of blood.

Alcoholics with a high tolerance to alcohol have a similar tolerance, or CROSS-TOLERANCE, to other sedatives. It takes a large amount of ether, for instance, to induce surgical anesthesia in an alcoholic. In addition, CROSS-ADDICTION occurs in alcoholics. One sedative drug (such as alcohol) is often replaced or used simultaneously with another (such as Valium) that produces approximately the same effects. The rate increase in the number of people, especially young women, addicted to both Valium and alcohol is alarming, especially in view of the high risk for fatalities when these substances are combined. Nevertheless many doctors continue to prescribe sedatives to patients with emotional problems, often without inquiring into their drinking habits. Complaints of anxiety, nervousness and insomnia may in fact reflect the early stages of alcoholism, and treatment with sedatives only exacerbates the problems of an alcoholic.

The easy availability of sedatives has made them a drug of abuse among high school students and young adults (this category includes people from one to four years beyond high school but not in college). NIDA (The National Institute on Drug Abuse) reported in 1993 that 44% of high school seniors reported that they could obtain barbiturates easily, and 41% reported the same for tranquilizers. High school seniors appear to have the highest rates of barbiturate abuse in the U.S. It was reported by NIDA that in a 1994 survey of high school students, 1.7% of seniors reported the nonprescribed use of barbiturates in the 30 days preceding the survey. This was up slightly from 1991 (1.4%); 4.1% of this group reported annual use, up from 3.4% in 1991. Young adults, the second-highest group of users, reported the same annual use in 1994 as in 1991, 1.8%; and a one-month use of 0.6% in 1994, an increase of 0.1% from 1991. In 1994 use of nonprescription tranquilizers was reported among young adults and in all grades of high school and college students. The rate was highest, however, among high school seniors (37% up from 36% in 1991). Young adults reported the second-highest annual use in 1991, 3.5%. However in 1994 10th graders had the second highest use, 3.3%, with young adults third in use, 2.9%. Attesting to its availability for illicit use, even children in the eighth grade reported increased annual tranquilizer abuse, 1.8% in 1991 and 2.4% in 1994. (See DRUGS and PHARMACOTHERAPY.)

P. M. Broughton, G. Higgins and J. R. P. O'Brien, "Acute Barbiturate Poisoning," *The Lancet* 1, no. 270 (1956): 180–184.

Stanley E. Gitlow, "A Pharmacological Approach to Alcoholism," *A. A. Grapevine* (October 1968).

R. C. Gupta and J. Kofold, "Toxicological Statistics for Barbiturates, Other Sedatives and Tranquilizers in Ontario: a 10-year Survey," *Canadian Medical Association Journal* 94 (1966): 863–865.

Frederick G. Hofmann, *A Handbook on Drug and Alcohol Abuse: The Biomedical Aspects* (New York: Oxford University Press, 1975).

Frank A. Seixas, "Alcohol and Its Drug Interactions," *Annals of Internal Medicine* 83, no. 1 (July 1975): 86–92.

sedativism   Addiction to one of the sedatives, which includes alcohol. The term "sedativism" also is used to describe dual or multiple addiction to sedatives. (See CROSS-ADDICTION.)

self-esteem   See PSYCHOLOGICAL MODELS OF ETIOLOGY.

self-help book publishing   Self-help books on alcoholism, drug addiction, child abuse, gambling,

codependence and any and all forms of addictive behavior or self-esteem issues are so prevalent now that, according to Edwin McDowell of the *New York Times,* "they have become known in publishing circles as *bibliotherapy* or the continuation of the recovery process through books." In fact, many bookstores have sections labeled *Recovery, Abuse* or *Addiction.* Linda Grey, president of Bantam Books, believes that "it speaks to something desperate in our society that there is such a demand."

It does indicate, among other things, that open and frank discussion of once-taboo subjects has now become socially acceptable. McDowell says that publishing companies are hesitant to estimate sales figures or revenues generated by the explosion of recovery books, but that they are in the "tens of millions of dollars, out of a $5 billion trade book industry."

In 1989 Dara Tyson, spokesperson for the huge Waldenbooks chain, stated that recovery and addiction books were among the company's fastest-growing categories and that the sale of audio cassettes based on such books was also on the rise.

A number of the biggest-selling books about substance abuse and recovery have been and are still being published by recognized recovery groups and rehabilitation centers, including Alcoholics Anonymous; Comprehensive Care of Newport Beach, California; Health Communications of Pompano Beach, Florida; and Fair Oaks Hospital of Summit, New Jersey, some of whose books are published by Villard Books, a division of Random House. Another important recovery book publisher is that of the Hazelden Foundation in Center City, Minnesota, which has been in existence for almost 50 years.

One of the most popular self-help books is *Adult Children of Alcoholics* by Janet Woititz (Health Communications, 1983). It has sold approximately 1.1 million copies in trade paperback. The book is an account of how to cope with alcoholic parents.

Edwin McDowell, "In Land of Addictions, Shelves Full of Solace," *New York Times* (June 21, 1989).

self reports   As defined by the Substance Abuse and Mental Health Services Administration (SAMHSA), self reports are "the information that the respondent gives directly." For example, self-reported substance use is that of alcohol and other drugs that the respondents themselves indicate they have used. In contrast, urinalysis and Breathalyzer readings provide information based on biological testing. Other sources of information on substance abuse and mental disorders are school, police and hospital records; biological and medical tests; reports from family and other informants; and physician assessments.

Accurate analysis of alcohol and other drug use data demands that there be a clear understanding of the distinctions between self-reported data and data collected from other sources. For example, drug users self-reporting the amount of drugs they use commonly underreport, but observations by others may be equally inaccurate since observers may not be aware of the frequency of the user's intake since many alcohol/other drug users become extremely adept at hiding their habit.

Beatrice A. Rouse, ed., *Substance Abuse and Mental Health Statistics Sourcebook* (Washington, D.C.: Substance Abuse and Mental Health Services Administration [SAMHSA], 1995).

sensitivity   The term *sensitivity* is sometimes used to explain why an individual may be prone to alcoholism. However, it generally is used without being well defined, and may refer to TOLERANCE or to an inability to abstain from drinking. There is usually a more precise alternate term. In the *Dictionary of Psychology*, J. P. Chaplin defines sensitivity as "the condition or ability involved in being receptive to stimuli."

James P. Chaplin, *Dictionary of Psychology*, 3rd rev. ed. (New York: Dell, 1985): 418.

Serax   A central nervous system (CNS) depressant that contains the BENZODIAZEPINE oxazepam and is used to treat anxiety and tension. Tolerance and both physical and psychological dependence can develop. When taken with alcohol or other CNS depressants it may have an ADDITIVE EFFECT.

Serenity Prayer   A prayer used by members of ALCOHOLICS ANONYMOUS (AA) and other 12-step groups in times of stress or anxiety. It is used to close AA/other meetings and often is analyzed in group discussions. The full text is as follows: "God grant me the serenity to accept the things I cannot change, the courage to change the things I can, and the wisdom to know the difference."

The prayer is based on one delivered by the Protestant theologian Reinhold Neibuhr (1892–

1971) at a church near Heath, Massachusetts, in the summer of 1934. Since then it has been widely quoted. It reads: "O God, give us serenity to accept what cannot be changed, courage to change what should be changed, and the wisdom to distinguish the one from the other."

sernyl   An anesthetic and analgesic containing PHENCYCLIDINE that was used in the past in veterinary medicine.

serotonin   A neurotransmitter, like adrenaline and ACETYLCHOLINE, that transmits messages in the brain. There are numerous theories about the relationship of serotonin and LSD; LSD seems either to inhibit the action of serotonin or to compete with it. One theory suggests that when LSD inhibits serotonin's orderly manner of transmitting messages, the brain is overcome with so many messages that it cannot handle them. Another theory posits that when serotonin is blocked, subconscious material takes over a person's consciousness and alters perception. A third premise is that LSD monopolizes the monoamine oxidase (MAO) enzymes that otherwise would be acting on serotonin to produce metabolites. Without normal metabolism there is a possibility that BUFOTENINE might develop as a byproduct and produce the hallucinations. All of these theories, especially the latter, are experimental and have yet to be proved, and the function of serotonin is still not completely understood. Serotonin activity is reduced in some types of depression.

Services for Drug and Alcohol Abuse and Alcoholism   The "Services for Drug and Alcohol Abuse and Alcoholism" section is the core feature of the *National Drug and Alcoholism Treatment Survey (NDATUS),* conducted by the National Institute on Alcohol Abuse and Alcoholism (NIAAA) and the National Institute on Drug Abuse (NIDA). The survey is designed to be a census of all known drug use and alcoholism treatment facilities in the U.S. Data include types of services provided, client capacity and census on the point-prevalence data, client demographic characteristics, and funding amounts and sources. The report is available from the National Clearinghouse for Alcohol and Drug Information (NCADI) and from the Substance Abuse and Mental Health Services Administration (SAMHSA).

Typical Effects of Alcohol on Sexual Functioning

ACUTE

1	May increase sexual desire, if taken in small quantities.
2	In larger quantities, sedates the cerebral cortex, reducing inhibitions, but also impeding translation of external sexual information for the hypothalamus.
3	Interferes with transfer of sexual functioning messages from the brain to other parts of the central nervous system and sex organs.
4	Relaxes necessary muscle tension.
5	In males, may impede or prevent erection; in females, may interfere with or prevent lubrication.
6	Reduces serum testosterone level.
7	Prevents orgasm.
8	Reduces sexual desire.
9	Produces sedation to the point of sleep.
10	In males, can aid in development of psychological impotence.

CHRONIC

1	Any of the above, occurring on a repeated basis, can become chronic and permanent.
2	Liver damage—reduces serum sex hormone levels.
3	Brain damage—prevents sexual messages from being transmitted and/or interpreted.
4	In males, may produce testicular atrophy.
5	In males, may produce permanent impotence.

Source: "Sexual Dysfunction and the Alcoholic," Focus on Alcohol and Drug Issues, July–August 1981.

sex   APHRODISIACS traditionally have been defined as substances that increase sexual drive and pleasure, and the search for effective aphrodisiacs has been going on since time immemorial. Folklore is full of references to foods, herbs, drinks, love potions and medications that are reputed to stimulate the sexual appetite. A modern redefinition of aphrodisiacs, however, takes into account the subjective pleasure experienced, not just changes in sex drive. Within this context, a number of drugs are believed to be aphrodisiacs. With a few exceptions, they do not directly affect the genitourinary tract but act on the brain in such a way as to relieve the user of social and sexual inhibitions, making him more apt to express sexual feelings. Research on the effects of such drugs has been limited by the small numbers of sample subjects, lack of control groups, reliance on drug-dependent subjects who are in treatment, and an under-representation of women. It is also difficult to give an accurate account of the specific effects that drugs have on sexual behavior and response, because they vary from person to person and from time to

Sex under the Influence of Alcohol and Other Drugs

Making the Link, Spring 1995, Center for Substance Abuse Prevention

"These [study] findings suggest a direct association between alcohol and other drug use and unsafe sexual behavior."

—Eighth Special Report to the
U.S. Congress on Alcohol and Health
(Secretary of Health and Human Services,
October 1993).

Alcohol and other drug use is linked to risky sexual behavior and poses significant threats to the health of adolescents. Substance abuse may impair adolescents' ability to make judgments about sex and contraception, placing them at increased risk for unplanned pregnancy, sexual assault, or becoming infected with a sexually transmitted disease (STD), including HIV/AIDS.

We know the AIDS virus can be transmitted through sharing hypodermic needles. Less is known about the dangerous role of alcohol and other drugs in sexual behavior that may lead to STDs and HIV/AIDS. To compound matters, there is also considerable evidence that alcohol and other drugs weaken the immune system, thereby increasing susceptibility to infection and disease.

Consider the following statistics:

The use of alcohol and other drugs can affect judgment and lead to taking serious sexual risks. There were 18,540 cases of AIDS among 13-24 year olds reported to the Centers for Disease Control and Prevention by the end of 1994.[1]

About 75% of high school seniors have had sexual intercourse at least once in their lives; about 20% have had more than four sexual partners by their senior year.[2]

Studies show that adolescents are less likely to use condoms when having sex after drinking alcohol than when sober. This places them at even higher risk for HIV infection, STDs, and unwanted pregnancy.[3]

A survey of high school students found that 18% of females and 39% of males say it is acceptable for a boy to force sex if the girl is stoned or drunk.[4]

According to the Centers for Disease Control and Prevention, HIV/AIDS has been the sixth leading cause of death among 15-20 year olds in the United States for over three years. One in five of the new AIDS cases diagnosed is in the 20 to 29 year age group, meaning that HIV transmission occurred during the teen years. Additionally, more than half of new cases of HIV infection in 1994 were related to drug use.[2]

There is still much to be learned about the relationship between alcohol and other drugs and sexual behavior. During the past decade, teens reported higher levels of sexual activity at earlier ages, experienced more unplanned pregnancies, and suffered higher rates of sexually transmitted diseases. To reduce the incidence of these problems in the future, prevention of alcohol and other drug abuse must be a top priority.

For more information, call the National Clearinghouse for Alcohol and Drug Information at 1-800-729-6686.

[1] Centers for Disease Control and Prevention, HIV/AIDS Surveillance Report 6, no. 2. Summary of Findings, 1994.

[2] Centers for Disease Control and Prevention, HIV/AIDS Prevention, Facts about: Adolescents and HIV/AIDS, December 1994.

[3] Strunin, L., and Hingson, R., Alcohol Use and Risk for HIV Infection, Alcohol and Health Research World 17, no. 1. National Institute on Alcohol Abuse and Alcoholism.

[4] Inspector General, U.S. Department of Health and Human Services, Youth and Alcohol: Dangerous and Deadly Consequences: Report to the Surgeon General, April 1992.

Source: Center for Substance Abuse Prevention. "Sex under the Influence of Alcohol and Other Drugs." *Making the Link, ML005.* Spring 1995. Substance Abuse and Mental Health Services Administration; U.S. Department of Health and Human Services.

time in the same individual, depending on the dose, the expectations and desires of the user and the setting in which the drugs are used.

Alcohol: While small doses of alcohol depress the cerebral cortex and provoke uninhibited behavior, larger doses and chronic use adversely affect neural control and coordination and inhibit sexual performance. Hormonal changes due to large amounts of alcohol include increased breakdown and reduced synthesis of testosterone, the male sex hormone that influences the development of masculine secondary sex characteristics, the lack of which makes sustained penile erection difficult. Alcohol also may stimulate the production of the leutinizing hormones that increase sexual drive, leaving the male user in the frustrating position of being sexually stimulated though unable to perform. Male alcoholics sometimes suffer from testicular atrophy and impotence, while female alcoholics may experience menstrual irregularity and even amenorrhea (absence of menses).

While small doses of alcohol may enhance sexual relations, after a number of drinks men may be unable to complete the sex act. Shakespeare noted the subject of alcohol vis-à-vis sexual activity in *MacBeth* (II, iii):

Macduff: What three things does drink especially provoke?
  Porter: Marry, sir, nose-painting, sleep and urine. Lechery, sir, it provokes and un-provokes; it provokes the desire, but it takes away the performance.

It is a tribute to Shakespeare's acute observation that after almost four centuries of further scientific endeavor, not much can be added to his description of the effects of alcohol on sexual activity.

Barbiturates, tranquilizers and other sedative hypnotics: Low doses of barbiturates and other sedative hypnotics affect the higher cortical functioning of the brain. This reduces anxiety about sexual matters, allowing some individuals to express themselves more freely. Many people are extremely sensitive to even low doses of these drugs, however, and experience a decrease in sexual drive, excitement and ability to achieve orgasm. As with most other substances, high doses and chronic use interfere with sexual pleasure.

Amphetamines and other stimulants: The use of STIMULANT drugs, especially amphetamines and cocaine, seems to increase sexual drive for many at low doses. In addition to enhancing sensory perception and heightening emotional response, this type of drug impedes the venous drainage of erectile tissue and thus prolongs sexual stimulation. (Cocaine is sometimes applied directly to the genitals to prolong intercourse, due to anesthetization.) However, at higher doses it decreases sensation, causing delay or failure to ejaculate in men and failure to achieve orgasm in women. Some consistent users of stimulant drugs report disinterest and distaste for sexual activity, especially those who administer amphetamines or cocaine intravenously.

Heroin: According to a 1982 research project conducted at the Haight-Ashbury Free Medical Clinic in San Francisco, a significant number of men and women who had suffered some sexual dysfunction prior to using heroin reported an improvement in sexual performance when they first began to use the drug. The women reported an increase in relaxation and a lessening of inhibitions, and the men reported delayed ejaculation. Long-term use of heroin, however, decreases sexual drive and generally impairs sexual functions. Menstrual irregularity, frigidity and reduced fertility are relatively common among female heroin addicts, while males commonly experience impotence due to decreased testosterone production. These problems occur with the use of heroin and with other opiate drugs, but usually cease after withdrawal.

Hallucinogens: The effect of hallucinogens on sexuality is inconsistent. Some users are completely uninterested in sex, consumed instead by more profound perceptions, while for others the pleasure of the sexual act is enhanced and heightened in intensity. Erotic feelings may remain on a mental level, with strong spiritual/mystical overtones, rather than on a purely physical plane.

Marijuana and other cannabis drugs relax the part of the brain that records and stores social inhibitions. Marijuana tends to enhance all sensory awareness, stimulating sexual pleasure, as well as the other sensory experiences, including taste, smell, sound, sight and touch. This is why it is common for smokers of marijuana, when "stoned," to get "the munchies" as the taste of food is heightened, to listen to music, or to engage in any activity involving the senses. The psychological effects of marijuana are not uniform, however, and the drug produces no direct physical reaction that stimulates sexual desire or performance. Like alcohol, large doses of cannabis affect the pituitary gland, which may lower the testosterone level. In women it can reduce the production of follicle-stimulating and leutinizing hormones, temporarily reducing sexual drive. Larger doses and/or chronic use may tend to produce a general lethargy.

Methaqualone and amyl nitrate: Two other substances that reputedly act as aphrodisiacs are methaqualone (Quaalude), and amyl nitrate, or "poppers." Although frequently used as sex-enhancing drugs, neither directly affects sexual functioning. Methaqualone dilates the capillaries just below the surface of the skin, producing a tingling sensation, which could, depending on the setting and the individual, enhance sexual enjoyment. Amyl nitrate is sold as an "incense" in HEAD SHOPS under a variety of brand names, such as Rush and Locker Room. A vasodilator, it produces a brief high and is alleged to subjectively prolong orgasm.

Yohimbe: One substance that has been used as an aphrodisiac for centuries is YOHIMBE, a crystalline alkaloid derivative isolated from the bark of the yohimbe tree, found in central Africa. While some researchers recognize this substance as an aphrodisiac, others believe that any increase in sexual powers is probably due to suggestion. Stimulant effects occur with high doses, which can also be highly toxic.

Drugs in general: The research that has been done seems to substantiate the idea that when drugs are used infrequently and at low doses, they can increase the sex drive and enhance sexual pleasure. But pleasure and performance diminish when individuals move from low to high doses and from infrequent to chronic use.

Sexual activity and AIDS: There is an increasing concern about the relationship of sexual activity and sexually transmitted diseases, particularly AIDS. The Research Institute of the New York State Office of Alcoholism and Substance Abuse Services, in a study of 802 adult men and women admitted to residential treatment facilities in New York State in 1992 and 1993, found that 60% had admitted to acquiring a sexually transmitted disease at least once. Only half of the participants in this study were aware of their HIV status and of those within this group who were identified as alcoholic, 6.7% admitted that they were infected with the virus. Dr. Douglas M. Scheidt, who authored the study with Dr. Michael Windle, has noted that studies using blood testing tend to find infection rates of 10% to 15% among alcoholics. In comparison, less than 1% of the population in the U.S. is infected with HIV. High rates for HIV in alcoholics can be related to sexual risk behaviors. Forty-six percent of the research sample reported that they had had multiple partners and failed to use a condom consistently within the past six months of the survey. Additionally, many severe alcoholics may be persons who are engaged in sex for money or drugs. Besides sexual risks, many alcoholics use illegal drugs, particularly injected drugs, which increases the risk for HIV. (See AIDS, REPRODUCTIVE FUNCTIONS and WOMEN.)

Research Institute on Addictions, "Alcoholic Inpatients at High Risk for HIV Infection," *Research in Brief* (New York State Department of Alcoholism and Substance Abuse Services, April 1995).

Shanghai Opium Commission of 1909 A meeting of thirteen nations, including the U.S., convened on the first day of 1909 to discuss issues related to narcotic control. The commission's nonbinding resolutions called for each country to gradually suppress opium smoking and to prohibit or regulate the nonmedical use of opium. Additionally, the resolutions sought an agreement that nations should not export opium to other nations where the laws prohibit the importing of this drug, and agreed that serious measures should be taken to control morphine and other opium derivatives. The Shanghai Commission led to the convening of the Hague Conference on Opium in 1911. (See HAGUE CONFERENCES OF 1911 AND 1914.)

sherry A fortified wine varying in color from amber to dark brown, sherry is the product of fermented palomino grapes to which spirits distilled from other wines have been added. Historically, Spanish sherry has been extremely popular in Britain since the 15th century, and the present name is an Anglicization of Jerez, or Jerez de La Frontera, a town in southern Spain where the wine was first produced. The name now is a generic designation, applied to specific wines made around the world, but purists insist that true sherry still is produced only in Jerez, Sanlucar de Barrameda and Puerto de Santa Maria, all just west of Gibraltar.

Palomino grapes for sherry production are allowed to stand for one day after harvesting to increase their acidity before crushing. After pressing, gypsum is added to the grape juice to increase acidity, and because of the technique it takes longer to ferment sherry than to ferment most other wines—about three months. After "racking" (when the clear liquid is siphoned off from the dregs), the fermented grape juice secretes a sediment known as *flor*, a fungus considered essential to the character of sherry wines.

Once filtered, sherries are fortified by the addition of Spanish brandies, or the distilled spirits of other wines, to give them an alcohol content between 15% and 20%. They then are aged in wood for up to two years. After this initial aging period, all sherries are blended in a *bodega* containing casks of different local varieties and vintages. Blended sherry is often shipped from Spain to Britain for final processing and bottling.

Sherry comes in two varieties, dry *(fino)* and sweet *(oloroso)*. The first sort, dry in taste and light in color, includes the varieties called Manzanilla and amontillado. The second sort, artificially sweetened and darker in color, includes the varieties called amorosa and "cream" sherry. Dry sherry is usually drunk as an aperitif, and *oloroso* generally is consumed as a dessert wine or a substitute for port. Marginal sherries commonly are used as cooking wines.

shot   A single drink of liquor, usually consumed in one swig. A shot glass or jigger generally holds one and one-half ounces of liquor.

simple phobia (specific phobia)   The essential feature of specific or simple phobias is marked and persistent fear of clearly discernible, circumscribed objects or situations. The fear-provoking object or situation is referred to as the phobic stimulus. Exposure to the object or situation almost invariably provokes an immediate anxiety response

sinsemilla   A Spanish word meaning seedless; *sin* (without) and *semilla* (seed). Sinsemilla is the seedless flowering top of the female cannabis plant, when it is unpollinated by the male plant. In 1988 sinsemilla accounted for 54% of the cannabis eradicated in the U.S., up from the 26% eradicated in 1983, according to the DEA (Drug Enforcement Administration). Additionally, in a 1995 report the agency indicated that most indoor cultivation operations now were growing sinsemilla. The THC (tetrahydrocannabinol, the principal psychoactive chemical) content of sinsemilla can be four to six times that of ordinary marijuana. Samples of sinsemilla analyzed by drug agents for their THC content in 1987 averaged 7.67%, with some samples as high as 20%.

Maurice L. Hill, "Marijuana," *DEA Briefing Book* (Washington, D.C. (April 17, 1989): 14.

Siva   A Hindu god who, among other things, is credited with bringing cannabis to the world.

skid row   The term "skid row" originated in Seattle, Washington. The city's first sawmill was built in 1852 in the Pioneer Square district near Puget Sound. The logs were dragged into the mill over a set of tracks, or skids, and the road along which they were dragged became known as Skid Road (which later was shortened to Skid Row). As Seattle grew, the Pioneer Square area became dilapidated and the term took on the meaning it has today: a hangout for alcoholics and vagrants. Now the term designates a condition of deterioration; a "hitting bottom," as well as basic homelessness or living the life of a hobo or a drifter.

One false stereotype of alcoholics is that they are mostly "skid row bums," sleeping in doorways without a home or job. In reality only about 3% to 5% of alcoholics are true skid row types, and many people living on skid row are not alcoholics.

skinning, skin popping   There are three methods of administering drugs parenterally (injecting hypodermically): intravenous injection into a vein; intramuscular injection into a muscle such as the buttocks or upper arm; and subcutaneous injection (skin-popping) under the skin. Injection into an artery is particularly dangerous and should never be attempted. The various methods of injection produce different effects. Intravenous injection (main-

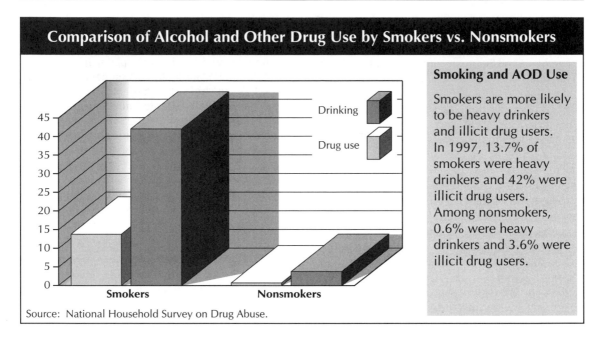

Comparison of Alcohol and Other Drug Use by Smokers vs. Nonsmokers

Drinking

Drug use

45
40
35
30
25
20
15
10
5
0

Smokers   Nonsmokers

Smoking and AOD Use

Smokers are more likely to be heavy drinkers and illicit drug users. In 1997, 13.7% of smokers were heavy drinkers and 42% were illicit drug users. Among nonsmokers, 0.6% were heavy drinkers and 3.6% were illicit drug users.

Source: National Household Survey on Drug Abuse.

lining) produces the quickest onset of effects using the least amount of the substance because it is injected directly into the vein. Heroin will be absorbed subcutaneously, but the rapid onset (rush) will be lost and more of the drug will be required to achieve the same effect. Cocaine, amphetamines and heroin are poorly absorbed from the intramuscular method and can cause painful abscesses. Cocaine and amphetamines have poor subcutaneous absorption. Abscess formation and, more rarely, tetanus are complications of subcutaneous use. Addicts usually begin by snorting a drug, move on to "skin popping" and then to "mainlining." See INTRAVENOUS DRUG-USE (IDU) and ADMINISTRATION.

Smith, Dr. Michael   Medical director of the drug treatment program at New York's Lincoln Hospital in the Bronx and chairman of the National Acupuncture Detoxification Association, Dr. Smith pioneered the incorporation of acupuncture into detoxification and treatment methods used to cure heroin, cocaine and alcohol addiction. Through his efforts, the practice is gaining acceptance by treatment professionals throughout the world.

Smith, Dr. Robert (1899–1970)   Cofounder with BILL WILSON of ALCOHOLICS ANONYMOUS (AA),

Robert Holbrook Smith (known to grateful AA members simply as Dr. Bob) was an Ohio surgeon, though a native of Vermont. He had become a desperately ill chronic drinker, without hope, until he met a stockbroker from New York, Bill W., who urgently needed a fellow alcoholic to help him maintain his own sobriety. They met in Akron, Ohio, in the spring of 1935, and out of that chance meeting there gradually developed the rough outlines of a concept that, through trial and error, was eventually to become AA. Through it all, Dr. Bob remained a poignant central figure. He died thirty-five years later on November 16, 1970, but his influence on the worldwide AA program was permanent and profound.

smoking and alcohol   People who drink heavily also tend to smoke heavily, and most alcoholics are heavy smokers. One study showed that more than 90% of male and female alcoholics were smokers. Another study found that 60% of all alcoholics smoked more than one pack of cigarettes a day and 30% smoked more than two packs.

There is a high incidence of pulmonary disease among alcoholics. It has been noted that in patients with severe alcoholism, chronic lung disorders, such as lung abscess, bronchitis and emphysema, are the most common problems other than liver disease.

Numerous studies have established the strong association between alcohol and tobacco consumption and CANCERS of the head and neck. It has been suggested that alcohol acts as a solvent and dissolves the tars in tobacco smoke, making them more available to the body tissues, particularly those in the head, neck and esophagus. Alcohol may alter the intracellular metabolism of the epithelial cells at cancer sites, resulting in an enhanced metabolic activation of tobacco-associated carcinogens. There is an apparent SYNERGY between alcohol and tobacco consumption that increases the risk of developing cancers of the upper alimentary tract and upper respiratory tract. According to some researchers, the risk of developing cancer of the mouth and throat among those who both smoke and drink is 15 times greater than the risk among those who neither smoke nor drink.

Heavy drinking appears to increase the urge to smoke, and therefore a high level of cigarette smoking may in some ways be attributable to the use of alcohol. Cigarette burns between the fingers are frequently exhibited by heavy drinkers who "nod off" while smoking, and many fires are caused this way as well.

According to the surgeon general's 1989 report on smoking and health, the prevalence of smoking among adults decreased from 40% in 1965 to 29% in 1987. Rates for smoking appear to have continued to decline. In the Substance Abuse and Health Service Administration's *1994 National Household Survey on Drug Abuse* the rate for past-month smoking was 26.0%. Former surgeon general C. Everett Koop has zealously campaigned in recent years for a "smoke-free society."

R. C. Bates, "Pathologies Associated with Alcoholism," *Quarterly Journal of Studies on Alcohol* 27 (1966): 110.

Charles S. Lieber et al., "Alcohol-Related Diseases and Carcinogenesis," *Cancer Research* 39, no. 7 (July 1979): 2863–2885.

A. B. Lowenfels, M. Mohman and K. Shibutani, "Surgical Consequences of Alcoholism." *Surgery, Gynecology and Obstetrics* 131 (July 1970): 129–138.

G. D. McCoy and E. L. Wynder, "Etiological and Preventive Implications in Alcohol Carcinogenesis," *Cancer Research* 39 (July 1979): 2844–2850.

H. M. Pollard, W. A. Gracie, and J. C. Sisson, "Extrahepatic Complications Associated with Cirrhosis of the Liver," *Journal of the American Medical Association* 169 (1959): 318.

smuggling   It has been estimated that over 90% of the illicit drugs consumed in the U.S. are produced in foreign countries. Supplies originate in diverse areas, but basically they come from Latin America, Southwest and Southeast Asia.

Shipment into the U.S. is accomplished in a variety of ways. Large-scale professional smugglers use commercial planes and ships for trafficking, but they also tend to use small private aircraft. A private plane often is used on a one-time-only basis to avoid detection, and landings are made at makeshift airfields in rural areas. Small boats also are used extensively for trafficking; often they are disguised as charter fishing craft. Drug trafficking networks are not always this sophisticated, however. Often amateur couriers are employed, who are relatively safe from arrest. The couriers are well paid and use every conceivable way of concealing drugs, either on their person or among their possessions. Drugs have been found in suitcases with hollow bottoms; in toy dolls and animals; pressed thin and placed in books. Other innovative smugglers have been known to hide drugs in body cavities; soak their clothes in a drug solution; or swallow balloons or condoms filled with a drug and later excrete them.

Most illicit drugs are smuggled into the U.S. by way of New York City, Florida, California and Texas. The Drug Enforcement Administration (DEA) is responsible for developing interdiction intelligence and participation in cooperative efforts with the U.S. Customs Service, the U.S. Coast Guard and the U.S. Border Patrol (part of the Immigration and Naturalization Service), which provide the principal anti-smuggling operations at ports of entry and along land and water borders. The South Florida Task Force, for example, which was established in 1982, may have reduced the flow into this key transshipment point, although smugglers appear to have simply diversified their traffic lanes into Texas, the Carolinas and the Northeast. The Task Force has, if nothing else, kept them off balance and similar task forces now are being established in these new areas.

In 1995 the DEA reported that the Southeastern high-purity heroin, produced by warlord armies, dominated the U.S. market. It was transported by independent suppliers who were overseas Chinese

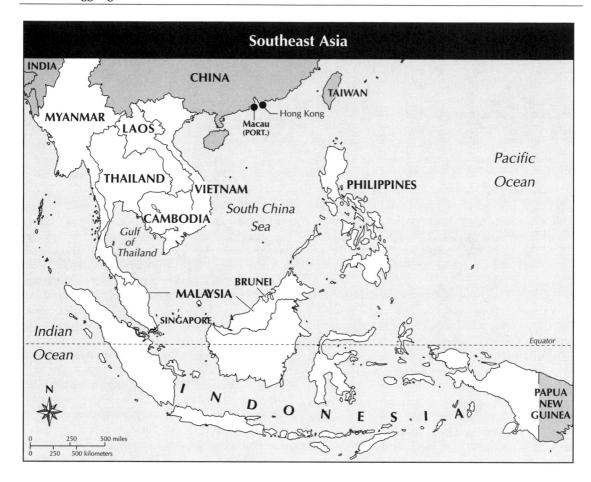

Southeast Asia

criminal elements and organized ethnic Chinese brokers groups in the U.S. The U.S. brokers group consorted with local criminal organizations through connections initially made in U.S. prisons. Additionally, Southeast Asian heroin was smuggled into the U.S. by Nigerian and West African groups. Middle Eastern traffickers smuggled Southwest Asian heroin to ethnic enclaves in the U.S. Virtually all heroin produced in Mexico was destined for the U.S. and was distributed primarily in the western states by Mexican-American criminal networks. Colombian heroin steadily increased in availability in eastern U.S. cities, as Colombian traffickers expanded their markets. In 1995 Colombia was the major producer and Colombian drug Mafiosi the major traffickers of cocaine into the U.S. Marijuana, was the most widely used and available drug in the U.S. with 50% of the total supply coming from Mexico. Increasing amounts also came from Colombia and Jamaica. There has also been an extensive increase in the amount of other dangerous drugs brought into the U.S. illegally—such as amphetamines, barbiturates, benzodiazepine and methaqualone—which have been diverted from legitimate sources or manufactured in highly sophisticated clandestine laboratories, many of which are in Europe. A large quantity of these drugs are channeled through Mexico and Colombia. In 1980 the Drug Enforcement Administration began to take note of large seizures of methaqualone tablets (loads of 1,000 or more pounds), which were arriving surreptitiously in the southeast U.S. The seizures often were the result of citizen complaints about mysterious aircraft landing on rural roads. The nature of these seizures suggest

Western Europe

that authorities are probably seeing only the tip of the iceberg in drug smuggling.

In 1994 two drugs—cocaine and heroin—constituted the most serious threat to the U.S. Virtually all cocaine in the U.S. is derived from coca grown in Peru (57%), Bolivia (30%) and Colombia (13%). Eighty percent of the cocaine in this country is processed in Colombia and shipped by Colombian drug traffickers.

Opium and its most dangerous derivative, heroin, are smuggled into the U.S. from major producer countries such as Burma (now Myanmar), Afghanistan, Iran, Laos, Pakistan and Thailand.

A subcommittee of the U.S. Senate estimated the global trade in illicit drugs at $500 billion a year. Of that, about $300 billion was earned by smugglers, dealers, wholesalers and money launderers—and roughly one-third of those drug sales are of cocaine.

sniff, sniffing   To inhale a drug through the nostrils. Usually referred to as SNORTING. (See ADMINISTRATION.)

snort, snorting   To inhale a drug through the nostrils. "Snort" is also a term for COCAINE and HEROIN. (See ADMINISTRATION.)

sober   A term used to describe a person who is not under the influence of alcohol or other psychoactive drugs. It also is used to describe an alcoholic who is no longer drinking. In some states, to be considered "legally sober" a person must have a blood alcohol concentration (BAC) of 0.05% or less. Such a person is not, however, as sober as one who has had nothing to drink. (See SOBRIETY.)

sobering pill   See L-DOPA and AMETHYSTIC.

sobering up   Detoxification after drinking. To date, no way of speeding up the detoxification process has been found, other than by kidney dialysis. Coffee or a cold shower may wake up someone who has passed out from excessive drinking, but he or she will still be intoxicated. It takes approximately an hour for a 150-lb. man to metabolize three-quarters of an ounce of absolute alcohol, though this rate can vary as much as +/-50%. (See METABOLISM.) Women metabolize alcohol in a slightly different way and at a different rate than men do. (See WOMEN.)

sobriety   Among alcoholics, and particularly among members of ALCOHOLICS ANONYMOUS, the word sobriety has a precise meaning. It refers to a state of abstinence in which the alcoholic is comfortable and secure, either free of a desire to drink or able to cope with such urges. The patient usually accepts outside help and support, including formal rehabilitation and therapy programs. AA insists upon the support systems of group fellowship and regular attendance at meetings as necessary to continuing sobriety.

The words SOBER and sobriety have been part of all languages as long as the words drunk and drunkenness have, but in AA jargon (and that of similar organizations) the definitions have now evolved to a more specific meaning. In this context sobriety does not mean a state characterized by moderation in drinking or one short of intoxication—it means total abstinence. AA, among others, is firm in its belief that an alcoholic can attain sobriety only through total abstinence, and that he or she can never resume "normal" or MODERATE DRINKING. If one resumes drinking, in AA's view, that first drink will trigger a chain of events that will lead, if not immediately then eventually, to a return to active alcoholic behavior.

In this belief they have followed the lead of the TEMPERANCE societies, without embracing the moral and religious tenets of that earlier movement. However, just as the temperance movement changed the meaning of the word temperance from moderation to prohibition, so AA has changed the meaning of the word sober from unaffected by liquor to absolutely free of liquor. (For information suggesting an alternative conclusion see RAND REPORT.)

In AA, sobriety begins after the alcoholic has taken his last drink, has admitted that she is "powerless over alcohol" and has begun to live a sober life. Length of sobriety, as counted in years, months and even days, looms large as a measure of the alcoholic's success in coping with his enemy—alcohol. Alcoholics joining the AA program are often urged to make "ninety meetings in ninety days," which translates into the equivalent of one meeting a day, every day for three months. Thereafter the number of meetings to be attended is up to the individual, although the recommended number continues to be high, indefinitely. Many AA groups call special attention to attendance achievements at their regular meetings and award "ninety day" pins. Anniversaries—a year's sobriety, two years' and so on—are faithfully remembered and celebrated. Length of sobriety is thus a major concern in the lives of AA members, and while the groups are informally democratic, longtime sobriety confers a measure of seniority. Thus a man or woman of 40 with 20 years of sobriety would have more of an "elder" status than would a man or woman of 60 with only two years of sobriety.

While length of sobriety is used as a major reinforcement factor in AA, fears concerning unremmitting sobriety are an ever present danger. The prospect of "never having another drink as long as I live" can be depressing, even terrifying, and can lead to disaster. To counter this danger, AA focuses on short-term sobriety. "One day at a time" is the motto used to help face down immediate desires to drink. The idea is to concentrate on remaining sober today, without worrying about tomorrow. The same procedure is followed tomorrow, and so on. Fears, doubts and anxieties must not be projected into the future. On the other hand, grandiose dreams and expectations of remaining sober are also considered dangerous. Sobriety is grounded in today, and in a realistic assessment of today's pitfalls and opportunities.

One measure of sobriety is quality. There is "good" sobriety and "poor" sobriety. Good sobriety consists of staying sober, attending meetings and functions and participating in the activities of the group—enjoying your sobriety and the fellowship of those like you. If you do these things, particularly if you make an effort to do them properly and systematically, you are said to be "following your program" and the prognosis is positive.

Poor sobriety is ignoring or fighting some, if not all, of the aspects of the program. This attitude may stem from a basic subconscious DENIAL of alcoholism, an inability to accept help or to face up to the reality of the situation. These are seen as symptoms of conflict and turmoil that may lead the alcoholic back to drinking. Another form of poor sobriety is "white-knuckled" sobriety, which means that the alcoholic stays sober only through grim determination. He or she lives in constant fear of a relapse and thinks incessantly of drinking, often with the feared result.

The term "dry drunk" is often applied to those with a poor sobriety record. The dry drunk has "dried out" and is no longer drinking but that is the only step he or she has taken. The implication is that the "dry" drunk will soon be "wet," or active, again, because although he has temporarily held in check the symptom of drinking, he has not as yet attended to the underlying problem, or attempted to instigate real change in his life, which would ultimately effect not only drinking behavior, but would lessen the desire to drink.

social class

Alcohol: There are different attitudes toward drug use among the various social classes in the U.S. For example, it has been found that as education and income rise, not only the number of drinkers, but the frequency of drinking rises as well (with the exception of young males). In general, upper-class groups have a more permissive attitude toward drinking. According to statistics in the first RAND REPORT (June 1976), there are more abstainers in the lower classes. (52% of the population in the lower social class were abstainers, compared with 34% in the middle class and 21% in the upper class.)

As education and income rise, there is less difference between the drinking styles and patterns of men and WOMEN. Drinking environments also differ according to class, with upper class groups drinking more often in restaurants, at dinner or at cocktail parties and lower class groups drinking more frequently in bars. Alcohol and other drug users in the middle and upper socioeconomic classes are generally under-reported in official statistics primarily due to the fact that their business and personal lifestyles sometimes shield them from public scrutiny. (See ALCOHOLIC.)

Drugs other than alcohol: Socioeconomic considerations do not appear to effect the use of amphetamines, which have been used by housewives (often by anorectics); by students studying for exams; by truckers needing to stay awake on prolonged trips; and by athletes wishing to excel.

The use of inhalants is not socially constricted. Certainly glue sniffing among children has not been confined to any particular class, although chronic inhalant abuse is found most often among Mexican-American and Native-American youngsters.

Barbiturate use generally is found in middle and upper class individuals, particularly women.

LSD and other hallucinogens first became popular among college students and thus can be linked to the middle and upper social classes. As they became readily obtainable on the illicit market, their use spread to all social classes. This phenomenon is not limited to hallucinogens but is seen in the increased popularity of many other drugs.

Though used extensively in the 1970s and 1980s mostly by the middle and upper classes, cocaine has customarily been used by heroin addicts and others across social lines since the early 1900s. Just when the negative effects of chronic use became known to the general public and cocaine use was leveling off in college student and middle class populations in the mid-1980s, the advent of inexpensive, smokable crack-cocaine resulted in an epidemic increase in cocaine use and addiction, especially among young and disadvantaged minority members.

Generally, there are a greater percent of heroin addicts among lower income groups centered in the metropolitan areas. This high incidence of abuse is in part attributed to the easy availability of narcotics "on the street" and to the lower quality of life available in lower income neighborhoods.

Marijuana, the most broadly used illicit drug in the U.S., is certainly not restricted to a particular social class; whether because of its availability or its relatively inexpensive cost, its use is far-reaching. Marijuana use is as prevalent among the teenage children of blue-collar workers as it is among college-educated adults in their 30s. Marijuana has been called "the opiate of the masses."

Treatment: Social class also may play a role in treatment. Upper middle and upper class individuals have superior health care insurance and greater expendable income, enabling easier access to private physicians, who often prescribe barbiturates or benzodiazepine as a sedative hypnotic to repress symptoms of anxiety or depression, rather than searching for solutions to the underlying problems. The authors of the first *Rand Report* found that lower-class patients drop out of therapy earlier than patients from the middle and upper class. The middle and upper classes, with greater access to treatment and fewer incidences of relapse than the lower social groups, have increased rates of rehabilitation. Consequently it is conjectured that social class may play a larger role in the course of addiction rather than in the cause of addiction. In other words, the middle and upper classes are more likely to seek treatment, to complete treatment and to benefit from treatment. Research has not yet analyzed the relationship of

addiction to the separate elements of social class, such as education, job classification and residential environment. Studies have tended to focus on income level, which is only one component of social orientation. (See HISPANICS [LATINOS], AFRICAN AMERICANS, and NATIVE AMERICANS [AMERICAN INDIANS].)

David J. Armor, J. Michael Polich and Harriet B. Stambul, *Alcoholism and Treatment* (New York: John Wiley & Sons, 1978): 61–77.

U.S. Department of Health and Human Services Office of Applied Studies, *Preliminary Estimates from the Drug Abuse Warning Network, 1994. Preliminary Estimates of Drug-Related Emergency Department Episodes,* advanced report (November 1995).

social drinking   The term "social drinking" usually refers to moderate drinking on social occasions. Alcohol stimulates sociability and relaxes inhibitions among people in groups. The term "social drinking" is also used to refer to drinking in any way that is found acceptable by a particular cultural group. Sometimes an individual participates in social drinking as a result of social pressures; at a cocktail party, for example, where one is urged to "have a drink" or to "have another."

social phobia   Social phobia is characterized by extreme anxiety about being judged by others, or fear that their behavior will cause one embarrassment or ridicule. Social phobia is not the same as shyness. Persons with social phobia may have such extreme anxiety that they experience panic attacks, which include such symptoms as heart palpitations, faintness, shortness of breath and profuse sweating.

social workers   Social workers who work in the field of alcoholism/other drug addiction are usually master's-level professionals who diagnose, treat and refer for special services individuals with problems related to drug use or abuse. Chemical dependency social workers work in family service centers, mental health programs, agencies that deal with populations associated with high rates of drug problems (such as adolescents, the homeless and the elderly), as well as in private practice. Many social workers in the field are specialists on family systems theory, a model that can be very effective in the treatment/or prevention of drug-use problems. The social work philosophy is based on the belief that individuals both shape and are shaped by their environments, that is, family, school or workplace, community and society. (By contrast, traditional psychiatry/psychology ascribes to a "medical model," wherein the client's problems are symptoms of an "illness" that needs to be treated, irrespective of environmental factors.) A master's degree in social work (M.S.W.) is the minimum credential required by most states for licensing or certification of professional social workers.

Society of Americans for Recovery, Inc. (SOAR)
A short-lived lobby group founded in the early 1990s and made up of individuals in recovery from alcoholism and/or other drug use, as well as their families and other concerned citizens. SOAR's objects were the empowerment of the recovery community to exercise it rights of citizenship and to educate the American public, news and entertainment media, employers, insurers, health care providers and all levels of government about the diseases of addiction and the possibilities of recovery.

sociocultural etiological theories   The many theories about what causes alcoholism and other drug use can generally be divided into three major groups: physiological, psychological and sociocultural. Sociocultural models of etiology postulate relationships between various factors in society and the incidence of alcohol and the use of at least some drugs other than alcohol (for example, the use of marijuana by Caribbeans). Ethnic and cultural differences in the use of alcohol suggest that society plays an important role in the development of alcoholism. Different cultures have different attitudes toward alcohol, set different standards for what constitutes appropriate use of intoxicants, and provide greater or lesser environmental support for drinking. Jews, Mormons and Muslims have very low rates of alcoholism, and the French have a very high rate. This disparity may be due to cultural proscriptions against alcohol in the case of the first three groups, and cultural support for high consumption of alcohol in the case of the last group. This same pattern is true of countries that have a long tradition of opiate use (Iran, Pakistan) and countries with a long history of coca use (Peru, Bolivia), whereas the abuse

of both cocaine (derived from coca) and opium is frowned upon in the U.S.

Cultural stress factors may also contribute to alcoholism and other drug use. Individuals may react to a crisis situation generated by external events with an increase in consumption of alcohol and other substances. There is a cyclical relationship between social instability and alcoholism/drug abuse: heavy consumption in reaction to social stress in turn increases the deterioration of the social environment.

Family patterns are another social factor contributing to alcoholism and other drug use. An unusually high incidence of familial alcoholism has been found in the backgrounds of alcoholics. While the part played by GENETICS cannot be ignored, there no doubt also is a strong social-learning factor involved in the development of alcoholism and the use of other drugs.

Sociocultural etiological theories of substance abuse receive wide support among experts in the field today. However, they are generally considered in conjunction with the two other etiological theories—physiological and psychological—since no single theory can independently explain the causes of alcoholism/other drug abuse.

sodium butabarbital   An intermediate-acting BARBITURATE, usually used to produce sedation and sleep.

Solfoton   A sedative hypnotic that contains 16 mg of the long-acting BARBITURATE phenobarbital. Used for sedation and to produce sleep, it has abuse potential with both physical and psychological dependence resulting. Respiratory depression and coma can occur with overdose.

solitary drinking   Solitary drinking often is distinguished from bar drinking, and the activities of many alcoholics tend to fall largely within one of these two categories. While individual behavior may vary from time to time, distinctions have been made between those who seek out public places to do their drinking and those who drink at home. It has been suggested, although more documentation is needed, that those who are more outwardly gregarious in their drinking habits are more likely to seek out and be more comfortable in highly supportive and organized groups, such as ALCOHOLICS ANONYMOUS, when attempting to resolve their drinking problems.

Those who often take a drink alone after work or before bed, or who drink a beer or two while mowing the lawn, are not classified as solitary drinkers. Drinking to excess is characteristic of solitary problem drinkers. Many solitary drinkers choose to be alone as a way of escaping from other problems. This can lead the solitary drinker into a cycle in which the seclusion, the drinking and the initial problems all feed on each other and contribute to a worsening of the original situation.

Sominex   An over-the-counter (OTC) sleep aid that can be potentially harmful because it contains the toxic substance SCOPOLAMINE. Some of the significant side effects of scopolamine are blurred vision, confusion, delirium and heart effects. Scopolamine generally is used to dry up secretions, and there is no evidence that the amount contained in Sominex functions as an aid to sleep. As far back as 1975 the FDA (Food and Drug Administration) recommended that scopolamine be removed from sleep aids but thus far no action has been taken.

sour mash   A particular grain mixture used to prepare the mash, or "wash," from which bourbon is distilled. The grain content of bourbon is at least 51% corn (Indian maize), with the remainder being made up of rye and malted barley. In sour mash bourbon this grain content is mixed with a residue from a previous distillation in order to encourage fermentation. The residue, called "slop," is acidic in taste and smell, and these characteristics, rather than the taste of the finished bourbon, give sour mash whiskey its name. The chief alternative to sour mash as an aid to fermentation is SWEET MASH, in which a high proportion of malted barley is blended with the corn and rye grains.

South Africa

Alcohol: In 1993 South Africa's annual per capita alcohol consumption was 4.6 liters, ranking it 24th among alcohol-consuming countries. The rate was down from a high of 5.1 liters in 1990. This country ranks 22 in annual per capita consumption of beer, which in 1993 was 54.9 liters.

Drugs other than alcohol: Marijuana (known as dagga in South Africa) has long been used, particu-

larly among the Bantu people. The South African mine workers often use dagga as an energizer during their work day. With the exception of alcohol, the abuse of other drugs was practically unknown in South Africa until the late 1960s, with the arrival of the age of narcotics, stimulants and depressants. However, with the fall of Apartheid, South Africa rejoined the world economy—and drug trafficking increased. In 1992 the police confiscated a mere 24 pounds of cocaine. By 1995 seizures had increased to 400 pounds. South Africa seems to have picked up quickly on drug-abuse trends, so that by 1995 government agencies were girding themselves for what they feared might become an epidemic of crack use in urban areas.

Cocaine from South America and heroin from Asia are smuggled in, both for sale and consumption in South Africa and its neighboring nations and for shipment to European destinations. As of 1995 South Africa is one of the largest cultivators of cannabis, but almost exclusively for domestic consumption. Additionally, the illicit use of Mandrax, a synthetic sleeping pill manufactured in South Africa and India, rose dramatically. (Mandrax is crushed, mixed with marijuana and smoked.)

Treatment: In 1969 the government appointed a committee of inquiry to investigate the extent of drug use. It was found that there was increasing experimentation among young people, and in 1971 the Substances and Rehabilitation Centers Act was passed. It provided penalties for drug dealing and use or possession of dangerous drugs. It also established a National Advisory Board on Rehabilitation Matters, which was instructed to plan and coordinate measures to combat drug use and provide treatment for drug-dependent individuals. The act also provided for the establishment of both government and private rehabilitation centers and their inspection. Anyone who voluntarily desires treatment may apply for admission to a center, but the 1971 act also provided for compulsory treatment in cases where a magistrate deemed it necessary. The provisions of the act apply not only to the abuse of dangerous drugs but also to alcohol abuse, which has long been recognized as a problem in South Africa.

Along with the establishment of treatment centers, the government is also establishing national drug-education programs. Voluntary welfare organizations are also working on the drug problem. The most active organization is the South African National Council on Alcoholism and Drug Dependence (SAN-CAD).

Spanish broom   *Spartium junceum,* a toxic plant containing CYTISINE.

sparkling wine   Wine has been produced in the Champagne district since the third century, but sparkling wine is a relatively recent invention of the region. By most accounts, it originated in the 1690s and, according to tradition, was the work of Dom Perignon, a monk in the Haut Villers Abbey. He also is credited with the first use of cork stoppers. Before this invention, carbonation of effervescent wines in bottles was not known.

The discovery of sparkling wine most likely occurred when a wine in the later stages of fermentation was bottled and stoppered with a cork. The effect of the carbonic gas produced by the continuing fermentation and retained in the bottle by a close-fitting cork would then have been obvious once the wine was opened. After it became desirable to produce such effervescent wines, the precise technique became a closely guarded secret. Sparkling wines did not gain in popularity until the end of the 18th century. Since then they have often been imitated in various fashions, which have included simply pumping a STILL WINE full of gas.

The traditional method of producing sparkling wines is to subject a chosen wine to a second fermentation in the bottle. In this case the chosen wine, called the cuvee, is bottled in especially thick glass, combined with controlled amounts of yeast and sugar and stoppered with a cork that is held in place by a wire wrapping. The wine is then aged for a period of between one and three years. With a minimum loss of pressure, the sediment produced by fermentation must be removed before shipment to market. For this reason the bottles temporarily are stored upside down, allowing the sediment to collect on the cork. The pressure in the bottle is reduced for a time by chilling it to about 25° F. Then, in a step called *degorgement,* the cork is pulled, the frozen yeast sediment is removed, the bottle is topped off with a clarified wine and sugar solution and a new cork is inserted.

Because of the costs involved in bottle fermentation many sparkling wines today are produced by subjecting the cuvee to a second fermentation in large closed stainless-steel tanks. Once fermentation has reached the desired level, the wine can be filtered in bulk, mixed with the clarified wine and sugar solution and then bottled. This method, called *cuvee close,* is considered inferior to bottle fermentation because of the different contact of the wine with the yeast in the second fermentation.

Sparkling wines from the French Champagne region are still considered to be the finest. The region has recently been broken into titular districts called Marne, Heute-Marne, Aube and Ardennes. Traditionally only sparkling wines from Champagne, France, would say "champagne," as opposed to "sparkling wine" on their labels, however, certain sparkling wines from other regions (such as upstate New York) now also print the word champagne on their labels.

Spain produces a greater quantity of sparkling wines than France, many of which are red or rose. The Panades district in northeastern Spain is particularly noted, and some argue that the sparkling wines produced at Cordorniu by the *cuvee close* method of second fermentation actually predate all French sparkling wines. Portugal is also known for its sparkling wines bottled in the southern Dao district, and in Germany such wines are bottled under the Perlwein and Sekt designations. Most of the wine regions of the U.S. produce the sparkling variety as well, with New York State being the leader. The alcohol content of sparkling wines is about 12% to 12.5%.

Special Action Office for Drug Abuse Prevention (SAODAP)   No longer in existence, this agency was established by the Office of the Presidency in 1972 to review and evaluate the functions and policies of all government agencies involved in the area of drug use and to establish policies and provide direction necessary to properly coordinate government efforts.

specialty substance abuse facilities   According to the Substance Abuse and Mental Health Services Administration, specialty substance abuse facilities are those "that provide only alcohol and/or drug-abuse treatment services." A specialty treatment provider meets the following criteria: (1) has a formal structured arrangement for substance-abuse treatment or recovery, using substance-abuse-specified personnel; (2) has a designated portion of the

Per Capita Spirits Consumption in Leading Countries

Consumption of spirits by country between 1992 and 1994 (in litres/inhabitant)

Country	1992	1993	1994	Country	1992	1993	1994
Russia	3.7	3.8	4.4	Uruguay	1.6	1.6	1.6
China	2.4	2.7	3.8	Luxembourg	1.60	1.60	1.60
Poland	3.5	3.8	3.5	United Kingdom	1.50	1.50	1.56
Cyprus	3.8	3.4	3.3	Switzerland	1.61	1.65	1.55
Hungary	3.40	3.05	3.06	Ukraine	2.6	2.5	1.5
Bulgaria	2.81	2.75	2.84	Sweden	1.60	1.51	1.50
Greece	2.7	2.8	2.8	Austria	1.26	1.5	1.4
Spain	2.7	2.5	2.5	Brazil	1.3	1.3	1.3
France	2.63	2.49	2.49	New Zealand	1.33	1.28	1.23
Germany	2.7	2.6	2.4	Belgium	1.20	1.2	1.2
Romania	3.5	3.5	2.2	Australia	1.16	1.16	?
Japan	2.1	2.1	2.0	Denmark	1.19	1.08	1.09
Cuba	2.0	2.0	2.0	South Africa	1	1	1
Slovak Republic	1.90	1.97	1.97	Italy	1	0.9	0.9
USA	2.12	2.01	1.96	Mexico	0.8	0.8	0.8
Chile	1.5	1.9	1.05	Portugal	0.8	0.8	0.8
Finland	2.25	1.98	1.85	Norway	0.85	0.77	0.75
Netherlands	1.90	1.88	1.77	Singapore	0.4	0.4	0.5
Canada	1.81	1.75	1.70	Turkey	0.4	0.4	0.4
Irish Republic	1.6	1.7	1.7	Argentina	0.2	0.3	0.3
Czech Republic	1.78	1.85	1.65	Thailand	0.08	0.08	0.09
Iceland	1.9	1.7	1.6	Ma[la]ysia	0.1	0.05	0.05

References: 1. World Drink Trends 1995, International Beverage Alcohol consumption and Production Trends.
   Produktschap voor Gedistilleerde Dranken, in association with NTC Publications LTD.
Source: *World Drink Trends,* 1995 edition

facility (or resources) for treatment services; and (3) has an allocated budget for such diagnosis of its clients and, thereafter, may include a wide range of treatment services, such as counseling and family therapy. Job placement or other rehabilitation services may also be offered.

Beatrice A. Rouse, ed., *Substance Abuse and Mental Health Statistics Sourcebook* (Washington, D.C.: Substance Abuse and Mental Health Services Administration, 1995).

spirit still   The second and smaller of the two stills employed in some double-distillation processes. The first and larger still, known as a WASH STILL, produces a weak and impure distillate called "low wine" that usually is strengthened and purified by further rectification in the spirit still. Passed once or repeatedly through the spirit still, the distillate is then collected in a final receiver vessel.

spirits   Originally the term "spirit" or "spirits" meant the essence of any substance. Now it is commonly used in this sense to refer to the alcoholic essence of a fermented substance from which it has been extracted. More generally speaking, the term "spirits" is a synonym for all alcoholic beverages, as distinguished from the many nonpotable varieties of chemical alcohols and denatured ethanols.

The alcohol content of all potable spirits is ethanol, a clear and colorless distillate. The variations in potable spirits are produced by impurities retained from the fermented mash, by flavorings added after distillation and by the containers used for aging. The purest are the so-called natural spirits, which are relatively flavorless and high in ethanol content.

The distinguishing feature of most common spirits is provided by the content of the fermented mash from which they are distilled. Gin and whiskey are spirits distilled from grains, brandy is a spirit distilled from wine, rum is a spirit distilled from sugarcane or molasses, and vodka is a spirit traditionally distilled from potatoes. A variety of other fermented substances, such as agave or dates, are distilled throughout the world to produce less-well-known potable spirits.

spontaneous recovery, spontaneous remission   A somewhat misleading term that refers to the cessation or positive modification of drug-abusing be-

havior by an individual who does so on their own, without professional treatment, meaning that they do not join a self-help group or seek professional counseling. The impetus to change may come as a result of maturity, changes in lifestyle or a new position of responsibility such as a career change, marriage or the birth of a child. Other factors that might precipitate a major turnabout are the fact that one's job, health or relationship is in jeopardy, or the reality of having sustained a loss due to one's actions or lifestyle. Sometimes regret, self-disgust or even "hitting bottom" is what is required to make the requisite decisions to induce change.

sports and drugs (including alcohol)   The use of drugs by competing athletes dates back a hundred years or more to a time when the popular drugs to use for increased performance were alcohol and caffeine. In present times, drug use by athletes is widespread and, while any number of drugs are used, the most popular drugs of abuse are amphetamines, steroids, cocaine, painkillers and alcohol. Drug use is not limited to professional athletes; it is also a problem at the college and high school levels.

The reasons for drug use vary. Amphetamines are taken to diminish pain or fatigue; to increase strength and endurance; to provide greater concentration; and to intensify aggressiveness and the desire to achieve. Steroids are taken during training in order to gain weight, pump up muscles and increase body mass. Other drugs are used during actual competition, either to enhance performance or to dull the pain of injuries. Drug use outside the playing arena is also a problem among athletes, many of whom may want to extend the exhilaration of play beyond the game; may have emotional problems from which they are seeking relief; or, in the case of the highly paid professionals, it may be an attempt to help ease, or escape from, the strain and responsibilities that accompany newfound power and wealth.

There has been a recent campaign among athletic organizations, particularly the National Football League and the International Olympic Committee, to eliminate the use of drugs. Olympic contestants are aware that they will be tested for evidence of drugs during the games. Professional football players are tested randomly (so players can never be sure when they will be tested). The use of drugs by football players was prohibited in 1972. Up to that time it was common practice for team doctors and trainers to hand out amphetamines and a 1970 survey showed that 60% of National Football League players took the drugs on a regular basis. Although heavy drug use was violently denied by football officials, a survey taken a year after use was prohibited suggested that many players were continuing to take amphetamines and turning to illicit sources when they were unable to obtain them legally. The testing controversy continues today, with many players protesting the practice as an "invasion of privacy."

Amphetamine use by athletes was first reported in the 1940s. They were used by top athletes primarily in endurance sports such as cycling, track, swimming and football. Amphetamines increase respiratory flow, the metabolic rate and cardiac output. They also increase alertness and intensify aggressiveness. In moderate to large doses, they also have an analgesic effect. This ability to relieve pain and increase drive and strength makes amphetamines extremely sought after by athletes involved in contact sports. Some of the adverse reactions to the use of amphetamines, however, are: irritability, restlessness, insomnia and impotence, not to mention dependence. Amphetamine deaths also have occurred in sports, usually as a result of the drug's cardiovascular effect in combination with heat and overexertion.

The International Olympic Committee defines "doping" as using substances alien to the body in abnormal amounts or by abnormal methods with the aim of taking unfair advantage during competition. If such a substance is used to treat an illness, the fact must be reported. Testing for drugs in Olympic competitions has become mandatory, and during the IX Pan American Games held in Caracas, Venezuela, in August 1983, tests proved positive in a number of cases. The presence of steroids was found in eight weight lifters, one an American, and they were stripped of their medals. When this was revealed, 12 U.S. track athletes left the games to return home. The reason for their departure and withdrawal from the games was not given and it is unsure at this time if it was a protest move or fear of exposure. All competitors were aware that they would be tested, but the equipment used was so sophisticated and advanced that for the first time it was possible to detect the use of steroids up to a year previously.

Ben Johnson, the Canadian sprinter who set a record at the 1988 Summer Olympics in South Korea, was ultimately disqualified for using anabolic steroids. In June 1989 he admitted for the first time that he had used performance-enhancing drugs starting as early as 1981.

The aim of an athlete who takes steroids is muscle hypertrophy. Steroids increase body mass because they improve nitrogen utilization and increase the appetite, though some authorities suggest that fluid retention rather than weight gain actually occurs. Steroids can have adverse reactions on liver function, can diminish libido and cause testicular atrophy along with hypertension. Steroids generally are taken during training periods and not just before a competition.

Testing at the Pan American Games was conducted by a highly advanced laboratory in East Germany (which also has the approval of the Olympics Committee) and involved a two-step procedure. First a urine sample was taken immediately after a competitor had taken part in an event. If the test was positive, the athlete's national Olympic Committee was notified and a second sample was taken in the presence of a committee member. If this test also proved positive, the Pan American Committee was notified and then had to decide on a course of action. The U.S. Olympic Committee has endorsed the testing and has announced that it will cooperate with the testing procedure in the future.

Narcotics sometimes are used by athletes when there is a need to perform in spite of pain. But the problem appears to be growing and is a matter of considerable concern by league officials and club owners in pro baseball, basketball and football. Alcohol, tranquilizers and other sedatives sometimes are abused because they have a calming effect on tension, anxiety and tremors. When they are employed it usually is with a certain amount of caution so that over-sedation is avoided.

In a June 1982 *Sports Illustrated* article, former Miami Dolphin, New Orleans Saint and San Diego Charger Don Reese described in graphic detail the course of his growing dependence on cocaine during his career with the National Football League. Stating that cocaine "controls and corrupts" professional football, Reese told the painful story of how he acquired an expensive habit and how it involved daily freebasing with other players and memory blackouts during games. Cocaine was readily available to NFL players, he said, not only from dealers who sometimes attend practices but also from respected veteran players.

Although it seems hard to believe now, reactions at the time to Reese's confession included accusations that he must be mentally unbalanced to have fallen prey to such a habit and that, accordingly, his allegations must be dismissed. Nevertheless, insiders' reports at the time reveal that as many as 60% of pro football players were snorting and/or freebasing cocaine regularly.

In June 1986 Len Bias, star basketball forward at the University of Maryland died of a cocaine reaction the day after he signed a lucrative professional contract with the Boston Celtics. Don Rogers of the Cleveland Browns professional football team died the same month of a similar drug overdose. In his 1987 autobiography, *L.T.: Living on the Edge* (written with David Falker), Lawrence Taylor, the legendary New York Giants linebacker, told of using drugs, particularly cocaine and crack, during the 1988 football season.

Drug abuse in baseball drew national attention in 1984 and 1985 with a sensational criminal trial of players with the Pittsburgh Pirates of the National League. Peter Ueberroth, the baseball commissioner at the time, proposed mandatory periodic random drug testing for major league players. During the 1987 season, the New York Met's star pitcher, Dwight Gooden, one of the most successful pitchers in the majors, returned to the game after a program of drug therapy at the Smithers Drug Rehabilitation Center. During spring training that year, Gooden had failed a routine urine test. He has since waged a successful battle against drug dependence and is now back pitching for the Yankees, though he continues to be tested regularly.

Under Commissioner Ueberroth's testing program, seven athletes were suspended in the 1986 season. They were allowed to return to play only if they donated 10% of their 1986 salaries to a substance-abuse prevention program, agreed to random drug testing and did 200 hours of drug-related community service. Since that time, several baseball teams have moved toward comprehensive drug-prevention and drug-testing programs. Some critics have attacked Ueberroth's drug-testing plan on grounds that its effectiveness is weakened or destroyed if results are made known to a third party. They believe that for testing to help the

user, findings must be kept confidential. Otherwise, the theory goes, the individual (player) loses trust in the process. Other skeptics say that baseball's drug-testing plan places all the emphasis on testing and eliminating drug users; it shows little or no concern for helping players who are "doing drugs." Still other critics say that any attempt to rehabilitate drug users is destined to fail if the drug-testing program is handled like a criminal procedure.

Enormous profits are generated by sports events in the U.S. Since sports fans encourage and demand victory and condone aggressiveness in athletes, it is not difficult to understand why competitors use drugs to achieve what the public wants. Nor is it hard to see why owners, trainers and officials in the various sports are willing to go to extraordinary and drastic lengths to please the public. The American College of Sports Medicine (ACSM), located in Indianapolis, Indiana, studied the effects of alcohol on physical performance. The *Position Stand Report* stated that,

> Although athletes may consume alcohol to improve psychological function, it is psychomotor performance that deteriorates most. Information processing is consistently impaired. Small to moderate amounts of alcohol impair reaction time, hand-eye coordination, accuracy, balance and complex coordination or gross motor skills. Performance will be most adversely affected in sports that require rapid reactions to changing stimuli, such as basketball, football, tennis, golf and auto racing. Thus, while some people believe alcohol may improve self-confidence, the available research reveals a deterioration in psychomotor performance.

In its 1988 publication, *Alcohol in Sports: Position Stand,* ACSM states that acute ingestion of alcohol appears to have no beneficial effect on the metabolic and physiological responses to exercise.

American College of Sports Medicine (ACSM), *Alcohol in Sports: Position Stand* (Indianapolis: ACSM, 1988).

Gilda Berger, *Drug Testing* (New York: Franklin Watts, 1987): 109–113.

Edward F. Dolan Jr., *Drugs in Sports* (New York: Franklin Watts, 1986): 74–75, 102–107.

Sports Drug Awareness Program Started by then attorney general William French Smith in June 1984, this program was developed in conjunction with the National High School Athletic Coaches

Factors Associated With Male Violence Against Their Partners

Minor Violence	Severe Violence
Husband high on drugs	Husband high on drugs
Wife drunk	Low family income
Husband drunk	Wife's father hit mother
Low family income	
Wife's father hit mother	
Violence approval norms	

Source: J. J. Collins and P. M. Messerschmidt, "Epidemiology of Alcohol-Related Volence," Alcohol Health & Research World 17 (1993): 93–99.

Association, the International Association of Chiefs of Police, the National Football League and the NFL Players Association to provide 5.5 million high school athletes with drug-abuse-prevention information. Additional organizations that have since joined in the program include: the Federal Bureau of Investigation, the Office of Juvenile Justice and Delinquency Prevention, the National Basketball Association, National Hockey League, the National Federation of Parents for Drug Free Youth, the National Association of Broadcasters, the National Federation of State High School Associations, the Sporting Goods Manufacturers Association and Major League Baseball. The goal of the program is to prevent drug use among school-age youth, with special emphasis on the role of the coach and the student-athlete (there are some 48,000 men and women coaches in 20,000 high schools across the country who are in a position to reach the 5.5 million student athletes). Each participating entity involved uses its unique constituency by directing prevention information and messages toward the 57 million young people now in kindergarten through college.

Department of Justice, Drug Enforcement Administration, "Sports Drug Awareness Program," *Demand Reduction Bulletin* (August 1986).

spouse abuse   Family violence in the U.S. is a significant and often ignored problem. American society tolerates a high level of violence in general and is usually unwilling to interfere in people's private lives. Spouse abuse consists of physical and mental injury of a wife or husband by a marital partner. The overwhelming majority of such abuse involves the battering of wives by husbands. A 1988–92 study compared women in upstate New York shelters, in an alcoholism outpatient treatment program, and women in the community at large. Forty-one percent of women in the outpatient program reported severe violence from pretreatment partners as compared to 9% of the women in the randomly selected households. (The rate for women in shelters was highest: an astonishing 96%.) A number of studies have concluded that a significant number of battered wives consider their husbands to have alcohol problems. Spousal abusers can be women as well as men, although wives are more often seriously injured because of their physical disadvantage. Women are statistically as likely to kill their spouses as are men, often citing the abuse they received from their husbands as the motive.

Spouse abuse frequently leads to child abuse. (See CHILDREN OF ALCOHOLICS AND SUBSTANCE ABUSERS.) A man who beats his wife may also beat his children; the abused wife may take out her anger and resentment on the children. A chain reaction may start, with each member in turn and in his or her own way provoking or imposing violence. Quarrels arise when one partner complains about the other's behavior, triggering a violent reaction in the partner, which leads the complainer to complain more, which can then trigger more violence. At one psychiatric clinic, it was discovered that 65% of the mothers who had abused their sons had been abused themselves by their husbands.

The link between family violence and alcoholism/other drug addiction (particularly to crack cocaine) has been established in several research studies. According to one estimate, up to 80% of all cases of family violence involve drinking or other drug taking, either before, during or after the incident. Spousal abuse related to abuse of drugs other than alcohol is less documented than that related solely to drinking, but it is generally assumed that most of the information about alcohol-related domestic violence applies equally to other mind-altering drugs.

Alcohol breaks down inhibitions, self-restraint and sound judgment, often resulting in violent behavior between husbands and wives. However, most research supports the conclusion that alcohol abuse does not itself *cause* family violence, but rather that the use of alcohol may be a catalyst, or even provide an excuse for violence. When intoxicated, the abuser may believe that normal rules for behavior do not apply. Moderate and problem drinkers are more frequently involved in such incidents than light drinkers.

Alcoholism and family abuse have many characteristics in common. Some consider family violence to be a disease, just as alcoholism is most often considered a disease. Both allow the subject to temporarily mask depression. Similarities have been found in the characters of spouse abusers and alcoholics, members of each group often are dependent, impulsive, frustrated, depressed and have low self-esteem. Both violence and alcoholism seem to provide coping mechanisms for abusers and alcoholics. More research is needed to uncover the particular circumstances leading to these traits.

Violence and drinking may be connected in several different ways. Perhaps the most common pattern is an eruption of violence that happens only when alcohol is consumed—either the abuser drinks and then hits, or the victim drinks until he or she becomes a target for abuse. The drinker, however, may drink to avoid a violent outburst or, in some instances, strike someone instead of taking a drink. Abuse occurs in a more subtle form when a heavy drinker neglects or disturbs his or her family to such an extent that it causes severe damage. Such behavior may create constant pressure within the family, which builds up and eventually erupts into violence. In addition, quarrels that begin over a spouse's drinking can result in physical abuse.

Because there is such a high threshold of violence in American society, and victims often hide the fact that they have been abused because of fear of reprisal or lack of understanding by the community, treatment of the dual problem of alcoholism and spouse abuse can be difficult. Women often do not report the beatings they receive because of a sense of helplessness, despair and/or fear. Instead of seeing alcoholism or their husband's violence as the crux of the problem, they may feel that they deserved it and are powerless to change things, or blaming themselves, that they have failed in their marriage and are incompetent as wives and mothers. Both alcoholism and family violence often are part of a repetitive cycle from generation to generation. Abusers and alcoholics have learned to abuse and drink in order to escape

their problems and reassert control. Children from abusive families learn these coping patterns from the same individuals who teach them to love. Thus loving and abuse become linked in their minds. It is therefore important to involve the whole family in treatment.

A problem in the treatment of alcohol-related abuse is that programs designed to deal with battered victims frequently are not capable of addressing alcohol problems, and alcohol counselors often remain ignorant about the mechanics of family violence. The two problems tend to be treated separately, although they are closely linked. It is therefore important to look for alcohol problems when dealing with family violence. Treating an alcoholism problem will not necessarily stop the violence, but it will aid in the process.

Robert J. Ackerman, Ph.D., *Let Go and Grow: Recovery for Adult Children* (Pompano Beach, Florida: Health Communications, Inc., 1987).

Jerry Flanzer, "The Vicious Circle of Alcoholism and Family Violence," *Alcoholism* 1, no. 3 (January/February 1981): 30–32.

Margaret H. Hindman, "Family Violence," *Alcohol Health & Research World* 4, no. 1 (Fall 1979).

K. Leonard and T. Jacob, "Alcoholism and Family Violence," in *Handbook of Family Violence* (New York: Plenum, 1988): 383–406.

Brenda A. Miller and William R. Downs, "The Impact of Family Violence on the Use of Alcohol by Women," *Alcohol Health & Research World* 17, no 2 (1993).

Judy Seixas and Geraldine Youcha, *Children of Alcoholics* (New York: Crown, 1985).

M. A. Stewart and C. S. de Blois, "Is Alcoholism Related to Physical Abuse of Wives and Children?" (paper presented at the National Council on Alcoholism Annual Meeting, St. Louis, 1978).

Ruth Sanchez-Dirks, "Reflections on Family Violence," *Alcohol Health & Research World* 4, no. 1 (Fall 1979).

M. A. Straus, "A Sociological Perspective in the Prevention and Treatment of Wifebeating," *Battered Women*, ed. M. Roy (New York: Van Nostrand Reinhold, 1977).

spree   A period of drug use, particularly one of prolonged, excessive use. It is usually associated with addiction.

spree drinking   Drinking characterized by periods of sobriety lasting weeks or months and drinking binges that continue for days or weeks. This type of periodic drinking is more common in the U.S. than in a country like FRANCE, where there is a higher percentage of steady drinkers.

While a spree drinker may not consume more alcohol over the space of a year than a steady moderate drinker, he or she is at more of a health risk. For expectant mothers particularly, a drinking spree may result in impairment to the fetus (FETAL ALCOHOL SYNDROME). E. M. JELLINEK, categorized this type of drinking as EPSILON ALCOHOLISM.

Sri Lanka

Alcohol: Some medical authorities in Sri Lanka, formerly known as Ceylon, argue that alcoholism is the single most important health and social problem facing the country. Heavy drinking is concentrated among a small segment of the population, but a pattern of excessive consumption appears to be spreading as the country becomes more urbanized and less rigorous in the observance of Buddhist and Hindu strictures on drinking.

Of legal liquors, the preferred beverages are arrack, a spirit made from rice or coconut milk with an alcohol content of 35%, and toddy, a beverage made from molasses and various beers with an alcohol content of 6% to 8%. In addition various wines, brandies, whiskeys and gins are imported. However, illegally produced alcoholic beverages are estimated to equal half the amount of legal alcohol available, and production of these home brews, which have an alcohol content ranging from 20% to 60%, has doubled in recent years. As is true throughout the world, illegal liquor in Sri Lanka often is based on methylated spirits, contains hazardous amounts of distillation by-products and has gained wide acceptance because it sells at a cheaper price than licensed, taxed liquors.

Statistics on per capita consumption indicate the presence of a large proportion of abstainers and, consequently, a small proportion of heavy drinkers. These figures, however, do not take into account illegal alcoholic beverages, and there is ample evidence to suggest a greater alcoholism problem than official estimates acknowledge. Consumption of home-brewed alcohol is especially high among the lower classes, whose members are unlikely ever to seek professional help. Alcohol has had no traditional place in the country's social or ceremonial

occasions, but in recent times drinking has become common at such events. Weekend drinking is also on the rise in urban areas and at agrarian celebrations in rural locations.

There has been an increase in physical complications, sometimes resulting in coma or death, associated with drinking illegal alcoholic beverages. Because of the lack of special hospital facilities for the treatment of alcoholism in Sri Lanka, statistics on the incidence of alcoholism are unavailable, but it is known that the incidence is higher in the capital city of Colombo than in other areas of the country.

The sole authority charged with alcoholism-prevention policies in Sri Lanka is the Department of Excise. This agency, assisted by the police, concentrates entirely on the licensing of public drinking places and the taxation of legally produced liquors. Neither of these efforts has had much impact because of the number of private drinking clubs in the country and the easy availability of illegal alcoholic beverages. There are at present no public education programs regarding the dangers of alcohol abuse, and the Department of Health has no alcoholism-related activities.

Drugs other than alcohol: According to the USDS (U.S. Department of State, 1996), Sri Lanka appeared to be a relatively minor player in the international drug-trafficking world. Although preoccupied with battling internal insurgency, it was maintaining a strong position against drug trafficking. Domestic drug use was containable, and sufficient treatment facilities existed for those in need.

stacking The process of combining different types of anabolic steroids so as to obtain maximum effectiveness and/or minimize side effects.

Stadol A narcotic AGONIST-ANTAGONIST that contains butorphanol tartrate. It is a potent analgesic, equivalent to morphine and is used for moderate to severe pain. Because of its antagonist properties it should not be given to patients with a physical dependence on narcotics, and it is not recommended for those who have a history of excessive drug use as it has a potential for both abuse and dependency. Adverse reactions to Stadol include sweating, nausea and sedation; overdosage can cause respiratory depression. Supplied in vials for intravenous and intramuscular injection, the onset of effects appears within 10 minutes when administered intravenously and last from three to four hours.

status epilepticus   Repetitive convulsive seizures that follow each other with no intervening periods of consciousness. These can result from rapid withdrawal from anticonvulsant or sedative drugs, or may be spontaneous. *Status epilepticus* is also possible during use of amphetamines and cocaine. In the case of *grand mal status epilepticus* the seizures may persist for hours or even days, and can be fatal.

steam beer   A bottom-fermented lager beer distinguished by a bitter, "hoppy" flavor similar to that of the ales. Steam beer is fermented at lower-than-normal temperatures and naturally carbonated. It is named for the fact that during its unique fermentation process the fermentation vat builds up pressure like a steam engine.

Steam beer is the only kind of beer entirely indigenous to the U.S. It originated in San Francisco in the mid-19th century, when the Gold Rush brought a sudden population explosion to the area. Lacking ice for the chilling required in normal fermentation, California brew masters were forced to experiment with fermentation at higher temperatures, and in the process they discovered a beer especially prized for its flavor by the working class of San Francisco. Steam beers were hurt by the shift in American taste to lighter, paler, lager beers and the status that was attached to them around the turn of the century. The final blow to the industry came from Prohibition, and today steam beer is brewed and bottled by only one company, Anchor, in San Francisco.

Steam beer is brewed exclusively from barley malt, unlike most lager beers, which use other cereal grains. It also has a far higher hop content, about four times the average of other beers. After a bottom-fermentation yeast has been added to the hop wort, fermentation of steam beer takes place at temperatures between 65° and 75° F, as opposed to the 40° to 60° F range for most lagers, and the fermentation tank usually is an exceptionally shallow one. Carbonation is entirely accomplished by "krausening" (the introduction of carbolic acid from a newly fermented and active wort), rather than by injection of artificially produced carbon dioxide. The result is a distinctive but rather fragile beer, one subject to clouding when excessively chilled, and often drunk at warmer-than-usual temperatures for that reason.

stereotyping   There are many stereotypes associated with alcoholics and users of other drugs. Stereotypes of male alcoholics include: "Bowery bums," men who "fell hard" after a major life stress. Women alcoholics are often viewed as slovenly, a gender-based negative that underscores the danger of stereotyping. Stereotypes of drug-addicted individuals are equally bias-ridden. In actuality, these rigid pictures are inaccurate and oversimplified explanations for chemical dependency, which is what is only half-jokingly referred to as an "equal opportunity disease." Alcoholism and dependency on drugs other than alcohol is a complex biopsychosocial disease, with no universal cause and no single treatment method appropriate for all people effected by it. Stereotypes are especially unfortunate, since they keep many people either from acknowledging that they need help (the businessman who denies his drinking problem by reassuring himself that he is not "one of those guys sleeping in the gutter") or going to get the help they need (the housewife who will not seek help lest she lose the respect of her family and of the community).

stereotypy   Persistent and often mechanical repetition of senseless words or acts. It is characteristic of schizophrenics and is sometimes seen in amphetamine, phencyclidine and cocaine users, as well as in alcoholics.

still, patent still   An apparatus used to distill alcohol from a fermented mash. In its simplest form a still consists of a vessel in which to heat the fermented mash, a collector in which to catch the alcohol vapor then given off, an exterior tube in which to cool and thus recondense the alcohol vapor and a receiving vessel in which to collect the liquid distillate.

The pot still is the oldest, the most traditional and the simplest type currently in use. It produces intermittent batches of distillate according to the process described above. In the years prior to legalization of private distilling, the pot still was prized because it was small, easily dismantled for hiding and extremely portable. The product of the pot still, however, was and remains erratic—subject to unintentional variations in temperature—and relatively impure. This "low-wine"

Common Drugs: Symptoms of Abuse of Stimulants

Stimulants. Drugs that stimulate the central nervous system.
*Includes lookalike drugs that contain caffeine, phenylpropanolamine (PBA), and ephedrine

Drug Name	Street Names	Method of Use	Sign and Symptoms	Hazards of Use
Amphetamines, Dextroamphetamine, Methamphetamine, Biphetamine	Speed, Uppers, Pep Pills, Bennies, Ice, Dexies, Moth, Crank, Crystal, Black Beauties	Smoked or swallowed in pill or capsule form; also injected.	Excess activity, irritability, restlessness, nervousness, and mood swings. Dilated pupils; needle marks.	Loss of appetitie, weight loss. Hallucinations; paranoia.
Nicotine–found in cigarettes, cigars pipe, and chewing tobacco.	Coffin Nail, Butt, Smoke, Cigarettes, Cigars, Chow, Snuff	Smoked, inhaled, or chewed.	Smell of tobacco, stained teeth and yellow fingers. High carbon monoxide levels.	Cancers of the lung, throat, mouth, esophagus. Heart disease, emphysema.

Source: New York State Office of Alcoholism and Substance Abuse Services.

distillate is weak in strength and heavy in taste unless further rectified by costly secondary distillations. However, the pot still remains the favorite of those who want the strong character and variable qualities of a single distiller's product. Most pot-still products, especially Scotch whiskies, enter the commercial marketplace only after being blended with other, lighter distillates.

The patent still, or continuous still, is the type most used today. It was invented in 1831 by Aeneas Coffey, an Irish exciseman, and has remained essential to commercially efficient distillation. The key advantage offered by the patent still is the fact that it combines twin distillation columns for semi-independent double distillations that can operate without halt. Although the product lacks the strong character of pot-still distillates, it can be mass-produced. Patent-still spirits generally are blended with small amounts of pot-still spirits to create a product that is distinctive and yet light enough to appeal to a broad market.

still wine   A noncarbonated wine. Still wine refers to any wine except SPARKLING WINE, which is carbonated and not "still" when poured in a glass.

stimulants   Drugs that stimulate the central nervous system and increase the activity of the brain or spinal cord. They produce greater energy, increase alertness and produce a feeling of euphoria. Am-phetamines, antiobesity agents and cocaine are stimulants. Caffeine and NICOTINE also are classified as stimulants but have a lesser immediate effect on the body, though the long-term effects of nicotine are extremely grave. Nicotine actually stimulates as well as depresses the central nervous system. Far more people have died or suffered from diseases directly related to the highly addictive, albeit legal substance tobacco than from all of the other available licit and illicit stimulants and depressants combined.

stomach   The stomach is the hollow muscular organ located between the esophagus and the upper small intestine (duodenum). It stores and dilutes ingested food, secretes gastric juices containing enzymes and other substances important to digestion and nutrition, and contracts to further hasten the breakdown of food through agitation.

Sedatives depress the entire metabolic and digestive process. The abuse of alcohol compounds this general disruption by directly damaging the stomach because it increases hydrochloric acid secretion. Factors such as stress and malnutrition often accompany alcoholism and can also contribute to its deleterious effects.

The ingestion of alcohol has been widely associated with inflammation of the stomach, especially its mucous membrane. The actual mechanism of damage has not been conclusively established, but it is generally accepted that alcohol stimulates secretion of stomach acid. Solutions of less than 10% ethanol stimulate the gastric glands to produce acid, and ingestion of higher concentrations of alcohol produces gastric irritation and reduces appetite. In addition, alcohol delays the emptying time of the stomach. These factors in combination may cause a hyper-acidic condition that in time could lead to stomach disorder. The most frequent symptoms are nausea, vomiting and diarrhea.

Irritation of the mucous membrane is common after a period of prolonged drinking. In most cases this subsides after alcohol consumption ceases, but prolonged and excessive use of alcohol may result in more serious erosion of the stomach membrane, ranging from inflammation to ulceration and hemorrhage. Excessive drinking frequently is associated with heavy smoking and together these abuses may have an ADDITIVE or synergistic effect, causing chronic inflammation of the stomach.

Stimulants resemble alcohol in their effect on the stomach. Abuse of this kind of drug increases gastric acid secretion, which, in turn, increases the risk of ulcers. Some individuals are so sensitive to caffeine, cocaine or even to herbs (such as herbal teas, which for centuries have been prescribed for medicinal purposes) that even small amounts of these substances can make them nauseous or induce vomiting, particularly when ingested on an "empty stomach."

Narcotic drugs generally slow digestion by reducing gastric secretion and decreasing motility. Heroin can induce spasms in the stomach's smooth muscle; in fact, addicts often exhibit increased muscular tone in the smooth muscle of the stomach, duodenum and intestines. Opiates produce constipation and are used to treat diarrhea. Heroin addicts also are susceptible to viral infections such as tetanus, which often involves gastrointestinal bleeding. Hypermotility, gastrointestinal cramps, nausea, vomiting and anorexia are all symptoms of opiate withdrawal.

Synthetic derivatives of belladonna, stramonium (jimson weed) and henbane—anticholinergics employed for centuries as poisons and as major components of "witches brews"—have been used to reduce gastric secretion and peristalsis in the treatment of gastritis and peptic ulcers. Psychedelic drugs do not seem to share this effect; instead they sometimes can cause nausea and vomiting (particularly peyote).

Cannabis derivatives are being used medically to control the nausea, vomiting and anorexia associated with chemotherapy. A few reports of inflammation of the stomach after long-term heavy use of strong cannabis preparations have emerged from eastern countries, but it is not known if this is due to extensive cannabis use, to diet or to other factors.

Sidney Cohen, *The Substance Abuse Problems* (New York: Haworth, 1981).

Frederick G. Hofmann, *A Handbook on Drug and Alcohol Abuse* (New York: Oxford University Press, 1977).

Esteban Mezey, "Effects of Alcohol on the Gastrointestinal System," chap 36. in *Practice of Medicine* VII (Hagerstown, Md.: Harper & Row, 1970).

Ralph W. Richter, ed., *Medical Aspects of Drug Abuse* (New York: Harper & Row, 1975).

stout A very dark and sweet variety of ale traditionally common in England but now associated mostly with Ireland. The grain content of stout has a far higher proportion of malted barley than that of other ales, and the maltose (a soluble sugar produced by malting) gives stout its distinctive taste and color. Stout is top fermented and processed in ways that are otherwise indistinguishable from those used in making ale.

stramonium Also called jimson weed, an alkaloid found in the DATURA plant. It has deliriant effects similar to BELLADONNA and belongs to the same plant family.

stroke Research by Lois Caplan, M.D., Tufts University, Boston, reveals that using common "street drugs" can increase the risk of stroke dramatically, sometimes after just one dose. Most often linked to strokes are cocaine in any form or dose, heroin and stimulants that are supplied in tablets or capsules but that are ground into powder and injected intravenously.

Stroke occurs when sudden increases in blood pressure ruptures blood vessels. Particles from crushed pills may lodge in capillaries; talc, used to dilute drugs, will over-stimulate the immune system, causing blood vessels to spasm and shut off the brain's blood flow.

Tim Friend, "Street Drugs Can Raise Stroke Risk," *USA Today* (January 19, 1989): 5D.

strychnine An extremely dangerous and toxic central nervous system stimulant that affects the spinal cord first and the cerebrum last. A highly poisonous, colorless, crystalline alkaloid obtained from *Nux*

Preliminary Data—						
Survey Sample Sizes for All Respondents [to SAMHSA National Household Survey on Drug Abuse]						
Demographic Characteristics	**1979**	**1982**	**1985**	**1988**	**1990**	**1991**
TOTAL	**7,224**	**5,624**	**8,021**	**8,814**	**9,259**	**32,594**
AGE GROUP						
12–17	2,165	1,581	2,230	3,095	2,177	8,005
18–25	2,044	1,283	1,812	1,505	2,052	7,937
26–34	1,064	1,571	2,166	1,987	2,355	8,126
>35	1,951	1,189	1,813	2,227	2,675	8,526
RACE/ETHNICITY						
White	5,862	4,532	3,960	4,551	5,241	15,648
Black	798	673	1,950	1,888	1,842	8,050
Hispanic	354	299	2,003	2,193	1,915	7,916
Other	210	120	108	182	261	980
SEX						
Male	3,357	2,637	3,516	3,938	4,165	14,422
Female	3,867	2,987	4,505	4,876	5,094	18,172

NOTE: The population distributions for the 1993 through 1997 NHSDAs are post-stratified to population projections of totals based on the 1990 decennial census. The 1979 NHSDA used population projections based on the 1970 census; NHSDAs from 1982 through 1992 used projections based on the 1980 census. The change from one census base to another has little effect on estimated percentages reporting drug use, but may have a significant effect on estimates of number of drug users in some subpopulation groups.

NOTE: Estimates for 1979 through 1993 may differ from estimates for these survey years that were published in other NHSDA reports. The estimates shown here for 1979 through 1993 have been adjusted to improve their com-

Source: SAMHSA, Office of Applied Studies, National Household Survey on Drug Abuse.

(continued on next page)

vomica and other similar plants. Rarely used today, it can cause debility and paralysis. Its medicinal value has been questioned because of the narrow margin between its therapeutic and toxic action.

Students against Drunk Driving (SADD)   Headquartered in Marlboro, Massachusetts, this program encourages students not to drink and drive, but, if they find that they have taken alcohol, to feel free to call their parents for a ride home. The program built itself around a signed contract between students and their parents. Similar to most antialcohol advocacy groups, SADD now incorporates a focus on drugs as well.

subculture, drug   An alternative lifestyle that centers around knowledge of, use of and availability of drugs. Members of a drug subculture share norms of behavior that are disapproved of by society at large, yet endow them with a certain respect and admiration among adherents.

As of June 1998						
Aged 12 and Older, by Age Group, Race/Ethnicity, and Sex: 1979–1997						
Demographic Characteristics	**1992**	**1993**	**1994**	**1995**	**1996**	**1997**
TOTAL	**28,832**	**26,489**	**17,809**	**17,747**	**18,269**	**24,505**
AGE GROUP						
12–17	7,254	6,978	4,698	4,595	4,538	7,844
18–25	7,721	5,531	3,706	3,963	4,366	6,239
26–34	7,516	8,342	5,223	5,213	5,262	4,387
>35	6,341	5,638	4,182	3,976	4,103	6,035
RACE/ETHNICITY						
White	14,080	12,478	8,663	8,459	8,481	12,443
Black	6,511	6,183	4,010	4,208	4,372	4,639
Hispanic	7,148	6,894	4,706	4,599	4,841	6,259
Other	1,093	934	430	481	575	1,164
SEX						
Male	12,988	12,059	7,950	7,652	7,774	10,836
Female	15,844	14,430	9,859	10,095	10,496	13,669

parability with estimates based on the new version of the NHSDA instrument that was fielded in 1994 and subsequent NHSDAs. For 1979 and 1982, estimates are not shown (as indicated by —) where (a) the relevant data were not collected, or (b) the data for those drugs were based on measures that differed appreciably from those used in the other survey years. Consequently, adjustments to the 1979 and 1982 data were made only for those drugs whose measures were comparable to those in the other survey years.

Because of the methodology used to adjust the 1979 through 1993 estimates, some logical inconsistency may exist between estimates for a given drug within the same survey year. For example, some adjusted estimates of past year use may appear to be greater than adjusted lifetime estimates. These inconsistencies tend to be small, rare and not statistically significant.

sublimaze A narcotic analgesic that contains fentanyl and whose activity is similar to that of MORPHINE and meperidine, but it is much faster-acting and its effect does not last as long. It is used as a pre- and postoperative sedation supplement. A potent analgesic, it has a high potential for abuse and dependency.

substance abuse A general term used to describe the abuse of drugs, including nicotine and alcohol. It refers to continuous and excessive use of a substance or chemical, often for other than its intended purpose, which results in emotional, cognitive, physical or social impairment of the user, the user's family or community. The term "substance abuse" refers to the inappropriate consumption of both illegal and legal substances, including prescription medications. In the case of a highly toxic carcinogen such as nicotine, even limited habitual usage would be appropriately classified as substance abuse.

Preliminary Data—
Adjusted 1979–1993 Estimates

Survey Sample Sizes for All Respondents [to SAMHSA National Household

Demographic Characteristics	12–17		18–25	
	1996	1997	1996	1997
TOTAL	4,538	7,844	4,366	6,239
RACE/ETHNICITY				
White	2,092	3,970	1,858	2,966
Black	1,073	1,346	1,134	1,062
Hispanic	1,225	2,086	1,213	1,863
Other	148	442	161	348
SEX				
Male	2,252	3,871	1,765	2,756
Female	2,286	3,973	2,601	3,483
POPULATION DENSITY[1]				
Large Metro	2,098	4,072	2,098	3,408
Small Metro	1,544	2,289	1,426	1,813
Nonmetro	896	1,483	842	1,018
REGION				
Northeast	719	834	697	618
North Central	916	992	838	731
South	1,810	2,226	1,751	1,733
West	1,093	3,783	1,080	3,157
ADULT EDUCATION[1]				
<High School	N/A	N/A	1,184	1,580
High School Grad	N/A	N/A	1,567	2,254
Some College	N/A	N/A	1,163	1,842
College Graduate	N/A	N/A	452	563
CURRENT EMPLOYMENT[2]				
Full-time	N/A	N/A	1,889	2,922
Part-time	N/A	N/A	927	1,257
Unemployed	N/A	N/A	432	602
Other[3]	N/A	N/A	1,118	1,458

N/A: Not applicable.

[1] Population density is based on 1990 MSA classifications and their 1990 Census of Population counts.

Source: SAMHSA, Office of Applied Studies, National Household Survey on Drug Abuse, 1996 and 1997.

(continued on next page)

As of June 1998

Survey on Drug Abuse] Aged 12 and Older, by Age Group and Demographic Characteristics: 1996 and 1997

26–34 Years		35 Years and Older		Total	
1996	**1997**	**1996**	**1997**	**1996**	**1997**
5,262	**4,387**	**4,103**	**6,035**	**18,269**	**24,505**
2,614	1,939	1,917	3,568	8,481	12,443
1,134	1,184	1,031	1,047	4,372	4,639
1,334	1,134	1,069	1,176	4,841	6,259
180	130	86	244	575	1,164
2,151	1,766	1,606	2,443	7,774	10,836
3,111	2,621	2,497	3,592	10,495	13,669
2,775	2,301	2,072	3,183	9,043	12,964
1,582	1,308	1,285	1,727	5,837	7,137
905	778	746	1,125	3,389	4,404
954	684	778	760	3,148	2,905
1,036	762	735	770	3,525	3,255
1,986	1,765	1,655	1,830	7,202	7,554
1,286	1,176	935	2,675	4,394	10,791
1,085	918	1,135	1,474	3,404	3,972
1,730	1,510	1,317	1,821	4,614	5,585
1,221	1,093	846	1,344	3,230	4,279
1,226	866	805	1,396	2,483	2,825
3,400	2,856	2,245	3,061	7,534	8,839
558	450	395	553	1,880	2,260
322	291	205	248	959	1,141
982	790	1,258	2,173	3,358	4,421

[2] Data on adult education and current employment not shown for persons aged 12–17. Estimates for both adult education and current employment are for persons aged >18.
[3] Retired, disabled, homemaker, student, "other."

Substance Abuse and Mental Health Services Administration (SAMHSA)   SAMHSA is the agency responsible for administering federal funding initiatives for prevention, intervention and treatment programs dealing with mental health, alcohol and drug use. SAMHSA is made up of three agencies: the Center for Substance Abuse Prevention, the Center for Substance Abuse Treatment and the Center for Mental Health Services.

Substance Abuse Narcotics Education Program (SANE)   A law enforcement and education effort similar to PROJECT DARE, in which police officers help to provide classes with presentations on drug abuse.

succinylcholine   A central nervous system depressant that acts as a skeletal muscle relaxant during surgery.

Sudan   The largest country in Africa, Sudan has a population of about 17 million. The Muslim religion, embraced by 85% of the population, is the single greatest restraint on drinking in the country, for the Koran prohibits consumption of alcoholic beverages and no Muslim in Sudan is permitted to hold a license for a drinking establishment or liquor store. As a result of the Koran's prohibition, there is virtually no drinking among the female Muslim population, but among the male Muslim population drinking may be on the rise lately, indicating that this religious ban may be losing its effect. Fifteen percent of the Sudanese population consists of Christians and persons belonging to no recognized sect on which the religious law against drinking has no effect.

The predominant legally produced liquors in Sudan are beer and sherry, and demand for both exceeds supply. Because of limited production and distribution problems restricting the availability of these beverages, there is widespread unregulated production—and consumption—of two illegal alcoholic beverages: marisa, a fermented sorghum, and aragi, a liquor distilled from either date or sorghum mashes. Marisa, which has alcohol content ranging from 1.8% to 5.1%, is common throughout the country. The date variety of aragi, with an alcohol content as high as 49%, is especially common in the northern districts of the country; the *aragi* distilled from sorghum has a lower alcohol content. Consumption of illegally produced aragi is an especially serious health problem in Sudan because this beverage often contains toxic by-products resulting from crude distillation processes.

Studies of drinking patterns in Sudan suggest that the drinking population is small and that excessive drinking is occasional. One survey of Khartoum province found that the rate of alcoholism among the male population was 1.8%, that less than half the male population drank and that of these drinkers only about 13% drank to excess. (Drinking to excess in this context meant taking a drink daily, for most drinkers surveyed drank only once or twice each month.) These statistics are thought to be above the national average because they include the country's largest urban population. Consequently the rate of alcoholism for the entire country is estimated to be somewhere below 1.8%.

Even this limited drinking, however, has a significant effect on the nation. Most excessive drinkers in Sudan suffer from symptoms of liver cirrhosis aggravated by endemic diseases, a high percentage of social drinkers suffer physical complications from illegally distilled alcohols, and as a result one-quarter of the hospital admissions in the entire country are either directly or indirectly related to alcohol abuse.

The only efforts to combat alcohol abuse in Sudan are nongovernmental, and it is generally agreed that what legal penalties exist for alcohol-related crimes are rarely enforced. The nation's general policy toward alcohol abuse is to encourage abstinence on religious rather than social grounds. Religious groups have begun to contribute to antialcohol campaigns, particularly in the country's most heavily populated areas to the north. These organizations, however, remain the sole source of preventative measures.

suicide   Suicide, the intentional taking of one's own life, generally is the result of a depressive state. Therefore, medical professionals must monitor individuals closely who are undergoing postwithdrawal depression symptoms from phencyclidine, amphetamines, cocaine or alcohol.

There are "accidental" as well as intentional suicides. A synergistic effect can be produced when depressant DRUGS are taken together; sometimes with fatal results. Combining drugs can also impair judgment and/or cause confusion—an individual may take additional and dangerous doses of a drug either without concern for, or without memory of, previous doses. The interaction of alcohol with other drugs is responsible for a large number of suicides and accidental deaths. Data from the Drug Abuse Warning Network (DAWN) indicated that in 1991 there were 175,203 emergency room drug-related episodes out of which .03% patients died and 69% were admitted to hospital inpatient units. Alcohol in combination with other drugs accounted for the highest rate of attempted suicide episodes (27.7%). The second leading cause was the non-narcotic acetaminophen (an aspirin alternative such as Tylenol) (14.1%), while the third highest rate of reported suicide cases was caused by aspirin overdose (9.7%). The rate of suicide attempts is higher for women than men, but the rate of completed suicides is higher for men. Alcoholic women are more likely to attempt suicide than nonalcoholic women, and the rate of completed suicides by female alcoholics is 23 times greater than that of nonalcoholic women.

Alcohol: Alcoholics of both genders are at particularly high risk of committing suicide. Although estimates of the level of risk vary, at least one study reported it to be 30 times greater than the risk of suicide among the general population. In a 30-year prospective study of 1,312 alcoholics, 88 (16%) of the 537 deaths were definite suicides. Alcoholics who commit suicide make more attempts than nonalcoholics who commit suicide, and alcoholic suicide attempts more closely resemble actual suicides than do nonalcoholic attempts. These findings suggest that alcoholics who try to kill themselves form a significant part of the population that eventually commits suicide. Studies show that between 15% and 64% of those who attempt suicide and up to 80% of completed suicides were committed by those who were drinking at the time. Other studies cited that 20% to 36% of suicide victims have a history of alcohol abuse or were drinking shortly before their suicides.

Barbiturates: Barbiturates are frequently responsible for suicide attempts, particularly among women. They are most often prescribed for insomnia, which is a likely indicator of depression. In a nontolerant person a small amount can constitute a lethal dose; consequently, doctors carefully prescribe no more than two week's supply at one time. In spite of this provision, there are no guarantees against suicide attempts. Accidental deaths from barbiturates combined with alcohol (both sedative drugs) are even more common than planned suicides using barbiturates alone.

The benzodiazepine derivatives, which are prescribed as tranquilizers, are very often used in suicide attempts. Valium, a minor tranquilizer, is one of the most widely prescribed drugs. The lethal dose of Valium alone is not known, and individuals ingesting 200 times the average dose have survived. Completed suicides involving Valium usually are a result of its being combined with another depressant.

Amphetamines and hallucinogens: Attempted or completed suicides from amphetamines and hallucinogens are generally not the result of an overdose of a particular drug, but are due to a psychotic state induced by taking the drug in the first place. When an individual's controls are diminished and a paranoid reaction sets in, he or she may impulsively attempt suicide. Accidental suicides have occurred when a person under the effects of a hallucinogen, particularly LSD, imagined that he could, for example, stop traffic or fly through the air.

A. Adelstein, "Alcoholism and Mortality," *Population Trends* 7 (1977).

M. Berglund, "Suicide in Alcoholism," *Archives of General Psychiatry* 41 (1984): 888–891.

Glen Evans & Norman L. Farberow, Ph.D., *The Encyclopedia of Suicide* (New York: Facts On File, 1988): 95–98.

D. M. Gallant, *Alcoholism: A Guide to Diagnosis, Intervention, and Treatment* (New York: W.W. Norton, 1987).

Enoch Gordis, M.D., ed., *Seventh Special Report to the U.S. Congress on Alcohol and Health* chapter 7 (Rockville, Md.: National Institute on Alcohol Abuse and Alcoholism [NIAAA], 1990).

A. Medhus, "Mortality among Female Alcoholics," *Scandinavian Journal of Social Medicine* 3 (1975): 111–115.

Robert O'Brien and Morris Chafetz, M.D., *The Encyclopedia of Alcoholism* (New York: Facts On File, 1983).

Division of Epidemiology and Prevention Research, *Annual Emergency Room Data 1991, Data from the Drug Abuse Warning Network* I, no. 11-A (Rockville, Md.: National Institute on Drug Abuse 1991).

supply reduction   Policies designed to reduce illicit drug use through legislation and police actions that reduce or eliminate the availability of that drug. Supply reduction can have unintended negative consequences (such as crime waves), as prices rise and addicts are pressed to pay more for their drugs; or cross-addiction by individuals who, unable to obtain their drug of choice, will switch to another drug of abuse. (See DEMAND REDUCTION and HARM REDUCTION.)

supra-additive   The synergistic or potentiating interaction of drugs whereby the effect of the two drugs in combination is greater than it would be if the effects were ADDITIVE. The chemical properties of one drug is causing the other drug to metabolize differently than it would if it were taken alone, thereby increasing its effects dramatically. (See SYNERGY.)

Supreme Court drug decisions, U.S.   In 1966 the Supreme Court ruled that compulsory blood tests are bodily searches. It said that the Fourth Amendment applied to such searches and that a compulsory blood test could be conducted only if there is "a clear indication that in fact . . . evidence will be found."

Prisons are the only institutions that have the Supreme Court's permission to conduct blanket searches. The decision stemmed from a 1984 federal case in New York's Southern District Court— *Storms v. Coughlin*. The Court determined that the constitutional right concerning privacy of prisoners gives way when it conflicts with prison security needs.

The only Supreme Court decision concerning the right to search students in public school involved a Piscataway, New Jersey, student. In *New Jersey v. T.L.O.*, January 1985, a teacher reported the case of a female student found smoking cigarettes in the girls' room. The student was in violation of a school rule that permitting smoking in designated areas only. The girl denied the charge and the assistant vice principal thereupon opened the student's purse and discovered a package of rolling papers. Suspecting possession of marijuana cigarettes, or "joints," the assistant vice principal then searched the student's purse and uncovered evidence of drug dealing. The Supreme Court stated that the Fourth Amendment prohibits unreasonable searches and seizures in public schools. But what constitutes "reasonable" depends upon the context in which a search is conducted. The assistant vice principal was deemed within his rights in searching the purse, because he had reasonable grounds to believe the student had "violated or [was] violating either the law or the rules of the school." In another case involving students, in 1995 the U.S. Supreme Court ruled that random drug testing of high school athletes was constitutional.

In regards to drug testing in the workplace, the Supreme Court has upheld an employer's right to randomly test employees. On December 1, 1986, the Supreme Court refused to hear a challenge brought by jockeys concerning the requirement that they submit to random testing. Some experts maintain that this ruling doesn't uphold mandatory drug testing and believe that the question one day must be heard and settled by the Supreme Court.

In March 1989 the Supreme Court upheld, by a 7-to-2 vote, the constitutionality of government regulations that require railroad crews involved in accidents to submit to prompt urinalysis and blood tests. The justices also upheld, 5 to 4, the legality of urine tests for U.S. Customs Service employees seeking drug enforcement posts. The decisions lent weight to the push by the Bush Administration for increased urine testing in the workplace.

A 1986 executive order by former president Reagan authorized drug testing throughout the federal government. Opponents of government screening tests argue that it is an "unreasonable search," prohibited by the Fourth Amendment.

Some legal scholars are concerned with the Court's direction in future cases. "Will it be limited to safety-sensitive positions, or broadened to include any public employee who is a role model?" asks Michigan Law Professor Yale Komisar. Other experts doubt that the Supreme Court will uphold random drug tests for a broad spectrum of government employees. Regarding the question of whether or not the government has the right to seize the assets of persons involved in federal drug crimes, in 1996 the Supreme Court ruled that the government did have the right and that this would not be considered double jeopardy. (See DRUG TESTING and LAUNDERING.)

Gilda Berger, *Drug Testing* (New York: Franklin Watts, 1987).

Alain Sanders, "A Boost for Drug Testing" *Time* (April 3, 1989): 62.

surgery Surgeons must be aware of a number of factors when operating on alcoholics/users of other drugs. The effects of general anesthesia can potentiate those of a number of other drugs (including alcohol), combining with them to produce potentially dangerous synergistic reactions. (See SYNERGY.) Chronic alcoholics, or individuals addicted to other sedative drugs, may have a CROSS-TOLERANCE to general anesthesia, requiring greater amounts to induce sleep. They also may undergo a prolonged second stage of anesthesia after the administration of inhalation anesthetics. In addition, there is the possibility of myocardial depression and altered blood volume in such patients.

Often drug-addicted individuals, most commonly alcoholics, appear healthy although their liver functions are severely impaired—a condition that can seriously affect the postoperative course. Even in the absence of liver damage, increased bleeding due to depleted platelet counts frequently complicates operations on drug-addicted patients. (Platelets, an important factor in blood clotting, are often impaired by poor nutrition and lack of overall self-maintenance common with substance users.)

DELIRIUM TREMENS (THE D.T.'S) is a serious potential complication specifically for alcoholic patients and some barbiturates users. Patients who drink the equivalent of one or more pints of whiskey per day, or who have a previous history of delirium tremens, are likely to develop this condition after the operation. The D.T.'s usually start within 48 to 72 hours after cessation of drinking, a period when it is wise to avoid operating on known heavy drinkers. (See DENTISTRY.)

Albert B. Lowenfels, Michael Rohman and Kinichi Shibutani, "Surgical Consequences of Alcoholism," *Surgery, Gynecology, and Obstetrics* 131 (July 1970): 129–138.

susceptibility Certain individuals may show a strong readiness to turn to alcohol or other mood-altering substances in times of stress. Such people are said to be susceptible to chemical dependency. "Susceptibility," however, is a vague term that does little to clarify or explain alcoholism/addiction to other drugs. GENETIC, hormonal, cultural, psychological and environmental factors all contribute to one's susceptibility to alcohol and other drug use, and one might be more susceptible at certain stressful periods during one's life than during other, more stable cycles. Physical conditions may also increase one's susceptibility. Vitamin deficiency and lack of a healthy balanced diet, exercise and sleeping regimen can all lead to susceptibility to substances that may temporarily appear to correct the imbalance. Overworking and/or sleep deprivation would increase one's susceptibility to caffeine, amphetamine, cocaine or other stimulant use for example.

Sweden In Sweden, as in most European countries, alcohol is the most widely abused substance. An estimated 10% of the population suffers from alcoholism. By contrast, according to a 1993 study by the Swedish government, approximately 14,000–20,000 people (about 2% of the population) used drugs other than alcohol, daily. Of these drugs, cannabis and amphetamines are the two most commonly used, although heroin and LSD use are significant enough to merit government concern. According to Thomas Nordegren of the nation's Committee on Health Education, 16 people die each day on average as a direct result of drug addiction.

Alcohol: In 1997, *World Drink Trends 1995* showed Sweden as 32nd out of 53 countries in per capita annual consumption of "pure alcohol." The average consumption per capita (for those aged 15 and above) was 5.3 liters, slightly greater than the amount consumed in neighboring Norway (4.1 liters), but less than consumption in the U.S. (6.8 liters).

Sweden has a long, impressive history of concern for abusers of drugs, including alcohol. In the 19th century some 400 temperance societies were in existence in Sweden, and this continuing voluntary movement receives government assistance and approval. Between 1922 and 1955 the government operated a passbook rationing system to moderate alcohol consumption. During that time men over 25 years of age were entitled to purchase up to three liters of spirits per month, while women of the same age could obtain that amount over a three-month period. Rationing was enforced by the adoption in 1922 of the Bratt system under which a state-owned company, Vin-Spritcentralen, was given control of all alcohol sales. This plan was adopted immediately after all-out prohibition was vetoed.

Parliament abandoned the rationing system in 1955 and transferred the burden of restricting alcohol use to the National Tax Board. Taxes were imposed according to the alcohol content of a beverage. (Today taxes on alcoholic beverages account for about 7% of the tax revenues.) The state-controlled company, Systembolaget, was given a monopoly on the retailing of alcoholic beverages, while Vin-Spritcentralen became responsible for the importation and wholesale trade.

Before 1978 public drunkenness was treated as a crime and offenders were arrested. Parliament then adopted a new strategy and legislation was enacted treating alcohol and other drug use as social problems rather than as criminal acts. Now, if offenders are taken into custody, they are dealt with leniently and usually turned over to counselors rather than jailers. The Government's primary task has been to educate the public about drug use and treatment for drug addiction. Public education is coordinated through a number of agencies, including a central Crime Prevention Council, which gathers statistics on alcohol and other drug use. The National Board of Education reports on drug use from sixth graders to high school sophomores; the National Defense Research Institute obtains similar information for 18-year-olds; and the Stockholm police are permitted to check for needle marks on people taken into custody. Armed with accurate statistics, the Government has been able to target segments of the population for special attention, such as the nearly three-fifths of all incarcerated criminals who are drug users.

Since 1978 alcoholism has been addressed as a small part of a larger social and sometimes medical problem. Drunk driving however, is taken very seriously; convicted offenders whose blood tests show an alcohol concentration of 1.5 promille or more may be incarcerated for 12 months.

Drugs other than alcohol: By the 1960s, Sweden had developed significant problems around abuse of drugs other than alcohol. Intravenous injection of central nervous system stimulants and opiates, smoking of marijuana and hashish, sniffing of solvents (mostly by teenagers) and the abuse of amphetamines and tranquilizers (which hit the market in the 1930s) were prevalent. With the failure of a brief attempt at drug legalization, the Swedish Parliament formed a tough plan of action in 1968 to cope with drug as well as alcohol abuse. Police and customs units were strengthened to keep drugs off the streets and out of the country. Stricter penal laws

were instituted, aimed at limiting imports from drug-producing countries in Asia, Europe and North Africa. The Government took an increasingly active role in international efforts to stem drug smuggling, including participation in the Single Convention of Narcotic Drugs established in 1961.

The addicts' "escape into abuse" is thought to result from Sweden's increasing industrialization and its accompanying ills: unemployment and the extreme pressure to increase productivity and efficiency. Because government statistics show that drug users are likely to attend school irregularly and eventually turn to criminal activities, parliament is committed to help alleviate the problem at its source. Offenders thought by police to pose a threat to themselves or others may be taken into immediate custody and given compulsory treatment and counseling on an intensive and/or long-term basis. Although forced into such programs, the long-range goal is for addicts to take voluntary control over their own recovery. As noted in the introduction to Sweden's Care of Alcoholics and Drug Abusers Act of 1982: "The possibility to inflict treatment on a person without his consent must never lead to the consequences that society takes over the individual's responsibility for his own life."

Sweden has also tightened up its laws against domestic drug dealers. Criminal acts are classified as misdemeanors, offenses and felonies, in ascending order of seriousness. Narcotics felonies are considered among the most serious offenses in Sweden's criminal justice system and convicted drug felons can be sentenced to a minimum of 10 years in prison. Wiretapping is now legal when considered necessary to track down drug dealers and there are stringent controls over the importation and sale of hypodermic syringes and needles used by "mainliners."

Treatment: Treatment has become a major element in Sweden's crackdown. This policy has resulted from the government's view that drug addicts and alcoholics are people whose abuse is often a consequence of their psychological and social difficulties.

In 1982 *The Fact Sheets on Sweden: Alcohol and Drug Abuse* noted Sweden's considerable help to people seeking to kick their abuse problems. The nation's mental hospitals include outpatient drug treatment units and beds in drug-addiction wards. Treatment facilities, including those in many prison wards, have specially trained addiction-care teams. Boarding institutes provide beds for addicts. Beds and care are also available at a number of private homes. Abusers almost ready to re-enter society can go to "halfway homes," where they associate almost exclusively with addicts and ex-addicts and receive the peer support needed to make the transition back to the "straight" world.

Swedish Council for Information on Alcohol and Other Drugs, "Alcohol Policy in Sweden," 2nd ed. (Stockholm, 1982).

Brewers and Licensed Retailers Association, *1993 Annual Report* (London, 1995).

Bureau of Narcotics and Law Enforcement Affairs, "Care of Alcoholics and Drug Abusers (Certain Cases) Act," Prepared by the Ministry of Social Affairs, International Secretariat. (Stockholm: Departementens Reprocentral, 1982).

"Fact Sheets on Sweden" (Stockholm: The Swedish Institute,: September 1982).

Narcotics Group of the Crime Prevention Council of the National Swedish Board of Health and Welfare, Committee on Health Education, *Facts on Narcotics and Narcotics Abuse* (Stockholm: Liberforlag, 1979).

Thomas Nordegren, "Alcohol and Alcoholism in Sweden," part of *Social Change in Sweden* Prepared for the Swedish Information Service, series no. 23 (New York: Swedish Consulate General, 1981).

Thomas Nordegren, "Narcotics Abuse and Care of Drug Addicts in Sweden: Problems and Development Tendencies," in *Social Change in Sweden* 21 (1980).

Report On the Alcohol and Drug Situation in Sweden 81 (Stockholm: Swedish Council for Information on Alcohol and Other Drugs, 1981).

sweet mash   A grain mixture used in preparation of the mash, or "wash," from which bourbon is distilled. The grain content of bourbon is at least 51% corn (Indian maize), with the remainder made up of rye and malted barley. In sweet mash bourbon there is an unusually high proportion of malted barley, which is rich in maltose, a soluble sugar that enhances fermentation by combining with yeast to produce alcohol. The chief alternative to sweet mash is SOUR MASH, in which a residue from a previous distillation is added as an aid to fermentation in the grain wash of bourbon.

Switzerland

Alcohol: Switzerland's consistently high rank worldwide in annual per capita consumption of alcohol may seem a little incongruous, given the country's reputation for precision, dispassion and neutrality. A progressive attitude toward alcoholism and alcohol-related problems, however, is a historical tradition in Switzerland: the first treatment center for alcoholics in Switzerland opened in Zurich before 1900, and the Swiss temperance movement is one of the oldest in Europe.

In the early 19th century the most prevalent drinking pattern was consumption of potato schnapps, a distilled alcohol that was produced in abundance because of surplus potato crops. When the Swiss Federal State was established in 1848, an indirect effect of its new constitution was increased availability of cheap potato schnapps because of liberalized trade controls. To change that situation, the government in 1885 introduced a constitutional amendment that imposed heavy taxes on potato schnapps, restricted sales of the liquor and created a state monopoly on its production. The result was an agricultural shift from potato production toward fruit production and a consequent rise in the distillation of various cider and fruit schnapps. In 1930 these products also were brought under the state alcohol monopoly and made subject to sales taxes and restrictions.

In modern times, the revenues of the state alcohol monopoly are distributed equally among the federal and canton, or provincial, authorities. The cantons are required to devote 10% of their share to programs aimed at combating alcoholism. Treatment of alcoholism in Switzerland is somewhat inhibited by the government's preference for a broad-based scientific, educational and economic initiative to reduce alcohol consumption over the more traditional public health model. Federal intervention is itself inhibited by the structure of the Swiss constitution, which grants some autonomy to individual cantons.

Three agencies in Switzerland address the problem of alcoholism: the Federal Commission Against Alcoholism, formed in 1947; the Swiss National Science Foundation, created in 1952, which has devoted a significant proportion of its energies to the country's alcohol-abuse problem; and the Swiss Institute for the Prevention of Alcoholism. Working in cooperation to emphasize the social causes of alcoholism, these agencies have the avowed purpose of creating "an intact alcohol legislation which is above all always aimed at the greatest possible efficiency on behalf of public welfare."

Drugs other than alcohol: The *International Narcotics Control Strategy Report March 1996* has described the status of narcotics in Switzerland as follows:

> *The Swiss government condemns the use of narcotics. Despite some doubt of its effectiveness, Swiss narcotics policy continues to rest on four pillars: prevention; therapy and rehabilitation; HARM REDUCTION; and law enforcement.*
>
> *Overall use of heroin and cocaine appears to be declining in Switzerland, but authorities are concerned about the rising abuse of hallucinogens—especially "ECSTASY (MDMA)." Switzerland pioneered methadone treatment programs in the late 1970s and adopted one of the first needle-exchange programs in the late 1980s to control the spread of the HIV virus. In 1994, shortly before closing one controversial and ultimately disastrous drug-control experiment (the notorious open-air drug market in a Zurich park), Switzerland introduced another controversial drug rehabilitation program, that includes delivery of narcotics to hard-core users under strict medical control. Under this program, addicts can obtain heroin, methadone, and morphine.*

Despite active government efforts to control the flow, Switzerland remains a critical transit point for narcotics bound for the European market.

Brewers and Licensed Retailers Association, *1993 Annual Report* (London: 1995).

United States Dept. of State, Bureau for International Narcotics and Law Enforcement Affairs, *International Narcotics Control Strategy Report March 1996.*

Hoeveel alcoholhoude dranken worden er in de wereld gedronken? (How many alcoholic beverages are being consumed throughout the world?), 27th ed. (Schiedam, Netherlands: Produktschap Voor Gedistilleerde Dranken, 1987).

sympathomimetic amines   Drugs that act on the autonomic nervous system that controls involuntary muscles. Sympathomimetic drugs are used in the treatment of a number of conditions, including bronchial asthma, glaucoma, respiratory failure, mucous membrane congestion and shock. Some of these drugs also act systemically as stimulants of the central nervous system, and they are the ones most sought after by drug users.

symptomatic alcoholism   Alcoholism that is secondary to another medical problem, such as psychoneurosis, psychosis or mental deficiency.

symptomatic drinking   Excessive drinking that is used as a way of handling tensions or unconscious problems. Also this can refer to drinking patterns that are symptoms of some mental disorder other than alcoholism.

synalgos   An analgesic containing drocode, promethazine hydrochloride, aspirin, caffeine and phenacetin. Used for the relief of minor to moderately severe pain in situations when a mild sedative also is needed; it may be habit-forming and has abuse potential. Tolerance, along with physical and psychological dependence, can occur. When taken with alcohol or other central nervous system depressants it has an ADDITIVE EFFECT.

Synanon   Founded in 1958 by Charles E. Dederich, the Synanon Church operates communities where people can learn a better way to live. Anyone with a problem of drug or alcohol addiction, delinquency, criminal behavior or any other character disorder is eligible for admission. There is no set entrance fee but individuals who can afford to contribute to their care are expected to do so. The first of its kind, Synanon once served as a model for numerous other therapeutic communities in the U.S. and abroad. Synanon communities still are located on two rural properties, one in central California and the other in Houston, Texas. The Synanon Church also acquires and distributes food to charitable organizations and has established the Synanon College, a California-approved vocational college offering a wide variety of classes.

Synar Amendment   Federal legislation passed in 1992 that requires states to have and enforce laws banning the sale and distribution of tobacco products to anyone under the age of 18.

Syndrome X   In *Licit & Illicit Drugs* (Little, Brown and Company, 1972), Edward M. Brecher and the editors of *Consumer Reports* used the term "Syndrome X" to describe the high incidence of deaths reportedly due to heroin overdose. Before 1943 few, if any, deaths among addicts were attributed to heroin overdose. During the 1950s, however, nearly 50% of such deaths were attributed to this cause, and by 1970, when some 800 addicts in New York City died, the figure had risen to 80%. According to Mr. Brecher, it is unlikely that these deaths were due to heroin overdose for several reasons. First, it is known that even large doses of heroin are not likely to kill. Second, most deaths attributed to heroin overdose occurred very suddenly; in true cases of heroin overdose the initial symptoms are stupor and lethargy, generally followed by coma—a process that can take up to 12 hours. Death can be forestalled effectively by administering a NARCOTIC ANTAGONIST, such as NALOXONE. And, third, says Brecher, most addicts whose deaths are reportedly due to overdose are individuals who have developed a tolerance to the drug so that even an extremely large dose of heroin would not necessarily cause their deaths.

If a person is known to be addicted to a particular drug and is suddenly found dead, the natural suspicion and assumption is that the drug caused the death. If a heroin addict dies with the syringe still in his arm, or witnesses report that just minutes before he died he was injecting heroin, the obvious conclusion is death by overdose. Such evidence would be circumstantial, however. According to Brecher "a conscientious search of the United States medical literature throughout recent decades has failed to turn up a single scientific paper reporting that heroin overdose . . . is in fact a cause of death among American addicts."

Brecher suggests several possible causes for Syndrome X deaths. Clearly, heroin itself could not be the cause, since the high incidence of deaths among addicts is a recent phenomenon and heroin has been used for a long time. The first Syndrome X deaths occurred in the early 1940s, when quinine first was added to heroin after an outbreak of malaria hit New York City addicts. More deaths occurred in the 1950s, when addicts began taking central nervous system depressants, especially barbiturates and alcohol. Previously, addicts generally had refrained from alcohol use, but after World War II, when heroin was in short supply many turned to alcohol as a substitute. A 1967 New York study involving the deaths of 588 addicts found alcohol to be present in 43% of the cases. At the Haight-Ashbury Medical Clinic in San Francisco, 37% of the addicts attending used barbiturates when withdrawal symptoms began; 24% used alcohol for the same reason.

A 1966 study by Dr. Milton Helpern, Chief Medical Examiner for New York City, found that massive pulmonary edema (flooding of the lungs with fluid) was a conspicuous condition in alleged overdose deaths, and that these deaths occurred very suddenly. It is these two characteristics that have been labeled Syndrome X. Dr. Michael M. Baden, an associate of Dr. Helpern, suggested that the majority of deaths are due to "an acute reaction to the intravenous injection of the heroin-quinine-sugar mixture" and to classify them as heroin overdose is a misnomer. There were also other factors suggesting that the deaths were not due to heroin overdose: most of the victims were long-term addicts, a fact which rules out the possibility that they had not developed tolerance; in some cases a number of addicts used the same heroin and only one died; there was an absence of high heroin concentration in tissue surrounding the point of injection and no evidence of heroin overdose in the urine of victims; and there was no evidence that the heroin was any "purer" than that which the addicts were accustomed to.

In 1970 two noted entertainers died of what was reported as "heroin overdose." The musician Jimi Hendrix was known to use both barbiturates and alcohol, and the singer Janis Joplin was known to be a heavy drinker. She had, in fact, been drinking heavily with friends the night she injected herself with heroin and died.

Great Britain also has studied the question of heroin overdose. The presence of quinine was all but ruled out since quinine is not used to "cut" heroin in Great Britain. However, although inconclusive, the British studies appear to confirm the alcohol-barbiturate-heroin theory.

Despite the accumulated evidence that there must be a cause other than heroin overdose for these deaths, research in the area is minimal and the classification remains.

synergy   When two or more drugs are taken together, the combined action can increase the normal effect of each drug. The condition is also referred to as POTENTIATION or supra-additive. Potentiation and synergy both refer to those occasions when you add one plus one and get three. The ADDITIVE EFFECT would give you two. Because of this phenomenon, a normally safe amount of a particular drug might have a devastating effect when taken with a drug that reacts synergistically to it.

For example, a small amount of alcohol combined with a very small dose of a barbiturate can have a much greater effect than either alcohol or a barbiturate taken alone. Due to competition for enzymes in the liver, when the two drugs are combined, the system cannot metabolize both at the same time. In this case, where both these drugs are competing for the same enzymes, the alcohol is always processed first. The barbiturate meanwhile accumulates in the blood, where its effects on the body and the mind are multiplied. This delayed metabolization of the barbiturate can result in a tripling or quadrupling of its potency when it enters the central nervous system.

The Third Special Report to the U.S. Congress on Alcohol and Health defined an interaction between alcohol (or other central nervous system depressants) and a drug as "any alteration in the pharmacologic properties of either due to the presence of the other." The report classified three different types by interactions:

> Antagonistic, in which the effects of one or both drugs are blocked or reduced;
> Additive, in which the effect is the sum of the effects of each;
> Supra-additive (synergistic or potentiating), in which the effect of the two drugs in combination is greater than it would be if the effects were additive.

The supra-additive effect is the most dangerous and, at times, can be fatal. Although not quite as dangerous, the antagonistic effect can be hazardous when the therapeutic effects of one drug are reduced by the presence of the other.

Drugs also have a half-life: this is the amount of time it takes for the body to remove half of the drug from the system. For drugs with a half-life of 24 hours or more, such as Valium, half of the first dose may still be in the body when the next is taken. After several days the buildup can be fairly extensive, and when alcohol or another central nervous system depressant is taken the unexpected result can be devastating.

synesthesia   The crossover of sensory effects. This phenomenon is most common during hallucinogenic use; colors may be smelled, sounds may be seen. Seeing stars after a blow on the head is a form of nondrug synesthesia.

synthetic marijuana   THC (TETRAHYDROCANNABINOL). THC is the psychoactive ingredient in marijuana. In the 1960s the term THC was often falsely used to refer to PCP.

synthetic narcotics   Narcotics that are produced entirely within a laboratory, as opposed to pharmaceutical products that are derived directly or indirectly from narcotics of natural origin. The two most widely used synthetic narcotics are meperidine and methadone. LAMM (levo-alpha-acetylmethadol) is only the second synthetic narcotic to be approved by the Food and Drug Administration to treat heroin addiction. As with methadone, it blocks the mood-altering effects of heroin and suppresses withdrawal symptoms. However, LAAM has a major advantage over methadone in that its effects last for 48 to 72 hours, while methadone's last for 24. Synthetic narcotics resemble morphine in their action and sometimes have an even greater analgesic potency. Consequently, tolerance and dependence can develop with their use, making them susceptible to abuse.

T

tachycardia An increase in heart rate. (See HEART.)

talbutal An intermediate-acting BARBITURATE usually used to produce sedation and sleep.

Talwin A potent analgesic that contains pentazocine and is equivalent in effect to CODEINE. It is an AGONIST-ANTAGONIST and is used as a preanesthetic as well as for moderate to severe pain relief. It has a high potential for abuse and both physical and psychological dependence occur. Its antagonist qualities are significant, and the drug will precipitate withdrawal in opiate-dependent people. In large doses, Talwin can cause acute central nervous system manifestations of hallucinations and disorientation. Its formulation has been altered by the addition of NALOXONE (Narcan), so that when illicit users inject it intravenously its euphoric effects are blocked.

tank From "drunk tank." Slang for a cell or jail where highly inebriated individuals are kept until sobered up. The term is also used to refer to an alcoholic, or to the state of being intoxicated (he/she was *tanked*).

taractan An antipsychotic that contains chlorprothixene and is used for the management of psychotic disorders. It has little potential for abuse or dependency. Respiratory depression, hypertension and convulsions can occur with overdosage. It is no longer distributed in the U.S.

TARGET A not-for-profit service organization dedicated to helping students cope with alcohol and other drugs. Associated with the National Federation of State High School Associations, TARGET's audience includes student-athletes, debaters, coaches, administrators, parents and others involved in extracurricular activities.

TCA Tricyclic ANTIDEPRESSANTS, the major category of antidepressants.

Tedral A bronchodilator containing theophylline, ephedrine hydrochloride and the sedative PHENOBARBITAL. It is used for bronchial asthma and other bronchospastic disorders. Because of the presence of the barbiturate phenobarbital, which is added to counteract the stimulant ephedrine, it may be habit-forming. It is no longer available in the U.S.

teetotal To be a *teetotaler, teetotaller, teetotalist.* From "tee-total," a local British colloquialism for "total." Advocating teetotalism—the principle or practice of total abstinence regarding alcoholic beverages.

temperance While the word temperance usually has been synonymous with moderation, in the 1800s it took on the narrower meaning of *abstinence.* Although as early as 1785 Dr. Benjamin Rush was presenting a strong scientific argument on the dangers of alcohol and the need for temperance, Americans were more receptive to moral pleas. The first temperance organization in the U.S. was founded in 1789 by some residents of Litchfield, Connecticut, who pledged never to drink. Similar groups began to operate on a local scale. The first national organization, the American Temperance Society, was formed in 1826. The movement was supported by Presbyterian and Methodist churches and drew its largest following from rural areas. By 1830 there were more than 1,000 temperance societies in existence and these organizations gained strength in rural communities between 1830 and 1860.

Temperance leaders used two techniques to persuade people to abstain: they advocated religious faith as a means for people to ease the anxieties that might lead them to drink, and they portrayed liquor as the agent of the devil and, therefore, a source of these anxieties. During this time a number of states adopted antialcohol measures ranging from licensing to complete prohibition. These measures lacked the support of the general nonrural populations and many were rapidly repealed. The earlier temperance groups (1825–40) were concerned with the plight of "drunkards" and many tried to help them to sobriety. After 1830, however, the societies began to stress that the "drunk" was a moral sinner who could stop drinking if he so desired. The goal of the groups changed from helping the alcoholic to removing the cause of his/her problem—alcohol. Soon, the idea of universal prohibition became prominent and all who drank were attacked as moral degenerates.

The Civil War divided the early and late temperance movements. After the war, the notion of temperance grew increasingly popular. More churches became directly involved in the movement. Catholics formed the Total Abstention Union in 1872, and the WOMAN'S CHRISTIAN TEMPERANCE UNION was founded in 1874. Eventually the movement shifted from moral attacks toward legislative measures, particularly PROHIBITION (THE VOLSTEAD ACT). On December 18, 1917, Congress submitted the Eighteenth Amendment to the states for ratification and on January 16, 1920, Prohibition went into effect.

Richard W. Howland and Joe W. Howland, "200 Years of Drinking in the United States: Evolution of the Disease Concept," in *Drinking,* ed. John A. Ewing and Beatrice A. Rouse (Chicago: Nelson-Hall, 1979): 39–60.

W. J. Rorabaugh, *The Alcoholic Republic* (New York: Oxford University Press, 1979): 187–222.

temposil   Temposil (the compound calcium carbamide) is used to produce an ANTABUSE effect in alcoholics participating in recovery programs. It differs from Antabuse in that its effect lasts only 12 to 24 hours, whereas that of Antabuse can extend four to five days before the danger of a reaction passes. Temposil is administered in alcohol treatment programs in Canada and Japan, but has not been approved for use in the U.S.

Tenuate   An ANORECTIC that contains diethylpropion hydrochloride and is used for weight control. Tolerance will develop and because it is chemically and pharmacologically similar to AMPHETAMINES it can produce psychological dependence, social dysfunction and has a high potential for abuse. Symptoms of overdosage are restlessness, rapid respiration, confusion and hallucinations.

tepanil   An ANORECTIC that contains diethylpropion hydrochloride and is used for weight control. Tolerance will develop and because it is chemically and pharmacologically similar to AMPHETAMINES it can produce psychological dependence, social dysfunction and has a high potential for abuse. Symptoms of overdosage are restlessness, rapid respiration, confusion and hallucinations. It is no longer available in the U.S.

tequila   A spirit distilled from a pulque, or fermented mash, of some species of agave plant, usually maguey. Its name derives from the district in the Mexican state of Jalisco where it originated. Tequila sometimes is referred to as "mescal."

The national alcoholic beverage of Mexico, tequila dates from the Spanish exploration of that country in the 15th and 16th centuries. Its production undoubtedly began when the Spanish, who already possessed knowledge of distillation, adapted distillation processes to the local vegetation most suitable for fermentation because of its natural sugar content. The maguey agave they employed is also known as blue agave. Now, because its principal use is distillation, it sometimes is called the tequilana plant.

Tequila is a strong spirit, ranging from 86 to 100 proof, traditionally drunk straight, preceded by a taste of salt and followed by a taste of lime. Since being mass-marketed in recent times, it now is also used in cocktails.

terpin hydrate A turpentine derivative and non-narcotic ANTITUSSIVE.

tetanus An acute infectious disease, commonly known as "lockjaw," which is caused by the bacillus *Clostridium tetani* found in the soil and in animal feces. It is usually transmitted through open wounds directly into the bloodstream, often by contaminated nails, knives or hypodermic needles. Tetanus is painful because it causes muscle spasms and is often fatal. Among addicts who regularly inject drugs, the chances of contracting the disease are well above average and the prognosis for recovery is less than average because of the frequency of injection, carelessness about the sterility of needles and the general poor health of the user.

Thai sticks Extremely potent, seedless or nearly seedless marijuana that is grown in Thailand and Vietnam and is packaged and tied in small stick-shaped bundles containing whole and complete "buds" of the plant. (See SINSEMILLA.)

Thailand Thailand, like many other countries in Southeast Asia, has been subjected to severe military conflicts and a general undermining of cultural stability by foreign influences, which in the case of Thailand includes drug traffickers. The effects of these factors are especially apparent in the rise in alcohol and narcotics consumption among the Thai people.

Alcohol: Thailand's population is 90% Buddhist, 4% Islamic and 2% Confucian. Although these religions have traditional strictures against alcohol consumption, alcohol-related job absenteeism produces daily expressions of concern from the business community. While in the past the country had little need for strict licensing of drinking places, the current situation appears to justify some control of drinking environments. One-third of the alcoholism cases in urban areas, such as Bangkok, where such estab-

lishments have proliferated, are estimated to be female employees of the various pubs, clubs and cafes that serve a clientele of national military officers. Importation of beer and whiskey remains relatively low, but there is an increasing daily use of such bootleg products as "Mekong whiskey" in both rural and urban areas.

The Thais have a tradition of limited alcohol consumption with evening meals. Over the last 20 years, however, authorities have noted a general trend toward consumption of alcohol with other meals, including, in rural areas, breakfast and a new pattern of continued drinking into the night in public places. Illegally distilled liquors comprise the primary alcoholic drinks for most of the population; during a typical drinking occasion, various alcoholic beverages are mixed. The increasing acceptance of alcohol as a social beverage has reached all levels of Thai society, from the military officers' clubs, stocked with imported brandy, to the rural villages, where rice whiskey is distilled.

The cost of alcoholism to Thailand is difficult to estimate due to a lack of data. The government's overriding concern at present is control of narcotic drugs.

Prevention of alcohol-related problems in Thailand is delegated to the Department of Treasury, with responsibility for educational programs left to the Ministry of Public Health. In February 1975 the International Congress on Alcohol and Drug Dependency met in Bangkok, and one year later the country established a Drug Education and Prevention Office. Each of the 72 provinces has its own Provincial Health Authority and mobile teams to treat health problems of all sorts in rural areas. There are 30 centers specifically designed for the treatment of alcohol and drug problems in Thailand.

Drugs other than alcohol: According to the USDS (U.S. Department of State, 1996), "Thailand remains the principal transit route for Southeast Asian heroin," and the cultivation of high-quality marijuana (known as *Thai* or *Thai sticks*) continues in northeastern Thailand, though on a smaller scale than in the past. "Opium and heroin production in the Golden Triangle have remained at very high levels . . . and continue to meet the demand of Thailand's drug addicts. Thailand's booming economy creates an expanding local market structure for traffickers. Heroin is replacing opium as the drug of choice among Thailand's hill tribes." Drug abuse is becoming an increasingly disturbing reality in Thailand, where according to a government-funded study completed in 1993, there are approximately 1.27 million addicts, or 2.2% of the population. Both government agencies and nongovernmental agencies working under the supervision of local officials are currently expanding efforts to carry out enforcement, prevention and demand-reduction policies.

THC (tetrahydrocannabinol)   THC (delta-9-tetrahydrocannabinol) is the psychoactive ingredient in MARIJUANA and is found in the resin of the hemp plant. It first was produced synthetically in 1966. The potency of hash or marijuana directly relates to the amount of THC contained therein. Although marijuana is presently classified as a hallucinogen and a Schedule I drug under the Controlled Substances Act (signifying that it has no known medical value), it should probably not be classified thus, although it can produce mildly psychedelic effects to a limited degree. A synthetic form of THC called Marinol was approved by the FDA initially as an antiemetic for chemotherapy patients and in 1993 as an appetite stimulant for AIDS patients. The psychoactive effects are more potent and long-lasting than that of marijuana.

thebaine   A principal alkaloid of OPIUM, thebaine was isolated in 1835, three years after the isolation of codeine. Because of its toxicity, thebaine itself has no medical use. Its conversion products, however, include the NARCOTIC ANTAGONISTS: NALOXONE, and NALTREXONE. Some codeine is made from thebaine. A series of other compounds that have analgesic properties many times more potent than morphine are also conversion products of thebaine, but their toxicity in humans limits their use to veterinary medicine.

therapeutic index   The average between an established effective dose of a drug and the LD50—the lethal dose for 50% of the population.

thiamine   Vitamin B1, occurring naturally and produced synthetically. It is found in a variety of plant and animal foods, including dried yeast, whole grains and cereals, nuts, legumes and meat (particularly liver and pork). It functions as a coenzyme in carbohydrate metabolism. Vitamin deficiency can result from inadequate intake, increased requirement, impaired absorption and impaired utilization. All of these metabolic impairments occur with alcoholism, which can lead to peripheral and central neuralgic and cardiac pathology. Peripheral signs include cramps and pain in the legs and feet, with decreased reflexes and muscle atrophy. Wernicke-Korsakoff syndrome, the CNS manifestation of thiamine deficiency, presents as confusion and confabulation in the early state, with nystagmus, paralysis of eye movement, cardiac failure, coma and eventually death if left untreated. Thiamine deficiency due to alcohol abuse is treated with replacement therapy—orally in mild cases, intramuscularly in more severe instances. (See WERNICKE'S ENCEPHALOPATHY SYNDROME and KORSAKOFF'S PSYCHOSIS.)

thin layer chromatography   TLC is a drug-testing process that can detect up to 40 different drugs in one urine sample. The process involves use of a glass plate covered with a thin layer of jellylike substance known as *gel.* Urine is applied as a spot near one edge of the gel surface. The glass plate then is placed upright in a closed container, with the edge adjacent to the spot at the bottom. The base of the container has just enough of a liquid solvent to wet that edge. By degrees, the solvent is carried up over the surface of the gel. When the solvent reaches the spot of urine, it pushes all the chemicals contained in the spot up along the surface. In most cases, the gel holds on to the different chemicals.

"The greater the attraction between each individual chemical and the gel," writes Berger, "the less it moves. The smaller the attraction, the farther up the glass it moves. After a period of time, the original spot is gone. Instead, there remains a series of spots called a *chromatogram,* going up along the surface of the gel. Each spot is made different by a different chemical that has been separated out of the spot of urine." Results of the TLC test depend on the skill and experience of the technician who reads the TLC plate. The technician uses his or her own judgment to determine which, if any, drugs are present. The subjectivity of interpretation is only one drawback of TLC. TLC techniques are not sufficiently sensitive for testing cocaine: positive tests frequently read as negative after only 48 hours. By contrast, enzyme multiplied immunoassay technique (EMIT) testing remains cocaine-sensitive for several days.

Gilda Berger, *Drug Testing* (New York: Franklin Watts, 1987): 37–38.

Thorazine   An antipsychotic brand of chlorpromazine, a phenothiazine derivative, used for the treatment of psychotic states. Not known to cause dependence or withdrawal, overdosage, however, can result in respiratory depression. When taken with alcohol or other central nervous system depressants it has an additive effect. It is available in tablets, capsules, suppositories, as a concentrate or in vials and ampules for injection.

tight   A slang term used to describe someone who is intoxicated on alcohol, perhaps even more intoxicated than someone who is HIGH or "tipsy."

TIPS (Training for Intervention Procedures by Servers of Alcohol)   National efforts to prevent alcohol abuse lack a coherent conceptual structure. Although many public service messages and pamphlets create awareness of the problem, informing drinkers of the consequences of heavy drinking (and particularly driving while intoxicated), the problems continue to mount.

One prevention approach with great potential is *server training*. Server training bridges the gap between messages designed to admonish and advise people and techniques designed to give people the skills they need to act. The skills of identification and intervention that servers acquire with this training method are designed to interrupt the patterns of alcohol use in order to prevent drunkenness and, failing that, to at least prevent the intoxicated person from driving.

Whereas public service announcements, slogans and pamphlets appear to be directed at those least likely to retain the information presented, the conceptual framework of server programs are based on the knowledge that alcohol taken in heavy doses undermines cognitive skills, interferes with recently learned information, sabotages plans to limit drinking and confounds the ability to keep track of the number of drinks consumed.

The concept is further based on the premise that behavioral change takes place in society where social values and limits of behavior are determined by the approval or disapproval of small groups of people in the social networks of the individual.

The best-known program of this type has the acronym TIPS—Training for Intervention Procedures by Servers of Alcohol—a program developed by the Health Education Foundation under the guidance of the founding director of the National Institute on Alcohol Abuse and Alcoholism, Morris E. Chafetz, M.D.

The program was initially designed to give servers of alcohol the skills needed to reduce the incidence of drunkenness and thereby the incidence of alcohol-related accidents or injury by patrons in commercial settings, including concessions, off-premise establishments and the like. The program's success in commercial areas led to the development of three prevention programs for the noncommercial arena: TIPS for Universities, TIPS for the Workplace and TIPS for Parents.

Thus far, TIPS is the only server-training program proven to be effective. One study by an independent university researcher group showed that not a single patron served by a TIPS-trained server achieved a blood-alcohol level of intoxication, whereas almost 50% of patrons served by non-TIPS-trained servers were tested to be legally intoxicated.

TIPS is a unique and valuable tool that can be used to help curb the excessive use of alcohol thereby promoting the health and safety of the public.

M. E. Chafetz, "Training in Intervention Procedures: A Prevention Program," *Abstracts and Reviews in Alcohol and Driving* 5, no. 4 (October–December 1984): 17–19.

W. Nason and E. S. Geller, "Training Bar Personnel to Prevent Drunk Driving: A Field Evaluation," *American Journal of Public Health* 77, no. 8 (August 1987).

E. S. Geller et al, "Does Server Training Make a Difference? An Empirical Field Evaluation," *Alcohol Health & Research World* 11, no. 4 (Summer 1987).

Enoch Gordis, M.D., ed., *Seventh Special Report to the U.S. Congress on Alcohol and Health* (January 1990).

TMA   A little-known synthetic HALLUCINOGEN (3, 4, 5-Trimethoxyphenyl-B-aminopropane) derived from MESCALINE. It is more potent than mescaline but less potent than LSD-25. TMA-2 and TMA-6 also are hallucinogenic substances.

Tokay   (In Hungarian, Tokaji.) A famous Hungarian wine named after Tokay, a village in northeast Hungary near the Carpathian mountains.

There are three basic types of Tokay wine: Tokay Essencia, Tokay Aszu and Tokay Szamorodini. With the exception of some of the Szamorodini and Aszu varieties, Tokay wines are generally sweet and thus used as dessert wines. The distinctive flavor of Tokay wines comes from aszu berries, which are grapes that have been allowed to remain on the vine until late autumn when they have shriveled and their juice has become very concentrated with sugar. The particular type of Tokay is determined by the amount of aszu berries used in making the wine.

Tokay Essencia is made entirely from aszu berries and is so rare that it is not marketed but used as private stock. Tokay Aszu is made from a carefully measured blend of normally ripened grapes and aszu berries. Aszu berries are added in amounts that vary from one to six puttonys, a puttony holding approximately 30 pounds of grapes. Tokay Aszu varies in taste from rather dry to extremely sweet, depending on the number of puttonys added. It is golden or amber in color and around 7 or 8 proof.

The term "Szamorodini" means "as it is grown," and it indicates that in making Tokay Szamorodini no special attention is given to the aszu berries. Whatever aszu berries get into the vats are pressed with the other grapes. If the result is a very dry wine, it is drunk as an aperitif rather than as a dessert wine.

tolerance   The variation in the effect on different individuals of a specific amount of alcohol (or any other consciousness-altering substance). Relating to alcohol, after a few drinks an inexperienced drinker may become intoxicated rapidly, while an experienced drinker can consume the same amount with little visible effect. The degree of intoxication exhibited at a given BLOOD ALCOHOL CONCENTRATION (BAC) varies widely among individuals.

The most significant factor in alcohol tolerance is the adaptation of the CENTRAL NERVOUS SYSTEM (CNS) to alcohol. Long-term alcoholics display higher-than-average CNS adaptation, which enables them to tolerate larger doses of all sedatives. They also have an increased ability to metabolize alcohol, but this is rapidly lost when drinking stops. One study showed that metabolic tolerance could be lost after three weeks of abstinence, even in those who had been severe alcoholics for five years or more.

Some alcoholics have reported losing their high tolerance to alcohol suddenly; in such cases a relatively small amount of alcohol would have an unexpectedly strong effect. This effect may be due to impaired METABOLISM or to the increased sensitivity of an organically damaged brain to alcohol.

While alcoholics may have a higher tolerance for alcohol than social drinkers or abstainers, the size of a lethal dose may not be much greater for alcoholics than for others.

toluene   A liquid aromatic hydrocarbon that is used chiefly as a solvent and is found in numerous common household products. It has an intoxicating effect when inhaled. (See INHALANTS.)

tooth grinding   Tooth grinding (bruxism) is relatively common among the general population during sleep. When it occurs during waking hours it can be an indication of chronic amphetamine or cocaine use.

top fermentation   Fermentation of a hop wort with a yeast that rises to the surface of the liquid in the course of brewing beer. Top fermentation is the process used in brewing ales, whereas BOTTOM FERMENTATION is used to brew lager beers. Beer yeasts are selected strains of bacterial enzymes that flocculate, or separate themselves, from the brewing beer so that they may be drawn off at the end of the process. Top fermentation, in conjunction with the blend of different cereal grains employed, accounts for the heavier flavor of ales in comparison with that of lagers. Typically, top fermentation is carried out at temperatures between 50° and 70° F and ordinarily takes between five and six days to produce the desired level of alcohol content.

toxic   Poisonous. Toxicity refers to the quality of being poisonous; toxicology is the science that deals with poisons and their effects.

trafficking   According to opinion polls, a majority of Americans believe that the sale and use of illegal drugs is the most serious law enforcement problem in the U.S. In fact, however, usage seems to be decreasing each year: The total annual expenditure

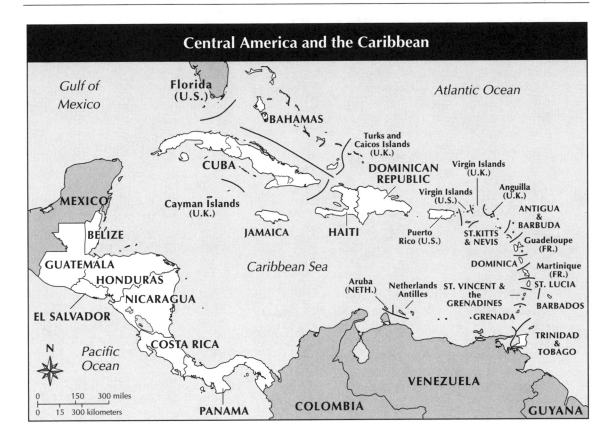

Central America and the Caribbean

Gulf of Mexico

Florida (U.S.)

Atlantic Ocean

BAHAMAS

Turks and Caicos Islands (U.K.)

CUBA

DOMINICAN REPUBLIC

Virgin Islands (U.K.)

Virgin Islands (U.S.)

Anguilla (U.K.)

Cayman Islands (U.K.)

MEXICO

JAMAICA

HAITI

Puerto Rico (U.S.)

ST. KITTS & NEVIS

ANTIGUA & BARBUDA

Guadeloupe (FR.)

BELIZE

GUATEMALA

HONDURAS

NICARAGUA

EL SALVADOR

Caribbean Sea

DOMINICA

Martinique (FR.)

ST. LUCIA

Aruba (NETH.)

Netherlands Antilles

ST. VINCENT & the GRENADINES

BARBADOS

GRENADA

COSTA RICA

N

Pacific Ocean

TRINIDAD & TOBAGO

VENEZUELA

0   150   300 miles

0   15   300 kilometers

PANAMA

COLOMBIA

GUYANA

on drugs in 1993 equaled $50.1 billion, a drop of more than 20% from 1988 when total expenditures equaled $65.7 billion. Expenditure on cocaine, the top illicit income producer, dropped from $41.9 billion in 1988 to $31.9 in 1993. In 1988 heroin generated an estimated $11.7 billion in sales but dropped to $7.4 billion in 1993. Other drugs, including amphetamines, methamphetamines, barbiturates, methaqualone and the hallucinogens, produced an estimated $3.2 billion in 1988 expenditures and dropped to $2.8 billion in 1988. Marijuana expenditures remained relatively stable: in 1988, $8.9 billion and in 1993, $9.0 billion. According to the White House (1995), no one really knows how much money the drug trade generates, and the above are simply "best estimates."

In 1993 shipments of consumable cocaine into the U.S. totaled between 243 and 340 metric tons (having dropped from previous higher rates). Availability is a major factor in the rise of cocaine abuse

and, unfortunately, supplies, though reduced, remain abundant. Coca cultivation is well established in COLOMBIA, PERU and BOLIVIA. Colombia is responsible for between 50% and 60% of the world's cocaine supply. Drugs from Colombia usually enter through south Florida, Southern California, New York City, Texas and in the 1990s through Puerto Rico as well. The U.S. government has made an attempt to reduce trafficking from South American countries through control of coca production but faces many barriers when trying to negotiate with these countries. Frequent changes in South American governments, local populations that are heavily dependent on coca sales for their principal income, and, until recently, indifference to U.S. interests, are just a few of the obstacles encountered.

In the 1980s, approximately 60% of the heroin imported into this country was refined from opium cultivated in Southwest Asia (the GOLDEN CRESCENT); 25% was from Mexico; and the balance was

Worldwide Illicit Drug				
	1997	**1996**	**1995**	**1994**
Country	**Hectares**	**Hectares**	**Hectares**	**Hectares**
Opium				
Afghanistan	39,150	37,950	38,740	29,180
India	2,050	3,100	4,750	5,500
Iran*	–	–	–	–
Pakistan	4,100	3,400	6,950	0
Total SW Asia	**45,300**	**44,450**	**50,440**	**34,680**
Burma	155,150	163,100	154,070	154,070
China	–	–	1,275	1,965
Laos	28,150	25,250	19,650	19,650
Thailand	1,650	2,170	1,750	2,110
Total SE Asia	**184,950**	**190,520**	**176,745**	**177,795**
Colombia	6,600	6,300	6,540	20,000
Lebanon	0	90	150	–
Guatemala	0	0	39	50
Mexico	4,000	5,100	5,050	5,795
Vietnam	6,150	3,150	–	–
Total Other	**16,750**	**14,640**	**11,779**	**25,845**
Total Opium	**247,000**	**249,610**	**238,964**	**238,320**
Coca				
Bolivia	45,800	48,100	48,600	48,100
Colombia	79,500	67,200	50,900	45,000
Peru	68,800	94,400	115,300	108,600
Ecuador	–	–	–	–
Total Coca	**194,100**	**209,700**	**214,800**	201,700
Cannabis				
Mexico	4,800	6,500	6,900	10,550
Colombia	5,000	5,000	5,000	4,986
Jamaica	317	527	305	308
Total Cannabis	**10,117**	**12,027**	**12,205**	**15,844**

* No firm data available. The United States government estimated in 1992 that Iran may have 3,500 hectares of opium poppy under cultivation. This estimate did not change in 1997.

(continued on next page)

Cultivation Totals						
1993	**1992**	**1991**	**1990**	**1989**	**1988**	**1987**
Hectares	Hectares	Hectares	Hectares	Hectares	Hectares	Hectares
21,080	19,470	17,190	12,370	18,650	23,000	18,500
4,400	–	–	–	–	–	–
–	–	–	–	–	–	–
0	8,170	8,205	8,220	6,050	11,588	9,970
25,480	**27,640**	**25,395**	**20,590**	**24,700**	**34,588**	**28,470**
146,600	153,700	160,000	150,100	143,000	104,200	76,021
–	–	–	–	–	–	–
18,520	25,610	29,625	30,580	42,130	40,400	0
2,110	2,050	3,000	3,435	4,075	2,843	2,934
167,230	**181,360**	**192,625**	**184,115**	**189,205**	**147,443**	**78,955**
20,000	20,000	1,160				
440	na	3,400	3,200	4,500	na	na
438	730	1,145	845	1,220	710	0
3,960	3,310	3,765	5,450	6,600	5,001	5,160
–	–	–	–	–	–	–
24,838	**24,040**	**9,470**	**9,495**	**12,320**	**5,711**	**5,160**
217,548	**233,040**	**227,490**	**214,200**	**226,225**	**187,742**	**112,585**
47,200	45,500	47,900	50,300	52,900	48,500	39,258
39,700	37,100	37,500	40,100	42,400	27,000	24,540
108,800	129,100	120,800	121,300	120,400	110,500	109,145
–	–	40	120	150	240	300
195,700	**211,700**	**206,240**	**211,820**	**215,850**	**186,240**	**173,243**
11,220	16,420	17,915	35,050	53,900	5,003	5,250
5,000	2,000	2,000	1,500	2,270	4,188	5,005
744	389	950	1,220	280	607	680
16,964	**18,809**	**20,865**	**37,770**	**56,450**	**9,798**	**10,935**

Source: United States Dept. of State, Bureau for International Narcotics and Law Enforcement Affairs, *International Narcotics Control Strategy Report,* March 1996.

South America

Caribbean Sea

Atlantic Ocean

BELIZE
GUATEMALA   HONDURAS
NICARAGUA
EL SALVADOR
COSTA RICA
PANAMA

VENEZUELA

TRINIDAD & TOBAGO

GUYANA
SURINAME
French Guiana (FRANCE)

COLOMBIA

ECUADOR

Galapagos Islands (ECUADOR)

Equator

Ucavali R.

Amazon R.

PERU

BRAZIL

BOLIVIA

PARAGUAY

Pacific Ocean

URUGUAY

CHILE

ARGENTINA

Atlantic Ocean

Falkland Islands (U.K.)

N

0   400   800 miles
0   400   800 kilometers

from Southeast Asia (the GOLDEN TRIANGLE). Since then, however, Southeast and Southwest Asia—most prominently, Burma (now Myanmar) and Afghanistan—have become major exporters of drugs worldwide. Imports into the U.S. from Mexico dropped significantly in the 1990s due to a newly aggressive eradication campaign against the opium poppy by the Mexican government. The major importation center for heroin in the U.S. is New York City, although Detroit has also become a major distribution center.

Although Mexico is still a source of marijuana, its overall share of the U.S. market has declined—from 18% in 1978 to 8% in the mid-1980s. In 1989, however, Mexico produced 4,750 metric tons of marijuana, 27.9% of the total sold in the U.S. In 1993 Mexico's potential net production increased to 6,280 metric tons, and its share of the U.S. market increased to 50%. South America and Colombia supplied 32.5% of the marijuana imported into the U.S. in 1989; Jamaica supplied 5% in 1989. Domestic cultivation rose in 1989 to about 25% and is centered in seven primary states: California (where it is estimated that marijuana is the state's largest cash crop, worth between $1 billion and $2 billion annually), Hawaii, Oregon, Arkansas, Missouri, Kentucky and Florida.

Other illicit drugs, such as amphetamines and barbiturates, come from several sources. Colombia is responsible for about 80% of these drugs, particularly methaqualone. The balance comes from Europe and often is diverted through Mexico. In 1989 there were an estimated 1.2 million addicts in the U.S. and 23 million "recreational" users spending more on drugs than a company such as General Motors earns. (See SMUGGLING, FRENCH CONNECTION and entries on individual countries.)

trancopal   A nonhypnotic antianxiety drug. It is a brand of chlormezanone and is used to improve the emotional state of patients by quieting them without impairing their clarity of consciousness.

transcendental meditation (TM)   TM is a form of meditation that can produce a dissociative state, interpreted as an out-of-the-body experience. Adherents often claim that TM decreases or eliminates the urge to use drugs.

Transportation System and Drug Abuse   The White House Conference for a Drug Free America's report in June 1988 stated: "Although no evidence exists to demonstrate that illicit drug use is more pervasive in transportation than in any other sector of society, the industry has an extraordinary obligation to ensure public safety and public trust. This obligation warrants that zero tolerance for drugs, on and off the job, must be the standard for the transportation industry, as it must be for private citizens who use our highways, waterways, and airways."

The conference made several recommendations pertinent to its goal of zero tolerance for drugs, including one to establish a drug-free working group composed of public- and private-sector experts, to address the long-range issues involving drug use and transportation.

Several programs already are in effect in private transportation companies, where both labor and management are taking steps to combat drug use and spread the antidrug message. Voluntary railroad employee-based drug prevention programs, such as "Operation Red Block" at Union Pacific and CSX Transportation, Inc., and "Operation Stop" at Burlington Northern, have initiated a wide variety of creative community activities that promote the policy of zero tolerance for drug use. Burns Brothers, Inc., owner of 23 truck stops west of the Mississippi River, sponsored a 300-truck convoy against drug use in 1987. The "world's largest truck convoy" crossed through seven states, conveying the trucking industry's concern. "Operation Full Ahead," sponsored by American Steamship Co., Buffalo, New York, is a joint labor-management program to promote the health, safety and well-being of the company's employees, with an emphasis on awareness, education and prevention of illicit drug use.

The U.S. Supreme Court in 1989 upheld the constitutionality of the federal government's regulations requiring railroad crews involved in accidents to submit to prompt urinalysis and blood tests. This ruling followed the January 4, 1987, Amtrak wreck near Baltimore that killed 16 and injured 176 people. After a urine test the train's engineer later admitted to drug use and pleaded guilty to manslaughter. Since November 1988 the U.S. Department of Transportation has mandated random drug tests for the nation's 4 million private transportation workers, including airline pilots and navigators, interstate truckers, bus drivers and railroad engineers and conductors.

While no precise statistics exist for prevalence of drug use among transportation workers in the U.S., a National Institute on Drug Abuse (NIDA) report on drug use in the industry as a whole projected that as many as 6 million employees may currently be engaged in drug use. Alcohol is still the nation's most serious drug problem in the industrial sector and affects transportation companies both large and small. However, focus on the risks of drinking and driving has impacted favorably on the commercial trucking system. According to the National Transportation Safety Board's 1992 study, drugs are involved in 22% of fatal traffic crashes. While still serious, this figure represents a significant decrease from 1985 figures.

White House Conference Report for a Drug Free America (Washington, D.C.: Government Printing Office, 1988): 95–103.

Tranxene   A sedative hypnotic that contains chlorazepate dipotassium, a BENZODIAZEPINE, and is used for the treatment of anxiety and for physical illnesses in which anxiety is manifested. When combined with alcohol or other central nervous system depressants it will have an ADDITIVE EFFECT. Overdosage results in varying degrees of central nervous system depression, from severe sedation to coma.

tranylcypromine   See MONOAMINE OXIDASE (MAO) INHIBITORS. It's trade name is Parnate.

Traynor v. Turnage   In a landmark decision handed down on April 20, 1988, the Supreme Court ruled 4 to 3 that the Veterans Administration can continue to deny disability and other benefits to most veterans disabled by alcoholism because their condition is caused by "willful misconduct."

The decision, which directly concerns only veterans, stressed the majority's view of what Congress intended in two ambiguously worded statutes (in 1977 and 1978) that define who is entitled to veterans' benefits and that prohibit discrimination against handicapped people.

Both the majority and the dissent stressed the view expressed by Associate Justice Byron R. White (who wrote for the majority) that "this litigation does not require the Court to decide whether alco-holism is a disease whose course its victims cannot control."

Writing for the majority in the case *Traynor* v. *Turnage* (no. 86-622 and 86-737), Justice White noted that the Veterans Administration policy with regard to alcoholism as a disability had been consistent since at least 1964.

Marcus A. Rothschild, M.D., editor of *Alcoholism: Clinical and Experimental Research,* the journal of the American Medical Society on Alcoholism, said that the Supreme Court decision was discouraging. "The ruling," he told the *New York Times,* "will lend itself to misinterpretation. To consider this genetic-inherited trait as willful misconduct is to deny all our more recent knowledge and advances."

Stuart Taylor Jr., "Denial of V.A. Benefits to Alcoholics Upheld," *New York Times* (April 21, 1988).

treatment   Treatment for drug use falls into various categories, including drug-free or maintenance; residential or ambulatory; medical or nonmedical; selective or nonselective; voluntary or involuntary. Treatment programs also offer virtually any combination of these methods.

The ANTABUSE maintenance program and drug-free programs such as ALCOHOLICS ANONYMOUS and its drug-related correlate, NARCOTICS ANONYMOUS, are aimed at abstinence. Abstinence-based residential approaches include drug-free therapeutic communities such as Synanon, Daytop, Odyssey House and numerous others; halfway houses; and rehabilitation programs of one to four months' duration. Involuntary treatment includes both medical and court authorizations that do not require the patient's consent and may compel an addict to start treatment, continue it, or both. Ambulatory treatment consists of programs in which a patient visits a treatment facility as an outpatient at periodic intervals. (See SMITH, DR. MICHAEL.)

Psychological dependency generally is believed to be more difficult to manage than physical dependency, and for this reason treatment programs employ a variety of methods. DETOXIFICATION programs, which often handle only physical dependency, are usually done in a hospital or other medically oriented facility. Upon discharge, a continuing program of treatment should be implemented or the incidence of RELAPSE will be high. Not all treatment programs will work for all patients. Upon detoxification some patients will benefit greatly from a program such as Alcoholics Anonymous or Narcotics Anonymous; others will benefit more from individual or GROUP THERAPY. Many times inpatient rehabilitation lasting one to four months is attempted. Intensive day treatment became increasingly popular in the 1990s as an alternative to inpatient rehabilitation. Some patients require the kind of drug-free supportive atmosphere provided by long-term therapeutic communities. The length of time addicted and the severity of illness often are used to determine the level of treatment offered, with those whose conditions are more severe needing the more supportive environments. However, little research has been conducted concerning the choice of treatment levels and methods of care, and only now are outcomes being examined in an organized manner.

In the past treatment programs have centered around the patient and have failed to consider his or her family. Rehabilitation programs now often involve the family, requiring family members to participate in parts of the addicted person's treatment, education and counseling.

tremor A shaking or trembling, usually from weakness or disease. Most withdrawal states as well as the use of stimulants (and sometimes hallucinogens) induce tremors. (See DELIRIUM TREMENS.)

trichloroethylene A hydrocarbon and volatile solvent, trichloroethylene is the ingredient in various cleaning fluids sometimes inhaled for their intoxicating effects. (See INHALANTS.)

triclofos sodium A depressant and sedative hypnotic generally used in the treatment of insomnia. It is a chloral derivative, and although it converts to chloral hydrate in the body, it is less potent and lacks its bitter taste and smell.

The drug reaches its peak level in one hour and has a half-life of 11 hours. It may be habit-forming, and dependency can develop. (See TRICLOSAN.)

triclosan A hypnotic agent that contains TRICLOFOS SODIUM. It is a chloral derivative generally used in the treatment of insomnia. It may be habit-forming and is conducive to dependency.

trimstat An ANORECTIC that contains phendimetrazine tartrate and is used for weight control. Users will develop tolerance, and because its activity is similar to that of AMPHETAMINES, it has a significant potential for abuse.

trimtabs An ANORECTIC that contains phendimetrazine tartrate and is used for weight control. Users will develop tolerance, and because its activity is similar to AMPHETAMINES it has a significant potential for abuse.

tripelennamine hydrochloride An antihistamine that recently has come into use in combination with pentazocine (TALWIN), a narcotic analgesic, as a substitute for heroin. "Cooked" and injected intravenously, the combination produces a "rush" described by users as equivalent to that of good-quality heroin. The slang name for the injected compound is "Ts and Blues"; it is experiencing increasing use nationally among heroin addicts because it costs less than one-quarter the price of heroin and, unlike street heroin, its potency can be determined and controlled. There are major health risks associated with its use, including damage to the small blood vessels of the lungs, eyes and brain; seizures and convulsions; and fatality due to overdose. Talwin has significant opiate antagonist qualities and precipitates withdrawal in narcotic-dependent individuals.

Synonyms: Other slang names include: tops and bottoms, Teddies and Betties, and Ts and Bs.

Jack E. Nelson et al., eds., *Guide to Drug Abuse Research Terminology,* Research Issue 26 (Department of Health and Human Services): 97.

tuinal A sedative hypnotic that contains the short- to intermediate-acting BARBITURATES secobarbital sodium and amobarbital sodium. A Schedule II drug, it is used for insomnia and as a preoperative medication. Tolerance and both physical and psychological dependence can develop. With a high potential for abuse, when taken with alcohol or other central nervous system depressants, it has an ADDITIVE or potentiating effect. Some of the symptoms of overdosage are respiratory depression, lowered body temperature and coma.

Synonyms: tooies, tuies, rainbows, red and blues.

Turkey   The use of alcohol in Turkey is minimal. The use of other drugs, however, particularly opium, marijuana and hashish, has long been a tradition. It has been customary for so long, in fact, that there is no stigma attached to the use and abuse of these drugs. Although Turkey has always been a heavy producer and consumer of opium, the use of heroin (which is also an opiate) has been rare—although the DEA (Drug Enforcement Administration) in 1996 reported a significant rise in domestic use due to increased trafficking. Opium generally is smoked or is used as opium gum (the final raw product) for strictly medicinal purposes.

Drugs other than alcohol: In 1923 the new republic, under the leadership of Ataturk (Mustafa Kemal), sought to modernize the nation, and programs were initiated to end many of the old customs, including the use of opium and hashish. Little was actually accomplished, and at the end of World War II the abuse of opium not only had increased but there was also an increase in the smuggling of illicit drugs. Stringent legislation was passed in 1953 to deter domestic use and illegal trade, but the government was aware that it would take time to become effective; there had been considerable opposition to legislation that would change long-established customs and dramatically affect the economy and welfare of the country. In 1971 further legislation was passed that banned opium production and, despite attempts for its repeal, the law still is in effect. The economic hardships caused by the 1971 legislation have led to compensation programs but it is an enormous undertaking because most of the former poppy farms must be rehabilitated and the social and economic structure of whole provinces must be reorganized.

Trafficking and production: There are very tough penalties in Turkey for the importation, exportation or manufacture of drugs without a license. In the case of morphine, cocaine, heroin or hashish the penalty can be life imprisonment, and Turkish jails have a considerable reputation for their extreme harshness and inhumane conditions.

Much of the opium that transits through Turkey is cultivated in Iran, Pakistan and Afghanistan (Southwest Asia). Despite the 1971 ban, which allowed opium production only for the scientific and medicinal markets, Turkish nationals play an important role both in refining and trafficking, particularly through Germany. These opiates are also smuggled into western Europe or the U.S. through Bulgaria and Yugoslavia, and in the 1990s the Ukraine as well. (See GOLDEN CRESCENT.) During the days of the FRENCH CONNECTION the U.S. Embassy, in an effort to assist the Turkish government's already vigorous narcotics laws, initiated a Protocol on Narcotics Cooperation that is designed to offer flexible and speedy commodity and training assistance to Turkish law enforcement officials.

Treatment: According to the U.S. DEA (1996) government officials in Turkey have begun to acknowledge increased drug use problems, but treatment programs are limited. Existing detoxification centers are run by the police. Drug abuse in Turkey has traditionally been considered a criminal rather than a social problem.

tussanil   A decongestant and ANTITUSSIVE that contains several ingredients, including the codeine derivative dihydrocodeinone bitartrate. It may be habit-forming, and both physical and psychological dependence can occur. It is no longer marketed in the U.S.

tussionex   An ANTITUSSIVE that contains resin complexes of hydrocodone and phenyltoloxamine. Potentially habit-forming; respiratory depression and convulsions can occur with overdosage.

Twenty-First Amendment   This amendment repealed the EIGHTEENTH AMENDMENT and returned to the states the right to make their own liquor laws. Michigan was the first state to approve the Twenty-First Amendment, and Utah was the 36th, completing the ratification process. On December 5, 1933, it became part of the Constitution and ended Prohibition.

tybamate   A sedative hypnotic that is similar structurally and pharmacologically to meprobamate, but is possibly more effective as a muscle relaxant. Tybamate resembles MEPROBAMATE in its effects, use and abuse potential.

Usage: Tybamate's medical application includes the treatment of tension, anxiety and insomnia resulting from psychoneurosis. (See TYBATRAN.)

Dosage: Tybamate is prescribed in oral doses of 20–35 mg per kilogram of body weight; in three or four daily doses for children aged 6–12; and in doses of 250–500 mg three or four times daily for adults. No more than 3 gm (3000 mg) should be administered per day.

Appearance and activity: Tybamate is a white crystalline powder that is soluble in alcohol and slightly soluble in water. Absorbed rapidly in the gastrointestinal tract and distributed evenly in the body, tybamate is metabolized in the liver and excreted by the kidneys. It acts on the thalmus and limbic systems of the brain, stabilizing the emotional circuits, but does not affect the cerebral cortex. The substance, which has a half-life of three hours, crosses the placental barrier and appears in mother's milk.

Effects: Like meprobamate, tybamate temporarily reduces tension and anxiety. Mild adverse reactions such as drowsiness and confusion usually can be controlled by adjusting the dose. Other negative side effects that have been reported include rash, nausea, anorexia and seizures.

Tolerance and dependence: Tolerance and psychological and physical dependence can occur, along with withdrawal symptoms. Barbiturates and tybamate display CROSS-TOLERANCE to each other, and tybamate is potentiated by alcohol and other depressants. Overdosage can cause stupor and death.

tybatran A sedative hypnotic that contains TYBAMATE and whose activity is similar to meprobamate. Tolerance and both physical and psychological dependence can occur.

Tylenol with Codeine An analgesic that contains acetaminophen and codeine phosphate. It is used for acute or chronic pain and to control a cough. Tolerance and both physical and psychological dependence can develop. Some results of overdosage are cardiorespiratory depression, circulatory collapse and coma.

U

Ulster Temperance Society   One of the earliest temperance organizations in Europe, it was founded in Northern Ireland in 1829. Thereafter, the organized temperance movement began to make effective progress.

uncontrolled drinking   A rather vague term generally used to refer to behavior that deliberately transgresses the social rules related to drinking. E. M. JELLINEK suggested the use of the term "undisciplined drinking" to describe such behavior. This behavior is not the same as LOSS OF CONTROL, which deprives the drinker of free choice.

under the influence of alcohol   When used in the general sense, this term refers to a mild disturbance of function caused by alcohol consumption. In many parts of the U.S. the condition is defined by the law in terms of specific concentrations of alcohol in the blood. The BLOOD ALCOHOL CONCENTRATION (BAC) of someone who is considered to be "under the influence of alcohol" is generally lower than that of someone classified as legally intoxicated. (See DRIVING WHILE IMPAIRED.)

United Kingdom

Alcohol: Alcohol has long been acknowledged as the leading drug of abuse in the United Kingdom. Despite the fact that in the late 19th century the government actively campaigned to shift the drinking pattern from gin to beer, both alcohol and to-

bacco consumption has increased. Beginning in the early part of this century, a "pub society" evolved in the UK with the result that drinking in public places has long been the primary form of entertainment. Thanks to the government intervention regarding gin, beer has dominated the English drinking scene as far and away the most popular alcoholic beverage. Annual per capita consumption of beer rose 3.9% between 1972 and 1978—the fourth highest per capita increase among western European countries. In addition, the income spent on beer (4.5% of household expenses) represented the highest proportion of any western European nation. In 1980 the average consumption per adult was: distilled spirits, 6 pints; wine, 15 pints; and beer, 270 pints. Economic factors such as high unemployment and poor housing are responsible in part, for increased alcohol consumption. While the cost of alcoholic beverages has risen, it has not risen as fast as other items in the economy. In 1985 UK beer consumption for persons 15 years and over was 109.2 liters. In 1994 the per capita rate of beer consumption remained high at 102.3 liters. The UK ranked ninth among 53 beer-consuming countries. Annual per capita consumption of alcohol was 7.2 liters in 1985. This increased slightly to 7.3 liters in 1995.

Government estimates report that 700,000 people suffer from alcohol-related problems. This figure is broken down geographically, as drinking patterns vary considerably within the UK. In Scotland and Northern Ireland there is a higher incidence of alcohol use than in England and Wales. Taking into account the impact of alcoholism on family and friends, the Department of Health and Social Services estimates that in England and Wales, 1 in 25 persons is affected by alcohol abuse; the figure is 1 in 10 in Scotland and Northern Ireland. The total impact alcohol-related incidents had on the economy (this included labor loss, health services, police and prison costs) was estimated to be $1.44 billion in 1979. That cost rose to more than $2 billion in 1989.

Government measures have attempted to reverse, or at least slow down, drinking trends. Legislative measures include public education, promotion of stricter laws for alcohol-related offenses, and revision of taxing and licensing laws affecting alcohol consumption. Some of these measures have met with strong opposition from the British Exchequer (the Treasury), the public (who oppose prohibitive taxes on alcoholic beverages) and the liquor industry—resisting efforts to restrain a trade that employs 700,000 people and exports $1.63 billion worth of goods.

Alcoholism treatment: Within the UK, both legislative controls on alcohol and treatment for alcohol-related problems are handled by specific divisions. In Scotland, alcohol problems fall under the authority of the Scottish Health Education Unit and the Scottish Council on Alcoholism. In Northern Ireland the sole autonomous agency handling alcohol issues is the Council on Alcohol-Related Problems. In England and Wales the Department of Health acts in cooperation with the National Council on Alcoholism, which is concerned primarily with preventative education, and with the Advisory Committee on Alcoholism, which deals mainly with clinical facilities. Treatment of alcohol-related problems is handled mostly by volunteer (nonprofit) organizations, assisted by the Department of Health and by substantial grants from the liquor industry.

The government's recent concern that the country's alcohol problems have indeed reached epidemic proportions is reflected in several white papers. (White papers are public documents issued by the government expressing their intended legislation on a particular subject.) Current reassessment of its responsibility to control alcohol problems among its citizens promises to result in a significant reorganization of governmental efforts to control alcohol abuse in the future.

Drugs other than alcohol: The use of drugs other than alcohol, though not as prevalent as in the U.S., has been a cause for concern in the UK since the 1920s, when the government first introduced policies aimed at controlling it. Drug addiction in the UK is treated as a medical rather than a criminal problem. A Ministry of Health committee in 1926 recommended that narcotic addicts (often people who had become addicted as a result of treatment for an illness) should receive narcotic prescriptions in the hope that they would gradually withdraw from the use of the drug. By 1960 the number of addicts had risen sharply and government committees undertook further studies. They reaffirmed the 1926 recommendations and established guidelines for what is now referred to as the "clinical system" or the "British system." A network of regular treatment centers was set up on both an inpatient and outpatient basis, and extremely controlled procedures were established for the prescribing of heroin and methadone to addicts. The number of drug-prescribing doctors also was restricted and controlled, and the recording and registering of addicts was made compulsory.

In 1967 the Dangerous Drugs Act was passed. As well as providing detention powers for illegal possession, use and sale of "notifiable" drugs, it also provides for a doctor's license to be revoked if he or she overprescribes. The extent of an addict's habit has been a controversy in the clinical system. Addicts obviously will try to convince a doctor that they have a strong, heavy habit in order to obtain larger doses. However, doctors are rationed as to the amount they may prescribe and urine tests frequently are employed to ascertain the extent of use. Once the existence of a habit has been established, those addicted to notifiable drugs are registered with the government and prescriptions are filed with a pharmacy, where they must then go on a *daily* basis to collect their designated dose.

In 1971 the Misuse of Drugs Act was passed and it came into full force in 1973. It modernized previous legislation and classified drugs according to the security required to prevent abuse and the penalties for illegal possession and sale. It also listed notifiable drugs as the following: cocaine, heroin, opium, methadone, morphine, diamorphine, dipipanone, hydrocodone, hydromorphone, dextromoramide, levorphanol, oxycodone, pethidine, piritramide and phenazocine.

The Misuse of Drugs Act also divided drugs into three categories according to their harmfulness. Maximum penalties for the chief types of offenses are related to the category of drugs involved. "Class A" drugs are the above-mentioned notifiable drugs, along with LSD; "class B" drugs include cannabis, cannabis plants, resin and liquid, amphetamines, dextroamphetamine, levamphetamine and methylamphetamine; while methaqualone and other miscellaneous drugs are categorized as "class C."

According to the Bureau for International Narcotics and Enforcement Affairs, marijuana was the illicit drug of choice in the UK during the mid-1990s. In 1995 the government set the number of marijuana users at approximately 100,000. Government attention has been focused on controlled heroin addiction. Although the anticipated influx of cocaine and crack-cocaine has not happened, amphetamines and ecstasy recently have attracted attention due to the highly publicized deaths of some young users.

Substance abuse treatment: The clinical system of drug treatment in the UK has been a controversial issue since first established. Opponents (including certain drug-treatment authorities in the UK and elsewhere) look on it as a "drugs-for-free" program and contend that it encourages drug use. Those who promote the system credit it with preventing the development of a black market, limiting narcotic use, reducing drug-related crime and enabling addicts to lead more useful lives. It has been suggested that the U.S. should adopt the system, but the usual medical and governmental response is to "wait and see." Though viewed as an interesting solution to the drug problem, it would seem that long-term positive results will have to be forthcoming before it is implemented.

In 1995 the British government issued a white paper entitled *Tackling Drugs Together* that launched a new drive against drugs. The aim of this initiative was to combine law enforcement with drug prevention in schools, in the community and in prison programs. The government also set up a 24-hour toll-free hot line that provides advice and information about drugs and inhalants. Rehabilitation programs for other drug-related problems are handled both through the Disabled Person's Resettlement Service of the Department of Employment and by volunteer organizations that run special hostels for addicts who have completed treatment in a hospital. Both the Phoenix House in London and the Alpha House in Portsmouth are rehabilitation hostels modeled after the Phoenix House in New York City.

Brewers and Licensed Retailers Association, *1993 Annual Report* (London, 1995).

United States Dept. of State, Bureau for International Narcotics and Law Enforcement Affairs, *International Narcotics Control Strategy Report March 1996.*

United States   In the 1990s the use of drugs, including alcohol, is so prevalent in the U.S. that it ranks as the number one topic of concern in a majority of public interest surveys. Drug use has been practiced on this continent since time immemorial, but was not regarded as a problem until the turn of the 20th century. The use of psychoactive substances predates the "discovery" of the North American continent by the Europeans, as many of the indigenous tribes included wine and other mood-altering plants, such as peyote, in their religious ceremonies. (It was from native peoples that the explorers learned to "drink the smoke" of burning tobacco, a habit they took with them when they returned to Europe.) (See SMOKING AND ALCOHOL.)

Historical overview: Alcohol use was common and tolerated in most of the first settlements. In many of the colonies, beverage alcohol was considered a staple. In general, the abuse of alcohol and even the existence of "the town drunk" were looked upon with benevolence. The early New Englanders, skilled at distilling grain into alcoholic beverages, created a flourishing RUM industry shortly upon their arrival.

At that time, MARIJUANA, known as hemp, was legally cultivated for its fiber, from which rope, paper and various other products were manufactured. Cannabis was used both recreationally and medicinally on a small scale throughout the 18th and 19th centuries. Cannabis cultivation was particularly extensive among the early Virginians and by the 19th century large plantations flourished throughout the south. Hemp production continued into the 1930s at which time commercial crops covered an estimated 10,000 acres nationally.

OPIUM use was common throughout the 19th century. Although mostly imported, opium poppies were also cultivated in the U.S. At that time "opium dens" (where paying customers came solely to smoke opium) were legal. Opium was a major ingredient of patent medications, such as LAUDANUM and PAREGORIC. These popular and affordable over-the-counter (OTC) tinctures were available at pharmacies. The history of the use and abuse of the opium derivative MORPHINE includes a disturbing episode in the American narrative. During the Civil War, wounded soldiers were treated with morphine on the battlefields and then sent home (many of them permanently disabled) with a syringe and a supply of the drug to kill the pain. The government, apparently unaware of the consequences of chronic use, inadvertently created a generation of morphine-addicted veterans. In the early years of the 20th century HEROIN virtually obliterated morphine and opium as drugs of abuse. It was not only a more refined and potent opium derivative, but it was smuggled into the U.S. in far greater quantities than opium or morphine, increasing its availability.

COCAINE was a relative latecomer to the U.S. Though its value as a stimulant was recognized years before, cocaine was popularized only in the late 1800s when it was introduced as an ingredient in many elixirs, including the fashionable new beverage Coca-Cola. Though the cocaine (coca) was removed from the recipe with the passage of the PURE FOOD AND DRUG ACT OF 1906, the COLA remains.

The history of drug control: Although the abuse of ALCOHOL was known throughout the U.S. from colonial times, PROHIBITION (THE VOLSTEAD ACT)—the first federal attempt to control alcohol consumption—was not enacted until 1919. It failed completely and was repealed in 1933. More recently, federal regulations, such as requiring states seeking federal highway funds to raise the minimum legal drinking age to reduce the number of fatalities as a result of alcohol-impairment, aimed at the reduction of particular alcohol-related problems have been more effective.

Legislation designed to control the production, distribution and use of drugs other than alcohol was introduced many years before Prohibition and achieved a relative amount of success. In 1895 San Francisco was the first of many cities to ban the opium smoking and opium dens that were popular among the Chinese immigrants who had been brought to America to build the railroads. This leg-islation may have been motivated more by racist sentiment than by concern about opium addiction, since no attempt was made until several years later to ban the sale of the readily available opium-based patent medicines. The Harrison Act of 1914 dealt the single greatest blow to unregulated distribution of mood-altering drugs in the U.S. It curtailed the sale of opiates and severely limited the circumstances under which physicians could prescribe them.

In the 1940s and 1950s, federal drug regulators grew concerned about newly discovered pharmaceuticals achieving popularity before their potential for abuse was acknowledged. One such group, sedatives, which were erroneously termed "minor tranquilizers," were prescribed by doctors for the treatment of anxiety. At the same time AMPHETAMINES, with their potential for cardiac damage and addiction, were prescribed as "energizers" and aids to weight loss. These pharmaceuticals are particularly harmful because patients using legitimate prescriptions often do not realize that they are every bit as vulnerable to dependence as illicit drug users. In the late 1960s and early 1970s, a time later romanticized as the "Woodstock Era," drug use took on a glamorous appeal when heralded by the Beatles, Timothy Leary and many other stars. Drug use decreased in the 1970s, but not for long. In the 1980s use of almost all drugs by young people was again on the rise. This fact, coupled with heightened national concern over drug-related violence, helped to launch the highly politicized campaign known as the "War on Drugs."

Alcohol: In our society there exists an acute awareness of the dangers of alcohol abuse. Equally deep-rooted, however, is the perception that drinking is not only socially acceptable but often a necessary reward for getting through the familial, social and occupational stresses of daily life. The consequence of these contradictory positions is the unsettling incongruity between values and drinking behavior. The message implicit in the inherited legacy from the 19th century temperance movement has evolved through the decades. Current factors contributing to antialcohol sentiment include both an awareness of the disastrous psychological and physical effects of chronic drinking as well as the potential loss to business profits (statistics reveal that alcohol abuse costs employers and tax payers and raises health insurance premiums). The religious right, with their

Preliminary Data—As of June 1996
Adjusted 1979–1993 Estimates

Estimated Numbers of Persons (in Thousands) in the U.S. Population Aged 12 and Older, by Age Group, Race/Ethnicity, and Sex: 1979–1997

Demographic Characteristics	1979	1982	1985	1988
TOTAL	180,343	186,440	192,605	198,347
AGE GROUP				
12–17	23,758	22,295	21,558	20,250
18–25	32,604	33,236	31,601	29,688
26–34	31,339	34,241	36,477	38,570
>35	92,641	96,669	102,969	109,839
RACE/ETHNICITY				
White	147,202	150,087	154,224	156,742
Black	19,271	20,134	21,332	22,271
Hispanic	10,586	11,834	13,256	14,925
Other	3,283	4,385	3,793	4,408
SEX				
Male	85,887	88,840	91,828	94,878
Female	94,456	97,600	100,776	103,468

NOTE: The population distributions for the 1993 through 1997 NHSDAs are post-stratified to population projections of totals based on the 1990 decennial census. The 1979 NHSDA used population projections based on the 1970 census; NHSDAs from 1982 through1992 used projections based on the 1980 census. The change from one census base to another has little effect on estimated percentages reporting drug use, but may have a significant effect on estimates of number of drug users in some subpopulation groups.

NOTE: Estimates for 1979 through 1993 may differ from estimates for these survey years that were published in other NHSDA reports. The estimates shown here for 1979 through 1993 have been adjusted to improve their comparability with estimates based on the new version of the NHSDA instrument that was fielded in 1994 and subsequent NHSDAs. For 1979 and 1982, estimates are not shown [as indicated by –] where (a) the relevant data were not collected, or (b) the date for those drugs were based on measures that differed appreciably from those used in the other survey years. Consequently, adjustments to the 1979 and 1982 data were made only for those drugs whose measures were comparable to those in the other survey years.

Source: SAMHSA, Office of Applied Studies, National Household Survey on Drug Abuse.

(continued on next page)

Preliminary Data—As of June 1996
Adjusted 1979–1993 Estimates (continued)

Estimated Numbers of Persons (in Thousands) in the U.S. Population Aged 12 and Older, by Age Group, Race/Ethnicity, and Sex: 1979–1997

Demographic Characteristics	1990	1991	1992	1993	1994	1995	1996	1997
TOTAL	**201,188**	**202,859**	**205,713**	**207,199**	**209,411**	**211,532**	**214,047**	**216,206**
AGE GROUP								
12–17	19,978	20,145	20,684	21,224	21,773	22,208	22,512	22,547
18–25	29,021	28,496	27,964	28,327	28,027	27,820	27,796	27,691
26–34	38,821	38,737	38,215	37,194	36,588	35,975	35,474	35,246
>35	113,368	115,481	118,850	120,453	123,023	125,529	128,265	130,722
RACE/ETHNICITY								
White	157,427	157,363	158,398	157,693	159,029	159,722	160,358	161,169
Black	22,779	23,030	23,649	23,002	23,365	23,686	24,053	24,406
Hispanic	15,734	161,178	16,849	18,501	19,112	19,736	20,813	21,578
Other	5,248	6,288	6,816	8,002	7,905	8,388	8,823	9,054
SEX								
Male	96,382	97,242	98,778	99,322	100,365	101,449	102,928	104,017
Female	104,806	105,617	106,935	107,877	109,046	110,083	111,120	112,189

Because of the methodology used to adjust the 1979 through 1993 estimates, some logical inconsistency may exist between estimates for a given drug within the same survey year. For example, some adjusted estimates of past year use may appear to be greater than adjusted lifetime estimates. These inconsistencies tend to be small, rare and not statistically significant.

[a] Difference between estimate and 1997 estimate is significant at the .05 level.
[b] Difference between estimate and 1997 estimate is significant at the .01 level.

powerful antidrinking message and grass roots organizations such as MOTHERS AGAINST DRUNK DRIVING, impact on public awareness. The gradual shift in awareness regarding alcohol's affects on individuals and society has led to much research on the causes of alcoholism, bringing many to accept the "disease concept" theory, which gave birth to ALCOHOLICS ANONYMOUS (AA). Membership in AA, or any other 12-Step program has become not only socially acceptable in many parts of the country, but attending a "meeting" is now a fashionable alternative to public socializing, such as going to a bar.

In spite of the inconsistencies in public sentiment, alcohol availability and CONSUMPTION has decreased since the 1980s. In a 1997 survey by *World Drink Trends 1995,* the U.S. ranked 24th out of the 53 leading alcohol-consuming countries and per capita consumption of alcohol stood at 6.8 liters (down from a high of 8.1 liters in 1980). Between 1990 and 1994, per capita beer consumption decreased almost 6%.

Among men in the U.S. with full-time jobs, statistics show that 14% are considered "heavier drinkers" (14 or more drinks per week), 36% are

Preliminary Data—

Survey Sample Sized for All Respondents Aged 12 and Older, by Age Group

Demographic Characteristics	12–17 Years		18–25 Years	
	1996	1997	1996	1997
TOTAL	22,512	22,547	27,796	27,691
RACE/ETHNICITY				
White	15,243	15,166	18,764	18,661
Black	3,288	3,227	3,778	3,874
Hispanic	2,909	3,007	3,882	3,807
Other	1,072	1,147	1,373	1,350
SEX				
Male	11,538	11,501	13,871	13,981
Female	10,974	11,047	13,925	13,710
POPULATION DENSITY[1]				
Large Metro	9,103	9,196	12,158	11,261
Small Metro	8,084	8,059	9,605	10,116
Nonmetro	5,324	5,292	6,033	6,314
REGION				
Northeast	3,738	3,825	4,661	4,408
North Central	5,863	5,154	6,740	6,309
South	7,946	8,492	9,546	11,147
West	4,964	5,076	6,849	5,826
ADULT EDUCATION[1]				
<High School	N/A	N/A	5,863	5,809
High School Grad	N/A	N/A	9,708	9,974
Some College	N/A	N/A	8,434	8,969
College Graduate	N/A	N/A	3,781	2,939
CURRENT EMPLOYMENT[2]				
Full-time	N/A	N/A	13,179	13,285
Part-time	N/A	N/A	6,417	6,293
Unemployed	N/A	N/A	2,227	2,316
Other[3]	N/A	N/A	5,973	5,797

N/A: Not applicable.

[1] Population density is based on 1990 MSA classifications and their 1990 Census of Population counts.

Source: SAMHSA, Office of Applied Studies, National Household Survey on Drug Abuse, 1996–1997.

(continued on next page)

As of June 1998

and Demographic Characteristcs: 1996 and 1997

26–34 Years		35 Years and Older		Total	
1996	**1997**	**1996**	**1997**	**1996**	**1997**
35,474	**35,246**	**128,265**	**130,722**	**214,047**	**216,206**
24,948	24,449	101,403	102,893	160,358	161,169
4,282	4,392	12,706	12,912	24,053	24,406
4,504	4,643	9,518	10,120	20,813	21,578
1,740	1,761	4,638	4,797	8,823	9,054
17,352	17,490	60,167	61,045	102,928	104,017
18,122	17,755	68,098	69,677	111,120	112,189
16,815	16,793	54,972	53,345	93,048	90,595
11,550	11,776	43,824	46,497	73,064	76.448
7,109	6,677	29,470	30,881	47,936	49,164
6,866	6,244	26.969	25,864	42,234	40,342
8,327	8,593	30,825	28,299	51,755	48,356
12,133	12,655	44,923	48,928	74,549	81,231
8,149	7,754	25,548	27,621	45,510	46,278
5,447	4,988	26,040	25,785	37,360	36,581
11,328	11,429	44,620	43,760	65,656	65,162
8,438	9,266	26,531	27,585	43,402	45,820
10,261	9,563	31.075	33,592	45,118	46,095
24,308	24,448	61,597	65,260	99,083	102,993
3,705	3,546	11,953	11,328	22,075	21,167
1,863	1,911	4,179	4,327	8,269	8,554
5,598	5,341	50,538	49,808	62,109	60,945

[2] Data on adult education and current employment not shown for persons aged 12–17. Estimates for both adult education and current employment are for persons aged >18.
[3] Retired, disabled, homemaker, student, "other."

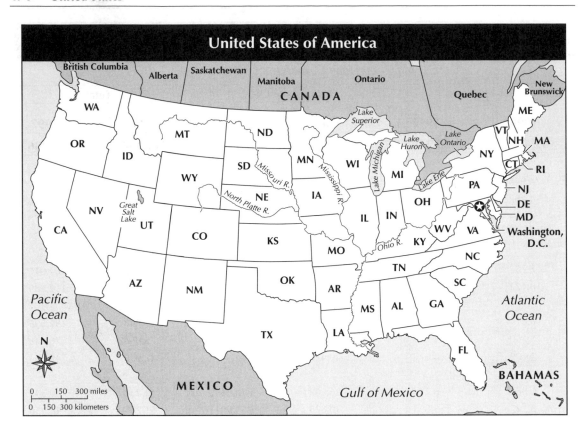

United States of America

"moderate drinkers" (4–13 drinks per week), 28% are "light drinkers" (3 drinks per week) and 22% are "abstainers." Among full-time employed women, 7% are heavier drinkers, 21% are moderate drinkers, 40% are light drinkers and 32% are abstainers. Among part-time workers, 35% of men and 4% of women are heavy drinkers. An unusually high proportion of the alcoholic beverages consumed in the U.S. are produced domestically: 95% of the beer, 85% of the wine and 68% of the distilled spirits.

Despite the drop in overall consumption, the costs to society of excessive drinking remain extremely high. In 1988 an estimated 18 million adults in the U.S. were problem drinkers; more than 10 million of them could be said to be suffering from alcoholism. Nearly 5 million ADOLESCENTS, or 3 in every 10, have drinking problems.

A 1988 Gallup Poll showed one in four families troubled by alcohol. Alcohol is the culprit in 40% of family court cases and accounts for between 25% and 50% of the violence between spouses. (See CHILDREN OF ALCOHOLICS AND SUBSTANCE ABUSERS and SPOUSE ABUSE.) In 1987 more than 1.4 million persons were treated for alcohol abuse and dependence. In 1985 an alcohol-related diagnosis was involved in 1.1 million (4%) cases. In 1986, of the 27.4 million short-stay hospital discharges (excluding those related to pregnancy) among Americans age 14 and older, there were more than 26,000 alcohol-related deaths caused by CIRRHOSIS. Drunk drivers were responsible for roughly half the 44,000 driving fatalities in 1988. Alcohol is a factor in nearly half of America's murders, suicides and accidental deaths. In all, chronic excessive drinking claims an estimated 100,000 lives per year, 20 times as many as do all illegal drugs combined. In 1990 alcoholism and alcohol abuse cost the U.S. an estimated $136 billion dollars. (See ACCIDENTS, CRIME, DISEASES, DRIVING WHILE IMPAIRED ECONOMIC IMPACT and SUICIDE.)

Alcoholism has been called the "equal opportunity disease" because it effects almost all ages, socio-economic levels, racial/ethnic groups and both genders. National Black Alcoholism Council chairperson Maxine Woman, summing up her belief about the vulnerability of her constituency, writes: "In the black community, the fire tends to spread much, much faster and burn a whole lot longer." (See AFRICAN AMERICANS.) The susceptibility of Native American and people of Irish descent is well known; however, high rates of alcoholism also occur among groups in which it was previously rare, such as among JEWS and ASIAN AMERICANS (Asian Americans are also prone to a skin flush reaction). In addition, as many as 45% of the country's more than 300,000 homeless individuals are alcoholics.

The various federal antialcohol programs—most of which were instituted in the 1960s—generally operate in conjunction with similar state and local programs. (Most of the state programs have operated since the 1950s.) The principal federal organization is the National Institute on Alcohol Abuse and Alcoholism (NIAAA), established in 1970. In addition to its own programs, this body operates the National Clearinghouse for Alcohol Information. The U.S. Department of Transportation has actively worked to reduce alcohol-related driving fatalities since the 1960s, and the Department of Education is responsible for school antialcohol programs.

Marijuana: Aside from alcohol, tobacco, caffeine and prescription medication, the major drug of use today in the U.S. is marijuana. It is the most widely used illegal drug in the U.S.—an estimated 62 million people have used marijuana (the actual number of users, whether regular or occasional, is impossible to verify). In 1994 the national drug-abuse survey estimated that 8.5% of the population had used marijuana in the year preceding the survey. Of major concern in the U.S. today is the early age at which drug users begin to experiment. Marijuana use, which declined among 12- to 17-year-olds between 1979 and 1992 (24.8% in 1979; 10.1% in 1991; and 8.1% in 1992), began edging back up in 1993 (10%). Since then, use by teenagers has continued to increase. The National Institute on Drug Abuse's 1994 *Monitoring the Future Study* reported that annual marijuana use among eighth graders rose 2.5 times its 1991 level (from 6% to 16%). During the same time period, annual usage among 10th graders rose

from 15% to 20%, and for 12th graders, from 22% to 35%. In 1995 nearly 1 in 20 (4.6%) seniors were using marijuana on a daily basis. In 1995 the U.S. government estimated that 25% of the available marijuana was cultivated domestically. Factoring in the number of people who grow plants in their backyard or in their homes for personal use, however, increases the percentage substantially. Marijuana is the second largest cash crop in California. Of the remaining 75% of the marijuana sold in the U.S., 50% is imported from Mexico and 25% from Jamaica and South America. The number of HEAD SHOPS that have sprung up around the country suggests that at some level the general public is willing to accept, if not condone, marijuana use. Head shops sell a wide variety of drug-related items, including rolling papers, pipes and water pipes, and even books on cultivating your own marijuana plants. (Many states have imposed interdictions on these shops, prohibiting the marketing of items specifically as "drug paraphernalia.")

Cocaine, heroin and polydrug use: Cocaine's potential as a drug of abuse may have previously been held in check by its relatively high price, but it became a leading recreational drug in the 1980s when prices dropped considerably. However, cocaine use since 1990, especially in the form of crack, has leveled off, possibly due to its impurity. The rate of heroin use remained relatively stable from the early 1900s until the mid-1980s, began a fairly steady rise until 1989, but declined again in the following year. The SAMHSA (Substance Abuse and Mental Health Services Administration) *1997 National Household Survey on Drug Abuse* estimated that 2,019,000 persons had used heroin in their lifetime and 597,000 (0.3% of the population) had used it in the year prior to the survey. POLYDRUG USE (the use of different classes of illicit drugs simultaneously) has been on the increase in recent years—often with disastrous results. The synergistic effects of certain drug combinations can be fatal. Alcohol is the most frequently involved primary or secondary drug in polydrug use, while many users regularly take an "upper" in the morning and a "downer" at night.

Trafficking: Although for many years south Florida was the hub of illicit drug trafficking, there has been a recent trend toward unloading drugs along the New England coastline, New York City, southern

California and Texas. This may be due to the fact that there has been increased surveillance by enforcement authorities in Florida. The high concentration of organized crime in the northeast and the desire by smugglers to land their products in densely populated areas where there is a larger market, allowing for quicker distribution, are certainly other possible factors. According to the U.S. Drug Enforcement Administration (DEA), in 1995 New York City was one of the major distribution points for Southeast Asian and South American heroin. However Florida and the southeastern region of the country remain prime importation areas simply because of their geographical relation to Latin America and the Caribbean.

The Midwest has recently developed its own distribution center: Chicago. Known for many years as the transportation capital of the U.S. (aircraft, trucking and railroad), Chicago's central location now is being exploited by drug traffickers. Drug gangs also are infiltrating midwestern cities such as Omaha, Des Moines, St. Louis, Cincinnati and Kansas City. Air smugglers have long been operating between the south-central U.S. and Latin America, usually using secondary roads and private airstrips, and because of the increased enforcement in South Florida in the mid-1990s, smugglers have turned to the Texas Gulf Coast for shipment by boat. In Texas, drugs coming in overland from Mexico have continued to be a major concern.

The western region of the U.S., which encompasses the area from Alaska to the California-Mexico border, faces three distinct drug-abuse problems: it is a source area, an importation point and a major distribution center. The majority of the country's clandestine drug labs are located in California, producing LSD, PCP and other chemical compounds, many of which gained popularity in this state. (See LSD, PCP, and CLANDESTINE LABORATORIES.) The area is convenient for smuggling not only because of its deep-water ports and rugged shoreline but also because of the proximity of LAX (Los Angeles International Airport). Geographically, California is a direct point of entry for both Southeast Asian and Mexican heroin.

Regional drug use: The primary drugs of abuse in the south-central region of the U.S. are marijuana and cocaine, followed by methamphetamine and heroin. The northeastern region, extending from Delaware to Maine, has more illicit drug users than any other part of the country. However, in 1994 it was estimated that at least half of the current heroin users lived in the western region of the country, while only a quarter lived in the northeast region.

The U.S. has the dubious distinction of being the world's leading consumer and "trend setter" for illicit drugs. This has been substantiated by the patterns of use for LSD, which was very popular during the 1960s, for crack in the 1980s and for the inhalants fad, which was short-lived, although use still continues on a smaller scale. As use of these substances became widespread in the U.S., within a matter of months (or in some cases it took up to a few years) their popularity spread to other countries.

For more detailed figures on the number of addicts, the sources of a drug, and the various treatment and prevention methods involved, see individual drug entries. For information on how drug use has affected the U.S. economy, see BUSINESS and ACCIDENTS.

urine screen   If a person has used a drug, either the drug itself or its metabolite will be present in the urine. Although other body fluids can be used to screen for the presence of drugs (blood, sweat, saliva, body tissue), urine testing has become the preferred procedure because specimens can be easily obtained with minimal facilities by an unskilled technician. The process also is relatively inexpensive and painless and provides highly reliable results. Urine testing for drugs first came into general use as a part of methadone maintenance and is now used routinely not only as a drug-abuse treatment procedure but in conjunction with military, sports, business and penal drug-screening programs as well.

The most widely used urine tests currently performed to detect the presence of drugs are: GAS CHROMATOGRAPHY/MASS SPECTOMETRY (GC-MS), RADIOIMMUNOASSAY (RIA) and ENZYME MULTIPLIED IMMUNOASSAY TECHNIQUE (EMIT). Two characteristics are basic to all the various urine tests—their sensitivity and their specificity. The sensitivity of a test is determined by the smallest concentration of a drug or metabolite that can be detected. The specificity of a test refers to the degree to which it can discriminate between closely related drugs, metabolites or naturally occurring substances.

The usual substances tested on a urine screen are THC (tetrahydrocannabinol, the active ingredient in marijuana), which appears as acid metabolites; heroin, which appears as morphine; amphetamines; cocaine; barbiturates and phencyclidine; though other compounds also can be detected. Methods for detecting LSD in urine are presently restricted to research laboratories.

The first over-the-counter urinalysis kit was marketed in early 1984 by Checkpoint Laboratories of Virginia. The kits are sold in drugstores and urine specimens are mailed to Checkpoint, which screens for traces of marijuana, cocaine and other drugs. (See DRUG TESTING.)

U.S. Coast Guard   A part of the Armed Forces, the Coast Guard is administered by the Department of Transportation in time of peace and the navy in time of war. It is the Coast Guard's responsibility to protect the shores and waters of the U.S. and its territories. Additionally this organization provides safety and enforces the laws and regulations in all maritime activities. In this capacity, the Coast Guard has been heavily involved in drug interdiction operations on the high seas as well as along the coast. Using ships, aircraft and personnel, they search for and seize ships and apprehend the crews suspected of smuggling contraband into the U.S.

U.S. Department of Education   Headed by a cabinet-level secretary, this department is engaged in several activities relating to alcohol and other drug use, including the development, funding and evaluation of school-based drug education and intervention programs.

U.S. Department of Health and Human Services (DHHS)   Headed by a cabinet-level secretary, this agency consists of units that include the U.S. Public Health Service, which is headed by an assistant secretary of DHHS. The six units that make up the service include

The Centers for Disease Control;
The Food and Drug Administration;
The Health Resources and Services Administration;
The National Institutes of Health;

The Alcohol, Drug Abuse, and Mental Health Administration;
The Agency for Toxic Substances and Disease Registry.

Because of its component agencies, DHHS has nominal oversight of program funding, research, regulation, enforcement, education and evaluation regarding drug and alcohol use and abuse.

U.S. Department of Labor   Among the many other issues that the U.S. Department of Labor addresses, are the issues of alcohol and other drug use. The department provides information on research and legislation related to substance abuse in the workplace and offers employers information that will assist them in the development of substance-abuse programs. This assistance is provided through the department's substance-abuse information database (SAID).

user   An individual who drinks alcoholic beverages or uses other mood-altering substances, as opposed to an "ABSTAINER."

U.S. Olympic Committee   Perhaps no organization has had more experience with preventing the use of illicit drugs by athletes than the U.S. Olympic Committee. The committee has for years worked extensively to make Olympic competition drug-free through the use of testing, prevention and education efforts.

In the 1988 Summer Olympics, Canada's Ben Johnson was forced to return his gold medal after his drug test revealed steroid use. The committee has achieved widespread international cooperation on these issues. Today, more than 300 drugs are banned at the Olympic Games by the International Olympic Committee.

U.S. Pharmacopeia (USP)   A legally recognized book of standards for drugs, published by the U.S. Pharmacopeia Convention, Inc. It contains standards for strength and purity and formulas for making nearly all drugs currently in use. The *USP,* first published in 1820, is revised every five years. Standards provided in the *USP* were given legal status under the National Food and Drug Act of 1967.

V

Valium A sedative hypnotic containing diazepam, a BENZODIAZEPINE derivative. Used in the treatment of tension, anxiety and seizures, as well as for alcohol withdrawal; tolerance can develop along with physical and psychological dependence. One of the most widely prescribed drugs in the U.S., Valium has a significant potential for abuse and when taken with alcohol or other central nervous system depressants it has an ADDITIVE effect.

Valmid A mild sedative hypnotic that contains ethinamate and is used when deep hypnosis is not needed. When taken with alcohol or other central nervous system depressants it can have an ADDITIVE effect. No longer available in the U.S., tolerance can develop along with dependency, and overdosage can cause respiratory depression.

vaporous anesthetics Liquid anesthetics that readily vaporize at relatively low temperatures. The two vaporous anesthetics that are sometimes abused as INHALANTS are CHLOROFORM and ETHER.

vascular system Several studies have shown associations between immoderate drinking and elevated blood pressure. One such study indicated a cause-and-effect relationship between alcohol consumption and hypertension, as well as a genetic factor that independently predisposes a person both to drinking and to hypertension. (See HEART.)

Diseases associated with blood clots, which obstruct blood vessels, are thought to be more common in alcoholics. Depressed platelet counts, a higher hematocrit (number of red blood cells) and decreased dissolution of fibrin, the basic element of blood clots, have been noted in the blood of alcoholics.

The *Eighth Special Report* notes that "while there is considerable evidence that moderate alcohol consumption decreases the risk of coronary artery disease (CAD), numerous studies have shown that chronic heavy drinking is associated with other cardiovascular diseases, such as cardiomyopathy (heart muscle disease), hypertension (high blood pressure), arrhythmias (disturbances in heart rhythm), and stroke (cerebrovascular hemorrhage)."

P. D. Arkwright et al., "Effects of Alcohol Use and Other Aspects of Lifestyle on Blood Pressure Levels and Prevalence of Hypertension in a Working Population," *Circulation* 66 (1982): 60–66.

P. D. Arkwright et al., "Alcohol and Hypertension," *Australian and New Zealand Journal of Medicine* 14 (1984): 463–469.

Enoch Gordis, M.D., ed., *Seventh Special Report to the U.S. Congress on Alcohol and Health* (Rockville, Md.: National Institute on Alcohol Abuse and Alcoholism [NIAAA], 1990).

Enoch Gordis, M.D., ed., *Eighth Special Report to the U.S. Congress on Alcohol and Health* (Rockville, Md.: NIAAA, 1993).

W. E. M. Lands and S. Zachari, "Alcohol and Cardiovascular Disease," *Alcohol Health & Research World* 14 (1990): 304–312.

Venezuela   Thanks to its vast oil resources, Venezuela experienced enormous economic growth during the 1970s, which resulted in a major increase in the availability of alcoholic beverages. This prosperity, along with Venezuela's location (its easy access by air, land and sea to major drug distribution and consumption sites), has made the country a major force in international drug trafficking.

Alcohol: Wine and beer production doubled in that decade, and the production of distilled spirits rose 500% between 1970 and 1976. Substantial increases also were reported in the importation of spirits, most of them entering the country through the duty-free port of Margarita. Available information suggests that the illegal production of alcoholic beverages also grew, despite this glut of regulated alcoholic beverages. The primary illegal drinks are *cocuy,* a distillate of cactus agave similar to Mexican tequila, and *guarapo fuerte,* a meadlike drink fermented from molasses.

In 1995 apparent Venezuelan per capita consumption of ABSOLUTE ALCOHOL, based on the total population, was measured at 5.3 liters, lower than that of countries in North America and western Europe, but second only to that of Brazil among the countries in South America surveyed. This figure probably is highly understated, however, as it does not include the consumption of illegal alcoholic beverages that is known to occur. In the year before, consumption of beer was measured at 76 liters per annum, and wine consumption apparently was too low for measurement.

Drugs other than alcohol: According to the Bureau of Narcotics and Law Enforcement Affairs, "Venezuela is a major transit country for cocaine, marijuana and heroin destined for the U.S. and Europe, and for chemicals diverted to Colombian drug laboratories." Faced with a growing drug-abuse problem—and a consequent surge in urban crime—Venezuelan government officials have intensified prevention and treatment efforts.

Brewers and Licensed Retailers Association, *1993 Annual Report* (London, 1995).

NTC Publications LTD, *World Drink Trends 1995* (London, 1997).

vermouth   A popular aperitif with a base of either red or white wine. During its manufacture vermouth is flavored with as many as 40 aromatic herbs, fortified with spirits, pasteurized, refrigerated and thoroughly filtered. In the U.S. and many other places, it is used mainly as an ingredient in cocktails. The lighter dry vermouth, known as French vermouth, frequently is combined with gin to make a martini. Italian vermouth, which is sweeter, is often served on the rocks. Vermouth contains up to 19% alcohol (38 proof).

Veronal   A long-acting BARBITURATE that contained BARBITAL. First manufactured in 1903, Veronal was the first barbiturate used in medicine but is no longer available.

vinbarbital   A short- to intermediate-acting BARBITURATE.

vinho de jurumena   A hallucinogenic beverage made from the seeds of *Mimosa hostilis,* a plant native to Brazil. It contains an organic form of DMT, the plant's active principle.

Violent Crime Control and Law Enforcement Act of 1994   The Violent Crime Control and Law Enforcement Act of 1994 represents a bipartisan product which took six years to enact. It is the largest crime bill in the history of the country and provided for 100,000 new police officers, $9.7 billion in funding for prisons and $6.1 billion in funding for prevention programs, which were designed with significant input from experienced police officers. The act also significantly expanded the government's ability to deal with problems caused by criminal aliens. The crime bill provided $2.6 billion in additional funding for the FBI (Federal Bureau of Investigation), DEA (Drug Enforcement Administration), INS (Immigration Naturalization Services), United States Attorneys, Treasury Department and other Justice Department components, as well as the federal courts. Some of the provisions of the bill that are relevant to AOD (alcohol and other drugs) are summarized below:

Provides new and stiffer penalties for violent and drug-trafficking crimes committed by gang members;

Triples the maximum penalties for using children to distribute drugs in or near a protected zone (schools, playgrounds, video arcades and youth centers);

Imposes mandatory life imprisonment without possibility of parole for federal offenders with three or more convictions for serious violent felonies or drug-trafficking crimes;

Sets up a competitive grant program to support state and local drug courts, which provide supervision and specialized services to offenders with rehabilitation potential ($29 million available in 1995; $971 million authorized for 1996–2000);

Provides $383 million for prison drug-treatment programs, including $270 million in formula grants for states.

virola   A tree belonging to the Myristicaceae family. The bark is made into a psychedelic snuff by the Yekwana Indians of Venezuela.

vision problems   Among the many physical problems evident in very young children of severely alcoholic mothers who drank during pregnancy are vision problems. Two reports by K. L. Jones and D.W. Smith and colleagues described, among other gross physical deformities in these children, short palpebral fissures (small eye openings), ptosis (drooping eyelids), microopthalmia (small eyes) and epicanthal folds (skin folds across the inner corners of the eyes, which are abnormal in Caucasians). A 1985 Swedish study confirmed that children of alcoholic mothers are likely to have severe distortions in visual perception. While there is much to be learned in this area, it is evident that FETAL ALCOHOL SYNDROME (FAS) is a major known cause of birth defects.

K. L. Jones and D. W. Smith, "Recognition of the Fetal Alcohol Syndrome in Early Infancy," *Lancet* 2 (1973): 999–1001.

K. L. Jones et al., "Pattern of Malformation in Offspring of Chronic Alcoholic Mothers," *Lancet* 1 (1973): 1267–1271.

vitamins and minerals   Vitamin and mineral deficiencies may occur in alcoholics and other drug users with or without an adequate food supply. According to an expert in the field, Dr. Esteban Mezey, "Alcoholism is probably the principal cause of vitamin and protein deficiencies among civilized people with adequate food supplies." (See NUTRITION.)

Nutritional deficiencies found in substance users can be attributed to a number of factors. One is malnutrition, commonly found in addicts in general and stemming from the poor eating habits and diminished self-care. Stimulants (cocaine and amphetamines) act as appetite suppressants, such that users of these drugs often forgo eating altogether for long periods. Alcoholics also are subject to nutritional deficiencies as a result of factors that are specific to excessive drinking. The consumption of ethanol causes impairment in the absorption and storage of ingested vitamins. Most vitamins are stored in the liver, but alcoholics with liver damage frequently lack the capacity to store them. Alcoholics frequently experience a diminished ability to convert vitamins into metabolically active cofactors, preventing the body from using vitamins properly. Excessive drinking also may increase the body's need for certain minerals to stimulate the specific enzymes required to metabolize excessive amounts of ingested ethanol, as well as to repair tissue damaged by ethanol. Zinc, for example, is needed for a number of enzymes. Excessive amounts of alcohol also affect mineral metabolism and cause excessive excretion of minerals in the urine.

Chronic alcoholism most frequently is associated with deficiencies of thiamine, vitamin B12 and folic acid. The minerals most commonly affected by excessive use of alcohol are magnesium, calcium and zinc.

Vitamins:

Thiamine: There is a direct connection between thiamine deficiency and alcoholism. Thiamine deficiency results from impaired absorption (from 40% to 60% of the body's ability to absorb thiamine is impaired by alcohol), decreased dietary intake and acute liver injury. Because a damaged liver lowers the body's response to administered thiamine, alcoholic patients need increasing amounts of thiamine in order to make certain enzymes react properly. Thiamine deficiency can cause beriberi, a condition associated with disease of the HEART muscle. It also appears to play a major role in WERNICKE'S ENCEPHALOPATHY syndrome.

Vitamin B12: Vitamin B12 is necessary for cell replication. High alcohol consumption causes impairment of vitamin B12 absorption, even with adequate intake of nutrients. Increased amounts of this vitamin are needed for metabolism of a high quantity of alcohol and for repair of tissue damage.

Folic Acid: Deficiencies of folic acid have been found in alcoholics, especially those with liver disease. Lack of folic acid, which is used in cell replication, may lead to impairment of DNA and protein synthesis.

Minerals:

Magnesium: An element involved in energy production of cells, magnesium plays an important role in the work of the central nervous system (CNS) and in the action of many body enzymes. During periods of alcohol ingestion there is a depletion of magnesium through urinary excretion. Because of magnesium's influence on the CNS this diminution may account in part for the irritability experienced after a period of drinking. Symptoms of WITHDRAWAL are similar to those of magnesium deficiency. Deficiencies of magnesium may play a role in cardiac arrhythmia and interfere with the body's response to thiamine.

Calcium: Acute ethanol consumption increases urinary excretion of calcium, particularly during withdrawal. Lack of calcium may be involved in alcoholic cardiomyopathy. Osteoporosis, a degeneration of bone tissue associated with calcium deficiency, is frequently found in alcoholics, as well as in users of drugs other than alcohol.

Zinc: Many enzymes associated with DNA synthesis and RNA metabolism require zinc. Zinc is important to the growth and repair of the liver. Alcohol/other drug users are often deficient in zinc, generally because of poor dietary habits. Zinc deficiency has been related to anorexia, which leads to further malnutrition.

Charles S. Lieber, "Alcohol-Nutrition Interactions: 1984 Update," *Alcohol* 1 (1984): 151–152.

Esteban Mezey, "Effects of Alcohol on the Gastrointestinal System," in *Practice of Medicine* 10, no. 7 (Hagerstown, Md.: Harper Medical, 1970): 1–9.

Gary and Steve Null, *Alcohol and Nutrition* (New York: Pyramid, 1977).

vodka A Russian word meaning "little water"; "the diminutive of *voda* (water). Vodka is the traditional alcoholic beverage of Russia, Poland and the Baltic states. In Russian the term sometimes is used to refer to any kind of distilled alcoholic beverage, which is compatible with the fact that vodka may be distilled from a wide variety of agricultural products. The substances from which vodka most often is distilled are rye, corn, barley, wheat, potatoes and, less frequently, sugar beets. In its history, however, vodka has been produced from whatever material was abundant and cheap at the time. The base from which vodka is made is not especially important because it is first distilled at or above 190 proof, which is almost pure alcohol.

Vodka was first produced in Russia during the 14th century, and up until World War II its production and consumption were limited almost exclusively to Russia, Poland and the Baltic states. After the war the production and consumption of vodka spread to other countries, particularly the U.S. but also Austria, Britain, the Netherlands, Finland, Denmark and Israel, where a kosher vodka has been produced.

The basic method currently used to make vodka was first developed in Russia and Poland; producers of vodka in other countries follow this basic method but have added their own variations. Today the distilling operation usually is dispensed with. Producers begin by buying distilled spirits that already have been highly rectified (or purified). These spirits are further rectified by filtration through beds of vegetable charcoal. The resultant liquid is at least 190 proof, which is reduced to a marketable strength by the addition of distilled water. Unlike other distilled alcoholic beverages, such as brandy or whiskey, vodka is not aged. Russian vodka is usually bottled at about 80 proof, and Polish vodka at around 90 proof. According to U.S. government regulations, vodka must be bottled at not less than 80 proof and not more than 110 proof.

In the U.S. federal regulations describe vodka as "neutral spirits . . . without distinctive character, aroma or taste." However, although vodka is usually colorless, contrary to popular opinion, it is not without odor or taste. Like any alcoholic beverage, it has both a taste and a smell. The absolute alcohol in vodka gives a mild burning sensation, or "sting," accompanied by an astringent taste. The CONGENERS present, depending on the particular type of vodka, also can contribute to the taste. The smell of vodka on the breath (or through the pores), while not so pronounced as that of whiskey, rum or, to a lesser extent, gin, is still detectable at close quarters, even when the vodka has been diluted by the addition of fruit juice, tonic or other mixers. While it does not change the basic taste of fruit juice or other mixers, vodka's presence is clearly detectable in such cocktails. Some varieties of vodka have additional coloring or flavoring added to them. One Polish vodka, for instance, is flavored with buffalo grass, which gives it a yellowish color and a somewhat bitter taste. Certain other foreign vodkas are colored brown (from walnut shells), blue and even lavender.

In the Soviet Union vodka is popular as an aperitif. It is swigged from a small glass and followed by hors d'oeuvres, such as caviar, herring and anchovies. In the U.S. vodka often is added to orange juice or tomato juice with a few other ingredients to make the drinks known respectively as a screwdriver and a Bloody Mary. (A Virgin Mary is the same drink without the vodka.) It is also sometimes used as a substitute for gin in mixed drinks. For example, it may be substituted for gin with tonic water or mixed with vermouth, in place of gin, to make a vodka martini.

voranil   An ANORECTIC that contains clortermine and is used for weight control. Tolerance can develop, and because its activity is similar to that of AMPHETAMINES both physical and psychological dependence can occur. It has a significant potential for abuse. Overdosage can result in restlessness, tremors, confusion and hallucinations. It is no longer legally available in the U.S.

voucher-based treatment   Behavioral model of treatment being tested on methadone-maintained heroin addicts to deter their use of cocaine. Early results are positive, with patients who receive vouchers for clean urine avoiding cocaine for more weeks and longer stretches of time than patients whose vouchers were not tied to the outcome of urine tests.

The treatment model has been the subject of a conservative backlash; their argument being that addicted individuals should not be "paid" for positive behaviors.

R. Mathias, "National Institute on Drug Abuse (NIDA) Program Promises Better Behavioral Treatment for Drug Abuse Patients," *NIDA Notes* (March/April, 1995).

wash still   The first and largest of the two stills employed in some double-distillation processes. The wash still produces a weak and impure distillate, known as "low wine," which usually is strengthened and purified by further rectification in a small and secondary SPIRIT STILL.

Washington, D.C., drug cases in   This is one of the major drug-infested cities in the U.S. Disruption of the lives of the capital's inhabitants due to drug use and drug-related crime is enormous. A recent survey found that 56% of criminal suspects tested were using drugs at the time of arrest. The city has earned the dubious honor of being dubbed the "Murder Capital" of the U.S.

In April 1989 after months of complaining by residents and some federal officials and lawmakers, then U.S. drug czar William Bennett unveiled an $80 million emergency plan for an assault on the city's drug-and-murder epidemic. Bennett's measures included: 82 additional federal agents to assist local police, a 500-bed detention facility to be built in the District and more beds available in a federal prison in nearby Maryland. Mayor Marion Barry (convicted in 1991 of drug possession) was snubbed by Bennett and was not invited to the press conference at which the plan was announced. Bennett said that Barry's administration "has failed to serve its citizens."

Urbanologists say the long-term solution is to create more and better jobs for youth in the inner city.

"Outline for a Skirmish," *Time* (April 24, 1989): 25.

Washingtonian movement   A 19th-century group that ALCOHOLICS ANONYMOUS (AA) came most to resemble. The temperance group swelled from a mere six alcoholics meeting in Baltimore in 1840 to 150,000 before the end of the decade. The Washingtonians, alone among such groups of that time, did not involve themselves with organized religion, politics or social reform. (Their later involvement in the abolitionist movement *did* lead to factions that split the group apart.) Nan Robertson, in her bestseller *Getting Better: Inside Alcoholics Anonymous,* writes: "Their purpose was remarkably single-minded, just like AA—sobered-up alcoholics saving other alcoholics who still drank, while teaching them to avoid the temptations that led them to drink in the first place." Abraham Lincoln said of the Washingtonians in 1842: "Those whom they desire to convince and persuade are their old friends and companions. They know they are not demons, not even the worst of men." Although short-lived, the Washingtonian movement had an impact and inspired other similar efforts in Boston, San Francisco and Chicago. By the late 1860s, the Washingtonians had, for the most part, passed from the American scene to be succeeded by a variety of new, secret temperance societies and fraternities.

Nan Robertson, *Getting Better: Inside Alcoholics Anonymous* (New York: William Morrow, 1988).

water of life   Any of several distilled spirits, the term "water of life" originally was used to refer to an elixir, probably not alcoholic, that would confer immortality or even perpetual youth on the drinker. The obsessive quest of mankind for such an elixir was probably best exemplified by Ponce de Leon's search for the Fountain of Youth. As early as Roman times, the term was associated with particularly strong forms of drink that would produce in the user a temporary feeling of blissful immortality. There was the added implication that life without this water was not worth living.

The Latin term was *aqua vitae* (water of life), which was translated into the Irish Gaelic *uisce beathadh* and the Scotch Gaelic *uisge beatha* and later anglicized to WHISKEY. It also became the Scandinavian AQUAVIT and the French EAU DE VIE.

Webb-Kenyon Law   Adopted by Congress in 1913, this law was designed to allow the dry states to exercise sovereignty over alcohol-related affairs within their borders. The law gave each state the right to make its own laws concerning mail-order shipments of liquor. It was approved by a large majority in both houses, vetoed by President William Howard Taft and passed over his veto.

Wernicke's encephalopathy (syndrome or disease)   Named after Carl Wernicke (1848–1905), a German neurologist who first described this condition, Wernicke's syndrome is a central nervous system disorder characterized by an acute confusional state, loss of balance and disorders of the eye nerves. It is often accompanied by ALCOHOLIC POLYNEUROPATHY and a high risk of congestive heart failure.

Wernicke's encephalopathy is caused by the combination of a thiamine deficiency and chronic heavy drinking. (See VITAMINS AND MINERALS.) Although victims of the disease require hospitalization, with the administration of thiamine, treatment is often successful if the condition is caught in its early stages. If not, it may progress into KORSAKOFF'S PSYCHOSIS, which has a much lower rate of cure. The signs of Wernicke's encephalopathy may coexist with those of Korsakoff's psychosis, and the two sometimes are linked together under the single designation Wernicke-Korsakoff syndrome.

whiskey (or whisky)   A potable alcoholic beverage distilled from the mash of fermented grains such as rye, wheat, corn, oats and barley in various combinations. The name is derived from the Irish Gaelic *uisce beathadh* and the Scottish Gaelic *uisge beatha,* meaning "water of life," shortened to *uisce* and then to the current pronunciation and spelling. "Whiskey" (plural "whiskeys") is the preferred spelling in Ireland and the U.S., and "whisky" (plural "whiskies") is the preferred spelling in Scotland and Canada. None of these countries produce a whiskey or whisky that remotely resembles the original beverage—a raw alcohol flavored with saffron, nutmeg and other spices to make it palatable. However, the whiskeys or whiskies they make are distinct, although the Canadian and American varieties may be considered together.

There are two types of Scotch whisky: pot still and patent still. Pot-still whiskies are made from malted barley only, and patent-still whiskies are made from a variety of cereal grains, including malted barley. Pot-still whiskies are the heaviest "malt" whiskies and are traditionally distinguished by their place of origin: the Highlands, the Lowlands, the Cambeltowns and the Islays. The distinct flavor created in each region is the result of the type of barley used, the method of curing, or "malting," the distillation process and the aging technique. Patent-still products are the lighter "grain" whiskies, which are generally less expensive and have a wider appeal than the pot-still types. In the production of patent-still whiskies the grain mixture is varied and the barley is cured without the traditional peat-drying, or turf-drying, process. These whiskies have lower levels of congeners because the rectification process used to make them takes longer than that employed to produce pot-still whiskies. Traditionalists sometimes object to the classification of these patent-still beverages as true Scotch whiskey.

For the past 100 years most Scotch whiskies have been blended for greater market appeal. This process has led to a more consistent and generally more palatable beverage at the cost of the local distinctions favored by traditionalists. All Scotch whiskey is aged for a minimum of three years, although a period of at least 12 years is favored. Aging for the most part takes place in wood casks of two sorts: "plain wood," seasoned oak that has never come in contact with another liquor; or "sherry wood," oak seasoned with that liquor and, in some cases, brandy or Madeira.

Irish whiskeys also are produced by the pot-still and patent-still techniques. However, unmalted grain and a different distilling process are used in their production. Irish pot-still whiskeys are made from a mash of less than 50% malted barley, supplemented by such grains as rye, wheat and oats. Irish patent-still whiskeys are made the same way as the Scotch varieties until the distillation stage: all Irish whiskeys are distilled three times, whereas Scotch whiskies are distilled twice. The result is a lower level of congeners and therefore a "cleaner" and "sweeter" beverage. Irish whiskeys are aged at least seven years, but longer aging periods are preferred.

The American and Canadian varieties of whiskey are bourbon, produced principally in the U.S, and rye, generally associated with Canada. The primary difference is that rye is blended from a mash in which rye predominates and bourbon is blended from a mash in which corn predominates. Both the distinctions in mash content and the aging of rye and bourbon in charred wood casks give the liquors a heavier body and a stronger taste than either Scotch whiskies or Irish whiskeys. The American and Canadian varieties are considered to have roughly twice the quantity of congeners and by-products as the Scotch and Irish varieties.

Many more countries than these four produce flavored neutral grain spirits that can be considered whiskey, but the products inevitably derive from and fall within one of the four principal categories discussed.

Whiskey Rebellion In 1794 western Pennsylvania farmers rose up against the imposition of a federal excise tax on liquor, which threatened the marketing of their grain in transportable liquid form. During the presidential terms of Thomas Jefferson and Andrew Jackson (1800–1808 and 1829–1837), personal freedom was popularized and rough frontier manners prevailed. Saloons were everywhere, and heavy drinking was commonplace. In reaction, temperance and prohibition sentiments grew and a vociferous minority concluded that distilled spirits were a "demon" and "destroyer." But it was the first internal revenue statute passed by Congress—the Revenue Act of 1791—calling for taxes on tobacco and distilled spirits that prompted the embattled farmers of Pennsylvania to armed struggle. They fought to preserve local "rights" to sell their untaxed whiskey, but the uprising was quelled after President Washington called out the militia. Jefferson repealed excises in 1802, referring to the "infernal" excise system "hostile to the genius of a free people." Federal taxes on alcohol and tobacco were not invoked again until 60 years later, in 1862.

Don Cahalan, *Understanding America's Drinking Problem: How to Combat the Hazards of Alcohol* (San Francisco: Jossey-Bass, 1988).

White House Conference for a Drug Free America
In 1986 the Congress passed and the president signed the Anti-Drug Abuse Act of 1986 (P.L. 99-576). One requirement of that legislation (Subtitle S of Title I) was the establishment of a White House Conference for a Drug Free America. The legislation was implemented by President Ronald Reagan through Executive Order No. 12595 on May 5, 1987, which added a new purpose for the conference: "To focus public attention on the importance of fostering a widespread attitude of intolerance for illegal drugs and their use throughout all segments of society."

Results of the conference were presented in a *Final Report to the president and the Congress,* signed by Lois Haight Herrington, June 1988. Herrington, a former deputy attorney general, noted that the "Conference met throughout the country in seven diverse cities. We asked questions, stimulated debate, and profited by the insight of national, state and local officials. We also heard from law enforcement, health care and research professionals, corporate and labor leaders, parents, educators, media and entertainment figures, and sports heroes. We involved both young and old whose lives are dedicated to fighting the scourge of illegal drugs as well as those who have been directly or indirectly tainted by drugs. We received the insight of our 127 distinguished presidential conferees."

More than 2,000 antidrug participants, over and above the president's appointees, took part in this historic conference. The point person of the Reagan administration's battle against illegal drugs, Nancy Reagan, spoke to the attendees, saying, "If you're a casual drug user, you're an accomplice to murder."

Much of the discussion appeared to critics to be simply a rehashing of old ideas—military intervention, crop eradication, drug testing, increased law-enforcement efforts—but most agreed that a significant first step would be to shift the focus of the drug war from trying to control and cut off the supplies to reducing the demand.

The conference's *Final Report,* issued in June 1988, submitted to the president's recommendations in 12 key areas relating to the overall drug problem. On one point, all the conferees seemed to agree—no single approach is going to reduce, let alone cure, the drug plague. There is no sure or quick fix.

White House Conference for a Drug Free America, Final Report (Washington, D.C.: Government Printing Office, June 1988).

White Mare   Code name for a 17-month investigation that resulted in late February 1989 in the biggest heroin bust ever in the U.S. FBI agents and police in New York arrested some 40 people, including the international drug ring's kingpin, Kok Leung Woo, 71. Also arrested were members of the ring in more than half a dozen cities around the world, including Canada, Singapore and Hong Kong. An astonishing 820 pounds of the narcotic, with an estimated street value of nearly $1 billion, was confiscated from three houses in New York City. The code name "White Mare" was inspired by the color of the drug and the fact that heroin often is known as "horse" on the street.

"Riding a White Mare," *Time* (March 6, 1989): 33.

white wine   An almost colorless wine produced by fermenting grape juice without the grape skins or stems, which give red and rose wines their color. Red wines are produced by fermenting grape juice with grape skins and stems, and rose wines are made by fermenting grape juice that usually has been allowed to soak for a period in grape skins. The alcohol content of white wines is about the same as that of red wines, ranging from 10% to 14%.

Once grapes intended for white wines have been gathered, they are crushed in an extractor or wine press to drain off their juice. The juice then is allowed to settle for a period of up to two days and decanted to ensure a product that is as clear as possible. The making of white wines differs from that of red wines in two other ways: a slightly higher proportion of antiseptic, usually sulfur dioxide, is used to eliminate all but the alcohol-tolerant natural yeasts, and additional active yeast cultures are added to assist fermentation.

White wines are fermented at low temperatures, ranging from 50° to 60° F. Fermentation is usually allowed to proceed until virtually all of the soluble sugars in the grape juice have been converted into alcohol and carbonic gas by the yeasts. The yeasts and sediments created by fermentation then are removed from the alcoholic grape juice, and the process continues through the same steps used in making red or rose wines. (See WINE.)

The most valued white wines currently produced are those from France. The white wines of the Bordeaux region are produced in Graves, south of the city of Bordeaux, and Sauterne, known for its sweeter, dessert wines. The most renowned white wine of the Burgundy region is Montrachet, produced in the southern areas of the Cote d'Or, but the most commonly known is Chablis, which has become a generic name for white wines made outside of France.

Other notable white wines include the Orvieto, Frascati and Soave varieties produced in Italy and the Rhine and Moselle wines of Germany, where far more white than red wines are made. Portugal's Dao wine district is known for white wines produced from the grapes of its mountain vineyards, and Hungary, which makes twice as much white wine as red wine, is known for white wines made from the Riesling grape, produced near Balaton Lake. Austria, Switzerland, The Czech Republic, Slovakia and Yugoslavia also produce significant quantities of white wine, as does the U.S., where far more white wine than red wine is consumed.

wild cucumber   *Exhinocystis lobata.* A vine native to the U.S. and a member of the melon family. There are claims that the seeds of the fruits can produce psychedelic effects.

wild fennel   *Foeniculum vulgare.* Though there are claims that when ingested psychedelic effects are produced, the plant is poisonous and can cause severe adverse reactions.

Wilson, Bill (1876–1971)   William Griffith Wilson, the man who shaped what has been called the greatest, most influential self-help group in the world, was born in East Dorset, Vermont, son of a marble quarry foreman. Cofounder with surgeon Dr. Robert SMITH of ALCOHOLICS ANONYMOUS (AA) in

Akron, Ohio (May 1935), Wilson, a New York stock-broker was a talker and a writer—the idea man of AA. He was impulsive, compassionate and a dreamer with intellectual pretensions who never completed his formal education. Nan Robertson writes of the two men that Dr. Bob "was the steady hand that held the cord of Bill Wilson's high-flying, erratic kite." Wilson married Lois Burnam WILSON, cofounder of the AL-ANON movement for families of alcoholics, in 1918. The marriage lasted until Bill W.'s death at age 75 in 1971. Upon his death, Bill Wilson's obituary ran with a full-face photograph across three columns of the front page of the *New York Times,* continuing inside for three columns. AA had almost a half-million membership in the U.S. and 88 other countries at the time of Wilson's death. Today worldwide membership is estimated at close to 2 million. Says Nan Robertson, "The only world in which Wilson succeeded was the world of Alcoholics Anonymous."

Nan Robertson, *Getting Better: Inside Alcoholics Anonymous* (New York: William Morrow, 1988).

Wilson, Lois Burnham (1892–1988) Cofounder of AL-ANON (the self-help movement for families of alcoholics) and wife of ALCOHOLICS ANONYMOUS cofounder Bill WILSON. Lois W., eldest of six children, was a graduate of the Packer Collegiate Institute in Brooklyn. From the time of her marriage in 1918, through Bill W.'s catastrophic drinking years in the late 1920s and early 1930s and beyond into sobriety, Lois W. often played the roles of confidante, nurse, family manager and breadwinner. Al-Anon, which today numbers roughly half a million members, was started in 1951. The organization uses AA's famed 12-step program for recovery, but is completely independent of AA. It was with the help of Anne B., who was a close friend, a Westchester (upstate New York) neighbor and, like Lois, the wife of an alcoholic, that Lois W. founded Al-Anon. Anne B. died in 1984 at the age of 84. Lois Wilson died in 1988 at the age of 96.

Nan Robertson, *Getting Better: Inside Alcoholics Anonymous* (New York: William Morrow, 1988).

wine From the Latin *vinum,* (wine). The fermented juice of grapes. The fermented juices of other fruits are designated as wines only when qualified by their basic raw material, such as "rice wine," "apple wine," "plum wine" and so forth. In addition to this etymological distinction grape juice is chemically distinct from other fruit juices by virtue of the presence of tartar, or potassium bitartrate, and natural yeasts that will produce fermentation without the addition of active cultures.

The history of wine making, or viticulture, began before the first Egyptian dynasty, around 4000 B.C., according to the first known hieroglyphic records on the subject, which were found in funereal carvings. Most historians agree that wine making postdates fermentation of grains for beer and honey for mead, both in Egypt and elsewhere. The discovery of the fermentative properties of grape juice in all likelihood occurred accidentally. The length of time required for grape vines to mature would have restricted their cultivation to settled rather than nomadic societies, suggesting that viticulture probably was a development of the later stages of early agrarian civilizations.

Because climate and soil conditions limited the yield of vineyards, wine was less a staple of Egyptian life than beer. Before 1000 B.C. viticulture was introduced in Greece, where the combination of better conditions for grape cultivation and a relatively advanced knowledge of botany brought wine, or *oinos,* a new prominence. Greek literature contains many tracts on the art of wine making, and Greek society was the first to ritualize and institutionalize wine drinking. Other Greek contributions to practical viticulture were the introduction of efficient pressing devices, flavoring methods and aging vessels. The Greeks invariably drank their wine mixed with water, suggesting that these beverages were somewhat lacking in palatability, but wine making nevertheless was an important part of their culture and was spread widely during the Greek age of exploration and conquest.

The Romans further advanced viticulture after it was introduced in Rome immediately prior to the advent of Christianity. They were the first to coat the insides of the *amphorae* (aging vessels) to prevent evaporation, and because of this superior aging technique they were the first to develop an appreciation of individual vintages. One of the earliest vintages to be stored for its special value was Opimian wine, fermented in individual seasons during the late second century B.C. and named for the reigning first consul. Like the Greeks before them, the Romans spread viticulture during reign of conquest and ex-

Per Capita Wine Consumption* by Country–1993 to 1995

1995 Rank per Capita		1995		1994		1993	
		Liters	Gallons	Liters	Gallons	Liters	Gallons
1	France	63.50	16.77	62.50	16.51	63.50	16.77
2	Italy	60.40	15.96	58.50	15.45	58.80	15.53
3	Portugal	58.40	15.43	57.00	15.06	56.00	14.79
4	Luxembourg	58.20	15.37	60.50	15.98	60.30	15.93
5	Argentina	43.80	11.57	43.20	11.41	44.40	11.73
6	Switzerland	43.60	11.52	44.30	11.70	46.00	12.15
7	Spain	36.30	9.59	32.20	8.51	34.10	9.01
8	Hungary	34.70	9.17	33.10	8.74	31.80	8.40
9	Greece	34.50	9.11	33.80	8.93	35.20	9.30
10	Austria	32.00	8.45	32.80	8.66	34.30	9.06
11	Uruguay	30.80	8.14	32.10	8.48	27.00	7.13
12	Denmark	27.60	7.29	26.21	6.92	25.19	6.65
13	Romania	25.30	6.68	18.80	4.97	19.10	5.05
14	Belgium	25.00	6.60	24.00	6.34	25.60	6.76
15	Germany	22.20	5.86	22.60	5.97	22.60	5.97
16	Bulgaria	21.80	5.76	22.00	5.81	22.10	5.84
17	Chile	21.70	5.73	21.40	5.65	20.30	5.36
18	Austarlia	18.20	4.81	18.50	4.89	18.20	4.81
19	Czech Republic	16.90	4.46	16.90	4.46	14.80	3.91
20	New Zealand	16.80	4.44	16.10	4.25	16.80	4.44
21	Netherlands	16.57	4.38	15.69	4.14	15.18	4.01
22	Republic of Ireland	16.10	4.25	12.70	3.35	13.50	3.57
23	Slovak Republic	14.90	3.94	13.90	3.67	14.30	3.78
24	Cyprus	13.70	3.62	13.70	3.62	12.80	3.38

(continued on next page)

Per Capita Wine Consumption* by Country–1993 to 1995 (continued)

1995 Rank per Capita	1995 Liters	1995 Gallons	1994 Liters	1994 Gallons	1993 Liters	1993 Gallons
25 United Kingdom	12.79	3.38	12.65	3.34	12.20	3.22
26 Sweden	12.70	3.35	12.60	3.33	12.67	3.35
27 South Africa	9.00	2.38	8.80	2.32	8.30	2.19
28 Canada	8.21	2.17	7.85	2.07	8.04	2.12
29 Finland	8.19	2.16	8.79	2.32	8.30	2.19
30 Norway	7.07	1.87	6.78	1.79	6.34	1.67
31 Poland	6.90	1.82	6.90	1.82	7.5	1.98
32 USA	6.76	1.79	6.68	1.77	6.60	1.74
33 Iceland	5.00	1.32	4.80	1.27	4.7	1.24
34 Israel	3.10	0.82	3.40	0.90	3.4	0.90
35 Russia	2.60	0.69	3.30	0.87	2.7	0.71

[*]NOTE: Per capita comsumption figures are based on resident population. Per capita consumption will be higher if based on legal drinking age population.

Source: Wine Institute/*World Drink Trends,* 1996.

pansion. Their introduction of wine grape vineyards in Spain was so successful that by the first century A.D. the Roman republic introduced trade controls to protect the domestic Spanish wine industry. The inception of the French and German wine industries also date from the Roman occupation. Wine making became common in the Rhone and Moselle valleys succeeding the Gallic Wars.

In the Dark Ages, following the collapse of the Roman Empire, viticulture declined, but in medieval times a slow rediscovery of wine making reemerged because of the demand for sacramental wines that accompanied the spread of Christianity. Fermentation practices during this time often were based on incomplete classical texts, thus, improvisations were introduced in France and Germany. Lacking ceramic vessels, for instance, wine makers substituted wooden casks, which now are considered essential for controlled aging of wines. Presented with other challenges, they devised fortified wines, dwarf grape vines, "plastering" (a method of producing good wine from thin grape juice) and a number of variations that have become standard steps in modernized wine making.

Production of wine begins with the cultivation of grapes, generally varieties of *Vinum vinifera.* Since fermentation processes are relatively uniform, the particular character of any distinct wine or vintage depends primarily on the choice of the grape variety, the composition of the soil and the weather during the growing season. The goal is to harvest a grape with a particular sugar content, generally between 18% and 24%, before the crop begins to deteriorate in early fall. Once harvested, grapes are crushed to release their juice, a step now accomplished by means of either roller crushers or rotary paddle crushers. In the production of WHITE WINE the skins then are separated from the juice; in the making of ROSE WINE the skins are generally allowed to soak in the juice for a day or two before separation; and in the manufacture of RED WINE the skins are allowed to remain in the juice. After an antiseptic, usually sulfur dioxide, has been introduced to kill all but the alcohol-tolerant natural yeasts in the grape juice, fermentation begins naturally, although sometimes it is assisted by the introduction of active yeast cultures. After fermentation, which can last anywhere from two days to two weeks, the alcoholic juice is subjected to "racking," a process that removes suspended yeasts and various sedimentary deposits. Further purification is achieved by filtration and "fining," in which substances are added to assist the separation of wine from deposits. All wines then are aged in wood for at least one year and often far longer before being bottled. Aging then continues in the bottle. The amount of aging that will produce the wine's finest quality depends both on its variety and on the character of its vintage.

wino   Slang term for an alcoholic who drinks wine only. Also, a person who drinks a large amount of wine because it can be obtained inexpensively, but will consume other alcoholic beverages when they are available.

withdrawal   A series of symptoms that appear when a drug on which the user is physically dependent is abruptly stopped or severely reduced is called a "withdrawal syndrome." Withdrawal occurs most dramatically and consistently in cases of addiction to sedatives (including alcohol) and narcotics. The syndrome consists of symptoms that are broadly opposite to the drugs' usual effects. This is called a "rebound" effect. There are different degrees of withdrawal, ranging from a severe hangover to the terrifying alcoholic hallucinosis accompanying DELIRIUM TREMENS (THE D.T.'S). The intensity and duration of withdrawal symptoms depends on the susceptibility of the user, the properties of the particular drug, the abruptness of the cessation and the degree of addiction. Longer-acting drugs have a longer-lasting psychoactive effect, take longer to eliminate from the system and are slower to metabo-

lize than shorter-acting substances. Generally speaking, shorter-acting substances, such as heroin, produce more severe withdrawal symptoms than longer-acting drugs, such as methadone. However, though the withdrawal from the shorter-acting drugs is more severe, it also develops more rapidly and is shorter in duration.

Sedatives including alcohol: The precise process of withdrawal from ALCOHOL and other sedatives is not completely understood, although the syndrome is well-documented. One explanation focuses on the manufacture and detoxification of small amounts of various alcohols in the body. These alcohols include ethanol, which is used in alcoholic beverages, and methanol, which is the main component in wood alcohol. Usually both are detoxified in the liver, with acetaldehyde produced from ethanol and formaldehyde produced from methanol. (See METABOLISM.) However, the liver enzymes involved in oxidation break down ethanol 16 times more rapidly than methanol. When ethanol is consumed, the liver, which has the capacity to handle all the alcohols that the body produces, becomes occupied with detoxifying it, and consequently there is a build up of methanol. After the ethanol has been disposed of the liver enzymes work on the methanol, manufacturing greatly increased amounts of formaldehyde, which is very toxic to the system. This may cause the withdrawal symptoms. Another explanation involves the central nervous system (CNS). Since alcohol impairs the normal functioning of the CNS, when one stops drinking, the CNS is no longer handicapped and a prolonged period of hyperactivity may occur causing the withdrawal effect. This interpretation provides insight into many of the symptoms and signs that are evoked.

It is unclear how quickly dependence on alcohol develops and exactly what symptoms constitute the first manifestations of withdrawal, but some symptoms usually appear within a few hours after the discontinuation of heavy and prolonged drinking. At this point the BLOOD ALCOHOL CONCENTRATION (BAC) may still be as high as 100 mg of ethanol per 100 ml of blood, or even higher. Usually the first signs to develop are weakness and tremulousness, possibly accompanied by anxiety, headache, nausea and abdominal cramps. Next, restlessness, agitation and cravings for alcohol or other SEDATIVES occur.

In time the tremors become more marked and one may begin to "see" or "hear" things

For an alcoholic with only a mild degree of physical dependence, the withdrawal syndrome may not extend beyond the duration of these symptoms, which disappear within a few days. However, in a minority of cases, alcoholics experience a second stage, marked by convulsive seizures known as RUM FITS. These seizures may occur as early as 12 hours after abstinence, but more often will manifest on the second or third day, and the number will vary depending on the individual. Medical intervention is always required as seizures may develop into STATUS EPILEPTICUS.

The third stage of withdrawal, consisting of alcohol hallucinosis and delirium tremens (the D.T.'s), is the most dangerous. The intense auditory, visual and tactile hallucinations can last three to four days and for the victim is the most dramatic and terrifying period. Along with severe agitation, disorientation and very little sleep, high fever and profuse sweating may occur, causing serious dehydration. As a rule, behavior becomes exceedingly aggressive and frequently self-destructive. Death from hyperthermia, peripheral vascular collapse or self-inflicted injury can take place during this stage of withdrawal: there is a 10% mortality rate for alcoholics suffering untreated delirium tremens.

Barbiturates, tranquilizers and other sedative hypnotics: Abrupt withdrawal from a sedative, rather than gradual detoxification, usually lasts 5–7 days and results in complete recovery from physical, though certainly not from psychological, dependence. In rare cases (due to unknown causes), patients have remained in chronic psychotic states resembling schizophrenia. Gradual detoxification is much safer than abrupt cessation, and convulsions can be avoided by the substitution of a drug that is CROSS-DEPENDENT with alcohol such as Librium or the early administration of large doses of an anticonvulsant, such as Dilantin. These drugs are used when an individual is detoxified in a hospital or treatment setting.

The addictive nature of barbiturates came to the attention of German chemists soon after the development of these drugs in the early 1900s, but the withdrawal syndrome was less consistent and even more puzzling than the one already known to occur with narcotics. Abrupt cessation of a regular intake of even large doses of sedative hypnotics did not *always* precipitate withdrawal symptoms, so evidence supporting the risk of addiction to these depressants remained inconclusive. The major difference, in fact, between depressants and narcotics is that dependence to depressants develops only above a certain threshold of daily intake. Even large amounts ingested below this threshold will not always cause physical addiction and, therefore, withdrawal. How slowly such dependence develops is not yet known, but the withdrawal syndrome brought about by the sharp reduction of intake or abstinence closely resembles an alcohol withdrawal syndrome. Withdrawal symptoms from depressants may occur within a few hours after the drug is stopped and are characterized by physical weakness, dizziness, sleeplessness, anxiety, nausea and vomiting. Hallucinations, delirium, delusions and convulsions may occur as long as three days to a week following withdrawal and may last for many days. Withdrawal from benzodiazepines (minor tranquilizers) is similar except that it may take longer to develop. The onset of withdrawal from tranquilizers with long half-lives is delayed but the withdrawal persists longer. Not all symptoms that emerge following cessation of tranquilizer use are withdrawal symptoms. Some represent emergent anxiety that was repressed by the medication. Withdrawal from barbiturates is dangerous and should be done either under the care of a physician or in a hospital setting.

Heroin and other narcotics: The duration and intensity of withdrawal symptoms from heroin and other narcotics is directly related to the quality of the drug and the quantity and frequency of use. Because of limited finances few addicts use more than 500 mg of morphine (125–150 mg of heroin) a day. Most addicts can afford to support only a relatively mild physical dependence and so are spared the most severe forms of opiate withdrawal. If an addict who uses low, regular, intermittent doses does not receive his regular fix at the expected time (usually every six to twelve hours), symptoms resembling the flu are likely to occur: uneasiness, yawning, nausea, sweating alternating with chills, various aches and pains, teary eyes and runny nose. Unless counteracted by a dose of heroin or a CROSS-TOLERANT drug, such as methadone, these symptoms gradually intensify and broaden to include a range of symptoms showing central nervous system excitation: pupillary dilation, increased heart rate and blood pressure, twitching, spasms, gooseflesh, diarrhea, sexual arousal and insomnia. Cardiovascular collapse is a risk. Withdrawal from a heavy chronic narcotic habit can be extremely severe and painful. Because narcotics readily cross the placental barrier, babies born of female addicts share their mothers' physical dependence and often exhibit withdrawal symptoms soon after birth.

Depending on the habit and on the quality of the heroin, heroin withdrawal generally peaks in 24 to 48 hours and is usually completed within a week. Certain effects, such as increased blood pressure and heart rate, can persist during a period of "protracted abstinence" of up to six months.

As previously mentioned, withdrawal from methadone is more prolonged but less severe than heroin withdrawal, since methadone is a longer acting, more slowly eliminated drug. If administered during heroin withdrawal, methadone can ease the intensity of the experience. Conversely, the administration of a group of drugs known as NARCOTIC ANTAGONISTS, of which NALORPHINE is an example, can precipitate the withdrawal process (and increase its unpleasantness).

Amphetamines and other stimulants: Stimulant drugs, such as amphetamines, caffeine and nicotine, are generally considered to be more psychologically than physically addictive. Nevertheless, sudden abstinence from amphetamines, cocaine and even coffee does produce symptoms in most people: headache, stomach cramps, lethargy, chronic fatigue and often severe emotional depression or irritability. Furthermore, abnormal electroencephalogram (EEG) patterns, which have been recorded during withdrawal from these drugs, stabilized after administration of the drug in question.

Hallucinogens: Neither hallucinogens nor cannabis are known to be physically addictive; abstinence or abrupt cessation of intake does not appear to produce recognizably distinct withdrawal symptoms.

Samuel Kaim, "The Acute Withdrawal Syndrome," *Alcoholism* 1, no. 5 (May/June, 1981.): 43.

Woman's Christian Temperance Union (WCTU)

Founded in Cleveland in 1874, this union grew out of a women's crusade to shut down saloons and promote morality and gradually developed into a national organization. In 1883 the organization was carried to other countries, increasing its total membership to a half-million. By 1907 the WCTU had branches in every state in the nation, with an aggregate national membership of 350,000.

The WCTU was a strong voice during the Prohibition era, and gradually it became concerned with other problems of society, particularly when Frances Willard became its president. The members spoke out on women's rights, civil reform and the general morals of society. As of 1992, the National WCTU had 50,000 members. It's official organ is the weekly *Union Signal.*

women Alcoholism traditionally has been considered a male problem though in the late 19th and early 20th centuries the use of patent medicines containing opiates and alcohol resulted in large numbers of addicts throughout American society—three times as many women as men developed such addictions. The typical addict was a middle-aged, middle to upper class housewife. Today illicit drug use and abuse is affecting women in all classes, ethnic groups and age categories.

The National Institute on Drug Abuse (NIDA) estimated that in 1997 at least 2 million women could be categorized as heavy drinkers (five or more drinks on five or more occasions in the past month from when the survey was taken). Studies have reported that there are fewer women heavy drinkers than men heavy drinkers and that a smaller percentage of women drink at all—(45.1% of women versus 58.2% of men, in 1988). Notwithstanding, statistics from the 1970s showed that nearly one-third of all alcoholics in the U.S. were women, and more recent estimates indicated that the figure is approaching 50%. Although some surveys showed that consumption rates for women were increasing in the 1970s and early 1980s, a series of studies in the 1987 *Sixth Special Report* uncovered no evidence of a major increase in consumption of alcohol by women in that period. Conclusive figures may be hard to arrive at due to the fact that so many women drink at home, and studies to date on women's drinking patterns have been fewer than on men's.

History: Women throughout history have been consumers as well as producers of alcohol. Babylonian women around 5000 B.C. brewed beer and ran

Preliminary Data—As of June 1998

Percentages Reporting Lifetime, Past Year, and Past Month Use of Illicit Drugs, Alcohol, and Tobacco in the U.S. Population of Females Aged 15 to 44, by Pregaancy Status and Parental Status: Annual Averages Based on 1996 and 1997 Samples

Drug	Females Aged 15–44			
		Used in Lifetime		
			Not Pregnant	
	Pregnant	No Children	Has Child Aged <2[1]	All Children Aged>2[1]
Any Illicit Drug[2]	41.4	43.1	41.0	47.7
Marijuana and Hashish	39.6	39.8	38.1	44.6
Cocaine	14.2	11.2	9.7	14.9
Crack	3.8	2.8	2.4	2.3
Inhalants	5.3	8.2	4.4	3.9
Hallucinogens	10.2	12.0	8.9	10.5
PCP	3.0	2.5	2.9	4.0
LSD	9.0	9.4	6.5	8.0
Heroin	2.2	1.0	1.0	0.7
Nonmedical Use of Any				
Psychotherapeutic[3]	9.1	11.1	8.6	11.7
Stimulants	3.8	4.4	3.8	5.7
Sedatives	1.1	2.0	1.4	2.9
Tranquilizers	3.3	4.5	2.9	4.5
Analgesics	4.7	6.9	5.4	6.0
Any Illicit Drug	20.0	23.1	18.7	23.5
other than Marijuana[2]				
Alcohol	78.3	79.5	81.5	87.5
"Binge" Alcohol Use[4]	–	–	–	–
Heavy Alcohol Use[4]	–	–	–	–
Cigarettes	62.3	64.5	65.7	73.9
Smokless Tobacco	4.4	7.0	4.6	4.5

* Low precision; no estimate reported.
– Not available.
[1] The respondent and the child(ren) both (all) reside int he same household.

(continued on next page)

Preliminary Data—As of June 1998 (continued)

Percentages Reporting Lifetime, Past Year, and Past Month Use of Illicit Drugs, Alcohol, and Tobacco in the U.S. Population of Females Aged 15 to 44, by Pregaancy Status and Parental Status: Annual Averages Based on 1996 and 1997 Samples

	Females Aged 15–44			
	Used in Past Year			
		Not Pregnant		
Drug	Pregnant	No Children	Has Child Aged <2[1]	All Children Aged>2[1]
Any Illicit Drug[2]	10.4	19.3	9.7	8.1
Marijuana and Hashish	8.1	16.2	7.5	5.7
Cocaine	2.8	3.5	1.7	1.5
Crack	0.8	1.2	0.6	0.5
Inhalants	0.3	2.2	0.3	0.2
Hallucinogens	1.5	3.7	0.9	0.5
PCP	0.2	0.3	0.3	0.0
LSD	1.2	2.5	0.2	0.1
Heroin	0.6	0.4	0.1	0.1
Nonmedical Use of Any				
Psychotherapeutic[3]	3.0	5.0	2.3	2.7
Stimulants	1.3	1.2	0.4	0.4
Sedatives	0.6	0.3	0.2	0.4
Tranquilizers	1.1	1.7	1.1	1.2
Analgesics	1.5	3.6	2.0	1.6
Any Illicit Drug	5.0	9.8	4.2	4.1
other than Marijuana[2]				
Alcohol	60.0	69.4	62.3	71.4
"Binge" Alcohol Use[4]	–	–	–	–
Heavy Alcohol Use[4]	–	–	–	–
Cigarettes	27.7	38.8	31.4	36.4
Smokless Tobacco	*	1.5	0.2	0.3

[2] Any Illicit Drug indicates use at least once of marijuana/hashish, cocaine (including crack), inhalants, hallucinogens (including PCP and LSD), heroin, or any prescription-type psychotherapeutic used nonmedically. Any Illicit Drug Other than Marijuana indicates use at least once of any of these listed drugs, regardless of marijuana/hashish use; marijuana/hashish users who also have used any of the other listed drugs are included.

(continued on next page)

Preliminary Data—As of June 1998 (continued)

Percentages Reporting Lifetime, Past Year, and Past Month Use of Illicit Drugs, Alcohol, and Tobacco in the U.S. Population of Females Aged 15 to 44, by Pregaancy Status and Parental Status: Annual Averages Based on 1996 and 1997 Samples

Drug		Females Aged 15–44		
		Used in Past Month		
			Not Pregnant	
	Pregnant	No Children	Has Child Aged <2[1]	All Children Aged>2[1]
Any Illicit Drug[2]	2.5	10.4	5.5	4.1
Marijuana and Hashish	1.5	8.3	4.2	2.9
Cocaine	0.2	1.4	0.5	0.6
Crack	0.1	0.6	0.3	0.2
Inhalants	*	0.7	0.2	0.1
Hallucinogens	0.1	1.3	0.6	0.1
PCP	*	0.0	0.3	*
LSD	*	0.6	*	*
Heroin	0.2	0.2	0.1	0.1
Nonmedical Use of Any				
Psychotherapeutic[3]	0.8	2.3	1.3	1.0
Stimulants	*	0.4	0.1	0.2
Sedatives	*	0.1	0.1	0.2
Tranquilizers	*	0.7	0.5	0.5
Analgesics	0.8	1.5	0.9	0.4
Any Illicit Drug other than Marijuana[2]	1.2	4.6	2.1	1.7
Alcohol	14.1	53.3	46.6	53.5
"Binge" Alcohol Use[4]	1.3	16.7	9.2	10.3
Heavy Alcohol Use[4]	0.3	4.6	2.0	2.3
Cigarettes	19.9	33.3	29.1	33.9
Smokless Tobacco	*	0.4	0.1	0.2

[3] Nonmedical use of any prescription-type stimulant, sedative, tranquilizer, or analgesic; does not include over-the-counter drugs.
[4] "Binge" Alcohol Use is defined as drinking five or more drinks on the same occasion on at least one day in the past 30 days. By "occasion" is meant at the same time or within a couple hours of each other. Heavy Alcohol Use is defined as drinking five or more drinks on the same occasion on each of five of more days in the past 30 days; all Heavy Alcohol Users are also "Binge" Alcohol Users.

Source: SAMHSA, Office of Applied Studies, National Household Survey on Drug Abuse, 1996 and 1997.

wine shops. To honor Bacchus, the god of wine and fertility, the ancient Greeks held drunken rites for women only. Nevertheless the double standard toward men's drinking and women's drinking began early. In ancient Rome a man could kill his wife if he smelled wine on her breath because drinking was thought to lead women to adultery. In the literature of the Middle Ages women's drinking is rarely discussed, but it is known that alcohol was given to women for medicinal purposes. Later, during the Renaissance, women were allowed to drink fairly openly. In London's GIN epidemic, between 1700 and 1750, women were blamed especially for the effect their drinking had on their children. (See FETAL ALCOHOL SYNDROME.) In colonial America, women often ran taverns and were allowed to enjoy alcohol at parties. Drunkenness, however, was not accepted and offenders were subject to punishment by being whipped publicly or forced to wear the letter "D." Victorian culture promoted the idea that women should be morally above reproach, and the use of alcohol did not conform to this mode of conduct. During the 1800s some women began to oppose the use of alcohol, and out of this grew the TEMPERANCE movement, which included such groups as the WOMAN'S CHRISTIAN TEMPERANCE UNION. Most historians feel that without women's involvement, PROHIBITION (THE VOLSTEAD ACT) in the early 20th century would never have gained momentum. The women of this movement felt that liquor led men to financial ruin and physical harm, which was inflicted on themselves, their wives and their children. One ironic aspect of the temperance movement was that many of the women who campaigned vehemently against the use of alcohol were at the same time consuming large amounts of patent medicines made up of opium and alcohol. In the 1920s women began to drink more openly and during Prohibition some women became bootleggers.

During this century and especially in the past few decades, women's consumption of alcohol and other drugs appears to have increased in relation to the past. This circumstance may be the result of social changes that have allowed women to be more open about their use of alcohol and other drugs. There was a particularly noticeable increase in drug use during World War II, when women joined the workforce in great numbers (as the majority of men were conscripted into the military).

Throughout history women have been expected to derive their sense of self-worth primarily through their relationships with men rather than through achievements and activities of their own. When something happens to the relationship, they may have little to fall back upon. Working women are often challenged by any number of stressors unique to their gender. Ambivalent or hostile feelings about women in management, for example, often lead women to think they must work harder than their male counterparts to prove their competency. Some women respond to this pressure by trying "to act like a man," and often to drink like one. Many women who work, particularly those with small children, are conflicted about not fulfilling all the roles of wife and mother, feeling that they should perform perfectly, both at work and at home. The additional stress of full-time employment compounding the responsibilities they have traditionally borne regarding home maintenance and child care may be a contributing factor to an increase in drug and alcohol consumption. New responsibilities are continually being added, but many of the old responsibilities have remained intact. Even fully employed women are still spending more time than men engaged in domestic responsibilities and child care. Working women who are divorced or separated often face enormous financial responsibilities as well as the burden of single parenthood—which is far more prevalent for women than men. In 1996 it was reported that many stress and anxiety-related ailments, particularly heart attacks and aggravated PMS (premenstrual syndrome), are on the rise for women.

Alcohol: Alcohol has different physical effects on women than on men. Women show higher BLOOD ALCOHOL CONCENTRATION (BAC) levels, adjusted for weight, than men for equivalent doses of alcohol. Initial absorption and metabolism of alcohol by stomach, or gastric, tissue diminishes toxicity, reducing the levels of alcohol in the bloodstream, thus reducing levels of intoxication. Alcohol dehydrogenase is the enzyme responsible for metabolizing alcohol. Studies have found that female social drinkers indicate less activity by this enzyme than do their male counterparts, and biopsies from female alcoholics revealed almost no gastric alcohol dehydrogenase activity. Another cause of this disparity in BAC levels is the fact that women have more fatty tissue and men have more muscle tissue, which contains more water than fatty tissue. Alcohol is distributed through the body in proportion to the water content of body tissue, therefore alcohol is diluted in the water contained in men's bodies and remains more potent in women's systems for longer periods of time. This process has been ignored by many researchers who have based their definition of alcoholism on the quantity of alcohol consumed and have used the same amounts for both sexes, also ignoring the fact that women are generally smaller, weighing less than men. In addition, since sex hormone levels apparently effect BAC and consequent behavioral effects—the same amount of alcohol will produce higher BACs during premenstrual phases than at other times.

Women alcoholics are very likely to have had either a father or other close male relative who was an alcoholic, and they first experience alcohol and begin to drink later than do men. Their drinking bouts are shorter than male drinking bouts. Unlike men, whose alcoholism generally progresses slowly, the symptoms of alcoholism appear rapidly in women. A period of 15 years or more leading up to severe alcoholism in men is condensed into a few years in women. Whereas women more often use alcohol to reduce stress on the job, men lose their jobs more frequently because of their drinking. More inclined than men to perceive their alcoholism as getting worse, women also are more prone to begin drinking after experiencing a severe crisis, such as divorce, death or separation. Periods of DEPRESSION prior to the onset of problem drinking occur far more frequently in women than in men. In the U.S. twice as many women as men suffer from depression. Another characteristic of alcoholic women is that they are more suicidal than alcoholic men.

Habitually women drink alone more often than men, probably because society still frowns on women going to bars alone. Consequently, when and if they do, they may find themselves accosted by various men, many of them not only inebriated, but making assumptions that if a woman goes to a bar alone she wants to be approached. Alcoholic males are publicly more visible and, as a result, receive treatment more often than females. Drinking, especially excessive drinking, has been and still is less acceptable for women than for men. Today women's social drinking is accepted, but female drunkenness is still looked upon with disdain. The consumption

of large amounts of alcohol by a man can be interpreted as a sign of coming of age or of masculinity; for a woman it is commonly seen as inappropriate behavior. A circle of family and friends are likely to hide or ignore a female problem drinker because they are embarrassed and ashamed. They often offer a form of "protection" or concealment rather than initiating a course of recovery. Consequently, women, more than men, have been likely to suffer their addictions in secret and not seek treatment. Although excessive drinking among women has been linked to promiscuity and neglect of the home, evidence to support these assumptions is often contradictory. Furthermore, women alcoholics generally show more concern for their children than do male alcoholics. Men are more likely to leave their alcoholic spouses than are women. Typically, the wives of alcoholics endure their husbands' problems and try to get them into treatment. Until recently, treatment programs specifically oriented toward assisting women have been rare, but more recent programs incorporating women's groups are proving successful.

Gynecological and obstetrical problems are relatively high among alcoholic women. They have a comparatively larger number of infertility problems, miscarriages and hysterectomies. (See REPRODUCTIVE FUNCTIONS.) However, these problems may sometimes precipitate the onset of alcoholism. Because of the high incidence of alcoholism in the families of alcoholic women, it is thought that a genetic component may be a contributing factor although it has been documented that excessive use of alcohol can damage a fetus. Nonetheless, it must be remembered that many alcoholic women also are heavy smokers and their diets are inadequate during pregnancy.

Women appear to be more susceptible than men to alcoholic CIRRHOSIS, and it has been hypothesized that there is an interaction between menopausal hormonal status and the susceptibility of the liver to the toxic effects of alcohol. Studies have shown that women die of cirrhosis earlier than men, even though they consume less alcohol, according to Judith Gavaler, an epidemiologist at the University of Pittsburgh Medical School.

Women are known to begin drinking alcohol at an earlier age now than in the past, and there has been a dramatic increase in alcohol consumption by adolescent girls. Studies conducted in San Mateo County, California, in 1968 showed that 15% of girls reported some alcohol use. Figures released by NIDA in 1990 indicate that among high school girls in the senior class of 1989, 81.4% had used alcohol in the past year, compared with 83.9% of senior boys. Regular drinking is now common among high school girls, and the number of young female drinkers is increasing more rapidly than the number of young male drinkers.

Minority women with drinking problems have received very little attention. Minority women have had to face discrimination because of both their race and their sex. They have higher unemployment rates than either white women or minority men and are far more likely to head families subsisting below the poverty level.

Alcoholism is a particularly severe problem for both male and female homosexuals as the percentage of homosexuals with alcohol problems is more than double that for the general population. According to a variety of estimates, one out of four homosexuals is an alcoholic as opposed to one out of 10 in the overall population. Lesbians are even more likely to have alcohol problems than homosexual men. A study in 1970 found that 35% of all lesbians had severe drinking problems, compared with 28% of homosexual men and only 5% of heterosexual women. This high rate has been attributed to the effects of an environment that is openly hostile to lesbians and forces isolation upon them. In many regions of the U.S. one of the few places where lesbians are socially accepted is the gay bar, where their isolation is reinforced in an atmosphere of alcohol. Outside of the homosexual environment, their sexual preference generally must be kept hidden for fear of losing their jobs, apartments or, in some cases, custody of their children. Lesbian alcoholics have even experienced discrimination in applying for treatment.

"SKID ROW" women have subsisted on the fringe of society and their problems are only now being studied. It is known that they usually are poorer than their male counterparts and end up on skid row at an earlier age. Many of these "bag ladies" wandering the streets of major cities are alcoholics. About two-thirds of them drink alone, as opposed to one-quarter of the destitute males. Little in the way of shelter or treatment has been offered to these women, and even when such services are provided temporarily, most of them have no place to return to other than the streets.

Causes: The causes and consequences of alcoholism are now acknowledged to be different for women than for men (in earlier research women were studied as a subgroup of men).

There is no single cause of alcoholism either for men or for women. Alcoholics of both sexes often suffer an unusual amount of stress and deprivation in their lives. It has been theorized that men drink because of dependency needs or to create an illusion of power over others. Neither of these theories seem to apply to women. Studies show that women drink primarily to relieve loneliness, feelings of inferiority and conflicts about their gender role regardless of their lifestyle. Those who subscribe to the traditionally "feminine" modes of behavior are forced to deny any supposedly "masculine" traits, and the women who consciously reject the feminine role may be ostracized by society. Many women who were sexually and psychologically abused as children, adolescents and even adults never overcome their feelings of shame and worthlessness. Drinking can be a means of escaping these and other conflicts.

One national survey focused on women who drank moderately or heavily. Identified within this group were specific demographic groups of women who displayed higher rates of drinking: (1) women who were unemployed; (2) women who were employed part-time outside the home; (3) divorced or separated women; (4) women who had never married; and (5) unmarried women who lived with a partner. Women in the fourth category had the highest incidence of drinking problems.

Treatment: Programs that admit women may offer them the same treatment they offer men, despite the fact that women have different histories and motivations for drinking. Child care rarely is provided by alcoholism programs. Follow-up support may be more important for alcoholic women than for alcoholic men, since women are less likely to receive support from their families (if they have not already lost them). Yet few alcohol treatment programs provide any sustained follow-up service, and as a result a large percentage of the women who complete treatment do not recover. If and when they do recover, the stigma attached to female alcoholism may make it difficult for these women to find jobs. More attention is now being paid to women alcoholics, and some therapy and support groups are designed specifically for them. These groups may make it easier for women to talk freely about issues such as sexuality and family relationships. NIDA has recommended the development of comprehensive treatment programs designed to meet the full range of women's needs: the provision of child care food, clothing, shelter, transportation, job counseling and training, legal assistance, educational programming, family planning, parenting training, family therapy, medical care, social services, psychological assessment, mental health care and assertiveness training. Recent figures from Alcoholics Anonymous indicate that women alcoholics are becoming more willing to seek help. The percentage of female members in AA has risen steadily, from 22% in 1968, to 29% in 1977, to 34% in 1986. There are now several hundred all-women's AA groups across the country. A national network designed specifically for alcoholic women, Women for Sobriety (WFS), was founded in 1975 by Jean Kirkpatrick, a sociologist who had been an alcoholic for 28 years. WFS is geared toward dealing with the different emotional needs of women, which are often neglected by AA. The WFS program is secular and offers 13 steps as guidelines in the affirmation of the value of each woman. Anonymity is left up to the individual. Many women are members of both WFS and AA.

Tobacco: The tobacco and alcoholic beverage industries have recognized women as a growing market, and many companies aim their advertising at women, using alluring marketing campaigns to entice them into tobacco use—not without results. There are approximately 200 million women smokers in the world today. Half of them are in developed countries; the other half are in developing countries (21% of women in developed countries and 8% in developing countries are smokers). Particularly in countries where women's roles are rapidly changing, smoking among older women is still rare, but among younger women it is increasing, and in such countries 30% to 50% of the younger women now smoke. In the U.S. and the UK lung cancer has replaced breast cancer as the most common form of cancer death for women. In many parts of India the use of chewing tobacco is widespread. This practice causes oral cancer and Indian women have the highest rate

of oral cancer among the world's female population. Risks for all smoking-related causes of death (lung cancer, other cancers, heart disease, stroke and chronic obstructive lung disease) are on the rise for both men and women, but the highest increases in risks are for female smokers. Results from two other studies that began in the 1970s confirm the results observed within the female smoking population in the American Cancer Society's (ACS) second *Cancer Prevention Study (CPS II)*. Statistics such as 36,035 women in the *Kaiser Permanente Study* and 121,700 women in the *Nurse's Health Study* show that women smokers had nearly twice the risk of death from all causes compared with women who did not smoke.

Half of the adolescents, whether male or female, who continue to smoke throughout their lives will be killed by tobacco. The number of male smokers in the U.S. has dropped sharply over the last 20 years yet there has been no similar decline for women. A 1989 government survey reported that 1.7 million teenage girls smoke as compared to 1.6 million boys. Statistics also indicate that men are twice as successful as women in their efforts to quit smoking.

Drugs other than alcohol: There are an estimated 2 to 3 million female prescription-drug addicts in the U.S. SEDATIVES are prescribed for women more than twice as often as for men, and women consume 71% of all antidepressant medications and 80% of all legal amphetamines (often in the form of diet pills). In 1980, 26 million Valium prescriptions were written for women. Since then, due to federal regulation, Valium has been prescribed less and is no longer among the 10 most frequently dispensed prescription drugs.

Numerous explanations for the high percentages of prescription drug use and abuse among women have been postulated. One theory is that drug use has been related to menstrual cycle reactions and to the fact that women see doctors more often than men and therefore are more likely to receive prescriptions. Some 67% of female problem drinkers correlate their drinking bouts with the days of the month when they are premenstrual, a time when many women experience emotional debility and depression. Doctors may be more inclined to pacify women with drugs, as they often do with the ELDERLY. Doctors frequently prescribe pills for the symptoms of alcoholism or other drug abuse instead of identifying the causes of the drug abuse. The high rate of prescriptions for antidepressants seems to be related to the fact that women are more likely than men to express their feelings and seek treatment from physicians. However, women are less likely to acknowledge their chemical dependency. Their drug-taking behavior exposes them to dangers that do not affect men, such as those imposed on the fetus during PREGNANCY. Almost half of all women in the 15-to-44 age group (the child-bearing years) have used illicit drugs at least once in their lives. Annual Emergency Room Data for 1991 from the Drug Abuse Warning Network (DAWN) reported that women account for 51% of all drug-related emergency room visits. Women with alcohol problems are much more likely to use prescribed drugs, particularly tranquilizers, than are men. The alcoholic woman often does not want her doctor to know about her drinking and thus exhibits the symptoms for which tranquilizers normally are prescribed: anxiety, tension, depression and so on. Use of tranquilizers, however, can lead to CROSS-ADDICTION and it can be harder to break a dual addiction than an addiction to alcohol alone. A 1983 survey of ALCOHOLICS ANONYMOUS (AA) members showed that 40% of the women (but only 27% of the men) were addicted to drugs other than alcohol. Three percent of the respondents were under the age of 21, and of this group 79% suffered from dual addiction. A 1986 survey of more than 15,000 AA members showed that 46% of the women but only 37% of the men were addicted to drugs other than alcohol. Taking alcohol with certain psychoactive drugs is also particularly dangerous, because of the synergistic reaction produced. (See SYNERGY.) A drug and alcohol, taken together, have a much greater effect than would be expected from either alone, and the chances of an overdose are increased severely. Most women are unaware of the grave and multitudinous side effects certain to occur with continued habitual use of either prescription or illicit drugs.

As of 1994, AIDS was the fourth leading cause of death among women of childbearing age in the U.S. Substance abuse is strongly related to AIDS because women who inject drugs transmit or are infected with the HIV virus by sharing needles and syringes. Of the 40,000 documented cases of AIDS in women in 1993, nearly 70% were connected to needle/syringe sharing or to having sex with the injecting drug user.

Holly Atkinson, M.D., "Women & Alcohol: The New Problem Drinkers," *New Woman* (September 1988).

Sheila B. Blume, "Diagnosis, Casefinding, and Treatment of Alcohol Problems in Women," *Alcohol Health & Research World* 2, no. 3 (Fall 1978): 10–22.

Ed Vasanti Burtle, *Women Who Drink* (Springfield, Ill.: Charles C. Thomas, 1979).

Health Communications, *An Emerging Issue: The Female Alcoholic* (Hollywood, Fla., 1977).

Edith Lynn Hornik, *The Drinking Woman* (New York: Association Press, 1977).

National Institute on Drug Abuse (NIDA), "Women and Drug Abuse" *NIDA Capsules* (March 1994).

E. R. Shore et al., "Arrests of Women for Driving Under the Influence," *Quarterly Journal of Studies on Alcohol* 49 (1988): 7–10.

Substance Abuse and Mental Health Services Administration, *National Household Survey on Drug Abuse: Main Findings 1993* (Rockville, Md.: Department of Health and Human Services [DHHS], June 1995).

R. W. Wilsnack et al., "Women's Drinking and Drinking Problems: Patterns from a 1981 National Survey," *American Journal of Public Health* 74 (1984): 1231–1238.

Marian Sandmaier, *The Invisible Alcoholics: Women and Alcohol Abuse in America* (New York: McGraw-Hill, 1980).

Geraline Youcha, *A Dangerous Pleasure* (New York: Hawthorn Books, 1978).

Enoch Gordis, M.D., ed., *Sixth Special Report to the U.S. Congress on Alcohol and Health,* (Rockville, Md.: National Institute on Alcohol Abuse and Alcoholism [NIAAA], 1987).

National Institute of Health (NIH), and National Cancer Institute, *Risks of Cigarette Smoking for Women on the Rise,* NIH press release (April 23, 1997): Online, http://www.nih.gov/news/pr/apr97/nci-23.htm.

World Health Organization (WHO), "Women Who Smoke Like Men Face the Same Risks As Men" press release (July 17, 1995): Online, http://www.who.ch/press/1995/ pr95-55.htm.

Women for Sobriety   A self-help organization that offers mutual support in the form of meetings exclusively for women. Women new to sobriety often feel vulnerable and stigmatized by the double standard against women who become alcoholic. WFS enables them to recover in a stigma free environment.

Women's Sports Foundation drug use program
An organization committed to the elimination of illicit drug use in amateur and professional athletics. The not-for-profit foundation fosters competitive opportunities for girls and women and has been in the forefront of efforts to protect athletes from illicit drug use as well as the abuse of legal drugs and alcohol.

workplace, antidrug policies and programs   A new office was created in February 1987 at NIDA (National Institute on Drug Abuse) called the Office of Workplace Initiatives (OWI) to raise awareness of drug-use issues among labor leaders, employers and employees and to foster the development of policy, effective employee education and supervisory training. OWI provides technical assistance to federal agencies and the private sector on the use of both drug-testing programs and Employee Assistance Programs (EAPs) to reduce drug use in the workplace.

The highest drug-using segment of the American work force is the young adult. (This category includes people from one to four years beyond high school but not in college.) The most recent SAMHSA (Substance Abuse and Mental Health Services Administration) *National Household Survey on Drug Abuse* revealed that of the 20- to 40-year-old population (those currently entering the workforce), 42% of young adults have used illicit drugs within the last year. Twenty-nine percent, or nearly a third of employed Americans in that age bracket, used an illicit drug in the past year, and 19% reported some illicit drug use at least once in the past month.

A survey on workplace drug use, conducted every five years since 1971 at Marquette University, reports that 95% of the companies surveyed reported direct experience with substance abuse in 1986, up from 82% in 1981 and 50% in 1976.

ATOD- (alcohol, tobacco and other drug) related problems are costing U.S. businesses over $100 billion a year in lost or impaired productivity, and these costs are increasing. Untold millions more dollars are lost as a result of problems often linked to substance abuse—seen as increased on-the-job accidents and security breaches. Lost productivity, absenteeism, and higher turnover costs, increased health-benefit utilization, accidents and losses stemming from impaired judgment and creativity are among the drug-related expenses not listed in the estimate. Still, the workplace is not being used optimally for prevention of these problems even though it would be a most effective way to reach Americans, their families and their communities, since a large majority of the adult population is employed. A growing number of companies now are looking to EMPLOYEE ASSISTANCE PROGRAMS to help control skyrocketing health care costs.

The Center for Substance Abuse Prevention (CSAP) has a toll-free help line to guide employers towards achieving a drug-free workplace (800-843-4971). Staff members provide consultation to employees about initiating a company policy that covers such efforts as employee education program, urine-testing programs and the establishment of an existing Employee Assistance Program (EAP) to deal directly with the drug-related problems of employees.

Individuals with personal questions related to substance abuse can call 800-662-HELP. Printed information about such matters also is available from the National Clearinghouse for Alcohol and Drug Information (NCADI) by calling 800-729-6686.

National Clearinghouse for Alcohol and Drug Information (NCADI), *Center for Substance Abuse Prevention (CSAP), Substance Abuse Resource Guide* (January 1993): Online, http://www.health.org/pubs/resguide/ wkplace. htm.

Dept. of Health and Human Services, Center for Substance Abuse Prevention, SAMHSA, "Alcohol, Tobacco and Other Drugs in the Workplace," *Making the Link* ML006 (Spring 1995).

National Institute on Drug Abuse, "Facts about Drugs in the Workplace," *NIDA Capsules,* cap 24, rev. (November 1987).

World Health Organization (WHO)   A specialized agency of the United Nations. WHO has the primary responsibility for international health matters and public health. Created in 1948, WHO has the benefit of 160 countries that exchange knowledge and experience with the aim of attaining a level of health that permits nations to lead socially and economically productive lives.

World War II, drug use in   By the beginning of the 1940s, large-scale illicit drug use in the U.S. had all but disappeared. Prescribed amphetamine use was increasing, however. Gilda Berger, writing about this in her book *Drug Abuse: The Impact on Society,* theorizes: "The success was not due to the various laws [that had been enacted] and treatment facilities that had been opened. Rather, World War II had cut off supply routes of drugs from Asia and Europe." As an editorial in *Time* stated in 1942, "The war is probably the best thing that ever happened to the U.S. drug addicts." This statement referred to the decline of heroin use. Alcoholism was unaffected by the war.

Gilda Berger, *Drug Abuse: The Impact on Society* (New York: Franklin Watts, 1988): 19.

Wo [sic] to Drunkards   A treatise written in 1673 by Increase Mather, the Puritan preacher and scholar, depicting the idea of drunkenness as a sinful disgrace. Said Mather: "Drink is in itself a good creature of God—but the abuse of drink is from Satan—and the Drunkard is from the Devil."

xylene   A volatile solvent. Although the vapors of this aromatic hydrocarbon are extremely irritating to the nasal membranes, it has some potential for INHALANT abuse.

Y

Yale University Center of Alcohol Studies   Established in 1943 as the School of Alcohol Studies in New Haven, Connecticut (now the Rutgers Center of Alcohol Studies at Rutgers University), it was the nation's first such formal educational program and almost immediately conferred a new respectability on the subject of alcoholism. E. M. JELLINEK, long the guru of those who assert that alcoholism is a disease, was one of the center's founders and its first director. The NATIONAL COUNCIL ON ALCOHOLISM (NCA) started as an offshoot of the National Committee for Education on Alcoholism (NCEA), which was founded in 1944 at the Yale Center of Alcohol Studies. Yale sponsored the *Quarterly Journal of Studies on Alcohol*, the Yale Summer School of Alcohol Studies (of which Professor Jellinek was director) and the Yale Plan Clinics (with its well-known research division). E. M. Jellinek was not a physician but a physiologist and biostatistician. At Yale he managed to collect and assemble the most advanced knowledge available on the subject. Consequently, he became, possibly, the world's foremost authority on alcoholism in his time.

Don Cahalan, *Understanding America's Drinking Problem: How to Combat the Hazards of Alcohol* (San Francisco: Jossey-Bass, 1988).

Nan Robertson, *Getting Better: Inside Alcoholics Anonymous* (New York: William Morrow, 1988).

yerba mate   A tea brewed from the leaves of *Ilex paraguariensis,* an evergreen shrub native to Paraguay and Brazil. It contains the stimulant CAFFEINE.

yohimbe   *Corynanthe yohimbe;* a tree native to West Africa whose bark and roots are purported to be an aphrodisiac. It produces hallucinations and mild euphoria, but is toxic in large doses. Though sold pharmaceutically in the U.S. as a treatment for impotence, it is still untested.

yopo beans   A hallucinogen used by the Guahibo Indians in South America.

Youth to Youth   An international not-for-profit drug-prevention education organization for youth in grades six to eight and grades nine through 12. College-age students act as group leaders. Youth to Youth conducts instructional seminars for youths and parents on forming their own drug-prevention programs and holds regional and national conferences yearly. A resource center provides training manuals, videos and other materials. A free quarterly newsletter is available upon request.

Z

zinc supplements   There are no controlled studies to substantiate improvement for alcohol-related diseases by taking vitamin supplements such as vitamin B. However, because of occasional episodes of night blindness and reports of ALCOHOL AMBLYOPIA (characterized by vision blurring due to central scotomas), vitamin A therapy and zinc supplements occasionally have been recommended by some clinicians. Though results are uncertain in this area of vitamin therapy, the supervised taking of vitamin and mineral supplements on a short-term basis will seldom be harmful to alcoholic patients who are undergoing the withdrawal syndrome. (See VITAMINS AND MINERALS.)

Donald M. Gallant, *Alcoholism: A Guide to Diagnosis, Intervention, and Treatment* (New York: W.W. Norton, 1987): 184.